★ 1998 ★ PEOPLE ENTERTAINMENT ALMANAC

★ 1998 ★

PEOPLE ENTERTAINMENT ALMANAC

CREATED AND PRODUCED BY
CADER BOOKS • NEW YORK

YEAR-IN-REVIEW
ROYALS
SCREEN
TUBE
SONG
PAGES
STAGE
20TH-CENTURY TIMELINE
PEOPLE EXTRAS
CELEB REGISTER

First Edition

10 9 8 7 6 5 4 3 2 1

Printed in the United States of America

CONTENTS

TUBE 153

SONG 215

PAGES 293

STAGE 355

THE PEOPLE TIMELINE 385

PEOPLE EXTRAS 415

THE PEOPLE REGISTER 459

PHOTO CREDITS

COVER

Front cover (clockwise from top): Gamma Liaison/Evan Agostini, Reuters/Kieran Doherty/Archive Photos, John Spellman/Retna Ltd. USA, Reuters/Fred Prouser/Archive, Gamma Liaison/Evan Agostini, Celebrity Photo, Bob Riha/Gamma Liaison, Archive Photos, AP Photo/Morry Gash, AP Photo/Marty Lederhandler, Nina Prommer/Globe Photos Inc., Spine: AP Photo/Bob D'Amico. Back cover: AP Photo/David Corio

YEAR IN REVIEW

p. 14 AP Photo/Kevork Djansezian; p. 15 Reuters/Mike Segar/Archive Photos; p. 16 Stephane Cardinale/Sygma; p. 17 AP Photo/APTV; p. 18 Eli Hersko/Retna Ltd. USA; p. 19 AP Photo/Ian Stewart/UK OUT; p. 20 Neshan H. Naltchayan/Reuters/Archive Photos; p. 21 Reuters/Jim Bourg/Archive Photos; p. 22 Reuters/Gary Hershorn/Archive Photos; p. 24 AP Photo/Lionel Cironneau; p. 25 FSP/Gamma Liaison

ROYALS

p. 57 Reuters/John Stillwell/Archive Photos; p. 59 Stewart Mark/Rota/Camerapress/Retna Ltd. USA; p. 63 AP Photo/ Jacqueline Arzt; p. 65 Pool Stills/Retna Ltd. USA; p. 67 FSP/Gamma Liaison; p. 68 Reuters/David Longstreath/Archive Photos; p. 69 Archive Photos/Barry Batchelor; p. 70 Reuters/Jim Bourg/Archive Photos; p. 71 Reuters/Kieran Doherty/ Archive Photos; p. 73 Reuters/Peter Morgan/Archive Photos

TUBE

p. 15 Randy Tepper/CBS; Fox Broadcasting Company; p. 183 DMB&B

SONG

p. 216, 217 Columbia; p. 218 Virgin;Warner Bros. Records; p. 219 Smithsonian Folkways Records; p. 220 Epic; p. 221 Warner Bros. Records; p. 222 Polygram; Columbia; p. 224 Capitol Records; p. 225 Island; p. 246 DGC Records; DGC/Geffen; Island; p. 247 Atlantic

PAGES

p. 294 Farrar, Straus & Giroux; p. 295 William Morrow; p. 296 HarperCollins; Pantheon; p. 297 W.W. Norton (2); Mysterious Press; p. 298 Riverhead Books; p. 299 Times Books; Scribner; p.300 Putnam; Pantheon; p. 301 Alfred A. Knopf; p. 302 Random House; p. 303 Hyperion; Henry Holt; p. 304 Little, Brown; Simon & Schuster; p. 305 Harcourt Brace; p. 306 Cader Books

TIMELINE

pp. 386, 387 (2), 388 Hulton Deutsch Collection; p. 389 (Archive Photos), pp. 390 (2), 391 (2), 392, 393, 396, 397 (2), 398, 400 (2), 401, 403, 404, 405 Hulton Deutsch Collection; p. 406 Holland/Retna Ltd.; p. 407 Archive Photos; p. 408 Hulton Deutsch Collection; p. 409 AP/Wide World; p. 412 Sarasota County Sheriff's Department/Meg Handler collection

PEOPLE EXTRAS

p. 442 AP Photo/Kevork Djansezian; Archive Photos/Popperfoto; p. 443 Walter McBride/Retna Ltd.; Reuters/ Fred Prouser/Archive Photos; p. 444 Archive Photos/Max B. Miller; Archive Photos/Popperfoto; p. 445 Archive Photos/ Popperfoto; Reuters/Jeff Vinnick/Archive Photos; p. 446 Archive Photos; Archive Photos/Popperfoto; p. 447 Reuters/ Archive Photos; Reuters/Jeff Christensen/Archive Photos; p. 448 Archive Photos/Fotos International; Archive Photos/ Bob Grant; p. 449 Archive Photos; Bill Davila/Retna Ltd.; p. 450 Andrea Renault/Globe Photos Inc.; Victor Malafronte/ Archive Photos; p. 451 AP Photo; Archive Photos/Jason Trigg; p. 452 Popperfoto/Archive Photos; AP Photo/Ken Cedeno; p. 453 Consolidated News/Archive Photos; AP Photo/Ken Cedeno; p. 454 Ron Phillips/Archive Photos (2); p. 455 AP Photo/Wade Payne; Steve Granitz/Retna Ltd.; p. 456 Frank Capri/Saga/Archive Photos; Archive Photos; p. 457 Popperfoto/ Archive Photos; Kosta Alexander/Fotos International/Archive Photos

THE PEOPLE REGISTER

p. 461 AP Photo/NBC; p. 467 Deidre Davidson/Saga/Archive Photos; p. 468 Fitzroy Barrett/Globe Photos Inc.; p. 474 Popperfoto/Archive Photos; p. 476 AP Photo/Rene Macura; p. 485 Lisa Rose/Globe Photos Inc.; p. 488 AP Photo/Marty Lederhandler; p. 490 AP Photo/Owen Connors Associates; p. 493 AP Photo/Las Vegas Review Journal/Jim Laurie; p. 495 Fitzroy Barrett/Globe Photos Inc.; p. 501 AP Photo/Michael Caulfield; p. 503 All Action/Retna Ltd. USA; p. 506 Armando Gallo/Retna Limited USA; p. 511 D. Benett; p. 515 Lisa Rose/Globe Photos Inc.; p. 520 Steve Granitz/Retna Limited USA; Kosta Alexander/Archive Photos; p. 521 Fotos International/Archive Photos; p. 527 Fitzroy Barrett/Globe Photos Inc.; p. 528 Armando Gallo/Retna Limited USA; p. 535 AP Photo/The Desert Sun/Steven Schretzmann; p. 536 John Spellman/ Retna Ltd. USA; p. 539 Reuters/Fred Prouser/Archive Photos; p. 544 Steve Granitz/Retna Ltd.; Theodore Wood/ Retna Ltd. USA; p. 550 Fitzroy Barrett/Globe Photos Inc.; p. 551 Lisa Rose/Globe Photos Inc.

STAFF

Editor-in-Chief
Michael Cader

Executive Editor
Camille N. Cline

Senior Editor
Steve Baumgartner

Design
Charles Kreloff, Orit Mardkha-Tenzer,
Stephen Hughes

Research
Cindy Achar, Daniel C. Bernstein, Meryl Davids,
Tracy Eberhart, Oren Rawls, Deborah E. Yeh

Consulting Editor
Seth Godin

PEOPLE Contributors
Eric Levin (Supervising Editor), Leslie Bonagura, Robert Britton, Robert Bronzo, Richard Burgheim, Steven Cook, Steven Dougherty, Nancy Eils, Jeremy Helligar, Ken Kantor, Maureen Kenna, Michael A. Lipton, Denise Lynch, Kristin McMurran, Samantha Miller, James Oberman, Vincent R. Peterson, Leah Rozen, Matthew Semble, Randy Vest, Paul Zelinski

Carol Wallace, Managing Editor; Ann S. Moore, President; Robert D. Jurgrau, Business Manager

ACKNOWLEDGMENTS

Many people and organizations have generously lent their time, resources, and expertise to help make this project possible. Special thanks go to: Sheri Abramson, Harcourt Brace; Academy of Recording Arts and Sciences; Jennifer Allen, PMK; Simon Applebaum, Cablevision; Stuart Applebaum, Bantam; Bridget Aschenberg, ICM; Alan Axelrod; Michael Barson, Putnam; Michelle Bega, Rogers & Cowan, Inc.; Jane Beirn, HarperCollins; Andi Berger, PMK; Cindi Berger; Marion Billings, M/S Billings Publicity, Ltd.; Helen Blake, National Infomercial Marketing Association; Judy Boals, Berman, Boals & Flynn; Elaine Bosman, HarperCollins; Matthew Bradley, Viking; Sandy Bresler, Bresler, Kelly, and Associates; Sarah Burns and Lee Butella, Knopf; Gerry Byrne, *Variety*; Brad Cafarelli, Bragman, Nyman, Cafarelli; Fr. John Catoir, Christophers; Center for the Book, Library of Congress; Center for Media and Public Affairs; Marylou Chlipala, Carnegie Mellon School of Drama; Bob Christie, National Academy of Television Arts and Sciences; Robert C. Christopher, The Pulitzer Prizes; Steve Clar; Rosie Cobbe, Fraser & Dunlop; Sam Cohn; Columbia University Graduate School of Journalism; Ace Collins; Sarah Cooper, O. W. Toad Ltd.; Don Corathers, *Dramatics* magazine; Angela Corio, Recording Industry Association of America; Marie Costanza, NYU Musical Theater Dept.; Crown; Louise Danton, National Academy of Television Arts and Sciences; Leslie Dart, PMK; Gary N. DaSilva; Joan Dim, NYU, Tisch School of the Arts; Alina Dinca, Nielsen Media Services; Heather Dinwiddie, American Symphony Orchestra League; Dramatists Guild; Steve Dworman, *Infomercial Marketing Report*; Larry Edwards, *Advertising Age*; Allen Eichhorn; Ed Enright, *Down Beat*; Kenneth Ewing; Charmaine Ferenczi, The Tantleff Office; Steve Fleming, HarperCollins; Karen Forester, Country Music Association; Susan Geller, Susan Geller & Associates; Heather Gifford, National Academy of Recording Artists; Debbie Gilwood; John Graff, Consulate of Luxembourg; Bob Gregg, Paramount; Amanda Grossman, Capitol Records; Cynthia Harris, Little, Brown; Ted Hearne, John D. and Catherine T. MacArthur Foundation; Tom Hill, Nick at Nite; Patricia Hodges, Time Warner; Sally Hoffman, Random House; Hollywood Chamber of Commerce; Hollywood Foreign Press Association; Dave Howard, Hofflund/Pollone Agency; Jane Huebsch, American Symphony Orchestra League; Patrick Ingram, Bantam; Gary Ink, *Publishers Weekly*; M. Jackson, AUDELCO; A. J. Jacobs; Elizabeth Jarret; Steve Jukes, Judy Daish Associates; Sue Kaplan, BPI; Joyce Ketay, Joyce Ketay Agency; Amanda Kimmel, Dell; John Kings, Texas Center for Writers; Pat Kingsley; Leonard Klady, *Variety*; Henry Kol, Consulate of the Netherlands; John Krier, Exhibitor Relations; Judy Krug, American Library Association; Ruth Levine, Penguin; Stacey Levitt, Rachel McCallister & Associates; Ed Limato, ICM; Elizabeth Maas, The League of American Theatres and Producers; Joe Marich; Howard Marcantel, National Academy of Cable Programming; Dan Mayer, Waldenbooks; Angela Medina, Juilliard School of Drama; Gilbert Medina, William Morris Agency; Lisa Meredith, National Cable Forum; Suzanne Mikesell, *Pulse!*; Jason Mitchell, Chronicle; T. J. Mitchell, Hofflund/Pollone Agency; Jessica Morell; Jamie Morris, *Soap Opera Digest*; Hirofumi Murabayashi, Consulate of Japan; Nara Nahm, Pantheon; The National Book Foundation; Karen Kriendler Nelson, Richard Tucker Foundation; David O'Connor; Catherine Olim, PMK; Bob Palmer; Charlotte Parker, Parker Public Relations; Gilbert Parker, William Morris; Karen Pascho; Jeffrey Pasternak, Simon & Schuster; Liz Perl, Berkley; Emmanuel Perrier, Consulate of Monaco; Ronnie Pugh, Country Music Hall of Fame; Myra Quinn, Peter Brown Agency; Joe Regal, Russell & Volkening; Tom Reidy, Tuneful Productions; Jonathan S. Renes, DMB&B; Andrew Rhodes, American Society of Magazine Editors; Sandy Rice, PMK; Rock and Roll Hall of Fame; Sandee Richardson, *Infomercial Marketing Report*; Richard Rodzinski, Van Cliburn Competition; Bradley Roberts, *Pollstar*; Cynthia Robinson, ALA; Susan Roman, American Library Association; Ami Roosevelt; Rachel Rosenberg, Northwestern University School of Speech; Howard Rosenstone, Rosenstone/Wender; Cari Ross; Jessica Rovins, MTV; Lucy Sabini, RCA; Heidi Schaeffer, ICM; Marly Rusoff, Doubleday; Bill Schelble; Ken Schneider, Knopf; Rachel Schnoll, Viking; Nancy Seltzer, Nancy Seltzer & Associates, Inc.; Greg Sharko, ATP Media Relations; John Sheehan, Center for Media and Public Affairs; Paul Shefrin, The Shefrin Company; Barry Sherman, University of Georgia; Jane Sindell, CAA; Smithsonian Institution, Division of Community Life; Eliza Sporn, Riverhead/Putnam; Robert Stein, United Talent Agency; Tracy Stevens, Quigley Publishing Company; Carol Stone, PMK; Laine Sutton, *Jeopardy!*; Jack Tantleff, The Tantleff Office; Jonathan Taylor, *Variety*; Prof. Mark Tucker, Columbia University; Terry Tuma, Yale School of Drama; Chris Upton, Knopf; Chris Vaccari, Harcourt Brace; Alexandra Vedel, Consulate of Denmark; John Walsh, Island Records; Sarah Webster, O. W. Toad Ltd.; Murray Weissman, Weissman Angellotti; Windi Wentworth, PBS; Moira Whalon; *Whitaker's Almanac*; Patricia Willis, Beinecke Library, Yale University; Staci Wolfe; Jennifer Wolfertz, Barnes & Noble.

THE YEAR IN REVIEW

JANUARY

Seinfeld sidekicks **Julia Louis-Dreyfus**, **Michael Richards**, and **Jason Alexander** each ask for $1 million per episode before they agree to another season of the No. 1–rated show. They reportedly settle in the $600,000 range, up from their current salary of $125Gs per. The guesstimate is that star **Jerry Seinfeld** will double his weekly take to $1 million, not counting the $40 million he was paid for rerun sales.

Superman sheds his 60-year-old trademark blue skivvies with red and yellow emblem, DC Comics reveals. In their place: streamlined blue and white tights. The "S" on his chest becomes more angular, and bullets no longer bounce off his chest; they pass right through it. The new costume draws fire from survivors of the '50s TV show. "It sounds horrible," Noel Neill (Lois Lane) tells the New York *Daily News*. Chimed in Jack Larson (Jimmy Olson), should fans not like the new look: "I'm sure Clark [Kent] will be able to rummage around [his closet] and find his old suit."

Monaco's royal family—**Prince Rainier** and those kids—celebrates the 700th anniversary of the dynasty, which is Europe's longest-running.

Frank Sinatra, 81, recovers at L.A.'s Cedars-Sinai Medical Center from an apparent heart attack. Paramedics brought the legendary singer and Oscar winner to the hospital following what was described as "an uncomplicated heart attack." This is the third time Ol' Blue Eyes was admitted to the hospital in three months. In November 1996, he'd spent eight days there due to what was described as a pinched nerve and mild pneumonia. In April, a bill to award Sinatra the Congressional Gold Medal clears Congress.

Bryant Gumbel ends his 15-year tenure on the *Today Show*. He had interviewed some 12,000 guests from former president **Richard Nixon** to **Miss Piggy** since he began on January 4, 1982. His last appearance on the show featured appearances from **Tom Cruise**, **Hillary Clinton**, and **The Artist Formerly Known As Prince**, among others. Gumbel is succeeded by **Matt Lauer**.

Catcher in the Rye author—and notorious New Hampshire recluse—**J.D. Salinger**, 78, publishes his first book in 34 years, *Hapworth 16, 1924*. The novel is in the form of a letter from 7-year-old Salinger hero Seymour Glass to his family. Originally published in *The New Yorker* in 1965, the

"You are sooo good-looking"—Seinfeld *cast's new salary raise is nothing to sneeze at.*

book is being issued by a small, Alexandria, Va.–based university imprint, Orchises Press.

Bill Cosby's only son, **Ennis William Cosby**, 27, is found shot to death near Bel Air, Calif. The young Cosby, a Columbia University doctoral student who assisted special education students, was changing a flat tire along the San Diego Freeway when he was killed.

In March, L.A. police arrest Mikail Markhasev, 18, a Ukranian immigrant. The suspect is found after police pursue a tip received by the *National Enquirer,* which offered a $100,000 reward. Markhasev pleads not guilty at his May arraignment. Also in May, Ennis Cosby is posthumously awarded a master's degree in education from the Teachers College at Columbia.

Camille and Bill Cosby en route from Manhattan to L.A. after hearing of the death of their son.

A few days after Cosby received the news of the murder of his son, a woman claiming to be the entertainer's illegitimate daughter and an accomplice are arrested in an unrelated attempt to extort $40 million from him. **Autumn Jackson**, 22, and **Jose Medina**, 51, reportedly threatened to sell Jackson's story to the tabloids if Cosby didn't comply. Cosby strongly denies her claim, although he admits that he had a 1973 "rendezvous" with Jackson's mother and that he set up a special trust fund for his alleged daughter. In August, a jury finds Jackson guilty of extortion, a crime carrying a maximum penalty of 12 years in prison and a $750,000 fine.

NBA rebound king **Dennis Rodman** is suspended for at least 11 games without pay for kicking a TV cameraman sitting courtside. The Chicago Bull is also fined and forks over $200,000 to the injured party.

Olympic figure skating champion **Oksana Baiul**, 19, crashes her Mercedes while reportedly driving 97 mph near her home in Connecticut. The Ukranian-born skater, who is two years younger than the state's drinking age, had a blood-alcohol content of 0.168 at the time of the accident. Baiul is ordered to attend an alcohol education program, but is allowed to keep her license.

FEBRUARY

A Santa Monica civil jury finds **O.J. Simpson** liable in the 1994 deaths of **Ron Goldman** and **Nicole Brown Simpson**. The jury awards Goldman's family $8.5 million in compensation. Ron Goldman's father, **Fred**, tells reporters outside the courthouse: "Our family is grateful for a verdict of responsibility, which is all we ever wanted.... Thank God."

La Liz's gutsy new look.

Later, the plaintiffs seek additional punitive damages, saying that O.J. Simpson is worth at least $15.7 million, which includes the $2 million to $3 million a year he could conceivably earn from signing autographs and writing another book. The defense protests that the earlier verdict left an already tapped-out Simpson $9.3 million in the hole. After nearly six hours of deliberation, the jury awards the estate of each victim $12.5 million from Simpson, for a total of $25 million.

Steffi Graf's father, **Peter Graf**, 58, is sentenced to three years and nine months in prison for evading $7.4 million in taxes on the tennis pro's earnings. The elder Graf had managed the career of his superstar daughter until he ran afoul of the law.

Elizabeth Taylor celebrates her 65th birthday at a star-studded ABC special tribute. Soon after, La Liz undergoes a four-hour operation, during which surgeons remove a 2-inch brain tumor from behind her left ear. "The tumor appears to be benign.... I believe everything went quite smoothly," reports Dr. Martin Cooper, the same neurosurgeon who successfully treated **George Burns** when he suffered head injuries in a 1994 fall.

Star Wars returns to the big screen for its 20th anniversary reissue. The 1977 sci-fi yarn demonstrates the timeless power of the Force as it snags $46.5 million in its first week, exceeding expectations by 40 percent. Licensing for *Star Wars* books, games, and action figures brings in a reported $4 billion more. The film is followed by the remainder of the trilogy, *The Empire Strikes Back* (1980) and *Return of the Jedi* (1983). A prequel trilogy is scheduled for 1999. Meanwhile, studio execs look for other vintage titles to dust off. In March, Paramount reissues *The Godfather* (1972).

Tara Lipinski, 14, becomes the youngest U.S. figure skating champion ever, after she nails a triple loop–triple loop combination during the National Championships. The 4' 8 3/4", 74-pound skater beats **Michelle Kwan**—the reigning champion—with a move never before performed by an American woman in competition.

Achieving what was previously believed as possible only in science fiction, Scottish researchers introduce a new star to biology: **Dolly**, a 7-month-old Finn-Dorset lamb which had begun life not like any other lamb but as a speck of DNA from a mature female sheep of which she is now a perfect copy.

MARCH

In Rancho Santa Fe, Calif., near San Diego, the bodies of 39 men and women are found after a mass suicide in a million-dollar mansion. The members of the **Heaven's Gate** cult, who came from nine states and ranged in ages from 28 to 72, believed their deaths would remove them from Earth, which they believed was corrupt, and give them passage aboard a UFO trailing the Hale-Bopp Comet. They killed themselves by ingesting a deadly cocktail of vodka and tranquilizers mixed with apple sauce or pudding. Plastic bags were placed over their heads to suffocate them. (The last two cultists to die went without the bags.) The victims—wearing matching dark pants and Nikes—were found lying on their backs on cots with large purple shrouds covering their chests and faces. All clutched $5 bills and coins in their hands.

Author-turned-recluse **Arthur C. Clarke**, 79, formally releases his latest novel, *3001: The Final Odyssey*, in a brief ceremony in Sri Lanka, where he has lived since 1956. Clarke's novel concludes the space epic he began in 1968 with *2001: A Space Odyssey*, starring his most famous creation, the psychotic computer HAL. In a live Internet "cybercast" commemorating HAL's birthday, Clarke chooses HAL's first words: "Good morning, doctors. I have taken the liberty of removing Windows 95 from my hard drive."

A New York judge returns custody of former *Home Alone* star **Macaulay Culkin** to his mother, **Patricia Brentrup**, after removing him from his parents' guardianship and turning his finances over to his longtime accountant, **Billy Brietner**. The judge had also declared that the 16-year-old star could use some of his $17 million to save his six siblings and estranged parents from being evicted from their respective homes. Before hearings were to begin at New York State's supreme court, **Kit Culkin** relinquishes custody of the children to their mother, saying that he did not want the children to have to choose.

Former Navy pilot and president of the United States **George Bush**, 72, turns skydiver in Yuma, Ariz., when he jumps from a plane for the first time since the war—that's WWII. The feat is said to have fulfilled a personal desire on the part of the former chief executive. Starting at 12,500 feet, Bush entered into a free fall before pulling the chord on his rainbow-colored parachute at the 4,500-ft. level. He landed perfectly and flashed observers—who included wife **Barbara**—a thumbs-up.

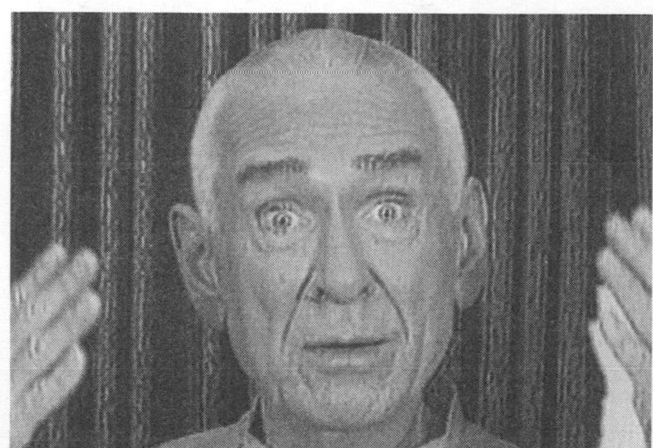

Marshall Applewhite, known as "Do" to his Heaven's Gate clan.

Current president **Bill Clinton** falls a shorter distance than his predecessor but injures his right knee at the Hobe Sound, Fla., home of golf pro **Greg Norman**.

Gangsta rapper **Notorious B.I.G.** is gunned down after a party in Los Angeles. The rapper, whose real name is Christopher Wallace, was leaving a *Soul Train* Awards party when gunfire erupted from a passing vehicle. Wallace, 24, was pronounced dead on arrival at a local hospital. Wallace's killing chillingly replayed the death of **Tupac Shakur**, a former friend turned bitter rival. The two rappers were the central figures of the feud much publicized in the music press between rap's East and West Coast factions. Days later, *Life After Death... 'Til Death Do Us Part* debuts as the last recording by Notorious B.I.G.

Retired pathologist and sometime flutist **Dr. Jack Kevorkian** releases a CD of his own music compositions, a mixture of acid jazz and hard bop. Its title: *A Very Still Life*.

Talk show host **Dick Cavett** suffers Job-like personal tragedy as he is sued for $35 million by a producer claiming Cavett had breached his contract by leaving his new syndicated radio show, apparently because of a recurrence of depression. Soon after, he and his wife **Carrie Nye** learn that their home of 30 years, a $3 million, 115-year-old Montauk, N.Y., mansion designed by the legendary **Stanford White**, had burned to the ground.

Slain gangsta rapper Notorious B.I.G.

APRIL

Per his last request, the ashes of **Timothy Leary**, '60s LSD guru and '90s Internet icon, are blasted into space aboard a Spanish satellite, along with the cremated remains of *Star Trek* creator **Gene Roddenberry** and 22 other extraterrestrial enthusiasts. It is said to be the world's first space funeral.

Trumpeter **Wynton Marsalis** becomes the first jazz musician ever to win a Pulitzer Prize, for the musical composition *Blood on the Fields*, his three-hour oratorio in poems and songs about the black experience.

Seattle-based grunge rock group **Soundgarden** splits up, terming the end of their 12-year union "mutual and amicable." The band, winner of several Grammy Awards, helped pave the way for grunge greats such as **Nirvana** and **Pearl Jam**.

Across the ocean, two French girls, ages 12 and 13, who were Nirvana fans, shoot themselves in the head in a copycat suicide modeled on the 1994 death of lead singer **Kurt Cobain**.

Fifty years after **Jackie Robinson** crossed baseball's color barrier, golf prodigy **Tiger Woods** becomes the first African-American to win a major golf championship. The 21-year-old Woods becomes the youngest person to win the Masters Tournament and, at 270 (and 18 strokes under par), breaks the previous Masters record of 271 that **Jack Nicklaus** and **Raymond Floyd** shared for more than 30 years. In July, Woods wins his fourth tournament of the year with a three-shot victory at the $2 million Western Open, held outside of Chicago.

MAY

Arnold Schwarzenegger undergoes open-heart surgery to replace a faulty aortic valve. "I've never felt sick or had any symptoms at all, but I know I'd have to take care of this condition sooner or later," Schwarzenegger says. The surgery is a success.

Veteran football star and *ABC Monday Night Football* commentator **Frank Gifford**, 66, is caught on hidden video in an intimate encounter with TWA flight attendant **Suzen Johnson**, 46. The incriminating video frames and Johnson's first-person account of the fling, published in the tabloid *Globe*, tarnish the image of Gifford's idyllic marriage to **Kathie Lee Gifford**.

The victim of alleged marital infidelities herself, Gifford's daughter, **Victoria Gifford Kennedy**, separates from husband **Michael Kennedy**, son of the late **Robert F. Kennedy**. Her husband allegedly had a five-year affair with his family's babysitter, which started when she was 14. The girl refused to press statutory rape charges.

Ellen Morgan, the fictional character played by **Ellen DeGeneres** on the ABC sitcom *Ellen*, comes out as a lesbian, and does it "with wit and poignancy," *The New York Times* declares in its lead editorial the following day. Before the "coming-out episode" even airs, the paparazzi probe into DeGeneres's off-screen life. Her relationship with *Volcano* star **Anne Heche** is thrust into the spotlight, and raises concerns about their future careers. Advertisers add further controversy when Wendy's, Chrysler, and J.C. Penney pull out of the breakthrough tube event. The

Tiger Woods masters the Masters.

Ellen DeGeneres and Anne Heche chat up President Clinton.

increased media attention converts into increased viewers for the show (42 million), more than twice its usual audience.

Fellow sportscaster **Marv Albert,** 53, is indicted on charges of sodomy and assault and battery stemming from an alleged incident in Arlington, Va., with a 41-year-old woman. The woman claimed that she was thrown down on the bed and bitten numerous times on her back after visiting Albert in his hotel room in February.

Before Albert's arraignment, he is allowed to wear his toupee while being photographed for mug shots. In August, DNA evidence shows it is virtually certain that Albert was the biter. The sportscaster had agreed to supply the imprint of his teeth for the DNA test. Despite the evidence, Albert's attorney says, "Marv continues to reassert his innocence and will establish it in court."

In late September, Albert changes his plea to guilty and is fired by NBC.

In a man-versus-machine epic, **Garry Kasparov**, 34, loses a six-game chess rematch with IBM's Deep Blue supercomputer, by a score of $3^1/2$–$2^1/2$.

"It's not the first hooker I've helped out," **Eddie Murphy** says after picking up a transvestite male prostitute as undercover sheriff's deputies look on in West Hollywood. Murphy tells *Entertainment Tonight,* "I've seen hookers on corners and I'll pull over and they'll go, 'Oh, you're Eddie Murphy, oh my God,' and I'll empty my wallet out to help. I'm just being a nice guy." Atisone Seiuli, 20, is arrested for prostitution, but authorities say that Murphy did not break the law.

Rock and Roll Hall of Fame icon **Bob Dylan** is hospitalized with a chest infection that causes him to cancel a European tour. The swelling around Dylan's heart is found not life-threatening. Dylan's son **Jakob Dylan**, lead singer of The Wallflowers, puts his own tour on hold to visit his father's bedside.

In August, the fully recovered songwriter is informed that he'll be playing for **Pope John Paul** at a youth rally in September. "The Pope, huh?" said Dylan, "I guess if the Vatican is reporting it, it must be happening. I'm not sure it's going to happen. I know I was the only American they asked, outside of Joni Mitchell." According to Monsignor Ernesto Vecchi, the event will not only be a concert, but "an occasion for the Pope to meet young people." Dylan is 56.

JUNE

After four days of deliberation, a Denver jury finds **Timothy McVeigh** guilty on all 11 federal charges, which included seven counts of first-degree murder as well as conspiracy and use of a weapon of mass destruction. McVeigh was being tried for the 1995 Oklahoma City blast that killed 168 people. At the site of the blast, the worst terrorist act on American soil, survivors and family members of victims greet the verdict with applause. One week later, he is sentenced to death.

Actors **Brad Pitt**, 33, and **Gwyneth Paltrow**, 24, end their Hollywood romance of 2 1/2 years. Although Pitt's publicist claimed the split was mutual, a friend of Pitt's insisted that "Brad called it off."

Luciano Pavarotti, Jose Carreras, and **Placido Domingo** reunite for another gala "Three Tenors" concert. The benefit performance in Pavarotti's home town of Modena, Italy, raises about $1.8 million to help rebuild opera houses devastated by fires in Venice and Barcelona. One face amid the 22,000 spectators belonged to **Michael Jackson**, who is reportedly planning to record a CD with Pavarotti.

In an echo of 1985's "We Are the World" recording extravaganza, music artists congregate at New York's Chelsea Piers to perform what is billed as an "all-star rendition" of **John Lennon**'s famous ballad "Imagine." The lineup includes **The Fugees, Joan Osborne, Busta Rhymes, Amy Grant, Jimmy Cliff, Liza Minnelli, Carole King, Spin Doctors, A Tribe Called Quest**, and model **Kate Moss**. The occasion inaugurates the John Lennon Songwriting Contest, a competition approved by Lennon's widow **Yoko Ono** to promote songwriting and the discovery of new talent.

Timothy McVeigh is convicted and sentenced to death for his role in the 1995 Oklahoma City bombing.

A judge in Ohio clears the way for a trial to determine whether the wrong man was convicted more than 40 years ago in the case of **Dr. Sam Sheppard**, whose story inspired *The Fugitive*. The Cleveland-area osteopath was convicted of second-degree murder in the 1954 death of his wife at their home. Unlike the movie's Richard Kimble, who escapes and finds the real killer, Sheppard did not flee custody. He served 16 years in prison, where he died in 1970.

First Daughter **Chelsea Clinton,** 17, graduates from the preppy Sidwell Friends School in Washington, D.C. After President Bill Clinton delivers a poignant yet concise commencement speech to her classmates, she attends the senior prom, an 11:30 p.m. cruise on the Potomac River. In September, Chelsea attends Stanford University.

Farrah Fawcett appears on *The Late Show with David Letterman* to promote her Playboy Channel TV special. The 50-year-old sex symbol rambles and strains to find simple words, prompting speculations of drug abuse. Fawcett denies the accusations, claiming that her behavior was intentional and meant to be playful.

Joan Lunden announces that she will split from the *Good Morning America* show after 17 years as co-host. While Lunden asserts that she is leaving to spend more time with her children, insiders suspect that ABC may have given her the boot since the show had been lagging in the ratings. She is replaced by Lisa McRee, 35, an anchor in the early '90s for *World News Now,* ABC News' overnight broadcast, and anchor of L.A. affiliate KABC's evening and night newscasts.

At its 6,139th performance, *Cats* celebrates becoming Broadway's longest-running enterprise with a spectacular show—after the theatrical performance. Laser drawings illustrating the history of **T. S. Eliot**'s *Old Possum's Book of Practical Cats* from its 1939 publication to its transformation into an **Andrew Lloyd Webber** musical are viewed over the Winter Garden theater building where *Cats* is performed. Some 8.25 million ticket-buyers have experienced the musical there for the past 15 years.

Matthew Perry, 27, voluntarily checks into a treatment center to battle an addiction to prescription painkillers. His publicist refused to say what medicine the *Friends* star was taking, but did say that he was in the "early stages of chemical dependency." The actor is discharged in early July.

Mike Tyson takes a bite during his rematch with Holyfield.

Tim Allen is placed on a year's probation and fined $500 for driving while impaired. The *Home Improvement* star, who pleaded guilty, was stopped for speeding in a ritzy Detroit suburb and arrested after failing sobriety tests. He called the sentence fair. "My inexcusable lapse in judgment is a mistake that is embarrassing to myself, my family and my associates," Allen said in a statement. "I have learned from this experience, and I am fortunate that my family and associates have forgiven me."

Stars from all fields turn out for a heavyweight bout between **Evander Holyfield** and **Mike Tyson** at Las Vegas's MGM Grand. Among the 16,000 fans: **Sylvester Stallone, Madonna, Tiger Woods, John F. Kennedy Jr.**, and the **Rev. Jesse Jackson**. Holyfield retains his title after Tyson is disqualified for twice biting Holyfield on the ear during the third round. In July, Tyson is banned from the ring and fined $3 million by the Nevada Athletic Commission. The boxer draws the maximum penalty for crossing the "fine line between boxing and chaos," according to the commission.

Prince Charles performs a last rite of empire, handing out British honors in the gilded ballroom of Hong Kong's Government House. Billionaire industrialist **Gordon Wu** and Financial Secretary **Donald Tsang** kneel on a stool specially imported from Buckingham Palace as they are knighted by the royal heir. During the knighting, a police band plays the Beatles' "Yesterday."

The next day, Hong Kong shakes its British rule, becoming a new, autonomous Special Administrative Region of China.

Betty Shabazz, the widow of Black Muslim leader **Malcolm X** and an icon of the civil rights movement, succumbs to burns suffered in a fire set in her Yonkers, N.Y., apartment by her 12-year-old grandson. A month later, **Malcolm Shabazz** enters a plea of guilty to the juvenile equivalent of manslaughter and arson. He faces 18 months or longer in detention.

JULY

Pete Sampras wins his fourth Wimbledon tournament, moving him to within two titles of emulating **Roy Emerson**'s all-time record of 12 grand slams. A month later, Sampras fails to close the gap at the new $254 million Arthur Ashe Stadium at the National Tennis Center in Queens, New York, when he loses to **Petr Korda** in the fourth round. Marking the official opening of the stadium and this year's U.S. Open were 22,000 fans and 38 former champs. Among those in attendance: **John McEnroe, Chris Evert, Billie Jean King, Ivan Lendl, Boris Becker, Steffi Graf**, and 1937 winner **Don Budge**.

The former **Ivana Trump**—whose second marriage was to New York real-estate developer **Donald Trump**—walks out on her third marriage, to Italian jet-setter **Riccardo Mazzucchelli**, less than two years after it began. Ivana's break-up comes only weeks after Donald and the woman who reportedly stole him away from Ivana, **Marla Maples Trump**, announced their own split. It came opportunely for the Donald, just shy of a milestone in their prenup agreement that would have upped Marla's settlement from $1 million to $5 million.

A Los Angeles jury unanimously rebuffs a drug user's claim that he'd been slandered by **Carroll O'Connor** when the television actor blamed him for his son's suicide. The jury deliberated for six hours over two days before finding in O'Connor's favor and against songwriter Harry Perzigian. Perzigian served a short jail sentence after he admitted he'd given cocaine to O'Connor's 32-year-old son, Hugh, who killed himself in 1995. A tearful O'Connor thanked jurors as he left the courtroom: "You did a great job. It cost me a bundle but I was willing to spend the dough. I knew a jury wasn't going to say I was wrong. I know a jury would back me up and you did. I'm very, very grateful."

Italian designer **Gianni Versace**, 50, is shot to death outside his South Beach mansion in Miami Beach, Fla. The renowned fashion figure was gunned down on the steps of his ornate home after he had been walking back from breakfast at a cafe a few blocks away. Suspected gay serial killer **Andrew Philip Cunanan**, 27, caught on tape running from the scene and whose handgun was "definitely" used in two other killings, shoots himself to death in a houseboat just 2½ miles from the Versace villa several days later.

Authorities say Cunanan, who eluded a nationwide manhunt for nearly three months, may have been stalking Versace out of jealousy because he had a crush on the fashion designer's boyfriend Antonio D'Amico, FBI agents, quoting sources, told news magazines. "A person who is using desperate means and exhibiting this kind of violent behavior, you have to be prepared for a very violent conclusion," comments FBI spokeswoman Colleen Crowley. A celebrity-studded memorial service for the designer is held in Milan, Italy at the end of the month.

The late Gianni Versace.

AUGUST

Box-office milestones are reached in the first weekend with *Men in Black* speeding past the $200-million mark and *Air Force One* hitting $55 million at U.S. ticket windows.

In the September issue of *George*, the magazine he founded and edits, **John F. Kennedy Jr.** calls two of his cousins "poster boys for bad behavior." Both **Rep. Joseph P. Kennedy II**, D-Mass., accused by his ex-wife of trying to have their marriage annulled for political expediency, and **Michael Kennedy**, accused of an affair with an underage baby-sitter, "chased an idealized alternative to their life," JFK Jr. says in the signed article. "I guess my first reaction was, 'Ask not what you can do for your cousin, but what you can do for his magazine,'" replies Joe Kennedy, in a reaction to the younger Kennedy's article. In the weeks following, the five-term congressman stuns political observers when he announces he will not run for governor in 1998, but will instead seek re-election to his current seat.

Actor **Christian Slater**, 27, is charged with three counts of assault with a deadly weapon and one count of battery after a quarrel with his girlfriend and a scuffle with Los Angeles police officers. When Slater allegedly punched girlfriend Michelle Jonas repeatedly in the face during a party, an acquaintance stepped in to help and the actor bit him on the abdomen. Police also report that the actor, who said he'd been drinking for days and had taken heroin and cocaine earlier in the day, tried to grab a gun away from an arresting officer. Slater was released on $50,000 bail. Five days after the brawl, Slater issues a statement that he "regrets the events" that led to his arrest and that he "is taking steps to ensure that this kind of thing will not happen again."

Two-time Oscar winner **Anthony Quinn**, 82, settles his bitter divorce case just hours after his son Danny testifies against his father. The proceedings involved Quinn and his second wife **Iolanda**, 62, who battled it out over Quinn's assets, reportedly worth $20 million. Their son, **Danny Quinn**, 33, testified that his father physically and verbally abused his mother whenever she brought up the actor's extramarital affairs. The terms of the settlement were not disclosed, but Mrs. Quinn was reported as being "very happy." Quinn, who has fathered 13 children by two wives and three mistresses, plans to marry a 35-year-old former secretary who is the mother of his two youngest children.

A few days later, Danny Quinn tells *USA Today* that he physically and verbally abused **Lauren Holly**, his former wife and soon-to-be former Mrs. **Jim Carrey**. He also says he deeply regrets his behavior and that now they have an amicable relationship.

Prince Philip, the Duke of Edinburgh, Prince William, Charles, Earl Spencer, Prince Harry, and Prince Charles (far right) march behind Princess Diana's coffin.

SEPTEMBER

Great Britain and the world mourn the death of **Princess Diana**, who died as the result of a car crash in Paris during the wee hours of August 31. Her companion, **Dodi Al Fayed** and the car's chauffeur, Henri Paul, also die in the crash in a tunnel along the Seine.

A week later, Diana's funeral is held at Westminster Abbey—2 billion TV viewers (the largest ever), tune in to watch **Princes William and Harry**, their father, **Prince Charles**, grandfather **Prince Philip**, and uncle, **Charles, Earl Spencer**, follow her casket from Kensington Palace to the Abbey.

Hours after Princess Diana's funeral, Buckingham Palace considered restoring her H.R.H. designation, but her Spencer "blood family" said she wouldn't have wanted to be known after her death as Her Royal Highness. (For more on the death of Princess Diana, see Royals, page 63.)

Church bells peal and anguished wails rise from mourners as **Mother Teresa**'s body is carried in a simple wooden coffin from the Calcutta headquarters of her worldwide charity to nearby St. Thomas's Catholic Church, where the Nobel laureate, who died Sept. 5 at age 87, lies in state. The open coffin in which she rested rode in an ambulance as the vehicle sped the 2 1/2 miles to St. Thomas's on streets cleared of traffic.

In March, Mother Teresa had chosen her successor at her Calcutta mission, the Missionaries of Charity: **Sister Nirmala**, 63, a Hindu convert to Catholicism. Mother Teresa remained in the humanitarian order until her death. First lady **Hillary Rodham Clinton** attends services for Mother Teresa while in New York. Forty-five hundred people—2,000 more than the cathedral's seats could accommodate—filled St. Patrick's Cathedral to celebrate the life and mourn the death of the angel of "God's poorest of the poor," as she was called by Cardinal John O'Connor, who led the service.

Radio host **Howard Stern** refuses to apologize for insulting French-speaking Quebequers on his show, saying, "I can't imagine anybody would take what I say seriously." Stern made his Canadian debut when his New York–based program was broadcast in Montreal and Toronto. He called Francophones "scumbags" and charged that the French collaborated with the Nazis during World War II. The broadcast prompted the Quebec government to suggest Stern was violating a law against stirring up ethnic hatred. At a news conference, Stern said, "The reason you guys have put me on the front page of your newspapers is because I'm the freshest, wildest radio host in the world. You've now been introduced to good radio."

O.J. Simpson moves out of the Brentwood mansion he once shared with his murdered ex-wife. The former football star leaves his home of 20 years for a gated community about a mile east of his old home, which he lost when he fell behind on mortgage payments.

Comedian **Drew Carey**, star of his own eponymous ABC sitcom, says he was sexually molested as a boy and believes the abuse contributed to his severe depression and two suicide attempts. Carey writes about his troubles in his book *Dirty Jokes and Beer: Stories of the Unrefined.* "When I was 9, I was sexually molested," the comedian writes. "Hey, that ought to sell some books, huh? Not even my family knows that."

TRIBUTES

WILLIAM J. BRENNAN JR.

Upon his death, retired Supreme Court Justice William Brennan left a legacy of judicial activism that, even his ideological opponents concede, qualified him as one of the most influential justices in U.S. history. During his 34 years on the high court, he was considered a great champion of individual rights and an unyielding yet genial warrior for the Constitution.

The son of Irish immigrant parents, Brennan was born as the second of eight children in Newark, N.J. His father, William Sr., was a laborer at a local brewery who rose to become a union leader. After graduating from the University of Pennsylvania and Harvard Law School, Brennan went into private practice, then served as a New Jersey jurist until President Eisenhower appointed him to the Supreme Court in 1956.

Brennan put his stamp on such landmark rulings as the doctrine of one person, one vote and the prohibition of prayer in public school. But he never lost his perspective as a man of the people. "He always spoke out for the little guy," Sen. Edward Kennedy said, "Because of Justice Brennan, they have more freedom in their lives."

Brennan died at 91 in a nursing home and was buried in the Arlington National Cemetery.

WILLIAM S. BURROUGHS

During a drunken game in Mexico City, William Burroughs accidentally shot and killed his second wife. The event turned his countenance dark even as it turned a self-indulgent sensualist into an author. "I had no choice," Burroughs once explained, "but to write my way out."

Burroughs's subsequent work included the 1959 experimental novel *Naked Lunch*—a horror account of life in the underworld of drug addiction and crime—and placed him at the center of the Beat Generation movement alongside novelist Jack Kerouac and poet Allen Ginsberg. He died of a heart attack in a Kansas hospital at the age of 83.

Burroughs, a gay, Harvard-educated drug addict whose works were so difficult to read that popular critics initially rejected him, came from prominent Midwestern and Southern families who represented the exact opposite of Burroughs's iconoclastic life. Though his attitude of revolt earned him an immediate place in literary history and a lasting appeal to youth, it was only after the mid-1960s that critics showed him any respect.

His reputation endured long after he left the literary limelight in Paris, London, and New York, and he turned into a recluse in Kansas. "To the end of his life," reported *The New York Times* in its obituary, "Mr. Burroughs remained pessimistic about the future for humankind."

JACQUES COUSTEAU

To Jacques-Yves Cousteau, being underwater was the closest place to heaven on earth. "When you dive," he said, "you begin to feel that you're an angel."

After more than half a century probing—and dramatizing—the secrets of the sea, the environmentalist, 87, succumbed to a respiratory infection and heart problems. More than 40 years after Cousteau's undersea film *The Silent World* won a 1956 Oscar (his TV documentaries also won 40 Emmy nominations), his waterborne achievements made him the most famous and beloved Frenchman on the globe. Called Le Commandant by his countrymen, Cousteau in 1980 was briefly urged to run for president. "His life," said French President Jacques Chirac, "resembles an adventure."

Born in the small town of Saint-André-de-Cubzac, near Bordeaux, Cousteau spent World War II in the Resistance, photographing underwater mine placements and codeveloping the Aqua-Lung, the first independent underwater breathing device. In 1950 Cousteau bought a refitted minesweeper, dubbed it the *Calypso* and used the ship as a command post.

The adventure was not without tragedy, and even a little *scandale.* Cousteau was devastated by the 1979 death, in a seaplane accident, of younger son and chosen heir Phillippe, and later feuded with elder son Jean-Michel, now 59, when the latter tried to put the family name on a resort in Fiji. Following the 1990 death of his first wife, Simone, at 72, the filmmaker wed former flight attendant Francine Triplet, now 45, who had by then given birth to two children by Cousteau (Diane, now 16, and Pierre-Yves, now 14).

Cousteau moved the frontiers of marine biology with only a camera, a boat, and an ocean of curiosity.

DAVID DOYLE

Although theater was his first love, Broadway-trained actor David Doyle never quibbled with the gig that fed him. "*Charlie's Angels* ain't Hamlet," he said about the TV jigglethon that made him famous 21 years ago, "but it sure is entertaining."

His bountifully tressed and scantily dressed costars, who included Farrah Fawcett, Kate Jackson, Cheryl Ladd, and Jaclyn Smith, came and went. But Doyle, who died of a heart attack in Encino, Calif., at age 67, played John Bosley, the avuncular go-between for the gal gumshoes and their unseen titular boss, for the entire series run from 1976 to 1981. As the ABC show became a pop-culture phenom—at its height, 20 million households tuned in—Doyle, as Charlie's only leading male character, was both envied and adored. "I found myself hugging him a lot," costar Jackson says of Doyle. "He was so quick to laugh and smile."

That joie de vivre was hard-won. The son a of a Lincoln, Neb., lawyer, Doyle began performing in community theater at age 10. In 1950 he moved to New York City and later made his Broadway debut in *Will Success Spoil Rock Hunter?* Tragedy struck in 1968 when his first wife, Rachel, died from an accidental staircase fall, leaving Doyle to care for the couple's daughter, Leah, now 35 and a mother of two living on Long Island, N.Y. After marrying Anne Nathan, his castmate in a Lincoln Center revival of *South Pacific,* Doyle moved his family to Los Angeles in 1972. Nathan, now 56, was diagnosed with retinitis pigmentosa, a disease that has left her nearly blind. Yet even in tough times, Doyle, known to a new generation as the voice of Grandpa on Nickelodeon's *Rugrats* cartoon, maintained his good humor. "This," he said of himself, "is one happy man."

CARLO FASSI

As the music ended, Nicole Bobek dropped to her knees on the ice at Lausanne, Switzerland, and buried her face in her hands. She had just finished out of contention for a medal at the World Figure Skating Championships, but that wasn't the source of her grief. Carlo Fassi, the celebrated coach who brought her to the Worlds, had died of a heart attack two days before.

Bobek said later, "I told Carlo I tried and that I loved him." She wasn't alone. Fassi's death at age 67 sent a shock wave through the insular world of figure skating. Peggy Fleming, one of his four Olympic gold medalists (the others were Dorothy Hamill and British skaters John Curry and Robin Cousins), says, "He touched more of my life than I had ever thought. Carlo had the ability to reach into our heads and draw the talent out of us."

Fassi's secret, it seems, was offering his charges unconditional support, along with an extended family that included Christa, his coaching partner and wife of 37 years, and their two sons and one daughter. Cousins says he chose Fassi as his coach not because he could turn him into a champion but because of "promises that I would be leaving my family to join his." Added Bobek, 19, "He took the place of being a dad. If I was dating, he wanted to know who it was—and he wanted to meet him."

A native of Milan and a bronze medalist at the 1953 world championships, Fassi, whose fractured English would remain a source of humor among his pupils and friends, came to the U.S. to help rebuild the national program after top American skaters, coaches, and judges died in a plane crash near Brussels in 1961. In 1968 he produced his first Olympic champion in Fleming. Eight years later Hamill and Curry struck gold, and Cousins won in 1980.

ALLEN GINSBERG

Ironically, the man who made his mark as an agent provocateur left the world as an éminence grise. Allen Ginsberg, 70, the quintessential Beat poet, died of liver cancer. A distinguished professor of English at Brooklyn College, he was a member of the American Academy of Arts and Letters, and charmed public figures from Bob Dylan to Czech President Vaclav Havel. The author of dozens of volumes of poetry, he collaborated with Paul McCartney and Philip Glass, and he was a finalist for the Pulitzer Prize for poetry in 1995. "He was torn between respectability and total rebellion," remarked longtime friend Charles Peters, editor of *The Washington Monthly*.

Ginsberg was the son of the poet and teacher Louis Ginsberg and his wife, Naomi, a Russian-born Marxist. While attending Columbia University, Ginsberg found literary soulmates in ex-jock Jack Kerouac and erudite junkie William S. Burroughs. On Oct. 13, 1955, he read his epic "Howl" in San Francisco, sparking the scandal that defined his life as an artist. A man whose "openness to experience" never faltered, Ginsberg savored his role as a social and political catalyst; after winning the 1957 obscenity trial sparked by "Howl," he was a tireless advocate of free speech. In the '60s he battled the cultural status quo—championing mind-altering drugs and demonstrating against the Vietnam War. A spiritual adventurer, he visited ashrams in India and studied Buddhism in Asia, but he never missed an opportunity to provoke: In 1965, he was deported from Cuba after declaring Ché Guevara to be "cute."

In the end, Ginsberg will be remembered for his selflessness as well as his gleeful spirit: In the '50s he edited and promoted the novels of Kerouac and Burroughs. He quietly supported financially strapped friends, and he always had time to connect with strangers. At a signing in San Francisco last October, Ginsberg (noticeably frail even then) was set to greet fans from noon until 2 p.m. But "people kept streaming in," reports Rani Singh, his assistant. Ginsberg stayed in his seat until 6 p.m.—and every last pilgrim had left with a signed book.

PAMELA HARRIMAN

At the White House Correspondents' Dinner in 1993, Barbra Streisand reportedly slipped into a chair next to the first woman U.S. Ambassador to France, a still-stunning septuagenarian, and whispered, "What's your secret?" Pamela Digby Churchill Hayward Harriman, 76, threw back her elegantly coiffed head and laughed. Whatever her secret was—and there was never any doubt that she had one—it was obviously unique and inimitable. When she died of a stroke after a swim at the venerable Ritz Hotel in Paris, she took that secret with her forever.

She leaves behind an almost mythic legacy of politics and passion, powerful husbands and paramours (Frank Sinatra, Aly Khan and Gianni Agnelli among them), fractious lawsuits and delicious innuendo that have echoed along the corridors of power for five decades. Poised and vivacious, Harriman once described her political influence as that of "a backroom girl."

She aimed high early on. Daughter of the 11th Baron Digby, she was taught that a woman's duty lay in getting and pleasing a husband. At 19, with her eye on greater things, she married Winston Churchill's dissolute son Randolph, 28, a union that produced her only child and secured her a name to open significant doors. At 10 Downing Street, she once said, "it seemed natural for me to be entertaining General Marshall or General Eisenhower." With Randolph away during the war, Pamela entertained more intimately: affairs with millionare diplomat Averell Harriman and newsman Edward R. Murrow, both married themselves.

Pamela divorced Churchill in 1945 and never looked back. In an earlier age she might have been called a courtesan, acquiring lovers from St. Moritz to Palm Springs and amassing money and power in the process. She settled into marriage again with Broadway producer Leland Hayward in 1960. Then, just six months after Hayward's death in 1971, Harriman, a 79-year-old widower, quietly wed the 51-year-old Pamela. When he died in 1986, Harriman left Pamela a sum estimated as high as $75 million.

Alone at 66, Pamela began wielding political clout in her own right. At her Virginia farm and Georgetown home, she charmed Democratic movers and shakers, raising some $12 million for the party. In Paris, after Bill Clinton rewarded Harriman with her ambassadorship in 1993, she entertained an estimated 60,000 people over four years, weaving a skein of friendships for U.S. interests that, says former assistant secretary of state Richard Holbrooke, "made her the best ambassador to France we've had in 30 years."

BRIAN KEITH

He played everything from a homicidal rancher to a stone-faced private detective, but the gruff, burly ex-Marine from Bayonne, N.J., was best known for the steady hand he kept on the family tiller in 1961's *The Parent Trap,* with Maureen O'Hara, and as kindly bachelor Uncle Bill, raising a pair of orphaned nieces and a nephew in his Manhattan apartment on TV's *Family Affair* (1966–71). Sadly, however, Brian Keith's trademark surety evidently faltered in the face of his advanced lung cancer and despair over the death by suicide of his 27-year-old actress daughter, Daisy. Keith, 75, died from the same means as his daughter—a self-inflicted gunshot wound. *Family Affair* alum Johnny Whitaker, 37, recalled Keith "making sure the set was a positive place" for his young costars. "He was as loving and curmudgeonly as always. He was a real Uncle Bill."

MURRAY KEMPTON

When big-city newspaper columnists die, the tributes that follow their passing tend toward adjectives like "colorful" or "two-fisted." When Murray Kempton died, though, his colleagues reached for other words. Kempton, said colorful, two-fisted columnist Jimmy Breslin, was "a lovely human being." And Jim Dwyer, in the *New York Daily News,* wrote of Kempton's mind as "a cabinet of brilliance."

For close to 50 years, Kempton, who was 79 when he died of an apparent heart attack in a Manhattan nursing home, was a beloved anachronism in the brawling world of New York City journalism. Where others scrambled into radio cars to race to a crime scene, Kempton, who had written for *Newsday* since 1981, mounted his three-speed bicycle and pedaled there at his own, more civilized pace. He covered trials and political conventions, funerals, murders, and mobsters. He had a devout mistrust of power and no tolerance at all for conventional wisdom. And he wrote in sentences that meandered elegantly through thickets of metaphor and allusion before returning gracefully to rest at whatever point Kempton had in mind.

The son of a stockbroker who died when Kempton was just 3 and a mother who counted George Mason, one of the authors of Virginia's

Bill of Rights, among her antecedents, Kempton was an only child, born in Baltimore. A 1939 graduate of Johns Hopkins University, he took a job at the *The New York Post*, served in the Pacific in World War II, then returned to the *Post,* where he began tilting at the forest of windmills that would preoccupy him for the rest of his life.

Kempton could find unexpected veins of good. Long after calling for Richard Nixon's resignation, he defended him in print. And the wife of mobster Carmine "The Snake" Persico sent a bouquet to the *Newsday* newsroom for Kempton's 75th birthday; it arrived at the same time as a letter from Cardinal John O'Connor. Said Breslin: "He put more honor in the newspaper business than anyone in our time."

CHARLES KURALT

Charles Kuralt's curiosity about the nooks and crannies of American life made him a standout in a medium that too often passes such places by. A rumpled populist who never lost his sense of wonder, Kuralt, 62, spent most of his 42-year career at CBS celebrating small amazements that others overlooked: the sharecropper who put nine children through college, the 104-year-old distance runner, the poet who spent his days pumping gas. "He did what he did better than anybody else possibly could have," said Charles Osgood, who succeeded Kuralt as host of *CBS News Sunday Morning* in 1994. "There was a humility in his demeanor and an elegance to the language he used."

As indifferent to his appearance as he was polished in his writing, Kuralt seemed an unlikely candidate for broadcast journalism. In the early '60s, Kuralt assuaged his "travel itch" by reporting from Latin America and Africa as well as Asia; he took four trips to Vietnam during the war. In 1967, at the height of the Vietnam War, Kuralt began contributing his "On the Road" segments to the *CBS Evening News*. During his 13-year stint on America's back roads, Kuralt wore out six campers and collected 12 Emmys.

But Kuralt's deteriorating health cut short the ride. Diagnosed with lupus, he died of heart failure at New York Hospital–Cornell Medical Center on Independence Day—a quintessentially American personality gone on the most quintessentially American day.

MARCELLO MASTROIANNI

As Marcello Mastroianni's coffin was carried to a hearse, more than 3,000 admirers jamming the square and adjacent streets burst into applause, and cries of "Ciao, Marcello!" drowned out the sobs. Perhaps it was only fitting that Mastroianni, who died of pancreatic cancer, would have such a Felliniesque farewell. It was his work in Federico Fellini's *La Dolce Vita* and *8 1/2* as well as starring roles in such other classic films as *Divorce—Italian Style* and *La Notte* that secured his reputation as the classically dashing (and, when the script called for it, comical) European lover. Only Mastroianni, who played opposite such exceptional beauties as Sophia Loren (11 times), Brigitte Bardot, and Claudia Cardinale, would ever object to that image and all that it implied. "I am not a sex addict," he once said on American television. For that matter, he claimed during the height of his fame in the late '60s, he was not even handsome: "I have a common face, anonymous—a little peasant face." In fact, Mastroianni was never aristocratic.

He was born in the impoverished village of Fontana Liri near Rome to a cabinetmaker father who went blind from diabetes and a mother who sufferd from arteriosclerosis and grew deaf. In 1950 he married fellow student Flora Carabella, but they separated some 20 years later because of his affairs. Over the course of making more than 130 films in 50 years, he took lovers, including actresses Anouk Aimée, Ursula Andress, Lauren Hutton, Catherine Deneuve, and Cardinale. Faye Dunaway, with whom he costarred in Vittorio De

Sica's 1969 film *A Place for Lovers,* wanted to marry him and have his children, but Mastroianni, a Catholic, refused to divorce his wife.

Shortly before finishing his final film, Manoel de Oliveira's *Journey to the Beginning of the World,* the dying Mastroianni gave an interview to the French magazine *Paris Match*. "I've loved [life] so much," he said. "When you get to my age, you realize life has slipped by...I just got here, and already I have to leave. It's absurd."

ROBERT MITCHUM

Charisma? Not exactly. Talent? Without a doubt. But what really set Robert Mitchum, 79, who succumbed to the effects of emphysema and lung cancer, apart from almost every actor of his or any other generation was a certain mystique. With his droopy bedroom eyes, lush baritone voice, and burly, don't tread-on-me physique, he embodied the scary, thrilling nexus where violence and sensuality become one. And somehow he did it with a cool nonchalance that never failed to charm. He has a secure reputation as one of the more venerated stars in the Hollywood firmament, an icon who never took himself or the movie business too seriously. Famously hard-drinking, profane, and with a love of fisticuffs, Mitchum nonetheless was sufficiently devoted to his craft that he continued to make movies right up to the time of his death. Perhaps more notable, the hunky sex symbol managed to stay married to his wife, Dorothy, for 57 years.

Mitchum received his only Oscar nomination for the heroic Lieutenant Walker in the 1945 film *The Story of G.I. Joe*. But his defining roles were in the noir classics *Crossfire* and *Out of the Past* and in his eerie portrayals of murderous psychopaths in *The Night of the Hunter* and *Cape Fear*. "You could say that Mitchum *was* film noir," says director Martin Scorsese.

In the end, Mitchum remained true to the persona he had worn as comfortably as an old trench coat throughout his life: unsentimental, but never humorless. In *Out of the Past* he utters one of the great fade-out lines in movie history, one that could serve not only as his own epitaph, but also of a bygone era. Jane Greer tells him, "I don't want to die." Replies the laconic Mitchum: "Neither do I, baby...But if I do, I want to die last."

MOTHER TERESA

Clad in the blue and white cotton sari of the Missionaries of Charity, the Roman Catholic order she founded in 1950, Mother Teresa was physically slight—she stood less than 5 feet tall—but tough as oak. Large, strong hands spoke of hard labor, and her stamina rarely flagged. She suffered heart attacks in 1983 and 1989, and both times was back at work within weeks. She was felled by cardiac arrest at the age of 87.

Born in Skopje, Macedonia, to an Albanian couple, Agnes Gonxha Bojaxhiu was one of three children. Her building-contractor father died when she was around 7, and her devout family, previously prosperous, was reduced to genteel poverty. At 12 Agnes felt a calling to help the poor; at 18, in 1928, she joined the Sisters of Loreto, a community of Irish nuns known for their missionary work. After taking the name of the 19th-century French nun St. Thérèse of Lisieux and training in Dublin and Darjeeling, India, the new Sister Teresa taught upper-class Bengali girls at St. Mary's High School in Calcutta, and eventually became the school's principal. In 1946, while on a train ride from Calcutta to Darjeeling, she received what she took to be a divine message. "I was to give up all," she wrote in her 1995 book *A Simple Path,* "and follow Jesus into the slums."

It took two years before she persuaded the Vatican to let her leave the cloister, live among the poor, and begin her work in Calcutta's streets. Her first Home for the Destitute and Dying, dedicated to providing compassionate care for the abandoned, was in the city's teeming Kalighat district. During the next 47 years, her order grew to include 5,000 nuns and brothers operating more than 2,500 orphanages, schools, clinics, and hospices in over 120 countries, including the U.S.

The reach of her influence seemed never to change her. Until illness forced her in 1996 to alter her daily routine, she rose at 4:30 each morning and kept to a frugal diet of rice and vegetables. All the donations and monetary awards that came to her—including the more than $190,000 that accompanied her 1979 Nobel Peace Prize—went to fund new orphanages, hospices, and homes for those suffering from leprosy.

Other sacrifices were more personal. When her mother lay dying in Albania in the 1970s, Mother Teresa decided, for the sake of her work, not to return home after Communist dictator Enver Hoxha refused to guarantee her safe passage out of the country. Not until 1989 did she return to Albania. Says biographer Kathryn Spink: "The first thing she did was to lay flowers on her mother's grave. She then laid flowers on Enver Hoxha's grave as a gesture of forgiveness and reconciliation."

"What one has to understand in Mother Teresa," Spink once added, "is that she sees Christ in every person she encounters. I have heard her say that every human being must be given the opportunity to do good." Certainly when her opportunity came, she made the most of it.

NOTORIOUS B.I.G.

You could tell by his funeral that Biggie Smalls was a complicated man. In 24 years he had already packed in three lives—as a shy, overweight kid, a small-time crack dealer, and a renowned rap artist—and two nicknames. Besides Biggie, Christopher Wallace was, of course, also known as the Notorious B.I.G. At his wake, hip-hop singer Faith Evans, Wallace's estranged widow and mother of one of his two children, belted a gospel tune while his rumored girlfriend, singer Lil' Kim, listened. And then there was the matter of his message. Wallace, who was shot dead on March 9 as he sat in a car in L.A., called his albums *Ready To Die* and *Life After Death... 'Til Death Do Us Part*. But his fans took away more from his music than danger and morbidity. As they waited for his hearse to pass, two little girls sat on a car roof across from the Brooklyn apartment where the late rapper had grown up, clutching a sign that said: "WE LOVE YOU BIGGIE, SAVE OUR YOUTH, STOP THE VIOLENCE."

Whatever the circumstances of his death, for many people Wallace remains a hero for symbolizing what is possible. "It's not good to glorify gangstas," said Cordell Patterson, 26, as he watched the rapper leaving his old neighborhood one last time. "But he showed a lot of people from the streets that you can change. And he was trying to make the biggest change in his life right at the time of his death."

COL. TOM PARKER

Col. Tom Parker liked to brag about his old carny days when he'd hide a $2 hot plate in a chicken cage, stick in the plug, and charge customers to see his incredible dancing birds. During the 22 years that Parker served as shot caller and dealmaker for Elvis Presley, he still liked to keep the heat on. When he died in Las Vegas of complications from a stroke, Presley's lifelong manager had become a sort of show business legend himself.

Famous for his flamboyantly bad taste (evident in the Hawaiian shirt he wore to Presley's 1977 funeral and the cheesy Elvis trinkets he sold by the truckload), Parker also tried to shroud his past in myth. It is believed he was born Andreas van Kuijk in Holland in 1909, that he entered the U.S. illegally around 1930 and joined a traveling carnival called the Great Parker Pony Circus. Turning his barker's skills to promoting country music acts on tour in Florida, the Colonel

—the title was an honorarium given him in 1948 by Louisiana Gov. Jimmie Davis, an ex-country singer he knew from his carny days—managed singers Eddy Arnold and Hank Snow before meeting Elvis in 1955. Then 20, acned, and unknown, Presley signed up after extolling the Colonel's virtues to his parents. Parker promptly moved the rocker from Sun Records to RCA; engineered three star-making TV appearances on *The Ed Sullivan Show*; and, before long, began mapping his way to Hollywood.

Yet while he brokered deals that would earn Presley $35 million by 1964, Parker's contracts steered up to 50 percent of his star's income into his own pockets. And for all his business savvy, he made some colossal blunders, especially in 1973 when he bargained off the rights to Presley's priceless music catalog for a paltry $5 million. He also encouraged Elvis to appear in a string of mindless, pretty-boy rock movies that both enriched and embarrassed the star. At the same time he toned down Presley's rebellious image and rocking sound, encouraging him to record only made-for-the-movies music.

In 1981, notorious gambler Parker was accused by the court-appointed guardian of Presley's daughter Lisa Marie of enriching himself at the singer's expense. Although a Memphis court stripped him of any legal rights to the Presley estate, Parker subsequently patched up his differences with Lisa Marie and her mother, Priscilla Presley.

Left a widower by the 1980 death of his first wife, Marie, Parker married a former RCA secretary, Loanne, now 61, and retired.

PAT PAULSEN

It was 1996. Bob Dole was running for president. So was Pat Paulsen. Again. Dole floated an idea he thought would put him into the White House—slash federal taxes by 15 percent. Paulsen had his own notion. "I think we should just tip the government if it does a good job," he said. "Fifteen percent is the standard tip, isn't it?"

For almost 30 years, Paulsen had a Pat solution to the nation's problems—or at least a memorable comment. When the dour-faced comic died at age 69 in Tijuana, Mexico, where he was undergoing alternative therapy for colon and brain cancer, he took an election-year institution with him. This was, after all, the man who once told reporters, "I've upped my standards. Now, up yours." During Watergate, Paulsen double-talked his way to the heart of the matter. "The fault lies not with the individual but with the system," he intoned, "and that system is Richard Nixon."

Paulsen's Stassen-esque political career—he ran for president five times—began in 1968 at the urging of Tom and Dick Smothers, on whose TV show he appeared. "Why not?" he responded. "I can't dance."

Running as the candidate of the Straight Talkin' American Government Party (the STAG party), "Pat would go into every city and tell the people how the rest of the country were jerks and how, when the campaign was over, he'd settle in their city," says Ken Kragen, Paulsen's former manager. "Toward the end of the '68 campaign we started worrying that Pat was going to get too many votes, so we went on the air and asked people not to vote for him. Despite that, he got like 200,000 votes."

Paulsen had a more colorful life than many of his backers imagined. Born in South Bend, Wash., and raised in Point Bonita, Calif., he served in the Marines during World War II. While at City College of San Francisco, where he majored in forestry, he joined the Ric-Y-Tic Players theater troupe. He was juggling stints as a gypsum miner, Fuller Brush man, and performer when he met the Smothers brothers in the mid-'60s. They hired him to write faux-folk songs, and in 1967 he became a regular on the their show. In 1968, Paulsen won an Emmy.

"He was like nobody else," says Tommy Smothers,

who remained a close friend. "He was a natural put-on artist."

MARGRET REY

A Cambridge, Mass., neighbor once asked Hans Rey how he survived life with his strong-willed wife, Margret, cocreator of the Curious George children's books. "Easy," replied the soft-spoken Hans, "Years ago, we decided that I make all the big decisions and she makes the small decisions. So far in our marriage, there haven't been any big decisions."

As an illustrator, Hans gave the trouble-prone George his mischievous look. But it was author Margret, who died at 90 following a heart attack, who endowed George with his irrepressible soul—having him blithely wreak havoc one moment, before saving the day in the next. Barely 5 feet tall, Rey posed as a human model for her husband's simian paintings, scrunching up her face and even jumping from chair to chair. "She was always unpredictable and doing things creatively," says Nader Darehshori of Houghton Mifflin, publisher of the series since 1941. "Often, I thought she *was* Curious George."

Born in Hamburg, Rey, the daughter of a German Parliament member, and her husband were living in Paris when a publisher asked them to write a children's book. When the Nazis invaded a year later, in 1940, the two fled by bicycle with their unsold manuscript and drawings stuffed in their pockets.

After Hans's death in 1977, Margret devoted herself to their only offspring—Curious George. With a new collaborator, she churned out 28 books and licensed the monkey's image for dolls and a TV show. She was inspired, it seemed, less by the money than by a romantic attachment to her late husband. Said Darehshori: "She looked at George as something special to both of them."

MIKE ROYKO

There's only one way to talk about Mike Royko, 62, and that's by telling a story. So here's the one about a young guy who drops out of college to join the Air Force in 1952. After he's given the choice of being a cook or an MP, he ends up editing the base newspaper. Why did he choose that, someone later asked? Because, Royko replied, "It struck me that any goof could write a newspaper story."

Perhaps. But no goof ever did it with the gritty brilliance of Mike Royko, the premier journalist of working-class America. Five times a week he gave his voice to the wage earner while scalding big business and political power brokers, most memorably former Chicago Mayor Richard J. Daley, whom he skewered in his 1971 book *Boss*. For 33 years his column, first in the *Chicago Daily News*, then the *Sun-Times* and finally the *Tribune* (and syndicated to 800 papers nationwide), was devoured as avidly as his city's deep-dish pizza. As his longtime friend and fellow Chicagoan Studs Terkel put it, "He wrote about those who keep the wheels of the world going." Royko knew that world firsthand.

Born to a Ukranian-immigrant father and a first-generation Polish-American mother, he grew up in a flat above the tavern in Chicago that his parents ran. A widower who remarried in 1986, Royko was devoted to his four children. But he also, famously, loved his drinking and gossiping sessions at his favorite watering hole, the Billy Goat Tavern, and he could throw a mean punch. Given his particular genius, it is tempting to regard Royko, a Pulitzer Prize winner, as a kind of blue-collar bard. He, of course, would have rejected that title as way too fancy. "You really can't take flattery or criticism too seriously," he once said. "We're talking about a newspaper column. Costs two bits...I'm just a part of it."

CARL SAGAN

When scientists announced last summer that they had potential evidence of ancient life on Mars, no one was more excited than Carl Sagan, 62. For decades he had scoured the heavens for any credible sign that life existed elsewhere in the vastness of the universe. Along the way he became America's best-known popularizer of science, an astronomer with a touch of the poet and a voice that seemed to have a separate control for "awe." In *Cosmos,* Sagan guided millions of people through the galaxies. "I like to explain science because it's like being in love," he once said. "When you're in love you want to tell the world."

And he did. Sagan wrote 22 books and won the Pulitzer Prize for *The Dragons of Eden: Speculations on the Evolution of Human Intelligence,* a 1978 nonfiction work. A screen adaption of his 1984 sci-fi novel, *Contact,* became a 1997 film starring Jodie Foster and Matthew McConaughey.

Sagan grew up in Brooklyn, "one step out of poverty," as he once put it, the son of a homemaker and a garment cutter. Earning undergraduate and graduate degrees from the University of Chicago, he established his credentials early with research that helped prove that the surface of Venus, despite its cloud cover, was burningly hot. He also distinguished himself as a teacher. "He had a wonderful enthusiasm and ability to communicate," recalls NASA space director David Morrison, who in the early '60s was one of Sagan's first graduate students. By 1969, Sagan had risen to the post he would occupy for the rest of his life, professor of astronomy and director of the Laboratory of Planetary Studies at Cornell University. He drew wide attention with his work for *Pioneer 10,* the 1972 NASA probe designed to depart the solar system and press on into interstellar space. Fixed to its exterior is a gold anodized plate that bears a greeting, in maps and symbols, to any extraterrestrials who might see it (it's now beyond the solar system). Sagan later took on crusades against nuclear weapons and environmental threats.

Even as he saw the end approaching, Sagan, who wrote the entry on "Life" in the *Encyclopedia Britannica,* held an unflinching notion of its eternity. He expected that his matter and energy would be dispersed after death throughout the cosmos. Given all that he was in life, that would be a lot of energy.

BETTY SHABAZZ

At the 1996 Democratic National Convention, a congressional aide was shocked to find Betty Shabazz, the widow of Black Muslim leader Malcolm X and an icon of the civil rights movement, standing in line to gain entry instead of avoiding the wait by using a VIP ticket. "That tells you something about her," says close friend Eleanor Holmes Norton, who adds, "It was not mandated that she get out and work every day as if her life depended on it. But that's what she did."

And more. For 32 years, Shabazz toiled tirelessly to preserve her late husband's legacy, his faith in the power of black self-sufficiency. That work ended when, at 63, she died from burns suffered in a fire apparently set in her Yonkers, N.Y., apartment by her 12-year-old grandson. Shabazz, who grew up in a middle-class Methodist home in Detroit, said it was by emulating her husband's self-discipline that she had succeeded in singlehandedly raising her six daughters after Malcolm was gunned down in front of her on Feb. 21, 1965, in New York City's Audubon Ballroom. She went on to earn a doctorate in education administration and to carve out a career as an educator at Medgar Evers College in Brooklyn, where she was known as Doctor Betty. "Our mother has made a transition—I like to think of it as that," says oldest daughter Attallah, 35. "She's boundless where she is."

JIMMY STEWART

When Jimmy Stewart died, some of the music of mid-century America died with him. He had suffered for years from failing health and heart problems, but friends say that Stewart, 89, had simply lost all interest in living since the death three years ago of his wife of 45 years, Gloria.

In 75 feature films, including *Mr. Smith Goes to Washington, Harvey, Rear Window, Vertigo,* and *Anatomy of a Murder,* Stewart took his place in the first rank of leading men of Hollywood's golden age. And with the classic *It's a Wonderful Life,* he became a staple of America's holiday season. Yet onscreen and in life, he appeared to be utterly unassuming, a man who made being ordinary the most appealing thing in the world.

He grew up the son of a prosperous hardware store owner in Indiana, Pa., and graduated Princeton with a degree in architecture.

To his female costars, Stewart's ordinariness was an irresistable appeal. He counted Loretta Young, Norma Shearer, Ginger Rogers, Marlene Dietrich, Olivia de Havilland, and Dinah Shore among his companions. Stewart's appeal extended to the Academy as well. His performance in *The Philadelphia Story* in 1940 brought him the Oscar for best actor. He followed the acclaimed hit with another stellar performance—in World War II. Stewart flew more than 20 missions over Germany and France, mostly as a squadron commander. He returned home a colonel with a Distinguished Flying Cross.

Stewart's first postwar project was *It's a Wonderful Life.* Although he received his third Oscar nomination, the movie was such a flop that critics heralded the collapse of Stewart's career. He replied with the comedy hit *Harvey,* the violent, angry Westerns of Anthony Mann (*Winchester '73, The Naked Spur*), the tilted dramas of Alfred Hitchcock (*Rear Window, Vertigo*), and Otto Preminger's *Anatomy of a Murder.*

These days a whole generation of young actors can be caught playing Jimmy Stewart. What they seem to want is to be like him—a man as simple and straightforward as the alphabet but with just as many possibilities. Jimmy Stewart once proposed his own epitaph: "He gave people a lot of pleasure." No matter what they may carve into his tombstone, those words will be his legacy.

BRANDON TARTIKOFF

Years before his brilliant 11-year run as president of NBC Entertainment, in a fiction-writing seminar at Yale, Brandon Tartikoff suggested how the plot of a D. H. Lawrence short story could be jazzed up. The professor, Pulitzer Prize–winning author Robert Penn Warren, said, "Young man, have you ever considered a career in television?"

Advice has seldom been sounder. In 1980, when he was 31, Tartikoff became the youngest person ever put in charge of network programming; he proceeded to take NBC from worst to first in the Nielsen ratings. Ideas for shows came to him in the middle of the night (*The Cosby Show*) or while visiting his elderly Aunt Lil in Miami (*The Golden Girls*). With *Hill Street Blues,* says NBC Sports' Dick Ebersol, "Brandon brought the great ensemble drama, with multiple story lines, to TV."

Following a head-on collision in 1991, Tartikoff made a career move that shocked Hollywood: he accepted a job as head of Paramount Pictures. But after running the studio for only a year and a half, he resigned to spend more time with his family. He eventually drifted back to work, creating shows with local TV stations and developing an entertainment Website site for America Online. In November 1996 he noticed a swelling on his neck.

The swelling was a recurrence of the lymphatic system cancer known as Hodgkin's disease. Tartikoff had battled the disease in 1974 and 1982; the cancer again went into remission, but his immune system was severely weakened. "None of us faced cancer three times and beat it," says Ebersol. "None of us had to go through the car accident. Yet he stayed warm, graceful and always funny. He was the gutsiest man I ever knew."

PAUL TSONGAS

More than anything, Paul Tsongas had a sense of responsibility. Struck by cancer in 1983, the U.S. senator walked away from his dream job and went home to

Lowell, Mass., with his wife and three daughters. As he launched his long-shot bid for the presidency in 1991, his lymphoma in remission, Tsongas made it clear that the issues of fiscal responsibility and personal sacrifice he chose to run on were inspired by the obligation he felt to that family. "They're going to lay me in the ground one day," he told *The Boston Globe*. "I want to do the things [that will make] my grandchildren feel good about me."

Tsongas, 55, died of pneumonia brought on by complications from his cancer treatment. "He battled through his own illness...to fight for America's well-being, and our country is deeply indebted to him," reflected President Bill Clinton. It was a gracious tribute to the socially liberal, economically conservative Tsongas, who once dismissed Clinton, running against him for president, as a fast-talking "panda-bear." Tsongas sharpened his wit—and his sense of morality—in a family of hard-working Greek immigrants. Educated at Dartmouth and Yale Law School, Tsongas was a moderate Republican until his opposition to the Vietnam War prodded him leftward. Elected to Congress as a Democrat in 1974, he moved to the Senate four years later and was on the fast track until cancer struck in 1983. Although it went into remission and he received bone-marrow transplants, the battle proved overwhelming. He will be remembered for his brave fight against illness, but Tsongas's greatest appeal was his decency.

GIANNI VERSACE

During two decades at the epicenter of the design world, Gianni Versace, 50, became known for a mischievous attitude almost as provocative as his cutting-edge clothes. After launching himself toward the fashion stratosphere with his first collection under his own name in 1978, Versace walked a tightrope between vulgarity and chic, opulence and camp. "If you're unhappy and you don't have a positive attitude, what good is being chic?" he once said.

It was a motto he lived by away from the catwalk as well as from his quiet retreat home in Italy to his flashy villa in Miami. In the last decade, Versace became known as "the rock and roll designer," partly due to his extensive use of leather, rubber, shiny metal, slits, and bondage design elements, and partly due to his friends (and sometimes ad campaign stars) Madonna, Courtney Love, The Artist Formerly Known As Prince, Sting, Jon Bon Jovi, and most famously and intimately, Elton John. Again, Versace knew his image even better—"half royalty, half rock and roll," he called his luxe mix—and indeed, his clothes also appealed to more regal types like Princess Diana, Warren Beatty, and Elizabeth Hurley.

The son of a seamstress and an appliance salesman from dirt-poor Reggio di Calabria in southern Italy, he had amassed a fortune estimated at $800 million with his off-the-rack evening fantasies that could sell for as much as $20,000.

Versace was possessed by a lifelong dream of beauty—which he shared with anyone who ever coveted the kitten-soft caress of velvet or the exquisite feel of silk against skin. "As a boy I dreamed of exactly what came to pass, of what I am doing now," Versace told PEOPLE in 1986. "I am happy, and every day I say, thanks, God, life is beautiful."

★

Edwin Haig Alberian, 77, who played Clarabelle the clown for a decade on TV's *Howdy Doody,* of pneumonia, in New Jersey.

Blues guitarist **Luther Allison**, 57, who played over his three-decade career with other greats of the genre, including Freddie King and Otis Rush, of lung and brain cancer in Madison, Wis.

Baseball's **Richie Ashburn**, 70, the Hall of Fame centerfielder who played with the Philadelphia Phillies most of his career, died of a heart attack in New York City. He had worked as a Phillies announcer for 35 years.

Thomas the Tank Engine author **Rev. Wilbert Awdry**, 85, in Stroud, England.

Songwriter **Mae Boren Axton**, 82, coauthor of "Heartbreak Hotel," and the mother of singer-songwriter Hoyt Axton, of undisclosed causes in Hendersonville, Tenn.

LaVern Baker, 67, the gutsy rhythm and blues belter who went to the top of the charts in the '50s and '60s with "Jim Dandy" and "Tweedle-Dee," in New York, of a heart ailment.

Jean-Dominique Bauby, 44, of complications from an infection. The *Elle* editor, who had been paralyzed by a stroke-induced trauma to the brain stem, passed away two days after completing a memoir of his "locked-in syndrome." The memoir, *The Diving Bell and the Butterfly*, was dictated through 200,000 blinks of his left eyelid—one of the only body parts still under his control.

Actor **John Beal**, 87, of complications from a stroke, in Santa Cruz, California. Beal, whose career on Broadway and in Hollywood spanned six decades, also appeared on TV shows including *The Waltons, Kojak*, and *Another World.*

Bebe, 40, the last of the seven bottlenose dolphins to star in the popular TV series *Flipper,* at the Miami Seaquarium. She gave birth to her eighth calf, Echo, last year.

Richard Berry, 61, who wrote the hypnotically choppy three-chord wonder, "Louie Louie," of an aortic aneurysm in L.A.

Actor **Donald T. Bexley**, 87, who played Redd Foxx's sidekick Bubba Hoover on the '70s sitcom *Sanford and Son,* of heart and kidney failure in Hampton, Va.

Sir Rudolf Bing, 95, of undisclosed causes in Yonkers, N.Y. Bing was general manager of the Metropolitan Opera in New York City from 1950 to 1972 and helped establish it as one of the world's pre-eminent opera companies.

Magician **Harry Blackstone**, 62, whose stage shows were a legacy of an earlier era, from complications of pancreatic cancer.

Actor **Sally Blane**, 87, who appeared in more than 80 movies from 1917 to 1954, of undisclosed causes in Palm Springs, Calif. She starred with Rudy Vallee in *The Vagabond Lover* (1929) and with Don Ameche and her sister Loretta Young in *The Story of Alexander Graham Bell* (1939).

Photojournalist **Horace Bristol**, 88, whose *LIFE* magazine photographs captured the suffering of migrant workers escaping the Oklahoma dust bowl in 1938, of colon cancer in Ojai, California. For the project, Bristol recruited author John Steinbeck, who later turned his notes into the 1939 novel *The Grapes of Wrath*.

Christopher Buckley, 81, who pioneered the use of aluminum cans for foods and beverages, in Cheshire, Connecticut.

Alternative rocker **Jeff Buckley**, 30, in Memphis. Buckley drowned while swimming in the Mississippi

River. Police saw no sign of drug or alcohol abuse, though his demise recalled that of his father, folk singer Tim Buckley, who died at 28 from an accidental overdose.

San Francisco Chronicle columnist **Herb Caen**, 80, whose daily jottings about life in the city won him a Pulitzer Prize in 1996, of lung cancer in San Francisco. Caen wrote his column for nearly 60 years and also produced 12 books.

Jeanne Calment, 122, whom the *Guinness Book of World Records* lists as the oldest person on the planet, in Arles, France. Calment credited her good health to olive oil and port wine.

Joe Camel, 23, cigarette trademark character. His creator, the R.J. Reynolds Co., pulled the plug.

Big band singer **Thelma Carpenter**, 77. Carpenter sang with jazz greats such as Coleman Hawkins and Count Basie, appeared in the film *The Wiz* (1978) and on Broadway as Pearl Bailey's standby in *Hello, Dolly!* in the 1968–69 production.

Adriana Caselotti, 80, the voice of Snow White in Disney's classic 1937 cartoon *Snow White and the Seven Dwarfs*, of cancer, in her L.A. home.

Cultural patron **Dorothy "Buffy" Chandler**, 96, widow of *Los Angeles Times* publisher Norman Chandler and mother of publisher Otis Chandler. The Dorothy Chandler Pavilion of the L.A. Music Center is where the Oscars are frequently held.

Aldolphus "Doc" Cheatham, 91, for seven decades an influential jazz trumpeter, in Washington, D.C., following a stroke.

Gerda Christian, 83, Adolf Hitler's favorite secretary because of her devotion and Aryan looks, of cancer in Dusseldorf, Germany. Christian, who was a Hitler loyalist to her death, once recalled, "I can't complain. Hitler wasn't such a bad boss to his staff."

Original *Romper Room* hostess (and Magic Mirror waver) **Nancy Claster**, 82, of cancer, in Baltimore.

Pat Collins, 62, the "hip hypnotist" who once hypnotized Lucille Ball on a segment of *The Lucy Show* and counted Ball, Robert Wagner, and other stars among her friends, in San Bernadino, Calif. She had been in ill-health for several years following a stroke.

Washington Redskins owner **Jack Kent Cooke**, 84, who in his 23 years as the football team's majority owner turned it into a three-time Super Bowl champion, after suffering a heart attack at his Washington home. A self-made millionare, Cooke started out selling encyclopedias door-to-door during the Depression, and by age 31, had amassed a media empire consisting of radio stations, newspapers, and magazines. A one-time owner of basketball's L.A. Lakers and hockey's L.A. Kings, he bought New York City's Chrysler Building.

Texas blues musician **Johnny Copeland**, 60, in New York, of complications during surgery to repair a heart valve.

Thalassa Cruso, 88, of gardening advice fame (she wrote 1960's wildly popular *Making Things Grow*), of complications from Alzheimer's, in Wellesley, Mass.

Bao Dai, 83, the last emperor of Vietnam, in Paris. After abdicating in 1945 under pressure from Ho Chi Minh, Dai was restored to power by the French in 1949, only to be deposed in 1955.

Actor **Gail Davis**, 71, who played TV's popular pigtailed title character in *Annie Oakley* from 1955-58, of cancer, in Los Angeles. She laid rightful claim to headlining the first Western to star a woman.

Charles Dederich, 83, a recovering alcoholic who in 1958 founded Synanon, the controversial drug rehabilitation program, of cardiorespiratory failure in Visalia, Calif. Although thousands of addicts eventually passed through his program, Dederich was fined, sentenced to five years' probation, and stripped of his role in running Synanon in 1980 after pleading no contest to charges that he had conspired to murder a lawyer who had sued the organization.

Willem de Kooning, 92, the abstract expressionist who became one of the 20th century's greatest painters, in his East Hampton, N.Y., studio, of complications from Alzheimer's. De Kooning's works stressed the depiction of emotion through shapes and colors, incorporating traces of the surrealist movement and prefiguring pop art. His meticulously composed 1944 *Pink Lady* sold for $3.63 million in 1987. Two years later his 1955 masterpiece *Interchange* sold for $20.6 million.

China's supreme leader, **Deng Xiaoping**, who by official accounts was 93, of respiratory and circulatory failure in Beijing. A lifelong Communist and onetime guerilla leader, he succeeded Mao Tse-tung as government head after a two-year power struggle following Mao's death in 1976. Deng is credited with opening China to foreign trade and private enterprise but is also believed to have ordered the brutal crackdown on prodemocracy student demonstrators in Tiananmen Square in 1989.

Poet, author, and critic **James Dickey**, 73, who wrote the bestselling novel *Deliverance* and the screenplay for the movie based on it, of complications from lung disease in Columbia, S.C. An Army pilot in World War II, Dickey was an avid outdoorsman and musician who produced some 20 volumes of poetry.

Astrologer and self-described psychic **Jeane Dixon**, 79, of a heart attack in Washington. In 1956, Dixon was quoted in *Parade* magazine as saying that a tall, young, brown-haired, blue-eyed Democrat would be elected president in 1960 and would die in office. While that prognostication later catapulted her to fame, some of Dixon's predictions—that World War III would break out in 1958 and that the Soviets would put the first person on the moon—came to naught.

Young readers author **Michael Dorris**, 52, who also wrote *The Broken Cord*, a memoir of his struggles with an adopted son with fetal alcohol syndrome. Dorris took his own life in Vermont.

Blondie illustrator **Stan Drake**, 75, in Connecticut, after a long illness.

Burlesque and Broadway performer **Joey Faye**, 87, of a heart attack in Englewood, N.J. Faye played second banana to such stars as Phil Silvers and Gypsy Rose Lee and appeared as the dancing grapes in Fruit of the Loom television commercials during the '80s.

Nigerian musician **Fela Anikulapo-Kuti**, 58, of AIDS complications. Fela was the creator of the genre known as Afro-beat, which combined traditional African music with American funk and jazz.

George Fenneman, 77, Groucho Marx's straight-faced sidekick on TV's *You Bet Your Life* (1950–61), of complications related to emphysema, in Los Angeles.

Italian director **Marco Ferreri**, 68, in Paris of a heart attack. *La Grande Bouffe* (1973) was the best known of his many films.

Former St. Louis Cardinals center fielder **Curt Flood**, 59, who fought one of the most significant legal battles in sports history, of throat cancer in Los Angeles. Though Flood's challenge to baseball's "reserve system," which bound players to their teams unless traded or sold, was rejected by the Supreme Court in 1972, it led eventually to free agency.

Edith Forc, 81, a retired school nurse who became

famous for uttering the line "I've fallen, and I can't get up" in nationally televised commercials for LifeCall, a medic-alert system.

"Wino Willie" Forkner, 76, the central figure in a biker gang that inspired the 1954 Marlon Brando movie *The Wild One,* of a ruptured aortic aneurysm in Santa Rosa, Calif.

Jolie Gabor, 97, socialite and mother of Hungarian-born actors Eva (*Green Acres*) and Zsa Zsa, in Rancho Mirage, Calif., of natural causes.

Magda Gabor, 79, the least famous member of the glamour-girl dynasty, of kidney failure in Rancho Mirage, Calif. Unlike her older siblings, Magda only had a brief acting career.

David Gallo, 57, the elder son of Ernest Gallo and co-president of the E&J Gallo Winery, of an apparent heart attack.

Former auto-leasing executive **Loras Goedken**, 52, the hemophiliac whose family is believed to be the hardest hit by the AIDS epidemic in America; Goedken had lost four brothers, his wife, and two other relatives to AIDS since 1987.

Billionaire financier **Sir James Goldsmith**, 64, who in 1994 founded and bankrolled Britain's Referendum Party to fight that country's move toward political and economic integration with Europe. After a long battle with cancer, he died of a heart attack in Spain.

Heidi Guenther, 22, a ballerina in the Boston Ballet; of cardiac arrest. While Guenther's weight was not unusual for a young dancer, and an autopsy showed no heart deformities and no unusual substances in her blood, many speculated that the dancer's sudden death was tied to an obsession with weight control. Friends, family, and the Boston Ballet had expressed concern at a sharp drop in weight over Guenther's last two years, to no avail. After her death, anecdotes about a suffering body image during adolescence surfaced, and a stash of over-the-counter laxatives was found; additionally, the driven dancer's weight had once been an issue in her demanding career.

Sydney Guilaroff, 89, the legendary movie hairdresser who designed "The Look" for MGM's greatest female stars, in Beverly Hills. Guilaroff began his MGM career on 1937's *Camille,* starring Greta Garbo. A courtly presence, he coiffed Marlene Dietrich for *Kismet,* Norma Shearer for *Marie Antoinette,* Vivien Leigh for *Gone with the Wind,* and Debbie Reynolds for *Singin' in the Rain.* He was also the perennial stylist of Joan Crawford, Ava Gardner, Marilyn Monroe, Natalie Wood, Shirley MacLaine, and Elizabeth Taylor and is credited with turning Lucille Ball into a redhead.

Former professional women's baseball player **Carol Habben**, 63, a center fielder and catcher whose team was featured in the 1992 film *A League of Their Own.*

Edward Hall, 67, a former model who worked as the Marlboro Man during the late '50s and early '60s, of lung cancer in Conn. Hall is at least the third Marlboro Man to succumb to lung cancer since 1992.

Writer **Helen Hanff**, 80, who came to prominence with her epistolary memoir *84 Charing Cross Road.* The book became a bestseller after its publication in 1970 and was turned into a hit Broadway show and a 1987 film starring Anne Bancroft and Anthony Hopkins.

Actor **Rita Morley Harvey**, 69, who was known as America's Most Televised Girl for her roles on such soap operas as *The Edge of Night* and *As the World Turns* during the 1950s and '60s, of cancer in Simsbury, Conn.

Bobby Helms, 61, whose "Jingle Bell Rock" was a Christmas 1957 hit, at his home near Indianapolis. The cause of death was not reported.

Billionare **Harry Helmsley**, 87, of pneumonia. Leona's husband of a quarter century began work as a $12-a-week office boy in New York City in 1925 and bought his first building for $1,000 during the depths of the Depression. The Helmsley partnership owns some 50,000 apartments and 27 hotels across the country, including the Empire State Building. When his wife was convicted of tax evasion in 1989, Harry, while indicted, was found mentally unfit to stand trial.

William Hickey, 69, acting teacher (of Barbra Streisand, Steve McQueen, and others) and scene-stealing Mafia don in 1985's *Prizzi's Honor,* of emphysema and bronchitis, in New York City.

Golfing great **Ben Hogan**, 84, who won 63 tournaments over three decades, of a stroke in Ft. Worth, Texas. The son of a blacksmith who committed suicide when Ben was 9, he learned to play while caddying for 65 cents a round. In 1949, after a near-fatal automobile collision, doctors told him he'd be lucky to walk again. Subsequently, Hogan played just a few tournaments a year, but in 1950 he won the U.S. Open. His total wins—including the Masters, the U.S. Open, the PGA Championship, and the British Open—rank him third of all time behind Sam Snead and Jack Nicklaus. Hogan's last competition was in 1971. He had fought Alzheimer's and cancer for the past few years.

Veteran TV and movie actor **Richard Jaeckel**, 70, of *Baywatch* and *Spenser: For Hire,* at the Motion Picture and Television Hospital in suburban Los Angeles, following an extended illness.

Original host of TV's *The Price Is Right* and *Name That Tune,* and on-air cigarette pitchman **Dennis James**, 79, of cancer in Palm Springs, Calif.

Cinematographer **Stuart Jewell**, 84, who popularized the use of time-lapse photography to reveal the wondrous workings of nature, of colon cancer in Sota Mesa, California. Jewell was one of six cameramen who filmed the Disney classic *The Living Desert,* which won the Academy Award for best documentary in 1953.

Josh the Wonder Dog, 16, holder of the *1997 Guinness Book of World Records* title as the world's most petted dog (478,000 pettings at the time of death), of cancer. Josh was the model for the mutt hero of four books by his owner, Richard Lynn Stack.

Composer **Burton Lane**, 84, of lung cancer in New York City. Lane wrote the music for such classic Broadway shows as *Finian's Rainbow* and *On a Clear Day You Can See Forever.*

British rock guitarist **Ronnie Lane**, 51, a founding member of the '60s group The Small Faces ("Itchycoo Park"), of multiple sclerosis. The Small Faces broke up in 1969 but quickly reformed as The Faces, revolving around future superstar Rod Stewart.

Actor **Rosina Lawrence**, 84, who starred in *Little Rascals* comedy shorts of the 1930s, in New York City. Lawrence also appeared in *A Connecticut Yankee* (1932) with Will Rogers and *Way Out West* (1937) with Laurel and Hardy.

Actor, TV producer, and director **Sheldon Leonard**, 89, a three-time Emmy winner who helped create some of the most popular shows of the 1960s. His acting roles included *Guys and Dolls* and *It's a Wonderful Life*. His productions included *The Dick Van Dyke Show*, *Gomer Pyle, U.S.M.C.*, and *I Spy*.

Songwriter **Irwin Jesse Levine**, 58, whose "Tie a Yellow Ribbon 'Round the Old Oak Tree" is second in the *Guinness Book of World Records* to The Beatles' "Yesterday" as the most recorded song in history, of complications from kidney failure in Livingston, N.J. "Yellow Ribbon," a 1973 No. 1 hit for Tony Orlando and Dawn, became an unofficial anthem during the 1979–81 Iran hostage crisis.

Attorney **Arthur Liman**, 64, who interrogated Lt. Col. Oliver North on national television in 1987 as lead counsel for the Senate committee investigating the Iran-Contra affair. He died of bladder cancer in New York City.

Oscar-winning costume designer **Jean Louis**, 89, at his home in Palm Springs, Calif. Besides making dresses for former first lady Nancy Reagan and nearly every top movie actress in Hollywood, he also did Rita Hayworth's signature strapless *Gilda* gown and Marilyn Monroe's 1962 sequined number when she sang "Happy Birthday" to JFK. He is survived by his widow (they married in 1993) Loretta Young, a lifetime friend and, in the '40s, perhaps the most beautiful woman on the screen.

French photographer and painter **Dora Maar**, 89, who was Picasso's lover and the model for many of his paintings in the 1930s and '40s, in Paris. Maar suffered from bouts of depression and became increasingly reclusive after the painter left her for a younger mistress, artist Françoise Gilot.

Bandleader **Harold Melvin**, 57, a prime practitioner of the Philly soul sound who recorded such '70s hits as "The Love I Lost" and "If You Don't Know Me By Now" with his group the Blue Notes, of an apparent stroke in Philadelphia.

Millie, 11, bestselling author and beloved pooch of George and Barbara Bush, of a stomach ailment in Kennebunkport, Maine. During her four years at the White House, the English springer spaniel had a knack for pawing her way into the limelight. *Millie's Book*, ghostwritten by Barbara Bush, raised $1.1 million for literacy programs.

Rose Will Monroe, 77, a.k.a. "Rosie the Riveter," the nation's poster girl for women joining the work force during World War II, in Clarksville, Ind.

Filmmaker **Carlton Moss**, 88, whose 1944 documentary *The Negro Soldier*, which the Army made to improve race relations, helped accelerate the drive for the desegregation of the armed services, of undisclosed causes in Los Angeles.

Edward Mulhare, 74, the Irish stage actor who gained fame in America in Broadway's *My Fair Lady* (when he replaced original star Rex Harrison) and on the TV series *The Ghost and Mrs. Muir* (in which he played the role Harrison originated in the movie) and *Knight Rider*, of lung cancer in Los Angeles.

Singer-songwriter **Laura Nyro**, 49, whose hits included "Wedding Bell Blues" by the Fifth Dimension and "Stoney End" by Barbara Streisand, of ovarian cancer in Danbury, Conn. A '60s contemporary of Joni Mitchell's, the Bronx native got one of her first big breaks in 1966 when Peter, Paul and Mary recorded her song "And When I Die." She went on to record 11 albums.

Social critic **Vance Packard**, 82, whose 1957 bestseller *The Hidden Persuaders* accused Madison Avenue of manipulating consumers through subtle, barely perceived messages meant to appeal to the subconscious, in Vineyard Haven, Mass., following a heart attack the previous week.

Former tennis star **Frank Parker**, 81, who won the U.S. Championships in 1944 and '45, in San Diego after undergoing surgery. Parker also captured two French national singles titles in 1948 and '49.

Lawrence Payton of The Four Tops music group, 59, of liver cancer, in Southfield, Mich. Fellow Top Levi Stubbs said that after 40 years together (and 50 million records sold), the group will not replace him. It will hereafter be called "The Tops."

Golfer **Henry Picard**, 90, a former Masters and PGA

champion, in Charleston, South Carolina.

Yiannis Pipis, 105, a violinist listed in the 1991 *Guinness Book of Records* as the world's most durable musician, in Cyprus.

Actor **Don Porter**, 84, of undisclosed causes at his home in Beverly Hills. He played Sally Field's father in the'60s sitcom *Gidget*.

English short-story writer **V. S. Pritchett**, 96, after a stroke.

Arthur Prysock, 74, balladeer ("Teach Me Tonight") and a two-time Grammy R&B nominee, while vacationing in Bermuda.

Actor **Marjorie Reynolds**, 75, who played William Bendix's super-tolerant wife Peg on the hit '50s sitcom *The Life of Riley*, of congestive heart failure in Manhattan Beach, Calif.

Sviatoslav Richter, 82, widely regarded as one of the greatest concert pianists of the 20th century, of a heart attack in Moscow.

Author **Leo Rosten**, 88, whose 1968 bestseller *The Joys of Yiddish* helped introduce words like yenta, chutzpah, shlemiel, and oy into the American vernacular, at his New York City home.

Former NBC president **Robert Sarnoff**, 78, who led the network into the color-TV era in the 1950s, of cancer in New York City. Sarnoff initiated the first televised presidential candidates' debate, between Vice President Richard Nixon and Sen. John F. Kennedy, in 1960.

Catherine Scorsese, 84, mother of film director Martin Scorsese, of complications from Alzheimer's disease in New York City. Scorsese appeared in a number of her son's movies, including *GoodFellas* and *Casino*, often improvising her own lines.

Reid Shelton, 72, who played Daddy Warbucks in the original productions of *Annie* with Andrea McArdle, of a stroke in Portland, Oregon.

University of Hawaii student **Shannon Smith**, 20, by drowning, in a successful rescue of his football coach's 6-year-old son.

Sir Georg Solti, 84, the Hungarian-born conductor who led the Chicago Symphony Orchestra from 1969 to 1991, of a heart attack in Antibes, France. Solti, whose vast range included mastery of 55 operas and 200 symphonies, won 30 Grammy awards over his lifetime—more than any other classical or pop artist. In 1977, Solti told reporters that Chicago should erect a statue to him for helping its orchestra gain international acclaim. Six years later, the city agreed and placed a bust of the conductor in Lincoln Park.

Television director **Larry Stewart**, 67, who worked on the hit series *Perry Mason, The Waltons,* and *Fantasy Island,* in Los Angeles. Stewart also served as the first president of the Academy of Television Arts and Sciences from 1976 to 1977.

Robert Switzer, 83, of Parkinson's disease in Shaker Heights, Ohio. Switzer was co-inventor of the fluorescent dyes and paints that were eventually marketed by his Day-Glo Color Corp.

Godzilla producer, **Tomoyuki Tanaka**, 86, of a stroke in Tokyo.

Tim Taylor, 28, lead singer of the alternative rock band Brainiac, in Dayton, Ohio, when the car he was driving missed a curve, hit two poles and a fire hydrant, and burst into flames.

Albert Thomas, 22, of the New Orleans rap group U.N.L.V., was found dead in a car from a gunshot wound.

Prince Charles's longtime friend and mentor, South African-born **Sir Laurens van der Post**, writer, explorer, philosopher, and war hero, at his home in London two days after his 90th birthday. Author of some 25 books, van der Post was imprisoned by the Japanese in Java during World War II, and his experiences were made into the 1983 film *Merry Christmas, Mr. Lawrence,* starring David Bowie.

Folk and country singer-songwriter **Townes Van Zandt**, 52, whose "Pancho and Lefty" became a No. 1 country hit for Willie Nelson and Merle Haggard in 1983, of an apparent heart attack in Mount Juliet, Tenn.

Augusta White, 91, who with her husband, John I. White (radio's Lonesome Cowboy on "Death Valley Days"), wrote the classic cowboy ballad "Get Along, Little Dogie," of natural causes. Despite their western reputation, Augusta and John, who died two years ago, spent most of their lives in New Jersey.

Character actor **Jesse White**, 79, who played the underworked Maytag washing machine repairman in TV commercials from 1967 to 1989.

Swedish director **Bo Widerberg**, 66, best known for his film *Elvira Madigan* (1967), in Angelholm, Sweden. the three-time Academy Award nominee's film *Raven's End* (1964) was named the best Swedish movie ever by a poll in a Swedish arts magazine.

Personal trainer **Cheryl Wilson**, 30, a regular competitor on TV's *American Gladiators,* died March 3 after her husband, Juan Minelli, 34, allegedly stabbed her to death in their home near Fort Lauderdale.

Theo Wilson, 78, who in her heyday with the *New York Daily News* became one of the nation's best-known trial reporters, covering—among others—the Charles Manson and Sirhan Sirhan murder trials, of a cerebral hemorrhage in L.A.

Bible-thumping minister **Glynn "Scotty" Wolfe**, 88, the world's most married man (according to the *Guinness Book of World Records*), in Redlands, Calif., of heart disease, just 10 days before his first wedding anniversary to wife No. 29, Linda Essex-Wolfe, the world's most married woman (23 husbands).

Boxer **Tony Zale**, 83, who battled Rocky Graziano for the middleweight title three times, twice successfully. Zale suffered from Parkinson's and Alzheimer's diseases and had been diagnosed with lymph node cancer.

Duke Zeibart, 86, whose restaurant near the White House served members of Washington's power and media elite from Harry Truman to Larry King, of heart disease and cancer in Bethesda, Md.

Film director **Fred Zinnemann**, who won Oscars for his *From Here to Eternity* and *A Man for All Seasons*—and made the classic *High Noon* and *A Nun's Story*—of a heart attack in his sleep at his London home, five weeks short of his 90th birthday. He was an artist and a gentleman.

MARRIAGES

Tennis ace **Andre Agassi**, 26, and actor **Brooke Shields**, 31, at St. John's Episcopal Chapel in Monterey. After the ceremony, the new Mr. and Mrs. Agassi and guests celebrated nearby at Carmel Valley's posh Stonepine Estate Resort. Brooke and Andre booked all 14 $300-to-$750-a-night suites. The couple had been introduced at a 1993 tennis match and kept in touch by fax until their first date.

Actors **Matthew Broderick**, 35, and **Sarah Jessica Parker**, 32, at New York's Anshe Slonim Synagogue on the historic Lower East Side. Society orchestra leader Peter Duchin provided the music—show tunes—for 100 surprised guests, who had been expecting a party. The bride wore a black and brown ruffled dress, and the groom wore a suit and tie. The next day, he reported back to work on the movie *Godzilla* and she to Broadway's *Once upon a Mattress*.

Filmmaker **Albert Brooks**, 49, and Kimberley Shlain, 31, a creative director of a multimedia company, in San Francisco. Guests included daredevil-comedian Super Dave Osborne (who is Brooks's brother), Garry Shandling, Carrie Fisher, and Penny Marshall.

Robert De Niro, 53, and Grace Hightower, 42, a former flight attendant, at a private ceremony in New York. It was De Niro's second marriage, Hightower's first. DeNiro has twin boys by his former girlfriend, former model Toukie Smith, and an adopted daughter with his first wife, actor Diahnne Abbott.

TV stars **David Duchovny**, 36, and **Téa Leoni**, 31, at the New York City prep school Duchovny attended until eighth grade. The couple exchanged self-penned vows in front of half a dozen witnesses. A quiet, informal meal at a French bistro followed, and then the couple returned to the posh Lowell Hotel on the Upper East Side. The couple had met in L.A. at the party of a mutual friend and had dated for four months.

Revlon model and ex-MTV veejay **Karen (Duff) Duffy**, 35, and investment banker John Lambrose, 31, in Jamaica.

Singer **Sheena Easton**, 38, and documentary director **Timothy Delarm**, 35, in Las Vegas. It is the third marriage for Easton, the first for Delarm.

British actor **Colin Firth**, 36, who played Mr. Darcy in the 1996 BBC adaptation of *Pride and Prejudice*, and Italian student Livia Giuggioli, 27, in a hilltop ceremony in Tuscany, Italy.

Ellen costar **Joely Fisher**, 29, and cinematographer Christopher Duddy, 35, on the soundstage of the Hollywood studio where they met. It was the first marriage for Fisher and the second for Duddy, who has two sons—8 and 11—from his first marriage.

Oasis singer **Liam Gallagher**, 24, and actor **Patsy Kensit**, 26, in a secretive civil ceremony witnessed only by a London registrar. The marriage—her third, his first—came two months after a previously announced service was canceled because the high-profile glam couple said the press was annoying them.

Oasis songwriter **Noel Gallagher**, 30, and record-company employee Meg Matthews, 31, in a private ceremony in Las Vegas. The couple tied the knot to the organ sounds of The Beatles' "Yesterday" and "All My Loving."

Actor **Robin Givens**, 32, and Yugoslavian-born tennis instructor Svetozar Marinkovic, 30, on Coronado Island, Calif. It is Givens's second marriage. She divorced boxer Mike Tyson in 1989.

Karenna Gore, 23, the eldest daughter of Vice President Al Gore, and Dr. Andrew Schiff, 31, at Washington's National Cathedral, where Al and Tipper Gore had wed 27 years earlier. The newlyweds had met at the Washington home of former congressman Tom Downey, a mutual family friend, and courted at the Clinton-Gore victory blowout in Little Rock.

Frasier star **Kelsey Grammer**, 42, and *Playboy* model Camille Donatacci, 28, in a sunset open-air wedding ceremony performed by two Catholic priests. A sit-down dinner reception followed at Saddlerock Ranch, a 1,000-acre Malibu spread featuring horses, ostriches, and llamas. Some 200 guests included *Cheers* costar John Ratzenberger and *Frasier* costar David Hyde Pierce. It was a third marriage for Grammer.

Federal Reserve Chairman **Alan Greenspan**, 71, and NBC's chief foreign affairs correspondent **Andrea Mitchell**, 50, in a garden ceremony at the Inn at Little Washington in Washington, Va. Supreme Court Associate Justice Ruth Bader Ginsberg presided over the ceremony, with 97 attendees, including Colin Powell, Henry Kissinger, and the groom's ex-flame Barbara Walters and her date, Virginia Senator John Warner. This was the second trip to the altar for both.

Former *L.A. Law* star **Harry Hamlin**, 44, and *Melrose Place* actor **Lisa Rinna**, 32, at their Hollywood Hills home. It was his third marriage and her first.

Dire Straits guitarist **Mark Knopfler**, 47, and actor Kitty Aldridge, 31, on Valentine's Day in Barbados. It was a second marriage for Aldridge and Knopfler's third.

Chrissie Hynde, 45, lead singer of The Pretenders, and Colombian sculptor Lucho Brieva, 32, in London. It was the second marriage for Hynde, who is divorced from Simple Minds singer Jim Kerr.

Country star **Tracy Lawrence**, 29 and Dallas Cowboys cheerleader Stephanie (Stacie) Drew, 27, in the Highland Park Presbyterian Church in Dallas. It was a second marriage for Lawrence. The evening candlelight ceremony was witnessed by 500 guests including quarterback Troy Aikman.

Frasier costar **Jane Leeves**, 35, and Paramount television executive **Marshall Coben**, 40, in England. It was the first marriage for Leeves and the second for Coben.

Actor **Jennifer Lopez**, 26, who played the slain Tejano singer in the film *Selena*, and model Ohani Noa, 23, in Miami.

Kimberly Michelle Mays, 18, who was somehow switched at birth with another baby and in 1993 successfully sued to remain with the man who reared her rather than with her biological parents (but later moved in with them for a time), married Jeremy Weeks, 19, a film-art student, in Orlando. Bob Mays, who cared for Kimberly from birth, gave the bride away.

Pugnacious TV pundit and ex-priest **John McLaughlin**, 70, and his producer, Cristina Vidal, 36, in Washington, D.C.

Former White House press secretary **Dee Dee Myers**, 35, and *New York Times* L.A. bureau chief Todd Purdum, 37, in Chicago. It was Myers's first marriage and Purdum's second.

Batman & Robin actor **Chris O'Donnell**, 26, and kindergarten teacher Caroline Fentress, 24, at St. Patrick's Church in Washington, D.C., her hometown. The large guest list included *Batman* director Joel Schumacher, Sen. Ted Kennedy and his wife Victoria, Ethel (Mrs. Robert) Kennedy, and O'Donnell's *In Love and War* costar Sandra Bullock. O'Donnell had met Fentress through her brother Andrew who attended Boston College with *Batman*'s sidekick.

Actor **Gary Oldman**, 38, and photographer Donya Fiorentino, 29, in L.A. It was a second marriage for Fiorentino and the third for Oldman.

Horse trainer **Mark Phillips**, 48, ex-husband of Britain's Princess Anne, and former U.S. Olympic equestrian Sandy Pflueger, 47, on the Hawaiian island of Oahu. It was the second marriage for both. Phillips and Anne divorced in 1992.

Chicago Bull **Scottie Pippen**, 31, and student Larsa Younan, 23, in Chicago. It was Pippen's second marriage and Younan's first.

Singer and chicken entrepreneur **Kenny Rogers**, 58, and longtime girlfriend Wanda Miller, 30, at his private estate in Lexington, Georgia. The wedding is Rogers' fifth, Miller's second. The two met in 1993 at the Atlanta restaurant where Miller worked as a host.

Author **Salman Rushdie**, 50, on whom a death sentence was pronounced in 1989 by the late Ayatolla Khomeini, on the grounds that passages in Rushdie's novel *The Satanic Verses* were blasphemous, married a British book editor who has been identified only as Elizabeth in East Hampton, N.Y. It is Rushdie's third marriage.

Two-time Grammy-winning singer **Jon Secada**, 35, and Maritere Vilar, 24, former publicist for the company that manages him, in a traditional Cuban Catholic ceremony in Coral Gables, Fla. It was a second marriage for Secada.

Country singer **Travis Tritt**, 34, and model Theresa Nelson, at his home outside Atlanta. More than 300 guests attended, including Tanya Tucker, Sam Cooke, Lari White, and Gary Rossington of the group Lynyrd Skynyrd.

Former heavyweight boxing champion **Mike Tyson**, 30, and physician **Monica Turner**, 31, in a private Muslim ceremony at her Bethesda, Md., home. It was a second marriage for Tyson, who was divorced from actor Robin Givens in 1989, and the first for Turner. The couple have a daughter, Rayna, 14 months.

Actor **Sylvester Stallone**, 50, and model **Jennifer Flavin**, 28, in a small but elaborate ceremony in London. The couple have a 9-month-old daughter together, Sophia Rose. Stallone was previously married to Sasha Czack and the formerly famous Brigitte Nielsen.

Richard B. Stolley, 68, founding managing editor of PEOPLE, and actor-journalist **Lise Hilboldt**, 45, in New York City.

Metallica drummer **Lars Ulrich**, 33, and medical student Skylar Satenstein, 25, in Las Vegas. It was the second marriage for Ulrich and the first for Saterstein.

Actors **Debra Winger** and **Arliss Howard**, both 41, in L.A. The couple met in 1993 while filming the movie *Wilder Napalm*.

Beverly Hills 90210 star **Ian Ziering**, 33, and *Playboy* playmate Nikke Schieler, 25, in L.A. It was the first marriage for both.

PARTINGS

Former *Cheers* actor **Kirstie Alley**, 42, and **Parker Stevenson**, 44, who starred in TV's *The Hardy Boys*, citing irreconcilable differences. The couple married in December 1983, but separated last year. They have two children: William True, 4, and Lillie, 3.

Figure skater **Tai Babilonia**, 37, and her husband, music producer **Cary Butler**, age unavailable; the couple married in 1991 and separated in 1995.

Actor **Kathy Bates**, 48, and her husband, actor **Anthony Campisi**, 48, after six years of marriage and 18 years together. They have no children.

Chicago Hope star **Peter Berg**, 35, and his wife, Calvin Klein executive Elizabeth Rogers. The couple, who married in 1993, have no children.

Television producer **Steven Bochco**, 53, and his wife, actor **Barbara Bosson**, 57, who costarred on her husband's series *Hill Street Blues* and *Murder One*, separated after 28 years of marriage. They have two grown children.

Motivational speaker **Les Brown**, 52, and singer **Gladys Knight**, 53. They were married for nearly two years.

Actor **Neve Campbell**, 23, and aspiring actor Jeff Colt, 33, separated after two years of marriage. He said he was disturbed by his wife's burgeoning fame.

Diva **Mariah Carey**, 28, and Sony Records chief **Tommy Mottola**, 47, filed for divorce after nearly four years of marriage. Carey has sold 75 million albums for Mottola's label since 1990. It was a second marriage for Mottola.

Funny man and cable guy **Jim Carrey**, 35, and former *Picket Fences* star **Lauren Holly**, 31, after 10 months of a tumultuous marriage. The couple had fallen in love on the set of '94's *Dumb and Dumber*, both soon after leaving a first marriage.

Action novelist and millionaire **Tom Clancy**, 51, and his wife, Wanda, after 26 years of marriage. When they also split two years prior, Wanda (temporarily) filed for divorce, claiming Clancy had "committed adultery with one Katherine Huang," a young New York assistant D.A. he met while surfing the Net.

New York Undercover star **Patti D'Arbanville**, 45, filed for divorce from bar owner Terry Quinn, 36. In round one of the messy split, the actor had Quinn arrested at the couple's Long Island home after telling police he had stolen $75,000 worth of her jewelry, including gifts from actor Don Johnson, the father of her son Jesse, 14. D'Arbanville and Quinn had been married since 1993.

Actor **Geena Davis**, 41, and director **Renny Harlin**, 39, after three years of marriage and some box-office disappointments. A spokesperson said the couple intends to remain close and in business together.

Reed Diamond, 29, of NBC's *Homicide: Life on the Street,* and wife Frederika Kesten, 30, filed for divorce in Los Angeles. The couple, who have no children, married in 1995.

Former *Charlie's Angels* star and poster girl **Farrah Fawcett**, 50, and actor **Ryan O'Neal**, 55, after a 17-year relationship. Though the couple never married, they were considered one of Hollywood's most celebrated pairs. The two will jointly participate in the upbringing of their 12-year-old son Redmond.

Lord of the Dance star **Michael Flatley**, 38, and his wife of 11 years, Beata Dziaba, 36. Flatley cited irreconcilable differences for the breakup. They have been separated since 1995 and have no children.

Former California Representative **Michael Huffington**, 49, who spent $29 million of his own money on an unsuccessful bid for a U.S. Senate seat, and his wife, Republican pundit and Picasso biographer **Arianna Huffington**, 46. The couple, who married in 1986, have two children, Christina, 8, and Isabella, 6.

Singer **LaToya Jackson**, 41, and Jack Gordon, 58, her husband of six years and former manager.

1994 Olympic gold medalist, skater **Dan Jansen**, and wife **Robin Jansen**, after seven years of marriage.

Opera diva **Dame Kiri Te Kanawa**, 53, who performed at the wedding of Prince Charles and Princess Diana, and husband and former manager Des Park, 54. Park broke off their 30-year marriage with a telegram while his wife was touring in Brazil.

Michael Kennedy, 39, fourth son of the late Robert F. Kennedy and head of the nonprofit Citizens Energy Corp. of Boston, and his wife, **Victoria Gifford Kennedy**, 40, daughter of sportscaster Frank Gifford, are separating after 16 years of marriage.

After 20 years of marriage, attorney Eileen McGann, 48, and President Clinton's former political advisor, **Dick Morris**, 48, who resigned in 1996 after his clandestine affair with a Washington call girl became public.

Actors **Brad Pitt**, 33, and **Gwyneth Paltrow**, 24, after a two and a half years. Their fairy-tale engagement lasted half a year.

Director **John Singleton**, 30, from his wife of five months, **Akousa Busia Singleton**, 30, a Ghanaian princess turned actor/writer. Their daughter Hadar was born just 13 days before the split.

In the Heat of the Night Oscar-winning actor **Rod Steiger**, 72, and his wife of 11 years, Paula, whom he recently credited for getting him through a decade of clinical depression. Citing irreconcilable differences, Steiger sought joint custody of the couple's 4-year-old son, Michael.

Billy Bob Thornton, and his fourth wife, Pietra Dawn Thornton. The 41-year-old actor has been linked to Laura Dern, who worked with him as a fellow guest star on TV's *Ellen* coming-out episode. Pietra Dawn Thornton claims her husband threatened to kill her and also punched, choked, and bit her during their four-year marriage.

Entrepreneur **Donald Trump**, 50, and **Marla Maples Trump**, 33. The pair separated just before their fifth anniversary, at which time their prenuptual agreement would have increased her settlement from one to five million dollars.

The former Mrs. Donald Trump, **Ivana**, 48, and international businessman **Riccardo Mazzuchelli**, 54, announced the end of their 20-month marriage. They had met in the wake of Ivana's humiliating 1990 divorce. The Italian jet-setter sent the home shopping huckstress a roomful of red roses after their first lunch date in 1991 and proposed later that year. Though the proposal was unsuccessful, three years later Mazzuchelli won her hand with an immense Burmese sapphire. It was Ivana's third marriage and Mazzuchelli's second. The breakup happened just weeks after Donald and Marla Maples announced their own split.

America's Funniest Home Videos host **Bob Saget**, 42, and wife Sherri, after nearly 15 years of marriage. The couple have three daughters ages 4, 7, and 10; irreconcilable differences were cited.

Actor **Ron Silver**, 51, and magazine editor Lynne Miller, divorced after 21 years of marriage. The couple, who separated in 1993, have two teenage children.

BIRTHS

Actor **Adrienne Barbeau**, 51, and husband **Billy Van Zandt**, 39, a producer and writer; their first children, identical twin boys, Walker Steven Barbeau Van Zandt and William Dalton Barbeau Van Zandt. Barbeau has a son from a previous marriage.

Actors **Annette Bening**, 39, and **Warren Beatty**, 60; their third child and second daughter, Isabel Ira Ashley.

Country singer **James Bonamy**, 25, and wife Amy Jane, 25; their first baby, James Daniel.

Actor **Pierce Brosnan**, 44, and his girlfriend, *Unsolved Mysteries* correspondent Keely Schaye Smith, 33; Dylan Thomas. Brosnan has two stepchildren—Charlotte, 23, and Christopher, 22—and a son, Sean William, 13, from his marriage to the late actor Cassandra Harris.

Kerry Kennedy Cuomo, 38, and her husband **Andrew Cuomo**, 39, Secretary of Housing and Urban Development; their third child.

Actor **Joan Cusack**, 34, and her husband, attorney Dick Burke, 33; their first child, Dylan John.

E! Entertainment correspondent **Kymberly Douglas**, 38, and *The Young and the Restless* star **Jerry Douglas**, 61; their first child, a boy, Hunter William. Douglas has two children from a previous marriage.

News anchor **Dina Ruiz**, 31, and husband **Clint Eastwood**, 66; a girl named Morgan, his fifth child and her first.

Rocker **Melissa Etheridge** and longtime companion, filmmaker **Julie Cypher,** 32; a daughter, Bailey Jean Cypher.

General Hospital star **Genie Francis**, 35, and her husband, *Star Trek: The Next Generation*'s **Jonathan Frakes**, 44; her second child, a girl. The couple also has a son, Jameson, 2.

Actor **Tracey Gold**, 27, and her husband, TV production assistant Roby Marshall, 31; their first child, a boy, Sage.

Courtney Kennedy Hill, 40, daughter of Ethel and Robert F. Kennedy, and her husband, **Paul Hill**, 42; their first child, a girl, Saoirse Roisin—the name is Gaelic. The Irish-born Hill, in a case that became the basis for the film *In the Name of the Father,* was one of the men who served 15 years in jail for allegedly bombing two English pubs. He was released in 1989 after a British court ruled police had altered evidence.

Country musician **Faith Hill**, 29, and **Tim McGraw**, 29; their first child, Gracie Katherine.

Singer **Julio Iglesias**, 53, and his girlfriend, Miranda Rijnsburger, 31; a boy, Michael Alexander. Divorced since 1979, Iglesias has three grown children from his marriage to journalist Isabel Preysler.

Country singer **Alan Jackson**, 38, and his wife, Denise, 37; a girl, Dani Grace. The couple have two other daughters, Mattie, 7, and Alexandra, 5.

Country star **Toby Keith**, 36, and his wife, **Tricia**, 34; their third child. Their other children are Shelley, 16, and Krystal, 11.

Former Olympic figure skater **Nancy Kerrigan**, 27, and her husband and manager, **Jerry Solomon**, 42; their first child, Matthew.

Actor/TV hostess **Ricki Lake**, 28, and her husband, **Rob Sussman**; their first child, Milo Sebastian Sussman.

Filmmaker **Spike Lee**, 40, and his wife, Tonya, 31, a lawyer; their second child, a boy, Jackson Lewis. Their daughter, Satchel, is 2.

Julia Louis-Dreyfus, 36, and husband **Brad Hall**, 39; their second child, Charles. Brother Henry is 5.

Sister Act costar **Kathy Najimy**, 35, and *Stomp* dancer **Dan Finnerty**, 26; their first child, daughter Samia Najimy Finnerty.

Baywatch costar **Gena Lee Nolin**, 25, and husband **Greg Fahlman**, 37; their first child, Spencer Michael.

Actor **Gary Oldman**, 39, and his wife, photographer **Donya Fiorentino**; their first child, a boy, Gulliver Flynn.

Ex-*90210* star **Luke Perry**, 30, and his wife, Minnie, 28; their first baby, a son, named Jack.

Tony Randall, 77, and his wife, actor **Heather Harlan**, 26; their first child, Julia Laurette.

1984 Olympic gold-winning gymnast (and current motivational speaker) **Mary Lou Retton**, 29, and husband Shannon Kelley, an investment broker; a second daughter, McKenna Lane Kelley. Daughter Shayla is 2.

Author **Salman Rushdie**, 50, who has been living under a death sentence imposed by the Iranian government since 1989; a second son in London. The mother, known only as Elizabeth to protect her identity, has been with the author for three years. Rushdie already has an adult son.

Olympic star and Houston Comet **Sheryl Swoopes**, 26, and husband Eric Jackson, 23; a boy, Jordan Eric.

Actor **Alan Thicke**, 50, and wife Gina, 28, a former Miss World; their first child, a boy, Carter William. Thicke has two adult sons from a previous marriage.

Former Olympic Skater **Debi Thomas**, 29, and husband Chris Bequette, 32, a lawyer; their first child, Christopher Jules II.

Actor **Ally Walker**, 36, star of the NBC series *Profiler*, and her husband, NBC executive **John Landgraf**; their first child, a boy.

Wheel of Fortune letter-turner **Vanna White,** 40, and husband George Santo Pietro, 50; a daughter, Giovanna, their second child. They have a son, Nicholas, 3.

Actor **Pia Zadora**, 38, and her husband, director **Jonathan Kaufer**, 42; their first baby, a boy, Jordan Maxwell. Zadora has two children from a previous marriage to businessman Meshulam Riklis.

CBS News anchor **Paula Zahn**, 40, and real estate developer Richard Cohen, 49; their third child, Austin Bryce. He joins Jared, 3, and Haley, 7.

ROYALS

THE ONCE MERRY MEN AND WOMEN OF WINDSOR

"I want to be as famous as the queen of England," the ambitious young Andy Warhol proclaimed back in the 1950s. He might as well have said that he wanted to be as famous as the Atlantic Ocean. The current British royal family has something that vast and immemorial about it. In the three centuries of its reign, other crowned families of Europe have been executed or packed off. But the Windsors still occupy the throne, as implacable and seemingly enduring as the planet Jupiter.

It hasn't been easy. The Windsors are expected to behave like the Cleavers even when they're feeling like the Simpsons. Being famous is more than their fate; in a sense it's their job. As the real decision-making power of the monarchy has dwindled, the public symbolism has become more important. On more than one occasion in the past, however, Britons have seemed ready to rid themselves of a dynasty that could look costly, shiftless, and Teutonic. The lessons of the past are not lost on the Windsors, who take their family history not just as a source of pride but also as a series of warnings to the present. Like her father, George VI, Elizabeth II has been a model of dignity and decorum. But a stroll among her ancestors in the National Portrait Gallery is enough to remind her of any number of hot-blooded blue bloods in her line.

Where does the Windsor saga begin? Actually, with the German Hanoverian kings. The royals like to consider Queen Victoria their matriarch because, while she was from the House of Hanover herself, her marriage to Prince Albert of Saxe-Coburg-Gotha established the present branch of the family tree. So emphasizing Albert's line allows the Windsors to distance themselves from Victoria's Hanoverian predecessors. Starting with **George I**, who was imported to England from Germany in 1714, the five increasingly preposterous rulers had made the British people rue almost the very idea of royalty.

After monarchs who alternated between extravagant skirt-chasing and outright incompetence, **Victoria** acceded to the crown in 1837, the niece of the last Hanoverian king, William IV. Immediately she made it her business to undo their legacy. She brought the monarchy a bit of wholesome romance through a devoted marriage to her German husband, **Prince Albert**. Indeed the transformation of the royal reputation may be Albert's achievement even more than Victoria's. With the middle classes taking power from the spoiled and lazy aristocrats, Albert gave them a royal family that the common man could both look up to and identify with: wreathed in pomp and ceremony but frugal, sober, dutiful, and monogamous.

Though Victoria's name has come to stand for prudishness, it was as much Albert who brought the moralizing strain to their marriage. As a young woman, the Queen didn't blush to size him up bluntly in her diary. ("Such a pretty mouth," she noted. "A beautiful figure, broad in the shoulders, and a fine waist.") But Albert worried that their children would take after his wayward parents, who had divorced in a tangle of adulteries. Above all he vowed that Edward, heir to the throne, would be raised in an atmosphere of hard schooling and abstinence. Naturally, Edward grew up to be dim, jolly, and goatish.

Upon Albert's death in 1861, Victoria, just 42 years old, plunged down a black hole of widowhood. Albert's bedroom was kept as it was on the day of his death, even to the extent of having fresh bedclothes laid out every night. She eventually roused herself sufficiently to regain the public's affection, and lived long enough to see her nine children and forty grandchildren married into most of the royal families of

Europe. On her deathbed she was supported by her grandson Kaiser Wilhelm of Germany, who 13 years later would lead his nation into war against hers.

When Victoria died in 1901, after the longest reign in her nation's history, her reputation for rectitude had become so stultifying that her womanizing heir, son **Edward VII**, found himself lionized for the same habits that had caused so much trouble for so many Hanoverian kings. Throughout his life the insatiable Edward conducted a series of lengthy affairs with some of the most celebrated beauties of the day, including the actresses Lillie Langtry and Sarah Bernhardt. With prosperity at home and vast empire abroad, the public was willing to overlook the moral lapses of a robust and even randy monarch. After nine popular years on the throne he was followed by **George V**, prim, exacting, and a stickler for impeccable dress. George led the country through World War I when he changed the family name from the Germanic Saxe-Coburg-Gotha to Windsor. He also encouraged closer ties between the royals and the people by allowing the Windsors to marry British nobles and commoners. Indeed among the first to benefit from this new trend was the present Queen Mother, a noblewoman who married George's son Albert, the future George VI.

George VI became the monarch, however, only after his elder brother abdicated. Crowned **Edward VIII** in 1936, the young man was already intent upon marriage to Wallis Warfield Simpson, a divorced American married to a British businessman. But the government would hear nothing of it and presented Edward with a choice—the lady or the land—hoping that he would choose the former and in the process remove a king who showed signs of Nazi sympathies. After a reign of almost a year, he resigned and, bearing the newly invented title of Duke of Windsor, he left England for the Continent and Wallis Simpson. They would return home only for rare visits—and, decades later, to be buried.

England was shaken—indeed on the night of Edward's abdication the sentries around Buckingham Palace were issued live ammunition for the first time in modern history. The public's reaction may have been overestimated, but when Edward's younger brother, Albert, now **George VI**, came to the throne in December 1936, all of Britain was poised for the worst.

For that matter, so was Albert. He had never expected to be king (formal speaking engagements left

The Queen Mother.

FOLLOW THE ROYAL LINE

The Windsors are but the latest of many families to rule the kingdom. Here is the complete lineage for Britain's crown according to *Whitaker's Almanac*, listed by year of accession.

Saxons and Danes

Egbert	827
Ethelwulf	839
Ethelbald	858
Ethelbert	858
Ethelred	866
Alfred the Great	871
Edward the Elder	899
Athelstan	925
Edmund	940
Edred	946
Edwy	955
Edgar	959
Edward the Martyr	975
Ethelred II	978
Edmund Ironside	1016
Canute the Dane	1017
Harold I	1035
Hardicanute	1040
Edward the Confessor	1042
Harold II	1066

The House of Normandy

William I	1066
William II	1087
Henry I	1100
Stephen	1135

The House of Plantagenet

Henry II	1154
Richard I	1189
John	1199
Henry III	1216
Edward I	1272
Edward II	1307
Edward III	1327
Richard II	1377

The House of Lancaster

Henry IV	1399
Henry V	1413
Henry VI	1422

The House of York

Edward IV	1461
Edward V	1483
Richard II	1483

The House of Tudor

Henry VII	1485
Henry VIII	1509
Edward VI	1547
Jane	1553
Mary I	1553
Elizabeth I	1558

The House of Stuart

James I (VI of Scotland)	1603
Charles I	1625

[Commonwealth declared, 1649]

The House of Stuart (restored)

Charles II	1660
James II (VII of Scotland)	1685
William II and Mary II	1689
Anne	1702

The House of Hanover

George I	1714
George II	1727
George III	1760
George IV	1820
William IV	1830
Victoria	1837

The House of Saxe-Coburg

Edward VII	1901

The House of Windsor

George V	1910
Edward VIII	1936
George VI	1936
Elizabeth II	1952

him shaken and depressed), and when he learned he was suddenly to take the throne, he went to his mother, Queen Mary, and wept for an hour. No wonder it was rumored that George VI was too frail to survive the coronation ceremony.

But his very narrowness and humility turned out to be qualities that were once again in favor among the British people. George VI and his wife, the current **Queen Mother**, Elizabeth, provided Britain with a center of gravity during the grim days of World War II, remaining in Buckingham Palace even when London was being fractured by German bombs and refusing to send Princesses Elizabeth and Margaret out of the country. No wonder Adolf Hitler called her "the most dangerous woman in Europe." King George's family represented what the English wanted during these terrible years: a conscientious and principled king, a winning queen, and two likable young princesses, Elizabeth and Margaret.

Still thriving at 97, the Queen Mother has become a beloved national institution. Adored for her approachability and cheerful mien, the QM was described by photographer Cecil Beaton as "the great mother figure and nanny of us all." A red-hot number in the '20s, she still likes "drinky-poos" (gin and tonic) before dinner, but she has never forgiven President Jimmy Carter for his shameful breach of etiquette: he kissed her on the lips.

London merchants quake when they see her coming. It's not her taste in tulle, it's that she reportedly rarely pays her accounts. And she's still keen as a tack. Says one old friend of her wicked wit: "She doesn't take prisoners."

Born Lady Elizabeth Bowes-Lyon, the serenely beautiful young woman was the Diana of her day. But fearing life in the royal fishbowl, she twice rejected marriage proposals from the painfully shy, stammering Prince Albert, who called her "the most wonderful person in the world."

It is amazing that this five-foot-tall aristocrat, the last Empress of India and the honorary colonel of 18 regiments, who has probably never cooked a meal or made a bed, is considered "everybody's mum." But the festivities surrounding her 90th birthday in 1990 confirmed the devotion she has long inspired.

When King George, a heavy smoker, died of lung cancer in 1952 at the age of 57, his daughter **Elizabeth II** took up the scepter knowing that her main job would be to preserve the gains her parents had made. Admittedly, Elizabeth is a figurehead, a constitutional monarch who reigns but does not rule. Yet no one trifles with the 71-year-old woman known at Buckingham Palace as The Boss. Part of her power is ex officio: It is bad form to contradict Her Most Excellent Majesty, Elizabeth the Second, by the Grace of God, of the United Kingdom of Great Britain and Northern Ireland and of Her other Realms and Territories, Queen, Head of the Commonwealth, Defender of the Faith. It is also hard to disagree with someone whom *Fortune* reckons as the world's richest woman.

Queen Elizabeth II and Prince Philip celebrate their fiftieth anniversary.

But much of Elizabeth's authority arises from the immovable force of her character. This is the monarch who at 27 overrode the objections of advisers and ordered her coronation to be televised because, she said, "I have to be seen to be believed." And who continued to appear in public and ride in open cars after her husband's favorite uncle, Lord Mountbatten, was assassinated by an IRA bomb in 1979. And who in 1982 coolly kept a disturbed intruder talking on the edge of her bed until she could summon help.

She grew up during the London blitz and matured in the ensuing period of austerity. The world's wealthiest woman still wanders around Buckingham Palace turning off lights. The heat is kept low and there are no objections; there never are. And when one of her favorite dogs killed a hare, the Queen carefully picked it up and presented it to the kitchen staff. "We can eat this," she announced.

When Elizabeth II rings, a staff of 300 jumps. When the queen is in London, the PM calls on her every Tuesday to brief her on government business. Though not a quick study, Elizabeth is assiduous, has a phenomenal memory, and frequently embarrasses ministers by knowing more about the issues than they do.

Elizabeth's hold on her subjects begins with her family. When as a 13-year-old she met a dashing cadet, she instantly decided that he was Midshipman Right. Five years later she had not changed her mind, and so in 1947 she married **Prince Philip** of Greece, a great-great-grandchild of Queen Victoria. Queen Elizabeth

THE VULGAR SUBJECT OF MONEY

Loaded as they are, money is something the Windsors prefer not to tarnish themselves with. They never carry cash, not a penny. And it's not because they carry American Express instead. Elizabeth's famous pocketbook is a stage prop. It sometimes contains only mints for her horses. Otherwise, the Windsors come in contact with currency the way other people encounter God—mostly on Sundays. Before church, Charles is reportedly provided with a £5 note for the collection plate; he likes to have it sprayed and ironed by his valet, then neatly creased and left for him beneath his clove box. You know, the box that holds your before-dinner clove. You probably have one around somewhere.

The Windsor wealth is complicated. A considerable portion is their own, acquired by them or their ancestors with personal funds. That would include Sandringham and Balmoral, two of the royal country estates, which they own the way the Cartwrights owned the Ponderosa. Both were purchased during Queen Victoria's reign. But the greater part of the wealth that surrounds them is held in trust for the nation. That means the Windsors can wear it, sit on it, eat off it, and go lightheartedly skipping down its glinting corridors. They just can't sew any name tags on it or cart it off to Christie's for auction.

If Britain should ever decide to get rid of the royal family, though, it would be a messy divorce. There's some confusion about which of their property belongs to the state and which is their own. In particular, who rightly possesses the lavish gifts from foreign potentates? Like the 2,000-year-old necklace from Egypt's former King Farouk?

And some of the royal's riches actually do benefit the public. It seems that Windsor Castle, their weekend residence, where construction began in the 11th century, may be perched atop oil deposits worth an estimated $1 billion. Queen Elizabeth II has given a white-gloved thumbs-up for exploratory drilling on a site somewhere between the royal household golf course and the royal household cricket ground. Any revenue generated will go directly to the Treasury.

By anyone's count, though, the total number is a whopper. *Fortune* has calculated that the Queen is one of the richest people in the world and four years ago they estimated her net worth at $7.8 billion. But a more recent London *Sunday Times* report placed her total at a paltry $680 million, though most surveys still put the Windsor wealth well into the billions. Charles, meanwhile, was believed to be worth about $400 million as of 1991, which would still place him among Britain's 40 wealthiest people. To paraphrase Mel Brooks: It is good to be Queen.

and Prince Phillip celebrated their golden wedding anniversary this year, reminding the world that marital happiness can indeed flourish in a royal family. The two attended a service of thanksgiving at Westminster Abbey where they were married, and later celebrated the occasion with a garden party at Buckingham Palace. Four thousand couples also marking their fiftieth anniversary were invited to share in the revelry.

Although Elizabeth has inevitably dominated her husband in the public realm, in the world of the Windsor family the duke of Edinburgh has had authority over educating the children: first Prince Charles and Princess Anne, later Princes Andrew and Edward. But Elizabeth's will is what holds the family and the royal public image together.

Her own image is not universally admired, at least from a fashion point of view. Dressing in a style that can be characterized as pseudo-frumpy, the queen stays out of the tabloids and gets her work done. While her hair is done every Monday at four p.m. by Charles Martyn, her hairdresser for the last two decades, she reads state papers and seldom glances in the mirror. Not everyone is happy about her diffidence. "I sometimes wish she had been a bit more of a clothes person," wistfully admits her couturier of four decades, Sir Hard Amies. "She doesn't care, basically. She listens to our advice, then goes off and wears shabby shoes because they're comfortable." But in fact Elizabeth does care about her appearance. Her outfits—the boxy, brightly colored clothes, clunky handbags, unfashionable reading glasses—are chosen with great deliberation to be unthreatening to women, unobtrusive to men, and easily seen by the crowds that line her path. If she were chic, she would be French, but this queen is British to her bones. That means a love of silver service and afternoon tea, bland food, sweetish wine, jigsaw puzzles, Dick Francis mysteries, and, most of all, tramps in the country amid her Thoroughbreds and her dogs. The Queen feeds her six corgis and two dorgis (a dachshund-corgi mix) herself, cutting up their meat and mixing it with biscuits in their separate bowls set out every afternoon by a footman.

No one takes better care of business than Her Majesty, who has long since realized that her maritally vexed offspring have created a throne-threatening PR problem for the House of Windsor. At the close of 1992, in a now-famous speech, she noted, "It has turned out to be an *annus horribilis*." If not the language of the common man, it was certainly a sentiment commonly understood. And things got even more horrible a few days after that speech. On the Queen's 45th wedding anniversary, a fire gutted a corner of Windsor Castle, causing damages of up to $60 million. As a debate brewed over who should bear the cost of repairs, Elizabeth, with her unerring sense for image damage control, proclaimed that she would give up a centuries-old royal perk by commencing to pay income tax on her private fortune, as well as pony up $8.5 million toward refurbishing the Castle. And perhaps most tellingly, the Queen announced that she was removing from the Civil List the Princes Andrew and Edward and the Princesses Anne and Margaret. That meant that she was switching from the public to her personal dole the annual upkeep of this spoiled quartet, not to mention their spendthrift spouses, present or future. And in 1993 she went one step further, conceding that marketing the mystique of the monarchy was in order. On August 7, 1996 she opened 19 state rooms in Buckingham Palace to public tours (leaving 631 rooms still off-limits) while she and the family were taking their annual summer retreat to Balmoral.

Her Majesty canceled her 70th birthday party in 1996 after the *Daily Mail* printed unauthorized details of what was to have been a private to-do near Windsor castle. It was an anti-climactic end to the matriarch's somber 70th year, over the course of which the Queen was assailed by the televised revelations of one daughter-in-law, the financial scandal of another, and the failure of two royal marriages. She watched Parliament erase the royal allowance, put her 80-foot yacht up for sale, and ground the royal planes.

Perhaps to counteract an image of the royals as freeloaders, the Queen set up a secret committee in 1996 to consider several astonishing reforms to the monarchy. The most startling change is already in effect. The "Family Firm" pays their own way with the $90 million earned annually from their estates, rather than collecting $12.75 million per year from taxpayers as they did in the past. Other proposals include streamlining the royal family to include only the monarch, the consort, and the children; lifting the 295-year-old ban on royals marrying Catholics; severing the formal links with the Church of England; and allowing the eldest child to succeed the throne regardless of gender. Many of these progressive suggestions need Parliament's stamp of approval, however, and British politicians' reluctance to tamper with tradition means that the Queen's proposals may remain just that for some time to come.

Despite her attempts to set things straight with the monarchy, Elizabeth has often been unpopular. In response to public outcry, she appeared on live television in an unprecedented effort to share her family's grief over the death of Princess Diana. And earlier in the year she launched a successful Web page that received over 12.5 million hits in its first two months. Though her popularity with the people took a hit when Diana died, Elizabeth's resolve rarely wavers, and she is always fully aware of her royal responsibilities. As former prime minister Margaret Thatcher said in a televised program screened on the Queen's 70th birthday, "She is the most conscientious lady. Whatever duty requires, she will do and will go on doing for the rest of her days."

THE DEATH OF A PRINCESS

The late Diana, Princess of Wales.

To her ex-husband, Prince Charles—as well as the rest of the world—the death of Diana, Princess of Wales, was an unimaginable shock. On Sept. 1, the day after Diana, 36, and her companion Dodi Al Fayed, 42, died in a cataclysmic car crash in Paris, the distraught Charles walked the hills surrounding Balmoral, the Queen's castle in Scotland. According to Britain's *Daily Mail,* the prince, 48, who had consoled himself with stiff martinis and late-night calls to friends including his mistress, Camilla Parker Bowles, was spotted wandering alone at 6:30 a.m. under dour gray skies. Over and over he asked himself how it could be that the fresh and uncomplicated girl he married when she was 20 should end her life in the mangled wreck of a car speeding through Paris.

With Diana's body lying in the Chapel Royal at St. James's Palace in London, the world seemed to be pondering the same question. If ever a life had seemed destined for greater things, it was Diana's. As the Lord Chamberlain's office and the Spencer family finalized plans for Diana's funeral at Westminster Abbey (a rite involving 1,900 mourners, including 70 representatives of Diana's favorite charities, and more than 2 billion television viewers) and her private burial on an island at her ancestral home, Althorp House, near the tiny village of Great Brington, her admirers were swept up in grief.

And there was anger as well: at the swarm of paparazzi who pursued the Mercedes in which she and Al Fayed had been riding into a tunnel alongside the Seine; at the driver, Henri Paul, a Ritz Hotel employee who, according to authorities, was legally drunk when the car flew out of control as it sped up to a reported 121 mph; and at the press in general, whom many blamed for the death of a woman who had lost all claim to privacy when she became a princess. Ironically, Diana's life had seemed full of promise at the time of her death. Publicly involved since July with the attentive Al Fayed, a splashy Egyptian-born businessman and movie producer (*Chariots of Fire*) who was the son of the controversial billionaire Mohamed Al Fayed, she had vacationed with him three times in five weeks. Dodi had also given Diana a reported $200,000 gold-and-diamond ring from Paris's Repossi jewelry boutique the afternoon before they were killed.

Earlier, Diana telephoned the *Daily Mail*'s Richard Kay, who reported that she "was as happy as I have ever known her. For the first time in years, all was well with her world." Exuberantly, Diana told Kay that she hoped to step back from charity work to concentrate on her private life. Branding the British press as "ferocious," she had earlier told the newspaper *Le Monde* that she would long since have fled the country if not for her sons. "Abroad it is different," she said. "There I am received with kindness."

In the evening before the fatal car crash, Diana and Al Fayed dined at the Ritz's luxurious L'Espadon restaurant. As they were preparing to leave, the maître d'hôtel whispered that about 30 photographers were massed outside the hotel. Dodi's Range Rover, with his regular chauffeur, sped away from the Ritz, followed by two more decoys. But most of the photographers didn't bite. When the couple finally left at around 12:15 a.m., it was in a black Mercedes S280 driven by Henri Paul, the hotel's assistant director of security. A stocky, balding Breton of 41, Paul was a former French Air Force commando who had twice completed a Mercedes-Benz training course. Scheduled to be off duty that night, Paul, whose blood alcohol level was later found to be triple the French legal limit, taunted photographers by announcing, "You won't catch up with us." On the mile-long stretch to the tunnel beside the Place de l'Alma, he picked up speed but lost none of their pursuers—at least seven cameramen on five motorcycles and scooters. Then it happened. Veering out of control on a slight curve, the Mercedes hurtled head-on into the 13th concrete support column inside the tunnel. Rolling over and slamming into the opposite wall, it came to a stop facing oncoming traffic.

The paparazzi descended seconds after the crash. With ambulances 15 minutes away, at least one cameraman began snapping the princess and Al Fayed, who died at the scene. Angry onlookers reportedly attacked the lensman before police arrived, and gendarmes confiscated his film. Rushed at 2 a.m. to the hospital La Pitié-Salpétrière, Diana, whose heart had been restarted once, was surrounded by a team of some 20 doctors and nurses. She quickly went into cardiac arrest; in surgery, physicians discovered a ruptured pulmonary vein and profuse bleeding into her chest cavity. At 4:57 a.m., Interior Minister Jean-Pierre Chevènement passed on the news of her death. (Trevor Rees-Jones, Al Fayed's Welsh bodyguard and the only occupant in the car wearing a seat belt, survived, but could not immediately recall the details of the crash.) That morning and throughout the week, public distress over the princess's death was most intense in London, where thousands of dazed mourners made pilgrimages to Buckingham Palace and Kensington Palace, Diana's home. They buried the wrought-iron gates in daisies and lilies and propped up hand-lettered signs: "Born a lady, became a princess, died a saint." Flags were lowered to half-mast, and services were held at churches including St. Paul's Cathedral, where the Waleses had wed on July 29, 1981. At St. James's Palace, the wait to sign the books of condolence lasted up to 11 hours.

Though their public demeanor was controlled as usual, the Windsors were profoundly shaken by the death of the woman they had so recently seen as an embarrassment. But the grief-wracked populace demanded that her former in-laws drop the stony silence of protocol and pub-

The princess and Dodi Al Fayed on vacation in the Mediterranean.

licly share the nation's sorrow. After the unrelenting barrage of criticism, the House of Windsor blinked. Queen Elizabeth took the extraordinary step of making a live, televised speech to assure her subjects that "we have all been trying in our different ways to cope." The Spencer side succeeded in shaping the kind of personalized funeral that the princess herself might have designed. Elton John was invited to sing. Princes William and Harry, who were told of their mother's death by Prince Charles while vacationing at Balmoral, were allowed to choose whether they would march behind her coffin.

On the day of the funeral, her coffin itself—drawn on a gun carriage—was draped with the Royal Standard and topped by three white wreaths: tulips from William, a large spray of lilies from Diana's brother Charles, Earl Spencer, 33, and from Harry, creamy Princess of Wales roses developed by a British botanist for his mother and available only this year. Nestled inside them was a card with MUMMY printed in a child's uncertain hand.

As the cortege neared Buckingham Palace, there in front of the gate stood Princes Edward and Andrew, Andrew's ex-wife, Sarah Ferguson, who had said earlier in a statement, "There are no words strong enough to describe the pain in [my] heart,"and their two daughters. As the gun carriage passed, the Queen bowed her head, a remarkable gesture written in no book of protocol.

Outside St. James's Palace, the principal mourners—Earl Spencer, William, and Harry—were joined not only by Prince Charles but also by his father, the 76-year-old Duke of Edinburgh. As the three men and two boys marched the last mile with many benefactors of Diana's charities, her mother, Frances Shand Kydd, 61, and her sisters, Lady Sarah McCorquodale and Lady Jane Fellowes—who had accompanied the red-eyed Prince Charles on his flight to Paris to retrieve Diana's remains—filed into the Abbey to the somber cadence of its tenor bell, tolling every minute.

During the funeral, both boys were overcome by Elton John's performance of his revamped "Candle in the Wind." Others were more pained by what followed—Earl Spencer's eloquent, outspoken speech to the royal family concerning their treatment of her and his nephews' future. In his eulogy to Diana, he promised that "we, your blood family, will do all we can to continue the imaginative and loving way in which you were steering these two exceptional young men so that their souls are not simply immersed by duty and tradition, but can sing openly as you planned." Another side of Diana's legacy was already being realized. In just the first two weeks after her death, more than $200 million from friends and strangers alike poured into the Diana, Princess of Wales Memorial Fund, set up by Kensington Palace to support her favorite charities. Mohamed Al Fayed pledged $7.5 million in donations to causes with which Diana had a personal connection.

The interment of Dodi, the man who had made Diana's last weeks so happy, took place on the day he died. Brought back to England, his body was buried expeditiously (according to Muslim custom) in Brookwood Cemetery near Woking, 35 miles southwest of London. After a prayer service at the London Central Mosque attended by 650 people, Dodi, the only son of Mohamed Al Fayed and the late Samira Khashoggi, sister of Saudi arms dealer Adnan, was laid to rest at 11:30 p.m.; shrouded in linen, the body was placed in a grave facing Mecca. "Diana and Dodi were made for each other," says photographer Terry O'Neill, one of the many friends who spoke of him warmly. "He offered the love, sympathy, understanding, quietness, and politeness she needed. Also, he had the peripheral things—the boats, houses, and security to give her the privacy she [craved]."

THE QUEEN OF PEOPLE'S HEARTS

In the end, it was the title she wore best. The fashion harbinger in glittering jewels and designer gowns was, in fact, more comfortable dealing with Mother Teresa than playing at Marie Antoinette. Using her celebrity to focus attention on breast cancer, AIDS, drug addiction, and most recently, the carnage wrought by land mines, she had, by the time of her death, largely fulfilled her goal to become the "queen of people's hearts." In her last interview, Diana told *Le Monde*, "Nothing gives me more happiness than to try to aid the most vulnerable of this society. Whoever is in distress who calls me, I will come running."

Some speculated it was her unhappy childhood that made her so sensitive to others' pain. She herself once suggested that her status as a royal outcast made her identify with the disenfranchised. "I was very confused by which area I should go into," she told the BBC two years ago. "Then I found myself being more and more involved with people who were rejected by society... and I found an affinity there." Though she cut the number of charities she actively supported from more than a hundred to six when her divorce was finalized last year, her intensity didn't slacken. "She would look you in the eye when she arrived as if to say, 'I'm yours for the evening. What do you want me to do?'" said Michael Watson, former chairman of the AIDS charity Crusaid.

Not that she ever had to. The mere sight of the world's most popular princess was enough to make the dollars—and the press—start pouring in. The auction of 79 of her evening gowns at Christie's last June—an idea first suggested by Prince William—raised more than $5.7 million for charity. After her death, Buckingham Palace had to set up a special memorial fund to accommodate the flood of money being donated for her causes. "No one could bring attention to an issue like she could," says Landmine Survivors Network head Ken Rutherford, 35, who accompanied Diana to Bosnia last month. "She was magic with these people."

But despite her high philanthropic profile, many of Diana's most moving gestures were made far from the cameras. Lord Thomas, a 37-year-old Londoner, recalls Diana often stopping by to serve lunch to the residents at the AIDS hospice where he volunteered "She wasn't there in any official capacity; she would come to visit completely on her own," he says. "She did things like this because she wanted to, from her heart."

THE WINDSORS CARRY ON

When **Charles, the Prince of Wales** walked beside his two sons, his father, Duke of Edinburgh, and his former brother-in-law, Charles, Earl Spencer, behind Princess Diana's cortege, savvy observers noticed something extraordinary. The future King of England, usually a pillar of protocol, had parted with tradition by wearing a blue Savile Row suit to the funeral. It was neither a symbol of disrespect nor a fickle fashion statement. Rather, says royal author Brian Hoey, "It was Diana's favorite blue suit, and she helped him choose it. She preferred him in blue [rather] than black or gray. It was a lovely, silent compliment to her."

The windsurfing-parachuting-scuba-diving Action Prince of the '70s and the oratorical Philosopher Prince of the '80s had morphed from the Self-absorbed Prince of the early '90s. Finally, perhaps, Charles might be finding his true colors. Already his comportment in the aftermath of Diana's death—tearfully receiving the coffin in France, tenderly consoling his sons, distraughtly walking alone in the misty Scottish highlands outside Balmoral—has helped soften his image as the poster boy for royal stoicism.

Routinely derided as both parent and public figure, he has never quite managed to capture the public's heart. But Charles has tried to please.

A distressed Prince Charles.

Until he was 32 years old he lived at home with his parents. Then he found a lovely bride and promptly fulfilled his duty to beget heirs. Now all he can do is wait for his mother to pass him the scepter. Elizabeth is ticking away better than Big Ben, and Charles could end up like his great-great-grandfather, King Edward VII, who held the title of Prince of Wales for almost 60 years before his mother, Queen Victoria, passed away.

So much of Charles's behavior, however, is a matter of upbringing and thankless experience. Just weeks after entering the world as heir to the throne in 1948, he was left in the care of nannies while his parents performed their endless royal duties. "There's a famous old photo," says royal author Anthony Holden, "of the Queen arriving home on a train after a coronation tour and greeting her mother and sister [Princess Margaret] with a kiss, then greeting Charles, who was about 4 years old, with a handshake and

Prince Charles and President Jiang Zemin of China in Hong Kong.

straightening his collar. That tells the whole story."

In 1971, a year after graduating from Trinity College in Cambridge, the prince enlisted in the Royal Navy, where he served for five years flying helicopters and serving on frigates. Already, at a polo match in the early '70s, he had met Camilla Shand, whose great-grandmother, Alice Keppel, had had an affair with Edward VII. Though they hit it off immediately, Camilla, reportedly having no interest in marrying Charles and becoming a public figure, wed cavalry officer Andrew Parker Bowles in 1973.

During the subsequent years, Charles has contributed eloquently and provocatively to the public discourse on the preservation of architecture, the environment, and the language. In 1997 he even fulfilled the grand though slightly depressing role of handing over Hong Kong and its 6.5 million imperial subjects to the Chinese government. On June 30 the prince joined Chinese president Jiang Zemin at a transition ceremony that marked a symbolic sunset over the British empire.

Preparing to ascend to the throne, however, wasn't enough to keep together his marriage with **Lady Diana Spencer**. In an excerpt of his diaries of 1986 and 1987, as reported in *The Prince of Wales,* an authorized biography by Jonathan Dimbleby, he wrote, "How awful incompatibility is... I never thought it would end up like this. How could I have got it all so wrong?"

As the world celebrated that fairy-tale marriage—seen by millions worldwide on July 29, 1981—the seeds of its failure began to become apparent. While the couple was touring Portugal in February 1987, photographers started to notice the first signs of marital strain—topped off by the pair taking separate suites at a palace in Lisbon.

Royal watchers maintain Prince Philip had urged his son to marry a quiet girl and produce an heir. Charles, though less cynical, certainly married a girl—and, at 20, 12 years his junior, that's what she was—for whom he was ill-suited. In December 1992 the Prince and Princess of Wales announced an official separation that finally ended the long charade of their once idealized marriage.

Shortly thereafter, the last hope of a happy ending quickly faded. A racy taped phone chat between Prince Charles and his then confidante and current love interest, Camilla Parker Bowles, was published worldwide. Charles revealed, among other steamy things, his surprising desire to live inside her "trousers or something." He purportedly declared his love for her and gushed, "In the next life, I should like to come back as your knickers."

Then came new revelations of a sexually charged phone conversation in which Diana discussed with *her* confidant, James Gilbey, her fear of getting pregnant. So in December 1993, when the tearful princess announced that she was greatly curtailing her public life, it appeared that the Palace had finally succeeded in reining her in.

"The dream is over. The people's darling will never become queen," proclaimed columnist John Casey in the *Evening Standard*.

In 1994, the second year of their official separation, the union of the prince and princess seemed to unspool with a special savagery and at indecent length in every possible medium. Worse, Charles and the House of Windsor itself seemed to lose in the process the public sympathy they so desperately tried to engender. The fire was fueled by the principals themselves, cooperating with unseemly disclosures and partisan biographies about lovers old and new, alienation of feelings, eating disorders, and suicide attempts. Caught in this murderous crossfire, Charles and Diana found themselves the villains of a klieg-lit reality that had finally, and sadly, overtaken the soft-focus fairy tale. In August of 1996, after much wrangling on both sides, the fairy tale legally ended in divorce.

Struggling to overcome his image as the diffident twit who allowed his marriage to founder, the prince rolled up his sleeves and wrestled with the demon of publicity. Charles maintained that he remained faithful to Diana "until it became clear that the marriage had irretrievably broken down." (But another '94 tome, *Camilla: The King's Mistress,* claims that Charles spent the night before his wedding with Parker Bowles.)

In January 1995, Camilla and her husband Andrew abandoned the charade that their union was intact, ending their 21-year marriage. Palace insiders were convinced that Charles's startling confessions and Camilla's split were part of an elaborate long-range plan designed to bring their 25-year relationship out of the shadows—and set the stage for another royal marriage. But it seems unlikely now that he could marry Camilla in the foreseeable future without deeply offending public opinion. Before Diana's death, Queen Elizabeth herself demanded that the prince scrap his dream of marrying Parker Bowles, warning him that it could cost him the throne. Royal insiders say that Charles will do whatever is necessary to ensure his family's continued reign, short of bowing to recent polls suggesting Britain's citizens would prefer to see the crown bypass Charles and go directly to William. "Diana's death will have many consequences," says Peter Archer, royal correspondent. "One will be that the royals will have to be responsive to the public. And it's a change he'll embrace. The Windsors are constantly reinventing themselves. For the moment, at least, the prince's role as Britain's next sovereign seems secure."

"Absolutely, he will be king if he outlives his mother," says Hoey. "There's no question of William

Camilla Parker Bowles.

Princess Diana's dresses on Christie's auction block.

bypassing him. William wouldn't want it, the Queen wouldn't want it, and I don't think the country would want it. It's his destiny."

With the death of his ex-wife, Charles's goal of distancing himself from her has been forever crushed. Earlier in the year Charles ditched the symbols of the Spencer family from his coat of arms and took up the coat of arms he used as a bachelor, which features his badge of three ostrich feathers and his motto "Ich dien" (I serve). In July he threw Camilla a lavish fiftieth birthday party on the grounds of Highgrove, the prince's Gloucestershire estate.

Upon learning of Diana's death, Camilla was reported to be "absolutely devastated." In early July Camilla herself had gotten into a car wreck while speeding off to Highgrove for a dinner with Charles. And while Charles himself did not gallop up on a shining steed to rescue her, Camilla did summon his royal staff on her cell phone to whisk her away from the scene of the crash. "The specter of Diana is going to haunt [Charles] until the day he dies," says Hoey. "We've seen the end to any possibility of a marriage [to Camilla] in the near future."

As for Diana, 36 and on her own for a year, her dramatic end was all the more tragic because she had just begun a new chapter in her life. Despite being stripped of the HRH status as part of the divorce settlement, the princess had become a magnetic presence in philanthropic efforts. Diana kicked off her revitalized mission with an auction of 79 of her designer dresses at Christie's auction house in New York.

Single-handedly she had lent fresh glamour and force to a fairly dowdy dynasty. As Princess of Wales she put her life and soul into the most wrenching social issues without ever flinching. "Against the advice of friends," adds author Hoey, "she was the first royal to shake hands without a glove with an AIDS patient. She knew that that photograph would help allay fears. It was a very brave thing to do."

Diana had begun with one overriding duty—to produce an heir, preferably male—and she was fortunate enough within two years of her marriage to produce two towheads, known as the heir and the spare—to whom she referred proudly, proprietarily as "my boys." Demonstrative where Charles was reserved, preferring fun to formality, she gave **Prince William**, 15, and **Prince Harry**, 13, a sense of childhood that no Windsor would have or could have. Harry felt the glare of the spotlight this year when it was reported that he has been having difficulty at school, perhaps because of a learning disability. And by all accounts, William, who lives with the burden of being Charles's heir, felt the pain of his parents breakup, and his mother's death, most acutely. "William already hates press photographers," says Judy Wade, a royals reporter. "This will deepen any anger he has."

Now 15, the boy who seems destined to be king is leaving childhood behind. A rambunctious toddler who grew into a reserved primary-schooler, William has been learning to cope with the peculiar demands of royal life. Like younger brother Harry, he must prepare for a role that will become more public over time, and one that will expose his every misstep. Upon the urging of his grandfather, Wills entered Eton, one of England's most exclusive public—meaning private—schools, and is the first heir to the British throne to do so. Eton has been educational home to many British luminaries, including Gladstone, Pitt the Elder, and 18 other prime ministers, since 1440. In March, William got a taste of the pomp and circumstance in his future when both parents stood by as he was confirmed as a member of the Anglican church in St. George's Chapel near Windsor Castle. The ceremony put him one step closer to the throne, as the King of England is also the Defender of the Faith.

Taller than his father at 6' 1", William has grown into a thoughtful young man with a strong sense of duty and little of the Windsors' emotional detachment. "When you discover you can give joy to people... there is nothing quite like it," Diana once told *The New Yorker.* "William has begun to understand that, too. And I am hoping it will grow in him." Though William could, as one royal watcher suggested half-seriously years ago, "decide to go backpacking in Nepal and not come back," that doesn't seem likely. After all, he is—and always will be—his mother's son. "He knows how much Diana would want him to do the job he was born to do," says Lord Jeffrey Archer, a close friend of Diana's. "He will be conscious of that and, in her memory, do it even better."

Diana and Charles were not the only royals having trouble making peace with the idea of separate households. Hitched for 16 years, Charles's younger sister, **Princess Anne**, and Captain Mark Phillips were initially drawn together by their passion for horses (both are extraordinary equestrians: Phillips coached America's Olympic team in 1996). But Anne's interests were much broader—she is president of the Save the Children Fund and was even nominated for the Nobel Peace Prize a few years back. Says Anne of her work, "You have to decide at the end of the day if you can live with yourself." You also have to decide if you can live with

Princes William and Harry at their beloved mother's funeral.

your husband, and the affirmative answer increasingly came into doubt. The couple finally separated in 1989, and after divorcing, Anne married long-time love Timothy Laurence, five years her junior, in December 1992. As close to her mother as any of her siblings, Anne staged her second wedding as an intimate family affair, attended by only a handful of relatives including her two children with Phillips, **Peter** and **Zara**.

Anne's second brother, rowdy **Prince Andrew, Duke of York**, has had his fair share of marital bad luck as well. After a plucky performance in the Falklands conflict, helicopter pilot Andy seemed interested mainly in oat-sowing and club-crawling with a string of steamy ladies, culminating with former soft-porn star Koo Stark. What well-bred English girl would marry Andrew and put up with him?

And so when the prince's roving eye fell upon Sarah Ferguson in 1985, the nation breathed a collective sigh of relief. A strapping, worldly wench who loved a good time, Fergie seemed perfectly suited to her happy-go-lucky hubby. But while **Sarah, Duchess of York**, produced two lovely daughters, **Princesses Beatrice** and **Eugenie**, she also committed gaffe after gaffe. If the Yorks often struck the public as a pair of heedless hedonists, at least they originally seemed besotted with each other. But Fergie's erratic behavior quickly brought that into doubt as well. After a series of romantic trysts and crass missteps on her part, the duchess was formally separated from the duke in 1992. Later that year London tabs were abrim with graphic photos of Fergie on the Riviera cavorting topless with her American-born "financial advisor," John Bryan, who was shown smooching the bare instep of her foot while her two young daughters looked on. She later confessed that the publication of those photos had been her "most humiliating experience."

Fergie was left scrambling to settle debts reaching more than $1.5 million by selling off the rights to her children's cartoon character, Budgie the Helicopter, opening a cable television channel, hosting a documentary in the Australian outback, and launching her own perfume. No stranger to the ups and downs of yo-yo diets, Fergie is well qualified for her current stint as a Weight Watchers spokeswoman. "My problem, you see, is the bum," she confided. "My daughters say, 'Give us your wiggle, Mummy.' " The duchess will collect $1 million for sharing such weighty confessions, and she also pocketed a cool $1.2 million for her tell-all book, *My Story*. Sarah swept through the talk show circuit promoting the book, offering tearjerking tidbits about life in her gilded cage. Oprah Winfrey lent a sympathetic ear as Fergie admitted, "I was never cut out for royalty."

In 1996 the Yorks finally decided to split officially, contending that, unlike the

A ROYAL CALENDAR

A listing of birthdays and other special royal milestones. (Source: *Whitaker's Almanac*)

Prince Andrew	February 19, 1960
Prince Edward	March 10, 1964
Princess Eugenie	March 23, 1990
Queen Elizabeth	April 21, 1926
The Queen's coronation	June 2, 1953
Prince Philip	June 10, 1921
Prince William	June 21, 1982
Queen Mother	August 4, 1900
Princess Beatrice	August 8, 1988
Princess Anne	August 15, 1950
Princess Margaret	August 21, 1930
Prince Henry	September 15, 1984
Duchess of York (Sarah)	October 15, 1959
Prince Charles	November 14, 1948
The Queen's wedding	November 20, 1947

Fergie as spokeswoman.

Waleses, their decision was "theirs alone," and not precipitated by a letter from the Queen. According to court insiders, however, Andrew and Fergie are still the closest of friends. In August of 1996 Andrew even threw the duchess a lavish party to "celebrate ten years of marriage," according to the *Daily Mirror*. The 200-guest bash, which followed Princess Beatrice's eighth birthday tea party, included old flame Koo Stark. The on-again, off-again duke and duchess have continued to send mixed messages: while Sarah acknowledged that they had agreed to see other people, she warned potential rivals not to cozy up too close to her ex, perhaps in response to Andrew's apparently romantic relationship with 29-year-old Henriette Peace.

Poor **Prince Edward**, Elizabeth's youngest and the only one never married, has never even been engaged, but the pressure is certainly on. The *Daily Mirror* reported that the Queen had invited Edward's girlfriend, Sophie Rhys-Jones, to her 70th birthday party, but had snubbed Diana and Sarah. Dating the 32-year-old London public relations rep—a Diana look alike who is distantly related to the princess—for over four years now, Edward has been trying to take things slowly. Given the failure of his three older siblings' marriages, it's hard to blame him for being a bit commitment-shy. "The Queen is happy with Sophie," says one Palace insider. "But she wants them to make up their minds. It's beginning to be make or break time."

Whether or not a royal alignment lies around the corner, the lovers are finding life together sweet. "Basically," said Rhys-Jones in 1995, "we are simply two people who are happy enjoying each other's company."

More underestimated than underdeveloped, Edward has blazed a difficult path that has brought him both criticism and success. Brits are ambivalent about his quitting the Royal Marines in 1987, a move that earned him the label "Wimp of Windsor" and that fueled speculation about his sexual preference. But Edward's independence of mind may make him the most interesting member of the royal family yet. He is, for instance, the first child of a reigning monarch to—*gulp*—take a real job, initially as a gofer with Andrew Lloyd Webber's Really Useful Theatre Company. After becoming overseas manager of *Cats* and *Starlight Express,* Edward

WORKING ROYALS

Not every crowned head lives off the tax revenue of their subjects. Here is a selection of royals who have been known to go through the nine-to-five grind like the rest of us.

Hereditary Prince Alois of Liechtenstein—works at a London auditing company

Queen Fabiola of Belgium—once worked as a nurse in a Madrid hospital

Prince Henrik of Denmark—once a secretary at the French embassy in London

Queen Noor of Jordan—worked as the Director of Planning and Design Projects at the Royal Jordanian Airline

Princess Masako of Japan—once trade specialist in the Japanese Foreign Ministry

Princess Alexandra of Denmark—once deputy head of marketing department of an investment firm

King Albert II of Belgium—served as president of the Belgian Red Cross

left Webber's company and now is joint managing director of a television production company, Ardent Productions, which produced a game show featuring off-color jokes about his mother, the Queen. His business cards read simply, "Edward Windsor." Loyal to his dreams as well as the British ideal of monarchy, the Queen's youngest child is, ran one editorial, "on the way to becoming the first really modern royal."

Edward's fascination with the theater is hardly unusual among the Windsors. Indeed, if the family reigned in Beverly Hills instead of Westminster, the Queen's younger sister, **Princess Margaret**, would be the family's Elizabeth Taylor. She has been onstage since age six, when she had a walk-on part in her father's coronation. With her theatrical props—a tortoise-shell cigarette holder, a tumbler of Famous Grouse whiskey, and a circle of intimates in the arts—the princess has played varied roles: tragic lover, wife, mother, divorcée, and regal grand dame. She emanates star quality, complete with romantic intrigues, erratic public behavior, mysterious health problems, and Sunset Boulevard brass. "I can't imagine anything more wonderful," she once said, "than being who I am."

Precocious and irrepressible as a child, the violet-eyed and theatrical Margaret wrapped George VI around her finger. Other men proved harder to keep. As a teenager she fell hard for a dashing fighter pilot named Peter Townsend, 16 years her senior, but finally passed him up at 22 when her union with the divorced Townsend was declared acceptable only if she gave up her claim to the throne and her royal income and if she would live abroad for five years.

Several years later Margaret walked the aisle with photographer Antony Armstrong-Jones (who became **Lord Snowdon** after the wedding). She produced two children with the artistic commoner: **David (Viscount Linley)** and **Lady Sarah Armstrong-Jones**. But their 18-year marriage was not a picture-book affair. Initially rejecting separation as too scandalous, both partners discreetly sizzled with old and new flames until the tabs ran pictures of Margaret and her lover Roddy Llewellyn, a gardener and wanna-be pop singer 17 years her junior. An uncontested divorce was granted in 1978.

But Margaret's son, David, did his part to show the happy side of royal life—his marriage in 1993 to Serena Stanhope, a blue blood with cover-girl looks, was a windfall for the monarchy, and their lavish nuptials at St. Margaret's Church were billed as the Wedding of the Year, drawing 650 guests.

As comfortable as the lives of the Windsors seem, ultimately being royal carries with it an incalculable personal price tag. Family members live with constant world scrutiny. And it's an irony of their station that even though they live their whole lives in public, they can barely speak their minds there. But the true value of the royal family lies in the realm of patriotic lumps in the throat. They have, at least until now, given Britain a symbol of nationhood.

CINDERELLA STORY

Don't have a fairy godmother to get you to the ball? Never fear; these days a commoner can snag her prince (or his princess) without magical intervention. Here's a list of royals who married outside of their blue blood background.

Prince Rainier of Monaco and Grace Kelly
King Edward VIII of England and Wallis Warfield Simpson
King Hussein of Jordan and Queen Noor (née Lisa Najeeb Halaby)
King Harald and Queen Sonja of Norway
Prince Joachim and Princess Alexandra of Denmark (née Alexandra Manley)
Princess Elena of Spain and businessman Jaime de Marichalar
King Carl XVI Gustav of Sweden and Silvia Sommerlath
Crown Prince Alexander of Yugoslavia and Crown Princess Katherine (née Katherine Batis)
Crown Prince Naruhito and Crown Princess Masako of Japan
Emperor Akihito and Empress Michiko of Japan

SUCCESSION: THE BUCK HOUSE BULLPEN

Under rules codified in the eighteenth century, rightful candidates to the British crown move up inexorably except for two disqualifiers: they cannot be Catholic (or marry into that faith) or be born out of wedlock. Unlike some European monarchies, which abide by the centuries-old Salic law—the exclusion of women from succession—the Court of St. James owes its vitality in great part to females. Victoria and the current Queen, for instance, are two of history's longest-reigning sovereigns. This is not to say that Britain's accession rules are not sexist: a monarch is succeeded by his or her eldest son, then by that son's sons in descending order of age, and only then by that son's daughters. The line starts again with the monarch's next youngest son, and so on, ending with the sovereign's daughters and their children. After the offspring are accounted for, the sovereign's brothers come next, followed finally by sisters. From there the line marches through uncles, aunts, and full courts of cousins, including, currently at No. 32, James Lascelles, 42, a onetime deejay in Albuquerque, N.M.

Herewith, the top 25 in the royal bullpen:

1. HRH The Prince of Wales, 48
   (Prince Charles)
2. HRH Prince William of Wales, 15
   (son of Prince Charles)
3. HRH Prince Henry of Wales, 13
   (second son of Prince Charles)
4. HRH The Duke of York (Prince Andrew), 37
   (second son of Queen Elizabeth)
5. HRH Princess Beatrice of York, 9
   (daughter of Prince Andrew)
6. HRH Princess Eugenie of York, 7
   (second daughter of Prince Andrew)
7. HRH Prince Edward, 33
   (third son of Queen Elizabeth)
8. HRH The Princess Royal (Princess Anne), 47
   (daughter of Queen Elizabeth)
9. Peter Phillips, 21
   (the highest-ranking commoner, son of Princess Anne)
10. Zara Phillips, 16
    (daughter of Princess Anne)
11. HRH Princess Margaret, Countess of Snowdon, 67
    (sister of Queen Elizabeth)
12. Viscount Linley (David), 35
    (son of Princess Margaret)
13. Lady Sarah Armstrong-Jones, 33
    (daughter of Princess Margaret)
14. Samuel David Benedict Chatto, 2
    (son of Lady Sarah Chatto)
15. HRH The Duke of Gloucester, 53
    (grandson of King George V, Queen Elizabeth's cousin)
16. The Earl of Ulster (Alexander), 23
    (son of the Duke of Gloucester)
17. Lady Davina Windsor, 20
    (daughter of the Duke of Gloucester)
18. Lady Rose Windsor, 17
    (second daughter of the Duke of Gloucester)
19. HRH The Duke of Kent (Edward), 62
    (cousin to both Queen Elizabeth and Prince Philip and son of George, Duke of Kent, younger brother of Kings Edward VII and George VI)
20. Baron Downpatrick, 9
    (son of the Duke of Kent's eldest son, the Earl of St. Andrews, who was dropped from the line when he married a Catholic)
21. Lord Nicholas Windsor, 27
    (second son of the Duke of Kent)
22. Lady Helen "Melons" Taylor, 33
    (daughter of the Duke of Kent)
23. Columbus George Donald Taylor, 2
    (son of Lady Helen Taylor)
24. Lord Frederick Windsor, 17
    (son of Prince Michael of Kent, who was dropped from the line for marrying a Catholic; Queen Elizabeth's cousin Prince Michael is the younger brother of the Duke of Kent)
25. Lady Gabriella Windsor, 16
    (daughter of Prince Michael)

ROYAL HOUSES AROUND THE WORLD

Though they rarely get the tabloid treatment of their British counterparts, less conspicuous royals do reign throughout the world. Herewith an international round-up of places where the crown still glitters.

BELGIUM

Current monarch: King Albert II (crowned 1993)

King Albert II, prince of Liège, was born on June 6, 1934. He is the son of King Leopold III and Queen Astrid, princess of Sweden, and the brother of the late King Baudouin of Belgium.

The Royal Family:

King Albert II was married to Paola Ruffo di Calabria, the daughter of a princely Italian family, in 1959. The king and queen have three children: Prince Philippe (b. 1960), Princess Astrid (b. 1962), who is now married to the Archduke Lorenz of East Austria, and Prince Laurent (b. 1963). The royal palace is in Brussels.

DENMARK

Current monarch: Queen Margrethe II (crowned 1972)

Margrethe Alexandrine Thorhildur Ingrid, the eldest daughter of King Frederik IX and Queen Ingrid of Denmark, was born on April 16, 1940.

The Royal Family:

Margrethe married French diplomat Henri-Marie-Jean-André, count de Laborde de Monpezat, in 1967 (he changed his name to Prince Henrik upon marriage). The queen and consort have two sons, Prince Frederik (b. 1968) and Prince Joachim (b. 1969; married in 1995 to Princess Alexandra). Crown Prince Frederik, as the official heir to the Danish throne, will eventually become King Frederik X. Besides the official residence in Copenhagen, the family also has a small mansion in southern France at Cahors, the home district of Prince Henrik.

JAPAN

Current monarch: Emperor Akihito (crowned 1989)

Born on December 23, 1933, Emperor Akihito is the eldest son of the late Emperor Hirohito (posthumously known as Emperor Showa) and Empress Nagako.

The Royal Family:

Emperor Akihito married Michiko Shoda in 1959. She is the eldest daughter of the Shoda family, a prominent name in Japanese industrial and academic circles. The emperor and empress live in the imperial palace in Tokyo, and they have three children: Crown Prince Naruhito (b. 1960; married in 1993 to Crown Princess Masako amid much public attention), Prince Akishino (b. 1965; married in 1990 to Princess Akishino), and Princess Sayako (b. 1969).

LIECHTENSTEIN

Current monarch: Prince Hans Adam II (crowned 1989)

His Serene Highness Prince Hans Adam II is the eldest son of the late Prince Franz Josef II of Liechtenstein and Countess Gina von Wilczek. He was born on February 14, 1945.

The Princial Family:

Hans Adam II married Countess Marie Kinsky von Wchinitz and Tettau of Prague in 1967. The couple has four children: Crown Prince Alois (b. 1968; married to Duchess Sophie of Bavaria in 1993; son Joseph Wenzel Maximilian Maria b. 1995; daughter Marie Caroline Immaculata b. 1996), Prince Maximilian (b. 1969), Prince Constantin (b. 1972), and Princess Tatjana (b. 1973). The royal family resides in the Vaduz Castle.

LUXEMBOURG

Current monarch: Grand Duke Jean (crowned 1964)

Grand Duke Jean was born on January 5, 1921. He is the eldest son of the late Grand Duchess Charlotte and Prince Felix of Luxembourg, prince of Bourbon Parma.

The Royal Family:

Grand Duke Jean was married to Princess Joséphine-Charlotte of Belgium in 1953. She is the daughter of Prince Leopold of Belgium and Princess Astrid of Sweden, and the sister of the late King Baudouin of Belgium. The royal couple resides in the Castle of Colmar-Berg in Luxembourg, and they have five children: Princess Marie-Astrid (b. 1954), Prince Henri (b. 1955; the hereditary grand duke of Luxembourg), Prince Jean and his twin sister Princess Margaretha (b. 1957), and Prince Guillaume (b. 1963).

MONACO

Current monarch: Prince Rainier III (crowned 1949)

The Sovereign Prince of Monaco and head of the House of Grimaldi, Prince Rainier III, was born on May 31, 1923. He is the grandson of the late Prince Louis II of Monaco and the son of Princess Charlotte and Prince Pierre, count of Polignac.

The Royal Family:

Prince Rainier III married American actress Grace Kelly (1929–1982) in 1956. She was the daughter of John B. and Margaret Kelly of Philadelphia. The couple had three children: Princess Caroline (b. 1957), Crown Prince Albert (b. 1958), and Princess Stephanie (b. 1965; married in 1995 to her French-born former bodyguard Daniel Ducruet, 31; now divorced). The royal palace is in Monte Carlo, and the family owns a private residence in Paris.

THE NETHERLANDS

Current monarch: Queen Beatrix (crowned 1980)

Beatrix Wilhemina Armgard was born on January 31, 1938, the first child of Queen Juliana and Prince Bernhard of the Netherlands.

The Royal Family:

Queen Beatrix was married to a German diplomat, Claus von Amsberg, in 1966, and the royal couple now resides in the Huis ten Bosch Palace in the Hague. The queen and prince have three sons: Prince Willem-Alexander Claus Georg Ferdinand (b. 1967), Prince Johan Friso Bernhard Christiaan David (b. 1968), and Prince Constantijn Christof Frederik Aschwin (b. 1969).

NORWAY

Current monarch: King Harald (crowned 1991)

Born on February 21, 1937, King Harald is the firstborn son of the late King Olav V and Princess Märtha.

The Royal Family:

The announcement that King Harald was to marry commoner Sonja Haraldsen in 1968 triggered much debate about the future of the Norwegian monarchy. Since their marriage, however, Queen Sonja has been accepted by the public. The king and queen, who reside in the royal palace in Oslo, have a daughter, Princess Märtha Louise (b. 1971), and a son, Crown Prince Haakon (b. 1973).

SPAIN

Current monarch: King Juan Carlos (crowned 1975)

Juan Carlos de Borbón y Borbón was born on January 5, 1938. He is the first son of Don Juan de Borbón y Battenberg and Doña María de las Mercedes de Borbón y Orleans, and the grandson of King Alfonso XIII and Queen Victoria Eugenia, who was herself the granddaughter of Queen Victoria of England.

The Royal Family:

King Juan Carlos married Princess Sofía, the daughter of King Paul I and Queen Fredericka of Greece, in 1962. The king and queen have three children: Princess Elena (b. 1963), Princess Cristina (b. 1965), and Crown Prince Felipe (b. 1968). Princess Elena, next in line for the throne, married banker Jaime de Marichalar, 31, in March 1995. It was Spain's first royal wedding since 1906. The Palacio de La Zarzuela, the family's official residence, is situated five kilometers outside of Madrid. Their summer residence, the Palace of Marivent, is in the city of Palma de Mallorca on the island of Mallorca.

SWEDEN

Current monarch: Carl XVI Gustaf (crowned 1973)

Carl XVI Gustaf was born on April 30, 1946, the youngest child and only son of hereditary Prince Gustaf Adolf of Sweden and Princess Sibylla of Sachsen-Coburg-Gotha.

The Royal Family:

Carl XVI Gustaf married commoner Silvia Renate Sommerlath, daughter of Walther and Alice Sommerlath of the Federal Republic of Germany, in 1976. The king and queen have three children: Princess Victoria (b. 1977), Prince Carl Philip (b. 1979), and Princess Madeleine (b. 1982). In 1980 the Swedish act of succession was changed to allow females the same rights of succession as males; the crown passes to the eldest child regardless of sex. Thus, eldest daughter Victoria has been named the crown princess and successor to Carl XVI Gustaf. The family lived in the royal palace in Stockholm until 1981, when they moved to Drottningholm Palace on the outskirts of the city.

SCREEN

PICKS & PANS 1997

Budgets got bigger, releases got wider, but stays at the cinema got shorter, as last week's feature got ousted by this Friday's spectacular...or spectacular flop. Asterisks mark the best blockbusters, as well as the gems you may have missed in the shuffle.

ABSOLUTE POWER
Clint Eastwood, Gene Hackman
Eastwood directs this gripping thriller in his usual expeditious, unadorned style, though the plot at times strains credulity. (R)

ADDICTED TO LOVE
Meg Ryan, Matthew Broderick
The fundamental problem with this oddly appealing, bruised valentine of a movie is that Ryan and Broderick are stalkers. If you can jump that hurdle, there is much to appreciate here. (R)

***AIR FORCE ONE**
Harrison Ford, Gary Oldman
A rousing thriller that hits cruising speed with its first scene and never slows down. (R)

ALBINO ALLIGATOR
Matt Dillon, Faye Dunaway, Gary Sinise, William Fichtner, Skeet Ulrich
This claustrophobic drama never moves beyond being a cinematic parlor trick showing how much one can accomplish in a restricted space. (R)

ANACONDA
Jennifer Lopez, Jon Voight
The title beast rams boats and coils and uncoils like some monstrous party favor in this preposterously amusing thriller. (PG-13)

AUSTIN POWERS: INTERNATIONAL MAN OF MYSTERY
Mike Myers, Elizabeth Hurley, Michael York, Mimi Rogers, Robert Wagner
Though the smutty humor gets excessive, this is an effervescent (but puny) spoof of all those swinging '60s secret agent movies. (PG-13)

B.A.P.S.
Halle Berry, Natalie Desselle
As a Black American Princess Berry sashays about in fabulously tasteless clothes with flair in this amiable but botched comedy. (PG-13)

BATMAN & ROBIN
George Clooney, Chris O'Donnell, Uma Thurman, Arnold Schwarzenegger
About what you've come to expect: loud, frenzied, brawling, and fixated on gadgetry. (PG-13)

THE BEAUTICIAN AND THE BEAST
Fran Drescher, Timothy Dalton
An excessively coiffed girl from Queens finds love when she's hired to tutor the offspring of a fictional nation's stern president. As Drescher herself has been known to say, "Oy." (PG)

BLISS
Craig Sheffer, Sheryl Lee, Terence Stamp
A painfully dull portrait of a marriage, *Bliss* is also a paean to the curative powers of sexual healing—but for all its frank talk and entwined limbs, there's no steam coming off this one. (Not rated)

BLOOD & WINE
Jack Nicholson, Steven Dorff, Judy Davis, Michael Caine, Jennifer Lopez
A dark domestic drama masquerading as a heist film, *Blood & Wine* makes for an often funny but uneven, and sometimes violent, film. (R)

BOX OF MOONLIGHT
John Turturro, Sam Rockwell
A straitlaced electrical engineer loosens up after spending time in the woods with a wacky forest sprite. An appealingly whimsical feel-good movie. (R)

BRASSED OFF
Ewan McGregor, Tara Fitzgerald, Pete Postlethwaite
While a proud bandleader dreams of winning a national competition, the government wants to shut down his small town's coal mine. This movie delivers way too much gloom-pah-pah. (R)

***BREAKDOWN**
Kurt Russell, Kathleen Quinlan
A graphic demonstration of the bad things that can happen to good people on our nation's highways, *Breakdown* will keep you on the edge of your seat for two hours. (R)

BROKEN ENGLISH
Aleksandra Vujcic, Rade Serbedzija, Julian Arahanga
A Croatian refugee waitress and a Maori cook fall in love in New Zealand, sparking objections of one group of outsiders against another. The setting, characters, and compelling performances make an old story new. (NC-17)

BUDDY
Rene Russo, Robbie Coltrane, Alan Cumming, Irma P. Hall
A 1920s socialite raises chimps as if they were her own kids. This sweet movie (based on a true story) should keep kids laughing, though adults will likely find it lacking spark. (PG)

***CAREER GIRLS**
Katrin Cartlidge, Lynda Steadman
Acted to perfection, this funny, touching movie has but one purpose: to let us draw close enough to two reunited college roommates so that we can hear their hearts beat. And break. (R)

CATS DON'T DANCE
Animated
Grim, mostly charmless, and overconceived, this film puts a politically correct overlay on a '30s musical plot about a movie-

crazed cat who takes a bus to Hollywood seeking stardom. (G)

***CHILDREN OF THE REVOLUTION**
Judy Davis, Geoffrey Rush, Sam Neill, F. Murray Abraham
An Australian communist has a one-night stand with Stalin; the love child grows to reject everything his mother stands for. A dizzyingly original comedy. (R)

COMMANDMENTS
Aidan Quinn, Courteney Cox
A black comedy with a surprisingly sentimental heart beneath a cynical veneer. Quinn shows just the right mix of outrage and loss as a doctor who tries to break all ten Commandments in retaliation against God. (R)

CON AIR
Nicolas Cage, John Cusack, John Malkovich, Steve Buscemi
This slick, violent, pumped-up action picture is loud in every sense of the word. (R)

CONSPIRACY THEORY
Mel Gibson, Julia Roberts
While the movie starts off promisingly with a yeasty fizz, it falls flat two thirds of the way through. (R)

CONTACT
Jodie Foster, Matthew McConaughey, Tom Skerritt, Angela Bassett
A plodding and uneven sci-fi drama with several redeeming moments of visual and emotional power. (PG)

COP LAND
Sylvester Stallone, Harvey Keitel, Ray Liotta, Robert De Niro
In the end, this small-scale film with big ambitions seems all too familiar. (R)

CRASH
James Spader, Holly Hunter, Elias Koteas, Deborah Kara Unger
The repellent *Crash* never develops its thesis or characters; instead it becomes a repetitive, boring blur of scenes that alternate between car crash, sex, car crash, sex, until you wonder whether there is a single traffic cop in all of Toronto. (NC-17)

DANTE'S PEAK
Pierce Brosnan, Linda Hamilton
What hath *Twister* wrought? Thanks to its predictable plot and boneheaded dialogue, this half-baked volcano picture never peaks. (PG-13)

THE DAYTRIPPERS
Anne Meara, Parker Posey
When a suburban schoolteacher discovers what she suspects is an extramarital love letter to her husband, who works in Manhattan, her whole family piles into the station wagon to drive into town for the day. A beautifully constructed little comedy. (Not rated)

THE DEVIL'S OWN
Harrison Ford, Brad Pitt, Margaret Colin, Natascha McElhone
This film can't make up its mind whether to be an American story, with chases and shootouts, or an Irish one, with heartbreak, insoluble conflict, and the pull of old ties too strong to break. (R)

***DONNIE BRASCO**
Al Pacino, Johnny Depp, Anne Heche
An FBI agent successfully infiltrates the Mafia in the 1970s. Pacino is achingly good as a wiseguy who is sadly anything but. (R)

DOUBLE TEAM
Jean-Claude Van Damme, Dennis Rodman, Mickey Rourke
A pointlessly packed action-thriller plot directed in overdrive. Vroom, vroom. (R)

DREAM WITH THE FISHES
David Arquette, Brad Hunt
Yet another comedy drama in which a straitlaced yuppie learns to loosen up only after being dragged through a string of misadventures by a freewheeling kook. Nothing here is sufficiently wild. (R)

8 HEADS IN A DUFFEL BAG
Joe Pesci, Andy Comeau, Kristy Swanson, George Hamilton, Dyan Cannon
A 79-cent plastic luggage tag would have eliminated the need for this piddling comedy. (R)

THE END OF VIOLENCE
Bill Pullman, Andie MacDowell
Meant to be a mosaic portrait of a criminally savage Hollywood on the cusp of the millenium, *Violence* is all very earnest, portentous, and more than a little annoying. (R)

THE EVENING STAR
Shirley MacLaine, Juliette Lewis, Miranda Richardson, Bill Paxton
Audiences who wept at *Terms of Endearment* come to this dumb sequel preconditioned to cry, but the story is so diffuse, they may be too distracted. (PG-13)

EVENT HORIZON
Laurence Fishburne, Sam Neill
This sci-fi horror film is a boring and blood-soaked mess. (R)

EVERYONE SAYS I LOVE YOU
Woody Allen, Goldie Hawn, Julia Roberts, Alan Alda, Drew Barrymore
The talented cast of this non-singers' musical is game enough, but what's missing is any real sense of purpose or moral weight. (R)

EXCESS BAGGAGE
Alicia Silverstone, Benicio Del Toro, Christopher Walken
There's one great gag in this muddleheaded kidnapping black comedy; after that, it's a long, hard sit. (PG-13)

***FACE/OFF**
John Travolta, Nicolas Cage
In addition to stunning action sequences, this taut psychological thriller (and meditation on the power of movie stars) has characters with intellect enough to reflect on their actions. (R)

FATHERS' DAY
Robin Williams, Billy Crystal
Williams does whatever he can

to breathe life into this premasticated comedy, which never rises above its *My Two Dads* sitcom premise. (PG-13)

FIERCE CREATURES
John Cleese, Kevin Kline, Jamie Lee Curtis, Michael Palin
A splendidly silly direct hit to the funny bone. (PG-13)

THE FIFTH ELEMENT
Bruce Willis, Gary Oldman, Ian Holm, Milla Jovovich, Luke Perry
A loud, shiny, easily forgettable-comic book of a sci-fi thriller, *Die Hard* in a *Blade Runner* wrapper. (PG-13)

FOOLS RUSH IN
Matthew Perry, Salma Hayek
This insipid romantic comedy has the leads flailing through a predictable plot that goes on far too long and substitutes high-energy antics for wit. (PG-13)

***FOR ROSEANNA**
Mercedes Ruehl, Jean Reno
This pleasant comic trifle eventually overstrains to amuse, but *Roseanna* pulls off a corker of a surprise, so all is forgiven. (PG-13)

***4 LITTLE GIRLS**
Documentary
Thirty-four years ago, four black girls were killed when a bomb exploded in the basement of a Baptist church in Birmingham. Spike Lee poignantly invokes the girls' lives and puts their shocking deaths in social and historical context, both then and now. (Not rated)

***THE FULL MONTY**
Robert Carlyle, Tom Wilkinson
A jolly, slick ensemble comedy about laid-off buddies doffing their clothes as the way to financial security. Completely, cheerfully inoffensive. (R)

THE GAME
Michael Douglas, Sean Penn
Douglas is trapped in an elaborate, potentially deadly game that has too few convincing twists. (R)

GENTLEMEN DON'T EAT POETS
Alan Bates, Theresa Russell, Sting
This disastrous little vanity production strives to parody all those chintzed-to-the-max British movies about murder among the landed, but instead plays like an interminable game of Clue. (R)

***GEORGE OF THE JUNGLE**
Brendan Fraser, Leslie Mann
This genial goofball of a movie wins you over with its silly, let's-just-have-some-fun charm. (PG)

GHOSTS OF MISSISSIPPI
Alec Baldwin, Whoopi Goldberg
The story behind white supremacist Byron De La Beckwith's belated conviction for shooting civil rights leader Medgar Evers has defeated director Rob Reiner; *Ghosts* is slow, reverent, and hushed. (PG-13)

G.I. JANE
Demi Moore, Viggo Mortensen, Anne Bancroft
Jane is short on plot beyond the obvious will-she-or-won't-she-survive-SEAL-school and long on *Flashdance*-like sequences of a sweaty Moore making like Jack Palance at the Oscars. (R)

GONE FISHIN'
Joe Pesci, Danny Glover
This dumb-buddies comedy flops about for a few minutes and dies. (PG)

GOOD BURGER
Kel Mitchell, Kenan Thompson
Lame comedy about teens who dish out chow at a burger joint. (PG)

***GOOD LUCK**
Gregory Hines, Vincent D'Onofrio
This comic drama follows two disabled men—one blind and the other in a wheelchair—as they journey from Seattle to Oregon to take part in a raft race. A small picture with a huge heart. (R)

GRAVESEND
Tony Tucci, Michael Parducci, Tom Malloy, Thomas Brandise, Macky Aquilino
Gravesend shows off a fine sense of drama and mordant humor as it tracks one very messed-up night in the lives of four young men after one of them fatally shoots the brother of another. (R)

GRIDLOCK'D
Tupac Shakur, Tim Roth
Two musicians try to go cold turkey. Solid work, but with the drugs, the scuzzy bonhomie, and the Roth, it all feels very Quentin Tarantino. (R)

***GROSSE POINTE BLANK**
John Cusack, Minnie Driver, Dan Aykroyd, Alan Arkin, Joan Cusack
Hit man Martin Blank discovers he can't leave his job behind during his 10th high school reunion. An invigoratingly fresh black comedy. (R)

***GUANTANAMERA**
Carlos Cruz, Mirtha Ibarra, Jorge Perugorria
A lively comedy from Cuba, *Guantanamera* doubles as a tasty travelogue, offering fascinating glimpses of contemporary Cuba. (Not rated)

HAMLET
Kenneth Branagh, Julie Christie, Sir Derek Jacobi, Kate Winslet
Even the most mediocre *Hamlet* is entertaining, and this production is hardly mediocre. (PG-13)

HERCULES
Animated, with voices by Tate Donovan, James Woods, Danny DeVito
In charting Hercules's rise from celebrity to true herodom, the movie displays style and sass even as it travels the well-worn Disney path—including bowdlerizing its source. (G)

***HOLLOW REED**
Martin Donovan, Joely Richardson
A father—who left his wife for a man—seeks custody after his son is battered by his ex-wife's live-in beau. Directed with great sensitivity, *Hollow Reed* is a hard-eyed look at how a curdled marriage's history continues to affect, and cloud, parental judgments. (Not rated)

HOODLUM
Laurence Fishburne, Tim Roth, Vanessa Williams, Andy Garcia
Ham-handedly ambitious, *Hoodlum* has stylish atmosphere, a sensational Fishburne—and *Godfather* influences that stop only with the theme music. (R)

IN AND OUT
Kevin Kline, Tom Selleck
Though not so great at fleshing out characters, this bright comedy is close to unbeatable on sharp, topical humor. (R)

IN LOVE AND WAR
Sandra Bullock, Chris O'Donnell
War is hell, love stinks, and that is why Hemingway ended up both a great writer and a rotten human being. Very dull. (PG-13)

***IN THE COMPANY OF MEN**
Aaron Eckhart, Stacy Edwards, Matt Malloy
Two junior executives plan to sweep a vulnerable young woman off her feet and then dump her. Either you will stay up half the night talking about this singularly chilling film, or you will feel too wrung out to talk about it at all. (R)

INVENTING THE ABBOTTS
Liv Tyler, Billy Crudup, Jennifer Connelly, Joaquin Phoenix, Joanna Going
A finely crafted but curiously old-fashioned coming-of-age drama set in an Illinois town in the late 1950s. (R)

JUNGLE 2 JUNGLE
Tim Allen, Sam Huntington
There's a lot that children will like in this story of an absentee father united with his jungle-raised son. Adults with more evolved senses of humor will find the movie cute but labored. (PG)

KAMA SUTRA: A TALE OF LOVE
Indira Varma, Sarita Choudhury, Ramon Tikaram, Naveen Andrews
Not a cheesy dirty movie—but there is still plenty to gape at in this flawed but frankly erotic tale of love and lust in 16th-century India. (Not rated)

KISS ME GUIDO
Nick Scotti, Anthony Barrile
A naive pizza maker from The Bronx discovers that his prospective new roomie is gay. A slight comedy that never overcomes its leering premise. (R)

***KOLYA**
Zdenek Sverak, Andrej Chalimon
An unwilling father slowly alters his perceptions about who he is and what he values. Quiet, understated, and profoundly moving, *Kolya* the movie proves as easy to love as Kolya the boy. (PG-13)

KULL THE CONQUEROR
Kevin Sorbo, Tia Carrere, Thomas Ian Griffith, Karina Lombard
This pectorial spectacular is so agreeably cheesy, it's pure Velveeta. (PG-13)

LEAVE IT TO BEAVER
Janine Turner, Christopher McDonald
Those who grew up on the original will get a big kick out of this, an appealing version that knowingly tweaks the series without undercutting its fundamental message. (PG)

LEO TOLSTOY'S ANNA KARENINA
Sophie Marceau, Sean Bean
Consider this movie the Cliffs Notes version; it hits all the novel's major plot points but fails to capture the depth of the characters' feelings. (PG-13)

LIAR LIAR
Jim Carrey, Maura Tierney, Jennifer Tilly, Justin Cooper, Cary Elwes
Think Ace Ventura, Attorney-at-Law, but with family values. (PG-13)

LOST HIGHWAY
Bill Pullman, Balthazar Getty
Once again David Lynch takes us into his dream world of madness and sexual violence. Get the man to a Starbucks. Now. (R)

***THE LOST WORLD: JURASSIC PARK**
Jeff Goldblum, Julianne Moore, Pete Postlethwaite, Vince Vaughn
A nonstop, 134-minute thrill ride. (PG-13)

LOVE AND OTHER CATASTROPHES
Frances O'Conner, Alice Garner
A bouncy Australian trifle about the college careers and love lives of five Melbourne students. (R)

***LOVE JONES**
Larenz Tate, Nia Long, Bill Bellamy
Minor carping about twenty-somethings' movie apartments aside, *love jones* is a smart, sassy romantic comedy. (R)

1997'S TOP TEN GROSSERS

Spielberg tops himself again: As of September 15, the only film bigger than his *Lost World* was *Men in Black* ... executive produced by Steven Spielberg. (Source: *Variety*)

1. *Men in Black*
2. *The Lost World: Jurassic Park*
3. *Liar Liar*
4. *Air Force One*
5. *My Best Friend's Wedding*
6. *Face/Off*
7. *Batman and Robin*
8. *Con Air*
9. *George of the Jungle*
10. *Contact*

LOVE! VALOUR! COMPASSION!
Jason Alexander, John Glover
Slow! Static! Annoying! Like watching the hit play—about eight gay men who share a vacation house—at too close a range. (R)

***MEN IN BLACK**
Tommy Lee Jones, Will Smith, Linda Fiorentino, Vincent D'Onofrio
A delightfully droll, deliciously quirky small film masquerading as a blockbuster—thanks to clever gags, imaginative effects, and snappy byplay. (PG-13)

METRO
Eddie Murphy, Michael Rapaport
A thumpingly loud but adrenaline-free action thriller. (R)

MICHAEL
John Travolta, Andie MacDowell, William Hurt, Robert Pastorelli
This movie trashes traditional religion, patronizes the Midwest, squeezes laughs out of a dying dog, scorns romance, and bashes men gleefully. Yet it buys into the notion that angels might really exist. Go figure. (PG-13)

MIMIC
Mira Sorvino, Jeremy Northam
A satisfyingly spooky giant bug time-waster. Think of *The Birds*, but dumber and set underground. (R)

MONEY TALKS
Chris Tucker, Charlie Sheen
Inconsequential, unoriginal cops-and-criminals comedy. Tucker ekes out a few laughs. (R)

***MOTHER**
Albert Brooks, Debbie Reynolds
Reynolds takes to director-writer Brooks's astringent (and very funny) comedy as if she had spent her life sipping vinegar. (PG-13)

***MOUTH TO MOUTH**
Javier Bardem, María Barranco, Aitana Sánchez-Gijón
This rollicking phone sex farce reminds you why Americans used to go to foreign movies in the first place: They were fun and had lots of sex. (R)

MRS. BROWN
Judi Dench, Billy Connolly
Widowed Queen Victoria is cheered by a Scottish horse groomer. A very slim chapter in British history, with a terribly one-dimensional Brown. (PG)

MURDER AT 1600
Wesley Snipes, Diane Lane, Alan Alda, Daniel Benzali, Dennis Miller
Snipes toils hard, but this White House murder mystery becomes increasingly preposterous with each new plot turn. (R)

MY BEST FRIEND'S WEDDING
Julia Roberts, Dermot Mulroney, Cameron Diaz, Rupert Everett
A frustratingly self-sabotaging movie. Why should we care about Julia Roberts's deceitful, nasty wedding-wrecker? (PG-13)

NIGHT FALLS ON MANHATTAN
Andy Garcia, Richard Dreyfuss, Lena Olin, Ian Holm, James Gandolfini
A provocative though clunkily plotted drama about the moral ambiguities confronting cops, lawyers, and politicians. (R)

NOTHING TO LOSE
Tim Robbins, Martin Lawrence
A broad, mechanical comedy about two guys who bond. Been there, done that. (R)

187
Samuel L. Jackson, John Heard, Kelly Rowan, Clifton Gonzalez Gonzalez
187 can't decide whether it's a valentine to courageous inner-city teachers or a revenge fantasy. Either way, it's a dog. (R)

OUT TO SEA
Jack Lemmon, Walter Matthau
Love Boat in which Lemmon and Matthau go hormonal. An agreeable bit of nonsense that will float the boats of the stars' fans. (PG-13)

PARADISE ROAD
Glenn Close, Pauline Collins, Frances McDormand, Julianna Margulies
Cliché prevents this film, based on the true stories of women imprisoned by the Japanese in Sumatra in 1942, from achieving the dramatic heft that was intended. (R)

***THE PEOPLE VS. LARRY FLYNT**
Woody Harrelson, Courtney Love
A high-spirited and unexpectedly entertaining celebration of the founder/publisher of *Hustler*. Love, as Flynt's late wife, Althea, steals the film. (R)

PICTURE PERFECT
Jennifer Aniston, Jay Mohr, Kevin Bacon, Olympia Dukakis
In the end, one can enjoy this savvy, insubstantial romantic comedy without buying into it. (PG-13)

THE PILLOW BOOK
Ewan McGregor, Vivian Wu
A fashion model with a fetish for full-body calligraphy decides to wield the brush herself. An exquisitely designed, sexually graphic visual feast that moves at a glacial but mesmerizing pace to a stomach-churning denouement. What gives? (Not rated)

THE PORTRAIT OF A LADY
Nicole Kidman, John Malkovich
Jane Campion's nervy but wacky version of Henry James's 1881 masterpiece has some sumptuously erotic moments, but its lead character lacks delicacy. (PG-13)

***PREFONTAINE**
Jared Leto, R. Lee Ermey
Unlike most sports movies, which have the artificial uplift of a pep rally, this movie about a defeated runner is small-scaled and quiet. A modest winner. (PG-13)

***PRIVATE PARTS**
Howard Stern, Mary McCormack, Robin Quivers, Fred Norris
The radio raunchmeister's sur-

prisingly droll bio-film does make you laugh. Out loud. A lot. (R)

ROMY AND MICHELE'S HIGH SCHOOL REUNION
Mira Sorvino, Lisa Kudrow
Cyndi Lauper's pop anthem "Girls Just Want To Have Fun" would be good match for the merry mood and message of this female buddy comedy. Not a good movie, but a fun one. (R)

ROSEWOOD
Ving Rhames, Jon Voight, Don Cheadle
The portentous would-be epic—about one of the more shameful episodes in America's tortured history of race relations—is too calculatedly mapped out to ever be quite as stirring as it wants to be. Still, this story needs telling, the narrative is inherently dramatic, and there are fervent performances. (R)

ROUGH MAGIC
Bridget Fonda, Russell Crowe
While on the run in Mexico, a magician's assistant in the early '50s falls for an American journalist and discovers she has potent magical powers of her own. It's all very odd, but not really very interesting. (PG-13)

THE SAINT
Val Kilmer, Elisabeth Shue
All the quick-change costume stuff can't disguise the fact that *The Saint* is a really big yawn and a sprawling mess to boot. (PG-13)

SELENA
Jennifer Lopez, Edward James Olmos, Jon Seda, Constance Marie
What can you say about a 23-year-old, mono-monikered, Tojano superstar who died? Not enough, these moviemakers seem to think, in a worshipful two-hour-plus movie. (PG)

SHADOW CONSPIRACY
Charlie Sheen, Linda Hamilton
An incompetent political thriller in which a White House assistant and a local reporter run breathlessly around Washington. (R)

SHALL WE DANCE?
Koji Yakusho, Tamiyo Kusakari
Instantly smitten by a glimpse of a melancholy dance teacher, a bored workaholic signs up for lessons, unbeknownst to his wife. This drama is so well acted that Western audiences should be able to see the poignant story at its heart. (PG)

SHE'S SO LOVELY
Sean Penn, Robin Wright Penn, John Travolta, Harry Dean Stanton
As softheaded as it is softhearted, *She's So Lovely* is by turns excessively sentimental, wildly comic, booze-soaked, sharply observed, compassionate, and irritatingly self-indulgent. (R)

SHILOH
Michael Moriarty, Blake Heron
An ingratiatingly old-fashioned kids' movie about a boy and his dog, *Shiloh* debates such big issues as what ownership really means and whether lying is ever justified, and does so without excessive preaching. (PG)

1996'S WORLDWIDE MONEYMAKERS

Forget about Peoria—will it play in Peru? Global grosses can cushion domestic disappointment or turn a homegrown hit into a bonanza. These members of the Class of '96 had the busiest box offices around the world. (Source: *Variety*)

Rank	Title	Gross (in millions)
1.	*Independence Day*	$808
2.	*Twister*	494
3.	*Mission: Impossible*	454
4.	*The Rock*	337
5.	*The Hunchback of Notre Dame*	323
6.	*101 Dalmatians*	314
7.	*Ransom*	307
8.	*Jerry Maguire*	271
9.	*The Nutty Professor*	270
10.	*Eraser*	235
11.	*Space Jam*	223
12.	*The Birdcage*	184
13.	*The First Wives Club*	183
14.	*Sleepers*	177
15.	*12 Monkeys*	164
16.	*Scream*	155
17.	*A Time To Kill*	154
18.	*Phenomenon*	153
19.	*Broken Arrow*	148
20.	*Star Trek: First Contact*	147

A SIMPLE WISH
Martin Short, Kathleen Turner
Half kiddie film, half adult satire, this unfocused comedy pits an unorthodox fairy godmother (Short) against a wicked witch with a heart of alum (Turner). (PG)

A SMILE LIKE YOURS
Greg Kinnear, Lauren Holly
A painfully strained comedy about the infertility woes of a married couple. (R)

SMILLA'S SENSE OF SNOW
Julia Ormond, Gabriel Byrne
A most disagreeable young woman tries to solve a murder in Copenhagen. Ormond is as ploddingly earnest as Nancy Drew. (R)

***SOME MOTHER'S SON**
Fionnula Flanagan, Helen Mirren, Aidan Gillen, David O'Hara
The least didactic and most compassionate of the '90s movies on Northern Ireland's "troubles," this film humanizes the politics by focusing on two Irish Catholic mothers. (R)

SPAWN
Michael Jai White, John Leguizamo
Phantasmagoric gobbledygook that only the most ardent fans of the comic book will willingly endure. (PG-13)

SPEED 2: CRUISE CONTROL
Sandra Bullock, Jason Patric
Like the mammoth cruise ship on which the movie is set, *Speed 2: Cruise Control* is big, bulky, and going nowhere. (PG-13)

SPRUNG
Tisha Campbell, Rusty Cundieff
This sweet-natured but perilously slight romantic comedy about four black twentysomethings could use a strong jolt of electric shock to quicken the pace. (R)

SUNDAY
David Suchet, Lisa Harrow
An out-of-work British actress living unhappily in Queens mistakes a homeless man for a famous English director. A delicate and affecting drama. (Not rated)

TEXAS CHAINSAW MASSACRE: THE NEXT GENERATION
Renee Zellweger, Matthew McConaughey, Robert Jacks
A gruesomely vile movie, shot in 1994 but released only now to cash in on the cast's newfound fame. (R)

THAT OLD FEELING
Bette Midler, Dennis Farina
This contrived fluffball of a comedy about reunited ex-spouses is hackneyed stuff, but it shows off Midler's marvelous comic abilities and supplies a good deal of broad fun. (PG-13)

THIS WORLD, THEN THE FIREWORKS
Billy Zane, Gina Gershon, Sheryl Lee
This overheated, plot-heavy noir confuses florid style with substance. (R)

'TIL THERE WAS YOU
Jeanne Tripplehorn, Dylan McDermott, Sarah Jessica Parker
The tangled film ultimately feels less like a romantic comedy than a game of cat's cradle. Its stars deserve better. (PG-13)

TIMOTHY LEARY'S DEAD
Documentary
Leary's colorful life (five wives, a jail escape, and more than 500 LSD trips) and prostate cancer death are traced; at 80 minutes, the film seems padded. (Not rated)

TOUCH
Skeet Ulrich, Bridget Fonda
Various unscrupulous folks in Los Angeles try to exploit a sketchily drawn miracle worker in this limp satire. (R)

TRAVELLER
Bill Paxton, Julianna Margulies
Despite the movie's colorful characters and cons, a violently nasty turn toward the end proves jolting and considerably dissipates one's feeling of goodwill toward *Traveller*. (R)

TRIAL AND ERROR
Michael Richards, Jeff Daniels, Charlize Theron, Jessica Steen
A passably amusing courtroom comedy about a high-powered lawyer (Daniels) who is impersonated, then replaced, by his out-of-work actor buddy (Richards). (PG-13)

TRUTH OR CONSEQUENCES, N.M.
Vincent Gallo, Kim Dickens, Kiefer Sutherland, Mykelti Williamson
A film that yearns to be a contemporary *Bonnie and Clyde*. It is neither compelling nor original. (R)

TURBO: A POWER RANGERS MOVIE
Jason David Frank, Hilary Shepard Turner, Catherine Sutherland
The second film featuring those helmet-headed teen superheros who karate-chop and kick-box the bad guys into submission. (G)

TURBULENCE
Ray Liotta, Lauren Holly
A luminous Holly turns in a strenuous performance that, at times, redeems the monumental banality of this tale, which amounts to *Airport 1975* meets *Passenger 57*. (R)

***TWIN TOWN**
Llyr Evans, Rhys Ifans
An unlikely but wildly enjoyable hybrid, this Welsh comedy combines the dopey humor of *Wayne's World*, the doped-up chic of *Trainspotting*, and, oddest of all, the sort of spectacularly violent revenge ethic that one associates with those unforgiving Corleones. (Not rated)

ULEE'S GOLD
Peter Fonda, Patricia Richardson
As a reclusive, widowed beekeeper taking care of his two

young granddaughters, Peter Fonda is powerfully good. (R)

UNDERWORLD
Denis Leary, Joe Mantegna, Larry Bishop
An awful patricidal fantasy story that combines dark atmospherics, elaborate plot, mysterious criminal kingpin, and heavy-handed psychology. (R)

***THE VAN**
Colm Meaney, Donal O'Kelly
A genial little character study about two middle-aged Irishmen dishing out fish, chips, and burgers from the back of a ramshackle van. In its own unassuming, men-behaving-daftly way, *Van* delivers. (R)

VOLCANO
Tommy Lee Jones, Anne Heche
When a movie is called *Volcano*, you want to see lava. Lots of it. Happily, *Volcano* pours on the magma. (PG-13)

***WAITING FOR GUFFMAN**
Christopher Guest, Catherine O'Hara, Fred Willard, Parker Posey
A spoof of community theater. These folks have no business being on a stage except that it leaves them flush with happiness; *Guffman* will do the same for its audience. (R)

WARRIORS OF VIRTUE
Mario Yedidia, Marley Shelton, Angus MacFadyen
This sometimes charming, sometimes vile, but always lively kids' action movie turns on the adventures of a 12-year-old schoolboy who is magically transported to the mystical subterranean kingdom of Tao. (PG)

WHEN THE CAT'S AWAY
Garance Clavel
A diverse search party seeks an escaped pet; more an exploration of Paris's changing character than a tale of cat and owner. Slight and charming. (R)

***WHEN WE WERE KINGS**
Documentary
Understated, witty, and fascinating, this film chronicles the Rumble in the Jungle—the 1974 heavyweight championship fight in Zaire between Muhammad Ali and the heavily favored George Foreman. (PG)

WILD AMERICA
Jonathan Taylor Thomas, Devon Sawa, Scott Bairstow
Three adventurous teenagers head across the country to film wild animals, primarily predators, in their natural habitats. Unfortunately, dopey subplots abound. (PG)

WORKING TITLES

At some point between the page and the public, the new releases and old favorites below had these unfamiliar labels:

What was once...	Eventually became...	What was once...	Eventually became...
Billy the Third	Tommy Boy	My Posse Don't Do Homework	Dangerous Minds
Black and White	Trading Places	Navy Cross	G.I. Jane
Bodily Harm	Malice	Paris Match	French Kiss
A Boy's Life	E. T., the Extra-Terrestrial	People Like Us	Philadelphia
Called Home	Witness	Prison Rodeo	Stir Crazy
Coma Guy	While You Were Sleeping	The Quest	Coming to America
Daddy's Home	Look Who's Talking	The Rainbow Warrior	On Deadly Ground
Extremely Violent	Last Action Hero	The Rest of Daniel	Forever Young
Father Goose	Fly Away Home	Shoeless Joe	Field of Dreams
Father's Day	Raising Cain	Simon Says	Die Hard With a Vengeance
Finished with Engines	No Way Out	Simple Simon	Mercury Rising
The Gaslight Addition	Now and Then	Space Cadet	Rocket Man
Going West in America	Switchback	The Soldier's Wife	The Crying Game
Hot and Cold	Weekend at Bernie's	Stray Dog	U-Turn
An Indian in the City	Jungle 2 Jungle	Teeny-Weenies	Honey, I Shrunk the Kids
I Was a Teenage Teenager	Clueless	Ten Soldiers	Red Dawn
Made Men	GoodFellas	3000	Pretty Woman
Man2Man	Man of the House		

THE TOP 100 FILMS OF ALL TIME

This list ranks the largest money-making movies of all time based on domestic (U.S. and Canada) box-office grosses. Figures include updated *Star Wars* grosses since the re-release and are accurate through September 14, 1997; summer blockbusters are still earning. (Source: *Variety*)

Rank	Film (year of release)	B.O. Gross
1.	*Star Wars* (1977)	$460,947,410
2.	*E.T., the Extra-Terrestrial* (1982)	399,804,539
3.	*Jurassic Park* (1993)	357,067,947
4.	*Forrest Gump* (1994)	329,689,600
5.	*The Lion King* (1994)	312,855,561
6.	*Return of the Jedi* (1983)	309,140,456
7.	*Independence Day* (1996)	306,155,579
8.	*The Empire Strikes Back* (1980)	290,178,670
9.	*Home Alone* (1990)	285,761,243
10.	*Jaws* (1975)	260,000,000
11.	*Batman* (1989)	251,188,924
12.	*Raiders of the Lost Ark* (1981)	242,374,454
13.	*Twister* (1996)	241,721,524
14.	*Men in Black* (1997)	239,354,920
15.	*Ghostbusters* (1984)	238,600,000
16.	*Beverly Hills Cop* (1984)	234,760,478
17.	*The Lost World: Jurassic Park* (1997)	228,467,634
18.	*Mrs. Doubtfire* (1993)	219,195,051
19.	*Ghost* (1990)	217,631,306
20.	*Aladdin* (1992)	217,350,219
21.	*Back to the Future* (1985)	208,242,016
22.	*Terminator 2: Judgment Day* (1991)	204,843,345
23.	*Indiana Jones and the Last Crusade* (1989)	197,171,806
24.	*Toy Story* (1995)	191,753,112
25.	*Gone with the Wind* (1939)	191,749,436
26.	*Dances with Wolves* (1990)	184,208,848
27.	*Batman Forever* (1995)	184,031,112
28.	*The Fugitive* (1993)	183,875,760
29.	*Mission: Impossible* (1996)	180,981,866
30.	*Liar Liar* (1997)	180,876,435
31.	*Indiana Jones and the Temple of Doom* (1984)	179,870,271
32.	*Pretty Woman* (1990)	178,406,268
33.	*Tootsie* (1982)	177,200,000
34.	*Top Gun* (1986)	176,781,728
35.	*Snow White and the Seven Dwarfs* (1937)	175,263,233
36.	*"Crocodile" Dundee* (1986)	174,634,806
37.	*Home Alone 2: Lost in New York* (1992)	173,585,516
38.	*Rain Man* (1988)	172,825,435
39.	*Apollo 13* (1995)	172,070,496
40.	*Three Men and a Baby* (1987)	167,780,960
41.	*Robin Hood: Prince of Thieves* (1991)	165,493,908
42.	*The Exorcist* (1973)	165,000,000
43.	*Air Force One* (1997)	163,224,275
44.	*Batman Returns* (1992)	162,831,698
45.	*The Sound of Music* (1965)	160,476,331
46.	*The Firm* (1993)	158,340,292
47.	*Fatal Attraction* (1987)	156,645,693
48.	*The Sting* (1973)	156,000,000
49.	*Who Framed Roger Rabbit* (1988)	154,112,492
50.	*Beverly Hills Cop II* (1987)	153,665,036
51.	*Jerry Maguire* (1996)	153,658,439
52.	*Grease* (1978)	153,112,492
53.	*Rambo: First Blood Part II* (1985)	150,415,432
54.	*Gremlins* (1984)	148,168,459
55.	*Lethal Weapon 2* (1989)	147,253,986
66.	*True Lies* (1994)	146,282,411
57.	*Beauty and the Beast* (1991)	145,863,363
58.	*The Santa Clause* (1994)	144,833,357
59.	*Lethal Weapon 3* (1992)	144,731,527
60.	*101 Dalmatians* (1961)	143,992,148
61.	*The Jungle Book* (1967)	141,843,612
62.	*National Lampoon's Animal House* (1978)	141,600,000
63.	*Pocahontas* (1995)	141,579,773
64.	*A Few Good Men* (1992)	141,340,178
65.	*Look Who's Talking* (1989)	140,088,813
66.	*Sister Act* (1992)	139,605,150
67.	*The Rocky Horror Picture Show* (1975)	138,929,642
68.	*Platoon* (1986)	137,963,328
69.	*Ransom* (1996)	136,458,966
70.	*101 Dalmatians* (1996)	136,189,294
71.	*Teenage Mutant Ninja Turtles* (1990)	135,265,915
72.	*The Godfather* (1972)	134,835,055
73.	*Superman* (1978)	134,218,018
74.	*The Rock* (1996)	134,069,511
75.	*The Silence of the Lambs* (1991)	130,726,716
76.	*Honey, I Shrunk the Kids* (1989)	130,724,172
77.	*The Flintstones* (1994)	130,531,208
78.	*An Officer and a Gentleman* (1982)	129,795,549
79.	*The Nutty Professor* (1996)	128,814,019
80.	*Close Encounters of the Third Kind* (1977)	128,290,347
81.	*Coming to America* (1988)	128,152,301
82.	*Rocky IV* (1985)	127,873,414
83.	*Dumb and Dumber* (1994)	127,175,374
84.	*Smokey and the Bandit* (1977)	126,737,428
85.	*Sleepless in Seattle* (1993)	126,680,884
86.	*City Slickers* (1991)	124,033,791
87.	*The Birdcage* (1996)	124,060,553
88.	*Good Morning Vietnam* (1987)	123,922,370
89.	*Rocky III* (1982)	122,823,192
90.	*Clear and Present Danger* (1994)	122,012,656
91.	*The Bodyguard* (1992)	121,945,720
92.	*Wayne's World* (1992)	121,697,323
93.	*Speed* (1994)	121,248,145
94.	*My Best Friend's Wedding* (1997)	121,104,309
95.	*The Hunt for Red October* (1990)	120,709,868
96.	*The Mask* (1994)	119,938,730
97.	*Hook* (1991)	119,654,823
98.	*Blazing Saddles* (1974)	119,500,000
99.	*Total Recall* (1990)	119,394,839
100.	*On Golden Pond* (1981)	118,710,777

THE TOP 100 FILMS OF 1996

Disaster movies featuring aliens and tornados drew audiences last year. Films are ranked according to their North American box-office grosses. (Starred films were released in 1995 but earned much of their income in 1996; grosses include 1996 only.) (Source: *Variety*)

Rank	Film	B.O. Gross
1.	*Independence Day*	306,155,579
2.	*Twister*	241,721,524
3.	*Mission: Impossible*	180,981,866
4.	*The Rock*	134,069,511
5.	*The Nutty Professor*	128,814,019
6.	*Ransom*	125,810,051
7.	*The Birdcage*	124,060,553
8.	*101 Dalmatians*	109,686,111
9.	*A Time to Kill*	108,766,007
10.	*Phenomenon*	104,464,977
11.	*The First Wives Club*	103,708,261
12.	*Eraser*	101,295,562
13.	*The Hunchback of Notre Dame*	99,931,320
14.	*Star Trek: First Contact*	86,249,815
15.	*Space Jam*	83,038,821
16.	*Mr. Holland's Opus*	82,569,971
17.	*Broken Arrow*	70,770,147
18.	*Jerry Maguire*	65,675,817
19.	*The Cable Guy*	60,240,295
20.	*Courage Under Fire*	59,031,057
21.	*Jack*	58,478,604
22.	*12 Monkeys**	56,988,975
23.	*Executive Decision*	56,679,192
24.	*Primal Fear*	56,116,183
25.	*Jingle All the Way*	54,460,867
26.	*Tin Cup*	53,888,896
27.	*Sleepers*	52,528,577
28.	*Dragonheart*	51,385,101
29.	*Up Close and Personal*	51,088,705
30.	*Jumanji**	46,730,884
31.	*Toy Story**	45,690,994
32.	*Beavis and Butt-head Do America*	44,547,878
33.	*William Shakespeare's Romeo & Juliet*	44,020,123
34.	*Grumpier Old Men**	43,513,780
35.	*The Mirror Has Two Faces*	40,466,068
36.	*Dead Man Walking**	39,329,753
37.	*Sense and Sensibility**	38,961,346
38.	*Happy Gilmore*	38,648,864
39.	*The Ghost and the Darkness*	37,746,329
40.	*Michael*	35,133,401
41.	*The Truth About Cats & Dogs*	34,848,673
42.	*A Thin Line Between Love and Hate*	34,767,836
43.	*Muppet Treasure Island*	34,326,951
44.	*Set It Off*	34,325,720
45.	*Waiting to Exhale**	33,695,953
46.	*Matilda*	33,498,222
47.	*Striptease*	33,190,858
48.	*Heat**	32,944,081
49.	*The Long Kiss Goodnight*	32,836,418
50.	*Homeward Bound II*	32,772,492
51.	*Black Sheep*	32,417,164
52.	*Rumble in the Bronx*	32,380,143
53.	*Eddie*	31,388,164
54.	*The Preacher's Wife*	30,783,747
55.	*Sgt. Bilko*	30,356,589
56.	*Leaving Las Vegas**	29,441,352
57.	*James and the Giant Peach*	28,946,127
58.	*Mars Attacks!*	28,075,674
59.	*The Island of Dr. Moreau*	27,682,712
60.	*Spy Hard*	26,960,191
61.	*Eye for an Eye*	26,877,589
62.	*Father of the Bride Part II**	26,713,095
63.	*Harriet the Spy*	26,567,568
64.	*First Kid*	26,154,472
65.	*Daylight*	26,070,220
66.	*From Dusk Till Dawn*	25,836,616
67.	*Down Periscope*	25,809,652
68.	*That Thing You Do!*	25,513,987
69.	*Escape from L.A.*	25,473,642
70.	*Kingpin*	25,020,036
71.	*The Craft*	24,881,502
72.	*Sabrina**	24,853,322
73.	*Scream*	24,464,954
74.	*Fly Away Home*	24,324,294
75.	*Fargo*	24,083,318
76.	*The English Patient*	23,951,352
77.	*The Juror*	22,754,727
78.	*One Fine Day*	22,722,971
79.	*Emma*	22,231,658
80.	*D3: The Mighty Ducks*	21,995,225
81.	*The Quest*	21,685,669
82.	*A Very Brady Sequel*	21,443,204
83.	*Bulletproof*	21,312,641
84.	*Multiplicity*	21,134,373
85.	*Oliver & Company*	20,872,291
86.	*Fear*	20,829,193
87.	*High School High*	20,737,241
88.	*Chain Reaction*	20,655,819
89.	*The Glimmer Man*	20,404,841
90.	*City Hall*	20,340,204
91.	*Don't Be a Menace to Society While Drinking Your Juice in the Hood*	20,109,115
92.	*Flipper*	20,080,020
93.	*Bed of Roses*	19,054,674
94.	*Kazaam*	18,937,264
95.	*The Fan*	18,626,419
96.	*Last Man Standing*	18,132,747
97.	*The Crow: City of Angels*	17,917,287
98.	*Extreme Measures*	17,380,126
99.	*The Phantom*	17,323,216
100.	*Fled*	17,201,404

THE TOP 50 FOREIGN-LANGUAGE FILMS

Audiences this year embraced *Kolya*, the Czech charmer that won over Oscar in March. *Shall We Dance?* waltzed to even greater success, quickstepping to No. 26 after only two months of release. In the meantime, final returns for *The Postman (Il Postino)* sent it to the top of the chart. (Source: *Variety*)

Rank	Film (year of U.S. release, director, country of origin)
1.	*The Postman (Il Postino)* (1995, Radford, Italy)
2.	*Like Water for Chocolate* (1993, Arau, Mexico)
3.	*I Am Curious (Yellow)* (1969, Sjoman, Sweden)
4.	*La Dolce Vita* (1960, Fellini, Italy)
5.	*La Cage aux folles* (1979, Molinaro, France/Italy)
6.	*Z* (1969, Costa-Gavras, France)
7.	*A Man and a Woman* (1966, Lelouch, France)
8.	*Cinema Paradiso* (1990, Tornatore, Italy/France)
9.	*Emmanuelle* (1975, Jaeckin, France)
10.	*Das Boot* (1982, Peterson, Germany)
11.	*8½* (1963, Fellini, Italy)
12.	*My Life as a Dog* (1987, Hallström, Sweden)
13.	*Elvira Madigan* (1967, Widerberg, Sweden)
14.	*The Story of O* (1975, Jaeckin, France)
15.	*Yesterday, Today and Tomorrow* (1964, de Sica, Italy)
16.	*Marriage Italian Style* (1964, de Sica, Italy)
17.	*Dear John* (1964, Lindgren, Sweden)
18.	*Cousin, Cousine* (1976, Tacchella, France)
19.	*Cyrano de Bergerac* (1990, Rappeneau, France)
20.	*Belle de Jour* (1967, Bunuel, France/Italy)
21.	*Women on the Verge of a Nervous Breakdown* (1988, Almodóvar, Spain)
22.	*Fanny and Alexander* (1983, Bergman, Sweden)
23.	*Eat Drink Man Woman* (1994, Lee, Taiwan)
24.	*Two Women* (1961, de Sica, Italy)
25.	*The Wedding Banquet* (1993, Lee, Taiwan)
26.	*Shall We Dance?* (1997, Suo, Japan)
27.	*Diva* (1982, Beineix, France)
28.	*Swept Away* (1975, Wertmüller, Italy)
29.	*Belle Epoque* (1993, Trueba, Spain)
30.	*The Garden of the Finzi-Continis* (1971, de Sica, Italy)
31.	*Mediterraneo* (1991, Salvatores, Italy)
32.	*La Cage aux folles II* (1981, Molinaro, France)
33.	*Kolya* (1997, Sverak, Czech Republic)
34.	*King of Hearts* (1967, de Broca, France/England)
35.	*Indochine* (1992, Wargnier, France)
36.	*Europa, Europa* (1991, Holland, France/Germany)
37.	*Jean de Florette* (1987, Berri, France)
38.	*Au revoir les enfants* (1988, Malle, France)
39.	*Farewell My Concubine* (1993, Chen, Hong Kong)
40.	*Madame Rosa* (1978, Mizrahi, France)
41.	*Babette's Feast* (1988, Axel, Denmark)
42.	*La Femme Nikita* (1990, Besson, France/Italy)
43.	*Wings of Desire* (1988, Wenders, Germany)
44.	*The Decline of the American Empire* (1986, Arcand, Canada)
45.	*Manon of the Spring* (1987, Berri, France)
46.	*Antonia's Line* (1995, Gorris, Belgium/UK/The Netherlands)
47.	*Tie Me Up! Tie Me Down!* (1990, Almodóvar, Spain)
48.	*Red* (1994, Kieslowski, France)
49.	*Camille Claudel* (1989, Nuytten, France)
50.	*Jesus of Montreal* (1989, Arcand, Canada)

ALL-TIME INTERNATIONAL BOX-OFFICE CHAMPS

After defending their turf from space invaders, the dinos keep stomping the competition. Despite *ID4* and the smash *Star Wars* reissues, *Jurassic Park* still rules the roost, while its *Lost World* sequel makes the biggest charge up the chart. (Source: *Variety*)

Rank	Film, Year of Release	B.O. Gross (millions)
1.	*Jurassic Park*, 1993	$913.1
2.	*Independence Day*, 1996	807.7
3.	*The Lion King*, 1994	772.3
4.	*Star Wars*, 1977	756.2
5.	*E.T., the Extra-Terrestrial*, 1982	701.1
6.	*Forrest Gump*, 1994	673.7
7.	*The Empire Strikes Back*, 1980	527.7
8.	*Ghost*, 1990	517.6
9.	*The Lost World: Jurassic Park*, 1997	502.6
10.	*Aladdin*, 1992	497.0
11.	*Indiana Jones and the Last Crusade*, 1989	494.8
12.	*Twister*, 1996	493.6
13.	*Terminator 2: Judgment Day*, 1991	490.0
14.	*Home Alone*, 1990	474.7
15.	*Return of the Jedi*, 1983	464.5
16.	*Jaws*, 1975	458.0
17.	*Pretty Woman*, 1990	454.4
18.	*Mission: Impossible*, 1996	453.9
19.	*Rain Man*, 1988	429.4
20.	*Mrs. Doubtfire*, 1993	423.1

THE TOP INDEPENDENT FILMS

Made outside the realm of the largest movie companies, independent films traditionally feature trimmer budgets, lesser-known talent, or an idiosyncratic vision. Yet these upstarts sometimes find their audiences. From art-house hits to drive-in classics, here are the "little" films that scored big. (Source: *Variety*)

Rank	Film (year of release)	B.O. Gross
1.	*Teenage Mutant Ninja Turtles* (1990)	$135,265,915
2.	*Dumb and Dumber* (1994)	127,175,374
3.	*The Mask* (1994)	119,938,730
4.	*Pulp Fiction* (1994)*	107,928,762
5.	*The Graduate* (1968)	104,397,102
6.	*Scream* (1996)*	102,962,881
7.	*Seven* (1995)*	100,082,393
8.	*Michael* (1996)*	95,353,936
9.	*The Amityville Horror* (1979)	86,432,519
10.	*Teenage Mutant Ninja Turtles II* (1991)	78,656,813
11.	*The English Patient* (1996)*	78,651,430
12.	*The Muppet Movie* (1979)	76,341,718
13.	*Mortal Kombat* (1995)*	70,433,227
14.	*Dirty Dancing* (1987)	63,892,689
15.	*The Crying Game* (1992)	62,548,947
16.	*In Search of Noah's Ark* (1977)	55,734,818
17.	*Austin Powers: International Man of Mystery* (1997)	53,809,420
18.	*Papillon* (1973)	53,267,431
19.	*Spawn* (1997)	52,909,350
20.	*Four Weddings and a Funeral* (1994)	52,700,832
21.	*The Crow* (1993)*	50,693,162
22.	*A Nightmare on Elm Street 4* (1988)	49,369,899
23.	*Halloween* (1978)	47,000,000
24.	*Grizzly Adams* (1975)	46,394,177
25.	*A Nightmare on Elm Street 3* (1987)	44,793,222
26.	*Love at First Bite* (1979)	43,884,929
27.	*Cabaret* (1972)	42,764,873
28.	*Time Bandits* (1981)	42,365,581
29.	*Cop Land* (1997)*	42,291,904
30.	*Teenage Mutant Ninja Turtles III* (1993)	42,273,609
31.	*The Piano* (1993)*	40,157,856
32.	*Benji* (1974)	39,522,601
33.	*Dead Man Walking* (1995)	39,387,284
34.	*The Sword and the Sorcerer* (1982)	39,103,425
35.	*Set It Off* (1996)*	36,059,911
36.	*Shine* (1996)*	35,780,120
37.	*Freddy's Dead: The Final Nightmare* (1991)	34,972,033
38.	*A Thin Line Between Love and Hate* (1996)*	34,753,692
39.	*Money Talks* (1997)*	34,205,257
40.	*Teen Wolf* (1985)	33,086,611
41.	*Rumble in the Bronx* (1996)*	32,348,738
42.	*The Lawnmower Man* (1992)	32,100,816
43.	*Dressed to Kill* (1980)	31,898,776
44.	*Adventures of the Wilderness Family* (1976)	31,223,187
45.	*The Texas Chainsaw Massacre* (1974)	30,859,623
46.	*A Nightmare on Elm Street, Part 2* (1985)	29,999,213
47.	*Carnal Knowledge* (1971)	28,623,684
48.	*National Lampoon's Loaded Weapon* (1993)	27,979,399
49.	*Menace II Society* (1993)	27,899,866
50.	*Soul Man* (1986)	27,820,000
51.	*The Island of Dr. Moreau* (1996)*	27,682,712
52.	*Friday* (1995)*	27,467,564
53.	*The Jazz Singer* (1980)	27,118,436
54.	*El Cid* (1961)	26,620,818
55.	*House Party* (1990)	26,385,627
56.	*Now and Then* (1995)*	26,342,995
57.	*Private Lessons* (1981)	26,278,365
58.	*Howards End* (1992)*	25,966,555
59.	*Chariots of the Gods* (1973)	25,948,371
60.	*Shadowlands* (1993)	25,842,377
61.	*From Dusk Till Dawn* (1996)*	25,753,840
62.	*A Nightmare on Elm Street* (1984)	25,504,513
63.	*Escape from New York* (1981)	25,244,626
64.	*sex, lies and videotape* (1989)	24,741,667
65.	*The Emerald Forest* (1985)	24,468,550
66.	*Fargo* (1996)	24,503,169
67.	*Sling Blade* (1996)*	24,486,049
68.	*Beyond and Back* (1978)	23,784,396
69.	*Caligula* (1980)	23,438,119
70.	*Circle of Friends* (1995)	23,397,365
71.	*Mimic* (1997)*	23,366,252
72.	*The Care Bears Movie* (1985)	22,934,622
73.	*The Usual Suspects* (1995)	23,290,959
74.	*Crimes of the Heart* (1986)	22,905,522
75.	*Missing in Action* (1984)	22,812,411
76.	*My Tutor* (1983)	22,587,834
77.	*Much Ado About Nothing* (1993)	22,550,957
78.	*In Search of Historic Jesus* (1980)	22,438,771
79.	*Emma* (1996)*	22,201,883
80.	*A Nightmare on Elm Street 5* (1989)	22,168,359
81.	*The Bermuda Triangle* (1978)	22,167,397
82.	*Don Juan DeMarco* (1995)*	22,150,451
83.	*The Player* (1992)	21,706,101
84.	*Like Water for Chocolate* (1993)	21,665,468
85.	*The Fog* (1980)	21,378,361
86.	*The Postman (Il Postino)** (1995)	21,640,564
87.	*Weekend Pass* (1984)	21,058,033
88.	*A Room with a View* (1986)	20,966,644
89.	*The Groove Tube* (1974)	20,447,386
90.	*Action Jackson* (1988)	20,256,955

Note: As the specialty-film scene has expanded, some indie production mainstays have linked up with major Hollywood houses. Movies from these "studio-affiliated indies" are noted by an asterisk.

Figures as of August 14, 1997.

THE TOP DOCUMENTARY FILMS

Times are tough for the "traditional" documentary. None since *Hoop Dreams* has cracked the chart, and even that popular and critical success didn't challenge the concert films, Cinerama spectacles, and tabloid-like exposés from days gone by. Perhaps doc lovers are settling for home viewing—which might explain why large-scale IMAX films, more commonly found at museums or amusement parks than in cinemas (and *never* on TV or video), continue to pull in crowds. (Source: *Variety*)

Rank	Film (year of release)	B.O. Gross
1.	*To Fly* (1976)	$82,500,000
2.	*In Search of Noah's Ark* (1977)	55,700,000
3.	*The Dream Is Alive* (1985)	55,200,000
4.	*Grand Canyon: The Hidden Secrets* (1984)	52,800,000
5.	*Raw* (1987)	50,500,000
6.	*This Is Cinerama* (1952)	41,600,000
7.	*Richard Pryor Live on the Sunset Strip* (1982)	36,300,000
8.	*Woodstock* (1970)	34,800,000
9.	*Seven Wonders of the World* (1956)	32,100,000
10.	*Cinerama Holiday* (1955)	29,600,000
11.	*Beavers* (1988)	26,400,000
12.	*Chariots of the Gods* (1973)	25,900,000
13.	*Beyond and Back* (1978)	23,800,000
14.	*To the Limit* (1989)	23,500,000
15.	*Blue Planet* (1990)	22,800,000
16.	*In Search of Historic Jesus* (1980)	22,400,000
17.	*The Bermuda Triangle* (1978)	22,200,000
18.	*The Late Great Planet Earth* (1977)	19,500,000
19.	*The Vanishing Wilderness* (1973)	17,000,000
20.	*Richard Pryor Here and Now* (1983)	16,200,000
21.	*Richard Pryor Live In Concert* (1979)	15,800,000
22.	*Truth or Dare* (1991)	15,000,000
23.	*You So Crazy* (1994)	10,200,000
24.	*Endless Summer* (1966)	9,400,000
25.	*Dirt* (1979)	9,200,000
26.	*U2: Rattle and Hum* (1988)	8,600,000
27.	*Hoop Dreams* (1994)	6,800,000
28.	*Roger & Me* (1989)	6,700,000

OLD MONEY WALLOPS THE NOUVEAU RICHE

The top-grossing domestic movies of all time are nearly all recently released films, thanks to ever-rising ticket prices. But what if the playing field is leveled? Exhibitor Relations Co., Inc. has compiled the following inflation-adjusted list of the highest-grossing films of all time. Figures are as of August, 1997.

Rank	Title	Opening Date	Adjusted Gross
1.	*Gone with the Wind*	1939	$871,189,902
2.	*Star Wars*	1977	774,992,216
3.	*E.T., the Extra-Terrestrial*	1982	559,706,809
4.	*The Ten Commandments*	1956	577,710,000
5.	*The Sound of Music*	1965	575,820,001
6.	*Jaws*	1975	564,827,586
7.	*Doctor Zhivago*	1965	547,437,359
8.	*The Jungle Book*	1967	489,710,821
9.	*Snow White*	1937	480,690,000
10.	*Ben-Hur*	1959	474,923,077
11.	*101 Dalmations*	1961	463,965,793
12.	*The Empire Strikes Back*	1980	431,571,424
13.	*The Exorcist*	1973	415,800,000
14.	*Return of the Jedi*	1983	412,803,112
15.	*The Sting*	1973	402,233,144
16.	*Raiders Of The Lost Ark*	1981	384,486,094
17.	*Jurassic Park*	1993	380,111,881
18.	*The Graduate*	1967	377,369,845
19.	*Fantasia*	1940	366,221,739
20.	*The Godfather*	1972	349,947,124

THE BIGGEST HITS, YEAR-BY-YEAR

The following are the top five movies of the year based on data from *Variety*, beginning with 1939, when a Hollywood legend, *Gone with the Wind*, hit the theaters. Dollar figures listed are rentals (the amount of money collected by the studio), rather than box-office grosses, a relatively new method of measuring a film's box-office strength. (Figures for 1941 films, with the exception of *Sergeant York*, are rough estimates.)

1939

1. *Gone with the Wind*	$77,641,106
2. *The Wizard of Oz*	4,544,851
3. *The Hunchback of Notre Dame* (tie)	1,500,000
3. *Jesse James* (tie)	1,500,000
3. *Mr. Smith Goes to Washington* (tie)	1,500,000

1940

1. *Fantasia*	$41,660,000
2. *Pinocchio*	40,442,000
3. *Boom Town*	4,586,415
4. *Rebecca* (tie)	1,500,000
4. *Santa Fe Trail* (tie)	1,500,000

1941

1. *Sergeant York*	$6,135,707
2. *Dive Bomber* (tie)	1,500,000
2. *Honky Tonk* (tie)	1,500,000
2. *The Philadelphia Story* (tie)	1,500,000
2. *A Yank in the R.A.F.* (tie)	1,500,000

1942

1. *Bambi*	$47,265,000
2. *Mrs. Miniver*	5,390,009
3. *Yankee Doodle Dandy*	4,719,681
4. *Random Harvest*	4,665,501
5. *Casablanca*	4,145,178

1943

1. *This Is the Army*	$8,301,000
2. *For Whom the Bell Tolls*	7,100,000
3. *The Outlaw*	5,075,000
4. *The Song of Bernadette*	5,000,000
5. *Stage Door Canteen*	4,339,532

1944

1. *Going My Way*	$6,500.000
2. *Meet Me in St. Louis*	5,132,202
3. *Since You Went Away*	4,924,756
4. *30 Seconds over Tokyo*	4,471,080
5. *White Cliffs of Dover*	4,045,250

1945

1. *The Bells of St. Mary's*	$8,000,000
2. *Leave Her to Heaven*	5,500,000
3. *Spellbound*	4,970,583
4. *Anchors Aweigh*	4,778,679
5. *The Valley of Decision*	4,566,374

1946

1. *Song of the South*	$29,228,717
2. *The Best Years of Our Lives* (tie)	11,300,000
2. *Duel in the Sun* (tie)	11,300,000
4. *The Jolson Story*	7,600,000
5. *Blue Skies*	5,700,000

1947

1. *Welcome Stranger*	$6,100,000
2. *The Egg and I*	5,500,000
3. *Unconquered*	5,250,000
4. *Life with Father*	5,057,000
5. *Forever Amber*	5,000,000

1948

1. *The Red Shoes*	$5,000,000
2. *Red River*	4,506,825
3. *The Paleface*	4,500,000
4. *The Three Musketeers*	4,306,876
5. *Johnny Belinda*	4,266,000

1949

1. *Samson and Delilah*	$11,500,000
2. *Battleground*	5,051,143
3. *Jolson Sings Again* (tie)	5,000,000
3. *The Sands of Iwo Jima* (tie)	5,000,000
5. *I Was a Male War Bride*	4,100,000

1950

1. *Cinderella*	$41,087,000
2. *King Solomon's Mines*	5,586,000
3. *Annie Get Your Gun*	4,919,394
4. *Cheaper by the Dozen*	4,425,000
5. *Father of the Bride*	4,054,405

1951

1. *Quo Vadis?*	$11,901,662
2. *Alice in Wonderland*	7,196,000
3. *Show Boat*	5,533,000
4. *David and Bathsheba*	4,720,000
5. *The Great Caruso*	4,531,000

1952

1. *This Is Cinerama*	$15,400,000
2. *The Greatest Show on Earth*	14,000,000
3. *The Snows of Kilimanjaro*	6,500,000
4. *Ivanhoe*	6,258,000
5. *Hans Christian Andersen*	6,000,000

1953

1. *Peter Pan*	$37,584,000
2. *The Robe*	17,500,000
3. *From Here to Eternity*	12,200,000
4. *Shane*	9,000,000
5. *How To Marry a Millionaire*	7,300,000

1954

1. *White Christmas*	$12,000,000
2. *20,000 Leagues Under the Sea*	11,267,000
3. *Rear Window*	9,812,271
4. *The Caine Mutiny*	8,700,000
5. *The Glenn Miller Story*	7,590,994

1955

1. *Lady and the Tramp*	$40,249,000
2. *Cinerama Holiday*	12,000,000
3. *Mister Roberts*	8,500,000
4. *Battle Cry*	8,100,000
5. *Oklahoma!*	7,100,000

1956

1. *The Ten Commandments*	$43,000,000
2. *Around the World in 80 Days*	23,120,000
3. *Giant*	14,000,000
4. *Seven Wonders of the World*	12,500,000
5. *The King and I*	8,500,000

1957

1. *The Bridge on the River Kwai*	$17,195,000
2. *Peyton Place*	11,500,000
3. *Sayonara*	10,500,000
4. *Old Yeller*	10,050,000
5. *Raintree County*	5,962,839

1958

1. *South Pacific*	$17,500,000
2. *Auntie Mame*	9,300,000
3. *Cat on a Hot Tin Roof*	8,785,162
4. *No Time for Sergeants*	7,500,000
5. *Gigi*	7,321.423

1959

1. *Ben-Hur*	$36,992,088
2. *Sleeping Beauty*	21,998,000
3. *The Shaggy Dog*	12,317,000
4. *Operation Petticoat*	9,321,555
5. *Darby O'Gill and the Little People*	8,336,000

1960

1. *Swiss Family Robinson*	$20,178,000
2. *Psycho*	11,200,000
3. *Spartacus*	10,300,454
4. *Exodus*	8,331,582
5. *The Alamo*	7,918,776

1961

1. *101 Dalmatians*	$68,648,000
2. *West Side Story*	19,645,570
3. *The Guns of Navarone*	13,000,000
4. *El Cid*	12,000,000
5. *The Absent-Minded Professor*	11,426,000

1962

1. *How the West Was Won*	$20,932,883
2. *Lawrence of Arabia*	20,310,000
3. *The Longest Day*	17,600,000
4. *In Search of the Castaways*	9,975,000
5. *The Music Man*	8,100,000

1963

1. *Cleopatra*	$26,000,000
2. *It's a Mad, Mad, Mad, Mad World*	20,849,786
3. *Tom Jones*	16,925,988
4. *Irma La Douce*	11,921,784
5. *The Sword in the Stone*	10,475,000

1964

1. *Mary Poppins*	$45,000,000
2. *Goldfinger*	22,997,706
3. *The Carpetbaggers*	15,500,000
4. *My Fair Lady*	12,000,000
5. *From Russia with Love*	9,924,279

1965

1. *The Sound of Music*	$79,975,000
2. *Doctor Zhivago*	47,116,811
3. *Thunderball*	28,621,434
4. *Those Magnificent Men in Their Flying Machines*	14,000,000
5. *That Darn Cat*	12,628,000

1966

1. *Hawaii*	$15,553,018
2. *The Bible*	15,000,000
3. *Who's Afraid of Virginia Woolf?*	14,500,000
4. *A Man for All Seasons*	12,750,000
5. *Lt. Robin Crusoe, USN*	10,164,000

1967

1. *The Jungle Book*	$60,964,000
2. *The Graduate*	44,090,729
3. *Guess Who's Coming to Dinner*	25,500,000
4. *Bonnie and Clyde*	22,800,000
5. *The Dirty Dozen*	20,403,826

1968

1. *Funny Girl*	$26,325,000
2. *2001: A Space Odyssey*	25,521,917
3. *The Odd Couple*	20,000,000
4. *Bullitt*	19,000,000
5. *Romeo and Juliet*	17,473,000

1969

1. *Butch Cassidy and the Sundance Kid*	$46,039,000
2. *The Love Bug*	23,150,000
3. *Midnight Cowboy*	20,499,282
4. *Easy Rider*	19,100,000
5. *Hello, Dolly!*	15,200,000

1970

1. *Love Story*	$50,000,000
2. *Airport*	45,220,118
3. *M*A*S*H*	36,720,000
4. *Patton*	28,100,000
5. *The Aristocats*	26,462,000

1971

1. *Fiddler on the Roof*	$38,251,196
2. *Billy Jack*	32,500,000
3. *The French Connection*	26,315,000
4. *Summer of '42*	20,500,000
5. *Diamonds Are Forever*	19,726,829

1972

1. *The Godfather*	$86,275,000
2. *The Poseidon Adventure*	42,000,000
3. *What's Up Doc?*	28,000,000
4. *Deliverance*	22,600,000
5. *Jeremiah Johnson*	21,900,000

1973

1. *The Exorcist*	$89,000,000
2. *The Sting*	78,212,000
3. *American Graffiti*	55,128,175
4. *Papillon*	22,500,000
5. *The Way We Were*	22,457,000

1974

1. *The Towering Inferno*	$52,000,000
2. *Blazing Saddles*	47,800,000
3. *Young Frankenstein*	38,823,000
4. *Earthquake*	35,849,994
5. *The Trial of Billy Jack*	31,100,000

1975

1. *Jaws*	$129,549,325
2. *One Flew over the Cuckoo's Nest*	59,939,701
3. *The Rocky Horror Picture Show*	40,020,000
4. *Shampoo*	23,822,000
5. *Dog Day Afternoon*	22,500,000

1976

1. *Rocky*	$56,524,972
2. *A Star Is Born*	37,100,000
3. *King Kong*	36,915,000
4. *Silver Streak*	30,018,000
5. *All the President's Men*	30,000,000

1977

1. *Star Wars*	$193,500,000
2. *Close Encounters of the Third Kind*	82,750,000
3. *Saturday Night Fever*	74,100,000
4. *Smokey and the Bandit*	58,949,939
5. *The Goodbye Girl*	41,839,170

1978

1. *Grease*	$96,300,000
2. *Superman*	82,800,000
3. *National Lampoon's Animal House*	70,826,000
4. *Every Which Way but Loose*	51,900,000
5. *Jaws 2*	50,431,964

1979

1. *Kramer vs. Kramer*	$59,986,335
2. *Star Trek: The Motion Picture*	56,000,000
3. *The Jerk*	42,989,656
4. *Rocky II*	42,169,387
5. *Alien*	40,300,000

1980

1. *The Empire Strikes Back*	$141,600,000
2. *9 to 5*	59,100,000
3. *Stir Crazy*	58,364,420
4. *Airplane!*	40,610,000
5. *Any Which Way You Can*	40,500,000

1981

1. *Raiders of the Lost Ark*	$115,598,000
2. *Superman II*	65,100,000
3. *On Golden Pond*	61,174,744
4. *Arthur*	42,000,000
5. *Stripes*	40,886,589

1982

1. *E.T., the Extra-Terrestrial*	$228,168,939
2. *Tootsie*	96,292,736
3. *Rocky III*	66,262,796
4. *An Officer and a Gentleman*	55,223,000
5. *Porky's*	54,000,000

1983

1. *Return of the Jedi*	$168,002,414
2. *Terms of Endearment*	50,250,000
3. *Trading Places*	40,600,000
4. *WarGames*	38,519,833
5. *Superman III*	37,200,000

1984

1. *Ghostbusters*	$130,211,324
2. *Indiana Jones and the Temple of Doom*	109,000,000
3. *Beverly Hills Cop*	108,000,000
4. *Gremlins*	79,500,000
5. *The Karate Kid*	43,432,881

1985

1. *Back to the Future*	$104,408,738
2. *Rambo: First Blood Part II*	78,919,250
3. *Rocky IV*	76,023,246
4. *The Color Purple*	47,900,000
5. *Out of Africa*	43,103,469

1986

1. *Top Gun*	$79,400,000
2. *"Crocodile" Dundee*	70,227,000
3. *Platoon*	69,742,143
4. *The Karate Kid, Part II*	58,362,026
5. *Star Trek IV: The Voyage Home*	56,820,071

1987

1. *Three Men and a Baby*	$81,313,000
2. *Beverly Hills Cop II*	80,857,776
3. *Fatal Attraction*	70,000,000
4. *Good Morning, Vietnam*	58,103,000
5. *The Untouchables*	36,866,530

1988

1. *Rain Man*	$86,813,000
2. *Who Framed Roger Rabbit*	81,244,000
3. *Coming to America*	65,000,000
4. *"Crocodile" Dundee II*	57,300,000
5. *Twins*	57,715,127

1989

1. *Batman*	$150,500,000
2. *Indiana Jones and the Last Crusade*	115,500,000
3. *Lethal Weapon 2*	79,500,000
4. *Back to the Future Part II*	72,319,630
5. *Honey, I Shrunk the Kids*	72,007,000

1990

1. *Home Alone*	$140,099,000
2. *Ghost*	98,200,000
3. *Pretty Woman*	81,905,530
4. *Dances with Wolves*	81,537,971
5. *Teenage Mutant Ninja Turtles*	67,650,000

1991

1. *Terminator 2: Judgment Day*	$112,500,000
2. *Robin Hood: Prince of Thieves*	86,000,000
3. *Beauty and the Beast*	69,415,000
4. *Hook*	65,000,000
5. *City Slickers*	60,750,000

1992

1. *Aladdin*	$111,740,683
2. *Home Alone 2: Lost in New York*	103,377,614
3. *Batman Returns*	100,100,000
4. *Lethal Weapon 3*	80,000,000
5. *A Few Good Men*	71,000,000

1993

1. *Jurassic Park*	$212,953,437
2. *Mrs. Doubtfire*	111,000,000
3. *The Fugitive*	97,000,000
4. *The Firm*	77,047,044
5. *Sleepless in Seattle*	64,930,137

1994

1. *The Lion King*	$173,057,366
2. *Forrest Gump*	156,000,000
3. *True Lies*	80,000,000
4. *The Santa Clause*	74,348,689
5. *The Flintstones*	70,753,383

1995

1. *Batman Forever*	$105,100,000
2. *Apollo 13*	87,412,631
3. *Toy Story*	82,342,480
4. *Pocahontas*	67,848,010
5. *Goldeneye*	49,847,866

1996

1. *Independence Day*	$177,200,000
2. *Twister*	113,500,000
3. *Mission: Impossible*	83,800,000
4. *Jerry Maguire*	74,900,000
5. *The Rock*	64,200,000

SEX FIRSTS ON THE SILVER SCREEN

- The first kiss appeared in *The Widow Jones* (1896).
- The first French kiss took place between Natalie Wood and Warren Beatty in *Splendor in the Grass* (1961).
- The first leading lady to kiss another was Marlene Dietrich in Josef von Sternberg's *Morocco* (1930).
- The first kiss in a Japanese film was finally allowed in *Twenty-Year-Old Youth* (1946).
- The longest single kiss on record took place between Regis Toomey and Jane Wyman in *You're in the Army Now* (1940); the smooch lasted three minutes and five seconds.
- The first leading lady to appear nude was Audrey Munson in *Inspiration* (1915).
- The first full male nudity featured Alan Bates and Oliver Reed in Ken Russell's *Women in Love* (1969).
- The first time sex was depicted was in *Ecstasy* with Hedy Lamarr (Czechoslovakia, 1932).
- The earliest known pornographic film was *A l'ecu d'or* (France, 1908).
- The first hard-core pornographic feature shown in American cinemas was *Deep Throat* (1972).
- The first film about homosexuality was Richard Oswald's *Anders als die Andern* (Germany, 1919).
- The first American film about homosexuality was Joseph Mankiewicz's *Suddenly Last Summer* (1959).

THE 100 BEST MOVIES OF ALL TIME

They are the celluloid touchstones of our inner life, the enduring echoes of various generations, and the most bittersweet of social commentaries played out 10 yards high. PEOPLE's movie critic Leah Rozen has selected 100 of the greatest, an assignment as agonizing as having to pick the 10 greatest home runs ever hit in baseball.

ACE IN THE HOLE (1951)
One of the most cynical movies ever made, about an ambitious reporter (Kirk Douglas) who, to milk the story and sell more newspapers, delays the rescue of a man trapped in a cave. Among director Billy Wilder's best work.

ADAM'S RIB (1949)
Katharine Hepburn and Spencer Tracy as married attorneys on opposite sides of an attempted murder case. The smartest and funniest of their five pairings.

THE ADVENTURES OF ROBIN HOOD (1938)
There have been other Robin Hoods, including Kevin Costner and Sean Connery, but never one as appealingly roguish as Errol Flynn. A rousing adventure.

THE AFRICAN QUEEN (1951)
In a splendidly comic and sweet romance, the mismatched Humphrey Bogart and Katharine Hepburn take a slow love boat up the river in steamy Africa.

ALL ABOUT EVE (1950)
Smart and tart. Director-writer Joseph Mankiewicz's acerbic masterpiece about theater folk, with Bette Davis at her caustic best.

AMERICAN GRAFFITI (1973)
In George Lucas's first hit film, a group of California teenagers, including Ron Howard and Richard Dreyfuss, spend one long night in 1962 cruising in cars and goofing off.

BACK STREET (1941)
A vintage weepie about a woman who gives up everything for love. This second of three filmed versions of Fannie Hurst's potboiler shines brightly thanks to the incomparable Margaret Sullavan and Charles Boyer.

BADLANDS (1973)
Martin Sheen and Sissy Spacek play a young couple who go on an aimless killing spree in a chilling cult film by director Terence Malick.

BEAUTY AND THE BEAST (1946)
French surrealist Jean Cocteau's sophisticated version of the classic fairy tale *La Belle et la bete* is for grown-up romantics. Then again, the 1991 Disney version, a musical, is pretty swell too.

BELLE DE JOUR (1967)
Director Luis Buñuel's deliciously creepy movie about a bourgeois Paris housewife, a radiant Catherine Deneuve, who spends her days working in a brothel. Or does she?

THE BEST YEARS OF OUR LIVES (1946)
A moving drama about the domestic and occupational difficulties facing three returning World War II vets, with Fredric March, Dana Andrews, and Harold Russell, a real vet who had lost both arms in the war.

THE BICYCLE THIEF (1948)
Director Vittorio de Sica's heartbreaking drama, a linchpin of Italian neo-realism, about a workman who loses everything when his bicycle is stolen.

THE BIRTH OF A NATION (1915)
The first blockbuster. Although parts now seem irredeemably racist, director D. W. Griffith's epic Civil War drama is still a sight to behold.

BLADE RUNNER (1982)
The future as you don't want it to be. Gruff guy Harrison Ford stars in director Ridley Scott's expert sci-fi drama.

BRINGING UP BABY (1938)
A ditzy Katharine Hepburn sets her sights on zoology professor Cary Grant in a delightful screwball comedy. And love that tiger.

BULL DURHAM (1988)
A great romance movie disguised as a baseball picture. Susan Sarandon gets to choose between minor leaguers Kevin Costner and Tim Robbins, both of whom pitch woo her way.

BUTCH CASSIDY AND THE SUNDANCE KID (1969)
In one of the all-time cool buddy movies, Paul Newman and Robert Redford display big star charisma and charm as gallivanting outlaws.

CAGED (1949)
If you see just one women-in-prison film, make it this one. Eleanor Parker stars as the good girl gone wrong.

CARNAL KNOWLEDGE (1971)
Unrelentlingly dark drama follows the sexual exploits and failures of two men (Art Garfunkel and Jack Nicholson) from college through middle age. Mike Nichols directed from Jules Feiffer's script.

CASABLANCA (1942)
A kiss is still a kiss, but the ones here have real staying power. This is Hollywood movie-making at its most stylishly satisfying, with Humphrey Bogart and Ingrid Bergman.

CHINATOWN (1974)
Jack Nicholson's nose gets sliced and lots of other nasty things happen in director Roman Polanski's jaundiced thriller set in '30s Los Angeles.

CITIZEN KANE (1941)
The granddaddy of all biopics, though innovative director-star Orson Welles had to change the name from William Randolph Hearst to Charles Foster Kane. A must-see for anyone interested in movies.

THE CROWD (1928)
This silent movie, directed by King Vidor, movingly depicts the everyday life of a young white-collar worker and his wife in New York City. It shows just how fluid and powerful the images in silent film had become right before sound took over.

DAVID COPPERFIELD (1934)
A perfect film adaptation of Charles Dickens's novel about the adventures of an orphaned youth. W. C. Fields is a hoot as Mr. Micawber.

DAY FOR NIGHT (1973)
French director François Truffaut's valentine to movie-making contains sly references and in-jokes to many of his earlier films. With Jacqueline Bisset and Jean-Pierre Léaud.

DEAD MAN WALKING (1995)
No matter where you stand on the death penalty, this powerful drama scores in telling the story of a nun (Susan Sarandon) who guides a murderer (Sean Penn) to contrition before his execution. Tim Robbins directed.

DO THE RIGHT THING (1989)
Director Spike Lee's street-smart drama about one very hot summer day in a tense Brooklyn neighborhood has plenty to say about race relations and the need for more and better communication.

DOUBLE INDEMNITY (1944)
Barbara Stanwyck, at her bad-girl best, sweet-talks Fred MacMurray into helping her kill her husband. Billy Wilder directed.

DR. STRANGELOVE (1962)
A savagely funny black comedy, though it's a tad dated now, about the nuclear bomb and world politics. Stanley Kubrick directed and Peter Sellers and George C. Scott star.

THE EMPIRE STRIKES BACK (1980)
The best of the *Star Wars* trilogy. Stars Harrison Ford, Carrie Fisher, and Mark Hamill.

E.T., THE EXTRA-TERRESTRIAL (1982)
It may be simple-minded and sentimental, but who can resist this sweet tale of the friendship between a suburban youth and an alien marooned on Earth?

FRANKENSTEIN (1931)
Still the scariest, and most humane, version of Mary Wollstonecraft Shelley's classic monster tale. With Boris Karloff as the big guy.

THE GENERAL (1926)
Buster Keaton, one of the comic glories of the silent era, piles on brilliant sight gag after sight gag in this Civil War comedy.

THE GODFATHER (1972)
A family drama about the troubled and violent Corleone clan. Director Francis Ford Coppola, with the help of Marlon Brando, James Caan, and a very young Al Pacino, made the ultimate gangster film.

THE GOLD RUSH (1925)
Charlie Chaplin's little tramp seeks his fortune in the Yukon. Watch for the justly famous shoe-eating scene in which Chaplin twirls shoelaces with a fork as if eating spaghetti.

GONE WITH THE WIND (1939)
This Civil War–era drama is big and long and we wouldn't change a minute of it. Except maybe the ending. But, tomorrow's another day, and maybe Rhett will come back then. With Clark Gable and Vivien Leigh.

THE GRADUATE (1968)
In a wonderfully wry comedy, Dustin Hoffman passes his first summer after college floating in his parents' pool and having a desultory affair with Anne Bancroft. Nearly 30 years later, this one still seems fresh.

THE GRAPES OF WRATH (1940)
Director John Ford's masterful adaptation of John Steinbeck's bleak novel about depression-era Oklahomans who head off for what they hope will be a better life in California. With Henry Fonda and Jane Darwell.

A HARD DAY'S NIGHT (1964)
The swinging '60s encapsulated, minus the politics. This first Beatles film is flat-out zany fun.

HIGH NOON (1952)
The Western pared to its bone. With Gary Cooper as the principled lawman who has to go it alone against the bad guys.

HIS GIRL FRIDAY (1940)
Speed is of the essence in this newspaper comedy, with Rosalind Russell and Cary Grant competing to see who can insult the other faster.

HOLIDAY INN (1942)
When Bing Crosby starts singing "White Christmas," you just know it's going to snow in time. Crosby and Fred Astaire costar in this chipper musical as the owners of a hotel where they put on shows with holiday themes.

HUD (1963)
Paul Newman as one of the screen's first anti-heroes, an amoral cowboy who brings no good to all whom he touches. With Melvyn Douglas and Patricia Neal.

INVASION OF THE BODY SNATCHERS (1955)
Low-budget, paranoid '50s sci-fi allegory about aliens taking over residents of a small town. The '78 remake can't hold a pod to it.

IT HAPPENED ONE NIGHT (1934)
Screwball comedy meets road picture in director Frank Capra's jaunty film about a runaway heiress who spars and sparks with a newspaperman. With Claudette Colbert and Clark Gable.

JAWS (1975)
Jumbo shark on the loose. Director Steven Spielberg scored his first blockbuster with this bloody thriller. Dig John Williams's carnivorous score.

THE LADY EVE (1941)
Wickedly entertaining comedy by director Preston Sturges about a con woman (Barbara Stanwyck) who hustles a youthful millionaire (Henry Fonda), only to realize almost too late that she's actually in love with the big lug.

THE LAST METRO (1980)
A moving drama about a French theatrical troupe in occupied Paris during World War II. François Truffaut directed, and Catherine Deneuve and Gérard Depardieu star.

LONE STAR (1996)
Director John Sayles's sweeping drama about fathers and sons, the past catching up to us, and cultural diversity, all crammed into the lives of folks in one small Texas border town.

LONG DAY'S JOURNEY INTO NIGHT (1962)
Playwright Eugene O'Neill's autobiographical masterpiece, brought to the screen with all the hurt showing. Katharine Hepburn digs deep as the morphine-addicted mother. Also stars Ralph Richardson and Jason Robards.

LONGTIME COMPANION (1990)
An AIDS drama about a tight-knit group of male friends in New York City in the 1980s which poignantly depicts just how devastating the disease is to both those who have it and those they leave behind.

THE MALTESE FALCON (1941)
Love that black bird. With Humphrey Bogart as private eye Sam Spade, who takes no guff from anyone, including conniving Mary Astor.

THE MANCHURIAN CANDIDATE (1962)
A sharp-witted political thriller, from which one suspects Oliver Stone learned much of what he knows. With Frank Sinatra, Laurence Harvey, and Angela Lansbury.

MCCABE AND MRS. MILLER (1971)
Director Robert Altman's lyrically haunting look at how the West was wasted, with Warren Beatty as a gunfighter who sets up a brothel and Julie Christie as his opium-addicted madam.

MEAN STREETS (1973)
Loyalty among thieves only goes so far, as a group of boyhood friends in Little Italy discover upon growing up. Martin Scorsese's breakthrough film, with Robert De Niro and Harvey Keitel.

MILDRED PIERCE (1945)
The ultimate Joan Crawford movie. She plays a suburban divorcée who makes a fortune as a hard-working restaurateur, only to see her spoiled daughter steal her beau.

NETWORK (1976)
Biliousness raised to high art. Paddy Chayefsky's sharp satire about the influence of the media. With Peter Finch, William Holden, and Faye Dunaway.

A NIGHT AT THE OPERA (1935)
The Marx Brothers reek loony havoc when—and before and after—the fat lady sings. Also stars Margaret Dumont, the matronly butt of so many of Groucho's jokes.

NOTORIOUS (1946)
Alfred Hitchcock at his perversely romantic best. Sexy and scary, with American agent Cary Grant sending lady love Ingrid Bergman to wed a covert Nazi.

PERSONA (1966)
The personalities of two women, a nurse and the mentally ill patient she is caring for, begin to overlap and mesh in Swedish filmmaker Ingmar Bergman's brooding, disturbing drama. With Liv Ullmann and Bibi Andersson.

PERSUASION (1995)
This pared-down rendering of Jane Austen's most mature novel perfectly serves the delicate tale of a woman (Amanda Root) who gets a second chance at finding love with the man (Ciaran Hinds) she rejected years before.

PICNIC AT HANGING ROCK (1975)
Spooky goings-on at a girls' school in turn-of-the-century Australia when several of the students mysteriously vanish, seemingly into thin air, while at a picnic. Peter Weir directed.

PLACES IN THE HEART (1984)
A lovely movie about human frailty and redemption from director Robert Benton. Sally Field stars as a newly widowed Texas farm woman who perseveres despite hard times.

THE PLAYER (1992)
Director Robert Altman zings Hollywood in a biting satire about a studio executive who gets away with murder. Tim Robbins has the lead, but masses of other big names show up for cameos.

PSYCHO (1960)
Janet Leigh, get away from that shower. Hitchcock's scalding shocker stars Tony Perkins as a

twisted hotel keeper who doesn't like his guests to check out.

PULP FICTION (1994)
Violent, amusing, and cleverly structured, director Quentin Tarantino's movie is vastly more entertaining that the horde of imitations it has spawned. With John Travolta, Bruce Willis, and Samuel L. Jackson.

THE PURPLE ROSE OF CAIRO (1984)
When the hero (Jeff Daniels) of a '30s movie steps out of the screen to begin making time with one of his biggest fans (Mia Farrow), the line between real life during the depression and movie fantasy becomes all too clear in Woody Allen's comic masterpiece.

QUEEN CHRISTINA (1937)
Greta Garbo is at her most androgynously alluring in a romanticized Hollywood biopic about a 17th-century Swedish queen. Check out Garbo's enigmatic expression in the famous final shot.

THE QUIET MAN (1952)
John Wayne and director John Ford left the Wild West behind for the greener fields of Ireland, with splendid results. In this boisterous, appealing love story, Wayne plays an American boxer who woos Irish lass Maureen O'Hara.

RAGING BULL (1980)
Director Martin Scorsese's penetrating look at the troubled life of pugilist Jake La Motta boasts one of Robert De Niro's finest performances.

RASHOMON (1950)
Truth proves elusive as four people involved each give differing accounts of a rape-murder in Japanese director Akira Kurosawa's brilliant drama.

REAR WINDOW (1954)
James Stewart and a sexy Grace Kelly star in Alfred Hitchcock's sophisticated thriller about an invalided photographer who spots a murder across his apartment courtyard.

REBEL WITHOUT A CAUSE (1955)
Alienated teens reign supreme as James Dean—who died before the movie was released—and Natalie Wood express the suffering of their generation.

ROMAN HOLIDAY (1953)
A charming romp with Audrey Hepburn at her most appealingly gamine as a princess who ditches her royal duties and takes up with Gregory Peck, an American newspaperman.

SCHINDLER'S LIST (1983)
Director Steven Spielberg's powerful retelling of the story of businessman Oskar Schindler, who saved hundreds of Jews from the Nazi gas chambers during World War II. With Liam Neeson as Schindler and Ben Kingsley as his Jewish factory foreman.

THE SEARCHERS (1956)
In a multilayered Western by director John Ford, John Wayne spends years searching for his niece, Natalie Wood, after her capture by Native Americans. One of the most influential films ever made.

SHANE (1953)
A retired gunfighter rides into town and helps out a homesteading couple and their young son. Sounds simple, but it's anything but. With Alan Ladd, Jean Arthur, and Brandon de Wilde.

THE SHOP AROUND THE CORNER (1940)
The famed "Lubitsch Touch," so named for the sophisticated comedy work of director Ernst Lubitsch, shines bright in a charming romance about two bickering shop clerks. With Jimmy Stewart and the matchless Margaret Sullavan.

SHOWBOAT (1936)
This classic musical about life aboard a Mississippi riverboat features dandy Jerome Kern tunes and a glimpse of why Paul Robeson and Helen Morgan were such electrifying performers in their day.

SINGIN' IN THE RAIN (1952)
A musical about Hollywood's awkward transition from silents to talkies, this one can't be beat, especially for Gene Kelly's singing and dancing of the damp title number.

SNOW WHITE AND THE SEVEN DWARFS (1937)
Walt Disney's first feature-length animated feature still shimmers brightly, though Snow White's brusque farewell to the dwarfs at the end seems a mite ungrateful.

SOME LIKE IT HOT (1959)
The funniest movie ever made about cross-dressing. Tony Curtis and Jack Lemmon star as musicians who, after witnessing a mob hit, go undercover with an all-girl band, whose members include Marilyn Monroe. Billy Wilder directed.

THE SOUND OF MUSIC (1965)
Sure, it's sugary, but any time Julie Andrews is on screen in this Rogers and Hammerstein musical about the would-be nun who comes to stay with the Von Trapp family, all is forgiven.

SULLIVAN'S TRAVELS (1941)
A Hollywood director (Joel McCrea) rediscovers the meaning of life while traveling across America in director Preston Sturges's quick-witted comedy drama. Watch for the automat scene.

SUNSET BOULEVARD (1950)
The original. In director Billy Wilder's savage look at the underbelly of Hollywood, silent star Gloria Swanson made her big comeback playing, appropriately

enough, a silent star hoping to make a comeback.

SWEET SMELL OF SUCCESS (1957)
Everyone's corrupt or corruptible in this atmospheric melodrama about nasty dealings between a Broadway press agent (Tony Curtis) and a powerful Manhattan newspaper columnist (Burt Lancaster).

TARZAN AND HIS MATE (1934)
The second of the Johnny Weissmuller films about Edgar Rice Borroughs' ape man, and the best of the series. Maureen O'Sullivan, dressed in next to nothing, makes a perky Jane.

THE TERMINATOR (1984)
Pure nihilistic fun, this sci-fi action thriller deservedly made muscleman Arnold Schwarzenegger, who plays a singularly focused android, into a big star.

THELMA AND LOUISE (1991)
Two good girls go wrong. A feminist firecracker of a movie, with strong performances by Susan Sarandon and Geena Davis. And check out the truly buff Brad Pitt.

THIS IS SPINAL TAP (1984)
This is a blast. Turn your amps up to 11 as you chuckle your way through this comic documentary about a heavy metal rock group and its hangers-on. Rob Reiner directed.

TO HAVE AND HAVE NOT (1944)
Romantic sparks fly in Humprey Bogart and Lauren Bacall's first pairing, a World War II drama that borrows more than a little from *Casablanca* but boasts a comic zing all its own.

TOP HAT (1935)
Fred Astaire and Ginger Rogers dance (and sing) "Cheek to Cheek" and other great Irving Berlin tunes in their most glorious teaming. Keep an eye peeled for a young Lucille Ball in the flower shop.

2001: A SPACE ODYSSEY (1968)
Director Stanley Kubrick's hauntingly beautiful and enormously influential science fiction thriller. And watch out for HAL.

UNFORGIVEN (1992)
Clint Eastwood directed and stars in a mature, meditative Western about an ex–hired gun turned farmer who goes on one last killing spree.

WHITE HEAT (1949)
Jimmy Cagney at his sinister best as a gangster who can't cut his ties to his mother's apron strings. Great ending.

WHO FRAMED ROGER RABBIT (1988)
It's 'toon time as animated characters and actors interact to solve a crime in a technological bit of trickery that shows just how far animation has come since the days of Gertie the Dinosaur. 'Toon or no 'toon, Jessica Rabbit (voiced by Kathleen Turner) is vavavoom.

THE WILD BUNCH (1969)
Director Sam Pekinpah's violent tale of revenge shakes the good ol' Western by its spurs. With William Holden, Ernest Borgnine, and Robert Ryan.

WITNESS (1985)
Cultures clash as a big-city detective (Harrison Ford) hides out among the Amish in order to protect a young Amish boy who has witnessed a murder.

THE WIZARD OF OZ (1939)
Is once a year often enough? This entertaining children's musical—assuming the kids are old enough to sit through the flying monkeys—features stellar performances by Judy Garland, Bert Lahr, Ray Bolger, and Jack Haley.

WRITTEN ON THE WIND (1956)
So bad it's good. A steamy melodrama about a very messed-up family, directed by Douglas Sirk, the master of glossy high camp, and starring Rock Hudson, Lauren Bacall, and Dorothy Malone.

TOP FILM SOUNDTRACKS

We love to go to the movies, but a good soundtrack means we can take them home with us, too. And fans do, as this list indicates. (Source: RIAA)

Soundtrack	Sales (in millions)
The Bodyguard	16
Purple Rain	13
Dirty Dancing	11
Saturday Night Fever	11
The Lion King	10
Footloose	8
Grease	8
Top Gun	7
Waiting To Exhale	7
Flashdance	6
Forrest Gump	5
The Jazz Singer	5

HOLLYWOOD'S FOOTPRINTS OF FAME

The first footprints at Grauman's Chinese Theater, as it was originally called, were made by Norma Talmadge in 1927 when, legend holds, she accidentally stepped in wet concrete outside the building. Since then over 180 stars have been immortalized, along with their hands, feet—and sometimes noses (Jimmy Durante), fists (John Wayne), and legs (Betty Grable). This year, director Robert Zemeckis made an impression, Jackie Chan put his best foot forward, and Michael Douglas joined father Kirk in the forecourt. The full Forecourt of the Stars at Mann's includes:

Abbott & Costello
Don Ameche
Julie Andrews
Edward Arnold
Fred Astaire
Gene Autry
John Barrymore
Freddie Bartholomew
Anne Baxter
Wallace Beery
Jack Benny
Edgar Bergen
Joan Blondell
Humphrey Bogart
Charles Boyer
Joe E. Brown
Yul Brynner
George Burns
Cantinflas
Eddie Cantor
Jim Carrey
Jackie Chan
Maurice Chevalier
Gary Cooper
Jackie Cooper
Jeanne Crain
Joan Crawford
Bing Crosby
Tom Cruise
Bebe Daniels
Linda Darnell
Marion Davies
Bette Davis
Doris Day
Olivia de Havilland
Cecil B. DeMille
Kirk Douglas
Michael Douglas
Marie Dressler
Donald Duck
Irene Dunne
Jimmie Durante
Deanna Durbin
Clint Eastwood
Nelson Eddy
Douglas Fairbanks
Alice Faye
Rhonda Fleming
Henry Fonda
Joan Fontaine
Harrison Ford
Clark Gable
Ava Gardner
Judy Garland
Greer Garson
Janet Gaynor
Mel Gibson
Whoopi Goldberg
Betty Grable
Cary Grant
Rosa Grauman (founder Sid Grauman's mother)
Sid Grauman
Ann Harding
Jean Harlow
Rex Harrison
William S. Hart
Susan Hayward
Rita Hayworth
Van Heflin
Sonja Henie
Jean Hersholt
Charlton Heston
Bob Hope
Rock Hudson
George Jessel
Van Johnson
Al Jolson
Danny Kaye
Michael Keaton
Gene Kelly
Deborah Kerr
Alan Ladd
Dorothy Lamour
Charles Laughton
Jack Lemmon
Mervyn LeRoy
Harold Lloyd
Sophia Loren
Myrna Loy
George Lucas
William Lundigan
Jeanette MacDonald
Ali MacGraw
Shirley MacLaine
Victor McLaglen
Steve McQueen
Fredric March
Dean Martin
Tony Martin
The Marx Brothers
James Mason
Marcello Mastroianni
Lauritz Melchior
Ray Milland
Hayley Mills
Carmen Miranda
Tom Mix
Marilyn Monroe
Colleen Moore
Eddie Murphy
George Murphy
Hildegarde Neff
Pola Negri
Paul Newman
Jack Nicholson
Jack Oakie
Margaret O'Brien
Donald O'Connor
Louella Parsons
Gregory Peck
Mary Pickford
Ezio Pinza
Sidney Poitier
Dick Powell
Eleanor Powell
William Powell
Tyrone Power
Anthony Quinn
George Raft
Burt Reynolds
Debbie Reynolds
The Ritz Brothers
Edward G. Robinson
May Robson
Ginger Rogers
Roy Rogers
Mickey Rooney
Jane Russell
Rosalind Russell
Arnold Schwarzenegger
Steven Seagal
Peter Sellers
Norma Shearer
Jean Simmons
Frank Sinatra
Red Skelton
Steven Spielberg
Sylvester Stallone
Barbara Stanwyck
Star Trek crew (William Shatner, Leonard Nimoy, DeForest Kelley, James Doohan, Nichelle Nichols, George Takei, Walter Koenig)
Star Wars characters
George Stevens
Jimmy Stewart
Meryl Streep
Gloria Swanson
Constance Talmadge
Norma Talmadge
Elizabeth Taylor
Robert Taylor
Shirley Temple
Danny Thomas
Gene Tierney
John Travolta
Lana Turner
Rudy Vallee
Dick Van Dyke
W. S. Van Dyke
Raoul Walsh
John Wayne
Clifton Webb
Oskar Werner
Richard Widmark
Esther Williams
Bruce Willis
Jane Withers
Natalie Wood
Joanne Woodward
Monty Woolley
Jane Wyman
Diana Wynyard
Loretta Young
Robert Zemeckis
Adolph Zukor

THE BRIGHTEST STARS, BY YEAR

In today's high-pressure movie business, the most valuable commodity is a star who shines so bright that he or she can "open" a movie—filling seats on the basis of pure popularity regardless of the allure of the film. Every year since 1933, Quigley Publishing has polled more than 500 moviehouse owners nationwide to determine which stars they regarded as the surest-fire box-office draw.

1933

1. Marie Dressler
2. Will Rogers
3. Janet Gaynor
4. Eddie Cantor
5. Wallace Beery
6. Jean Harlow
7. Clark Gable
8. Mae West
9. Norma Shearer
10. Joan Crawford

1934

1. Will Rogers
2. Clark Gable
3. Janet Gaynor
4. Wallace Beery
5. Mae West
6. Joan Crawford
7. Bing Crosby
8. Shirley Temple
9. Marie Dressler
10. Norma Shearer

1935

1. Shirley Temple
2. Will Rogers
3. Clark Gable
4. Fred Astaire & Ginger Rogers
5. Joan Crawford
6. Claudette Colbert
7. Dick Powell
8. Wallace Beery
9. Joe E. Brown
10. James Cagney

1936

1. Shirley Temple
2. Clark Gable
3. Fred Astaire and Ginger Rogers
4. Robert Taylor
5. Joe E. Brown
6. Dick Powell
7. Joan Crawford
8. Claudette Colbert
9. Jeanette MacDonald
10. Gary Cooper

1937

1. Shirley Temple
2. Clark Gable
3. Robert Taylor
4. Bing Crosby
5. William Powell
6. Jane Withers
7. Fred Astaire & Ginger Rogers
8. Sonja Henie
9. Gary Cooper
10. Myrna Loy

1938

1. Shirley Temple
2. Clark Gable
3. Sonja Henie
4. Mickey Rooney
5. Spencer Tracy
6. Robert Taylor
7. Myrna Loy
8. Jane Withers
9. Alice Faye
10. Tyrone Power

1939

1. Mickey Rooney
2. Tyrone Power
3. Spencer Tracy
4. Clark Gable
5. Shirley Temple
6. Bette Davis
7. Alice Faye
8. Errol Flynn
9. James Cagney
10. Sonja Henie

1940

1. Mickey Rooney
2. Spencer Tracy
3. Clark Gable
4. Gene Autry
5. Tyrone Power
6. James Cagney
7. Bing Crosby
8. Wallace Beery
9. Bette Davis
10. Judy Garland

1941

1. Mickey Rooney
2. Clark Gable
3. Abbott & Costello
4. Bob Hope
5. Spencer Tracy
6. Gene Autry
7. Gary Cooper
8. Bette Davis
9. James Cagney
10. Spencer Tracy

1942

1. Abbott & Costello
2. Clark Gable
3. Gary Cooper
4. Mickey Rooney
5. Bob Hope
6. James Cagney
7. Gene Autry
8. Betty Grable
9. Greer Garson
10. Spencer Tracy

1943

1. Betty Grable
2. Bob Hope
3. Abbott & Costello
4. Bing Crosby
5. Gary Cooper
6. Greer Garson
7. Humphrey Bogart
8. James Cagney
9. Mickey Rooney
10. Clark Gable

1944

1. Bing Crosby
2. Gary Cooper
3. Bob Hope
4. Betty Grable
5. Spencer Tracy
6. Greer Garson
7. Humphrey Bogart
8. Abbott & Costello
9. Cary Grant
10. Bette Davis

1945

1. Bing Crosby
2. Van Johnson
3. Greer Garson
4. Betty Grable
5. Spencer Tracy
6. Humphrey Bogart (tie)
6. Gary Cooper (tie)
8. Bob Hope
9. Judy Garland
10. Margaret O'Brien

1946

1. Bing Crosby
2. Ingrid Bergman
3. Van Johnson
4. Gary Cooper
5. Bob Hope
6. Humphrey Bogart
7. Greer Garson
8. Margaret O'Brien
9. Betty Grable
10. Roy Rogers

1947

1. Bing Crosby
2. Betty Grable
3. Ingrid Bergman
4. Gary Cooper
5. Humphrey Bogart
6. Bob Hope
7. Clark Gable
8. Gregory Peck
9. Claudette Colbert
10. Alan Ladd

1948

1. Bing Crosby
2. Betty Grable
3. Abbott & Costello
4. Gary Cooper
5. Bob Hope

6. Humphrey Bogart
7. Clark Gable
8. Cary Grant
9. Spencer Tracy
10. Ingrid Bergman

1949

1. Bob Hope
2. Bing Crosby
3. Abbott & Costello
4. John Wayne
5. Gary Cooper
6. Cary Grant
7. Betty Grable
8. Esther Williams
9. Humphrey Bogart
10. Clark Gable

1950

1. John Wayne
2. Bob Hope
3. Bing Crosby
4. Betty Grable
5. James Stewart
6. Abbott & Costello
7. Clifton Webb
8. Esther Williams
9. Spencer Tracy
10. Randolph Scott

1951

1. John Wayne
2. Dean Martin & Jerry Lewis
3. Betty Grable
4. Abbott & Costello
5. Bing Crosby
6. Bob Hope
7. Randolph Scott
8. Gary Cooper
9. Doris Day
10. Spencer Tracy

1952

1. Dean Martin & Jerry Lewis
2. Gary Cooper
3. John Wayne
4. Bing Crosby
5. Bob Hope
6. James Stewart
7. Doris Day
8. Gregory Peck
9. Susan Hayward
10. Randolph Scott

1953

1. Gary Cooper
2. Dean Martin & Jerry Lewis
3. John Wayne
4. Alan Ladd
5. Bing Crosby
6. Marilyn Monroe
7. James Stewart
8. Bob Hope
9. Susan Hayward
10. Randolph Scott

1954

1. John Wayne
2. Dean Martin & Jerry Lewis
3. Gary Cooper
4. James Stewart
5. Marilyn Monroe
6. Alan Ladd
7. William Holden
8. Bing Crosby
9. Jane Wyman
10. Marlon Brando

1955

1. James Stewart
2. Grace Kelly
3. John Wayne
4. William Holden
5. Gary Cooper
6. Marlon Brando
7. Dean Martin & Jerry Lewis
8. Humphrey Bogart
9. June Allyson
10. Clark Gable

1956

1. William Holden
2. John Wayne
3. James Stewart
4. Burt Lancaster
5. Glenn Ford
6. Dean Martin & Jerry Lewis
7. Gary Cooper
8. Marilyn Monroe
9. Kim Novak
10. Frank Sinatra

1957

1. Rock Hudson
2. John Wayne
3. Pat Boone
4. Elvis Presley
5. Frank Sinatra
6. Gary Cooper
7. William Holden
8. James Stewart
9. Jerry Lewis
10. Yul Brynner

1958

1. Glenn Ford
2. Elizabeth Taylor
3. Jerry Lewis
4. Marlon Brando
5. Rock Hudson
6. William Holden
7. Brigitte Bardot
8. Yul Brynner
9. James Stewart
10. Frank Sinatra

1959

1. Rock Hudson
2. Cary Grant
3. James Stewart
4. Doris Day
5. Debbie Reynolds
6. Glenn Ford
7. Frank Sinatra
8. John Wayne
9. Jerry Lewis
10. Susan Hayward

1960

1. Doris Day
2. Rock Hudson
3. Cary Grant
4. Elizabeth Taylor
5. Debbie Reynolds
6. Tony Curtis
7. Sandra Dee
8. Frank Sinatra
9. Jack Lemmon
10. John Wayne

1961

1. Elizabeth Taylor
2. Rock Hudson
3. Doris Day
4. John Wayne
5. Cary Grant
6. Sandra Dee
7. Jerry Lewis
8. William Holden
9. Tony Curtis
10. Elvis Presley

1962

1. Doris Day
2. Rock Hudson
3. Cary Grant
4. John Wayne
5. Elvis Presley
6. Elizabeth Taylor
7. Jerry Lewis
8. Frank Sinatra
9. Sandra Dee
10. Burt Lancaster

1963

1. Doris Day
2. John Wayne
3. Rock Hudson
4. Jack Lemmon
5. Cary Grant
6. Elizabeth Taylor
7. Elvis Presley
8. Sandra Dee
9. Paul Newman
10. Jerry Lewis

1964

1. Doris Day
2. Jack Lemmon
3. Rock Hudson
4. John Wayne
5. Cary Grant
6. Elvis Presley
7. Shirley MacLaine
8. Ann-Margret
9. Paul Newman
10. Jerry Lewis

1965

1. Sean Connery
2. John Wayne
3. Doris Day
4. Julie Andrews
5. Jack Lemmon
6. Elvis Presley
7. Cary Grant
8. James Stewart
9. Elizabeth Taylor
10. Richard Burton

1966

1. Julie Andrews
2. Sean Connery
3. Elizabeth Taylor
4. Jack Lemmon
5. Richard Burton
6. Cary Grant
7. John Wayne
8. Doris Day
9. Paul Newman
10. Elvis Presley

1967

1. Julie Andrews
2. Lee Marvin
3. Paul Newman
4. Dean Martin
5. Sean Connery
6. Elizabeth Taylor
7. Sidney Poitier
8. John Wayne
9. Richard Burton
10. Steve McQueen

1968

1. Sidney Poitier
2. Paul Newman
3. Julie Andrews
4. John Wayne
5. Clint Eastwood
6. Dean Martin
7. Steve McQueen
8. Jack Lemmon
9. Lee Marvin
10. Elizabeth Taylor

1969

1. Paul Newman
2. John Wayne
3. Steve McQueen
4. Dustin Hoffman
5. Clint Eastwood
6. Sidney Poitier
7. Lee Marvin
8. Jack Lemmon
9. Katharine Hepburn
10. Barbra Streisand

1970

1. Paul Newman
2. Clint Eastwood
3. Steve McQueen
4. John Wayne
5. Elliott Gould
6. Dustin Hoffman
7. Lee Marvin
8. Jack Lemmon
9. Barbra Streisand
10. Walter Matthau

1971

1. John Wayne
2. Clint Eastwood
3. Paul Newman
4. Steve McQueen
5. George C. Scott
6. Dustin Hoffman
7. Walter Matthau
8. Ali MacGraw
9. Sean Connery
10. Lee Marvin

1972

1. Clint Eastwood
2. George C. Scott
3. Gene Hackman
4. John Wayne
5. Barbra Streisand
6. Marlon Brando
7. Paul Newman
8. Steve McQueen
9. Dustin Hoffman
10. Goldie Hawn

1973

1. Clint Eastwood
2. Ryan O'Neal
3. Steve McQueen
4. Burt Reynolds
5. Robert Redford
6. Barbra Streisand
7. Paul Newman
8. Charles Bronson
9. John Wayne
10. Marlon Brando

1974

1. Robert Redford
2. Clint Eastwood
3. Paul Newman
4. Barbra Streisand
5. Steve McQueen
6. Burt Reynolds
7. Charles Bronson
8. Jack Nicholson
9. Al Pacino
10. John Wayne

1975

1. Robert Redford
2. Barbra Streisand
3. Al Pacino
4. Charles Bronson
5. Paul Newman
6. Clint Eastwood
7. Burt Reynolds
8. Woody Allen
9. Steve McQueen
10. Gene Hackman

1976

1. Robert Redford
2. Jack Nicholson
3. Dustin Hoffman
4. Clint Eastwood
5. Mel Brooks
6. Burt Reynolds
7. Al Pacino
8. Tatum O'Neal
9. Woody Allen
10. Charles Bronson

1977

1. Sylvester Stallone
2. Barbra Streisand
3. Clint Eastwood
4. Burt Reynolds
5. Robert Redford
6. Woody Allen
7. Mel Brooks
8. Al Pacino
9. Diane Keaton
10. Robert De Niro

1978

1. Burt Reynolds
2. John Travolta
3. Richard Dreyfuss
4. Warren Beatty
5. Clint Eastwood
6. Woody Allen
7. Diane Keaton
8. Jane Fonda
9. Peter Sellers
10. Barbra Streisand

1979

1. Burt Reynolds
2. Clint Eastwood
3. Jane Fonda
4. Woody Allen
5. Barbra Streisand
6. Sylvester Stallone
7. John Travolta
8. Jill Clayburgh
9. Roger Moore
10. Mel Brooks

1980

1. Burt Reynolds
2. Robert Redford
3. Clint Eastwood
4. Jane Fonda
5. Dustin Hoffman
6. John Travolta
7. Sally Field
8. Sissy Spacek
9. Barbra Streisand
10. Steve Martin

1981

1. Burt Reynolds
2. Clint Eastwood
3. Dudley Moore
4. Dolly Parton
5. Jane Fonda
6. Harrison Ford
7. Alan Alda
8. Bo Derek
9. Goldie Hawn
10. Bill Murray

1982

1. Burt Reynolds
2. Clint Eastwood
3. Sylvester Stallone
4. Dudley Moore
5. Richard Pryor
6. Dolly Parton
7. Jane Fonda
8. Richard Gere
9. Paul Newman
10. Harrison Ford

1983

1. Clint Eastwood
2. Eddie Murphy
3. Sylvester Stallone
4. Burt Reynolds
5. John Travolta
6. Dustin Hoffman
7. Harrison Ford
8. Richard Gere
9. Chevy Chase
10. Tom Cruise

1984

1. Clint Eastwood
2. Bill Murray
3. Harrison Ford
4. Eddie Murphy
5. Sally Field
6. Burt Reynolds
7. Robert Redford
8. Prince
9. Dan Aykroyd
10. Meryl Streep

1985

1. Sylvester Stallone
2. Eddie Murphy
3. Clint Eastwood
4. Michael J. Fox
5. Chevy Chase
6. Arnold Schwarzenegger
7. Chuck Norris
8. Harrison Ford
9. Michael Douglas
10. Meryl Streep

1986

1. Tom Cruise
2. Eddie Murphy
3. Paul Hogan
4. Rodney Dangerfield
5. Bette Midler
6. Sylvester Stallone
7. Clint Eastwood
8. Whoopi Goldberg
9. Kathleen Turner
10. Paul Newman

1987

1. Eddie Murphy
2. Michael Douglas
3. Michael J. Fox
4. Arnold Schwarzenegger
5. Paul Hogan
6. Tom Cruise
7. Glenn Close
8. Sylvester Stallone
9. Cher
10. Mel Gibson

1988

1. Tom Cruise
2. Eddie Murphy
3. Tom Hanks
4. Arnold Schwarzenegger
5. Paul Hogan
6. Danny DeVito
7. Bette Midler
8. Robin Williams
9. Tom Selleck
10. Dustin Hoffman

1989

1. Jack Nicholson
2. Tom Cruise
3. Robin Williams
4. Michael Douglas
5. Tom Hanks
6. Michael J. Fox
7. Eddie Murphy
8. Mel Gibson
9. Sean Connery
10. Kathleen Turner

1990

1. Arnold Schwarzenegger
2. Julia Roberts
3. Bruce Willis
4. Tom Cruise
5. Mel Gibson
6. Kevin Costner
7. Patrick Swayze
8. Sean Connery
9. Harrison Ford
10. Richard Gere

1991

1. Kevin Costner
2. Arnold Schwarzenegger
3. Robin Williams
4. Julia Roberts
5. Macaulay Culkin
6. Jodie Foster
7. Billy Crystal
8. Dustin Hoffman
9. Robert De Niro
10. Mel Gibson

1992

1. Tom Cruise
2. Mel Gibson
3. Kevin Costner
4. Jack Nicholson
5. Macaulay Culkin
6. Whoopi Goldberg
7. Michael Douglas
8. Clint Eastwood
9. Steven Seagal
10. Robin Williams

1993

1. Clint Eastwood
2. Tom Cruise
3. Robin Williams
4. Kevin Costner
5. Harrison Ford
6. Julia Roberts
7. Tom Hanks
8. Mel Gibson
9. Whoopi Goldberg
10. Sylvester Stallone

1994

1. Tom Hanks
2. Jim Carrey
3. Arnold Schwarzenegger
4. Tom Cruise
5. Harrison Ford
6. Tim Allen
7. Mel Gibson
8. Jodie Foster
9. Michael Douglas
10. Tommy Lee Jones

1995

1. Tom Hanks
2. Jim Carrey
3. Brad Pitt
4. Harrison Ford
5. Robin Williams
6. Sandra Bullock
7. Mel Gibson
8. Demi Moore
9. John Travolta
10. Kevin Costner (tie)
10. Michael Douglas (tie)

1996

1. Tom Cruise (tie)
1. Mel Gibson (tie)
3. John Travolta
4. Arnold Schwarzenegger
5. Sandra Bullock
6. Robin Williams
7. Sean Connery
8. Harrison Ford
9. Kevin Costner
10. Michelle Pfeiffer

STAR LIGHT, STAR BRIGHT

Awarding points on a descending scale of 10, PEOPLE has analyzed Quigley Publishing's yearly film stars rankings to determine the most popular screen actors of all time.

Rank	Actor	Score
1.	John Wayne	172
2.	Clint Eastwood	165
3.	Bing Crosby	111
4.	Gary Cooper	102
5.	Clark Gable	91
6.	Burt Reynolds	90
7.	Bob Hope	84
8.	Paul Newman	76
9.	Doris Day	72
10.	Rock Hudson	69
11.	Betty Grable	66
12.	Tom Cruise (tie)	62
12.	Cary Grant (tie)	62
14.	Eddie Murphy (tie)	57
14.	Abbott & Costello (tie)	57
16.	James Stewart	56
17.	Robert Redford	55
18.	Arnold Schwarzenegger	53
19.	Sylvester Stallone	50
20.	Shirley Temple	49
21.	Spencer Tracy (tie)	48
21.	Barbra Streisand (tie)	48
23.	Steve McQueen	47
24.	Dean Martin & Jerry Lewis (tie)	46
24.	Mickey Rooney (tie)	46
26.	Harrison Ford	45
27.	Elizabeth Taylor	44
28.	Dustin Hoffman	42
29.	Mel Gibson	41
30.	Jack Lemmon	40
31.	Robin Williams	39
32.	Tom Hanks	38
33.	Sean Connery	36
34.	Julie Andrews	35
35.	Humphrey Bogart (tie)	34
35.	Gary Cooper (tie)	34
35.	John Travolta (tie)	34
38.	Kevin Costner (tie)	33
38.	William Holden (tie)	33
40.	Elvis Presley (tie)	29
40.	Jack Nicholson (tie)	29
42.	Jane Fonda (tie)	28
42.	Will Rogers (tie)	28
44.	Michael Douglas	25
45.	Garson Greer	24
46.	Woody Allen (tie)	22
46.	Jerry Lewis (tie)	22
48.	Glenn Ford (tie)	21
48.	Julia Roberts (tie)	21
50.	Michael J. Fox (tie)	20
50.	Paul Hogan (tie)	20
50.	Lee Marvin (tie)	20
50.	Robert Taylor (tie)	20

THE HOLLYWOOD BLACKLIST

The House Committee on Un-American Activities investigated the entertainment business for subversive activities—i.e., communist connections—starting in 1947. By the end of the hearings in 1958, roughly 100 film, television, radio, theater, and music industry figures had been questioned. Approximately one-third of them provided the committee with the names of others who were alleged sympathizers. The remainder, insisting that their political beliefs were a private matter, took either the First or the Fifth Amendment and refused to name names; some of these men and women were jailed, almost all were blacklisted, and many had their careers ruined.

The following were some of the most well known of the informers who identified over 300 supposed communist sympathizers:

Lee J. Cobb, actor (*On the Waterfront, Twelve Angry Men, Death of a Salesman, Exodus,* "The Virginian")

Sterling Hayden, actor (*The Asphalt Jungle, Johnny Guitar, Dr. Strangelove*)

Roy Huggins, writer/director/producer ("Cheyenne," "Maverick," "The Rockford Files")

Elia Kazan, director (*Gentleman's Agreement, On the Waterfront, A Streetcar Named Desire*)

Isobel Lennert, screenwriter (*East Side, West Side, Anchors Aweigh, Meet Me in Las Vegas*)

Clifford Odets, playwright (*Waiting for Lefty, Golden Boy*)

Jerome Robbins, dancer/choreographer/assoc. director, New York City Ballet (*Fancy Free, Interplay, Dances at a Gathering*)

Robert Rossen, director (*Body and Soul, All the King's Men*)

Budd Schulberg, screenwriter/novelist (*On the Waterfront*)

Leo Townsend, screenwriter (*Night and Day, Beach Blanket Bingo, Bikini Beach*)

The following, six of them Oscar winners, refused to incriminate themselves or to inform on others, and as a result were either jailed, blacklisted, or forced to leave the country:

Herschel Bernardi, actor (*The Front*)

Howard Da Silva, actor (*Mommy Dearest*)

Carl Foreman, director/screenwriter (screenwriter, *High Noon*)

Dashiell Hammett, novelist (*The Thin Man, The Maltese Falcon*)

Lillian Hellman, playwright/screenwriter (*The Little Foxes, The Watch on the Rhine*)

Howard Koch, radio writer/screenwriter/playwright ("War of the Worlds," *Casablanca*)

Ring Lardner Jr., screenwriter (*Woman of the Year, Laura, M*A*S*H*)

Philip Loeb, actor ("The Goldbergs")

Joseph Losey, director (*The Concrete Jungle, The Damned, The Servant, Modesty Blaise, Boom!, The Go-Between*)

Albert Maltz, screenwriter/playwright (*This Gun for Hire, Destination Tokyo, The House I Live In, Pride of the Marines, The Robe*)

Arthur Miller, playwright/screenwriter (*The Crucible, Death of a Salesman, The Misfits*)

Zero Mostel, actor/comedian (*A Funny Thing Happened on the Way to the Forum, The Producers, Fiddler on the Roof*)

Dorothy Parker, short-story writer/screenwriter

("Laments for the Living," *A Star is Born*)

John Randolph, actor (*Come Back, Little Sheba, Serpico*)

Paul Robeson, actor/singer (*Show Boat, The Emperor Jones*)

Waldo Salt, screenwriter (*Midnight Cowboy, Serpico, Coming Home*)

Robert Adrian Scott, screenwriter/producer (producer, *Murder, My Sweet, Crossfire*)

Pete Seeger, musician (coauthor, "If I Had a Hammer")

Gale Sondergaard, actress (*Anthony Adverse, A Night To Remember, The Spider Woman*)

Dalton Trumbo, screenwriter (*Kitty Foyle, Thirty Seconds over Tokyo, The Brave One* [under the name of Robert Rich], *Exodus, Hawaii, Spartacus*)

Sam Wanamaker, actor (*The Spy Who Came in from the Cold, Private Benjamin*)

Nedrick Young, screenwriter (*The Defiant Ones, Inherit the Wind*)

The following have received belated credit from the Writers Guild of America for films previously attributed to other scribes or written under pseudonyms:

The Brave One (1956), screenplay by Harry Franklin and Merrill G. White, story by Dalton Trumbo. Original credit: screenplay, Franklin and White, based on a story by Robert Rich

The Bridge on the River Kwai (1957), screenplay by Carl Foreman and Michael Wilson, based on the novel by Pierre Boulle. Original credit: screenplay, Boulle, from his own novel

Broken Arrow (1950), screenplay by Albert Maltz, based on the novel Blood Brother"by Elliot Arnold. Original credit: screenplay, Michael Blankfort, based on the novel by Arnold

The Day of the Triffids (1963), screenplay by Bernard Gordon, based on the novel by John Wyndham. Original credit: screenplay, Philip Yordan, based on the novel by Wyndham

Deadly Is the Female ("Gun Crazy") (1949), screenplay by MacKinlay Kantor and Dalton Trumbo, based on a *Saturday Evening Post* story "Gun Crazy" by Kantor. Original credit: screenplay, Kantor and Millard Kaufman, from *Post* story "Gun Crazy" by Kantor

The Defiant Ones (1958), written by Nedrick Young and Harold Jacob Smith. Original credit: screenplay, Nathan E. Douglas and Smith

Friendly Persuasion (1956), screenplay by Michael Wilson. Original credit: based on the novel by Jessamyn West

Lawrence of Arabia (1962), screenplay by Robert Bolt and Michael Wilson, based on the life and writings of T. H. Lawrence. Original credit: screenplay by Robert Bolt

Odds Against Tomorrow (1959), screenplay by Abraham Polonsky and Nelson Gidding, based on the novel by William P. McGivern. Original credit: screenplay, John O. Killens and Gidding, based on the novel by McGivern

Roman Holiday (1953), screenplay by Ian McLellan Hunter and John Dighton, story by Dalton Trumbo. Original credit: screenplay, Hunter and Dighton, story by Hunter

SIX DEGREES OF KEVIN BACON

There's no escapin' Kevin Bacon and the game that's swept parties, film schools, and the Internet. Now you can flex your memory for movies with the Kevin Bacon game. The objective is to connect Kevin Bacon to any other screen actor through a network of common costars. Listed below are the best known, along with their Bacon link.

Jennifer Aniston, *Picture Perfect*
Anne Archer, *Hero at Large*
Alec Baldwin, *She's Having a Baby*
William Baldwin, *Flatliners*
Ellen Barkin, *Diner*
John Belushi, *National Lampoon's Animal House*
Candice Bergen, Starting Over
Wilford Brimley, *End of the Line*
John Candy, *Planes, Trains and Automobiles*
John Cleese, *The Big Picture*
Kevin Costner, *JFK*
Tom Cruise, *A Few Good Men*
Jamie Lee Curtis, *Queens Logic*
Robert de Niro, *Sleepers*
Minnie Driver, *Sleepers*
Olympia Dukakis, *Picture Perfect*
Linda Fiorentino, *Queens Logic*
Laurence Fishburne, *Quicksilver*
Elliott Gould, *The Big Picture*
Steve Guttenberg, *Diner*
Tom Hanks, *Apollo 13*
Ed Harris, *Apollo 13*
Teri Hatcher, *The Big Picture*
Dustin Hoffman, *Sleepers*
Holly Hunter, *End of the Line*
Tommy Lee Jones, *JFK*
Bruno Kirby, *Sleepers*
Nathan Lane, *He Said, She Said*
Jennifer Jason Leigh, *The Big Picture*
Jack Lemmon, *JFK*
John Lithgow, *Footloose*
John Malkovich, *Queens Logic*
Joe Mantegna, *Queens Logic*
Steve Martin, *Planes, Trains and Automobiles*
Marsha Mason, *Only When I Laugh*
Walter Matthau, *JFK*
Elizabeth McGovern, *She's Having a Baby*
Kristy McNichol, *Only When I Laugh*
Demi Moore, *A Few Good Men*
Jack Nicholson, *A Few Good Men*
Gary Oldman, *Criminal Law*
Sarah Jessica Parker, *Footloose*
Bill Paxton, *Apollo 13*
Joe Pesci, *JFK*
Brad Pitt, *Sleepers*
Kevin Pollak, *A Few Good Men*
Paul Reiser, *Diner*
Burt Reynolds, *Starting Over*
John Ritter, *Hero at Large*
Julia Roberts, *Flatliners*
Mickey Rourke, *Diner*
Kyra Sedgwick, *Pyrates*
Martin Short, *The Big Picture*
Gary Sinise, *Apollo 13*
Christian Slater, *Murder in the First*
Sissy Spacek, *JFK*
Mary Steenburgen, *End of the Line*
Daniel Stern, *Diner*
Sharon Stone, *He Said, She Said*
Meryl Streep, *The River Wild*
Donald Sutherland, *National Lampoon's Animal House*
Kiefer Sutherland, *Flatliners*
Tom Waits, *Queens Logic*
Dianne Wiest, *Footloose*

BACK TO BACON

A wide range of starting points, along with short and dizzyingly twisted paths, are offered below.

Louis Armstrong was in *Hello, Dolly!* with **Walter Matthau**, who was in *JFK* with **Kevin Bacon**.

Al Pacino was in *Sea of Love* with **Michael Rooker**, who was in *JFK* with **Kevin Bacon**.

Uma Thurman was in *Henry and June* with **Fred Ward**, who was in *Tremors* with **Kevin Bacon**.

Katharine Hepburn was in *Guess Who's Coming to Dinner* with **Sidney Poitier**, who was in *Sneakers* with **David Strathairn**, who was in *The River Wild* with **Kevin Bacon**.

Flea was in *My Own Private Idaho* with **Grace Zabrieskie**, who was in *Twin Peaks: Fire Walk with Me* with **Kiefer Sutherland**, who was in *A Few Good Men* with **Kevin Bacon**.

Shirley Temple was in *That Hagen Girl* with **Rory Calhoun**, who was in *Motel Hell* with **Nancy Parsons**, who was in *Porky's* with **Dan Monahan**, who was in *Up the Creek* with **Tim Matheson**, who was in *National Lampoon's Animal House* with **Kevin Bacon**.

SUPERSTAR FILMOGRAPHIES

The filmographies for some of Hollywood's most important, most popular people list only full-length feature films to which these actors and directors contributed significantly. Included are some early works released directly onto video years after completion.

WOODY ALLEN
Director/screenwriter/actor

What's New, Pussycat? (screenwriter/actor, 1965)
What's Up, Tiger Lily? (director/screenwriter/actor, 1966)
Casino Royale (co-screenwriter/actor, 1967)
Take the Money and Run (director/co-screenwriter/actor, 1969)
Bananas (director/screenwriter/actor, 1971)
Play It Again, Sam (screenwriter/actor, 1972)
Everything You Always Wanted To Know About Sex (*but were afraid to ask)* (director/co-screenwriter/actor, 1972)
Sleeper (director/screenwriter/actor, 1973)
Love and Death (director/screenwriter/actor, 1975)
The Front (actor, 1976)
Annie Hall (director/co-screenwriter/actor, 1977; Academy Awards for best picture, best director, best original screenplay)
Interiors (director/screenwriter/actor, 1978)
Manhattan (director/co-screenwriter/actor, 1979)
Stardust Memories (director/screenwriter/actor, 1980)
A Midsummer Night's Sex Comedy (director/screenwriter/actor, 1982)
Zelig (director/screenwriter/actor, 1983)
Broadway Danny Rose (director/screenwriter/actor, 1984)
The Purple Rose of Cairo (director/screenwriter, 1985)
Hannah and Her Sisters (director/screenwriter/actor, 1986; Academy Award for best original screenplay)
Radio Days (director/screenwriter/actor, 1987)
King Lear (actor, 1987)
September (director/screenwriter, 1987)
Another Woman (director/screenwriter, 1988)
"Oedipus Wrecks," in *New York Stories* (director/co-screenwriter/actor, 1989)
Crimes and Misdemeanors (director/screenwriter/actor, 1989)
Alice (director/screenwriter, 1990)
Scenes from a Mall (actor, 1991)
Shadows and Fog (director/screenwriter/actor, 1992)
Husbands and Wives (director/screenwriter/actor, 1992)
Manhattan Murder Mystery (director/screenwriter/actor, 1993)
Bullets over Broadway (director/co-screenwriter, 1994)
Mighty Aphrodite (director/screenwriter/actor, 1995)
Everyone Says I Love You (director/screenwriter/actor, 1996)
Deconstructing Harry (director/screenwriter/actor, 1997)

SANDRA BULLOCK
Actor

Who Shot Patakango? (1990)
Religion, Inc. (1990—videotape)
When the Party's Over (1992)
Who Do I Gotta Kill? (1992)
Love Potion No. 9 (1992)
The Vanishing (1993)
Fire on the Amazon (1992—videotape)
Demolition Man (1993)
The Thing Called Love (1993)
Wrestling Ernest Hemingway (1993)
Speed (1994)
While You Were Sleeping (1995)
The Net (1995)
Two If by Sea (1996)
A Time To Kill (1996)
In Love and War (1997)
Speed 2: Cruise Control (1997)

GLENN CLOSE
Actor

The World According to Garp (1982)
The Big Chill (1983)
The Stone Boy (1984)
Greystoke: The Legend of Tarzan, Lord of the Apes (Voice, 1984)
The Natural (1984)
Jagged Edge (1985)
Maxie (1985)
Fatal Attraction (1987)
Dangerous Liaisons (1988)
Light Years (cartoon voice, 1988)
Immediate Family (1989)
Hamlet (1990)
Reversal of Fortune (1990)
Meeting Venus (1991)
The Paper (1994)
The House of the Spirits (1994)
Mary Reilly (1996)
101 Dalmatians (1996)
Mars Attacks! (1996)
Paradise Road (1997)
Air Force One (1997)

SEAN CONNERY
Actor

No Road Back (1956)
Action of the Tiger (1957)
Another Time, Another Place (1958)
Hell Drivers (1957)
Time Lock (1957)
A Night to Remember (1958)
Tarzan's Greatest Adventure (1959)
Darby O'Gill and the Little People (1959)
On the Fiddle (1961)
The Frightened City (1961)
The Longest Day (1962)
Dr. No (1962)
From Russia with Love (1963)
Goldfinger (1964)
Woman of Straw (1964)
Marnie (1964)
Thunderball (1965)
The Hill (1965)
A Fine Madness (1966)
You Only Live Twice (1967)
Shalako (1968)
Bowler and Bonnet (1969, director)
The Molly Maguires (1970)
The Red Tent (1971)
The Anderson Tapes (1971)
Diamonds Are Forever (1971)
The Offence (or *Something like the Truth,* 1973)
Zardoz (1974)
Murder on the Orient Express (1974)
Ransom (1974)
The Wind and the Lion (1975)
The Man Who Would Be King (1975)
The Terrorists (1975)
Robin and Marian (1976)
The Next Man (1976)
A Bridge Too Far (1977)
The Great Train Robbery (1979)
Meteor (1979)
Cuba (1979)
Outland (1981)
Time Bandits (1981)
Wrong Is Right (1981)
G'ole (1982)
Five Days One Summer (1982)
Never Say Never Again (1983)
Sword of the Valiant (1984)
Highlander (1985)
The Name of the Rose (1986)
The Untouchables (1987; Academy Award for best supporting actor)
The Presidio (1988)
Memories of Me (1988)
Indiana Jones and the Last Crusade (1989)
Family Business (1989)
The Hunt for Red October (1990)
The Russia House (1990)
Highlander II: The Quickening (1991)

Robin Hood: Prince of Thieves (1991)

Medicine Man (1992)

Rising Sun (1993)

A Good Man in Africa (1994)

Just Cause (1995)

First Knight (1995)

Dragonheart (voice, 1996)

The Rock (1996)

FRANCIS FORD COPPOLA

Director/producer/screenwriter

Dementia 13 (director/screenwriter, 1963)

Is Paris Burning? (screenwriter, 1966)

This Property Is Condemned (screenwriter, 1966)

You're a Big Boy Now (director/screenwriter, 1966)

Finian's Rainbow (director, 1968)

The Rain People (director/screenwriter, 1969)

Patton (co-screenwriter, 1970; Academy Award for best screenplay)

The Godfather (director/co-screenwriter, 1972; Academy Award for best screenplay)

The Conversation (director/co-producer/screenwriter, 1974)

The Godfather, Part II (director/co-producer/coscreenwriter, 1974; Academy Awards for best director, best picture, best screenplay)

The Great Gatsby (screenwriter, 1974)

Apocalypse Now (director/producer/co-screenwriter/musical co-composer, 1979)

One from the Heart (director/co-screenwriter, 1982)

The Outsiders (director/producer, 1983)

Rumble Fish (director/co-screenwriter, 1983)

The Cotton Club (director/co-screenwriter, 1984)

Captain EO (director, 1986)

Peggy Sue Got Married (director, 1986)

Gardens of Stone (director/co-producer, 1987)

Tucker: The Man and His Dream (director, 1988)

"Life Without Zoe," in *New York Stories* (director/co-screenwriter, 1989)

The Godfather, Part III (director/producer/co-screenwriter, 1990)

Bram Stoker's Dracula (director/producer, 1992)

Mary Shelley's Frankenstein (producer, 1994)

Don Juan DeMarco (co-producer, 1995)

Jack (director, 1996)

Buddy (executive producer, 1997)

KEVIN COSTNER

Actor/director/producer

Shadows Run Black (actor, 1981)

Night Shift (actor, 1982)

Stacy's Knights (actor, 1982)

The Big Chill (played corpse, all other scenes edited out, 1983)

The Gunrunner (actor, 1983)

Table for Five (actor, 1983)

Testament (actor, 1983)

American Flyers (actor, 1985)

Fandango (actor, 1985)

Silverado (actor, 1985)

Sizzle Beach, U.S.A. (actor, 1986)

No Way Out (actor, 1987)

The Untouchables (actor, 1987)

Bull Durham (actor, 1988)

Chasing Dreams (actor, 1989)

Field of Dreams (actor, 1989)

Dances with Wolves (actor/director/producer, 1990; Academy Awards for best picture, best director)

Revenge (actor, 1990)

Robin Hood: Prince of Thieves (actor, 1991)

JFK (actor, 1991)

The Bodyguard (actor/producer, 1992)

A Perfect World (actor, 1993)

Wyatt Earp (actor/producer, 1994)

Rapa Nui (co-producer, 1994)

The War (actor, 1994)

Waterworld (actor/producer, 1995)

Tin Cup (1996)

TOM CRUISE

Actor

Endless Love (1981)

Taps (1981)

Losin' It (1983)

The Outsiders (1983)

Risky Business (1983)

All the Right Moves (1983)

Legend (1986)

Top Gun (1986)

The Color of Money (1986)

Cocktail (1988)

Rain Man (1988)

Born on the Fourth of July (1989)

Days of Thunder (1990)

Far and Away (1992)

A Few Good Men (1992)

The Firm (1993)

Interview with the Vampire (1994)

Mission: Impossible (actor/co-producer, 1996)

Jerry Maguire (1996)

CLINT EASTWOOD

Actor/director/producer

Francis in the Navy (actor, 1955)

Lady Godiva (actor, 1955)

Never Say Goodbye (actor,1955)

Revenge of the Creature (actor, 1955)

Tarantula (actor, 1955)

The Traveling Saleslady (actor, 1956)

Star in the Dust (actor, 1956)

Escapade in Japan (actor, 1957)

Ambush at Cimarron Pass (actor, 1958)

Lafayette Escadrille (actor, 1958)

A Fistful of Dollars (actor, 1964)

For a Few Dollars More (actor, 1965)

The Good, the Bad, and the Ugly (actor, 1966)

Coogan's Bluff (actor, 1968)

Hang 'Em High (actor, 1968)

The Witches (actor, 1968)

Where Eagles Dare (actor, 1968)

Paint Your Wagon (actor, 1969)

Kelly's Heroes (actor, 1970)

Two Mules for Sister Sara (actor, 1970)

The Beguiled (actor, 1971)

Dirty Harry (actor, 1971)

Play Misty For Me (actor/director, 1971)

Joe Kidd (actor, 1972)

Breezy (actor, 1973)

High Plains Drifter (actor/director, 1973)

Magnum Force (actor, 1973)

Thunderbolt and Lightfoot (actor, 1974)

The Eiger Sanction (actor/director, 1974)

The Outlaw Josey Wales (actor/director, 1975)

The Enforcer (actor, 1976)

The Gauntlet (actor/director, 1977)

Every Which Way but Loose (actor, 1978)

Escape from Alcatraz (actor, 1979)

Any Which Way You Can (actor, 1980)

Bronco Billy (actor/director, 1980)

Firefox (actor/director/producer, 1982)

Honkytonk Man (actor/director/producer, 1982)

Sudden Impact (actor/director/producer, 1983)

City Heat (actor, 1984)

Tightrope (actor/producer, 1984)

Pale Rider (actor/director/producer, 1985)

Heartbreak Ridge (actor/director/producer, 1986)

Bird (director/producer, 1988)

The Dead Pool (actor/producer, 1988)

Pink Cadillac (actor, 1989)

The Rookie (actor/director, 1990)

White Hunter, Black Heart (actor/director/producer, 1990)

Unforgiven (actor/director/producer, 1992; Academy Awards for best director and best film)

In the Line of Fire (actor/producer, 1993)

A Perfect World (actor/director, 1993)

The Bridges of Madison County (actor/director, 1995)

Absolute Power (actor/director, 1997)

JODIE FOSTER

Actor/director

Napoleon and Samantha (1972)

Kansas City Bomber (1972)

Tom Sawyer (1973)
One Little Indian (1973)
Alice Doesn't Live Here Anymore (1974)
Echoes of a Summer (1976)
Bugsy Malone (1976)
Taxi Driver (1976)
The Little Girl Who Lives Down the Lane (1976)
Freaky Friday (1977)
Candleshoe (1977)
Moi, fleur bleue (1977)
Il Casotto (1977)
Carny (1980)
Foxes (1980)
O'Hara's Wife (1982)
Les Sang des autres (*The Blood of Others*) (1984)
The Hotel New Hampshire (1984)
Mesmerized (actor/co-producer, 1986)
Siesta (1987)
Five Corners (1988)
The Accused (1988; Academy Award for best actress)
Stealing Home (1988)
Backtrack (1989)
The Silence of the Lambs (1991; Academy Award for best actress)
Little Man Tate (actor/director, 1991)
Shadows and Fog (1992)
Sommersby (1993)
Maverick (1994)
Nell (1994)
Home for the Holidays (director, 1995)
Contact (1997)

MEL GIBSON
Actor/director

Summer City (1977)
Tim (1979)
Mad Max (1979)
Attack Force Z (1981)
Gallipoli (1981)
The Road Warrior (1981)
The Year of Living Dangerously (1982)
The Bounty (1984)
Mrs. Soffel (1984)
The River (1984)
Mad Max Beyond Thunderdome (1985)
Lethal Weapon (1987)
Tequila Sunrise (1988)
Lethal Weapon 2 (1989)
Air America (1990)
Bird on a Wire (1990)
Hamlet (1990)
Forever Young (1992)
Lethal Weapon 3 (1992)
The Man Without a Face (actor/director, 1993)
Maverick (1994)
Braveheart (actor/director/producer, 1995; Academy Awards for best director and best picture)
Pocahontas (cartoon voice, 1995)
Ransom (1996)
Conspiracy Theory (1997)

WHOOPI GOLDBERG
Actor

The Color Purple (1985)
Jumpin' Jack Flash (1986)
Burglar (1987)
Fatal Beauty (1987)
Clara's Heart (1988)
The Telephone (1988)
Beverly Hills Brats (1989)
Homer and Eddie (1989)
Ghost (1990; Academy Award for best supporting actress)
The Long Walk Home (1990)
Soapdish (1991)
The Player (1992)
Sarafina! (1992)
Sister Act (1992)
Made in America (1993)
Sister Act 2: Back in the Habit (1993)
Corrina, Corrina (1994)
The Lion King (cartoon voice, 1994)
The Pagemaster (cartoon voice, 1994)
The Little Rascals (1994)
Star Trek: Generations (1994)
Boys on the Side (1995)
Moonlight & Valentino (1995)
Theodore Rex (1996—videotape)
Eddie (1996)
Bogus (1996)
The Associate (1996)

TOM HANKS
Actor

He Knows You're Alone (1980)
Splash (1984)
Bachelor Party (1984)
The Man with One Red Shoe (1985)
Volunteers (1985)
The Money Pit (1986)
Nothing in Common (1986)
Every Time We Say Goodbye (1986)
Dragnet (1987)
Big (1988)
Punchline (1988)
The Burbs (1989)
Turner and Hooch (1989)
Joe Versus the Volcano (1990)
The Bonfire of the Vanities (1990)
Radio Flyer (1992)
A League of Their Own (1992)
Sleepless in Seattle (1993)
Philadelphia (1993; Academy Award for best actor)
Forrest Gump (1994; Academy Award for best actor)
Apollo 13 (1995)
Toy Story (cartoon voice, 1995)
That Thing You Do! (writer/director/actor, 1996)

ANTHONY HOPKINS
Actor

The Lion in Winter (1968)
Hamlet (1969)
The Looking Glass War (1970)
When Eight Bells Toll (1971)
Young Winston (1972)
A Doll's House (1973)
The Girl From Petrovka (1974)
Juggernaut (1974)
All Creatures Great and Small (1975)
Audrey Rose (1977)
A Bridge Too Far (1977)
International Velvet (1978)
Magic (1978)
A Change of Seasons (1980)
The Elephant Man (1980)
The Bounty (1984)
Blunt (1986)
The Good Father (1986)
84 Charing Cross Road (1987)
The Dawning (1988)
A Chorus of Disapproval (1987)
Desperate Hours (1990)
The Silence of the Lambs (1991; Academy Award for best actor)
The Remains of the Day (1993)
Shadowlands (1993)
The Trial (1993)
The Road to Wellville (1994)
Legends of the Fall (1994)
Nixon (1995)
August (actor/director, 1996)
Surviving Picasso (1996)
Amistad (1997)

SPIKE LEE
Director/producer/screenwriter/actor

She's Gotta Have It (director/producer/screenwriter/actor, 1986)
School Daze (director/producer/screenwriter/actor, 1988)
Do the Right Thing (director/producer/screenwriter/actor, 1989)
Mo' Better Blues (director/producer/screenwriter/actor, 1990)
Lonely in America, (actor, 1990)
Jungle Fever (director/producer/screenwriter/actor, 1991)
Malcolm X (director/producer/co-screenwriter/actor, 1992)
Crooklyn (director/producer/co-screenwriter/actor, 1994)
Clockers (director/co-producer/co-screenwriter, 1995)
Girl 6 (director/producer, 1996)
Get On The Bus (director/producer, 1996)
When We Were Kings (interviewee, 1996)
4 Little Girls (director/producer, 1997)

DEMI MOORE
Actor/Producer

Choices (1981)
Parasite (1982)
Young Doctors in Love (1982)
Blame It on Rio (1984)
No Small Affair (1984)
St. Elmo's Fire (1985)
About Last Night (1986)
One Crazy Summer (1986)

Wisdom (1986)
The Seventh Sign (1988)
We're No Angels (1989)
Ghost (1990)
Mortal Thoughts (actor/co-producer, 1991)
Nothing but Trouble (1991)
The Butcher's Wife (1991)
A Few Good Men (1992)
Indecent Proposal (1993)
Disclosure (1994)
The Scarlet Letter (1995)
Now and Then (1995)
The Juror (1996)
The Hunchback of Notre Dame (cartoon voice, 1996)
Striptease (1996)
Austin Powers: International Man of Mystery (co-producer, 1997)
G.I. Jane (1997)
Deconstructing Harry (1997)

JACK NICHOLSON
Actor/producer/screenwriter/director

Cry Baby Killer (1958)
Studs Lonigan (1960)
Too Soon To Love (1960)
The Wild Ride (1960)
Little Shop of Horrors (1961)
The Broken Land (1962)
The Raven (1963)
The Terror (1963)
Thunder Island (screenwriter, 1963)
Ensign Pulver (1964)
Back Door to Hell (1964)
The Fortune (1965)
Flight to Fury (actor/screenwriter, 1966)
Ride in the Whirlwind (actor/producer/screenwriter, 1966)
Hell's Angels on Wheels (1966)
The Shooting (actor/producer, 1967)
The Trip (screenwriter, 1967)
St. Valentine's Day Massacre (1967)
Head (actor/producer/screenwriter, 1968)
Psych-Out (1968)
Easy Rider (1969)
Five Easy Pieces (1970)
On a Clear Day You Can See Forever (1970)
Rebel Rousers (1970)
Carnal Knowledge (1971)
Drive, He Said (director/producer/screenwriter, 1971)
A Safe Place (1971)
The King of Marvin Gardens (1972)
The Last Detail (1973)
Chinatown (1974)
The Fortune (1975)
One Flew over the Cuckoo's Nest (1975; Academy Award for best actor)
The Passenger (1975)
Tommy (1975)
The Last Tycoon (1976)
The Missouri Breaks (1976)
Goin' South (actor/director, 1978)
The Shining (1980)
The Border (1981)
The Postman Always Rings Twice (1981)
Reds (1981)
Terms of Endearment (1983; Academy Award for best supporting actor)
Prizzi's Honor (1985)
Heartburn (1986)
Broadcast News (1987)
Ironweed (1987)
The Witches of Eastwick (1987)
Batman (1989)
The Two Jakes (actor/director, 1990)
Man Trouble (1992)
A Few Good Men (1992)
Hoffa (1992)
Wolf (1994)
The Crossing Guard (1995)
Mars Attacks! (1996)
The Evening Star (1996)
Blood and Wine (1997)

MICHELLE PFEIFFER
Actor

The Hollywood Knights (1980)
Falling in Love Again (1980)
Charlie Chan and the Curse of the Dragon Queen (1981)
Grease 2 (1982)
Scarface (1983)
Into the Night (1985)
Ladyhawke (1985)
Sweet Liberty (1986)
Amazon Women on the Moon (1987)
The Witches of Eastwick (1987)
Dangerous Liaisons (1988)
Married to the Mob (1988)
Tequila Sunrise (1988)
The Fabulous Baker Boys (1989)
The Russia House (1990)
Frankie and Johnny (1991)
Batman Returns (1992)
Love Field (1992)
The Age of Innocence (1993)
Wolf (1994)
Dangerous Minds (1995)
Up Close and Personal (1996)
To Gillian on Her 37th Birthday (1996)
One Fine Day (1996)
A Thousand Acres (1997)

JULIA ROBERTS
Actor

Satisfaction (1988)
Mystic Pizza (1988)
Blood Red (1989)
Steel Magnolias (1989)
Pretty Woman (1990)
Flatliners (1990)
Sleeping with the Enemy (1991)
Dying Young (1991)
Hook (1991)
The Player (1992)
The Pelican Brief (1993)
I Love Trouble (1994)
Ready to Wear (1994)
Something To Talk About (1995)
Mary Reilly (1996)
Everyone Says I Love You (1996)
My Best Friend's Wedding (1997)
Conspiracy Theory (1997)

MEG RYAN
Actor

Rich and Famous (1981)
Amityville 3-D (1983)
Armed and Dangerous (1986)
Top Gun (1986)
Innerspace (1987)
Promised Land (1987)
D.O.A. (1988)
The Presidio (1988)
When Harry Met Sally . . . (1989)
Joe Versus the Volcano (1990)
The Doors (1991)
Prelude to a Kiss (1992)
Sleepless in Seattle (1993)
Flesh and Bone (1993)
When a Man Loves a Woman (1994)
I.Q. (1994)
French Kiss (actor/coproducer, 1995)
Restoration (1995)
Courage Under Fire (1996)
Addicted to Love (1997)
Anastasia (cartoon voice, 1997)

ARNOLD SCHWARZENEGGER
Actor

Hercules in New York (1974)
Stay Hungry (1976)
Pumping Iron (1977)
The Villain (1979)
Conan the Barbarian (1982)
Conan the Destroyer (1984)
The Terminator (1984)
Commando (1985)
Red Sonja (1985)
Raw Deal (1986)
Predator (1987)
The Running Man (1987)
Red Heat (1988)
Twins (1988)
Total Recall (1989)
Kindergarten Cop (1990)
Terminator 2: Judgment Day (1991)
Last Action Hero (1993)
True Lies (1994)
Junior (1994)
Eraser (1996)
Jingle All the Way (1996)
Batman and Robin (1997)

MARTIN SCORSESE
Director/producer/screenwriter

Who's That Knocking at My Door? (director/screenwriter/actor, 1969)
Street Scenes 1970 (director/actor, 1970)
Boxcar Bertha (director, 1972)
Mean Streets (director/screenwriter, 1973)
Alice Doesn't Live Here Anymore

(director, 1974)

Taxi Driver (director, 1976)

New York, New York (director, 1977)

American Boy: A Profile of Steven Prince (director, 1978)

The Last Waltz (director/actor, 1978)

Raging Bull (director/actor, 1980)

The King of Comedy (director/actor, 1983)

After Hours (director, 1985)

The Color of Money (director, 1986)

The Last Temptation of Christ (director, 1988)

"Life Lessons," in *New York Stories* (director, 1989)

GoodFellas (director/co-screenwriter, 1990)

Made in Milan (director, 1990)

The Grifters (producer, 1990)

Cape Fear (director, 1991)

The Age of Innocence (director/co-screenwriter, 1993)

Clockers (co-producer, 1995)

Casino (director/co-screenwriter, 1995)

Kundun (director, 1997)

STEVEN SPIELBERG

Director/producer/screenwriter

Duel (director, telefilm, 1971; U.S. theatrical release, 1984)

The Sugarland Express (director/co-screenwriter,1974)

Jaws (director, 1975)

Close Encounters of the Third Kind (director/screenwriter, 1977)

1941 (director, 1979)

Raiders of the Lost Ark (director, 1981)

E.T., the Extra-Terrestrial (director/co-producer, 1982)

Poltergeist (co-producer/co-screenwriter, 1982)

"Kick the Can," in *Twilight Zone—The Movie* (director/co-producer, 1983)

Indiana Jones and the Temple of Doom (director, 1984)

The Color Purple (director/co-producer, 1985)

Special Academy Award presented in 1986, the Irving G. Thalberg Award, for consistently high quality of filmmaking

Empire of the Sun (director/co-producer, 1987)

Always (director/co-producer, 1989)

Indiana Jones and the Last Crusade (director, 1989)

Hook (director, 1991)

An American Tail II: Fievel Goes West (co-producer, 1991)

Jurassic Park (director, 1993)

Schindler's List (director/producer, 1993; Academy Awards for best director, best picture)

The Lost World: Jurassic Park (director, 1997)

Men in Black (executive producer, 1997)

Amistad (director, 1997)

SYLVESTER STALLONE

Actor/director/screenwriter

A Party at Kitty and Stud's (reissued as *The Italian Stallion)* (actor, 1970)

Bananas (actor, 1971)

The Lords of Flatbush (actor/co-screenwriter, 1974)

Capone (actor, 1975)

Death Race 2000 (actor, 1975)

Farewell, My Lovely (actor, 1975)

No Place to Hide (actor, 1975)

The Prisoner of Second Avenue (actor, 1975)

Cannonball (actor, 1976)

Rocky (actor/screenwriter/fight choreographer, 1976)

F.I.S.T. (actor/co-screenwriter, 1978)

Paradise Alley (actor/director/screenwriter, 1978)

Rocky II (actor/director/screenwriter/fight choreographer, 1979)

Victory (actor, 1981)

Nighthawks (actor, 1981)

First Blood (actor/co-screenwriter, 1982)

Rocky III (actor/director/screenwriter/fight choreographer, 1982)

Staying Alive (director/co-producer/co-screenwriter, 1983)

Rhinestone (actor/co-screenwriter, 1984)

Rambo: First Blood, Part II (actor/co-screenwriter, 1985)

Rocky IV (actor/director/screenwriter, 1985)

Cobra (actor/screenwriter, 1986)

Over the Top (actor/co-screenwriter, 1987)

Rambo III (actor/co-screenwriter, 1988)

Lock Up (actor, 1989)

Tango and Cash (actor, 1989)

Rocky V (actor/screenwriter, 1990)

Oscar (actor, 1991)

Stop! or My Mom Will Shoot (actor, 1992)

Cliffhanger (actor/co-screenwriter, 1993)

Demolition Man (actor, 1993)

The Specialist (actor, 1994)

Judge Dredd (actor, 1995)

Assassins (actor, 1995)

Daylight (actor, 1996)

Cop Land (actor, 1997)

SHARON STONE

Actor

Stardust Memories (1980)

Deadly Blessing (1981)

Bolero (France) (1981)

Irreconcilable Differences (1984)

King Solomon's Mines (1985)

Allan Quartermain and the Lost City of Gold (1987)

Action Jackson (1988)

Above the Law (1988)

Personal Choice (Beyond the Stars) (1989)

Blood and Sand (1989)

Total Recall (1990)

He Said, She Said (1991)

Scissors (1991)

Year of the Gun (1991)

Basic Instinct (1992)

Where Sleeping Dogs Lie (1992)

Diary of a Hitman (1992)

Sliver (1993)

Intersection (1994)

The Specialist (1994)

The Quick and the Dead (1995)

Casino (1995)

Diabolique (1996)

Last Dance (1996)

MERYL STREEP

Actor

Julia (1977)

The Deer Hunter (1978)

Manhattan (1979)

The Seduction of Joe Tynan (1979)

Kramer vs. Kramer (1979; Academy Award for best supporting actress)

The French Lieutenant's Woman (1981)

Sophie's Choice (1982; Academy Award for best actress)

Still of the Night (1982)

Silkwood (1983)

Falling in Love (1984)

Plenty (1985)

Out of Africa (1985)

Heartburn (1986)

Ironweed (1987)

A Cry in The Dark (1988)

She-Devil (1989)

Postcards from the Edge (1990)

Defending Your Life (1991)

Death Becomes Her (1992)

The House of the Spirits (1994)

The River Wild (1994)

The Bridges of Madison County (1995)

Before and After (1996)

Marvin's Room (1996)

EMMA THOMPSON

Actor/screenwriter

Henry V (1989)

The Tall Guy (1989)

Impromptu (1990)

Dead Again (1991)

Howard's End (1992)

Peter's Friends (1992)

Much Ado About Nothing (1993)

The Remains of the Day (1993)

In the Name of the Father (1993)

Junior (1994)

Carrington (1995)

Sense and Sensibility (actor/screenwriter, 1995; Academy Award for best adapted screenplay)

DENZEL WASHINGTON

Actor

Carbon Copy (1981)

A Soldier's Story (1984)

Power (1986)

Cry Freedom (1987)

Glory (1989; Academy Award for best supporting actor)

For Queen and Country (1989)

Reunion (1989)

The Mighty Quinn (1989)

Mo' Better Blues (1990)

Heart Condition (1990)

Ricochet (1991)

Mississippi Masala (1991)

Malcolm X (1992)

Much Ado About Nothing (1993)

The Pelican Brief (1993)

Philadelphia (1993)

Crimson Tide (1995)

Virtuosity (1995)

Devil in a Blue Dress (1995)

Courage Under Fire (1996)

The Preacher's Wife (1996)

THE TOP VIDEOS, YEAR-BY-YEAR

Billboard magazine has been tracking bestselling videos since 1980 and started ranking video rentals in 1982. In 1996, two-tape behemoths *Braveheart*, *Heat*, and *Casino* performed even better at rental counters than they had in theaters—suggesting that many prefer long films with a La-Z-Boy and pause button.

1980

Sales

1. *The Godfather*
2. *Saturday Night Fever*
3. *Superman*
4. *M*A*S*H*
5. *The Godfather, Part II*
6. *Blazing Saddles*
7. *10*
8. *Grease*
9. *The Sound of Music*
10. *Halloween*

1981

Sales

1. *Airplane!*
2. *Caddyshack*
3. *9 to 5*
4. *Superman*
5. *Alien*
6. *Star Trek*
7. *Fame*
8. *Ordinary People*
9. *The Elephant Man*
10. *Popeye*

1982

Sales

1. *Clash of the Titans*
2. *An American Werewolf in London*
3. *Atlantic City*
4. *Stir Crazy*
5. *The Jazz Singer*
6. The *Blue Lagoon*
7. *Kramer vs. Kramer*
8. *Casablanca*
9. *Raging Bull*
10. *Jane Fonda's Workout*

Rentals

1. *Clash of the Titans*
2. *An American Werewolf in London*
3. *Arthur*
4. *Star Wars*
5. *Fort Apache, the Bronx*
6. *For Your Eyes Only*
7. *On Golden Pond*
8. *Stripes*
9. *The Cannonball Run*
10. *Superman II*

1983

Sales

1. *Jane Fonda's Workout*
2. *Star Trek II: The Wrath of Khan*
3. *An Officer and a Gentleman*
4. *The Compleat Beatles*
5. *Rocky III*
6. *Playboy Vol. I*
7. *Poltergeist*
8. *Star Wars*
9. *Blade Runner*
10. *The Road Warrior*

Rentals

1. *An Officer and a Gentleman*
2. *Star Trek II: The Wrath of Khan*
3. *The Road Warrior*
4. *Rocky III*
5. *Poltergeist*
6. *First Blood*
7. *Das Boot*
8. *Night Shift*
9. *Blade Runner*
10. *Sophie's Choice*

1984

Sales

1. *Jane Fonda's Workout*
2. *Raiders of the Lost Ark*
3. *Making Michael Jackson's "Thriller"*
4. *Flashdance*
5. *Duran Duran*
6. *Risky Business*
7. *48 Hrs.*
8. *Do It Debbie's Way*
9. *Trading Places*
10. *The Jane Fonda Workout Challenge*

Rentals

1. *Raiders of the Lost Ark*
2. *Risky Business*
3. *Flashdance*
4. *48 Hrs.*
5. *Tootsie*
6. *Mr. Mom*
7. *Sudden Impact*
8. *Trading Places*
9. *Blue Thunder*
10. *Making Michael Jackson's "Thriller"*

1985

Sales

1. *Jane Fonda's Workout*
2. *Prime Time*
3. *Making Michael Jackson's "Thriller"*
4. *Purple Rain*
5. *Gone with the Wind*
6. *The Jane Fonda Workout Challenge*
7. *Raiders of the Lost Ark*
8. *Raquel, Total Beauty and Fitness*
9. *We Are the World—The Video Event*
10. *Wham! The Video*

Rentals

1. *The Karate Kid*
2. *The Terminator*
3. *Police Academy*
4. *Romancing the Stone*
5. *Revenge of the Nerds*
6. *The Natural*
7. *Starman*
8. *The Empire Strikes Back*
9. *Bachelor Party*
10. *Splash*

1986

Sales

1. *Jane Fonda's New Workout*
2. *Jane Fonda's Workout*
3. *Pinocchio*
4. *Beverly Hills Cop*
5. *The Sound of Music*
6. *Jane Fonda's Prime Time Workout*
7. *Casablanca*
8. *Gone with the Wind*
9. *The Wizard of Oz*
10. *The Best of John Belushi*

Rentals

1. *Back to the Future*
2. *Beverly Hills Cop*
3. *Prizzi's Honor*
4. *Witness*
5. *Ghostbusters*
6. *Rambo: First Blood Part II*
7. *Return of the Jedi*
8. *Cocoon*
9. *Mask*
10. *Gremlins*

1987

Sales

1. *Jane Fonda's Low Impact Aerobic Workout*
2. *Jane Fonda's New Workout*
3. *Sleeping Beauty*
4. *Top Gun*
5. *Callanetics*
6. *The Sound of Music*
7. *Kathy Smith's Body Basics*
8. *Indiana Jones and the Temple of Doom*
9. *Star Trek III: The Search for Spock*
10. *Star Trek II: The Wrath of Khan*

Rentals

1. *Short Circuit*
2. *Top Gun*
3. *Back to School*
4. *Indiana Jones and the Temple of Doom*
5. *Down and Out in Beverly Hills*
6. *The Color of Money*
7. *Ferris Bueller's Day Off*
8. *Stand By Me*
9. *Ruthless People*
10. *Aliens*

1988

Sales

1. *Lady and the Tramp*
2. *Callanetics*
3. *Jane Fonda's Low Impact Aerobic Workout*
4. *Star Trek IV: The Voyage Home*
5. *Start Up with Jane Fonda*
6. *An American Tail*
7. *Jane Fonda's New Workout*
8. *Pink Floyd: The Wall*
9. *Dirty Dancing*
10. *Sleeping Beauty*

Rentals

1. *Dirty Dancing*
2. *Lethal Weapon*
3. *Fatal Attraction*
4. *The Untouchables*
5. *The Witches of Eastwick*
6. *No Way Out*
7. *Outrageous Fortune*

8. *Robocop*
9. *Stakeout*
10. *Tin Men*

1989

Sales

1. *Cinderella*
2. *E.T., the Extra-Terrestrial*
3. *Jane Fonda's Complete Workout*
4. *Moonwalker*
5. *Callanetics*
6. *Dirty Dancing*
7. *The Wizard of Oz: The Fiftieth Anniversary Edition*
8. *Lethal Weapon*
9. *U2 Rattle and Hum*
10. *Pink Floyd: The Delicate Sound of Thunder*

Rentals

1. *Big*
2. *Die Hard*
3. *A Fish Called Wanda*
4. *Three Men and a Baby*
5. *Beetlejuice*
6. *Coming to America*
7. *Cocktail*
8. *Twins*
9. *Bull Durham*
10. *"Crocodile" Dundee II*

1990

Sales

1. *Bambi*
2. *New Kids on the Block: Hangin' Tough Live*
3. *The Little Mermaid*
4. *Lethal Weapon 2*
5. *The Wizard of Oz: The Fiftieth Anniversary Edition*
6. *Batman*
7. *Honey, I Shrunk the Kids*
8. *The Land Before Time*
9. *Who Framed Roger Rabbit*
10. *Teenage Mutant Ninja Turtles: Cowabunga, Shredhead*

Rentals

1. *Look Who's Talking*
2. *When Harry Met Sally*
3. *Parenthood*
4. *K-9*
5. *Dead Poets Society*
6. *Steel Magnolias*
7. *Sea of Love*
8. *Turner & Hooch*
9. *Black Rain*
10. *Internal Affairs*

1991

Sales

1. *Pretty Woman*
2. *The Little Mermaid*
3. *Peter Pan*
4. *The Jungle Book*
5. *The Three Tenors in Concert*
6. *Richard Simmons: Sweatin' to the Oldies*
7. *Teenage Mutant Ninja Turtles: The Movie*
8. *The Terminator*
9. *Ducktales: The Movie*
10. *Total Recall*

Rentals

1. *Ghost*
2. *Pretty Woman*
3. *GoodFellas*
4. *Bird on a Wire*
5. *Flatliners*
6. *The Hunt for Red October*
7. *Kindergarten Cop*
8. *Total Recall*
9. *Sleeping with the Enemy*
10. *Another 48 Hrs.*

1992

Sales

1. *Fantasia*
2. *101 Dalmations*
3. *The Jungle Book*
4. *Robin Hood: Prince of Thieves*
5. *Cherfitness: A New Attitude*
6. *Fievel Goes West*
7. *1992 Playboy Video Playmate Calendar*
8. *Home Alone*
9. *The Rescuers Down Under*
10. *Playboy: Sexy Lingerie IV*

Rentals

1. *Thelma and Louise*
2. *The Silence of the Lambs*
3. *The Fisher King*
4. *City Slickers*
5. *Backdraft*
6. *Cape Fear*
7. *The Hand That Rocks the Cradle*
8. *Father of the Bride*
9. *Deceived*
10. *What About Bob?*

1993

Sales

1. *Beauty and the Beast*
2. *Pinocchio*
3. *101 Dalmatians*
4. *Playboy Celebrity Centerfold: Jessica Hahn*
5. *Sister Act*
6. *Playboy Playmate of the Year 1993: Anna Nicole Smith*
7. *Cindy Crawford/Shape Your Body Workout*
8. *Home Alone 2: Lost in New York*
9. *Disney's Sing Along Songs: Friend Like Me*
10. *Beethoven*

Rentals

1. *Sister Act*
2. *Patriot Games*
3. *Under Siege*
4. *A League of Their Own*
5. *A Few Good Men*
6. *Scent of a Woman*
7. *Unforgiven*
8. *Sneakers*
9. *Passenger 57*
10. *The Bodyguard*

1994

Sales

1. *Aladdin*
2. *Playboy Celebrity Centerfold: Dian Parkinson*
3. *Yanni: Live at the Acropolis*
4. *Free Willy*
5. *Mrs. Doubtfire*
6. *The Fugitive*
7. *The Return of Jafar*
8. *The Fox and the Hound*
9. *Ace Ventura: Pet Detective*
10. *Beauty and the Beast*

Rentals

1. *Sleepless in Seattle*
2. *Philadelphia*
3. *In the Line of Fire*
4. *The Pelican Brief*
5. *The Fugitive*
6. *The Firm*
7. *Carlito's Way*
8. *Sliver*
9. *Ace Ventura: Pet Detective*
10. *Mrs. Doubtfire*

1995

Sales

1. *The Lion King*
2. *Forrest Gump*
3. *Speed*
4. *Jurassic Park*
5. *The Mask*
6. *Playboy: The Best of Pamela Anderson*
7. *Snow White and the Seven Dwarfs*
8. *The Crow*
9. *Pink Floyd: Pulse*
10. *Yanni: Live at the Acropolis*

Rentals

1. *The Shawshank Redemption*
2. *True Lies*
3. *Disclosure*
4. *Speed*
5. *The Client*
6. *Clear and Present Danger*
7. *When a Man Loves a Woman*
8. *Dumb and Dumber*
9. *Just Cause*
10. *Outbreak*

1996

Sales

1. *Babe*
2. *Apollo 13*
3. *Pulp Fiction*
4. *Playboy: The Best of Jenny McCarthy*
5. *The Aristocats*
6. *Batman Forever*
7. *Jumanji*
8. *Pocahontas*
9. *Cinderella*
10. *Heavy Metal*

Rentals

1. *Braveheart*
2. *The Usual Suspects*
3. *Seven*
4. *Heat*
5. *12 Monkeys*
6. *Get Shorty*
7. *Crimson Tide*
8. *Casino*
9. *Executive Decision*
10. *The Net*

EXTRA! EXTRA! HOW TO GET IN THE BIG PICTURE

Can you pretend to see a spaceship *and* drop your jaw? Or is normalcy in the presence of stars more your forté? Either way, don't sit around waiting to be discovered. Here's how to get your face on the silver screen (or at least in a car commercial). (For more detailed information, check *Back to One*, by Cullen Chambers.)

CASTING AGENCIES

The easiest way to land a bit part in the movies, on TV, or on the radio is to register with a casting agency. There are hundreds of these in the L.A. area. Most charge a modest registration fee of $20 or under, or no fee at all. The following are some of the best known and reputed. The proper registration procedure is noted at the end of each entry.

Academy Kids Management
(casts children and young adults only)
Vineland Studios
4942 Vineland Ave. #103
N. Hollywood, Calif. 91601
(818) 769-8091
Walk-ins on selected Sundays

Anna Miller Casting
P.O. Box 66
Sunland, Calif. 91041
(213) 957-4696
Walk-in dates, times, and locations updated on the fourth of each month

Bill Dance Casting
(must be 18 or older)
3518 W. Cahuenga Blvd. #210
Los Angeles, Calif. 90068
(213) 878-1131
Walk-ins Monday through Thursday from noon to 1 p.m.

Cast of Thousands
P.O. Box 1899
Burbank, Calif. 91507
(818) 985-9995
By appointment only

Central/Cenex Casting
The largest casting agency in the entertainment industry. Central Casting handles union actors; Cenex handles non-union actors.
1700 W. Burbank Blvd.
Burbank, Calif. 91506
Central: (818) 562-2700
Cenex: (818) 562-2800
Central: walk-ins Tuesday (last name A through L) and Thursday (last name M through Z) from 2 to 3:30 p.m.
Cenex: walk-ins Monday, Wednesday, and Friday from 10 to 11:30 a.m.

Lane Model and Talent Agency
14071 Windsor Place
Santa Ana, Calif. 92705
(714) 731-1420 or
(714) 731-4560
Send photo and resumé with self-addressed stamped envelope.

HOW THE MIGHTY HAVE RISEN

They're big stars now—but they weren't born that way. These Hollywood idols began their movie careers as lowly extras.

Lucille Ball
Gary Cooper
Bill Cosby
Kevin Costner
Robert De Niro
Robert Duvall
Clark Gable
Teri Garr
Janet Gaynor
Whoopi Goldberg
Mark Harmon
Dustin Hoffman
Bob Hope
Casey Kasem
Michael Landon
Sophia Loren
Marilyn Monroe
Mary Tyler Moore
Ronald Reagan
Burt Reynolds
Tom Selleck
Suzanne Somers
Sylvester Stallone
Donald Sutherland
John Wayne

Messenger Associates Casting
P.O. Box 2380
Toluca Lake, Calif. 91610
(818) 508-5486
Call to find out registration times between 10:00 and 10:30 a.m. on weekdays.

Rainbow Casting
12501 Chandler Blvd. #204
N. Hollywood, Calif. 91607
(818) 752-2278
Walk-ins Monday through Thursday from 11 a.m. to 2 p.m.

Screen Children Agency
(casts children and young adults only)
4000 Riverside Drive
Suite A
Burbank, Calif. 91505
(818) 846-4300
Send photo and resumé

PAYMENT

Extra work may be a rich experience, but it's not a very lucrative one. A typical salary for eight hours is $40; children can claim somewhat higher wages. The money's a little better if you're in Actors Equity, Screen Actors Guild, or the American Federation of Television and Radio Artists—yet you needn't join a union to get in on the action, and you'll still get salary "bumps" for almost anything you do beyond standing around in a crowd scene. Time-and-a-half is paid for shifts between eight and 10 hours; double time is paid for anything over 10 hours.

TRADE SOURCES

These magazines list casting calls and give up-to-the-minute facts on current films and theater productions.

Backstage
1515 Broadway 14th floor
New York, N.Y. 10036-8986
(212) 764-7300
published: weekly
cost per issue: $2.25

Backstage West
5055 Wilshire Blvd.
Los Angeles, Calif. 90036
(213) 525-2356
published: weekly
cost per issue: $2.00

Dramalogue
1456 N. Gordon St.
Los Angeles, Calif. 90028
(213) 464-5079
published: weekly
cost per issue: $1.85

Hollywood Reporter
5055 Wilshire Blvd.
Los Angeles, Calif. 90036
(213) 525-2000
published: weekdays
cost per issue: $1.75 every day except Tuesday
cost per Tuesday issue: $2.50

Daily Variety
5700 Wilshire Blvd.
Suite 120
Los Angeles, Calif. 90036
(213) 857-6600
published: weekdays
cost per issue: $1.75

TALKING THE TALK

On the set, what separates the men from the boys (or the women from the girls) is whether they know how to separate the "gaffer" from the "flipper."

craft services
on-set catering

flipper
cosmetic false teeth for children

gaffer
lighting and electrical equipment crew member

golden time
overtime after the 16th hour for theatrical talent

honey wagon
truck or towed vehicle containing dressing rooms, production offices, and/or mobile restrooms

hot set
a set that is ready for use and is not to be disturbed

P&G
performers with a clean-cut, all-American look like that favored by Proctor & Gamble for its ads

sight-and-sound
parents' right under union contract to be within sight and sound of their child performer at all times

wild track
soundtrack with no apparent relationship to the picture it accompanies

FAVORITE FICTIONAL CHARACTERS FROM FILM

The silver screen is, literally, a land of giants; yet in the dark, a moviegoer can share in all the gigantic experiences and emotions. Here's a close-up on some celluloid individuals who are truly larger than life. (Source: *The Encyclopedia of Fictional Characters*, Berkley Publishing Corp. and Seth Godin Productions)

Max Bialystock
The Producers
A down-and-out (but still pompous) theater producer who desperately wants to regain his former glory. He schemes with his accountant, Leo Bloom, to win the backing of every spinster in New York for a play that is guaranteed to fail, therefore keeping most of the money for himself. He produces "Springtime for Hitler," written by a Nazi fanatic, directed by an inept transvestite, and starring a mindless, drug-bombed hippie.

Rick Blaine
Casablanca
Cynical, hard-boiled owner of successful bistro Rick's Café Américain in World War II–era Casablanca, Morocco. Rick formerly worked as a gunrunner in Ethiopia and mercenary with Spanish Loyalists, though he keeps his past deeply buried. Also deeply buried under his thick hide is a sensitive heart, capable of being wounded. He has a love-hate relationship with many people in this spy-and-intrigue-infested town, including corrupt Inspector Louis Renault, officer of the Vichy government police. Has no respect for Nazi occupiers and openly disdains their rules and pretensions to a "thousand-year reich." Refuses to drink with customers, though when alone he drowns his sorrows in bourbon. Once involved with Ilsa Lund during brief whirlwind affair in Paris. Claims he sticks his neck out for no one, though actions often prove otherwise, particularly with regard to Ilsa's husband, Victor Laszlo. Wears white tuxedo jacket at work, rumpled trench coat and fedora when traveling through fog, an unexpected but apparently common phenomenon in this desert locale. A cigarette is usually between his fingers or hanging off his lower lip. Has strong aversion to the song "As Time Goes By." "I'm no good at being noble, but it doesn't take much to see that the problems of three little people don't amount to a hill of beans in this crazy world."

Benjamin Braddock
The Graduate
He is a postgraduate everyman; now that he has graduated from college, he has no idea of what to do next. For now, he's living at home in California, under the comfortable roof of his suburban upper-class socialite parents, who want him to find a job and follow in their conservative footsteps. Awkward, gangly, and shy, Braddock is given a taste of the less conventional aspects of upper-class suburban life by the family's old friend Mrs. Robinson. He subsequently gets at least a sense of what he might want out of life when he encounters the Robinsons's daughter, Elaine. His feelings for her catalyze hitherto-untapped reserves of strong will and guts which belie his placid, phlegmatic facade. Is doubtful about his future in plastics.

Bubba
Forrest Gump
Mildly retarded resident of small town along a Louisiana bayou. He's a close friend of Forrest Gump during military basic training and combat in Vietnam. While he has a pleasant personality, Bubba's mouth and protruding lower lip are constantly hanging open. He dreams of opening up his own shrimping business and knows endless ways to cook shrimp and talk about them.

Chance "the Gardener"
Being There
The ultimate naïf. Totally, absurdly absorbed in his profession of gardening, to the point that he knows literally nothing else. But amazingly, people take his simplistic comments as being full of ironic wisdom about the world. Catapulted to national fame, he appears on talk shows and advises the president on issues of the day. "I like to watch."

Cruella De Vil
101 Dalmatians
A tall, gaunt, flamboyant femme with a mean greedy streak, whose get-rich scheme involves turning Dalmatian puppies into fur coats. A scratchy-voiced diva with shaggy black and white hair, she wears a red dress, matching gloves and a rug-like fur coat. She can berate her two dim-witted henchmen one minute and purringly coax dogs from their owners the next.

Frank N. Furter
The Rocky Horror Picture Show
He's "just a sweet transvestite, from Transsexual, Transylvania." Well, actually, he's more like an alien from another planet. Furter

is a mad scientist, an inventor who is demented, perverted, and oversexed. He's got great powers of persuasion and virtually no morals at all. He takes great pleasure in seducing innocent victims like Brad Majors and Janet Weiss, when they wander within reach. Frank lives in a dark, old castle with a staff of eccentric and oversexed servants. He wears six-inch platform shoes, a garter belt, bright red lipstick, black gloves and a cape, and has beautifully manicured fingernails. He's built himself a man, a technological hunk with blond hair and a tan, called Rocky Horror, who is "good for relieving my tension." Frank is intelligent and sharp-tongued. His entire body is an erogenous zone. Frank is also given to killing people who annoy him. The facts that he's power-mad and has discovered the secret to life itself make him very dangerous. "There's no crime in giving yourself over to pleasure."

Pippi Longstocking
Pippi Longstocking
The freest spirit and self-proclaimed "strongest girl in the world." A freckled nine-year-old with carrot-colored hair worn in tight braids, Pippi gets her last name from wearing one black and one brown stocking with black shoes that are twice as long as her feet. Her mother died when she was very young, and so Pippi has had to learn to fend for herself. Living alone in her little ramshackle house called Villa Villekulla, Pippi's only companions are a horse who lives on her porch and a monkey named Mr. Nilsson. "Don't you worry about me. I'll always come out on top."

Michael Myers
Halloween
Tight-lipped, determined, and homicidally psychotic, Myers was born in 1957 in Haddonfield, Illinois, where he was raised until October 31, 1963. At that time, he took a large kitchen knife and stabbed sister Judith to death. He was a resident of a mental health facility from that day on until October 30, 1978, when he received an unintentional early release. Extremely intelligent and physically fit, he avoids contact with others whenever possible. When last seen, he was walking around with six bullets inside him, courtesy of his primary caregiver, psychiatrist Dr. Loomis.

Mildred Pierce
Mildred Pierce
A rags-to-riches-to-rags restaurateur, doting mother, and baker extraordinaire from Southern California. When her first marriage to Bert Pierce turns sour, she slaves as a waitress and sells pies on the side to keep her two daughters in good schools and fine clothes. Obsessed with her haughty elder daughter, Veda, Mildred tries to buy her love with money and music lessons. She starts keeping company with breakfast customer and socially prominent playboy Monty Beragon. When her younger daughter, Kay, dies suddenly, she's secretly thankful it wasn't Veda. Mildred has a pair of fabulous "immoral" legs and is apparently great in the sack. Through tenacious hard work, she opens a successful chicken place in Glendale, derogatorily nicknamed the Pie Wagon by Monty and Veda. With her new money, Mildred tries to control others and marries Monty in order to appear "good enough" in Veda's eyes. She's shattered to discover Veda in Monty's bed, tries to strangle her daughter, and then tries to put the pieces of her life together again—without Monty and Veda. "To hell with her!"

Sonny
Dog Day Afternoon
He's a foulmouthed Italian American Vietnam veteran in an unhappy marriage and desperate for money. In addition to his heterosexual marriage, he has been unofficially married to his neurotic homosexual partner, Leon, a preoperative transsexual. Sonny's attempting to turn his life around by robbing a Brooklyn bank with Sal. Is constantly running into Murphy's law in everything he undertakes. An unlikely media darling, whose mind is always racing, plotting, planning. "Attica! Attica!"

Jeff Spicoli
Fast Times at Ridgemont High
Way cool surfin' dude and perennial student at Ridgemont High School, where he's known to have pizzas delivered to the classroom. His dreams are often about getting national media recognition by riding the perfect wave on his surfboard. Wears his hair shoulder length and clothes distinctively casual. Jeff's brain is usually tuned into an alternative outlet from those surrounding him, which doesn't seem to bother him in the least. All in all, a totally awesome guy. "Whoa!"

Ted Striker
Airplane!
Former pilot, scarred by post-traumatic stress resulting from wartime action. He remains a determined individual and a romantic. When the going gets tough, he takes control of a commercial jetliner. Manages to rise above mechanical failures, the presence of lunatics and incompetents all around him, a steady stream of bad puns, and a truly horrendous perspiration problem.

OSCAR—DECADE-BY-DECADE

For sixty-nine years Oscar has been handed out—now he's at an age for savoring life's achievements. "He rattles," says Olivia de Havilland, holding her 1949 Oscar to the phone receiver and shaking him to illustrate. Ernest Borgnine, a 1955 winner, complains that his Oscar "flakes." Jack Lemmon, who took his *Mr. Roberts* Oscar home in 1956, says the statue rusted: "I had to send him back to the Academy to be redipped." But, ah, how nice to have the old guy around.

Sure, like any sexagenarian, Oscar has taken his lumps. He's been called "a cruel joke" (Marion Davies), "a heartbreaker" (Orson Welles), and "something to be feared" (George C. Scott). But don't count him out. Oscar's imprimatur can add $25 million or more to a winning film's gross, double an actor's salary, and at least triple the size of his ego.

What a shock, then, to learn that Oscar started life as a patsy. In 1927, MGM kingpin Louis B. Mayer and 35 cronies decided to form an Academy of Motion Picture Arts and Sciences. Forget the high-toned blather of the first charter seeking "the improvement and advancement of the...profession." What Mayer really wanted was to stop the advance of film unions. An Academy would keep labor disputes in the hands of the studios. As a carrot to actors, writers, directors, and technicians, Mayer formed a committee to find "some little way" of rewarding merit in film.

While Mayer finagled, MGM art director Cedric Gibbons doodled a sketch of a naked man with a sword, standing on a reel of film. Today Oscar is a thirteen-and-a-half inch, eight-and-a-half pound trophy cast in a metal alloy, then plated in turn with copper, nickel, silver, and finally gold. At Oscar's debut in 1929, some laughed. Screenwriter Frances (*The Champ*) Marion believed Hollywood had found its ideal symbol, "an athletic body . . . with half his head, that part which held his brains, completely sliced off."

But, hey, Oscar didn't need brains. The studio bosses controlled the nominations and virtually handpicked the winners. It took years for Oscar to clean house—the Academy did not even start using sealed envelopes until 1941. Since then the Academy, which has grown from a scant 36 members in 1927 to the 4,523 voting members of today, has tried to discourage machinations, especially ad campaigns, to influence voting. It hasn't succeeded, of course. But Oscar, by dint of sheer perseverance, has become, in the words of 1957 winner Alec (*The Bridge on the River Kwai*) Guinness, "the most highly prized [award] of all." At this point, the grandstanding and costuming have become as much a reason for tuning in the Oscars as finding out the winners. "Well, hell—let's face it," says Katharine Hepburn, recipient of a record four Oscars for acting, "It's our track meet. It's painful but it's thrilling."

THE FIRST DECADE

1927-1936

Oscar threw his first party in 1929. The press stayed away. A black-tie crowd clapped politely as all 12 awards were distributed in under five minutes. The three Best Actor nominees didn't bother to show up. Janet Gaynor, first Best Actress winner, gamely tried to act thrilled. "Had I known what it would come to mean in the next few years," she said later, "I'm sure I'd have been overwhelmed." It was the first and last Oscar bust. The Depression and the sound era soon made movies into the ideal escapism, and Oscar's touch came to mean box-office gold. Some aspired to win. Others conspired. As ever in Hollywood, greed, jealousy, and raw ambition added up to a helluva show.

The first Best Actor winner, Emil Jannings, had scooted home to Germany before collecting his Oscar scroll. His later Nazi propaganda films—

done, he said, under duress—made him a favorite with Hitler. Marlene Dietrich disputed the Führer on the talents of her *Blue Angel* costar: "He was a terrible ham."

★

First ceremony: Hollywood's elite jammed the Roosevelt Hotel to hear Al Jolson put down the Oscar as a "paperweight." Jolie's film, *The Jazz Singer*—an early talkie—had been disqualified; only silent films were eligible. The Academy was suspicious of new trends. Some things never change.

★

The WWI air extravaganza *Wings*, starring Buddy Rogers, Clara Bow, and Richard Arlen, was the first Best Picture winner. With tinted color in the battle scenes and noise machines in the theaters to simulate plane crashes, here was a primitive *Top Gun* that showed the Academy's early fondness for spectacle.

★

In 1930, Norma Shearer, winner for *The Divorcée*, posed for a photograph with Oscar two days *before* the ceremony. "She sleeps with the boss," sniped Joan Crawford. Rumor had it that MGM's Irving Thalberg pressured employees to vote for his wife.

★

Oscar's first tie: Fredric March (*Dr. Jekyll and Mr. Hyde*) and Wallace Beery (*The Champ*) shared the 1931 gold. Both had recently adopted children. "Odd," said March, "that Wally and I were given awards for best male performance."

★

Clark Gable and Claudette Colbert both took Oscars for Frank Capra's 1934 comedy, *It Happened One Night*, as did Capra and the film—the only clean sweep in Academy history until *One Flew over the Cuckoo's Nest* duplicated the feat in 1975. No one expected it. Everybody still thinks Gable won for *Gone with the Wind*.

★

The Academy invented a new category, Best Song, prompted by Fred Astaire & Ginger Rogers's dancing and singing of "The Continental" in 1934's *The Gay Divorcee*.

★

Bette Davis collected an award for 1935's *Dangerous*, and gave the statue its name. Reflecting that the trophy "resembled the backside" of her first husband, bandleader Harmon Oscar Nelson Jr., she dubbed her prize Oscar. The moniker stuck.

THE SECOND DECADE

1937–1946

The Oscar ceremony was establishment now, broadcast on radio. In 1939 Gone with the Wind *became the most popular and profitable film ever. But this was also a time of war, as reflected in movies from* Mrs. Miniver *to* The Best Years of Our Lives. *Winston Churchill hailed* Miniver *as "propaganda worth a hundred battleships." As a wartime cost-cutting measure, the Academy ended its elaborate banquets and took the show inside a theater, where food and drink could no longer distract from the ego battles.*

Walt Disney is given a special honorary award for 1938's *Snow White and the Seven Dwarfs*, featuring one large Oscar and seven tiny ones.

★

Gone with the Wind, then the costliest movie in history ($3,957,000) wins eight Oscars, a record not broken until 1958's *Gigi*. Leigh was the triumphant victor, Gable the disgruntled loser. "This was my last chance," he groaned. He was right.

Hattie McDaniel, Miss Scarlett's maid, was the first black actor to win an Oscar. Hattie sobbed on accepting her plaque (supporting players didn't receive full statues until 1943).

★

Playing George M. Cohan in 1942, James Cagney—America's favorite tough guy—became the first actor to win an Oscar for a musical. "Don't forget," said Jimmy in his acceptance speech, "it was a pretty good part."

★

Bogie told Ingrid Bergman in *Casablanca* that their wartime love story "didn't amount to a hill of beans in this crazy world." Except for winning the Best Picture

Oscar of 1943 and the hearts of all romantics.

★

Barry Fitzgerald's role as a twinkly old priest in 1944's *Going My Way* made him a popular winner. But at home a few days later, he forgot that wartime Oscars were made of plaster instead of bronze and decapitated his prize with a golf club.

★

The Lost Weekend, the Best Picture of 1945, offered an unsparing portrait of an alcoholic, by Ray Milland. "I gave it everything I had," said the actor. He must have. Accepting the Oscar, a speechless Milland simply bowed and departed.

THE THIRD DECADE

1947–1956

No sooner had the war ended over there than the Academy embarked on its own war at home. The enemy? Television. The little black box was emptying movie theaters at an alarming rate. The studios retaliated at first with sex, violence and Cinemascope, then gave in. So did Oscar. The Academy Awards were telecast for the first time in 1953. Variety*'s headline heralded a new era: "1ST MAJOR PIX-TV WEDDING BIG CLICK."*

Many years prior, actor Walter Huston said he asked his son, John, "If you ever become a writer or director, please find a good part for your old man." John complied with *The Treasure of the Sierra Madre* and won 1948 Oscars for them both.

★

Joseph Mankiewicz's crackerjack 1950 comedy *All About Eve* still holds the record—14 nominations. Though *Eve* won six Oscars, including Best Picture, co-stars Bette Davis and Anne Baxter both lost to *Born Yesterday*'s Judy Holliday.

★

Vivien Leigh copped her second Best Actress Oscar in 1951 for *A Streetcar Named Desire*. When the award was announced in Hollywood, Leigh was in New York starring in *Antony and Cleopatra* with then-husband Laurence Olivier.

★

In Hollywood, Donald O'Connor watched Shirley Booth's reaction in New York on being named 1952's Best Actress for *Come Back, Little Sheba*. Meanwhile, the largest single audience (about 80 million) in TV's five-year history saw the first Oscarcast.

★

Having fought to play Maggio in 1953's *From Here to Eternity*, Frank Sinatra triumphed. Said the Best Supporting Actor, "I ducked the party and took a walk. Just me and Oscar." The salty version of James Jones's Army-barracks novel won a whopping eight Oscars, including Best Picture. And Deborah Kerr's sexy roll on the sand with Burt Lancaster cracked her saintly image.

★

A year before her royal wedding in 1956, *The Country Girl*'s Grace Kelly scored an upset victory over Judy Garland in *A Star is Born*. Kelly confided: "I wanted to win so badly, I was afraid that I would stand up no matter which name was read out."

★

First-time film producer Michael Todd nabbed the 1956 Best Picture Oscar with his star-studded *Around the World in 80 Days*. "Imagine this—and being married to Liz, too," he enthused.

THE FOURTH DECADE

1957–1966

The times they were a-changing. Drugs, hippies, the youth movement, civil rights demonstrations, the Kennedy assassination: Many films dealt with these social and political upheavals. But you couldn't tell by Oscar. Relevant was out; big was in. The Academy awarded either historical epics (Ben-Hur, The Bridge on the River Kwai, Lawrence of Arabia, A Man for All Seasons) *or blockbuster musicals* (Gigi, West Side Story, My Fair Lady, The Sound of Music). *The most controversial move on the Academy's part was to issue a formal slap to those who tried to "buy" Oscar nominations by purchasing self-congratulatory ads in the trade papers. Few paid heed.*

Joanne Woodward, the new Mrs. Paul Newman, collected her 1957 Oscar for *The Three*

Faces of Eve in a $100 dress she made herself. Joan Crawford claimed Hollywood glamour "had been set back twenty years." When Paul finally won his Oscar, twenty-nine years later, clothes weren't a problem. He didn't show up at all.

★

In 1959, Best Picture *Ben-Hur* took a record eleven Oscars, including Best Actor for Charlton Heston, who got the part after Burt Lancaster dropped out. "It was hard work," said Chuck, who drove a mean chariot. But some questioned his talents. "That Heston," said actor Aldo Ray, "what a hamola."

★

Denounced in Congress in 1950 for her adulterous affair with Roberto Rossellini, Ingrid Bergman ended her decade-long Hollywood exile by presenting a 1959 Best Picture Oscar to *Gigi* producer Arthur Freed. She said her recipe for happiness was "good health and a poor memory."

★

Sporting a tracheotomy scar from a near-fatal bout of pneumonia, Liz Taylor scored a sympathy Oscar for 1960's *Butterfield 8*. In 1966 Liz won Oscar No. 2 for *Who's Afraid of Virginia Woolf?*, but railed at the Academy when fifth husband Richard Burton failed to win too.

★

"I'd like to think it will help," said Sidney Poitier after Anne Bancroft opened the envelope and, for 1963's *Lilies of the Field*, he became the first black Best Actor winner. "But I don't believe my Oscar will be a magic wand that will wipe away the restrictions on job opportunities for Negro actors."

★

Sisters and Best Actress nominees Lynn and Vanessa Redgrave, cited respectively for 1966's *Georgy Girl* and *Morgan!*, were only the second sister nominees in Oscar history. And they came from a notable British acting family to boot. Maybe so. But Liz Taylor still whupped them both.

THE FIFTH DECADE

1967–1976

Oscar neared its half-century mark in a reactionary mood. Breakthrough films such as Bonnie and Clyde, The Graduate, *and* Easy Rider *ended up losers. In 1968, the year of* 2001: A Space Odyssey, Oliver! *won the Best Picture prize. Yikes. No wonder a streaker felt the need to defame one of the decade's Academy telecasts. Then, a rebel cry was heard in filmland. Newcomers Dustin Hoffman and Jon Voight dared to duke it out with the Duke, John Wayne, for the statue. They failed, but their X-rated* Midnight Cowboy *took the Best Picture prize in 1969. Jane Fonda raised hackles with her Vietnam views and won anyway. The warring factions of the Academy were creating sparks.*

For the second time in Oscar history, a tie was declared. *Funny Girl*'s Barbra Streisand and *The Lion in Winter*'s Katharine Hepburn received the same number of votes from the 1968 Academy's 3,030 members. Designer Edith Head was "shocked," not by the tie but by Streisand's tacky peekaboo pantsuit.

★

John Wayne had to let it all hang out in 1969 as bloated, one-eyed Rooster Cogburn to finally collect his first Oscar at 62 after 250 movies. "Wow," drawled the Duke, "if I had known, I would have put that eye patch on 35 years earlier."

★

Deriding the Oscars as a "meat parade," George C. Scott declined his nomination as 1970's Best Actor. "My God!" exclaimed Goldie Hawn as she opened the envelope and read the winner's name, "It's George C. Scott."

★

When Marlon Brando was voted 1972's Best Actor, he sent Apache Sacheen Littlefeather to reject the Oscar for all the Native Americans Hollywood had demeaned. "Childish," scowled Charlton Heston. "Wonderful," gushed Jane Fonda.

★

Would-be comic Robert Opel snuck backstage at the 1974 Oscars ceremony, flustering emcee David Niven as the cameras cut away to spare home viewers the streaker's shortcomings. The hit of a dull show, Opel was found murdered five years later in his San Francisco sex shop.

★

Struggling actor Sylvester Stallone took half a week to write a script for himself about an underdog fighter. He lost the Best Actor Oscar, but the sleeper film won the title as Best Picture of 1976. "*Rocky* will be remembered," said Sly with typical modesty.

THE SIXTH DECADE

1977–1986

Oscar had a goal now. Ignoring the films of George Lucas and Steven Spielberg became a full-time job. The Hardy Boys of the zap-happy set combined their youthful fantasies with dazzling special effects to create eight of the top 10 box office hits of all time (E.T., Star Wars, Return of the Jedi, The Empire Strikes Back, Jaws, Raiders of the Lost Ark, Indiana Jones, *and* Back to the Future). *Not a Best Picture winner in the bunch. The Academy, doing penance for scorning Vietnam in the previous decade, anointed politically themed films from* The Deer Hunter *to* Platoon. *A vote for* Gandhi, *the movie, was a vote for Gandhi, the man. Oscar, typically late, began sporting a social conscience.*

Accepting her Best Supporting Actress Oscar for 1976's *Julia*, Vanessa Redgrave dismissed as "Zionist hoodlums" those who showed up to protest her politics. The audience booed, Vanessa had to dine later with her two bodyguards, and a confused Jack Nicholson cracked, "What are these Zionists? I've been skiing."

★

"It's simply terrific. This is something," sputtered Diane Keaton after accepting the 1977 Best Actress prize for *Annie Hall* from first winner Janet Gaynor. Her co-star and former boyfriend Woody Allen stayed home and shrugged off the Academy as meaningless: "I just don't think they know what they're doing."

★

Robert Redford and Warren Beatty have never won Oscars for their acting. That might make sense. Instead, each (Redford for 1980's *Ordinary People* and Beatty for 1981's *Reds*) took the prize as Best Director—a pinnacle Hitchcock, Bergman, Fellini, and Welles never reached. Go figure.

★

Jane Fonda rushed from the 1982 Academy Awards show to present her ailing father and *On Golden Pond* costar, Henry, with the long-overdue first Oscar of his 47-year career. "Hell, if I hadn't won, I wouldn't be able to walk with my head up anymore," Fonda said to his wife, Shirlee. He died five months later.

★

Gidget gets respect: For 1984's *Places in the Heart*, Sally Field won a second Oscar and spoke the words that will haunt her forever: "You like me! You like me!"

★

Perennial also-ran Paul Newman won for reprising his 1961 *Hustler* role in 1986's *The Color of Money*. "After losing six times, I felt it cruel and unusual punishment to attend," said the no-show.

★

Writer-director Oliver Stone took the 1986 Best Picture Oscar for *Platoon*, based on his wartime experiences in Vietnam—a film almost no studio wanted to make.

★

In 1987 Marlee Matlin of *Children of a Lesser God* became the first hearing-impaired Best Actress winner. "After I'm alone I'm going to scream," she said.

THE SEVENTH DECADE

1987–1996

Oscar continues his old traditions by heaping awards on elder statesmen—from Clint Eastwood, Paul Newman, and Sean Connery to Jack Palance, Jessica Tandy, and Martin Landau—who should have been recognized long before. Best Director continues to be a fickle category—how could *Oscar recognize* Apollo 13 *for seemingly everything except Ron Howard's direction? But the drought finally ends for traditional punching bag Steven Spielberg. Of course it took the culturally significant* Schindler's List *to get the Oscar monkey off of Spielberg's back (after three previ-*

ous Best Director nominations), rather than his second-highest grossing movie of all time, Jurassic Park*—making it clear that he was chosen as best director, not most successful. In 1995,* Forrest Gump *bucks the conventional wisdom that box-office favorites don't play well in Academy-land, becoming the highest-grossing picture ever to claim the Best Picture Award.*

In 1988, a barely dressed, slightly tattooed Cher wins Best Actress and announces, "I don't think that this means I am somebody, but I guess I'm on my way."

★

The telecast hits new lows in production values in 1989, with the dreadful Snow White musical opening giving Oscar a black eye.

★

Whoopi Goldberg becomes only the second African-American woman to claim an acting award, as Best Supporting Actress for her role in 1990's *Ghost*.

★

Jack Palance shows he's no old-timer by performing one-handed push-ups by way of accepting his Best Supporting Actor statuette for *City Slickers*. And he provides Oscar host Billy Crystal with a year's worth of material.

★

Lizzy Gardiner, the winner for best costume design on *Priscilla, Queen of the Desert,* makes a memorable imprint on the 1995 ceremonies in her dress fashioned from American Express gold cards.

★

Jessica Lange is 1995's Best Actress for a 1991 performance: Trapped for years by Orion Pictures' financial woes, her *Blue Sky* languished on a bank vault's floor.

★

In 1996, actors get tougher to categorize. Mel Gibson wins trophies for producing and directing—but not acting in—*Braveheart.* Similarly, first-time scripter Emma Thompson takes Best Adapted Screenplay honors for her *Sense and Sensibility*.

★

As Decade Seven closes, the academy's love for independent film burns brighter than ever. *The English Patient*'s sweep makes it an all-time champ; trophies not taken by the big-studio reject go to the off-Hollywood likes of *Fargo, Sling Blade*, and *Shine*. Were it not for Cuba Gooding Jr.'s *Jerry Maguire* win, no major Oscar would have stayed in Tinseltown.

IN THE NAME OF PRODUCTION

More and more celebrity actors are starting their own production companies. But how did they get such funny names? Here's a list of some luminary-owned companies and the inspiration behind their appellations.

Actor	Production Company	Where the Name Came From
Kevin Costner	TIG Productions	The nickname of his grandmother
Clint Eastwood	Malpaso Productions	A creek in Carmel, Calif., and a Spanish expression meaning "dangerous step," which critics mistakenly assumed he made in forming the company
Jodie Foster	Egg Pictures	The egg as a symbol of protection
Tom Hanks	Clavius Base	The otherworldly planet in Stanley Kubrick's *2001: A Space Odyssey*
Dustin Hoffman	Punch Productions	After the Punchinello character in *Punch and Judy* shows
Meg Ryan	Prufrock Pictures	Alluding to one of her favorite poems, T. S. Eliot's "Love Song of J. Alfred Prufrock"

THE ACADEMY AWARDS

	1927–28	1928–29	1929–30
Picture	*Wings*	*Broadway Melody*	*All Quiet on the Western Front*
Actor	Emil Jannings, *The Last Command; The Way of All Flesh*	Warner Baxter, *In Old Arizona*	George Arliss, *Disraeli*
Actress	Janet Gaynor, *Seventh Heaven; Street Angel; Sunrise*	Mary Pickford, *Coquette*	Norma Shearer, *The Divorcée*
Director	Frank Borzage, *Seventh Heaven*; Lewis Milestone, *Two Arabian Knights*	Frank Lloyd, *The Divine Lady; Weary River; Drag*	Lewis Milestone, *All Quiet on the Western Front*
Adapted Screenplay	Benjamin Glazer, *Seventh Heaven*	—	—
Original Story	Ben Hecht, *Underworld*	Hans Kraly, *The Patriot*	Frances Marion, *The Big House*
Cinematography	*Sunrise*	*White Shadows in the South Seas*	*With Byrd at the South Pole*
Interior Decoration	*The Dove* and *The Tempest*	*The Bridge of San Luis Rey*	*King of Jazz*
Sound	—	—	*The Big House*

OSCAR RECORDS

Most awards in any category: Walt Disney, 27 regular and six special

Most honored films: *Ben-Hur* in 1959, with 11 and *West Side Story* in 1961, with 10

Most nominated films: *All About Eve*, with 14, and *Gone with the Wind, From Here to Eternity, Mary Poppins, Who's Afraid of Virginia Woolf?*, and *Forrest Gump* with 13 each

Most nominated films to receive no awards: *The Turning Point* and *The Color Purple*, with 11 each

Most Best Actor awards: Spencer Tracy, Fredric March, Gary Cooper, Marlon Brando, Dustin Hoffman, and Tom Hanks, with two each

Most Best Director awards: John Ford with four, for *The Informer, The Grapes of Wrath, How Green Was My Valley*, and *The Quiet Man*

Most Best Actress awards: Katharine Hepburn with four, for *Morning Glory, Guess Who's Coming to Dinner, The Lion in Winter*, and *On Golden Pond*

Best Actress awards for debut performances: Shirley Booth for *Come Back, Little Sheba*, Barbra Streisand for *Funny Girl*, and Marlee Matlin for *Children of a Lesser God*

First African American Oscar winner: Hattie McDaniel, Best Supporting Actress, in *Gone with the Wind*

	1930–31	1931–32	1932–33
Picture	*Cimarron*	*Grand Hotel*	*Cavalcade*
Actor	Lionel Barrymore, *A Free Soul*	Wallace Beery, *The Champ*; Fredric March, *Dr. Jekyll and Mr. Hyde*	Charles Laughton, *The Private Life of Henry VIII*
Actress	Marie Dressler, *Min and Bill*	Helen Hayes, *The Sin of Madelon Claudet*	Katharine Hepburn, *Morning Glory*
Supporting Actor	—	—	—
Supporting Actress	—	—	—
Director	Norman Taurog, *Skippy*	Frank Borzage, *Bad Girl*	Frank Lloyd, *Cavalcade*
Adapted Screenplay/ Screenplay	Howard Estabrook, *Cimarron*	Edwin Burke, *Bad Girl*	Victor Heerman and Sarah Y. Mason, *Little Women*
Original Story	John Monk Saunders, *The Dawn Patrol*	Francis Marion, *The Champ*	Robert Lord, *One Way Passage*
Song	—	—	—
Score	—	—	—
Cinematography	*Tabu*	*Shanghai Express*	*A Farewell to Arms*
Interior Decoration	*Cimarron*	*Transatlantic*	*Cavalcade*
Film Editing	—	—	—
Sound	Paramount Studio Sound Department	Paramount Studio Sound Department	*A Farewell to Arms*
Short Films	—	*Flower and Trees* (Cartoons); *The Music Box* (Comedy); *Wrestling Swordfish* (Novelty)	*The Three Little Pigs* (Cartoons); *So This Is Harris* (Comedy); *Krakatoa* (Novelty)

POPULAR AND PRAISED

Few films claim the hearts of both the moviegoing public and the majority of the Academy of Motion Picture Arts and Sciences. In fact, only 10 of the top 100 money-makers of all time have won best-picture Oscars. Those films are listed below, ranked in order of amount grossed. (Source: *Variety*)

1.	*Forrest Gump*	1994
2.	*Gone with the Wind*	1939
3.	*Dances with Wolves*	1990
4.	*Rain Man*	1988
5.	*The Sound of Music*	1965
6.	*The Sting*	1973
7.	*Platoon*	1986
8.	*The Godfather*	1972
9.	*The Silence of the Lambs*	1991
10.	*Rocky*	1976

1934	1935	1936	1937
It Happened One Night	*Mutiny on the Bounty*	*The Great Ziegfeld*	*The Life of Emile Zola*
Clark Gable, *It Happened One Night*	Victor McLaglen, *The Informer*	Paul Muni, *The Story of Louis Pasteur*	Spencer Tracy, *Captains Courageous*
Claudette Colbert, *It Happened One Night*	Bette Davis, *Dangerous*	Luise Rainer, *The Great Ziegfeld*	Luise Rainer, *The Good Earth*
—	—	Walter Brennan, *Come and Get It*	Joseph Schildkraut, *The Life of Emile Zola*
—	—	Gale Sondergaard, *Anthony Adverse*	Alice Brady, *In Old Chicago*
Frank Capra, *It Happened One Night*	John Ford, *The Informer*	Frank Capra, *Mr. Deeds Goes to Town*	Leo McCarey, *The Awful Truth*
Robert Riskin, *It Happened One Night*	Dudley Nichols, *The Informer*	Pierre Collings and Sheridan Gibney, *The Story of Louis Pasteur*	Heinz Herald, Geza Herczeg, and Norman Reilly Raine, *The Life of Emile Zola*
Arthur Caesar, *Manhattan Melodrama*	Ben Hecht and Charles MacArthur, *The Scoundrel*	Pierre Collings and Sheridan Gibney, *The Story of Louis Pasteur*	William A. Wellman and Robert Carson, *A Star is Born*
"The Continental" *(The Gay Divorcée)*	"Lullaby of Broadway" *(Gold Diggers of 1935)*	"The Way You Look Tonight" *(Swing Time)*	"Sweet Leilani" *(Waikiki Wedding)*
One Night of Love	*The Informer*	*Anthony Adverse*	*100 Men and a Girl*
Cleopatra	*A Midsummer Night's Dream*	*Anthony Adverse*	*The Good Earth*
The Merry Widow	*The Dark Angel*	*Dodsworth*	*Lost Horizon*
Eskimo	*A Midsummer Night's Dream*	*Anthony Adverse*	*Lost Horizon*
One Night of Love	*Naughty Marietta*	*San Francisco*	*The Hurricane*
The Tortoise and the Hare (Cartoons); *La Cucaracha* (Comedy); *City of Wax* (Novelty)	*Three Orphan Kittens* (Cartoons); *How To Sleep* (Comedy); *Wings over Mt. Everest* (Novelty)	*Country Cousin* (Cartoons); *Bored of Education* (One-Reel); *The Public Pays* (Two-Reel); *Give Me Liberty* (Color)	*The Old Mill* (Cartoons); *Private Life of the Gannetts* (One-Reel); *Torture Money* (Two-Reel); *Penny Wisdom* (Color)

DISNEY'S WINNING TUNES

Disney has dominated the Oscar Best Song category in recent years, winning seven out of eight times since 1989. In total, the studio has won 10 times in this category; Paramount still leads with 15 wins, while 20th Century Fox's 10 wins ties it with Disney for second place.

Song	Film	Year
"When You Wish Upon a Star"	*Pinocchio*	1940
"Zip-a-Dee-Doo-Dah"	*Song of the South*	1947
"Chim Chim Cher-ee"	*Mary Poppins*	1964
"Under the Sea"	*The Little Mermaid*	1989
"Sooner or Later"	*Dick Tracy*	1990
"Beauty and the Beast"	*Beauty and the Beast*	1991
"A Whole New World"	*Aladdin*	1992
"Can You Feel the Love Tonight"	*The Lion King*	1994
"Colors of the Wind"	*Pocahontas*	1995
"You Must Love Me"	*Evita*	1996

	1938	1939	1940
Picture	*You Can't Take It with You*	*Gone with the Wind*	*Rebecca*
Actor	Spencer Tracy, *Boys Town*	Robert Donat, *Goodbye, Mr. Chips*	James Stewart, *The Philadelphia Story*
Actress	Bette Davis, *Jezebel*	Vivien Leigh, *Gone with the Wind*	Ginger Rogers, *Kitty Foyle*
Supporting Actor	Walter Brennan, *Kentucky*	Thomas Mitchell, *Stagecoach*	Walter Brennan, *The Westerner*
Supporting Actress	Fay Bainter, *Jezebel*	Hattie McDaniel, *Gone with the Wind*	Jane Darwell, *The Grapes of Wrath*
Director	Frank Capra, *You Can't Take It with You*	Victor Fleming, *Gone with the Wind*	John Ford, *The Grapes of Wrath*
Screenplay	Ian Dalrymple, Cecil Lewis, and W. P. Lipscomb, *Pygmalion*	Sidney Howard, *Gone with the Wind*	Donald Ogden Stewart, *The Philadelphia Story*
Original Screenplay/ Original Story	Eleanore Griffin and Dore Schary, *Boys Town*	Lewis R. Foster, *Mr. Smith Goes to Washington*	Preston Sturges, *The Great McGinty;* Benjamin Glazer and John S. Toldy, *Arise, My Love*
Song	"Thanks for the Memory" *(Big Broadcast of 1938)*	"Over the Rainbow" *(The Wizard of Oz)*	"When You Wish upon a Star" *(Pinocchio)*
Score/Original Score	*Alexander's Ragtime Band*; *The Adventures of Robin Hood*	*Stagecoach*; *The Wizard of Oz*	*Tin Pan Alley; Pinocchio*
Cinematography	*The Great Waltz*	*Wuthering Heights* (B&W); *Gone with the Wind* (Color)	*Rebecca* (B&W); *The Thief of Bagdad* (Color)
Interior Decoration	*The Adventures of Robin Hood*	*Gone with the Wind*	*Pride and Prejudice* (B&W); *The Thief of Bagdad* (Color)
Film Editing	*The Adventures of Robin Hood*	*Gone with the Wind*	*North West Mounted Police*
Sound	*The Cowboy and the Lady*	*When Tomorrow Comes*	*Strike Up the Band*
Special Effects	—	*The Rains Came*	*The Thief of Bagdad*
Short Films	*Ferdinand the Bull* (Cartoons); *That Mothers Might Live* (One-Reel); *Declaration of Independence* (Two-Reel)	*The Ugly Duckling* (Cartoons); *Busy Little Bears* (One-Reel); *Sons of Liberty* (Two-Reel)	*Milky Way* (Cartoons); *Quicker 'N a Wink* (One-Reel); *Teddy, the Rough Rider* (Two-Reel)
Documentaries	—	—	—

> “The Oscar is the most valuable, but least expensive, item of world-wide public relations ever invented in any industry.”
>
> —Frank Capra,
> Best Director, 1934
> Best Director, 1936
> Best Director, 1938

1941	1942	1943	1944
How Green Was My Valley	*Mrs. Miniver*	*Casablanca*	*Going My Way*
Gary Cooper, *Sergeant York*	James Cagney, *Yankee Doodle Dandy*	Paul Lukas, *Watch on the Rhine*	Bing Crosby, *Going My Way*
Joan Fontaine, *Suspicion*	Greer Garson, *Mrs. Miniver*	Jennifer Jones, *The Song of Bernadette*	Ingrid Bergman, *Gaslight*
Donald Crisp, *How Green Was My Valley*	Van Heflin, *Johnny Eager*	Charles Coburn, *The More the Merrier*	Barry Fitzgerald, *Going My Way*
Mary Astor, *The Great Lie*	Teresa Wright, *Mrs. Miniver*	Katina Paxinou, *For Whom the Bell Tolls*	Ethel Barrymore, *None but the Lonely Heart*
John Ford, *How Green Was My Valley*	William Wyler, *Mrs. Miniver*	Michael Curtiz, *Casablanca*	Leo McCarey, *Going My Way*
Sidney Buchman and Seton I. Miller, *Here Comes Mr. Jordan*	George Froeschel, James Hilton, Claudine West, and Arthur Wimperis, *Mrs. Miniver*	Julius J. Epstein, Philip G. Epstein, and Howard Koch, *Casablanca*	Frank Butler and Frank Cavett, *Going My Way*
Harry Segall, *Here Comes Mr. Jordan*; Herman J. Mankiewicz and Orson Welles, *Citizen Kane*	Michael Kanin and Ring Lardner Jr., *Woman of the Year*; Emeric Pressburger, *The Invaders*	Norman Krasna, *Princess O'Rourke;* William Saroyan, *The Human Comedy*	Lamar Trotti, *Wilson;* Leo McCarey, *Going My Way*
"The Last Time I Saw Paris" *(Lady Be Good)*	"White Christmas" *(Holiday Inn)*	"You'll Never Know" *(Hello, Frisco, Hello)*	"Swinging on a Star" *(Going My Way)*
All That Money Can Buy (Dramatic); *Dumbo* (Musical)	*Now, Voyager* (Dramatic or Comedy); *Yankee Doodle Dandy* (Musical)	*The Song of Bernadette* (Dramatic or Comedy); *This Is the Army* (Musical)	*Since You Went Away* (Dramatic or Comedy); *Cover Girl* (Musical)
How Green Was My Valley (B&W); *Blood and Sand* (Color)	*Mrs. Miniver* (B&W); *The Black Swan* (Color)	*The Song of Bernadette* (B&W); *The Phantom of the Opera* (Color)	*Laura* (B&W); *Wilson* (Color)
How Green Was My Valley (B&W) *Blossoms in the Dust* (Color)	*This Above All* (B&W); *My Gal Sal* (Color)	*The Song of Bernadette* (B&W); *The Phantom of the Opera* (Color)	*Gaslight* (B&W); *Wilson* (Color)
Sergeant York	*The Pride of the Yankees*	*Air Force*	*Wilson*
That Hamilton Woman	*Yankee Doodle Dandy*	*This Land Is Mine*	*Wilson*
I Wanted Wings	*Reap the Wild Wind*	*Crash Dive*	*Thirty Seconds over Tokyo*
Lend a Paw (Cartoons); *Of Pups and Puzzles* (One-Reel); *Main Street on the March* (Two-Reel)	*Der Fuehrer's Face* (Cartoons); *Speaking of Animals and Their Families* (One-Reel); *Beyond the Line of Duty* (Two-Reel)	*Yankee Doodle Mouse* (Cartoons); *Amphibious Fighters* (One-Reel); *Heavenly Music* (Two-Reel)	*Mouse Trouble* (Cartoons); *Who's Who in Animal Land* (One-Reel); *I Won't Play* (Two-Reel)
Churchill's Island	*Battle of Midway; Kokoda Front Line; Moscow Strikes Back; Prelude to War*	*December 7th* (Short); *Desert Victory* (Feature)	*With the Marines at Tarawa* (Short); *The Fighting Lady* (Feature)

	1945	1946	1947
Picture	*The Lost Weekend*	*The Best Years of Our Lives*	*Gentleman's Agreement*
Actor	Ray Milland, *The Lost Weekend*	Fredric March, *The Best Years of Our Lives*	Ronald Colman, *A Double Life*
Actress	Joan Crawford, *Mildred Pierce*	Olivia de Havilland, *To Each His Own*	Loretta Young, *The Farmer's Daughter*
Supporting Actor	James Dunn, *A Tree Grows in Brooklyn*	Harold Russell, *The Best Years of Our Lives*	Edmund Gwenn, *Miracle on 34th Street*
Supporting Actress	Anne Revere, *National Velvet*	Anne Baxter, *The Razor's Edge*	Celeste Holm, *Gentleman's Agreement*
Director	Billy Wilder, *The Lost Weekend*	William Wyler, *The Best Years of Our Lives*	Elia Kazan, *Gentleman's Agreement*
Screenplay	Charles Brackett and Billy Wilder, *The Lost Weekend*	Robert E. Sherwood, *The Best Years of Our Lives*	George Seaton, *Miracle on 34th Street*
Original Screenplay/ Original Story	Richard Schweizer, *Marie-Louise*; Charles G. Booth, *The House on 92nd Street*	Muriel and Sydney Box, *The Seventh Veil;* Clemence Dane, *Vacation from Marriage*	Sidney Sheldon, *The Bachelor and the Bobby-Soxer*; Valentine Davies, *Miracle on 34th Street*
Song	"It Might As Well Be Spring" *(State Fair)*	"On the Atchison, Topeka and Santa Fe" *(The Harvey Girls)*	"Zip-A-Dee-Doo-Dah" *(Song of the South)*
Score—Dramatic or Comedy/ Musical	*Spellbound*; *Anchors Aweigh*	*The Best Years of Our Lives; The Jolson Story*	*A Double Life; Mother Wore Tights*
Cinematography	*The Picture of Dorian Gray* (B&W); *Leave Her to Heaven* (Color)	*Anna and the King of Siam* (B&W); *The Yearling* (Color)	*Great Expectations* (B&W); *Black Narcissus* (Color)
Costume Design	—	—	—
Interior Decoration, through 1946; Art Direction—Set Decoration, from 1947	*Blood on the Sun* (B&W); *Frenchman's Creek* (Color)	*Anna and the King of Siam* (B&W); *The Yearling* (Color)	*Great Expectations* (B&W); *Black Narcissus* (Color)
Film Editing	*National Velvet*	*The Best Years of Our Lives*	*Body and Soul*
Sound	*The Bells of St. Mary's*	*The Jolson Story*	*The Bishop's Wife*
Special Effects	*Wonder Man*	*Blithe Spirit*	*Green Dolphin Street*
Short Films	*Quiet Please* (Cartoons); *Stairway to Light* (One-Reel); *Star in the Night* (Two-Reel)	*The Cat Concerto* (Cartoons); *Facing Your Danger* (One-Reel); *A Boy and His Dog* (Two-Reel)	*Tweetie Pie* (Cartoons); *Goodbye Miss Turlock* (One-Reel); *Climbing the Matterhorn* (Two-Reel)
Documentaries	*Hitler Lives?* (Short); *The True Glory* (Feature)	*Seeds of Destiny* (Short)	*First Steps* (Short); *Design for Death* (Feature)

> “The only honest way to find the best actor would be to let everybody play Hamlet and let the best man win.”
>
> —Humphrey Bogart,
> Best Actor, 1951

1948	1949	1950	1951
Hamlet	*All the King's Men*	*All About Eve*	*An American in Paris*
Laurence Olivier, *Hamlet*	Broderick Crawford, *All the King's Men*	José Ferrer, *Cyrano de Bergerac*	Humphrey Bogart, *The African Queen*
Jane Wyman, *Johnny Belinda*	Olivia de Havilland, *The Heiress*	Judy Holliday, *Born Yesterday*	Vivien Leigh, *A Streetcar Named Desire*
Walter Huston, *The Treasure of the Sierra Madre*	Dean Jagger, *Twelve O'Clock High*	George Sanders, *All About Eve*	Karl Malden, *A Streetcar Named Desire*
Claire Trevor, *Key Largo*	Mercedes McCambridge, *All the King's Men*	Josephine Hull, *Harvey*	Kim Hunter, *A Streetcar Named Desire*
John Huston, *The Treasure of the Sierra Madre*	Joseph L. Mankiewicz, *A Letter to Three Wives*	Joseph L. Mankiewicz, *All About Eve*	George Stevens, *A Place in the Sun*
John Huston, *The Treasure of the Sierra Madre*	Joseph L. Mankiewicz, *A Letter to Three Wives*	Joseph L. Mankiewicz, *All About Eve*	Michael Wilson and Harry Brown, *A Place in the Sun*
Richard Schweizer and David Wechsler, *The Search*	Douglas Morrow, *The Stratton Story* (Motion Picture Story); Robert Pirosh, *Battleground* (Story and Screenplay)	Edna & Edward Anhalt, *Panic in the Streets* (Motion Picture Story); Charles Brackett, Billy Wilder, and D.M. Marshman Jr., *Sunset Boulevard* (Story and Screenplay)	Paul Dehn and James Bernard, *Seven Days to Noon* (Motion Picture Story); Alan Jay Lerner, *An American in Paris* (Story and Screenplay)
"Buttons and Bows" *(The Paleface)*	"Baby, It's Cold Outside" *(Neptune's Daughter)*	"Mona Lisa" *(Captain Carey, USA)*	"In the Cool, Cool, Cool of the Evening" *(Here Comes the Groom)*
The Red Shoes; *Easter Parade*	*The Heiress; On the Town*	*Sunset Boulevard*; *Annie Get Your Gun*	*A Place in the Sun*; *An American in Paris*
The Naked City (B&W); *Joan of Arc* (Color)	*Battleground* (B&W); *She Wore a Yellow Ribbon* (Color)	*The Third Man* (B&W); *King Solomon's Mines* (Color)	*A Place in the Sun* (B&W); *An American in Paris* (Color)
Hamlet (B&W); *Joan of Arc* (Color)	*The Heiress* (B&W); *Adventures of Don Juan* (Color)	*All About Eve* (B&W); *Samson and Delilah* (Color)	*A Place in the Sun* (B&W); *An American in Paris* (Color)
Hamlet (B&W); *The Red Shoes* (Color)	*The Heiress* (B&W); *Little Women* (Color)	*Sunset Boulevard* (B&W); *Samson and Delilah* (Color)	*A Streetcar Named Desire* (B&W); *An American in Paris* (Color)
The Naked City	*Champion*	*King Solomon's Mines*	*A Place in the Sun*
The Snake Pit	*Twelve O'Clock High*	*All About Eve*	*The Great Caruso*
Portrait of Jennie	*Mighty Joe Young*	*Destination Moon*	*When Worlds Collide*
The Little Orphan (Cartoons); *Symphony of a City* (One-Reel); *Seal Island* (Two-Reel)	*For Scent-imental Reasons* (Cartoons); *Aquatic House Party* (One-Reel); *Van Gogh* (Two-Reel)	*Gerald McBoing-Boing* (Cartoons); *Grandad of Races* (One-Reel); *In Beaver Valley* (Two-Reel)	*Two Mouseketeers* (Cartoons); *World of Kids* (One-Reel); *Nature's Half Acre* (Two-Reel)
Toward Independence (Short); *The Secret Land* (Feature)	*A Chance To Live* and *So Much for So Little* (Short); *Daybreak in Udi* (Feature)	*Why Korea?* (Short); *The Titan: Story of Michelangelo* (Feature)	*Benjy* (Short); *Kon-Tiki* (Feature)

> "This is one night I wish I smoked and drank."
>
> —Grace Kelly,
> Best Actress, 1954

	1952	1953	1954
Picture	*The Greatest Show on Earth*	*From Here to Eternity*	*On the Waterfront*
Actor	Gary Cooper, *High Noon*	William Holden, *Stalag 17*	Marlon Brando, *On the Waterfront*
Actress	Shirley Booth, *Come Back, Little Sheba*	Audrey Hepburn, *Roman Holiday*	Grace Kelly, *The Country Girl*
Supporting Actor	Anthony Quinn, *Viva Zapata!*	Frank Sinatra, *From Here to Eternity*	Edmond O'Brien, *The Barefoot Contessa*
Supporting Actress	Gloria Grahame, *The Bad and the Beautiful*	Donna Reed, *From Here to Eternity*	Eva Marie Saint, *On the Waterfront*
Director	John Ford, *The Quiet Man*	Fred Zinnemann, *From Here to Eternity*	Elia Kazan, *On the Waterfront*
Screenplay	Charles Schnee, *The Bad and the Beautiful*	Daniel Taradash, *From Here to Eternity*	George Seaton, *The Country Girl*
Story/Story and Screenplay	Frederic M. Frank, Theodore St. John, and Frank Cavett, *The Greatest Show on Earth*; T.E.B. Clarke, *The Lavender Hill Mob*	Ian McLellan Hunter, *Roman Holiday*; Charles Brackett, Walter Reisch, and Richard Breen, *Titanic*	Philip Yordan, *Broken Lance*; Budd Schulberg, *On the Waterfront*
Song	"High Noon (Do Not Forsake Me, Oh My Darlin')" *(High Noon)*	"Secret Love" *(Calamity Jane)*	"Three Coins in the Fountain" *(Three Coins in the Fountain)*
Score—Dramatic or Comedy/ Musical	*High Noon; With a Song in My Heart*	*Lili; Call Me Madam*	*The High and the Mighty*; *Seven Brides for Seven Brothers*
Cinematography	*The Bad and the Beautiful* (B&W); *The Quiet Man* (Color)	*From Here to Eternity* (B&W); *Shane* (Color)	*On the Waterfront* (B&W); *Three Coins in the Fountain* (Color)
Costume Design	*The Bad and the Beautiful* (B&W); *Moulin Rouge* (Color)	*Roman Holiday* (B&W); *The Robe* (Color)	*Sabrina* (B&W); *Gate of Hell* (Color)
Art Direction—Set Decoration	*The Bad and the Beautiful* (B&W); *Moulin Rouge* (Color)	*Julius Caesar* (B&W); *The Robe* (Color)	*On the Waterfront* (B&W); *20,000 Leagues Under the Sea* (Color)
Film Editing	*High Noon*	*From Here to Eternity*	*On the Waterfront*
Foreign Language Film	—	—	—
Sound	*Breaking the Sound Barrier*	*From Here to Eternity*	*The Glenn Miller Story*
Special Effects	*Plymouth Adventure*	*The War of the Worlds*	*20,000 Leagues Under the Sea*
Short Films	*Johann Mouse* (Cartoons); *Light in the Window* (One-Reel); *Water Birds* (Two-Reel)	*Toot, Whistle, Plunk and Boom* (Cartoons); *The Merry Wives of Windsor Overture* (One-Reel); *Bear Country* (Two-Reel)	*When Magoo Flew* (Cartoons); *This Mechanical Age* (One-Reel); *A Time Out of War* (Two-Reel)
Documentaries	*Neighbours* (Short); *The Sea Around Us* (Feature)	*The Alaskan Eskimo* (Short); *The Living Desert* (Feature)	*Thursday's Children* (Short); *The Vanishing Prairie* (Feature)

1955	1956	1957	1958
Marty	*Around the World in 80 Days*	*The Bridge on the River Kwai*	*Gigi*
Ernest Borgnine, *Marty*	Yul Brynner, *The King and I*	Alec Guinness, *The Bridge on the River Kwai*	David Niven, *Separate Tables*
Anna Magnani, *The Rose Tattoo*	Ingrid Bergman, *Anastasia*	Joanne Woodward, *The Three Faces of Eve*	Susan Hayward, *I Want to Live!*
Jack Lemmon, *Mister Roberts*	Anthony Quinn, *Lust for Life*	Red Buttons, *Sayonara*	Burl Ives, *The Big Country*
Jo Van Fleet, *East of Eden*	Dorothy Malone, *Written on the Wind*	Miyoshi Umeki, *Sayonara*	Wendy Hiller, *Separate Tables*
Delbert Mann, *Marty*	George Stevens, *Giant*	David Lean, *The Bridge on the River Kwai*	Vincente Minnelli, *Gigi*
Paddy Chayefsky, *Marty*	James Poe, John Farrow, and S.J. Perelman, *Around the World in 80 Days* (Adapted)	Pierre Boulle, *The Bridge on the River Kwai* (Adapted)	Alan Jay Lerner, *Gigi* (Adapted)
Daniel Fuchs, *Love Me or Leave Me*; William Ludwig and Sonya Levien, *Interrupted Melody*	Dalton Trumbo (aka Robert Rich), *The Brave One*; Albert Lamorisse, *The Red Balloon* (Original)	George Wells, *Designing Woman*	Nathan E. Douglas and Harold Jacob Smith, *The Defiant Ones*
"Love is a Many-Splendored Thing" *(Love Is a Many-Splendored Thing)*	"Whatever Will Be, Will Be (Que Será, Será)" *(The Man Who Knew Too Much)*	"All the Way" *(The Joker Is Wild)*	"Gigi" *(Gigi)*
Love is a Many-Splendored Thing; *Oklahoma!*	*Around the World in 80 Days*; *The King and I*	*The Bridge on the River Kwai*	*The Old Man and the Sea*; *Gigi*
The Rose Tattoo (B&W); *To Catch a Thief* (Color)	*Somebody up There Likes Me* (B&W); *Around the World in 80 Days* (Color)	*The Bridge on the River Kwai*	*The Defiant Ones* (B&W); *Gigi* (Color)
I'll Cry Tomorrow (B&W); *Love Is a Many-Splendored Thing* (Color)	*The Solid Gold Cadillac* (B&W); *The King and I* (Color)	*Les Girls*	*Gigi*
The Rose Tattoo (B&W); *Picnic* (Color)	*Somebody up There Likes Me* (B&W); *The King and I* (Color)	*Sayonara*	*Gigi*
Picnic	*Around the World in 80 Days*	*The Bridge on the River Kwai*	*Gigi*
—	*La Strada* (Italy)	*The Nights of Cabiria* (Italy)	*My Uncle* (France)
Oklahoma!	*The King and I*	*Sayonara*	*South Pacific*
The Bridges at Toko-Ri	*The Ten Commandments*	*The Enemy Below*	*tom thumb*
Speedy Gonzales (Cartoon); *Survival City* (One-Reel); *The Face of Lincoln* (Two-Reel)	*Mister Magoo's Puddle Jumper* (Cartoons); *Crashing the Water Barrier* (One-Reel); *The Bespoke Overcoat* (Two-Reel)	*Birds Anonymous* (Cartoons); *The Wetback Hound* (Live Action)	*Knighty Knight Bugs* (Cartoons); *Grand Canyon* (Live Action)
Men Against the Arctic (Short); *Helen Keller in Her Story* (Feature)	*The True Story of the Civil War* (Short); *The Silent World* (Feature)	*Albert Schweitzer* (Feature)	*AMA Girls* (Short); *White Wilderness* (Feature)

	1959	1960	1961
Picture	*Ben-Hur*	*The Apartment*	*West Side Story*
Actor	Charlton Heston, *Ben-Hur*	Burt Lancaster, *Elmer Gantry*	Maximilian Schell, *Judgment at Nuremburg*
Actress	Simone Signoret, *Room at the Top*	Elizabeth Taylor, *Butterfield 8*	Sophia Loren, *Two Women*
Supporting Actor	Hugh Griffith, *Ben-Hur*	Peter Ustinov, *Spartacus*	George Chakiris, *West Side Story*
Supporting Actress	Shelley Winters, *The Diary of Anne Frank*	Shirley Jones, *Elmer Gantry*	Rita Moreno, *West Side Story*
Director	William Wyler, *Ben-Hur*	Billy Wilder, *The Apartment*	Robert Wise and Jerome Robbins, *West Side Story*
Adapted Screenplay	Neil Paterson, *Room at the Top*	Richard Brooks, *Elmer Gantry*	Abby Mann, *Judgment at Nuremberg*
Story and Screenplay	Russell Rouse and Clarence Greene, story; Stanley Shapiro and Maurice Richlin, screenplay, *Pillow Talk*	Billy Wilder and I.A.L. Diamond, *The Apartment*	William Inge, *Splendor in the Grass*
Song	"High Hopes" *(A Hole in the Head)*	"Never on Sunday" *(Never on Sunday)*	"Moon River" *(Breakfast at Tiffany's)*
Score	*Ben-Hur* (Dramatic or Comedy); *Porgy and Bess* (Musical)	*Exodus* (Dramatic or Comedy); *Song Without End (The Story of Franz Liszt)* (Musical)	*Breakfast at Tiffany's* (Dramatic or Comedy); *West Side Story* (Musical)
Cinematography	*The Diary of Anne Frank* (B&W); *Ben-Hur* (Color)	*Sons and Lovers* (B&W); *Spartacus* (Color)	*The Hustler* (B&W); *West Side Story* (Color)
Costume Design	*Some Like It Hot* (B&W); *Ben-Hur* (Color)	*The Facts of Life* (B&W); *Spartacus* (Color)	*La Dolce Vita* (B&W); *West Side Story* (Color)
Art Direction—Set Decoration	*The Diary of Anne Frank* (B&W); *Ben-Hur* (Color)	*The Apartment* (B&W); *Spartacus* (Color)	*The Hustler* (B&W); *West Side Story* (Color)
Film Editing	*Ben-Hur*	*The Apartment*	*West Side Story*
Foreign Language Film	*Black Orpheus* (France)	*The Virgin Spring* (Sweden)	*Through a Glass Darkly* (Sweden)
Sound	*Ben-Hur*	*The Alamo*	*West Side Story*
Sound Effects (Editing)	—	—	—
Visual Effects	—	—	—
Special Effects	*Ben-Hur*	*The Time Machine*	*The Guns of Navarone*
Short Films	*Moonbird* (Cartoons); *The Golden Fish* (Live Action)	*Munro* (Cartoons); *Day of the Painter* (Live Action)	*Ersatz (The Substitute)* (Cartoons); *Seawards the Great Ships* (Live Action)
Documentaries	*Glass* (Short); *Serengeti Shall Not Die* (Feature)	*Giuseppina* (Short); *The Horse with the Flying Tail* (Feature)	*Project Hope* (Short); *Le Ciel et la boue (Sky Above and Mud Beneath)* (Feature)

	1962	1963	1964	1965
	Lawrence of Arabia	*Tom Jones*	*My Fair Lady*	*The Sound of Music*
	Gregory Peck, *To Kill a Mockingbird*	Sidney Poitier, *Lilies of the Field*	Rex Harrison, *My Fair Lady*	Lee Marvin, *Cat Ballou*
	Anne Bancroft, *The Miracle Worker*	Patricia Neal, *Hud*	Julie Andrews, *Mary Poppins*	Julie Christie, *Darling*
	Ed Begley, *Sweet Bird of Youth*	Melvyn Douglas, *Hud*	Peter Ustinov, *Topkapi*	Martin Balsam, *A Thousand Clowns*
	Patty Duke, *The Miracle Worker*	Margaret Rutherford, *The V.I.P.s*	Lila Kedrova, *Zorba the Greek*	Shelley Winters, *A Patch of Blue*
	David Lean, *Lawrence of Arabia*	Tony Richardson, *Tom Jones*	George Cukor, *My Fair Lady*	Robert Wise, *The Sound of Music*
	Horton Foote, *To Kill a Mockingbird*	John Osborne, *Tom Jones*	Edward Anhalt, *Beckett*	Robert Bolt, *Doctor Zhivago*
	Ennio de Concini, Alfredo Giannetti, and Pietro Germi, *Divorce—Italian Style*	James R. Webb, *How the West Was Won*	S. H. Barnett, story; Peter Stone and Frank Tarloff, screenplay, *Father Goose*	Frederic Raphael, *Darling*
	"Days of Wine and Roses" *(Days of Wine and Roses)*	"Call Me Irresponsible" *(Papa's Delicate Condition)*	"Chim Chim Cher-ee" *(Mary Poppins)*	"The Shadow of Your Smile" *(The Sandpiper)*
	Lawrence of Arabia (Original); *The Music Man* (Adaptation)	*Tom Jones* (Original); *Irma La Douce* (Adaptation)	*Mary Poppins* (Original); *My Fair Lady* (Adaptation)	*Doctor Zhivago* (Original); *The Sound of Music* (Adaptation)
	The Longest Day (B&W); *Lawrence of Arabia* (Color)	*Hud* (B&W); *Cleopatra* (Color)	*Zorba the Greek* (B&W); *My Fair Lady* (Color)	*Ship of Fools* (B&W); *Doctor Zhivago* (Color)
	Whatever Happened to Baby Jane? (B&W); *The Wonderful World of the Brothers Grimm* (Color)	*8½* (B&W); *Cleopatra* (Color)	*The Night of the Iguana* (B&W); *My Fair Lady* (Color)	*Darling* (B&W); *Doctor Zhivago* (Color)
	To Kill a Mockingbird (B&W); *Lawrence of Arabia* (Color)	*America America* (B&W); *Cleopatra* (Color)	*Zorba the Greek* (B&W); *My Fair Lady* (Color)	*Ship of Fools* (B&W); *Doctor Zhivago* (Color)
	Lawrence of Arabia	*How the West Was Won*	*Mary Poppins*	*The Sound of Music*
	Sundays and Cybèle (France)	*8½* (Italy)	*Yesterday, Today and Tomorrow* (Italy)	*The Shop on Main Street* (Czechoslovakia)
	Lawrence of Arabia	*How the West Was Won*	*My Fair Lady*	*The Sound of Music*
	—	*It's a Mad, Mad, Mad, Mad World*	*Goldfinger*	*The Great Race*
	—	*Cleopatra*	*Mary Poppins*	*Thunderball*
	The Longest Day	—	—	—
	The Hole (Cartoons); *Heureux Anniversaire* (Live Action)	*The Critic* (Cartoons); *An Occurrence at Owl Creek Bridge* (Live Action)	*The Pink Phink* (Cartoons); *Casals Conducts: 1964* (Live Action)	*The Dot and the Line* (Cartoons); *The Chicken* (*Le Poulet*) (Live Action)
	Dylan Thomas (Short); *Black Fox* (Feature)	*Chagall* (Short); *Robert Frost: A Lover's Quarrel with the World* (Feature)	*Nine from Little Rock* (Short); *Jacques-Yves Cousteau's World Without Sun* (Feature)	*To Be Alive!* (Short); *The Eleanor Roosevelt Story* (Feature)

	1966	1967	1968
Picture	*A Man for All Seasons*	*In the Heat of the Night*	*Oliver!*
Actor	Paul Scofield, *A Man for All Seasons*	Rod Steiger, *In the Heat of the Night*	Cliff Robertson, *Charly*
Actress	Elizabeth Taylor, *Who's Afraid of Virginia Woolf?*	Katharine Hepburn, *Guess Who's Coming to Dinner*	Katharine Hepburn, *The Lion in Winter;* Barbra Streisand, *Funny Girl*
Supporting Actor	Walter Matthau, *The Fortune Cookie*	George Kennedy, *Cool Hand Luke*	Jack Albertson, *The Subject Was Roses*
Supporting Actress	Sandy Dennis, *Who's Afraid of Virginia Woolf?*	Estelle Parsons, *Bonnie and Clyde*	Ruth Gordon, *Rosemary's Baby*
Director	Fred Zinnemann, *A Man for All Seasons*	Mike Nichols, *The Graduate*	Carol Reed, *Oliver!*
Adapted Screenplay	Robert Bolt, *A Man for All Seasons*	Stirling Silliphant, *In the Heat of the Night*	James Goldman, *The Lion in Winter*
Story and Screenplay	Claude Lelouch, story; Pierre Uytterhoeven and Claude Lelouch, screenplay, *A Man and a Woman*	William Rose, *Guess Who's Coming to Dinner?*	Mel Brooks, *The Producers*
Song	"Born Free" *(Born Free)*	"Talk to the Animals" *(Doctor Dolittle)*	"The Windmills of Your Mind" *(The Thomas Crown Affair)*
Score	*Born Free* (Original); *A Funny Thing Happened on the Way to the Forum* (Adaptation)	*Thoroughly Modern Millie* (Original); *Camelot* (Adaptation)	*The Lion in Winter* (Nonmusical); *Oliver!* (Musical)
Cinematography	*Who's Afraid of Virginia Woolf?* (B&W); *A Man for All Seasons*	*Bonnie and Clyde*	*Romeo and Juliet*
Costume Design	*Who's Afraid of Virginia Woolf?* (B&W); *A Man for All Seasons* (Color)	*Camelot*	*Romeo and Juliet*
Art Direction—Set Decoration	*Who's Afraid of Virginia Woolf?* (B&W); *Fantastic Voyage* (Color)	*Camelot*	*Oliver!*
Film Editing	*Grand Prix*	*In the Heat of the Night*	*Bullitt*
Foreign Language Film	*A Man and a Woman* (France)	*Closely Watched Trains* (Czechoslovakia)	*War and Peace* (U.S.S.R.)
Sound	*Grand Prix*	*In the Heat of the Night*	*Oliver!*
Sound Effects (Editing)	*Grand Prix*	*The Dirty Dozen*	—
Visual Effects	*Fantastic Voyage*	*Doctor Dolittle*	*2001: A Space Odyssey*
Short Films	*Herb Alpert and the Tijuana Brass Double Feature* (Cartoons); *Wild Wings* (Live Action)	*The Box* (Cartoons); *A Place to Stand* (Live Action)	*Winnie the Pooh and the Blustery Day* (Cartoons); *Robert Kennedy Remembered* (Live Action)
Documentaries	*A Year Toward Tomorrow* (Short); *The War Game* (Feature)	*The Redwoods* (Short); *The Anderson Platoon* (Feature)	*Why Man Creates* (Short); *Journey into Self* (Feature)

1969	1970	1971	1972
Midnight Cowboy	*Patton*	*The French Connection*	*The Godfather*
John Wayne, *True Grit*	George C. Scott, *Patton*	Gene Hackman, *The French Connection*	Marlon Brando, *The Godfather*
Maggie Smith, *The Prime of Miss Jean Brodie*	Glenda Jackson, *Women in Love*	Jane Fonda, *Klute*	Liza Minnelli, *Cabaret*
Gig Young, *They Shoot Horses, Don't They?*	John Mills, *Ryan's Daughter*	Ben Johnson, *The Last Picture Show*	Joel Grey, *Cabaret*
Goldie Hawn, *Cactus Flower*	Helen Hayes, *Airport*	Cloris Leachman, *The Last Picture Show*	Eileen Heckart, *Butterflies Are Free*
John Schlesinger, *Midnight Cowboy*	Franklin J. Schaffner, *Patton*	William Friedkin, *The French Connection*	Bob Fosse, *Cabaret*
Waldo Salt, *Midnight Cowboy*	Ring Lardner Jr., *M*A*S*H*	Ernest Tidyman, *The French Connection*	Mario Puzo and Francis Ford Coppola, *The Godfather*
William Goldman, *Butch Cassidy and the Sundance Kid*	Francis Ford Coppola and Edmund H. North, *Patton*	Paddy Chayefsky, *The Hospital*	Jeremy Larner, *The Candidate*
"Raindrops Keep Fallin' on My Head" *(Butch Cassidy and the Sundance Kid)*	"For All We Know" *(Lovers and Other Strangers)*	"Theme from *Shaft*" *(Shaft)*	"The Morning After" *(The Poseidon Adventure)*
Butch Cassidy and the Sundance Kid (Nonmusical); *Hello Dolly!* (Musical)	*Love Story* (Original Score); *Let It Be* (Original Song Score)	*Summer of '42* (Dramatic); *Fiddler on the Roof* (Adapted)	*Limelight* (Dramatic); *Cabaret* (Adapted)
Butch Cassidy and the Sundance Kid	*Ryan's Daughter*	*Fiddler on the Roof*	*Cabaret*
Anne of the Thousand Days	*Cromwell*	*Nicholas and Alexandra*	*Travels with My Aunt*
Hello Dolly!	*Patton*	*Nicholas and Alexandra*	*Cabaret*
Z	*Patton*	*The French Connection*	*Cabaret*
Z (Algeria)	*Investigation of a Citizen Above Suspicion* (Italy)	*The Garden of the Finzi-Continis* (Italy)	*The Discreet Charm of the Bourgeoisie* (France)
Hello Dolly!	*Patton*	*Fiddler on the Roof*	*Cabaret*
—	—	—	—
Marooned	*Tora! Tora! Tora!*	*Bedknobs and Broomsticks*	—
It's Tough to Be a Bird (Cartoons); *The Magic Machines* (Live Action)	*Is It Always Right To Be Right?* (Cartoons); *The Resurrection of Broncho Billy* (Live Action)	*The Crunch Bird* (Animated); *Sentinels of Silence* (Live Action)	*A Christmas Carol* (Animated); *Norman Rockwell's World . . . An American Dream* (Live Action)
Czechoslovakia 1968 (Short); *Arthur Rubinstein—The Love of Life* (Feature)	*Interviews with My Lai Veterans* (Short) *Woodstock* (Feature)	*Sentinels of Silence* (Short); *The Hellstrom Chronicle* (Feature)	*This Tiny World* (Short); *Marjoe* (Feature)

	1973	1974	1975
Picture	*The Sting*	*The Godfather Part II*	*One Flew over the Cuckoo's Nest*
Actor	Jack Lemmon, *Save the Tiger*	Art Carney, *Harry and Tonto*	Jack Nicholson, *One Flew over the Cuckoo's Nest*
Actress	Glenda Jackson, *A Touch of Class*	Ellen Burstyn, *Alice Doesn't Live Here Anymore*	Louise Fletcher, *One Flew over the Cuckoo's Nest*
Supporting Actor	John Houseman, *The Paper Chase*	Robert De Niro, *The Godfather Part II*	George Burns, *The Sunshine Boys*
Supporting Actress	Tatum O'Neal, *Paper Moon*	Ingrid Bergman, *Murder on the Orient Express*	Lee Grant, *Shampoo*
Director	George Roy Hill, *The Sting*	Francis Ford Coppola, *The Godfather Part II*	Milos Forman, *One Flew over the Cuckoo's Nest*
Adapted Screenplay	William Peter Blatty, *The Exorcist*	Francis Ford Coppola and Mario Puzo, *The Godfather Part II*	Lawrence Hauben and Bo Goldman, *One Flew over the Cuckoo's Nest*
Original Screenplay	David S. Ward, *The Sting*	Robert Towne, *Chinatown*	Frank Pierson, *Dog Day Afternoon*
Song	"The Way We Were" *(The Way We Were)*	"We May Never Love Like This Again" *(The Towering Inferno)*	"I'm Easy" *(Nashville)*
Score	*The Way We Were* (Original); *The Sting* (Adaptation)	*The Godfather Part II* (Original); *The Great Gatsby* (Adaptation)	*Jaws* (Original); *Barry Lyndon* (Adaptation)
Cinematography	*Cries and Whispers*	*The Towering Inferno*	*Barry Lyndon*
Costume Design	*The Sting*	*The Great Gatsby*	*Barry Lyndon*
Art Direction—Set Decoration	*The Sting*	*The Godfather Part II*	*Barry Lyndon*
Film Editing	*The Sting*	*The Towering Inferno*	*Jaws*
Foreign Language Film	*Day for Night* (France)	*Amarcord* (Italy)	*Dersu Uzala* (U.S.S.R.)
Sound	*The Exorcist*	*Earthquake*	*Jaws*
Visual Effects	—	—	—
Short Films	*Frank Film* (Animated); *The Bolero* (Live Action)	*Closed Mondays* (Animated); *One-Eyed Men Are Kings* (Live Action)	*Great* (Animated); *Angel and Big Joe* (Live Action)
Documentaries	*Princeton: A Search for Answers* (Short); *The Great American Cowboy* (Feature)	*Don't* (Short); *Hearts and Minds* (Feature)	*The End of the Game* (Short); *The Man Who Skied down Everest* (Feature)

“Raquel, you open the envelope; my eyes are busy.”

—Dean Jones,
Presenter, 1966

1976	1977	1978	1979
Rocky	*Annie Hall*	*The Deer Hunter*	*Kramer vs. Kramer*
Peter Finch, *Network*	Richard Dreyfuss, *The Goodbye Girl*	Jon Voight, *Coming Home*	Dustin Hoffman, *Kramer vs. Kramer*
Faye Dunaway, *Network*	Diane Keaton, *Annie Hall*	Jane Fonda, *Coming Home*	Sally Field, *Norma Rae*
Jason Robards, *All the President's Men*	Jason Robards, *Julia*	Christopher Walken, *The Deer Hunter*	Melvyn Douglas, *Being There*
Beatrice Straight, *Network*	Vanessa Redgrave, *Julia*	Maggie Smith, *California Suite*	Meryl Streep, *Kramer vs. Kramer*
John G. Avildsen, *Rocky*	Woody Allen, *Annie Hall*	Michael Cimino, *The Deer Hunter*	Robert Benton, *Kramer vs. Kramer*
William Goldman, *All the President's Men*	Alvin Sargent, *Julia*	Oliver Stone, *Midnight Express*	Robert Benton, *Kramer vs. Kramer*
Paddy Chayefsky, *Network*	Woody Allen and Marshall Brickman, *Annie Hall*	Nancy Dowd, story; Waldo Salt and Robert C. Jones, screenplay, *Coming Home*	Steve Tesich, *Breaking Away*
"Evergreen" *(A Star Is Born)*	"You Light Up My Life" *(You Light Up My Life)*	"Last Dance" *(Thank God It's Friday)*	"It Goes Like It Goes" *(Norma Rae)*
The Omen (Original); *Bound for Glory* (Adaptation)	*Star Wars* (Original); *A Little Night Music* (Adaptation)	*Midnight Express* (Original); *The Buddy Holly Story* (Adaptation)	*A Little Romance* (Original); *All That Jazz* (Adaptation)
Bound for Glory	*Close Encounters of the Third Kind*	*Days of Heaven*	*Apocalypse Now*
Fellini's Casanova	*Star Wars*	*Death on the Nile*	*All That Jazz*
All the President's Men	*Star Wars*	*Heaven Can Wait*	*All That Jazz*
Rocky	*Star Wars*	*The Deer Hunter*	*All That Jazz*
Black and White in Color (Ivory Coast)	*Madame Rosa* (France)	*Get Out Your Handkerchiefs* (France)	*The Tin Drum* (Federal Republic of Germany)
All the President's Men	*Star Wars*	*The Deer Hunter*	*Apocalypse Now*
—	*Star Wars*	—	*Alien*
Leisure (Animated); *In the Region of Ice* (Live Action)	*Sand Castle* (Animated); *I'll Find a Way* (Live Action)	*Special Delivery* (Animated); *Teenage Father* (Live Action)	*Every Child* (Animated); *Board and Care* (Live Action)
Number Our Days (Short); *Harlan County, U.S.A.* (Feature)	*Gravity Is My Enemy* (Short); *Who Are the DeBolts? And Where Did They Get Nineteen Kids?* (Feature)	*The Flight of the Gossamer Condor* (Short); *Scared Straight!* (Feature)	*Paul Robeson: Tribute to an Artist* (Short); *Best Boy* (Feature)

"Marlon Brando very regretfully cannot accept this very generous award. And the reasons for this being are the treatment of American Indians today by the film industry."

—Sacheen Littlefeather, refusing Brando's 1972 Best Actor Award

	1980	1981	1982
Picture	*Ordinary People*	*Chariots of Fire*	*Gandhi*
Actor	Robert De Niro, *Raging Bull*	Henry Fonda, *On Golden Pond*	Ben Kingsley, *Gandhi*
Actress	Sissy Spacek, *Coal Miner's Daughter*	Katharine Hepburn, *On Golden Pond*	Meryl Streep, *Sophie's Choice*
Supporting Actor	Timothy Hutton, *Ordinary People*	John Gielgud, *Arthur*	Louis Gossett Jr., *An Officer and a Gentleman*
Supporting Actress	Mary Steenburgen, *Melvin and Howard*	Maureen Stapleton, *Reds*	Jessica Lange, *Tootsie*
Director	Robert Redford, *Ordinary People*	Warren Beatty, *Reds*	Richard Attenborough, *Gandhi*
Adapted Screenplay	Alvin Sargent, *Ordinary People*	Ernest Thompson, *On Golden Pond*	Costa-Gavras and Donald Stewart, *Missing*
Original Screenplay	Bo Goldman, *Melvin and Howard*	Colin Welland, *Chariots of Fire*	John Briley, *Gandhi*
Song	"Fame" *(Fame)*	"Arthur's Theme (Best That You Can Do)" *(Arthur)*	"Up Where We Belong" *(An Officer and a Gentleman)*
Original Score	*Fame*	*Chariots of Fire*	*E.T., the Extra-Terrestrial*, *Victor/Victoria* (Song Score/Adaptation)
Cinematography	*Tess*	*Reds*	*Gandhi*
Costume Design	*Tess*	*Chariots of Fire*	*Gandhi*
Art Direction—Set Decoration	*Tess*	*Raiders of the Lost Ark*	*Gandhi*
Film Editing	*Raging Bull*	*Raiders of the Lost Ark*	*Gandhi*
Foreign Language Film	*Moscow Does Not Believe in Tears* (U.S.S.R.)	*Mephisto* (Hungary)	*Volver A Empezar (To Begin Again)* (Spain)
Sound	*The Empire Strikes Back*	*Raiders of the Lost Ark*	*Gandhi*
Sound Effects (Editing)	—	—	*E.T., the Extra-Terrestrial*
Makeup	—	*An American Werewolf in London*	*Quest for Fire*
Visual Effects	—	*Raiders of the Lost Ark*	*E.T., the Extra-Terrestrial*
Short Films	*The Fly* (Animated); *The Dollar Bottom* (Live Action)	*Crac* (Animated); *Violet* (Live Action)	*Tango* (Animated); *A Shocking Accident* (Live Action)
Documentaries	*Karl Hess: Toward Liberty* (Short); *From Mao to Mozart: Isaac Stern in China* (Feature)	*Genocide* (Short); *Close Harmony* (Feature)	*If You Love This Planet* (Short); *Just Another Missing Kid* (Feature)

1983	1984	1985	1986
Terms of Endearment	*Amadeus*	*Out of Africa*	*Platoon*
Robert Duvall, *Tender Mercies*	F. Murray Abraham, *Amadeus*	William Hurt, *Kiss of the Spider Woman*	Paul Newman, *The Color of Money*
Shirley MacLaine, *Terms of Endearment*	Sally Field, *Places in the Heart*	Geraldine Page, *The Trip to Bountiful*	Marlee Matlin, *Children of a Lesser God*
Jack Nicholson, *Terms of Endearment*	Haing S. Ngor, *The Killing Fields*	Don Ameche, *Cocoon*	Michael Caine, *Hannah and Her Sisters*
Linda Hunt, *The Year of Living Dangerously*	Peggy Ashcroft, *A Passage to India*	Anjelica Huston, *Prizzi's Honor*	Dianne Wiest, *Hannah and Her Sisters*
James L. Brooks, *Terms of Endearment*	Milos Forman, *Amadeus*	Sydney Pollack, *Out of Africa*	Oliver Stone, *Platoon*
James L. Brooks, *Terms of Endearment*	Peter Shaffer, *Amadeus*	Kurt Luedtke, *Out of Africa*	Ruth Prawer Jhabvala, *A Room with a View*
Horton Foote, *Tender Mercies*	Robert Benton, *Places in the Heart*	William Kelley, Pamela Wallace, and Earl W. Wallace, *Witness*	Woody Allen, *Hannah and Her Sisters*
"Flashdance . . . What a Feeling" *(Flashdance)*	"I Just Called To Say I Love You" *(The Woman in Red)*	"Say You, Say Me" *(White Nights)*	"Take My Breath Away" *(Top Gun)*
The Right Stuff; Yentl (Song Score/Adaptation)	*A Passage to India*; *Purple Rain* (Song Score)	*Out of Africa*	*'Round Midnight*
Fanny & Alexander	*The Killing Fields*	*Out of Africa*	*The Mission*
Fanny & Alexander	*Amadeus*	*Ran*	*A Room with a View*
Fanny & Alexander	*Amadeus*	*Out of Africa*	*A Room with a View*
The Right Stuff	*The Killing Fields*	*Witness*	*Platoon*
Fanny & Alexander (Sweden)	*Dangerous Moves* (Switzerland)	*The Official Story* (Argentina)	*The Assault* (The Netherlands)
The Right Stuff	*Amadeus*	*Out of Africa*	*Platoon*
The Right Stuff	—	*Back to the Future*	*Aliens*
—	*Amadeus*	*Mask*	*The Fly*
Return of the Jedi	*Indiana Jones and the Temple of Doom*	*Cocoon*	*Aliens*
Sundae in New York (Animated); *Boys and Girls* (Live Action)	*Charade* (Animated); *Up* (Live Action)	*Anna & Bella* (Animated); *Molly's Pilgrim* (Live Action)	*A Greek Tragedy* (Animated); *Precious Images* (Live Action)
Flamenco at 5:15 (Short); *He Makes Me Feel Like Dancin'* (Feature)	*The Stone Carvers* (Short); *The Times of Harvey Milk* (Feature)	*Witness to War: Dr. Charlie Clements* (Short); *Broken Rainbow* (Feature)	*Women—For America, for the World* (Short); *Artie Shaw: Time Is All You've Got* and *Down and out in America* (Feature)

	1987	1988	1989
Picture	*The Last Emperor*	*Rain Man*	*Driving Miss Daisy*
Actor	Michael Douglas, *Wall Street*	Dustin Hoffman, *Rain Man*	Daniel Day-Lewis, *My Left Foot*
Actress	Cher, *Moonstruck*	Jodie Foster, *The Accused*	Jessica Tandy, *Driving Miss Daisy*
Supporting Actor	Sean Connery, *The Untouchables*	Kevin Kline, *A Fish Called Wanda*	Denzel Washington, *Glory*
Supporting Actress	Olympia Dukakis, *Moonstruck*	Geena Davis, *The Accidental Tourist*	Brenda Fricker, *My Left Foot*
Director	Bernardo Bertolucci, *The Last Emperor*	Barry Levinson, *Rain Man*	Oliver Stone, *Born on the Fourth of July*
Adapted Screenplay	Mark Peploe and Bernardo Bertolucci, *The Last Emperor*	Christopher Hampton, *Dangerous Liaisons*	Tom Schulman, *Dead Poets Society*
Original Screenplay	John Patrick Shanley, *Moonstruck*	Ronald Bass and Barry Morrow, *Rain Man*	Alfred Uhry, *Driving Miss Daisy*
Song	"(I've Had) The Time of My Life" *(Dirty Dancing)*	"Let the River Run" *(Working Girl)*	"Under the Sea" *(The Little Mermaid)*
Original Score	*The Last Emperor*	*The Milagro Beanfield War*	*The Little Mermaid*
Cinematography	*The Last Emperor*	*Mississippi Burning*	*Glory*
Costume Design	*The Last Emperor*	*Dangerous Liaisons*	*Henry V*
Art Direction—Set Decoration	*The Last Emperor*	*Dangerous Liaisons*	*Batman*
Film Editing	*The Last Emperor*	*Who Framed Roger Rabbit*	*Born on the Fourth of July*
Foreign Language Film	*Babette's Feast* (Denmark)	*Pelle the Conqueror* (Denmark)	*Cinema Paradiso* (Italy)
Sound	*The Last Emperor*	*Bird*	*Glory*
Sound Effects (Editing)	—	*Who Framed Roger Rabbit*	*Indiana Jones and the Last Crusade*
Makeup	*Harry and the Hendersons*	*Beetlejuice*	*Driving Miss Daisy*
Visual Effects	*Innerspace*	*Who Framed Roger Rabbit*	*The Abyss*
Short Films	*The Man Who Planted Trees* (Animated); *Ray's Male Heterosexual Dance Hall* (Live Action)	*Tin Toy* (Animated); *The Appointments of Dennis Jennings* (Live Action)	*Balance* (Animated); *Work Experience* (Live Action)
Documentaries	*Young at Heart* (Short); *The Ten-Year Lunch: The Wit and the Legend of the Algonquin Round Table* (Feature)	*You Don't Have To Die* (Short); *Hotel Terminus: The Life and Times of Klaus Barbie* (Feature)	*The Johnstown Flood* (Short); *Common Threads: Stories from the Quilt* (Feature)

> “I do the Oscar show every five years to remind people out here I'm still alive.”
>
> —Paul Newman,
> Honorary Award, 1985
> Best Actor, 1986

1990	1991	1992	1993
Dances with Wolves	*The Silence of the Lambs*	*Unforgiven*	*Schindler's List*
Jeremy Irons, *Reversal of Fortune*	Anthony Hopkins, *The Silence of the Lambs*	Al Pacino, *Scent of a Woman*	Tom Hanks, *Philadelphia*
Kathy Bates, *Misery*	Jodie Foster, *The Silence of the Lambs*	Emma Thompson, *Howards End*	Holly Hunter, *The Piano*
Joe Pesci, *GoodFellas*	Jack Palance, *City Slickers*	Gene Hackman, *Unforgiven*	Tommy Lee Jones, *The Fugitive*
Whoopi Goldberg, *Ghost*	Mercedes Ruehl, *The Fisher King*	Marisa Tomei, *My Cousin Vinny*	Anna Paquin, *The Piano*
Kevin Costner, *Dances with Wolves*	Jonathan Demme, *The Silence of the Lambs*	Clint Eastwood, *Unforgiven*	Steven Spielberg, *Schindler's List*
Michael Blake, *Dances with Wolves*	Ted Tally, *The Silence of the Lambs*	Ruth Prawer Jhabvala, *Howards End*	Steven Zaillian, *Schindler's List*
Bruce Joel Rubin, *Ghost*	Callie Khouri, *Thelma & Louise*	Neil Jordan, *The Crying Game*	Jane Campion, *The Piano*
"Sooner or Later (I Always Get My Man)" *(Dick Tracy)*	"Beauty and the Beast" *(Beauty and the Beast)*	"A Whole New World" *(Aladdin)*	"Streets of Philadelphia" (*Philadelphia*)
Dances with Wolves	*Beauty and the Beast*	*Aladdin*	*Schindler's List*
Dances with Wolves	*JFK*	*A River Runs Through It*	*Schindler's List*
Cyrano de Bergerac	*Bugsy*	*Bram Stoker's Dracula*	*The Age of Innocence*
Dick Tracy	*Bugsy*	*Howards End*	*Schindler's List*
Dances with Wolves	*JFK*	*Unforgiven*	*Schindler's List*
Journey of Hope (Switzerland)	*Mediterraneo* (Italy)	*Indochine* (France)	*Belle Epoque* (Spain)
Dances with Wolves	*Terminator 2: Judgment Day*	*The Last of the Mohicans*	*Jurassic Park*
The Hunt for Red October	*Terminator 2: Judgment Day*	*Bram Stoker's Dracula*	*Jurassic Park*
Dick Tracy	*Terminator 2: Judgment Day*	*Bram Stoker's Dracula*	*Mrs. Doubtfire*
Total Recall	*Terminator 2: Judgment Day*	*Death Becomes Her*	*Jurassic Park*
Creature Comforts (Animated); *The Lunch Date* (Live Action)	*Manipulation* (Animated); *Session Man* (Live Action)	*Mona Lisa Descending a Staircase* (Animated); *Omnibus* (Live Action)	*The Wrong Trousers* (Animated); *Black Rider* (Live Action)
Days of Waiting (Short); *American Dream* (Feature)	*Deadly Deception: General Electric, Nuclear Weapons and Our Environment* (Short); *In the Shadow of the Stars* (Feature)	*Educating Peter* (Short); *The Panama Deception* (Feature)	*Defending Our Lives* (Short); *I Am a Promise: The Children of Stanton Elementary School* (Feature)

"Good evening, Hollywood phonies."

—Chevy Chase, Host, 1987

	1994	1995	1996
Picture	*Forrest Gump*	*Braveheart*	*The English Patient*
Actor	Tom Hanks, *Forrest Gump*	Nicolas Cage, *Leaving Las Vegas*	Geoffrey Rush, *Shine*
Actress	Jessica Lange, *Blue Sky*	Susan Sarandon, *Dead Man Walking*	Frances McDormand, *Fargo*
Supporting Actor	Martin Landau, *Ed Wood*	Kevin Spacey, *The Usual Suspects*	Cuba Gooding Jr., *Jerry Maguire*
Supporting Actress	Dianne Wiest, *Bullets over Broadway*	Mira Sorvino, *Mighty Aphrodite*	Juliette Binoche, *The English Patient*
Director	Robert Zemeckis, *Forrest Gump*	Mel Gibson, *Braveheart*	Anthony Minghella, *The English Patient*
Adapted Screenplay	Eric Roth, *Forrest Gump*	Emma Thompson, *Sense and Sensibility*	Billy Bob Thornton, *Sling Blade*
Original Screenplay	Roger Avary and Quentin Tarantino, *Pulp Fiction*	Christopher McQuarrie, *The Usual Suspects*	Ethan Coen and Joel Coen, *Fargo*
Best Song	"Can You Feel the Love Tonight" (*The Lion King*)	"Colors of the Wind" (*Pocahontas*)	"You Must Love Me" (*Evita*)
Original Score	*The Lion King*	*The Postman (Il Postino)*	*Emma* (Musical or Comedy); *The English Patient* (Drama)
Cinematography	*Legends of the Fall*	*Braveheart*	*The English Patient*
Costume Design	*The Adventures of Priscilla, Queen of the Desert*	*Restoration*	*The English Patient*
Art Direction—Set Decoration	*The Madness of King George*	*Restoration*	*The English Patient*
Film Editing	*Forrest Gump*	*Apollo 13*	*The English Patient*
Foreign Language Film	*Burnt by the Sun* (Russia)	*Antonia's Line* (Netherlands)	*Kolya* (Czech Republic)
Sound	*Speed*	*Apollo 13*	*The English Patient*
Sound Effects (Editing)	*Speed*	*Braveheart*	*The Ghost and the Darkness*
Makeup	*Ed Wood*	*Braveheart*	*The Nutty Professor*
Visual Effects	*Forrest Gump*	*Babe*	*Independence Day*
Short Films	*Bob's Birthday* (Animated); *Franz Kafka's It's a Wonderful Life* and *Trevor* (Live Action)	*A Close Shave* (Animated); *Lieberman in Love* (Live Action)	*Quest* (Animated); *Dear Diary* (Live Action)
Documentaries	*A Time for Justice* (Short); *Maya Lin: A Strong Clear Vision* (Feature)	*One Survivor Remembers* (Short); *Anne Frank Remembered* (Feature)	*Breathing Lessons: The Life and Work of Mark O'Brien* (Short); *When We Were Kings* (Feature)

MORE OSCAR RECORDS

Oldest Best Actor winner:
Henry Fonda, 76, for *On Golden Pond*

Oldest Best Actress winner:
Jessica Tandy, 80, for *Driving Miss Daisy*

Youngest Best Supporting Actress winners:
Tatum O'Neal for *Paper Moon* and Anna Paquin for *The Piano*, both at age 11

Most nominations before winning an Oscar:
Geraldine Page, with eight

Most nominations, without winning an Oscar:
Roland Anderson and Alex North, with 15
George Folsey, with 13
Federico Fellini and Loren L. Ryder, with 12

Women directors whose films were nominated for Best Picture:
Randa Haines for *Children of a Lesser God*
Penny Marshall for *Awakenings*
Barbra Streisand for *The Prince of Tides*
Jane Campion for *The Piano*

Two-time Best Supporting Actresses:
Shelley Winters for *The Diary of Anne Frank* and *A Patch of Blue*
Dianne Wiest for *Hannah and Her Sisters* and *Bullets over Broadway*

Most popular Oscar-winning film genre:
drama (46% of all winners)

Least popular Oscar-winning film genre:
suspense-thriller (two winners: *Rebecca* in 1940 and *The Silence of the Lambs* in 1991)

Films that swept the top five Oscars:
It Happened One Night in 1934
One Flew over the Cuckoo's Nest in 1975
The Silence of the Lambs in 1991

Shortest Best Picture winner:
Annie Hall (94 minutes)

Westerns that won Best Picture:
Cimarron in 1930/1
Dances With Wolves in 1990
Unforgiven in 1992

FILM AWARDS

NATIONAL SOCIETY OF FILM CRITICS

Annual Awards for Best Film

1966 Blow-Up
1967 Persona
1968 Shame
1969 Z
1970 M*A*S*H
1971 Claire's Knee
1972 The Discreet Charm of the Bourgeoisie
1973 Day for Night
1974 Scenes from a Marriage
1975 Nashville
1976 All The President's Men
1977 Annie Hall
1978 Get Out Your Handkerchiefs
1979 Breaking Away
1980 Melvin and Howard
1981 Atlantic City
1982 Tootsie
1983 Night of the Shooting Stars
1984 Stranger Than Paradise
1985 Ran
1986 Blue Velvet
1987 The Dead
1988 The Unbearable Lightness of Being
1989 Drugstore Cowboy
1990 GoodFellas
1991 Life Is Sweet
1992 Unforgiven
1993 Schindler's List
1994 Pulp Fiction
1995 Babe
1996 Breaking the Waves

SUNDANCE FILM FESTIVAL

GRAND JURY PRIZE

1978 Girlfriends
1979 Spirit in the Wind
1981 Heartland
Gal Young Un

Dramatic

1982 Street Music
1983 Purple Haze
1984 Old Enough
1985 Blood Simple
1986 Smooth Talk
1987 Waiting for the Moon
Trouble with Dick
1988 Heat and Sunlight
1989 True Love
1990 Chameleon Street
1991 Poison
1992 In the Soup
1993 Ruby in Paradise
Public Access
1994 What Happened Was . . .
1995 The Brothers McMullen
1996 Welcome to the Dollhouse
1997 Sunday

FILMMAKERS TROPHY

Dramatic

1989 Powwow Highway
1990 House Party
1991 Privilege
1992 Zebrahead
1993 Fly By Night
1994 Clerks
1995 Angela
1996 Girls Town
1997 In the Company of Men

AUDIENCE AWARD

Dramatic

1989 sex, lies and videotape
1990 Longtime Companion
1991 One Cup of Coffee (released as "Pastime")
1992 The Waterdance
1993 El Mariachi
1994 Spanking the Monkey
1995 Picture Bride
1996 Care of the Spitfire Grill (released as "The Spitfire Grill")
1997 Hurricane
love jones

CANNES FILM FESTIVAL

Palme d'Or for Best Film

1946 La Bataille du rail (France)
1947 Antoine et Antoinette (France)
1948 No festival
1949 The Third Man (G.B.)
1950 No festival
1951 Miracle in Milan (Italy)
Miss Julie (Sweden)
1952 Othello (Morocco)
Two Cents Worth of Hope (Italy)
1953 Wages of Fear (France)
1954 Gate of Hell (Japan)
1955 Marty (U.S.)
1956 World of Silence (France)
1957 Friendly Persuasion (U.S.)
1958 The Cranes are Flying (U.S.S.R.)
1959 Black Orpheus (France)
1960 La Dolce Vita (Italy)
1961 Viridiana (Spain)
Une Aussi longue absence (France)
1962 The Given Word (Brazil)
1963 The Leopard (Italy)
1964 The Umbrellas of Cherbourg (France)
1965 The Knack (G.B.)
1966 A Man and a Woman (France)
Signore e Signori (Italy)
1967 Blow-Up (G.B.)
1968 Festival disrupted; no awards
1969 If . . . (G.B.)
1970 M*A*S*H (U.S.)
1971 The Go-Between (G.B.)
1972 The Working Class Goes to Paradise (Italy)
The Mattei Affair (Italy)
1973 Scarecrow (U.S.)
The Hireling (G.B.)
1974 The Conversation (U.S.)
1975 Chronicle of the Burning Years (Algeria)
1976 Taxi Driver (U.S.)
1977 Padre Padrone (Italy)
1978 L'Albero Degli Zoccoli (Italy)
1979 The Tin Drum (Germany)
Apocalypse Now (U.S.)
1980 All That Jazz (U.S.)
Kagemusha (Japan)
1981 Man of Iron (Poland)
1982 Missing (U.S.)
Yol (Turkey)
1983 The Ballad of Narayama (Japan)
1984 Paris, Texas (Germany)
1985 When Father Was Away On Business (Yugoslavia)
1986 The Mission (G.B.)
1987 Under the Sun of Satan (France)
1988 Pelle the Conqueror (Denmark)
1989 sex, lies and videotape (U.S.)
1990 Wild at Heart (U.S.)
1991 Barton Fink (U.S.)
1992 The Best Intentions (Denmark)
1993 The Piano (New Zealand)
Farewell My Concubine (Hong Kong)
1994 Pulp Fiction (U.S.)
1995 Underground (Bosnia)
1996 Secrets and Lies (G.B.)
1997 The Taste of Cherry (Iran)
The Eel (Japan)

VENICE FILM FESTIVAL

Golden Lion [for Best Film or Best Foreign Film]

1932 No official award
1933 No festival
1934 Man of Aran (G.B.)
1935 Anna Karenina (U.S.)
1936 Der Kaiser von Kalifornien (Germany)

1937 Un Carnet debal (France)
1938 Olympia (Germany)
1939 No award given
1940 Der Postmeister (Germany)
1941 Ohm Kruger (Germany)
1942 Der grosse König (Germany)
1943 No festival
1944 No festival
1945 No festival
1946 The Southerner (U.S.)
1947 Sirena (Czechoslovakia)
1948 Hamlet (G.B.)
1949 Manon (France)
1950 Justice is Done (France)
1951 Rashomon (Japan)
1952 Forbidden Games (France)
1953 No award given
1954 Romeo and Juliet (Italy/G.B.)
1955 Ordet (Denmark)
1956 No award given
1957 Aparajito (India)
1958 Muhomatsu no Issho (Japan)
1959 Il Generale della Rovere (Italy)
1960 Le Passage du Rhin (France)
1961 Last Year at Marienbad (France)
1962 Childhood of Ivan (U.S.S.R.)
1963 Le Mani sulla città (Italy)
1964 Red Desert (Italy)
1965 Of a Thousand Delights (Italy)
1966 Battle of Algiers (Italy)
1967 Belle de Jour (France)
1968 Die Aristen in der Zirkuskuppel (Germany)

Jury and award system discontinued 1969–79

1980 Gloria (U.S.)
Atlantic City (France/Canada)
1981 Die Bleierne Zeit (Germany)
1982 The State of Things (Germany)
1983 Prénom Carmen (France/Switzerland)
1984 Year of the Quiet Sun (Poland)
1985 Sans toit ni loi (Vagabonde) (France)
1986 Le Rayon vert (France)
1987 Au revoir, les enfants (France)
1988 The Legend of the Holy Drinker (Italy)
1989 A City of Sadness (Taiwan)
1990 Rosencrantz and Guildenstern Are Dead (G.B.)
1991 Urga (U.S.S.R./France)
1992 The Story of Qiu Ju (China)
1993 Blue (France)
Short Cuts (U.S.)
1994 Before the Rain (Macedonia)
Vive L'Amour (Taiwan)
1995 Cyclo (France-Vietnam)1996 Michael Collins (Great Britain-U.S.)
1997 Hana-bi (Fireworks) (Japan)

BERLIN FILM FESTIVAL AWARD

Golden Bear Award for Best Film

1953 The Wages of Fear (France)
1954 Hobson's Choice (G.B.)
1955 The Rats (Germany)
1956 Invitation to the Dance (G.B.)
1957 Twelve Angry Men (U.S.)
1958 The End of the Day (Sweden)
1959 The Cousins (France)
1960 Lazarillo de Tormes (Spain)
1961 La Notte (Italy)
1962 A Kind of Loving (G.B.)
1963 Oath of Obedience (Germany)
The Devil (Italy)
1964 Dry Summer (Turkey)
1965 Alphaville (France)
1966 Cul-de-Sac (G.B.)
1967 Le Depart (Belgium)
1968 Ole Dole Duff (Sweden)
1969 Early Years (Yugoslavia)
1970 No award
1971 The Garden of the Finzi-Continis (Italy)
1972 The Canterbury Tales (Italy)
1973 Distant Thunder (India)
1974 The Apprenticeship of Duddy Kravitz (Canada)
1975 Orkobefogadas (Hungary)
1976 Buffalo Bill and the Indians (U.S.) [award declined]
1977 The Ascent (U.S.S.R.)
1978 The Trouts (Spain)
The Words of Max (Spain)
1979 David (Germany)
1980 Heartland (U.S.)
Palermo Oder Wolfsburg (Germany)
1981 Di Presa Di Presa (Spain)
1982 Die Sehnsucht der Veronica Voss (Germany)
1983 Ascendancy (G.B.)
The Beehive (Spain)
1984 Love Streams (U.S.)
1985 Wetherby (G.B.)
Die Frau und der Fremde (Germany)
1986 Stammheim (Germany)
1987 The Theme (U.S.S.R.)
1988 Red Sorghum (China)
1989 Rain Man (U.S.)
1990 Music Box (U.S.)
Larks on a String (Czechoslovakia)
1991 House of Smiles (Italy)
1992 Grand Canyon (U.S.)
1993 The Woman from the Lake of Scented Souls (China)
The Wedding Banquet (Taiwan/U.S.)
1994 In the Name of the Father (UK/Ireland)
1995 Live Bait (France)
1996 Sense and Sensibility (G.B.)
1997 The People vs. Larry Flynt (U.S.)

INDEPENDENT SPIRIT AWARDS

These prizes are considered the Oscars of the independent film world.

Best Feature

1986 After Hours
1987 Platoon
1988 River's Edge
1989 Stand and Deliver
1990 sex, lies and videotape
1991 The Grifters
1992 Rambling Rose
1993 The Player
1994 Short Cuts
1995 Pulp Fiction
1996 Leaving Las Vegas
1997 Fargo

Best First Feature

1987 Spike Lee, director
She's Gotta Have It
1988 Emile Ardolino, director
Dirty Dancing
1989 Donald Petrie, director
Mystic Pizza
1990 Michael Lehmann, director
Heathers
1991 Whit Stillman, producer/director
Metropolitan
1992 Matty Rich, director
Straight Out of Brooklyn
1993 Neal Jimenez and Michael Steinberg, directors
The Waterdance
1994 Robert Rodriguez, director
El Mariachi
1995 David O. Russell, director
Spanking the Monkey
1996 Edward Burns, director
The Brothers McMullen
1997 Billy Bob Thornton, director
Sling Blade

Best Director

1986 Martin Scorsese
After Hours
1987 Oliver Stone
Platoon
1988 John Huston
The Dead
1989 Ramon Menendez
Stand and Deliver
1990 Steven Soderbergh
sex, lies and videotape
1991 Charles Burnett
To Sleep with Anger

1992 Martha Coolidge
Rambling Rose
1993 Carl Franklin
One False Move
1994 Robert Altman
Short Cuts
1995 Quentin Tarantino
Pulp Fiction
1996 Mike Figgis
Leaving Las Vegas
1997 Joel Coen, director
Fargo

Best Screenplay
1986 Horton Foote
The Trip to Bountiful
1987 Oliver Stone
Platoon
1988 Neal Jimenez
River's Edge
1989 Ramon Menendez and Tom Musca
Stand and Deliver
1990 Gus Van Sant Jr. and Daniel Yost
Drugstore Cowboy
1991 Charles Burnett
To Sleep with Anger
1992 Gus Van Sant Jr.
My Own Private Idaho
1993 Neal Jimenez
The Waterdance
1994 Robert Altman and Frank Barhydt
Short Cuts
1995 David O. Russell
Spanking the Monkey
1996 Christopher McQuarrie
The Usual Suspects
1997 Joel Coen and Ethan Coen
Fargo

Best Cinematographer
1986 Toyomichi Kurita
Trouble In Mind
1987 Bob Richardson
Platoon
1988 Haskell Wexler
Matewan
1989 Sven Nykvist
The Unbearable Lightness of Being
1990 Robert Yeoman
Drugstore Cowboy
1991 Fred Elmes
Wild at Heart
1992 Walt Lloyd
Kafka
1993 Frederick Elmes
Night on Earth
1994 Lisa Rinzler
Menace II Society
1995 John Thomas
Barcelona
1996 Declan Quinn
Leaving Las Vegas
1997 Roger Deakins
Fargo

Best Actor
1986 M. Emmet Walsh
Blood Simple
1987 James Woods
Salvador
1988 Dennis Quaid
The Big Easy
1989 Edward James Olmos
Stand and Deliver
1990 Matt Dillon
Drugstore Cowboy
1991 Danny Glover
To Sleep with Anger
1992 River Phoenix
My Own Private Idaho
1993 Harvey Keitel
Bad Lieutenant
1994 Jeff Bridges
American Heart
1995 Samuel L. Jackson
Pulp Fiction
1996 Sean Penn
Dead Man Walking
1997 William H. Macy
Fargo

Best Actress
1986 Geraldine Page
The Trip to Bountiful
1987 Isabella Rossellini
Blue Velvet
1988 Sally Kirkland
Anna
1989 Jodie Foster
Five Corners
1990 Andie MacDowell
sex, lies and videotape
1991 Anjelica Huston
The Grifters
1992 Judy Davis
Impromptu
1993 Fairuza Balk
Gas, Food, Lodging
1994 Ashley Judd
Ruby in Paradise
1995 Linda Fiorentino
The Last Seduction
1996 Elisabeth Shue
Leaving Las Vegas
1997 Frances McDormand
Fargo

Best Supporting Actor
1988 Morgan Freeman
Street Smart
1989 Lou Diamond Phillips
Stand and Deliver
1990 Max Perlich
Drugstore Cowboy
1991 Bruce Davison
Longtime Companion
1992 David Strathairn
City of Hope
1993 Steve Buscemi
Reservoir Dogs
1994 Christopher Lloyd
Twenty Bucks
1995 Chazz Palmintieri
Bullets over Broadway
1996 Benicio Del Toro
The Usual Suspects
1997 Benecio Del Toro
Basquiat

Best Supporting Actress
1988 Anjelica Huston
The Dead
1989 Rosanna De Soto
Stand and Deliver
1990 Laura San Giacomo
sex, lies and videotape
1991 Sheryl Lee Ralph
To Sleep with Anger
1992 Diane Ladd
Rambling Rose
1993 Alfre Woodard
Passion Fish
1994 Lili Taylor
Household Saints
1995 Dianne Wiest
Bullets over Broadway
1996 Mare Winningham
Georgia
1997 Elizabeth Pena
Lone Star

Best Foreign Film
1986 Kiss of the Spider Woman
1987 A Room with a View
1988 My Life as a Dog
1989 Wings of Desire
1990 My Left Foot
1991 Sweetie
1992 An Angel at My Table
1993 The Crying Game
1994 The Piano
1995 Red
1996 Before the Rain
1997 Secrets and Lies

MTV MOVIE AWARDS

Best Movie
1992 Terminator 2: Judgment Day
1993 A Few Good Men
1994 Menace II Society
1995 Pulp Fiction

1996 Seven
1997 Scream

Best Male Performance
1992 Arnold Schwarzenegger
Terminator 2: Judgment Day
1993 Denzel Washington
Malcolm X
1994 Tom Hanks
Philadelphia
1995 Brad Pitt
Interview with the Vampire
1996 Jim Carrey
Ace Ventura: When Nature Calls
1997 Tom Cruise
Jerry Maguire

Best Female Performance
1992 Linda Hamilton
Terminator 2: Judgment Day
1993 Sharon Stone
Basic Instinct
1994 Janet Jackson
Poetic Justice
1995 Sandra Bullock
Speed
1996 Alicia Silverstone
Clueless
1997 Claire Danes
William Shakespeare's Romeo and Juliet

Most Desirable Male
1992 Keanu Reeves
Point Break
1993 Chistian Slater
Untamed Heart
1994 William Baldwin
Sliver
1995 Brad Pitt
Legends of the Fall
1996 Brad Pitt
Seven

Most Desirable Female
1992 Linda Hamilton
Terminator 2: Judgment Day
1993 Sharon Stone
Basic Instinct
1994 Janet Jackson
Poetic Justice
1995 Sandra Bullock
Speed
1996 Alicia Silverstone
Clueless

Breakthrough Performance
1992 Edward Furlong
Terminator 2: Judgment Day
1993 Marisa Tomei
My Cousin Vinny
1994 Alicia Silverstone
The Crush
1995 Kirsten Dunst
Interview with the Vampire
1996 George Clooney
From Dusk Till Dawn
1997 Matthey McConaughey
A Time To Kill

Best On-Screen Duo
1992 Mike Myers and Dana Carvey
Wayne's World
1993 Mel Gibson and Danny Glover
Lethal Weapon 3
1994 Harrison Ford and Tommy Lee Jones
The Fugitive
1995 Keanu Reeves and Sandra Bullock
Speed
1996 Chris Farley and David Spade
Tommy Boy
1997 Sean Connery and Nicolas Cage
The Rock

Best Villain
1992 Rebecca DeMornay
The Hand That Rocks the Cradle
1993 Jennifer Jason Leigh
Single White Female
1994 Alicia Silverstone
The Crush
1995 Dennis Hopper
Speed
1996 Kevin Spacey
Seven
1997 Jim Carrey
The Cable Guy

Best Comedic Performance
1992 Billy Crystal
City Slickers
1993 Robin Williams
Aladdin
1994 Robin Williams
Mrs. Doubtfire
1995 Jim Carrey
Dumb and Dumber
1996 Jim Carrey
Ace Ventura: When Nature Calls
1997 Jim Carrey
The Cable Guy

Best Song
1992 Bryan Adams
"(Everything I Do) I Do It For You" (*Robin Hood: Prince of Thieves*)
1993 Whitney Houston
"I Will Always Love You" (*The Bodyguard*)
1994 Michael Jackson
"Will You Be There" (*Free Willy*)
1995 Stone Temple Pilots
"Big Empty" (*The Crow*)
1996 Brandy
"Sittin' up in My Room" (*Waiting To Exhale*)
1997 Bush
"Machinehead" (*Fear*)

Best Kiss
1992 Macaulay Culkin and Anna Chlumsky
My Girl
1993 Marisa Tomei and Christian Slater
Untamed Heart
1994 Woody Harrelson and Demi Moore
Indecent Proposal
1995 Jim Carrey and Lauren Holly
Dumb and Dumber
1996 Natasha Henstridge and Anthony Guidere
Species
1997 Will Smith and Vivica A. Fox
Independence Day

Best Action Sequence
1992 Terminator 2: Judgment Day
1993 Lethal Weapon 3
1994 The Fugitive
1995 Speed
1996 Braveheart
1997 Twister

Best New Filmmaker Award
1992 John Singleton
Boyz N the Hood
1993 Carl Franklin
One False Move
1994 Steven Zaillian
Searching for Bobby Fischer
1995 Steve James
Hoop Dreams
1996 Wes Anderson
Bottle Rocket
1997 Doug Liman
Swingers

Best Fight
1996 Adam Sandler and Bob Barker
Happy Gilmore
1997 Fairuza Balk and Robin Tunney
The Craft

Lifetime Achievement Award
1992 Jason Voorhees
Friday the 13th
1993 The Three Stooges
1994 Richard Roundtree
Shaft film series
1995 Jackie Chan
1996 Godzilla
1997 Chewbacca

DIRECTOR'S GUILD AWARDS

Year	Film	Director
1948–49	A Letter to Three Wives	Joseph Mankiewicz
1949–50	All the King's Men	Robert Rossen
1950–51	All About Eve	Joseph Mankiewicz
1951	A Place in the Sun	George Stevens
1952	The Quiet Man	John Ford
1953	From Here to Eternity	Fred Zinnemann
1954	On the Waterfront	Elia Kazan
1955	Marty	Delbert Mann
1956	Giant	George Stevens
1957	Bridge on the River Kwai	David Lean
1958	Gigi	Vincente Minnelli
1959	Ben-Hur	William Wyler
1960	The Apartment	Billy Wilder
1961	West Side Story	Robert Wise and Jerome Robbins
1962	Lawrence of Arabia	David Lean
1963	Tom Jones	Tony Richardson
1964	My Fair Lady	George Cukor
1965	The Sound of Music	Robert Wise
1966	A Man for All Seasons	Fred Zinnemann
1967	The Graduate	Mike Nichols
1968	The Lion in Winter	Anthony Harvey
1969	Midnight Cowboy	John Schlesinger
1970	Patton	Franklin J. Schaffner
1971	The French Connection	William Friedkin
1972	The Godfather	Francis Ford Coppola
1973	The Sting	George Roy Hill
1974	The Godfather, Part II	Francis Ford Coppola
1975	One Flew over the Cuckoo's Nest	Milos Forman
1976	Rocky	John G. Avildsen
1977	Annie Hall	Woody Allen
1978	The Deer Hunter	Michael Cimino
1979	Kramer vs. Kramer	Robert Benton
1980	Ordinary People	Robert Redford
1981	Reds	Warren Beatty
1982	Gandhi	Richard Attenborough
1983	Terms of Endearment	James L. Brooks
1984	Amadeus	Milos Forman
1985	The Color Purple	Steven Spielberg
1986	Platoon	Oliver Stone
1987	The Last Emperor	Bernardo Bertolucci
1988	Rain Man	Barry Levinson
1989	Born on the Fourth of July	Oliver Stone
1990	Dances with Wolves	Kevin Costner
1991	The Silence of the Lambs	Jonathan Demme
1992	Unforgiven	Clint Eastwood
1993	Schindler's List	Steven Spielberg
1994	Forrest Gump	Robert Zemeckis
1995	Apollo 13	Ron Howard
1996	The English Patient	Anthony Minghella

TUBE

PICKS & PANS 1996-97

It was a lackluster season of low ratings and executive shake-ups for the broadcast networks. A few new series offered a glimmer of hope, while others bit the dust. PEOPLE's team of TV critics grade the new class:

Show	Network	Grade	Review
EZ Streets	CBS	A+	Brilliant TV-noir innovation pairs a police detective and an ex-con in a murky urban setting with a haunting score. An instant classic.
American Visions	PBS	A	TIME magazine critic Robert Hughes evinces strong opinions, a sense of humor, and a way with words as he covers three centuries of American art.
Gun	ABC	A	This anthology series follows a high-caliber semiautomatic as it passes from owner to owner.
Millennium	Fox	A	A creepy soundtrack, terrifying visuals, and ingenious plot twists make this brainchild of *X-Files* creator Chris Carter one of the best new shows of the year.
Dangerous Minds	ABC	A-	Actually inspiring. An ex-Marine-turned-English-teacher has gutsy intensity, and the students seem authentic.
Mr. Rhodes	NBC	A-	A *Welcome Back, Kotter* for the gentry. Good cast, good writing, with a hip but intelligent star (Tom Rhodes).
Buffy the Vampire Slayer	WB	B+	War against a league of vampires can interfere with a girl's social life, but such is the duty of California teen Buffy Summers. With a smooth ensemble, only the vampires disappoint.
Fired Up	NBC	B+	Axed from her public relations firm, a self-absorbed career woman evokes empathy despite a prima donna act.
La Femme Nikita	USA	B+	Derived from the 1990 French movie thriller, this lively series about a sexy assassin manages to appeal.
Oz	HBO	B+	There's nary a ray of sunshine at the Oswald Maximum Security Penitentiary, but the Big House is full of fine actors.
The Practice	ABC	B+	This lawyer series is like its workaholic characters—taking on too much, trying too hard.
Sabrina, the Teenage Witch	ABC	B+	Clever writing and the delightful Melissa Joan Hart make this unlikely plot a high schooler's witch fulfillment.
Spy Game	ABC	B+	A happy rehash of those agent series from the 1960s. The violence is of the chop-socko martial-arts kind. Knowingly dumb-funny.
Daria	MTV	B	Spun off from a character on *Beavis and Butthead,* this animated series follows the nonadventures of a poisonously sarcastic teen. As Daria's voice, Tracy Grandstaff has just the right tone.
Dead Man's Gun	Showtime	B	Though not of the same caliber as ABC's *Gun,* this anthology promises to keep viewers reasonably entertained as it follows a gun from owner to owner in the Old West.
Everybody Loves Raymond	CBS	B	Life on Long Island becomes a cross between *Seinfeld* and *Home Improvement* in this sitcom with stand-up Ray Romano.
Orleans	CBS	B	Larry Hagman (*Dallas*) returns to series television as a judge and the head of a prominent metropolitan family. *Orleans* might develop into something good.
Prince Street	NBC	B	For now, this slick series about youngish undercover cops is enjoyable as an exercise in precinct glamour.
Public Morals	CBS	B	Producer Steven Bochco has described this sitcom as a *Barney Miller* for the '90s, but it is more like *NYPD Blue* on holiday.

The Ruby Wax Show	Fox	B	The actress-comedian (and cowriter of *Absolutely Fabulous*) refreshes the talk show routine with her irreverent, extremely forward way of chatting up celebrities.
The Steve Harvey Show	WB	B	Harvey plays a onetime minor R&B star starting over as a high school music teacher. Not the freshest setup, but by TV standards Harvey is convincing as an actual person.
7th Heaven	WB	B-	While a combination of *The Waltons* and *Dynasty* could have been successful, instead Aaron Spelling gives us a bland family drama about a minister, his wife, and five kids.
Arliss	HBO	B-	We can always count on a major-league effort from Robert Wuhl, who plays an ego-stroking sports agent. But the show as a whole lacks the consistency of a championship series.
Arsenio	ABC	B-	Though boyish and bouncy, Arsenio Hall fails to bring strong comic personality to this sitcom about a newly married sportscaster.
Coast to Coast	CBS	B-	Celebrates small-town Americana's unaffected quirkiness, good hearts, and the humble courage of ordinary people. Pleasant enough, though slightly condescending.
Feds	CBS	B-	*Law & Order* at a higher level of government, as New York City federal prosecutors and FBI agents join to fight crime. Unfortunately, something is lost in the enlargement.
Just Shoot Me	NBC	B-	Playing a conniving secretary, David Spade is demonically sarcastic. The problem: The rest of the cast can't match him.
The RuPaul Show	VH1	B-	Well, a talk show hosted by a 6' 5" drag queen certainly makes a change from those *American Bandstand* reruns.
Spin City	ABC	B-	In his return to TV, Michael J. Fox retains his wonderful timing and delivery, but the political satire is toothless, corny, and passé.
Stargate SG-1	Showtime	B-	It's likely that fans of the big-screen epic will be satisfied with the TV version starring Richard Dean Anderson (*MacGyver*). Sci-fi devotees will probably be holding conventions any day now.
Claude's Crib	USA	C+	To make ends meet, Claude Brooks lets rooms to an interracial group of twentysomethings. Neither upsetting nor interesting.
Life...And Stuff	CBS	C+	He's not Ray Romano; stand-up comic Rick Reynolds has a lot to say, but a family sitcom may be the wrong place to say it.
Oddville MTV	MTV	C+	The novelty of this talk-variety spoof wears thin. Your jaded ears may not detect a significant difference between the woman who imitates a seagull and the woman who imitates a dolphin.

Everybody Loves Raymond.

King of the Hill.

Roar	Fox	C+	Features clangorous combat scenes in which 5th-century warriors emit fierce, throaty sounds while having at one another with swords, spears, and fists. Your only defense: Turn down the volume.
Win Ben Stein's Money	Comedy	C+	A capital idea for a quiz show: A celebrity brain must defend the prize money against average citizens. But as Stein straddles roles as host and contestant, the concept doesn't quite pay off.
Chicago Sons	NBC	C	There's nothing familial about these three brothers starring Jason Bateman—except their identically slick sitcom patter. They could just as easily be fraternity brothers or fellow Shriners.
Crisis Center	NBC	C	Cops, doctors, social workers, and just about every group who advertises in the Yellow Pages crowd this unfocused ensemble drama.
Early Edition	CBS	C	What would you do if you knew one day in advance everything that would happen in the world? Hopefully something better than watch this series.
Fast Track	Showtime	C	A doctor and former race-car driver becomes a track physician in a 600-horsepower *General Hospital*. This vehicle is overheated.
King of the Hill	Fox	C	De-fanged of their usual satire and sick humor, the creator of *Beavis and Butthead* and a writer for *The Simpsons* give us a harmless and pointless animated series.
Pearl	CBS	C	A loading-dock-manager-turned-student (Rhea Perlman) and her arrogant professor (Malcolm McDowell) make an appealingly odd couple, but before their worlds collide, they need to have worlds.
Relativity	ABC	C	Kimberly Williams from *Father of the Bride* stars in a wispy series about star-crossed lovers.
Sunset Beach	NBC	C	From the producer of *Melrose Place*, a predictable assortment of boy-men with impeccable musculature and girl-women in thigh-high shifts.
Temporarily Yours	CBS	C	Does the world need another Fran Drescher? Playing a Brooklyn-raised working girl, Debi Mazar has presence but is wasting her time.
Todd McFarlane's "Spawn"	HBO	C	In the bleak, violent, paranoid world of this adult animated series, it seems the only bright color is blood-red—or, in the case of the superhuman title character, blood-green.
Homeboys in Outer Space	UPN	C-	A sloppy parody of *Star Trek* and *Star Wars*. Willingly stupid.
Make Me Laugh	Comedy	C-	Updated from the '50s, this game show doesn't work with comics from the '90s. Must be depreciation.
Mission Genesis	Sci-Fi	C-	Crew members on a mission to repopulate plague-devastated Earth look like the *Saved by the Bell* kids in low-rent *Star Trek* costumes.
The Hunger	Showtime	D+	Bizarre yarns, such as a woman who grows a tail during sex, add up to an anthology series that is all style, no sense.
Pauly	Fox	D	Crude humor from Pauly Shore, who plays a spoiled slacker who initially mistakes his rich father's fiancée (Charlotte Ross) for a hooker because, well, she looks like one.
The Jenny McCarthy Show	MTV	F	The former cohost of *Singled Out* has yet to learn that being funny and idiotic aren't the same thing.

THE CABLE DIRECTORY

The following is a complete list of all national cable television networks, as of our press date, according to the 1997 National Cable Television Association guide, *Cable Television Developments*. In many cases, the networks on-the-air are also on-line.

A&E Television Network (A&E)
original biographies, mysteries, and specials
www.biography.com

Action Pay Per View
independent action, sci-fi, thriller movies
www.msbet.com

Adam & Eve
adult movies
www.cyberspice.com

Adultvision
erotic movies

All News Channel
continuous newscasts
www.allnews.com

AMC (American Movie Classics)
Hollywood's greatest films
www.amctv.com

America's Health Network
health information, using call-in format

ANA Television
programming in Arabic and English for Arab-Americans

Animal Planet
animal and natural history documentaries
www.discovery.com

Asian American Satellite TV
Chinese-language news, drama, movies, sports, education, and entertainment

BET (Black Entertainment Television)
music videos, sports, drama, sitcoms, concerts, specials, talk shows, gospel, news
www.betnetworks.com

BET On Jazz: The Cable Jazz Channel
jazz productions, films, and documentaries
www.betnetworks.com

Bloomberg Information Television
financial markets, news, sports, and weather in "multi-screen" format
www.bloomberg.com

The Box
viewer-programmed music videos of all types

Bravo Cable Network
cultural offerings including films, arts specials, interviews
www.bravotv.com

Cable Video Store
movies and special events

Canal de Noticias NBC
Spanish-language news

Canal Sur
Latin American newscasts, entertainment, and sports

Cartoon Network
cartoons

Channel America Television Network
sports, music, talk shows, movies

Children's Cable Network
nonviolent educational programming
www.oeg-ccn.com

Cine Latino
original Spanish-language movies

Cinemax
contemporary and classic films

Classic Arts Showcase
nonprofit arts programming

Classic Sports Network
sporting events, interviews, series, and documentaries

CMT: Country Music Television)
country music videos

CNBC
business, money, and talk programming
www.cnbc.com

c/net: The Computer Network
computers, on-line services, interactive media, and video games

CNN (Cable News Network)
news, weather, sports
www.cnn.com

CNNfn
market and business news
www.cnnfn.com

CNN International (CNNI)
global news, business, weather, and sports
www.cnn.com/CNNI

CNN/SI
24-hour sports news

Comedy Central
all-comedy programming
www.comcentral.com

Consumer Resource Network (CRN)
www.crninfo.com
marketer-supported information

Continuous Hits 1, 2, 3, 4
the latest Hollywood films
www.ppv.com

Courtroom Television Network (Court TV)
live and taped trial coverage and legal features
www.courttv.com

The Crime Channel
crime-related programming, including series, movies, and news

C-SPAN (Cable Satellite Public Affairs Network)
straight news from Washington and around the nation
www.c-span.org

C-SPAN2
live coverage of the U.S. Senate and public affairs programming

Deep Dish TV
educational programming

The Discovery Channel
nature, history, technology, and adventure
www.discovery.com

Discovery Civilization
documentaries on the people, places, and events from pre-history to the 21st century

Discovery Kids
nonfiction for young people and parents

Discovery Science
high technology and how things work

Discovery Travel & Living
programming on life off the job

The Disney Channel
family entertainment
www.disney.com

E! Entertainment Television
celebrity interviews, news, features

The ECOLOGY Channel
trends, news, fiction, and nonfiction about the environment
www.ecology.com

ENCORE
films of the '60s–'80s

ENCORE Thematic Multiplex SM
movies, with "mood on demand" viewing options

ESPN
broad appeal and narrow interest sports programming
ESPNET.SportsZone.com

ESPN2
live and original sports programming

ESPNEWS
continuous scores, highlights, analyses, interviews, and live press conferences

Ethnic-American Broadcasting Co. L.P.
targeted ethnic programming

EWTN: Global Catholic Network
religious programming in English and Spanish
www.etwn.com

The Family Channel
varied programming for children and families. www.famfun.com

The Filipino Channel
news, drama, sitcoms, and cultural programs from the Philippines. www.abs-cbn.com

Fit TV
health and fitness

Flix
movies from the '60s–'90s

FoxNet
regular Fox network programs
www.foxnet.com

Fox News Channel
general news service
www.foxnews.com

Fox Sports Americas
Spanish-language sports

FREE SPEECH TV (FStv)
experimental media and progressive programming
www.freespeech.org

fX (Fox Basic Cable)
entertainment and lifestyle programming for ages 18–49

fXM: Movies from Fox
movies scheduled by genre

Galavisión
Spanish-language movies, sports, news

Game Show Network
new and classic game shows
www.sony.com

Gay Entertainment Television
gay talk, style, and variety programming getv.com

GEMS International Television
Spanish-language women's programming

CABLEACE WINNERS

The CableACE Award recognizes excellence in original program achievement at both the national and local level. Here are the major 1996 winners. (Source: National Academy of Cable Programming)

Dramatic Series	Showtime	*The Outer Limits*
Talk Show Series	Comedy Central	*Politically Incorrect with Bill Maher*
Comedy Series	HBO	*The Larry Sanders Show*
Variety Special/Series	HBO	*Tracey Takes On...*
Movie/Miniseries	HBO	*Truman*
Actor, Movie/Miniseries	HBO	Gary Sinise, *Truman*
Actress, Movie/Miniseries	Lifetime	Sela Ward, *Almost Golden: The Jessica Savitch Story*
Actor, Comedy Series	HBO	Garry Shandling, *The Larry Sanders Show*
Actress, Comedy Series	HBO	Tracey Ullman, *Tracey Takes On...*

Global Shopping Network
electronic retailing
globalshopping.com

The Golf Channel
golf tournaments and instruction
www.thegolfchannel.com

Great American Country
country music videos

HBO (Home Box Office)
films, specials, sports
www.hbohomevideo.com

Headline News
half-hour newscasts, from CNN
www.cnn.com/HLN

The History Channel
historical documentaries, movies, and mini-series
www.historychannel.com

Home & Garden Television
lifestyle programming
www.hgtv.com

Home Shopping Network (HSN)
discount shopping at home

Home Shopping Spree (Spree!)
more shopping at home

Hot Choice
action-adventure and adult movies
www.ppv.com

HTV
Spanish-language music videos
www.htv.com

The Idea Channel
leading scholars in discussions on a variety of topics

The Independent Film Channel
independent films
www.ifctv.com

The Inspirational Network (INSP)
interdenominational family programming

International Channel
multinational programming in 22 different languages
www.i-channel.com

INTRO TELEVISION
program showcases and new network previews

Jewish Television Network
news, public affairs, arts, and entertainment

Jones Computer Network (JCN)
computer instruction, news, commentary, courses
www.jec.edu

KALEIDOSCOPE
programming by and for people with disabilities

Knowledge TV
programming for personal growth
www.jec.edu

Ladbroke Racing Channel/Meadows Racing Network
live thoroughbred and harness racing

Las Vegas Television Network
entertainment/lifestyle programs on Las Vegas scene

The Learning Channel
educational programming for all ages
www.discovery.com

Lifetime Television (LIFE)
entertainment and information programming aimed at women
www.lifetimetv.com

M2: Music Television
music videos

MOR Music TV
music entertainment, information, and sales of recorded music

The Movie Channel (TMC)
current and classic movies

MSNBC
all news with online resources

MTV: Music Television
music videos and pop culture programming
www.mtv.com

MTV Networks Latin America
Spanish-language music videos

MuchMusic USA
rock, rap, country, and alternative videos
www.muchmusic-usa.com

The Music Zone
global music video network

My Pet TV
animal information and entertainment

NASA Television
space program coverage and other educational material
www.hq.nasa.gov/office/pao/ntv.html

National & International Singles Television Network
variety entertainment and matching service
net.fcref.org

NET—Political NewsTalk Network
original programming focusing on Washington's intrigue and issues
net.fcref.org

Network One
interactive entertainment including movies, action and adventure, and music

NewSport
sports news and scores
www.rainbow-networks.com

NewsTalk Television
news-based interactive talk channel
www.newstalk.com

Newsworld International
news from the United States and around the world

Nick at Nite's TV Land
America's favorite classic television programs

Nickelodeon/Nick at Nite
kids' programming during the day; TV classics after hours
www.nick-at-nite.viacom.com

Nostalgia Television
entertainment, lifestyle, and information for adults

Odyssey
diverse religious and family programming
www.odysseychannel.com

The Outdoor Channel
outdoor lifestyle programming-
www.outdoorchannel.com

Outdoor Life Network
outdoor recreation, conservation, wilderness, and adventure programming

OVATION
visual and performing arts
www.ovationtv.com

Planet Central Television
environmentally themed programming
www.pctvi.com

Playboy TV
adult entertainment
www.playboy.com/PlayboyTV

Plex
seven movie channels in one

Prime Network
national sports

Product Information Network (PIN)
infomercials

Q2
QVC highlights

QVC
home-shopping service
www.qvc.com

Request Television
pay-per-view movies and events
www.requesttv.com

Sci-Fi Channel
fantasy, horror, and sci-fi series, movies, originals
www.scifi.com

SCOLA
international TV news, broadcast to schools

Shop at Home
electronic retailing

Showtime
movies, series, specials, boxing, other entertainment
www.showtimeonline.com

SingleVision
lifestyle and infotainment programming for singles
www.singlestv.com

Speedvision Network
automotive, marine, and aviation programming

Spice
adult movies
www.cyberspice.com

STARZ!
first-run movie releases from Universal, Miramax, Columbia, and other leading distributors

STARZ! 2
more movies

Student Film Network
short length films, alternative and experimental work

Sundance Channel
independent film and documentaries
www.sundancechannel.com

TBS
movies, sports, comedies, kids' shows

Telemundo
Spanish-language programming with movies, game shows, news, music, soap operas, and sports

TNN: The Nashville Network
country music and lifestyle programming

TNT (Turner Network Television)
vintage and original films, sports, kids' shows, specials

Total Communication Network
programming for hearing-impaired
www.paccenter.com/tcn

The Travel Channel
travel news, documentaries, live events
www.travelchannel.com

Trinity Broadcasting Network
religious programming
www.tbn.org

CABLE'S BIGGEST NETWORKS

Ranked by number of subscribers, these cable channels are found in the most American homes. (Source: National Cable Television Association)

1. ESPN
2. CNN (Cable News Network)
3. TNT (Turner Network Television)
4. TBS
5. C-SPAN
6. USA Network
7. The Discovery Channel
8. The Nashville Network (TNN)
9. Lifetime Television (LIFE)
10. The Family Channel
11. A&E Television Network
12. MTV: Music Television
13. Nickelodeon/Nick at Nite
14. The Weather Channel
15. Headline News
16. AMC (American Movie Classics)
17. CNBC
18. QVC
19. VH1(Music First)
20. The Learning Channel

Trio
family entertainment

Tropical Television Network
programming from the Caribbean, Central and South America

Turner Classic Movies (TCM)
nearly 400 movies per month
www.turner.com/tcm/index/htm

TV Asia
programming from the Asian subcontinent, mostly in English

TV Food Network (TVFN)
food, fitness, health, nutrition
www2.foodtv.com/index/htm

TV-JAPAN
news, sports, drama, education, and kids' shows from Japan

U Network
student-produced programming in all genres

Univision
Spanish-speaking programs, with movies, sports, national newscasts

USA Network
all-entertainment network

UVTV/KTLA
Los Angeles station featuring Dodgers baseball
www.uvsg.com/pr/uv/ktlahome.htm

UVTV/WGN
Chicago station featuring Cubs and White Sox baseball, Bulls and NCAA basketball
www.uvsg.com/wgnhome.htm

UVTV/WPIX
New York station featuring New York Yankees baseball and pre-season Giants and Jets football
www.uvsg.com/pr/uv/wpix-home.htm

ValueVision: The Brand Name Channel
home shopping

VHI (Music First)
music videos targeted to the 25- to 44-year-old audience
www.vh1.com

Via TV Network
television shopping network

Video Catalog Channel
home shopping for antiques and collectibles

Viewer's Choice
films, sports, musical events
www.ppv.com

The Weather Channel
local, national, and international weather information
www.weather.com

WGN/UV
Chicago station featuring specials, news, movies, local sports

WorldJazz
jazz for national and international audiences

The Worship Network
Christian worship and music set to scenic videos

WSBK
Boston station offering movies, specials, and local sports

WWOR/AEC Service
New York station featuring action and adventure plus the Mets

Z Music Television
Christian videos, specials, news, and entertainment

CABLE'S MOST POPULAR NETWORKS

These are the most-watched cable channels in America. (Source: Nielsen Media Research)

1. Home Box Office (HBO)
2. Turner Network Televison (TNT)
3. USA Network
4. TBS
5. Nickelodeon/Nick at Nite
6. ESPN
7. Lifetime Television
8. A&E Television Network
9. The Discovery Channel
10. The Family Channel
11. TNN: The Nashville Network
12. Cable News Network (CNN)
13. Cinemax
14. The Disney Channel
15. American Movie Classics (AMC)
16. Showtime
17. The Cartoon Network
18. Music Television (MTV)
19. The Learning Channel
20. WGN

THE MOST POPULAR SHOWS ON TV

The following chart shows America's TV favorites every year beginning in 1949. (Sources: *Variety* [1949–50, month of October] and Nielsen Media Research)

1949–50

1. The Texaco Star Theater — NBC
2. Toast of the Town (Ed Sullivan) — CBS
3. Arthur Godfrey's Talent Scouts — CBS
4. Fireball Fun for All — NBC
5. Philco Television Playhouse — NBC
6. Fireside Theatre — NBC
7. The Goldbergs — CBS
8. Suspense — CBS
9. The Ford Television Theater — CBS
10. Cavalcade of Stars — DUMONT

1950–51

1. The Texaco Star Theater — NBC
2. Fireside Theatre — NBC
3. Your Show of Shows — NBC
4. Philco Television Playhouse — NBC
5. The Colgate Comedy Hour — NBC
6. Gillette Cavalcade of Sports — NBC
7. Arthur Godfrey's Talent Scouts — CBS
8. Mama — CBS
9. Robert Montgomery Presents — NBC
10. Martin Kane, Private Eye — NBC
11. Man Against Crime — CBS
12. Somerset Maugham Theatre — NBC
13. Kraft Television Theatre — NBC
14. Toast of the Town (Ed Sullivan) — CBS
15. The Aldrich Family — NBC
16. You Bet Your Life — NBC
17. Armstrong Circle Theater (tie) — NBC
17. Big Town (tie) — CBS
17. Lights Out (tie) — NBC
20. The Alan Young Show — CBS

1951–52

1. Arthur Godfrey's Talent Scouts — CBS
2. The Texaco Star Theater — NBC
3. I Love Lucy — CBS
4. The Red Skelton Show — NBC
5. The Colgate Comedy Hour — NBC
6. Fireside Theatre — NBC
7. The Jack Benny Program — CBS
8. Your Show of Shows — NBC
9. You Bet Your Life — NBC
10. Arthur Godfrey and His Friends — CBS
11. Mama — CBS
12. Philco Television Playhouse — NBC
13. Amos 'n' Andy — CBS
14. Big Town — CBS
15. Pabst Blue Ribbon Bouts — CBS
16. Gillette Cavalcade of Sports — NBC
17. The Alan Young Show — CBS
18. All-Star Revue (tie) — NBC
18. Dragnet (tie) — NBC
20. Kraft Television Theatre — NBC

1952–53

1. I Love Lucy — CBS
2. Arthur Godfrey's Talent Scouts — CBS
3. Arthur Godfrey and His Friends — CBS
4. Dragnet — NBC
5. The Texaco Star Theater — NBC
6. The Buick Circus Hour — NBC
7. The Colgate Comedy Hour — NBC
8. Gangbusters — NBC
9. You Bet Your Life — NBC
10. Fireside Theatre — NBC
11. The Red Buttons Show — CBS
12. The Jack Benny Program — CBS
13. Life with Luigi — CBS
14. Pabst Blue Ribbon Bouts — CBS
15. Goodyear Television Playhouse — NBC
16. The Life of Riley — NBC
17. Mama — CBS
18. Your Show of Shows — NBC
19. What's My Line? — CBS
20. Strike It Rich — CBS

1953–54

1. I Love Lucy — CBS
2. Dragnet — NBC
3. Arthur Godfrey's Talent Scouts (tie) — CBS
3. You Bet Your Life (tie) — NBC
5. The Bob Hope Show — NBC
6. The Buick-Berle Show — NBC
7. Arthur Godfrey and His Friends — CBS
8. The Ford Television Theater — NBC
9. The Jackie Gleason Show — CBS
10. Fireside Theatre — NBC
11. The Colgate Comedy Hour (tie) — NBC
11. This Is Your Life (tie) — NBC
13. The Red Buttons Show — CBS
14. The Life of Riley — NBC
15. Our Miss Brooks — CBS
16. Treasury Men in Action — NBC
17. All-Star Revue (Martha Raye) — NBC
18. The Jack Benny Program — CBS
19. Gillette Cavalcade of Sports — NBC
20. Philco Television Playhouse — NBC

1954–55

1. I Love Lucy — CBS
2. The Jackie Gleason Show — CBS
3. Dragnet — NBC
4. You Bet Your Life — NBC
5. Toast of the Town (Ed Sullivan) — CBS
6. Disneyland — ABC
7. The Bob Hope Show — NBC
8. The Jack Benny Program — CBS
9. The Martha Raye Show — NBC
10. The George Gobel Show — NBC
11. The Ford Television Theater — NBC
12. December Bride — CBS
13. The Buick-Berle Show — NBC
14. This Is Your Life — NBC
15. I've Got a Secret — CBS
16. Two for the Money — CBS
17. Your Hit Parade — NBC
18. The Millionaire — CBS
19. General Electric Theater — CBS
20. Arthur Godfrey's Talent Scouts — CBS

1955–56

1.	The $64,000 Question	CBS
2.	I Love Lucy	CBS
3.	The Ed Sullivan Show	CBS
4.	Disneyland	ABC
5.	The Jack Benny Program	CBS
6.	December Bride	CBS
7.	You Bet Your Life	NBC
8.	Dragnet	NBC
9.	I've Got a Secret	CBS
10.	General Electric Theater	CBS
11.	Private Secretary (tie)	CBS
11.	The Ford Television Theater (tie)	NBC
13.	The Red Skelton Show	CBS
14.	The George Gobel Show	NBC
15.	The $64,000 Challenge	CBS
16.	Arthur Godfrey's Talent Scouts	CBS
17.	The Lineup	CBS
18.	Shower of Stars	CBS
19.	The Perry Como Show	NBC
20.	The Honeymooners	CBS

1956–57

1.	I Love Lucy	CBS
2.	The Ed Sullivan Show	CBS
3.	General Electric Theater	CBS
4.	The $64,000 Question	CBS
5.	December Bride	CBS
6.	Alfred Hitchcock Presents	CBS
7.	I've Got a Secret (tie)	CBS
7.	Gunsmoke (tie)	CBS
9.	The Perry Como Show	NBC
10.	The Jack Benny Program	CBS
11.	Dragnet	NBC
12.	Arthur Godfrey's Talent Scouts	CBS
13.	The Millionaire (tie)	CBS
13.	Disneyland (tie)	ABC
15.	Shower of Stars	CBS
16.	The Lineup	CBS
17.	The Red Skelton Show	CBS
18.	You Bet Your Life	NBC
19.	The Life and Legend of Wyatt Earp	ABC
20.	Private Secretary	CBS

1957–58

1.	Gunsmoke	CBS
2.	The Danny Thomas Show	CBS
3.	Tales of Wells Fargo	NBC
4.	Have Gun, Will Travel	CBS
5.	I've Got a Secret	CBS
6.	The Life and Legend of Wyatt Earp	ABC
7.	General Electric Theater	CBS
8.	The Restless Gun	NBC
9.	December Bride	CBS
10.	You Bet Your Life	NBC
11.	Alfred Hitchcock Presents (tie)	CBS
11.	Cheyenne (tie)	ABC
13.	The Tennessee Ernie Ford Show	NBC
14.	The Red Skelton Show	CBS
15.	Wagon Train (tie)	NBC
15.	Sugarfoot (tie)	ABC
15.	Father Knows Best (tie)	CBS
18.	Twenty-One	NBC
19.	The Ed Sullivan Show	CBS
20.	The Jack Benny Program	CBS

1958–59

1.	Gunsmoke	CBS
2.	Wagon Train	NBC
3.	Have Gun, Will Travel	CBS
4.	The Rifleman	ABC
5.	The Danny Thomas Show	CBS
6.	Maverick	ABC
7.	Tales of Wells Fargo	NBC
8.	The Real McCoys	ABC
9.	I've Got a Secret	CBS
10.	Wyatt Earp	ABC
11.	The Price Is Right	NBC
12.	The Red Skelton Show	CBS
13.	Zane Grey Theater (tie)	CBS
13.	Father Knows Best (tie)	CBS
15.	The Texan	CBS
16.	Wanted: Dead or Alive (tie)	CBS
16.	Peter Gunn (tie)	NBC
18.	Cheyenne	ABC
19.	Perry Mason	CBS
20.	The Tennessee Ernie Ford Show	NBC

1959–60

1.	Gunsmoke	CBS
2.	Wagon Train	NBC
3.	Have Gun, Will Travel	CBS
4.	The Danny Thomas Show	CBS
5.	The Red Skelton Show	CBS
6.	Father Knows Best (tie)	CBS
6.	77 Sunset Strip (tie)	ABC
8.	The Price Is Right	NBC
9.	Wanted: Dead or Alive	CBS
10.	Perry Mason	CBS
11.	The Real McCoys	ABC
12.	The Ed Sullivan Show	CBS
13.	The Bing Crosby Show	ABC
14.	The Rifleman	ABC
15.	The Tennessee Ernie Ford Show	NBC
16.	The Lawman	ABC
17.	Dennis the Menace	CBS
18.	Cheyenne	ABC
19.	Rawhide	CBS
20.	Maverick	ABC

1960–61

1.	Gunsmoke	CBS
2.	Wagon Train	NBC
3.	Have Gun, Will Travel	CBS
4.	The Andy Griffith Show	CBS
5.	The Real McCoys	ABC
6.	Rawhide	CBS
7.	Candid Camera	CBS
8.	The Untouchables (tie)	ABC
8.	The Price Is Right (tie)	NBC
10.	The Jack Benny Program	CBS
11.	Dennis the Menace	CBS
12.	The Danny Thomas Show	CBS
13.	My Three Sons (tie)	ABC
13.	77 Sunset Strip (tie)	ABC
15.	The Ed Sullivan Show	CBS
16.	Perry Mason	CBS
17.	Bonanza	NBC
18.	The Flintstones	ABC
19.	The Red Skelton Show	CBS
20.	Alfred Hitchcock Presents	CBS

1961–62

1.	Wagon Train	NBC
2.	Bonanza	NBC
3.	Gunsmoke	CBS
4.	Hazel	NBC
5.	Perry Mason	CBS
6.	The Red Skelton Show	CBS
7.	The Andy Griffith Show	CBS
8.	The Danny Thomas Show	CBS
9.	Dr. Kildare	NBC
10.	Candid Camera	CBS
11.	My Three Sons	ABC
12.	The Garry Moore Show	CBS
13.	Rawhide	CBS
14.	The Real McCoys	ABC
15.	Lassie	CBS
16.	Sing Along with Mitch	NBC
17.	Dennis the Menace (tie)	CBS
17.	Marshal Dillon (tie) (Gunsmoke reruns)	CBS
19.	Ben Casey	ABC
20.	The Ed Sullivan Show	CBS

1962–63

1.	The Beverly Hillbillies	CBS
2.	Candid Camera (tie)	CBS
2.	The Red Skelton Show (tie)	CBS
4.	Bonanza (tie)	NBC
4.	The Lucy Show (tie)	CBS
6.	The Andy Griffith Show	CBS
7.	Ben Casey (tie)	ABC
7.	The Danny Thomas Show (tie)	CBS
9.	The Dick Van Dyke Show	CBS
10.	Gunsmoke	CBS
11.	Dr. Kildare (tie)	NBC
11.	The Jack Benny Program (tie)	CBS
13.	What's My Line?	CBS
14.	The Ed Sullivan Show	CBS
15.	Hazel	NBC
16.	I've Got a Secret	CBS
17.	The Jackie Gleason Show	CBS
18.	The Defenders	CBS
19.	The Garry Moore Show (tie)	CBS
19.	To Tell the Truth (tie)	CBS

1963–64

1.	The Beverly Hillbillies	CBS
2.	Bonanza	NBC
3.	The Dick Van Dyke Show	CBS
4.	Petticoat Junction	CBS
5.	The Andy Griffith Show	CBS
6.	The Lucy Show	CBS
7.	Candid Camera	CBS
8.	The Ed Sullivan Show	CBS
9.	The Danny Thomas Show	CBS
10.	My Favorite Martian	CBS
11.	The Red Skelton Show	CBS
12.	I've Got a Secret (tie)	CBS
12.	Lassie (tie)	CBS
12.	The Jack Benny Program (tie)	CBS
15.	The Jackie Gleason Show	CBS
16.	The Donna Reed Show	ABC
17.	The Virginian	NBC
18.	The Patty Duke Show	ABC
19.	Dr. Kildare	NBC
20.	Gunsmoke	CBS

1964–65

1.	Bonanza	NBC
2.	Bewitched	ABC
3.	Gomer Pyle, U.S.M.C.	CBS
4.	The Andy Griffith Show	CBS
5.	The Fugitive	ABC
6.	The Red Skelton Hour	CBS
7.	The Dick Van Dyke Show	CBS
8.	The Lucy Show	CBS
9.	Peyton Place (II)	ABC
10.	Combat	ABC
11.	Walt Disney's Wonderful World of Color	NBC
12.	The Beverly Hillbillies	CBS
13.	My Three Sons	ABC
14.	Branded	NBC
15.	Petticoat Junction (tie)	CBS
15.	The Ed Sullivan Show (tie)	CBS
17.	Lassie	CBS
18.	The Munsters (tie)	CBS
18.	Gilligan's Island (tie)	CBS
20.	Peyton Place (V)	ABC

1965–66

1.	Bonanza	NBC
2.	Gomer Pyle, U.S.M.C.	CBS
3.	The Lucy Show	CBS
4.	The Red Skelton Hour	CBS
5.	Batman (II)	ABC
6.	The Andy Griffith Show	CBS
7.	Bewitched (tie)	ABC
7.	The Beverly Hillbillies (tie)	CBS
9.	Hogan's Heroes	CBS
10.	Batman (I)	ABC
11.	Green Acres	CBS
12.	Get Smart	NBC
13.	The Man from U.N.C.L.E.	NBC
14.	Daktari	CBS
15.	My Three Sons	CBS
16.	The Dick Van Dyke Show	CBS
17.	Walt Disney's Wonderful World of Color (tie)	NBC
17.	The Ed Sullivan Show (tie)	CBS
19.	The Lawrence Welk Show (tie)	ABC
19.	I've Got a Secret (tie)	CBS

1966–67

1.	Bonanza	NBC
2.	The Red Skelton Hour	CBS
3.	The Andy Griffith Show	CBS
4.	The Lucy Show	CBS
5.	The Jackie Gleason Show	CBS
6.	Green Acres	CBS
7.	Daktari (tie)	CBS
7.	Bewitched (tie)	ABC
7.	The Beverly Hillbillies (tie)	CBS
10.	Gomer Pyle, U.S.M.C. (tie)	CBS
10.	The Virginian (tie)	NBC
10.	The Lawrence Welk Show (tie)	ABC
10.	The Ed Sullivan Show (tie)	CBS
14.	The Dean Martin Show (tie)	CBS
14.	Family Affair (tie)	CBS
16.	Smothers Brothers Comedy Hour	CBS
17.	The CBS Friday Night Movie (tie)	CBS
17.	Hogan's Heroes (tie)	CBS
19.	Walt Disney's Wonderful World of Color	NBC
20.	Saturday Night at the Movies	NBC

1967–68

1. The Andy Griffith Show CBS
2. The Lucy Show CBS
3. Gomer Pyle, U.S.M.C. CBS
4. Gunsmoke (tie) CBS
4. Family Affair (tie) CBS
4. Bonanza (tie) NBC
7. The Red Skelton Hour CBS
8. The Dean Martin Show NBC
9. The Jackie Gleason Show CBS
10. Saturday Night at the Movies NBC
11. Bewitched ABC
12. The Beverly Hillbillies CBS
13. The Ed Sullivan Show CBS
14. The Virginian NBC
15. The CBS Friday Night Movie (tie) CBS
15. Green Acres (tie) CBS
17. The Lawrence Welk Show ABC
18. Smothers Brothers Comedy Hour CBS
19. Gentle Ben CBS
20. Tuesday Night at the Movies NBC

1968–69

1. Rowan and Martin's Laugh-In NBC
2. Gomer Pyle, U.S.M.C. CBS
3. Bonanza NBC
4. Mayberry R.F.D. CBS
5. Family Affair CBS
6. Gunsmoke CBS
7. Julia NBC
8. The Dean Martin Show NBC
9. Here's Lucy CBS
10. The Beverly Hillbillies CBS
11. Mission: Impossible (tie) CBS
11. Bewitched (tie) ABC
11. The Red Skelton Hour (tie) CBS
14. My Three Sons CBS
15. The Glen Campbell Goodtime Hour CBS
16. Ironside NBC
17. The Virginian NBC
18. The F.B.I. ABC
19. Green Acres CBS
20. Dragnet NBC

1969–70

1. Rowan and Martin's Laugh-In NBC
2. Gunsmoke CBS
3. Bonanza NBC
4. Mayberry R.F.D. CBS
5. Family Affair CBS
6. Here's Lucy CBS
7. The Red Skelton Hour CBS
8. Marcus Welby, M.D. ABC
9. The Wonderful World of Disney NBC
10. The Doris Day Show CBS
11. The Bill Cosby Show NBC
12. The Jim Nabors Hour CBS
13. The Carol Burnett Show CBS
14. The Dean Martin Show NBC
15. My Three Sons (tie) CBS
15. Ironside (tie) NBC
15. The Johnny Cash Show (tie) ABC
18. The Beverly Hillbillies CBS
19. Hawaii Five-O CBS
20. Glen Campbell Goodtime Hour CBS

1970–71

1. Marcus Welby, M.D. ABC
2. The Flip Wilson Show NBC
3. Here's Lucy CBS
4. Ironside NBC
5. Gunsmoke CBS
6. The ABC Movie of the Week ABC
7. Hawaii Five-O CBS
8. Medical Center CBS
9. Bonanza NBC
10. The F.B.I. ABC
11. The Mod Squad ABC
12. Adam-12 NBC
13. Rowan and Martin's Laugh-In (tie) NBC
13. The Wonderful World of Disney (tie) NBC
15. Mayberry R.F.D. CBS
16. Hee Haw CBS
17. Mannix CBS
18. The Men from Shiloh NBC
19. My Three Sons CBS
20. The Doris Day Show CBS

1971–72

1. All in the Family CBS
2. The Flip Wilson Show NBC
3. Marcus Welby, M.D. ABC
4. Gunsmoke CBS
5. The ABC Movie of the Week ABC
6. Sanford and Son NBC
7. Mannix CBS
8. Funny Face (tie) CBS
8. Adam-12 (tie) NBC
10. The Mary Tyler Moore Show CBS
11. Here's Lucy CBS
12. Hawaii Five-O CBS
13. Medical Center CBS
14. The NBC Mystery Movie NBC
15. Ironside NBC
16. The Partridge Family ABC
17. The F.B.I. ABC
18. The New Dick Van Dyke Show CBS
19. The Wonderful World of Disney NBC
20. Bonanza NBC

1972–73

1. All in the Family CBS
2. Sanford and Son NBC
3. Hawaii Five-O CBS
4. Maude CBS
5. Bridget Loves Bernie (tie) CBS
5. The NBC Sunday Mystery Movie (tie) NBC
7. The Mary Tyler Moore Show (tie) CBS
7. Gunsmoke (tie) CBS
9. The Wonderful World of Disney NBC
10. Ironside NBC
11. Adam-12 NBC
12. The Flip Wilson Show NBC
13. Marcus Welby, M.D. ABC
14. Cannon CBS
15. Here's Lucy CBS
16. The Bob Newhart Show CBS
17. ABC Tuesday Movie of the Week ABC
18. NFL Monday Night Football ABC
19. The Partridge Family (tie) ABC
19. The Waltons (tie) CBS

1973–74

1.	All in the Family	CBS
2.	The Waltons	CBS
3.	Sanford and Son	NBC
4.	M*A*S*H	CBS
5.	Hawaii Five-O	CBS
6.	Maude	CBS
7.	Kojak (tie)	CBS
7.	The Sonny and Cher Comedy Hour (tie)	CBS
9.	The Mary Tyler Moore Show (tie)	CBS
9.	Cannon (tie)	CBS
11.	The Six Million Dollar Man	ABC
12.	The Bob Newhart Show (tie)	CBS
12.	The Wonderful World of Disney (tie)	NBC
14.	The NBC Sunday Mystery Movie	NBC
15.	Gunsmoke	CBS
16.	Happy Days	ABC
17.	Good Times (tie)	CBS
17.	Barnaby Jones (tie)	CBS
19.	NFL Monday Night Football (tie)	ABC
19.	The CBS Friday Night Movie (tie)	CBS

1974–75

1.	All in the Family	CBS
2.	Sanford and Son	NBC
3.	Chico and the Man	NBC
4.	The Jeffersons	CBS
5.	M*A*S*H	CBS
6.	Rhoda	CBS
7.	Good Times	CBS
8.	The Waltons	CBS
9.	Maude	CBS
10.	Hawaii Five-O	CBS
11.	The Mary Tyler Moore Show	CBS
12.	The Rockford Files	NBC
13.	Little House on the Prairie	NBC
14.	Kojak	CBS
15.	Police Woman	NBC
16.	S.W.A.T.	ABC
17.	The Bob Newhart Show	CBS
18.	The Wonderful World of Disney (tie)	NBC
18.	The Rookies (tie)	ABC
20.	Mannix	CBS

1975–76

1.	All in the Family	CBS
2.	Rich Man, Poor Man	ABC
3.	Laverne and Shirley	ABC
4.	Maude	CBS
5.	The Bionic Woman	ABC
6.	Phyllis	CBS
7.	Sanford and Son (tie)	NBC
7.	Rhoda (tie)	CBS
9.	The Six Million Dollar Man	ABC
10.	The ABC Monday Night Movie	ABC
11.	Happy Days	ABC
12.	One Day at a Time	CBS
13.	The ABC Sunday Night Movie	ABC
14.	The Waltons (tie)	CBS
14.	M*A*S*H (tie)	CBS
16.	Starsky and Hutch (tie)	ABC
16.	Good Heavens (tie)	ABC
18.	Welcome Back, Kotter	ABC
19.	The Mary Tyler Moore Show	CBS
20.	Kojak	CBS

1976–77

1.	Happy Days	ABC
2.	Laverne and Shirley	ABC
3.	The ABC Monday Night Movie	ABC
4.	M*A*S*H	CBS
5.	Charlie's Angels	ABC
6.	The Big Event	NBC
7.	The Six Million Dollar Man	ABC
8.	The ABC Sunday Night Movie (tie)	ABC
8.	Baretta (tie)	ABC
8.	One Day at a Time (tie)	CBS
11.	Three's Company	ABC
12.	All in the Family	CBS
13.	Welcome Back, Kotter	ABC
14.	The Bionic Woman	ABC
15.	The Waltons (tie)	CBS
15.	Little House on the Prairie (tie)	NBC
17.	Barney Miller	ABC
18.	60 Minutes (tie)	CBS
18.	Hawaii Five-O (tie)	CBS
20.	NBC Monday Night at the Movies	NBC

1977–78

1.	Laverne and Shirley	ABC
2.	Happy Days	ABC
3.	Three's Company	ABC
4.	Charlie's Angels (tie)	ABC
4.	All in the Family (tie)	CBS
4.	60 Minutes (tie)	CBS
7.	Little House on the Prairie	NBC
8.	M*A*S*H (tie)	CBS
8.	Alice (tie)	CBS
10.	One Day at a Time	CBS
11.	How the West Was Won	ABC
12.	Eight Is Enough	ABC
13.	Soap	ABC
14.	The Love Boat	ABC
15.	NBC Monday Night Movie	NBC
16.	NFL Monday Night Football	ABC
17.	Barney Miller (tie)	ABC
17.	Fantasy Island (tie)	ABC
19.	The Amazing Spider-Man (tie)	CBS
19.	Project U.F.O. (tie)	NBC

1978–79

1.	Laverne and Shirley	ABC
2.	Three's Company	ABC
3.	Mork & Mindy	ABC
4.	Happy Days (tie)	ABC
4.	The Ropers (tie)	ABC
6.	What's Happening!! (tie)	ABC
6.	Alice (8:30) (tie)	CBS
8.	M*A*S*H	CBS
9.	One Day at a Time (Monday)	CBS
10.	Taxi	ABC
11.	60 Minutes (tie)	CBS
11.	Charlie's Angels (tie)	ABC
13.	Angie	ABC
14.	Alice (9:30)	CBS
15.	All in the Family	CBS
16.	WKRP in Cincinnati (tie)	CBS
16.	Soap (tie)	ABC
18.	Eight Is Enough	ABC
19.	All in the Family	CBS
20.	Barney Miller (tie)	ABC
20.	CBS Sunday Night Movie (tie)	CBS

1979–80

1.	60 Minutes	CBS
2.	Three's Company	ABC
3.	That's Incredible	ABC
4.	M*A*S*H	CBS
5.	Alice	CBS
6.	Dallas	CBS
7.	Flo	CBS
8.	The Jeffersons	CBS
9.	The Dukes of Hazzard	CBS
10.	One Day at a Time	CBS
11.	WKRP in Cincinnati	CBS
12.	Goodtime Girls	ABC
13.	Archie Bunker's Place	CBS
14.	Taxi	ABC
15.	Eight Is Enough	ABC
16.	Little House on the Prairie	NBC
17.	House Calls	CBS
18.	Real People	NBC
19.	CHiPs	NBC
20.	Happy Days	ABC

1980–81

1.	Dallas	CBS
2.	60 Minutes	CBS
3.	The Dukes of Hazzard	CBS
4.	Private Benjamin	CBS
5.	M*A*S*H	CBS
6.	The Love Boat	ABC
7.	The NBC Tuesday Night Movie	NBC
8.	House Calls	CBS
9.	The Jeffersons (tie)	CBS
9.	Little House on the Prairie (tie)	NBC
11.	The Two of Us	CBS
12.	Alice	CBS
13.	Real People (tie)	NBC
13.	Three's Company (tie)	ABC
15.	The NBC Movie of the Week (tie)	NBC
15.	One Day at a Time (tie)	CBS
17.	Too Close for Comfort (tie)	ABC
17.	Magnum, P.I. (tie)	CBS
19.	Diff'rent Strokes (tie)	NBC
19.	NFL Monday Night Football (tie)	ABC

1981–82

1.	Dallas (9:00)	CBS
2.	Dallas (10:00)	CBS
3.	60 Minutes	CBS
4.	Three's Company (tie)	ABC
4.	CBS NFL Football Post 2 (tie)	CBS
6.	The Jeffersons	CBS
7.	Joanie Loves Chachi	ABC
8.	The Dukes of Hazzard (9:00)	CBS
9.	Alice (tie)	CBS
9.	The Dukes of Hazzard (8:00) (tie)	CBS
11.	The ABC Monday Night Movie (tie)	ABC
11.	Too Close for Comfort (tie)	ABC
13.	M*A*S*H	CBS
14.	One Day at a Time	CBS
15.	NFL Monday Night Football	ABC
16.	Falcon Crest	CBS
17.	Archie Bunker's Place (tie)	CBS
17.	The Love Boat (tie)	ABC
19.	Hart to Hart	ABC
20.	Trapper John, M.D.	CBS

1982–83

1.	60 Minutes	CBS
2.	Dallas	CBS
3.	M*A*S*H (tie)	CBS
3.	Magnum, P.I. (tie)	CBS
5.	Dynasty	ABC
6.	Three's Company	ABC
7.	Simon & Simon	CBS
8.	Falcon Crest	CBS
9.	NFL Monday Night Football	ABC
10.	The Love Boat	ABC
11.	One Day at a Time (Sunday)	CBS
12.	Newhart (Monday)	CBS
13.	The Jeffersons (tie)	CBS
13.	The A Team (tie)	NBC
15.	The Fall Guy (9:00)	ABC
16.	Newhart (Sunday, 9:30)	CBS
17.	The Mississippi	CBS
18.	9 to 5	ABC
19.	The Fall Guy	ABC
20.	The ABC Monday Night Movie	ABC

1983–84

1.	Dallas	CBS
2.	Dynasty	ABC
3.	The A Team	NBC
4.	60 Minutes	CBS
5.	Simon & Simon	CBS
6.	Magnum, P.I.	CBS
7.	Falcon Crest	CBS
8.	Kate & Allie	CBS
9.	Hotel	ABC
10.	Cagney & Lacey	CBS
11.	Knots Landing	CBS
12.	The ABC Sunday Night Movie (tie)	ABC
12.	The ABC Monday Night Movie (tie)	ABC
14.	TV's Bloopers & Practical Jokes	NBC
15.	AfterMASH	CBS
16.	The Fall Guy	ABC
17.	The Four Seasons	CBS
18.	The Love Boat	ABC
19.	Riptide	NBC
20.	The Jeffersons	CBS

1984–85

1.	Dynasty	ABC
2.	Dallas	CBS
3.	The Cosby Show	NBC
4.	60 Minutes	CBS
5.	Family Ties	NBC
6.	The A Team (tie)	NBC
6.	Simon & Simon (tie)	CBS
8.	Knots Landing	CBS
9.	Murder, She Wrote	CBS
10.	Falcon Crest (tie)	CBS
10.	Crazy Like a Fox (tie)	CBS
12.	Hotel	ABC
13.	Cheers	NBC
14.	Riptide (tie)	NBC
14.	Who's the Boss? (tie)	ABC
16.	Magnum, P.I.	CBS
17.	Hail to the Chief	ABC
18.	Newhart	CBS
19.	Kate & Allie	CBS
20.	The NBC Monday Night Movie	NBC

1985–86

1.	The Cosby Show	NBC
2.	Family Ties	NBC
3.	Murder, She Wrote	CBS
4.	60 Minutes	CBS
5.	Cheers	NBC
6.	Dallas (tie)	CBS
6.	Dynasty (tie)	ABC
6.	The Golden Girls (tie)	NBC
9.	Miami Vice	NBC
10.	Who's the Boss?	ABC
11.	Perfect Strangers	ABC
12.	Night Court	NBC
13.	The CBS Sunday Night Movie	CBS
14.	Highway to Heaven (tie)	NBC
14.	Kate & Allie (tie)	CBS
16.	NFL Monday Night Football	ABC
17.	Newhart	CBS
18.	Knots Landing (tie)	CBS
18.	Growing Pains (tie)	ABC
20.	227	NBC

1986–87

1.	The Cosby Show	NBC
2.	Family Ties	NBC
3.	Cheers	NBC
4.	Murder, She Wrote	CBS
5.	Night Court	NBC
6.	The Golden Girls	NBC
7.	60 Minutes	CBS
8.	Growing Pains	ABC
9.	Moonlighting	ABC
10.	Who's the Boss?	ABC
11.	Dallas	CBS
12.	Nothing in Common	NBC
13.	Newhart	CBS
14.	Amen	NBC
15.	227	NBC
16.	Matlock (tie)	NBC
16.	CBS Sunday Night Movie (tie)	CBS
16.	NBC Monday Night Movie (tie)	NBC
19.	NFL Monday Night Football (tie)	ABC
19.	Kate & Allie (tie)	CBS

1987–88

1.	The Cosby Show	NBC
2.	A Different World	NBC
3.	Cheers	NBC
4.	Growing Pains (Tuesday)	ABC
5.	Night Court	NBC
6.	The Golden Girls	NBC
7.	Who's the Boss?	ABC
8.	60 Minutes	CBS
9.	Murder, She Wrote	CBS
10.	The Wonder Years	ABC
11.	Alf	NBC
12.	Moonlighting (tie)	ABC
12.	L.A. Law (tie)	NBC
14.	NFL Monday Night Football	ABC
15.	Matlock (tie)	NBC
15.	Growing Pains (Wednesday) (tie)	ABC
17.	Amen	NBC
18.	Family Ties	NBC
19.	Hunter	NBC
20.	The CBS Sunday Night Movie	CBS

1988–89

1.	Roseanne (9:00) (tie)	ABC
1.	The Cosby Show (tie)	NBC
3.	Roseanne (8:30) (tie)	ABC
3.	A Different World (tie)	NBC
5.	Cheers	NBC
6.	60 Minutes	CBS
7.	The Golden Girls	NBC
8.	Who's the Boss?	ABC
9.	The Wonder Years	ABC
10.	Murder, She Wrote	CBS
11.	Empty Nest	NBC
12.	Anything but Love	ABC
13.	Dear John	NBC
14.	Growing Pains	ABC
15.	Alf (tie)	NBC
15.	L.A. Law (tie)	NBC
17.	Matlock	NBC
18.	Unsolved Mysteries (tie)	NBC
18.	Hunter (tie)	NBC
20.	In the Heat of the Night	NBC

1989–90

1.	Roseanne	ABC
2.	The Cosby Show	NBC
3.	Cheers	NBC
4.	A Different World	NBC
5.	America's Funniest Home Videos	ABC
6.	The Golden Girls	NBC
7.	60 Minutes	CBS
8.	The Wonder Years	ABC
9.	Empty Nest	NBC
10.	Chicken Soup	ABC
11.	NFL Monday Night Football	ABC
12.	Unsolved Mysteries	NBC
13.	Who's the Boss?	ABC
14.	L.A. Law (tie)	NBC
14.	Murder, She Wrote (tie)	CBS
16.	Grand	NBC
17.	In the Heat of the Night	NBC
18.	Dear John	NBC
19.	Coach	ABC
20.	Matlock	NBC

1990–91

1.	Cheers	NBC
2.	60 Minutes	CBS
3.	Roseanne	ABC
4.	A Different World	NBC
5.	The Cosby Show	NBC
6.	NFL Monday Night Football	ABC
7.	America's Funniest Home Videos	ABC
8.	Murphy Brown	CBS
9.	America's Funniest People (tie)	ABC
9.	Designing Women (tie)	CBS
9.	Empty Nest (tie)	NBC
12.	Golden Girls	NBC
13.	Murder, She Wrote	CBS
14.	Unsolved Mysteries	NBC
15.	Full House	ABC
16.	Family Matters	ABC
17.	Coach (tie)	ABC
17.	Matlock (tie)	NBC
19.	In the Heat of the Night	NBC
20.	Major Dad	CBS

1991–92

1.	60 Minutes	CBS
2.	Roseanne	ABC
3.	Murphy Brown	CBS
4.	Cheers	NBC
5.	Home Improvement	ABC
6.	Designing Women	CBS
7.	Coach	ABC
8.	Full House	ABC
9.	Murder, She Wrote (tie)	CBS
9.	Unsolved Mysteries (tie)	NBC
11.	Major Dad (tie)	CBS
11.	NFL Monday Night Football (tie)	ABC
13.	Room For Two	ABC
14.	The CBS Sunday Night Movie	CBS
15.	Evening Shade	CBS
16.	Northern Exposure	CBS
17.	A Different World	NBC
18.	The Cosby Show	NBC
19.	Wings	NBC
20.	America's Funniest Home Videos (tie)	ABC
20.	Fresh Prince of Bel Air (tie)	NBC

1992–93

1.	60 Minutes	CBS
2.	Roseanne	ABC
3.	Home Improvement	ABC
4.	Murphy Brown	CBS
5.	Murder, She Wrote	CBS
6.	Coach	ABC
7.	NFL Monday Night Football	ABC
8.	The CBS Sunday Night Movie (tie)	CBS
8.	Cheers (tie)	NBC
10.	Full House	ABC
11.	Northern Exposure	CBS
12.	Rescue: 911	CBS
13.	20/20	ABC
14.	The CBS Tuesday Night Movie (tie)	CBS
14.	Love & War (tie)	CBS
16.	Fresh Prince of Bel Air (tie)	NBC
16.	Hangin' with Mr. Cooper (tie)	ABC
16.	The Jackie Thomas Show (tie)	ABC
19.	Evening Shade	CBS
20.	Hearts Afire (tie)	CBS
20.	Unsolved Mysteries (tie)	NBC

1993–94

1.	Home Improvement	ABC
2.	60 Minutes	CBS
3.	Seinfeld	NBC
4.	Roseanne	ABC
5.	Grace Under Fire	ABC
6.	These Friends of Mine	ABC
7.	Frasier	NBC
8.	Coach (tie)	ABC
8.	NFL Monday Night Football (tie)	ABC
10.	Murder, She Wrote	CBS
11.	Murphy Brown	CBS
12.	Thunder Alley	ABC
13.	The CBS Sunday Night Movie	CBS
14.	20/20	ABC
15.	Love & War	CBS
16.	Primetime Live (tie)	ABC
16.	Wings (tie)	NBC
18.	NYPD Blue	ABC
19.	Homicide: Life on the Street	NBC
20.	Northern Exposure	CBS

1994–95

1.	Seinfeld	NBC
2.	ER	NBC
3.	Home Improvement	ABC
4.	Grace Under Fire	ABC
5.	NFL Monday Night Football	ABC
6.	60 Minutes	CBS
7.	NYPD Blue	ABC
8.	Friends	NBC
9.	Roseanne (tie)	ABC
9.	Murder, She Wrote (tie)	CBS
11.	Mad About You	NBC
12.	Madman of the People	NBC
13.	Ellen	ABC
14.	Hope & Gloria	NBC
15.	Frasier	NBC
16.	Murphy Brown	CBS
17.	20/20	ABC
18.	CBS Sunday Movie	CBS
19.	NBC Monday Night Movies	NBC
20.	Dave's World	CBS

1995–96

1.	ER	NBC
2.	Seinfeld	NBC
3.	Friends	NBC
4.	Caroline in the City	NBC
5.	NFL Monday Night Football	ABC
6.	The Single Guy	NBC
7.	Home Improvement	ABC
8.	Boston Common	NBC
9.	60 Minutes	CBS
10.	NYPD Blue	ABC
11.	Frasier (tie)	NBC
11.	20/20 (tie)	ABC
13.	Grace Under Fire	ABC
14.	Coach (tie)	ABC
14.	NBC Monday Night Movies (tie)	NBC
16.	Roseanne	ABC
17.	The Nanny	CBS
18.	Murphy Brown (tie)	CBS
18.	Primetime Live (tie)	ABC
18.	Walker, Texas Ranger (tie)	CBS

1996–97

1.	ER	NBC
2.	Seinfeld	NBC
3.	Suddenly Susan	NBC
4.	Friends (tie)	NBC
4.	The Naked Truth (tie)	NBC
6.	Fired Up	NBC
7.	NFL Monday Night Football	ABC
8.	The Single Guy	NBC
9.	Home Improvement	ABC
10.	Touched by an Angel	CBS
11.	60 Minutes	CBS
12.	20/20	ABC
13.	NYPD Blue	ABC
14.	CBS Sunday Movie	CBS
15.	Primetime Live	ABC
16.	Frasier	NBC
17.	Spin City	ABC
18.	NBC Sunday Night Movie (tie)	NBC
18.	The Drew Carey Show (tie)	NBC
20.	The X-Files	FOX

1996-97 SPECIAL RATINGS

The following are Nielsen ratings for a variety of special categories for the most recent season. (Source: Nielsen Media Research)

SYNDICATED TALK SHOWS

	Show	Distributor
1.	The Oprah Winfrey Show	Kingworld/ Camelot
2.	The Rosie O'Donnell Show	Warner Brothers/ Turner
3.	The Montel Williams Show	Paramount/ Premier
4.	Live with Regis and Kathie Lee	Buena Vista
5.	The Jenny Jones Show	Warner Brothers
6.	Sally Jessy Raphael	Multimedia
7.	The Maury Povich Show	Paramount/ Premier
8.	Ricki Lake	Columbia Tristar
9.	Jerry Springer	Universal
10.	Geraldo	Tribune
11.	The Gordon Elliott Show	20th Television

SOAPS

	Show	Network
1.	The Young and the Restless	CBS
2.	Days of Our Lives	NBC
3.	The Bold and the Beautiful	CBS
4.	General Hospital	ABC
5.	All My Children	ABC
6.	As the World Turns	CBS
7.	One Life To Live	ABC
8.	Guiding Light	CBS
9.	Another World	NBC
10.	The City	ABC

QUIZ AND GAME SHOWS

	Show	Distributor
1.	Wheel of Fortune	Kingsworld/ Camelot
2.	Jeopardy!	Kingsworld/ Camelot
3.	The Price Is Right (11:30 a.m.)	CBS
4.	Wheel of Fortune (Weekend)	Kingsworld/ Camelot
5.	The Price Is Right (11:00 a.m.)	CBS CBS

SATURDAY MORNING CHILDREN'S PROGRAMS

	Show	Network
1.	Eerie, Indiana	Fox
2.	Goosebumps (10:00 a.m.)	Fox
3.	Life with Louie	Fox
4.	X-Men	Fox
5.	Goosebumps (10:30 a.m.)	Fox
6.	Spider-Man	Fox
7.	Casper	Fox
8.	The Tick	Fox
9.	Bugs Bunny/ Tweety Show (10:30 a.m.) (tie)	ABC
9.	Saved by the Bell (11:00 a.m.) (tie)	NBC
11.	California Dreams (tie)	NBC
11.	Power Rangers Turbo (tie)	Fox
13.	Hang Time (tie)	NBC
13.	Schoolhouse Rock (10:55 a.m.) (tie)	ABC
15.	Saved by the Bell (10:00 a.m.) (tie)	NBC
15.	Schoolhouse Rock (10:25 a.m.) (tie)	ABC

TRIVIAL TRIUMPHS

The answer: See below. The question? Who are *Celebrity Jeopardy!*'s all-time-highest earners? (P.S. *CBS This Morning* anchor Mark McEwen won the 1997 tourney.) (Source: *Jeopardy!*)

Name	Earnings	Name	Earnings
Jerry Orbach	$34,000	LeVar Burton	$14,500
Charles Shaughnessy	$31,800	David Hyde Pierce	$13,600
Norman Schwarzkopf	$28,000	Markie Post	$12,400
Mark McEwen	$26,700	Charles Kimbrough	$12,000
Cheech Marin	$25,000	Kareem Abdul-Jabbar	$11,900
Laura Innes	$24,400	Jason Alexander	$11,800
Sam Waterston	$23,800	Lou Diamond Phillips	$11,400
Mike Piazza	$17,900	Stephen King	$11,400
Chris Hardwick	$15,800	Ed Asner	$10,900
Benjamin Salisbury	$15,000	Isaac Mizrahi	$10,900

PBS'S MOST POPULAR PROGRAMS

Viewers often associate PBS with children's programming, but in fact, PBS is a variety service offering a mix of nature, history, arts, news, and public affairs programming. It is PBS's diverse schedule of quality programming that draws the viewers. (Source: Nielsen Television Index)

1. *National Geographic Specials:* "Island of the Giant Bears" (1994)
2. *The American Experience:* "The Kennedys" (1992)
3. *National Geographic Specials:* "Reflections on Elephants" (1994)
4. *Carerras Domingo Pavarotti with Mehta—Three Tenors* (1994)
5. *NOVA:* "The Ice Man" (1992)
6. *National Geographic Specials:* "Lost Kingdoms of the Maya" (1993)
7. *National Geographic Specials:* "Mysteries Underground" (1992) (tie)
7. *I'll Fly Away: Then and Now* (1993) (tie)
9. *NOVA:* "The Codebreakers" (1994)
10. *Nature:* "Pandas of the Sleeping Dragon" (1994) (tie)
10. *The Living Edens:* "Denali: Alaska's Great Wilderness" (1997) (tie)
12. *Baseball* (1994) (tie)
12. *NOVA:* "This Old Pyramid" (1992) (tie)
12. *NOVA:* "Secret of the Wild Child" (1994) (tie)
15. *Frontline:* "The Secret File on J. Edgar Hoover" (1993)

WHAT'S IN A NAME?

Is a favorite show any less sweet by a different name? The creators often thought so. And so many of the most popular shows of all time began with names other than those that became familiar to millions. A sampling follows (when a show had multiple names, they are listed in sequence).

Original Name	Final Name
The Alley Cats	Charlie's Angels
The Brady Brood	The Brady Bunch
45 Minutes from Harlem	Diff'rent Strokes
Country Cousins/ The Eddie Albert Show	Green Acres
Cyborg	The Six Million Dollar Man
Danny Doyle	I Spy
Eye-Opener	CBS Morning Show
Family Business	The Partridge Family
The Flagstones	The Flintstones
McHale's Men	McHale's Navy
Head of the Family	The Dick Van Dyke Show
McHale's Men	McHale's Navy
Mr. Solo/Solo	The Man From U.N.C.L.E.
Occupation Unknown	What's My Line?
Oil	Dynasty
Ozark Widow/Dern Tootin'/ Whistle Stop	Petticoat Junction
The Rise and Shine Revue	Today
Spencer's Mountain	The Waltons
Sunset 77	77 Sunset Strip
Those Were the Days	All in the Family
Wally and the Beaver	Leave It to Beaver

THE TOP 50 TELEVISION SHOWS

These single broadcasts drew the largest audiences in TV history. Recently, only sporting events have scored on this list. (Source: Nielsen Media Research)

Rank	Program	Date
1.	M*A*S*H	February 28, 1983
2.	Dallas (Who Shot J.R.?)	November 21, 1980
3.	Roots, Part 8 (conclusion)	January 30, 1977
4.	Super Bowl XVI	January 24, 1982
5.	Super Bowl XVII	January 30, 1983
6.	Winter Olympics	February 23, 1994
7.	Super Bowl XX	January 26, 1986
8.	Gone with the Wind, Part 1	November 7, 1976
9.	Gone with the Wind, Part 2	November 8, 1976
10.	Super Bowl XII	January 15, 1978
11.	Super Bowl XIII	January 21, 1979
12.	Bob Hope Christmas Show	January 15, 1970
13.	Super Bowl XVIII (tie)	January 22, 1984
13.	Super Bowl XIX (tie)	January 20, 1985
15.	Super Bowl XIV	January 20, 1980
16.	Super Bowl XXX	January 28, 1996
17.	ABC Theater (The Day After)	November 20, 1983
18.	Roots, Part 6 (tie)	January 28, 1977
18.	The Fugitive (tie)	August 29, 1967
20.	Super Bowl XXI	January 25, 1987
21.	Roots, Part 5	January 27, 1977
22.	Super Bowl XXVIII (tie)	January 29, 1994
22.	Cheers (tie)	May 20, 1993
24.	The Ed Sullivan Show (TV debut of The Beatles)	February 9, 1964
25.	Super Bowl XXVII	January 31, 1993
26.	Bob Hope Christmas Show	January 14, 1971
27.	Roots, Part 3	January 25, 1977
28.	Super Bowl XI (tie)	January 9, 1977
28.	Super Bowl XV (tie)	January 25, 1981
30.	Super Bowl VI	January 16, 1972
31.	Winter Olympics (tie)	January 24, 1994
31.	Roots, Part 2 (tie)	January 24, 1977
33.	The Beverly Hillbillies	January 8, 1964
34.	Roots, Part 4 (tie)	January 26, 1977
34.	The Ed Sullivan Show (with The Beatles) (tie)	February 16, 1964
36.	Super Bowl XXIII	January 22, 1989
37.	The 43rd Academy Awards	April 7, 1970
38.	Super Bowl XXXI	January 26, 1997
39.	The Thorn Birds, Part 3	March 29, 1983
40.	The Thorn Birds, Part 4	March 30, 1983
41.	NFC championship game	January 10, 1982
42.	The Beverly Hillbillies	January 15, 1964
43.	Super Bowl VII	January 14, 1973
44.	Thorn Birds, Part 2	March 28, 1983
45.	Super Bowl IX (tie)	January 12, 1975
45.	The Beverly Hillbillies (tie)	February 26, 1964
47.	Super Bowl X (tie)	January 18, 1976
47.	Airport (tie)	November 11, 1973
47.	Love Story (tie)	October 1, 1972
47.	Cinderella (tie)	February 22, 1965
47.	Roots, Part 7 (tie)	January 29, 1977
52.	The Beverly Hillbillies	February 26, 1964

MOST WATCHED MOVIES ON TELEVISION

This list includes network prime-time feature films, both those made for theaters and those (including miniseries) made specifically for TV (*). Although *The Wizard of Oz*'s best showing misses our list at No. 34, many years of high ratings have made it overall the most popular movie ever shown on TV. (Source: Nielsen Media Research)

Rank	Movie	Air Date
1.	Roots, Part 8*	January 30, 1977
2.	Gone with the Wind, Part 1	November 7, 1976
3.	Gone with the Wind, Part 2	November 8, 1976
4.	The Day After*	November 20, 1983
5.	Roots, Part 6*	January 28, 1977
6.	Roots, Part 5*	January 27, 1977
7.	Roots, Part 3*	January 25, 1977
8.	Roots, Part 2*	January 24, 1977
9.	Roots, Part 4*	January 26, 1977
10.	The Thorn Birds, Part 3*	March 29, 1983
11.	The Thorn Birds, Part 4*	March 30, 1983
12.	The Thorn Birds, Part 2*	March 28, 1983
13.	Love Story (tie)	October 1, 1972
13.	Airport (tie)	November 11, 1973
13.	Roots, Part 7*	January 29, 1977
16.	The Winds of War, Part 7*	February 13, 1983
17.	Roots, Part 1	January 23, 1977
18.	The Winds of War, Part 2*	February 7, 1983
19.	The Thorn Birds, Part 1*	March 27, 1983
20.	The Godfather, Part 2	November 18, 1974
21.	Jaws	November 4, 1979
22.	The Poseidon Adventure	October 27, 1974
23.	The Birds (tie)	January 16, 1968
23.	True Grit (tie)	November 12, 1972
25.	Patton	November 19, 1972
26.	The Bridge on the River Kwai	September 25, 1966
27.	Jeremiah Johnson (tie)	January 18, 1976
27.	Helter Skelter, Part 2 (tie)*	April 2, 1976
29.	Rocky (tie)	February 4, 1979
29.	Ben-Hur (tie)	February 14, 1971

PEOPLE'S FAVORITE 50 TV STARS

The most popular TV personalities are not necessarily the most influential or prestigious. Often, they're performers who evoke smiles, empathy, good vibes—in short, the sort of folks you'd like to know in real life. This year, Farrah's out and Rosie's in. PEOPLE's deputy television editor, Michael A. Lipton, presents his all-star team:

JAMES ARNESS
With his weatherbeaten face, loping gait, and laconic delivery, he stood alone as TV's last—and best—Western hero when the gunsmoke finally cleared.

BEA ARTHUR
The first sitcom feminist: her foghorn voice, bristly authority, and, er, Maude-lin wit reduced mere men to spineless jellyfish.

LUCILLE BALL
Those lips (pouting ruefully), those eyes (pop-eyed with surprise), that voice ("Rick-kkkkky!"). Ay-yi-yi, since 1951, this kooky carrot-top always delivered 24-karat comedy.

JACK BENNY
Well! He got more laughs with That Look than Uncle Miltie ever did in a dress or Benny's old crony Burns did waving his cigar.

VALERIE BERTINELLI
She grew up, one day at a time, the achingly nubile girl next door, and blossomed into an empathetic TV-movie princess.

BILL BIXBY
A Martian's best friend, Eddie's widowed father, the Hulk's gentle alter ego, the ingratiating Bixby never seemed to wear out his welcome.

TOM BROKAW
With his genial smile and drawling delivery, he's more of an anchor *guy*, blessed with a straightforward self-assuredness that cements his credibility.

RAYMOND BURR
With his imposing baritone and X-ray eyes that penetrated the most ingenious alibis, Burr's Perry Mason never rested his defense till the guilty party (never, of course, his poor, framed client) confessed on the stand.

JOHNNY CARSON
Silver-haired, silver-tongued paterfamilias to Jay and Dave, this wise old night owl could give a hoot about returning to the throne he held for four glorious decades.

RICHARD CHAMBERLAIN
Let's see: '60s dreamboat Dr. Kildare leaves TV to Hamlet it up on the British stage, then triumphantly returns as the King of the Miniseries. There's gotta be a movie of the week here...

KATIE COURIC
She's your tomboyish kid sister all grown up, and while there's a mule-like kick to her interviews, her big heart and feisty twinkle keep her warm.

TONY DANZA
This onetime boxer rode a *Taxi* to fame, then showed *Who's the Boss* as star of his own long-running sitcom.

PHIL DONAHUE
"Caller, are you there?" Earnest, excitable, daring, and dashing (literally, into the audience), the snow-thatched maestro of daytime talk left no taboo unturned, no trauma untreated.

DAVID DUCHOVNY
A minimalist actor with sad, basset eyes and a sly-like-a-Fox sense of humor, he is the exemplar of '90s cool and cynicism. The Truth is not so far Out There.

LINDA EVANS
Prime-time soaps' poor little rich girl, she more than held her own against mean old Alexis. Even while (literally) slinging mud, her wholesome sexiness remained Krystle-clear.

PETER FALK
As the raincoat-rumpled detective with the frog-horn voice, Falk brought an ironic sense of mischief to his role as a regular guy besting the arrogant elites.

DENNIS FRANZ
The blustery, beer-bellied blue-collar joe as macho sex symbol. You got a problem with dat?

JAMES GARNER
Despite a body wracked by wear and tear, and a face etched with wisdom and woe, Garner remains TV's most credible—and comedic—action star.

JACKIE GLEASON
How sweet it was to see The Great One storm, scheme, and suffer as Ralph Kramden, the Willy Loman of bus drivers.

JOHN GOODMAN
As Roseanne's better—and slightly bigger—half, he is in many ways Gleason's heir as the hearty har-har working stiff, only blessed with an earthy realism that's hard to resist.

LARRY HAGMAN
So gleefully villainous, he made the viewer his grinning accomplice. We were completely in thrall of devilish J.R., TV's most hissable, kissable anti-hero.

ALFRED HITCHCOCK
TV transformed the film name into a household face—an erudite gargoyle whose drollery and drop-dead delivery made for a murderously marvelous one-man-show-within-the-show.

DAVID JANSSEN
A haggard, haunted underdog whose raspy voice and soulful brow served him brilliantly, whether playing fugitives or feds.

MICHAEL LANDON
From Little Joe Cartwright to big man on the prairie to angelic emissary, Landon made sentimentality a virtue, wrung drama out of decency, and rang true with each heartfelt performance.

ANGELA LANSBURY
How did Cabot Cove manage to rack up the nation's highest murder rate? Ask this nebbishy doyenne of TV crimesolvers.

LASSIE
The wonder dog of our childhood dreams.

JAY LENO
The hardest-working man in showbiz sweated bullets to show us he was as good as—or, as his ratings would indicate, better than—Letterman.

HEATHER LOCKLEAR
Her simultaneous stints as *Dynasty*'s vixenette and *T.J. Hooker*'s rookie cop in the '80s gave no hint she'd blossom (like poison ivy) into *Melrose Place*'s mellifluous villainess.

ELIZABETH MONTGOMERY
Sure, she bewitched us with that wiggly nose, but beyond the levity (and levitation), a serious TV-movie actress was in the wings.

MARY TYLER MOORE
She can still turn the world on with her smile. Yet for most of us, she'll always remain winsome single girl Mary Richards, her cap forever aloft, frozen in time.

LEONARD NIMOY
Who says a pointy-eared intellectual can't be a sex symbol? Star Trekkers melded their minds with Spock's and became one with the sci-fi universe.

ROSIE O'DONNELL
Okay, so she's no Oprah. But with her showbiz connections, breezy banter, and self-effacing, seat-of-the-pants wit, O'Donnell has revitalized daytime talk virtually overnight.

REGIS PHILBIN
Morning TV's twinkle-eyed curmudgeon, the perfect complement (and, perhaps, antidote) to self-absorbed Kathie Lee.

GILDA RADNER
The madcap heart and soul of the original *Saturday Night Live*.

DONNA REED
A suburban TV mom for the ages—smart, beautiful and sunny.

MICHAEL RICHARDS
A maniac for all seasons: all he has to do to get laughs is walk/stagger/glide/boogie/tumble through Seinfeld's door.

FRED ROGERS
It really was a beautiful day in the neighborhood when this genial, sweet, protective grown-up first sat down 30 years ago, laced up his sneakers, and became every kid's best friend.

ROY ROGERS
The quintessential TV cowboy, tall in the saddle, handy with a six-shooter, yet for the most part, just plain Trigger-happy.

FRED SAVAGE
The joys and agonies of adolescence were wonderfully expressed in Savage's tender, perpetually wide-eyed visage.

TOM SELLECK
TV's merriest manchild, he spent his Magnum opus living out every guy's fantasies—and has a bright new career in sitcoms.

JANE SEYMOUR
The queen of miniseries has settled down for a spell as a frontier sawbones—and is still elegance personified.

PHIL SILVERS
Ten-HUT! His Sgt. Bilko was a fast-squawking, never-balking con artist supreme who tweaked authority and energized '50s TV.

HOMER SIMPSON
Slobbus americanus, he eclipses his bratty son Bart, and has even been known to dispense pearls of Homer-spun wisdom.

SUZANNE SOMERS
A sitcom sexpot turned infomericial empress—no ifs, ands, or buttmasters about it.

RICHARD THOMAS
Forever boyish, dreamy-eyed, sensitively staring out moonlit windows, pen held to lips: the good son, the stalwart sib. G'night, John-Boy!

DICK VAN DYKE
Limber-limbed, rubber-faced, G-rated precursor to Jim Carrey, he could trip the light fantastic (even while tripping over an ottoman).

JUDGE JOSEPH WAPNER
Stern, wise, impartial, and impatient. The very model of a Supreme Court justice? Yes, and case closed.

VANNA WHITE
Fortune smiles on all who gaze upon the lovely Vanna. She turns letters—and heads—with a sensual body language all her own.

OPRAH WINFREY
So empathetic is this talk-show tsarina with her guests—and so upfront about herself it's scary—that she could be having a ball one day, and bawling the next.

HENRY WINKLER
Aaaaaaay! This retro '70s-cum-'50s sitcom star exuded the cool we all wished we'd had in our not-so-happy high school days.

PEOPLE'S 50 FORMATIVE SHOWS

The mark of all great television shows is their profound, or at least pervasive, impact on the pop culture. No sooner are they on the air than it's impossible to remember how we got along without them. Herewith, PEOPLE's shows of shows.

THE ADVENTURES OF SUPERMAN

More than 40 years later, this show starring George Reeves as the Man of Steel is still the only good superhero series TV has ever produced.

ALL IN THE FAMILY

At the heart of this epochal sitcom were the corrosive working-class prejudices of Archie Bunker, a Northern redneck. His political arguments with his liberal live-in son-in-law make *Crossfire* seem tame.

ALL MY CHILDREN

The soap trend-setter has tackled big social and medical issues without ever losing a grip on its primary imperative: addictive story-telling.

THE ANDY GRIFFITH SHOW

The precursor of the so-called rusticoms of the '60s, this quiet masterpiece had heart, humor, wisdom, and—often overlooked— an outstanding cast. The launching pad for *Gomer Pyle, U.S.M.C* and *Mayberry R.F.D.*

THE BEVERLY HILLBILLIES

Yee ha! The most outrageous yokel yuk-fest this side of *Li'l Abner.* Bonus points for TV's most recognizable theme song.

BONANZA

It was that larger-than-life clan, the Cartwrights, that made the Ponderosa worth visiting every week.

THE BULLWINKLE SHOW

Jay Ward's kaleidoscopic, pun-crammed cartoon about a dense moose and a plucky flying squirrel delighted kids of all ages.

BURNS AND ALLEN

This iconoclastic '50s show gleefully disregarded TV tradition, including the observance of "the fourth wall." The comic chemistry between this old vaudeville team has never been duplicated.

CANDID CAMERA

"When you least expect it/You're elected/You're the star today." Alan Funt milked hilarious results from simply filming people in situations when they thought no one was watching.

CHARLIE'S ANGELS

A brilliant TV concept: staff a standard detective show with a gorgeous trio (Farrah Fawcett, Kate Jackson, and Jaclyn Smith) in sausage-skin clothing. This was producer Aaron Spelling's first megahit and his finest hour.

CHEERS

The pluperfect pinnacle of the sitcom genre.

THE COSBY SHOW

Witty, warm, and winning, the domestic experiences of the Huxtables touted family values without sermonizing.

THE DICK VAN DYKE SHOW

The first TV comedy to thoroughly exploit dual settings. For the first half of the '60s, the only place on the planet funnier than the Petrie household was Rob's office at the apocryphal *Alan Brady Show.*

DRAGNET

The show's deliberately laconic style ("Just the facts, ma'am") only underscored the gritty power of its tales of cops and miscreants.

DYNASTY

The squabbles of the Carringtons proved that the rich really are different than you and me: they dress swankily while hatching Byzantine plots of revenge against one another.

FAWLTY TOWERS

John Cleese starred as an apoplectic innkeeper in this import, a remarkably seamless slapstick farce.

GUNSMOKE

TV's archetypal and longest running Western.

HILL STREET BLUES

Creator Steven Bochco spiced up his precinct house gumbo with a rich slate of characters, multi-tiered narratives, wry humor and a dash of fatalism.

THE HONEYMOONERS

The antics of a bus driver and a sewer worker in a Brooklyn tenement yielded a priceless vein of American humor. Jackie Gleason and Art Carney were sublime.

JEOPARDY

The thinking person's game show.

L.A. LAW

A powerhouse legal drama complex, unpredictable, imaginative and always rewarding.

THE LARRY SANDERS SHOW

This sardonic backstage tour of a talk show is TV's funniest satire, perhaps because we love to see the medium mock itself.

LEAVE IT TO BEAVER

Took the familiar family sitcom formula of the '50s and gave it a devious adolescent twist. Show stealer: Eddie Haskell

MARY HARTMAN, MARY HARTMAN
And now for something completely different. This soap opera spoof presented everyday life in Fernwood, Ohio as a pastiche of country song, floor wax commercial, and Kurt Vonnegut novel.

THE MARY TYLER MOORE SHOW
A magical confluence of concept, cast, and material made this the high watermark of '70s television.

M*A*S*H
Hands-down, the most successful series ever spun off from a feature film. The comedy lasted eight years longer than the Korean War had.

MIAMI VICE
Against a gaudy SoFlo backdrop of neon and pastels, cute cops chase after well-armed cocaine cowboys in flashy sport scars and cigarette boats. The only reason TV has ever furnished to stay home on Friday nights.

MISSION: IMPOSSIBLE
Your mission, should you decide to accept it, is to name a better adventure series than this taut, gripping espionage exercise.

THE MONKEES
Rock music reared its unruly head in primetime with this madcap, faux-psychedelic '60s comedy about a perky pop quartet. Groundbreaking for its time, even if the show soon settled into lame Stooges schtick.

NIGHTLINE
A provident opportunity to hash out the day's big news event.

N.Y.P.D. BLUE
The most electrifying cop show since *Naked City* (1958-63). Acute and suspenseful, *Blue* roars by like a runaway train.

THE ODD COUPLE
Opposites amuse, but never so much as in this impeccably cast, tone-perfect comedy about a pair of mismatched, middle-aged, Manhattan neo-bachelors.

THE ROCKFORD FILES
The couch potato's choice: a sly, undemanding, endlessly entertaining delight.

ROSEANNE
An adventurous, abrasive, authentic and always amusing examination of the struggles of a working-class family.

ROWAN AND MARTIN'S LAUGH-IN
With zany banter, double entendres, and go-go dancers (including Goldie Hawn), this late-'60s comedy cavalcade nudged TV into the age of hipsters.

ST. ELSEWHERE
Piquant and volatile, this Jack-in-the-box drama about a lesser Boston hospital ran from intense tragedy to bawdy comedy.

SEINFELD
An hermetic, exquisitely maintained comedy of contemporary urban manners and mores.

SESAME STREET
This jauntily educational PBS series for pre-schoolers is culturally diverse, inventive and altogether admirable.

77 SUNSET STRIP
The most influential of the Sputnik-era private eye series was this ultra-cool conceit which starred Efrem Zimbalist Jr. and Roger Smith as a pair of suave, college-educated judo experts.

THE SIMPSONS
You'd need a shelf full of books like this Almanac and a crack research staff to run down all the pop culture references in a single episode of this puckish cartoon about the post-nuclear family.

60 MINUTES
The ultimate news magazine.

STAR TREK
This notorious cult favorite was little-honored during its original '60s run but became a rerun staple and has launched a thriving industry of spin-offs.

THIRTYSOMETHING
Though dismissed by cynics as yuppie whining, this was in fact a drama of rare pathos, complexity and insight.

TODAY
The oldest, and in our book, the best of the matinal infotainment bandwagons.

THE TONIGHT SHOW
It's a tradition as comfortable as flannel pajamas: awaiting the Sandman while watching Johnny's (and now Jay's) guests play musical chairs.

THE TWILIGHT ZONE
This spine-tingling supernatural anthology was penetrating, often profound, but above all, singularly spooky.

WALT DISNEY PRESENTS
Over four decades, under a variety of banners and working alternately for each of the three major networks, the Disney studio consistently turned out the tube's finest, most indelible family fare.

THE X-FILES
"The truth is out there." Really out there. But week after week, this suspenseful series transforms paranormal and outright bizarre concepts into gripping, credible drama.

YOU BET YOUR LIFE
This '50s series was ostensibly a quiz show, but in fact that was merely a pretext for host Groucho Marx to sharpen his legendary wit on a succession of contestants.

YOUR SHOW OF SHOWS
The apex of the variety show, this '50s favorite thrived on the astoundingly versatile comedic talents of Sid Caesar and Imogene Coca and a stable of writers that included Mel Brooks, Larry Gelbart, Neil Simon, and Woody Allen.

NICK AT NITE'S CLASSIC TV COUNTDOWN

In the land of reruns, 1996 was a breakthrough year. Retro-TV references abounded in pop culture, and Nick at Nite led the way, spinning off a new 24-hour network: TV Land. This new trove of TV rarities led to a fresh "Top 25" slate of honorees in the eighth annual Classic TV Countdown. As always, the selections are based on viewer requests, ratings, critical favor, pre-fame celebrity guest stars, show landmarks (first episodes, marriages, and births), and quintessential moments or bizarre plot twists.

1996 SELECTIONS

1 *The Odd Couple,* "Password"

Well, now everybody does know that Aristophanes wrote a famous play called *The Birds,* and it's a well-known fact that Abraham Lincoln loved mayonnaise, but when Felix offered these clues to Oscar, it led only to an unforgettable episode, named by both Jack Klugman and Tony Randall as one of their all-time favorites.

2 *Happy Days,* "Richie Fights Back"

There's only so tough you can be with a "Howdy-Doody" face, but the classic performances by Ron Howard and Henry Winkler create a quintessential episode as Richie attempts to remake himself in the Fonz's image.

3 *I Love Lucy,* "Lucy Makes a TV Commercial"

It's "Vitameatavegamin" (in case you've always wondered how to spell it) and perhaps the single greatest comic soliloquy in TV history.

4 *Green Acres,* "How To Succeed in Television Without Really Trying"

From a show that explored the postmodern territory of self-referential and surrealist comedy comes the ultimate paradigm: a show in which Oliver accidentally makes a TV show, and lights up Hooterville's Nielsen ratings, too!

5 *The Dick Van Dyke Show,* "Coast to Coast Big Mouth"

A perennial on the Countdown charts, this masterpiece features Laura Petrie's accidental revelation on national TV that Alan Brady wears a toupee and the hilarious apology scene that is perhaps writer-producer-actor Carl Reiner's single finest on-screen performance.

6 *Taxi,* "Love Un-American Style"

Another classic example of the comic sparks that can result "When Sitcoms Collide!" Latka and Simka celebrate their love with a traditional matchmaking event called a Schloogel. In it, Rev. Jim's dream date is none other than actress Marcia Wallace—Dr. Bob Hartley's receptionist, "Carol."

7 *The Bob Newhart Show,* "Ex-Con Job"

This episode features one of the most unforgettable moments of the many that this show created—when Howard enters Bob and Emily's apartment, sees them with their hands against the wall being held at gunpoint, and immediately surmises that there is a hold-up in progress...and runs over to help them "hold-up" the wall.

8 *The Sonny & Cher Show,* "Smothers Brothers Guest"

Two giants of comedy-variety, actually two pairs of two giants each, making four giants of comedy-variety on one show.

9 *Happy Days,* "The Deadly Dares"

From Uncle Miltie to Flip's Geraldine to Bosom Buddies, men wearing dresses has been a staple of television comedy. In this episode not only do Richie and Ralph don women's clothing, but the Fonz does too! (A nightie no less.)

10 *Bewitched,* "Divided, He Falls"

Dick York at his gawky, sputtering best—split into two Darrins—the fun-loving one who suggests that Sam "whap up some champagne" and the hard-working one who bores poor Larry Tate to tears with his unrelenting marketing suggestions.

11 *The Phil Silvers Show,* "The Eating Contest"

One of the many fine Bilko shows, this one stands out both for Silver's usual hilarious conniving and the small-screen debut of Fred Gwynne, who went on to play Muldoon in *Car 54* and then effectively ended his TV career by becoming nationally recognized as Herman Munster.

12 *The Munsters,* "Movie Star Munster"

A classic show meets a classic TV plotline—an unlikely character suddenly thrust into potential movie stardom. In this case, who else but Herman?

13 *The Odd Couple,* "Songwriter"

Wolfman Jack guest stars, as does Jaye P. Morgan, but most importantly, Felix pens the immortal lyrics: "Happy and peppy and bursting with love."

14 *Rhoda,* "Rhoda's Wedding, Part 2"

Of TV's many famous on-screen weddings—from Mr. Peepers to Luke and Laura—this one stands out above all. Of course, as we all know, the marriage only lasted about 40 episodes.

15 *Rhoda,* "Rhoda's Wedding, Part 1"

It was created as a single hour-long episode. At the time it originally aired, this episode set a ratings record, becoming the most-watched sitcom ever.

16 *Mary Tyler Moore,* "Chuckles Bites the Dust"

Though it slipped down to #16 on these charts, this classic among classics was later named by TV Land and *TV Guide* as the #1 episode of all time in the "100 All-Time Greatest Episodes" issue.

17 *The Addams Family,* "Amnesia in the Family"

It's the single most popular neurological disorder in TV Land—Superman, Lucy, Rob Pertrie, even Flipper have suffered bouts of memory loss following blows to the head. And in this memorable episode, it's Gomez who takes the hit.

18 *I Dream of Jeannie,* "My Master the Weakling"

There's nothing like a classic TV guest star—Paul Lynde, Sammy Davis Jr., or in this case, Don Rickles. He plays a sadistic and maniacal physical fitness instructor with his irresistible rubber-faced scowl.

19 *The Odd Couple,* "Subway Story"

After a debate about the basic goodness of New York City's people, Felix and Oscar find themselves trapped on a subway with a random assortment of the citizenry and get to test their hypotheses. Felix introduces "Harvey Hankie" to his fellow straphangers.

20 *Mister Ed,* "Leo Durocher Meets Mr. Ed"

America's favorite talking horse is an observant baseball fan, whose phone calls offering advice to Leo Durocher lead to a visit to Dodger Stadium, many guest-starring roles by the 1963 Dodgers, and a memorable trot around the basepaths by Ed himself.

21 *I Love Lucy,* "Job Switching"

With *I Love Lucy* running in syndication ever since it went off the air—both years and in countries throughout the world—we estimate there are approximately one billion people alive today who still know what episode you mean when you say "the chocolate factory."

22 *Happy Days,* "Date with Fonzie"

Garry Marshall's hit creation spawned a number of spin-offs—*Mork and Mindy* and *Joanie Loves Chachi* were two—but the best-loved spin-off of them all began with this episode, as the world met Shirley and her pal Laverne for the very first time.

23 *Mary Tyler Moore,* "Ted Baxter's Famous Broadcasters' School"

The pompous newscaster is talked into a money-making scheme and drags the entire newsroom down with him. As the "school song" puts it: "We have no gym, we have no pool, but we have heart, at Ted Baxter's Famous Broadcasters' School."

24 *That Girl,* "This Little Piggy Had a Ball"

The classic "big toe stuck in a bowling ball" storyline—and not only that, but this episode is peppered with tasty cameo appearances. Dabney Coleman, Rob Reiner, and Teri Garr all appear in bit parts—but of course the bowling ball is the star.

25 *I Dream of Jeannie,* "Jeannie the Hip Hippie"

There's nothing funnier than the sitcoms in which 1960s establishment Hollywood tried to portray "Hippie" culture, and no show did it with more frequency or verve than "Jeannie."

...U GET TICKETS TO TELEVISION SHOWS

...what you want about television, but at least it's free (more or less). Not only that, ...ut you can also obtain free tickets to see talk shows, game shows, and situation comedies, most of which tape in New York, Chicago, or Los Angeles. Here's how.

NEW YORK

THE DAILY SHOW

Speak with a show representative at (212) 560-3135 between 11 a.m. and 5 p.m., or visit www.comedycentral.com/dailyshow to order tickets electronically. Ticket requests are handled ...wo to three months ahead of the ...aping. *The Daily Show* generally ...es in the evening, Monday ...gh Thursday. You may ...st up to four tickets. You ...e 18 or older to attend.

...LDO

... self-addressed stamped ...ope with your ticket ...st to *Geraldo* Tickets, CBS ...ision, 524 W. 57th Street, ... York, NY 10019. For ...rded information about tick... and the taping schedule, call ...2) 265-1283.

...ATE NIGHT WITH CONAN O'BRIEN

Mail one postcard per show (no ...etters) with name, address, and ...umber of tickets desired (a max...um of eight on Tuesday to ...ursday tapings, five on Friday ...ngs): *Late Night* Tickets, c/o ...C, 30 Rockefeller Plaza, New ...k, NY 10112. The wait list is ...ut one month, and the ticket ...ill ... ...ir best to accom... ... lim-

(same address as above). Standbys are given out one per person on a first-come–first-serve basis and do not guarantee admission. Minimum age is 16. For more information call (212) 664-3057 or (212) 664-3056 for an updated schedule of shows.

LATE SHOW WITH DAVID LETTERMAN

Send a postcard with name and address to *Late Show* Tickets, Ed Sullivan Theater, 1697 Broadway, New York, NY 10019. Tickets are usually mailed within six months; if no response is received, another card should be sent. Only two tickets are issued per request, and specific dates cannot generally be accommodated. There are, however, about 100 tickets available at the theater each day of taping, with a waiting line forming very early in the morning; veterans arrive before 6 a.m. In addition, standby numbers are issued each day at noon. It is recommended that the studio audience dress warmly since the studio is kept cold during taping. Minimum age is 16.

LIVE WITH REGIS AND KATHIE LEE

Send a postcard with your name, address, phone number, and the number of tickets desired (limit of four per request) to *Live* Tickets, Ansonia Station, P.O. Box 777, New York, NY 10023-0777. There is a twelve-month wait for tickets. On show days, a limited number of standby tickets are issued on a first-come–first-serve basis on West 67th Street and Columbus Avenue at 8 a.m., but these tickets do not guarantee admission. Minimum age is 18. Ticket holders may be required to show ID before entering the studio, and it is suggested that you dress warmly to attend the taping, as the studio is kept cold. For more ticket and taping information call (212) 456-3537.

THE MAURY POVICH SHOW

For ticket information and taping schedules call the ticket hotline, (212) 989-3622, and leave a message indicating your name, address, phone number, the number of tickets (maximum of two), and dates desired. Booking is generally done one month in advance, and a representative will mail the tickets and information to you. Once you have received the tickets, call (212) 989-8800 to confirm or cancel your reservations. Standby tickets are available starting at 9:15 a.m. on the day of the taping at the studio on 221 West 26th Street. You must be at least 16 to attend.

THE MONTEL WILLIAMS SHOW

Send your name, address, phone number, and the number of tickets desired to Montel Williams Tickets, 433 W. 53rd St., New York, NY 10019. Tickets are also available by phone request. Call the ticket line at (212) 830-0364 for more information. There is a minimum age of 18 and a dressy-casual dress code; no white shirts, hats, or scarves on the head are permitted.

RICKI LAKE

Send a postcard with your address and number of tickets desired to *The Ricki Lake Show,* Ticket Office, 401 Fifth Avenue, 7th Floor, New York, NY 10016. Tickets are distributed on a first-come–first-serve basis two to three weeks before the show and do not guarantee admission. There is a limit of four tickets per request. Standby tickets are also available at the studio, 2 East 37th Street, one hour before taping. You must be at least 18 to attend. For further information and schedules of topics, speak with a representative at (212) 889-6767.

THE ROSIE O'DONNELL SHOW

Send a postcard requesting tickets to *The Rosie O'Donnell Show,* c/o NBC, 30 Rockefeller Plaza, New York, NY 10012. There is a waiting list approximately one year long. However, standby tickets are available on the day of the show at the side entrance of the GE Building on West 49th Street, opposite the Rockefeller Center Garage. These tickets are distributed at 8 a.m. Minimum age is five years old.

SALLY JESSY RAPHAEL

Send a postcard with your address and the number of tickets desired to *Sally Jessy Raphael* Tickets, P.O. Box 1400, Radio City Station, New York, NY 10101. Or call (212) 582-1722, ext. 213 or 272, for ticket and taping information between 8:30 a.m. and 5:00 p.m., Monday through Friday. Standby tickets are also available on taping days at 8:30 a.m. at 515 West 57th Street.

SATURDAY NIGHT LIVE

To obtain tickets for next season, send one postcard (no letters) with your name and address to *Saturday Night Live* Tickets, c/o NBC, 30 Rockefeller Plaza, New York, NY 10112. NBC accepts postcards during the month of August only, and these requests will be entered into a lottery drawing. If you are are selected, you will be notified by mail two weeks in advance that you have received two tickets to either the dress rehearsal or the live broadcast. *SNL* tapes only from September to May. It is not possible to request specific dates, but about 100 standby tickets are available on the Saturdays of original shows at 9:15 a.m. at the side entrance of the GE Building on West 49th Street, opposite the Rockefeller Center Garage. Standbys are given on a first-come–first-serve basis, and only one per person; they do not guarantee admission. You must be 16 or over to attend. For more information call (212) 664-3057 or 664-3056. Phone reservations are not available.

THE VICKI LAWRENCE SHOW

Send a postcard to *The Vicki Lawrence Show,* P.O. Box 900 Madison Square Station, New York, NY 10059. You may also call (212) 802-4052 or fax (212) 802-4207. Include your name, address, daytime phone, and requested show date. Tickets are distributed on a first-come–first-serve basis. The show is taped live on weekdays at 9:00 a.m. A standby line forms before that time at the studio at 212 Fifth Avenue. Minimum age is 10.

CHICAGO

THE JENNY JONES SHOW

Call (312) 836-9485 to make reservations at least six to eight weeks in advance or to obtain standby information. Callers should be prepared to provide the specific date they would like to attend. The minimum age is 18.

THE JERRY SPRINGER SHOW

Write 454 North Columbus Drive, Chicago, IL 60611 with your name, address, local phone number, number of tickets, and date desired, or call (312) 32 5365. Requests should be ma at least one month in advanc Tickets are generally maile one to three weeks before t taping, and there is a minim age of 18 required to atten Audience members may no shorts and must present prop identification before entering studio for the taping.

OPRAH

Tickets are not available by ma but reservations to appear in th studio audience can be made by calling (312) 591-9222. These lines are often busy as soon as the caller line opens at 9 a.m. Central Time. Reservations are taken no more than 30 days in advance of the show. Audience members must be 18 years old over with a photo ID. Children 16 and 17 may attend only if accompanied by a parent with birth certificate identification.

LOS ANGELES

THE KEENEN IVORY WAYANS SHOW

Call the ticket line at (213) 769-5538 and leave your name and telephone number. The show tapes Monday through Friday at 3 p.m. You must be 18 to attend.

THE TONIGHT SHOW WITH JAY LENO

Send a self-addressed, stamped envelope with the date of the show you would like to see and the number of tickets desired (requests are limited to four per card) to NBC Tickets, 3000 W. Alameda Ave., Burbank, CA 91523. Tickets will be sent two to three weeks before the show. On the day of tapings, tickets are also available at the Burbank ticket counter off the California Street side of the studio facility. Hours are 8 a.m.–5 p.m., Monday through Friday, but arrive early as tickets are distributed on a first-come–first-serve basis. The minimum age to attend is 16. For recorded ticket information, taping schedules, group bookings, and directions to the Burbank, California studios, call NBC Studios at (818) 840-3537.

VIBE

Call the hotline at (213) 520-1201 or write 7800 Beverly Blvd., East Building, Room 258, CA 90036. The show tapes Monday through Friday at 4:30 p.m.

LEEZA, FRASIER, FIRED UP, AND MORE

Paramount Guest Relations handles the reservations for shows such as *Jenny, Moesha, In the House, Home Team with Terry Bradshaw, Late Line, Sister, Sister, Hitz, George & Leo, Dharma & Greg*, and *Union Square*. A limited number of priority admission reservations are available by calling Paramount Guest Relations at (213) 956-1777 between 9 a.m. and 6 p.m., Monday through Friday. Reservations are taken on a first-come–first-serve basis while the supply lasts. Reservations become available beginning five working days in advance of each scheduled show. Production schedules vary from week to week. For recorded ticket and taping information call the Paramount Studio guest relations line at (213) 956-5575.

FRIENDS AND OTHER SERIES

Audiences Unlimited distributes limited numbers of tickets for many of the situation comedies shot before live audiences in the Los Angeles area. They have tickets for favorites such as *Friends, Home Improvement, Mad About You, Murphy Brown, 3rd Rock from the Sun, Caroline in the City, Cybill, Everybody Loves Raymond, Family Matters, Suddenly Susan, The Drew Carey Show, The Naked Truth,* and *Ellen*. They also distribute tickets for new shows like *Veronica's Closet* and *The Gregory Hines Show,* and even award shows.

For a recorded message giving a weekly list of tickets available, the times and locations of taping, call (818) 753-3470. A one-month advance show taping-filming schedule is available by phone or by sending a self-addressed, stamped envelope to Audiences Unlimited, 100 Universal City Plaza, Building 153, Universal City, CA 91608. Tickets are available by mail from the same address.

Some shows, such as *Friends* and *Home Improvment,* are available by mail order only, and there is typically a four- to six-month wait. Tickets are mailed ten days to two weeks prior to show date and are limited for all shows, so include alternate choices.

The Audiences Unlimited Website, www.tvtickets.com, is another source of information. Tickets can be distributed for most shows by e-mail.

There is a six-ticket maximum per request. Minimum age is generally 16 or 18, depending on the show. No standby tickets are available.

HOW TO GET ON AUDIENCE-PARTICIPATION SHOWS

We all play along with the game shows when we watch at home, but only a few of us make it onto the air to play the games for real. Here are the wheres and hows on becoming a contestant on the leading shows.

JEOPARDY!

Every year, over 15,000 trivia buffs apply for some 400 contestant slots. All contestants must first pass a fifty-question test. Los Angeles test dates are available from the *Jeopardy!* contestant line, (310) 280-5367, Monday through Friday from 10:00 to 4:30. The test dates are scheduled intermittently throughout the year, so call two to three weeks prior to being in the Los Angeles area to schedule an appointment. For information about out-of-town and tournament contestant searches watch your local *Jeopardy!* station for announcements. Successful test-takers are invited to play a mock version of the game, and if that goes well they may be called to be scheduled as a contestant, up to one month to one year after the tryout.

To participate in the studio audience, send a self-addressed stamped envelope to *Jeopardy!* Tickets, 10202 W. Washington Boulevard, Culver City, CA 90232. Neither phone reservations nor standby tickets are available. *Jeopardy!* is generally taped Tuesdays and Wednesdays, with five shows each day. For recorded information about taping and schedules, call (310) 280-8856

MTV

MTV airs several shows with audience participants, contestants, and dancers, among them *Singled Out, The Grind,* and the annual spring break and summertime specials. Many of these shows require auditions and/or advance reservations. MTV sets up individual audience participation hotlines for each show that will be taped. Hotline numbers are broadcast on MTV and on local radio stations approximately one month to two weeks before each event. Shows involving extensive participation, such as *Real World* and *Road Rules,* generally require a 10-minute audition video. More information can be found on the MTV Website (www.mtv.com) or by calling the Viewer Service Hotline at (212) 258-8700.

THE PRICE IS RIGHT

Since all of the contestants on *The Price Is Right* are selected from the audience, call CBS Tickets in Los Angeles at (213) 852-2449 for the most up-to-date taping schedule and ticket information. Tickets can be requested by sending a card noting your preferred date and number of tickets and a self-addressed, stamped envelope to *The Price Is Right* Tickets, Television City, 7800 Fairfax Boulevard, Los Angeles, CA 90036. Allow four to six weeks for delivery. Tickets are also available from the ticket window at the above address on the day of the taping; priority numbers are distributed starting at 7:30 a.m. *The Price Is Right* is usually taped on Mondays, Tuesdays, and Wednesdays at 1:15 and 4:45. Ticketholders are processed several hours before each taping begins for name tag distribution, interviews, and admission to the studio. You must be 18 or older.

WHEEL OF FORTUNE

To try out as a contestant, send a postcard with your name, address, and phone number to *Wheel of Fortune*, 10202 Washington Boulevard, Room 5300, Culver City, CA 90232. Candidates whose postcards are randomly selected will be given auditions. Contestant auditions are held sporadically throughout the year, both in Los Angeles and during contestant searches around the U.S. Auditions involve a fill-in-the-blank test and a mock game. The most up-to-date information on auditions is available by calling (213) 520-5555, Monday through Friday, from 10:00 a.m. to 6:00 p.m. Pacific Standard Time. For information on attending the show as an audience member call (800) 482-9840.

STARS WITH SOAPY ROOTS

Many of the most familiar faces in the entertainment world first appeared on the small screen of daytime TV. Test your soap-opera memory against our list.

Actor	Character	Soap
Richard Dean Anderson	Dr. Jeff Webber	General Hospital
Armand Assante	Dr. Mike Powers	The Doctors
Kevin Bacon	Tim Werner	Guiding Light
Alec Baldwin	Billy Allison Aldrich	The Doctors
Bonnie Bedelia	Sandy Porter	Love of Life
Tom Berenger	Timmy Siegel	One Life To Live
Corbin Bernsen	Kenny Graham	Ryan's Hope
Yasmine Bleeth	Ryan Fenelli	Ryan's Hope
Carol Burnett	Verla Grubbs	All My Children
Ellen Burstyn	Dr. Kate Bartok	The Doctors
Kate Capshaw	Jinx Avery Mallory	The Edge of Night
Tia Carrere	Jade Soong	General Hospital
Dixie Carter	Olivia Brandeis "Brandy" Henderson	The Edge of Night
Nell Carter	Ethel Green	Ryan's Hope
Shaun Cassidy	Dusty Walker	General Hospital
Lacey Chabert	Bianca Montgomery	All My Children
Jill Clayburgh	Grace Bolton	Search for Tomorrow
Dabney Coleman	Dr. Tracy Brown	Bright Promise
Courteney Cox	Bunny	As the World Turns
Ted Danson	Tim Conway	Somerset
Olympia Dukakis	Barbara Moreno	Search for Tomorrow
Morgan Fairchild	Jennifer Phillips	Search for Tomorrow
Laurence Fishburne	Joshua West	One Life To Live
Vivica A. Fox	Dr. Stephanie Simmons	The Young and the Restless
Morgan Freeman	Roy Bingham	Another World
Sarah Michelle Gellar	Kendall Hart	All My Children
Kelsey Grammer	Dr. Canard	Another World

Marisa Tomei on As the World Turns.

Courteney Cox on As the World Turns.

Actor	Character	Soap
Charles Grodin	Matt Crane	The Young Marrieds
Larry Hagman	Ed Gibson	The Edge of Night
Mark Hamill	Kent Murray	General Hospital
David Hasselhoff	Bill "Snapper" Foster	The Young and the Restless
Anne Heche	Marley Hudson	Another World
Lauren Holly	Julie Chandler	All My Children
Kate Jackson	Daphne Harridge	Dark Shadows
James Earl Jones	Dr. Jim Frazier	Guiding Light
Tommy Lee Jones	Dr. Mark Toland	One Life To Live
Raul Julia	Miguel Garcia	Love of Life
Kevin Kline	Woody Reed	Search for Tomorrow
Don Knotts	Wilbur Peabody	Search for Tomorrow
Téa Leoni	Lisa Di Napoli	Santa Barbara
Judith Light	Karen Martin	One Life To Live
Hal Linden	Larry Carter	Search for Tomorrow
Ray Liotta	Joey Perini	Another World
Marsha Mason	Judith Cole	Love of Life
Demi Moore	Jackie Templeton	General Hospital
Kate Mulgrew	Mary Ryan Fenelli	Ryan's Hope
Luke Perry	Ned Bates	Loving
Regis Philbin	Malachy Malone	Ryan's Hope
Phylicia Rashad	Courtney Wright	One Life To Live
Christopher Reeve	Benno ("Beanie" or "Ben") Harper	Love of Life
Eric Roberts	Ted Bancroft	Another World
Meg Ryan	Betsy Stewart	As the World Turns
Pat Sajak	Kevin Hathaway	Days of Our Lives
Susan Sarandon	Sarah	Search for Tomorrow
Kyra Sedgwick	Julia Shearer	Another World
Tom Selleck	Jed Andrews	The Young and the Restless
Christian Slater	D. J. LaSalle	Ryan's Hope
Rick Springfield	Dr. Noah Drake	General Hospital
John Stamos	Blackie Parrish	General Hospital
Marisa Tomei	Marcy Thompson	As the World Turns
Janine Turner	Laura Templeton	General Hospital
Kathleen Turner	Nola Dancy Aldrich	The Doctors
Cicely Tyson	Martha Frazier	Guiding Light
Blair Underwood	Bobby Blue	One Life To Live
Jack Wagner	Frisco Jones	General Hospital
Christopher Walken	Michael Bauer	Guiding Light
Sigourney Weaver	Avis Ryan	Somerset
Billy Dee Williams	Dr. Jim Frazier	Guiding Light
JoBeth Williams	Brandy Sheloo	Guiding Light
Robin Wright	Kelly Capwell	Santa Barbara

PRIME TIME'S TOP 40

There's something infectious about television theme songs. Here are the ones that hit highest on the *Billboard* charts. (The list excludes songs that were hits prior to their adoption as television anthems.)

Song	Show	Performer	Chart Position/Year
I'll Be There for You*	Friends	The Rembrandts	1/1995
S.W.A.T.	S.W.A.T.	Rhythm Heritage	1/1975
Welcome Back	Welcome Back, Kotter	John Sebastian	1/1976
Miami Vice	Miami Vice	Jan Hammer	1/1985
Believe It or Not	The Greatest American Hero	Joey Scarbury	2/1981
Dragnet	Dragnet	Ray Anthony Orchestra	3/1953
Secret Agent Man	Secret Agent Man	Johnny Rivers	3/1966
Hawaii Five-O	Hawaii Five-O	The Ventures	4/1969
Happy Days	Happy Days	Pratt and McClain	5/1976
Makin' It	Makin' It	David Naughton	5/1979
Peter Gunn	Peter Gunn	Ray Anthony Orchestra	8/1959
Three Stars Will Shine Tonight	Dr. Kildare	Richard Chamberlain	10/1962
The Rockford Files	The Rockford Files	Mike Post	10/1975
Hill Street Blues	Hill Street Blues	Mike Post and Larry Carlton	10/1981
Zorro	Zorro	The Chordettes	17/1958
Batman	Batman	The Marketts	17/1966
Different Worlds	Angie	Maureen McGovern	18/1979
Bonanza	Bonanza	Al Caiola	19/1961
Keep Your Eye on the Sparrow	Baretta	Rhythm Heritage	20/1976
Mr. Lucky	Mr. Lucky	Henry Mancini Orchestra	21/1960
The Dukes of Hazzard	The Dukes of Hazzard	Waylon Jennings	21/1980
Moonlighting	Moonlighting	Al Jarreau	23/1987
Making Our Dreams Come True	Laverne & Shirley	Cyndi Grecco	25/1976
Magnum, P.I.	Magnum, P.I.	Mike Post	25/1982
Ben Casey	Ben Casey	Valjean	28/1962
Blue Star	Medic	Felicia Sanders	29/1955
Route 66	Route 66	Nelson Riddle Orchestra	30/1962
Ballad of Paladin	Have Gun Will Travel	Duane Eddy	33/1962
Seattle	Here Come the Brides	Perry Como	38/1969
The Men	The Men	Isaac Hayes	38/1972
Mission: Impossible	Mission: Impossible	Lalo Schifrin	41/1968
Those Were the Days	All in the Family	Carroll O'Connor and Jean Stapleton	43/1971
The Ballad of Jed Clampett	Beverly Hillbillies	Lester Flatt and Earl Scruggs	44/1962
Charlie's Angels	Charlie's Angels	Henry Mancini	45/1977
Dynasty	Dynasty	Bill Conti	52/1982
My Three Sons	My Three Sons	Lawrence Welk Orchestra	55/1961

*Reached No. 1 on *Billboard's* Hot 100 Airplay Chart before release as an A-side single; upon release, reached No. 17 on *Billboard's* Hot 100 Singles Chart.

THE GREATEST COMMERCIALS OF ALL TIME

To commemorate the TV ad's first five decades, the editors of *Advertising Age* have selected the era's 50 finest spots. Judged on the basis of their creativity, durability, and longevity, these are the commercials that made us laugh, cry, and—most importantly—buy. Source: © Crain Communications Inc., Spring 1995 and May 26, 1997 issues

1940s

Gillette
A well-recognized radio jingle—"Look sharp, feel sharp..." is put to animation in one of the first regularly run TV commercials.

Lucky Strike
Dancing cigarettes twirl and swing and wind up in the Luckies pack for the concluding L.S.M.F.T. slogan—Lucky Strike Means Fine Tobacco.

Texaco
The be-all and end-all of the early days of commercial TV, with the singing "men from Texaco... who work from Maine to Mexico" getting every product plug imaginable into their weekly song.

1950s

Alka-Seltzer
Speedy Alka-Seltzer, the walking, talking tablet from early '50s-style "stop motion" became a certified classic before giving way to the creative revolution of the '60s.

Anacin
This early spot positioned Anacin as a "tension headache" remedy by fancifully diagramming a tension headache—and probably causing them all over America.

Chevrolet
When Dinah Shore sang "See the USA in your Chevrolet" on her popular TV show, America made the car the No. 1 name plate on the new interstate highway system and in suburbia.

Timex
The famous "takes a licking and keeps on ticking" watch torture test began its 20-year-plus run.

1960s

Maxwell House
With the catchy "Good to the Last Drop" slogan and a catchier audiovisual mnemonic (the bubbling coffee sound), Maxwell House evoked the smell and flavor of brewed coffee, and sales percolated from the very start.

Lyndon Johnson
This seminal political commercial—a young girl picking petals from a daisy along with the countdown to a nuclear explosion—ran only once before it was withdrawn by the candidate.

Marlboro
Rugged cowboys and theme music from the movie *The Magnificent Seven* drove the campaign that revived sagging Marlboro, previously a brand targeted to women.

Noxzema
One of the earliest examples of overtly sexy TV advertising has former Miss Sweden Gunilla Knutson eyeing the camera and cooing the double-entendre "Take it off, take it all off" for Noxzema shave cream while the music from "The Stripper" plays.

Cracker Jack
Character actor Jack Gilford walks through a sleeping railcar when a hand pops out from an upper-berth curtain with a box of Cracker Jack, intended for someone on the other side of the aisle. But deadpan Gilford intercepts it, helps himself and passes it back and forth to the unknowing passengers in a hilarious routine.

Hertz
People glide through the air and into a moving open convertible as "Hertz puts you in the driver's seat." Its endurance was enhanced by later parodies.

Benson & Hedges
To tout the cigarette brand's 100-millimeter size, the "disadvantages" of length are humorously demonstrated—popping a balloon, getting caught in an elevator door, etc.

Alka-Seltzer
"Mamma Mia, atsa some spicy meatball!" From the first frame to the last, the heartburn joke is propelled ever forward.

1970s

Budweiser
This classic annual TV Christmas card lives on as the beer-wagon team of Clydesdales trots through a picturesque snow-covered small town.

Volkswagen
"Funeral" has a deceased tycoon reading his will as limos enter the cemetery. He berates his spendthrift wife, partner, and sons—whom we see in limos—and leaves them almost nothing.

To his nephew, who's driving a VW Beetle, he gives "my entire fortune of $100 billion dollars."

Coca-Cola
Bill Backer and Billy Davis's "I'd Like To Buy the World a Coke," sung by young people from numerous nations on a hilltop in Italy in 1971, became the pop song, "I'd Like To Teach the World To Sing."

Lite Beer from Miller
Who more natural to turn a "female-oriented" low-calorie beer called Lite into a manly brew? Ex-jocks. And with this long-running "Everything you ever wanted in a beer—and less" campaign, Miller Lite beer shot to the top of the market.

Xerox
Could Brother Dominick produce 500 more sets of his hand-lettered manuscript? Yes, with the "miracle" coming from the Xerox 9200 copier.

Life Cereal
Two brothers get their younger sibling Mikey to try Life and, surprise, he likes it. "Hey, Mikey" entered the lexicon.

American Express
With competition from bank charge cards increasing, American Express began its "Do you know me?" campaign to suggest empowerment through the Green Card.

American Express
For its Travelers Cheques, Karl Malden brought his *Streets of San Francisco* detective persona to these AmEx commercials. But the spots ran far longer than the TV series, and "Don't leave home without 'em" became embedded in the collective American consciousness.

McDonald's
With an energetic crew cleaning and singing "You deserve a break today," McDonald's established two themes: (1) its outlets were not "greasy spoons" and (2) mothers weren't short-changing their families by patronizing the quick-service restaurant leader.

Dannon
"In [what was then Soviet] Georgia, where they eat a lot of yogurt, a lot of people live past 100," says one spot from a series for Dannon yogurt, which fondly filmed a village of centenarians enjoying free samples. One ends: "eighty-nine-year-old Renan Topagua...ate two cups. That pleased his mother very much."

Southern Airways
Possibly the funniest spot ever filmed, this one for a now-defunct airline portrays coach-class travel as akin to transatlantic steerage, in contrast to the Roman orgy going on in first class.

7UP
Geoffrey Holder's deep voice and a tropical setting were just the right touches to introduce the "uncola nut," 7UP's answer to Coke and Pepsi's key ingredient. A palpably refreshing point of differentiation.

Sunsweet
Opens with an arrogant man saying, "I warn you in advance, I'm not going to like your prunes." He says prunes are both pitted and wrinkled. A hand holds out a box of Sunsweet prunes and the man discovers they don't have pits. He finds them sweet and moist, but still complains about the wrinkles. Closing stentorian VO: "Today the pits, tomorrow the wrinkles."

Polaroid
When Mariette Hartley joined James Garner for these repartee-filled spots, Polaroid and its One-Step and SX-70 moved from novelty to mainstream in the camera business.

Chanel
This 1979 work from director Ridley Scott was one of the first in a "new wave" of highly visual "graphics" approaches that swept in from the U.K. A woman lolls by a swimming pool; a man dives, emerges at her feet; an airplane's shadow passes—for the simple message: "Chanel...share the fantasy."

1980s

Bartles & Jaymes
Classic "plain folks" approach features homespun codgers Frank Bartles and Ed Jaymes on a porch as Frank (Ed never speaks) introduces the product in staccato monotone and ends with the campaign tagline "Thank you for your support."

Chrysler
One of the most effective executive ad spokesmen ever, Chrysler's Lee Iacocca helped bring his company back from the brink of bankruptcy with blunt-talking commercials challenging consumers: "If you can find a better car, buy it."

Wendy's
"Where's the beef?!" Clara Peller barked and a pop culture phenomenon was born.

Eastman Kodak
In "Daddy's Little Girl," snapshots record a child's life up to her wedding, whereupon no father of daughters can keep from choking up. Sentimental yet restrained, this masterpiece reminds parents to capture Kodak memories while they can.

Eveready Energizer
One of TV's cleverest campaigns made its debut in '89 with the first Energizer Bunny parodies. The pink drum-thumper, itself a parody of one used by rival Duracell, romps through three

15 second "commercials"—dead-on sendups of coffee, wine, and decongestant spots.

Federal Express
Fast-talker John Moschitta humorously sets FedEx's role in a fast-paced world.

Ronald Reagan
This "feel-good" spot for his 1984 reelection campaign shows patriotic vignettes while musing on the theme "It's Morning Again in America."

Coca-Cola
The fearsome brute, Pittsburgh Steelers' defender Mean Joe Greene, took a long swig of Coca-Cola and suddenly was humanized enough to toss his jersey to a young fan. Maudlin or no, the 1980 vignette is perhaps the most beloved of all commercials.

AT&T
One of the best in the AT&T series stressing the human side of long-distance calling, the husband asks his crying wife what's wrong. "Joey called. Is everything alright? Yes. Then why are you crying? 'Cause Joey said, 'I called just to say I love you, Mom.' "

Isuzu
Nobody had ever heard of Isuzu before "lying" car salesman (correct information was simultaneously shown) David Leisure became one of the most popular characters in America.

Nike
Bo Diddley strums his guitar and then athlete Bo Jackson does the same with far less success, causing the legendary musician to intone, "Bo, you don't know diddley." A takeoff on earlier "Bo knows" spots in which Jackson is shown to excel in a variety of athletics.

Cheer
In a departure from staid Procter & Gamble's messages, this spot features a silent deadpan presenter smudging a handkerchief and putting it in a cocktail shaker with water, ice, and a dash of Cheer. As an opera aria plays, he removes the hanky, shows it's now spotless, hangs it on a line to dry, and marches off-camera.

Apple Macintosh
Ridley Scott also directed this Orwellian nightmare of tyranny and enslavement, broadly suggesting that Big Brother and IBM were one and the same. "1984" is the greatest commercial ever.

Pepsi-Cola
After being the "Pepsi generation" for one generation, at least, Pepsi-Cola signed the pop music icon of the '80s, Michael Jackson, to position the soft drink as "the choice of a new generation," in one of the largest celebrity endorsement agreements in advertising history.

Calvin Klein
Teen-age supermodel Brooke Shields took Calvin Klein (and the jeans market in general) to new heights of sophistication in this campaign, done by noted photographer Richard Avedon, as she purred, "Know what comes between me and my Calvins? Nothing!"

California Raisins
Hip Claymation raisins, some wearing sunglasses, shuffle to Marvin Gaye's '60s hit, "I Heard It Through the Grapevine."

1990s

Bud Light
The spot that made "Yes...I AM!" the first big advertising catch phrase of the '90s, this has a cheeky young man talking his way into a limousine reserved for a Dr. Galazkiewicz by claiming to be "Dr. Gally-wick-its," first making certain the driver had stocked the limo with Bud Light.

Hallmark
Long a user of emotion-evoking advertising, Hallmark Cards pulled out all the stops in this two-minute spot centered on a "surprise" one hundreth birthday party (she knows). Noteworthy, too, is the mainstreaming of the African-American family; the appeal here is universal.

Levi's for Women
Breathtaking painted-glass animation expressed a distinctly female perspective, and by the time women viewers filtered the message through their own psyches, Levi's for Women was given credit for truly understanding them.

Coca-Cola
It was advertising done by a Hollywood talent agency, Creative Artists Agency. It was computer-animated imagery such as never seen before. It was a heartstopper for Madison Avenue and a heart-warmer for American viewers. The Coca-Cola "Polar Bears" spot was a carbonated watershed, part of an "Always"-themed, logo-centered effort featuring one of the best jingles ever.

THE BEST COMMERCIALS OF 1996

Although these ads have not yet stood the test of time, they won high praise from a panel of advertisers, ad agency representatives, and *Advertising Age* editors. Here are some of the Best Awards for 1996:

Snickers
The endzone painter for the Chiefs makes the finishing touches to the "S" in the team moniker. A big lineman compliments him on his work, adding "But who are the 'Chefs'? " The exasperated painter's not going anywhere for a while, so he gnaws disgustedly on a Snickers.

Nissan Motor Corp.
With Barbie and Ken lookalikes cruising around in a toy convertible, this fun spot is a welcome break from dull car ads.

McDonald's Corp.
A swinging baby smiles when he can see the McDonald's sign outside his window, then cries when the swing goes backward and the windowsill blocks his view.

Pepsi-Cola Co.
A security camera spots a Coke driver loading up a store's cooler with his product. He sneaks a hand into the adjoining Pepsi shelves to grab a can, triggering an avalanche of Pepsi cans.

Anheuser-Busch
It's a tearful departure at a train station, with the man pleading by holding up notes for the woman seated on the train. "At least leave me the Bud Light," he scribbles. She shakes her head no, but writes "Pole" in response as he runs alongside—smack into a pole.

Centraal Beheer
President Clinton suffers a little voodoo magic, and Centraal Beheer, the European insurance company, advises, "Just call us."

Polaroid Corp.
A harried architect tells his wife on the phone that he can't meet her for lunch. But when he sees the Polaroid she left in his briefcase, he says, "I'll be there in 10 minutes."

Eveready Battery Co.
A spoof of those documentaries on chasing and filming rare animals, this ad successfully keeps the Energizer Bunny going and going.

Reebok
Twenty celebrities, including Sting, Richard Attenborough, Jose Carreras, Quentin Crisp, and Tom Jones, are shown passing a soccer ball. End frame shows a Reebok shoe and logo.

Partnership for a Drug-Free America
A pretty young woman removes one facial enhancement after another—to show the unglamorous drug addict underneath. Tagline is "It's hard to face what heroin can do to you."

Levi Strauss & Co.
Jean-clad strangers on an elevator eye each other, then share the same daydream of love, marriage, and family. But when the ride ends, they hesitate, then silently go their separate ways.

E. McIlhenny Sons Corp.
A tough hombre eating Tabasco-laced pizza acts unfazed as a mosquito bites him. The pest flies off and then explodes, as the man smiles with satisfaction.

THE TOP INFOMERCIALS

This unique form of advertising in the guise of programming was first seen on American television in 1984 when advertising was deregulated, and the affliction has metastasized since. The following is a list of 1996's 10 most profitable infomercials, based exclusively on the shows' sales. (Source: *Steve Dworman's Infomercial Marketing Report*)

1. AbRoller Plus (fitness product)
2. Trudeau Marketing Group (business opportunity)
3. Psychic Friends (psychic line)
4. Dick Clark's Rock n' Roll Era (music compilation)
5. Quick Study (self-improvement)
6. Mega Reading (self-improvement)
7. Power Rider (fitness product)
8. Perfect Abs (fitness product)
9. Ellen Kreidman (relationship)
10. AbTrainer (fitness product)

FAVORITE FICTIONAL CHARACTERS FROM TV

Perhaps more than any other entertainment, television relies on irresistable characters—even the scoundrels have charm. Here are 12 personages not just invited into our living room, but who we happily absorbed into our routine. (Source: *The Encyclopedia of Fictional Characters*, Berkley Publishing Corp. and Seth Godin Productions)

Agent 99

Get Smart

Femme fatale secret agent. Crack espionage agent for the U.S. intelligence agency CONTROL in Washington, D.C. She usually and unaccountably defers to slightly more senior (male) Agent 86, Maxwell Smart, whom she loves. 99 is often chosen by the Chief to work with Max and usually ends up saving the operation he has botched. She has style, wit, intelligence, and the lean beauty of a model. Her poses and disguises often lead powerful bad men to fall in love with her, much to Max's dismay and jealousy. Even KAOS's Siegfried finds her attractive. Her knowledge of esoteric cultures and historical events is often the key to discovering the evil plans of Siegfried. She likes to let Max feel he has saved the day. "Oh, Max! Hurry, Max, hurry!"

Master Sergeant Ernie Bilko

The Phil Silvers Show

With little more than ingenuity, bluster, and an ability to think fast on his feet, World War II vet Bilko virtually has the run of Fort Baxter, Kansas, the sleepy military base at which he's stationed. The con man's con man, he runs gambling games, concocts various money-making schemes, and manipulates his immediate superiors, all while running the Company B Motor Pool. He occasionally romances Joan Hogan, a WAC. Stationed in New Guinea during the war, he sold nylons to USO girls at an absurd profit.

Johnny "Dr. Johnny Fever" Caravella

WKRP in Cincinnati

The doctor is an aging rock 'n' roller. Once he hit the radio heights, but now he works for ailing Cincinnati radio station WKRP. He's been around the rock 'n' roll block but doesn't remember most of it. His personality is droll and dry. He makes out that he's just too cool to really care. There's still some residual hippie in Johnny; even if he's lost the edge, he isn't quite ready to conform. He has little patience for the establishment authority figures at WKRP, his boss, Arthur Carlson, newsman Les Nesman, and advertising man Herb Tarlek. He lusts after bombshell receptionist Jennifer Marlowe.

Carlton "the Doorman"

Rhoda

The doorman in Rhoda Morgenstern's apartment building, he is never seen but often heard over the intercom. He suffers from a chronic identity crisis and is always fearful that people will forget who he is. Thus he seems compelled to reintroduce himself every time he buzzes Rhoda's apartment. "Hi, this is Carlton...your doorman."

Laverne De Fazio

Laverne and Shirley

She's a wisecracking, guy-hungry, working girl. Laverne works at the Shotz Brewery in Milwaukee with best friend and roommate Shirley Feeney. Tall, big-haired, and not gorgeous, Laverne favors tight monogrammed sweaters with her skirts and saddle shoes. Loud and obnoxious, she's really defensive and insecure. She and Shirley fight a lot, but they always make up in the end. Spends her free time bowling and eating pizza. Trying to get ahead and make a life for herself.

Fat Albert

Fat Albert and the Cosby Kids

A majorly obese kid with an even bigger heart, Fat Albert lives in a Philadelphia ghetto and is the de facto leader of a friendly neighborhood gang. Other members of this group include young Bill Cosby and Old Weird Harold. For reasons that don't need elaborating, Fat Albert is the undisputed and obvious world champion of buck-buck, a game where players jump on opposing players' backs. "Hey, hey, hey!"

Jonas "The Skipper" Grumby

Gilligan's Island

Well-meaning, oafish ship's skipper. Carries the burden of not having saved the SS Minnow from a wreck but retains a good sense of humor. His perennial outfit consists of white pants and blue shirt. While best pals with crewman Gilligan, or "little buddy," he can get bossy. The Skipper hopes to rebuild the ship and get off the island. He reveres the Professor, has a lust-fear relationship with Ginger, and has a liking for Mary Ann. Bunks with Gilligan. Constantly disappointed with Gilligan's antics. "Oh, Gilligan, not again!"

Mary Hartman

Mary Hartman, Mary Hartman

Sweet but slow-witted stereotypical American housewife who lives in Fernwood, Ohio. She married Tom Hartman when she was 17 years old. A true naïf, she believes everything she sees on television and is obsessed with the prospect of "waxy yellow buildup" on her kitchen floor. Something is always going wrong in Mary's life: her father, George Shumway, disappears; her somewhat senile grandfather Raymond Larkin is known as the Fernwood Flasher; her daughter, Heather, is kidnapped by the town's mass murderer; her husband, Tom, is impotent but cheats on her anyway; and her best friend, Loretta, is paralyzed. She also has an affair with local cop Dennis Foley. She eventually suffers a nervous breakdown.

Erica Kane

All My Children

Gorgeous, glamorous, and totally self-involved, Erica is the biggest star living in suburban Pine Valley—and she'll never let you forget it. Model, actress, cosmetics executive, talk-show host, whatever Erica does she does big. (Her autobiography is called "Raising Kane.") Daughter of motherly Mona and jet-setting film director Eric—who abandoned her—Erica is always looking for love, hence her full name: Erica Kane Martin Brent Cudahy Chadler Montgomery Montgomery Marick Marick. And those are only the ones she married; other "great loves" include Nick Davis, Jeremy Hunter, and one of her husband's brothers, Jackson Montgomery. She has two daughters, beloved Bianca and devilish Kendall, whom she gave up for adoption as a teen. "I'm Erica Kane!"

Fred Sanford

Sanford and Son

Crotchety and misanthropic senior citizen Fred Sanford runs a Los Angeles junkyard with his beloved son, Lamont Sanford. Fred can be quick-witted and amusing, but that's only on occasion. His usual demeanor is ornery and nasty to everyone around him, including his son. His particular target is sister-in-law Esther, with whom he has a continually fractious relationship. He does seem to like Donna Harris, a nurse, although he never makes good on his promise to marry her. A widower, Fred has a controlling hold on his pride and joy, Lamont; whenever Lamont threatens to move on, Fred fakes a heart attack and screams for his dead wife: "I'm coming, Elizabeth, I'm coming!"

Luke Spencer

General Hospital

Roguish, wry, bad boy Luke doesn't have the looks of a matinee idol, but he does have the charm and the swagger, and so he gets away with murder—or close to it. After raping Laura Vining, he ends up marrying her, and theirs is a romance for the ages. Never one to walk the straight and narrow, Luke's owned a nightclub, gotten messed up with the mob, and still managed to become Mayor of Port Charles. His sister is Bobbie. When Laura disappeared for a while, he romanced Holly Sutton. He and Laura have a son, Lucky.

Cosmo G. Spacely

The Jetsons

The mean-spirited, not-too-bright CEO of Spacely Sprockets. Spacely constantly battles his archcompetitor, Cogswell Cogs. His small body houses a very loud voice. Mr. Spacely has a pronounced Napoleon complex and is very demanding of his employees. One harassed employee is nice guy George Jetson, of whom Cosmo constantly takes advantage, often nagging him on his way home via TV phone.

THE EMMY AWARDS

As the television industry has grown, so has the business of television awards—so much so that the Emmys are now presented in two separate ceremonies to accommodate the wealth of categories. The following presents a wide selection of winners in major areas through the years.

	1949	1950
Actor	—	Alan Young
Actress	—	Gertrude Berg
Drama	—	*Pulitzer Prize Playhouse*, ABC
Variety Program	—	*The Alan Young Show*, CBS
Game Show	—	*Truth or Consequences*, CBS
Children's Show	*Time for Beany*, KTLA	*Time for Beany*, KTLA

	1951	1952	1953
Actor	Sid Caesar	Thomas Mitchell	Donald O'Connor, *Colgate Comedy Hour*, NBC
Actress	Imogene Coca	Helen Hayes	Eve Arden, *Our Miss Brooks*, CBS
Drama	*Studio One*, CBS	*Robert Montgomery Presents*, NBC	*U.S. Steel Hour*, ABC
Mystery, Action, or Adventure	—	*Dragnet*, NBC	*Dragnet*, NBC
Comedy	*Red Skelton Show*, NBC	*I Love Lucy*, CBS	*I Love Lucy*, CBS
Comedian	Red Skelton, NBC	Lucille Ball, CBS; Jimmy Durante, NBC	—
Variety Program	*Your Show of Shows*, NBC	*Your Show of Shows*, NBC	*Omnibus*, CBS
Game Show	—	*What's My Line?*, CBS	*This is Your Life*, NBC; *What's My Line?*, CBS
Children's Program	—	*Time for Beany*, KTLA	*Kukla, Fran & Ollie*, NBC

	1954	1955	1956
Actor	Danny Thomas, *Make Room for Daddy*, ABC	Phil Silvers, *The Phil Silvers Show*, CBS	Robert Moss, *Father Knows Best*, NBC
Actress	Loretta Young, *The Loretta Young Show*, NBC	Lucille Ball, *I Love Lucy*, CBS	Loretta Young, *The Loretta Young Show*, NBC
Drama	*U.S. Steel Hour*, ABC	*Producers' Showcase*, NBC	*Playhouse 90*, CBS
Mystery, Action, or Adventure	*Dragnet*, NBC	*Disneyland*, ABC	—
Comedy	*Make Room for Daddy*, ABC	*The Phil Silvers Show*, CBS	—
Comedian	—	Phil Silvers, CBS; Nanette Fabray, NBC	Sid Caesar, *Caesar's Hour*, NBC; Nanette Fabray, *Caesar's Hour*, NBC
Variety Series	*Disneyland*, ABC	*The Ed Sullivan Show*, CBS	—
Game Show	*This Is Your Life*, NBC	*The $64,000 Question*, CBS	—
Children's Program	*Lassie*, CBS	*Lassie*, CBS	—

	1957	1958–59	1959–60
Drama	*Gunsmoke*, CBS	*The Alcoa Hour/Goodyear Playhouse*, NBC; *Playhouse 90*, CBS	*Playhouse 90*, CBS
Actor—Series	—	Raymond Burr, *Perry Mason*, CBS (Drama)	Robert Stack, *The Untouchables*, ABC
Actress—Series	—	Loretta Young, *The Loretta Young Show*, NBC (Drama)	Jane Wyatt, *Father Knows Best*, CBS
Supporting Actor—Series	—	Dennis Weaver, *Gunsmoke*, CBS	—
Supporting Actress—Drama Series	—	Barbara Hale, *Perry Mason*, CBS	—
Director—Drama	—	George Schaefer, *Little Moon of Aloban*, NBC; Jack Smight, *Eddie*, NBC	Robert Mulligan, *The Moon and Sixpence*, NBC
Writer—Drama	—	James Costigan, *Little Moon of Alban*, NBC; Alfred Brenner and Ken Hughes, *Eddie*, NBC	Rod Serling, *The Twilight Zone*, CBS
Comedy	*The Phil Silvers Show*, CBS	*The Jack Benny Show*, CBS	*Art Carney Special*, NBC
Actor—Comedy Series	Robert Young, *Father Knows Best*, NBC	Jack Benny, *The Jack Benny Show*, CBS	Dick Van Dyke, *The Dick Van Dyke Show*, CBS
Actress—Comedy Series	Jane Wyatt, *Father Knows Best*, NBC	Jane Wyatt, *Father Knows Best*, CBS & NBC	Jane Wyatt, *Father Knows Best*, CBS
Supporting Actor—Comedy Series	Carl Reiner, *Caesar's Hour*, NBC	Tom Poston, *The Steve Allen Show*, NBC	—
Supporting Actress—Comedy Series	Ann B. Davis, *The Bob Cummings Show*, CBS and NBC	Ann B. Davis, *The Bob Cummings Show*, NBC	—
Director—Comedy/Comedy Series	—	Peter Tewksbury, *Father Knows Best*, CBS	Ralph Levy and Bud Yorkin, *The Jack Benny Hour Specials*, CBS
Writer—Comedy/Comedy Series	Nat Hiken, Billy Friedberg, Phil Sharp, Terry Ryan, Coleman Jacoby, Arnold Rosen, Sidney Zelinko, A.J. Russell, and Tony Webster, *The Phil Silvers Show*, CBS	Sam Perrin, George Balzer, Hal Goldman, and Al Gordon, *The Jack Benny Show*, CBS	Sam Perrin, George Balzer, Hal Goldman, and Al Gordon, *The Jack Benny Show*, CBS
Variety Program	*The Dinah Shore Chevy Show*, NBC	*The Dinah Shore Chevy Show*, NBC	*The Fabulous Fifties*, CBS
Game Show	—	*What's My Line?*, CBS	—
Children's Program	—	—	*Huckleberry Hound*, SYN

	1960–61	1961–62	1962–63
Actor	Raymond Burr, *Perry Mason,* CBS	E.G. Marshall, *The Defenders,* CBS	E.G. Marshall, *The Defenders,* CBS
Actress	Barbara Stanwyck, *The Barbara Stanwyck Show,* NBC	Shirley Booth, *Hazel,* NBC	Shirley Booth, *Hazel,* NBC
Drama	*Macbeth,* NBC	*The Defenders,* CBS	*The Defenders,* CBS
Director—Drama	George Schaefer, *Macbeth,* NBC	Franklin Schaffner, *The Defenders,* CBS	Stuart Rosenberg, *The Defenders,* CBS
Writer—Drama	Rod Serling, *The Twilight Zone,* CBS	Reginald Rose, *The Defenders,* CBS	Robert Thorn, Reginald Rose, *The Defenders,* CBS
Comedy	*The Jack Benny Show,* CBS	*The Bob Newhart Show,* NBC	*The Dick Van Dyke Show,* CBS
Director—Comedy	Sheldon Leonard, *The Danny Thomas Show,* CBS	Nat Hiken, *Car 54, Where Are You?,* NBC	John Rich, *The Dick Van Dyke Show,* CBS
Writer—Comedy	Sherwood Schwartz, Dave O'Brien, Al Schwartz, Martin Ragaway, and Red Skelton, *The Red Skelton Show,* CBS	Carl Reiner, *The Dick Van Dyke Show,* CBS	Carl Reiner, *The Dick Van Dyke Show,* CBS
Variety Program	*Astaire Time,* NBC	*The Garry Moore Show,* CBS	*The Andy Williams Show,* NBC
Individual Performance—Variety or Music Program/Series	Fred Astaire, *Astaire Time,* NBC	Carol Burnett, *The Garry Moore Show,* CBS	Carol Burnett, *Julie and Carol at Carnegie Hall,* CBS; *Carol and Company,* CBS
Panel, Quiz or Audience Participation	—	—	*College Bowl,* CBS
Children's Program	*Young People's Concert: Aaron Copland's Birthday Party,* CBS	*New York Philharmonic Young People's Concerts with Leonard Bernstein,* CBS	*Walt Disney's Wonderful World of Color,* NBC

THE RATINGS CONNECTION

Having the No. 1 rated show for a season doesn't necessarily guarantee Emmy success…or does it? Here is a list of the No. 1 shows that have also won the top honors—along with those that have achieved the dubious distinction of winning the ratings race but losing the Emmy battle.

EMMY WINNERS

Texaco Star Theatre
I Love Lucy
The $64,000 Question
Gunsmoke
Rowan and Martin's Laugh-In
All in the Family
60 Minutes
The Cosby Show
Cheers
Seinfeld
ER

EMMY LOSERS

Arthur Godfrey's Talent Scouts
Wagon Train
The Beverly Hillbillies
Bonanza
The Andy Griffith Show
Marcus Welby, M.D.
Happy Days
Laverne & Shirley
Three's Company
Dallas
Dynasty
Roseanne
Home Improvement

	1963–64	1964–65	1965–66
Drama	*The Defenders*, CBS	In 1964–65 the entire award system was changed for one year, and there were no awards given in individual categories that in any way match the categories from other years.	*The Fugitive*, ABC
Actor—Drama Series	Jack Klugman, *The Defenders*, CBS		Bill Cosby, *I Spy*, NBC
Actress—Drama Series	Shelley Winters, *Two Is The Number*, NBC		Barbara Stanwyck, *The Big Valley*, ABC
Supporting Actor—Drama Series	Albert Parker, *One Day In The Life of Ivan Denisovich*, NBC	—	James Daly, *Eagle in a Cage*, NBC
Supporting Actress—Drama Series	Ruth White, *Little Moon of Alban*, NBC	—	Lee Grant, *Peyton Place*, ABC
Writer—Drama	Ernest Kinay, *The Defenders*, CBS	—	Sydney Pollack, *The Game*, NBC
Director—Drama	Tom Gries, *East Side/West Side*, CBS	—	Millard Lampell, *Eagle in a Cage*, NBC
Comedy	*The Dick Van Dyke Show*, CBS	—	*The Dick Van Dyke Show*, CBS
Actor—Comedy Series	Dick Van Dyke, *The Dick Van Dyke Show*, CBS	—	Dick Van Dyke, *The Dick Van Dyke Show*, CBS
Actress—Comedy Series	Mary Tyler Moore, *The Dick Van Dyke Show*, CBS	—	Mary Tyler Moore, *The Dick Van Dyke Show*, CBS
Supporting Actor—Comedy Series	—	—	Don Knotts, *The Andy Griffith Show*, CBS
Supp. Actress—Comedy Series	—	—	Alice Pearce, *Bewitched*, ABC
Director—Comedy	Jerry Paris, *The Dick Van Dyke Show*, CBS	—	William Asher, *Bewitched*, ABC
Writer—Comedy	Carl Reiner, Sam Denoff, and Bill Penky, *The Dick Van Dyke Show*, CBS	—	Bill Persky, Sam Denoff, *The Dick Van Dyke Show*, CBS
Variety Program	*The Danny Kaye Show*, CBS	—	*The Andy Williams Show*, NBC
Director—Variety or Music	Robert Scheerer, *The Danny Kaye Show*, CBS	—	Alan Handley, *The Julie Andrews Show*, NBC
Writer—Variety	—	—	Al Gordon, Hal Goldman, and Sheldon Keller, *An Evening with Carol Channing*, CBS
Children's Program	*Discovery '63-'64*, ABC	—	*A Charlie Brown Christmas*, CBS

WINNING TEAMS

Looking for a rare wedding gift? Consider his-and-hers Emmies: Only six married couples have ever sported matching trophies. One duo, *St. Elsewhere*'s Daniels and Bartlett, won for playing a husband and wife onscreen.

Hume Cronyn & Jessica Tandy
William Daniels & Bonnie Bartlett
Danny DeVito & Rhea Perlman
Phil Donahue & Marlo Thomas
Alfred Lunt & Lynn Fontanne
George C. Scott & Colleen Dewhurst

	1966–67	1967–68	1968–69
Drama Series	*Mission: Impossible*, CBS	*Mission: Impossible*, CBS	*NET Playhouse*, NET
Actor—Drama Series	Bill Cosby, *I Spy*, NBC	Bill Cosby, *I Spy*, NBC	Carl Betz, *Judd, for the Defense*, ABC
Actress—Drama Series	Barbara Bain, *Mission: Impossible*, CBS	Barbara Bain, *Mission: Impossible*, CBS	Barbara Bain, *Mission: Impossible*, CBS
Supporting Actor—Drama	Eli Wallach, *The Poppy Is Also a Flower*, ABC	Milburn Stone, *Gunsmoke*, CBS	—
Supporting Actress—Drama	Agnes Moorehead, *The Wild, Wild West*, CBS	Barbara Anderson, *Ironside*, NBC	Susan Saint James, *The Name of the Game*, NBC
Director—Drama	Alex Segal, *Death of a Salesman*, CBS	Paul Bogart, *Dear Friends*, CBS	David Green, *The People Next Door*, CBS
Writer—Drama	Bruce Geller, *Mission: Impossible*, CBS	Loring Mandel, *Do Not Go Gentle into That Good Night*, CBS	J.P. Miller, *The People Next Door*, CBS
Comedy	*The Monkees*, NBC	*Get Smart*, NBC	*Get Smart*, NBC
Actor—Comedy Series	Don Adams, *Get Smart*, NBC	Don Adams, *Get Smart*, NBC	Don Adams, *Get Smart*, NBC
Actress—Comedy Series	Lucille Ball, *The Lucy Show*, CBS	Lucille Ball, *The Lucy Show*, CBS	Hope Lange, *The Ghost and Mrs. Muir*, NBC
Supporting Actor—Comedy Series	Don Knotts, *The Andy Griffith Show*, CBS	Werner Klemperer, *Hogan's Heroes*, CBS	Werner Klemperer, *Hogan's Heroes*, CBS
Supporting Actress—Comedy Series	Frances Bavier, *The Andy Griffith Show*, CBS	Marion Lorne, *Bewitched*, ABC	—
Director—Comedy/ Comedy Series	James Frawley, *The Monkees*, NBC	Bruce Bilson, *Get Smart*, NBC	—
Writer—Comedy/ Comedy Series	Buck Henry and Leonard Stern, *Get Smart*, NBC	Allan Burns and Chris Hayward, *He and She*, CBS	Alan Blye, Bob Einstein, Murray Roman, Carl Gottlieb, Jerry Music, Steve Martin, Cecil Tuck, Paul Wayne, Cy Howard, and Mason Williams, *The Smothers Brothers Comedy Hour*, CBS
Variety Program	*The Andy Williams Show*, NBC	*Rowan and Martin's Laugh-In*, NBC	*Rowan and Martin's Laugh-In*, NBC
Director—Variety or Music	Fielder Cook, *Brigadoon*, ABC	Jack Haley, Jr., *Movin' with Nancy*, NBC	—
Writer—Variety or Music	Mel Brooks, Sam Denoff, Bill Persky, Carl Reiner, and Mel Tolkin, *The Sid Caesar, Imogene Coca, Carl Reiner, Howard Morris Special*, CBS	Chris Beard, Phil Hahn, Jack Hanrahan, Coslough Johnson, Paul Keyes, Marc London, Allan Manings, David Panich, Hugh Wedlock, and Digby Wolfe, *Rowan and Martin's Laugh-In*, NBC	—
Children's Program	*Jack and the Beanstalk*, NBC	—	—

	1969–70	1970–71	1971–72
Drama	*Marcus Welby, M.D.*, ABC	*The Bold Ones: The Senator*, NBC	*Elizabeth R*, PBS
Actor—Drama Series	Robert Young, *Marcus Welby, M.D.*, ABC	Hal Holbrook, *The Bold Ones: The Senator*, NBC	Peter Falk, *Columbo*, NBC
Actress—Drama Series	Susan Hampshire, *The Forsyte Saga*, NET	Susan Hampshire, *The First Churchills*, PBS	Glenda Jackson, *Elizabeth R.*, PBS
Supporting Actor—Drama Series	James Brolin, *Marcus Welby, M.D.*, ABC	David Burns, *The Price*, NBC	Jack Warden, *Brian's Song*, ABC
Supporting Actress—Drama Series	Gail Fisher, *Mannix*, CBS	Margaret Leighton, *Hamlet*, NBC	Jenny Agutter, *The Snow Goose*, NBC
Director—Drama Series	—	Daryl Duke, *The Bold Ones: The Senator*, NBC	Alexander Singer, *The Bold Ones: The Lawyers*, NBC
Writer—Drama	Richard Levinson and William Link, *My Sweet Charlie*, NBC	Joel Oliansky, *The Bold Ones: The Senator*, NBC	Richard L. Levinson and William Link, *Columbo*, NBC
Comedy	*My World and Welcome to It*, NBC	*All in the Family*, CBS	*All in the Family*, CBS
Actor—Comedy Series	William Windom, *My World and Welcome to It*, NBC	Jack Klugman, *The Odd Couple*, ABC	Carroll O'Connor, *All in the Family*, CBS
Actress—Comedy Series	Hope Lange, *The Ghost and Mrs. Muir*, ABC	Jean Stapleton, *All in the Family*, CBS	Jean Stapleton, *All in the Family*, CBS
Supporting Actor—Comedy Series	Michael Constantine, *Room 222*, ABC	Edward Asner, *The Mary Tyler Moore Show*, CBS	Edward Asner, *The Mary Tyler Moore Show*, CBS
Supporting Actress—Comedy Series	Karen Valentine, *Room 222*, ABC	Valerie Harper, *The Mary Tyler Moore Show*, CBS	Valerie Harper, *The Mary Tyler Moore Show*, CBS; Sally Struthers, *All in the Family, CBS*
Director—Comedy Series	—	Jay Sandrich, *The Mary Tyler Moore Show*, CBS	John Rich, *All in the Family*, CBS
Writer—Comedy Series	—	James L. Brooks and Allan Burns, *The Mary Tyler Moore Show*, CBS	Burt Styler, *All in the Family*, CBS
Drama/Comedy Special	—	—	*Brian's Song*, ABC
Variety or Music Series	*The David Frost Show*, SYN	*The David Frost Show, SYN (Talk), The Flip Wilson Show*, NBC (Music)	*The Dick Cavett Show, ABC* (Talk), *The Carol Burnett Show*, CBS (Music)
Director—Variety or Music	—	Mark Warren, *Rowan and Martin's Laugh-In*, NBC	Art Fisher, *The Sonny & Cher Comedy Hour*, CBS
Writer—Variety or Music	—	Herbert Baker, Hal Goodman, Larry Klein, Bob Weiskopf, Bob Schiller, Norman Steinberg, and Flip Wilson, *The Flip Wilson Show*, NBC	Don Hinkley, Stan Hart, Larry Siegel, Woody Kling, Roger Beatty, Art Baer, Ben Joelson, Stan Burns, Mike Marmer, and Arnie Rosen, *The Carol Burnett Show*, CBS
Daytime Drama Series	—	—	*The Doctors*, NBC
Children's Program	*Sesame Street*, NET	*Sesame Street*, PBS	*Sesame Street*, PBS

	1972–73	1973–74	1974–75
Drama	*The Waltons*, CBS	*Upstairs, Downstairs*, PBS	*Upstairs, Downstairs*, PBS
Actor—Drama Series	Richard Thomas, *The Waltons*, CBS	Telly Savalas, *Kojak*, CBS	Robert Blake, *Baretta*, ABC
Actress—Drama Series	Michael Learned, *The Waltons*, CBS	Michael Learned, *The Waltons*, CBS	Jean Marsh, *Upstairs, Downstairs*, PBS
Supporting Actor—Drama/Drama Series	Scott Jacoby, *That Certain Summer*, ABC	Michael Moriarty, *The Glass Menagerie*, ABC	Will Geer, *The Waltons*, CBS
Supporting Actress—Drama/Drama Series	Ellen Corby, *The Waltons*, CBS	Joanna Miles, *The Glass Menagerie*, ABC	Ellen Corby, *The Waltons*, CBS
Director—Drama	Joseph Sargent, *The Marcus Nelson Murders*, CBS	John Korty, *The Autobiography of Miss Jane Pittman*, CBS	George Cukor, *Love Among the Ruins*, ABC
Director—Drama Series	Jerry Thorpe, *Kung Fu*, ABC	Robert Butler, *The Blue Knight*, NBC	Bill Bain, *Upstairs, Downstairs*, PBS
Writer—Drama Series	John McGreevey, *The Waltons*, CBS	Joanna Lee, *The Waltons*, CBS	Howard Fast, *Benjamin Franklin*, CBS
Comedy	*All in the Family*, CBS	*M*A*S*H*, CBS	*The Mary Tyler Moore Show*, CBS
Actor—Comedy Series	Jack Klugman, *The Odd Couple*, ABC	Alan Alda, *M*A*S*H*, CBS	Tony Randall, *The Odd Couple*, ABC
Actress—Comedy Series	Mary Tyler Moore, *The Mary Tyler Moore Show*, CBS	Mary Tyler Moore, *The Mary Tyler Moore Show*, CBS	Valerie Harper, *Rhoda*, CBS
Supporting Actor—Comedy Series	Ted Knight, *The Mary Tyler Moore Show*, CBS	Rob Reiner, *All in the Family*, CBS	Ed Asner, *The Mary Tyler Moore Show*, CBS
Supporting Actress—Comedy Series	Valerie Harper, *The Mary Tyler Moore Show*, CBS	Cloris Leachman, *The Mary Tyler Moore Show*, CBS	Betty White, *The Mary Tyler Moore Show*, CBS
Director—Comedy Series	Jay Sandrich, *The Mary Tyler Moore Show*, CBS	Jackie Cooper, *M*A*S*H*, CBS	Gene Reynolds, *M*A*S*H*, CBS
Writer—Comedy Series	Michael Ross, Bernie West, and Lee Kalcheim, *All in the Family*, CBS	Treva Silverman, *The Mary Tyler Moore Show*, CBS	Ed. Weinberger and Stan Daniels, *The Mary Tyler Moore Show*, CBS
Drama/Comedy Special	*A War of Children*, CBS	*The Autobiography of Miss Jane Pittman*, CBS	*The Law*, NBC
Variety Series	*The Julie Andrews Hour*, ABC	*The Carol Burnett Show*, CBS	*The Carol Burnett Show*, CBS
Director—Variety or Music	Bill Davis, *The Julie Andrews Hour*, ABC	Dave Powers, *The Carol Burnett Show*, CBS	Dave Powers, *The Carol Burnett Show*, CBS

	1972–73	1973–74	1974–75
Writer—Variety or Music Series	Stan Hart, Larry Siegel, Gail Parent, Woody Kling, Roger Beatty, Tom Patchett, Jay Tarses, Robert Hilliard, Arnie Kogen, Bill Angelos, and Buz Kohan, *The Carol Burnett Show*, CBS	Ed Simmons, Gary Belkin, Roger Beatty, Arnie Kogen, Bill Richmond, Gene Perret, Rudy De Luca, Barry Levinson, Dick Clair, Jenna McMahon, and Barry Harman, *The Carol Burnett Show*, CBS	Ed Simmons, Gary Belkin, Roger Beatty, Arnie Kogen, Bill Richmond, Gene Perret, Rudy De Luca, Barry Levinson, Dick Clair, and Jenna McMahon, *The Carol Burnett Show*, CBS
Variety, Music, or Comedy Special	*Singer Presents Liza with a "Z"*, CBS	*Lily Tomlin*, CBS	*An Evening with John Denver*, ABC
Miniseries/Limited Series	*Tom Brown's Schooldays*, PBS	*Columbo*, NBC	*Benjamin Franklin*, CBS
Actor—Miniseries/ Limited Series	Anthony Murphy, *Tom Brown's Schooldays*, PBS	William Holden, *The Blue Knight*, NBC	Peter Falk, *Columbo*, NBC
Actress—Miniseries/ Limited Series	Susan Hampshire, *Vanity Fair*, PBS	Mildred Natwick, *The Snoop Sisters*, NBC	Jessica Walter, *Amy Prentiss*, NBC
Daytime Drama Series	*The Edge of Night*, CBS	*The Doctors*, NBC	*The Young and the Restless*, CBS
Actor—Daytime Drama Series	—	Macdonald Carey, *Days of Our Lives*, NBC	Macdonald Carey, *Days of Our Lives*, NBC
Actress—Daytime Drama Series	—	Elizabeth Hubbard, *The Doctors*, NBC	Susan Flannery, *Days of Our Lives*, NBC
Host—Game Show	—	Peter Marshall, *The Hollywood Squares*, NBC	Peter Marshall, *The Hollywood Squares*, NBC
Host—Talk or Service	—	Dinah Shore, *Dinah's Place*, NBC	Barbara Walters, *Today*, NBC
Game Show	—	*Password*, ABC	*Hollywood Squares*, NBC
Talk, Service or Variety Series	—	*The Merv Griffin Show*, SYN	*Dinah!*, SYN
Children's Special	—	*Marlo Thomas and Friends in Free To Be . . . You and Me*, ABC	*Yes, Virginia, There Is a Santa Claus*, ABC
Children's Entertainment Series	—	*Zoom, PBS*	*Star Trek*, NBC

	1975–76	1976–77	1977–78
Drama	*Police Story*, NBC	*Upstairs, Downstairs*, PBS	*The Rockford Files*, NBC
Actor—Drama Series	Peter Falk, *Columbo*, NBC	James Garner, *The Rockford Files*, NBC	Edward Asner, *Lou Grant*, CBS
Actress—Drama Series	Michael Learned, *The Waltons*, CBS	Lindsay Wagner, *The Bionic Woman*, ABC	Sada Thompson, *Family*, ABC
Supporting Actor—Drama Series	Anthony Zerbe, *Harry-O*, ABC	Gary Frank, *Family*, ABC	Robert Vaughn, *Washington: Behind Closed Doors*, ABC
Supp. Actress—Drama Series	Ellen Corby, *The Waltons*, CBS	Kristy McNichol, *Family*, ABC	Nancy Marchand, *Lou Grant*, CBS
Director—Drama Series	David Greene, *Rich Man, Poor Man*, ABC	David Greene, *Roots*, ABC	Marvin J. Chomsky, *Holocaust*, NBC
Writer—Drama Series	Sherman Yellen, *The Adams Chronicles*, PBS	Ernest Kinoy and William Blinn, *Roots*, ABC	Gerald Green, *Holocaust*, NBC
Comedy	*The Mary Tyler Moore Show*, CBS	*The Mary Tyler Moore Show*, CBS	*All in the Family*, CBS
Actor—Comedy Series	Jack Albertson, *Chico and the Man*, NBC	Carroll O'Connor, *All in the Family*, CBS	Carroll O'Connor, *All in the Family*, CBS
Actress—Comedy Series	Mary Tyler Moore, *The Mary Tyler Moore Show*, CBS	Beatrice Arthur, *Maude*, CBS	Jean Stapleton, *All in the Family*, CBS

	1975–76	1976–77	1977–78
Supporting Actor—Comedy Series	Ted Knight, *The Mary Tyler Moore Show*, CBS	Gary Burghoff, *M*A*S*H*, CBS	Rob Reiner, *All in the Family*, CBS
Supporting Actress—Comedy Series	Betty White, *The Mary Tyler Moore Show*, CBS	Mary Kay Place, *Mary Hartman, Mary Hartman*, SYN	Julie Kavner, *Rhoda*, CBS
Director—Comedy/Comedy Series	Gene Reynolds, *M*A*S*H*, CBS	Alan Alda, *M*A*S*H*, CBS	Paul Bogart, *All in the Family*, CBS
Writer—Comedy Series	David Lloyd, *The Mary Tyler Moore Show*, CBS	Allan Burns, James L. Brooks, Ed. Weinberger, Stan Daniels, David Lloyd, and Bob Ellison, *The Mary Tyler Moore Show*, CBS	Bob Weiskopf and Bob Schiller (Teleplay); Barry Harman and Harve Brosten (Story), *All in the Family*, CBS
Drama/Comedy Special	*Eleanor and Franklin*, ABC	*Eleanor and Franklin: The White House Years*, ABC	*The Gathering*, ABC
Variety Series	*NBC's Saturday Night*, NBC	*Van Dyke and Company*, NBC	*The Muppet Show*, SYN
Limited Series	*Upstairs, Downstairs*, PBS	*Roots*, ABC	*Holocaust*, NBC
Actor—Limited Series	Hal Holbrook, *Sandburg's Lincoln*, NBC	Christopher Plummer, *The Moneychangers*, NBC	Michael Moriarty, *Holocaust*, NBC
Actress—Limited Series	Rosemary Harris, *Notorious Women*, PBS	Patty Duke Astin, *Captains and the Kings*, NBC	Meryl Streep, *Holocaust*, NBC
Daytime Drama Series	*Another World*, NBC	*Ryan's Hope*, ABC	*Days of Our Lives*, NBC
Actor—Daytime Drama Series	Larry Haines, *Search for Tomorrow*, CBS	Val Dufour, *Search for Tomorrow*, CBS	James Pritchett, *The Doctors*, NBC
Actress—Daytime Drama Series	Helen Gallagher, *Ryan's Hope*, ABC	Helen Gallagher, *Ryan's Hope*, ABC	Laurie Heinemann, *Another World*, NBC
Host—Game Show	Allen Ludden, *Password*, ABC	Bert Convy, *Tattletales*, CBS	Richard Dawson, *Family Feud*, ABC
Host—Talk or Service Series	Dinah Shore, *Dinah!*, SYN	Phil Donahue, *Donahue*, SYN	Phil Donahue, *Donahue*, SYN
Game Show	*The $20,000 Pyramid*, ABC	*Family Feud*, ABC	*The Hollywood Squares*, NBC
Talk, Service or Variety Series	*Dinah!*, SYN	*The Merv Griffin Show*, SYN	*Donahue*, SYN
Children's Entertainment Series	*Big Blue Marble*, SYN	*Zoom*, PBS	*Captain Kangaroo*, CBS

	1978–79	1979–80	1980–81
Drama	*Lou Grant*, CBS	*Lou Grant*, CBS	*Hill Street Blues*, NBC
Actor—Drama Series	Ron Leibman, *Kaz*, CBS	Ed Asner, *Lou Grant*, CBS	Daniel J. Travanti, *Hill Street Blues*, NBC
Actress—Drama Series	Mariette Hartley, *The Incredible Hulk*, CBS	Barbara Bel Geddes, *Dallas*, CBS	Barbara Babcock, *Hill Street Blues*, NBC
Supporting Actor—Drama Series	Stuart Margolin, *The Rockford Files*, NBC	Stuart Margolin, *The Rockford Files*, NBC	Michael Conrad, *Hill Street Blues*, NBC
Supporting Actress—Drama Series	Kristy McNichol, *Family*, ABC	Nancy Marchand, *Lou Grant*, CBS	Nancy Marchand, *Lou Grant*, CBS
Director—Drama Series	Jackie Cooper, *The White Shadow*, CBS	Roger Young, *Lou Grant*, CBS	Robert Butler, *Hill Street Blues*, NBC
Writer—Drama Series	Michele Gallery, *Lou Grant*, CBS	Seth Freeman, *Lou Grant*, CBS	Michael Kozoll and Steven Bochco, *Hill Street Blues*, NBC
Comedy	*Taxi*, ABC	*Taxi*, ABC	*Taxi*, ABC
Actor—Comedy Series	Carroll O'Connor, *All in the Family*, CBS	Richard Mulligan, *Soap*, ABC	Judd Hirsch, *Taxi*, ABC
Actress—Comedy Series	Ruth Gordon, *Taxi*, ABC	Cathryn Damon, *Soap*, ABC	Isabel Sanford, *The Jeffersons*, CBS
Supporting Actor—Comedy Series	Robert Guillaume, *Soap*, ABC	Harry Morgan, *M*A*S*H*, CBS	Danny De Vito, *Taxi*, ABC
Supporting Actress—Comedy Series	Sally Struthers, *All in the Family*, CBS	Loretta Swit, *M*A*S*H*, CBS	Eileen Brennan, *Private Benjamin*, CBS
Director—Comedy Series	Noam Pitlik, *Barney Miller*, ABC	James Burrows, *Taxi*, ABC	James Burrows, *Taxi*, ABC
Writer—Comedy Series	Alan Alda, *M*A*S*H*, CBS	Bob Colleary, *Barney Miller*, ABC	Michael Leeson, *Taxi*, ABC
Drama/Comedy Special	*Friendly Fire*, ABC	*The Miracle Worker*, NBC	*Playing for Time*, CBS
Variety Program	*Steve & Eydie Celebrate Irving Berlin*, NBC	*Baryshnikov on Broadway*, ABC	*Lily: Sold Out*, CBS
Director—Variety or Music	—	Dwight Hemion, *Baryshnikov on Broadway*, ABC	Don Mischer, *The Kennedy Center Honors: A National Celebration of the Performing Arts*, CBS

	1978–79	1979–80	1980–81
Writer—Variety or Music	—	Buz Kohan, *Shirley MacLaine... Every Little Movement*, CBS	Jerry Juhl, David Odell, Chris Langham, *The Muppet Show*, SYN
Limited Series	*Roots: The Next Generations*, ABC	*Edward & Mrs. Simpson*, SYN	*Shogun*, NBC
Actor—Limited Series	Peter Strauss, *The Jericho Mile*, ABC	Powers Boothe, *Guyana Tragedy: The Story of Jim Jones*, CBS	Anthony Hopkins, *The Bunker*, CBS
Actress—Limited Series	Bette Davis, *Strangers: The Story of a Mother and Daughter*, CBS	Patty Duke Astin, *The Miracle Worker*, NBC	Vanessa Redgrave, *Playing for Time*, CBS
Supporting Actor—Limited Series or Special	Marlon Brando, *Roots: The Next Generations*, ABC	George Grizzard, *The Oldest Living Graduate*, NBC	David Warner, *Masada*, ABC
Supporting Actress—Limited Series or Special	Esther Rolle, *Summer of My German Soldier*, NBC	Mare Winningham, *Amber Waves*, ABC	Jane Alexander, *Playing for Time*, CBS
Director—Limited Series or Special	David Greene, *Friendly Fire*, ABC	Marvin J. Chomsky, *Attica*, ABC	James Goldstone, *Kent State*, NBC
Writer—Limited Series or Special	Patrick Nolan and Michael Mann, *The Jericho Mile*, ABC	David Chase, *Off the Minnesota Strip*, ABC	Arthur Miller, *Playing for Time*, CBS
Daytime Drama Series	*Ryan's Hope*, ABC	*Guiding Light*, CBS	*General Hospital*, ABC
Actor—Daytime Drama Series	Al Freeman, Jr., *One Life to Live*, ABC	Douglass Watson, *Another World*, NBC	Douglass Watson, *Another World*, NBC
Actress—Daytime Drama Series	Irene Dailey, *Another World*, NBC	Judith Light, *One Life to Live*, ABC	Judith Light, *One Life to Live*, ABC
Supporting Actor—Daytime Drama Series	Peter Hansen, *General Hospital*, ABC	Warren Burton, *All My Children*, ABC	Larry Haines, *Search for Tomorrow*, CBS
Supporting Actress—Daytime Drama Series	Suzanne Rogers, *Days of Our Lives*, NBC	Francesca James, *All My Children*, ABC	Jane Elliot, *General Hospital*, ABC
Host—Game Show	Dick Clark, *The $20,000 Pyramid*, ABC	Peter Marshall, *The Hollywood Squares*, NBC	Peter Marshall, *The Hollywood Squares*, NBC
Host—Talk or Service	Phil Donahue, *Donahue*, SYN	Phil Donahue, *Donahue*, SYN	Hugh Downs, *Over Easy*, PBS
Game Show	*The Hollywood Squares*, NBC	*The Hollywood Squares*, NBC; *The $20,000 Pyramid*, ABC	*The $20,000 Pyramid*, ABC
Talk, Service or Variety Series	*Donahue*, SYN	*Donahue*, SYN	*Donahue*, SYN
Children's Special	*Christmas Eve on Sesame Street*, PBS	—	*Donahue and Kids*, NBC
Children's Entertainment Series	*Kids Are People Too*, ABC	*Hot Hero Sandwich*, NBC	*Captain Kangaroo*, CBS

	1981–82	1982–83	1983–84
Drama	*Hill Street Blues*, NBC	*Hill Street Blues*, NBC	*Hill Street Blues*, NBC
Actor—Drama Series	Daniel J. Travanti, *Hill Street Blues*, NBC	Ed Flanders, *St. Elsewhere*, NBC	Tom Selleck, *Magnum, P.I.*, CBS
Actress—Drama Series	Michael Learned, *Nurse*, CBS	Tyne Daly, *Cagney & Lacey*, CBS	Tyne Daly, *Cagney & Lacey*, CBS
Supporting Actor—Drama Series	Michael Conrad, *Hill Street Blues*, NBC	James Coco, *St. Elsewhere*, NBC	Bruce Weitz, *Hill Street Blues*, NBC
Supporting Actress—Drama Series	Nancy Marchand, *Lou Grant*, CBS	Doris Roberts, *St. Elsewhere*, NBC	Alfre Woodard, *Hill Street Blues*, NBC
Director—Drama Series	Harry Harris, *Fame*, NBC	Jeff Bleckner, *Hill Street Blues*, NBC	Corey Allen, *Hill Street Blues*, NBC
Writer—Drama Series	Steven Bochco, Anthony Yerkovich, Jeffrey Lewis and Michael Wagner (Teleplay); Michael Kozoll, and Steven Bochco (Story), *Hill Street Blues*, NBC	David Milch, *Hill Street Blues*, NBC	John Ford Noonan (Teleplay); John Masius and Tom Fontana (Story), *St. Elsewhere*, NBC
Comedy	*Barney Miller*, ABC	*Cheers*, NBC	*Cheers*, NBC
Actor—Comedy Series	Alan Alda, *M*A*S*H*, CBS	Judd Hirsch, *Taxi*, NBC	John Ritter, *Three's Company*, ABC
Actress—Comedy Series	Carol Kane, *Taxi*, ABC	Shelley Long, *Cheers*, NBC	Jane Curtin, *Kate & Allie*, CBS
Supporting Actor—Comedy Series	Christopher Lloyd, *Taxi*, ABC	Christopher Lloyd, *Taxi*, NBC	Pat Harrington, Jr., *One Day at a Time*, CBS
Supp. Actress—Comedy Series	Loretta Swit, *M*A*S*H*, CBS	Carol Kane, *Taxi*, NBC	Rhea Perlman, *Cheers*, NBC
Director—Comedy Series	Alan Rafkin, *One Day at a Time*, CBS	James Burrows, *Cheers*, NBC	Bill Persky, *Kate & Allie*, CBS
Writer—Comedy Series	Ken Estin, *Taxi*, ABC	Glen Charles, Les Charles, *Cheers*, NBC	David Angel, *Cheers*, NBC
Drama/Comedy Special	*A Woman Called Golda*, SYN	*Special Bulletin*, NBC	*Something About Amelia*, ABC
Variety, Music, or Comedy Program	*Night of 100 Stars*, ABC	*Motown 25: Yesterday, Today, Forever*, NBC	*The 6th Annual Kennedy Center Honors: A Celebration of the Performing Arts*, CBS
Individual Performance—Variety or Music Program	—	Leontyne Price, *Live From Lincoln Center: Leontyne Price, Zubin Mehta, and the New York Philharmonic*, PBS	Cloris Leachman, *Screen Actors Guild 50th Anniversary Celebration*, CBS
Director—Variety or Music	Dwight Hemion, *Goldie and Kids Listen to Us*, ABC	Dwight Hemion, *Sheena Easton Act I*, NBC	Dwight Hemion, *Here's Television Entertainment*, NBC
Writer—Variety or Music	John Candy, Joe Flaherty, Eugene Levy, Andrea Martin, Rick Moranis, Catherine O'Hara, Dave Thomas, Dick Blasucci, Paul Flaherty, Bob Dolman, John McAndrew, Doug Steckler, M. Bert Rich, Jeffrey Barron, Michael Short, Chris Cluess, Stuart Kreisman, and Brian McConnachie, *SCTV Comedy Network*, NBC	John Candy, Joe Flaherty, Eugene Levy, Andrea Martin, Martin Short, Dick Blasucci, Paul Flaherty, John McAndrew, Doug Steckler, Bob Dolman, Michael Short, and Mary Charlotte Wilcox, *SCTV Network*, NBC	Steve O'Donnell, Gerard Mulligan, Sanford Frank, Joseph E. Toplyn, Christopher Elliott, Matt Wickline, Jeff Martin, Ted Greenberg, David Yazbek, Merrill Markoe, and David Letterman, *Late Night with David Letterman*, NBC

	1981–82	1982–83	1983–84
Limited Series	*Marco Polo*, NBC	*Nicholas Nickleby*, SYN	*Concealed Enemies*, PBS
Actor—Limited Series or Special	Mickey Rooney, *Bill*, CBS	Tommy Lee Jones, *The Executioner's Song*, NBC	Laurence Olivier, *King Lear*, SYN
Actress—Limited Series or Special	Ingrid Bergman, *A Woman Called Golda*, SYN	Barbara Stanwyck, *The Thorn Birds*, ABC	Jane Fonda, *The Dollmaker*, ABC
Supporting Actor—Limited Series or Special	Laurence Olivier, *Brideshead Revisited*, PBS	Richard Kiley, *The Thorn Birds*, ABC	Art Carney, *Terrible Joe Moran*, CBS
Supporting Actress—Limited Series or Special	Penny Fuller, *Elephant Man*, ABC	Jean Simmons, *The Thorn Birds*, ABC	Roxana Zal, *Something About Amelia*, ABC
Director—Limited Series or Special	Marvin J. Chomsky, *Inside the Third Reich*, ABC	John Erman, *Who Will Love My Children?*, ABC	Jeff Bleckner, *Concealed Enemies*, PBS
Writer—Limited Series or Special	Corey Blechman (Teleplay); Barry Morrow (Story), *Bill*, CBS	Marshall Herskovitz (Teleplay); Edward Zwick, Marshall Herskovitz (Story), *Special Bulletin*, NBC	William Hanley, *Something About Amelia*, ABC
Daytime Drama Series	*Guiding Light*, CBS	*The Young & The Restless*, CBS	*General Hospital*, ABC
Actor—Daytime Drama Series	Anthony Geary, *General Hospital*, ABC	Robert S. Woods, *One Life to Live*, ABC	Larry Bryggman, *As the World Turns*, CBS
Actress—Daytime Drama Series	Robin Strasser, *One Life To Live*, ABC	Dorothy Lyman, *All My Children*, ABC	Erika Slezak, *One Life To Live*, ABC
Supporting Actor—Daytime Drama Series	David Lewis, *General Hospital*, ABC	Darnell Williams, *All My Children*, ABC	Justin Deas, *As the World Turns*, CBS
Supporting Actress—Daytime Drama Series	Dorothy Lyman, *All My Children*, ABC	Louise Shaffer, *Ryan's Hope*, ABC	Judi Evans, *The Guiding Light*, CBS
Host—Game Show	Bob Barker, *The Price Is Right*, CBS	Betty White, *Just Men!*, NBC	Bob Barker, *The Price Is Right*, CBS
Host—Talk or Service	Phil Donahue, *Donahue*, SYN	Phil Donahue, *Donahue*, SYN	Gary Collins, *Hour Magazine*, SYN
Game Show	*Password Plus*, NBC	*The New $25,000 Pyramid*, CBS	*The $25,000 Pyramid*, CBS
Talk or Service Series	*The Richard Simmons Show*, SYN	*This Old House*, PBS	*Woman to Woman*, SYN
Children's Special	*The Wave*, ABC	*Big Bird in China*, NBC	*He Makes Me Feel Like Dancin'*, NBC
Children's Series	*Captain Kangaroo*, CBS	*Smurfs*, NBC	*Captain Kangaroo*, CBS

	1984–85	1985–86	1986–87
Drama	*Cagney and Lacey,* CBS	*Cagney & Lacey,* CBS	*L. A. Law,* NBC
Actor—Drama Series	William Daniels, *St. Elsewhere,* NBC	William Daniels, *St. Elsewhere,* NBC	Bruce Willis, *Moonlighting,* ABC
Actress—Drama Series	Tyne Daly, *Cagney & Lacey,* CBS	Sharon Gless, *Cagney & Lacey,* CBS	Sharon Gless, *Cagney & Lacey,* CBS
Supporting Actor—Drama Series	Edward James Olmos, *Miami Vice,* NBC	John Karlen, *Cagney & Lacey,* CBS	John Hillerman, *Magnum, P.I.,* CBS
Supporting Actress—Drama Series	Betty Thomas, *Hill Street Blues,* NBC	Bonnie Bartlett, *St. Elsewhere,* NBC	Bonnie Bartlett, *St. Elsewhere,* NBC
Director—Drama Series	Karen Arthur, *Cagney & Lacey,* CBS	Georg Stanford Brown, *Cagney & Lacey,* CBS	Gregory Hoblit, *L.A. Law,* NBC
Writer—Drama Series	Patricia M. Green, *Cagney & Lacey,* CBS	Tom Fontana, John Tinker, and John Masius, *St. Elsewhere,* NBC	Steven Bochco, Terry Louise Fisher, *L.A. Law,* NBC
Comedy	*The Cosby Show,* NBC	*The Golden Girls,* NBC	*The Golden Girls,* NBC
Actor—Comedy Series	Robert Guillaume, *Benson,* ABC	Michael J. Fox, *Family Ties,* NBC	Michael J. Fox, *Family Ties,* NBC
Actress—Comedy Series	Jane Curtin, *Kate & Allie,* CBS	Betty White, *The Golden Girls,* NBC	Rue McClanahan, *The Golden Girls,* NBC
Supporting Actor—Comedy Series	John Larroquette, *Night Court,* NBC	John Larroquette, *Night Court,* NBC	John Larroquette, *Night Court,* NBC
Supporting Actress—Comedy Series	Rhea Perlman, *Cheers,* NBC	Rhea Perlman, *Cheers,* NBC	Jackée Harry, *227,* NBC
Director—Comedy Series	Jay Sandrich, *The Cosby Show,* NBC	Jay Sandrich, *The Cosby Show,* NBC	Terry Hughes, *The Golden Girls,* NBC
Writer—Comedy Series	Ed. Weinberger, Michael Leeson, *The Cosby Show,* NBC	Barry Fanaro and Mort Nathan, *The Golden Girls,* NBC	Gary David Goldberg, Alan Uger, *Family Ties,* NBC
Drama/Comedy Special	*Do You Remember Love,* CBS	*Love Is Never Silent,* NBC	*Promise,* CBS
Variety, Music, or Comedy Program	*Motown Returns to the Apollo,* NBC	*The Kennedy Center Honors: A Celebration of the Performing Arts,* CBS	*The 1987 Tony Awards,* CBS
Individual Performance—Variety or Music Program	George Hearn, *Sweeney Todd,* PBS	Whitney Houston, *The 28th Annual Grammy Awards,* CBS	Robin Williams, *A Carol Burnett Special: Carol, Carl, Whoopi & Robin,* ABC
Director—Variety or Music	Terry Hughes, *Sweeney Todd,* PBS	Waris Hussein, *Copacabana,* CBS	Don Mischer, *The Kennedy Center Honors: A Celebration of the Performing Arts,* CBS
Writer—Variety or Music	Gerard Mulligan, Sandy Frank, Joe Toplyn, Chris Elliott, Matt Wickline, Jeff Martin, Eddie Gorodetsky, Randy Cohen, Larry Jacobson, Kevin Curran, Fred Graver, Merrill Markoe, and David Letterman, *Late Night with David Letterman,* NBC	David Letterman, Steve O'Donnell, Sandy Frank, Joe Toplyn, Chris Elliott, Matt Wickline, Jeff Martin, Gerard Mulligan, Randy Cohen, Larry Jacobson, Kevin Curran, Fred Graver, and Merrill Markoe, *Late Night with David Letterman,* NBC	Steve O'Donnell, Sandy Frank, Joe Toplyn, Chris Elliott, Matt Wickline, Jeff Martin, Gerard Mulligan, Randy Cohen, Larry Jacobson, Kevin Curran, Fred Graver, Adam Resnick, and David Letterman, *Late Night with David Letterman,* NBC

	1984–85	1985–86	1986–87
Miniseries	*The Jewel in the Crown*, PBS	*Peter the Great*, NBC	*A Year in the Life*, NBC
Actor—Miniseries	Richard Crenna, *The Rape of Richard Beck*, ABC	Dustin Hoffman, *Death of a Salesman*, CBS	James Woods, *Promise*, CBS
Actress—Miniseries	Joanne Woodward, *Do You Remember Love*, CBS	Marlo Thomas, *Nobody's Child*, CBS	Gena Rowlands, *The Betty Ford Story*, ABC
Supporting Actor—Miniseries or Special	Karl Malden, *Fatal Vision*, NBC	John Malkovich, *Death of a Salesman*, CBS	Dabney Coleman, *Sworn to Silence*, ABC
Supporting Actress—Miniseries/ Limited Series or Special	Kim Stanley, *Cat on a Hot Tin Roof*, PBS	Colleen Dewhurst, *Between Two Women*, ABC	Piper Laurie, *Promise*, CBS
Director—Miniseries or Special	Lamont Johnson, *Wallenberg: A Hero's Story*, NBC	Joseph Sargent, *Love Is Never Silent*, NBC	Glenn Jordan, *Promise*, CBS
Writer—Miniseries or Special	Vickie Patik, *Do You Remember Love*, CBS	Ron Cowen and Daniel Lipman (Teleplay); Sherman Yellen (Story), *An Early Frost*, NBC	Richard Friedenberg (Teleplay); Kenneth Blackwell, Tennyson Flowers, and Richard Friedenberg (Story), *Promise*, CBS
Daytime Drama Series	*The Young and the Restless*, CBS	*The Young and the Restless*, CBS	*As the World Turns*, CBS
Actor—Daytime Drama Series	Darnell Williams, *All My Children*, ABC	David Canary, *All My Children*, ABC	Larry Bryggman, *As the World Turns*, CBS
Actress—Daytime Drama Series	Kim Zimmer, *Guiding Light*, CBS	Erika Slezak, *One Life To Live*, ABC	Kim Zimmer, *Guiding Light*, CBS
Supporting Actor—Daytime Drama Series	Larry Gates, *Guiding Light*, CBS	John Wesley Shipp, *As the World Turns*, CBS	Gregg Marx, *As the World Turns*, CBS
Supporting Actress—Daytime Drama Series	Beth Maitland, *The Young and the Restless*, CBS	Leann Hunley, *Days of Our Lives*, NBC	Kathleen Noone, *All My Children*, ABC
Ingenue— Daytime Drama Series	Tracey E. Bregman, *The Young and the Restless*, CBS	Ellen Wheeler, *Another World*, NBC	Martha Byrne, *As the World Turns*, CBS
Younger Leading Man— Daytime Drama Series	Brian Bloom, *As the World Turns*, CBS	Michael E. Knight, *All My Children*, ABC	Michael E. Knight, *All My Children*, ABC
Host—Game Show	Dick Clark, *The $25,000 Pyramid*, CBS	Dick Clark, *The $25,000 Pyramid*, CBS	Bob Barker, *The Price Is Right*, CBS
Host—Talk or Service	Phil Donahue, *Donahue*, SYN	Phil Donahue, *Donahue*, SYN	Oprah Winfrey, *The Oprah Winfrey Show*, SYN
Game Show	*The $25,000 Pyramid*, CBS	*The $25,000 Pyramid*, CBS	*The $25,000 Pyramid*, CBS
Talk, Service or Variety Series	*Donahue*, SYN	*Donahue*, SYN	*The Oprah Winfrey Show*, SYN
Children's Special	*Displaced Person*, PBS	*Anne of Green Gables*, PBS	*Jim Henson's The Storyteller: Hans My Hedgehog*, NBC
Children's Series	*Sesame Street*, PBS	*Sesame Street*, PBS	*Sesame Street*, PBS

	1987–88	1988–89	1989–90
Drama	*thirtysomething*, ABC	*L.A. Law*, NBC	*L.A. Law*, NBC
Actor—Drama Series	Richard Kiley, *A Year in the Life*, NBC	Carroll O'Connor, *In the Heat of the Night*, NBC	Peter Falk, *Columbo*, ABC
Actress—Drama Series	Tyne Daly, *Cagney & Lacey*, CBS	Dana Delany, *China Beach*, ABC	Patricia Wettig, *thirtysomething*, ABC
Supporting Actor—Drama Series	Larry Drake, *L.A. Law*, NBC	Larry Drake, *L.A. Law*, NBC	Jimmy Smits, *L.A. Law*, NBC
Supporting Actress—Drama Series	Patricia Wettig, *thirtysomething*, ABC	Melanie Mayron, *thirtysomething*, ABC	Marg Helgenberger, *China Beach*, ABC
Director—Drama Series	Mark Tinker, *St. Elsewhere*, NBC	Robert Altman, *Tanner '88*, HBO	Thomas Carter, *Equal Justice*, ABC; Scott Winant, *thirtysomething*, ABC
Writer—Drama Series	Paul Haggis, Marshall Herskovitz, *thirtysomething*, ABC	Joseph Dougherty, *thirtysomething*, ABC	David E. Kelley, *L.A. Law*, NBC
Comedy	*The Wonder Years*, ABC	*Cheers*, NBC	*Murphy Brown*, CBS
Actor—Comedy Series	Michael J. Fox, *Family Ties*, NBC	Richard Mulligan, *Empty Nest*, NBC	Ted Danson, *Cheers*, NBC
Actress—Comedy Series	Beatrice Arthur, *The Golden Girls*, NBC	Candice Bergen, *Murphy Brown*, CBS	Candice Bergen, *Murphy Brown*, CBS
Supporting Actor—Comedy Series	John Larroquette, *Night Court*, NBC	Woody Harrelson, *Cheers*, NBC	Alex Rocco, *The Famous Teddy Z*, CBS
Supporting Actress—Comedy Series	Estelle Getty, *The Golden Girls*, NBC	Rhea Perlman, *Cheers*, NBC	Bebe Neuwirth, *Cheers*, NBC
Director—Comedy Series	Gregory Hoblit, *Hooperman*, ABC	Peter Baldwin, *The Wonder Years*, ABC	Michael Dinner, *The Wonder Years*, ABC
Writer—Comedy Series	Hugh Wilson, *Frank's Place*, CBS	Diane English, *Murphy Brown*, CBS	Bob Brush, *The Wonder Years*, ABC
Drama/Comedy Special	*Inherit the Wind*, NBC	*Day One*, CBS	*Caroline?*, CBS; *The Incident*, CBS
Variety, Music, or Comedy Program	*Irving Berlin's 100th Birthday Celebration*, CBS	*The Tracey Ullman Show*, FOX	*In Living Color*, FOX
Individual Performance—Variety or Music Program	Robin Williams, *ABC Presents a Royal Gala*, ABC	Linda Ronstadt, *Canciones de Mi Padre*, PBS	Tracey Ullman, *The Best of the Tracey Ullman Show*, FOX
Director—Variety or Music	Patricia Birch and Humphrey Burton, *Celebrating Gershwin*, PBS	Jim Henson, *The Jim Henson Hour*, NBC	Dwight Hemion, *The Kennedy Center Honors: A Celebration of the Performing Arts*, CBS

	1987–88	1988–89	1989–90
Writer—Variety or Music	Jackie Mason, *Jackie Mason on Broadway*, HBO	James Downey, head writer; John Bowman, A. Whitney Brown, Gregory Daniels, Tom Davis, Al Franken, Shannon Gaughan, Jack Handey, Phil Hartman, Lorne Michaels, Mike Myers, Conan O'Brien, Bob Odenkirk, Herb Sargent, Tom Schiller, Robert Smigel, Bonnie Turner, Terry Turner, and Christine Zander, writers; George Meyer, additional sketches, *Saturday Night Live*, NBC	Billy Crystal, *Billy Crystal: Midnight Train to Moscow*, HBO; James L. Brooks, Heide Perlman, Sam Simon, Jerry Belson, Marc Flanagan, Dinah Kirgo, Jay Kogen, Wallace Wolodarsky, Ian Praiser, Marilyn Suzanne Miller, and Tracey Ullman, *The Tracey Ullman Show*, FOX
Miniseries	*The Murder of Mary Phagan*, NBC	*War and Remembrance*, ABC	*Drug Wars: The Camarena Story*, NBC
Actor—Miniseries or Special	Jason Robards, *Inherit the Wind*, NBC	James Woods, *My Name is Bill W.*, ABC	Hume Cronyn, *Age-Old Friends*, HBO
Actress—Miniseries or Special	Jessica Tandy, *Foxfire*, CBS	Holly Hunter, *Roe vs. Wade*, NBC	Barbara Hershey, *A Killing in a Small Town*, CBS
Supporting Actor—Miniseries or Special	John Shea, *Baby M*, ABC	Derek Jacobi, *The Tenth Man*, CBS	Vincent Gardenia, *Age-Old Friends*, HBO
Supporting Actress—Miniseries or Special	Jane Seymour, *Onassis: The Richest Man in the World*, ABC	Colleen Dewhurst, *Those She Left Behind*, NBC	Eva Marie Saint, *People Like Us*, NBC
Director—Miniseries or Special	Lamont Johnson, *Gore Vidal's Lincoln*, NBC	Simon Wincer, *Lonesome Dove*, CBS	Joseph Sargent, *Caroline?*, CBS
Writer—Miniseries or Special	William Hanley, *The Attic: The Hiding of Anne Frank*, CBS	Abby Mann, Robin Vote, and Ron Hutchison, *Murderers Among Us: The Simon Wiesenthal Story*, HBO	Terrence McNally, *Andre's Mother*, PBS
Daytime Drama Series	*Santa Barbara*, NBC	*Santa Barbara*, NBC	*Santa Barbara*, NBC
Actor—Daytime Drama Series	David Canary, *All My Children*, ABC	David Canary, *All My Children*, ABC	A Martinez, *Santa Barbara*, NBC
Actress—Daytime Drama Series	Helen Gallagher, *Ryan's Hope*, ABC	Marcy Walker, *Santa Barbara*, NBC	Kim Zimmer, *Guiding Light*, CBS
Supp. Actor—Daytime Drama	Justin Deas, *Santa Barbara*, NBC	Justin Deas, *Santa Barbara*, NBC	Henry Darrow, *Santa Barbara*, NBC
Supporting Actress—Daytime Drama Series	Ellen Wheeler, *All My Children*, ABC	Debbi Morgan, *All My Children*, ABC; Nancy Lee Grahn, *Santa Barbara*, NBC	Julia Barr, *All My Children*, ABC
Ingenue—Daytime Drama Series	Julianne Moore, *As the World Turns*, CBS	Kimberly McCullough, *General Hospital*, ABC	Cady McClain, *All My Children*, ABC
Younger Leading Man—Daytime Drama Series	Billy Warlock, *Days of Our Lives*, NBC	Justin Gocke, *Santa Barbara*, NBC	Andrew Kavovit, *As the World Turns*, CBS
Host—Game Show	Bob Barker, *The Price Is Right*, CBS	Alex Trebek, *Jeopardy!*, SYN	Alex Trebek, *Jeopardy!*, SYN; Bob Barker, *The Price Is Right*, CBS
Host—Talk or Service Show	Phil Donahue, *Donahue*, SYN	Sally Jessy Raphael, *Sally Jessy Raphael*, SYN	Joan Rivers, *The Joan Rivers Show*, SYN
Game Show	*The Price Is Right*, CBS	*The $25,000 Pyramid*, CBS	*Jeopardy!*, SYN
Talk, Service, or Variety Series	*The Oprah Winfrey Show*, SYN	*The Oprah Winfrey Show*, SYN	*Sally Jessy Raphael*, SYN
Children's Special	*The Secret Garden*, CBS	*Free To Be ... A Family*, ABC	*A Mother's Courage: The Mary Thomas Story*, NBC
Children's Series	*Sesame Street*, PBS	*Newton's Apple*, PBS	*Reading Rainbow*, PBS

	1990–91	1991–92	1992–93
Drama	*L.A. Law*, NBC	*Northern Exposure*, CBS	*Picket Fences*, CBS
Actor—Drama Series	James Earl Jones, *Gabriel's Fire*, ABC	Christopher Lloyd, *Avonlea*, DIS	Tom Skerritt, *Picket Fences*, CBS
Actress—Drama Series	Patricia Wettig, *thirtysomething*, ABC	Dana Delany, *China Beach*, ABC	Kathy Baker, *Picket Fences*, CBS
Supporting Actor—Drama Series	Timothy Busfield, *thirtysomething*, ABC	Richard Dysart, *L.A. Law*, NBC	Chad Lowe, *Life Goes On*, ABC
Supporting Actress—Drama Series	Madge Sinclair, *Gabriel's Fire*, ABC	Valerie Mahaffey, *Northern Exposure*, CBS	Mary Alice, *I'll Fly Away*, NBC
Director—Drama Series	Thomas Carter, *Equal Justice*, ABC	Eric Laneuville, *I'll Fly Away*, NBC	Barry Levinson, *Homicide—Life on the Street*, NBC
Writer—Drama Series	David E. Kelley, *L.A. Law*, NBC	Andrew Schneider and Diane Frolov, *Northern Exposure*, CBS	Tom Fontana, *Homicide—Life on the Street*, NBC
Comedy	*Cheers*, NBC	*Murphy Brown*, CBS	*Seinfeld*, NBC
Actor—Comedy Series	Burt Reynolds, *Evening Shade*, CBS	Craig T. Nelson, *Coach*, ABC	Ted Danson, *Cheers*, NBC
Actress—Comedy Series	Kirstie Alley, *Cheers*, NBC	Candice Bergen, *Murphy Brown*, CBS	Roseanne Arnold, *Roseanne*, ABC
Supporting Actor—Comedy Series	Jonathan Winters, *Davis Rules*, ABC	Michael Jeter, *Evening Shade*, CBS	Michael Richards, *Seinfeld*, NBC
Supp. Actress—Comedy Series	Bebe Neuwirth, *Cheers*, NBC	Laurie Metcalf, *Roseanne*, ABC	Laurie Metcalf, *Roseanne*, ABC
Director—Comedy Series	James Burrows, *Cheers*, NBC	Barnet Kellman, *Murphy Brown*, CBS	Betty Thomas, *Dream On*, HBO
Writer—Comedy Series	Gary Dontzig and Steven Peterman, *Murphy Brown*, CBS	Elaine Pope and Larry Charles, *Seinfeld*, NBC	Larry David, *Seinfeld*, NBC
Variety, Music, or Comedy Program	*The 63rd Annual Academy Awards*, ABC	*The Tonight Show Starring Johnny Carson*, NBC	*Saturday Night Live*, NBC
Individual Performance—Variety or Music Program	Billy Crystal, *The 63rd Annual Academy Awards*, ABC	Bette Midler, *The Tonight Show Starring Johnny Carson*, NBC	Dana Carvey, *Saturday Night Live*, NBC
Director—Variety or Music	Hal Gurnee, *Late Night with David Letterman*, NBC	Patricia Birch, *Unforgettable with Love: Natalie Cole Sings the Songs of Nat King Cole*, PBS	Walter C. Miller, *The 1992 Tony Awards*, CBS
Writer—Variety or Music	Hal Kanter and Buz Kohan, writers; Billy Crystal, David Steinberg, Bruce Vilanch, and Robert Wuhl (Special Material), *The 63rd Annual Academy Awards*, ABC	Hal Kanter and Buz Kohan, writers); Billy Crystal, Marc Shaiman, David Steinberg, Robert Wuhl, and Bruce Vilanch, special material, *The 64rd Annual Academy Awards*, ABC	Judd Apatow, Robert Cohen, David Cross, Brent Forrester, Jeff Kahn, Bruce Kirschbaum, Bob Odenkirk, Sultan Pepper, Dino Stamatopoulos, and Ben Stiller, *The Ben Stiller Show*, FOX
Made for Television Movie	—	*Miss Rose White*: Hallmark Hall of Fame, NBC	*Barbarians at the Gate*, HBO; *Stalin*, HBO
Miniseries	*Separate but Equal*, ABC	*A Woman Named Jackie*, NBC	*Prime Suspect 2*, PBS

	1990–91	1991–92	1992–93
Actor—Miniseries or Special	John Gielgud, *Summer's Lease*, PBS	Beau Bridges, *Without Warning: The James Brady Story*, HBO	Robert Morse, *Tru*, PBS
Actress—Miniseries or Special	Lynn Whitfield, *The Josephine Baker Story*, HBO	Gena Rowlands, *Face of a Stranger*, CBS	Holly Hunter, *The Positively True Adventures of the Alleged Texas Cheerleader-Murdering Mom*, HBO
Supporting Actor—Miniseries or Special	James Earl Jones, *Heat Wave*, TNT	Hume Cronyn, *Neil Simon's Broadway Bound*, ABC	Beau Bridges, *The Positively True Adventures of the Alleged Texas Cheerleader-Murdering Mom*, HBO
Supporting Actress—Miniseries or Special	Ruby Dee, *Decoration Day*, NBC	Amanda Plummer, *Miss Rose White*, NBC	Mary Tyler Moore, *Stolen Babies*, LIF
Director—Miniseries or Special	Brian Gibson, *The Josephine Baker Story*, HBO	Daniel Petrie, *Mark Twain and Me*, DIS	James Sadwith, *Sinatra*, CBS
Writer—Miniseries or Special	Andrew Davies, *House of Cards*, PBS	John Falsey and Joshua Brand, *I'll Fly Away*, NBC	Jane Anderson, *The Positively True Adventures of the Alleged Texas Cheerleader-Murdering Mom*, HBO
Daytime Drama Series	*As the World Turns*, CBS	*All My Children*, ABC	*The Young and the Restless*, CBS
Actor—Daytime Drama Series	Peter Bergman, *The Young and the Restless*, CBS	Peter Bergman, *The Young and the Restless*, CBS	David Canary, *All My Children*, ABC
Actress—Daytime Drama Series	Finola Hughes, *General Hospital*, ABC	Erika Slezak, *One Life to Live*, ABC	Linda Dano, *Another World*, NBC
Supporting Actor—Daytime Drama Series	Bernie Barrow, *Loving*, ABC	Thom Christopher, *One Life to Live*, ABC	Gerald Anthony, *General Hospital*, ABC
Supporting Actress—Daytime Drama Series	Jess Walton, *The Young and the Restless*, CBS	Maeve Kinkead, *Guiding Light*, CBS	Ellen Parker, *Guiding Light*, CBS
Younger Actress—Daytime Drama Series	Anne Heche, *Another World*, NBC	Tricia Cast, *The Young and the Restless*, CBS	Heather Tom, *The Young and the Restless*, CBS
Younger Leading Man—Daytime Drama Series	Rick Hearst, *Guiding Light*, CBS	Kristoff St. John, *The Young and the Restless*, CBS	Monti Sharp, *Guiding Light*, CBS
Host—Game Show	Bob Barker, *The Price Is Right*, CBS	Bob Barker, *The Price Is Right*, CBS	Pat Sajak, *Wheel of Fortune*, SYN
Host—Talk or Service Show	Oprah Winfrey, *The Oprah Winfrey Show*, SYN	Oprah Winfrey, *The Oprah Winfrey Show*, SYN	Oprah Winfrey, *The Oprah Winfrey Show*, SYN
Game Show	*Jeopardy!*, SYN	*Jeopardy!*, SYN	*Jeopardy!*, SYN
Talk, Service, or Variety Series	*The Oprah Winfrey Show*, SYN	*The Oprah Winfrey Show*, SYN	*Good Morning America*, ABC
Children's Special	*You Can't Grow Home Again: A 3-2-1 Contact Extra*, PBS	*Mark Twain and Me*, DIS	*Shades of a Single Protein*, ABC
Children's Series	*Sesame Street*, PBS	*Sesame Street*, PBS	*Reading Rainbow*, PBS; *Tiny Toon Adventures*, SYN (Animated)

	1993-94	1994-95
Drama	*Picket Fences,* CBS	*NYPD Blue,* ABC
Actor—Drama Series	Dennis Franz, *NYPD Blue,* ABC	Mandy Patinkin, *Chicago Hope,* CBS
Actress—Drama Series	Sela Ward, *Sisters,* NBC	Kathy Baker, *Picket Fences,* CBS
Supporting Actor—Drama Series	Fyvush Finkel, *Picket Fences,* CBS	Ray Walston, *Picket Fences,* CBS
Supporting Actress—Drama Series	Leigh Taylor-Young, *Picket Fences,* CBS	Julianna Margulies, *ER,* NBC
Director—Drama Series	Daniel Sackheim, *NYPD Blue,* ABC	Mimi Leder, *ER,* NBC
Writer—Drama Series	Ann Biderman, *NYPD Blue,* ABC	Michael Crichton, *ER,* NBC
Comedy	*Frasier,* NBC	*Frasier,* NBC
Actor—Comedy Series	Kelsey Grammer, *Frasier,* NBC	Kelsey Grammer, *Frasier,* NBC
Actress—Comedy Series	Candice Bergen, *Murphy Brown,* CBS	Candice Bergen, *Murphy Brown,* CBS
Supporting Actor—Comedy Series	Michael Richards, *Seinfeld,* NBC	David Hyde Pierce, *Frasier,* NBC
Supp. Actress—Comedy Series	Laurie Metcalf, *Roseanne,* ABC	Christine Baranski, *Cybill,* CBS
Director—Comedy Series	James Burrows, *Frasier,* NBC	David Lee, *Frasier,* NBC
Writer—Comedy Series	David Angel, Peter Casey, and David Lee, *Frasier,* NBC	Chuck Ranberg, Anne Flett-Giordano, *Frasier,* NBC
Variety, Music, or Comedy Program	*Late Show With David Letterman,* CBS	*The Tonight Show with Jay Leno,* NBC
Individual Performance—Variety or Music Program	Tracey Ullman, *Tracey Ullman Takes On New York,* HBO	Barbra Streisand, *Barbra Streisand: The Concert,* HBO
Director—Variety or Music	Walter C. Miller, *The Tony Awards,* CBS	Jeff Margolis, *The 67th Annual Academy Awards,* ABC
Writer—Variety or Music	Jeff Cesario, Mike Dugan, Eddie Feldmann, Gregory Greenberg, Dennis Miller, Kevin Rooney, *Dennis Miller Live,* HBO	Jeff Cesario, Ed Driscoll, David Feldman, Eddie Feldmann, Gregory Greenberg, Dennis Miller, Kevin Rooney, *Dennis Miller Live,* HBO
Made for Television Movie	*And the Band Played On,* HBO	*Indictment: The McMartin Trial,* HBO
Miniseries	*Mystery: Prime Suspect 3,* PBS	*Joseph,* TNT

	1993-94	1994-95
Actor—Miniseries or Special	Hume Cronyn, *Hallmark Hall of Fame: To Dance With the White Dog,* CBS	Raul Julia, *The Burning Season,* HBO
Actress—Miniseries or Special	Kirstie Alley, *David's Mother,* CBS	Glenn Close, *Serving in Silence: The Margarethe Cammermeyer Story,* NBC
Supporting Actor—Miniseries or Special	Michael Goorjian, *David's Mother,* CBS	Donald Sutherland, *Citizen X,* HBO
Supporting Actress—Miniseries or Special	Cicely Tyson, *Oldest Living Confederate Widow Tells All,* CBS	Judy Davis, *Serving in Silence: The Margarethe Cammemeyer Story,* NBC
Director—Miniseries or Special	John Frankenheimer, *Against the Wall,* HBO	John Frankenheimer, *The Burning Season,* HBO
Writer—Miniseries or Special	Bob Randall, *David's Mother,* CBS	Alison Cross, *Serving in Silence: The Margarethe Cammermeyer Story,* NBC
Daytime Drama Series	*All My Children,* ABC	*General Hospital,* ABC
Actor—Daytime Drama Series	Michael Zaslow, *Guiding Light,* CBS	Justin Deas, *Guiding Light,* CBS
Actress—Daytime Drama Series	Hillary B. Smith, *One Life to Live,* ABC	Erika Slezak, *One Life to Live,* ABC
Supporting Actor—Daytime Drama Series	Justin Deas, *Guiding Light,* CBS	Jerry Ver Dorn, *Guiding Light,* CBS
Supporting Actress—Daytime Drama Series	Susan Haskell, *One Life to Live,* ABC	Rena Sofer, *General Hospital,* ABC
Younger Actress—Daytime Drama Series	Melissa Hayden, *Guiding Light,* CBS	Sarah Michelle Gellar, *All My Children,* ABC
Younger Leading Man—Daytime Drama Series	Roger Howarth, *One Life to Live,* ABC	Jonathan Jackson, *General Hospital,* ABC
Host—Talk or Service Show	Oprah Winfrey, *The Oprah Winfrey Show,* SYN	Oprah Winfrey, *The Oprah Winfrey Show,* SYN
Game Show	*Jeopardy!,* SYN	*Jeopardy!,* SYN
Talk, Service, or Variety Series	*The Oprah Winfrey Show,* SYN-	*The Oprah Winfrey Show,* SYN
Children's Special	*Dead Drunk: The Kevin Tunell Story,* HBO	*A Child Betrayed: The Calvin Mire Story,* HBO
Children's Series	*Sesame Street,* PBS; *Rugrats,* Nick (Animated)	*Nick News,* Nickelodeon; *Where on Earth is Carmen San Diego?,* Fox (Animated)

	1995-96	1996-97
Drama	*ER,* NBC	*Law & Order,* NBC
Actor—Drama Series	Dennis Franz, *NYPD Blue,* ABC	Dennis Franz, *NYPD Blue,* ABC
Actress—Drama Series	Kathy Baker, *Picket Fences,* CBS	Gillian Anderson, *The X-Files,* Fox
Supporting Actor—Drama Series	Ray Walston, *Picket Fences,* CBS	Hector Elizondo, *Chicago Hope,* CBS
Supporting Actress—Drama Series	Tyne Daly, *Christy,* CBS	Kim Delaney, *NYPD Blue,* ABC
Director—Drama Series	Jeremy Kagan, *Chicago Hope,* CBS	Mark Tinker, *NYPD Blue,* ABC
Writer—Drama Series	Darin Morgan, *The X-Files,* Fox	David Milch, Stephen Gaghan, Michael R. Perry, *NYPD Blue,* ABC
Comedy	*Frasier,* NBC	*Frasier,* NBC
Actor—Comedy Series	John Lithgow, *3rd Rock from the Sun,* NBC	John Lithgow, *3rd Rock from the Sun,* NBC
Actress—Comedy Series	Helen Hunt, *Mad About You,* NBC	Helen Hunt, *Mad About You,* NBC
Supporting Actor—Comedy Series	Rip Torn, *The Larry Sanders Show,* HBO	Michael Richards, *Seinfeld,* NBC
Supporting Actress—Comedy Series	Julia Louis-Dreyfuss, *Seinfeld,* NBC	Kristen Johnston, *3rd Rock from the Sun,* NBC
Director—Comedy Series	Michael Lembeck, *Friends,* NBC	David Lee, *Frasier,* NBC
Writer—Comedy Series	Joe Keenan, Christopher Lloyd, Rob Greenberg, Jack Burditt, Chuck Ranberg, Anne Flett-Giordano, Linda Morris, and Vic Rauseo, *Frasier,* NBC	Ellen DeGeneres, Mark Driscoll, Dava Savel, Tracy Newman, and Jonathan Stark, *Ellen,* ABC
Variety, Music, or Comedy Program	*Dennis Miller Live,* HBO	*Tracey Takes On...,* HBO (series) *Chris Rock: Bring the Pain,* HBO (special)
Individual Performance—Variety or Music Program	Tony Bennett, *Tony Bennett Live by Request: A Valentine Special,* A&E	Bette Midler, *Bette Midler: Diva Las Vegas,* HBO
Director—Variety or Music	Louis J. Horvitz, *The Kennedy Center Honors,* CBS	Don Mischer, *Centennial Olympic Games, Opening Ceremonies,* NBC
Writer—Variety or Music	Eddie Feldmann, David Feldmann, Mike Gandolfini, Tom Hertz, Leah Krinsky, Dennis Miller, Rick Overton, *Dennis Miller Live,* HBO	Chris Rock, *Chris Rock: Bring the Pain,* HBO
Made for Television Movie	*Truman,* HBO	*Miss Evers' Boys,* HBO
Miniseries	*Gulliver's Travels,* NBC	*Prime Suspect 5: Errors of Judgment,* PBS

	1995-96	1996-97
Actor—Miniseries or Special	Alan Rickman, *Rasputin,* HBO	Armand Assante, *Gotti,* HBO
Actress—Miniseries or Special	Helen Mirren, *Prime Suspect: Scent of Darkness,* PBS	Alfre Woodard, *Miss Evers' Boys,* HBO
Supporting Actor—Miniseries or Special	Tom Hulce, *The Heidi Chronicles,* TNT	Beau Bridges, *The Second Civil War,* HBO
Supporting Actress—Miniseries or Special	Greta Scacchi, *Rasputin,* HBO	Diana Rigg, *Rebecca,* PBS
Director—Miniseries or Special	John Frankenheimer, *Andersonville,* TNT	Andrei Konchalovsky, *The Odyssey, Part I and II,* NBC
Writer—Miniseries or Special	Simon Moore, *Gulliver's Travels,* NBC	Horton Foote, *William Faulkner's Old Man,* CBS
Daytime Drama Series	*General Hospital,* ABC	*General Hospital,* ABC
Actor—Daytime Drama Series	Charles Keating, *Another World,* NBC	Justin Deas, *Guiding Light,* CBS
Actress—Daytime Drama Series	Erika Slezak, *One Life to Live,* ABC	Jess Walton, *The Young and the Restless,* CBS
Supporting Actor—Daytime Drama Series	Jerry Ver Dorn, *Guiding Light,* CBS	Ian Buchanan, *The Bold and the Beautiful,* CBS
Supporting Actress—Daytime Drama Series	Anna Holbrook, *Another World,* NBC	Michelle Stafford, *The Young and the Restless,* CBS
Younger Actress—Daytime Drama Series	Kimberly McCullough, *General Hospital,* ABC	Sarah Brown, *General Hospital,* ABC
Younger Leading Man—Daytime Drama Series	Kevin Mambo, *Guiding Light,* CBS	Kevin Mambo, *Guiding Light,* CBS
Host—Talk or Service Show	Montel Williams, *The Montel Williams Show,* SYN	Rosie O'Donnell, *The Rosie O'Donnell Show,* SYN
Game Show	*The Price Is Right,* CBS	*The Price Is Right,* CBS
Talk, Service, or Variety Series	*The Oprah Winfrey Show,* SYN	*The Oprah Winfrey Show,* SYN
Children's Special	*Stand Up,* CBS	*Elmo Saves Christmas,* PBS
Children's Series	*Sesame Street,* PBS; *Animaniacs,* WB (Animated)	*Reading Rainbow,* PBS; *Animaniacs,* WB (Animated)

SONG

PICKS & PANS 1997

From the teen-MMMboppers Hanson to the late, great Woody Guthrie, the year's releases ranged from chart-topping debuts to compilations and rereleases of legends from an era past. PEOPLE reviewed them all for your listening pleasure, with the finest offerings earning an asterisk.

NINE LIVES
Aerosmith
Although perfectly acceptable, Aerosmith isn't getting all those millions just to be that.

RECKLESS
Luther Allison
From uptempo rockers to contemplative acoustic blues, the late Allison performed with the fiery energy of a teenager and the grizzled soul of a veteran.

PAY BEFORE YOU PUMP
Al Anderson
He may not be the flashiest of guys, but this country-fried rocker knows how to tinker around and get the job done.

BACKSTREET BOYS
Backstreet Boys
Their debut CD fares best when the funk flows; the ballads are so peppy, one can't help smiling despite the tinge of melancholy in the harmonies—though such cheer renders hyperbole like "Without you I don't think I can live" all the more cringe-inducing.

BADUIZM
Erykah Badu
Despite her best intentions, Badu's neo-bohemian stylings quickly become as formulaic as the claustrophobic R&B she's trying to avoid.

***L'AMOUR OU LA FOLIE**
BeauSoleil
For the hippest back-porch dance party your block has ever seen, toss on this zesty gumbo of zydeco, Creole, southern two-step, Gulf Coast swamp-pop, Cajun wedding ballads, and French country and western.

STILL WATERS
Bee Gees
Not since their '70s heyday has sweet harmony sounded quite so spine-tingling.

***WHATEVER AND EVER AMEN**
Ben Folds Five
The band sounds sort of like Squeeze meets Freddie Mercury—at a George Gershwin tribute. The smart sound is a perfect match for the group's wry, home-spun lyrics.

DAN BERN
Dan Bern
With his guitar and harmonica and nasal twang, Bern may sound as if he has listened to too many Bob Dylan albums—but his biting, accessible sense of humor is his own.

BEAUTIFUL WORLD
Big Head Todd & the Monsters
BHT&M stumble when they try their hand at funk, and occasionally succumb to mid-tempo blahs, but when the band hits its country-sparked stride their world is a beautiful one indeed.

***BIG HOUSE**
Big House
With several Don Henley-esque ballads, blues funk, and an irresistible head-out-on-the-highway anthem, this high-octane CD finds the group breezing toward a sunny future.

***LEAVIN' THIS TOWN**
Terri Binion
Graced by great songs, tasteful production, razor-sharp rhythm section, and Binion's warm, honey-tinged voice, *Leavin'* is a knockout piece of modern country-rock.

TELEGRAM
Björk
The Icelandic sprite has enlisted various cutting-edge collaborators to rework nine songs from her 1995 *Post*. As intriguing as such radical reinvention might be, it doesn't always fly.

NOTHIN' BUT THE TAILLIGHTS
Clint Black
Steady, reliable Black brings a homegrown touch of class to his projects, and rarely sacrifices texture or tradition.

***SHARE MY WORLD**
Mary J. Blige
Mary J. effortlessly shifts gears from fly-girl throw-downs to sultry love songs without breaking a press-on nail.

STRAIGHT ON TILL MORNING
Blues Traveler
Beyond virtuoso harmonica, this watery jam will leave the uninitiated wondering whether this band, as one song puts it, justifies the thrill.

BLUR
Blur
Abandoning smart, catchy songs, Blur vacillates wildly from drowsy, tuneless psychedelia to

trashy punk to jangly sing-along pop-rock without ever committing to—or excelling at—any particular genre.

BRIGID BODEN
Brigid Boden
If the world's top scientists decided to blend the genes of Madonna and Enya, the result would probably be Boden. Her lullaby-ready voice and thumping disco instincts make for an engaging mix.

ROOTS AND WINGS
James Bonamy
Bonamy almost sets himself apart from country music's ever-expanding pack of pleasant-voiced, guitar-strummin' pretty boys—yet there's an overriding sameness to many of his songs.

***BOOK OF SPELLS**
The Boneshakers
There's a funky, vibrant bounce to much of the material on the duo's debut disc—a little Philly soul here, some Muscle Shoals-style horns there—that paints *Book of Spells* a warmer color than traditional blues.

THE ART OF WAR
Bone Thugs-N-Harmony
The unique blend of bullet-fast rhymes and smooth R&B crooning quickly runs out of ammo here.

DESTINATION ANYWHERE
Jon Bon Jovi
Whether with a haunting ballad delivered sotto voce or a buoyant rocker at full vocal throttle, Bon Jovi demonstrates that his songwriting is as diverse as his ever-changing hairstyles.

PAT BOONE IN A METAL MOOD: NO MORE MR. NICE GUY
Pat Boone
The only metal in Boone's mood is in the big-band horns and arrangements on nearly every track of this kitschy collection.

***EARTHLING**
David Bowie
After 30-odd albums in a dazzling 30-year career, the former space oddity begins his reentry and winds up, of all places, in the jungle. Major Tom has fallen to Earth, and it's good to have him back.

***BR5-49**
BR5-49
This debut is a much-needed reminder that country music's traditions run deeper than 10-gallon hats and pickup trucks.

SHELTER
The Brand New Heavies
Talented singer Siedah Garrett rarely breaks out and establishes her own identity—and without a distinctive diva at the helm, this acid-jazz combo's not much more than a hip lounge act.

***GATE SWINGS**
Clarence "Gatemouth" Brown
Versatile bluesman Gatemouth swings for the big-band fences on one swinging, graceful solo after another and only whiffs once.

***STILL CLIMBING**
Brownstone
Unlike many of their counterparts, who seem too attached to mechanical, mid-tempo beats, Brownstone's three-part harmony nails the emotional bull's-eye with their torchy, slow rhythm and blues.

***DEVOTION + DOUBT**
Richard Buckner
An all-night traveler on the Heartache Highway, this San Franciscan with a bourbon-and-smoke voice sings some of the most haunting tales of lost love you're likely to cry over in this lifetime.

MUSIC EVOLUTION
Buckshot LeFonque
Branford Marsalis throws together jazz, drum and bass, samba, rock, R&B, and a few mutations that fall in between. The end result is a sonic explosion that, even when it falters, is infused with the joy of playing.

THE DEFINITION OF SOUL
Solomon Burke
They don't call Burke the King of Rock 'n' Soul for nothing. While he is strictly an old-school soul man, the present gospel-friendly R&B climate should welcome his wistfully sensual offerings.

IN THIS WORLD
The Burns Sisters
The Sisters impress with an ingratiating, eccentric, seemingly natural-born style—more folk than rock, more singer-songwriter than country, more old-time than New Age.

***THE NOTORIOUS BYRD BROTHERS**
***SWEETHEART OF THE RODEO**
***DR. BYRDS AND MR. HYDE**
***BALLAD OF EASY RIDER**
The Byrds
It's difficult to imagine discs as stylistically opposed as these four reissues. All, however, are still somehow the Byrds, who continue to shimmer after all these years.

***FEELINGS**
David Byrne
Smoothly showing off his range with an assortment of dance-

savvy grooves, Byrne has pulled off a neat trick in this digitally enhanced age: He has found a soul within the machine.

*EVERYTHING I TOUCH RUNS WILD
Lori Carson

On this rambling soft-rock collection recorded with just a guitar, an accordion, and a few other acoustic instruments, unadorned songs about loneliness, loss, and the unpredictability of love allow Carson's radiant voice to shine through.

*ADAM AND EVE
Catherine Wheel

Catherine Wheel subtly weaves its inspiration (most notably Pink Floyd) into a more contemporary fabric. This is truly ambitious music-making, with an ethereal spell that lingers.

*DOC CHEATHAM AND NICHOLAS PAYTON
Doc Cheatham and Nicholas Payton

Some seven decades after his debut, Cheatham teams with 23-year-old fellow trumpet maestro Payton for an intimate, extremely satisfying set of jazz standards.

*DIG YOUR OWN HOLE
The Chemical Brothers

The musical progeny of Black Sabbath and Public Enemy concoct a noisy pastiche of breakbeats, synth blips, sequencers and guitar loops—it's a danceable explosion that rocks the party.

*KEEPERS
Guy Clark

On his formidable first live recording, Clark rebuilds personal favorites and classics from the first two-thirds of his career as the models of simplicity he'd always thought they were. Just when you think it can't get any better, it often does.

THE CHARITY OF NIGHT
Bruce Cockburn

At his most droning, Cockburn raises the dread specter of inept rap, but at his best, he's a talking bluesman for our time.

STARDUST
Natalie Cole

Cole is a gifted performer, her voice an arresting mix of cream and crinoline rustle. She ought to stop singing with her father—it's creepy, especially when we're talking love songs.

THIS FIRE
Paula Cole

Cole has released an often powerful collection that examines the emotional facets of being a woman.

DISCIPLINED BREAKDOWN
Collective Soul

Has enough sing-along pop on it for a *Party of Five* soundtrack.

*MY SOUL
Coolio

Coolio's hip-hop is loaded with rugged, no-nonsense performances and smart, pointed lyrics.

*THE DANDY WARHOLS COME DOWN
The Dandy Warhols

Embracing delicate, almost surreal sonics, alternative rockers the Dandy Warhols wallow in beautiful, chilled-out sounds.

*SOME OTHER SUCKER'S PARADE
Del Amitri

Del Amitri has always had a gift for irresistible pop, but this time the quintet has really produced something special.

*LIVING IN CLIP
Ani DiFranco

Those offended by strong language might have trouble getting past the words, but the message is worth the effort.

HAND IT OVER
Dinosaur Jr

J Mascis's dizzying virtuousity has made him the idol of guitar geeks from Chapel Hill to Tokyo; still, his band's lack of lyrical hooks make this record best for those who think an amp is wasted unless its volume is set to 10.

WHERE I STAND
George Ducas

Ducas lacks that last ounce of individuality to push him past artisanry into genuine creativity.

THE COLOUR OF LOVE
Ronnie Earl and the Broadcasters

Jazz and blues instrumentals with equal parts verve and soul, *The Colour of Love* is a flavorful musical ragout.

EVERGREEN
Echo & The Bunnymen

Always skilled at mixing sweet pop melodies with a shading of moodiness, the reunited alt-rockers opt for more of the former this time out.

WEST
Mark Eitzel

Eitzel's voice has a careworn quality that works well when bolstered by a solid melody, but too many other songs meander into a lugubrious, jazz-tinged swamp.

THE THREE AMERICAS
Elaine Elias
Cuban *montunos* embrace Brazilian sambas, and both join forces in straight-ahead jazz drawn from *el norte;* pianist-composer Elias crosses borders with élan.

***SUPA DUPA FLY**
Missy "Misdemeanor" Elliott
Missy takes stripped-down hooks, grooves, and attitude, then fills them with jagged, herky-jerky drum-and-bass patterns that are as melodic as they are funky. Add Missy's witty, off-kilter lyrics and her refreshingly down-to-earth image and you have the arrival of a true R&B force.

EV3
En Vogue
The girl group that once set the standard for elegant yet in-your-face pop offers an uneven and remarkably spiritless effort.

20TH CENTURY BLUES
Marianne Faithfull
Performing haunting songs evoking Germany's Weimar Republic, Faithfull sounds as if she not only understands her dark, moody material but has lived it.

PORTRAIT: THE MUSIC OF DAN FOGELBERG 1972-1997
Dan Fogelberg
Fogelberg comes across less as a country boy than a closet rock and roller disguised as an easy-listening smoothie on this career-spanning 4-CD set.

THE COLOUR AND THE SHAPE
Foo Fighters
Brasher and more four-on-the-floor assertive than their 1995 debut, *The Colour and the Shape* also contains some of modern rock's most melodic tantrums since Nirvana's *Nevermind.*

***FOUNTAINS OF WAYNE**
Fountains of Wayne
An irresistable album studded with smart-funny lyrics, amiable melodies toughened up by gravelly guitars, and more hooks than a Peter Pan audition.

BUTCH
The Geraldine Fibbers
A little bit country and a little bit rock and roll; a band to be reckoned with.

FRESH!
Gina G
A squeaky-clean Eurodisco blend of rushing synth melodies, chirpy vocals, and dial-a-hook lyrics with a winsome ballad or two thrown in for variety.

TAKE A LOOK OVER YOUR SHOULDER (REALITY)
Warren G
Aided by the mellifluous-voiced Nate Dogg and Ronnie Isley, Warren stirs up chewy, chunky tracks that keep the heads bobbing and the Jeeps bouncing.

***SHADY GROVE**
Jerry Garcia and David Grisman
On the first album in a series culled from spontaneous sessions, the interplay between Garcia's guitar and Grisman's mandolin imparts new musical nuances to 13 traditional folk songs.

DRAWN TO THE DEEP END
Gene
The album's one-two opening punch gets you all revved up, but the remainder of the disc goes way over the deep end with mopey melodies and navel-gazing babble.

GOD'S PROPERTY FROM KIRK FRANKLIN'S NU NATION
God's Property
The Christian group behind the rousing, catchy "Stomp" does a nice job of blurring the divisions between church and record chart.

***THE LAST ROCK N' ROLL TOUR**
Graham Parker & the Figgs
On this live CD, Parker artfully kicks out the jams, revivifying and unifying a selection of his work dating from 1976 to last year's *Acid Bubblegum.*

BROKEN CIRCLE
Jerry Granelli & UFB
Circle's first half consists mostly of imaginative covers; on the second, Granelli and UFB's jazz-rock beautifully conveys the depth, complexity, and plight of Native American culture.

***AL GREEN ANTHOLOGY**
Al Green
Not many artists deserve an anthology as much as Green. His songs come "right out of the air" and give the listener a rare glimpse into a love-man's soul.

BLUE ROSES FROM THE MOONS
Nanci Griffith
Griffith's supple and expressive voice, with a few exceptions, sounds lackluster and strained, disappearing at times behind lush arrangements.

***THIS LAND IS YOUR LAND: THE ASCH RECORDINGS VOL. 1**
Woody Guthrie
Volume 1 of The Asch Recordings suggests that the projected four-CD set will be one of the indispensable documents of 20th-century American music.

BEYOND THE MISSOURI SKY (SHORT STORIES)
Charlie Haden & Pat Metheny
The country-flavored collaboration between Haden and Metheny is a mixed success, most affecting when it's terse and bluesy.

7 PARK AVENUE
Pete Ham
Even in bare-bones demo state, these songs by the late Badfinger guitarist-composer reveal his gift for bittersweet melodies and terrific hooks.

MIDDLE OF NOWHERE
Hanson
The boys have a knack for bright and bouncy teeny-bop fare. Not all their tunes have the snap of first-rate bubblegum, but who's quibbling? Since *Nowhere* is everywhere these days, why not enjoy it?

***THE WILL TO LIVE**
Ben Harper
On his remarkable third album, this singer-guitarist proves he has never met a musical style he doesn't like. What keeps the mosaic together is Harper's pleasingly mellow vocal style and seemingly sincere lyrics about lost love and spiritual longing.

***LITTLE HEAD**
John Hiatt
Prolific song craftsman Hiatt is also a funky, soulful singer who consistently generates solid, good-time, bass-drums-and-guitar-driven pop as well as searing ballads that—depending on your age—are either timeless or Jurassic.

***PROMISED LAND**
The Holmes Brothers
The real article: rugged, honest, and undeniably soulful.

***OUT OF MY WAY**
Peter Holsapple
Less grandiose than R.E.M., more offbeat than Hootie & The Blowfish, Holsapple's debut solo album jumps styles and moods without losing its emotional intimacy.

DON'T LOOK BACK
John Lee Hooker
Occasionally the music sounds a bit thin, and studio effects strain to beef up Hooker's sometimes rickety voice, but where else are you going to find a septuagenarian nimbly tearing through Jimi Hendrix's "Red House"?

***THE PREACHER'S WIFE* ORIGINAL SOUNDTRACK**
Whitney Houston
For the first time in her 12-year recording career, Houston sounds genuinely moved by her material. Still, for all of Houston's newly acquired grit, she's no Mahalia Jackson.

***LOVE TRAKTOR AND OTHER SONGS**
Hummingfish
While not all of Hummingfish's tunes live up to the album's highlights, this fish is definitely swimming in the right direction.

SHAMING OF THE SUN
Indigo Girls
Intelligent lyrics, rich harmonies, and intertwining voices set against homespun, melodic folk are what the Indigo Girls do best.

ELEGANTLY WASTED
INXS
Plenty of tunes that would have sounded right a decade ago, but if you've heard this music before, which plenty of people have, there's not that much reason to listen to it again.

BLOOD ON THE DANCE FLOOR—HISTORY IN THE MIX
Michael Jackson
Most of *Blood*'s dance versions of *HIStory* tracks are no match for the thumping cuts that currently rule club music, but five new tunes are thrillers of the highest order.

***WHIPLASH**
James
The tunes are about mood as much as melody: they float along gently on a cushion of guitars and keyboards, creating a blissful feeling.

***LOVE'S BEEN ROUGH ON ME**
Etta James
After forty-three years, this truly great soul singer still sounds as if she's living, eating, breathing, and dying every syllable she sings.

***TRAVELLING WITHOUT MOVING**
Jamiroquai
Travelling cranks out the sort of intricate yet freewheeling tunes that were Stevie Wonder's specialty during his creative heyday.

SOUND OF LIES
The Jayhawks
Following the departure of a cofounder, *Sound of Lies* proves that the remaining Jayhawks have wings of their own.

***WYCLEF JEAN PRESENTS THE CARNIVAL**
Wyclef Jean
From Creole folk to the Havana-meets-Harlem vibe of "Guantanamera," Jean gleefully incorporates a myriad of styles, all tied together by rap's rhythm.

***NEVER HOME**
Freedy Johnston
Johnston's voice is, as usual, a bit thin; the characters in his songs are still mainly blue-collar; his music remains your basic hook-heavy pop-rock. But these elements combine to make *Never Home* one of the most mesmerizing, personable CDs this year.

GHOSTY HEAD
Rickie Lee Jones
Jones forges a daring alliance between lo-fi folk-jazz and high-tech rhythm surges. Unfortunately, much of the album is

filled with meandering, inscrutable pieces that ultimately leave you exasperated.

***LOVE ALWAYS**
K-Ci & JoJo
Taking a cue from the romantic, restrained approach of Babyface, this excellent project from Jodeci's Hailey brothers offers acoustic arrangements and well-crafted songs paying homage to monogamy, commitment, and adult behavior.

PICNIC
Robert Earl Keen
Keen crafts songs somewhere between rock and country, with lyrics squarely in the bleak terrain of unlimited horizons and hemmed-in dreams—but his deadpan humor keeps the ants out of this *Picnic*.

STANDING IN MY SHOES
Leo Kottke
With a disco-ful of drums, percussion, and synthesized rhythm tracks, Kottke's album—soaring acoustic guitar lines above, a jungle of thudding beats below— is an eagle in combat boots.

CITIZEN WAYNE
Wayne Kramer
A founder of the influential MC5, one of punk's most political bands, Kramer still has big issues on his mind. Thanks to a healthy dose of humor, this CD is a riot, in both senses of the word.

SO LONG SO WRONG
Allison Krauss & Union Station
So Long So Wrong showcases the angelic soprano's crackerjack band and artfully blends traditional bluegrass with touching ballads.

UNDER THESE ROCKS AND STONES
Chantal Kreviazuk
Alanis Morissette, Rickie Lee Jones, Joan Osborne—on these dozen varied tracks, Kreviazuk exhibits more personalities than Sybil. Only time will tell if she can stand apart from the crowd.

LIE TO ME
Jonny Lang
By not trying to sound like either a guitar god or a Mississippi cotton-field laborer, Lang comes up with a pleasing blues-pop.

***DRAG**
k. d. lang
Lang creates mysterious, mesmerizing pop as seductive as the addictions she explores.

SISTERS OF AVALON
Cyndi Lauper
Employing a weathered vibrato at the low end of her vocal range, Lauper offers hip-hop with a world beat. But for all her bold experimentation, Lauper seems to be trying too hard.

***SONGS & MORE SONGS BY TOM LEHRER**
Tom Lehrer
The title of this anthology by America's satirist emeritus is nearly the only thing about it that isn't brilliantly original and hugely entertaining.

SECRET SAMADHI
Live
Live's agonized howling makes for a remarkable noise, but at times one begins to feel like a therapist witnessing a nervous breakdown.

***COMING UP**
The London Suede
This English-accented glam rock is one of the most exciting albums to cross the Atlantic in years, injecting madcap exuberance into a genre that has damn near overdosed on melancholy and infinite sadness.

LOVE, PEACE & NAPPINESS
Lost Boyz
On their second album, these Queens, N.Y.–based rappers have found their way clear to a compelling vision of hip-hop unity.

***CELEBRATING SINATRA**
Joe Lovano
This beautifully textured salute to the greatest pop singer of all time is, in a word, great.

THE BEAUTY PROCESS: TRIPLE PLATINUM
L7
This almost sounds like a new start; aural assaulters L7 soften and prove they understand pop craftsmanship as well as volume.

***MESSENGER**
Luciano
The singer many consider the heir to the late Bob Marley is back with an album that delivers a universal mantra of faith, self-determination, and irresistible spirituality.

***SEÑOR BLUES**
Taj Mahal
Mahal's broad vocal range and excellent backup band make this album of diverse styles pulsate.

FALLEN IS BABYLON
Ziggy Marley & the Melody Makers
The pop-flavored reggae group successfully pushes its sound into new directions.

***LOVE TRAVELS**
Kathy Mattea
Mattea's landmark album proves that country music can promote variety and rise above all that hackneyed lyin', cheatin', woman-chasin', honky-tonkin', whiskey-drinkin' stuff.

***FLAMING PIE**
Paul McCartney
As he once did with The Beatles, Sir Paul weaves music and words into strands of hope in a collection of intimate, introspective songs.

EVERYWHERE
Tim McGraw
Although McGraw has a distinctive voice, his performances on these state-of-the-heart trifles are so polished that he winds up sounding like just another handsome, hat-happy hunk.

LIVE IN TIME
Mingus Big Band
Plenty of meaty, memorable solos, but the real star is this world-class band, swinging through Mingus's music with an ease that masks the pieces' difficulty.

ANIMAL RIGHTS
Moby
Moby has ditched the haunting, strobe-lit club groove of techno and joined the headbangers' ball. Problem is, things get overblown and rote when he kicks out the jams.

MONK ON MONK
T. S. Monk
A deft but underrated drummer in his own right, T .S. Monk's star-studded tribute to his father often feels more like a showcase than a record.

STRANGEST PLACES
Abra Moore
A successful amalgam of seeming disparate musical styles, highlighted by the unaffected honesty of Moore's performance.

LIKE SWIMMING
Morphine
The sing-speak vocals continue to sound as if they've been recorded off a bad phone connection, but the songs themselves radiate a jazzy sensuality.

MALADJUSTED
Morrissey
After 13 years spent documenting his teen angst on record, it's time for the former Smiths frontman to change his tune.

THE HEALING GAME
Van Morrison
The disc will satisfy those too eager for the consolations of familiar-sounding music to spend much time remembering the heights to which their man once soared.

GENERATION SWINE
Mötley Crüe
The Crüe delivers only a handful of fired-up tunes; the rest sound bloated and inert.

YOU WILL GO TO THE MOON
Moxy Früvous
This is often an ingratiatingly playful-going-on-vapid pseudo-'60s album by a band that doesn't take itself too seriously, an all-too-uncommon trait in these self-important times.

HAPPY BIRTHDAY TO ME
The Muffs
Cross-breed The Ramones with The Bangles and you might get this feisty Los Angeles trio, who deliver a sound that is roughed-up enough to annoy deserving neighbors, melodic enough to please the rest.

THE KING AND I
The New Broadway Cast Recording
It would take a very, very cold heart not to be enchanted by Donna Murphy as teacher Anna Leonownes, but try as he does, Lou Diamond Phillips cannot emerge from Yul Brynner's long shadow.

***LIFE AFTER DEATH**
The Notorious B.I.G.
The rap sensation's last recording is a series of cautionary tales that are offensive, exciting, disturbing, funky, and undeniably the product of a serious talent.

SCHIZOPHONIC
Nuno
Schizophonic sounds like musical candy: crunchy hard rock on the outside with plenty of sweet, chewy, jangly pop hooks on the inside.

STONED SOUL PICNIC: THE BEST OF LAURA NYRO
Laura Nyro
Soul Picnic's second disc, laden with Nyro's newer songs, meanders. The first disc, however, glows, lit by six songs from *Eli and the Thirteenth Confession*—one of the greatest albums from the brief era when music was a religion, a communal rite.

BE HERE NOW
Oasis
A few songs drag and meander, and talented songwriter Noel Gallagher is now even stealing from himself—yet the band excels at delivering taut, melodic pop anthems that immediately stick in your head.

***IXNAY ON THE HOMBRE**
The Offspring
Blasting enough sonic energy to stun small animals at 10 paces and offering plenty of smart-ass

rebellion, these rough boys bury a catchy riff that softens the assault in each 75-mph song.

***TITANIC: A NEW MUSICAL**
Original Broadway Cast Recording
Rich orchestration and somber lyrics keep this big, moving score shipshape.

***LIVE 1973**
Gram Parsons & the Fallen Angels
A welcome recapturing of the late country-rock pioneer's glory.

RAHSAAN PATTERSON
Rahsaan Patterson
The R&B Romeo has a playful sexiness, a soaring tenor, and a serious skill for coming up with catchy, funky songs that avoid formula.

***BRIGHTEN THE CORNERS**
Pavement
All the familiar Pavement elements are here: guitar riffs that shift adroitly from spacey to propulsive; wonderfully off-key vocals; goofy lyrics and baffling song titles. While perhaps not 100 percent pure genius, *Brighten* affirms Pavement as one of the best indie bands around.

RESIGNED
Michael Penn
Yearning for more snap and crackling intelligence in your pop? Penn—who puts equal emphasis on both confessional content and entertainment value—may offer what you crave.

***ARKOLOGY**
Lee "Scratch" Perry
This long-overdue collection of stripped-down, psychedelic reggae heavy on the reverb is a must for hard-core fans and rhythm neophytes alike.

SONDHEIM, ETC.: BERNADETTE PETERS LIVE AT CARNEGIE HALL
Bernadette Peters
Acolytes of the Broadway star adore her every bit of breathiness and archly etched intonation. It's really too bad, because when Peters reins it in and just sings, she is darn fine.

MICHAEL PETERSON
Michael Peterson
Peterson has a good ear for honky-tonk material and a hearty, rough-and-tumble way of performing it.

***OUR LOVE IS HERE TO STAY**
John Pizzarelli
Backed by a 17-piece orchestra, Pizzarelli swings and sways through 12 eclectic tunes with an eagerness and accessibility other crooners often lack, and he never allows slickness to override substance. This splendid CD will leave you breathless.

VANISHING POINT
Primal Scream
Trip-pop? Sci-fi disco? Whatever—Primal Scream's wonderful hallucinogenic aura is the result of genuine musical smarts.

THE FAT OF THE LAND
Prodigy
It takes more than shrieked vocals and sledgehammer sonics to stir up real musical momentum; in the end, much of *Fat* sounds like well-orchestrated noise.

NO WAY OUT
Puff Daddy & the Family
To purists, Sean "Puffy" Combs relies a little too much on other musicians' work. There's no denying, though, that he knows how to make hits.

***OK COMPUTER**
Radiohead
Radiohead unleashes perfectly crafted pop songs that are as unnerving as they are lovely.

RESTRAINING BOLT
Radish
Restraining Bolt's dozen cuts are robust sugar metal, melodic songs abuzz with six-string pyrotechnics and teen-pleasing lyrics about unrequited love, making music, and being a nerd—but Radish's sound is less an original one than a collage of its teen songwriter's influences.

INDESTRUCTIBLE
Reign
This isn't music meant for deep thought. If club-friendly ear candy is your thing, this album could satisfy your cravings.

FEEL LIKE GOING HOME: THE ESSENTIAL CHARLIE RICH
Charlie Rich
With its curious selections, this collection ends up being far from complete.

BITTER SWEET
Kim Richey
The album merges lonesome blues and rural sensibility with quiet introspection and uncluttered production, but Richey's no-frills singing lacks theatrical punch and pitch-perfect clarity.

***DIARY OF A MOD HOUSEWIFE**
Amy Rigby
Rigby has transformed her early arriving midlife crisis and her fraying marriage into 12 songs that hang intricately crafted stories upon irresistible melodic hooks.

***SWEET POTATO PIE**
The Robert Cray Band
Cray, the blues guitarist's guitarist, has increasingly showcased his skills as a soul songwriter and vocalist—and never more so than here.

***ROBYN IS HERE**
Robyn
Listening to the assured manner with which her voice glides over swaggering, syncopated funk, there's no denying that a major talent has arrived.

***UNDER ONE ROOF**
Roomful of Blues
Roomful of Blues' crisp, taut horn section keeps the joint jumping and, if you're in the

mood, can turn a dull evening at home into a heel-clicking night of fun.

***THE LONG WAY AROUND**
Tom Russell
Russell demonstrates a poet's eye and a storyteller's ear in this captivating folk-country album.

FROM NOW ON
Robin S.
What happened to all that contagious joy? On her second album, Robin seems more concerned with vocal gymnastics than spreading delight.

IT MEANS EVERYTHING
Save Ferris
This plucky ska-pop-swing band shows just what a can-do attitude can do.

***COME ON HOME**
Boz Scaggs
A combo of R&B standards and Scaggs originals that often already sound like classics.

SECADA
Jon Secada
With romantic male pop singers in short supply, Secada should retain his position as one of pop's premier "love men"—especially with a Spanish version of the album hitting stores as well.

***DUST BUNNIES**
Bettie Serveert
The appealing counterpoint of the Dutch foursome's crunching guitars and lilting vocals evokes the soul-pleasing moodiness of rainy afternoons among the lovelorn.

***OTHER SONGS**
Ron Sexsmith
Ron Sexsmith sure has a knack for romanticism without sentimentality—and with this fine follow-up he's fast proving himself worthy of the raves.

***DVORAK FOR TWO**
Gil Shaham/Orli Shaham
The talented, showy violin soloist Gil and his pianist sister Orli are no mere brother-and-sister act. This is a lovely, lively recording.

***BRAND NEW KNIFE**
Shonen Knife
From the opening song, the band merrily skips through the rock riff book singing about robot toys, fresh produce, roller coasters, and fear of frogs.

FREAK SHOW
Silverchair
For such grunge-oriented music, the album is surprisingly polished, with razor-sharp melodies, sturdy hooks, and moments of poignant beauty.

SMALL REVELATIONS
Chris Smither
Smither's eighth album is refreshingly spare, featuring stellar guitar playing set against his sometimes quirky, sometimes heady lyrics and offhand, raspy baritone.

STRAIGHTAWAYS
Son Volt
It's hard not to like the band's raw country sound, with its blend of fiddles, lap steel, and crunchy guitar. Yet the relentless desolation eventually makes for a monotonous ride.

SPIDERS
Space
Space's music stays in your head (like it or not), thanks to the weird but infectious pop veneer with which they cover their crypt-kicking tracks.

SPICE
Spice Girls
Spice is smart—well-crafted, well-produced, and keenly radio-friendly. So while it's true that *Spice* isn't a work of great and meaningful artistic importance, it sure is a lot of fun.

LISA STANSFIELD
Lisa Stansfield
With her up-to-the-second R&B sound, Stansfield never resorts to gut-busting theatrics. One gets the impression that she's singing to an actual person and not just a cold, lifeless microphone; her peers should listen and learn.

***SPIRITUALS & GOSPEL**
Mavis Staples and Lucky Peterson
In an age of high-concept partnerships and mega-platinum acts, the disc stands out because it's so obviously a labor of love and because it is so very good.

***TELEPATHY**
Bill Stewart
When Stewart's music works, this is forward-looking '90s jazz at its best: five skillful players who treat structure as a launching pad, not a prison; who stay in sync through sheer mutual receptivity—that's right, telepathy.

CARRYING YOUR LOVE WITH ME
George Strait
This release is business as usual—but a satisfying enterprise it is. The expected mix of bittersweet ballads, soft-swayin' rockers, and boot-scootin' twang are all delivered in Strait's easy-going, dependable style.

MACK DIVA SAVES THE WORLD
Sandra St. Victor
Even while indulging her vocal whimsy, St. Victor displays a coolly seductive self-possession here that makes this the most unified and satisfying set of music she's recorded.

THE BLUE ONENESS OF DREAMS
Sekou Sundiata
Sekou has made a record that

flows jazzily and resonates with the seductiveness of a smoky soul song.

BLUE SKY ON MARS
Matthew Sweet
There are occasional flashes of the old brilliance, but toothless lyrics and sub-wizardly guitar work ultimately render this a semi-Sweet effort.

***HOURGLASS**
James Taylor
Emotional depth makes *Hourglass* Taylor's best work in 20 years.

LOVE AMONG THE RUINS
10,000 Maniacs
Mary Ramsey's voice is harmonious, though it lacks original vocalist Natalie Merchant's range and emotional urgency. A bigger problem is the band's new material—mostly mid-tempo drones, all air and no grit.

***WHITE ON BLONDE**
Texas
A melting pot of rock and roll grit, hip-hop ambience, Motown soul, and good old pop hooks.

***RETREAT FROM THE SUN**
That Dog
Like a politician in October, That Dog wants to be all things to all people. But this group actually delivers on its platform, doling out a little bit of pop, folk, alternative rock, and even a dollop of country in one of the year's most compelling recordings.

THEN: THE EARLIER YEARS
They Might Be Giants
This retrospective is a testament to what two guys (John Flansburgh and John Linnell) with a warped sense of humor, a gift for melody, plus some cheap synths and drum machines can achieve.

***THIRD EYE BLIND**
Third Eye Blind
This San Francisco quartet's fully charmed debut serves up a mélange of guitars, keyboards, and percussion in a seductive collection of punk-flavored pop—sans repetitive riffs and vocal vapidity.

THE STORY OF MY LIFE
Irma Thomas
Provides an idea of what Aretha Franklin might sound like today had she kept her feet planted in Southern soul.

COIL
Toad the Wet Sprocket
This upbeat, riff-roaring quartet is the alternative rock equivalent of a college applicant's "safety" school: not the pulse-quickening, everything-I-ever-hoped-for favorite, but a solid runner-up that you'll learn to enjoy, and perhaps even love.

***GUN SHY TRIGGER HAPPY**
Jen Trynin
Hypnotic vocals, gritty guitar, and grown-up lyrics: A musical tour de force.

BROADWAY & 52ND
Us3
This pulsating, fluid jazz-rap pastiche is sonically pleasing but verbally vacant.

POP
U2
For an album long rumored to be a radical reinvention of a great band, *Pop* turns out to be surprisingly tame.

THE HIGHWAY KIND
Townes Van Zandt
The Highway Kind is in some ways almost unlistenable, and in others, near great; in Van Zandt's shockingly intimate versions of country classics, you can almost smell the whiskey, feel the pain.

REAR VIEW MIRROR
Townes Van Zandt
A live, best-of album of the late troubled Texas troubadour.

***CLUB VERBOTEN**
various artists
This eclectic anthology based on music historically popular with the homosexual community is entertaining listening, no matter what your lifestyle preferences.

***FOLK LIVE FROM MOUNTAIN STAGE**
***GOSPEL LIVE FROM MOUNTAIN STAGE**
various artists
These outstanding collections of "roots music" breathe new life into our cultural legacy.

MUSIC FROM AND INSPIRED BY THE *BATMAN & ROBIN* MOTION PICTURE
various artists
Let's hope "inspired by" means much of this joyless stuff didn't make the movie's final cut.

***FIRE ON THE MOUNTAIN: REGGAE CELEBRATES THE GRATEFUL DEAD, VOL. 2**
various artists
This feel-good disc makes the sky a little bluer, the grass a little greener, and the world a little happier.

MEN IN BLACK—THE ALBUM
various artists
There are worse sins than being unoriginal, and this is one soundtrack that adds up to more than just a commercial.

MUSIC FROM THE MOTION PICTURE *WILLIAM SHAKESPEARE'S ROMEO & JULIET*
various artists
The disc is a potent, cohesive collection that stands on its own thematically while doing old Willy proud.

***NUYORICAN SOUL**
various artists
Brimming with great tunes, stellar playing, and an infectious attitude, the album is a tribute to the timeless power of rhythm—and proof that it don't mean a thing if it ain't got that swing.

THE PLANET SLEEPS ON A STARRY NIGHT
various artists
Planet presents lullabies from around the globe; the cheerier but less compelling *Starry* does the same, using jazz and New Age performers instead of the songs' countrymen.

SPAWN—THE ALBUM
various artists
Modern rock and electronica have united, and the genres complement each other rather than crash and burn.

***THE SUGAR HILL RECORDS STORY**
various artists
Documenting what was arguably rap's most influential label, *Story* is a butt-shaking tribute to a genre that changed America's cultural fabric.

'S WONDERFUL—CONCORD JAZZ SALUTES IRA GERSHWIN
various artists
Hardly definitive, as it is limited to tunes culled from Concord recordings, but is nonetheless pure Gershwin gold.

TIME AND LOVE: THE MUSIC OF LAURA NYRO
various artists
This all-star homage to a mold-breaking songwriter works on a variety of levels—each solidifying Nyro's legacy as one of American pop's more underrated masters.

A TRIBUTE TO OSCAR PETERSON LIVE AT THE TOWN HALL
various artists
While this offering doesn't have the turbocharged velocity and often breathtaking authority of the jazz pianist's earlier recordings, the music still happens to be very good.

******WHEN WE WERE KINGS*** **SOUNDTRACK**
various artists
The soundtrack to the award-winning documentary about the festivities surrounding the Muhammad Ali and George Foreman "Rumble in the Jungle" in Zaire is a soulful history lesson that packs a wallop.

***LIVE AT CARNEGIE HALL**
Stevie Ray Vaughan and Double Trouble
This 1984 event produced a fuller, richer sound and a radical alteration of the electric guitarist's Texas roadhouse music.

AXE TO GRIND
Monster Mike Welch
Welch isn't ready to be the star of the show and would be better served by laboring in someone's band and mastering the subtleties inherent in all great blues.

STRANGERS ALMANAC
Whiskeytown
Hailed as the rough-hewn spawn of neo-punk's Replacements and Merle Haggard, Whiskeytown almost lives up to the hype.

TERRA INCOGNITA
Chris Whitley
Whitley's lyrical themes remain existentially heavy, covering alienation, addiction, and powerlessness. Fortunately, his highly original mix of blues, funk, groove-rock, and folk regains some breathing room and buoyancy.

***BOMBS & BUTTERFLIES**
Widespread Panic
Echoes of the Allman Brothers Band, Grateful Dead, and Jefferson Airplane continue to ricochet around them, but Widespread Panic increasingly sound like themselves.

***TURNING POINT**
David Wilcox
As adept with irony as he is with melody, this excellent singer-guitarist explores life's rougher edges and earns a place among rock's finer songwriters.

END OF THE SUMMER
Dar Williams
With a little luck, this engaging album may propel Williams to the same heights recently enjoyed by her fellow folkie Shawn Colvin.

***EGYPTOLOGY**
World Party
Writer/performer/producer Karl Wallinger, hiding behind the collective moniker World Party, once again excavates high-level, evocative pop-rock.

WU-TANG FOREVER
Wu-Tang Clan
Listening to the Clan's unsettling sound is no easy task. Most of its 120 minutes fulfill fans' expectations, but few groups, no matter how strong, can sustain their creativity for such a long stretch.

UNDER THE COVERS
Dwight Yoakam
Yoakam covers his impeccably cool favorites, but eventually the production's razzle-dazzle and leaps of genre get tiresome.

I CAN HEAR THE HEART BEATING AS ONE
Yo La Tengo
Long known for their whimsical lyrics, off-kilter harmonies, and affinity for brain-piercing guitar feedback, Yo La Tengo have added new layers to their dense atmospherics.

BOP LUAKA
Zap Mama
Essentially a solo effort (with instrumental support) by vocalist Marie Daulne, *Bop Luaka* is filled with lush, category-defying blends of African, European, American, and Jamaican motifs.

ROCK AND ROLL HALL OF FAME

The Rock and Roll Hall of Fame in Cleveland continues to select the greatest rock and roll musicians for induction. A nominee must have released a record at least 25 years prior to induction; Early Influences honors the formative figures in rock.

1986

Chuck Berry
James Brown
Ray Charles
Sam Cooke
Fats Domino
The Everly Brothers
Buddy Holly
Jerry Lee Lewis
Elvis Presley
Little Richard

Early Influences
Robert Johnson
Jimmie Rodgers
Jimmy Yancey

Nonperformers
Alan Freed
Sam Phillips

Lifetime Achievement
John Hammond

1987

The Coasters
Eddie Cochran
Bo Diddley
Aretha Franklin
Marvin Gaye
Bill Haley
B. B. King
Clyde McPhatter
Ricky Nelson
Roy Orbison
Carl Perkins
Smokey Robinson
Big Joe Turner
Muddy Waters
Jackie Wilson

Early Influences
Louis Jordan
T-Bone Walker
Hank Williams

Nonperformers
Leonard Chess
Ahmet Ertegun
Jerry Leiber and Mike Stoller
Jerry Wexler

1988

The Beach Boys
The Beatles
The Drifters
Bob Dylan
The Supremes

Early Influences
Woody Guthrie
Leadbelly
Les Paul

Nonperformer
Berry Gordy Jr.

1989

Dion
Otis Redding
The Rolling Stones
The Temptations
Stevie Wonder

Early Influences
The Ink Spots
Bessie Smith
The Soul Stirrers

Nonperformer
Phil Spector

1990

Hank Ballard
Bobby Darin
The Four Seasons
The Four Tops
The Kinks
The Platters
Simon & Garfunkel
The Who

Early Influences
Louis Armstrong
Charlie Christian
Ma Rainey

Nonperformers
Lamont Dozier
Gerry Goffin and Carole King
Brian Holland and Eddie Holland

1991

LaVern Baker
The Byrds
John Lee Hooker
The Impressions
Wilson Pickett
Jimmy Reed
Ike and Tina Turner

Early Influence
Howlin' Wolf

Nonperformers
Dave Bartholomew
Ralph Bass

Lifetime Achievement
Nesuhi Ertegun

1992

Bobby "Blue" Bland
Booker T & The MG's
Johnny Cash
Jimi Hendrix Experience
The Isley Brothers
Sam and Dave
The Yardbirds

Early Influences
Elmore James
Professor Longhair

Nonperformers
Leo Fender
Doc Pomus
Bill Graham

1993

Ruth Brown
Cream
Creedence Clearwater Revival
The Doors
Etta James
Frankie Lymon & The Teenagers
Van Morrison
Sly & The Family Stone

Early Influence
Dinah Washington

Nonperformers
Dick Clark
Milt Gabler

1994

The Animals
The Band
Duane Eddy
Grateful Dead
Elton John
John Lennon
Bob Marley
Rod Stewart

Early Influence
Willie Dixon

Nonperformer
Johnny Otis

1995

The Allman Brothers Band
Al Green
Janis Joplin
Led Zeppelin
Martha & The Vandellas
Neil Young
Frank Zappa

Early Influence
The Orioles

Nonperformer
Paul Ackerman

1996

David Bowie
Gladys Knight and the Pips
Jefferson Airplane
Little Willie John
Pink Floyd
The Shirelles
The Velvet Underground

Early Influence
Pete Seeger

Nonperformer
Tom Donahue

1997

Joni Mitchell
Buffalo Springfield
The Young Rascals
Parliament/Funkadelic
The Jackson Five
The Bee Gees
Crosby, Stills and Nash

Early Influences
Bill Monroe
Mahalia Jackson

Nonperformer
Syd Nathan

JAZZ HALL OF FAME

Down Beat magazine, America's leading jazz publication, conducts an annual poll of both readers and critics to determine the greatest luminaries of the jazz world. The honorees:

	Readers poll	Critics poll
1952	Louis Armstrong	—
1953	Glenn Miller	—
1954	Stan Kenton	—
1955	Charlie Parker	—
1956	Duke Ellington	—
1957	Benny Goodman	—
1958	Count Basie	—
1959	Lester Young	—
1960	Dizzy Gillespie	—
1961	Billie Holiday	Coleman Hawkins
1962	Miles Davis	Bix Beiderbecke
1963	Thelonious Monk	Jelly Roll Morton
1964	Eric Dolphy	Art Tatum
1965	John Coltrane	Earl Hines
1966	Bud Powell	Charlie Christian
1967	Billy Strayhorn	Bessie Smith
1968	Wes Montgomery	Sidney Bechet, Fats Waller
1969	Ornette Coleman	Pee Wee Russell, Jack Teagarden
1970	Jimi Hendrix	Johnny Hodges
1971	Charles Mingus	Roy Eldridge, Django Reinhardt
1972	Gene Krupa	Clifford Brown
1973	Sonny Rollins	Fletcher Henderson
1974	Buddy Rich	Ben Webster
1975	Cannonball Adderley	Cecil Taylor
1976	Woody Herman	King Oliver
1977	Paul Desmond	Benny Carter
1978	Joe Venuti	Rahsaan Roland Kirk
1979	Ella Fitzgerald	Lennie Tristano
1980	Dexter Gordon	Max Roach
1981	Art Blakey	Bill Evans
1982	Art Pepper	Fats Navarro
1983	Stephane Grappelli	Albert Ayler
1984	Oscar Peterson	Sun Ra
1985	Sarah Vaughan	Zoot Sims
1986	Stan Getz	Gil Evans
1987	Lionel Hampton	Johnny Dodds, Thad Jones, Teddy Wilson
1988	Jaco Pastorius	Kenny Clarke
1989	Woody Shaw	Chet Baker
1990	Red Rodney	Mary Lou Williams
1991	Lee Morgan	John Carter
1992	Maynard Ferguson	James P. Johnson
1993	Gerry Mulligan	Edward Blackwell
1994	Dave Brubeck	Frank Zappa
1995	J. J. Johnson	Julius Hemphill
1996	Horace Silver	Artie Shaw
1997		Tony Williams

COUNTRY MUSIC HALL OF FAME

Located in Nashville along with everything else in country music, the Country Music Hall of Fame inducts its honorees each autumn. The enshrined elite:

1962 Roy Acuff
1963 (elections held but no one candidate received enough votes)
1964 Tex Ritter
1965 Ernest Tubb
1966 James R. Denny, George D. Hay, Uncle Dave Macon, Eddy Arnold
1967 Red Foley, J. L. Frank, Jim Reeves, Stephen H. Sholes
1968 Bob Wills
1969 Gene Autry
1970 Original Carter Family (A. P. Carter, Maybelle Carter, Sara Carter), Bill Monroe
1971 Arthur Edward Satherley
1972 Jimmie Davis
1973 Patsy Cline, Chet Atkins
1974 Owen Bradley, Frank "Pee Wee" King
1975 Minnie Pearl
1976 Paul Cohen, Kitty Wells
1977 Merle Travis
1978 Grandpa Jones
1979 Hubert Long, Hank Snow
1980 Connie B. Gay, Original Sons of the Pioneers, Johnny Cash
1981 Vernon Dalhart, Grant Turner
1982 Lefty Frizzell, Marty Robbins, Roy Horton
1983 Little Jimmy Dickens
1984 Ralph Peer, Floyd Tillman
1985 Lester Flatt and Earl Scruggs
1986 Wesley Rose, The Duke of Paducah
1987 Rod Brasfield
1988 Roy Rogers, Loretta Lynn
1989 Jack Stapp, Hank Thompson, Cliffie Stone
1990 Tennessee Ernie Ford
1991 Boudleaux and Felice Bryant
1992 George Jones, Frances Preston
1993 Willie Nelson
1994 Merle Haggard
1995 Roger Miller and Jo Walker-Meador
1996 Patsy Montana, Buck Owens, Ray Price

TOP CONCERT APPEARANCES

The following survey lists the most successful North American individual concert appearances, based on box-office grosses, for 1996 and for all time. A concert appearance is defined here as all performances in a visit to a single town. (Source: Pollstar)

1996

	Artist	Location
1.	"3 Tenors"/Jose Carreras/ Placido Domingo/ Luciano Pavarotti	East Rutherford, New Jersey
2.	"The Who's Quadrophenia"/ Joan Osborne/ Me'shell Ndegeocello	New York City
3.	Bob Seger & The Silver Bullet Band/John Hiatt	Auburn Hills, Michigan
4.	"The Clifford Ball"/Phish	Plattsburgh, New York
5.	KISS/D Generation/ CIV/311/The Nixons	New York City
6.	"Tibetan Freedom Concert"/ Smashing Pumpkins/ Beastie Boys/ Red Hot Chili Peppers/ A Tribe Called Quest	San Francisco
7.	Jimmy Buffett	Mansfield, Massachusetts
8.	The Eagles	Clemson, South Carolina
9.	Gloria Estefan	New York City
10.	The Eagles	Uniondale, New York
11.	Garth Brooks	Auburn Hills, Michigan
12.	Rod Stewart	New York City
13.	Garth Brooks	Landover, Maryland
14.	KISS	Philadelphia
15.	Juan Gabriel	Mexico City
16.	Neil Diamond	Boston
17.	Gloria Estefan	Miami
18.	KISS/Stabbing Westward/ Red 5	Inglewood, California
19.	Pearl Jam/Ben Harper/ Fastbacks	New York City
20.	"Country America"	Oshkosh, Wisconsin

ALL TIME

	Artist	Location
1.	Barbra Streisand	New York City, 1994
2.	Elton John/Billy Joel	East Rutherford, New Jersey, 1994
3.	Barbra Streisand	Las Vegas, 1993
4.	"3 Tenors"/Jose Carreras/ Placido Domingo/ Luciano Pavarotti	East Rutherford, New Jersey, 1996
5.	Barbra Streisand	Anaheim, California, 1994
6.	The Rolling Stones	Mexico City, 1995
7.	The Rolling Stones/ Living Colour/ Mar & Magette/ Dou Dov n' Diaye Rose	New York City, 1989
8.	Bette Midler	New York City, 1993
9.	The Rolling Stones	East Rutherford, New Jersey, 1994
10.	The Rolling Stones/ Seal	Oakland, California, 1994
11.	The Rolling Stones/ Guns N' Roses/ Living Colour	Los Angeles, 1989
12.	Madonna	Mexico City, 1993
13.	Paul Simon/Simon & Garfunkel	New York City, 1993
14.	Barbra Streisand	Auburn Hills, Michigan, 1994
15.	Elton John/Billy Joel	Philadelphia, 1994
16.	Bruce Springsteen & the E Street Band	East Rutherford, New Jersey, 1985
17.	Paul McCartney	Mexico City, 1993
18.	Bruce Springsteen	East Rutherford, New Jersey, 1992
19.	The Rolling Stones/ Buddy Guy/ Red Hot Chili Peppers	Pasadena, California, 1994
20.	Bruce Springsteen & the E Street Band	Los Angeles, 1985

TOP CONCERT TOURS

These are the most successful North American tours of all time, along with year-by-year leaders since 1987. The rankings are based on grosses rather than attendance. (Source: Pollstar)

ALL TIME

Rank	Artist	Year of tour
1.	The Rolling Stones	1994
2.	Pink Floyd	1994
3.	The Rolling Stones	1989
4.	The Eagles	1994
5.	New Kids on the Block	1990
6.	U2	1992
7.	The Eagles	1995
8.	Barbra Streisand	1994
9.	Grateful Dead	1994
10.	Elton John/Billy Joel	1994
11.	Grateful Dead	1993
12.	Boyz II Men	1995
13.	Billy Joel	1990
14.	The Who	1989
15.	Bruce Springsteen & the E Street Band	1985
16.	R.E.M.	1995
17.	Paul McCartney	1990
18.	Bon Jovi	1989
19.	U2	1987
20.	Grateful Dead	1991

1987

Rank	Artist	Cities/Shows
1.	U2	50/79
2.	Bon Jovi	104/130
3.	Pink Floyd	28/60
4.	Grateful Dead	37/84
5.	David Bowie	31/45
6.	Mötley Crüe	92/100
7.	Whitney Houston	77/89
8.	Huey Lewis & the News	89/101
9.	Boston	37/69
10.	Alabama	117/127
11.	Genesis	18/30
12.	Heart	82/88
13.	Madonna	19/22
14.	Billy Joel	42/57
15.	Kenny Rogers	78/99
16.	Luther Vandross	51/65
17.	Tina Turner	71/78
18.	Bryan Adams	81/84
19.	Def Leppard	58/59
20.	Fleetwood Mac	45/48

1988

Rank	Artist	Cities/Shows
1.	Pink Floyd	23/35
2.	Van Halen's "Monsters of Rock"	23/26
3.	Def Leppard	94/112
4.	Grateful Dead	33/80
5.	Aerosmith	96/105
6.	Michael Jackson	19/54
7.	AC/DC	105/110
8.	Rod Stewart	82/88
9.	"Rat Pack/Ultimate Event"	23/41
10.	George Michael	32/46
11.	Whitesnake	83/84
12.	Bruce Springsteen & the E Street Band	21/43
13.	Robert Plant	88/92
14.	Luther Vandross/Anita Baker	26/42
15.	INXS	75/81
16.	John Cougar Mellencamp	45/54
17.	Kenny Rogers	88/167
18.	New Edition	67/70
19.	Randy Travis	98/119
20.	Sting	75/79

1989

Rank	Artist	Cities/Shows
1.	The Rolling Stones	33/60
2.	The Who	27/39
3.	Bon Jovi	129/143
4.	Grateful Dead	33/73
5.	New Kids on the Block	112/143
6.	Neil Diamond	29/69
7.	Metallica	134/140
8.	Elton John	32/47
9.	Rod Stewart	61/71
10.	Beach Boys/Chicago	57/59
11.	Poison	82/83
12.	R.E.M.	84/87
13.	Cinderella	135/136
14.	Barry Manilow	44/123
15.	George Strait	90/104
16.	New Edition	48/49
17.	Kenny Rogers	85/115
18.	Alabama	77/79
19.	Reba McEntire	111/126
20.	Randy Travis	88/105

1990

Rank	Artist	Cities/Shows
1.	New Kids on the Block	122/152
2.	Billy Joel	53/95
3.	Paul McCartney	21/32
4.	Grateful Dead	27/63
5.	Janet Jackson	62/89
6.	Aerosmith	92/101
7.	M. C. Hammer	132/138
8.	Mötley Crüe	103/108
9.	Phil Collins	27/56
10.	Eric Clapton	48/57
11.	David Bowie	41/51
12.	Madonna	12/32
13.	KISS	121/121
14.	Rush	56/63
15.	Depeche Mode	32/33
16.	Randy Travis	98/125
17.	Whitesnake	99/101
18.	Fleetwood Mac	54/62
19.	Kenny Rogers	66/105
20.	Alabama	102/103

1991

Rank	Artist	Cities/Shows
1.	Grateful Dead	27/76
2.	ZZ Top	85/106
3.	The Judds	116/126
4.	Rod Stewart	47/59
5.	Paul Simon	72/76
6.	Guns N' Roses	30/43
7.	Bell Biv Devoe/Johnny Gill/Keith Sweat	66/72
8.	Michael Bolton	70/103
9.	Garth Brooks	94/111
10.	Clint Black	92/100
11.	AC/DC	57/60
12.	Sting	64/81
13.	Luther Vandross	50/60
14.	Scorpions	90/93
15.	Van Halen	42/46
16.	Frank Sinatra	30/53
17.	Randy Travis	93/107
18.	Jimmy Buffett	37/51
19.	Jane's Addiction (includes "Lollapalooza")	56/66
20.	Yes	55/57

1992

Rank	Artist	Cities/Shows
1.	U2	61/73
2.	Grateful Dead	23/55
3.	Guns N' Roses/Metallica	25/25
4.	Neil Diamond	26/69
5.	Bruce Springsteen	36/59
6.	Genesis	24/28
7.	Elton John	32/49
8.	Metallica	87/102
9.	Eric Clapton	30/37
10.	Hammer	123/130
11.	Bryan Adams	92/94
12.	Jimmy Buffett	43/64
13.	"Lollapalooza II"	29/35
14.	Garth Brooks	78/79
15.	Reba McEntire	102/111
16.	Ozzy Osbourne	80/88
17.	John Mellencamp	44/55
18.	Harry Connick Jr.	43/87
19.	Def Leppard	72/77
20.	Rush	52/55

1993

Rank	Artist	Cities/Shows
1.	Grateful Dead	29/81
2.	Rod Stewart	54/68
3.	Neil Diamond	43/75
4.	Paul McCartney	23/23
5.	Bette Midler	29/71
6.	Billy Joel	22/39
7.	Garth Brooks	29/54
8.	Jimmy Buffett	32/52
9.	Reba McEntire	97/105
10.	Kenny G	82/97
11.	"Lollapalooza III"	29/34
12.	Aerosmith	61/66
13.	Clint Black/Wynonna	70/73
14.	Van Halen	32/40
15.	Alan Jackson	98/105
16.	Luther Vandross	42/49
17.	Peter Gabriel	31/38
18.	Def Leppard	90/91
19.	Depeche Mode	40/49
20.	Elton John	27/34

1994

Rank	Artist	Cities/Shows
1.	The Rolling Stones	43/60
2.	Pink Floyd	39/59
3.	The Eagles	32/54
4.	Barbra Streisand	6/22
5.	Grateful Dead	29/84
6.	Elton John/Billy Joel	14/21
7.	Aerosmith	71/76
8.	"Lollapalooza IV"	33/43
9.	Phil Collins	41/59
10.	Reba McEntire	96/102
11.	Bette Midler	44/54
12.	Billy Joel	40/49
13.	Michael Bolton	84/93
14.	Metallica	49/50
15.	ZZ Top	93/96
16.	Janet Jackson	63/72
17.	Brooks & Dunn	95/99
18.	Alan Jackson	93/99
19.	Jimmy Buffett	25/43
20.	Rod Stewart	33/34

1995

Rank	Artist	Cities/Shows
1.	The Eagles	46/58
2.	Boyz II Men	133/134
3.	R.E.M.	63/81
4.	Grateful Dead	20/45
5.	Jimmy Page/Robert Plant	56/68
6.	Van Halen	85/94
7.	Tom Petty and the Heartbreakers	80/89
8.	Reba McEntire	91/101
9.	Elton John	27/41
10.	Elton John/Billy Joel	10/12
11.	Alan Jackson	95/97
12.	Jimmy Buffett	37/52
13.	Yanni	50/59
14.	Vince Gill	82/90
15.	Phish	67/79
16.	Brooks & Dunn	91/91
17.	George Strait	48/49
18.	Live	79/81
19.	"Lollapalooza '95"	26/29
20.	Amy Grant	79/80

1996

Rank	Artist	Cities/Shows
1.	KISS	75/92
2.	Garth Brooks	41/121
3.	Neil Diamond	49/72
4.	Rod Stewart	62/65
5.	Bob Seger	57/64
6.	Jimmy Buffett	28/44
7.	Reba McEntire	83/86
8.	Alanis Morissette	88/98
9.	Hootie & The Blowfish	73/80
10.	Ozzy Osbourne	100/100
11.	AC/DC	74/81
12.	Dave Matthews Band	78/81
13.	George Strait	53/58
14.	Sting	51/56
15.	The Smashing Pumpkins	68/79
16.	"The H.O.R.D.E. Festival"	40/42
17.	The Who	22/31
18.	Phish	42/50
19.	"Lollapallooza '96"	20/22
20.	Alan Jackson	71/71

BILLBOARD'S TOP 10 SINGLES

These listings start before rap, soul, and rock; but whether the singer's a "Prisoner of Love" (1946) or just plain "Twisted" (1997), the latest sound keeps redefining the oldest emotion. The more things change...

1946

1. "Prisoner of Love," Perry Como
2. "To Each His Own," Eddy Howard
3. "The Gypsy," Ink Spots
4. "Five Minutes More," Frank Sinatra
5. "Rumors Are Flying," Frankie Carle
6. "Oh! What It Seemed To Be," Frankie Carle
7. "Personality," Johnny Mercer & The Pied Pipers
8. "South America, Take It Away," Bing Crosby & The Andrews Sisters
9. "The Gypsy," Dinah Shore
10. "Oh! What It Seemed To Be," Frank Sinatra

1947

1. "Near You," Francis Craig
2. "Peg O' My Heart," Harmonicats
3. "Heartaches," Ted Weems
4. "Linda," Ray Noble Orchestra & Buddy Clark (tie)
4. "Smoke, Smoke, Smoke (That Cigarette)," Tex Williams (tie)
6. "I Wish I Didn't Love You So," Vaughn Monroe
7. "Peg O' My Heart," Three Suns
8. "Anniversary Song," Al Jolson
9. "Near You," Larry Green Orchestra
10. "That's My Desire," Sammy Kaye

1948

1. "Twelfth Street Rag," Pee Wee Hunt
2. "Manana," Peggy Lee
3. "Now Is the Hour," Bing Crosby
4. "A Tree in the Meadow," Margaret Whiting
5. "My Happiness," Jon & Sandra Steele
6. "You Can't Be True, Dear," Ken Griffin & Jerry Wayne
7. "Little White Lies," Dick Haymes
8. "You Call Everybody Darlin'," Al Trace
9. "My Happiness," Pied Pipers
10. "I'm Looking Over a Four Leaf Clover," Art Mooney

1949

1. "Riders in the Sky," Vaughn Monroe Orchestra
2. "That Lucky Old Sun," Frankie Laine
3. "You're Breaking My Heart," Vic Damone
4. "Some Enchanted Evening," Perry Como
5. "Slipping Around," Jimmy Wakely & Margaret Whiting
6. "I Can Dream, Can't I?" Andrews Sisters & Gordon Jenkins
7. "Cruising Down the River," Russ Morgan Orchestra
8. "A Little Bird Told Me," Evelyn Knight & The Stardusters
9. "Mule Train," Frankie Laine
10. "Jealous Heart," Al Morgan

1950

1. "Goodnight Irene," Gordon Jenkins & The Weavers
2. "Mona Lisa," Nat King Cole
3. "Third Man Theme," Anton Karas
4. "Sam's Song," Gary & Bing Crosby
5. "Simple Melody," Gary & Bing Crosby
6. "Music, Music, Music," Teresa Brewer
7. "Third Man Theme," Guy Lombardo
8. "Chattanoogie Shoe Shine Boy," Red Foley
9. "Harbor Lights," Sammy Kaye
10. "It Isn't Fair," Sammy Kaye & Don Cornell

1951

1. "Too Young," Nat King Cole
2. "Because of You," Tony Bennett
3. "How High the Moon," Les Paul & Mary Ford
4. "Come On-A My House," Rosemary Clooney
5. "Be My Love," Mario Lanza
6. "On Top of Old Smoky," Weavers
7. "Cold, Cold Heart," Tony Bennett
8. "If," Perry Como
9. "Loveliest Night of the Year," Mario Lanza
10. "Tennessee Waltz," Patti Page

1952

1. "Blue Tango," Leroy Anderson
2. "Wheel of Fortune," Kay Starr
3. "Cry," Johnnie Ray
4. "You Belong to Me," Jo Stafford
5. "Auf Wiederseh'n, Sweetheart," Vera Lynn
6. "I Went to Your Wedding," Patti Page
7. "Half as Much," Rosemary Clooney
8. "Wish You Were Here," Eddie Fisher & Hugo Winterhalter
9. "Here in My Heart," Al Martino
10. "Delicado," Percy Faith

1953

1. "Song From Moulin Rouge," Percy Faith
2. "Vaya con Dios," Les Paul & Mary Ford
3. "Doggie in the Window," Patti Page
4. "I'm Walking Behind You," Eddie Fisher
5. "You, You, You," Ames Brothers
6. "Till I Waltz Again with You," Teresa Brewer
7. "April in Portugal," Les Baxter
8. "No Other Love," Perry Como
9. "Don't Let the Stars Get in Your Eyes," Perry Como
10. "I Believe," Frankie Laine

1954

1. "Little Things Mean a Lot," Kitty Kallen
2. "Wanted," Perry Como
3. "Hey, There," Rosemary Clooney
4. "Sh-Boom," Crew Cuts
5. "Make Love to Me," Jo Stafford
6. "Oh! My Pa-Pa," Eddie Fisher
7. "I Get So Lonely," Four Knights
8. "Three Coins in the Fountain," Four Aces
9. "Secret Love," Doris Day
10. "Hernando's Highway," Archie Bleyer

1955

1. "Cherry Pink and Apple Blossom White," Perez Prado
2. "Rock Around the Clock," Bill Haley & His Comets
3. "The Yellow Rose of Texas," Mitch Miller
4. "Autumn Leaves," Roger Williams
5. "Unchained Melody," Les Baxter
6. "The Ballad of Davy Crockett," Bill Hayes
7. "Love Is a Many-Splendored Thing," Four Aces
8. "Sincerely," McGuire Sisters

9. "Ain't That a Shame," Pat Boone
10. "Dance with Me Henry," Georgia Gibbs

1956

1. "Heartbreak Hotel," Elvis Presley
2. "Don't Be Cruel," Elvis Presley
3. "Lisbon Antigua," Nelson Riddle
4. "My Prayer," Platters
5. "The Wayward Wind," Gogi Grant
6. "Hound Dog," Elvis Presley
7. "The Poor People of Paris," Les Baxter
8. "Whatever Will Be Will Be (Que Sera Sera)," Doris Day
9. "Memories Are Made of This," Dean Martin
10. "Rock and Roll Waltz," Kay Starr

1957

1. "All Shook Up," Elvis Presley
2. "Love Letters in the Sand," Pat Boone
3. "Little Darlin'," Diamonds
4. "Young Love," Tab Hunter
5. "So Rare," Jimmy Dorsey
6. "Don't Forbid Me," Pat Boone
7. "Singing the Blues," Guy Mitchell
8. "Young Love," Sonny James
9. "Too Much," Elvis Presley
10. "Round and Round," Perry Como

1958

1. "Volare (Nel Blu Dipinto Di Blu)," Domenico Modugno
2. "All I Have To Do Is Dream/ Claudette," Everly Brothers
3. "Don't/I Beg of You," Elvis Presley
4. "Witch Doctor," David Seville
5. "Patricia," Perez Prado
6. "Sail Along Silvery Moon/Raunchy," Billy Vaughn
7. "Catch a Falling Star/Magic Moments," Perry Como
8. "Tequila," Champs
9. "It's All in the Game," Tommy Edwards
10. "Return to Me," Dean Martin

1959

1. "The Battle of New Orleans," Johnny Horton
2. "Mack the Knife," Bobby Darin
3. "Personality," Lloyd Price
4. "Venus," Frankie Avalon
5. "Lonely Boy," Paul Anka
6. "Dream Lover," Bobby Darin
7. "The Three Bells," Browns
8. "Come Softly to Me," Fleetwoods
9. "Kansas City," Wilbert Harrison
10. "Mr. Blue," Fleetwoods

1960

1. "Theme from *A Summer Place*," Percy Faith
2. "He'll Have To Go," Jim Reeves
3. "Cathy's Clown," Everly Brothers
4. "Running Bear," Johnny Preston
5. "Teen Angel," Mark Dinning
6. "It's Now or Never," Elvis Presley
7. "Handy Man," Jimmy Jones
8. "I'm Sorry," Brenda Lee
9. "Stuck on You," Elvis Presley
10. "The Twist," Chubby Checker

1961

1. "Tossin' and Turnin'," Bobby Lewis
2. "I Fall to Pieces," Patsy Cline
3. "Michael," Highwaymen
4. "Cryin'," Roy Orbison
5. "Runaway," Del Shannon
6. "My True Story," Jive Five
7. "Pony Time," Chubby Checker
8. "Wheels," String-a-Longs
9. "Raindrops," Dee Clark
10. "Wooden Heart (Muss I Denn)," Joe Dowell

1962

1. "Stranger on the Shore," Mr. Acker Bilk
2. "I Can't Stop Loving You," Ray Charles
3. "Mashed Potato Time," Dee Dee Sharp
4. "Roses Are Red," Bobby Vinton
5. "The Stripper," David Rose
6. "Johnny Angel," Shelley Fabares
7. "Loco-motion," Little Eva
8. "Let Me In," Sensations
9. "The Twist," Chubby Checker
10. "Soldier Boy," Shirelles

1963

1. "Sugar Shack," Jimmy Gilmer & The Fireballs
2. "Surfin' USA," Beach Boys
3. "The End of the World," Skeeter Davis
4. "Rhythm of the Rain," Cascades
5. "He's So Fine," Chiffons
6. "Blue Velvet," Bobby Vinton
7. "Hey Paula," Paul & Paula
8. "Fingertips II," Little Stevie Wonder
9. "Washington Square," Village Stompers
10. "It's All Right," Impressions

1964

1. "I Want To Hold Your Hand," Beatles
2. "She Loves You," Beatles
3. "Hello, Dolly!" Louis Armstrong
4. "Oh, Pretty Woman," Roy Orbison
5. "I Get Around," Beach Boys
6. "Everybody Loves Somebody," Dean Martin
7. "My Guy," Mary Wells
8. "We'll Sing in the Sunshine," Gale Garnett
9. "Last Kiss," J. Frank Wilson & The Cavaliers
10. "Where Did Our Love Go," Supremes

1965

1. "Wooly Bully," Sam the Sham & The Pharaohs
2. "I Can't Help Myself," Four Tops
3. "(I Can't Get No) Satisfaction," Rolling Stones
4. "You Were on My Mind," We Five
5. "You've Lost That Lovin' Feelin'," Righteous Brothers
6. "Downtown," Petula Clark
7. "Help!," Beatles
8. "Can't You Hear My Heartbeat," Herman's Hermits
9. "Crying in the Chapel," Elvis Presley
10. "My Girl," Temptations

1966

1. "The Ballad of the Green Berets," S/Sgt. Barry Sadler
2. "Cherish," Association
3. "(You're My) Soul and Inspiration," Righteous Brothers
4. "Reach Out I'll Be There," Four Tops
5. "96 Tears," ? & the Mysterians
6. "Last Train to Clarksville," Monkees
7. "Monday, Monday," Mamas & the Papas
8. "You Can't Hurry Love," Supremes
9. "Poor Side of Town," Johnny Rivers
10. "California Dreamin'," Mamas & the Papas

1967

1. "To Sir with Love," Lulu
2. "The Letter," Box Tops
3. "Ode to Billie Joe," Bobby Gentry
4. "Windy," Association
5. "I'm a Believer," Monkees
6. "Light My Fire," Doors
7. "Somethin' Stupid," Nancy Sinatra & Frank Sinatra
8. "Happy Together," Turtles

9. "Groovin'," Young Rascals
10. "Can't Take My Eyes Off You," Frankie Valli

1968

1. "Hey Jude," Beatles
2. "Love Is Blue (L'Amour Est Blue)," Paul Mauriat
3. "Honey," Bobby Goldsboro
4. "(Sittin' on) The Dock of the Bay," Otis Redding
5. "People Got To Be Free," Rascals
6. "Sunshine of Your Love," Cream
7. "This Guy's in Love with You," Herb Alpert
8. "The Good, the Bad and the Ugly," Hugo Montenegro
9. "Mrs. Robinson," Simon & Garfunkel
10. "Tighten Up," Archie Bell & The Drells

1969

1. "Sugar, Sugar," Archies
2. "Aquarius/Let the Sunshine In," Fifth Dimension
3. "I Can't Get Next to You," Temptations
4. "Honky Tonk Women," Rolling Stones
5. "Everyday People," Sly & the Family Stone
6. "Dizzy," Tommy Roe
7. "Hot Fun in the Summertime," Sly & the Family Stone
8. "I'll Never Fall in Love Again," Tom Jones
9. "Build Me Up Buttercup," Foundations
10. "Crimson and Clover," Tommy James & The Shondells

1970

1. "Bridge over Troubled Water," Simon & Garfunkel
2. "(They Long To Be) Close to You," Carpenters
3. "American Woman/No Sugar Tonight," Guess Who
4. "Raindrops Keep Fallin' on My Head," B. J. Thomas
5. "War," Edwin Starr
6. "Ain't No Mountain High Enough," Diana Ross
7. "I'll Be There," Jackson 5
8. "Get Ready," Rare Earth
9. "Let It Be," Beatles
10. "Band of Gold," Freda Payne

1971

1. "Joy to the World," Three Dog Night
2. "Maggie May/Reason To Believe," Rod Stewart
3. "It's Too Late/I Feel the Earth Move," Carole King
4. "One Bad Apple," Osmonds
5. "How Can You Mend a Broken Heart," Bee Gees
6. "Indian Reservation," Raiders
7. "Go Away Little Girl," Donny Osmond
8. "Take Me Home, Country Roads," John Denver with Fat City
9. "Just My Imagination (Running Away with Me)," Temptations
10. "Knock Three Times," Dawn

1972

1. "The First Time Ever I Saw Your Face," Roberta Flack
2. "Alone Again (Naturally)," Gilbert O'Sullivan
3. "American Pie," Don McLean
4. "Without You," Nilsson
5. "Candy Man," Sammy Davis Jr.
6. "I Gotcha," Joe Tex
7. "Lean on Me," Bill Withers
8. "Baby Don't Get Hooked on Me," Mac Davis
9. "Brand New Key," Melanie
10. "Daddy Don't You Walk So Fast," Wayne Newton

1973

1. "Tie a Yellow Ribbon 'Round the Ole Oak Tree," Tony Orlando & Dawn
2. "Bad, Bad Leroy Brown," Jim Croce
3. "Killing Me Softly with His Song," Roberta Flack
4. "Let's Get It On," Marvin Gaye
5. "My Love," Paul McCartney & Wings
6. "Why Me," Kris Kristofferson
7. "Crocodile Rock," Elton John
8. "Will It Go Round in Circles," Billy Preston
9. "You're So Vain," Carly Simon
10. "Touch Me in the Morning," Diana Ross

1974

1. "The Way We Were," Barbra Streisand
2. "Seasons in the Sun," Terry Jacks
3. "Love's Theme," Love Unlimited Orchestra
4. "Come and Get Your Love," Redbone
5. "Dancing Machine," Jackson 5
6. "The Loco-motion," Grand Funk Railroad
7. "TSOP," MFSB
8. "The Streak," Ray Stevens
9. "Bennie and the Jets," Elton John
10. "One Hell of a Woman," Mac Davis

1975

1. "Love Will Keep Us Together," Captain & Tennille
2. "Rhinestone Cowboy," Glen Campbell
3. "Philadelphia Freedom," Elton John
4. "Before the Next Teardrop Falls," Freddy Fender
5. "My Eyes Adored You," Frankie Valli
6. "Shining Star," Earth, Wind & Fire
7. "Fame," David Bowie
8. "Laughter in the Rain," Neil Sedaka
9. "One of These Nights," Eagles
10. "Thank God I'm a Country Boy," John Denver

1976

1. "Silly Love Songs," Wings
2. "Don't Go Breaking My Heart," Elton John & Kiki Dee
3. "Disco Lady," Johnnie Taylor
4. "December, 1963 (Oh, What a Night)," Four Seasons
5. "Play That Funky Music," Wild Cherry
6. "Kiss and Say Goodbye," Manhattans
7. "Love Machine, Pt. 1," Miracles
8. "50 Ways To Leave Your Lover," Paul Simon
9. "Love Is Alive," Gary Wright
10. "A Fifth of Beethoven," Walter Murphy & The Big Apple Band

1977

1. "Tonight's the Night (Gonna Be Alright)," Rod Stewart
2. "I Just Want To Be Your Everything," Andy Gibb
3. "Best of My Love," Emotions
4. "Love Theme from *A Star Is Born* (Evergreen)" Barbra Streisand
5. "Angel in Your Arms," Hot
6. "I Like Dreamin'," Kenny Nolan
7. "Don't Leave Me This Way," Thelma Houston
8. "(Your Love Has Lifted Me) Higher and Higher," Rita Coolidge
9. "Undercover Angel," Alan O'Day
10. "Torn Between Two Lovers," Mary MacGregor

1978

1. "Shadow Dancing," Andy Gibb
2. "Night Fever," Bee Gees
3. "You Light Up My Life," Debby Boone
4. "Stayin' Alive," Bee Gees
5. "Kiss You All Over," Exile
6. "How Deep Is Your Love," Bee Gees
7. "Baby Come Back," Player
8. "Love Is Thicker Than Water," Andy Gibb

9. "Boogie Oogie Oogie," A Taste of Honey
10. "Three Times a Lady," Commodores

1979

1. "My Sharona," Knack
2. "Bad Girls," Donna Summer
3. "Le Freak," Chic
4. "Da Ya Think I'm Sexy," Rod Stewart
5. "Reunited," Peaches & Herb
6. "I Will Survive," Gloria Gaynor
7. "Hot Stuff," Donna Summer
8. "Y.M.C.A.," Village People
9. "Ring My Bell," Anita Ward
10. "Sad Eyes," Robert John

1980

1. "Call Me," Blondie
2. "Another Brick in the Wall," Pink Floyd
3. "Magic," Olivia Newton-John
4. "Rock with You," Michael Jackson
5. "Do That to Me One More Time," Captain & Tennille
6. "Crazy Little Thing Called Love," Queen
7. "Coming Up," Paul McCartney
8. "Funkytown," Lipps, Inc.
9. "It's Still Rock and Roll to Me," Billy Joel
10. "The Rose," Bette Midler

1981

1. "Bette Davis Eyes," Kim Carnes
2. "Endless Love," Diana Ross & Lionel Richie
3. "Lady," Kenny Rogers
4. "(Just Like) Starting Over," John Lennon
5. "Jessie's Girl," Rick Springfield
6. "Celebration," Kool & the Gang
7. "Kiss on My List," Daryl Hall & John Oates
8. "I Love a Rainy Night," Eddie Rabbitt
9. "9 to 5," Dolly Parton
10. "Keep On Loving You," REO Speedwagon

1982

1. "Physical," Olivia Newton-John
2. "Eye of the Tiger," Survivor
3. "I Love Rock 'n' Roll," Joan Jett & the Blackhearts
4. "Ebony and Ivory," Paul McCartney & Stevie Wonder
5. "Centerfold," The J. Geils Band
6. "Don't You Want Me," Human League
7. "Jack and Diane," John Cougar
8. "Hurts So Good," John Cougar
9. "Abracadabra," Steve Miller Band
10. "Hard To Say I'm Sorry," Chicago

1983

1. "Every Breath You Take," The Police
2. "Billie Jean," Michael Jackson
3. "Flashdance... What a Feeling," Irene Cara
4. "Down Under," Men at Work
5. "Beat It," Michael Jackson
6. "Total Eclipse of the Heart," Bonnie Tyler
7. "Maneater," Daryl Hall & John Oates
8. "Baby Come to Me," Patti Austin with James Ingram
9. "Maniac," Michael Sembello
10. "Sweet Dreams (Are Made of This)," Eurythmics

1984

1. "When Doves Cry," Prince
2. "What's Love Got To Do with It," Tina Turner
3. "Say Say Say," Paul McCartney & Michael Jackson
4. "Footloose," Kenny Loggins
5. "Against All Odds (Take a Look at Me Now)," Phil Collins
6. "Jump," Van Halen
7. "Hello," Lionel Richie
8. "Owner of a Lonely Heart," Yes
9. "Ghostbusters," Ray Parker Jr.
10. "Karma Chameleon," Culture Club

1985

1. "Careless Whisper," Wham! featuring George Michael
2. "Like a Virgin," Madonna
3. "Wake Me Up Before You Go-Go," Wham!
4. "I Want To Know What Love Is," Foreigner
5. "I Feel for You," Chaka Khan
6. "Out of Touch," Daryl Hall & John Oates
7. "Everybody Wants To Rule the World," Tears for Fears
8. "Money for Nothing," Dire Straits
9. "Crazy for You," Madonna
10. "Take on Me," a-ha

1986

1. "That's What Friends Are For," Dionne & Friends
2. "Say You, Say Me," Lionel Richie
3. "I Miss You," Klymaxx
4. "On My Own," Patti LaBelle & Michael McDonald
5. "Broken Wings," Mr. Mister
6. "How Will I Know," Whitney Houston
7. "Party All the Time," Eddie Murphy
8. "Burning Heart," Survivor
9. "Kyrie," Mr. Mister
10. "Addicted to Love," Robert Palmer

1987

1. "Walk Like an Egyptian," Bangles
2. "Alone," Heart
3. "Shake You Down," Gregory Abbott
4. "I Wanna Dance with Somebody (Who Loves Me)," Whitney Houston
5. "Nothing's Gonna Stop Us Now," Starship
6. "C'est La Vie," Robbie Nevil
7. "Here I Go Again," Whitesnake
8. "The Way It Is," Bruce Hornsby & the Range
9. "Shakedown," Bob Seger
10. "Livin' On a Prayer," Bon Jovi

1988

1. "Faith," George Michael
2. "Need You Tonight," INXS
3. "Got My Mind Set on You," George Harrison
4. "Never Gonna Give You Up," Rick Astley
5. "Sweet Child o' Mine," Guns N' Roses
6. "So Emotional," Whitney Houston
7. "Heaven Is a Place on Earth," Belinda Carlisle
8. "Could've Been," Tiffany
9. "Hands to Heaven," Breathe
10. "Roll with It," Steve Winwood

1989

1. "Look Away," Chicago
2. "My Prerogative," Bobby Brown
3. "Every Rose Has Its Thorn," Poison
4. "Straight Up," Paula Abdul
5. "Miss You Much," Janet Jackson
6. "Cold Hearted," Paula Abdul
7. "Wind Beneath My Wings," Bette Midler
8. "Girl You Know It's True," Milli Vanilli
9. "Baby, I Love Your Way/Freebird Medley," Will to Power
10. "Giving You the Best That I Got," Anita Baker

1990

1. "Hold On," Wilson Phillips
2. "It Must Have Been Love," Roxette
3. "Nothing Compares 2 U," Sinéad O'Connor
4. "Poison," Bell Biv Devoe
5. "Vogue," Madonna
6. "Vision of Love," Mariah Carey

7. "Another Day in Paradise," Phil Collins
8. "Hold On," En Vogue
9. "Cradle of Love," Billy Idol
10. "Blaze of Glory," Jon Bon Jovi

1991

1. "(Everything I Do) I Do It for You," Bryan Adams
2. "I Wanna Sex You Up," Color Me Badd
3. "Gonna Make You Sweat," C+C Music Factory
4. "Rush Rush," Paula Abdul
5. "One More Try," Timmy T.
6. "Unbelievable," EMF
7. "More Than Words," Extreme
8. "I Like the Way (The Kissing Game)," Hi-Five
9. "The First Time," Surface
10. "Baby Baby," Amy Grant

1992

1. "End of the Road," Boyz II Men
2. "Baby Got Back," Sir Mix-A-Lot
3. "Jump," Kris Kross
4. "Save the Best for Last," Vanessa Williams
5. "Baby-Baby-Baby," TLC
6. "Tears in Heaven," Eric Clapton
7. "My Lovin' (You're Never Gonna Get It)," En Vogue
8. "Under the Bridge," Red Hot Chili Peppers
9. "All 4 Love," Color Me Badd
10. "Just Another Day," Jon Secada

1993

1. "I Will Always Love You," Whitney Houston
2. "Whoomp! (There It Is)," Tag Team
3. "Can't Help Falling in Love," UB40
4. "That's the Way Love Goes," Janet Jackson
5. "Freak Me," Silk
6. "Weak," SWV
7. "If I Ever Fall in Love," Shai
8. "Dreamlover," Mariah Carey
9. "Rump Shaker," Wreckx-N-Effect
10. "Informer," Snow

1994

1. "The Sign," Ace of Base
2. "I Swear," All-4-One
3. "I'll Make Love to You," Boyz II Men
4. "The Power of Love," Céline Dion
5. "Hero," Mariah Carey
6. "Stay (I Missed You)," Lisa Loeb & Nine Stories
7. "Breathe Again," Toni Braxton
8. "All for Love," Bryan Adams/Rod Stewart/Sting
9. "All That She Wants," Ace of Base
10. "Don't Turn Around," Ace of Base

1995

1. "Gangsta's Paradise," Coolio featuring L.V.
2. "Waterfalls," TLC
3. "Creep," TLC
4. "Kiss from a Rose," Seal
5. "On Bended Knee," Boyz II Men
6. "Another Night," Real McCoy
7. "Fantasy," Mariah Carey
8. "Take A Bow," Madonna
9. "Don't Take It Personal (Just One of Dem Days)," Monica
10. "This Is How We Do It," Montell Jordan

1996

1. "Macarena (Bayside Boys Mix)," Los Del Rio
2. "One Sweet Day," Mariah Carey & Boyz II Men
3. "Because You Loved Me," Celine Dion
4. "Nobody Knows," The Tony Rich Project
5. "Always Be My Baby," Mariah Carey
6. "Give Me One Reason," Tracy Chapman
7. "Tha Crossroads," Bone Thugs-N-Harmony
8. "I Love You Always Forever," Donna Lewis
9. "You're Makin' Me High/Let It Flow," Toni Braxton
10. "Twisted," Keith Sweat

RAP WRAPPED UP

Nearly 20 years after its commercial breakthrough, rap has become a dominant part of the pop music landscape. Here, selected by PEOPLE music critic Jeremy Helligar, are some of the genre's essential albums.

1. Arrested Development, *3 Years, 5 Months and 2 Days in the Life of...* (1992)
2. Beastie Boys, *Licensed to Ill* (1986)
3. Beastie Boys, *Paul's Boutique* (1989)
4. De La Soul, *3 Feet High & Rising* (1989)
5. Digable Planets, *Blowout Comb* (1994)
6. Dr. Dre, *The Chronic* (1993)
7. Missy "Misdemeanor" Elliot, *Supa Dupa Fly* (1997)
8. Grandmaster Flash & The Furious Five, *Greatest Messages* (1987)
9. Lil' Kim, *Hard Core* (1996)
10. L.L. Cool J, *All World* (1996)
11. Naughty By Nature, *Poverty's Paradise* (1995)
12. N.W.A., *Straight Outta Compton* (1989)
13. Public Enemy, *Fear of a Black Planet* (1990)
14. Run-D.M.C., *Run-D.M.C.* (1984)
15. Run-D.M.C., *Greatest Hits (1983-1991)* 1991
16. Salt-N-Pepa, *Hot, Cool & Vicious* (1986)
17. A Tribe Called Quest, *Beats, Rhymes and Life* (1996)
18. various artists, *The First 10 Years of Def Jam Classics* (1995)
19. Whodini, *Escape* (1984)
20. Wu-Tang Clan, *Enter the Wu-Tang (36 Chambers)* (1994)

BILLBOARD'S TOP 10 ALBUMS

Forty years ago, the only women on these charts were relegated to soundtracks; in 1992, *no* ladies joined the guys at the top. Times have changed. From blue chip divas to the angsty Alanis, female musicians today are heard like never before.

1957

1. *My Fair Lady*, original cast
2. *Hymns*, Tennessee Ernie Ford
3. *Oklahoma!*, soundtrack
4. *Around the World in 80 Days*, soundtrack
5. *The King and I*, soundtrack
6. *Calypso*, Harry Belafonte
7. *Love Is the Thing*, Nat King Cole
8. *The Eddy Duchin Story*, soundtrack
9. *Songs of the Fabulous Fifties*, Roger Williams
10. *Film Encores*, Mantovani

1958

1. *My Fair Lady*, original cast
2. *The Music Man*, original cast
3. *Johnny's Greatest Hits*, Johnny Mathis
4. *South Pacific*, soundtrack
5. *Come Fly with Me*, Frank Sinatra
6. *Around the World in 80 Days*, soundtrack
7. *Warm*, Johnny Mathis
8. *South Pacific*, original cast
9. *Ricky*, Ricky Nelson
10. *The King and I*, soundtrack

1959

1. *Music from "Peter Gunn,"* Henry Mancini
2. *Gigi*, soundtrack
3. *South Pacific*, soundtrack
4. *From the Hungry i*, Kingston Trio
5. *The Kingston Trio at Large*, Kingston Trio
6. *Sing Along with Mitch*, Mitch Miller
7. *Inside Shelley Berman*, Shelley Berman
8. *Exotica, Vol. 1*, Martin Denny
9. *My Fair Lady*, original cast
10. *Flower Drum Song*, original cast

1960

1. *The Sound of Music*, original cast
2. *Inside Shelley Berman*, Shelley Berman
3. *The Button-Down Mind of Bob Newhart*, Bob Newhart
4. *Sixty Years of Music America Loves Best, Vol. I*, various artists
5. *Here We Go Again*, Kingston Trio
6. *Sold Out*, Kingston Trio
7. *Heavenly*, Johnny Mathis
8. *South Pacific*, soundtrack
9. *Faithfully*, Johnny Mathis
10. *Outside Shelley Berman*, Shelley Berman

1961

1. *Camelot*, original cast
2. *Great Motion Picture Themes*, various artists
3. *Never on Sunday*, soundtrack
4. *The Sound of Music*, original cast
5. *Exodus*, soundtrack
6. *Knockers Up*, Rusty Warren
7. *G.I. Blues*, Elvis Presley/soundtrack
8. *Sing Along with Mitch*, Mitch Miller
9. *Calcutta*, Lawrence Welk
10. *Tonight in Person*, Limeliters

1962

1. *West Side Story*, soundtrack
2. *Breakfast at Tiffany's*, Henry Mancini
3. *Blue Hawaii*, Elvis Presley/soundtrack
4. *West Side Story*, original cast
5. *The Sound of Music*, original cast
6. *Time Out*, Dave Brubeck
7. *Camelot*, original cast
8. *Your Twist Party*, Chubby Checker
9. *Knockers Up*, Rusty Warren
10. *Judy at Carnegie Hall*, Judy Garland

1963

1. *West Side Story*, soundtrack
2. *Peter, Paul and Mary*, Peter, Paul and Mary
3. *Moving*, Peter, Paul and Mary
4. *Joan Baez in Concert*, Joan Baez
5. *I Left My Heart in San Francisco*, Tony Bennett
6. *Moon River and Other Great Movie Themes*, Andy Williams
7. *Lawrence of Arabia*, soundtrack
8. *Days of Wine and Roses*, Andy Williams
9. *Oliver*, original cast
10. *Modern Sounds in Country and Western Music, Vol. 2*, Ray Charles

1964

1. *Hello, Dolly!*, original cast
2. *In the Wind*, Peter, Paul and Mary
3. *Honey in the Horn*, Al Hirt
4. *The Barbra Streisand Album*, Barbra Streisand
5. *West Side Story*, soundtrack
6. *Peter, Paul and Mary*, Peter, Paul & Mary
7. *The Second Barbra Streisand Album*, Barbra Streisand
8. *Meet the Beatles*, Beatles
9. *The Third Barbra Streisand Album*, Barbra Streisand
10. *Moon River and Other Great Movie Themes*, Andy Williams

1965

1. *Mary Poppins*, soundtrack
2. *Beatles '65*, Beatles
3. *The Sound of Music*, soundtrack
4. *My Fair Lady*, soundtrack
5. *Fiddler on the Roof*, original cast
6. *Goldfinger*, soundtrack
7. *Hello, Dolly!*, original cast
8. *Dear Heart*, Andy Williams
9. *Introducing Herman's Hermits*, Herman's Hermits
10. *Beatles VI*, Beatles

1966

1. *Whipped Cream and Other Delights*, Herb Alpert & the Tijuana Brass
2. *The Sound of Music*, soundtrack
3. *Going Places*, Herb Alpert & the Tijuana Brass
4. *Rubber Soul*, Beatles
5. *What Now My Love*, Herb Alpert & the Tijuana Brass
6. *If You Can Believe Your Eyes and Ears*, Mamas & the Papas
7. *Dr. Zhivago*, soundtrack
8. *Revolver*, Beatles
9. *Color Me Barbra*, Barbra Streisand
10. *Ballad of the Green Berets*, S/Sgt. Barry Sadler

1967

1. *More of the Monkees*, Monkees
2. *The Monkees*, Monkees
3. *Dr. Zhivago*, soundtrack
4. *The Sound of Music*, soundtrack
5. *The Temptations' Greatest Hits*, Temptations
6. *A Man and a Woman*, soundtrack
7. *S.R.O.*, Herb Alpert & the Tijuana Brass
8. *Whipped Cream and Other Delights*, Herb Alpert & the Tijuana Brass
9. *Going Places*, Herb Alpert & the Tijuana Brass
10. *Sgt. Pepper's Lonely Hearts Club Band*, Beatles

1968

1. *Are You Experienced?*, Jimi Hendrix Experience
2. *The Graduate*, Simon & Garfunkel/soundtrack
3. *Disraeli Gears*, Cream
4. *Magical Mystery Tour*, Beatles/soundtrack
5. *Diana Ross and the Supremes' Greatest Hits*, Diana Ross & The Supremes
6. *Sgt. Pepper's Lonely Hearts Club Band*, Beatles
7. *The Doors*, The Doors
8. *Parsley, Sage, Rosemary and Thyme*, Simon & Garfunkel
9. *Vanilla Fudge*, Vanilla Fudge
10. *Blooming Hits*, Paul Mauriat & His Orchestra

1969

1. *In-a-Gadda-Da-Vida*, Iron Butterfly
2. *Hair*, original cast
3. *Blood, Sweat and Tears*, Blood, Sweat and Tears
4. *Bayou Country*, Creedence Clearwater Revival
5. *Led Zeppelin*, Led Zeppelin
6. *Johnny Cash at Folsom Prison*, Johnny Cash
7. *Funny Girl*, soundtrack
8. *The Beatles (The White Album)*, Beatles
9. *Donovan's Greatest Hits*, Donovan
10. *The Association's Greatest Hits*, Association

1970

1. *Bridge over Troubled Water*, Simon & Garfunkel
2. *Led Zeppelin II*, Led Zeppelin
3. *Chicago*, Chicago
4. *Abbey Road*, Beatles
5. *Santana*, Santana
6. *Get Ready*, Rare Earth
7. *Easy Rider*, soundtrack
8. *Butch Cassidy and the Sundance Kid*, soundtrack
9. *Joe Cocker!*, Joe Cocker
10. *Three Dog Night Was Captured Live at the Forum*, Three Dog Night

1971

1. *Jesus Christ Superstar*, various artists
2. *Tapestry*, Carole King
3. *Close to You*, Carpenters
4. *Pearl*, Janis Joplin
5. *Abraxas*, Santana
6. *The Partridge Family Album*, Partridge Family
7. *Sweet Baby James*, James Taylor
8. *Tea for the Tillerman*, Cat Stevens
9. *Greatest Hits*, Sly & the Family Stone
10. *Chicago III*, Chicago

1972

1. *Harvest*, Neil Young
2. *Tapestry*, Carole King
3. *American Pie*, Don McLean
4. *Teaser and the Firecat*, Cat Stevens
5. *Hot Rocks, 1964–71*, Rolling Stones
6. *Killer*, Alice Cooper
7. *First Take*, Roberta Flack
8. *America*, America
9. *Music*, Carole King
10. *Madman Across the Water*, Elton John

1973

1. *The World Is a Ghetto*, War
2. *Summer Breeze*, Seals & Crofts
3. *Talking Book*, Stevie Wonder
4. *No Secrets*, Carly Simon
5. *Lady Sings the Blues*, Diana Ross
6. *They Only Come Out at Night*, Edgar Winter Group
7. *I Am Woman*, Helen Reddy
8. *Don't Shoot Me, I'm Only the Piano Player*, Elton John
9. *I'm Still in Love with You*, Al Green
10. *Seventh Sojourn*, Moody Blues

1974

1. *Goodbye Yellow Brick Road*, Elton John
2. *John Denver's Greatest Hits*, John Denver
3. *Band on the Run*, Paul McCartney & Wings
4. *Innervisions*, Stevie Wonder
5. *You Don't Mess Around with Jim*, Jim Croce
6. *American Graffiti*, soundtrack
7. *Imagination*, Gladys Knight & The Pips
8. *Behind Closed Doors*, Charlie Rich
9. *The Sting*, soundtrack
10. *Tres Hombres*, ZZ Top

1975

1. *Elton John—Greatest Hits*, Elton John
2. *John Denver's Greatest Hits*, John Denver
3. *That's the Way of the World*, Earth, Wind & Fire
4. *Back Home Again*, John Denver
5. *Phoebe Snow*, Phoebe Snow
6. *Heart Like a Wheel*, Linda Ronstadt
7. *Captain Fantastic and the Brown Dirt Cowboy*, Elton John
8. *An Evening with John Denver*, John Denver
9. *AWB*, Average White Band
10. *On the Border*, Eagles

1976

1. *Frampton Comes Alive*, Peter Frampton
2. *Fleetwood Mac*, Fleetwood Mac
3. *Wings at the Speed of Sound*, Wings
4. *Greatest Hits, 1971–1975*, Eagles
5. *Chicago IX—Chicago's Greatest Hits*, Chicago
6. *The Dream Weaver*, Gary Wright
7. *Desire*, Bob Dylan
8. *A Night at the Opera*, Queen
9. *History—America's Greatest Hits*, America
10. *Gratitude*, Earth, Wind & Fire

1977

1. *Rumours*, Fleetwood Mac
2. *Songs in the Key of Life*, Stevie Wonder
3. *A Star Is Born*, Barbra Streisand/Kris Kristofferson/soundtrack
4. *Hotel California*, Eagles
5. *Boston*, Boston
6. *A New World Record*, Electric Light Orchestra
7. *Part 3*, K.C. & the Sunshine Band
8. *Silk Degrees*, Boz Scaggs
9. *Night Moves*, Bob Seger & the Silver Bullet Band
10. *Fleetwood Mac*, Fleetwood Mac

1978

1. *Saturday Night Fever*, Bee Gees/various artists/soundtrack
2. *Grease*, John Travolta/Olivia Newton-John/soundtrack
3. *Rumours*, Fleetwood Mac
4. *The Stranger*, Billy Joel
5. *Aja*, Steely Dan
6. *Feels So Good*, Chuck Mangione
7. *The Grand Illusion*, Styx
8. *Simple Dreams*, Linda Ronstadt
9. *Point of Know Return*, Kansas
10. *Slowhand*, Eric Clapton

1979

1. *52nd Street*, Billy Joel
2. *Spirits Having Flown*, Bee Gees
3. *Minute by Minute*, Doobie Brothers
4. *The Cars*, The Cars
5. *Breakfast in America*, Supertramp
6. *Live and More*, Donna Summer
7. *Pieces of Eight*, Styx
8. *Bad Girls*, Donna Summer
9. *Parallel Lines*, Blondie
10. *Blondes Have More Fun*, Rod Stewart

1980

1. *The Wall*, Pink Floyd
2. *The Long Run*, Eagles
3. *Off the Wall*, Michael Jackson

4. *Glass Houses,* Billy Joel
5. *Damn the Torpedoes,* Tom Petty & the Heartbreakers
6. *Against the Wind,* Bob Seger & the Silver Bullet Band
7. *In the Heat of the Night,* Pat Benatar
8. *Eat to the Beat,* Blondie
9. *In Through the Out Door,* Led Zeppelin
10. *Kenny,* Kenny Rogers

1981

1. *Hi Infidelity,* REO Speedwagon
2. *Double Fantasy,* John Lennon & Yoko Ono
3. *Greatest Hits,* Kenny Rogers
4. *Christopher Cross,* Christopher Cross
5. *Crimes of Passion,* Pat Benatar
6. *Paradise Theatre,* Styx
7. *Back in Black,* AC/DC
8. *Voices,* Daryl Hall & John Oates
9. *Zenyatta Mondatta,* The Police
10. *The River,* Bruce Springsteen

1982

1. *Asia,* Asia
2. *Beauty and the Beat,* The Go-Go's
3. *4,* Foreigner
4. *American Fool,* John Cougar
5. *Freeze-Frame,* The J. Geils Band
6. *Escape,* Journey
7. *Get Lucky,* Loverboy
8. *Bella Donna,* Stevie Nicks
9. *Chariots of Fire,* Vangelis/soundtrack
10. *Ghost in the Machine,* The Police

1983

1. *Thriller,* Michael Jackson
2. *Business as Usual,* Men at Work
3. *Synchronicity,* The Police
4. *H2O,* Daryl Hall & John Oates
5. *1999,* Prince
6. *Lionel Richie,* Lionel Richie
7. *Jane Fonda's Workout Record,* Jane Fonda
8. *Pyromania,* Def Leppard
9. *Kissing To Be Clever,* Culture Club
10. *Olivia's Greatest Hits, Vol. 2,* Olivia Newton-John

1984

1. *Thriller,* Michael Jackson
2. *Sports,* Huey Lewis & the News
3. *Can't Slow Down,* Lionel Richie
4. *An Innocent Man,* Billy Joel
5. *Colour by Numbers,* Culture Club
6. *1984,* Van Halen
7. *Eliminator,* ZZ Top
8. *Synchronicity,* The Police
9. *Footloose,* soundtrack
10. *Seven and the Ragged Tiger,* Duran Duran

1985

1. *Born in the U.S.A.,* Bruce Springsteen
2. *Reckless,* Bryan Adams
3. *Like a Virgin,* Madonna
4. *Make It Big,* Wham!
5. *Private Dancer,* Tina Turner
6. *No Jacket Required,* Phil Collins
7. *Beverly Hills Cop,* soundtrack
8. *Suddenly,* Billy Ocean
9. *Purple Rain,* Prince & the Revolution
10. *Songs from the Big Chair,* Tears for Fears

1986

1. *Whitney Houston,* Whitney Houston
2. *Heart,* Heart
3. *Scarecrow,* John Cougar Mellencamp
4. *Afterburner,* ZZ Top
5. *Brothers in Arms,* Dire Straits
6. *Control,* Janet Jackson
7. *Welcome to the Real World,* Mr. Mister
8. *Promise,* Sade
9. *No Jacket Required,* Phil Collins
10. *Primitive Love,* Miami Sound Machine

1987

1. *Slippery When Wet,* Bon Jovi
2. *Graceland,* Paul Simon
3. *Licensed To Ill,* Beastie Boys
4. *The Way It Is,* Bruce Hornsby & the Range
5. *Control,* Janet Jackson
6. *The Joshua Tree,* U2
7. *Fore!,* Huey Lewis & the News
8. *Night Songs,* Cinderella
9. *Rapture,* Anita Baker
10. *Invisible Touch,* Genesis

1988

1. *Faith,* George Michael
2. *Dirty Dancing,* soundtrack
3. *Hysteria,* Def Leppard
4. *Kick,* INXS
5. *Bad,* Michael Jackson
6. *Appetite for Destruction,* Guns N' Roses
7. *Out of the Blue,* Debbie Gibson
8. *Richard Marx,* Richard Marx
9. *Tiffany,* Tiffany
10. *Permanent Vacation,* Aerosmith

1989

1. *Don't Be Cruel,* Bobby Brown
2. *Hangin' Tough,* New Kids on the Block
3. *Forever Your Girl,* Paula Abdul
4. *New Jersey,* Bon Jovi
5. *Appetite for Destruction,* Guns N' Roses
6. *The Raw & the Cooked,* Fine Young Cannibals
7. *GNR Lies,* Guns N' Roses
8. *Traveling Wilburys,* Traveling Wilburys
9. *Hysteria,* Def Leppard
10. *Girl You Know It's True,* Milli Vanilli

1990

1. *Janet Jackson's Rhythm Nation 1814,* Janet Jackson
2. *. . . But Seriously,* Phil Collins
3. *Soul Provider,* Michael Bolton
4. *Pump,* Aerosmith
5. *Please Hammer Don't Hurt 'Em,* M.C. Hammer
6. *Forever Your Girl,* Paula Abdul
7. *Dr. Feelgood,* Mötley Crüe
8. *The End of Innocence,* Don Henley
9. *Cosmic Thing,* The B-52's
10. *Storm Front,* Billy Joel

1991

1. *Mariah Carey,* Mariah Carey
2. *No Fences,* Garth Brooks
3. *Shake Your Money Maker,* The Black Crowes
4. *Gonna Make You Sweat,* C+C Music Factory
5. *Wilson Phillips,* Wilson Phillips
6. *To the Extreme,* Vanilla Ice
7. *Please Hammer Don't Hurt 'Em,* M.C. Hammer
8. *The Immaculate Collection,* Madonna
9. *Empire,* Queensryche
10. *I'm Your Baby Tonight,* Whitney Houston

1992

1. *Ropin' the Wind,* Garth Brooks
2. *Dangerous,* Michael Jackson
3. *Nevermind,* Nirvana
4. *Some Gave All,* Billy Ray Cyrus
5. *Achtung Baby,* U2
6. *No Fences,* Garth Brooks
7. *Metallica,* Metallica
8. *Time, Love, & Tenderness,* Michael Bolton
9. *Too Legit To Quit,* Hammer
10. *Totally Krossed Out,* Kris Kross

1993

1. *The Bodyguard,* soundtrack
2. *Breathless,* Kenny G
3. *Unplugged,* Eric Clapton
4. *janet.,* Janet Jackson
5. *Some Gave All,* Billy Ray Cyrus
6. *The Chronic,* Dr. Dre
7. *Pocket Full of Kryptonite,* Spin Doctors
8. *Ten,* Pearl Jam
9. *The Chase,* Garth Brooks
10. *Core,* Stone Temple Pilots

1994

1. *The Sign,* Ace of Base
2. *Music Box,* Mariah Carey
3. *Doggystyle,* Snoop Doggy Dogg
4. *The Lion King* soundtrack
5. *August & Everything After,* Counting Crows
6. *VS.,* Pearl Jam
7. *Toni Braxton,* Toni Braxton
8. *janet.,* Janet Jackson
9. *Bat out of Hell II: Back into Hell,* Meat Loaf
10. *The One Thing,* Michael Bolton

1995

1. *Cracked Rear View,* Hootie & The Blowfish
2. *The Hits,* Garth Brooks
3. *II,* Boyz II Men
4. *Hell Freezes Over,* Eagles
5. *Crazysexycool,* TLC
6. *Vitalogy,* Pearl Jam
7. *Dookie,* Green Day
8. *Throwing Copper,* Live
9. *Miracles: The Holiday Album,* Kenny G
10. *The Lion King* soundtrack

1996

1. *Jagged Little Pill,* Alanis Morissette
2. *Daydream,* Mariah Carey
3. *Falling into You,* Celine Dion
4. *Waiting To Exhale,* soundtrack
5. *The Score,* Fugees
6. *The Woman in Me,* Shania Twain
7. *Fresh Horses,* Garth Brooks
8. *Anthology 1,* The Beatles
9. *Cracked Rear View,* Hootie & The Blowfish
10. *Mellon Collie and the Infinite Sadness,* The Smashing Pumpkins

BILLBOARD NUMBER ONES FOR 1997

Week by week, here are the most popular albums and songs so far in 1997. (Source: *Billboard*)

Tragic Kingdom, No Doubt — January 4
"Un-Break My Heart," Toni Braxton

Tragic Kingdom, No Doubt — January 11
"Un-Break My Heart," Toni Braxton

Tragic Kingdom, No Doubt — January 18
"Un-Break My Heart," Toni Braxton

Tragic Kingdom, No Doubt — January 25
"Un-Break My Heart," Toni Braxton

Tragic Kingdom, No Doubt — February 1
"Un-Break My Heart," Toni Braxton

Tragic Kingdom, No Doubt — February 8
"Un-Break My Heart," Toni Braxton

Gridlock'd soundtrack — February 15
"Un-Break My Heart," Toni Braxton

Tragic Kingdom, No Doubt — February 22
"Wannabe," Spice Girls

Unchained Melody/The Early Years, LeAnn Rimes — March 1
"Wannabe," Spice Girls

Secret Samadhi, Live — March 8
"Wannabe," Spice Girls

Howard Stern Private Parts: The Album soundtrack — March 15
"Wannabe," Spice Girls

Pop, U2 — March 22
"Can't Nobody Hold Me Down," Puff Daddy (Featuring Mase)

The Untouchable, Scarface — March 29
"Can't Nobody Hold Me Down," Puff Daddy (Featuring Mase)

Nine Lives, Aerosmith — April 5
"Can't Nobody Hold Me Down," Puff Daddy (Featuring Mase)

Life After Death, The Notorious B.I.G. — April 12
"Can't Nobody Hold Me Down," Puff Daddy (Featuring Mase)

Life After Death, The Notorious B.I.G. — April 19
"Can't Nobody Hold Me Down," Puff Daddy (Featuring Mase)

Life After Death, The Notorious B.I.G. — April 26
"Can't Nobody Hold Me Down," Puff Daddy (Featuring Mase)

Life After Death, The Notorious B.I.G. — May 3
"Hypnotize," The Notorious B.I.G.

Share My World, Mary J. Blige — May 10
"Hypnotize," The Notorious B.I.G.

Carrying Your Love with Me, George Strait — May 17
"Hypnotize," The Notorious B.I.G.

Spice, Spice Girls — May 24
"MMMbop," Hanson

Spice, Spice Girls — May 31
"MMMbop," Hanson

Spice, Spice Girls — June 7
"MMMbop," Hanson

Spice, Spice Girls — June 14
"I'll Be Missing You," Puff Daddy & Faith Evans (Featuring 112)

Wu-Tang Forever, Wu-Tang Clan — June 21
"I'll Be Missing You," Puff Daddy & Faith Evans (Featuring 112)

Butterfly Kisses (Shades of Grace), Bob Carlisle — June 28
"I'll Be Missing You," Puff Daddy & Faith Evans (Featuring 112)

Butterfly Kisses (Shades of Grace), Bob Carlisle — July 5
"I'll Be Missing You," Puff Daddy & Faith Evans (Featuring 112)

Spice, Spice Girls — July 12
"I'll Be Missing You," Puff Daddy & Faith Evans (Featuring 112)

The Fat of the Land, Prodigy — July 19
"I'll Be Missing You," Puff Daddy & Faith Evans (Featuring 112)

Men in Black soundtrack — July 26
"I'll Be Missing You," Puff Daddy & Faith Evans (Featuring 112)

Men in Black soundtrack — August 2
"I'll Be Missing You," Puff Daddy & Faith Evans (Featuring 112)

No Way Out, Puff Daddy & the Family — August 9
"I'll Be Missing You," Puff Daddy & Faith Evans (Featuring 112)

The Art of War, Bone Thugs-N-Harmony — August 16
"I'll Be Missing You," Puff Daddy & Faith Evans (Featuring 112)

No Way Out, Puff Daddy & the Family — August 23
"I'll Be Missing You," Puff Daddy & Faith Evans (Featuring 112)

No Way Out, Puff Daddy & the Family — August 30
"Mo Money Mo Problems," The Notorious B.I.G. (Featuring Puff Daddy & Mase)

The Dance, Fleetwood Mac — September 6
"Mo Money Mo Problems," The Notorious B.I.G. (Featuring Puff Daddy & Mase)

No Way Out, Puff Daddy & the Family — September 13
"Honey," Mariah Carey

Ghetto D, Master P — September 20
"Honey," Mariah Carey

DESERT ISLAND DISCS

Since 1983, *Pulse!* (the magazine published by Tower Records/Video) has been asking major recording artists, "If you were stranded on a desert island, what 10 records would you want with you?" The following is a sampling from its archives.

BECK

Dust Bowl Ballads	Woody Guthrie
Outer Space	Toby Rean and the Common People
The Flasher	Soundtrack
Getz/Gilberto	Stan Getz and Joao Gilberto
Moog: The Eclectic Electrics of	Dick Hyman
Any compilation by	Carter Family
Any compilation by	Mississippi Fred McDowell
Comic Strip	Serge Gainsbourg
Songs From A Room	Leonard Cohen
Right Now!	Pussy Galore

EMMYLOU HARRIS

Nebraska	Bruce Springsteen
Neil Young	Neil Young
Dancer With Bruised Knees	Kate and Anna McGarrigle
Will the Circle Be Unbroken	The Staple Singers
Ballroom	De Danann
Dreamin' My Dreams	Waylon Jennings
Gilded Palace of Sin	The Flying Burrito Brothers
Famous Blue Raincoat	Jennifer Warnes
Music From Big Pink	The Band
Acadie	Daniel Lanois

TOM PETTY

Good Vibrations: Thirty Years of The Beach Boys	The Beach Boys
The Byrds	The Byrds
Greatest Hits	The Searchers
Rainin' in My Heart	Slim Harpo
The Chess Box	Howlin' Wolf
Elvis—The King of Rock & Roll:The Complete '50s Masters	Elvis Presley
Grevious Angel	Gram Parsons
Greatest Hits	Wilson Pickett
$1,000,000 Worth of Twang	Duane Eddy
A Date With the Everly Brothers	The Everly Brothers

ANTHONY KIEDIS (RED HOT CHILI PEPPERS)

I Against I	Bad Brains
Talking Book	Stevie Wonder
Anything by	Bob Marley and the Wailers
Hardcore Jollies	Funkadelic
Greatest Hits	James Brown
Greatest Hits	Marvin Gaye
Greatest Hits	Billie Holiday
Are You Experienced?	Jimi Hendrix Experience

SUZANNE VEGA

Eli and the 13th Confession	Laura Nyro
Songs of Leonard Cohen	Leonard Cohen
The Velvet Underground and Nico	The Velvet Underground
Sounds of Silence	Simon and Garfunkel
Synchronicity (side 2)	The Police
Hatful of Hollow	The Smiths
Somebody's Got To Do It	Frank Christian
Working on Wings to Fly	Cindy Kallet
2	Cindy Kallet

MICHAEL STIPE (R.E.M.)

Pink Flag	Wire
Marquee Moon	Television
Horses	Patti Smith
Rhapsody in Blue	George Gershwin
Experiment in Terror	Henry Mancini
Fellini Satyricon	soundtrack
The Velvet Underground	The Velvet Underground
154	Wire
Exotica 2	Martin Denny
Sound of the Sand	David Thomas & the Pedestrians

ICE-T

On Fire	Stetsasonic
Yo! Bum Rush the Show	Public Enemy
Salt-N-Pepa	Salt-N-Pepa
Licensed to Ill	Beastie Boys
Motor-Booty Affair	Parliament
The Best of the Delfonics	The Delfonics
Down by Law	MC Shan
All LPs	AC/DC
All LPs	Judas Priest

BILLY JOEL

Take Five	Dave Brubeck
Rubber Soul	The Beatles
Hot Rocks, 1964–69	The Rolling Stones
Adagio for Strings	Samuel Barber, performed by Leonard Bernstein and the New York Philharmonic
Led Zeppelin	Led Zeppelin
Axis: Bold As Love	Jimi Hendrix Experience
The Complete Tatum Solo Masterpieces, Volumes 1–9	Art Tatum
John Barleycorn Must Die	Traffic
Otis Redding's Greatest Hits	Otis Redding
The Genius of Ray Charles	Ray Charles

CARLY SIMON

Tea for the Tillerman	Cat Stevens
Caverna Magica	Andreas Vollenweider
Midnight Love	Marvin Gaye
Alchemy—Live	Dire Straits
Winter	George Winston
Water Music	George Frideric Handel
Porgy and Bess	any version
Puccini Arias	Kiri Te Kanawa
Paradise and Lunch	Ry Cooder
Greatest Hits	The Temptations
I Musici, Concerto in A Minor, Concerto in D Minor, Brandenburg Concertos	Johann Sebastian Bach

K.D. LANG

The Patsy Cline Story	Patsy Cline
Hard Hitting Songs for Hard Hit People	Hazel Dickens
Season of Glass	Yoko Ono
Country Hits, Vol. 7 (K-Tel)	various artists
Mingus	Joni Mitchell
Latin à la Lee	Peggy Lee
Any album by	Kate Bush
Wild, Wild Young Women	various artists
Ella and Oscar	Ella Fitzgerald and Oscar Peterson
Rickie Lee Jones	Rickie Lee Jones

DWIGHT YOAKAM

The Best of Buck Owens, Vols. I, II, III	Buck Owens
Buckaroo	Buck Owens
The Songs That Made Him Famous	Johnny Cash
The Columbia Sessions	Stanley Brothers
The Best of Merle Haggard	Merle Haggard
The Georgia Satellites	The Georgia Satellites
Can't Stand the Weather	Stevie Ray Vaughan
. . . And a Time To Dance	Los Lobos
Rockin' George Jones	George Jones
Get Yer Ya-Ya's Out	The Rolling Stones
Green River	Creedence Clearwater Revival
Riptide	Robert Palmer

JOE ELLIOTT (DEF LEPPARD)

Listen Like Thieves	INXS
Electric Warrior	T. Rex
"Angel No. 9"	Mick Ronson
"Elected"	Alice Cooper
"Livin' on a Prayer"	Bon Jovi
All the Young Dudes ("and all other LP's")	Mott the Hoople
Montrose	Montrose
The Unforgettable Fire	U2
All LP's by	Psychedelic Furs
English Settlement	XTC

LENNY KRAVITZ

Kaya	Bob Marley and the Wailers
Catch a Fire	Bob Marley and the Wailers
Electric Ladyland	Jimi Hendrix Experience
Smash Hits	Jimi Hendrix Experience
Plastic Ono Band	John Lennon
Innervisions	Stevie Wonder
Houses of the Holy	Led Zeppelin
Untitled	Led Zeppelin
Past Masters	The Beatles
What's Going On	Marvin Gaye

DOLLY PARTON

Any album by	George Jones
Any album by	Linda Ronstadt
Any album by	Cat Stevens
Any album by	Otis Redding
Tracy Chapman	Tracy Chapman
Kenny and Dolly's Christmas Album	Kenny Rogers and Dolly Parton
Trio	Dolly Parton, Emmylou Harris, Linda Ronstadt
"Sometimes When We Touch"	Dan Hill
"Hitchin' a Ride"	Vanity Fare
Any album by	Doug Kershaw

DAVE PIRNER (SOUL ASYLUM)

Bitches Brew	Miles Davis
The Complete Recordings	Robert Johnson
Out of Step	Minor Threat
Exile on Main Street	The Rolling Stones
Loaded	The Velvet Underground
Horses	Patti Smith
The Stooges	The Stooges
Poor Boy	Woodie Guthrie
Pearl	Janis Joplin
Up on the Sun	Meat Puppets

JOAN BAEZ

The Brandenburg Concertos	Johann Sebastian Bach
The Beethoven String Quartets	various artists
The Final Cut	Pink Floyd
Brahms Alto Rhapsody, Op. 53	Kathleen Ferrier
Jussi Bjoerling Arias Vols. I & II	
Tristan und Isolde	Wagner, sung by Birgit Nilsson
Chopin Etudes	Maurizio Pollini
Blonde on Blonde	Bob Dylan
Scottish Fantasy	Max Bruch, performed by Jascha Heifetz
Compilation "Dance" tape	Steve Winwood, Stevie Wonder, Ruben Blades, U2, Peter Gabriel, Talk Talk, Tears for Fears, Foreigner, Eurythmics

ROSANNE CASH

Atlantic Rhythm and Blues 1947–1974	various artists
Paradise and Lunch	Ry Cooder
A Hard Day's Night	The Beatles
Graceland	Paul Simon
Gorilla	James Taylor
Blonde on Blonde	Bob Dylan
Desire	Bob Dylan
Infidels	Bob Dylan
King of America	Elvis Costello
My Aim Is True	Elvis Costello
Born To Run	Bruce Springsteen
Hard Promises	Tom Petty

KEITH RICHARDS (ROLLING STONES)

"Little Queenie"	Chuck Berry
Any album of	Johann Sebastian Bach
Any album of	Wolfgang Amadeus Mozart
"Key to the Highway"	Little Walter with Jimmy Rogers
"Still a Fool"	Muddy Waters
"Reach Out"	Four Tops
"Mystery Train"	Elvis Presley
"Come on Everybody"	Eddie Cochran
"That'll Be the Day"	Buddy Holly

Some doo-wop by the Jive Five, or maybe a bit of Segovia.

ICE CUBE

To the East, Blackwards	X-Clan
Fear of a Black Planet	Public Enemy
Any album by	K-Solo
Holy Intellect	Poor Righteous Teachers
Greatest Hits	Marvin Gaye
Greatest HIts	Harold Melvin & the Blue Notes
Greatest Hits	Parliament
Greatest Hits	James Brown
AmeriKKKa's Most Wanted	Ice Cube

BARRY GIBB (THE BEE GEES)

"Wake Up Little Susie"	The Everly Brothers
"Crying"	Roy Orbison
"In Dreams"	Roy Orbison
"Missing You"	Ray Peterson
"Keep Right on A'Hurtin' "	Johnny Tillotson
"White Christmas"	Bing Crosby
"Are You Lonesome Tonight"	Elvis Presley
"Jailhouse Rock"	Elvis Presley
"I Can't Stop Loving You"	Ray Charles
"Worried Man"	Ray Charles

SIMON LEBON (DURAN DURAN)

Inti Illimani	Canto de Pueblos Andinos
Tantalizing with the Blues	John Lee Hooker
Nocturnes	Chopin
Mirror Moves	Psychedelic Furs
Nightclubbing	Grace Jones
The Idiot	Iggy Pop
Big Science	Laurie Anderson
Man with a Horn	Miles Davis
Welcome to the Pleasuredome (sides 1 and 2)	Frankie Goes to Hollywood

AIMEE MANN

Plants & Birds & Rocks & Things	The Loud Family
Mellow Gold	Beck
Exile in Guyville	Liz Phair
Frosting on the Beater	The Posies
Odessey & Oracle	The Zombies
Sgt. Pepper's Lonely Hearts Club Band	The Beatles
Good Old Boys	Randy Newman
Straight Up	Badfinger
Imperial Bedroom	Elvis Costello
Walk Across the Rooftops	The Blue Nile

BELLY (entire band)

Miss America	Mary Margaret O'Hara
Murmur	R.E.M.
Midnight Cowboy sountrack	John Barry
I Against I	Bad Brains
Under the Big Black Sun	X
The Beatles	The Beatles
Exile on Main Street	The Rolling Stones
Low	David Bowie
Government Issue	Government Issue
Trial	Verbal Assault

DION

Slow Turning	John Hiatt
The Joshue Tree	U2
Night Moves	Bob Seger
The Freewheelin' Bob Dylan	Bob Dylan
Greatest Hits	Creedence Clearwater Revival
King of the Delta Blues	Robert Johnson
The Great 28	Chuck Berry
Born in the USA	Bruce Springsteen
Rickie Lee Jones	Rickie Lee Jones
Graceland	Graceland

THE BESTSELLING ALBUMS OF ALL TIME

The Recording Industry Association of America tracks monthly album sales and awards gold and platinum certification based on the sale of 500,000 units for gold, one million units for platinum, and two million units or more for multiplatinum. Here are the albums which top the lists, organized by category, as of August 28, 1997.

ROCK/POP

25 million
Michael Jackson, *Thriller,* 1982

24 million
Eagles, *Their Greatest Hits, 1971–1975,* 1977

17 million
Fleetwood Mac, *Rumours,* 1977

16 million
The Beatles, *The Beatles,* 1968
Boston, *Boston,* 1976
Led Zeppelin, *Untitled,* 1971
Whitney Houston/various artists, *The Bodyguard* soundtrack, 1992

15 million
Hootie & The Blowfish, *Cracked Rear View,* 1994
Bruce Springsteen, *Born in the U.S.A.,* 1984
Alanis Morissette, *Jagged Little Pill,* 1995

14 million
The Beatles, *1967–1970,* 1993
Eagles, *Hotel California,* 1976
Guns N' Roses, *Appetite for Destruction,* 1987

13 million
The Beatles, *1962–1966,* 1993
Elton John, *Greatest Hits,* 1974
Meat Loaf, *Bat out of Hell,* 1977
Pink Floyd, *The Dark Side of the Moon,* 1973
Prince & the Revolution, *Purple Rain,* 1984

12 million
AC/DC, *Back in Black,* 1980
Bon Jovi, *Slippery When Wet,* 1986
Boyz II Men, *II,* 1994
Whitney Houston, *Whitney Houston,* 1985
Bruce Springsteen, *Bruce Springsteen & the E Street Band Live, 1975–1985,* 1986

11 million
The Beatles, *Abbey Road,* 1969
The Beatles, *Sgt. Pepper's Lonely Hearts Club Band,* 1967
Bee Gees/various artists, *Saturday Night Fever* soundtrack, 1977
Def Leppard, *Hysteria,* 1987
Pink Floyd, *The Wall,* 1979
James Taylor, *Greatest Hits,* 1976
various artists, *Dirty Dancing* soundtrack, 1987

10 million
Eric Clapton, *Unplugged,* 1992
Doobie Brothers, *Best of the Doobies,* 1976
Carole King, *Tapestry,* 1971
George Michael, *Faith,* 1987
Pearl Jam, *Ten,* 1991
Lionel Richie, *Can't Slow Down,* 1984
TLC, *CrazySexyCool,* 1994
U2, *The Joshua Tree,* 1987
Van Halen, *Van Halen,* 1978
various artists, *The Lion King* soundtrack, 1994
ZZ Top, *Eliminator,* 1983

9 million
Ace of Base, *The Sign,* 1993
Aerosmith, *Greatest Hits,* 1980
Boyz II Men, *Cooleyhighharmony,* 1991
Mariah Carey, *Daydream,* 1995
Mariah Carey, *Music Box,* 1993
Def Leppard, *Pyromania,* 1983
Celine Dion, *Falling into You,* 1996
Dire Straits, *Brothers in Arms,* 1985
Eagles, *Eagles Greatest Hits Volume II,* 1982
Green Day, *Dookie,* 1994
Whitney Houston, *Whitney,* 1987
Billy Joel, *Greatest Hits Volume I & II,* 1985
Billy Joel, *The Stranger,* 1977
Journey, *Escape,* 1981
Journey, *Journey's Greatest Hits,* 1988
Madonna, *Like a Virgin,* 1984
Bob Marley and the Wailers, *Legend,* 1984
Metallica, *Metallica,* 1991
Nirvana, *Nevermind,* 1991
R.E.O. Speedwagon, *Hi-Infidelity,* 1982
Van Halen, *1984,* 1984

8 million
The Beatles, *The Beatles Anthology Volume 1,* 1995
Michael Bolton, *Time, Love and Tenderness,* 1991
Toni Braxton, *Toni Braxton,* 1993
Mariah Carey, *Mariah Carey,* 1991
Michael Jackson, *Bad,* 1987
New Kids on the Block, *Hangin' Tough,* 1988
No Doubt, *Tragic Kingdom,* 1995
Olivia Newton-John/John Travolta, *Grease* soundtrack, 1972
Smashing Pumpkins, *Mellon Collie and the Infinite Sadness,* 1996
various artists, *Footloose* soundtrack, 1984
Whitesnake, *Whitesnake,* 1987

COUNTRY

13 million
Garth Brooks, *No Fences,* 1990

12 million
Kenny Rogers, *Greatest Hits,* 1980

11 million
Garth Brooks, *Ropin' the Wind,* 1991

9 million
Billy Ray Cyrus, *Some Gave All,* 1992
Garth Brooks, *The Hits,* 1994
Shania Twain, *The Woman in Me,* 1995

7 million
Garth Brooks, *Garth Brooks,* 1989
Patsy Cline, *Greatest Hits,* 1967

6 million
Garth Brooks, *In Pieces,* 1993
Garth Brooks, *The Chase,* 1991
Alan Jackson, *A Lot About Livin' (And a Little About Love),* 1992

5 million
Alabama, *Alabama's Greatest Hits,* 1986
Brooks & Dunn, *Brand New Man,* 1991
Tim McGraw, *Not a Moment Too Soon,* 1994
Bonnie Raitt, *Luck of the Draw,* 1991
Kenny Rogers, *The Gambler,* 1978

George Strait, *Pure Country,* 1992
Randy Travis, *Always and Forever,* 1987
Wynonna, *Wynonna,* 1992

4 million
Alabama, *Feels So Right,* 1981
Alabama, *Mountain Music,* 1982
Garth Brooks, *Fresh Horses,* 1995
Brooks & Dunn, *Hard Workin' Man,* 1993
Alan Jackson, *Don't Rock the Jukebox,* 1991
Waylon Jennings, *Greatest Hits,* 1979
Reba McEntire, *Greatest Hits, Vol. 2,* 1993
John Michael Montgomery, *Kickin' It Up,* 1994
Anne Murray, *Greatest Hits,* 1980
Willie Nelson, *Always on My Mind,* 1982
Willie Nelson, *Stardust,* 1990
Bonnie Raitt, *Nick of Time,* 1989
Kenny Rogers, *Ten Years of Gold,* 1978
Kenny Rogers, *20 Greatest Hits,* 1983

3 million
Alabama, *The Closer You Get,* 1983
Alabama, *Roll On,* 1984
Clint Black, *Killin' Time,* 1989
Clint Black, *Put Yourself in My Shoes,* 1990
Garth Brooks, *Beyond the Season,* 1992
Garth Brooks, *The Garth Brooks Collection,* 1994
Deana Carter, *Did I Shave My Legs For This?,* 1996
Charlie Daniels Band, *Million Mile Reflections,* 1978
Vince Gill, *I Still Believe in You,* 1992
Vince Gill, *When Love Finds You,* 1994
Alan Jackson, *Who I Am,* 1994
Alan Jackson, *Greatest Hits Collection,* 1995
Reba McEntire, *It's Your Call,* 1992
Reba McEntire, *For My Broken Heart,* 1991
Reba McEntire, *Greatest Hits,* 1987
Reba McEntire, *Read My Mind,* 1994
John Michael Montgomery, *John Michael Montgomery,* 1995
John Michael Montgomery, *Life's a Dance,* 1992
LeAnn Rimes, *Blue,* 1996
Kenny Rogers, *Kenny,* 1979
The Statler Brothers, *Best of The Statler Brothers,* 1975
George Strait, *Strait out of the Box,* 1995
Randy Travis, *Storms of Life,* 1992
Travis Tritt, *It's All About To Change,* 1991
Dwight Yoakam, *This Time,* 1994

JAZZ

11 million
Kenny G, *Breathless,* 1992

7 million
Kenny G, *Miracles,* 1994

5 million
Kenny G, *Duotones,* 1986

4 million
Kenny G, *Silhouette,* 1988

3 million
Kenny G, *Kenny G Live,* 1989
Kenny G, *The Moment,* 1996
George Benson, *Breezin',* 1984

Platinum
George Benson, *Weekend in L.A.,* 1978
George Benson, *Give Me the Night,* 1980
George Benson, *In Flight,* 1977
Kenny G, *Gravity,* 1985
Herbie Hancock, *Future Shock,* 1983
Bob James/David Sanborn, *Double Vision,* 1991
Al Jarreau, *Breakin' Away,* 1982
Chuck Mangione, *Feels So Good,* 1977
Spyro Gyra, *Morning Dance,* 1979

RAP

10 million
M.C. Hammer, *Please Hammer Don't Hurt 'Em,* 1990

7 million
2Pac, *All Eyez On Me,* 1996
Vanilla Ice, *To the Extreme,* 1990

6 million
Notorious B.I.G., *Life After Death,* 1997

5 million
Beastie Boys, *Licensed To Ill,* 1986
Fugees, *The Score,* 1996
Salt-N-Pepa, *Very Necessary,* 1993

4 million
Arrested Development, *3 Years, 5 Months and 2 Days in the Life of...,* 1992
Bone Thugs-N-Harmony, *E. 1999 Eternal,* 1995
The Fugees, *The Score,* 1996
Kris Kross, *Totally Krossed Out,* 1992
Snoop Doggy Dogg, *Doggystyle,* 1993

3 million
D.J. Jazzy Jeff and The Fresh Prince, *He's the D.J., I'm the Rapper,* 1988
Dr. Dre, *The Chronic,* 1992
Warren G., *Regulate ... G Funk Era,* 1994
Hammer, *Too Legit To Quit,* 1992
Run-D.M.C., *Raising Hell,* 1986
Wu-Tang Clan, *Wu-Tang Forever,* 1997

CLASSICAL

2 million
Benedictine Monks of Santo Domingo de Silos, *Chant,* 1994
Carreras, Domingo, Pavarotti, *The Three Tenors in Concert,* 1990

Platinum
Wendy Carlos, *Switched on Bach,* 1986
Carreras, Domingo, Pavarotti with Mehta, *The Three Tenors in Concert 1994,* 1994
London Symphony Orchestra for Victoria's Secret, *Classics by Request, Volumes I-V,* 1988–1992*
Luciano Pavarotti, *O Holy Night,* London, 1985
Royal Philharmonic Orchestra, *Hooked on Classics,* 1982
Piotr Tchaikovsky performed by Van Cliburn with the RCA Symphony Orchestra/Kirill Kondrashin, *Piano Concerto No. 1 in B-flat Minor, Op. 23,* 1982

*These albums are sold exclusively through Victoria's Secret stores and catalogs and are therefore not eligible for certification by the RIAA.

THE ROCK OF AGES: PEOPLE'S FAVORITE 50

Steve Dougherty has been PEOPLE's chief music writer since 1985. Herewith, his completely subjective list of the 50 albums he'd stock in his personal jukebox.

THE BAND (1969)
The Band
Rock 'n' roll's Great American Novel came with a backbeat and Robbie Robertson's story songs, told by Richard Manuel, Levon Helm, and Rick Danko, whose straight-to-the-heart and heartland vocals would make Mark Twain proud.

A HARD DAY'S NIGHT (1964),
RUBBER SOUL (1965),
THE BEATLES (1969)
The Beatles
Lennon, at the height of his vocal and writing powers, dominates all three discs; and for a change, the Cute One rocks as well.

ODELAY (1996)
Beck
An album from pop's beat-crazy, wordy rapping kid, Beck Hansen (no relation to the Oklahoma teen trio), that shows off his heightened senses of rhythm and humor.

CHUCK BERRY'S GOLDEN HITS (1967)
Chuck Berry
The brown-eyed handsome man told Tchaikovsky the news: There is indeed such a thing as a three-minute masterpiece.

THE RISE AND FALL OF ZIGGY STARDUST AND THE SPIDERS FROM MARS (1972)
David Bowie
Music had never glittered quite like this before and glam rock never sounded so good again.

20 ALL-TIME GREATEST HITS! (1991)
James Brown
You'll feel good! But then, you knew that you would.

BUFFALO SPRINGFIELD 1958–77 (1976)
Buffalo Springfield
This is evidence of why many a hippie tear spilled at the breakup of the supergroup that spawned Neil Young, Stephen Stills, and Jim Messina.

LONDON CALLING (1979)
The Clash
They pronounced rock dead, then celebrated its resurrection on this, a double album without a lame cut in the lot.

MY AIM IS TRUE (1977)
Elvis Costello
He looked punk, acted mean, sounded nasty, and hit right on target in his album debut.

LAYLA AND OTHER ASSORTED LOVE SONGS (1970)
Derek and the Dominoes
Eric Clapton and Duane Allman. 'Nuff said.

THE CHRONIC (1992)
Dr. Dre (with Snoop Doggy Dogg)
Hip-hop's auteur and his pet rapper share their bemused family values.

BRINGING IT ALL BACK HOME (1965),
HIGHWAY 61 REVISITED (1965),
JOHN WESLEY HARDING (1968)
Bob Dylan
For all who question the lasting fuss over the rheumy rock laureate, three masterworks.

I NEVER LOVED A MAN (THE WAY I LOVE YOU) (1967)
Aretha Franklin
They invented soul so she could be queen.

WHAT'S GOING ON (1971)
Marvin Gaye
Motown's sex star made hearts and minds quicken with this ambitious song cycle.

ARE YOU EXPERIENCED? (1967)
Jimi Hendrix Experience
That voice. Those songs. That guitar. We're still asking, "Where did this guy come from?"

Beck, *Odelay*

Nirvana, *Nevermind*

U2, *Achtung Baby*

ARTHUR (DECLINE AND FALL OF THE BRITISH EMPIRE) (1969), **MUSWELL HILLBILLIES** (1971)
The Kinks
Tommy without the pretensions: these are two of plaintive mod genius Ray Davies's brilliantly realized theme albums.

ORIGINAL GOLDEN HITS, VOLS. 1 AND 2 (1969)
Jerry Lee Lewis
Killer tracks from The Killer: all is forgiven.

GROOVIEST 17 ORIGINAL HITS (1959)
Little Richard
"Good Golly Miss Molly," "Tutti Fruiti," "Lucille," "Long Tall Sally," "Rip It Up." Macon, Ga.'s absolutely fabulous former dishwasher screamed 'em all to life at New Orleans's Specialty Records studio.

COURT AND SPARK (1974)
Joni Mitchell
The ultimate chick singer whips one on the boys.

MOBY GRAPE (1967)
Moby Grape
San Francisco's one-masterpiece wonder squeezed all their juice into this ignored collection.

THE BEST OF VAN MORRISON (1990)
Van Morrison
Romance for the soul.

NEVERMIND (1991)
Nirvana
Full of as much old-fashioned tube amplifier feedback as neo-punk martyr Kurt Cobain's fabled rage, this is a call to get with it for all classic rock-fixated geezers who insist that the music ain't what it used to be.

TEAR THE ROOF OFF (1993)
Parliament Funkadelic
So they did and something memorable was born.

THE 10 MOST OVERRATED ALBUMS

For those contrarians who would rather smash discs than play them, here is a flip-side list of legendary non-legends in the annals of rock.

THE CARS (1978)
The Cars
Great rock bands give exhilarating rides; this sleek clunker bores.

4 WAY STREET (1971)
Crosby, Stills, Nash and Young
They could have used a stop sign.

THE DOORS (1967)
The Doors
As an icon, Jim Morrison can't be beat; but his great looks, leather pants, and lucrative afterlife make people forget he was a mediocre singer and pretentious poet masquerading as a rock star.

TAPESTRY (1971)
Carole King
The immortal author of "Will You Still Love Me Tomorrow" and "(You Make Me Feel Like) a Natural Woman" sinned by making the pop charts safe for the legion of self-indulgent, sentimental singer-songwriter solo acts who followed.

UNTITLED (1971)
Led Zeppelin
The album that gave us "Stairway to Heaven" and other artifacts of arena-ready blowhard rock.

(WHAT'S THE STORY) MORNING GLORY? (1995)
Oasis
They like to compare themselves to the Beatles and Stones, but prove with this album's lame lyrics and hand-me-down sound to be in the same league with neither.

ELVIS (TV SPECIAL) (1968)
Elvis Presley
The gig that was trumpeted as his return to '50s form. Leatherclad in Vegas a year after the Summer of Love, The King was already out of touch with current culture and his music.

THE DREAM OF THE BLUE TURTLES (1985)
Sting
The Police man lured listeners with his pop status, then stung them with stingy jazz.

TOMMY (1969)
The Who
Maybe if Pete had left it to critics to call his own composition "A Rock Opera," it wouldn't make us want to gag.

And, finally: **THE COMPACT DISC ITSELF**
It's not the pop, scratch,and hum we miss—it's what's lost in the digital mix. Sound waves, like rock, should roll, rather than get chopped up into chewy bytes.

G. P./GRIEVOUS ANGEL (1990)
Gram Parsons
The high priest of such current alternative country-rock acts as Wilco and Son Volt, Parsons invented the genre he called "Cosmic American Music" and served up these two ageless solo albums of rocking country soul before his death at 26.

THE SUN SESSIONS (1987), **ELVIS' GOLDEN RECORDS, VOL. 1** (1958)
Elvis Presley
Rock and roll at its best.

1999 (1982)
Prince
From when he had a name and all the critics loved him in New York, and everywhere else.

MURMUR (1983)
R.E.M.
The debut album that brought "Radio Free Europe" to the promised land. What's it about? Who knows? Who cares?

HISTORY OF OTIS REDDING (1968)
Otis Redding
The greatest soul ever told.

TIM (1985)
The Replacements
Put "Swingin' Party" on replay, never let it stop.

BEGGAR'S BANQUET (1968), **STICKY FINGERS** (1971), **THE SINGLES COLLECTION** (1989)
The Rolling Stones
The first two are mid-career classics. In the last, an obscure collection of mostly mono, many never released in the U.S. singles, finds the Stones paying tribute to their black American heroes.

NEVER MIND THE BOLLOCKS, HERE'S THE SEX PISTOLS (1977)
Sex Pistols
Unlistenable then, unbeatable now, it mocks, it taunts, it screams, and you can dance to it!

BETWEEN HEAVEN AND HELL (1992)
Social Distortion
Tatooed frontman Mike Ness looks like he stepped from the gates of San Quentin; he sings Patsy Cline's "Making Believe (You Still Love Me)" like a prison-yard angel.

BACK TO MONO (1991)
Phil Spector
Actually four CDs, offering unforgettable visits by (mostly) girl groups to the little man's Great Wall of Sound.

BORN TO RUN (1975)
Bruce Springsteen
The Boss as rock and roll tradesman, redefining the exuberant yearning to get out on the highway with a guitar strapped 'cross his back.

STORYTELLER (Boxed Set, 1992)
Rod Stewart
Remember that before he turned out the lights and cuddled up to the Manilow inside him, Rod the mod was an underrated lyricist who rivaled Van Morrison in the U.K. soul crooner department.

HITSVILLE USA: THE MOTOWN SINGLES COLLECTION (1992)
The Supremes, The Four Tops, Smokey Robinson & The Miracles, The Jackson Five, The Temptations, et al.
The soundtrack of the '60s, courtesy of Detroit's big wheel, Berry Gordy. (And it's got Mary Wells and Marvin Gaye too.)

GIRLFRIEND (1991)
Matthew Sweet
With former Television star Richard Lloyd, Sweet made the album of the year only to be ignored by radio and its customers, who didn't buy it.

TALKING HEADS 77 (1977)
Talking Heads
Leading the punk revolt from these shores, art school misfit David Byrne makes his bow as one of rock's strangest, and most talented, characters.

ACHTUNG BABY (1991)
U2
The Dubliners finally drop the earnest facade, as well as the endlessly repeated rhythm guitar riff that launched them, and deliver a sonic treat recorded in the cold war capital of Berlin.

ATLANTIC R&B 1947–1974 (1991)
various artists
Before they named it Rock, it was spelled R&B. A chest of pop's buried treasures.

MEATY BEATY BIG AND BOUNCY (1971)
The Who
Known for their big productions, including the overrated *Tommy* and underrated *Quadrophenia*, the London mods rocked Top 40 radio with these high explosives.

AFTER THE GOLD RUSH (1970)
Neil Young
One nugget from four brilliant decades of work by the once and current rocker.

ABSOLUTELY FREE (1967)
Frank Zappa
Innovative, mocking, shocking, and funny as hell.

THE NAME OF THIS BAND IS . . .

From Abba to ZZ Top, here's the scoop on how our favorite bands came up with their famous names.

Abba: an acronym made up of the first initials of the band members' names—Agnetha Fältskog, Benny Andersson, Björn Ulvaeus, and Anni-Frid Lyngstad.

Black Sabbath: an ocult thriller by novelist Denis Wheatley.

Depeche Mode: a French magazine (which means "fast fashion).

Duran Duran: took the name from the villain in the 1967 science fiction film *Barbarella*.

Bob Dylan: Robert Zimmerman took his new last name not from Dylan Thomas, as is often assumed, but from an uncle "Dillion."

Eurythmics: the name is defined in the *American Heritage Dictionary* a "the choreographic art of interpreting musical composition by a rhythmical, free-style graceful movement of the body in response to the rhythm of the music.

Grateful Dead: an English folk ballad archetype involving karma and the life cycle.

Hole: band leader Courtney Love chose the name after a line in the Greek tragedy *Medea*: "There's a hole burning deep inside of me." She says she picked it because "I knew it would confuse people."

The Hollies: after music legend and icon Buddy Holly.

Jane's Addiction: allegedly, Jane is a Hollywood hooker through whom the band members met in Los Angeles.

Living Colour: inspired by the introduction to the old Walt Disney TV show: "The following program is brought to you in living color."

The Meat Puppets: from the idea that the musicians are only vehicles of their music's will.

Pearl Jam: named after Eddie Vedder's grandmother Pearl, who was married to a Native American and made hallucinogenic preserves from peyote.

Pink Floyd: a combination of the names of two Georgia bluesmen, Pink Anderson and Floyd Council.

The Police: an ironic reference to drummer Stewart Copeland's father, former chief of the CIA's Political Action Staff.

Soundgarden: named after a beach sculpture by Lake Washington in Seattle which hums in the wind.

They Might Be Giants: a 1971 film title cribbed from *Don Quixote;* band members liked its curiosity and paranoia.

UB40: since the band members were all unemployed, they chose the name of the British unemployment benefit card.

Velvet Underground: from the title of an obscure book about sadomasochism.

ZZ Top: after Texas bluesman Z. Z. Hill.

CHANGE OF TUNE

Like the best-laid plans, the best-named bands often went astray before deciding on a final moniker. Here are some enduring groups with their long lost early names.

Final Name	Original Name	Final Name	Original Name
The Bangles	Supersonic Bangs; Bangs	Journey	Golden Gate Rhythm Section
The Beach Boys	Carl and the Passions	Led Zeppelin	New Yardbirds
The Beatles	Johnny and the Moondogs	Lynyrd Skynyrd	My Backyard
The Bee Gees	Rattlesnakes	The Mamas and the Papas	New Journeymen
Black Sabbath	Earth	The Righteous Brothers	Paramours
Buffalo Springfield	The Herd	Salt-N-Pepa	Supernature
The Byrds	Beefeaters	Simon and Garfunkel	Tom and Jerry
Creedence Clearwater Revival	The Golliwogs	Styx	Trade Winds; TW4
Culture Club	Praise of Lemmings	Sonny and Cher	Caesar and Cleo
The Cure	Obelisk; Goat Band	Steppenwolf	Sparrow
Depeche Mode	Composition of Sound	The Supremes	Primettes
Dire Straits	Cafe Racers	Talking Heads	Artistics
Earth Wind & Fire	Salty Peppers	The Temptations	The Elgins
Grateful Dead	Warlocks	U2	Feedback; the Hype

THE 50 BEST COUNTRY ALBUMS

PEOPLE's Randy Vest touts this country album starter set, with additional tips of the Stetson to Webb Pierce, Ernest Tubb, Kitty Wells, Bob Wills and many others.

THE BEST OF EDDY ARNOLD (1967)
Eddy Arnold
The Tennessee Plowboy shows his smoother side on these (mostly) '60s tracks.

THINKIN' PROBLEM (1994)
David Ball
Among a sea of hat acts, Ball's topper stands out in the crowd, thanks to this twangy tour de force.

KILLIN' TIME (1989)
Clint Black
An incredible, play-it-over-and-over-again debut that garnered Black five No. 1 singles.

NO FENCES (1990)
Garth Brooks
Pure, heartfelt songs recorded just before Garth became GARTH.

HIGH AND DRY (1991)
Marty Brown
Of all the pretenders to Hank's throne, Brown is the real deal.

COME ON COME ON (1992)
Mary Chapin Carpenter
A blissful fusion of country, folk, and rock from the "hometown girl."

I FELL IN LOVE (1990)
Carlene Carter
After years of dabbling in rock, June Carter and Carl Smith's little girl finds her roots in country.

JOHNNY CASH AT FOLSOM PRISON (1968)
Johnny Cash
Cash's live performance for a throng of inmates remains a milestone. "Folsom Prison Blues" can still evoke chills.

KING'S RECORD SHOP (1987)
Rosanne Cash
Produced by then hubby Rodney Crowell, this Grammy-winning album is right on the money.

THE PATSY CLINE STORY (1963)
Patsy Cline
Sublime sounds from country's high priestess of female vocalists.

DIAMONDS AND DIRT (1988)
Rodney Crowell
Singer-songwriter Crowell hit a home run with this critically lauded and commercially successful release.

GUITAR TOWN (1986)
Steve Earle
Rough-housin' Earle found himself a spot on country's crowded map with this inspired outing.

THE BEST OF LEFTY FRIZZELL (1991)
Lefty Frizzell
His style influenced everyone from Willie to Merle to George Jones. Here's the evidence.

WHEN I CALL YOUR NAME (1989)
Vince Gill
The sweetest pipes this side of heaven, caressing material that's just as heavenly.

CHISELED IN STONE (1987)
Vern Gosdin
A hard-edged voice that's packed with pathos.

TRIO (1987)
Emmylou Harris, Dolly Parton, Linda Ronstadt
Three distinct song stylists in a perfect, harmonious blend.

DOWN EVERY ROAD 1962–1994 (1996)
Merle Haggard
A four-disc anthology shows why the Hag is one of country's enduring legends.

HIGHWAYMAN (1985)
The Highwaymen (Johnny Cash, Waylon Jennings, Kris Kristofferson, Willie Nelson)
An inspired collaboration between some of country's elder statesmen.

ROCKIN' IN THE COUNTRY: THE BEST OF WANDA JACKSON (1990)
Wanda Jackson
From rockabilly to Nash-pop, Jackson growls and purrs up a storm.

SHE THINKS I STILL CARE: THE GEORGE JONES COLLECTION (1997)
George Jones
A two-disc set chronicling Jones's often overlooked years with the United Artists label in the '60s.

THE JUDDS (WYNONNA & NAOMI) (1984)
The Judds
Wynonna and her mater never sounded quite as honest or engaging after this memorable debut.

PICKIN' ON NASHVILLE (1989)
Kentucky Headhunters
Raucous rock from the Bluegrass State's (and Arkansas') impish, redneck sons.

SHADOWLAND (1988)
k.d. lang
Lang teams up with legendary producer Owen Bradley to create studio magic.

ANTHOLOGY 1956–80 (1991)
Brenda Lee
The songs are mostly pop, but the pipes are pure country all the way.

20 GREATEST HITS (1987)
Loretta Lynn
From givin' a carousin' hubby

what-fer to wardin' off a would-be man-stealer, the coal miner's daughter is a tough lady to top.

GOLDEN HITS (1965)
Roger Miller
The King of the Road's loopy takes on booze, buffalo, and Britain.

COUNTRY MUSIC HALL OF FAME (1991)
Bill Monroe
The father of bluegrass and his mandolin. Need we say more?

LEAVE THE LIGHT ON (1989)
Lorrie Morgan
George Morgan's daughter takes center stage and stakes a claim on country's landscape.

WHY LADY WHY (1983)
Gary Morris
A voice of operatic strength surrounding some mighty sturdy songs.

JUST LIKE OLD TIMES (1992)
Heather Myles
A rousing, Bakersfield-influenced sleeper by a dynamic singer.

RED HEADED STRANGER (1975)
Willie Nelson
Bare-bones country by the genre's celebrated redneck outlaw.

WILL THE CIRCLE BE UNBROKEN (1972)
The Nitty Gritty Dirt Band
An historic summit with the likes of Roy Acuff and Mother Maybelle Carter.

THE NEW NASHVILLE CATS (1991)
Mark O'Connor
The country fiddler/classical composer is joined by some 50 heavyweight pickers on this Grammy-winning set.

80'S LADIES (1987)
K. T. Oslin
Sassy and bittersweet songs truthfully sung by a seasoned survivor.

THE BUCK OWENS COLLECTION, 1959–1990 (1992)
Buck Owens
Three CDs worth of classic tunes from the king of the Bakersfield sound and his stalwart Buckaroos.

THE COMPLETE 50'S MASTERS (1992)
Elvis Presley
The King's earliest sides (8 CDs!) before Hollywood and mediocrity beckoned.

THE ESSENTIAL RAY PRICE, 1951–62 (1991)
Ray Price
Raw performances from the man once known as the "Cherokee Cowboy" who later found success crooning pop-styled ballads.

FOUR WALLS: THE LEGEND BEGINS (1991)
Jim Reeves
An early, mostly harder-edged Reeves, already showing signs of that vocal "touch of velvet."

THE ESSENTIAL MARTY ROBBINS, 1951–82 (1991)
Marty Robbins
The King of the Balladeers lends his distinct tenor to storytelling songs and country-pop.

WHAT A WOMAN WANTS TO HEAR (1991)
Dawn Sears
Shamefully overlooked powerhouse vocalist whose followup, *Nothin' but Good*, was equally as memorable.

THE ESSENTIAL CONNIE SMITH (1996)
Connie Smith
One of country's greatest female singers of the '60s, '70s, or for that matter, any decade.

STRAIT OUT OF THE BOX (1995)
George Strait
From a winning 16-year career, here are the cream of the crop.

STORMS OF LIFE (1986)
Randy Travis
With this debut album, Travis helped to restore country music's heart and soul. He's never equalled it.

THE VERY BEST OF CONWAY TWITTY (1978)
Conway Twitty
Once called "the best friend a song ever had," Twitty put his own indelible stamp on the country genre.

KEVIN WELCH (1990)
Kevin Welch
Call it alterna-country. This singer-songwriter from Oklahoma brings a poet's sensibility to his work.

THE ESSENTIAL DOTTIE WEST (1996)
Dottie West
West's husky vocals were never better than on these defining 1960s and '70s tracks.

I WONDER DO YOU THINK OF ME (1989)
Keith Whitley
The title cut alone by the late, lamented Whitley will break your heart.

40 GREATEST HITS (1978)
Hank Williams
The Daddy...the King...the Master.

ANNIVERSARY: TWENTY YEARS OF HITS (1987)
Tammy Wynette
Wynette conveys more pain in "Til I Get it Right" than most artists can in their entire repertoire.

GUITARS, CADILLACS, ETC., ETC. (1986)
Dwight Yoakam
California honky-tonk collides with Nashville tradition. A rouser of a debut.

GREAT TITLES TO COUNTRY SONGS

A case could be made that the aptest aphorists of pop culture are country songwriters. Herewith, some of C & W's quirkier titles.

"Divorce Me C.O.D.," Merle Travis

"Don't You Think This Outlaw Bit's Done Got Out of Hand," Waylon Jennings

"Heaven's Just a Sin Away," The Kendells

"I Cheated Me Right Out of You," Moe Bandy

"I Forgot More Than You'll Ever Know," Davis Sisters

"I'll Never Get Out of This World Alive," Hank Williams Sr.

"I'm Gonna Hire a Wino to Decorate Our Home," David Frizzell

"I'm the Only Hell (Mama Ever Raised)," Johnny Paycheck

"It's Not Love (But It's Not Bad)," Merle Haggard

"I've Enjoyed About as Much of This as I Can Stand," Porter Wagoner

"The Lord Knows I'm Drinkin'," Cal Smith

"Mama's in the Graveyard, Papa's in the Pen (Papa Loved Mama and Mama Loved Men)," Garth Brooks

"Marriage Has Ruined More Good Love Affairs," Jan Howard

"Maximum Security to Minimum Wage," Don King

"Now I Lay Me Down To Cheat," David Allan Coe

"She's Actin' Single (I'm Drinkin' Doubles)," Gary Stewart

"She Got the Goldmine (I Got the Shaft)," Jerry Reed

"She Was Bitten on the Udder by an Adder," Jethro Burns

"Sleeping Single (in a Double Bed)," Barbara Mandrell

"Take an Old Cold Tater and Wait," Little Jimmy Dickens

"Take This Job and Shove It," Johnny Paycheck

"Yonder Comes a Sucker," Jim Reeves

"You Just Hurt My Last Feeling," Sammi Smith

"You're Gonna Ruin My Bad Reputation," Ronnie McDowell

"You're Out Doing What I'm Here Doing Without," Gene Watson

"You're the Reason Our Kids Are Ugly," Loretta Lynn

"Waitin' in Your Welfare Line," Buck Owens

"What's Made Milwaukee Famous (Has Made a Loser Out of Me)," Jerry Lee Lewis

"When It's Springtime in Alaska (It's Forty Below)," Johnny Horton

PEOPLE'S 20 TRAILBLAZERS OF C & W MUSIC

Many of these legendary divas and dudes of the Grand Ole Opry are now dead, but their music and influence live forever—from Nashville to Austin to Bakersfield, wherever country artists are at work.

Roy Acuff
Eddy Arnold
Gene Autry
Boudleaux Bryant
The Carter Family
Patsy Cline
Spade Cooley
Tennessee Ernie Ford
Lefty Frizzell
Bill Monroe
Minnie Pearl
Tex Ritter
Marty Robbins
Jimmie Rodgers
Roy Rogers
Hank Snow
Ernest Tubb
Kitty Wells
Hank Williams Sr.
Bob Wills

JAZZ: ESSENTIAL LISTENING

Not encyclopedic or definitive, this is simply a list of 50 marvelous jazz albums. The recordings here date from the '20s to the '90s, and they cover a range of styles. Any jazz purist, or for that matter, impurist, will find sins of omission and commission on this list. All we, the jazz jury at PEOPLE, can say is that these albums have enriched our lives immeasurably and given us an almost embarrassing amount of pleasure. To us, these recordings are the easiest sort of listening, full of wit, passion, invention, and beauty.

Louis Armstrong	*Hot Fives and Sevens,* Vol. II or III (1926–27)
Chet Baker	*My Funny Valentine* (1954)
Count Basie	*The Original American Decca Recordings* (1937–39)
Bix and Tram Beiderbecke	*The Bix Beiderbecke Story,* Vol. II (1927–28)
Art Blakey & The Jazz Messengers	*Buhaina's Delight* (1961)
Clifford Brown and Max Roach	*Clifford Brown and Max Roach* (1954–55)
Betty Carter	*Betty Carter* (1966)
Ornette Coleman	*The Shape of Jazz To Come* (1959–60)
Ornette Coleman	*Free Jazz* (1960)
John Coltrane	*Coltrane* (1957)
John Coltrane	*Meditations* (1965)
Miles Davis	*Kind of Blue* (1959)
Miles Davis and Gil Evans	*Porgy and Bess* (1958)
Paul Desmond and Gerry Mulligan	*Two of a Mind* (1962)
Eric Dolphy	*Out to Lunch* (1964)
Duke Ellington	*The Blanton-Webster Band* (1940-42)
Duke Ellington & The Jungle Band	*Rockin' in Rhythm,* Vol. III (1929–31)
Bill Evans	*The Village Vanguard Sessions* (1961)
Art Farmer	*Something To Live For* (1987)
Ella Fitzgerald	*The Gershwin Songbook* (1959)
Ella Fitzgerald	*The Intimate Ella* (1960)
Stan Getz	*The Roost Quartets 1950-51* (1950–51)
Benny Goodman	*Carnegie Hall Concert* (1938)
Charlie Haden & Quartet	*Haunted Heart* (1990)
Lionel Hampton	*The Complete Lionel Hampton* (1937–41)
Herbie Hancock	*Maiden Voyage* (1965)
Coleman Hawkins	*Body and Soul: The Complete Coleman Hawkins,* Vol. I (1929–40)
Coleman Hawkins	*The Complete Coleman Hawkins* (1944)
Fletcher Henderson and Don Redman	*Developing an American Orchestra, 1923–1937* (1923–37)
Billie Holiday	*The Quintessential Billie Holiday,* Vol. III, IV, or V (1937–39)
James P. Johnson	*Snowy Morning Blues* (1930, 1944)
Abbey Lincoln	*The World Is Falling Down* (1990)
Charles Mingus	*New Tijuana Moods* (1957)
Thelonious Monk	*The Unique Thelonious Monk* (1956)
Thelonious Monk	*Alone in San Francisco* (1959)
Thelonious Monk	*Monk's Dream* (1962)
Gerry Mulligan	*What Is There To Say?* (1958–59)

Oliver Nelson	*Blues and the Abstract Truth* (1961)
King Oliver	*King Oliver's Jazz Band 1923* (1923)
Charlie Parker	*The Charlie Parker Story* (1945)
Charlie Parker (with Dizzy Gillespie, Max Roach, Bud Powell, and Charles Mingus)	*The Greatest Jazz Concert Ever* (1953)
Bud Powell	*The Amazing Bud Powell*, Vol. I (1949–51)
Bud Powell	*The Genius of Bud Powell* (1951)
Sonny Rollins	*A Night at the Village Vanguard*, Vols. I and II (1957)
John Scofield (1989)	*Time on My Hands*
Art Tatum	*The Tatum Solo Masterpieces*, Vol. III (1953–55)
Cecil Taylor	*Unit Structures* (1966)
Sarah Vaughan and Clifford Brown	*Sarah Vaughan With Clifford Brown* (1954)
Fats Waller	*The Joint Is Jumpin'* (1929–43)
Lester Young	*The Complete Lester Young* (1943–44)

JAZZ TODAY

A new generation of stars is emerging in jazz. Steeped in tradition, technically prodigious, often daring, and always fired by the energy and passion of youth, they are a formidable lot, as varied in style as they are united in their allegiance to the verities of swing, the blues, and improvisation. Here are some standout albums by the the new school.

Geri Allen, *Twenty One* (1994)
(piano)

James Carter, *The Real Quietstorm* (1995)
(saxophone/flute/clarinet)

Marty Ehrlich, *Can You Hear A Motion?* (1994)
(various instruments)

Kenny Garrett, *Triology* (1995)
(alto sax)

Javon Jackson, *For One Who Knows* (1995)
(saxophone)

Hank Jones and Charlie Haden, *Steal Away: Spirituals, Hymns, and Folk Songs* (1995)
(piano; bass)

Leroy Jones, *Mo' Cream From The Crop* (1994)
(trumpet)

Keb' Mo', *Keb' Mo'* (1994)
(guitar)

Abbey Lincoln, *A Turtle's Dream* (1994)
(vocals)

Marcus Printup, *Song for the Beautiful Woman* (1995)
(trumpet)

Eric Reed, *The Swing And I* (1995)
(piano)

Jacky Terrasson, *Jacky Terrasson* (1995)
(piano)

Steve Turre, *Rhythm Within* (1995)
(trombone)

Cassandra Wilson, *Blue Skies* (1988)
(vocals)

50 GREAT CLASSICAL RECORDINGS

We can't really presume to pick a classical library for all tastes, but PEOPLE's editors will hazard this tendentious consensus of outstanding recordings.

Johann Sebastian Bach	*Brandenburg Concertos*, Munich Bach Orchestra/Karl Richter
Johann Sebastian Bach	*The Well-Tempered Clavier*, BWV 846-893, Davitt Moroney
Samuel Barber	*Adagio for Strings*, Saint Louis Symphony Orchestra/Leonard Slatkin
Béla Bartók	*String Quartets Nos. 1–6*, Emerson Quartet
Ludwig van Beethoven	*Symphonies Nos. 1–9, Complete Cycles*, Berlin Philharmonic/Herbert von Karajan
Ludwig van Beethoven	*Piano Sonata in C Minor, Op. 13, "Pathétique,"* Wilhelm Kempff
Ludwig van Beethoven	*Piano Sonata in C-sharp Minor, Op. 27, No. 2, "Moonlight,"* Wilhelm Kempff
Hector Berlioz	*Symphonie fantastique*, French National Radio Orchestra/Sir Thomas Beecham
Leonard Bernstein	*Chichester Psalms*, John Paul Bogart; Camerata Singers, New York Philharmonic/ Leonard Bernstein
Georges Bizet	*Carmen*, Agnes Baltsa, José Carreras; Chorus of the Paris Opéra, Berlin Philharmonic/Herbert von Karajan
Johannes Brahms	*Violin Concerto in D, Op. 77*, Itzhak Perlman; Chicago Symphony Orchestra/Carlo Maria Giulini
Benjamin Britten	*War Requiem, Op. 66*, Lorna Haywood, Anthony Rolfe Johnson, Benjamin Luxon; Atlanta Boy Choir, Atlanta Symphony Orchestra & Chorus/Robert Shaw
Frédéric Chopin	*26 Preludes*, Dmitri Alexeev
Aaron Copland	*Appalachian Spring*, New York Philharmonic/Leonard Bernstein
Claude Debussy	*Images*, Claudio Arrau
Antonín Dvorák	*Symphony No. 9 in E Minor, Op. 95, "From the New World,"* London Symphony Orchestra/István Kertész
César Franck	*Symphony in D Minor*, Berlin Radio Symphony Orchestra/Vladimir Ashkenazy
George Gershwin	*Rhapsody in Blue*, Columbia Symphony Orchestra, New York Philharmonic/ Leonard Bernstein
George Gershwin	*Porgy and Bess*, Willard White, Leona Mitchell; Cleveland Orchestra & Chorus/ Lorin Maazel
George Frideric Handel	*Messiah*, Heather Harper, Helen Watts, John Wakefield, John Shirley-Quirk; London Symphony Orchestra & Choir/Sir Colin Davis
Joseph Haydn	*Symphonies Nos. 93-104, "London,"* Royal Concertgebouw Orchestra/Sir Colin Davis
Joseph Haydn	*String Quartets, Op. 76, "Erdödy,"* Takács Quartet
Charles Ives	*Three Places in New England*, Boston Symphony Orchestra/Michael Tilson Thomas
Franz Liszt	*Les Préludes*, Philadelphia Orchestra/Riccardo Muti
Gustav Mahler	*Symphony No. 9 in D*, Vienna Philharmonic/Bruno Walter
Felix Mendelssohn	*Violin Concerto in E Minor, Op. 64*, Kyung Wha Chung; Montreal Symphony Orchestra/ Charles Dutoit

Wolfgang Amadeus Mozart	*Symphony No. 41 in C, K. 551, "Jupiter,"* Columbia Symphony Orchestra/Bruno Walter
Wolfgang Amadeus Mozart	*A Little Night Music, K. 525*, Prague Chamber Orchestra/Sir Charles Mackerras
Wolfgang Amadeus Mozart	*The Marriage of Figaro*, Samuel Ramey, Lucia Popp; London Opera Chorus, London Philharmonic Orchestra/Sir George Solti
Wolfgang Amadeus Mozart	*Don Giovanni*, Eberhard Wächter, Joan Sutherland, Elisabeth Schwarzkopf; Philharmonia Orchestra & Chorus/Carlo Maria Giulini
Modest Mussorgsky	*Pictures at an Exhibition*, Montreal Symphony Orchestra/Charles Dutoit
Giacomo Puccini	*La Bohème*, Mirella Freni, Luciano Pavarotti; Chorus of the Deutsche Oper Berlin, Berlin Philharmonic/Herbert von Karajan
Sergei Prokofiev	*Symphony No. 1 in D, Op. 25, "Classical,"* Berlin Philharmonic/Herbert von Karajan
Sergei Rachmaninoff	*Piano Concerto No. 2 in C Minor, Op. 18*, Vladimir Ashkenazy; London Symphony Orchestra/André Previn
Nikolai Rimsky-Korsakov	*Scheherazade, Op. 35*, Royal Concertgebouw Orchestra/Kirill Kondrashin
Gioacchino Rossini	*The Barber of Seville*, Leo Nucci, William Matteuzzi, Cecilia Bartoli; Chorus & Orchestra of the Teatro Comunale di Bologna/Giuseppe Patanè
Camille Saint-Saëns	*The Carnival of the Animals*, Montreal Symphony Orchestra, London Sinfonietta/ Charles Dutoit
Domenico Scarlatti	*Keyboard Sonatas*, Vladimir Horowitz
Arnold Schoenberg	*Verklärte Nacht (Transfigured Night), Op. 4*, Jiri Najnar, Vaclav Bernasek; Talich Quartet
Franz Schubert	*Die Schöne Müllerin, D. 795; Winterreise, D. 911*, Dietrich Fischer-Dieskau, Gerald Moore
Robert Schumann	*Op. 19, "Carnaval: Pretty Scenes on Four Notes,"* Artur Rubinstein
Dmitri Shostakovich	*Symphony No. 5 in D Minor, Op. 47*, Royal Concertgebouw Orchestra/Bernard Haitink
Jean Sibelius	*Symphony No. 5 in E-flat, Op. 82*, Boston Symphony Orchestra/Sir Colin Davis
Igor Stravinsky	*The Rite of Spring*, New York Philharmonic, Cleveland Orchestra/Pierre Boulez
Piotr Ilyich Tchaikovsky	*Symphony No. 6 in B Minor, Op. 74, "Pathétique,"* Leningrad Philharmonic/Evgeny Mravinsky
Piotr Ilyich Tchaikovsky	*Piano Concerto No. 1 in B-flat Minor, Op. 23*, Van Cliburn; RCA Symphony Orchestra/Kirill Kondrashin
Giuseppe Verdi	*Requiem*, Elisabeth Schwarzkopf, Christa Ludwig, Nicolai Gedda, Nicolai Ghiaurov; Philharmonia Orchestra & Chorus/Carlo Maria Giulini
Giuseppe Verdi	*La Traviata*, Joan Sutherland, Luciano Pavarotti; London Opera Chorus, National Philharmonic Orchestra/Richard Bonynge
Antonio Vivaldi	*Concertos for Violin, Strings, and Continuo, Op. 8, Nos. 1–4, "The Four Seasons,"* Alan Loveday; Academy of St. Martin-in-the-Fields/Sir Neville Marriner
Richard Wagner	*The Ring of the Nibelung*, Birgit Nilsson, Wolfgang Windgassen; Chorus & Orchestra of the Bayreuth Festival/Karl Böhm

THE 50 GREATEST CLASSICAL COMPOSERS

They're all dead white men, but they sure could write a tune. Here are the classics of the classical composers as selected by PEOPLE:

Johann Sebastian Bach (German, 1685–1750)
Samuel Barber (American, 1910–81)
Béla Bartók (Hungarian, 1881–1945)
Ludwig van Beethoven (German, 1770–1827)
Hector Berlioz (French, 1803–69)
Leonard Bernstein (American, 1918–90)
Georges Bizet (French, 1838–75)
Johannes Brahms (German, 1833–97)
Benjamin Britten (British, 1913–76)
John Cage (American, 1912–92)
Elliott Carter (American, b. 1908)
Frédéric Chopin (Polish, 1810–49)
Aaron Copland (American, 1900–90)
François Couperin (French, 1668–1733)
Claude Debussy (French, 1862–1918)
Antonín Dvorák (Czech, 1841–1904)
Gabriel Fauré (French, 1845–1924)
César Franck (Belgian/French, 1822–90)
George Gershwin (American, 1898–1937)
George Frideric Handel (German/British, 1685–1759)
Franz Joseph Haydn (Austrian, 1732–1809)
Paul Hindemith (German, 1895–1963)
Charles Ives (American, 1874–1954)
Leos Janácek (Czech, 1854–1928)
Franz Liszt (Hungarian, 1811–86)
Gustav Mahler (Bohemian/Austrian, 1860–1911)
Felix Mendelssohn (German, 1809–47)
Claudio Monteverdi (Italian, 1567–1643)
Wolfgang Amadeus Mozart (Austrian, 1756–91)
Giovanni da Palestrina (Italian, c. 1525–94)
Sergei Prokofiev (Russian, 1891–1953)
Giacomo Puccini (Italian, 1858–1924)
Sergei Rachmaninoff (Russian, 1873–1943)
Jean-Philippe Rameau (French, 1683–1764)
Maurice Ravel (French, 1875–1937)
Camille Saint-Saëns (French, 1835–1921)
Domenico Scarlatti (Italian, 1685–1757)
Arnold Schoenberg (Austrian, 1874–1951)
Franz Schubert (Austrian, 1797–1828)
Dmitri Shostakovich (Russian, 1906–75)
Jean Sibelius (Finnish, 1865–1957)
Johann Strauss (Austrian, 1825–99)
Richard Strauss (German, 1864–1949)
Igor Stravinsky (Russian, 1882–1971)
Piotr Ilyitch Tchaikovsky (Russian, 1840–93)
Georg Philipp Telemann (German, 1681–1767)
Ralph Vaughan Williams (British, 1872–1958)
Giuseppe Verdi (Italian, 1813–1901)
Antonio Vivaldi (Italian, 1678–1741)
Richard Wagner (German, 1813–83)

MAJOR AMERICAN SYMPHONY ORCHESTRAS

From Miami to Seattle, American cities are supporting some of the finest symphonies in the world. The following orchestras, 25 of the most important in the U.S., are listed with their conductors or music directors.

Atlanta Symphony Orchestra	Yoel Levi	Atlanta, GA
Baltimore Symphony Orchestra	David Zinman	Baltimore, MD
Boston Symphony Orchestra	Seiji Ozawa	Boston, MA
Chicago Symphony Orchestra	Daniel Barenboim	Chicago, IL
Cincinnati Symphony Orchestra	Jesús Lopez-Cobos	Cincinnati, OH
Cleveland Orchestra	Christoph von Dohnányi	Cleveland, OH
Columbus Symphony	Alessandro Siciliani	Columbus, OH
Dallas Symphony Orchestra	Andrew Litton	Dallas, TX
Detroit Symphony Orchestra	Neeme Järvi	Detroit, MI
Florida Philharmonic Orchestra	James Judd	Fort Lauderdale, FL
Houston Symphony	Christoph Eschenbach	Houston, TX
Indianapolis Symphony Orchestra	Raymond Leppard	Indianapolis, IN
Los Angeles Philharmonic	Esa-Pekka Salonen	Los Angeles, CA
Milwaukee Symphony Orchestra	Andreas Delfs	Milwaukee, WI
Minnesota Orchestra	Eiji Oue	Minneapolis, MN
National Symphony Orchestra	Leonard Slatkin	Washington, DC
New World Symphony	Michael Tilson Thomas	Miami Beach, FL
New York Philharmonic	Kurt Masur	New York, NY
Oregon Symphony	James DePreist	Portland, OR
Philadelphia Orchestra	Wolfgang Sawallisch	Philadelphia, PA
Pittsburgh Symphony Orchestra	Mariss Jansons	Pittsburgh, PA
St. Louis Symphony Orchestra	Hans Vonk	St. Louis, MO
San Francisco Symphony	Michael Tilson Thomas	San Francisco, CA
Seattle Symphony	Gerard Schwarz	Seattle, WA
Utah Symphony Orchestra	Joseph Silverstein	Salt Lake City, UT

MUSICAL PERIODS

As it turns out, classical music isn't all classical. To help you sort out baroque quartets and romantic symphonies from classical sonatas and modern operas, here's the chronological breakdown of musical periods:

PERIOD	DATES
Renaissance	1450–1600
Baroque	1600–1750
Classical	1750–1825
Romantic	1825–1910
Modern	1910–present

CLIFFS' CLUES TO OPERA PLOTS

Opera is drama expressed musically, verbally, and visually—the ultimate experience for ears, eyes, and emotions. If you're intimidated by the prospect of sitting through three or more hours of heightened drama in a foreign language, but are intrigued by the passionate, mysterious world of divas and Don Juans, start here, with our summaries of 10 classics. (Dates given indicate the first staged production.)

THE BARBER OF SEVILLE (1782)
Composed by Gioacchino Rossini, text by Sterbini. Based on the novel by Beaumarchais. Set in Seville, Spain, in the 17th century.
Count Almaviva, a Grandee of Spain, loves Rosina, the young ward and bride-to-be of Dr. Bartolo. With the help of Figaro, the town barber and busybody, the Count enters his rival's home disguised as a drunken soldier, then as a music teacher. Having gained access to Rosina, he easily persuades her to take his hand. Almaviva then convinces a notary, procured by Bartolo for his own marriage to Rosina, to marry him to Rosina in Bartolo's absence.

LA BOHÈME (1896)
Composed by Giacomo Puccini, text by Luigi Illica and Giuseppe Giacosa. Based on the novel Scènes de la vie de Bohème *by Henri Murger. Set in Paris, France, in the 17th century.*
Rodolfo, a poet, lives in the Latin Quarter of Paris with his dear friends—a painter, a philosopher, and a musician—who defy their hunger with cheerfulness and pranks. The quartet of friends is so poor that they resort to burning Rodolfo's poetry to keep warm. But Rodolfo's heart is soon warmed by the frail and consumptive Mimi, who knocks on his door one night, her candle extinguished by a winter draft. The two fall in love, but Mimi grows weaker and weaker. Eventually, her sickness and Rodolfo's overprotectiveness drive the two apart. Mimi's last request is to return to Rodolfo's attic room, where they first met, and where she will die in his arms.

DON CARLOS (1867)
Composed by Giuseppe Verdi, text by G. Méry and C. du Locle. Based on the play by Friedrich von Schiller. Set in France and Spain, during the Spanish Inquisition.
Don Carlos, infante of Spain, is torn between a futile love for Queen Elizabeth, his stepmother, to whom he was once engaged, and a fierce desire to bring freedom to Flanders, a Protestant country under Spanish (Catholic) domain. The queen's attendant, who is deeply in love with Carlos, tells the king, untruthfully, that Carlos and Elizabeth have been unfaithful to him. Carlos is sent to death, ostensibly for demanding to be let go to Flanders. Elizabeth remains at her husband's side, and Carlos escapes his death in the last moments of the opera, saved by the King's father, who takes Carlos into the cloister.

DON GIOVANNI (1787)
Composed by Wolfgang Amadeus Mozart, text by Lorenzo da Ponte. Based on the text Il Convitato *by Giovanni Bertati. Set in Seville at the end of the 18th century.*
The insatiable lover, Don Juan, jaunts from lass to lass, breaking hearts and wreaking havoc before he is finally dragged into Hell by the statue of the Commendatore who he killed in a duel after attempting to seduce his daughter, Doña Anna.

ELEKTRA (1909)
Composed by Richard Strauss, text by Hugo von Hofmannsthal. Adapted from the play by Sophocles. Set in ancient Mycenae.
Her soul withered by grief, Elektra is bent on avenging the seven-year-old murder of her father, Agamemnon, at the hands of her mother, Klytämnestra, and her mother's lover, Aegisth. Elektra persuades her brother Orest to murder Klytämnestra and Aegisth. The murders send Elektra into a dance of joy that becomes a frenzied

dance of death, ending in the explosion of her heart.

LUCIA DI LAMMERMOOR (1835)
Composed by Gaetano Donizetti, text by Salvatore Cammarano. Based on the novel The Bride of Lammermoor *by Sir Walter Scott. Set in Scotland in 1700.*
Her mother's death is slowly but inexorably driving the tragic Lucia to madness. She loves Edgardo, but their promised union is sabotaged by her brother, who forces her to marry Arturo, a wealthy man she does not love. Tormented by visions of ghosts and spirits and devastated over the loss of Edgardo, Lucia murders her groom on their wedding night, then experiences a series of hallucinations before collapsing and dying of a broken heart.

RIGOLETTO (1851)
Composed by Giuseppe Verdi, text by Francesco Maria Piave. Based on Victor Hugo's Le Roi s'amuse. *Set Mantua, Italy, in the 16th century.*
Rigoletto, a court jester, intends to have the Duke of Mantua murdered for seducing his daughter, Gilda, but brings about the murder of the girl, instead.

The first of a "romantic trilogy," *Rigoletto* is followed by *Il Trovotore* and *La Traviata.*

TOSCA (1900)
Composed by Giacomo Puccini, text by Giuseppe Giacosa and Luigi Illica. Based on the play La Tosca *by Victorien Sardou. Set in Rome, in 1800.*
Floria Tosca, a prima donna, is passionately pursued by the evil Scarpia, chief of the Roman police. Yet Tosca loves Cavaradossi, a painter and a liberal patriot. She attempts to save her lover from execution when he is accused of aiding a fugitive, by pretending to yield to Scarpia's wishes, then killing him. But her actions unwittingly help to destroy her true love, Cavaradossi.

LA TRAVIATA (1853)
Composed by Giuseppe Verdi, text by Francesco Maria Piave. Based on Alexandre Dumas's play La Tame aux Camélias. *Set in Paris and vicinity in 1850.*
Violetta, a courtesan, renounces her life of pleasure in order to be with her gentlemanly lover, Alfredo. But Alfredo's father persuades Violetta that she is a blight on his family and that she must leave Alfredo for the good of his career. She returns to her former protector, with whom Alfredo fights a duel. Alfredo is subsequently forced to flee the country, and will return only to find Violetta dying of consumption.

TRISTAN AND ISOLDE (1865)
Composed and written by Richard Wagner. Set in a ship at sea, in England, and in Ireland, in a legendary time.
Tristan is dispatched to Ireland by his uncle, King Marke, to win him Isolde's hand. Yet Tristan and Isolde have long loved one another, each believing their love to be unrequited. On board the vessel that brings them to Cornwall, they drink what they believe to be a death potion, but is in fact a love potion. King Marke later discovers them in a midnight embrace. Tristan, wounded by one of the king's knights, flees to France. Isolde follows, finds him dying, and she too dies by his side.

THE WORLD'S LARGEST OPERA HOUSES

These houses showcase the world's best singers and stand as monuments to the grandeur of opera.

Opera House	Location	Total Capacity
The Metropolitan Opera	New York, NY	4,065
Cincinnati Opera	Cincinnati, OH	3,630
Lyric Opera of Chicago	Chicago, IL	3,563
San Francisco Opera	San Francisco, CA	3,476
The Dallas Opera	Dallas, TX	3,420

MTV VIDEO MUSIC AWARDS

BEST VIDEO OF THE YEAR

1984	The Cars	*You Might Think*
1985	Don Henley	*The Boys of Summer*
1986	Dire Straits	*Money for Nothing*
1987	Peter Gabriel	*Sledgehammer*
1988	INXS	*Need You Tonight/Mediate*
1989	Neil Young	*This Note's for You*
1990	Sinead O'Connor	*Nothing Compares 2 U*
1991	R.E.M.	*Losing My Religion*
1992	Van Halen	*Right Now*
1993	Pearl Jam	*Jeremy*
1994	Aerosmith	*Cryin'*
1995	TLC	*Waterfalls*
1996	The Smashing Pumpkins	*Tonight, Tonight*
1997	Jamiroquai	*Virtual Insanity*

BEST MALE VIDEO

1984	David Bowie	*China Girl*
1985	Bruce Springsteen	*I'm on Fire*
1986	Robert Palmer	*Addicted to Love*
1987	Peter Gabriel	*Sledgehammer*
1988	Prince	*U Got the Look*
1989	Elvis Costello	*Veronica*
1990	Don Henley	*The End of the Innocence*
1991	Chris Isaak	*Wicked Game* (Concept)
1992	Eric Clapton	*Tears in Heaven* (Performance)
1993	Lenny Kravitz	*Are You Gonna Go My Way*
1994	Tom Petty and the Heartbreakers	*Mary Jane's Last Dance*
1995	Tom Petty and the Heartbreakers	*You Don't Know How It Feels*
1996	Beck	*Where It's At*
1997	Beck	*The Devil's Haircut*

BEST FEMALE VIDEO

1984	Cyndi Lauper	*Girls Just Want To Have Fun*
1985	Tina Turner	*What's Love Got To Do with It*
1986	Whitney Houston	*How Will I Know*
1987	Madonna	*Papa Don't Preach*
1988	Suzanne Vega	*Luka*
1989	Paula Abdul	*Straight Up*
1990	Sinead O'Connor	*Nothing Compares 2 U*
1991	Janet Jackson	*Love Will Never Do Without You*
1992	Annie Lennox	*Why*
1993	k.d. lang	*Constant Craving*
1994	Janet Jackson	*If*
1995	Madonna	*Take a Bow*
1996	Alanis Morissette	*Ironic*
1997	Jewel	*You Were Meant for Me*

BEST CONCEPT VIDEO

1984	Herbie Hancock	*Rockit*
1985	Glenn Frey	*Smuggler's Blues*
1986	a-ha	*Take On Me*
1987	Peter Gabriel/ Stephen Johnson	*Sledgehammer*
1988	Pink Floyd	*Learning To Fly*

BEST GROUP VIDEO

1984	ZZ Top	*Legs*
1985	USA for Africa	*We Are the World*
1986	Dire Straits	*Money for Nothing*
1987	Talking Heads	*Wild Wild Life*
1988	INXS	*Need You Tonight/Mediate*
1989	Living Colour	*Cult of Personality*
1990	The B-52's	*Love Shack*
1991	R.E.M.	*Losing My Religion*
1992	U2	*Even Better Than the Real Thing*
1993	Pearl Jam	*Jeremy*
1994	Aerosmith	*Cryin'*
1995	TLC	*Waterfalls*
1996	Foo Fighters	*Big Me*
1997	No Doubt	*Don't Speak*

BEST NEW ARTIST IN A VIDEO

1984	Eurythmics	*Sweet Dreams (Are Made of This)*
1985	'Til Tuesday	*Voices Carry*
1986	a-ha	*Take On Me*
1987	Crowded House	*Don't Dream It's Over*
1988	Guns N' Roses	*Welcome to the Jungle*
1989	Living Colour	*Cult of Personality*
1990	Michael Penn	*No Myth*
1991	Jesus Jones	*Right Here, Right Now*
1992	Nirvana	*Smells Like Teen Spirit*
1993	Stone Temple Pilots	*Plush*
1994	Counting Crows	*Mr. Jones*
1995	Hootie & The Blowfish	*Hold My Hand*
1996	Alanis Morissette	*Ironic*
1997	Fiona Apple	*Sleep to Dream*

BEST RAP VIDEO

1989	D.J. Jazzy Jeff & The Fresh Prince	*Parents Just Don't Understand*
1990	M.C. Hammer	*U Can't Touch This*
1991	L.L. Cool J	*Mama Said Knock You Out*
1992	Arrested Development	*Tennessee*
1993	Arrested Development	*People Everyday*

1994	Snoop Doggy Dogg	*Doggy Dogg World*
1995	Dr. Dre	*Keep Their Heads Ringin'*
1996	Coolio featuring LV	*Gangsta's Paradise*
1997	The Notorious B.I.G.	*Hypnotize*

BEST DANCE VIDEO

1989	Paula Abdul	*Straight Up*
1990	M.C. Hammer	*U Can't Touch This*
1991	C+C Music Factory	*Gonna Make You Sweat (Everybody Dance Now)*
1992	Prince & the New Power Generation	*Cream*
1993	En Vogue	*Free Your Mind*
1994	Salt-N-Pepa w/ En Vogue	*Whatta Man*
1995	Michael and Janet Jackson	*Scream*
1996	Coolio	*1, 2, 3, 4 (Sumpin' New)*
1997	Spice Girls	*Wannabe*

BEST METAL/HARD ROCK VIDEO

1989	Guns N' Roses	*Sweet Child o' Mine*
1990	Aerosmith	*Janie's Got a Gun*
1991	Aerosmith	*The Other Side*
1992	Metallica	*Enter Sandman*
1993	Pearl Jam	*Jeremy*
1994	Soundgarden	*Black Hole Sun*
1995	White Zombie	*More Human Than Human*
1996	Metallica	*Until It Sleeps*
1997	Aerosmith	*Falling in Love (Is Hard on the Knees)*

BEST R&B VIDEO

1993	En Vogue	*Free Your Mind*
1994	Salt-N-Pepa w/ En Vogue	*Whatta Man*
1995	TLC	*Waterfalls*
1996	The Fugees	*Killing Me Softly*
1997	Puff Daddy and the Family	*I'll Be Missing You*

BEST VIDEO FROM A FILM

1987	Talking Heads	*Wild Wild Life [True Stories}*
1988	Los Lobos	*La Bamba [La Bamba]*
1989	U2 with B.B. King	*When Love Comes to Town [U2 Rattle and Hum]*
1990	Billy Idol	*Cradle of Love [The Adventures of Ford Fairlaine]*
1991	Chris Isaak	*Wicked Game [Wild at Heart]*
1992	Queen	*Bohemian Rhapsody [Wayne's World]*
1993	Alice in Chains	*Would? [Singles]*
1994	Bruce Springsteen	*Streets of Philadelphia [Philadelphia]*
1995	Seal	*Kiss from a Rose [Batman Forever]*
1996	Coolio	*Gangsta's Paradise [Dangerous Minds]*
1997	Will Smith	*Men in Black [Men in Black]*

BEST CHOREOGRAPHY IN A VIDEO

1994	Salt-N-Pepa w/ En Vogue; Frank Gatson/Randy Connors	*Whatta Man*
1995	Michael and Janet Jackson; Lavelle Smith, Travis Payne, Tina Landon, Sean Cheeseman	*Scream*
1996	Bjork; Michael Rooney	*It's Oh So Quiet*
1997	Beck	*The New Pollution*

BEST ALTERNATIVE VIDEO

1991	Jane's Addiction	*Been Caught Stealing*
1992	Nirvana	*Smells Like Teen Spirit*
1993	Nirvana	*In Bloom* (Version 1—Dresses)
1994	Nirvana	*Heart-Shaped Box*
1995	Weezer	*Buddy Holly*
1996	The Smashing Pumpkins	*1979*
1997	Sublime	*What I Got*

BEST SPECIAL EFFECTS IN A VIDEO

1984	Herbie Hancock	*Rockit*
1985	Tom Petty & the Heartbreakers Tony Mitchell, Kathy Dougherty, Peter Cohen	*Don't Come Around Here No More*
1986	a-ha; Michael Patterson	*Take On Me*
1987	Peter Gabriel; Stephen Johnson, Peter Lord	*Sledgehammer*
1988	Squeeze; Jim Francis, Dave Barton	*Hourglass*
1989	Michael Jackson; Jim Blashfield	*Leave Me Alone*
1990	Tears For Fears; Jim Blashfield	*Sowing the Seeds of Love*
1991	Faith No More; David Faithful, Ralph Ziman	*Falling to Pieces*

1992	U2; Simon Taylor	*Even Better Than the Real Thing*
1993	Peter Gabriel; Real World Productions/ Colossal Pictures	*Steam*
1994	Peter Gabriel; Brett Leonard/ Angel Studios	*Kiss That Frog*
1995	The Rolling Stones; Fred Raimondi	*Love Is Strong*
1996	The Smashing Pumpkins; Chris Staves	*Tonight, Tonight*
1997	Jamiroquai	*Virtual Insanity*

BEST DIRECTION IN A VIDEO

1984	ZZ Top; Tim Newman	*Sharp Dressed Man*
1985	Don Henley; John Baptiste Mondino	*The Boys of Summer*
1986	a-ha; Steven Barron	*Take On Me*
1987	Peter Gabriel; Stephen Johnson	*Sledgehammer*
1988	George Michael; Andy Morahan, George Michael	*Father Figure*
1989	Madonna; David Fincher	*Express Yourself*
1990	Madonna; David Fincher	*Vogue*
1991	R.E.M.; Tarsem	*Losing My Religion*
1992	Van Halen; Mark Fenske	*Right Now*
1993	Pearl Jam; Mark Pellington	*Jeremy*
1994	R.E.M.; Jake Scott	*Everybody Hurts*
1995	Weezer; Spike Jonze	*Buddy Holly*
1996	The Smashing Pumpkins; Jonathan Dayton and Valerie Faris	*Tonight, Tonight*
1997	Beck; Beck Hansen	*The New Pollution*

BREAKTHROUGH VIDEO

1988	INXS	*Need You Tonight/Mediate*
1989	Art of Noise, featuring Tom Jones	*Kiss*
1990	Tears for Fears; Jim Blashfield	*Sowing the Seeds of Love*
1991	R.E.M.; Tarsem	*Losing My Religion*
1992	Red Hot Chili Peppers; Stephane Sednaoui	*Give It Away*
1993	Los Lobos; Ondrej Rudavsky, Axel Erickson	*Kiko & The Lavender Moon*
1994	R.E.M.; Jane Gutterman	*Everybody Hurts*
1995	Weezer; Spike Jonze	*Buddy Holly*
1996	The Smashing Pumpkins; Jonathan Dayton and Valerie Faris	*Tonight, Tonight*
1997	Jamiroquai; Jonathan Glazer	*Virtual Insanity*

VIDEO VANGUARD AWARD

1984 The Beatles, David Bowie, Richard Lester
1985 David Byrne, Kevin Godley and Lol Creme, Russell Mulcahy
1986 Madonna and Zbigniew Rybeznski
1987 Julien Temple and Peter Gabriel
1988 Michael Jackson
1989 George Michael
1990 Janet Jackson
1991 no award given
1992 no award given
1993 no award given
1994 Tom Petty
1995 R.E.M.
1996 no award given
1997 Mark Romanek, L. L. Cool J

MICHAEL JACKSON VIDEO VANGUARD AWARD

1991 Bon Jovi, Wayne Isham
1992 Guns N' Roses

VIEWER'S CHOICE AWARD

1984	Michael Jackson	*Thriller*
1985	USA for Africa	*We Are the World*
1986	a-ha	*Take On Me*
1987	U2	*With or Without You*
1988	INXS	*Need You Tonight/Mediate*
1989	Madonna	*Like a Prayer*
1990	Aerosmith	*Janie's Got a Gun*
1994	Aerosmith	*Cryin'*
1995	TLC	*Waterfalls*
1996	Bush	*Glycerine*
1997	Prodigy	*Breathe*

THE GRAMMY AWARDS

Even more so than most award-giving bodies, the National Academy of Recording Arts and Sciences has switched, added, deleted, and renamed its various award categories on a regular basis. The following chart gathers the majority of continuing categories that honor mainstream musical achievement. This means you won't find the awards for polka or jacket liner notes, but you will find years of musical greats (and electorate gaffes) in an easy-to-follow format.

	1958	1959	1960
Record of the Year	Domenico Modugno, "Nel Blu Dipinto Di Blu (Volare)"	Bobby Darin, "Mack the Knife"	Percy Faith, "Theme from *A Summer Place*"
Album of the Year	Henry Mancini, *The Music from Peter Gunn*	Frank Sinatra, *Come Dance with Me*	Bob Newhart, *Button Down Mind*
Song of the Year	Domenico Modugno, "Nel Blu Dipinto Di Blu (Volare)"	Jimmy Driftwood, "The Battle of New Orleans"	Ernest Gold, "Theme from *Exodus*"
Pop Vocal, Female	Ella Fitzgerald, *Ella Fitzgerald Sings the Irving Berlin Song Book*	Ella Fitzgerald, "But Not for Me"	Ella Fitzgerald, *Mack the Knife, Ella in Berlin*
Pop Vocal, Male	Perry Como, "Catch a Falling Star"	Frank Sinatra, *Come Dance with Me*	Ray Charles, *Genius of Ray Charles*
New Artist	—	Bobby Darin	Bob Newhart
Pop Vocal, Duo or Group with Vocal	Louis Prima and Keely Smith, "That Old Black Magic"	Mormon Tabernacle Choir, "Battle Hymn of the Republic"	Eydie Gormé and Steve Lawrence, "We Got Us"
Rhythm and Blues Song	Champs, "Tequila"	Dinah Washington, "What a Diff'rence a Day Makes"	Ray Charles, "Let the Good Times Roll"
Jazz, Soloist	—	Ella Fitzgerald, *Ella Swings Lightly*	—
Jazz, Group	Count Basie, *Basie*	Jonah Jones, *I Dig Chicks*	André Previn, *West Side Story*
Jazz, Big Band/ Large Ensemble Performance	—	—	Henry Mancini, *The Blues and the Beat*
Folk Recording	—	Kingston Trio, *The Kingston Trio at Large*	Harry Belafonte, *Swing Dat Hammer*
Cast Show Album	*The Music Man*	*Porgy and Bess*	*The Sound of Music*
Comedy Recording (Spoken Word/Musical)	David Seville, "The Chipmunk Song"	Shelley Berman, *Inside Shelley Berman;* Homer & Jethro, *The Battle of Kookamonga*	Bob Newhart, *Button Down Mind Strikes Back;* Paul Weston and Jo Stafford, *Jonathan and Darlene Edwards in Paris*
Classical Orchestral Performance	Felix Slatkin, Hollywood Bowl Symphony, *Gaîeté Parisienne*	Charles Munch, conductor, Boston Symphony, *Debussy: Images for Orchestra*	Fritz Reiner, conductor, Chicago Symphony, *Bartók: Music for Strings, Percussion and Celeste*
Opera Recording	Roger Wagner Chorale, *Virtuoso*	Erich Leinsdorf, conductor, Vienna Philharmonic, *Mozart: The Marriage of Figaro*	Erich Leinsdorf, conductor, Rome Opera House Chorus and Orchestra, *Puccini: Turandot* (Solos: Tebaldi, Nilsson, Bjoerling, Tozzi)
Chamber Music Performance	Hollywood String Quartet, *Beethoven: Quartet 130*	Artur Rubinstein, *Beethoven: Sonata No. 21 in C, Op. 53; "Waldstein" Sonata No. 18 in E Flat, Op. 53, No. 3*	Laurindo Almeida, *Conversations with the Guitar*

	1961	1962	1963
Record of the Year	Henry Mancini, "Moon River"	Tony Bennett, "I Left My Heart in San Francisco"	Henry Mancini, "The Days of Wine and Roses"
Album of the Year	Judy Garland, *Judy at Carnegie Hall*	Vaughn Meader, *The First Family*	Barbra Streisand, *The Barbra Streisand Album*
Song of the Year	Henry Mancini and Johnny Mercer, "Moon River"	Leslie Bricusse and Anthony Newley, "What Kind of Fool Am I"	Johnny Mercer and Henry Mancini, "The Days of Wine and Roses"
(Pop) Vocal, Female	Judy Garland, *Judy at Carnegie Hall*	Ella Fitzgerald, *Ella Swings Brightly with Nelson Riddle*	Barbra Streisand, *The Barbra Streisand Album*
(Pop) Vocal, Male	Jack Jones, "Lollipops and Roses"	Tony Bennett, "I Left My Heart in San Francisco"	Jack Jones, "Wives and Lovers"
New Artist	Peter Nero	Robert Goulet	Swingle Singers
Pop Vocal, Duo or Group with Vocal	Lambert, Hendricks & Ross, *High Flying*	Peter, Paul & Mary, "If I Had a Hammer"	Peter, Paul & Mary, "Blowin' in the Wind"
Rhythm and Blues Song	Ray Charles, "Hit the Road, Jack"	Ray Charles, "I Can't Stop Loving You"	Ray Charles, "Busted"
Jazz, Soloist/Small Group	André Previn, *André Previn Plays Harold Arlen*	Stan Getz, *Desafinado*	Bill Evans, *Conversations with Myself*
Jazz, Big Band/Large Ensemble Performance	Stan Kenton, *West Side Story*	Stan Kenton, *Adventures in Jazz*	Woody Herman Band, *Encore: Woody Herman, 1963*
Contemporary Folk	Belafonte Folk Singers, *Belafonte Folk Singers at Home and Abroad*	Peter, Paul & Mary, "If I Had a Hammer"	Peter, Paul & Mary, "Blowin' in the Wind"
Cast Show Album	*How To Succeed in Business Without Really Trying*	*No Strings*	*She Loves Me*
Comedy Recording	Mike Nichols and Elaine May, *An Evening with Mike Nichols and Elaine May*	Vaughn Meader, *The First Family*	Allen Sherman, *Hello Mudduh, Hello Faddah*
Classical Album	Igor Stravinsky, conductor, Columbia Symphony, *Stravinsky Conducts, 1960: Le Sacre du Printemps; Petruchka*	Vladimir Horowitz, *Columbia Records Presents Vladimir Horowitz*	Benjamin Britten, conductor, London Symphony Orchestra and Chorus, *Britten: War Requiem*
Classical Orchestral Performance	Charles Munch, conductor, Boston Symphony, *Ravel: Daphnis et Chloe*	Igor Stravinsky, conductor, Columbia Symphony, *Stravinsky: The Firebird Ballet*	Erich Leinsdorf, conductor, Boston Symphony, *Bartók: Concerto for Orchestra*
Opera Recording	Gabriele Santini, conductor, Rome Opera Chorus and Orchestra, *Puccini: Madama Butterfly*	Georg Solti, conductor, Rome Opera House Orchestra and Chorus (Solos: Price, Vickers, Gorr, Merrill, Tozzi), *Verdi: Aïda*	Erich Leinsdorf, conductor, RCA Italiana Orchestra and Chorus (Solos: Price, Tucker, Elias), *Puccini: Madama Butterfly*
Chamber Music Performance	Jascha Heifetz, Gregor Piatigorsky, William Primrose, *Beethoven: Serenade, Op. 8; Kodaly: Duo for Violin & Cello, Op. 7*	Jascha Heifetz, Gregor Piatigorsky, William Primrose, *The Heifetz-Piatigorsky Concerts with Primrose, Pennario and Guests*	Julian Bream Consort, *An Evening of Elizabethan Music*

	1964	1965	1966
Record of the Year	Stan Getz and Astrud Gilberto, "The Girl from Ipanema"	Herb Alpert & The Tijuana Brass, "A Taste of Honey"	Frank Sinatra, "Strangers in the Night"
Album of the Year	Stan Getz and Joao Gilberto, *Getz/Gilberto*	Frank Sinatra, *September of My Years*	Frank Sinatra, *Sinatra: A Man & His Music*
Song of the Year	Jerry Herman, "Hello, Dolly!"	Paul Francis Webster and Johnny Mandel, "The Shadow of Your Smile (Love Theme from *The Sandpiper*)"	John Lennon and Paul McCartney, "Michelle"
Pop Vocal, Female	Barbra Streisand, "People"	Barbra Streisand, *My Name Is Barbra*	Eydie Gorme, "If He Walked into My Life"
Pop Vocal, Male	Louis Armstrong, "Hello, Dolly!"	Frank Sinatra, "It Was a Very Good Year"	Frank Sinatra, "Strangers in the Night"
Rock Vocal Female, Male	Petula Clark, "Downtown"	Petula Clark, "I Know a Place"; Roger Miller, "King of the Road"	Paul McCartney, "Eleanor Rigby"
New Artist	The Beatles	Tom Jones	—
Pop Vocal, Duo or Group	The Beatles, *A Hard Day's Night*	Anita Kerr Quartet, *We Dig Mancini*	Anita Kerr Quartet, "A Man and a Woman"
Rock Performance, Duo or Group with Vocal	—	Statler Brothers, "Flowers on the Wall"	The Mamas & The Papas, "Monday, Monday"
Rhythm and Blues Song	Nancy Wilson, "How Glad I Am"	James Brown, "Papa's Got a Brand New Bag"	Ray Charles, "Crying Time"
R&B Vocal	—	—	Ray Charles, "Crying Time"
R&B Duo or Group with Vocal	—	—	Ramsey Lewis, "Hold It Right There"
Country Song	Roger Miller, "Dang Me"	Roger Miller, "King of the Road"	Bill Sherrill and Glenn Sutton, "Almost Persuaded"
Country Vocal, Female	Dottie West, "Here Comes My Baby"	Jody Miller, "Queen of the House"	Jeannie Seely, "Don't Touch Me"
Country Vocal, Male	Roger Miller, "Dang Me"	Roger Miller, "King of the Road"	David Houston, "Almost Persuaded"
Jazz, Group	Stan Getz, *Getz/Gilberto*	Ramsey Lewis Trio, *The "In" Crowd*	Wes Montgomery, *Goin' Out of My Head*
Jazz, Big Band/ Large Ensemble Performance	Laurindo Almeida, *Guitar from Ipanema*	Duke Ellington Orchestra, *Ellington '66*	—
Gospel Performance, Duo, Group, Choir or Chorus	—	George Beverly Shea and Anita Ker Quartet, *Southland Favorites*	Porter Wagoner & the Blackwood Bros., *Grand Old Gospel*
Folk Recording	Gale Garnett, *We'll Sing in the Sunshine*	Harry Belafonte, Miriam Makeba, *An Evening with Belafonte/Makeba*	Cortelia Clark, *Blues in the Street*
Cast Show Album	*Funny Girl*	*On a Clear Day You Can See Forever*	*Mame*
Comedy Recording	Bill Cosby, *I Started Out as a Child*	Bill Cosby, *Why Is There Air?*	Bill Cosby, *Wonderfulness*

	1964	1965	1966
Classical Album	Leonard Bernstein, conductor, New York Philharmonic, *Bernstein: Symphony No. 3*	Vladimir Horowitz, *Horowitz at Carnegie Hall: An Historic Return*	Morton Gould conductor, Chicago Symphony, *Ives: Symphony No. 1 in D Minor*
Classical Orchestral Performance	Erich Leinsdorf, conductor, Boston Symphony, *Mahler: Symphony No. 5 in C Sharp Minor;* Berg: *Wozzeck Excerpts*	Leopold Stokowski, conductor, American Symphony, *Ives: Symphony No. 4*	Erich Leinsdorf, conductor, Boston Symphony, *Mahler: Symphony No. 6 in A Minor*
Opera Recording	Herbert von Karajan, conductor, Vienna Philharmonic and Chorus (Solos: Price, Corelli, Merrill, Freni), *Bizet: Carmen*	Karl Bohm, conductor, Orchestra of German Opera, Berlin, (Solos: Fischer-Dieskau, Lear, Wunderlich), *Berg: Wozzeck*	Georg Solti, conductor, Vienna Philharmonic (Solos: Nilsson, Crespin, Ludwig, King, Hotter), *Wagner: Die Walküre*
Chamber Music Performance	Jascha Heifetz, Gregor Piatigorsky (Jacob Lateiner, piano), *Beethoven: Trio No. 1 in E Flat, Op. 1, No. 1*	Juilliard String Quartet, *Bartók: The Six String Quartets*	Boston Symphony Chamber Players, *Boston Symphony Chamber Players*

	1967	1968	1969
Record of the Year	5th Dimension, "Up, Up and Away"	Simon & Garfunkel, "Mrs. Robinson"	5th Dimension, "Aquarius/Let the Sunshine In"
Album of the Year	The Beatles, *Sgt. Pepper's Lonely Hearts Club Band*	Glen Campbell, *By the Time I Get to Phoenix*	Blood, Sweat & Tears, *Blood, Sweat & Tears*
Song of the Year	Jim Webb, "Up, Up and Away"	Bobby Russell, "Little Green Apples"	Joe South, "Games People Play"
Pop Vocal, Female	Bobbie Gentry, "Ode to Billie Joe"	Dionne Warwick, "Do You Know the Way To San Jose"	Peggy Lee, "Is That All There Is"
Pop Vocal, Male	Glen Campbell, "By the Time I Get to Phoenix"	José Feliciano, "Light My Fire"	Harry Nilsson, "Everybody's Talkin"
New Artist	Bobbie Gentry	José Feliciano	Crosby, Stills & Nash
Pop Vocal	5th Dimension, "Up, Up and Away"	Simon & Garfunkel, "Mrs. Robinson"	5th Dimension, "Aquarius/Let the Sunshine In"
Rock Performance, Duo or Group	5th Dimension, "Up, Up and Away"	—	—
Rhythm and Blues Song	Aretha Franklin, "Respect"	Otis Redding and Steve Cropper, "(Sittin' On) the Dock of the Bay"	Richard Spencer, "Color Him Father"
R&B Vocal, Female	Aretha Franklin, "Respect"	Aretha Franklin, "Chain of Fools"	Aretha Franklin, "Share Your Love With Me"
R&B Vocal, Male	Lou Rawls, "Dead End Street"	Otis Redding, "(Sittin' On) the Dock of the Bay"	Joe Simon, "The Chokin' Kind"

	1967	1968	1969
R&B Duo or Group with Vocal	Sam & Dave, "Soul Man"	The Temptations, "Cloud Nine"	The Isley Brothers, "It's Your Thing"
Country Song	John Hartford, "Gentle on My Mind"	Bobby Russell, "Little Green Apples"	Shel Silverstein, "A Boy Named Sue"
Country Vocal, Female	Tammy Wynette, "I Don't Wanna Play House"	Jeannie C. Riley, "Harper Valley P.T.A."	Tammy Wynette, "Stand By Your Man"
Country Vocal, Male	Glen Campbell, "Gentle on My Mind"	Johnny Cash, "Folsom Prison Blues"	Johnny Cash, "A Boy Named Sue"
Country Performance, Duo or Group with Vocal	Johnny Cash and June Carter, "Jackson"	Flatt & Scruggs, "Foggy Mountain Breakdown"	Waylon Jennings & The Kimberlys, "MacArthur Park"
Jazz, Group	Cannonball Adderley Quintet, *Mercy, Mercy, Mercy*	Bill Evans Trio, *Bill Evans at the Montreux Jazz Festival*	Wes Montgomery, *Willow Weep For Me*
Jazz, Big Band/ Large Ensemble Performance	Duke Ellington, *Far East Suite*	Duke Ellington, *And His Mother Called Him Bill*	Quincy Jones, "Walking in Space"
Gospel Performance, Duo, Group, Choir or Chorus	Porter Wagoner & The Blackwood Bros. Quartet, *More Grand Old Gospel*	Happy Goodman Family, *The Happy Gospel of the Happy Goodmans*	Porter Wagoner & the Blackwood Bros., *In Gospel Country*
Folk Recording	John Hartford, "Gentle on My Mind"	Judy Collins, "Both Sides Now"	Joni Mitchell, *Clouds*
Cast Show Album	*Cabaret*	*Hair*	*Promises, Promises*
Comedy Recording	Bill Cosby, *Revenge*	Bill Cosby, *To Russell, My Brother, Whom I Slept With*	Bill Cosby, *The Best of Bill Cosby*
Classical Album	Pierre Boulez, conductor, Orchestra and Chorus of Paris National Opera (Solos: Berry, Strauss, Uhl, Doench), *Berg: Wozzeck;* Leonard Berstein, conductor, London Symphony, *Mahler: Symphony No. 8 in E Flat Major ("Symphony of a Thousand")*	—	Walter Carlos, *Switched-On Bach*
Classical Orchestral Performance	Igor Stravinsky, conductor, Columbia Symphony, *Stravinsky: Firebird & Petrouchka Suites*	Pierre Boulez, conductor, New Philharmonic Orchestra, *Boulez Conducts Debussy*	Pierre Boulez, conductor, Cleveland Orchestra, *Boulez Conducts Debussy, Vol. 2: "Images Pour Orchestre"*
Opera Recording	Pierre Boulez, conductor, Orchestra and Chorus of Paris National Opera (Solos: Berry, Strauss, Uhl, Doench), *Berg: Wozzeck*	Erich Leinsdorf, conductor, New Philharmonic Orchestra and Ambrosian Opera Chorus (Soloists: Price, Troyanos, Raskin, Milnes, Shirley, Flagello), *Mozart: Cosi fan tutte*	Herbert von Karajan, conductor, Berlin Philharmonic (Soloists: Thomas, Stewart, Stolze, Dernesch, Keleman, Dominguez, Gayer, Ridderbusch), *Wagner: Siegfried*
Chamber Music Performance	Ravi Shankar and Yehudi Menuhin, *West Meets East*	E. Power Biggs with Edward Tarr Brass Ensemble and Gabrieli Consort, Vittorio Negri, conductor, *Gabrieli: Canzoni for Brass, Winds, Strings & Organ*	The Philadelphia, Cleveland, and Chicago Brass Ensembles, *Gabrieli: Antiphonal Music of Gabrieli (Canzoni for Brass Choirs)*

	1970	1971	1972
Record of the Year	Simon & Garfunkel, "Bridge Over Troubled Water"	Carole King, "It's Too Late"	Roberta Flack, "The First Time Ever I Saw Your Face"
Album of the Year	Simon & Garfunkel, *Bridge Over Troubled Water*	Carole King, *Tapestry*	George Harrison and Friends (Ravi Shankar, Bob Dylan, Leon Russell, Ringo Starr, Billy Preston, Eric Clapton, Klaus Voorman, others), *The Concert for Bangladesh*
Song of the Year	Paul Simon, "Bridge Over Troubled Water"	Carole King, "You've Got a Friend"	Ewan MacColl, "The First Time Ever I Saw Your Face"
Pop Vocal, Female	Dionne Warwick, "I'll Never Fall In Love Again"	Carole King, "Tapestry"	Helen Reddy, "I Am Woman"
Pop Vocal, Male	Ray Stevens, "Everything Is Beautiful"	James Taylor, "You've Got a Friend"	Nilsson, "Without You"
New Artist	The Carpenters	Carly Simon	America
Pop Vocal, Duo or Group with Vocal	Carpenters, "Close to You"	Carpenters, *Carpenters*	Roberta Flack and Donny Hathaway, "Where Is the Love"
Rhythm and Blues Song	Ronald Dunbar, General Johnson, "Patches"	Bill Withers, "Ain't No Sunshine"	Barrett Strong and Norman Whitfield, "Papa Was a Rolling Stone"
R&B Vocal, Female	Aretha Franklin, "Don't Play That Song"	Aretha Franklin, "Bridge Over Troubled Water"	Aretha Franklin, "Young, Gifted & Black"
R&B Vocal, Male	B.B. King, "The Thrill Is Gone"	Lou Rawls, "A Natural Man"	Billy Paul, "Me and Mrs. Jones"
R&B Duo or Group with Vocal	The Delfonics, "Didn't I (Blow Your Mind This Time)"	Ike and Tina Turner, "Proud Mary"	The Temptations, "Papa Was a Rolling Stone"
Country Song	Marty Robbins, "My Woman, My Woman, My Wife"	Kris Kristofferson, "Help Me Make It Through the Night"	Ben Peters, "Kiss an Angel Good Mornin' "
Country Vocal, Female	Lynn Anderson, "Rose Garden"	Sammi Smith, "Help Me Make It Through the Night"	Donna Fargo, "Happiest Girl in the Whole U.S.A."
Country Vocal, Male	Ray Price, "For the Good Times"	Jerry Reed, "When You're Hot, You're Hot"	Charley Pride, *Charley Pride Sings Heart Songs*
Country Performance, Duo or Group with Vocal	Johnny Cash and June Carpenter, "If I Were a Carpenter"	Conway Twitty and Loretta Lynn, "After the Fire Is Gone"	The Statler Brothers, "Class of '57"
Traditional Blues Recording	T-Bone Walker, "Good Feelin' "	Muddy Waters, *They Call Me Muddy Waters*	Muddy Waters, *The London Muddy Waters Session*
Jazz, Soloist	—	Bill Evans, *The Bill Evans Album*	Gary Burton, *Alone at Last*
Jazz, Group	Bill Evans, *Alone*	Bill Evans Trio, *The Bill Evans Album*	Freddie Hubbard, *First Light*
Jazz, Big Band/ Large Ensemble Performance	Miles Davis, *Bitches Brew*	Duke Ellington, *New Orleans Suite*	Duke Ellington, *Togo Brava Suite*
Gospel Performance, Duo, Group, Choir or Chorus	Oak Ridge Boys, "Talk About the Good Times"	Charley Pride, "Let Me Live"	Blackwood Brothers, *L-O-V-E*
Cast Show Album	*Company*	*Godspell*	*Don't Bother Me, I Can't Cope*
Comedy Recording	Flip Wilson, *The Devil Made Me Buy This Dress*	Lily Tomlin, *This Is a Recording*	George Carlin, *FM & AM*

	1970	1971	1972
Classical Album	Colin Davis, conductor, Royal Opera House Orchestra and Chorus (Solos: Vickers, Veasey Lindholm), *Berlioz: Les Troyens*, Philips	Vladimir Horowitz, *Horowitz Plays Rachmaninoff*	Georg Solti, conductor, Chicago Symphony, Vienna Boys Choir, Vienna State Opera Chorus, Vienna Singverein Chorus and soloists, *Mahler: Symphony No. 8 in E Flat Major (Symphony of a Thousand)*
Classical Orchestral Performance	Pierre Boulez, conductor, Cleveland Orchestra, *Stravinsky: Le Sacre du printemps*	Carlo Maria Giulini, conductor, Chicago Symphony, *Mahler: Symphony No. 1 in D Major*	Georg Solti, conductor, Chicago Symphony, *Mahler: Symphony No. 7 in E Minor*
Opera Recording	Colin Davis, conductor, Royal Opera House Orchestra and Chorus (Solos: Vickers, Veasey, Lindholm), *Berlioz: Les Troyens*	Erich Leinsdorf, conductor, London Symphony and John Alldis Choir (Solos: Price, Domingo, Milnes, Bumbry, Raimondi), *Verdi: Aïda*	Colin Davis, conductor, BBC Symphony/Chorus of Covent Garden (Solos: Gedda, Eda-Pierre, Soyer, Berbie), *Berlioz: Benvenuto Cellini*
Chamber Music Performance	Eugene Istomin, Isaac Stern, Leonard Rose, *Beethoven: The Complete Piano Trios*	Juilliard Quartet, *Debussy: Quartet in G Minor/Ravel: Quartet in F Major*	Julian Bream and John Williams, *Julian & John*

	1973	1974	1975
Record of the Year	Roberta Flack, "Killing Me Softly with His Song"	Olivia Newton-John, "I Honestly Love You"	Captain & Tennille, "Love Will Keep Us Together"
Album of the Year	Stevie Wonder, *Innervisions*	Stevie Wonder, *Fulfillingness' First Finale*	Paul Simon, *Still Crazy After All These Years*
Song of the Year	Norman Gimbel and Charles Fox, "Killing Me Softly with His Song"	Marilyn and Alan Bergman, Marvin Hamlisch, "The Way We Were"	Stephen Sondheim, "Send In the Clowns"
Pop Vocal, Female	Roberta Flack, "Killing Me Softly with His Song"	Olivia Newton-John, "I Honestly Love You"	Janis Ian, "At Seventeen"
Pop Vocal, Male	Stevie Wonder, "You Are the Sunshine of My Life"	Stevie Wonder, *Fulfillingness' First Finale*	Paul Simon, *Still Crazy After All These Years*
New Artist	Bette Midler	Marvin Hamlisch	Natalie Cole
Pop Vocal, Duo or Group with Vocal	Gladys Knight & The Pips, "Neither One of Us (Wants To Be the First To Say Goodbye)"	Paul McCartney & Wings, "Band on the Run"	Eagles, "Lyin' Eyes"
Rhythm and Blues Song	Stevie Wonder, "Superstition"	Stevie Wonder, "Living for the City"	H. W. Casey, Richard Finch, Willie Clarke, and Betty Wright, "Where Is the Love"
R&B Vocal, Female	Aretha Franklin, "Master of Eyes"	Aretha Franklin, "Ain't Nothing Like the Real Thing"	Natalie Cole, "This Will Be"
R&B Vocal, Male	Stevie Wonder, "Superstition"	Stevie Wonder, "Boogie On Reggae Woman"	Ray Charles, "Living for the City"

	1973	1974	1975
R&B Duo or Group with Vocal	Gladys Knight & The Pips, "Midnight Train to Georgia"	Rufus, "Tell Me Something Good"	Earth, Wind & Fire, "Shining Star"
Country Song	Kenny O'Dell, "Behind Closed Doors"	Norris Wilson and Bill Sherrill, "A Very Special Love Song"	Chips Moman and Larry Butler, "(Hey Won't You Play) Another Somebody Done Somebody Wrong Song"
Country Vocal, Female	Olivia Newton-John, "Let Me Be There "	Anne Murray, "Love Song"	Linda Ronstadt, "I Can't Help It (If I'm Still in Love with You)"
Country Vocal, Male	Charlie Rich, "Behind Closed Doors"	Ronnie Milsap, "Please Don't Tell Me How the Story Ends"	Willie Nelson, "Blue Eyes Crying in the Rain"
Country Performance, Duo or Group with Vocal	Kris Kristofferson and Rita Coolidge, "From the Bottle to the Bottom"	The Pointer Sisters, "Fairytale"	Kris Kristofferson and Rita Coolidge, "Lover Please"
Traditional Blues Recording	Doc Watson, *Then and Now*	Doc and Merle Watson, *Two Days in November*	Muddy Waters, *Thc Muddy Waters Woodstock Album*
Jazz, Soloist	Art Tatum, *God Is in the House*	Charlie Parker, *First Recordings!*	Dizzy Gillespie, *Oscar Peterson and Dizzy Gillespie*
Jazz, Group	Supersax, *Supersax Plays Bird*	Oscar Peterson, Joe Pass, and Niels Pedersen, *The Trio*	Return to Forever featuring Chick Corea, *No Mystery*
Jazz, Big Band/ Large Ensemble Performance	Woody Herman, *Giant Steps*	Woody Herman, *Thundering Herd*	Phil Woods with Michel Legrand & His Orchestra, *Images*
Cast Show Album	*A Little Night Music*	*Raisin*	*The Wiz*
Comedy Recording	Cheech & Chong, *Los Cochinos*	Richard Pryor, *That Nigger's Crazy*	Richard Pryor, *Is It Something I Said?*
Classical Album	Pierre Boulez, conductor, New York Philharmonic, *Bartók: Concerto for Orchestra*	Georg Solti, conductor, Chicago Symphony, *Berlioz: Symphonie Fantastique*	Georg Solti, conductor, Chicago Symphony, *Beethoven: Symphonies (9) Complete*
Classical Orchestral Performance	Pierre Boulez, conductor, New York Philharmonic, *Bartók: Concerto for Orchestra*	Georg Solti, conductor, Chicago Symphony, *Berlioz: Symphonie Fantastique*	Pierre Boulez, conductor, New York Philharmonic, *Ravel: Daphnis et Chloë*
Opera Recording	Leonard Bernstein, conductor, Metropolitan Opera Orchestra and Manhattan Opera Chorus (Solos: Horne, McCracken, Maliponte, Krause), *Bizet: Carmen*	Georg Solti, conductor, London Philharmonic (Soloists: Caballé, Domingo, Milnes, Blegen, Raimondi), *Puccini: La Bohème*	Colin Davis, conductor, Royal Opera House, Covent Garden (Solos: Caballé, Baker, Gedda, Ganzarolli, Van Allen, Cotrubas), *Mozart: Cosi fan tutte*
Chamber Music Performance	Gunther Schuller and New England Ragtime Ensemble, *Joplin: The Red Back Book*	Artur Rubinstein, Henryk Szeryng, and Pierre Fournier, *Brahms: Trios (complete)/ Schumann: Trio No. 1 in D Minor*	Artur Rubinstein, Henryk Szeryng, and Pierre Fournier, *Shubert: Trios Nos. 1 in B Flat Major Op. 99 & 2 in E Flat Major Op. 100*

	1976	1977	1978
Record of the Year	George Benson, "This Masquerade"	Eagles, "Hotel California"	Billy Joel, "Just the Way You Are"
Album of the Year	Stevie Wonder, *Songs in the Key of Life*	Fleetwood Mac, *Rumours*	The Bee Gees and others, *Saturday Night Fever*
Song of the Year	Bruce Johnston, "I Write the Songs"	Joe Brooks, "You Light Up My Life"; Barbra Streisand, "Love Theme from *A Star Is Born* (Evergreen)"	Billy Joel, "Just the Way You Are"
(Pop) Vocal, Female	Linda Ronstadt, *Hasten Down the Wind*	Barbra Streisand, "Love Theme from *A Star Is Born* (Evergreen)"	Anne Murray, "You Needed Me"
(Pop) Vocal, Male	Stevie Wonder, *Songs in the Key of Life*	James Taylor, "Handy Man"	Barry Manilow, "Copacabana (At the Copa)"
New Artist	Starland Vocal Band	Debby Boone	A Taste of Honey
Pop Vocal, Duo or Group with Vocal	Chicago, "If You Leave Me Now"	The Bee Gees, "How Deep Is Your Love"	The Bee Gees, *Saturday Night Fever*
Rhythm and Blues Song	Boz Scaggs and David Paich, "Lowdown"	Leo Sayer and Vini Poncia, "You Make Me Feel Like Dancing"	Paul Jabara, "Last Dance"
R&B Vocal, Female	Natalie Cole, "Sophisticated Lady (She's a Different Lady)"	Thelma Houston, "Don't Leave Me This Way"	Donna Summer, "Last Dance"
R&B Vocal, Male	Stevie Wonder, "I Wish"	Lou Rawls, *Unmistakably Lou*	George Benson, "On Broadway"
R&B Duo or Group with Vocal	Marilyn McCoo and Billy Davis, Jr., "You Don't Have To Be a Star (To Be in My Show)"	Emotions, "Best of My Love"	Earth, Wind & Fire, "All 'n All"
Country Song	Larry Gatlin, "Broken Lady"	Richard Leigh, "Don't It Make My Brown Eyes Blue"	Don Schlitz, "The Gambler"
Country Vocal, Female	Emmylou Harris, *Elite Hotel*	Crystal Gayle, "Don't It Make My Brown Eyes Blue"	Dolly Parton, *Here You Come Again*
Country Vocal, Male	Ronnie Milsap, "(I'm a) Stand by My Woman Man"	Kenny Rogers, "Lucille"	Willie Nelson, "Georgia on My Mind"
Country Performance, Duo or Group with Vocal	Amazing Rhythm Aces, "The End Is Not in Sight (The Cowboy Tune)"	The Kendalls, "Heaven's Just a Sin Away"	Waylon Jennings and Willie Nelson, "Mamas Don't Let Your Babies Grow Up To Be Cowboys"
Ethnic or Traditional Recording	John Hartford, *Mark Twang*	Muddy Waters, *Hard Again*	Muddy Waters, *I'm Ready*
Jazz, Soloist	Count Basie, *Basie & Zoot*	Oscar Peterson, *The Giants*	Oscar Peterson, *Montreux '77, Oscar Peterson Jam*
Jazz, Group	Chick Corea, *The Leprechaun*	Phil Woods, *The Phil Woods Six—Live from the Showboat*	Chick Corea, *Friends*
Jazz, Big Band/ Large Ensemble Performance	Duke Ellington, *The Ellington Suites*	Count Basie & His Orchestra, *Prime Time*	Thad Jones and Mel Lewis, *Live in Munich*
Cast Show Album	*Bubbling Brown Sugar*	*Annie*	*Ain't Misbehavin'*
Comedy Recording	Richard Pryor, *Bicentennial Nigger*	Steve Martin, *Let's Get Small*	Steve Martin, *A Wild and Crazy Guy*
Classical Album	Artur Rubinstein with Daniel Barenboim, conductor, London Philharmonic, *Beethoven: The Five Piano Concertos*	Leonard Bernstein, Vladimir Horowitz, Isaac Stern, Mstislav Rostropovich, Dietrich Fischer-Dieskau, Yehudi Menuhin, Lyndon Woodside, *Concert of the Century* (recorded live at Carnegie Hall May 18, 1976)	Itzhak Perlman with Carlo Maria Giulini, conductor, Chicago Symphony, *Brahms: Concerto for Violin in D Major*

	1976	1977	1978
Classical Orchestral Performance	Georg Solti, conductor, Chicago Symphony, *Strauss: Also Sprach Zarathustra*	Carlo Maria Giulini, conductor, Chicago Symphony, *Mahler: Symphony No. 9 in D Major*	Herbert von Karajan, conductor, Berlin Philharmonic, *Beethoven: Symphonies (9) Complete*
Opera Recording	Lorin Maazel conductor, Cleveland Orchestra and Chorus (Solos: Mitchell, White), *Gershwin: Porgy & Bess*	John De Main, conductor, Houston Grand Opera Production (Solos: Albert, Dale, Smith, Shakesnider, Lane, Brice, Smalls), *Gershwin: Porgy & Bess*	Julius Rudel, conductor, New York City Opera Orchestra and Chorus (Solos: Sills, Titus), *Lehar: The Merry Widow*
Chamber Music Performance	David Munrow, conductor, The Early Music Consort of London, *The Art of Courtly Love*	Juilliard Quartet, *Schöenberg: Quartets for Strings*	Itzhak Perlman and Vladimir Ashkenazy, *Beethoven: Sonatas for Violin and Piano*

GRAMMY AWARD RECORDS

In 1957, the newly-formed National Academy of Recording Arts & Sciences first conceived of a peer award to recognize outstanding achievement in the recording field. The Grammys, named after the gramophone statuette, have since expanded from 28 categories to 81. The following artists have all set records in the annals of Grammy history:

Youngest "Album of the Year" winner:
Alanis Morissette, age 21 when *Jagged Little Pill* was named 1995's best LP

Winningest winner:
Georg Solti, the conductor of the Chicago Symphony, has won 30 awards

Winningest female:
Aretha Franklin, with 15 awards (and an uninterrupted winning streak from 1967 to 1974)

Most awards in a single year:
Michael Jackson in 1983, with seven for Album of the Year *Thriller* and one for *E.T., the Extra-Terrestrial* as Best Recording for Children

Most country awards:
Chet Atkins with 14

Most jazz awards:
Ella Fitzgerald with 13

Most comedy awards:
Bill Cosby with 9

Most opera awards:
Leontyne Price with 13

	1979	1980	1981
Record of the Year	The Doobie Brothers, "What a Fool Believes"	Christopher Cross, "Sailing"	Kim Carnes, "Bette Davis Eyes"
Album of the Year	Billy Joel, *52nd Street*	Christopher Cross, *Christopher Cross*	John Lennon and Yoko Ono, *Double Fantasy*
Song of the Year	Kenny Loggins and Michael McDonald, "What a Fool Believes"	Christopher Cross, "Sailing"	Donna Weiss and Jackie DeShannon, "Bette Davis Eyes"
Pop Vocal, Female	Dionne Warwick, "I'll Never Love This Way Again"	Bette Midler, "The Rose"	Lena Horne, *Lena Horne: The Lady and Her Music Live on Broadway*
Pop Vocal, Male	Billy Joel, *52nd Street*	Kenny Loggins, "This Is It"	Al Jarreau, *Breakin' Away*
Rock Vocal, Female	Donna Summer, "Hot Stuff"	Pat Benatar, *Crimes of Passion*	Pat Benatar, "Fire and Ice"
Rock Vocal, Male	Bob Dylan, "Gotta Serve Somebody"	Billy Joel, *Glass Houses*	Rick Springfield, "Jessie's Girl"
New Artist	Rickie Lee Jones	Christopher Cross	Sheena Easton
Pop Vocal, Duo or Group with Vocal	The Doobie Brothers, *Minute by Minute*	Barbra Streisand and Barry Gibb, "Guilty"	The Manhattan Transfer, "Boy from New York City"
Rock Performance, Duo or Group with Vocal	The Eagles, "Heartache Tonight"	Bob Seger & the Silver Bullet Band, *Against the Wind*	The Police, "Don't Stand So Close to Me"
Rhythm and Blues Song	David Foster, Jay Graydon, and Bill Champlin, "After the Love Has Gone"	Reggie Lucas and James Mtume, "Never Knew Love Like This Before"	Bill Withers, William Salter, and Ralph MacDonald, "Just the Two of Us"
R&B Vocal, Female	Dionne Warwick, "Déjà Vu"	Stephanie Mills, "Never Knew Love Like This Before"	Aretha Franklin, "Hold On, I'm Comin' "
R&B Vocal, Male	Michael Jackson, "Don't Stop 'Til You Get Enough"	George Benson, *Give Me the Night*	James Ingram, "One Hundred Ways"
R&B Duo or Group with Vocal	Earth, Wind & Fire, "After the Love Has Gone"	Manhattans, "Shining Star"	Quincy Jones, *The Dude*
Country Song	Bob Morrison and Debbie Hupp, "You Decorated My Life"	Willie Nelson, "On the Road Again"	Dolly Parton, "9 to 5"
Country Vocal, Female	Emmylou Harris, *Blue Kentucky Girl*	Anne Murray, "Could I Have This Dance"	Dolly Parton, "9 to 5"
Country Vocal, Male	Kenny Rogers, "The Gambler"	George Jones, "He Stopped Loving Her Today"	Ronnie Milsap, "(There's) No Gettin' Over Me"
Country Performance, Duo or Group with Vocal	Charlie Daniels Band, "The Devil Went Down to Georgia"	Roy Orbison and Emmylou Harris, "That Lovin' You Feelin' Again"	Oak Ridge Boys, "Elvira"
Ethnic or Traditional Recording	Muddy Waters, *Muddy "Mississippi" Waters Live*	Dr. Isaiah Ross, Maxwell Street Jimmy, Big Joe William, Son House, Rev. Robert Wilkins, Little Brother Montgomery, and Sunnyland Slim, *Rare Blues*	B. B. King, *There Must Be a Better World Somewhere*
Jazz Vocal, Female	Ella Fitzgerald, *Fine and Mellow*	Ella Fitzgerald, *A Perfect Match/Ella & Basie*	Ella Fitzgerald, *Digital III at Montreux*
Jazz Vocal, Male	—	George Benson, "Moody's Mood"	Al Jarreau, "Blue Rondo à la Turk"
Jazz, Soloist	Oscar Peterson, *Jousts*	Bill Evans, *I Will Say Goodbye*	John Coltrane, *Bye, Bye Blackbird*

	1979	1980	1981
Jazz, Group	Gary Burton and Chick Corea, *Duet*	Bill Evans, *We Will Meet Again*	Chick Corea and Gary Burton, *Chick Corea and Gary Burton in Concert, Zurich, October 28, 1979*
Jazz, Big Band/ Large Ensemble Performance	Duke Ellington, *At Fargo, 1940 Live*	Count Basie and Orchestra, *On the Road*	Gerry Mulligan & His Orchestra, *Walk on the Water*
Jazz Fusion Performance, Vocal or Instrumental	Weather Report, *8:30*	Manhattan Transfer, "Birdland"	Grover Washington Jr., *Winelight*
Cast Show Album	*Sweeney Todd*	*Evita*	*Lena Horne: The Lady and Her Music Live on Broadway*
Comedy Recording	Robin Williams, *Reality...What a Concept*	Rodney Dangerfield, *No Respect*	Richard Pryor, *Rev. Du Rite*
Classical Album	Georg Solti, conductor, Chicago Symphony Orchestra, *Brahms: Symphonies (4) Complete*	Pierre Boulez, conductor, Orchestre d l'Opera de Paris (Solos: Stratas, Minton, Mazura, Toni Blankenheim), *Berg: Lulu*	Georg Solti, conductor, Chicago Symphony Orchestra and Chorus (Solos: Buchanan, Zakai), *Mahler: Symphony No. 2 in C Minor*
Classical Orchestral Performance	Georg Solti, conductor, Chicago Symphony, *Brahms: Symphonies (4) Complete*	Georg Solti, conductor, Chicago Symphony, *Bruckner: Symphony No. 6 in A Major*	Georg Solti, conductor, Chicago Symphony, *Mahler: Symphony No. 2 in C Minor*
Opera Recording	Colin Davis, conductor, Orchestra and Chorus of the Royal Opera House, Covent Garden (Solos: Vickers, Harper, Summers), *Britten: Peter Grimes*	Pierre Boulez, conductor, Orchestre d l'Opera de Paris (Solos: Stratas, Minton, Mazura, Blankenheim), *Berg: Lulu*	Charles Mackerras, conductor, Vienna Philharmonic (Solos: Zahradnicek, Zitek, Zidek), *Janacek: From the House of the Dead*
Chamber Music Performance	Dennis Russel Davies, conductor, St. Paul Chamber Orchestra, *Copland: Appalachian Spring*	Itzhak Perlman and Pinchas Zukerman, *Music for Two Violins (Moszkowski: Suite for Two Violins/Shostakovich: Duets/ Prokofiev: Sonata for Two Violins)*	Itzhak Perlman, Lynn Harrell, and Vladimir Ashkenazy, *Tchaikovsky: Piano Trio in A Minor*

FAMOUS LOSERS

The following artists have never won a Grammy in a competitive category, although many have been nominated. Asterisks indicate that the performers have, however, belatedly received the NARAS Lifetime Achievement Award.

AC/DC
Beach Boys
Chuck Berry*
Jackson Browne
The Byrds
Cher
Patsy Cline*
Sam Cooke
Elvis Costello
Creedence Clearwater Revival
Cream
Bing Crosby*
Fats Domino*
The Doors
The Drifters
The Four Tops
Peter Frampton
Benny Goodman*
Grateful Dead
Jimi Hendrix*
The Jackson 5
Janis Joplin
Led Zeppelin
Little Richard
Pretenders
Queen
Cat Stevens
Diana Ross
Lawrence Welk
Kitty Wells*
The Who
Hank Williams, Sr.*
Ncil Young

	1982	1983	1984
Record of the Year	Toto, "Rosanna"	Michael Jackson, "Beat It"	Tina Turner, "What's Love Got To Do with It"
Album of the Year	Toto, *Toto IV*	Michael Jackson, *Thriller*	Lionel Richie, *Can't Slow Down*
Song of the Year	Johnny Christopher, Mark James, and Wayne Thompson, "Always on My Mind"	Sting, "Every Breath You Take"	Graham Lyle and Terry Britten, "What's Love Got To Do with It"
Pop Vocal, Female	Melissa Manchester, "You Should Hear How She Talks About You"	Irene Cara, "Flashdance...What a Feeling"	Tina Turner, "What's Love got To Do with It"
Pop Vocal, Male	Lionel Richie, "Truly"	Michael Jackson, *Thriller*	Phil Collins, "Against All Odds (Take a Look at Me Now)"
Rock Vocal, Female	Pat Benatar, "Shadows of the Night"	Pat Benatar, "Love Is a Battlefield"	Tina Turner, "Better Be Good to Me"
Rock Vocal, Male	John Cougar, "Hurts So Good"	Michael Jackson, "Beat It"	Bruce Springsteen, "Dancing in the Dark"
New Artist	Men at Work	Culture Club	Cyndi Lauper
Pop Vocal, Duo or Group with Vocal	Joe Cocker and Jennifer Warnes, "Up Where We Belong"	The Police, "Every Breath You Take"	Pointer Sisters, "Jump (For My Love)"
Rock Performance, Duo or Group with Vocal	Survivor, "Eye of the Tiger"	The Police, *Synchronicity*	Prince and the Revolution, *Purple Rain*
Rhythm and Blues Song	Jay Graydon, Steve Lukather, and Bill Champlin, "Turn Your Love Around"	Michael Jackson, "Billie Jean"	Prince, "I Feel for You"
R&B Vocal, Female	Jennifer Holliday, "And I Am Telling You I'm Not Going"	Chaka Khan, *Chaka Khan*	Chaka Khan, "I Feel for You"
R&B Vocal, Male	Marvin Gaye, "Sexual Healing"	Michael Jackson, "Billie Jean"	Billy Ocean, "Caribbean Queen (No More Love on the Run)"
R&B Duo or Group with Vocal	Dazz Band,"Let It Whip"; Earth, Wind & Fire, "Wanna Be With You"	Rufus & Chaka Khan, "Ain't Nobody"	James Ingram and Michael McDonald, "Yah Mo B There"
Country Song	Johnny Christopher, Wayne Thompson, and Mark James, "Always on My Mind"	Mike Reed, "Stranger in My House"	Steve Goodman, "City of New Orleans"
Country Vocal, Female	Juice Newton, "Break It To Me Gently"	Anne Murray, "A Little Good News"	Emmylou Harris, "In My Dreams"
Country Vocal, Male	Willie Nelson, "Always on My Mind"	Lee Greenwood, "I.O.U."	Merle Haggard, "That's the Way Love Goes"
Country Performance, Group	Alabama, *Mountain Music*	Alabama, *The Closer You Get*	The Judds, "Mama He's Crazy"
Traditional Blues Recording	Clarence "Gatemouth" Brown, *Alright Again*	B. B. King, *Blues 'n' Jazz*	John Hammond, Stevie Ray Vaughan & Double Trouble, Sugar Blue, Koko Taylor & The Blues Machine, Luther "Guitar Junior" Johnson, and J. B. Hutto & The New Hawks, *Blues Explosion*
Reggae Recording	—	—	Black Uhuru, *Anthem*
Jazz Vocal, Female	Sarah Vaughan, *Gershwin Live!*	Ella Fitzgerald, *The Best Is Yet to Come*	—
Jazz Vocal, Male	Mel Torme, *An Evening with George Shearing and Mel Torme*	Mel Torme, *Top Drawer*	Joe Williams, *Nothin' but the Blues*
Jazz, Soloist	Miles Davis, *We Want Miles*	Wynton Marsalis, *Think of One*	Wynton Marsalis, *Hot House Flowers*

	1982	1983	1984
Jazz, Group	Phil Woods Quartet, *"More" Live*	The Phil Woods Quartet, *At the Vanguard*	Art Blakey & The Jazz Messengers, *New York Scene*
Jazz, Big Band/ Large Ensemble Performance	Count Basie & His Orchestra, *Warm Breeze*	Rob McConnell and The Boss Brass, *All in Good Time*	Count Basie & His Orchestra, *88 Basie Street*
Jazz Fusion Performance	Pat Metheny Group, *Offramp*	Pat Metheny Group, *Travels*	Pat Metheny Group, *First Circle*
Gospel Performance, Female	—	Amy Grant, "Ageless Medley"	Amy Grant, "Angels"
Gospel Performance, Male	—	Russ Taff, *Walls of Glass*	Michael W. Smith, *Michael W. Smith 2*
Gospel Performance, Duo, Group, Choir or Chorus	—	Sandi Patti and Larnelle Harris, "More Than Wonderful"	Debby Boone and Phil Driscoll, "Keep the Flame Burning"
Ethnic or Traditional Folk Recording	Queen Ida, *Queen Ida and the Bon Temps Zydeco Band on Tour*	Clifton Chenier & His Red Hot Louisiana Band, *I'm Here*	Elizabeth Cotten, *Elizabeth Cotten Live!*
Cast Show Album	*Dreamgirls*	*Cats (Complete Original Broadway Cast Recording)*	*Sunday in the Park with George*
Comedy Recording	Richard Pryor, *Live on the Sunset Strip*	Eddie Murphy, *Eddie Murphy: Comedian*	"Weird Al" Yankovic, "Eat It"
Classical Album	Glenn Gould, *Bach: The Goldberg Variations*	Georg Solti, conductor, Chicago Symphony, *Mahler: Symphony No. 9 in D Major*	Neville Marriner, conductor, Academy of St. Martin-in-the-Fields/Ambrosian Opera Chorus/Choristers of Westminster Abbey, *Amadeus (Original Soundtrack)*
Classical Orchestral Performance	James Levine, conductor, Chicago Symphony, *Mahler: Symphony No. 7 in E Minor (Song of the Night)*	Georg Solti, conductor, Chicago Symphony, *Mahler: Symphony No. 9 in D Major*	Leonard Slatkin, conductor, St. Louis Symphony, *Prokofiev: Symphony No. 5 in B Flat, Op. 100*
Opera Recording	Pierre Boulez, conductor, Bayreuth Festival Orchestra (Solos: Jones, Altmeyer, Wenkel, Hofmann, Jung, Jerusalem, Zednik, McIntyre, Salminen, Becht), *Wagner: Der Ring des Nibelungen*	James Levine, conductor, The Metropolitan Opera Orchestra and Chorus (Solos: Stratas, Domingo, MacNeill), *Verdi: La Traviata*	Lorin Maazel, conductor, Orchestre National de France/Choeurs et Maitrise de Radio France (Solos: Johnson, Esham, Domingo, Raimondi), *Bizet: Carmen*
Chamber Music Performance	Richard Stoltzman and Richard Goode, *Brahms: The Sonatas for Clarinet & Piano, Op. 120*	Mstislav Rostropovich and Rudolph Serkin, *Brahms: Sonata for Cello & Piano in E Minor, Op. 38 & Sonata in F Major, Op. 99*	Juilliard String Quartet, *Beethoven: The Late String Quartets*

	1985	1986	1987
Record of the Year	USA for Africa, "We Are the World"	Steve Winwood, "Higher Love"	Paul Simon, "Graceland"
Album of the Year	Phil Collins, *No Jacket Required*	Paul Simon, *Graceland*	U2, *The Joshua Tree*
Song of the Year	Michael Jackson and Lionel Richie, "We Are the World"	Burt Bacharach and Carole Bayer Sager, "That's What Friends Are For"	James Horner, Barry Mann, and Cynthia Weil, "Somewhere Out There"
Pop Vocal, Female	Whitney Houston, "Saving All My Love for You"	Barbra Streisand, *The Broadway Album*	Whitney Houston, "I Wanna Dance with Somebody (Who Loves Me)"
Pop Vocal, Male	Phil Collins, *No Jacket Required*	Steve Winwood, "Higher Love"	Sting, *Bring on the Night*
Rock Vocal, Female	Tina Turner, "One of the Living"	Tina Turner, "Back Where You Started"	—
Rock Vocal, Male	Don Henley, "The Boys of Summer"	Robert Palmer, "Addicted to Love"	Bruce Springsteen, *Tunnel of Love*
New Artist	Sade	Bruce Hornsby and the Range	Jody Watley
Pop Vocal, Duo or Group with Vocal	USA for Africa, "We Are the World"	Dionne Warwick & Friends featuring Elton John, Gladys Knight, and Stevie Wonder, "That's What Friends Are For"	Bill Medley and Jennifer Warnes, "(I've Had) The Time of My Life"
Rock Performance, Group	Dire Straits, "Money for Nothing"	Eurythmics, "Missionary Man"	U2, *The Joshua Tree*
New Age Recording	—	Andreas Vollenweider, *Down to the Moon*	Yusef Lateef, *Yusef Lateef's Little Symphony*
Rhythm and Blues Song	Narada Michael Walden and Jeffrey Cohen, "Freeway of Love"	Anita Baker, Louis A. Johnson, Gary Bias, "Sweet Love"	Bill Withers, "Lean on Me"
R&B Vocal, Female	Aretha Franklin, "Freeway of Love"	Anita Baker, *Rapture*	Aretha Franklin, *Aretha*
R&B Vocal, Male	Stevie Wonder, *In Square Circle*	James Brown, "Living in America"	Smokey Robinson, "Just To See Her"
R&B Duo or Group with Vocal	Commodores, "Nightshift"	Prince & The Revolution, "Kiss"	Aretha Franklin and George Michael, "I Knew You Were Waiting (For Me)"
Country Song	Jimmy L. Webb, "Highwayman"	Jamie O'Hara, "Grandpa (Tell Me 'Bout the Good Old Days)"	Paul Overstreet and Don Schlitz, *Forever and Ever, Amen*
Country Vocal, Female	Rosanne Cash, "I Don't Know Why You Don't Want Me"	Reba McEntire, "Whoever's in New England"	K. T. Oslin, "80's Ladies"
Country Vocal, Male	Ronnie Milsap, "Lost in the Fifties Tonight (In the Still of the Night)"	Ronnie Milsap, *Lost in the Fifties Tonight*	Randy Travis, *Always & Forever*
Country Performance, Duo or Group with Vocal	The Judds, *Why Not Me*	The Judds, "Grandpa (Tell Me 'Bout the Good Old Days)"	Dolly Parton, Linda Ronstadt, and Emmylou Harris, *Trio*
Country Vocal, Collaboration	—	—	Ronnie Milsap and Kenny Rogers, "Make No Mistake, She's Mine"
Traditional Blues Recording	B. B. King, "My Guitar Sings the Blues"	Albert Collins, Robert Cray, and Johnny Copeland, *Showdown*	Professor Longhair, *Houseparty New Orleans Style*
Contemporary Blues	—	—	Robert Cray Band, *Strong Persuader*

	1985	1986	1987
Reggae Recording	Jimmy Cliff, *Cliff Hanger*	Steel Pulse, *Babylon the Bandit*	Peter Tosh, *No Nuclear War*
Jazz Vocal, Female	Cleo Laine, *Cleo at Carnegie, the 10th Anniversary Concert*	Diane Schuur, *Timeless*	Diane Schuur, *Diane Schuur & The Count Basie Orchestra*
Jazz Vocal, Male	Jon Hendricks and Bobby McFerrin, "Another Night in Tunisia"	Bobby McFerrin, " 'Round Midnight"	Bobby McFerrin, "What Is This Thing Called Love"
Jazz, Soloist	Wynton Marsalis, *Black Codes from the Underground*	Miles Davis, *Tutu*	Dexter Gordon, *The Other Side of 'Round Midnight*
Jazz, Group	Wynton Marsalis Group, *Black Codes from the Underground*	Wynton Marsalis, *J Mood*	Wynton Marsalis, *Marsalis Standard Time, Volume I*
Jazz, Big Band/ Large Ensemble Performance	John Barry and Bob Wilber, *The Cotton Club*	The Tonight Show Band with Doc Severinsen, *The Tonight Show Band with Doc Severinsen*	The Duke Ellington Orchestra, conducted by Mercer Ellington, *Digital Duke*
Jazz Fusion Performance, Vocal or Instrumental	David Sanborn, *Straight to the Heart*	Bob James and David Sanborn, *Double Vision*	Pat Metheny Group, *Still Life (Talking)*
Gospel Performance, Female	Amy Grant, *Unguarded*	Sandi Patti, *Morning Like This*	Deniece Williams, "I Believe in You"
Gospel Performance, Male	Larnelle Harris, "How Excellent Is Thy Name"	Philip Bailey, *Triumph*	Larnelle Harris, *The Father Hath Provided*
Gospel Performance, Duo, Group, Choir or Chorus	Larnelle Harris and Sandi Patti, "I've Just Seen Jesus"	Sandi Patti & Deniece Williams, "They Say"	Mylon LeFevre & Broken Heart, *Crack the Sky*
Traditional Folk Recording	Rockin' Sidney, "My Toot Toot"	Doc Watson, *Riding the Midnight Train*	Ladysmith Black Mambazo, *Shaka Zulu*
Contemporary Folk Recording	—	Arlo Guthrie, John Hartford, Richie Havens, Bonnie Koloc, Nitty Gritty Dirt Band, John Prine and others, *Tribute to Steve Goodman*	Steve Goodman, *Unfinished Business*
Cast Show Album	*West Side Story*	*Follies in Concert*	*Les Misérables*
Comedy Recording	Whoopi Goldberg, *Whoopi Goldberg*	Bill Cosby, *Those of You With or Without Children, You'll Understand*	Robin Williams, *A Night at the Met*
Classical Album	Robert Shaw, conductor, Atlanta Symphony Orchestra and Chorus, (Solo: Aler) *Berlioz: Requiem*	Vladimir Horowitz, *Horowitz: The Studio Recordings, New York 1985*	Vladimir Horowitz, *Horowitz in Moscow*
Classical Orchestral Performance	Robert Shaw, conductor, Atlanta Symphony Orchestra, *Fauré: Pelléas et Mélisande*	Georg Solti, conductor, Chicago Symphony Orchestra, *Liszt: A Faust Symphony*	Georg Solti, conductor, Chicago Symphony Orchestra, *Beethoven: Symphony No. 9 in D Minor*
Opera Recording	Georg Solti, conductor, Chicago Symphony Orchestra and Chorus (Solos: Mazura, Langridge), *Schoenberg: Moses und Aaron*	John Mauceri, conductor, New York City Opera Chorus and Orchestra (Solos: Mills, Clement, Eisler, Lankston, Castle, Reeve, Harrold, Billings), *Bernstein: Candide*	James Levine, conductor, Vienna Philharmonic (Solos: Tomowa-Sintow, Battle, Baltsa, Lakes, Prey), *R. Strauss: Ariadne auf Naxos*
Chamber Music Performance	Emanuel Ax and Yo-Yo Ma, *Brahms: Cello and Piano Sonatas in E Major & F Major*	Yo-Yo Ma and Emanuel Ax, *Beethoven: Cello & Piano Sonata No. 4 in C and Variations*	Itzhak Perlman, Lynn Harrell, and Vladimir Ashkenazy, *Beethoven: The Complete Piano Trios*

	1988	1989	1990
Record of the Year	Bobby McFerrin, "Don't Worry, Be Happy"	Bette Midler, "Wind Beneath My Wings"	Phil Collins, "Another Day in Paradise"
Album of the Year	George Michael, *Faith*	Bonnie Raitt, *Nick of Time*	Quincy Jones, *Back on the Block*
Song of the Year	Bobby McFerrin, "Don't Worry, Be Happy"	Larry Henley and Jeff Silbar, "Wind Beneath My Wings"	Julie Gold, "From a Distance"
Pop Vocal, Female	Tracy Chapman, "Fast Car"	Bonnie Raitt, "Nick of Time"	Mariah Carey, "Vision of Love"
Pop Vocal, Male	Bobby McFerrin, "Don't Worry, Be Happy"	Michael Bolton, "How Am I Supposed to Live Without You"	Roy Orbison, "Oh, Pretty Woman"
Rock Vocal, Female	Tina Turner, *Tina Live in Europe*	Bonnie Raitt, *Nick of Time*	Alannah Myles, "Black Velvet"
Rock Vocal, Male	Robert Palmer, "Simply Irresistible"	Don Henley, *The End of the Innocence*	Eric Clapton, "Bad Love"
New Artist	Tracy Chapman	No award (Milli Vanilli)	Mariah Carey
Pop Vocal, Duo or Group with Vocal	The Manhattan Transfer, *Brasil*	Linda Ronstadt and Aaron Neville, "Don't Know Much"	Linda Ronstadt with Aaron Neville, "All My Life"
Rock Performance, Duo or Group with Vocal	U2, "Desire"	Traveling Wilburys, *Traveling Wilburys, Volume I*	Aerosmith, "Janie's Got a Gun"
New Age Recording	Shadowfax, *Folksongs for a Nuclear Village*	Peter Gabriel, *Passion (Music from The Last Temptation of Christ)*	Mark Isham, *Mark Isham*
Hard Rock	Jethro Tull, *Crest of a Knave*	Living Colour, "Cult of Personality"	Living Colour, *Time's Up*
Metal	—	Metallica, "One"	Metallica, "Stone Cold Crazy"
Alternative	—	—	Sinéad O'Connor, *I Do Not Want What I Haven't Got*
Rap Performance, Solo	D.J. Jazzy Jeff & The Fresh Prince, "Parents Just Don't Understand"	Young MC, "Bust a Move"	M.C. Hammer, "U Can't Touch This"
Rap Performance by a Duo or Group	—	—	Ice-T, Melle Mel, Big Daddy Kane, Kool Moe Dee, and Quincy Jones III, "Back on the Block"
Rhythm and Blues Song	Anita Baker, Skip Scarborough, and Randy Holland, "Giving You the Best That I Got"	Kenny Gamble and Leon Huff, "If You Don't Know Me By Now"	Rick James, Alonzo Mille, and M.C. Hammer, "U Can't Touch This"
R&B Vocal, Female	Anita Baker, "Giving You the Best That I Got"	Anita Baker, *Giving You the Best That I Got*	Anita Baker, *Compositions*
R&B Vocal, Male	Terence Trent D'Arby, *Introducing the Hardline According to Terence Trent D'Arby*	Bobby Brown, "Every Little Step"	Luther Vandross, "Here and Now"
R&B Duo or Group with Vocal	Gladys Knight & The Pips, "Love Overboard"	Soul II Soul featuring Caron Wheeler, "Back to Life"	Ray Charles and Chaka Khan, "I'll Be Good to You"
Country Song	K. T. Oslin, "Hold Me"	Rodney Crowell, "After All This Time"	Jon Vezner and Don Henry, "Where've You Been"

	1988	1989	1990
Country Vocal, Female	K. T. Oslin, "Hold Me"	k.d. lang, *Absolute Torch and Twang*	Kathy Mattea, "Where've You Been"
Country Vocal, Male	Randy Travis, *Old 8 x 10*	Lyle Lovett, *Lyle Lovett and His Large Band*	Vince Gill, "When I Call Your Name"
Country Performance, Duo or Group with Vocal	The Judds, "Give a Little Love"	The Nitty Gritty Dirt Band, *Will the Circle Be Unbroken, Volume 2*	The Kentucky Headhunters, *Pickin' on Nashville*
Country Vocal, Collaboration	Roy Orbison and k.d. lang, "Crying"	Hank Williams Jr. and Hank Williams Sr., "There's a Tear in My Beer"	Chet Atkins and Mark Knopfler, "Poor Boy Blues"
Traditional Blues Recording	Willie Dixon, *Hidden Charms*	John Lee Hooker and Bonnie Raitt, "I'm in the Mood"	B.B. King, *Live at San Quentin*
Contemporary Blues	The Robert Cray Band, "Don't Be Afraid of the Dark"	Stevie Ray Vaughan & Double Trouble, *In Step*	The Vaughan Brothers, *Family Style*
Reggae Recording	Ziggy Marley & The Melody Makers, *Conscious Party*	Ziggy Marley & The Melody Makers, *One Bright Day*	Bunny Wailer, *Time Will Tell—A Tribute to Bob Marley*
Jazz Vocal, Female	Betty Carter, *Look What I Got!*	Ruth Brown, *Blues on Broadway*	Ella Fitzgerald, *All That Jazz*
Jazz Vocal, Male	Bobby McFerrin, "Brothers"	Harry Connick Jr., *When Harry Met Sally...*	Harry Connick Jr., *We Are in Love*
Jazz, Soloist	Michael Brecker, *Don't Try This at Home*	Miles Davis, *Aura*	Oscar Peterson, *The Legendary Oscar Peterson Trio Live at the Blue Note*
Jazz, Group	McCoy Tyner, Pharaoh Sanders, David Murray, Cecil McBee, and Roy Haynes, *Blues for Coltrane: A Tribute to John Coltrane*	Chick Corea Akoustic Band, *Chick Corea Akoustic Band*	Oscar Peterson Trio, *The Legendary Oscar Peterson Trio Live at the Blue Note*
Jazz, Big Band/ Large Ensemble Performance	Gil Evans & The Monday Night Orchestra, *Bud & Bird*	Miles Davis, *Aura*	George Benson featuring the Count Basie Orchestra; Frank Foster, conductor, "Basie's Bag"
Jazz Fusion Performance, Vocal or Instrumental	Yellowjackets, *Politics*	Pat Metheny Group, *Letter from Home*	Quincy Jones, "Birdland"
Gospel Performance, Female	Amy Grant, *Lead Me On*	CeCe Winans, "Don't Cry"	—
Gospel Performance, Male	Larnelle Harris, *Christmas*	BeBe Winans, "Meantime"	—
Gospel Performance, Duo, Group, Choir or Chorus	The Winans, *The Winans Live at Carnegie Hall*	Take 6, "The Savior Is Waiting"	Rev. James Cleveland, *Having Church*
Traditional Folk Recording	Various artists, *Folkways: A Vision Shared—A Tribute to Woody Guthrie and Leadbelly*	Bulgarian State Female Vocal Choir, *Le Mystère des voix bulgares, Vol. II*	Doc Watson, *On Praying Ground*
Contemporary Folk Recording	Tracy Chapman, *Tracy Chapman*	Indigo Girls, *Indigo Girls*	Shawn Colvin, *Steady On*
Cast Show Album	*Into the Woods*	*Jerome Robbins' Broadway*	*Les Misérables, The Complete Symphonic Recording*

	1988	1989	1990
Comedy Recording	Robin Williams, *Good Morning, Vietnam*	"Professor" Peter Schickele, *P.D.Q. Bach: 1712 Overture and Other Musical Assaults*	"Professor" Peter Schickele, *P.D.Q. Bach: Oedipus Tex & Other Choral Calamities*
Classical Album	Robert Shaw, conductor, Atlanta Symphony Orchestra and Chorus, *Verdi: Requiem and Operatic Choruses*	Emerson String Quartet, *Bartók: 6 String Quartets*	Leonard Bernstein, conductor, New York Philharmonic, *Ives: Symphony No. 2 (and Three Short Works)*
Classical Orchestral Performance	Robert Shaw, conductor, Atlanta Symphony Orchestra, *Rorem: String Symphony;* Louis Lane, conductor, Atlanta Symphony Orchestra, *Sunday Morning* and *Eagles*	Leonard Bernstein, conductor, New York Philharmonic, *Mahler: Sym. No. 3 in D Min.*	Leonard Bernstein, conductor, Chicago Symphony, *Shostakovich: Symphonies No. 1, Op. 10, and No. 7, Op. 60*
Opera Recording	Georg Solti, conductor, Vienna State Opera Choir & Vienna Philharmonic (Solos: Domingo, Norman, Randova, Nimsgern, Sotin, Fischer-Dieskau), *Wagner: Lohengrin*	James Levine, conductor, Metropolitan Opera Orchestra (Solos: Lakes, Moll, Morris, Norman, Behrens, Ludwig), *Wagner: Die Walküre*	James Levine, conductor, Metropolitan Opera Orchestra (Solos: Morris, Ludwig, Jerusalem, Wlaschiha, Moll, Zednik, Rootering), *Wagner: Das Rheingold*
Chamber Music Performance	Murray Perahia and Sir Georg Solti, pianos, with David Corkhill and Evelyn Glennie, percussion, *Bartók: Sonata for Two Pianos and Percussion; Brahms: Variations on a Theme by Joseph Haydn for Two Pianos*	Emerson String Quartet, *Bartók: 6 String Quartets*	Itzhak Perlman, violin; Daniel Barenboim, piano, *Brahms: The Three Violin Sonatas*

GRAMMY CHAMPS

Thanks to The Beatles' "Free as a Bird," George and John join Sir Paul among the National Academy of Recording Arts and Sciences' most honored musicians. Contenting himself with nine trophies, Ringo just misses the cutoff; he's positioned where new entry Eric Clapton sat last year.

Sir Georg Solti	30
Quincy Jones	26
Vladimir Horowitz	25
Henry Mancini	20
Stevie Wonder	20
Pierre Boulez	19
Leonard Bernstein	16
Paul Simon (including Simon & Garfunkel)	16
John T. Williams	16
Aretha Franklin	15
Itzhak Perlman	15
Chet Atkins	14
Ella Fitzgerald	13
David Foster	13
Michael Jackson	13
Paul McCartney (including The Beatles and Wings)	13
Leontyne Price	13
Robert Shaw (including Robert Shaw Chorale)	13
Ray Charles	12
Eric Clapton	12
Thomas Z. Shepard	12
Sting (including The Police)	12
Duke Ellington	11
James Mallinson	11
Roger Miller	11
George Harrison (including The Beatles and Travelling Wilburys)	10
John Lennon (including The Beatles)	10
Yo-Yo Ma	10
Bobby McFerrin	10
Alan Menken	10
Artur Rubinstein	10
Robert Woods	10

	1991	1992	1993
Record of the Year	Natalie Cole (with Nat "King" Cole), "Unforgettable"	Eric Clapton, "Tears in Heaven"	Whitney Houston, "I Will Always Love You"
Album of the Year	Natalie Cole, *Unforgettable*	Eric Clapton, *Unplugged*	Whitney Houston and others, *The Bodyguard—Original Soundtrack*
Song of the Year	Irving Gordon, "Unforgettable"	Eric Clapton and Will Jennings, "Tears in Heaven"	Alan Menken and Tim Rice, "A Whole New World"
Pop Vocal, Female	Bonnie Raitt, "Something to Talk About"	k.d. lang, "Constant Craving"	Whitney Houston, "I Will Always Love You"
Pop Vocal, Male	Michael Bolton, "When a Man Loves a Woman"	Eric Clapton, "Tears in Heaven"	Sting, "If I Ever Lose My Faith In You"
Rock Vocal, Female	Bonnie Raitt, *Luck of the Draw*	Melissa Etheridge, "Ain't It Heavy"	—
Rock Vocal, Male	—	Eric Clapton, *Tears in Heaven*	—
Rock Song/ Rock Vocal Performance, Solo	Sting, "Soul Cages"	Eric Clapton and Jim Gordon, *Layla*	Meat Loaf, "I'd Do Anything for Love (But I Won't Do That)"
New Artist	Mark Cohn	Arrested Development	Toni Braxton
Pop Vocal, Duo or Group with Vocal	R.E.M., "Losing My Religion"	Celine Dion and Peabo Bryson, "Beauty and the Beast"	Peabo Bryson and Regina Belle, "A Whole New World"
Rock Performance, Duo or Group with Vocal	Bonnie Raitt and Delbert McClinton, "Good Man, Good Woman"	U2, *Achtung Baby*	Aerosmith, "Living on the Edge"
New Age Recording	Mannheim Steamroller, *Fresh Aire 7*	Enya, *Sheperd Moons*	Paul Winter Consort, *Spanish Angel*
Hard Rock	Van Halen, *For Unlawful Carnal Knowledge*	Red Hot Chili Peppers, "Give It Away"	Stone Temple Pilots, "Plush"
Metal	Metallica, *Metallica*	Nine Inch Nails, "Wish"	Ozzy Ozbourne, "I Don't Want To Change the World"
Alternative	R.E.M., *Out of Time*	Tom Waits, *Bone Machine*	U2, *Zooropa*
Rap Performance, Solo	L.L. Cool J, "Mama Said Knock You Out"	Sir Mix-A-Lot, "Baby Got Back"	Dr. Dre, "Let Me Ride"
Rap Performance by a Duo or Group	D.J. Jazzy Jeff & The Fresh Prince, "Summertime"	Arrested Development, "Tennessee"	Digable Planets, "Rebirth of Slick (Cool Like Dat)"
Rhythm and Blues Song	Luther Vandross, Marcus Miller, and Teddy Vann, "Power of Love/Love Power"	L.A. Reid, Babyface, and Daryl Simmons, "End of the Road"	Janet Jackson, James Harris III, and Terry Lewis, "That's the Way Love Goes"
R&B Vocal, Female	Patti LaBelle, *Burnin'*; Lisa Fischer; "How Can I Ease the Pain"	Chaka Khan, *The Woman I Am*	Toni Braxton, "Another Sad Love Song"
R&B Vocal, Male	Luther Vandross, *Power of Love*	Al Jarreau, *Heaven and Earth*	Ray Charles, "A Song For You"
R&B Duo or Group with Vocal	Boyz II Men, *Cooleyhighharmony*	Boyz II Men, "End of the Road"	Sade, "No Ordinary Love"
Country Song	Naomi Judd, John Jarvis, and Paul Overstreet, "Love Can Build a Bridge"	Vince Gill and John Barlow Jarvis, "I Still Believe in You"	Lucinda Williams, "Passionate Kisses"
Country Vocal, Female	Mary-Chapin Carpenter, "Down at the Twist and Shout"	Mary-Chapin Carpenter, "I Feel Lucky"	Mary-Chapin Carpenter, "Passionate Kisses"
Country Vocal, Male	Garth Brooks, *Ropin' the Wind*	Vince Gill, *I Still Believe in You*	Dwight Yoakam, "Ain't That Lonely Yet"

	1991	1992	1993
Country Performance, Duo or Group with Vocal	The Judds, "Love Can Build a Bridge"	Emmylou Harris & The Nash Ramblers, *Emmylou Harris & The Nash Ramblers at the Ryman*	Brooks & Dunn, "Hard Workin' Man"
Country Vocal, Collaboration	Steve Wariner, Ricky Skaggs, and Vince Gill, "Restless"	Travis Tritt and Marty Stuart, "The Whiskey Ain't Workin' "	Reba McEntire and Linda Davis, "Does He Love You"
Traditional Blues Recording	B. B. King, *Live at the Apollo*	Dr. John, *Goin' Back to New Orleans*	B.B. King, *Blues Summit*
Contemporary Blues	Buddy Guy, *Damn Right, I've Got the Blues*	Stevie Ray Vaughan & Double Trouble, *The Sky Is Crying*	Buddy Guy, *Feels Like Rain*
Reggae Recording	Shabba Ranks, *As Raw as Ever*	Shabba Ranks, *X-tra Naked*	Inner Circle, *Bad Boys*
Jazz, Soloist	Stan Getz, "I Remember You"	Joe Henderson, "Lush Life"	Joe Henderson, "Miles Ahead"
Jazz, Group	Oscar Peterson Trio, *Saturday Night at the Blue Note*	Branford Marsalis, *I Heard You Twice the First Time*	Joe Henderson, *So Near, So Far (Musings for Miles)*
Jazz, Big Band/ Large Ensemble Performance	Dizzy Gillespie & The United Nation Orchestra, *Live at the Royal Festival Hall*	McCoy Tyner Big Band, *The Turning Point*	Miles Davis and Quincy Jones, *Miles and Quincy Live at Montreaux*
Jazz Fusion Performance	—	Pat Metheny, *Secret Story*	—
Gospel Performance, Duo, Group, Choir or Chorus	Sounds of Blackness, *The Evolution of Gospel*	Music & Arts Seminar Mass Choir; Edwin Hawkins, choir director, *Edwin Hawkins Music & Arts Seminar Mass Choir: Recorded Live in Los Angeles*	Brooklyn Tabernacle Choir; Carol Cymbala, choir director, *Live ... We Come Rejoicing*
Traditional Folk Recording	Ken Burns and John Colby, *The Civil War*	The Chieftains, *Another Country*	The Chieftains, *The Celtic Harp*
Contemporary Folk Recording	John Prine, *The Missing Years*	The Chieftains, *An Irish Evening Live at the Grand Opera House, Belfast*	Nanci Griffith, *Other Voices/Other Rooms*
Cast Show Album	*The Will Rogers Follies*	*Guys and Dolls*	*The Who's Tommy*
Comedy Recording	"Professor" Peter Schickele, *P.D.Q. Bach: WTWP Classical Talkity-Talk Radio*	"Professor" Peter Schickele, *P.D.Q. Bach: Music for an Awful Lot of Winds & Percussion*	George Carlin, *Jammin' in New York*
Classical Album	Leonard Bernstein, conductor, London Symphony Orchestra (Solos: Hadley, Anderson, Ludwig, Green, Gedda, Jones), *Bernstein: Candide*	Leonard Bernstein, conductor, Berlin Philharmonic Orchestra, *Mahler: Symphony No. 9*	Pierre Boulez, conductor, Chicago Symphony Orchestra and Chorus; John Alen John Tomlinson, baritone, *Bartók: The Wooden Prince & C*
Classical Orchestral Performance	Daniel Barenboim, conductor, Chicago Symphony Orchestra, *Corigliano: Symphony No. 1*	Leonard Bernstein, conductor, Berlin Philharmonic Orchestra, *Mahler: Symphony No. 9*	Pierre Boulez, conductor, Chicago Symphony, *Bartók: The Wooden Prince*
Opera Recording	James Levine, conductor, Metropolitan Opera Orchestra and Chorus (Solos: Behrens, Studer, Schwarz, Goldberg, Weikl, Wlaschiha, Salminen), *Wagner: Götterdämmerung*	Georg Solti conductor, Vienna Philharmonic (Solos: Domingo, Varady, Van Dam, Behrens, Runkel, Jo), *R. Strauss: Die Frau Ohne Schatten*	John Nelson, conductor, English Chamber Orchestra and Ambrosian Opera Chorus (Solos: Battle, Horne, Ramey, Aler, McNair, Chance, Mackie, Doss); *Handel: Semele*
Chamber Music Performance	Isaac Stern and Jamie Laredo, violins; Yo-Yo Ma, cello; Emanuel Ax, piano, *Brahms: Piano Quartets*	Yo-Yo Ma, cello; Emanuel Ax, piano, *Brahms: Sonatas for Cello & Piano*	Anne-Sophie Mutter, violin, and James Levine, conductor, Chicago Symphony, *Berg: Violoin Concerto/Rihm: Time Chant*

	1994	1995	1996
Record of the Year	Sheryl Crow, "All I Wanna Do"	Seal, "Kiss From a Rose"	Eric Clapton, "Change the World"
Album of the Year	Tony Bennett, *MTV Unplugged*	Alanis Morissette, *Jagged Little Pill*	Celine Dion, *Falling Into You*
Song of the Year	Bruce Springsteen, "Streets of Philadelphia"	Seal, "Kiss From a Rose"	Gordon Kennedy, Wayne Kirkpatrick & Tommy Sims, "Change the World"
Pop Vocal, Female	Sheryl Crow, "All I Wanna Do"	Annie Lennox, "No More 'I Love You's' "	Toni Braxton, "Un-Break My Heart"
Pop Vocal, Male	Elton John, "Can You Feel the Love Tonight"	Seal, "Kiss From a Rose"	Eric Clapton, "Change the World"
Rock Vocal, Female	Melissa Etheridge, "Come to My Window"	Alanis Morissette, "You Oughta Know"	Sheryl Crow, "If It Makes You Happy"
Rock Vocal, Male	Bruce Springsteen, "Streets of Philadelphia"	Tom Petty, "You Don't Know How It Feels"	Beck, "Where It's At"
Rock Song/ Rock Vocal Performance, Solo	Bruce Springsteen, "Streets of Philadelphia"	Glen Ballard and Alanis Morissette, "You Oughta Know"	Tracy Chapman, "Give Me One Reason"
New Artist	Sheryl Crow	Hootie & The Blowfish	LeAnn Rimes
Pop Vocal, Duo or Group with Vocal	All-4-One, "I Swear"	Hootie & The Blowfish, "Let Her Cry"	The Beatles, "Free As a Bird"
Rock Performance, Duo or Group with Vocal	Aerosmith, "Crazy"	Blues Traveler, "Run-Around"	Dave Matthews Band, "So Much To Say"
New Age Recording	Paul Winter, "Prayer for the Wild Thing"	George Winston, *Forest*	Enya, *The Memory of Trees*
Hard Rock	Soundgarden, "Black Hole Sun"	Pearl Jam, "Spin the Black Circle"	The Smashing Pumpkins, "Bullet with Butterfly Wings"
Metal	Soundgarden, "Spoonman"	Nine Inch Nails, "Happiness in Slavery"	Rage Against the Machine, "Tire Me"
Alternative	Green Day, *Dookie*	Nirvana, *MTV Unplugged in New York*	Beck, *Odelay*
Rap Performance, Solo	Queen Latifah, "U.N.I.T.Y."	Coolio, "Gangsta's Paradise"	L.L. Cool J, "Hey Lover"
Rap Performance by a Duo or Group	Salt-N-Pepa, "None of Your Business"	Method Man Featuring Mary J. Blige, "I'll Be There for You"/ "You're All I Need to Get By"	Bone Thugs-N-Harmony, "Tha Crossroads"
Rhythm and Blues Song	Babyface, "I'll Make Love to You"	Stevie Wonder, "For Your Love"	Babyface, "Exhale (Shoop Shoop)"
R&B Vocal, Female	Toni Braxton, "Breathe Again"	Anita Baker, "I Apologize"	Toni Braxton, "You're Makin' Me High"
R&B Vocal, Male	Babyface, "When Can I See You"	Stevie Wonder, "For Your Love"	Luther Vandross, "Your Secret Love"
R&B Duo or Group with Vocal	Boyz II Men, "I'll Make Love to You"	TLC, "Creep"	The Fugees, "Killing Me Softly"
Country Song	Gary Baker and Frank J. Myers, "I Swear"	Vince Gill, "Go Rest High on That Mountain"	Bill Mack, "Blue"
Country Vocal, Female	Mary Chapin Carpenter, "Shut Up and Kiss Me"	Alison Krauss, "Baby, Now That I've Found You"	LeAnn Rimes, "Blue"
Country Vocal, Male	Vince Gill, "When Love Finds You"	Vince Gill, "Go Rest High on That Mountain"	Vince Gill, "Worlds Apart"

	1994	1995	1996
Country Performance, Duo or Group with Vocal	Asleep at the Wheel with Lyle Lovett, "Blues for Dixie"	The Mavericks, "Here Comes the Rain"	Brooks & Dunn, "My Maria"
Country Vocal, Collaboration	Aaron Neville and Trisha Yearwood, "I Fall to Pieces"	Shenandoah & Alison Krauss, "Somewhere in the Vicinity of the Heart"	Vince Gill featuring Alison Krauss & Union Station, "High Lonesome Sound"
Traditional Blues Recording	Eric Clapton, *From the Cradle*	John Lee Hooker, *Chill Out*	James Cotton, *Deep in the Blues*
Contemporary Blues	Pops Staples, *Father Father*	Buddy Guy, *Slippin' In*	Keb' Mo', *Just Like You*
Reggae Recording	Bunny Wailer, *Crucial! Roots Classics*	Shaggy, *Boombastic*	Bunny Wailer, *Hall of Fame—A Tribute to Bob Marley's 50th Anniversary*
Jazz, Soloist	Benny Carter, "Prelude to a Kiss"	Lena Horne, *An Evening With Lena Horne* (vocals); Michael Brecker, *Impressions* (instrumental)	Cassandra Wilson, *New Moon Daughter* (vocals); Michael Brecker, "Cabin Fever" (instrumental)
Jazz, Group/ Jazz, Instrumental Performance, Individual or Group	Ron Carter, Herbie Hancock, Wallace Roney, Wayne Shorter & Tony Williams, *A Tribute to Miles*	McCoy Tyner Trio Featuring Michael Brecker, *Infinity*	Michael Brecker, *Tales from the Hudson*
Jazz, Big Band/ Large Ensemble Performance	McCoy Tyner Big Band, *Journey*	GRP All-Star Big Band & Tom Scott, "All Blues"	Count Basie Orchestra (with The New York Voices), *Live at Manchester Craftsmen's Guild*
Contemporary Jazz Performance	—	Pat Metheny Group, *We Live Here*	Wayne Shorter, *High Life*
Gospel Performance, Duo, Group, Choir or Chorus	The Thompson Community Singers, Rev. Milton Brunson, choir director, *Through God's Eyes* and The Love Fellowship Crusade Choir, Hezekiah Walker, choir director, *Live in Atlanta at Morehouse College* (tie)	The Brooklyn Tabernacle Choir, *Praise Him...Live!*	Shirley Caesar's Outreach Convention Choir, *Just a Word*
Traditional Folk Recording	Bob Dylan, *World Gone Wrong*	Ramblin' Jack Elliott, *South Coast*	Pete Seeger, *Pete*
Contemporary Folk Recording	Johnny Cash, *American Recordings*	Emmylou Harris, *Wrecking Ball*	Bruce Springsteen, *The Ghost of Tom Joad*
Cast Show Album	*Passion*	*Smokey Joe's Cafe—The Songs of Leiber and Stoller*	*Riverdance*
Comedy Recording	Sam Kinison, *Live From Hell*	Jonathan Winters, *Crank Calls*	Al Franken, *Rush Limbaugh Is a Big Fat Idiot*
Classical Album	Pierre Boulez, conductor, Chicago Symphony Orchestra, *Bartok: Concerto for Orch.; Four Orchestral Pieces, Op. 12*	Pierre Boulez, conductor, Cleveland Orchestra and Chorus, *Debussy: La Mer; Nocturnes; Jeux, etc.*	Leonard Slatkin, conductor, various artists, *Corigliano: Of Rage and Remembrance*
Classical Orchestral Performance	Pierre Boulez, conductor, Chicago Symphony Orchestra, *Bartok: Concerto for Orch.; Four Orchestral Pieces, Op. 12*	Pierre Boulez, conductor, Cleveland Orchestra and Chorus, *Debussy: La Mer; Nocturnes; Jeux, etc.*	Michael Tilson Thomas, conductor, San Francisco Symphony, *Prokofiev: Romeo and Juliet (Scenes from the Ballet)*
Opera Recording	Kent Nagano, conductor, Orchestra and Chorus of Opera de Lyon (Solos: Cheryl Struder, Jerry Hadley, Samuel Ramey, Kenn Chester), *Floyd: Susannah*	Charles Dutoit, conductor, Montreal Symphony Orchestra & Chorus, *Berlioz: Les Troyens*	Richard Hickox, conductor, Opera London, London Symphony Chorus, City of London Sinfonia (Solos: Philip Langridge, Alan Opie, Janice Watson), *Britten: Peter Grimes*
Chamber Music Performance	Daniel Barenboim, piano; Dale Clevenger, horn; Larry Combs, clarinet (Chicago Symphony), Daniele Damiano, bassoon; Hansjorg Schellenberger, oboe (Berlin Philharmonic), *Beethoven/Mozart: Quintets*	Emanuel Ax, piano; Yo-Yo Ma, cello; Richard Stoltzman, clarinet, *Brahms/Beethoven/Mozart: Clarinet Trios*	Cleveland Quartet, "Corigliano: String Quartet"

THE COUNTRY MUSIC ASSOCIATION AWARDS

	1967	1968	1969
Entertainer	Eddy Arnold	Glen Campbell	Johnny Cash
Song	Dallas Frazier, "There Goes My Everything"	Bobby Russell, "Honey"	Bob Ferguson, "Carroll County Accident"
Female Vocalist	Loretta Lynn	Tammy Wynette	Tammy Wynette
Male Vocalist	Jack Greene	Glen Campbell	Johnny Cash
Album	Jack Greene, *There Goes My Everything*	Johnny Cash, *Johnny Cash at Folsom Prison*	Johnny Cash, *Johnny Cash at San Quentin Prison*
Single	Jack Greene, "There Goes My Everything"	Jeannie C. Riley, "Harper Valley P.T.A."	Johnny Cash, "A Boy Named Sue"
Vocal Group	The Stoneman Family	Porter Wagoner and Dolly Parton	Johnny Cash and June Carter
Musician	Chet Atkins	Chet Atkins	Chet Atkins

	1970	1971	1972
Entertainer	Merle Haggard	Charley Pride	Loretta Lynn
Song	Kris Kristofferson, "Sunday Morning Coming Down"	Freddie Hart, "Easy Loving"	Freddie Hart, "Easy Loving"
Female Vocalist	Tammy Wynette	Lynn Anderson	Loretta Lynn
Male Vocalist	Merle Haggard	Charley Pride	Charley Pride
Album	Merle Haggard, *Okie from Muskogee*	Ray Price, *I Won't Mention It Again*	Merle Haggard, *Let Me Tell You About a Song*
Single	Merle Haggard, "Okie From Muskogee"	Sammi Smith, "Help Me Make It Through the Night"	Donna Fargo, "The Happiest Girl in the Whole U.S.A."
Vocal Group	The Glaser Brother	The Osborne Brothers	The Statler Brothers
Vocal Duo	Porter Wagoner and Dolly Parton	Porter Wagoner and Dolly Parton	Conway Twitty and Loretta Lynn
Musician	Jerry Reed	Jerry Reed	Charlie McCoy

QUEENS OF COUNTRY

Critically lauded and popularly applauded, women crooners were and are fundamental to the success of country music. Here are the genre's leading ladies:

Mary Chapin Carpenter
With over eight million albums sold worldwide, five Grammy Awards and two CMA Awards, Carpenter is one of the preeminent singer-songwriters in the business.

Deana Carter
The child of session-guitarist extraordinaire Fred Carter Jr. sings with a frankness that transforms her music into profound poetry.

Patsy Cline
Though she was killed in a 1963 plane crash at age 30, her *Greatest Hits* went multiplatinum in 1992.

Patty Loveless
Patty's music is about emotion. She exposes her rawest nerves, bruises, and doubts for the sake of reaching the core of her songs.

Reba McEntire
As the seller of more than 35 million records, the star of country music's greatest roadshow, and five triple platinum albums to her credit, Reba is the most successful female country star in history.

LeAnn Rimes
The Patsy Cline reincarnation was the youngest singer, at age 13, to debut in the country chart's Top 50.

Kitty Wells
Country's first major female star; she was the first woman to have a No. 1 country single in 1952 with the song "It Wasn't God Who Made Honky Tonk Angels."

Trisha Yearwood
One of music's finest interpretive vocalists, Trisha worked her way up from an intern to multiple platinum-selling albums.

	1973	1974	1975
Entertainer	Roy Clark	Charlie Rich	John Denver
Song	Kenny O'Dell, "Behind Closed Doors"	Don Wayne, "Country Bumpkin"	John Denver, "Back Home Again"
Female Vocalist	Loretta Lynn	Olivia Newton-John	Dolly Parton
Male Vocalist	Charlie Rich	Ronnie Milsap	Waylon Jennings
Album	Charlie Rich, *Behind Closed Doors*	Charlie Rich, *A Very Special Love Song*	Ronnie Milsap, *A Legend in My Time*
Single	Charlie Rich, "Behind Closed Doors"	Cal Smith, "Country Bumpkin"	Freddy Fender, "Before the Next Teardrop Falls"
Vocal Group	The Statler Brothers	The Statler Brothers	The Statler Brothers
Vocal Duo	Conway Twitty and Loretta Lynn	Conway Twitty and Loretta Lynn	Conway Twitty and Loretta Lynn
Musician	Charlie McCoy	Don Rich	Johnny Gimble

	1976	1977	1978
Entertainer	Mel Tillis	Ronnie Milsap	Dolly Parton
Song	Larry Weiss, "Rhinestone Cowboy"	Roger Bowling & Hal Bynum, "Lucille"	Richard Leigh, "Don't It Make My Brown Eyes Blue"
Female Vocalist	Dolly Parton	Crystal Gayle	Crystal Gayle
Male Vocalist	Ronnie Milsap	Ronnie Milsap	Don Williams
Album	Waylon Jennings, Willie Nelson, Tompall Glaser, Jessi Colter, *Wanted—The Outlaws*	Ronnie Milsap, *Ronnie Milsap Live*	Ronnie Milsap, *It Was Almost Like a Song*
Single	Waylon Jennings & Willie Nelson, "Good Hearted Woman"	Kenny Rogers, "Lucille"	The Kendalls, "Heaven's Just a Sin Away"
Vocal Group	The Statler Brothers	The Statler Brothers	The Oak Ridge Boys
Vocal Duo	Waylon Jennings & Willie Nelson	Jim Ed Brown & Helen Cornelius	Kenny Rogers and Dottie West
Musician	Hargus "Pig" Robbins	Roy Clark	Roy Clark

	1979	1980	1981
Entertainer	Willie Nelson	Barbara Mandrell	Barbara Mandrell
Song	Don Schlitz, "The Gambler"	Bobby Braddock & Curly Putman, "He Stopped Loving Her Today"	Bobby Braddock & Curly Putman, "He Stopped Loving Her Today"
Female Vocalist	Barbara Mandrell	Emmylou Harris	Barbara Mandrell
Male Vocalist	Kenny Rogers	George Jones	George Jones
Album	Kenny Rogers, *The Gambler*	Original Motion Picture Soundtrack, *Coal Miner's Daughter*	Don Williams, *I Believe in You*
Single	Charlie Daniels Band, "The Devil Went Down to Georgia"	George Jones, "He Stopped Loving Her Today"	Oak Ridge Boys, "Elvira"
Vocal Group	The Statler Brothers	The Statler Brothers	Alabama
Horizon Award	—	—	Terri Gibbs
Vocal Duo	Kenny Rogers and Dottie West	Moe Bandy and Joe Stampley	David Frizzell and Shelly West
Musician	Charlie Daniels	Roy Clark	Chet Atkins

	1982	1983	1984
Entertainer	Alabama	Alabama	Alabama
Song	Johnny Christopher, Wayne Carson, Mark James, "Always On My Mind"	Johnny Christopher, Wayne Carson, Mark James, "Always On My Mind"	Larry Henley, Jeff Silbar, "Wind Beneath My Wings"
Female Vocalist	Janie Fricke	Janie Fricke	Reba McEntire
Male Vocalist	Ricky Skaggs	Lee Greenwood	Lee Greenwood
Album	Willie Nelson, *Always on My Mind*	Alabama, *The Closer You Get*	Anne Murray, *A Little Good News*
Single	Willie Nelson, "Always on My Mind"	John Anderson, "Swingin' "	Anne Murray, "A Little Good News"
Vocal Group	Alabama	Alabama	The Statler Brothers
Horizon Award	Ricky Skaggs	John Anderson	The Judds
Vocal Duo	David Frizzell and Shelly West	Merle Haggard and Willie Nelson	Willie Nelson & Julio Iglesias
Musician	Chet Atkins	Chet Atkins	Chet Atkins

	1985	1986	1987
Entertainer	Ricky Skaggs	Reba McEntire	Hank Williams Jr.
Song	Lee Greenwood, "God Bless the USA"	Paul Overstreet, Don Schlitz, "On the Other Hand"	Paul Overstreet, Don Schlitz, "Forever and Ever, Amen"
Female Vocalist	Reba McEntire	Reba McEntire	Reba McEntire
Male Vocalist	George Strait	George Strait	Randy Travis
Album	George Strait, *Does Fort Worth Ever Cross Your Mind*	Ronnie Milsap, *Lost in the Fifties Tonight*	Randy Travis, *Always and Forever*
Single	The Judds, "Why Not Me"	Dan Seals, "Bop"	Randy Travis, "Forever and Ever, Amen"
Vocal Group	The Judds	The Judds	The Judds
Horizon Award	Sawyer Brown	Randy Travis	Holly Dunn
Vocal Duo	Anne Murray and Dave Loggins	Dan Seals and Marie Osmond	Ricky Skaggs and Sharon White
Musician	Chet Atkins	Johnny Gimble	Johnny Gimble
Music Video	Hank Williams Jr., *All My Rowdy Friends Are Comin' Over Tonight*	George Jones, *Who's Gonna Fill Their Shoes*	Hank Williams Jr., *My Name Is Bocephus*

	1988	1989	1990
Entertainer	Hank Williams Jr.	George Strait	George Strait
Song	K.T. Oslin, "80's Ladies"	Max D. Barnes, Vern Gosdin, "Chiseled in Stone"	Jon Vezner, Don Henry, "Where've You Been"
Female Vocalist	K.T. Oslin	Kathy Mattea	Kathy Mattea
Male Vocalist	Randy Travis	Ricky Van Shelton	Clint Black
Album	Hank Williams Jr., *Born to Boogie*	Nitty Gritty Dirt Band, *Will the Circle Be Unbroken, Vol. II*	Kentucky HeadHunters, *Pickin' on Nashville*
Single	Kathy Mattea, "Eighteen Wheels and a Dozen Roses"	Keith Whitley, "I'm No Stranger to the Rain"	Vince Gill, "When I Call Your Name"
Vocal Group	Highway 101	Highway 101	Kentucky HeadHunters
Vocal Event	Dolly Parton, Emmylou Harris, Linda Ronstadt, *Trio*	Hank Williams Jr., Hank Williams Sr.	Lorrie Morgan, Keith Whitley
Horizon Award	Ricky Van Shelton	Clint Black	Garth Brooks
Vocal Duo	The Judds	The Judds	The Judds
Musician	Chet Atkins	Johnny Gimble	Johnny Gimble
Music Video	—	Hank Williams Jr., Hank Williams Sr., *There's a Tear in My Beer*	Garth Brooks, *The Dance*

	1991	1992
Entertainer	Garth Brooks	Garth Brooks
Song	Vince Gill, Tim DuBois, "When I Call Your Name"	Vince Gill, Max D. Barnes, "Look at Us"
Female Vocalist	Tanya Tucker	Mary-Chapin Carpenter
Male Vocalist	Vince Gill	Vince Gill
Album	Garth Brooks, *No Fences*	Garth Brooks, *Ropin' the Wind*
Single	Garth Brooks, "Friends in Low Places"	Billy Ray Cyrus, "Achy Breaky Heart"
Vocal Group	Kentucky HeadHunters	Diamond Rio
Vocal Event	Mark O'Connor & The New Nashville Cats (featuring Vince Gill, Ricky Skaggs, and Steve Wariner)	Marty Stuart, Travis Tritt
Horizon Award	Travis Tritt	Suzy Bogguss
Vocal Duo	The Judds	Brooks & Dunn
Musician	Mark O'Connor	Mark O'Connor
Music Video	Garth Brooks, *The Thunder Rolls*	Alan Jackson, *Midnight in Montgomery*

	1993	1994
Entertainer	Vince Gill	Vince Gill
Song	Vince Gill, John Barlow Jarvis, "I Still Believe in You"	Alan Jackson, Jim McBride, "Chattahoochee"
Female Vocalist	Mary-Chapin Carpenter	Pam Tillis
Male Vocalist	Vince Gill	Vince Gill
Album	Vince Gill, *I Still Believe in You*	*Common Thread: The Songs of the Eagles*
Single	Alan Jackson, "Chattahoochee"	John Michael Montgomery, "I Swear"
Vocal Group	Diamond Rio	Diamond Rio
Vocal Event	George Jones with Vince Gill, Mark Chesnutt, Garth Brooks, Travis Tritt, Joe Diffie, Alan Jackson, Pam Tillis, T. Graham Brown, Patty Loveless, Clint Black, *I Don't Need Your Rockin' Chair*	Reba McEntire with Linda Davis, "Does He Love You"
Horizon Award	Mark Chesnutt	John Michael Montgomery
Vocal Duo	Brooks & Dunn	Brooks & Dunn
Musician	Mark O'Connor	Mark O'Connor
Music Video	Alan Jackson, *Chattahoochee*	Martina McBride, *Independence Day*

	1995	1996	1997
Entertainer of the Year	Alan Jackson	Brooks & Dunn	Garth Brooks
Song of the Year	Gretchen Peters, "Independence Day"	Vince Gill, "Go Rest High on That Mountain"	Matraca Berg and Gary Harrison, "Strawberry Wine"
Female Vocalist of the Year	Alison Krauss	Patty Loveless	Trisha Yearwood
Male Vocalist of the Year	Vince Gill	George Strait	George Strait
Album of the Year	Patty Loveless, *When Fallen Angels Fly*	George Strait, *Blue Clear Sky*	George Strait, *Carrying Your Love With Me*
Single of the Year	Alison Krauss and the Union Station, "When You Say Nothing at All"	George Strait, "Check Yes or No"	Deana Carter, "Strawberry Wine"
Vocal Group of the Year	The Mavericks	The Mavericks	Diamond Rio
Vocal Event of the Year	Shenandoah with Alison Krauss, "Somewhere in the Vicinity of the Heart"	Dolly Parton with Vince Gill, "I Will Always Love You"	Tim McGraw with Faith Hill, "It's Your Love"
Horizon Award	Alison Krauss	Bryan White	LeAnn Rimes
Vocal Duo of the Year	Brooks & Dunn	Brooks & Dunn	Brooks & Dunn
Musician of the Year	Mark O'Connor	Mark O'Connor	Brent Mason
Music Video of the Year	The Tractors, *Baby Likes to Rock It*	Junior Brown, *My Wife Thinks You're Dead*	Kathy Mattea, *455 Rocket*

PAGES

PICKS & PANS 1997

From the books you read cover to cover to the books that make you run for cover, PEOPLE's discerning critics read 'em and rated 'em. Picks marked with an asterisk are the cream of 1997's literary offerings.

***DENIAL**
Keith Ablow
A forensic psychiatrist helps track a killer while nursing his own frailties: using cocaine, gambling, and booze.

***A SLENDER THREAD**
Diane Ackerman
The astonishing, sensitive, and sharply observed account of one year the author spent answering phones for a suicide-prevention hotline.

MEDICINE MAN
Alice Adams
Adams's novel begins promisingly but soon derails into a predictable litany of doctor bashing. This *Medicine* doesn't go down well.

PROUD SPIRIT
Rosemary Altea
The popular British medium's conversations with the great beyond.

LAUGHTER'S GENTLE SOUL
Billy Altman
This biography of Robert Benchley, one of the more generous-spirited members of the 1920s celebrated Algonquin Round Table, is earnest and diligent, but not nearly as much fun as it ought to be.

YO!
Julia Alvarez
The book's fractured structure overshadows Alvarez's ability to capture the complexities of Dominican family life.

AN AFFAIR TO REMEMBER: THE REMARKABLE LOVE STORY OF KATHARINE HEPBURN AND SPENCER TRACY
Christopher Andersen
A moving reminder of how much damage grown-up romance can sustain, filled with moving anecdotes and gossipy details.

***ALIAS GRACE**
Margaret Atwood
The novel offers a gripping narrative combined with the author's characteristically acute psychological and social observations.

AS FRANCESCA
Martha Baer
Baer writes with a certain raw briskness. But like previous exercises in technosex, her sexcapade is flat. Details are left blank to mimic the anonymity of cyberspace, but the book mostly comes off as vague.

NAMING THE NEW WORLD
Calvin Baker
Baker spins a multigenerational saga about one African-American family's journey from preslavery to the present.

***LIVES OF THE MONSTER DOGS**
Kirsten Bakis
This poignant, mostly magnificent book inspires all sorts of wild wonderment about man's best friend. What do dogs think about? What would they say if they could talk? What if dogs were more like us?

BREAKING THE RULES
Laura Banks and Janette Barber
There's a laugh or two to be had, but not nearly enough to justify breaking Rule No. 1 regarding rushed-to-print parodies: Save your money and skim through them in the bookstore.

THE UNTOUCHABLE
John Banville
What makes a spy? This thriller engagingly searches for fictional answers among the real English university pals who rose to political and cultural power while spying for the U.S.S.R. A poetic and deeply affecting portrait of arrogance born of privilege.

***COLD CASE**
Linda Barnes
Some of the twists prove a tad melodramatic, but with a stylish pro like Barnes doing the plotting, this chilling case won't leave you cold.

LADYFINGERS & NUN'S TUMMIES: A LIGHTHEARTED LOOK AT HOW FOODS GOT THEIR NAMES
Martha Barnette
After reading Martha Barnette's amusing new book, listening to a waiter's recitation of the day's specials will never be the same.

***RISING TIDE: THE GREAT MISSISSIPPI FLOOD OF 1927 AND HOW IT CHANGED AMERICA**
John M. Barry
Readers may grow impatient with the exhaustive detail, but Barry's book is a valuable study of the ways in which man and nature conspire to wreak damage that lasts for generations.

OUT OF BODY
Thomas Baum
How can a murder suspect explain his increasingly vivid sensation of traveling outside his body? A chilling, twilight-zone thriller, subtle enough to seduce even those who normally shun the paranormal.

STEVEN SPIELBERG: THE UNAUTHORIZED BIOGRAPHY
John Baxter
Fragmented and far from comprehensive.

WITHOUT LYING DOWN: FRANCES MARION AND THE POWERFUL WOMEN OF EARLY HOLLYWOOD
Cari Beauchamp
Though her portrait of Marion remains a bit sketchy, Beauchamp gives us a dense and panoramic view of the studio system, of early Hollywood society, and the importance of female friendships in that fascinating era—the old-girl network that sustained a group of creative women through the infancy of American film.

***JOY SCHOOL**
Elizabeth Berg
Berg once again manages to deliver a story that tugs at the heartstrings while largely avoiding canned sentiment.

1,003 GREAT THINGS ABOUT GETTING OLDER
Lisa Birnbach
The book is worth a few chuckles.

LOVE INVENTS US
Amy Bloom
The premise of this lyrical but flawed first novel: people are not only made for each other, but also made by each other.

BLUE GUIDE: FRANCE
Less a travel guide than an architectural lesson, this brick-like volume offers no hints on where to eat or stay but drones on in numbing detail about every historic pile of bricks.

***MIDWIVES**
Chris Bohjalian
A superbly crafted and astonishingly powerful novel, this small-town drama will thrill readers who cherish their worn copies of *To Kill a Mockingbird.*

ANYTHING YOUR LITTLE HEART DESIRES: AN AMERICAN FAMILY STORY
Patricia Bosworth
This bittersweet tribute to the author's father explores the chasm between public success and private failure, between political achievement and domestic disaster.

ROUGH MIX
Jimmy Bowen and Jim Jerome
The deliciously gossipy memoir of a music-industry boss, whose ego rivals his knack for choosing hits.

BEFORE I WAKE
Eric Bowman
An ingeniously constructed murder mystery, filled with fascinating forensic details and mesmerizing cop/killer mind games.

***YAK BUTTER AND BLACK TEA**
Wade Brackenbury
Brackenbury lacks the descriptive powers and cultural insights of the great travel writers. But his straightforward, unpretentious narrative allows us to accompany him vicariously on a journey that will fascinate—and terrify—even the bravest armchair traveler.

FURTHER LANE
James Brady
A dish-seeking journalist in exclusive East Hampton seeks a murderer. This romp is spiced with delicious insider references and celebrity cameos.

***VOWS: WEDDINGS OF THE NINETIES FROM THE NEW YORK TIMES**
Lois Smith Brady with photographs by Edward Keating
Brady's columns read like short stories—true romance stories, to be exact. Even those who resolutely don't cry at weddings will be charmed and moved.

THE FIRST $20 MILLION IS ALWAYS THE HARDEST
Po Bronson
This Silicon Valley black comedy offers plenty of vanities, but no bonfire.

ALTERED STATES
Anita Brookner
Though impressive for its craftsmanship, the novel is unremittingly dark, turning the thrill of romance into a shudder.

***FATHER AND SON**
Larry Brown
The book succeeds as a thriller, but it's also a compelling meditation on father-son relationships. Brown shows us that the powerful bond between men and their boys can thrive on love or, in its absence, turn dangerously to ashes.

FAT TUESDAY
Sandra Brown
With deft, breakneck pacing, heaping doses of local color, and a story that gets more intriguing with every page, Brown turns an oft-trod premise into a surprisingly affecting thriller.

WRY MARTINIS
Christopher Buckley
Knock back *Wry Martinis* all at once and you'll end up woozy and regretful. Best to savor it. Small sips will make you feel civilized and smart and just a little giddy—sort of like Chris Buckley himself.

***CIMARRON ROSE**
James Lee Burke
To defend his teenaged stepson from murder charges, an abusive stepfather hires a troubled attorney—the boy's biological father—and ignites a tinderbox of family secrets, class hatred, and criminal psychosis.

***TABLOID DREAMS**
Robert Olen Butler
An inventive and surprisingly straight-faced collection of short stories that takes an imaginative leap into the tales that could lie behind the attention-grabbing headlines.

WRITERS HARVEST
edited by Ethan Canin
This collection of new short fiction is a very politically correct patchwork. Still, it's an engaging assortment that touches upon virtually all of life's tidemarks.

BRAIN DROPPINGS
George Carlin
No matter how funny a joke is, reading it isn't nearly as enjoyable an experience as hearing it expertly told.

THE GENESIS CODE
John Case
Sharply written with great sense of style and suspense, despite annoying attempts at symbolism.

THE PROJECT
Zev Chafets
A well-paced thriller about the first Jewish president's bid for re-election.

MONKEY KING
Patricia Chao
Though the story, which unfolds both forward and backward in time, is at points too elliptical, the pace is quick, the writing artful. Readers will hope to hear from Chao again.

***KILLING FLOOR**
Lee Child
From its jolting opening scene to its fiery final confrontation, this suspenseful actioner is irresistible.

PRETEND YOU DON'T SEE HER
Mary Higgins Clark
Although Clark is known for her multilayered plots, this is perhaps her most convoluted yet, with more than a few incredible twists and implausible turns.

***3001: THE FINAL ODYSSEY**
Arthur C. Clarke
Clarke, one of the last surviving grand masters of science fiction, continues to dazzle with his meticulously detailed, and scientifically plausible, vision of mankind's future.

COMEDY CENTRAL: THE ESSENTIAL GUIDE TO COMEDY
Christopher Claro and Julie Klam
Thoughtfully designed to help laugh-starved readers separate the comedic wheat from the chaff.

THE MORAL INTELLIGENCE OF CHILDREN
Robert Coles
Intelligent, accessible, and compelling, the book effectively captures the challenge, for children and parents alike, of struggling with life's ironies and ambiguities.

WILLIE: RAISING AND LOVING A CHILD WITH ATTENTION DEFICIT DISORDER
Ann Colin
Colin skillfully conveys the isolation, uncertainty, and pressures that affect so many parents as they struggle to do what's right for their children.

VENDETTA: LUCKY'S REVENGE
Jackie Collins
Embarrassing to pick up, impossible to put down. It's a miniseries waiting to happen.

TRUNK MUSIC
Michael Connelly
For those seeking the kind of action that takes more turns than a roulette wheel, this jazzy joyride is a sure bet.

WHAT GIRLS LEARN
Karin Cook
Cook skillfully captures the stumbling steps young girls take toward adulthood and describes the need they have for mothers during these often painful years.

HORNET'S NEST
Patricia Cornwell
With numerous flaws, it's unlikely that *Hornet's Nest* will create the usual Cornwell buzz.

THE KILLING SEASON
Miles Corwin
An engaging nonfiction account of life and death in a tough urban homicide department.

INDIGO SLAM
Robert Crais
A detective story starring a cool, wise-guy L.A. private eye, *Slam* is filled with suspenseful action, though some of the writer's distinctive snap is missing.

***WALTER CRONKITE: A REPORTER'S LIFE**
Walter Cronkite
Cronkite has forsaken all pretense of objectivity in a spirited memoir about covering the tragicomic 20th century. National institutions aren't supposed to have such fun—or produce such an entertaining book.

***THE COLLECTED STORIES**
Amanda Cross
The 10 tales here are as tonic as a palate-cleansing sorbet.

THE WOMAN WHO SPILLED WORDS ALL OVER HERSELF
Rosemary Daniell
The Southern poet's memoir-as-writing-manual proves just how earthy, inspiring, and even rapturous her take on the creative process can be.

***THE BONE COLLECTOR**
Jeffery Deaver
Mixing fascinating forensics, quirky characters, and stunning plot surprises, Deaver gives new meaning to the phrase "chilled to the bone."

THE COMPLETE GEEK (AN OPERATING MANUAL)
by Johnny Deep, illustrated by Bruce Tinsley
A misguided effort to define—and elevate—the geek beast.

THE MISTRESS OF SPICES
Chitra Banerjee Divakaruni
In this wry, sometimes elliptical first novel, a story of Indian immigrants in America unfolds as an extraordinary fairy tale of portents and promises, desires and destiny.

COMMON CARNAGE
Stephen Dobyns
Two owls ruminate about philosophy while disemboweling a mouse; a man gives his wife a bottle fished from a dumpster. These dark, humorous poems address the difficulty of living moral, conscious lives in a world that is both flawed and violent.

THE MOTHER-DAUGHTER BOOK CLUB
Shireen Dodson with Teresa Barker
Practical suggestions for ways mothers and daughters can read together, presented in a down-to-earth, commonsensical manner.

MOTHER LOVE
Rita Dove
In these insightful sonnets, a former poet laureate examines the bonds between mothers and daughters.

THE BIBLE CODE
Michael Drosnin
An astonishing computer program uncovers linked groups of letters concealed in biblical texts that spell out eerily accurate predictions.

***LOVE WARPS THE MIND A LITTLE**
John Dufresne
Dufresne paints no fancy pictures, but he succeeds in depicting life as it is really lived.

***MONSTER**
John Gregory Dunne
Dunne's scathing—and funny—recollections cast piercing light on the curious rituals and practices of corporate Hollywood.

A CUP OF TEA
Amy Ephron
With deceptive simplicity and appealingly uncluttered prose, Ephron weaves a morality tale that moves inexorably from mannered start to jarring finish.

***NEVER STREET**
Loren D. Estleman
About the only thing as satisfying as the rococo plot twists are

the writer's equally graceful turns of phrase.

***LIKELY TO DIE**
Linda Fairstein
Step aside, Marple and Millhone: Here comes sleek and single Manhattan sex-crimes prosecutor Alexandra Cooper in a whopping whodunit.

AN INDEPENDENT WOMAN
Howard Fast
The sixth and final volume of Fast's century-long California family saga is eventful and well-crafted, enlivened by a large and diverse cast of characters and a keen understanding of the dynamics of a complex extended family.

TOMBSTONES
Gregg Felsen
Though filled with macabre illuminating death trivia, this book turns out to be an uplifting tribute to the human spirit, despite its undeniably grave subject matter.

FIELDING'S EUROPEAN CRUISES
Ship-by-ship charts together with brief reports-of-call on topics from hiking to Vikings, reveal that—surprise!—nicer trips cost more.

***STAR WARS* CHRONICLES**
Deborah Fine and Aeon Inc
An oversize, lushly illustrated, trivia-laden tome—the Imperial Star Destroyer of coffee-table books.

THE COLLECTOR COLLECTOR
Tibor Fischer
A daring novel in which inanimate objects take their revenge: a high-priced piece of ancient pottery narrates the surreal, comedic story.

THE OXFORD MARK TWAIN
edited by Shelley Fishkin
Samuel Clemens's complete works in a set of 29 illustrated volumes, introduced by such Twainiacs as Toni Morrison, Roy Blount Jr., and Walter Mosley.

THE BLUE FLOWER
Penelope Fitzgerald
This book leaves you with more than just a soggy hankie. You learn that love is stranger—and sturdier—than anyone might have guessed.

WOMEN WITH MEN
Richard Ford
A master of the finely observed detail, Ford renders his fictional terrain with such power that one is quickly seduced—even if the action sometimes feels forced and two of the protagonists are annoyingly solipsistic.

ALL FALL DOWN
Zachary Alan Fox
A single mother and cop matches wits with a kidnapper.

FAITH AND TREASON
Antonia Fraser
Combining her skills as a novelist with those of historian, Fraser uses a foiled Catholic conspiracy to blow up James I in 1605 to focus on the penalties—fines, imprisonment, sometimes death—suffered by Catholics in early Jacobean England.

COLD MOUNTAIN
Charles Frazier
A stirring Civil War tale that, like Homer's *Odyssey*, is the story of a soldier slowly making his way home from war to the woman he left behind.

AT LARGE: THE STRANGE CASE OF THE WORLD'S BIGGEST INTERNET INVASION
David H. Freedman and Charles C. Mann
A genuinely intriguing and oddly moving true-life whodunit about the most successful computer cracker in history.

TRUE LOVE
Stories told to and by Robert Fulghum
Caution: This book will cause the reader to have an insatiable urge to strangle a small pet.

BECAUSE THEY WANTED TO
Mary Gaitskill
Gaitskill plumbs the psyches of people who think they're acting only out of want and not need.

ICEBREAKER: THE AUTOBIOGRAPHY OF RUDY GALINDO
Rudy Galindo with Eric Marcus
The giddy and breathless story of the figure skater's personal tragedies and setbacks.

***THE COLLECTED STORIES OF MAVIS GALLANT**
Mavis Gallant
Gallant's stories are shifting blends of the dark and the comic—each a precise, almost clinical exploration of the joy, fear, hope, and indifference that fill her characters' souls.

***THE BEACH**
Alex Garland
Generation X meets *Lord of the Flies* in this ripping good adventure yarn.

***THIRTEEN WAYS OF LOOKING AT A BLACK MAN**
Henry Louis Gates Jr.
Profiling eight African-American men, this collection asks critical questions about this diverse group's common ground.

DECEPTION ON HIS MIND
Elizabeth George
This ninth volume of George's

mystery series conveys its suspects' wrenching stories with exceptional grace.

MEADOWLANDS
Louise Glück
At once mythic and contemporary, chatty and intense, this cycle of poems offers a wry, fresh take on the long-delayed reunion of Penelope and Odysseus—and a portrait of a modern marriage on the edge of dissolution.

HIS NAME IS RON: OUR SEARCH FOR JUSTICE
The Family of Ronald Goldman, with William and Marilyn Hoffer
Especially moving when describing the ordinary rituals of grief, the Goldmans recount their ordeal all the way through the civil trial verdict.

THE MANSION ON THE HILL
Fred Goodman
After reading this book, you still won't be happy paying $15.98 for that new CD, but at least you'll understand where the money is going

***THERE AND GONE**
Photographs by John Gossage
Gossage finds triggers for the complex emotions that lurk within his tense and often startling compositions.

NO BRAKES
Lois Gould
This slim book revs with eroticism and suspense, lyrical prose, and spectral characters that linger in the imagination.

THE DREAM OF THE UNIFIED FIELD
Jorie Graham
These dense, philosophical, rewarding poems push—with a transfixed intensity—against the limits of language and experience to explore the uneasy transactions between the self and the world.

MY DROWNING
Jim Grimsley
The lack of complexity and individualizing detail makes this book more like a catalog of woes than a fully realized work of art.

THE PARTNER
John Grisham
A deliciously complicated tale of legal intrigue and life on the lam.

ONE MAN'S AMERICA
Henry Grunwald
There's enough material here for many thoughtful books, and one hopes that Grunwald will narrow his scope and write them.

NEW YEAR'S EVE
Lisa Grunwald
This book is like a New Year's resolution—good while it lasts, but it doesn't stick with you for long.

THE LAST PARTY
Anthony Haden-Guest
An evocative description of the rise and fall of Studio 54, a converted TV studio turned into a sanctum of unrivaled revelry.

RED SKY AT NIGHT
James W. Hall
A first-rate thriller in which the action hero is confined to a wheelchair throughout the bulk of the book.

***HIGH LONESOME**
Barry Hannah
Hannah captures the patois of the swamp and palmetto lands but wisely lets his own voice resonate the loudest. Bold and original, he explores the lives of his eccentrics without exploiting them.

OUR WAR: WHAT WE DID IN VIETNAM AND WHAT IT DID TO US
David Harris
Harris's fervor is admirable, but his analysis stays on the surface.

THE KISS
Kathryn Harrison
For readers willing to accompany her across some difficult terrain, Harrison offers a haunting journey not easily forgotten.

SUN UNDER WOOD
Robert Hass
Images from nature, from religion, and from art are interwoven with personal history to illuminate the meaning of language, of happiness, and of the ties that bind us to family, lovers, and friends.

DO THE WINDOWS OPEN?
Julie Hecht
Nine comic private monologues that are a mix of deadpan wit at despair and fleeting moments of joy.

PRINCESS CHARMING
Jane Heller
A seamless read that blends romance, mystery, and wit.

***TUMBLE HOME**
Amy Hempel
Seven short stories and a bravely hopeful novella about a woman recovering from an emotional

breakdown; Hempel makes haunting bits of beauty out of motley scraps.

SWIMMING ACROSS THE HUDSON
Joshua Henkin
In a first novel of unusual grace and resonance, Henkin achieves a voice at once sweet and tormented.

THE REAR VIEW: A BRIEF AND ELEGANT HISTORY OF BOTTOMS THROUGH THE AGES
Jean-Luc Hennig
Hennig locates the history of our culture in an erotically and symbolically charged portion of female flesh.

JOYSTICK NATION
J. C. Herz
This witty treatise chronicles how deeply video games tap into our basic instincts and have become a part of our psyche.

NAKED CAME THE MANATEE
Carl Hiaasen et al.
Anyone who contends that truth is stranger than fiction has clearly not read this madcap crime farce, written in installments by 13 top Florida talents.

THE PRESIDENT'S DAUGHTER
Jack Higgins
Plenty of old-fashioned intrigue, thrilling chase scenes, and moral tough guys just on the edge of respectability.

GUILTY AS SIN
Tami Hoag
Hoag has thrown in too much, miring the reader in a multitude of plot lines.

THE WOMAN AND THE APE
Peter Hoeg
Hoeg manages to direct our attention to the mysterious qualities that define us as human.

THE MAGICIAN'S TALE
David Hunt
A murder mystery created with mesmerizing sleight of hand.

INSIGHT COMPACT GUIDES: LAS VEGAS
A nifty, well-illustrated booklet with useful advice on games, hotels, and shows.

***THE VIEW FROM HERE**
Brian Keith Jackson
Jackson crafts a 1950s Mississippi mother of five's odyssey from voicelessness to authority with daring, assigning much of the narrating duty to her unborn baby. The result, with nods to works by Alice Walker and Toni Morrison, is a triumph.

JUST AN ORDINARY DAY
Shirley Jackson
Jackson fans will be dismayed; new readers will wonder why her reputation has survived for so long.

LE DIVORCE
Diane Johnson
For the most part *Le Divorce* is le champagne cocktail with more than a *petit* kick.

LOS ALAMOS
Joseph Kanon
A murder mystery that vividly evokes the time and place of the atomic bomb's birth.

HOLE IN THE WATER
Robert Kearney
Compressing his tale of crime and punishment into 17 taut hours, first-time novelist Kearney stages some hold-your-breath suspense.

PAYBACK
Thomas Kelly
Part crime tale, part coming-of-age saga, this richly observed first novel is a supple blend of trade-union strife, family dysfunction, ethnic loyalty, and the grim toll of manual labor.

***THE BIG PICTURE**
Douglas Kennedy
While smoothly navigating the plot's many hairpin curves, Kennedy provides a thoughtful meditation about learning what really matters.

DEATH DUTY
Stephen Kimball
There are enough plot snafus and emotional dullness here to make a reader think this book was the product of a government agency.

L.A. BIZARRO! THE INSIDER'S GUIDE TO THE OBSCURE, THE ABSURD, AND THE PERVERSE IN LOS ANGELES
A fun, ribald compendium of the kitschy-kitschy cool.

CROOKED LITTLE HEART
Anne Lamott
In a sense, nothing much happens in this book, yet everything

does. But that's life, and Lamott deserves praise for telling it like it is.

THREE CHORDS AND THE TRUTH
Laurence Leamer
A behind-the-scenes picture of a mediocre and greedy country music industry.

BEST SEAT IN THE HOUSE
Spike Lee with Ralph Wiley
A jazzy yet serious examination of the filmmaker's deep-rooted devotion to basketball.

SACRED
Dennis Lehane
A dark maelstrom of pulp fiction, crackling with enough suspense to make for many a night's screams.

LET'S GO: THE BUDGET GUIDE TO EUROPE 1997
So authentically gritty with information about under-moneyed travel that you feel like taking a shower after reading it.

THE LIFE AND DEATH OF PETER SELLERS
Roger Lewis
An occasionally excessive biography that includes accounts of oddball and infantile behavior and an especially telling look at the actor's early years.

GOOD HAIR
Benilde Little
In his first novel, Little examines the caste consciousness of the black bourgeoisie.

HEAT WAVE
Penelope Lively
This satisfying novel tells the story of a divorced, middle-aged editor who believes her son-in-law is deceiving her daughter just as she was once betrayed.

LONDON: THE ROUGH GUIDE
Impressive research on architecture and history but poorly organized.

***THE SUNDAY MACARONI CLUB**
Steve Lopez
With al dente dialogue and a savory cast of engaging miscreants, *Macaroni* does for machine politics what Elmore Leonard's works do for unorganized crime.

***THE UNDERTAKING: LIFE STUDIES FROM THE DISMAL TRADE**
Thomas Lynch
A memoir lively with passing fancies, alternately sad and sadly funny, on a funeral director's encounters with death.

UNDERBOSS
Peter Maas
An absorbing, intimate, alluring tale of power, greed, and Mob intrigue that tells the story of Sammy "The Bull" Gravano's transformation from a murderous mobster into the federal informant who helped jail John Gotti.

THE GOSPEL ACCORDING TO THE SON
Norman Mailer
Written as Jesus's autobiography, this novel might have been much more fascinating, but Mailer demurs with uncharacteristic timidity in the face of his imposing protagonist.

PERFECT ANGEL
Seth Margolis
A fast-paced psychopathic killer thriller with a surprising twist at the end.

THE SECRET TO TENDER PIE
Mindy Marin
A quaint, handsome and high-cal collection of favorite recipes from grandmothers across America.

***NEWS OF A KIDNAPPING**
Gabriel García Márquez
Márquez abandons fiction for fact in this terse, journalistic account of the taking of 10 hostages in his native Colombia.

THE LIST
Steve Martini
A swiftly paced murder mystery that doubles as a critque of what the author sees as an increasingly superficial publishing industry.

***CHASING CEZANNE**
Peter Mayle
Easygoing wit and dead-on satire directed at a gallery of rich people and even richer food.

NOCTURNE
Ed McBain
Though at times overwhelmingly grim, the author showcases his unparalleled gift for showing the world through the weary eyes of cops.

STEVEN SPIELBERG: A BIOGRAPHY
Joseph McBride
Dishes without sneering and admires without fawning, but dries up once the director makes it big.

BEEN THERE, HAVEN'T DONE THAT: A VIRGIN'S MEMOIR
Tara McCarthy
Smug, dreary, and self-righteous.

SUSPICION
Robert McCrum
A deftly written tale of betrayal and guilt that chronicles the wildly different but inextricably linked lives of two brothers.

SKYLAR IN YANKEELAND
Gregory McDonald
A mystery saturated with a fine sense of social pretensions and dark humor.

A FACE AT THE WINDOW
Dennis McFarland
A phantasmagoric and frustrating focus on a fragile family and the way it's all but undone by a troubling clan of ghosts.

***ASYLUM**
Patrick McGrath
A beautifully written, morally complex, and utterly convincing tale of madness and violent death, desperate love, lust, and hatred.

BRIGHT ANGEL TIME
Martha McPhee
An original, peculiarly American story of a family unhappy in its own way, but the conclusion lacks conviction.

HUNGER POINT
Jillian Medoff
An affecting first novel that captures the angst of female Gen-X-ers as manifested in eating disorders, random sexual encounters, and a vague sense of hopelessness.

DREAMING OF HITLER: PASSIONS & PROVOCATIONS
Daphne Merkin
Though one can only marvel at the author's Olympic-caliber self-absorption, Merkin does have an extraordinary ability to write about embarrassing subjects with calm and clarity. Regrettably, though, the collection has an everything-and-the-kitchen-sink quality.

ANDREW WYETH: A SECRET LIFE
Richard Meryman
A soap opera sketch instead of a balanced portrait, this biography follows Wyeth's life from his youth living with a tyannical father to his marriage to his overbearing wife to a possible affair with neighbor Helga Testorf.

THE SISTAHS' RULES
Denene Millner
This guide—"Secrets for Meeting, Getting, and Keeping a Good Black Man"—is mainly commonsensical and often hilarious.

A DRY SPELL
Susie Moloney
Four years into a drought choking the life out of a town, a handsome, mysterious rainmaker drifts into town. A spellbinding start, a stock finish.

BEHIND THE OVAL OFFICE: WINNING THE PRESIDENCY IN THE NINETIES
Dick Morris
Aside from a brief explanation of Morris's affair with Sherry Rowlands, the book is pure, albeit fascinating, politics.

THE MOST SCENIC DRIVES IN AMERICA
Gorgeous photos of magnificent vistas make this a coffee-table book as well as a how-to, with maps and directions for those who enjoy spending days behind the wheel.

LEAVE IT TO ME
Bharati Mukherjee
Leave challenges us to sympathize with an angry young woman whose overwhelming sense of entitlement leads her to play judge and jury, devouring all in her quest for a new identity.

JANE AUSTEN: OBSTINATE HEART
Valerie Crosvenor Myer
Hollywood's favorite 19th-century novelist emerges as a stubborn iconoclast in this bracingly unsentimental biography.

MEDUSA'S CHILD
John J. Nance
An airborne thriller that snares the reader eearly and doesn't let go.

IMAGINING ROBERT
Jay Neugeboren
In this unflinching memoir the author details his younger brother's struggle to survive mental illness.

***SEA CHANGE**
Peter Nichols
An account of the author's thrilling attempt to cross the Atlantic in a 27-foot, engineless wooden sailboat, merged with captivating flashbacks of his recent ill-fated marriage.

DINOSAURS OF THE FLAMING CLIFFS
Michael Novacek
An action-packed account of pioneering road trips to the wasteland of Mongolia's Gobi Desert where the author discovered the mother of all animal graveyards.

POINT LAST SEEN
Hannah Nyala
The moving *Point* interweaves compelling accounts of Nyala's Mississippi upbringing and evolution into an expert missing-

persons tracker with harrowing stories of domestic violence.

MAN CRAZY
Joyce Carol Oates
A sexually burgeoning 21-year-old becomes the slave of a satanic biker-cult leader. The prose is mesmerizing and powerful, but the reader becomes numbed.

***KIDS ARE PUNNY**
compiled by Rosie O'Donnell
A sweet, chuckle-filled collection of jokes, puns, and riddles sent to Rosie's show by kids, at her request.

***THE GOOD BROTHER**
Chris Offutt
In this powerful first novel, the sound of regional voices—flat and spare in the Rockies, baroque in the Appalachians—makes the idea of community real to readers.

THE SPEED QUEEN
Stewart O'Nan
This fictional memoir of a woman facing execution offers a dexterous blend of suspense and social commentary.

THE PLEASURE OF YOUR COMPANY
Molly O'Neill
The *New York Times Magazine*'s food columnist whips up a cast of fictional characters who form a food group to discuss the basic problem of cooking in the '90s: so many dishes, not enough time.

MARTHA STEWART: JUST DESSERTS
Jerry Oppenheimer
A wicked debunking of Stewart's carefully crafted persona based on interviews with close to 400 on-the-record sources.

LOITERING WITH INTENT: THE APPRENTICE
Peter O'Toole
Crackling with the energy of a life lived to the hilt, the author revisits his years as a young student at London's Royal Academy of Dramatic Arts.

OUT & ABOUT GAY TRAVEL GUIDES: USA CITIES
This frank and funny guide has straight talk on where to go and how to get there for singles, couples, the shy, and the sociable, but the three male authors mostly write about outings for men.

PIMPS, WHORES AND WELFARE BRATS: THE STUNNING CONSERVATIVE TRANSFORMATION OF A FORMER WELFARE QUEEN
Star Parker with Lorenzo Benet
An autobiography-cum-manifesto narrating one woman's rise from public assistance to publisher of a magazine for Christian singles.

SILENT WITNESS
Richard North Patterson
In the hands of the psychological-thriller master, there are no easy or expected answers, and the finale is as startling as the bang of a gavel.

PARENTS' GUIDE TO HIKING & CAMPING
Or how to tell the theme parks to hit the road and detox your kids from Nintendo and TV, saving a bundle to boot.

THE CLUB DUMAS
Arturo Perez-Reverte
Pleasant enough entertainment for the reader who likes spooky thrills mixed with serious edification.

THE FIGURED WHEEL, NEW AND SELECTED POEMS 1966–1996
Robert Pinsky
Exuberantly thoughtful poems from our current poet laureate that mix memory and meditation, autobiography and history.

SECRECY
Belva Plain
Plain seems to breeze through her writing with no regard for literary flourishes. Instead, she delivers another compelling story about women coping with life's crises.

JACKIE BY JOSIE
Caroline Preston
A grad student unexpectedly discovers that elements of her own life subtly echo those of Jackie O's in this engrossing yet lighthearted drama.

MASON & DIXON
Thomas Pynchon
An imaginative epic that seeks to define today's America via yesterday's, with varying success.

BAD LAND
Jonathan Raban
Subtitled *An American Romance,* this engaging history of Montana, like many a love affair, is a story of dreams, deceit, and heartbreak.

FAMILY TRAVELS: AROUND THE WORLD IN 30 (OR SO) DAYS
Richard Reeves and family
The account of how a newspaper columnist and clan spent their summer vacation traversing the world.

LOCKED IN THE CABINET
Robert B. Reich
An appealing yet ultimately disheartening memoir of what the idealistic economist endured between his arrival in Washington and his resignation four years later.

MANOR HOUSE
Paige Rense
The editor-in-chief of *Architectural Digest* may know her chintz, but she's pretty chintzy on details to flesh out paper-thin characters.

LIVING THE DREAM
Dot Richardson with Don Yaeger
Though some of Richardson's motivational chat about playing your hardest seems a little familiar, the woman whose home run won America the '96 women's softball gold medal has penned an inspirational book.

TYCOON
Harold Robbins
A cartoonish sex-and-greed potboiler.

SANCTUARY
Nora Roberts
The successful portrayal of a family's slow healing.

FRUITFUL: A REAL MOTHER IN THE MODERN WORLD
Anne Roiphe
Captures the feeling of ambivalence that many women have about motherhood.

EVE'S APPLE
Jonathan Rosen
An impressive yet uneven first novel concerning a pair of twenty-something New York City neurotics.

ABUSE OF POWER
Nancy Taylor Rosenberg
The troubles of a rookie cop keep the tension high, but the maudlin finish may leave you more exhausted than enthralled.

SOME OF ME
Isabella Rossellini
Though at times coy and withholding, this memoir includes a private and loving view of her parents' lives.

AMERICAN PASTORAL
Philip Roth
A gripping, emotionally charged, and penetrating look at the domestic effects of Vietnam.

GOD OF SMALL THINGS
Arundhati Roy
A lushly romantic first novel with an occasionally feverish tone and shaky plot, but also filled with wondrous imagination.

THE ISLAND OF THE COLORBLIND
Oliver Sacks
Compassionate and awestruck portrait of an isolated Micronesian community afflicted with color-blindness.

THE NIGHT CREW
John Sanford
The story of a freelance news crew that cruises L.A. in search of carnage to tape and sell.

***ROUGH JUSTICE**
Lisa Scottoline
A wonderfully engrossing, sometimes hilarious thriller that will delight courtroom junkies.

DEEPER: MY TWO-YEAR ODYSSEY IN CYBERSPACE
John Seabrook
This analysis of today's cyberculture makes a few good points about the Net's shortcomings, but remains underwhelming.

SEATTLE ACCESS
This volume adroitly covers each neighborhood with history, trivia, and plenty of tips on dining and nightlife.

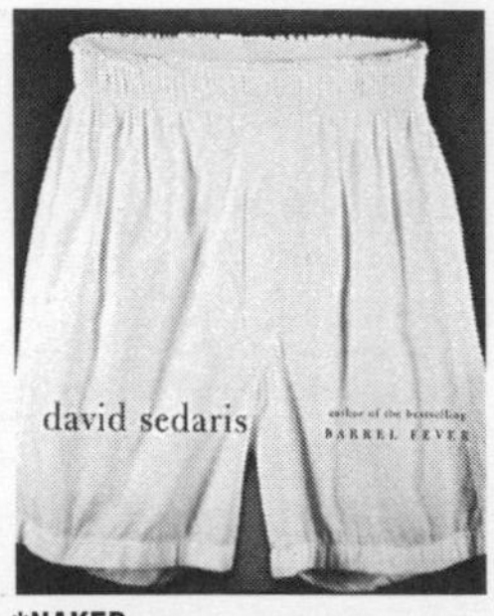

***NAKED**
David Sedaris
A brilliant collection of autobiographical essays with a mordant edge and ripe with wisdom.

HIGH-HEEL BLUE
Diane K. Shah
A seductive chiller with a devious, double-barreled plot set in the LAPD.

WEIRD ROOMS
Mal and Sandra Sharpe; photographs by Alexander Vertikoff
If you're in the market for a few sensible decorating tips, steer way clear of this endearingly whimsical picture book.

UP ISLAND
Anne Rivers Siddons
Heroine Molly Redwine escapes to Martha's Vineyard to cope with a spate of midlife woes.

THE UNLIKELY SPY
Daniel Silva
An Oxford history professor must ferret out German agents to ensure the success of the landing at Normandy.

WALKING THE BLACK CAT
Charles Simic
These mysterious, haunting poems evoke a remarkable world of ghosts, ventriloquists, and gypsy fortune-tellers.

OVITZ: THE INSIDE STORY OF HOLLYWOOD'S MOST CONTROVERSIAL POWER BROKER
Robert Slater
Hardly an unkind word in the entire book, and the subject remains mysterious and unrevealed.

***SPARES**
Michael Marshall Smith
This darkly atmospheric sci-fi thriller masterfully moves the whodunit toward the future.

MRS. KEPPEL AND HER DAUGHTER
Diana Souhami
Strangely poignant, Diana Souhami's portrait of the struggle between two strong-willed women is a compelling study of post-Victorian British society.

SOUTH-EAST ASIA ON A SHOESTRING
This literate, not-just-for-backpackers series features an excellent new edition on such challenging destinations as Vietnam and Thailand, but the information is not updated yearly.

***REALITY AND DREAMS**
Muriel Spark
Spark examines the peculiar and mystical connections between reality and fantasy, between life and art, in a voice quite unlike any other writer's: elegant, wise, sympathetic, satiric—at once darkly sinister and brightly chipper.

BOGART
A. M. Sperber and Eric Lax
A graceful, compelling narrative based on interviews with over 200 of Bogie's cronies and colleagues.

NOTORIOUS
Donald Spoto
A sympathetic biography of Ingrid Bergman with several undocumented tidbits and selective omissions, such as the actor's Nazi films.

TO DANCE WITH THE DEVIL: THE NEW WAR ON BREAST CANCER: POLITICS, POWER AND PEOPLE
Karen Stabiner
Although some stories are harrowing, the account of one doctor's near-visionary dedication is uplifting; most women will be comforted to know that someone is working tirelessly and selflessly to improve—and prolong—their lives.

DEAL ON ICE
Les Standiford
An action mystery novel featuring a contractor-cum-detective as the engaging main character—hard-boiled, yes, but in deference to the '90s, soft around the edges.

GLUED TO THE SET: THE 60 TELEVISION SHOWS AND EVENTS THAT MADE US WHO WE ARE TODAY
Steven D. Stark
A provocative book about a subject on which nearly every American, not unjustly, considers himself an expert.

EAT YOUR WAY ACROSS THE USA
Jane and Michael Stern
A cross-country culinary guide that should be stashed in every food lover's glove compartment.

***BEAR AND HIS DAUGHTER**
Robert Stone
A powerful collection of seven short stories that depict ordinary people ripped apart by spiritual crisis.

THE CONTINUOUS LIFE
Mark Strand
Melancholy evocations joined with hilarious mini-narratives, reflections on mortality and on "the small tremors of love" that resonate beyond death.

CATS IN LOVE
J. C. Suares and Jane Martin
Evidence that felines can be affectionate.

VIEW WITH A GRAIN OF SAND
Wislawa Szymborska
With the lightest touch, this wise and witty Polish poet—the 1995 Nobel laureate—tackles the mystery of love at first sight, the joy of self-pity, the ravages of war, and the small miracle of an onion.

***THE RULES FOR CATS**
Bradford Telford and Michael Cader
Guidelines to help cats assert their rightful place as head of the household.

HOME BODY
John Thorne
Thorne's whimsical mini-essays transform the ordinary household into an enchanted landscape crowded with odd and wonderful objects we once knew as stove, sink, or chest of drawers.

AFTER RAIN
William Trevor
A collection of poignant stories that proves the most effective drama comes from the aftermath of events and not from the events themselves.

A SPANISH LOVER
Joanna Trollope
The forceful story of the passions that rage beneath the surface serenity of a pair of twin sisters' lives.

MURDER IN THE HOUSE
Margaret Truman
Truman's prose is stodgy, and there are occasional bits of flossy over-reach, but this presidential daughter has staked out interesting territory, and she tells her story well.

HEART OF WAR
Lucian K. Truscott IV
If the subject of old-style treachery in the New Army sounds a tad tedious for dog day afternoons—surprise! Bursting with sex, murder, and assorted mayhem, this military thriller packs more firepower than the Fourth of July.

THE UNOFFICIAL GUIDE TO WALT DISNEY WORLD 1997
This exhaustive study of every WDW hotel, ride and, seemingly, rest station makes the D-Day invasion plan look like a whim cooked up over a couple of martinis.

BLACK LEOPARD
Steven Voien
A mystery adventure that evokes a West Africa rarely seen by tourists: AIDS-ridden, poverty-stricken, and violent.

THE VON HOFFMAN BROS.' BIG DAMN BOOK OF SHEER MANLINESS
Todd and Brant von Hoffman, Colby Allerton & Some Other Wiseguys
A big damn spoof of all things manly, an over-the-top commentary on our gender-confused culture with one sorry conclusion: Being a real man means having really bad taste.

AFTER THE MADNESS: A JUDGE'S OWN PRISON MEMOIR
Sol Wachtler
Wachtler's compassion for the other prisoners and his newly reconsidered ideas about the injustices of our legal system make one think it might be salutary for other judges to do some hard time.

ANDRE TALKS HAIR!
Andre Walker
A handsome book, full of pretty women and commonsense advice from Oprah's stylist.

***CAR: A DRAMA OF THE AMERICAN WORKPLACE**
Mary Walton
Fascinating without being overly technical, this account of the Ford Taurus's redesign describes how the rides of our dreams are really assembled.

WICKED WOMEN
Fay Weldon
In this often-caustic collection, Weldon's heroines become downright malicious while making sure their betrayers get their just desserts—and then some.

THE AX
Donald E. Westlake
The story of one man's murder spree, told in the aggrieved voice of a loving husband and father chillingly unaware that he has gone mad.

MRS. WHALEY AND HER CHARLESTON GARDEN
Emily Whaley in conversation with William Baldwin
If we can't actually spend an afternoon strolling amid the camellias in Emily Whaley's Charleston garden, the next-best thing is stretching out with her delightful book that guides us through the 30-by-110-foot plot that she has nurtured for six decades.

WEEDING OUT THE TEARS: A MOTHER'S STORY OF LOVE, LOSS AND RENEWAL
Jeanne White with Susan Dworkin
Jeanne White's comforting and painful account of the much-publicized illness and death from AIDS of her son Ryan—and of the strength and sense of purpose that she has gained as a legacy of Ryan's brief life.

NORTH OF HAVANA
Randy Wayne White
A naturalist's eye and an ironic sensibility make this mystery novel add up to more than the sum of its parts.

SIBERIAN LIGHT
Robin White
White employs every plot device and stock character in the genre. *Light* manages to be a decent thriller despite the overkill.

JOHN WAYNE'S AMERICA: THE POLITICS OF CELEBRITY
Garry Wills
A fascinatingly obsessive book that considers the film career of this iconic figure and the nature of the myth that continues to outlive him.

***HEADLINE JUSTICE**
Theo Wilson
The keenly observant memoir of a fireball reporter who spent four decades covering some of the most sensational trials of New York.

THE DEATH AND LIFE OF BOBBY Z
Don Winslow
An inmate impersonates a smuggler for the DEA. Any lapses in credibility are outweighed by the cinematic pacing, potent irony, and great escapes.

GIRLS ONLY
Alex Witchel
Pleasant but disappointingly light memoir of the distaff half of the author's family.

DRACULA: THE CONNOISSEUR'S GUIDE
Leonard Wolf
For anything less than a devout Draculaphile, this book is not only excessively bloody, but also bloody excessive.

THE NIGHT IN QUESTION
Tobias Wolff
Parents, siblings, and friends brush up against one another in poignant and often absurd scenarios.

A HISTORY OF THE BREAST
Marilyn Yalom
Covers 25,000 years of changing attitudes towards the secondary sexual characteristics of the female of the species.

FICTION AND NONFICTION BESTSELLERS

Publishers Weekly began charting the nation's top-selling hardcover fiction in 1895. The first nonfiction lists were published regularly beginning in 1917, and during World War I the trade magazine even tracked the most popular war books. (The Winston Churchill on the fiction lists, by the way, was an American novelist who died in 1947; his British statesman namesake was, of course, a bestselling and Nobel Prize–winning writer of nonfiction.) These rankings are not based on net sales figures but rather on publishers' reports of copies shipped and billed.

1900

Fiction

1. *To Have and To Hold*, Mary Johnston
2. *Red Pottage*, Mary Cholmondeley
3. *Unleavened Bread*, Robert Grant
4. *The Reign of Law*, James Lane Allen
5. *Eben Holden*, Irving Bacheller
6. *Janice Meredith*, Paul Leicester Ford
7. *The Redemption of David Corson*, Charles Frederic Goss
8. *Richard Carvel*, Winston Churchill
9. *When Knighthood Was in Flower*, Charles Major
10. *Alice of Old Vincennes*, Maurice Thompson

1901

Fiction

1. *The Crisis*, Winston Churchill
2. *Alice of Old Vincennes*, Maurice Thompson
3. *The Helmet of Navarre*, Bertha Runkle
4. *The Right of Way*, Gilbert Parker
5. *Eben Holden*, Irving Bacheller
6. *The Visits of Elizabeth*, Elinor Glyn
7. *The Puppet Crown*, Harold MacGrath
8. *Richard Yea-and-Nay*, Maurice Hewlett
9. *Graustark*, George Barr McCutcheon
10. *D'ri and I*, Irving Bacheller

1902

Fiction

1. *The Virginian*, Owen Wister
2. *Mrs. Wiggs of the Cabbage Patch*, Alice Caldwell Hegan
3. *Dorothy Vernon of Haddon Hall*, Charles Major
4. *The Mississippi Bubble*, Emerson Hough
5. *Audrey*, Mary Johnston
6. *The Right of Way*, Gilbert Parker
7. *The Hound of the Baskervilles*, A. Conan Doyle
8. *The Two Vanrevels*, Booth Tarkington
9. *The Blue Flower*, Henry van Dyke
10. *Sir Richard Calmady*, Lucas Malet

1903

Fiction

1. *Lady Rose's Daughter*, Mary Augusta Ward
2. *Gordon Keith*, Thomas Nelson Page
3. *The Pit*, Frank Norris
4. *Lovey Mary*, Alice Hegan Rice
5. *The Virginian*, Owen Wister
6. *Mrs. Wiggs of the Cabbage Patch*, Alice Hegan Rice
7. *The Mettle of the Pasture*, James Lane Allen
8. *Letters of a Self-Made Merchant to His Son*, George Horace Lorimer
9. *The One Woman*, Thomas Dixon Jr.
10. *The Little Shepherd of Kingdom Come*, John Fox Jr.

1904

Fiction

1. *The Crossing*, Winston Churchill
2. *The Deliverance*, Ellen Glasgow
3. *The Masquerader*, anonymous (Katherine Cecil Thurston)
4. *In the Bishop's Carriage*, Miriam Michelson
5. *Sir Mortimer*, Mary Johnston
6. *Beverly of Graustark*, George Barr McCutcheon
7. *The Little Shepherd of Kingdom Come*, John Fox Jr.
8. *Rebecca of Sunnybrook Farm*, Kate Douglas Wiggin
9. *My Friend Prospero*, Henry Harland
10. *The Silent Places*, Stewart Edward White

1905

Fiction

1. *The Marriage of William Ashe*, Mary Augusta Ward
2. *Sandy*, Alice Hegan Rice
3. *The Garden of Allah*, Robert Hichens
4. *The Clansman*, Thomas Dixon Jr.
5. *Nedra*, George Barr McCutcheon
6. *The Gambler*, Katherine Cecil Thurston
7. *The Masquerader*, anonymous (Katherine Cecil Thurston)
8. *The House of Mirth*, Edith Wharton
9. *The Princess Passes*, C. N. and A. M. Williamson
10. *Rose o' the River*, Kate Douglas Wiggin

1906

Fiction

1. *Coniston*, Winston Churchill
2. *Lady Baltimore*, Owen Wister
3. *The Fighting Chance*, Robert W. Chambers
4. *The House of a Thousand Candles*, Meredith Nicholson
5. *Jane Cable*, George Barr McCutcheon
6. *The Jungle*, Upton Sinclair
7. *The Awakening of Helena Ritchie*, Margaret Deland
8. *The Spoilers*, Rex Beach
9. *The House of Mirth*, Edith Wharton
10. *The Wheel of Life*, Ellen Glasgow

1907

Fiction

1. *The Lady of the Decoration*, Frances Little
2. *The Weavers*, Gilbert Parker
3. *The Port of Missing Men*, Meredith Nicholson
4. *The Shuttle*, Frances Hodgson Burnett
5. *The Brass Bowl*, Louis J. Vance
6. *Satan Sanderson*, Hallie Erminie Rives
7. *The Daughter of Anderson Crow*, George Barr McCutcheon
8. *The Younger Set*, Robert W. Chambers
9. *The Doctor*, Ralph Connor
10. *Half a Rogue*, Harold MacGrath

1908

Fiction

1. *Mr. Crewe's Career,* Winston Churchill
2. *The Barrier,* Rex Beach
3. *The Trail of the Lonesome Pine,* John Fox Jr.
4. *The Lure of the Mask,* Harold MacGrath
5. *The Shuttle,* Frances Hodgson Burnett
6. *Peter,* F. Hopkinson Smith
7. *Lewis Rand,* Mary Johnston
8. *The Black Bag,* Louis J. Vance
9. *The Man from Brodney's,* George Barr McCutcheon
10. *The Weavers,* Gilbert Parker

1909

Fiction

1. *The Inner Shrine,* anonymous (Basil King)
2. *Katrine,* Elinor Macartney Lane
3. *The Silver Horde,* Rex Beach
4. *The Man in Lower Ten,* Mary Roberts Rinehart
5. *The Trail of the Lonesome Pine,* John Fox Jr.
6. *Truxton King,* George Barr McCutcheon
7. *54-40 or Fight,* Emerson Hough
8. *The Goose Girl,* Harold MacGrath
9. *Peter,* F. Hopkinson Smith
10. *Septimus,* William J. Locke

1910

Fiction

1. *The Rosary,* Florence Barclay
2. *A Modern Chronicle,* Winston Churchill
3. *The Wild Olive,* anonymous (Basil King)
4. *Max,* Katherine Cecil Thurston
5. *The Kingdom of Slender Swords,* Hallie Erminie Rives
6. *Simon the Jester,* William J. Locke
7. *Lord Loveland Discovers America,* C. N. and A. M. Williamson
8. *The Window at the White Cat,* Mary Roberts Rinehart
9. *Molly Make-Believe,* Eleanor Abbott
10. *When a Man Marries,* Mary Roberts Rinehart

1911

Fiction

1. *The Broad Highway,* Jeffrey Farnol
2. *The Prodigal Judge,* Vaughan Kester
3. *The Winning of Barbara Worth,* Harold Bell Wright
4. *Queed,* Henry Sydnor Harrison
5. *The Harvester,* Gene Stratton Porter
6. *The Iron Woman,* Margaret Deland
7. *The Long Roll,* Mary Johnston
8. *Molly Make-Believe,* Eleanor Abbott
9. *The Rosary,* Florence Barclay
10. *The Common Law,* Robert W. Chambers

1912

Fiction

1. *The Harvester,* Gene Stratton Porter
2. *The Street Called Straight,* Basil King
3. *Their Yesterdays,* Harold Bell Wright
4. *The Melting of Molly,* Maria Thompson Daviess
5. *A Hoosier Chronicle,* Meredith Nicholson
6. *The Winning of Barbara Worth,* Harold Bell Wright
7. *The Just and the Unjust,* Vaughan Kester
8. *The Net,* Rex Beach
9. *Tante,* Anne Douglas Sedgwick
10. *Fran,* J. Breckenridge Ellis

MOST CHALLENGED (NOT BANNED) BOOKS

Books enrich our lives, but to a certain vocal part of the population they can enrage as well. While the intention of those challenging these books *was* to ban them, most of the books stayed on the shelves because of the efforts of librarians, teachers, parents, and students. Here are the most challenged books in school libraries and curriculums, in the last year, according to the American Library Association's Office for Intellectual Freedom (Jan. 1–Dec. 31, 1996) and over the last 14 years, according to People for the American Way.

1982–96

1. *Of Mice and Men,* John Steinbeck
2. *The Catcher in the Rye,* J.D. Salinger
3. *The Chocolate War,* Robert Cormier
4. *I Know Why the Caged Bird Sings,* Maya Angelou
5. *Scary Stories To Tell in the Dark,* Alvin Schwartz
6. *The Adventures of Huckleberry Finn,* Mark Twain
7. *More Scary Stories To Tell in the Dark,* Alvin Schwartz
8. *Go Ask Alice,* anonymous
9. *Bridge to Terabithia,* Katherine Paterson
10. *The Witches,* Roald Dahl

1996

1. *Goosebumps Series,* R. L. Stine
2. *The Adventures of Huckleberry Finn,* Mark Twain
3. *I Know Why the Caged Bird Sings,* Maya Angelou
4. *It's Perfectly Normal,* Robbie Harris
5. *The Chocolate War,* Robert Cormier
6. *The Catcher in the Rye,* J.D. Salinger
7. *Bridge to Terabithia,* Katherine Paterson
8. *Forever,* Judy Blume
9. *My Brother Sam Is Dead,* Christopher and James Lincoln Collier

Nonfiction
1. *The Promised Land*, Mary Antin
2. *The Montessori Method*, Maria Montessori
3. *South America*, James Bryce
4. *A New Conscience and an Ancient Evil*, Jane Addams
5. *Three Plays*, Eugène Brieux
6. *Your United States*, Arnold Bennett
7. *Creative Evolution*, Henri Bergson
8. *How to Live on Twenty-Four Hours a Day*, Arnold Bennett
9. *Woman and Labor*, Olive Schreiner
10. *Mark Twain*, Albert Bigelow Paine

1913

Fiction
1. *The Inside of the Cup*, Winston Churchill
2. *V. V.'s Eyes*, Henry Sydnor Harrison
3. *Laddie*, Gene Stratton Porter
4. *The Judgment House*, Sir Gilbert Parker
5. *Heart of the Hills*, John Fox Jr.
6. *The Amateur Gentleman*, Jeffrey Farnol
7. *The Woman Thou Gavest Me*, Hall Caine
8. *Pollyanna*, Eleanor H. Porter
9. *The Valiants of Virginia*, Hallie Erminie Rives
10. *T. Tembarom*, Frances Hodgson Burnett

Nonfiction
1. *Crowds*, Gerald Stanley Lee
2. *Germany and the Germans*, Price Collier
3. *Zone Policeman 88*, Harry A. Franck
4. *The New Freedom*, Woodrow Wilson
5. *South America*, James Bryce
6. *Your United States*, Arnold Bennett
7. *The Promised Land*, Mary Antin
8. *Auction Bridge To-Day*, Milton C. Work
9. *Three Plays*, Eugène Brieux
10. *Psychology and Industrial Efficiency*, Hugo Munsterberg

1914

Fiction
1. *The Eyes of the World*, Harold Bell Wright
2. *Pollyanna*, Eleanor H. Porter
3. *The Inside of the Cup*, Winston Churchill
4. *The Salamander*, Owen Johnson
5. *The Fortunate Youth*, William J. Locke
6. *T. Tembarom*, Frances Hodgson Burnett
7. *Penrod*, Booth Tarkington
8. *Diane of the Green Van*, Leona Dalrymple
9. *The Devil's Garden*, W. B. Maxwell
10. *The Prince of Graustark*, George Barr McCutcheon

1915

Fiction
1. *The Turmoil*, Booth Tarkington
2. *A Far Country*, Winston Churchill
3. *Michael O'Halloran*, Gene Stratton Porter
4. *Pollyanna Grows Up*, Eleanor H. Porter
5. *K*, Mary Roberts Rinehart
6. *Jaffery*, William J. Locke
7. *Felix O'Day*, F. Hopkinson Smith
8. *The Harbor*, Ernest Poole
9. *The Lone Star Ranger*, Zane Grey
10. *Angela's Business*, Henry Sydnor Harrison

1916

Fiction
1. *Seventeen*, Booth Tarkington
2. *When a Man's a Man*, Harold Bell Wright
3. *Just David*, Eleanor H. Porter
4. *Mr. Britling Sees It Through*, H. G. Wells
5. *Life and Gabriella*, Ellen Glasgow
6. *The Real Adventure*, Henry Kitchell Webster
7. *Bars of Iron*, Ethel M. Dell
8. *Nan of Music Mountain*, Frank H. Spearman
9. *Dear Enemy*, Jean Webster
10. *The Heart of Rachael*, Kathleen Norris

1917

Fiction
1. *Mr. Britling Sees It Through*, H. G. Wells
2. *The Light in the Clearing*, Irving Bacheller
3. *The Red Planet*, William J. Locke
4. *The Road to Understanding*, Eleanor H. Porter
5. *Wildfire*, Zane Grey
6. *Christine*, Alice Cholmondeley
7. *In the Wilderness*, Robert S. Hichens
8. *His Family*, Ernest Poole
9. *The Definite Object*, Jeffrey Farnol
10. *The Hundredth Chance*, Ethel M. Dell

General Nonfiction
1. *Rhymes of a Red Cross Man*, Robert W. Service
2. *The Plattsburg Manual*, O. O. Ellis and E. B. Garey
3. *Raymond*, Sir Oliver Lodge
4. *Poems of Alan Seeger*, Alan Seeger
5. *God the Invisible King*, H. G. Wells
6. *Laugh and Live*, Douglas Fairbanks
7. *Better Meals for Less Money*, Mary Green

War Books
1. *The First Hundred Thousand*, Ian Hay
2. *My Home in the Field of Honor*, Frances W. Huard
3. *A Student in Arms*, Donald Hankey
4. *Over the Top*, Arthur Guy Empey
5. *Carry On*, Coningsby Dawson
6. *Getting Together*, Ian Hay
7. *My Second Year of the War*, Frederick Palmer
8. *The Land of Deepening Shadow*, D. Thomas Curtin
9. *Italy, France and Britain at War*, H. G. Wells
10. *The Worn Doorstep*, Margaret Sherwood

1918

Fiction
1. *The U. P. Trail*, Zane Grey
2. *The Tree of Heaven*, May Sinclair
3. *The Amazing Interlude*, Mary Roberts Rinehart
4. *Dere Mable*, Edward Streeter
5. *Oh, Money! Money!*, Eleanor H. Porter
6. *Greatheart*, Ethel M. Dell
7. *The Major*, Ralph Connor
8. *The Pawns Count*, E. Phillips Oppenheim
9. *A Daughter of the Land*, Gene Stratton Porter
10. *Sonia*, Stephen McKenna

General Nonfiction
1. *Rhymes of a Red Cross Man*, Robert W. Service
2. *Treasury of War Poetry*, G. H. Clark
3. *With the Colors*, Everard J. Appleton
4. *Recollections*, Viscount Morley
5. *Laugh and Live*, Douglas Fairbanks
6. *Mark Twain's Letters*, Albert Bigelow Paine, editor
7. *Adventures and Letters of Richard Harding Davis*, Richard Harding Davis
8. *Over Here*, Edgar Guest
9. *Diplomatic Days*, Edith O'Shaughnessy
10. *Poems of Alan Seeger*, Alan Seeger

War Books
1. *My Four Years in Germany*, James W. Gerard
2. *The Glory of the Trenches*, Coningsby Dawson
3. *Over the Top*, Arthur Guy Empey

4. *A Minstrel in France*, Harry Lauder
5. *Private Peat*, Harold R. Peat
6. *Outwitting the Hun*, Lieut. Pat O'Brien
7. *Face to Face with Kaiserism*, James W. Gerard
8. *Carry On*, Coningsby Dawson
9. *Out to Win*, Coningsby Dawson
10. *Under Fire*, Henri Barbusse

1919

Fiction

1. *The Four Horsemen of the Apocalypse*, V. Blasco Ibañez
2. *The Arrow of Gold*, Joseph Conrad
3. *The Desert of Wheat*, Zane Grey
4. *Dangerous Days*, Mary Roberts Rinehart
5. *The Sky Pilot in No Man's Land*, Ralph Connor
6. *The Re-Creation of Brian Kent*, Harold Bell Wright
7. *Dawn*, Gene Stratton Porter
8. *The Tin Soldier*, Temple Bailey
9. *Christopher and Columbus*, "Elizabeth"
10. *In Secret*, Robert W. Chambers

Nonfiction

1. *The Education of Henry Adams*, Henry Adams
2. *The Years Between*, Rudyard Kipling
3. *Belgium*, Brand Whitlock
4. *The Seven Purposes*, Margaret Cameron
5. *In Flanders Fields*, John McCrae
6. *Bolshevism*, John Spargo

1920

Fiction

1. *The Man of the Forest*, Zane Grey
2. *Kindred of the Dust*, Peter B. Kyne
3. *The Re-Creation of Brian Kent*, Harold Bell Wright
4. *The River's End*, James Oliver Curwood
5. *A Man for the Ages*, Irving Bacheller
6. *Mary-Marie*, Eleanor H. Porter
7. *The Portygee*, Joseph C. Lincoln
8. *The Great Impersonation*, E. Phillips Oppenheim
9. *The Lamp in the Desert*, Ethel M. Dell
10. *Harriet and the Piper*, Kathleen Norris

Nonfiction

1. *Now It Can Be Told*, Philip Gibbs
2. *The Economic Consequences of the Peace*, John M. Keynes
3. *Roosevelt's Letters to His Children*, Joseph B. Bishop, editor
4. *Theodore Roosevelt*, William Roscoe Thayer
5. *White Shadows in the South Seas*, Frederick O'Brien
6. *An American Idyll*, Cornelia Stratton Parker

1921

Fiction

1. *Main Street*, Sinclair Lewis
2. *The Brimming Cup*, Dorothy Canfield
3. *The Mysterious Rider*, Zane Grey
4. *The Age of Innocence*, Edith Wharton
5. *The Valley of Silent Men*, James Oliver Curwood
6. *The Sheik*, Edith M. Hull
7. *A Poor Wise Man*, Mary Roberts Rinehart
8. *Her Father's Daughter*, Gene Stratton Porter
9. *The Sisters-in-Law*, Gertrude Atherton
10. *The Kingdom Round the Corner*, Coningsby Dawson

Nonfiction

1. *The Outline of History*, H. G. Wells
2. *White Shadows in the South Seas*, Frederick O'Brien
3. *The Mirrors of Downing Street*, A Gentleman with a Duster (pseudonym for Harold Begbie)
4. *The Autobiography of Margot Asquith*, Margot Asquith
6. *Peace Negotiations*, Robert Lansing

1922

Fiction

1. *If Winter Comes*, A.S.M. Hutchinson
2. *The Sheik*, Edith M. Hull
3. *Gentle Julia*, Booth Tarkington
4. *The Head of the House of Coombe*, Frances Hodgson Burnett
5. *Simon Called Peter*, Robert Keable
6. *The Breaking Point*, Mary Roberts Rinehart
7. *This Freedom*, A.S.M. Hutchinson
8. *Maria Chapdelaine*, Louis Hémon
9. *To the Last Man*, Zane Grey
10. *Babbitt*, Sinclair Lewis (tie)
10. *Helen of the Old House*, Harold Bell Wright (tie)

Nonfiction

1. *The Outline of History*, H. G. Wells
2. *The Story of Mankind*, Hendrik Willem Van Loon
3. *The Americanization of Edward Bok*, Edward Bok
4. *Diet and Health*, Lulu Hunt Peters
5. *The Mind in the Making*, James Harvey Robinson
6. *The Outline of Science*, J. Arthur Thomson
7. *Outwitting Our Nerves*, Josephine A. Jackson and Helen M. Salisbury
8. *Queen Victoria*, Lytton Strachey
9. *Mirrors of Washington*, anonymous (Clinton W. Gilbert)
10. *Painted Windows*, A Gentleman with a Duster (pseudonym for Harold Begbie)

1923

Fiction

1. *Black Oxen*, Gertrude Atherton
2. *His Children's Children*, Arthur Train
3. *The Enchanted April*, "Elizabeth"
4. *Babbitt*, Sinclair Lewis
5. *The Dim Lantern*, Temple Bailey
6. *This Freedom*, A.S.M. Hutchinson
7. *The Mine with the Iron Door*, Harold Bell Wright
8. *The Wanderer of the Wasteland*, Zane Grey
9. *The Sea-Hawk*, Rafael Sabatini
10. *The Breaking Point*, Mary Roberts Rinehart

Nonfiction

1. *Etiquette*, Emily Post
2. *The Life of Christ*, Giovanni Papini
3. *The Life and Letters of Walter H. Page*, Burton J. Hendrick, editor
4. *The Mind in the Making*, James Harvey Robinson
5. *The Outline of History*, H. G. Wells
6. *Diet and Health*, Lulu Hunt Peters
7. *Self-Mastery Through Conscious Auto-Suggestion*, Emile Coué
8. *The Americanization of Edward Bok*, Edward Bok
9. *The Story of Mankind*, Hendrik Willem Van Loon
10. *A Man from Maine*, Edward Bok

1924

Fiction

1. *So Big*, Edna Ferber
2. *The Plastic Age*, Percy Marks
3. *The Little French Girl*, Anne Douglas Sedgwick
4. *The Heirs Apparent*, Philip Gibbs
5. *A Gentleman of Courage*, James Oliver Curwood
6. *The Call of the Canyon*, Zane Grey
7. *The Midlander*, Booth Tarkington
8. *The Coast of Folly*, Coningsby Dawson
9. *Mistress Wilding*, Rafael Sabatini
10. *The Homemaker*, Dorothy Canfield Fisher

Nonfiction

1. *Diet and Health*, Lulu Hunt Peters
2. *The Life of Christ*, Giovanni Papini
3. *The Boston Cooking School Cook Book*, Fannie Farmer, editor
4. *Etiquette*, Emily Post
5. *Ariel*, André Maurois
6. *The Cross Word Puzzle Books*, Prosper Buranelli, et al.
7. *Mark Twain's Autobiography*, Mark Twain
8. *Saint Joan*, Bernard Shaw
9. *The New Decalogue of Science*, Albert E. Wiggam
10. *The Americanization of Edward Bok*, Edward Bok

1925

Fiction

1. *Soundings*, A. Hamilton Gibbs
2. *The Constant Nymph*, Margaret Kennedy
3. *The Keeper of the Bees*, Gene Stratton Porter
4. *Glorious Apollo*, E. Barrington
5. *The Green Hat*, Michael Arlen
6. *The Little French Girl*, Anne Douglas Sedgwick
7. *Arrowsmith*, Sinclair Lewis
8. *The Perennial Bachelor*, Anne Parrish
9. *The Carolinian*, Rafael Sabatini
10. *One Increasing Purpose*, A.S.M. Hutchinson

Nonfiction

1. *Diet and Health*, Lulu Hunt Peters
2. *The Boston Cooking School Cook Book*, rev. ed., Fannie Farmer, editor
3. *When We Were Very Young*, A. A. Milne
4. *The Man Nobody Knows*, Bruce Barton
5. *The Life of Christ*, Giovanni Papini
6. *Ariel*, André Maurois
7. *Twice Thirty*, Edward Bok
8. *Twenty-Five Years*, Lord Grey
9. *Anatole France Himself*, J. J. Brousson
10. *The Cross Word Puzzle Books*, Prosper Buranelli, et al.

1926

Fiction

1. *The Private Life of Helen of Troy*, John Erskine
2. *Gentlemen Prefer Blondes*, Anita Loos
3. *Sorrell and Son*, Warwick Deeping
4. *The Hounds of Spring*, Sylvia Thompson
5. *Beau Sabreur*, P. C. Wren
6. *The Silver Spoon*, John Galsworthy
7. *Beau Geste*, P. C. Wren
8. *Show Boat*, Edna Ferber
9. *After Noon*, Susan Ertz
10. *The Blue Window*, Temple Bailey

Nonfiction

1. *The Man Nobody Knows*, Bruce Barton
2. *Why We Behave Like Human Beings*, George A. Dorsey
3. *Diet and Health*, Lulu Hunt Peters
4. *Our Times*, Vol. I, Mark Sullivan
5. *The Boston Cooking School Cook Book*, rev. ed., Fannie Farmer, editor
6. *Auction Bridge Complete*, Milton C. Work
7. *The Book Nobody Knows*, Bruce Barton
8. *The Story of Philosophy*, Will Durant
9. *The Light of Faith*, Edgar A. Guest
10. *Jefferson and Hamilton,* Claude G. Bowers

1927

Fiction

1. *Elmer Gantry*, Sinclair Lewis
2. *The Plutocrat*, Booth Tarkington
3. *Doomsday*, Warwick Deeping
4. *Sorrell and Son*, Warwick Deeping
5. *Jalna*, Mazo de la Roche
6. *Lost Ecstasy*, Mary Roberts Rinehart
7. *Twilight Sleep*, Edith Wharton
8. *Tomorrow Morning*, Anne Parrish
9. *The Old Countess*, Anne Douglas Sedgwick
10. *A Good Woman*, Louis Bromfield

Nonfiction

1. *The Story of Philosophy*, Will Durant
2. *Napoleon*, Emil Ludwig
3. *Revolt in the Desert*, T. E. Lawrence
4. *Trader Horn,* Vol. I, Alfred Aloysius Horn and Ethelreda Lewis
5. *We*, Charles A. Lindbergh
6. *Ask Me Another*, Julian Spafford and Lucien Esty
7. *The Royal Road to Romance*, Richard Halliburton
8. *The Glorious Adventure*, Richard Halliburton
9. *Why We Behave Like Human Beings*, George A. Dorsey
10. *Mother India*, Katherine Mayo

1928

Fiction

1. *The Bridge of San Luis Rey*, Thornton Wilder
2. *Wintersmoon*, Hugh Walpole
3. *Swan Song*, John Galsworthy
4. *The Greene Murder Case*, S. S. Van Dine
5. *Bad Girl*, Viña Delmar
6. *Claire Ambler*, Booth Tarkington
7. *Old Pybus*, Warwick Deeping
8. *All Kneeling*, Anne Parrish
9. *Jalna*, Mazo de la Roche
10. *The Strange Case of Miss Annie Spragg*, Louis Bromfield

Nonfiction

1. *Disraeli*, André Maurois
2. *Mother India*, Katherine Mayo
3. *Trader Horn*, Vol. I, Alfred Aloysius Horn and Ethelreda Lewis
4. *Napoleon*, Emil Ludwig
5. *Strange Interlude*, Eugene O'Neill
6. *We*, Charles A. Lindbergh
7. *Count Luckner, the Sea Devil*, Lowell Thomas
8. *Goethe*, Emil Ludwig
9. *Skyward*, Richard E. Byrd
10. *The Intelligent Woman's Guide to Socialism and Capitalism*, George Bernard Shaw

1929

Fiction

1. *All Quiet on the Western Front*, Erich Maria Remarque
2. *Dodsworth*, Sinclair Lewis
3. *Dark Hester*, Anne Douglas Sedgwick
4. *The Bishop Murder Case*, S. S. Van Dine
5. *Roper's Row*, Warwick Deeping
6. *Peder Victorious*, O. E. Rölvaag
7. *Mamba's Daughters*, DuBose Heyward
8. *The Galaxy*, Susan Ertz
9. *Scarlet Sister Mary*, Julia Peterkin
10. *Joseph and His Brethren*, H. W. Freeman

Nonfiction

1. *The Art of Thinking*, Ernest Dimnet
2. *Henry the Eighth*, Francis Hackett
3. *The Cradle of the Deep*, Joan Lowell
4. *Elizabeth and Essex*, Lytton Strachey
5. *The Specialist*, Chic Sale
6. *A Preface to Morals*, Walter Lippmann
7. *Believe It or Not*, Robert L. Ripley
8. *John Brown's Body*, Stephen Vincent Benét
9. *The Tragic Era*, Claude G. Bowers
10. *The Mansions of Philosophy*, Will Durant

1930

Fiction

1. *Cimarron*, Edna Ferber
2. *Exile*, Warwick Deeping
3. *The Woman of Andros*, Thornton Wilder
4. *Years of Grace*, Margaret Ayer Barnes
5. *Angel Pavement*, J. B. Priestley
6. *The Door*, Mary Roberts Rinehart

7. *Rogue Herries*, Hugh Walpole
8. *Chances*, A. Hamilton Gibbs
9. *Young Man of Manhattan*, Katharine Brush
10. *Twenty-Four Hours*, Louis Bromfield

Nonfiction

1. *The Story of San Michele*, Axel Munthe
2. *The Strange Death of President Harding*, Gaston B. Means and May Dixon Thacker
3. *Byron*, André Maurois
4. *The Adams Family*, James Truslow Adams
5. *Lone Cowboy*, Will James
6. *Lincoln*, Emil Ludwig
7. *The Story of Philosophy*, Will Durant
8. *The Outline of History*, H. G. Wells
9. *The Art of Thinking*, Ernest Dimnet
10. *The Rise of American Civilization*, Charles and Mary Beard

1931

Fiction

1. *The Good Earth*, Pearl S. Buck
2. *Shadows on the Rock*, Willa Cather
3. *A White Bird Flying*, Bess Streeter Aldrich
4. *Grand Hotel*, Vicki Baum
5. *Years of Grace*, Margaret Ayer Barnes
6. *The Road Back*, Erich Maria Remarque
7. *The Bridge of Desire*, Warwick Deeping
8. *Back Street*, Fannie Hurst
9. *Finch's Fortune*, Mazo de la Roche
10. *Maid in Waiting*, John Galsworthy

Nonfiction

1. *Education of a Princess*, Grand Duchess Marie
2. *The Story of San Michele*, Axel Munthe
3. *Washington Merry-Go-Round*, anonymous (Drew Pearson and Robert S. Allen)
4. *Boners: Being a Collection of Schoolboy Wisdom, or Knowledge as It Is Sometimes Written*, compiled by Alexander Abingdon; illustrated by Dr. Seuss
5. *Culbertson's Summary*, Ely Culbertson
6. *Contract Bridge Blue Book*, Ely Culbertson
7. *Fatal Interview*, Edna St. Vincent Millay
8. *The Epic of America*, James Truslow Adams
9. *Mexico*, Stuart Chase
10. *New Russia's Primer*, Mikhail Ilin

1932

Fiction

1. *The Good Earth*, Pearl S. Buck
2. *The Fountain*, Charles Morgan
3. *Sons*, Pearl S. Buck
4. *Magnolia Street*, Louis Golding
5. *The Sheltered Life*, Ellen Glasgow
6. *Old Wine and New*, Warwick Deeping
7. *Mary's Neck*, Booth Tarkington
8. *Magnificent Obsession*, Lloyd C. Douglas
9. *Inheritance*, Phyllis Bentley
10. *Three Loves*, A. J. Cronin

Nonfiction

1. *The Epic of America*, James Truslow Adams
2. *Only Yesterday*, Frederick Lewis Allen
3. *A Fortune to Share*, Vash Young
4. *Culbertson's Summary*, Ely Culbertson
5. *Van Loon's Geography*, Hendrik Willem Van Loon
6. *What We Live By*, Ernest Dimnet
7. *The March of Democracy*, James Truslow Adams
8. *Washington Merry-Go-Round*, anonymous (Drew Pearson and Robert S. Allen)
9. *The Story of My Life*, Clarence Darrow
10. *More Merry-Go-Round*, anonymous (Drew Pearson and Robert S. Allen)

1933

Fiction

1. *Anthony Adverse*, Hervey Allen
2. *As the Earth Turns*, Gladys Hasty Carroll
3. *Ann Vickers*, Sinclair Lewis
4. *Magnificent Obsession*, Lloyd C. Douglas
5. *One More River*, John Galsworthy
6. *Forgive Us Our Trespasses*, Lloyd C. Douglas
7. *The Master of Jalna*, Mazo de la Roche
8. *Miss Bishop*, Bess Streeter Aldrich
9. *The Farm*, Louis Bromfield
10. *Little Man, What Now?*, Hans Fallada

Nonfiction

1. *Life Begins at Forty*, Walter B. Pitkin
2. *Marie Antoinette*, Stefan Zweig
3. *British Agent*, R. H. Bruce Lockhart
4. *100,000,000 Guinea Pigs*, Arthur Kallet and F. J. Schlink
5. *The House of Exile*, Nora Waln
6. *Van Loon's Geography*, Hendrik Willem Van Loon
7. *Looking Forward*, Franklin D. Roosevelt
8. *Contract Bridge Blue Book of 1933*, Ely Culbertson
9. *The Arches of the Years*, Halliday Sutherland
10. *The March of Democracy*, Vol. II, James Truslow Adams

1934

Fiction

1. *Anthony Adverse*, Hervey Allen
2. *Lamb in His Bosom*, Caroline Miller
3. *So Red the Rose*, Stark Young
4. *Good-Bye, Mr. Chips*, James Hilton
5. *Within This Present*, Margaret Ayer Barnes
6. *Work of Art*, Sinclair Lewis
7. *Private Worlds*, Phyllis Bottome
8. *Mary Peters*, Mary Ellen Chase
9. *Oil for the Lamps of China*, Alice Tisdale Hobart
10. *Seven Gothic Tales*, Isak Dinesen

Nonfiction

1. *While Rome Burns*, Alexander Woollcott
2. *Life Begins at Forty*, Walter B. Pitkin
3. *Nijinsky*, Romola Nijinsky
4. *100,000,000 Guinea Pigs*, Arthur Kallet and F. J. Schlink
5. *The Native's Return*, Louis Adamic
6. *Stars Fell on Alabama*, Carl Carmer
7. *Brazilian Adventure*, Peter Fleming
8. *Forty-two Years in the White House*, Ike Hoover
9. *You Must Relax*, Edmund Jacobson
10. *The Life of Our Lord*, Charles Dickens

1935

Fiction

1. *Green Light*, Lloyd C. Douglas
2. *Vein of Iron*, Ellen Glasgow
3. *Of Time and the River*, Thomas Wolfe
4. *Time Out of Mind*, Rachel Field
5. *Good-Bye, Mr. Chips*, James Hilton
6. *The Forty Days of Musa Dagh*, Franz Werfel
7. *Heaven's My Destination*, Thornton Wilder
8. *Lost Horizon*, James Hilton
9. *Come and Get It*, Edna Ferber
10. *Europa*, Robert Briffault

Nonfiction

1. *North to the Orient*, Anne Morrow Lindbergh
2. *While Rome Burns*, Alexander Woollcott

3. *Life with Father*, Clarence Day
4. *Personal History*, Vincent Sheean
5. *Seven Pillars of Wisdom*, T. E. Lawrence
6. *Francis the First*, Francis Hackett
7. *Mary Queen of Scotland and the Isles*, Stefan Zweig
8. *Rats, Lice and History*, Hans Zinsser
9. *R. E. Lee*, Douglas Southall Freeman
10. *Skin Deep*, M. C. Phillips

1936

Fiction

1. *Gone with the Wind*, Margaret Mitchell
2. *The Last Puritan*, George Santayana
3. *Sparkenbroke*, Charles Morgan
4. *Drums Along the Mohawk*, Walter D. Edmonds
5. *It Can't Happen Here*, Sinclair Lewis
6. *White Banners*, Lloyd C. Douglas
7. *The Hurricane*, Charles Nordhoff and James Norman Hall
8. *The Thinking Reed*, Rebecca West
9. *The Doctor*, Mary Roberts Rinehart
10. *Eyeless in Gaza*, Aldous Huxley

Nonfiction

1. *Man the Unknown*, Alexis Carrel
2. *Wake Up and Live!*, Dorothea Brande
3. *The Way of a Transgressor*, Negley Farson
4. *Around the World in Eleven Years*, Patience, Richard, and Johnny Abbe
5. *North to the Orient*, Anne Morrow Lindbergh
6. *An American Doctor's Odyssey*, Victor Heiser
7. *Inside Europe*, John Gunther
8. *Live Alone and Like It*, Marjorie Hillis
9. *Life with Father*, Clarence Day
10. *I Write As I Please*, Walter Duranty

1937

Fiction

1. *Gone with the Wind*, Margaret Mitchell
2. *Northwest Passage*, Kenneth Roberts
3. *The Citadel*, A. J. Cronin
4. *And So—Victoria*, Vaughan Wilkins
5. *Drums Along the Mohawk*, Walter D. Edmonds
6. *The Years*, Virginia Woolf
7. *Theatre*, W. Somerset Maugham
8. *Of Mice and Men*, John Steinbeck
9. *The Rains Came*, Louis Bromfield
10. *We Are Not Alone*, James Hilton

Nonfiction

1. *How To Win Friends and Influence People*, Dale Carnegie
2. *An American Doctor's Odyssey*, Victor Heiser
3. *The Return to Religion*, Henry C. Link
4. *The Arts*, Hendrik Willem Van Loon
5. *Orchids on Your Budget*, Marjorie Hillis
6. *Present Indicative*, Noel Coward
7. *Mathematics for the Million*, Lancelot Hogben
8. *Life with Mother*, Clarence Day
9. *The Nile*, Emil Ludwig
10. *The Flowering of New England*, Van Wyck Brooks

1938

Fiction

1. *The Yearling*, Marjorie Kinnan Rawlings
2. *The Citadel*, A. J. Cronin
3. *My Son, My Son!*, Howard Spring
4. *Rebecca*, Daphne du Maurier
5. *Northwest Passage*, Kenneth Roberts
6. *All This, and Heaven Too*, Rachel Field
7. *The Rains Came*, Louis Bromfield
8. *And Tell of Time*, Laura Krey
9. *The Mortal Storm*, Phyllis Bottome
10. *Action at Aquila*, Hervey Allen

Nonfiction

1. *The Importance of Living*, Lin Yutang
2. *With Malice Toward Some*, Margaret Halsey
3. *Madame Curie*, Eve Curie
4. *Listen! The Wind*, Anne Morrow Lindbergh
5. *The Horse and Buggy Doctor*, Arthur E. Hertzler
6. *How To Win Friends and Influence People*, Dale Carnegie
7. *Benjamin Franklin*, Carl Van Doren
8. *I'm a Stranger Here Myself*, Ogden Nash
9. *Alone*, Richard E. Byrd
10. *Fanny Kemble*, Margaret Armstrong

1939

Fiction

1. *The Grapes of Wrath*, John Steinbeck
2. *All This, and Heaven Too*, Rachel Field
3. *Rebecca*, Daphne du Maurier
4. *Wickford Point*, John P. Marquand
5. *Escape*, Ethel Vance
6. *Disputed Passage*, Lloyd C. Douglas
7. *The Yearling*, Marjorie Kinnan Rawlings
8. *The Tree of Liberty*, Elizabeth Page
9. *The Nazarene*, Sholem Asch
10. *Kitty Foyle*, Christopher Morley

Nonfiction

1. *Days of Our Years*, Pierre van Paassen
2. *Reaching for the Stars*, Nora Waln
3. *Inside Asia*, John Gunther
4. *Autobiography with Letters*, William Lyon Phelps
5. *Country Lawyer*, Bellamy Partridge
6. *Wind, Sand and Stars*, Antoine de St. Exupéry
7. *Mein Kampf*, Adolf Hitler
8. *A Peculiar Treasure*, Edna Ferber
9. *Not Peace but a Sword*, Vincent Sheean
10. *Listen! The Wind*, Anne Morrow Lindbergh

1940

Fiction

1. *How Green Was My Valley*, Richard Llewellyn
2. *Kitty Foyle*, Christopher Morley
3. *Mrs. Miniver*, Jan Struther
4. *For Whom the Bell Tolls*, Ernest Hemingway
5. *The Nazarene*, Sholem Asch
6. *Stars on the Sea*, F. van Wyck Mason
7. *Oliver Wiswell*, Kenneth Roberts
8. *The Grapes of Wrath*, John Steinbeck
9. *Night in Bombay*, Louis Bromfield
10. *The Family*, Nina Fedorova

Nonfiction

1. *I Married Adventure*, Osa Johnson
2. *How to Read a Book*, Mortimer Adler
3. *A Smattering of Ignorance*, Oscar Levant
4. *Country Squire in the White House*, John T. Flynn
5. *Land Below the Wind*, Agnes Newton Keith
6. *American White Paper*, Joseph W. Alsop Jr. and Robert Kintnor
7. *New England: Indian Summer*, Van Wyck Brooks
8. *As I Remember Him*, Hans Zinsser
9. *Days of Our Years*, Pierre van Paassen
10. *Bet It's a Boy*, Betty B. Blunt

1941

Fiction

1. *The Keys of the Kingdom*, A. J. Cronin
2. *Random Harvest*, James Hilton
3. *This Above All*, Eric Knight
4. *The Sun Is My Undoing*, Marguerite Steen
5. *For Whom the Bell Tolls*, Ernest Hemingway
6. *Oliver Wiswell*, Kenneth Roberts

7. *H. M. Pulham, Esquire*, John P. Marquand
8. *Mr. and Mrs. Cugat*, Isabel Scott Rorick
9. *Saratoga Trunk*, Edna Ferber
10. *Windswept*, Mary Ellen Chase

Nonfiction

1. *Berlin Diary*, William L. Shirer
2. *The White Cliffs*, Alice Duer Miller
3. *Out of the Night*, Jan Valtin
4. *Inside Latin America*, John Gunther
5. *Blood, Sweat and Tears*, Winston S. Churchill
6. *You Can't Do Business with Hitler*, Douglas Miller
7. *Reading I've Liked*, Clifton Fadiman, editor
8. *Reveille in Washington*, Margaret Leech
9. *Exit Laughing*, Irvin S. Cobb
10. *My Sister and I*, Dirk van der Heide

1942

Fiction

1. *The Song of Bernadette*, Franz Werfel
2. *The Moon Is Down*, John Steinbeck
3. *Dragon Seed*, Pearl S. Buck
4. *And Now Tomorrow*, Rachel Field
5. *Drivin' Woman*, Elizabeth Pickett
6. *Windswept*, Mary Ellen Chase
7. *The Robe*, Lloyd C. Douglas
8. *The Sun Is My Undoing*, Marguerite Steen
9. *Kings Row*, Henry Bellamann
10. *The Keys of the Kingdom*, A. J. Cronin

Nonfiction

1. *See Here, Private Hargrove*, Marion Hargrove
2. *Mission to Moscow*, Joseph E. Davies
3. *The Last Time I Saw Paris*, Elliot Paul
4. *Cross Creek*, Marjorie Kinnan Rawlings
5. *Victory Through Air Power*, Major Alexander P. de Seversky
6. *Past Imperfect*, Ilka Chase
7. *They Were Expendable*, W. L. White
8. *Flight to Arras*, Antoine de St. Exupéry
9. *Washington Is Like That*, W. M. Kiplinger
10. *Inside Latin America*, John Gunther

1943

Fiction

1. *The Robe*, Lloyd C. Douglas
2. *The Valley of Decision*, Marcia Davenport
3. *So Little Time*, John P. Marquand
4. *A Tree Grows in Brooklyn*, Betty Smith
5. *The Human Comedy*, William Saroyan
6. *Mrs. Parkington*, Louis Bromfield
7. *The Apostle*, Sholem Asch
8. *Hungry Hill*, Daphne du Maurier
9. *The Forest and the Fort*, Hervey Allen
10. *The Song of Bernadette*, Franz Werfel

Nonfiction

1. *Under Cover*, John Roy Carlson
2. *One World*, Wendell L. Willkie
3. *Journey Among Warriors*, Eve Curie
4. *On Being a Real Person*, Harry Emerson Fosdick
5. *Guadalcanal Diary*, Richard Tregaskis
6. *Burma Surgeon*, Lt. Col. Gordon Seagrave
7. *Our Hearts Were Young and Gay*, Cornelia Otis Skinner and Emily Kimbrough
8. *U. S. Foreign Policy*, Walter Lippmann
9. *Here Is Your War*, Ernie Pyle
10. *See Here, Private Hargrove*, Marion Hargrove

1944

Fiction

1. *Strange Fruit*, Lillian Smith
2. *The Robe*, Lloyd C. Douglas
3. *A Tree Grows in Brooklyn*, Betty Smith
4. *Forever Amber*, Kathleen Winsor
5. *The Razor's Edge*, W. Somerset Maugham
6. *The Green Years*, A. J. Cronin
7. *Leave Her to Heaven*, Ben Ames Williams
8. *Green Dolphin Street*, Elizabeth Goudge
9. *A Bell for Adano*, John Hersey
10. *The Apostle*, Sholem Asch

Nonfiction

1. *I Never Left Home*, Bob Hope
2. *Brave Men*, Ernie Pyle
3. *Good Night, Sweet Prince*, Gene Fowler
4. *Under Cover*, John Roy Carlson
5. *Yankee from Olympus*, Catherine Drinker Bowen
6. *The Time for Decision*, Sumner Welles
7. *Here Is Your War*, Ernie Pyle
8. *Anna and the King of Siam*, Margaret Landon
9. *The Curtain Rises*, Quentin Reynolds
10. *Ten Years in Japan*, Joseph C. Grew

1945

Fiction

1. *Forever Amber*, Kathleen Winsor
2. *The Robe*, Lloyd C. Douglas
3. *The Black Rose*, Thomas B. Costain
4. *The White Tower*, James Ramsey Ullman
5. *Cass Timberlane*, Sinclair Lewis
6. *A Lion Is in the Streets*, Adria Locke Langley
7. *So Well Remembered*, James Hilton
8. *Captain from Castile*, Samuel Shellabarger
9. *Earth and High Heaven*, Gwethalyn Graham
10. *Immortal Wife*, Irving Stone

Nonfiction

1. *Brave Men*, Ernie Pyle
2. *Dear Sir*, Juliet Lowell
3. *Up Front*, Bill Mauldin
4. *Black Boy*, Richard Wright
5. *Try and Stop Me*, Bennett Cerf
6. *Anything Can Happen*, George and Helen Papashvily
7. *General Marshall's Report*, U.S. War Department General Staff
8. *The Egg and I*, Betty MacDonald
9. *The Thurber Carnival*, James Thurber
10. *Pleasant Valley*, Louis Bromfield

1946

Fiction

1. *The King's General*, Daphne du Maurier
2. *This Side of Innocence*, Taylor Caldwell
3. *The River Road*, Frances Parkinson Keyes
4. *The Miracle of the Bells*, Russell Janney
5. *The Hucksters*, Frederic Wakeman
6. *The Foxes of Harrow*, Frank Yerby
7. *Arch of Triumph*, Erich Maria Remarque
8. *The Black Rose*, Thomas B. Costain
9. *B. F.'s Daughter*, John P. Marquand
10. *The Snake Pit*, Mary Jane Ward

Nonfiction

1. *The Egg and I*, Betty MacDonald
2. *Peace of Mind*, Joshua L. Liebman
3. *As He Saw It*, Elliott Roosevelt
4. *The Roosevelt I Knew*, Frances Perkins
5. *Last Chapter*, Ernie Pyle
6. *Starling of the White House*, Thomas Sugrue and Col. Edmund Starling
7. *I Chose Freedom*, Victor Kravchenko
8. *The Anatomy of Peace*, Emery Reves
9. *Top Secret*, Ralph Ingersoll
10. *A Solo in Tom-Toms*, Gene Fowler

1947

Fiction

1. *The Miracle of the Bells*, Russell Janney
2. *The Moneyman*, Thomas B. Costain
3. *Gentleman's Agreement*, Laura Z. Hobson

4. *Lydia Bailey*, Kenneth Roberts
5. *The Vixens*, Frank Yerby
6. *The Wayward Bus*, John Steinbeck
7. *House Divided*, Ben Ames Williams
8. *Kingsblood Royal*, Sinclair Lewis
9. *East Side, West Side*, Marcia Davenport
10. *Prince of Foxes*, Samuel Shellabarger

Nonfiction

1. *Peace of Mind*, Joshua L. Liebman
2. *Information Please Almanac, 1947*, John Kieran, editor
3. *Inside U.S.A.*, John Gunther
4. *A Study of History*, Arnold J. Toynbee
5. *Speaking Frankly*, James F. Byrnes
6. *Human Destiny*, Pierre Lecomte du Noüy
7. *The Egg and I*, Betty MacDonald
8. *The American Past*, Roger Butterfield
9. *The Fireside Book of Folk Songs*, Margaret B. Boni, editor
10. *Together*, Katharine T. Marshall

1948

Fiction

1. *The Big Fisherman*, Lloyd C. Douglas
2. *The Naked and the Dead*, Norman Mailer
3. *Dinner at Antoine's*, Frances Parkinson Keyes
4. *The Bishop's Mantle*, Agnes Sligh Turnbull
5. *Tomorrow Will Be Better*, Betty Smith
6. *The Golden Hawk*, Frank Yerby
7. *Raintree County*, Ross Lockridge Jr.
8. *Shannon's Way*, A. J. Cronin
9. *Pilgrim's Inn*, Elizabeth Goudge
10. *The Young Lions*, Irwin Shaw

Nonfiction

1. *Crusade in Europe*, Dwight D. Eisenhower
2. *How to Stop Worrying and Start Living*, Dale Carnegie
3. *Peace of Mind*, Joshua L. Liebman
4. *Sexual Behavior in the Human Male*, A. C. Kinsey, et al.
5. *Wine, Women and Words*, Billy Rose
6. *The Life and Times of the Shmoo*, Al Capp
7. *The Gathering Storm*, Winston Churchill
8. *Roosevelt and Hopkins*, Robert E. Sherwood
9. *A Guide to Confident Living*, Norman Vincent Peale
10. *The Plague and I*, Betty MacDonald

1949

Fiction

1. *The Egyptian*, Mika Waltari
2. *The Big Fisherman*, Lloyd C. Douglas
3. *Mary*, Sholem Asch
4. *A Rage to Live*, John O'Hara
5. *Point of No Return*, John P. Marquand
6. *Dinner at Antoine's*, Frances Parkinson Keyes
7. *High Towers*, Thomas B. Costain
8. *Cutlass Empire*, Van Wyck Mason
9. *Pride's Castle*, Frank Yerby
10. *Father of the Bride*, Edward Streeter

Nonfiction

1. *White Collar Zoo*, Clare Barnes Jr.
2. *How to Win at Canasta*, Oswald Jacoby
3. *The Seven Storey Mountain*, Thomas Merton
4. *Home Sweet Zoo*, Clare Barnes Jr.
5. *Cheaper by the Dozen*, Frank B. Gilbreth Jr. and Ernestine Gilbreth Carey
6. *The Greatest Story Ever Told*, Fulton Oursler
7. *Canasta, the Argentine Rummy Game*, Ottilie H. Reilly
8. *Canasta*, Josephine Artayeta de Viel and Ralph Michael
9. *Peace of Soul*, Fulton J. Sheen
10. *A Guide to Confident Living*, Norman Vincent Peale

1950

Fiction

1. *The Cardinal*, Henry Morton Robinson
2. *Joy Street*, Frances Parkinson Keyes
3. *Across the River and into the Trees*, Ernest Hemingway
4. *The Wall*, John Hersey
5. *Star Money*, Kathleen Winsor
6. *The Parasites*, Daphne du Maurier
7. *Floodtide*, Frank Yerby
8. *Jubilee Trail*, Gwen Bristow
9. *The Adventurer*, Mika Waltari
10. *The Disenchanted*, Budd Schulberg

Nonfiction

1. *Betty Crocker's Picture Cook Book*
2. *The Baby*
3. *Look Younger, Live Longer*, Gayelord Hauser
4. *How I Raised Myself from Failure to Success in Selling*, Frank Bettger
5. *Kon-Tiki*, Thor Heyerdahl
6. *Mr. Jones, Meet the Master*, Peter Marshall
7. *Your Dream Home*, Hubbard Cobb
8. *The Mature Mind*, H. A. Overstreet
9. *Campus Zoo*, Clare Barnes Jr.
10. *Belles on Their Toes*, Frank Gilbreth Jr. and Ernestine Gilbreth Carey

1951

Fiction

1. *From Here to Eternity*, James Jones
2. *The Caine Mutiny*, Herman Wouk
3. *Moses*, Sholem Asch
4. *The Cardinal*, Henry Morton Robinson
5. *A Woman Called Fancy*, Frank Yerby
6. *The Cruel Sea*, Nicholas Monsarrat
7. *Melville Goodwin, U.S.A.*, John P. Marquand

THE LONGEST WORDS

Though most of us will never attempt to use them, these are the longest unhyphenated words in that linguists' Bible, the *Oxford English Dictionary*.

	WORD	LETTERS
1.	pneumonoultramicroscopicsilicovolcanoconiosis	45
2.	supercalifragilisticexpialidocious	34
3.	pseudopseudohypoparathyroidism	30
4.	floccinaucinihilipilification	29
4.	triethylsulphonemethylmethane	29
6.	antidisestablishmentarianism	28
6.	octamethylcyclotetrasiloxane	28
6.	tetrachlorodibenzoparadioxin	28
9.	hepaticocholangiogastronomy	27
10.	radiommunoelectrophoresis	26
10.	radioimmunoelectrophoretic	26

8. *Return to Paradise*, James A. Michener
9. *The Foundling*, Cardinal Spellman
10. *The Wanderer*, Mika Waltari

Nonfiction

1. *Look Younger, Live Longer*, Gayelord Hauser
2. *Betty Crocker's Picture Cook Book*
3. *Washington Confidential*, Jack Lait and Lee Mortimer
4. *Better Homes and Gardens Garden Book*
5. *Better Homes and Gardens Handyman's Book*
6. *The Sea Around Us*, Rachel L. Carson
7. *Thorndike-Barnhart Comprehensive Desk Dictionary*, Clarence L. Barnhart, editor
8. *Pogo*, Walt Kelly
9. *Kon-Tiki*, Thor Heyerdahl
10. *The New Yorker Twenty-Fifth Anniversary Album*

1952

Fiction

1. *The Silver Chalice*, Thomas B. Costain
2. *The Caine Mutiny*, Herman Wouk
3. *East of Eden*, John Steinbeck
4. *My Cousin Rachel*, Daphne du Maurier
5. *Steamboat Gothic*, Frances Parkinson Keyes
6. *Giant*, Edna Ferber
7. *The Old Man and the Sea*, Ernest Hemingway
8. *The Gown of Glory*, Agnes Sligh Turnbull
9. *The Saracen Blade*, Frank Yerby
10. *The Houses in Between*, Howard Spring

Nonfiction

1. *The Holy Bible: Revised Standard Version*
2. *A Man Called Peter*, Catherine Marshall
3. *U.S.A. Confidential*, Jack Lait and Lee Mortimer
4. *The Sea Around Us*, Rachel L. Carson
5. *Tallulah*, Tallulah Bankhead
6. *The Power of Positive Thinking*, Norman Vincent Peale
7. *This I Believe*, Edward P. Morgan, editor; Edward R. Murrow, foreword
8. *This Is Ike*, Wilson Hicks, editor
9. *Witness*, Whittaker Chambers
10. *Mr. President*, William Hillman

1953

Fiction

1. *The Robe*, Lloyd C. Douglas
2. *The Silver Chalice*, Thomas B. Costain
3. *Désirée*, Annemarie Selinko
4. *Battle Cry*, Leon M. Uris
5. *From Here to Eternity*, James Jones
6. *The High and the Mighty*, Ernest K. Gann
7. *Beyond This Place*, A. J. Cronin
8. *Time and Time Again*, James Hilton
9. *Lord Vanity*, Samuel Shellabarger
10. *The Unconquered*, Ben Ames Williams

Nonfiction

1. *The Holy Bible: Revised Standard Version*
2. *The Power of Positive Thinking*, Norman Vincent Peale
3. *Sexual Behavior in the Human Female*, Alfred C. Kinsey, et al.
4. *Angel Unaware*, Dale Evans Rogers
5. *Life Is Worth Living*, Fulton J. Sheen
6. *A Man Called Peter*, Catherine Marshall
7. *This I Believe*, Edward P. Morgan, editor; Edward R. Murrow, foreword
8. *The Greatest Faith Ever Known*, Fulton Oursler and G.A.O. Armstrong
9. *How to Play Your Best Golf*, Tommy Armour
10. *A House Is Not a Home*, Polly Adler

1954

Fiction

1. *Not as a Stranger*, Morton Thompson
2. *Mary Anne*, Daphne du Maurier
3. *Love Is Eternal*, Irving Stone
4. *The Royal Box*, Frances Parkinson Keyes
5. *The Egyptian*, Mika Waltari
6. *No Time for Sergeants*, Mac Hyman
7. *Sweet Thursday*, John Steinbeck
8. *The View from Pompey's Head*, Hamilton Basso
9. *Never Victorious, Never Defeated*, Taylor Caldwell
10. *Benton's Row*, Frank Yerby

Nonfiction

1. *The Holy Bible: Revised Standard Version*
2. *The Power of Positive Thinking*, Norman Vincent Peale
3. *Better Homes and Gardens New Cook Book*
4. *Betty Crocker's Good and Easy Cook Book*
5. *The Tumult and the Shouting*, Grantland Rice
6. *I'll Cry Tomorrow*, Lillian Roth, Gerold Frank, and Mike Connolly
7. *The Prayers of Peter Marshall*, Catherine Marshall, editor
8. *This I Believe, 2*, Raymond Swing, editor
9. *But We Were Born Free*, Elmer Davis
10. *The Saturday Evening Post Treasury*, Roger Butterfield, editor

1955

Fiction

1. *Marjorie Morningstar*, Herman Wouk
2. *Auntie Mame*, Patrick Dennis
3. *Andersonville*, MacKinlay Kantor
4. *Bonjour Tristesse*, Françoise Sagan
5. *The Man in the Gray Flannel Suit*, Sloan Wilson
6. *Something of Value*, Robert Ruark
7. *Not As a Stranger*, Morton Thompson
8. *No Time for Sergeants*, Mac Hyman
9. *The Tontine*, Thomas B. Costain
10. *Ten North Frederick*, John O'Hara

Nonfiction

1. *Gift from the Sea*, Anne Morrow Lindbergh
2. *The Power of Positive Thinking*, Norman Vincent Peale
3. *The Family of Man*, Edward Steichen
4. *A Man Called Peter*, Catherine Marshall
5. *How to Live 365 Days a Year*, John A. Schindler
6. *Better Homes and Gardens Diet Book*
7. *The Secret of Happiness*, Billy Graham
8. *Why Johnny Can't Read*, Rudolf Flesch
9. *Inside Africa*, John Gunther
10. *Year of Decisions*, Harry S Truman

1956

Fiction

1. *Don't Go Near the Water*, William Brinkley
2. *The Last Hurrah*, Edwin O'Connor
3. *Peyton Place*, Grace Metalious
4. *Auntie Mame*, Patrick Dennis
5. *Eloise*, Kay Thompson
6. *Andersonville*, MacKinlay Kantor
7. *A Certain Smile*, Françoise Sagan
8. *The Tribe That Lost Its Head*, Nicholas Monsarrat
9. *The Mandarins*, Simone de Beauvoir
10. *Boon Island*, Kenneth Roberts

Nonfiction

1. *Arthritis and Common Sense*, rev. ed., Dan Dale Alexander
2. *Webster's New World Dictionary of the American Language*, concise ed., David B. Guralnik
3. *Betty Crocker's Picture Cook Book*, 2nd. ed.
4. *Etiquette*, Frances Benton
5. *Better Homes and Gardens Barbecue Book*
6. *The Search for Bridey Murphy*, Morey Bernstein
7. *Love or Perish*, Smiley Blanton, M.D.
8. *Better Homes and Gardens Decorating Book*
9. *How To Live 365 Days a Year*, John A. Schindler
10. *The Nun's Story*, Kathryn Hulme

1957

Fiction

1. *By Love Possessed*, James Gould Cozzens
2. *Peyton Place*, Grace Metalious
3. *Compulsion*, Meyer Levin
4. *Rally Round the Flag, Boys!*, Max Shulman
5. *Blue Camellia*, Frances Parkinson Keyes
6. *Eloise in Paris*, Kay Thompson
7. *The Scapegoat*, Daphne du Maurier
8. *On the Beach*, Nevil Shute
9. *Below the Salt*, Thomas B. Costain
10. *Atlas Shrugged*, Ayn Rand

Nonfiction

1. *Kids Say the Darndest Things!*, Art Linkletter
2. *The FBI Story*, Don Whitehead
3. *Stay Alive All Your Life*, Norman Vincent Peale
4. *To Live Again*, Catherine Marshall
5. *Better Homes and Gardens Flower Arranging*
6. *Where Did You Go? Out. What Did You Do? Nothing*, Robert Paul Smith
7. *Baruch: My Own Story*, Bernard M. Baruch
8. *Please Don't Eat the Daisies*, Jean Kerr
9. *The American Heritage Book of Great Historic Places*
10. *The Day Christ Died*, Jim Bishop

1958

Fiction

1. *Doctor Zhivago*, Boris Pasternak
2. *Anatomy of a Murder*, Robert Traver
3. *Lolita*, Vladimir Nabokov
4. *Around the World with Auntie Mame*, Patrick Dennis
5. *From the Terrace*, John O'Hara
6. *Eloise at Christmastime*, Kay Thompson
7. *Ice Palace*, Edna Ferber
8. *The Winthrop Woman*, Anya Seton
9. *The Enemy Camp*, Jerome Weidman
10. *Victorine*, Frances Parkinson Keyes

Nonfiction

1. *Kids Say the Darndest Things!*, Art Linkletter
2. *'Twixt Twelve and Twenty*, Pat Boone
3. *Only in America*, Harry Golden
4. *Masters of Deceit*, Edgar Hoover
5. *Please Don't Eat the Daisies*, Jean Kerr
6. *Better Homes and Gardens Salad Book*
7. *The New Testament in Modern English*, J. P. Phillips, trans.
8. *Aku-Aku*, Thor Heyerdahl
9. *Dear Abby*, Abigail Van Buren
10. *Inside Russia Today*, John Gunther

1959

Fiction

1. *Exodus*, Leon Uris
2. *Doctor Zhivago*, Boris Pasternak
3. *Hawaii*, James Michener
4. *Advise and Consent*, Allen Drury
5. *Lady Chatterley's Lover*, D. H. Lawrence
6. *The Ugly American*, William J. Lederer and Eugene L. Burdick
7. *Dear and Glorious Physician*, Taylor Caldwell
8. *Lolita*, Vladimir Nabokov
9. *Mrs. 'Arris Goes to Paris*, Paul Gallico
10. *Poor No More*, Robert Ruark

Nonfiction

1. *'Twixt Twelve and Twenty*, Pat Boone
2. *Folk Medicine*, D. C. Jarvis
3. *For 2¢ Plain*, Harry Golden
4. *The Status Seekers*, Vance Packard
5. *Act One*, Moss Hart
6. *Charley Weaver's Letters from Mamma*, Cliff Arquette
7. *The Elements of Style*, William Strunk Jr. and E. B. White
8. *The General Foods Kitchens Cookbook*
9. *Only in America*, Harry Golden
10. *Mine Enemy Grows Older*, Alexander King

1960

Fiction

1. *Advise and Consent*, Allen Drury
2. *Hawaii*, James A. Michener
3. *The Leopard*, Giuseppe di Lampedusa
4. *The Chapman Report*, Irving Wallace
5. *Ourselves To Know*, John O'Hara
6. *The Constant Image*, Marcia Davenport
7. *The Lovely Ambition*, Mary Ellen Chase
8. *The Listener*, Taylor Caldwell
9. *Trustee from the Toolroom*, Nevil Shute
10. *Sermons and Soda-Water*, John O'Hara

Nonfiction

1. *Folk Medicine*, D. C. Jarvis
2. *Better Homes and Gardens First Aid for Your Family*
3. *The General Foods Kitchens Cookbook*
4. *May This House Be Safe from Tigers*, Alexander King
5. *Better Homes and Gardens Dessert Book*
6. *Better Homes and Gardens Decorating Ideas*
7. *The Rise and Fall of the Third Reich*, William L. Shirer
8. *The Conscience of a Conservative*, Barry Goldwater
9. *I Kid You Not*, Jack Paar
10. *Between You, Me and the Gatepost*, Pat Boone

1961

Fiction

1. *The Agony and the Ecstasy*, Irving Stone
2. *Franny and Zooey*, J. D. Salinger
3. *To Kill a Mockingbird*, Harper Lee
4. *Mila 18*, Leon Uris
5. *The Carpetbaggers*, Harold Robbins
6. *Tropic of Cancer*, Henry Miller
7. *Winnie Ille Pu*, Alexander Lenard, trans.
8. *Daughter of Silence*, Morris West
9. *The Edge of Sadness*, Edwin O'Connor
10. *The Winter of Our Discontent*, John Steinbeck

Nonfiction

1. *The New English Bible: The New Testament*
2. *The Rise and Fall of the Third Reich*, William Shirer
3. *Better Homes and Gardens Sewing Book*

4. *Casserole Cook Book*
5. *A Nation of Sheep*, William Lederer
6. *Better Homes and Gardens Nutrition for Your Family*
7. *The Making of the President, 1960*, Theodore H. White
8. *Calories Don't Count*, Dr. Herman Taller
9. *Betty Crocker's New Picture Cook Book: New Edition*
10. *Ring of Bright Water*, Gavin Maxwell

1962

Fiction

1. *Ship of Fools*, Katherine Anne Porter
2. *Dearly Beloved*, Anne Morrow Lindbergh
3. *A Shade of Difference*, Allen Drury
4. *Youngblood Hawke*, Herman Wouk
5. *Franny and Zooey*, J. D. Salinger
6. *Fail-Safe*, Eugene Burdick and Harvey Wheeler
7. *Seven Days in May*, Fletcher Knebel and Charles W. Bailey II
8. *The Prize*, Irving Wallace
9. *The Agony and the Ecstasy*, Irving Stone
10. *The Reivers*, William Faulkner

Nonfiction

1. *Calories Don't Count*, Dr. Herman Taller
2. *The New English Bible: The New Testament*
3. *Better Homes and Gardens Cook Book: New Edition*
4. *O Ye Jigs & Juleps!*, Virginia Cary Hudson
5. *Happiness Is a Warm Puppy*, Charles M. Schulz
6. *The Joy of Cooking: New Edition*, Irma S. Rombauer and Marion Rombauer Becker
7. *My Life in Court*, Louis Nizer
8. *The Rothschilds*, Frederic Morton
9. *Sex and the Single Girl*, Helen Gurley Brown
10. *Travels with Charley*, John Steinbeck

1963

Fiction

1. *The Shoes of the Fisherman*, Morris L. West
2. *The Group*, Mary McCarthy
3. *Raise High the Roof Beam, Carpenters, and Seymour—An Introduction*, J. D. Salinger
4. *Caravans*, James A. Michener
5. *Elizabeth Appleton*, John O'Hara
6. *Grandmother and the Priests*, Taylor Caldwell
7. *City of Night*, John Rechy
8. *The Glass-Blowers*, Daphne du Maurier
9. *The Sand Pebbles*, Richard McKenna
10. *The Battle of the Villa Fiorita*, Rumer Godden

LITERATURE GOES TO THE MOVIES

It's no secret that many movies, both good and bad, are based on books. This list presents a small sampling of unusual, delightful, and surprising books by leading writers that were turned into well-known movies. (The dates after the titles indicate the year of the film version's release.)

Awakenings (1990), Oliver Sacks
The Blue Angel (1930, 1959), Heinrich Mann
The Body Snatcher (1945), Robert Louis Stevenson
Breakfast at Tiffany's (1961), Truman Capote
Chitty, Chitty, Bang, Bang (1968), Ian Fleming
The Death and Life of Dith Pran (released as *The Killing Fields*, 1984), Sidney Schanberg
Deliverance (1972), James Dickey
Do Androids Dream of Electric Sheep? (released as *Blade Runner*, 1982), Philip K. Dick
Don't Look Now (1971), Daphne du Maurier
The Executioners (released as *Cape Fear*, 1962, 1991), J. D. MacDonald
The Grifters (1990), Jim Thompson
The Hamlet (originally *The Long, Hot Summer*, 1957) William Faulkner
Jumanji (1995), Chris Van Allsburg
The Killer Angels (released as *Gettysburg*, 1993), Michael Shaara
The Last Picture Show (1971), Larry McMurtry
Legends of the Fall (1994), Jim Harrison
Lost Moon (released as *Apollo 13*, 1995), Jim Lovell and Jeffrey Kluger
The Magnificent Ambersons (1942), Booth Tarkington
The Maltese Falcon (1941; also released as *Satan Met a Lady*, 1937), Dashiell Hammett
Mildred Pierce (1945), James M. Cain
The Natural (1984), Bernard Malamud
Burning Patience (released as *Il Postino (The Postman)*,1995), Antonio Skarmeta
The Postman Always Rings Twice (1946, 1981), James M. Cain
Rum Punch (released as *Jackie Brown*), Elmore Leonard
The Seven Pillars of Wisdom (released as *Lawrence of Arabia*, 1962), T. E. Lawrence
Tales from the South Pacific (produced as the musical *South Pacific* and later released as a film, 1958), James Michener
The Turn of the Screw (released as *The Innocents*, 1961), Henry James
Two Hours to Doom (released as *Dr. Strangelove*, 1964), Peter George

Nonfiction

1. *Happiness Is a Warm Puppy*, Charles M. Schulz
2. *Security Is a Thumb and a Blanket*, Charles M. Schulz
3. *J.F.K.: The Man and the Myth*, Victor Lasky
4. *Profiles in Courage: Inaugural Edition*, John F. Kennedy
5. *O Ye Jigs & Juleps!*, Virginia Cary Hudson
6. *Better Homes and Gardens Bread Cook Book*
7. *The Pillsbury Family Cookbook*
8. *I Owe Russia $1200*, Bob Hope
9. *Heloise's Housekeeping Hints*
10. *Better Homes and Gardens Baby Book*

1964

Fiction

1. *The Spy Who Came in from the Cold*, John Le Carré
2. *Candy*, Terry Southern and Mason Hoffenberg
3. *Herzog*, Saul Bellow
4. *Armageddon*, Leon Uris
5. *The Man*, Irving Wallace
6. *The Rector of Justin*, Louis Auchincloss
7. *The Martyred*, Richard E. Kim
8. *You Only Live Twice*, Ian Fleming
9. *This Rough Magic*, Mary Stewart
10. *Convention*, Fletcher Knebel and Charles W. Bailey II

Nonfiction

1. *Four Days*, American Heritage and United Press International
2. *I Need All the Friends I Can Get*, Charles M. Schulz
3. *Profiles in Courage: Memorial Edition*, John F. Kennedy
4. *In His Own Write*, John Lennon
5. *Christmas Is Together-Time*, Charles M. Schulz
6. *A Day in the Life of President Kennedy*, Jim Bishop
7. *The Kennedy Wit*, compiled by Bill Adler
8. *A Moveable Feast*, Ernest Hemingway
9. *Reminiscences*, General Douglas MacArthur
10. *The John F. Kennedys*, Mark Shaw

1965

Fiction

1. *The Source*, James A. Michener
2. *Up the Down Staircase*, Bel Kaufman
3. *Herzog*, Saul Bellow
4. *The Looking Glass War*, John Le Carré
5. *The Green Berets*, Robin Moore
6. *Those Who Love*, Irving Stone
7. *The Man with the Golden Gun*, Ian Fleming
8. *Hotel*, Arthur Hailey
9. *The Ambassador*, Morris West
10. *Don't Stop the Carnival*, Herman Wouk

Nonfiction

1. *How To Be a Jewish Mother*, Dan Greenburg
2. *A Gift of Prophecy*, Ruth Montgomery
3. *Games People Play*, Eric Berne, M.D.
4. *World Aflame*, Billy Graham
5. *Happiness Is a Dry Martini*, Johnny Carson
6. *Markings*, Dag Hammarskjöld
7. *A Thousand Days*, Arthur Schlesinger Jr.
8. *My Shadow Ran Fast*, Bill Sands
9. *Kennedy*, Theodore C. Sorensen
10. *The Making of the President, 1964*, Theodore H. White

1966

Fiction

1. *Valley of the Dolls*, Jacqueline Susann
2. *The Adventurers*, Harold Robbins
3. *The Secret of Santa Vittoria*, Robert Crichton
4. *Capable of Honor*, Allen Drury
5. *The Double Image*, Helen MacInnes
6. *The Fixer*, Bernard Malamud
7. *Tell No Man*, Adela Rogers St. Johns
8. *Tai-Pan*, James Clavell
9. *The Embezzler*, Louis Auchincloss
10. *All in the Family*, Edwin O'Connor

Nonfiction

1. *How to Avoid Probate*, Norman F. Dacey
2. *Human Sexual Response*, William Howard Masters and Virginia E. Johnston
3. *In Cold Blood*, Truman Capote
4. *Games People Play*, Eric Berne, M.D.
5. *A Thousand Days*, Arthur M. Schlesinger Jr.
6. *Everything but Money*, Sam Levenson
7. *The Random House Dictionary of the English Language*
8. *Rush to Judgment*, Mark Lane
9. *The Last Battle*, Cornelius Ryan
10. *Phyllis Diller's Housekeeping Hints*, Phyllis Diller

1967

Fiction

1. *The Arrangement*, Elia Kazan
2. *The Confessions of Nat Turner*, William Styron (tie)
2. *The Chosen*, Chaim Potok (tie)
4. *Topaz*, Leon Uris
5. *Christy*, Catherine Marshall
6. *The Eighth Day*, Thornton Wilder
7. *Rosemary's Baby*, Ira Levin
8. *The Plot*, Irving Wallace
9. *The Gabriel Hounds*, Mary Stewart
10. *The Exhibitionist*, Henry Sutton

Nonfiction

1. *Death of a President*, William Manchester
2. *Misery Is a Blind Date*, Johnny Carson
3. *Games People Play*, Eric Berne, M.D.
4. *Stanyan Street & Other Sorrows*, Rod McKuen
5. *A Modern Priest Looks at His Outdated Church*, Father James Kavanaugh
6. *Everything but Money*, Sam Levenson
7. *Our Crowd*, Stephen Birmingham
8. *Edgar Cayce—The Sleeping Prophet*, Jess Stearn (tie)
8. *Better Homes and Gardens Favorite Ways with Chicken* (tie)
8. *Phyllis Diller's Marriage Manual*, Phyllis Diller (tie)

1968

Fiction

1. *Airport*, Arthur Hailey
2. *Couples*, John Updike
3. *The Salzburg Connection*, Helen MacInnes
4. *A Small Town in Germany*, John Le Carré
5. *Testimony of Two Men*, Taylor Caldwell
6. *Preserve and Protect*, Allen Drury
7. *Myra Breckinridge*, Gore Vidal
8. *Vanished*, Fletcher Knebel
9. *Christy*, Catherine Marshall
10. *The Tower of Babel*, Morris L. West

Nonfiction

1. *Better Homes and Gardens New Cook Book*
2. *The Random House Dictionary of the English Language: College Edition*, Laurence Urdang, editor
3. *Listen to the Warm*, Rod McKuen
4. *Between Parent and Child*, Haim G. Ginott
5. *Lonesome Cities*, Rod McKuen

6. *The Doctor's Quick Weight Loss Diet*, Erwin M. Stillman and Samm Sinclair Baker
7. *The Money Game*, Adam Smith
8. *Stanyan Street & Other Sorrows*, Rod McKuen
9. *The Weight Watcher's Cook Book*, Jean Nidetch
10. *Better Homes and Gardens Eat and Stay Slim*

1969

Fiction

1. *Portnoy's Complaint*, Philip Roth
2. *The Godfather*, Mario Puzo
3. *The Love Machine*, Jacqueline Susann
4. *The Inheritors*, Harold Robbins
5. *The Andromeda Strain*, Michael Crichton
6. *The Seven Minutes*, Irving Wallace
7. *Naked Came the Stranger*, Penelope Ashe
8. *The Promise*, Chaim Potok
9. *The Pretenders*, Gwen Davis
10. *The House on the Strand*, Daphne du Maurier

Nonfiction

1. *American Heritage Dictionary of the English Language*, William Morris, editor
2. *In Someone's Shadow*, Rod McKuen
3. *The Peter Principle*, Laurence J. Peter and Raymond Hull
4. *Between Parent and Teenager*, Dr. Haim G. Ginott
5. *The Graham Kerr Cookbook*, the Galloping Gourmet
6. *The Selling of the President 1968*, Joe McGinniss
7. *Miss Craig's 21-Day Shape-Up Program for Men and Women*, Marjorie Craig
8. *My Life and Prophecies*, Jeane Dixon with René Noorbergen
9. *Linda Goodman's Sun Signs*, Linda Goodman
10. *Twelve Years of Christmas*, Rod McKuen

1970

Fiction

1. *Love Story*, Erich Segal
2. *The French Lieutenant's Woman*, John Fowles
3. *Islands in the Stream*, Ernest Hemingway
4. *The Crystal Cave*, Mary Stewart
5. *Great Lion of God*, Taylor Caldwell
6. *QB VII*, Leon Uris
7. *The Gang That Couldn't Shoot Straight*, Jimmy Breslin
8. *The Secret Woman*, Victoria Holt
9. *Travels with My Aunt*, Graham Greene
10. *Rich Man, Poor Man*, Irwin Shaw

Nonfiction

1. *Everything You Always Wanted To Know About Sex but Were Afraid To Ask*, David Reuben, M.D.
2. *The New English Bible*
3. *The Sensuous Woman*, "J"
4. *Better Homes and Gardens Fondue and Tabletop Cooking*
5. *Up the Organization*, Robert Townsend
6. *Ball Four*, Jim Bouton
7. *American Heritage Dictionary of the English Language*, William Morris
8. *Body Language*, Julius Fast
9. *In Someone's Shadow*, Rod McKuen
10. *Caught in the Quiet*, Rod McKuen

1971

Fiction

1. *Wheels*, Arthur Hailey
2. *The Exorcist*, William P. Blatty
3. *The Passions of the Mind*, Irving Stone
4. *The Day of the Jackal*, Frederick Forsyth
5. *The Betsy*, Harold Robbins
6. *Message from Malaga*, Helen MacInnes
7. *The Winds of War*, Herman Wouk
8. *The Drifters*, James A. Michener
9. *The Other*, Thomas Tryon
10. *Rabbit Redux*, John Updike

Nonfiction

1. *The Sensous Man*, "M"
2. *Bury My Heart at Wounded Knee*, Dee Brown
3. *Better Homes and Gardens Blender Cook Book*
4. *I'm O.K., You're O.K.*, Thomas Harris
5. *Any Woman Can!*, David Reuben, M.D.
6. *Inside the Third Reich*, Albert Speer
7. *Eleanor and Franklin*, Joseph P. Lash
8. *Wunnerful, Wunnerful!*, Lawrence Welk
9. *Honor Thy Father*, Gay Talese
10. *Fields of Wonder*, Rod McKuen

1972

Fiction

1. *Jonathan Livingston Seagull*, Richard Bach
2. *August, 1914*, Alexander Solzhenitsyn
3. *The Odessa File*, Frederick Forsyth
4. *The Day of the Jackal*, Frederick Forsyth
5. *The Word*, Irving Wallace
6. *The Winds of War*, Herman Wouk
7. *Captains and the Kings*, Taylor Caldwell
8. *Two from Galilee*, Marjorie Holmes
9. *My Name Is Asher Lev*, Chaim Potok
10. *Semi-Tough*, Dan Jenkins

Nonfiction

1. *The Living Bible*, Kenneth Taylor
2. *I'm O.K., You're O.K.*, Thomas Harris
3. *Open Marriage*, Nena and George O'Neill
4. *Harry S. Truman*, Margaret Truman
5. *Dr. Atkins' Diet Revolution*, Robert C. Atkins
6. *Better Homes and Gardens Menu Cook Book*
7. *The Peter Prescription*, Laurence J. Peter
8. *A World Beyond*, Ruth Montgomery
9. *Journey to Ixtlan*, Carlos Castaneda
10. *Better Homes and Gardens Low-Calorie Desserts*

1973

Fiction

1. *Jonathan Livingston Seagull*, Richard Bach
2. *Once Is Not Enough*, Jacqueline Susann
3. *Breakfast of Champions*, Kurt Vonnegut
4. *The Odessa File*, Frederick Forsyth
5. *Burr*, Gore Vidal
6. *The Hollow Hills*, Mary Stewart
7. *Evening in Byzantium*, Irwin Shaw
8. *The Matlock Paper*, Robert Ludlum
9. *The Billion Dollar Sure Thing*, Paul E. Erdman
10. *The Honorary Consul*, Graham Greene

Nonfiction

1. *The Living Bible*, Kenneth Taylor
2. *Dr. Atkins' Diet Revolution*, Robert C. Atkins
3. *I'm O.K., You're O.K.*, Thomas Harris
4. *The Joy of Sex*, Alex Comfort
5. *Weight Watchers Program Cookbook*, Jean Nidetch
6. *How To Be Your Own Best Friend*, Mildred Newman, et al.
7. *The Art of Walt Disney*, Christopher Finch
8. *Better Homes and Gardens Home Canning Cookbook*
9. *Alistair Cooke's America*, Alistair Cooke
10. *Sybil*, Flora R. Schreiber

1974

Fiction

1. *Centennial*, James A. Michener
2. *Watership Down*, Richard Adams
3. *Jaws*, Peter Benchley
4. *Tinker, Tailor, Soldier, Spy*, John Le Carré
5. *Something Happened*, Joseph Heller
6. *The Dogs of War*, Frederick Forsyth
7. *The Pirate*, Harold J. Robbins
8. *I Heard the Owl Call My Name*, Margaret Craven
9. *The Seven-Per-Cent Solution*, John H. Watson, M.D., Nicholas Meyer, editor
10. *The Fan Club*, Irving Wallace

Nonfiction

1. *The Total Woman*, Marabel Morgan
2. *All the President's Men*, Carl Bernstein and Bob Woodward
3. *Plain Speaking: An Oral Biography of Harry S. Truman*, Merle Miller
4. *More Joy: A Lovemaking Companion to The Joy of Sex*, Alex Comfort
5. *Alistair Cooke's America*, Alistair Cooke
6. *Tales of Power*, Carlos A. Castaneda
7. *You Can Profit from a Monetary Crisis*, Harry Browne
8. *All Things Bright and Beautiful*, James Herriot
9. *The Bermuda Triangle*, Charles Berlitz with J. Manson Valentine
10. *The Memory Book*, Harry Lorayne and Jerry Lucas

AMERICA'S POETS LAUREATE

To honor America's greatest poets, the Librarian of Congress names a poet laureate. The anointed:

Robert Penn Warren	1986–87
Richard Wilbur	1987–88
Howard Nemerov	1988–90
Mark Strand	1990–91
Joseph Brodsky	1991–92
Mona Van Duyn	1992–93
Rita Dove	1993–95
Robert Hass	1995–97
Robert Pinsky	1997–

1975

Fiction

1. *Ragtime*, E. L. Doctorow
2. *The Moneychangers*, Arthur Hailey
3. *Curtain*, Agatha Christie
4. *Looking for Mister Goodbar*, Judith Rossner
5. *The Choirboys*, Joseph Wambaugh
6. *The Eagle Has Landed*, Jack Higgins
7. *The Greek Treasure: A Biographical Novel of Henry and Sophia Schliemann*, Irving Stone
8. *The Great Train Robbery*, Michael Crichton
9. *Shogun*, James Clavell
10. *Humboldt's Gift*, Saul Bellow

Nonfiction

1. *Angels: God's Secret Agents*, Billy Graham
2. *Winning Through Intimidation*, Robert Ringer
3. *TM: Discovering Energy and Overcoming Stress*, Harold H. Bloomfield
4. *The Ascent of Man*, Jacob Bronowski
5. *Sylvia Porter's Money Book*, Sylvia Porter
6. *Total Fitness in 30 Minutes a Week*, Laurence E. Morehouse and Leonard Gross
7. *The Bermuda Triangle*, Charles Berlitz with J. Manson Valentine
8. *The Save-Your-Life Diet*, David Reuben
9. *Bring on the Empty Horses*, David Niven
10. *Breach of Faith: The Fall of Richard Nixon*, Theodore H. White

1976

Fiction

1. *Trinity*, Leon Uris
2. *Sleeping Murder*, Agatha Christie
3. *Dolores*, Jacqueline Susann
4. *Storm Warning*, Jack Higgins
5. *The Deep*, Peter Benchley
6. *1876*, Gore Vidal
7. *Slapstick: or, Lonesome No More!*, Kurt Vonnegut
8. *The Lonely Lady*, Harold Robbins
9. *Touch Not the Cat*, Mary Stewart
10. *A Stranger in the Mirror*, Sidney Sheldon

Nonfiction

1. *The Final Days*, Bob Woodward and Carl Bernstein
2. *Roots*, Alex Haley
3. *Your Erroneous Zones*, Dr. Wayne W. Dyer
4. *Passages: The Predictable Crises of Adult Life*, Gail Sheehy
5. *Born Again*, Charles W. Colson
6. *The Grass Is Always Greener over the Septic Tank*, Erma Bombeck
7. *Angels: God's Secret Agents*, Billy Graham
8. *Blind Ambition: The White House Years*, John Dean
9. *The Hite Report: A Nationwide Study of Female Sexuality*, Shere Hite
10. *The Right and the Power: The Prosecution of Watergate*, Leon Jaworski

1977

Fiction

1. *The Silmarillion*, J.R.R. Tolkien; Christopher Tolkien
2. *The Thorn Birds*, Colleen McCullough
3. *Illusions: The Adventures of a Reluctant Messiah*, Richard Bach
4. *The Honourable Schoolboy*, John Le Carré
5. *Oliver's Story*, Erich Segal
6. *Dreams Die First*, Harold Robbins
7. *Beggarman, Thief*, Irwin Shaw
8. *How To Save Your Own Life*, Erica Jong
9. *Delta of Venus: Erotica*, Anaïs Nin
10. *Daniel Martin*, John Fowles

Nonfiction

1. *Roots*, Alex Haley
2. *Looking Out for #1*, Robert Ringer
3. *All Things Wise and Wonderful*, James Herriot
4. *Your Erroneous Zones*, Dr. Wayne W. Dyer
5. *The Book of Lists*, David Wallechinsky, Irving Wallace, and Amy Wallace
6. *The Possible Dream: A Candid Look at Amway*, Charles Paul Conn
7. *The Dragons of Eden: Speculations on the Evolution of Human Intelligence*, Carl Sagan
8. *The Second Ring of Power*, Carlos Castaneda
9. *The Grass Is Always Greener over the Septic Tank*, Erma Bombeck
10. *The Amityville Horror*, Jay Anson

1978

Fiction

1. *Chesapeake*, James A. Michener
2. *War and Remembrance*, Herman Wouk
3. *Fools Die*, Mario Puzo

4. *Bloodlines*, Sidney Sheldon
5. *Scruples*, Judith Krantz
6. *Evergreen*, Belva Plain
7. *Illusions: The Adventures of a Reluctant Messiah*, Richard Bach
8. *The Holcroft Covenant*, Robert Ludlum
9. *Second Generation*, Howard Fast
10. *Eye of the Needle*, Ken Follett

Nonfiction

1. *If Life Is a Bowl of Cherries—What Am I Doing in the Pits?*, Erma Bombeck
2. *Gnomes*, Wil Huygen and Rien Poortvliet
3. *The Complete Book of Running*, James Fixx
4. *Mommie Dearest*, Christina Crawford
5. *Pulling Your Own Strings*, Dr. Wayne W. Dyer
8. *RN: The Memoirs of Richard Nixon*, Richard Nixon
7. *A Distant Mirror: The Calamitous Fourteenth Century*, Barbara Tuchman
8. *Faeries*, Brian Froud and Alan Lee
9. *In Search of History: A Personal Adventure*, Theodore H. White
10. *The Muppet Show Book*, the Muppet People

1979

Fiction

1. *The Matarese Circle*, Robert Ludlum
2. *Sophie's Choice*, William Styron
3. *Overload*, Arthur Hailey
4. *Memories of Another Day*, Harold Robbins
5. *Jailbird*, Kurt Vonnegut
6. *The Dead Zone*, Stephen King
7. *The Last Enchantment*, Mary Stewart
8. *The Establishment*, Howard Fast
9. *The Third World War: August 1985*, Gen. Sir John Hackett, et al.
10. *Smiley's People*, John Le Carré

Nonfiction

1. *Aunt Erma's Cope Book*, Erma Bombeck
2. *The Complete Scarsdale Medical Diet*, Herman Tarnower, M.D., and Samm Sinclair Baker
3. *How to Prosper During the Coming Bad Years*, Howard J. Ruff
4. *Cruel Shoes*, Steve Martin
5. *The Pritikin Program for Diet and Exercise*, Nathan Pritikin and Patrick McGrady Jr.
6. *White House Years*, Henry Kissinger
7. *Lauren Bacall By Myself*, Lauren Bacall
8. *The Brethren: Inside the Supreme Court*, Bob Woodward and Scott Armstrong
9. *Restoring the American Dream*, Robert J. Ringer
10. *The Winner's Circle*, Charles Paul Conn

1980

Fiction

1. *The Covenant*, James A. Michener
2. *The Bourne Identity*, Robert Ludlum
3. *Rage of Angels*, Sidney Sheldon
4. *Princess Daisy*, Judith Krantz
5. *Firestarter*, Stephen King
6. *The Key to Rebecca*, Ken Follett
7. *Random Winds*, Belva Plain
8. *The Devil's Alternative*, Frederick Forsyth
9. *The Fifth Horseman*, Larry Collins and Dominique Lapierre
10. *The Spike*, Arnaud de Borchgrave and Robert Moss

Nonfiction

1. *Crisis Investing: Opportunities and Profits in the Coming Great Depression*, Douglas R. Casey
2. *Cosmos*, Carl Sagan
3. *Free to Choose: A Personal Statement*, Milton and Rose Friedman
4. *Anatomy of an Illness as Perceived by the Patient*, Norman Cousins
5. *Thy Neighbor's Wife*, Gay Talese
6. *The Sky's the Limit*, Dr. Wayne W. Dyer
7. *The Third Wave*, Alvin Toffler
8. *Craig Claiborne's Gourmet Diet*, Craig Claiborne with Pierre Franey
9. *Nothing Down*, Robert Allen
10. *Shelley: Also Known as Shirley*, Shelley Winters

1981

Fiction

1. *Noble House*, James Clavell
2. *The Hotel New Hampshire*, John Irving
3. *Cujo*, Stephen King
4. *An Indecent Obsession*, Colleen McCullough
5. *Gorky Park*, Martin Cruz Smith
6. *Masquerade*, Kit Williams
7. *Goodbye, Janette*, Harold Robbins
8. *The Third Deadly Sin*, Lawrence Sanders
9. *The Glitter Dome*, Joseph Wambaugh
10. *No Time for Tears*, Cynthia Freeman

Nonfiction

1. *The Beverly Hills Diet*, Judy Mazel
2. *The Lord God Made Them All*, James Herriot
3. *Richard Simmons' Never-Say-Diet Book*, Richard Simmons
4. *A Light in the Attic*, Shel Silverstein
5. *Cosmos*, Carl Sagan
6. *Better Homes & Gardens New Cook Book*
7. *Miss Piggy's Guide to Life*, Miss Piggy as told to Henry Beard
8. *Weight Watchers 365-Day Menu Cookbook*
9. *You Can Negotiate Anything*, Herb Cohen
10. *A Few Minutes with Andy Rooney*, Andrew A. Rooney

1982

Fiction

1. *E.T., the Extra-Terrestrial Storybook*, William Kotzwinkle
2. *Space*, James A. Michener
3. *The Parsifal Mosaic*, Robert Ludlum
4. *Master of the Game*, Sidney Sheldon
5. *Mistral's Daughter*, Judith Krantz
6. *The Valley of Horses*, Jean M. Auel
7. *Different Seasons*, Stephen King
8. *North and South*, John Jakes
9. *2010: Odyssey Two*, Arthur C. Clarke
10. *The Man from St. Petersburg*, Ken Follett

Nonfiction

1. *Jane Fonda's Workout Book*, Jane Fonda
2. *Living, Loving and Learning*, Leo Buscaglia
3. *And More by Andy Rooney*, Andrew A. Rooney
4. *Better Homes & Gardens New Cookbook*
5. *Life Extension: Adding Years to Your Life And Life to Your Years—A Practical Scientific Approach*, Durk Pearson and Sandy Shaw
6. *When Bad Things Happen to Good People*, Harold S. Kushner
7. *A Few Minutes with Andy Rooney*, Andrew A. Rooney
8. *The Weight Watchers Food Plan Diet Cookbook*, Jean Nidetch
9. *Richard Simmons' Never-Say-Diet Cookbook*, Richard Simmons
10. *No Bad Dogs: The Woodhouse Way*, Barbara Woodhouse

1983

Fiction

1. *Return of the Jedi Storybook*, Joan D. Vinge, adapt.
2. *Poland*, James A. Michener
3. *Pet Sematary*, Stephen King
4. *The Little Drummer Girl*, John Le Carré
5. *Christine*, Stephen King
6. *Changes*, Danielle Steel
7. *The Name of the Rose*, Umberto Eco
8. *White Gold Wielder: Book Three of The Second Chronicles of Thomas Covenant*, Stephen R. Donaldson
9. *Hollywood Wives*, Jackie Collins
10. *The Lonesome Gods*, Louis L'Amour

Nonfiction

1. *In Search of Excellence: Lessons from America's Best-Run Companies*, Thomas J. Peters and Robert H. Waterman Jr.
2. *Megatrends: Ten New Directions Transforming Our Lives*, John Naisbitt
3. *Motherhood: The Second Oldest Profession*, Erma Bombeck
4. *The One Minute Manager*, Kenneth Blanchard and Spencer Johnson
5. *Jane Fonda's Workout Book*, Jane Fonda
6. *The Best of James Herriot*, James Herriot
7. *The Mary Kay Guide to Beauty: Discovering Your Special Look*
8. *On Wings of Eagles*, Ken Follett
9. *Creating Wealth*, Robert G. Allen
10. *The Body Principal: The Exercise Program for Life*, Victoria Principal

1984

Fiction

1. *The Talisman*, Stephen King and Peter Straub
2. *The Aquitaine Progression*, Robert Ludlum
3. *The Sicilian*, Mario Puzo
4. *Love and War*, John Jakes
5. *The Butter Battle Book*, Dr. Seuss
6. *". . . And the Ladies of the Club,"* Helen Hooven Santmyer
7. *The Fourth Protocol*, Frederick Forsyth
8. *Full Circle*, Danielle Steel
9. *The Life and Hard Times of Heidi Abromowitz*, Joan Rivers
10. *Lincoln: A Novel*, Gore Vidal

Nonfiction

1. *Iacocca: An Autobiography*, Lee Iacocca with William Novak
2. *Loving Each Other*, Leo Buscaglia
3. *Eat to Win: The Sports Nutrition Bible*, Robert Haas, M.D.
4. *Pieces of My Mind*, Andrew A. Rooney
5. *Weight Watchers Fast and Fabulous Cookbook*
6. *What They Don't Teach You at Harvard Business School: Notes from a Street-Smart Executive*, Mark H. McCormack
7. *Women Coming of Age*, Jane Fonda with Mignon McCarthy
8. *Moses the Kitten*, James Herriot
9. *The One Minute Salesperson*, Spencer Johnson, M.D., and Larry Wilson
10. *Weight Watchers Quick Start Program Cookbook*, Jean Nidetch

1985

Fiction

1. *The Mammoth Hunters*, Jean M. Auel
2. *Texas*, James A. Michener
3. *Lake Wobegon Days*, Garrison Keillor
4. *If Tomorrow Comes*, Sidney Sheldon
5. *Skeleton Crew*, Stephen King
6. *Secrets*, Danielle Steel
7. *Contact*, Carl Sagan
8. *Lucky*, Jackie Collins
9. *Family Album*, Danielle Steel
10. *Jubal Sackett*, Louis L'Amour

Nonfiction

1. *Iacocca: An Autobiography*, Lee Iacocca with William Novak
2. *Yeager: An Autobiography*, Gen. Chuck Yeager and Leo Janos
3. *Elvis and Me*, Priscilla Beaulieu Presley with Sandra Harmon
4. *Fit for Life*, Harvey and Marilyn Diamond
5. *The Be-Happy Attitudes*, Robert Schuller
6. *Dancing in the Light*, Shirley MacLaine
7. *A Passion for Excellence: The Leadership Difference*, Thomas J. Peters and Nancy K. Austin
8. *The Frugal Gourmet*, Jeff Smith
9. *I Never Played the Game*, Howard Cosell with Peter Bonventre
10. *Dr. Berger's Immune Power Diet*, Stuart M. Berger, M.D.

1986

Fiction

1. *It*, Stephen King
2. *Red Storm Rising*, Tom Clancy
3. *Whirlwind*, James Clavell
4. *The Bourne Supremacy*, Robert Ludlum
5. *Hollywood Husbands*, Jackie Collins
6. *Wanderlust*, Danielle Steel
7. *I'll Take Manhattan*, Judith Krantz
8. *Last of the Breed*, Louis L'Amour
9. *The Prince of Tides*, Pat Conroy
10. *A Perfect Spy*, John Le Carré

Nonfiction

1. *Fatherhood*, Bill Cosby
2. *Fit for Life*, Harvey and Marilyn Diamond
3. *His Way: The Unauthorized Biography of Frank Sinatra*, Kitty Kelley
4. *The Rotation Diet*, Martin Katahn
5. *You're Only Old Once*, Dr. Seuss
6. *Callanetics: Ten Years Younger in Ten Hours*, Callan Pinckney
7. *The Frugal Gourmet Cooks with Wine*, Jeff Smith
8. *Be Happy—You Are Loved!*, Robert H. Schuller
9. *Word for Word*, Andrew A. Rooney
10. *James Herriot's Dog Stories*, James Herriot

1987

Fiction

1. *The Tommyknockers*, Stephen King
2. *Patriot Games*, Tom Clancy
3. *Kaleidoscope*, Danielle Steel
4. *Misery*, Stephen King
5. *Leaving Home: A Collection of Lake Wobegon Stories*, Garrison Keillor
6. *Windmills of the Gods*, Sidney Sheldon
7. *Presumed Innocent*, Scott Turow
8. *Fine Things*, Danielle Steel
9. *Heaven and Hell*, John Jakes
10. *The Eyes of the Dragon*, Stephen King

Nonfiction

1. *Time Flies*, Bill Cosby
2. *Spycatcher: The Candid Autobiography of a Senior Intelligence Officer*, Peter Wright with Paul Greengrass
3. *Family: The Ties That Bind . . . and Gag!*, Erma Bombeck
4. *Veil: The Secret Wars of the CIA, 1981–1987*, Bob Woodward
5. *A Day in the Life of America*, Rick Smolan and David Cohen
6. *The Great Depression of 1990*, Ravi Batra
7. *It's All in the Playing*, Shirley MacLaine
8. *Man of the House: The Life and Political Memoirs of Speaker Tip O'Neill*, Thomas P. O'Neill Jr. with William Novak
9. *The Frugal Gourmet Cooks American*, Jeff Smith
10. *The Closing of the American Mind*, Allan Bloom

1988

Fiction

1. *The Cardinal of the Kremlin*, Tom Clancy
2. *The Sands of Time*, Sidney Sheldon
3. *Zoya*, Danielle Steel
4. *The Icarus Agenda*, Robert Ludlum
5. *Alaska*, James A. Michener
6. *Till We Meet Again*, Judith Krantz
7. *The Queen of the Damned*, Anne Rice
8. *To Be the Best*, Barbara Taylor Bradford
9. *One: A Novel*, Richard Bach
10. *Mitla Pass*, Leon Uris

Nonfiction

1. *The 8-Week Cholesterol Cure*, Robert E. Kowalski
2. *Talking Straight*, Lee Iacocca with Sonny Kleinfield
3. *A Brief History of Time: From the Big Bang to Black Holes*, Steven W. Hawking
4. *Trump: The Art of the Deal*, Donald J. Trump with Tony Schwartz
5. *Gracie: A Love Story*, George Burns
6. *Elizabeth Takes Off*, Elizabeth Taylor
7. *Swim with the Sharks without Being Eaten Alive*, Harvey MacKay
8. *Christmas in America*, David Cohen, editor
9. *Weight Watchers Quick Success Program Book*, Jean Nidetch
10. *Moonwalk*, Michael Jackson

1989

Fiction

1. *Clear and Present Danger*, Tom Clancy
2. *The Dark Half*, Stephen King
3. *Daddy*, Danielle Steel
4. *Star*, Danielle Steel
5. *Caribbean*, James A. Michener
6. *The Satanic Verses*, Salman Rushdie
7. *The Russia House*, John Le Carré
8. *The Pillars of the Earth*, Ken Follet
9. *California Gold*, John Jakes
10. *While My Pretty One Sleeps*, Mary Higgins Clark

Nonfiction

1. *All I Really Need To Know I Learned in Kindergarten: Uncommon Thoughts on Common Things*, Robert Fulghum
2. *Wealth Without Risk: How To Develop a Personal Fortune Without Going Out on a Limb*, Charles J. Givens
3. *A Woman Named Jackie*, C. David Heymann
4. *It Was on Fire When I Lay Down on It*, Robert Fulghum
5. *Better Homes and Gardens New Cook Book*
6. *The Way Things Work*, David Macaulay
7. *It's Always Something*, Gilda Radner
8. *Roseanne: My Life as a Woman*, Roseanne Barr
9. *The Frugal Gourmet Cooks Three Ancient Cuisines: China, Greece, and Rome*, Jeff Smith
10. *My Turn: The Memoirs of Nancy Reagan*, Nancy Reagan with William Novak

1990

Fiction

1. *The Plains of Passage*, Jean M. Auel
2. *Four Past Midnight*, Stephen King
3. *The Burden of Proof*, Scott Turow
4. *Memories of Midnight*, Sidney Sheldon
5. *Message from Nam*, Danielle Steel
6. *The Bourne Ultimatum*, Robert Ludlum
7. *The Stand: The Complete and Uncut Edition*, Stephen King
8. *Lady Boss*, Jackie Collins
9. *The Witching Hour*, Anne Rice
10. *September*, Rosamunde Pilcher

Nonfiction

1. *A Life on the Road*, Charles Kuralt
2. *The Civil War*, Geoffrey C. Ward with Ric Burns and Ken Burns
3. *The Frugal Gourmet on Our Immigrant Heritage: Recipes You Should Have Gotten from Your Grandmother*, Jeff Smith
4. *Better Homes and Gardens New Cook Book*
5. *Financial Self-Defense: How To Win the Fight for Financial Freedom*, Charles J. Givens
6. *Homecoming: Reclaiming and Championing Your Inner Child*, John Bradshaw
7. *Wealth Without Risk: How To Develop a Personal Fortune Without Going Out on a Limb*, Charles J. Givens
8. *Bo Knows Bo*, Bo Jackson and Dick Schaap
9. *An American Life: An Autobiography*, Ronald Reagan
10. *Megatrends 2000: Ten New Directions for the 1990s*, John Naisbitt and Patricia Aburdene

1991

Fiction

1. *Scarlett: The Sequel to Margaret Mitchell's "Gone with the Wind,"* Alexandra Ripley
2. *The Sum of All Fears*, Tom Clancy
3. *Needful Things*, Stephen King
4. *No Greater Love*, Danielle Steel
5. *Heartbeat*, Danielle Steel
6. *The Doomsday Conspiracy*, Sidney Sheldon
7. *The Firm*, John Grisham
8. *Night Over Water*, Ken Follet
9. *Remember*, Barbara Taylor Bradford
10. *Loves Music, Loves to Dance*, Mary Higgins Clark

Nonfiction

1. *Me: Stories of My Life*, Katharine Hepburn
2. *Nancy Reagan: The Unauthorized Biography*, Kitty Kelley
3. *Uh-Oh: Some Observations from Both Sides of the Refrigerator Door*, Robert Fulghum
4. *Under Fire: An American Story*, Oliver North with William Novak
5. *Final Exit: The Practicalities of Self-Deliverance and Assisted Suicide for the Dying*, Derek Humphry
6. *When You Look Like Your Passport Photo, It's Time to Go Home*, Erma Bombeck
7. *More Wealth Without Risk*, Charles J. Givens
8. *Den of Thieves*, James B. Stewart
9. *Childhood*, Bill Cosby
10. *Financial Self-Defense*, Charles J. Givens

1992

Fiction

1. *Dolores Claiborne*, Stephen King
2. *The Pelican Brief*, John Grisham
3. *Gerald's Game*, Stephen King
4. *Mixed Blessings*, Danielle Steel
5. *Jewels*, Danielle Steel
6. *The Stars Shine Down*, Sidney Sheldon
7. *Tale of the Body Thief*, Anne Rice
8. *Mexico*, James A. Michener
9. *Waiting to Exhale*, Terry McMillan
10. *All Around the Town*, Mary Higgins Clark

Nonfiction

1. *The Way Things Ought To Be*, Rush Limbaugh
2. *It Doesn't Take a Hero: The Autobiography*, Gen. H. Norman Schwarzkopf

3. *How to Satisfy a Woman Every Time*, Naura Hayden
4. *Every Living Thing*, James Herriot
5. *A Return to Love*, Marianne Williamson
6. *Sam Walton: Made in America*, Sam Walton
7. *Diana: Her True Story*, Andrew Morton
8. *Truman*, David McCullough
9. *Silent Passage*, Gail Sheehy
10. *Sex*, Madonna

1993

Fiction

1. *The Bridges of Madison County*, Robert James Waller
2. *The Client*, John Grisham
3. *Slow Waltz at Cedar Bend*, Robert James Waller
4. *Without Remorse*, Tom Clancy
5. *Nightmares and Dreamscapes*, Stephen King
6. *Vanished*, Danielle Steel
7. *Lasher*, Anne Rice
8. *Pleading Guilty*, Scott Turow
9. *Like Water for Chocolate*, Laura Esquivel
10. *The Scorpio Illusion*, Robert Ludlum

Nonfiction

1. *See, I Told You So*, Rush Limbaugh
2. *Private Parts*, Howard Stern
3. *Seinlanguage*, Jerry Seinfeld
4. *Embraced by the Light*, Betty J. Eadie with Curtis Taylor
5. *Ageless Body, Timeless Mind*, Deepak Chopra
6. *Stop the Insanity*, Susan Powter
7. *Women Who Run with the Wolves*, Clarissa Pinkola Estes
8. *Men Are from Mars, Women Are from Venus*, John Gray
9. *The Hidden Life of Dogs*, Elizabeth Marshall Thomas
10. *And If You Play Golf, You're My Friend*, Harvey Penick with Bud Shrake

1994

Fiction

1. *The Chamber*, John Grisham
2. *Debt of Honor*, Tom Clancy
3. *The Celestine Prophecy*, James Redfield
4. *The Gift*, Danielle Steel
5. *Insomnia*, Steven King
6. *Politically Correct Bedtime Stories*, James Finn Garner
7. *Wings*, Danielle Steel
8. *Accident*, Danielle Steel
9. *The Bridges of Madison County*, Robert James Waller
10. *Disclosure*, Michael Crichton

Nonfiction

1. *In the Kitchen with Rosie*, Rosie Daley
2. *Men Are from Mars, Women Are from Venus*, John Gray
3. *Crossing the Threshold of Hope*, John Paul II.
4. *Magic Eye I*, N.E. Thing Enterprises
5. *The Book of Virtues*, William J. Bennett
6. *Magic Eye II*, N.E. Thing Enterprises
7. *Embraced by the Light*, Betty J. Eadie with Curtis Taylor
8. *Don't Stand Too Close to a Naked Man*, Tim Allen
9. *Couplehood*, Paul Reiser
10. *Magic Eye III*, N.E. Thing Enterprises

1995

Fiction

1. *The Rainmaker*, John Grisham
2. *The Lost World*, Michael Crichton
3. *Five Days in Paris*, Danielle Steel
4. *The Christmas Box*, Richard Paul Evans
5. *Lightning*, Danielle Steel
6. *The Celestine Prophecy*, James Redfield
7. *Rose Madder*, Stephen King
8. *Silent Night*, Mary Higgins Clark
9. *Politically Correct Holiday Stories*, James Finn Garner
10. *The Horse Whisperer*, Nicholas Evans

Nonfiction

1. *Men Are from Mars, Women Are from Venus*, John Gray
2. *My American Journey*, Colin Powell with Joseph Perisco
3. *Miss America*, Howard Stern
4. *The Seven Spiritual Laws of Success*, Deepak Chopra
5. *The Road Ahead*, Bill Gates
6. *Charles Kuralt's America*, Charles Kuralt
7. *Mars and Venus in the Bedroom*, John Gray
8. *To Renew America*, Newt Gingrich
9. *My Point...and I Do Have One*, Ellen DeGeneres
10. *The Moral Compass*, William J. Bennett

1996

Fiction

1. *The Runaway Jury*, John Grisham
2. *Executive Orders*, Tom Clancy
3. *Desperation*, Stephen King
4. *Airframe*, Michael Crichton
5. *The Regulators*, Richard Bachman
6. *Malice*, Danielle Steele
7. *Silent Honor*, Danielle Steel
8. *Primary Colors*, anonymous
9. *Cause of Death*, Patricia Cornwell
10. *The Tenth Insight*, James Redfield
11. *The Deep End of the Ocean*, Jaquelyn Mitchard
12. *How Stella Got Her Groove Back*, Terry McMillan
13. *Moonlight Becomes You*, Mary Higgins Clark
14. *My Gal Sunday*, Mary Higgins Clark
15. *The Celestine Prophesy*, James Redfield

Nonfiction

1. *Make the Connection*, Oprah Winfrey and Bob Greene
2. *Men Are from Mars, Women Are from Venus*, John Gray
3. *The Dilbert Principle*, Scott Adams
4. *Simple Abundance*, Sarah Ban Breathnach
5. *The Zone*, Barry Sears with Bill Lawren
6. *Bad As I Wanna Be*, Dennis Rodman
7. *In Contempt*, Christopher Darden
8. *A Reporter's Life*, Walter Cronkite
9. *Dogbert's Top Secret Management Handbook*, Scott Adams
10. *My Sergei: A Love Story*, Ekaterina Gordeeva with E. M. Swift
11. *Gift and Mystery*, Pope John Paul II
12. *I'm Not Really Here*, Tim Allen
13. *Rush Limbaugh Is a Big Fat Idiot and Other Observations*, Al Franken
14. *James Herriot's Favorite Dog Stories*, James Herriot
15. *My Story*, The Duchess of York

BESTSELLING CHILDREN'S BOOKS

Publishers Weekly started breaking out a separate children's bestseller list recently; here are results from the past four decidedly Disney-dominated years.

1993

1. *Barney's Farm Animals,* Kimberly Kearns and Marie O'Brien, illustrated by Karen Malzeke-McDonald
2. *Barney's Favorite Mother Goose Rhymes,* Stephen White, illustrated by Mary Grace Eubank
3. *Baby Bop's Toys,* Kimberly Kearns and Marie O'Brien
4. *Barney's Color Surprise,* Mary Ann Dudko and Margie Larsen
5. *Baby Bop's Counting Book,* Mary Ann Dudko and Margie Larsen
6. *Where's Waldo? In Hollywood,* Martin Handford
7. *Aladdin (Disney Classic)*
8. *Baby Bop Discovers Shapes,* Stephen White, illustrated by Larry Daste
9. *Poky Puppy's First Christmas,* Justine Korman, illustrated by Jean Chandler
10. *Beauty and the Beast: Teapot's Tale,* Justine Korman, illustrated by Peter Emslie

1994

1. *The Lion King (Classic),* Disney/Mouse Works
2. *The Lion King (Little Golden Book),* Justine Korman, illustrated by D. Williams
3. *The Lion King (Big Golden Book),* Justine Korman, illustrated by H.R. Russell
4. *Simba Roars!,* Disney/Mouse Works
5. *Aladdin's Magic Carpet Ride,* T. Slater Margulies
6. *The Christmas Bunny,* Arnold Rabin, illustrated by Carolyn Ewing
7. *The Lion King Illustrated Classic,* illustrated by Michael Humphries and Marshall Toomey
8. *The Lion King (Sturdy Shape),* Mary Packard, illustrated by Darrell Baker
9. *The Sorcerer's Apprentice,* Don Ferguson
10. *The Very Hungry Caterpillar Board Book,* Eric Carle

1995

1. *Pocahontas (Classic),* Disney/Mouse Works
2. *Pocahontas,* Justine Korman, illustrated by D. Williams
3. *The Children's Book of Virtues,* William J. Bennett, illustrated by Michael Hague
4. *Guess How Much I Love You,* Sam McBratney, illustrated by Anita Jeram
5. *Pocahontas: Wind's Lullaby,* Justine Korman, illustrated by Peter Emslie and D. Williams
6. *Daisy-Head Mayzie,* Dr. Seuss
7. *Winnie the Pooh: The Grand and Wonderful Day,* Mary Packard, illustrated by Darrell Baker
8. *Rainbow Fish to the Rescue!,* Marcus Pfister
9. *Hide & Squeak, Meeko!,* Disney/Mouse Works
10. *Pocahontas (Sturdy Shape),* Mary Packard, illustrated by Darrell Baker

1996

1. *Falling Up,* Shel Silverstein
2. *The Hunchback of Notre Dame,* Disney/Mouse Works
3. *Disney's Hunchback of Notre Dame,* adapted by Justine Korman, illustrated by Don Williams
4. *My Many Colored Days,* Dr. Seuss, illustrated by Steve Johnson and Lou Fancher
5. *Disney's Hunchback of Notre Dame: Quasimodo the Hero,* Barbara Bazaldua, illustrated by Don Williams
6. *Disney's 101 Dalmatians: Snow Puppies,* Barbara Bazaldua, illustrated by Don Williams
7. *Disney's Winnie the Pooh: The Sweetest Christmas,* Ann Braybrooks, illustrated by Josie Yee
8. *Guess How Much I Love You,* Sam McBratney, illustrated by Anita Jeram
9. *The Hunchback of Notre Dame,* Disney/Mouse Works
10. *Djali's Jolly Day,* Disney/Mouse Works

LITERARY LISTENING

Americans have been doing a lot of reading behind the wheel, and as this list of bestselling books on tape reveals, our tastes are pretty broad. Based on 1996's most successful audio books at Waldenbooks and Barnes & Noble, this list gives us a good gauge of the year's most popular listening.

1. *Men Are from Mars, Women Are from Venus,* John Gray
2. *The Runaway Jury,* John Grisham
3. *Seven Habits of Highly Effective People,* Stephen Covey
4. *The Seven Spiritual Laws of Success,* Deepak Chopra
5. *Executive Orders,* Tom Clancy
6. *The Celestine Prophesy,* James Redfield
7. *Way of the Wizard,* Deepak Chopra
8. *Primary Colors,* anonymous
9. *Make the Connection,* Oprah Winfrey/Bob Greene
10. *Emotional Intelligence,* Daniel Goleman
11. *The Road Ahead,* Bill Gates
12. *Anthony Robbins Power To Succeed,* Anthony Robbins
13. *The Rainmaker,* John Grisham
14. *Charles Kuralt's America,* Charles Kuralt
15. *How To Argue and Win Everytime,* Jerry Spence

BESTSELLING CHILDREN'S BOOKS OF ALL TIME

The following is a list of the 100 bestselling hardcover children's books. The figures reflect domestic sales from the original date of publication through the end of 1996. (Source: *Publishers Weekly*)

Rank	Book, Author (original publication date)
1.	*The Poky Little Puppy*, Janette Sebring Lowrey (1942)
2.	*The Tale of Peter Rabbit*, Beatrix Potter (1902)
3.	*Tootle*, Gertrude Crampton (1945)
4.	*Saggy Baggy Elephant*, Kathryn and Byron Jackson (1947)
5.	*Scuffy the Tugboat*, Gertrude Crampton (1955)
6.	*Pat the Bunny*, Dorothy Kunhardt (1940)
7.	*Green Eggs and Ham*, Dr. Seuss (1960)
8.	*The Cat in the Hat*, Dr. Seuss (1957)
9.	*The Littlest Angel*, Charles Tazewell (1946)
10.	*One Fish, Two Fish, Red Fish, Blue Fish*, Dr. Seuss (1960)
11.	*Where the Sidewalk Ends*, Shel Silverstein (1974)
12.	*Hop on Pop*, Dr. Seuss (1963)
13.	*Dr. Seuss's ABC*, Dr. Seuss (1960)
14.	*The Tale of Benjamin Bunny*, Beatrix Potter (1904)
15.	*The Giving Tree*, Shel Silverstein (1964)
16.	*The Children's Bible* (1965)
17.	*Disney's The Lion King*, adapted by Justine Korman (1994)
18.	*The Tale of Jemima Puddle-Duck*, Beatrix Potter (1908)
19.	*Richard Scarry's Best Word Book Ever*, Richard Scarry (1963)
20.	*The Real Mother Goose*, illus. by Blanche F. Wright (1989)
21.	*The Cat in the Hat Comes Back*, Dr. Seuss (1958)
22.	*A Light in the Attic*, Shel Silverstein (1981)
23.	*Are You My Mother?*, P.D. Eastman (1960)
24.	*The Tale of Squirrel Nutkin*, Beatrix Potter (1903)
25.	*The Tale of Tom Kitten*, Beatrix Potter (1907)
26.	*Fox In Socks*, Dr. Seuss (1965)
27.	*Where's Waldo*, Martin Handford (1987)
28.	*The Great Waldo Search*, Martin Handford (1989)
29.	*The Polar Express*, Chris Van Allsburg (1985)
30.	*Winnie-the-Pooh*, A.A. Milne, illus. by Ernest Shepard (1926)
31.	*Find Waldo Now*, Martin Handford (1989)
32.	*Go, Dog Go!*, P.D. Eastman (1961)
33.	*Oh, the Places You'll Go!*, Dr. Seuss (1990)
34.	*Macmillan Dictionary for Children*, edited by Judith Levey (1975)
35.	*My Book About Me (by Me, Myself)*, Dr. Seuss, illus. by Roy McKie (1969)
36.	*Walt Disney's Storyland*, Walt Disney (1962)
37.	*The Cat in the Hat Beginner Book Dictionary*, P.D. Eastman (1964)
38.	*How the Grinch Stole Christmas*, Dr. Seuss (1957)
39.	*The Rainbow Fish*, Marcus Pfister (1992)
40.	*Richard Scarry's Best Mother Goose Ever*, Richard Scarry (1964)
41.	*The Touch Me Book*, Pat and Eve Witte (1961)
42.	*Goodnight Moon*, Margaret Wise Brown, illus. by Clement Hurd (1947)
43.	*I Am a Bunny*, Ole Risom, illus. by Richard Scarry (1963)
44.	*The Little Engine That Could*, Watty Piper (1930)
45.	*Charlotte's Web*, E.B. White, illus. by Garth Williams (1952)
46.	*Never Talk to Strangers*, Irma Joyce (1967)
47.	*When We Were Very Young*, A.A. Milne, illus. by Ernest Shepard (1924)
48.	*Richard Scarry's Best Storybook Ever*, Richard Scarry (1968)
49.	*Barney's Magical Picnic*, Stephen White (1993)
50.	*I Can Read with My Eyes Shut*, Dr. Seuss (1978)
51.	*The Secret of the Old Clock* (Nancy Drew #1), Carolyn Keene (1930)
52.	*The Tower Treasure* (Hardy Boys #1), Franklin Dixon (1927)
53.	*Just Imagine* (1992)
54.	*Put Me In the Zoo*, Robert Lopshire (1960)
55.	*Disney's 101 Dalmations*, adapted by Ronald Kidd (1991)
56.	*The Very Hungry Caterpillar*, Eric Carle (1969)
57.	*Barney's Farm Animals* (1993)
58.	*Where the Wild Things Are*, Maurice Sendak (1964)
59.	*Richard Scarry's Cars and Trucks and Things That Go*, Richard Scarry (1968)
60.	*Disney's Beauty and the Beast*, adapted by Ronald Kidd (1992)
61.	*The Little Prince*, Antoine de Saint Exupery (1943)
62.	*Eloise Wilkin's Mother Goose*, Eloise Wilkin (1961)
63.	*Disney's The Little Mermaid*, adapted by Ronald Kidd (1991)
64.	*Oh, The Things You Can Think!*, Dr. Seuss (1975)
65.	*Love Is a Special Way of Feeling*, Joan Walsh Anglund (1960)
66.	*Big Bird's Color Game*, Children's Television Workshop (1980)
67.	*Disney's Aladdin*, adapted by Ronald Kidd (1992)
68.	*The Hidden Staircase* (Nancy Drew #2), Carolyn Keene (1930)
69.	*The House on the Cliff* (Hardy Boys #2), Franklin Dixon (1927)
70.	*Meet Samantha*, Susan Adler (1986)
71.	*Animalia*, Graeme Base (1987)
72.	*Barney's Favorite Mother Goose Rhymes Vol. 1* (1993)
73.	*Disney's The Lion King*, adapted by Ronald Kidd (1994)
74.	*Meet Andy*, Connie Porter (1993)
75.	*Oh Say Can You Say?*, Dr. Seuss (1979)
76.	*Barney's Color Surprise* (1993)
77.	*The Way Things Work*, David Macaulay (1988)
78.	*Tawny Scrawny Lion*, Kathryn Jackson (1952)
79.	*Make Way for Ducklings*, Robert McCloskey (1941)
80.	*Meet Kirsten*, Janet Shaw (1986)
81.	*There's A Wocket in My Pocket*, Dr. Seuss (1974)
82.	*Millions of Cats*, Wanda Gag (1928)
83.	*E.T., the Extra-Terrestrial Story Book*, William Kotzwinkle (1992)
84.	*A Fly Went By*, Mike McClintock (1958)
85.	*The Bungalow Mystery* (Nancy Drew #3), Carolyn Keene (1930)
86.	*Santa Mouse*, Elfrieda Dewitt (1966)
87.	*The Magic Locket*, Elizabeth Koda-Callan (1988)
88.	*The Secret of the Old Mill* (Hardy Boys #3), Franklin Dixon (1930)
89.	*Mr. Brown Can Moo! Can You?*, Dr. Seuss (1970)
90.	*If You Give a Mouse a Cookie*, Laura Numeroff, illus. by Felicia Bond (1985)
91.	*Richard Scarry's What Do People Do All Day?*, Richard Scarry (1968)
92.	*Where's Spot?*, Eric Hill (1980)
93.	*House at Pooh Corner*, A.A. Milne, illus. by Ernest Shepard (1928)
94.	*The Tall Book of Nursery Tales*, illus. by Feodor Rojankovsky (1944)
95.	*Yertle the Turtle and Other Stories*, Dr. Seuss (1958)
96.	*Richard Scarry's Early Words*, Richard Scarry (1976)
97.	*The Jolly Postman*, Janet and Allan Ahlberg (1986)
98.	*The Mystery of Lilac Inn* (Nancy Drew #4), Carolyn Keene (1930)
99.	*Dr. Seuss's Sleep Book*, Dr. Seuss (1962)
100.	*Baby Bop's Counting Book* (1993)

THE PEOPLE BOOKSHELF

PEOPLE hasn't been reviewing books long enough to hazard a best-of-the-century list, but here are the books we loved the most over the past two decades.

FICTION

Absolute Power, David Baldacci
The Accidental Tourist, Anne Tyler
All the Pretty Horses, Cormac McCarthy
Anagrams, Lorrie Moore
Anton the Dove Fancier, Bernard Gotfryd
August, Judith Rossner
Before and After, Rosellen Brown
Beloved, Toni Morrison
Birdy, William Wharton
The Blooding, Joseph Wambaugh
The Blue Afternoon, William Boyd
Body and Soul, Frank Conroy
The Bonfire of the Vanities, Tom Wolfe
Breathing Lessons, Anne Tyler
Cat's Eye, Margaret Atwood
A Civil Action, Jonathan Harr
Clockers, Richard Price
The Cloister Walk, Kathleen Norris
Collaborators, Janet Kauffman
The Collected Stories, Isaac Bashevis Singer
The Color Purple, Alice Walker
Come to Grief, Dick Francis
A Confederacy of Dunces, John Kennedy Toole
Dinner at the Homesick Restaurant, Anne Tyler
The Dragons of Eden, Carl Sagan
Dutch Shea Jr., John Gregory Dunne
East Is East, T. Coraghessan Boyle
Ellis Island, Mark Helprin
Enchantment, Daphne Merkin
Eye of the Needle, Ken Follett
Fanny, Erica Jong
Final Payments, Mary Gordon
The Firm, John Grisham
The First Man in Rome, Colleen McCullough
For Love, Sue Miller
Foreign Affairs, Alison Lurie
Get Shorty, Elmore Leonard
The Glass House, Laura Furman
The Good Mother, Sue Miller
Gorky Park, Martin Cruz Smith
The Green Mile, Stephen King
Happy To Be There, Garrison Keillor
Her First American, Lore Segal
The Honourable Schoolboy, John Le Carré
The House of the Spirits, Isabel Allende
Illumination Night, Abbie Hoffman
An Indecent Obsession, Colleen McCollough
Independence Day, Richard Ford
Kolymsky Heights, Lionel Davidson
Labrava, Elmore Leonard
Lake Wobegon Days, Garrison Keillor
Lancelot, Walker Percy
A Lesson Before Dying, Ernest J. Gaines
The Liar's Club, Mary Karr
Libra, Don DeLillo
A Light in the Attic, Shel Silverstein
Life Its Ownself, Dan Jenkins
Love in the Time of Cholera, Gabriel García Márquez
The Love Letter, Cathleen Schine
Machine Dreams, Jayne Anne Phillips
The Mambo Kings Play Songs of Love, Oscar Hijuelos
A Map of the World, Jane Hamilton
Maus: A Survivor's Tale, II: And Here My Troubles Begin, Art Spiegelman
Me and My Baby View the Eclipse, Lee Smith
Memoirs of an Invisible Man, H. F. Saint
Monkeys, Susan Minot
Monsignor Quixote, Graham Greene
More Die of Heartbreak, Saul Bellow
Music for Chameleons, Truman Capote
The Natural Man, Ed McClanahan
Noble House, James Clavell
Owning Jolene, Shelby Hearon
The Palace Thief, Ethan Canin
Patrimony, Philip Roth
Perfume, Patrick Süskind
Poodle Springs, Raymond Chandler and Robert B. Parker
The Pope of Greenwich Village, Vincent Park
Presumed Innocent, Scott Turow
The Progress of Love, Alice Munro
Quinn's Book, William Kennedy
Rabbit at Rest, John Updike
The Robber Bride, Margaret Atwood
Roger's Version, John Updike
Rose, Martin Cruz Smith
The Russia House, John Le Carré
Salvador, Joan Didion
The Secret History, Donna Tartt
Seventh Heaven, Alice Hoffman
She's Come Undone, Wally Lamb
The Sicilian, Mario Puzo
Smilla's Sense of Snow, Peter Hoeg
A Soldier of the Great War, Mark Helprin
Sophie's Choice, William Styron
Stormy Weather, Carl Hiaasen
Talking to the Dead, Sylvia Watanabe
Tooth Imprints on a Corn Dog, Mark Leyner
Tracks, Louise Erdrich
The Tree of Life, Hugh Nissenson
True Confessions, John Gregory Dunne
The Twenty-Seventh City, Jonathan Franzen
Typical American, Gish Jen

Waiting to Exhale, Terry McMillan
The White Hotel, D. M. Thomas
Who Will Run the Frog Hospital?, Lorrie Moore
Winter's Tale, Mark Helprin
World's Fair, E. L. Doctorow
The Yellow Wind, David Grossman

NONFICTION

American Caesar, William Manchester
American Prospects, Joel Sternfeld
Backlash, Susan Faludi
Best Intentions, Robert Sam Anson
The Best of Dear Abby, Abigail Van Buren
Blood Sport, James B. Stewart
Blue Highways, William Least Heat Moon
The Bookmakers's Daughter, Shirley Abbott
The Box: An Oral History of Television 1920-61, Jeff Kisseloff
Cameraworks, David Hockney
The Chimpanzees of Gombe, Jane Goodall
Colored People: A Memoir, Henry Louis Gates Jr.
The Culture of Narcissism, Christopher Lasch
Dave Barry is Not Making This Up, Dave Barry
Dave Barry Slept Here, Dave Barry
Den of Thieves, James B. Stewart
The Devil's Candy, Julie Salamon
A Distant Mirror, Barbara Tuchman
Dreaming: Hard Luck and Good Times in America, Carolyn See
The Duke of Deception, Geoffrey Wolff
Edie, Jean Stein, edited with George Plimpton
Edith Sitwell, Victoria Glendinning
The Fatal Shore, Robert Hughes
Fatal Vision, Joe McGinniss
Fatherhood, Bill Cosby
The Forbidden Experiment, Roger Shattuck
Fungus the Bogeyman, Raymond Briggs
Gal, Ruthie Bolton
The Girl I Left Behind, Jane O'Reilly
The Glass House, Laura Furman
Goldwyn: A Biography, A. Scott Berg
A Good Life, Ben Bradlee
"The Good War," Studs Terkel
The Hidden Life of Dogs, Elizabeth Marshall
Home Before Dark, Susan Cheever
Hometown, Peter Davis
The Hot Zone, Richard Preston
House, Tracy Kidder
I Dream s World, Brian Lanker
In and Out of the Garden, Sara Midda
In Contempt, Christopher Darden
Ingrid Bergman: My Story, Ingrid Bergman and Alan Burgess
Inside Edge: A Revealing Journey into the Secret World of Figure Skating, Christine Brennan
Into the Wild, Jon Krakauer
January Sun, Richard Stengel
The Kennedys: An American Dream, Peter Collier and David Horowitz
Kissinger, Walter Isaacson
The Knife and Gun Club, Eugene Richards
Krik? Krak!, Edwidge Danticat
The Last Lion, William Manchester
Laura Z., A Life, Laura Z. Hobson
Lauren Bacall By Myself, Lauren Bacall
Lenin's Tomb, David Remnick
A Life of Picasso, John Richardson
Little League Confidential, Bill Geist
The Lives of John Lennon, Albert Goldman
Loitering with Intent, Peter O'Toole
Maida Heatter's Book of Great Chocolate Desserts, Maida Heatter
The Man Who Mistook His Wife for a Hat, Oliver Sacks
Means of Ascent, Robert A. Caro
The Medusa and the Snail, Lewis Thomas
Midair, Frank Conroy
Miss Manners' Guide to Excruciatingly Correct Behavior, Judith Martin
Mister Rogers Talks with Parents, Fred Rogers and Barry Head
Moonshine, Alec Wilkinson
The Non-Runner's Book, Vic Ziegel and Lewis Grossberger
No Ordinary Time, Doris Kearns Goodwin
On Boxing, Joyce Carol Oates
On Photography, Susan Sontag
Outrage, Vincent Bugliosi
Pablo Picasso, A Retrospective, edited by William Rubin
Payback, Joe Klein
Photoportraits, Henri Cartier-Bresson
President Kennedy, Richard Reeves
The Ragman's Son, Kirk Douglas
The Rise of Theodore Roosevelt, Edmund Morris
A Rumor of War, Philip Caputo
Saul Steinberg, Harold Rosenberg
Serpentine, Thomas Thompson
Side Effects, Woody Allen
The Sketchbooks of Picasso, Pablo Picasso
The Snow Leopard, Peter Mathiessen
The Story of English, Robert McCrum, William Cran, and Robert MacNeil
Sylvia Plachy's Unguided Tour, Sylvia Plachy
The Teamsters, Steven Brill
Thank You for Smoking, Christopher Buckley
Truman, David McCullough
Why Are They Weeping?, photographed by David C. Turnley and written by Alan Cowell
Workers, Sebastião Salgado
A Writer's Beginnings, Eudora Welty
The Years of Lyndon Johnson: The Path to Power, Robert A. Caro

THE PEOPLE TRASH HEAP

PEOPLE's reviewers read these books because they had to—it's their job. But you have a choice. The following is a selection of books Picks & Pans reviewers judged as the worst—or most over-rated—from the past two decades.

FICTION

Alnilam, James Dickey
American Psycho, Bret Easton Ellis
Ancient Evenings, Norman Mailer
Answer as a Man, Taylor Caldwell
Any Woman's Blues, Erica Jong
Ascent Into Hell, Andrew M. Greeley
Beast, Peter Benchley
The Big Hype, Avery Corman
A Bloodsmoor Romance, Joyce Carol Oates
The Bourne Ultimatum, Robert Ludlum
Brain, Robin Cook
Children of Light, Robert Stone
The Children's Story, James Clavell
Christine, Stephen King
The Coup, John Updike
Daddy, Danielle Steel
The Devil's Alternative, Frederick Forsyth
Doctors, Erich Segal
Elvis, Albert Goldman
Empress, Sylvia Wallace
Fever, Robin Cook
Floating Dragon, Peter Straub
.44, Jimmy Breslin and Dick Schaap
Free to Love, Ivana Trump
Friends in High Places, John Weitz
The Girl of the Sea of Cortez, Peter Benchley
Godplayer, Robin Cook
Gumpisms, Winston Groom
Happy Endings, Sally Quinn
Heartburn, Nora Ephron
The Holcroft Covenant, Robert Ludlum
Hollywood Kids, Jackie Collins
Home Front, Patti Davis with Maureen Strange Foster
The Hope, Herman Wouk
A House of Secrets, Patti Davis
I Dream a World, Brian Lanker
Illusions: The Adventures of a Reluctant Messiah, Richard Bach
In Praise of the Stepmother, Mario Vargas Llosa
Inside, Outside, Herman Wouk
The Island, Peter Benchley
Lace, Shirley Conran
Lasher, Anne Rice
The Last Days of America, Paul Erdman
Legion, William Peter Blatty
Life After God, Douglas Coupland
Lord of the Dance, Andrew M. Greeley
Love and War, John Jakes
Lucky, Jackie Collins
Lust, Susan Minot
The Mammoth Hunters, Jean M. Auel
Manhattan, Neal Travis
A Matter of Honor, Jeffrey Archer
Maybe, Lillian Hellman
Megan's Book of Divorce, Erica Jong
Memories of Another Day, Harold Robbins
Men in Love, Nancy Friday
The Men's Club, Leonard Michaels
Message from Nam, Danielle Steel
Mindbend, Robin Cook
The Minstrel, Bernard Benson
Monímbo, Robert Moss and Arnaud de Borchgrave
The Mosquito Coast, Paul Theroux
The Mummy, Anne Rice
Murder in the White House, Margaret Truman
Nature's End, Whitley Streiber and James Kunetka
The Ninth Configuration, William Peter Blatty
Of Love and Shadows, Isabel Allende
The Old Neighborhood, Avery Corman
Oliver's Story, Erich Segal
The Origin, Irving Stone
Outbreak, Robin Cook
The Paper Men, William Golding
Parachutes and Kisses, Erica Jong
The Pigeon, Patrick Süskind
The Pillars of the Earth, Ken Follett
Pinball, Jerzy Kosinski
The Plagiarist, Benjamin Cheever
Postcards from the Edge, Carrie Fisher
A Prayer for Owen Meany, John Irving
Prime Time, Joan Collins
"Q" Clearance, Peter Benchley
Queen of the Damned, Anne Rice
Regrets Only, Sally Quinn
Rock Star, Jackie Collins
The Runaway Soul, Harold Brodkey
S., John Updike
Sailor Song, Ken Kesey
Savages, Shirley Conran
Scruples, Judith Krantz
See You Later, Alligator, William F. Buckley Jr.
Singing Songs, Meg Tilly
Slaves of New York, Tama Janowitz
Slow Waltz at Cedar Bend, Robert James Waller
Smart Women, Judy Blume
Spellbinder, Harold Robbins
Sphinx, Robin Cook
Spring Collection, Judith Krantz
Star, Danielle Steel
The Story of Henri Todd, William F. Buckley Jr.
Story of My Life, Jay McInerney
The Talisman, Stephen King and Peter Straub
The Temple of My Familiar, Alice Walker
Texas, James Michener
Tinsel, William Goldman
Vox, Nicholson Baker
The Walnut Door, John Hersey
West of Sunset, Dirk Bogarde
Where Love Goes, Joyce Maynard
Whirlwind, James Clavell
The Winners, Dominick Dunne

NONFICTION

An Affair to Remember, Maureen Donaldson and William Royce
Among the Porcupines, Carol Matthau
Andrew Wyeth: The Helga Pictures, John Wilmerding
Bardot Deneuve Fonda, Roger Vadim
Better than Sex, Hunter Thompson
The Beverly Hills Diet, Judy Mazel
Beyond Reason, Margaret Trudeau
Blown Away, A. E. Hotchner
The Book of Lists, David Wallechinsky, Irving Wallace, and Amy Wallace
Brando for Breakfast, Anna Kashfi and E. P. Stein
Brother Billy, Ruth Carter Stapleton
Bus 9 to Paradise, Leo Buscaglia
Cary Grant: The Lonely Heart, Charles Higham and Roy Moseley
Character: America's Search for Leadership, Gail Sheehy
Cruel Shoes, Steve Martin
Dance with the Devil, Kirk Douglas
Dancing in the Light, Shirley MacLaine
Diana Alone, Nicholas Davies
Driving Under the Affluence, Julia Phillips
Elizabeth Taylor: The Last Star, Kitty Kelley
Elvis Aaron Presley: Revelations from the Memphis Mafia, Alanna Nash, with Billy Smith, Marty Lacker and Lamar Fike
Enter Whining, Fran Drescher
Family—The Ties That Bind . . . and Gag!, Erma Bombeck
Feminine Force: Release the Power Within to Create the Life You Deserve, Georgette Mosbacher
Find O.J.: The Juice is Loose, Peter Wood and Jeff Vaughn
Flight of the Avenger: George Bush at War and in Love, Joe Hyams
Garbo: Her Story, Antoni Gronowicz
Give War a Chance, P. J. O'Rourke
Glory Days: Bruce Springsteen in the 1980s, Dave Marsh
Good Guys, Bad Guys, Shere Hite and Kate Colleran
Having It All, Helen Gurley Brown
The Hite Report on Male Sexuality, Shere Hite
How to Take Charge of Your Life, Bernard Berkowitz and Mildred Newman
In the American West, Richard Avedon
The Informers, Bret Easton Ellis
I Remember, Dan Rather
It's All in the Playing, Shirley MacLaine
I Want to Tell You, O.J. Simpson
Jack and Jackie: Portrait of an American Marriage, Christopher Andersen
The Jackson Phenomenon, Elizabeth O. Colton
Just Between Us Girls, Sydney Biddle Barrows
Just Enough Rope, Joan Braden
The Killing of the Unicorn, Peter Bogdanovich
The Last Brother, Joe McGinniss
Laurence Olivier: A Biography, Donald Spoto
Life's Little Instruction Book, H. Jackson Brown Jr.
The Linda Evans Beauty and Exercise Book, Linda Evans
The Lives of John Lennon, Albert Goldman
Marcia Clark: Her Private Trials and Public Triumphs, Clifford L. Linedecker
Metropolitan Life, Fran Lebowitz
Mistrial of the Century, Tracy Kennedy
More Memories, Ralph Emery
Mountain Get Out of My Way, Montel Williams with Daniel Paisner
Mutant Message Down Under, Marlo Morgan
My Lives, Roseanne
Nice Work if You Can Get It, Michael Feinstein
1945, Newt Gingrich and William R. Forstchen
Not That You Asked, Andrew A. Rooney
Now You Know, Kitty Dukakis
Number One, Billy Martin and Peter Golenboch
O.J.: 101 Theories, Conspiracies & Alibis, Peter Roberts
On Your Own, Brooke Shields
The One Minute Father, Spencer Johnson, M.D.
The One Minute Mother, Spencer Johnson, M.D.
Out on a Limb, Shirley MacLaine
A Place at the Table, Bruce Bawer
The Power to Heal, edited by Rick Smolan, Phillip Moffitt, and Matthew Naythons, M.D.
Princess in Love, Anna Pasternak
Pulling Your Own Strings, Dr. Wayne Dyer
The Rants, Dennis Miller
Real Moments, Barbara DeAngelis
Restoring the American Dream, Robert Ringer
Revolution from Within, Gloria Steinem
RN: The Memoirs of Richard Nixon, Richard Nixon
Running and Being, Dr. George Sheehan
The Second Seduction, Frances Lear
Secrets of a Sparrow, Diana Ross
Sex, Madonna
The Search for Justice, Robert Shapiro with Larkin Warren
Shelley: Also Known As Shirley, Shelley Winters
Social Studies, Fran Lebowitz
Tennessee: Cry of the Heart, Dotson Rader
Thy Neighbor's Wife, Gay Talese
Transformation, Whitley Streiber
Uh-Oh, Robert Fulghum
Wasted: The Preppie Murder, Linda Wolfe
Willie, Willie Nelson with Bud Shrake
Women and Love, Shere Hite
Women's Work, Anne Tolstoi Wallach
Woody Allen: A Biography, Eric Lax

BIBLIOGRAPHIES OF LEADING AUTHORS

These are complete listings for a broad selection of the most popular, most admired, most discussed, and most eagerly devoured authors today. For each, all full-length works, poetry, and plays are listed, followed by the year of publication.

ISABEL ALLENDE

Fiction
The House of the Spirits (1985)
Eva Luna (1988)
Of Love and Shadows (1988)
The Infinite Plan (1993)
Paula (1995)

MARGARET ATWOOD

Fiction
The Edible Woman (1969)
Surfacing (1972)
Lady Oracle (1976)
Dancing Girls (1977)
Life Before Man (1979)
Bodily Harm (1981)
Murder in the Dark (1983)
Bluebeard's Egg (1983)
The Handmaid's Tale (1985)
Cat's Eye (1988)
Wilderness Tips (1991)
Good Bones and Simple Murders (1992)
The Robber Bride (1993)
Alias Grace (1996)

Poetry
The Circle Game (1964)
The Animals in That Country (1968)
The Journals of Susanna Moodie (1970)
Procedures for Underground (1970)
Power Politics (1971)
You Are Happy (1974)
Two-Headed Poems (1978)
True Stories (1981)
Snake Poems (1983)
Interlunar (1984)
Morning in the Burned House (1995)

Children's books
Up in the Tree (1978)
Anna's Pet (1980)
For the Birds (1990)
Princess Prunella and the Purple Peanut (1995)

Nonfiction
Survival: A Thematic Guide to Canadian Literature (1972)
Days of the Rebels, 1815–1840 (1977)
Second Words (1982)
Strange Things: The Malevolent North in Canadian Literature (1996)

SAUL BELLOW

Fiction
Dangling Man (1944)
The Victim (1947)
The Adventures of Augie March (1953; National Book Award)
Seize the Day (1956)
Henderson the Rain King (1959)
Herzog (1964; National Book Award)
Mr. Sammler's Planet (1970; National Book Award)
Humbolt's Gift (1975; Pulitzer Prize)
The Dean's December (1982)
Mosby's Memoirs & Other Stories (1984)
A Theft (1989)
Something to Remember Me By (1991)
More Die of Heartbreak (1987)
The Actual (1997)

Nonfiction
To Jerusalem and Back: A Personal Account (1976)
It All Adds Up (1994)

Play
The Last Analysis, a Play (produced 1964)

Nobel Prize for Literature, 1976

TOM CLANCY

Fiction
The Hunt for Red October (1984)
Red Storm Rising (1986)
Patriot Games (1987)
The Cardinal of the Kremlin (1988)
Clear and Present Danger (1989)
The Sum of All Fears (1991)
Without Remorse (1993)
Debt of Honor (1994)
Executive Orders (1996)

Nonfiction
Submarine: A Guided Tour Inside a Nuclear Warship (1993)
Armored Cav: A Guided Tour of an Armored Cavalry Regiment (1994)
Fighter Wing: A Guided Tour of an Air Force Combat Wing (1995)
Reality Check: What's Going On Out There? (1995)
Marine: A Guided Tour of a Marine Expeditionary Unit (1996)
Airborne: A Guided Tour of an Airborne Taskforce (1997)

PAT CONROY

Fiction
The Boo (1970)
The Water Is Wide (1972)
The Great Santini (1976)
The Lords of Discipline (1980)
The Prince of Tides (1986)
Beach Music (1995)

MICHAEL CRICHTON

Fiction
The Andromeda Strain (1969)
The Terminal Man (1972)
Westworld (screenplay, 1975)
The Great Train Robbery (1975)
Eaters of the Dead (1976)
Congo (1980)
Sphere (1987)
Jurassic Park (1990)
Rising Sun (1992)
Disclosure (1994)
The Lost World (1995)
Airframe (1996)
Twister (1996)

Fiction written as John Lange
Odds On (1966)
Scratch One (1967)
Easy Go (1968; re-published as *The Last Tomb*, 1974)
The Venom Business (1969)
Zero Cool (1970)
Drug of Choice (1970)
Grave Descend (1970)
Binary (1972)

Fiction written as Jeffrey Hudson
A Case of Need (1968)

Fiction written as Michael Douglas (with brother Douglas Crichton)
Dealing, Or the Berkeley-to-Boston Forty-Brick Lost-Bag Blues (1971)

Nonfiction
Five Patients: The Hospital Explained (1970)
Jasper Johns (1977)
Electronic Life: How To Think about Computers (1983)
Travels (autobiography, 1988)

E. L. DOCTOROW

Fiction
Welcome to Hard Times (1960)
Big as Life (1966)
The Book of Daniel (1971)
Ragtime (1975; National Book Critics Circle Award)
Loon Lake (1980)
World's Fair (1985; National Book Award)
Billy Bathgate (1989; National Book Critics Circle Award; PEN/Faulkner Award)
The Waterworks (1994)

Nonfiction
Jack London, Hemingway, and the Constitution: Selected Writings, 1977–1992 (1993)
The Lives of Poets (1997)

LOUISE ERDRICH

Fiction

Love Medicine (1984; National Book Critics Circle Award)

The Beet Queen (1986)

Tracks (1988)

The Crown of Columbus (coauthor, 1991)

The Bingo Palace (1994)

The Blue Jay's Dance (1995)

Tales of Burning Love (1996)

Poetry

Jacklight (1984)

Baptism of Desire (1989)

Children's books

Grandmother's Pidgeon (1996)

JOHN GRISHAM

Fiction

A Time to Kill (1988)

The Firm (1990)

The Pelican Brief (1990)

The Client (1993)

The Chamber (1994)

The Rainmaker (1995)

The Runaway Jury (1996)

The Partner (1997)

MARK HELPRIN

Fiction

Winter's Tale (1983)

Refiner's Fire (1990)

Dove of the East and Other Stories (1990)

A Soldier of the Great War (1991)

Memoir from Antproof Case (1995)

The Veil of Snows (1997)

Children's books

Swan Lake (1989)

A City in Winter (1996)

STEPHEN KING

Fiction

Carrie (1975)

Salem's Lot (1976)

The Shining (1977)

The Stand (1978)

The Dead Zone (1979)

Firestarter (1980)

Cujo (1981)

The Dark Tower: The Gunslinger (1982)

Christine (1983)

Pet Sematary (1983)

The Talisman (coauthor, 1984)

Cycle of the Werewolf (1985)

It (1986)

The Eyes of the Dragon (1987)

Misery (1987)

The Tommyknockers (1987)

The Dark Half (1989)

The Dark Tower II: The Drawing of Three (1989)

The Dark Tower III: The Waste Lands (1991)

Needful Things (1991)

Gerald's Game (1992)

Dolores Claiborne (1992)

Insomnia (1994)

Rose Madder (1995)

The Green Mile (serial novel, 1996)

Desperation (1996)

Fiction written as Richard Bachman

Rage (1977)

The Long Walk (1979)

Roadwork: A Novel of the First Energy Crisis (1981)

The Running Man (1982)

Thinner (1984)

The Regulators (1996)

Nonfiction

Danse Macabre (1981)

JOHN LE CARRÉ
(nom de plume of David Cornwell)

Fiction

Call for the Dead (1960)

A Murder of Quality (1962)

The Spy Who Came in from the Cold (1964)

The Incongruous Spy (1964)

The Looking Glass War (1965)

A Small Town in Germany (1968)

The Naive and Sentimental Lover (1971)

Tinker, Tailor, Soldier, Spy (1977)

Smiley's People (1980)

The Honourable Schoolboy (1982)

The Little Drummer Girl (1983)

A Perfect Spy (1986)

The Russia House (1989)

The Secret Pilgrim (1991)

The Night Manager (1993)

Our Game (1995)

The Naive and Sentimental Lover (1997)

Tinker Tailor Soldier (1997)

ROBERT LUDLUM

Fiction

The Scarlatti Inheritance (1971)

The Osterman Weekend (1972)

The Matlock Paper (1973)

The Rhineman Exchange (1974)

The Gemini Contenders (1976)

The Chancellor Manuscript (1977)

The Holcroft Covenant (1978)

The Matarese Circle (1979)

The Bourne Identity (1980)

The Parsifal Mosaic (1982)

The Aquitaine Progression (1984)

The Bourne Supremacy (1986)

The Icarus Agenda (1988)

The Bourne Ultimatum (1990)

The Road to Omaha (1992)

The Scorpio Illusion (1993)

The Apocalypse Watch (1995)

Fiction written as Jonathan Ryder

Trevayne (1973; reissued under Robert Ludlum, 1992)

The Cry of the Halidon (1974; reissued under Robert Ludlum, 1996)

Fiction written as Michael Shepherd

The Road to Gandolfo (1975; reissued under Robert Ludlum, 1992)

NORMAN MAILER

Fiction

The Naked and the Dead (1948)

Barbary Shore (1951)

The Deer Park (1955; screenplay, *Wild 90*, 1967)

Advertisements for Myself (1959)

Deaths for the Ladies (1962)

The Presidential Papers (1963)

An American Dream (1965)

Cannibals and Christians (1966)

Existential Errands (1972)

Genius and Lust (1976)

The Executioner's Song (1979; Pulitzer Prize; screenplay 1982)

Ancient Evenings (1983)

Tough Guys Don't Dance (1984; screenplay 1987)

Huckleberry Finn, Alive at One Hundred (1984)

Harlot's Ghost (1992)

The Gospel According To The Son (1996)

Nonfiction

Why Are We in Vietnam? (1967)

The Armies of the Night: History as a Novel, the Novel as History (1968; Pulitzer Prize; National Book Award)

Miami and the Siege of Chicago (1968; National Book Award)

Of a Fire on the Moon (1970)

King of the Hill: On the Fight of the Century (1971)

St. George and the Godfather (1971)

The Prisoner of Sex (1971)

Marilyn: A Biography (1973)

The Faith of Graffiti (1974)

The Fight (1975)

Of Women and Their Elegance (1980)

Of a Small and Modest Malignancy, Wicked and Bristling with Dots (1980)

Pieces and Pontifications (1982)

Oswald's Tale (1995)

Portrait of Picasso as a Young Man (1995)

JAMES A. MICHENER

Fiction

Tales of the South Pacific (1947; Pulitzer Prize)

The Fires of the Spring (1949)

Return To Paradise (1951)

The Bridges of Toko-Ri (1953)

Sayonara (1954)

Hawaii (1959)

Caravans (1963)

The Source (1965)

The Drifters (1971)

Centennial (1974)

Chesapeake (1978)

The Covenant (1980)

Space (1982)

Poland (1983)

Texas (1985)

Legacy (1987)

Alaska (1988)

Caribbean (1989)

Journey (1989)

The Eagle and the Raven (1990)

The Novel (1991)

Mexico (1992)

Recessional (1994)

Miracle in Seville (1995)

Children's book
South Pacific (1992)

Nonfiction
The Voice of Asia (1951)

The Floating World (1954)

The Bridge at Andau (1957)

Facing East (1961)

Iberia: Spanish Travels and Reflections (1968)

America vs. America: The Revolution in Middle-Class Values (1969)

Presidential Lottery: The Reckless Gamble in Our Electoral System (1969)

A Study of the Art of Jack Levine (1970)

Kent State: What Happened and Why (1971)

Sports in America (1976)

The World Is My Home (memoirs, 1992)

Literary Reflections: Michener on Michener, Hemingway, Capote, and Others (1993)

My Lost Mexico (1995)

This Noble Land (1996)

TONI MORRISON

Fiction
The Bluest Eye (1969)

Sula (1973)

Song of Solomon (1977; National Book Critics Circle Award)

Tar Baby (1981)

Beloved (1987; Pulitzer Prize)

Jazz (1992)

Nonfiction
Playing in the Dark: Whiteness and the Literary Imagination (1992)

Play
Dreaming Emmett (1986)

Nobel Prize for Literature, 1993

THOMAS PYNCHON

Fiction
V (1963)

The Crying of Lot 49 (1965)

Gravity's Rainbow (1973; National Book Award)

Vineland (1990)

Mason & Dixon (1997)

ANNE RICE

Fiction
Interview with the Vampire (1976)

The Feast of All Saints (1980)

Cry to Heaven (1982)

The Vampire Lestat (1985)

The Queen of the Damned (1988)

The Mummy or *Ramses the Damned* (1989)

The Witching Hour (1990)

Tale of the Body Thief (1992)

Lasher (1993)

Taltos (1994)

Memnoch the Devil (1995)

Servant of the Bone (1996)

Violin (1997)

Fiction written as A. N. Roquelaure
The Claiming of Sleeping Beauty (1983)

Beauty's Punishment (1984)

Beauty's Release: The Continued Erotic Adventures of Sleeping Beauty (1985)

Fiction written as Anne Rampling
Exit to Eden (1985)

Belinda (1986)

PHILIP ROTH

Fiction
Goodbye, Columbus (1959; National Book Award)

Letting Go (1962)

When She Was Good (1967)

Portnoy's Complaint (1969)

Our Gang (1971)

The Breast (1972)

The Great American Novel (1973)

My Life as a Man (1974)

Reading Myself and Others (1975)

The Professor of Desire (1977)

The Ghost Writer (1979)

Zuckerman Unbound (1981)

The Anatomy Lesson (1983)

Zuckerman Bound (1985)

The Counterlife (1987; National Book Critics Circle Award)

Deception (1990)

Operation Shylock (1993; PEN/Faulkner Award)

Sabbath's Theater (1995; National Book Award)

The Prague Orgy (1996)

American Pastoral (1997)

Nonfiction
The Facts: A Novelist's Autobiography (1988)

Patrimony: A True Story (memoirs, 1991; National Book Critics Circle Award)

SALMAN RUSHDIE

Fiction
Grimus (1975)

Midnight's Children (1981; Booker Prize)

Shame (1983)

The Satanic Verses (1989)

Haroun and the Sea of Stories (1991)

The Moor's Last Sigh (1995)

East, West: Stories (1995)

Nonfiction
The Jaguar Smile: A Nicaraguan Journey (1987)

Imaginary Homelands (1992)

MAURICE SENDAK

Children's books
Kenny's Window (1956)

Very Far Away (1957)

The Sign on Rosie's Door (1960)

Chicken Soup with Rice (1962)

One Was Johnny (1962)

Alligators All Around (1962)

Pierre (1962)

Where the Wild Things Are (1963; Caldecott Medal)

Hector Protector [and] As I Went Over the Water (1965)

Higglety Pigglety Pop! or, There Must Be More to Life (1967)

In the Night Kitchen (1970)

Ten Little Rabbits: A Counting Book with Mino the Magician (1970)

Maurice Sendak's Really Rosie (1975)

Some Swell Pup; or Are You Sure You Want a Dog? (1976)

Seven Little Monsters (1977)

Outside Over There (1981)

We Are All in the Dumps with Jack and Guy (1993)

Bernard (1994)

Max (1994)

Moishe (1994)

Tsippi (1994)

The Miami Giant (coauthor, 1995)

Hans Christian Anderson Award, 1970

DANIELLE STEEL

Fiction
Going Home (1973)

Passion's Promise (1977)

Now and Forever (1978)

The Promise (1978)

Season of Passion (1979)

Summer's End (1979)

To Love Again (1980)

The Ring (1980)

Loving (1980)

Remembrance (1981)

Palomino (1981)

Once in a Lifetime (1982)

Crossings (1982)

A Perfect Stranger (1982)

Thurston House (1983)

Changes (1983)

Full Circle (1984)

Family Album (1985)

Secrets (1985)

Wanderlust (1986)

Fine Things (1987)

Kaleidoscope (1987)

Zoya (1988)

Star (1989)

Daddy (1989)

Message from Nam (1990)

Heartbeat (1991)

No Greater Love (1991)

Jewels (1992)

Mixed Blessings (1992)
Vanished (1993)
Accident (1994)
The Gift (1994)
Wings (1994)
Silent Honor (1995)
Lightning (1995)
Five Days in Paris (1995)
Malice (1996)
Days of Shame (1996)

Children's books
Max and the Babysitter (1989)
Martha's Best Friend (1989)
Max's Daddy Goes to the Hospital (1989)
Martha's New Daddy (1989)
Max's New Baby (1989)
Martha's New School (1989)
Max Runs Away (1990)
Martha's New Puppy (1990)
Max and Grandma and Grandpa Winky (1991)
Martha and Hilary and the Stranger (1991)
Freddie's Trip (1992)
Freddie's First Night Away (1992)
Freddie and the Doctor (1992)
Freddie's Accident (1992)

Poetry
Love Poems by Danielle Steel (1981)

Nonfiction
Having a Baby (1984)

ANNE TYLER

Fiction
If Morning Ever Comes (1964)
The Tin Can Tree (1965)
A Slipping-Down Life (1970)
The Clock Winder (1972)
Celestial Navigation (1974)
Searching for Caleb (1976)
Earthly Possessions (1977)
Morgan's Passing (1980)
Dinner at the Homesick Restaurant (1982)
The Accidental Tourist (1985; National Book Critics Circle Award)
Breathing Lessons (1988; Pulitzer Prize)
Saint Maybe (1991)
Ladder of Years (1995)
A Slipping-Down Life (1997)

Children's book
Tumble Tower (1993)

JOHN UPDIKE

Fiction
The Poorhouse Fair (1959)
Rabbit, Run (1960)
The Centaur (1963; National Book Award)
Of the Farm (1965)
Couples (1968)
Rabbit Redux (1971)
A Month of Sundays (1975)
Marry Me: A Romance (1976)
The Coup (1978)
Rabbit Is Rich (1981; Pulitzer Prize; National Book Award; National Book Critics Circle Award)
The Witches of Eastwick (1984)
Roger's Version (1986)
S. (1988)
Rabbit at Rest (1990; Pulitzer Prize; National Book Critics Circle Award)
Memoirs of the Ford Administration (1992)
Brazil (1994)
In the Beauty of the Lilies (1996)

Nonfiction
Self Consciousness (memoirs, 1989)
Golf Dreams (1996)

Play
Buchanan Dying (1974)

Children's books
The Magic Flute (1962)
The Ring (1964)
A Child's Calendar (1965)
Bottom's Dream (1969)

ALICE WALKER

Fiction
The Third Life of Grange Copeland (1970)
Meridian (1976)
The Color Purple (1982; Pulitzer Prize; National Book Award)
The Temple of My Familiar (1989)
Possessing the Secret of Joy (1992)

Nonfiction
Warrior Marks (1993)
The Same River Twice (memoirs, 1996)

Poetry
Once (1976)
Revolutionary Petunias and Other Poems (1973)
Goodnight, Willie Lee, I'll See You in the Morning (1984)
Horses Make a Landscape Look More Beautiful (1984)
Her Blue Body Everything We Know: Earthling Poems, 1965-1990 (1990)

Children's books
Langston Hughes, American Poet (1974)
To Hell With Dying (1988)
Finding the Green Stone (1991)

TRY ANOTHER TITLE

A title can make or break a book. Had these literary masterpieces gone to press with their original tags, who knows where they, or we, would be now.

The Title That Made History	The Rejected Title
All Things Bright and Beautiful, James Harriot	*It Shouldn't Happen to a Vet*
East of Eden, John Steinbeck	*The Salinas Valley*
The Man with the Golden Arm, Nelson Algren	*The Neon Wilderness; Night without Mercy*
The Mill on the Floss, George Eliot	*St. Ogg's on the Floss; The House of Tullever; Sister Maggie*
Moby Dick, Herman Melville	*The Whale*
Roots, Alex Haley	*Before This Anger*
The Rose Tattoo, Tennessee Williams	*The Eclipse of May 29, 1919*
Valley of the Dolls, Jacqueline Susann	*They Don't Build Statues to Businessmen*
War and Peace, Leo Tolstoy	*All's Well That Ends Well*

FROM GREAT BEGINNINGS, GREAT NOVELS GROW

Every great book has to start somewhere—this is how selected authors began some of their most enduring tales.

"At a village of la Mancha, whose name I do not wish to remember, there lived a little while ago one of those gentlemen who are wont to keep a lance in the rack, an old buckler, a lean horse, and a swift greyhound."
— *The Adventures of Don Quixote de la Mancha*, Miguel de Cervantes

"Alice was beginning to get very tired of sitting by her sister on the bank and of having nothing to do: once or twice she had peeped into the book her sister was reading, but it had no pictures or conversations in it, 'and what is the use of a book,' thought Alice, 'without pictures or conversations?' "
— *Alice in Wonderland*, Lewis Carroll

"Happy families are all alike, but an unhappy family is unhappy in its own way."
— *Anna Karenina*, Leo Tolstoy

"It was a queer, sultry summer, the summer they electrocuted the Rosenbergs, and I didn't know what I was doing in New York."
— *The Bell Jar*, Sylvia Plath

"There are songs that come free from the blue-eyed grass, from the dust of a thousand country roads."
— *The Bridges of Madison County*, Robert James Waller

"Buck did not read the newspapers, or he would have known that trouble was brewing, not alone for himself, but for every tide-water dog, strong of muscle and with warm, long hair, from Puget Sound to San Diego."
— *The Call of the Wild*, Jack London

"I have noticed that when someone asks for you on the telephone and, finding you out, leaves a message begging you to call him up the moment you come in, and it's important, the matter is more often important to him than to you."
— *Cakes and Ale*, W. Somerset Maugham

"Nobody was really surprised when it happened, not really, not at the subconscious level where savage things grow."
— *Carrie*, Stephen King

"It was love at first sight."
— *Catch-22*, Joseph Heller

"If you really want to hear about it, the first thing you'll probably want to know is where I was born, and what my lousy childhood was like, and how my parents were occupied and all before they had me, and all that David Copperfield kind of crap, but I don't feel like going into it, if you want to know the truth."
— *The Catcher in the Rye*, J. D. Salinger

" 'Where's Papa going with that ax?' said Fern to her mother as they were setting the table for breakfast."
— *Charlotte's Web*, E. B. White

"What's it going to be then, eh?"
— *A Clockwork Orange*, Anthony Burgess

"AAA CON is the first name in the phone book of most large American cities."
— *Dad*, William Wharton

"You will see, my dear, that I have kept my word and that bonnets and pom-poms do not take up all my time—there will always be some left over for you."
— *Dangerous Liaisons*, Choderlos de Laclos

"Whether I shall turn out to be the hero of my own life, or whether that station will be held by anybody else, these pages must show."
— *David Copperfield*, Charles Dickens

"I hope I will be able to confide everything to you, as I have never been able to confide in anyone, and I hope you will be a great source of comfort and support."
— *The Diary of a Young Girl*, Anne Frank

"The lady was extraordinarily naked."
— *Eight Black Horses*, Ed McBain

"There were 117 psychoanalysts on the Pan Am flight to Vienna and I'd been treated by at least six of them."
— *Fear of Flying*, Erica Jong

"riverrun, past Eve and Adam's, from swerve of shore to bend of bay, brings us by a commodius

vicus of recirculation back to Howth Castle and Environs."
— *Finnegan's Wake*, James Joyce

"This is the saddest story I have ever heard."
— *The Good Soldier*, Ford Maddox Ford

"To the red country and part of the gray country of Oklahoma, the last rains came gently, and they did not cut the scarred earth."
— *The Grapes of Wrath*, John Steinbeck

"In my younger and more vulnerable years my father gave me some advice that I've been turning over in my mind ever since."
— *The Great Gatsby*, F. Scott Fitzgerald

"It is three hundred forty-eight years, six months, and nineteen days ago today that the citizens of Paris were awakened by the pealing of all the bells in the triple precincts of the City, the University, and the Town."
— *The Hunchback of Notre-Dame*, Victor Hugo

"—Something is a little strange, that's what you notice, that she's not a woman like all the others."
— *Kiss of the Spider Woman*, Manuel Puig

"Whenever my mother talks to me, she begins the conversation as if we were already in the middle of an argument."
— *The Kitchen God's Wife*, Amy Tan

"I shook the rain from my hat and walked into the room."
— *I, The Jury,* Mickey Spillane

"He did not expect to see blood."
— *Kramer Versus Kramer,* Avery Corman

"Lolita, light of my life, fire of my loins."
— *Lolita*, Vladimir Nabokov

"What can you say about a twenty-five-year-old girl who died?"
— *Love Story*, Erich Segal

"When Gregor Samsa woke up one morning from unsettling dreams, he found himself changed in his bed into a monstrous vermin."
— *Metamorphosis*, Franz Kafka

"Call me Ishmael."
— *Moby Dick*, Herman Melville

"The sun shone, having no alternative, on the nothing new."
— *Murphy*, Samuel Beckett

"It was a bright cold day in April, and the clocks were striking thirteen."
— *1984*, George Orwell

"Died on me finally."
— *Oldest Living Confederate Widow Tells All,* Allan Gurganus

"To have reason to get up in the morning, it is necessary to possess a guiding principle."
— *Ordinary People* Judith Guest

"Jinn and Phyllis were spending a wonderful holiday, in space, as far away as possible from the inhabited stars."
— *Planet of the Apes*, Pierre Boulle

"She was so deeply imbedded in my consciousness that for the first year of school I seem to have believed that each of my teachers was my mother in disguise."
— *Portnoy's Complaint*, Philip Roth

"Under certain circumstances there are few hours in life more agreeable than the hour dedicated to the ceremony known as afternoon tea."
— *The Portrait of a Lady*, Henry James

"It began as a mistake."
— *Post Office,* Charles Bukowski

"For a long time I used to go to bed early."
— *Remembrance of Things Past* (Vol. I, *Swann's Way*), Marcel Proust

"In our family, there was no clear line between religion and fly fishing."
— *A River Runs Through It*, Norman MacLean

"It was the best of times, it was the worst of times, it was the age of wisdom, it was the age of foolishness, it was the epoch of belief, it was the epoch of incredulity, it was the season of Light, it was the season of Darkness, it was the spring of hope, it was the winter of despair, we had everything before us, we had nothing before us, we were all going direct to Heaven, we were all going direct the other way—in short, the period was so far like the present period, that some of its noisiest authorities insisted on its being received, for good or for evil, in the superlative degree of comparison only."
— *A Tale of Two Cities*, Charles Dickens

FAMOUS LAST WORDS

All good books come to an end—often, a good one. Here are some of the more memorable.

"But I reckon I got to light out for the territory ahead of the rest, because Aunt Sally she's going to adopt me and sivilize me, and I can't stand it. I been there before."
— *The Adventures of Huckleberry Finn,* Mark Twain

"The creatures outside looked from pig to man, and from man to pig, and from pig to man again; but already it was impossible to say which was which."
— *Animal Farm,* George Orwell

"The eyes and the faces all turned themselves toward me, and guiding myself by them, as by a magical thread, I stepped into the room."
— *The Bell Jar,* Sylvia Plath

"'Hurrah for Karamazov!'"
— *The Brothers Karamazov,* Fyodor Dostoevsky

"With relief, with humiliation, with terror, he understood that he too was a mere appearance, dreamt by another."
— *The Circular Ruins,* Jorge Luis Borges

"Oedipa settled back to await the crying of lot 49."
— *The Crying of Lot 49,* Thomas Pynchon

"History will call us wise."
— *Dune,* Frank Herbert

"I'll think of some way to get him back. After all, tomorrow is another day."
— *Gone with the Wind,* Margaret Mitchell

"So we beat on, boats against the current, born back ceaselessly into the past."
— *The Great Gatsby,* F. Scott Fitzgerald

"The offing was barred by a black bank of clouds, and the tranquil waterway leading to the uttermost ends of the earth flowed sombre under an overcast sky—seemed to lead into the heart of an immense darkness."
— *Heart of Darkness,* Joseph Conrad

" . . . and thence we came forth to see again the stars."
— *The Inferno,* Dante

"Who knows but that, on the lower frequencies, I speak for you?"
— *Invisible Man,* Ralph Ellison

"Florentino Ariza had kept his answer ready for 53 years, seven months, and eleven days and nights. 'Forever,' he said."
— *Love in the Time of Cholera,* Gabriel García Márquez

"For man himself is a mystery, and all humanity rests upon reverence before the mystery that is man."
— *The Magic Mountain,* Thomas Mann

"*Hot dog!*"
— *The Naked and the Dead,* Norman Mailer

"So [said the doctor]. Now vee may perhaps to begin. Yes?"
— *Portnoy's Complaint,* Philip Roth

"The God-damned fools."
— *The Reprieve,* Jean-Paul Sartre

"For now he knew what Shalimar knew: If you surrendered to the air, you could *ride* it."
— *Song of Solomon,* Toni Morrison

"He walked towards the faintly murmuring, glowing town, quickly."
— *Sons and Lovers,* D. H. Lawrence

"They endured."
— *The Sound and the Fury,* William Faulkner

"For all to be accomplished, for me to feel less lonely, all that remained to hope was that on the day of my execution there should be a huge crowd of spectators and that they should greet me with howls of execration."
— *The Stranger,* Albert Camus

"'It is a far, far better thing that I do, than I have ever done. It is a far, far better rest that I go to, than I have ever known.'"
— *A Tale of Two Cities,* Charles Dickens

"A Cock and a Bull, said Yorick— And one of the best of its kind, I ever heard."
— *The Life and Opinions of Tristram Shandy,* Laurence Sterne

"Yes I said yes I will yes."
— *Ulysses,* James Joyce

BOOKS OF THE CENTURY

To commemorate the New York Public Library's 100th anniversary, the librarians of this venerable institution identified books that, from their varying perspectives, have played defining roles in the making of the 20th century. Included are books that influenced the course of events, for good and for bad; books that interpreted new worlds; and books that simply delighted millions of patrons.

LANDMARKS OF MODERN LITERATURE

The Three Sisters, Anton Chekhov (1901)
Remembrance of Things Past, Marcel Proust (1913-27)
Tender Buttons, Gertrude Stein (1914)
The Metamorphosis, Franz Kafka (1915)
Renascence and Other Poems, Edna St. Vincent Millay (1917)
The Wild Swans at Coole, William Butler Yeats (1917)
Six Characters in Search of an Author, Luigi Pirandello (1921)
The Waste Land, T. S. Eliot (1922)
Ulysses, James Joyce (1922)
The Magic Mountain, Thomas Mann (1924)
The Great Gatsby, F. Scott Fitzgerald (1925)
To the Lighthouse, Virginia Woolf (1927)
Gypsy Ballads, Frederico García Lorca (1928)
Native Son, Richard Wright (1940)
The Age of Anxiety: A Baroque Eclogue, W. H. Auden (1947)
Invisible Man, Ralph Ellison (1952)
Lolita, Vladimir Nabokov (1955)
Fictions, Jorge Luis Borges (1944; 2nd augmented edition 1956)
One Hundred Years of Solitude, Gabriel García Márquez (1967)
Song of Solomon, Toni Morrison (1977)

PROTEST AND PROGRESS

The Battle with the Slum, Jacob Ritts (1902)
The Souls of Black Folk, W.E.B. Du Bois (1903)
The Jungle, Upton Sinclair (1906)
Twenty Years at Hull-House, Jane Addams (1910)
The House on Henry Street, Lillian Wald (1915)
The Autobiography of Lincoln Steffens, Lincoln Steffens (1931)
U.S.A., John Dos Passos (1937)
The Grapes of Wrath, John Steinbeck (1939)
Let Us Now Praise Famous Men, James Agee and Walker Evans (1941)
Strange Fruit, Lillian Smith (1944)
Growing Up Absurd, Paul Goodman (1960)
The Fire Next Time, James Baldwin (1963)
The Autobiography of Malcolm X, Malcolm X (1965)
And the Band Played On, Randy Shilts (1987)
There Are No Children Here, Alex Kotlowitz (1991)

POPULAR CULTURE & MASS ENTERTAINMENT

Dracula, Bram Stoker (1897)
The Turn of the Screw, Henry James (1898)
The Hound of the Baskervilles, Arthur Conan Doyle (1902)
Tarzan of the Apes, Edgar Rice Burroughs (1912)
Riders of the Purple Sage, Zane Grey (1912)
The Mysterious Affair at Styles, Agatha Christie (1920)
How To Win Friends and Influence People, Dale Carnegie (1936)
Gone with the Wind, Margaret Mitchell (1936)
The Big Sleep, Raymond Chandler (1939)
The Day of the Locust, Nathanael West (1939)
Peyton Place, Grace Metalious (1956)
The Cat in the Hat, Dr. Seuss (1957)
Stranger in a Strange Land, Robert A. Heinlein (1961)
Catch-22, Joseph Heller (1961)
In Cold Blood: A True Account of a Multiple Murder and Its Consequences, Truman Capote (1965)
Ball Four: My Life and Times Throwing the Knuckleball in the Big Leagues, Jim Bouton (1970)
Carrie, Stephen King (1974)
The Bonfire of the Vanities, Tom Wolfe (1987)

WOMEN RISE

The Age of Innocence, Edith Wharton (1920)
Woman Suffrage and Politics: The Inner Story of the Suffrage Movement, Carrie Chapman Catt and Nettie Rogers Shuler (1923)
My Fight for Birth Control, Margaret Sanger (1931)
Dust Tracks on a Dirt Road, Zora Neale Hurston (1942)
The Second Sex, Simone de Beauvoir (1949)
The Golden Notebook, Doris Lessing (1962)

The Feminine Mystique, Betty Friedan (1963)
I Know Why the Caged Bird Sings, Maya Angelou (1969)
Sisterhood Is Powerful: An Anthology of Writings from the Women's Liberations Movement, edited by Robin Morgan (1970)
Against Our Will: Men, Women and Rape, Susan Brownmiller (1975)
The Color Purple, Alice Walker (1982)

ECONOMICS & TECHNOLOGY

The Theory of the Leisure Class: An Economic Study of Institutions, Thorstein Veblen (1899)
The Protestant Ethic and the Spirit of Capitalism, Max Weber (1904–5)
The Education of Henry Adams, Henry Adams (1907)
The General Theory of Employment, Interest and Money, John Meynard Keynes (1936)
A Theory of the Consumption Function, Milton Friedman (1957)
The Affluent Society, John Kenneth Galbraith (1958)
The Death and Life of Great American Cities, Jane Jacobs (1961)
Superhighway—Super Hoax, Helen Leavitt (1970)
Small Is Beautiful: A Study of Economics as if People Mattered, E. F. Schumacher (1973)
The Whole Internet: User's Guide and Catalogue, Ed Krol (1992)

MIND & SPIRIT

Suicide: A Study in Sociology, Emile Durkheim (1897)
The Interpretation of Dreams, Sigmund Freud (1900)
Studies in the Psychology of Sex, Havelock Ellis (1901–28)
The Varieties of Religious Experience: A Study in Human Nature, Wiilliam James (1902)
The Prophet, Kahlil Gibran (1923)
Why I Am Not a Christian, Bertrand Russell (1927)
Coming of Age in Samoa, Margaret Mead (1928)
Being and Nothingness, Jean-Paul Sartre (1943)
The Common Sense Book of Baby Care, Dr. Benjamin Spock (1946)
The Holy Bible, Revised Standard Version (1952)
The Courage to Be, Paul Tillich (1952)
One Flew Over the Cuckoo's Nest, Ken Kesey (1962)
The Politics of Ecstasy, Timothy Leary (1968)
On Death and Dying, Elisabeth Kübler-Ross (1969)
The Uses of Enchantment, Bruno Bettelheim (1976)

MORE BOOKS THAT SHAPE LIVES

The Library of Congress established its Center for the Book in 1977 to stimulate public interest in books, reading, and libraries. Here is its list of the 25 books that have had the greatest impact on readers' lives.

The Adventures of Huckleberry Finn, Mark Twain
Atlas Shrugged, Ayn Rand
The Autobiography of Benjamin Franklin
The Bible
The Catcher in the Rye, J. D. Salinger
Charlotte's Web, E. B. White
The Diary of a Young Girl, Anne Frank
Don Quixote, Miguel de Cervantes
Gone with the Wind, Margaret Mitchell
Hiroshima, John Hersey
How To Win Friends and Influence People, Dale Carnegie
I Know Why the Caged Bird Sings, Maya Angelou
Invisible Man, Ralph Ellison
The Little Prince, Antoine de Saint Exupéry
Little Women, Louisa May Alcott
The Lord of the Rings, J.R.R. Tolkien
Roots, Alex Haley
The Secret Garden, Frances Hodgson Burnett
To Kill a Mockingbird, Harper Lee
Treasure Island, Robert Louis Stevenson
Walden, Henry David Thoreau
War and Peace, Leo Tolstoy
What Color Is Your Parachute? Richard Nelson Bolles

FAVORITE FICTIONAL CHARACTERS FROM BOOKS

Sometimes, the most vivid characters one encounters emerge only from words: from the mind of an author, the pages of a book, and a reader's own imagination. Here are a dozen of the most remarkable. (Source: *The Encyclopedia of Fictional Characters*, Berkley Publishing Corp. and Seth Godin Productions)

Chief Bromden
One Flew over the Cuckoo's Nest
The Chief is a towering, powerful, but slow-moving Native American who pretends to be a mute, to escape the world that has so harmed him and his people. His size, if not athletic ability, makes him a natural on the basketball court. He grows to love Randle Patrick McMurphy, the new patient who suspects he's faking his muteness, and who exhorts his fellows to defy Mildred Ratched, the nurse who oppressively oversees the ward. Finally, he breaks his silence when McMurphy is lobotomized, helps McMurphy to achieve a kind of liberty, and overcomes his personal inertia enough to make his escape from the prisonlike hospital.

Daisy Buchanan
The Great Gatsby
Impressionable and weak-willed Daisy Fay, a society girl from Louisville, Kentucky, marries Tom Buchanan of Chicago. It's done on the rebound after a thwarted wartime love affair with Jay Gatsby. Beautiful, vacuous, and selfish, she and Tom have one child, a daughter, Pamela. She appears to tolerate her husband's extramarital affairs and indulges in one of her own with Gatsby, whom she meets again through the combined efforts of her friend Jordan Baker and her distant cousin Nick Carraway. The greatest attraction of this otherwise unexceptionable woman, to both Buchanan and Gatsby, is her position in society. "Her voice is full of money," Gatsby says. The crux of her life is having to choose between her husband and her lover.

Jenny Fields
The World According to Garp
Jenny Fields is a no-nonsense nurse who cares nothing about other people's morals and expectations. Neither does she care that she puzzles her traditional family by a total lack of interest in marriage and settling down. That doesn't mean, however, that she doesn't want a child, and when the opportunity arises, in the form of a severely wounded ball turret gunner, Jenny proceeds to get herself pregnant, to the shock and distress of the family. She hires on as nurse at a private school for boys to support herself and her son, whom she names after his father, T. S. (for Technical Sergeant) Garp. When she writes her life story, she becomes a huge success and rallying point for a feminist movement, which really wasn't what she intended at all.

Jean Louise "Scout" Finch
To Kill a Mockingbird
This scrappy little tomboy has a propensity for getting into fistfights and consequently gets into constant trouble at school. She's the kid sister of Jem Finch, who helps to look after her, and the daughter of lawyer Atticus Finch, whose words and actions teach her a great deal about the evils of prejudice and the importance of having an open mind and treating others with respect. Though, like the other local children, she initially fears weird local recluse Boo Radley, she ultimately learns better, with her father's help. She also unwittingly defuses a potentially dangerous situation involving a lynch mob. She is still at the point in her life when she's revolted by the prospect of wearing a dress or behaving like a little lady.

Miss Lonelyhearts
Miss Lonelyhearts
The "agony aunt" for the New York Post-Dispatch, Miss Lonelyhearts started his (that's right—his) career as a reporter. After spending months as Miss Lonelyhearts, he suffers daily as he reads the private griefs of those seeking his advice. He takes his job too seriously, for which he is ridiculed by Shrike, the feature editor.

Ezekiel "Easy" Rawlins
Devil in a Blue Dress
Down the mean streets of Watts he goes, wary, wisecracking, and usually up to his neck in trouble. Like his spiritual progenitor, Philip Marlowe, he's too cagey to believe in much of anything, but too smart and honorable to believe in nothing at all. He keeps an eye on several apartment buildings he secretly owns by working as their janitor. Easy has a reputation for fairness and integrity among the poor, hard-pressed African Americans of 1950s Los Angeles, for whom he often does unpaid favors, asking only that they return the favor when they can—"a real country way of doing business." His mistrust of authority was confirmed by his time in the army. "Somewhere along the line I had slipped into

the role of a confidential agent who represented people when the law broke down. And the law broke down often enough to keep me busy."

Santiago
The Old Man and the Sea
He is an elderly Cuban fisherman and widower. Santiago loves the New York Yankees and, above all, the great DiMaggio. With advancing age, he feels his life and energy slipping away and yearns for the virile potency he felt as a younger man. Even though he hasn't landed a fish in more than eighty days, he puts to sea at the urging of the little boy who is his only real friend. This time, in an effort to change his fortune, he goes far out at sea, where, to his delight, he hooks the biggest marlin he's ever seen. There ensues an epic battle, as Santiago desperately wants one last great triumph over the forces of age and time. First, he must fight the great fish, and then he must fight hordes of ravenous sharks for possession of his catch, as he tries to get the marlin back to shore intact. But nature has no respect for age.

Sam Spade
The Maltese Falcon
The original tough guy in a cruel world, Sam Spade knows that when the chips are down, we all stand alone. By turns seething with righteous anger or coolly calculating, Sam is a steely-eyed private investigator in San Francisco in the 1920s. Caught in a web of intrigue following the murder of his partner, Miles Archer, Sam ultimately reveals a practical code of justice that underlies his bitter cynicism about human nature. The trouble begins when a beautiful young woman calling herself Miss Wonderly hires the partners to follow a man named Floyd Thursby. Miles accepts the job and is found murdered later that night in Chinatown; Thursby's body is discovered half an hour later. Sam becomes the prime suspect when the police find out that he not only loathed his late partner but was having an affair with Archer's wife, Iva. Soon, Miss Wonderly reappears, reveals herself as Brigid O'Shaughnessy and begs Sam to help her. Even though Sam knows Brigid is full of lies, he agrees to work for her and ultimately begins a romantic involvement with her as well. The plot thickens with unseemly characters all in pursuit of a mysterious statuette of a falcon, and Sam expertly plays them off against each other until he is the only one left standing or not in jail. Even his beloved Brigid is left to dangle in the breeze when he learns that she killed his partner. After all, what does love mean in a world of lies?

Carrie White
Carrie
A pathologically shy, emotionally sheltered, and physically immature high school senior who sits at the bottom of the social pecking order. Her pale complexion, stringy hair, and dowdy clothes also set her apart. Singled out by a popular clique of girls, Carrie becomes the object of their petty spite. Shielded as she is from the world by her fanatically religious mother, the innocent Carrie is ill-equipped to understand the motives of her classmates. However, Carrie's outwardly harmless demeanor masks a frightening inner power of which she is unaware, until a cruel trick is played on her by classmates on prom night. Then her psychokinetic strength is suddenly and fearsomely displayed.

Nero Wolfe
The Rubber Band
As well known for his corpulence as he is for his brilliance at solving crimes, private detective Wolfe loves gourmet food and his greenhouse full of orchids as much as he detests exercise. Fortunately he has his assistant Archie Goodwin, a sprightly, young man-about-town, to run his errands for him.

Jing-Mei "June" Woo
The Joy Luck Club
June, whose parents left China bent on finding a new life in America, has spent her life in an effort at total assimilation—turning her back on her heritage and becoming more American than any fifth-generation San Franciscan. But she finally learns about her mother's painful life in China and, with this knowledge, seeks a new balance between her family's past and her own present and comes to accept what and whom she comes from.

Yurii Andreievich Zhivago
Doctor Zhivago
A man caught on the rocks of Mother Russia, battered by the tides of history. Orphaned at ten, Zhivago is sent to Moscow to study medicine. After attaining his degree, he marries Antonina Gromeko. Despite his marriage, his life is intertwined with that of Lara Guishar, the great love of his life. Zhivago, a dreamer and romantic, writes a series of poems about Lara, a work that takes a place in the higher works of Russian literature. He serves as a doctor in the Czar's army during World War I, and then for Communist partisans during the Russian Civil War. Zhivago has a son, Sashenka, and a daughter, Tania. Following Lara's departure to Vladivostok, Zhivago becomes depressed and dissolute. He dies in Moscow in 1929.

LITERARY AWARDS

NATIONAL BOOK AWARDS

Fiction

1950 Nelson Algren
The Man with the Golden Arm
1951 William Faulkner
The Collected Stories of William Faulkner
1952 James Jones
From Here to Eternity
1953 Ralph Ellison
Invisible Man
1954 Saul Bellow
The Adventures of Augie March
1955 William Faulkner
A Fable
1956 John O'Hara
Ten North Frederick
1957 Wright Morris
The Field of Vision
1958 John Cheever
The Wapshot Chronicle
1959 Bernard Malamud
The Magic Barrel
1960 Philip Roth
Goodbye, Columbus
1961 Conrad Richter
The Waters of Kronos
1962 Walker Percy
The Moviegoer
1963 J. F. Powers
Morte D'Urban
1964 John Updike
The Centaur
1965 Saul Bellow
Herzog
1966 Katherine Anne Porter
The Collected Stories of Katherine Anne Porter
1967 Bernard Malamud
The Fixer
1968 Thornton Wilder
The Eighth Day
1969 Jerzy Kosinski
Steps
1970 Joyce Carol Oates
Them
1971 Saul Bellow
Mr. Sammler's Planet
1972 Flannery O'Connor
The Complete Stories of Flannery O'Connor
1973 John Barth
Chimera
John Williams
Augustus
1974 Thomas Pynchon
Gravity's Rainbow
Isaac Bashevis Singer
A Crown of Feathers and Other Stories
1975 Robert Stone
Dog Soldiers
Thomas Williams
The Hair of Harold Roux
1976 William Gaddis
JR
1977 Wallace Stegner
The Spectator Bird
1978 Mary Lee Settle
Blood Ties
1979 Tim O'Brien
Going After Cacciato
1980 William Styron (hardcover)
Sophie's Choice
John Irving (paperback)
The World According to Garp
1981 Wright Morris (hardcover)
Plains Song
John Cheever (paperback)
The Stories of John Cheever
1982 John Updike (hardcover)
Rabbit Is Rich
William Maxwell (paperback)
So Long, See You Tomorrow
1983 Alice Walker (hardcover)
The Color Purple
Eudora Welty (paperback)
Collected Stories of Eudora Welty
1984 Ellen Gilchrist
Victory over Japan: A Book of Stories
1985 Don DeLillo
White Noise
1986 E. L. Doctorow
World's Fair
1987 Larry Heinemann
Paco's Story
1988 Pete Dexter
Paris Trout
1989 John Casey
Spartina
1990 Charles Johnson
Middle Passage
1991 Norman Rush
Mating
1992 Cormac McCarthy
All the Pretty Horses
1993 E. Annie Proulx
The Shipping News
1994 William Gaddis
A Frolic of His Own
1995 Philip Roth
Sabbath's Theater
1996 Andrea Barrett
Ship Fever and Other Stories

Nonfiction

1950 Ralph L. Rusk
Ralph Waldo Emerson
1951 Newton Arvin
Herman Melville
1952 Rachel Carson
The Sea Around Us
1953 Bernard A. De Voto
The Course of an Empire
1954 Bruce Catton
A Stillness at Appomattox
1955 Joseph Wood Krutch
The Measure of Man
1956 Herbert Kubly
An American in Italy
1957 George F. Kennan
Russia Leaves the War
1958 Catherine Drinker Bowen
The Lion and the Throne
1959 J. Christopher Herold
Mistress to an Age: A Life of Madame de Stael
1960 Richard Ellmann
James Joyce
1961 William L. Shirer
The Rise and Fall of the Third Reich
1962 Lewis Mumford
The City in History: Its Origins, Its Transformations and Its Prospects
1963 Leon Edel
Henry James, Vol. II: The Conquest of London. Henry James, Vol. III: The Middle Years
1980 Tom Wolfe (hardcover)
The Right Stuff
Peter Matthiessen (paperback)
The Snow Leopard
1981 Maxine Hong Kingston (hardcover)
China Men
Jane Kramer (paperback)
The Last Cowboy
1982 Tracy Kidder (hardcover)
The Soul of a New Machine
Victor S. Navasky (paperback)
Naming Names
1983 Fox Butterfield
China: Alive in the Bitter Sea
James Fallows (paperback)
National Defense
1984 Rovert V. Remini
Andrew Jackson and the Course of American Democracy, 1833–1845
1985 J. Anthony Lukas
Common Ground: A Turbulent Decade in the Lives of Three American Families

1986 Barry Lopez
Arctic Dreams
1987 Richard Rhodes
The Making of the Atom Bomb
1988 Neil Sheehan
A Bright Shining Lie: John Paul Vann and America in Vietnam
1989 Thomas L. Friedman
From Beirut to Jerusalem
1990 Ron Chernow
The House of Morgan: An American Banking Dynasty and the Rise of Modern Finance
1991 Orlando Patterson
Freedom
1992 Paul Monette
Becoming a Man: Half a Life Story
1993 Gore Vidal
United States: Essays 1952–1992
1994 Sherwin B. Nuland
How We Die: Reflections on Life's Final Chapter
1995 Tina Rosenberg
The Haunted Land: Facing Europe's Ghosts After Communism
1996 James Caroll
An American Requiem

Poetry

1950 William Carlos Williams
Paterson: Book III and Selected Poems
1951 Wallace Stevens
The Auroras of Autumn
1952 Marianne Moore
Collected Poems
1953 Archibald MacLeish
Collected Poems, 1917–1952
1954 Conrad Aiken
Collected Poems
1955 Wallace Stevens
The Collected Poems of Wallace Stevens
1956 W. H. Auden
The Shield of Achilles
1957 Richard Wilbur
Things of This World
1958 Robert Penn Warren
Promises: Poems, 1954–1956
1959 Theodore Roethke
Words for the Wind
1960 Robert Lowell
Life Studies
1961 Randall Jarrell
The Woman at the Washington Zoo
1962 Alan Dugan
Poems
1963 William Strafford
Traveling Through the Dark
1964 John Crowe Ransom
Selected Poems
1965 Theodore Roethke
The Far Field
1966 James Dickey
Buckdancer's Choice: Poems
1967 James Merrill
Nights and Days
1968 Robert Bly
The Light Around the Body
1969 John Berryman
His Toy, His Dream, His Rest
1970 Elizabeth Bishop
The Complete Poems
1971 Mona Van Duyn
To See, To Take
1972 Howard Moss
Selected Poems
Frank O'Hara
The Collected Poems of Frank O'Hara
1973 A. R. Ammons
Collected Poems, 1951–1971
1974 Allen Ginsberg
The Fall of America: Poems of These States
Adrienne Rich
Diving into the Wreck: Poems 1971–1972
1975 Marilyn Hacker
Presentation Piece
1976 John Ashbery
Self-Portrait in a Convex Mirror
1977 Richard Eberhart
Collected Poems, 1930–1976
1978 Howard Nemerov
The Collected Poems of Howard Nemerov
1979 James Merrill
Mirabell: Book of Numbers
1980 Philip Levine
Ashes
1981 Lisel Mueller
The Need To Hold Still
1982 William Bronk
Life Supports: New and Collected Poems
1983 Galway Kinnell
Selected Poems
Charles Wright
Country Music: Selected Early Poems
1991 Philip Levine
What Work Is
1992 Mary Oliver
New & Selected Poems
1993 A. R. Ammons
Garbage
1994 James Tate
A Worshipful Company of Fletchers
1995 Stanley Kunitz
Passing Through: The Later Poems New and Selected
1996 Hayden Carruth
Scrambled Eggs & Whiskey

Young People's Literature

1996 Victor Martinez
Parrot in the Oven: Mi Vida

NEWBERY MEDAL BOOKS

For children's literature

1922 Hendrik van Loon
The Story of Mankind
1923 Hugh Lofting
The Voyages of Doctor Dolittle
1924 Charles Hawes
The Dark Frigate
1925 Charles Finger
Tales from Silver Lands
1926 Arthur Chrisman
Shen of the Sea
1927 Will James
Smoky, the Cowhorse
1928 Dhan Mukerji
Gay Neck, the Story of a Pigeon
1929 Eric P. Kelly
The Trumpeter of Krakow
1930 Rachel Field
Hitty, Her First Hundred Years
1931 Elizabeth Coatsworth
The Cat Who Went to Heaven
1932 Laura Armer
Waterless Mountain
1933 Elizabeth Lewis
Young Fu of the Upper Yangtze
1934 Cornelia Meigs
Invincible Louisa
1935 Monica Shannon
Dobry
1936 Carol Brink
Caddie Woodlawn
1937 Ruth Sawyer
Roller Skates
1938 Kate Seredy
The White Stag
1939 Elizabeth Enright
Thimble Summer
1940 James Daugherty
Daniel Boone
1941 Armstrong Sperry
Call It Courage
1942 Walter Edmonds
The Matchlock Gun
1943 Elizabeth Gray
Adam of the Road
1944 Esther Forbes
Johnny Tremain
1945 Robert Lawson
Rabbit Hill

1946 Lois Lenski
Strawberry Girl

1947 Carolyn Bailey
Miss Hickory

1948 William Pène du Bois
The Twenty-One Balloons

1949 Marguerite Henry
King of the Wind

1950 Marguerite de Angeli
The Door in the Wall

1951 Elizabeth Yates
Amos Fortune, Free Man

1952 Eleanor Estes
Ginger Pye

1953 Ann Nolan Clark
Secret of the Andes

1954 Joseph Krumgold
...And Now Miguel

1955 Meindert DeJong
The Wheel on the School

1956 Jean Lee Latham
Carry On, Mr. Bowditch

1957 Virginia Sorenson
Miracles on Maple Hill

1958 Harold Keith
Rifles for Watie

1959 Elizabeth George Speare
The Witch of Blackbird Pond

1960 Joseph Krumgold
Onion John

1961 Scott O'Dell
Island of the Blue Dolphins

1962 Elizabeth George Speare
The Bronze Bow

1963 Madeleine L'Engle
A Wrinkle in Time

1964 Emily Neville
It's Like This, Cat

1965 Maia Wojciechowska
Shadow of a Bull

1966 Elizabeth Borton de Trevino
I, Juan de Pareja

1967 Irene Hunt
Up a Road Slowly

1968 E. L. Konigsburg
From the Mixed-Up Files of Mrs. Basil E. Frankweiler

1969 Lloyd Alexander
The High King

1970 William H. Armstrong
Sounder

1971 Betsy Byars
Summer of the Swans

1972 Robert C. O'Brien
Mrs. Frisby and the Rats of NIMH

1973 Jean Craighead George
Julie of the Wolves

1974 Paula Fox
The Slave Dancer

1975 Virginia Hamilton
M. C. Higgins, the Great

1976 Susan Cooper
The Grey King

1977 Mildred D. Taylor
Roll of Thunder, Hear My Cry

1978 Katherine Paterson
Bridge to Terabithia

1979 Ellen Raskin
The Westing Game

1980 Joan W. Blos
A Gathering of Days

1981 Katherine Paterson
Jacob Have I Loved

1982 Nancy Willard
A Visit to William Blake's Inn: Poems for Innocent and Experienced Travelers

1983 Cynthia Voight
Dicey's Song

1984 Beverly Cleary
Dear Mr. Henshaw

1985 Robin McKinley
The Hero and the Crown

1986 Patricia MacLachlan
Sarah, Plain and Tall

1987 Sid Fleischman
The Whipping Boy

1988 Russell Freedman
Lincoln: A Photobiography

1989 Paul Fleischman
Joyful Noise: Poems for Two Voices

1990 Lois Lowry
Number the Stars

1991 Jerry Spinelli
Maniac Magee

1992 Phyllis Reynolds Naylor
Shiloh

1993 Cynthia Rylant
Missing May

1994 Lois Lowry
The Giver

1995 Sharon Creech
Walk Two Moons

1996 Karen Cushman
The Midwife's Apprentice

1997 E. L. Konigsburg
The View from Saturday

CALDECOTT MEDAL BOOKS

For children's picture books

1938 Helen Dean Fish, ill. by Dorothy P. Lathrop
Animals of the Bible

1939 Thomas Handforth
Mei Li

1940 Ingri and Edgar Parin d'Aulaire
Abraham Lincoln

1941 Robert Lawson
They Were Strong and Good

1942 Robert McCloskey
Make Way for Ducklings

1943 Virginia Lee Burton
The Little House

1944 James Thurber, ill. by Louis Slobodkin
Many Moons

1945 Rachel Field, ill. by Elizabeth Orton Jones
Prayer for a Child

1946 Maude and Mishka Petersham
The Rooster Crows

1947 Golden MacDonald, ill. by Leonard Weisgard
The Little Island

1948 Alvin Tresselt, ill. by Roger Duvoisin
White Snow, Bright Snow

1949 Berta and Elmer Hader
The Big Snow

1950 Leo Politi
Song of the Swallows

1951 Katherine Milhous
The Egg Tree

1952 Will Lipkind, ill. by Nicolas Mordvinoff
Finders Keepers

1953 Lynd Ward
The Biggest Bear

1954 Ludwig Bemelmans
Madeline's Rescue

1955 Marcia Brown
Cinderella

1956 John Langstaff, ill. by Feodor Rojankovsky
Frog Went A-Courtin'

1957 Janice Udry, ill. by Marc Simont
A Tree Is Nice

1958 Robert McCloskey
Time of Wonder

1959 Barbara Cooney
Chanticleer and the Fox

1960 Marie Hall Ets and Aurora Labastida
Nine Days to Christmas

1961 Ruth Robbins, ill. by Nicolas Sidjakov
Baboushka and the Three Kings

1962 Marcia Brown
Once a Mouse

1963 Ezra Jack Keats
The Snowy Day

1964 Maurice Sendak
Where the Wild Things Are

1965 Beatrice Schenk de Regniers, ill. by Beni Montresor
May I Bring a Friend?

1966 Sorche Nic Leodhas, ill. by Nonny Hogrogian
Always Room for One More

1967 Evaline Ness
Sam, Bangs & Moonshine

1968 Barbara Emberley, ill. by Ed Emberley
Drummer Hoff

1969 Arthur Ransome, ill. by Uri Shulevitz
The Fool of the World and the Flying Ship
1970 William Steig
Sylvester and the Magic Pebble
1971 Gail E. Haley
A Story a Story
1972 Nonny Hogrogian
One Fine Day
1973 Lafcadio Hearn, retold by Arlene Mosel, ill. by Blair Lent
The Funny Little Woman
1974 Harve Zemach, picts. by Margot Zemach
Duffy and the Devil
1975 Gerald McDermott
Arrow to the Sun
1976 Verna Aardema, picts. by Leo and Diane Dillon
Why Mosquitoes Buzz in People's Ears
1977 Margaret Musgrove, picts. by Leo and Diane Dillon
Ashanti to Zulu
1978 Peter Spier
Noah's Ark
1979 Paul Goble
The Girl Who Loved Wild Horses
1980 Donald Hall, picts. by Barbara Cooney
Ox-Cart Man
1981 Arnold Lobel
Fables
1982 Chris Van Allsburg
Jumanji
1983 Blaise Cendrars, trans. and ill. by Marcia Brown
Shadow
1984 Alice and Martin Provensen
The Glorious Flight: Across the Channel with Louis Blériot
1985 Margaret Hodges, ill. by Trina Schart Hyman
Saint George and the Dragon
1986 Chris Van Allsburg
The Polar Express
1987 Arthur Yorinks, ill. by Richard Egielski
Hey, Al
1988 Jane Yolen, ill. by John Schoenherr
Owl Moon
1989 Karen Ackerman, ill. by Stephen Gammell
Song and Dance Man
1990 Ed Young
Lon Po Po
1991 David Macaulay
Black and White
1992 David Wiesner
Tuesday
1993 Emily Arnold McCully
Mirette on the High Wire
1994 Allen Say
Grandfather's Journey
1995 Eve Bunting, ill. by David Diaz
Smoky Night
1996 Peggy Rathmann
Officer Buckle and Gloria
1997 David Wisniewski
Golem

BOLLINGEN PRIZE IN POETRY

1949 Wallace Stevens
1950 John Crowe Ransom
1951 Marianne Moore
1952 Archibald MacLeish
William Carlos Williams
1953 W. H. Auden
1954 Leonie Adams
Louise Bogan
1955 Conrad Aiken
1956 Allen Tate
1957 e. e. cummings
1958 Theodore Roethke
1959 Delmore Schwartz
1960 Yvor Winters
1961 Richard Eberhart
John Hall Wheelock
1962 Robert Frost
1965 Horace Gregory
1967 Robert Penn Warren
1969 John Berryman
Karl Shapiro
1971 Richard Wilbur
Mona Van Duyn
1973 James Merrill
1975 A. R. Ammons
1977 David Ignatow
1979 W. S. Merwin
1981 May Swenson
Howard Nemerov
1983 Anthony E. Hecht
John Hollander
1985 John Ashbery
Fred Chappell
1987 Stanley Kunitz
1989 Edgar Bowers
1991 Laura (Riding) Jackson
Donald Justice
1993 Mark Strand
1995 Kenneth Koch
1996 Gary Snyder

PEN/FAULKNER AWARD

Best American work of fiction

1981 Walter Abish
How German Is It?
1982 David Bradley
The Chaneysville Incident
1983 Toby Olson
Seaview
1984 John Edgar Wideman
Sent for You Yesterday
1985 Tobias Wolff
The Barracks Thief
1986 Peter Taylor
The Old Forest
1987 Richard Wiley
Soldiers in Hiding
1988 T. Coraghessan Boyle
World's End
1989 James Salter
Dusk
1990 E. L. Doctorow
Billy Bathgate
1991 John Edgar Wideman
Philadelphia Fire
1992 Don DeLillo
Mao II
1993 E. Annie Proulx
Postcards
1994 Philip Roth
Operation Shylock
1995 David Guterson
Snow Falling on Cedars
1996 Richard Ford
Independence Day
1997 Gina Berriault
Women in Their Beds

BOOKER PRIZE

British award for fiction

1969 P. H. Newby
Something To Answer For
1970 Bernice Rubens
The Elected Member
1971 V. S. Naipaul
In a Free State
1972 John Berger
G
1973 J. G. Farrell
The Siege of Krishnapur
1974 Nadine Gordimer
The Conservationist
1975 Ruth Prawer Jhabvala
Heat and Dust
1976 David Storey
Saville
1977 Paul Scott
Staying On
1978 Iris Murdoch
The Sea, the Sea
1979 Penelope Fitzgerald
Offshore
1980 William Golding
Rites of Passage
1981 Salman Rushdie
Midnight's Children
1982 Thomas Keneally
Schindler's Ark
1983 J. M. Coetzee
Life & Times of Michael K
1984 Anita Brookner
Hotel du Lac

1985 Keri Hulme
The Bone People
1986 Kingsley Amis
The Old Devils
1987 Penelope Lively
Moon Tiger
1988 Peter Carey
Oscar and Lucinda
1989 Kazuo Ishiguro
The Remains of the Day
1990 A. S. Byatt
Possession
1991 Ben Okri
The Famished Road
1992 Michael Ondaatje
The English Patient
Barry Unsworth
Sacred Hunger
1993 Roddy Doyle
Paddy Clark Ha Ha Ha
1994 James Kelman
How Late It Was, How Late
1995 Pat Barker
The Ghost Road
1996 Graham Swift
Last Orders

NOBEL PRIZE FOR LITERATURE

1901 Rene-Francois-Armend Prudhomme
France
1902 Bjornstjerne Bjornson
Norway
1903 Christian Mommsen
Germany
1904 Jose Echegaray y Eizaguirre
Spain
Frederic Mistral
France
1905 Henryk Sienkiewicz
Poland
1906 Giosue Carducci
Italy
1907 Joseph Rudyard Kipling
Great Britain
1908 Rudolph Eucker
Germany
1909 Selma Lagerlof
Sweden
1910 Paul Ludwig von Heyse
Germany
1911 Maurice Maeterlinck
Belgium
1912 Gerhart Hauptmann
Germany
1913 Sir Rabindranath Tagore
India
1915 Roland Romain
France
1916 Carl Gustof Verner Von Heidenstam
Sweden
1917 Karl Adolph Gjellerup
Denmark
Henrik Pontoppidan
Denmark
1918 Erik Axel Karlfeldt
Sweden
1919 Carl Spitteler
Switzerland
1920 Knut Hamsun
Norway
1921 Anatole France
France
1922 Jacinto Benaventi y Martinez
Spain
1923 William Butler Yeats
Ireland
1924 Wladylaw Reymont
Poland
1925 George Bernard Shaw
Ireland
1926 Grazia Deledda
Italy
1927 Henri Bergson
France
1928 Sigrid Undset
Norway
1929 Paul Mann
Germany
1930 Henry Sinclair Lewis
United States
1931 Erik Axel Karlfeldt
Sweden
1932 John Galsworthy
Great Britain
1933 Ivan Bunin
Russia
1934 Luigi Pirandello
Italy
1936 Eugene O'Neill
United States
1937 Roger Martin du Gard
France
1938 Pearl S. Buck
United States
1939 Frans Sillanpaa
Finland
1944 Johannes Jensen
Denmark
1945 Gabriela Mistral
Chile
1946 Herman Hesse
Germany
1947 Andre Gide
France
1948 Thomas Stearns Eliot
United States
Isaac Singer
Poland
1949 William Faulkner
United States
1950 Bertrand Russell
Great Britain
1951 Par Fabian Lagerkirst
Sweden
1952 Francois Mauriac
France
1953 Sir Winston Churchill
Great Britain
1954 Ernest Hemingway
United States
1955 Halldor Laxness
Iceland
1956 Juan Jimenez
Spain
1957 Albert Camus
France
1958 Boris Pasternak
Russia
1959 Salvatore Quasimodo
Italy
1960 Saint-John Perse
France
1961 Ivo Andric
Yugoslavia
1962 John Steinbeck
United States
1963 Giorgos Seferis
Greece
1964 Jean-Paul Sartre
France
1965 Mikhail Sholokov
Russia
1966 Shmuel Agnon
Austria
Leonie Sachs
Germany
1967 Miguel Asturias
Guatemala
1968 Yasunari Kawabata
Japan
1969 Samuel Beckett
Ireland
1970 Alexander Solzhenitsyn
Russia
1971 Pablo Neruda
Chile
1972 Heinrich Boll
Germany
1973 Patrick White
Australia
1974 Euyind Johnson
Sweden
1975 Eugenio Montale
Italy
1976 Saul Bellow
Canada
1977 Vicente Aleixandre y Merlo
Spain
1978 Isaac Bashevis Singer
United States
1979 Odysseus Elytis
Greece
1980 Czeslaw Milosz
Poland
1981 Elias Canetti
Bulgaria

1982 Gabriel Jose Garcia Marquez
Colombia
1983 William Golding
Great Britain
1984 Jaroslav Seifert
Czechoslovakia
1985 Claude Simon
France
1986 Wole Soyinka
Nigeria
1987 Joseph Brodsky
Russia
1988 Naguib Mahfouz
Egypt
1989 Camilo Jose Cela
Spain
1990 Octavio Paz
Mexico
1991 Nadine Gordimer
South Africa
1992 Derek Walcott
St. Lucia
1993 Toni Morrison
United States
1994 Kenzaburo Oe
Japan
1995 Seamus Heaney
Ireland
1996 Wislawa Szymborska
Poland

NATIONAL MAGAZINE AWARD

Public Service/Public Interest

1970 Life
1971 The Nation
1972 Philadelphia
1973 [not awarded]
1974 Scientific American
1975 Consumer Reports
1976 Business Week
1977 Philadelphia
1978 Mother Jones
1979 New West
1980 Texas Monthly
1981 Reader's Digest
1982 The Atlantic Monthly
1983 Foreign Affairs
1984 The New Yorker
1985 The Washingtonian
1986 Science 85
1987 Money
1988 The Atlantic Monthly
1989 California
1990 Southern Exposure
1991 Family Circle
1992 Glamour
1993 The Family Therapy Network
1994 Philadelphia
1995 The New Republic
1996 Texas Monthly
1997 Fortune

Specialized Journalism

1970 Philadelphia
1971 Rolling Stone
1972 Architectural Record
1973 Psychology Today
1974 Texas Monthly
1975 Medical Economics
1976 United Mine Workers Journal
1977 Architectural Record
1978 Scientific American
1979 National Journal
1980 IEEE Spectrum

Design/Visual Excellence

1970 Look
1971 Vogue
1972 Esquire
1973 Horizon
1974 Newsweek
1975 Country Journal
National Lampoon
1976 Horticulture
1977 Rolling Stone
1978 Architectural Digest
1979 Audubon
1980 GEO
1981 Attenzione
1982 Nautical Quarterly
1983 New York
1984 House & Garden
1985 Forbes
1986 Time
1987 Elle
1988 Life
1989 Rolling Stone
1990 Esquire
1991 Condé Nast Traveler
1992 Vanity Fair
1993 Harper's Bazaar
1994 Allure
1995 Martha Stewart Living
1996 Wired
1997 I.D. Magazine

Reporting (Excellence)/News Reporting

1970 The New Yorker
1971 The Atlantic Monthly
1972 The Atlantic Monthly
1973 New York
1974 The New Yorker
1975 The New Yorker
1976 Audubon
1977 Audubon
1978 The New Yorker
1979 Texas Monthly
1980 Mother Jones
1981 National Journal
1982 The Washingtonian
1983 Institutional Investor
1984 Vanity Fair
1985 Texas Monthly
1986 Rolling Stone
1987 Life
1988 Baltimore Magazine
The Washingtonian
1989 The New Yorker
1990 The New Yorker
1991 The New Yorker
1992 The New Republic
1993 IEEE Spectrum
1994 The New Yorker
1995 The Atlantic Monthly
1996 The New Yorker
1997 Outside

General Excellence (Under 100,000 circulation)

1981 ARTnews
1982 Camera Arts
1983 Louisiana Life
1984 The American Lawyer
1985 Manhattan, inc.
1986 New England Monthly
1987 New England Monthly
1988 The Sciences
1989 The Sciences
1990 7 Days
1991 The New Republic
1992 The New Republic
1993 Lingua Franca
1994 Print
1995 I.D. Magazine
1996 The Sciences
1997 I.D. Magazine

General Excellence (100,000–400,000)

1981 Audubon
1982 Rocky Mountain Magazine
1983 Harper's Magazine
1984 Outside
1985 American Heritage
1986 3-2-1 Contact
1987 Common Cause
1988 Hippocrates
1989 American Heritage
1990 Texas Monthly
1991 Interview
1992 Texas Monthly
1993 American Photo
1994 Wired
1995 Men's Journal
1996 Civilization
1997 Wired

General Excellence (400,000–1,000,000)

1981 Business Week
1982 Science 81
1983 Science 82
1984 House & Garden
1985 American Health
1986 Discover
1987 Elle
1988 Fortune
1989 Vanity Fair

1990 Metropolitan Home
1991 Condé Nast Traveler
1992 Mirabella
1993 The Atlantic Monthly
1994 Health
1995 The New Yorker
1996 Outside
1997 Outside

General Excellence (over 1,000,000)

1981 Glamour
1982 Newsweek
1983 Life
1984 National Geographic
1985 Time
1986 Money
1987 People Weekly
1988 Parents
1989 Sports Illustrated
1990 Sports Illustrated
1991 Glamour
1992 National Geographic
1993 Newsweek
1994 Business Week
1995 Entertainment Weekly
1996 Business Week
1997 Vanity Fair

Essays and Criticism

1978 Esquire
1979 Life
1980 Natural History
1981 Time
1982 The Atlantic Monthly
1983 The American Lawyer
1984 The New Republic
1985 Boston
1986 The Sciences
1987 Outside
1988 Harper's Magazine
1989 Harper's Magazine
1990 Vanity Fair
1991 The Sciences
1992 The Nation
1993 The American Lawyer
1994 Harper's Magazine
1995 Harper's Magazine
1996 The New Yorker
1997 The New Yorker

Fiction

1978 The New Yorker
1979 The Atlantic Monthly
1980 Antaeus
1981 The North American Review
1982 The New Yorker
1983 The North American Review
1984 Seventeen
1985 Playboy
1986 The Georgia Review
1987 Esquire
1988 The Atlantic
1989 The New Yorker
1990 The New Yorker
1991 Esquire
1992 Story
1993 The New Yorker
1994 Harper's Magazine
1995 Story
1996 Harper's Magazine
1997 The New Yorker

Single Topic Issue

1979 Progressive Architecture
1980 Scientific American
1981 Business Week
1982 Newsweek
1983 IEEE Spectrum
1984 Esquire
1985 American Heritage
1986 IEEE Spectrum
1987 Bulletin of the Atomic Scientists
1988 Life
1989 Hippocrates
1990 National Geographic
1991 The American Lawyer
1992 Business Week
1993 Newsweek
1994 Health
1995 Discover
1996 Bon Appétit
1997 Scientific American

Personal Service/Service to the Individual

1974 Sports Illustrated
1975 Esquire
1976 Modern Medicine
1977 Harper's Magazine
1978 Newsweek
1979 The American Journal of Nursing
1980 Saturday Review
1982 Philadelphia
1983 Sunset
1984 New York
1985 The Washingtonian
1986 Farm Journal
1987 Consumer Reports
1988 Money
1989 Good Housekeeping
1990 Consumer Reports
1991 New York
1992 Creative Classroom
1993 Good Housekeeping
1994 Fortune
1995 SmartMoney
1996 SmartMoney
1997 Glamour

Special Interests

1986 Popular Mechanics
1987 Sports Afield
1988 Condé Nast Traveler
1989 Condé Nast Traveler
1990 Arts & Antiques
1991 New York
1992 Sports Afield
1993 Philadelphia
1994 Outside
1995 Gentlemen's Quarterly
1996 Saveur
1997 Smithsonian Magazine

Photography

1985 Life
1986 Vogue
1987 National Geographic
1988 Rolling Stone
1989 National Geographic
1990 Texas Monthly
1991 National Geographic
1992 National Geographic
1993 Harper's Bazaar
1994 Martha Stewart Living
1995 Rolling Stone
1996 Saveur
1997 National Geographic

Feature Writing

1988 The Atlantic Monthly
1989 Esquire
1990 The Washingtonian
1991 U.S. News & World Report
1992 Sports Illustrated
1993 The New Yorker
1994 Harper's Magazine
1995 Gentlemen's Quarterly
1996 Gentlemen's Quarterly
1997 Sports Illustrated

PULITZER PRIZE

Fiction

1918 Ernest Poole
His Family
1919 Booth Tarkington
The Magnificent Ambersons
1920 No award
1921 Edith Wharton
The Age of Innocence
1922 Booth Tarkington
Alice Adams
1923 Willa Cather
One of Ours
1924 Margaret Wilson
The Able McLaughlins
1925 Edna Ferber
So Big
1926 Sinclair Lewis (refused prize)
Arrowsmith
1927 Louis Bromfield
Early Autumn
1928 Thornton Wilder
Bridge of San Luis Rey

1929 Julia M. Peterkin
Scarlet Sister Mary
1930 Oliver LaFarge
Laughing Boy
1931 Margaret Ayer Barnes
Years of Grace
1932 Pearl S. Buck
The Good Earth
1933 T. S. Stribling
The Store
1934 Caroline Miller
Lamb in His Bosom
1935 Josephine W. Johnson
Now in November
1936 Harold L. Davis
Honey in the Horn
1937 Margaret Mitchell
Gone with the Wind
1938 John P. Marquand
The Late George Apley
1939 Marjorie Kinnan Rawlings
The Yearling
1940 John Steinbeck
The Grapes of Wrath
1941 No award
1942 Ellen Glasgow
In This Our Life
1943 Upton Sinclair
Dragon's Teeth
1944 Martin Flavin
Journey in the Dark
1945 John Hersey
A Bell for Adano
1946 No Award
1947 Robert Penn Warren
All thc King's Men
1948 James A. Michener
Tales of the South Pacific
1949 James Gould Cozzens
Guard of Honor
1950 A. B. Guthrie, Jr.
The Way West
1951 Conrad Richter
The Town
1952 Herman Wouk
The Caine Mutiny
1953 Ernest Hemingway
The Old Man and the Sea
1954 No award
1955 William Faulkner
A Fable
1956 MacKinlay Kantor
Andersonville
1957 No award
1958 James Agee
A Death in the Family
1959 Robert Lewis Taylor
The Travels of Jaimie McPheeters
1960 Allen Drury
Advise and Consent
1961 Harper Lee
To Kill a Mockingbird
1962 Edwin O'Connor
The Edge of Sadness
1963 William Faulkner
The Reivers
1964 No award
1965 Shirley Ann Grau
The Keepers of the House
1966 Katherine Anne Porter
Collected Stories of
1967 Bernard Malamud
The Fixer
1968 William Styron
The Confessions of Nat Turner
1969 N. Scott Momaday
House Made of Dawn
1970 Jean Stafford
Collected Stories
1971 No award
1972 Wallace Stegner
Angle of Repose
1973 Eudora Welty
The Optimist's Daughter
1974 No award
1975 Michael Shaara
The Killer Angels
1976 Saul Bellow
Humboldt's Gift
1977 No award
1978 James Alan McPherson
Elbow Room
1979 John Cheever
The Stories of John Cheever
1980 Norman Mailer
The Executioner's Song
1981 John Kennedy Toole
A Confederacy of Dunces
1982 John Updike
Rabbit Is Rich
1983 Alice Walker
The Color Purple
1984 William Kennedy
Ironweed
1985 Alison Lurie
Foreign Affairs
1986 Larry McMurtry
Lonesome Dove
1987 Peter Taylor
A Summons to Memphis
1988 Toni Morrison
Beloved
1989 Anne Tyler
Breathing Lessons
1990 Oscar Hijuelos
The Mambo Kings Play Songs of Love
1991 John Updike
Rabbit at Rest
1992 Jane Smiley
A Thousand Acres
1993 Robert Olen Butler
A Good Scent from a Strange Mountain
1994 E. Annie Proulx
The Shipping News
1995 Carol Shields
The Stone Diaries
1996 Richard Ford
Independence Day
1997 Steven Millhauser
Martin Dressler: The Tale of an American Dreamer

Nonfiction

1962 Theodore H. White
The Making of the President 1960
1963 Barbara W. Tuchman
The Guns of August
1964 Richard Hofstadter
Anti-Intellectualism in American Life
1965 Howard Mumford Jones
O Strange New World
1966 Edwin Way Teale
Wandering Through Winter
1967 David Brion Davis
The Problem of Slavery in Western Culture
1968 Will Durant and Ariel Durant
Rousseau and Revolution: The tenth and concluding volume of The Story of Civilization
1969 Norman Mailer
The Armies of the Night
Rene Jules Dubos
So Human an Animal
1970 Erik H. Erikson
Gandhi's Truth
1971 John Toland
The Rising Sun

1972 Barbara W. Tuchman
Stilwell and the American Experience in China 1911–1945
1973 Robert Coles
Children of Crisis, Vols. II and III
Francis FitzGerald
Fire in the Lake: The Vietnamese and the Americans in Vietnam
1974 Ernest Becker
The Denial of Death
1975 Annie Dillard
Pilgram at Tinker Creek
1976 Robert N. Butler
Why Survive? Being Old in America
1977 William W. Warner
Beautiful Swimmers
1978 Carl Sagan
The Dragons of Eden
1979 Edward O. Wilson
On Human Nature
1980 Douglas R. Hofstadter
Gödel, Escher, Bach: An Eternal Golden Braid
1981 Carl E. Schorske
Fin-de-Siecle Vienna: Politics and Culture
1982 Tracy Kidder
The Soul of a New Machine
1983 Susan Sheehan
Is There No Place on Earth for Me ?
1984 Paul Starr
The Social Transformation of American Medicine
1985 Studs Terkel
The Good War: An Oral History of World War Two
1986 J. Anthony Lukas
Common Ground: A Turbulent Decade in the Lives of Three American Families
Joseph Lelyveld
Move Your Shadow
1987 David K. Shipler
Arab and Jew: Wounded Spirits in a Promised Land
1988 Richard Rhodes
The Making of the Atomic Bomb
1989 Neil Sheehan
A Bright Shining Lie: John Paul Vann and America in Vietnam
1990 Dale Maharidge and Michael Williamson
And Their Children After Them
1991 Bert Holdobler and Edward O. Wilson
The Ants
1992 Daniel Yergin
The Prize: The Epic Quest for Oil, Money, and Power
1993 Garry Wills
Lincoln at Gettysburg
1994 David Remnick
Lenin's Tomb
1995 Jonathan Weiner
The Beak of the Finch: A Story of Evolution in Our Time
1996 Tina Rosenberg
The Haunted Land: Facing Europe's Ghosts After Communism
1997 Richard Kluger
Ashes to Ashes: America's Hundred-Year Cigarette War, the Public Health, and the Unabashed Triumph of Philip Morris

Poetry

1918 Sara Teasdale
Love Songs
1919 Carl Sandburg
Corn Huskers
Margaret Widemer
Old Road to Paradise
1920 No award
1921 No award
1922 Edwin Arlington Robinson
Collected Poems
1923 Edna St. Vincent Millay
The Ballad of the Harp-Weaver; A Few Figs from Thistles; Eight Sonnets in American Poetry, 1922; A Miscellany
1924 Robert Frost
New Hampshire: A Poem with Notes and Grace Notes
1925 Edwin Arlington Robinson
The Man Who Died Twice
1926 Amy Lowell
What's O'Clock
1927 Leonora Speyer
Fiddler's Farewell
1928 Edwin Arlington Robinson
Tristram
1929 Stephen Vincent Benet
John Brown's Body
1930 Conrad Aiken
Selected Poems
1931 Robert Frost
Collected Poems
1932 George Dillon
The Flowering Stone
1933 Archibald MacLeish
Conquistador
1934 Robert Hillyer
Collected Verse
1935 Audrey Wurdemann
Bright Ambush
1936 Robert P. Tristram Coffin
Strange Holiness
1937 Robert Frost
A Further Range
1938 Marya Zaturenska
Cold Morning Sky
1939 John Gould Fletcher
Selected Poems
1940 Mark Van Doren
Collected Poems
1941 Leonrard Bacon
Sunderland Capture
1942 William Rose Benet
The Dust Which Is God
1943 Robert Frost
A Witness Tree
1944 Stephen Vincent Benet
Western Star
1945 Karl Shapiro
V-Letter and Other Poems
1946 No award
1947 Robert Lowell
Lord Weary's Castle
1948 W. H. Auden
The Age of Anxiety
1949 Peter Viereck
Terror and Decorum
1950 Gwendolyn Brooks
Annie Allen
1951 Carl Sandburg
Complete Poems
1952 Marianne Moore
Collected Poems
1953 Archibald MacLeish
Collected Poems 1917–1952
1954 Theodore Roethke
The Waking
1955 Wallace Stevens
Collected Poems
1956 Elizabeth Bishop
Poems, North and South
1957 Richard Wilbur
Things of This World
1958 Robert Penn Warren
Promises: Poems 1954–1956
1959 Stanley Kunitz
Selected Poems 1928–1958

1960 W. D. Snodgrass
Heart's Needle
1961 Phyllis McGinley
Times Three: Selected Verse from Three Decades
1962 Alan Dugan
Poems
1963 William Carlos Williams
Pictures from Breughel
1964 Louis Simpson
At the End of the Open Road
1965 John Berryman
77 Dream Songs
1966 Richard Eberhart
Selected Poems
1967 Anne Sexton
Live or Die
1968 Anthony Hecht
The Hard Hours
1969 George Oppen
Of Being Numerous
1970 Richard Howard
Untitled Subjects
1971 W. S. Merwin
The Carrier of Ladders
1972 James Wright
Collected Poems
1973 Maxine Kumin
Up Country
1974 Robert Lowell
The Dolphin
1975 Gary Snyder
Turtle Island
1976 John Ashbery
Self-Portrait in a Convex Mirror
1977 James Merrill
Divine Comedies
1978 Howard Nemerov
Collected Poems
1979 Robert Penn Warren
Now and Then
1980 Donald Justice
Selected Poems
1981 James Schuyler
The Morning of the Poem
1982 Sylvia Plath
The Collected Poems
1983 Galway Kinnell
Selected Poems
1984 Mary Oliver
American Primitive
1985 Carolyn Kizer
Yin
1986 Henry Taylor
The Flying Change
1987 Rita Dove
Thomas and Beulah
1988 William Meredith
Partial Accounts: New and Selected Poems
1989 Richard Wilbur
New and Collected Poems
1990 Charles Simic
The World Doesn't End
1991 Mona Van Duyn
Near Changes
1992 James Tate
Selected Poems
1993 Louise Gluck
The Wild Iris
1994 Yusef Komunyakaa
Neon Vernacular
1995 Philip Levine
The Simple Truth
1996 Jorie Graham
The Dream of the Unified Field
1997 Lisel Mueller
Alive Together

STAGE

BROADWAY SHOWS OF THE 1996–97 SEASON

Audiences flocked to the Great White Way this year: The total 10,318,217 tickets sold helped *Cats* creep past *A Chorus Line* as Broadway's longest-running show, and kept lavish productions like *Titanic* afloat. (Source: *Variety*)

NEW PRODUCTIONS

A Doll's House (R)
A Thousand Clowns (R)
An American Daughter
Annie (M-R)
Barrymore
Candide (M-R)
Chicago (M-R)
Dream: A Johnny Mercer Musical (M)
Hugie (R)
Into the Whirlwind
It's a Slippery Slope (So)
Jekyll & Hyde (M)
John Gray: Men Are from Mars, Women Are from Venus (Sp)
Juan Darien: A Carnival Mass (M)
Julia Sweeney's God Said "Ha!" (So)
King David (Sp)
London Assurance (R)
Once upon a Mattress (M-R)
Play On! (M)
Present Laughter (R)
Sex and Longing
Skylight (P)
Stanley
Steel Pier (M)
Summer and Smoke (R)
Taking Sides
Tartuffe, Born Again (R)
The Gin Game (R)
The Last Night of Ballyhoo
The Life (M)
The Little Foxes (R)
The Rehearsal (R)
The Young Man from Atlanta
Three Sisters (R)
Titanic (M)

HOLDOVERS

A Delicate Balance (R)
A Funny Thing Happened on the Way to the Forum (M-R)
An Ideal Husband (R)
Beauty and the Beast (M)
Big (M)
Bring in 'Da Noise, Bring in 'Da Funk (M)
Buried Child
Cats (M)
Grease (M-R)
How To Succeed in Business Without Really Trying (M-R)
Les Miserables (M)
Love Thy Neighbor (Sp-So)
Master Class
Miss Saigon (M)
Rent (M)
Rob Becker's Defending the Caveman (Sp-So)
Seven Guitars
Show Boat (M-R)
Smokey Joe's Cafe (M-Rev)
State Fair (M-R)
Sunset Boulevard (M)
The King and I (M-R)
The Phantom of the Opera (M)
Victor/Victoria (M)

(M) denotes musical.
(R) denotes revival.
(So) denotes solo performance.
(Rev) denotes revue.
(Sp) denotes special attraction.

ON THE ROAD

Road shows may not boast the most lavish stagings, but these productions can meet a wider audience and consistently give Broadway a run for its money. (Source: *Variety*)

Season	Broadway box office/ total shows during most profitable week	Road box office/ total shows during most profitable week
1981–82	$221.2 million/31 shows	$249.5 million/30 shows
1986–87	$207.2 million/28 shows	$224.3 million/21 shows
1991–92	$292.4 million/28 shows	$502.7 million/25 shows
1992–93	$327.7 million/21 shows	$620.6 million/34 shows
1993–94	$356.0 million/21 shows	$687.7 million/30 shows
1994–95	$406.3 million/23 shows	$694.6 million/33 shows
1995–96	$436.1 million/28 shows	$762.3 million/27 shows
1996–97	$499.4 million/27 shows	$752.9 million/27 shows

LONGEST-RUNNING SHOWS ON BROADWAY

The following is a list of the longest-running shows on Broadway (as of September 7, 1997) based on the number of performances.

(M) stands for musical and (R) for revival. (Source: *Variety*)

Show	Performances
Cats (M) (1982–)	6,229
A Chorus Line (M) (1975–90)	6,137
Oh! Calcutta! (M-R) (1976–89)	5,852
Les Misérables (M) (1987–)	4,337
The Phantom of the Opera (M) (1988–)	4,037
42nd Street (M) (1980–89)	3,486
Grease (M) (1972–80)	3,388
Fiddler on the Roof (M) (1964–72)	3,242
Life with Father (1939–47)	3,224
Tobacco Road (1933–41)	3,182
Hello, Dolly! (M) (1964–70)	2,844
My Fair Lady (M) (1956–62)	2,717
Miss Saigon (M) (1991–)	2,670
Annie (M) (1977–83)	2,377
Man of La Mancha (M) (1965–71)	2,328
Abie's Irish Rose (1922–27)	2,327
Oklahoma! (M) (1943–48)	2,212
Pippin (M) (1972–77)	1,944
South Pacific (M) (1949–54)	1,925
The Magic Show (M) (1974–78)	1,920
Deathtrap (1978–82)	1,792
Gemini (1977–81)	1,788
Harvey (1944–49)	1,775
Dancin' (M) (1978–82)	1,774
La Cage aux folles (M) (1983–87)	1,761
Hair (M) (1968–72)	1,750
The Wiz (M) (1975–79)	1,672
Born Yesterday (1946–49)	1,642
Crazy for You (1992-96)	1,622
Ain't Misbehavin' (M) (1978–82)	1,604
Best Little Whorehouse in Texas (M) (1978–82)	1,584
Mary, Mary (1961–64)	1,572
Evita (M) (1979–83)	1,567
Voice of the Turtle (1943–48)	1,557
Barefoot in the Park (1963–64)	1,530
Brighton Beach Memoirs (1983–86)	1,530
Dreamgirls (M) (1981–85)	1,521
Mame (M) (1966–70)	1,508
Same Time, Next Year (1976–78)	1,453
Arsenic and Old Lace (1941–44)	1,444
The Sound of Music (M) (1959–63)	1,443
Beauty and the Beast (1994–)	1,418
How To Succeed in Business Without Really Trying (M) (1961–65)	1,417
Hellzapoppin (M) (1938–41)	1,404
The Music Man (M) (1957–61)	1,375
Funny Girl (M) (1964–67)	1,348
Grease (M-R) (1993–)	1,343
Mummenschanz (M) (1977–80)	1,326
Oh! Calcutta! (M) (1969–72)	1,314
Angel Street (1941–44)	1,295
Lightnin' (1918–21)	1,291
Promises, Promises (M) (1968–72)	1,281
The King and I (M) (1951–54)	1,246
Cactus Flower (1965–68)	1,234
Torch Song Trilogy (1982–85)	1,222
Sleuth (1970–73)	1,222
1776 (M) (1969–72)	1,217
Equus (1974–77)	1,209
Sugar Babies (M) (1979–82)	1,208
Guys and Dolls (M) (1950–53)	1,200
Amadeus (1980–83)	1,181
Cabaret (M) (1966–69)	1,165
Mister Roberts (1948–51)	1,157
Annie Get Your Gun (M) (1946–49)	1,147
Guys and Dolls (M-R) (1992–95)	1,143
The Seven Year Itch (1952–55)	1,141
Butterflies Are Free (1969–72)	1,128
Pins and Needles (M) (1937–40)	1,108
Plaza Suite (1968–70)	1,097
They're Playing Our Song (M) (1979–81)	1,082
Kiss Me, Kate (M) (1948–51)	1,070
Don't Bother Me, I Can't Cope (M) (1972–74)	1,065
The Pajama Game (M) (1954–56)	1,063
Shenandoah (M) (1975–77)	1,050
Smokey Joe's Cafe (1995–)	1,045
Teahouse of the August Moon (1953–56)	1,027

BROADWAY'S FAVORITES: PLACE THAT TUNE

Know the song but can't place the musical in which it originally appeared? Here is a checklist of some Great White Way melodies that linger on.

SONG	SHOW
"Almost Like Being in Love"	Brigadoon
"And I Am Telling You I'm Not Going"	Dreamgirls
"Anything You Can Do"	Annie Get Your Gun
"Bali Ha'i"	South Pacific
"The Ballad of Mack the Knife"	The Threepenny Opera
"Bewitched, Bothered, and Bewildered"	Pal Joey
"A Bushel and a Peck"	Guys and Dolls
"Climb Ev'ry Mountain"	The Sound of Music
"Everything's Coming Up Roses"	Gypsy
"Getting To Know You"	The King and I
"I Am What I Am"	La Cage aux folles
"I Cain't Say No"	Oklahoma!
"I Could Have Danced All Night"	My Fair Lady
"I Don't Know How To Love Him"	Jesus Christ Superstar
"I Feel Pretty"	West Side Story
"I Get a Kick out of You"	Anything Goes
"I Got Plenty o' Nothin' "	Porgy and Bess
"I Got Rhythm"	Girl Crazy
"I Got the Sun in the Morning"	Annie Get Your Gun
"I Whistle a Happy Tune"	The King and I
"If Ever I Would Leave You"	Camelot
"It Ain't Necessarily So"	Porgy and Bess
"I've Grown Accustomed to Her Face"	My Fair Lady
"Let the Sunshine In"	Hair
"Lover, Come Back to Me"	The New Moon
"Luck Be a Lady"	Guys and Dolls
"Maria"	West Side Story
"Memory"	Cats
"The Music of the Night"	The Phantom of the Opera
"My Favorite Things"	The Sound of Music
"Oh, What a Beautiful Mornin' "	Oklahoma!
"Ol' Man River"	Show Boat
"One Night in Bangkok"	Chess
"On the Street Where You Live"	My Fair Lady
"The Quest (The Impossible Dream)"	Man of La Mancha
"Seventy-Six Trombones"	The Music Man
"Shall We Dance?"	The King and I
"Smoke Gets in Your Eyes"	Roberta
"Some Enchanted Evening"	South Pacific
"The Sound of Music"	The Sound of Music
"Summertime"	Porgy and Bess
"Sunrise, Sunset"	Fiddler on the Roof
"Tea for Two"	No, No, Nanette
"Thank Heaven for Little Girls"	Gigi
"There Is Nothin' Like a Dame"	South Pacific
"There's No Business Like Show Business"	Annie Get Your Gun
"This Is the Army, Mr. Jones"	This Is the Army
"Till There Was You"	The Music Man
"Tonight"	West Side Story
"You'll Never Walk Alone"	Carousel
"You're the Top"	Anything Goes
"We Need a Little Christmas"	Mame
"What I Did for Love"	A Chorus Line

SCHOOLS FOR STARS

Even some of the most talented thespians have honed their skills in the classroom, as indicated by the alumni rolls of these five career nurturing institutions.

CARNEGIE MELLON SCHOOL OF DRAMA

Shari Belafonte, actor
Steven Bochco, producer
Albert Brooks, actor/director
Ted Danson, actor
Iris Rainier Dart, novelist
Barbara Feldon, actor
Mark Frost, producer
Mariette Hartley, actor
Holly Hunter, actor
Jack Klugman, actor
Judith Light, actor
Burke Moses, actor
John Pasquin, director
George Peppard, actor
George Romero, director
Laura San Giacomo, actor
Ellen Travolta, actress
Michael Tucker, actor
Blair Underwood, actor
John Wells, producer

JUILLIARD SCHOOL DRAMA DIVISION

Christine Baranski, actor
Andre Braugher, actor
Kelsey Grammer, actor
William Hurt, actor
Laura Linney, actor
Patti LuPone, actor/singer
Val Kilmer, actor
Kevin Kline, actor/director
Linda Kozlowski, actor
Kelly McGillis, actor
Elizabeth McGovern, actor
Mandy Patinkin, actor/singer
Christopher Reeve, actor
Ving Rhames, actor
Kevin Spacey, actor
Jeanne Tripplehorn, actor
Robin Williams, actor

NEW YORK UNIVERSITY, TISCH SCHOOL OF THE ARTS

Alec Baldwin, actor
Barry Bostwick, actor
Billy Crudup, actor
Kathryn Erbe, actor
Bridget Fonda, actor
Marcia Gay Harden, actor
Kristen Johnson, actor
Tony Kushner, playwright
Eriq LaSalle, actor
Andrew McCarthy, actor
Jerry O'Connell, actor
Adam Sandler, actor
Kevin Spacey, actor
Stephen Spinella, actor
D. B. Sweeney, actor
Skeet Ulrich, actor
George C. Wolfe, director

NORTHWESTERN UNIVERSITY SCHOOL OF SPEECH

Ann-Margret, actor/dancer
Warren Beatty, actor
Richard Benjamin, actor
Karen Black, actor
Brad Hall, actor
Charlton Heston, actor
Sherry Lansing, producer
Shelly Long, actor
Julia Louis-Dreyfus, actor
Dermot Mulroney, actor
Patricia Neal, actor
Jerry Orbach, actor
Paula Prentiss, actor
Tony Randall, actor
Tony Roberts, actor
David Schwimmer, actor
Peter Strauss, actor
Kimberly Williams, actor

YALE SCHOOL OF DRAMA

Angela Bassett, actor
Robert Brustein, director/writer
Christopher Durang, playwright
Charles S. Dutton, actor
Jill Eikenberry, actor
David Alan Grier, actor
John Guare, playwright
A. R. Gurney, playwright
Julie Harris, actor
Tama Janowitz, writer
Elia Kazan, director
Stacy Keach, actor
Mark Linn-Baker, actor
Santo Loquasto, set designer
Frances McDormand, actor
Paul Newman, actor
Carrie Nye, actor
Tony Shaloub, actor
Talia Shire, actor
Meryl Streep, actor
Ted Tally, playwright/screenwriter
John Turturro, actor/director
Joan Van Ark, actor
Wendy Wasserstein, playwright
Sigourney Weaver, actor
Edmund Wilson, writer
Henry Winkler, actor/director

THEATER'S LEADING LIGHTS

Selected for their contributions to today's theater, the following artists are responsible for many of the most important and popular plays currently being produced in the English language. Each list of works notes every play, screenplay, or teleplay created by the artist (aside from one-acts), as well as major awards won by the work and the year of its first production.

BETH HENLEY
playwright/screenwriter

Parade (1975)
Crimes of the Heart (1979; Pulitzer Prize; screenplay, 1987)
The Moon Watch (screenplay, 1983)
The Miss Firecracker Contest (1984; screenplay 1986)
The Wake of Jamey Foster (1984)
The Debutante Ball (1985)
The Lucky Spot (1986)
True Stories (coauthor, screenplay, 1986)
Nobody's Fool (screenplay, 1987)
Abundance (1989)
Signature (1990)
Control Freaks (1992)
Revelers (1994)
L-Play (1995)

TONY KUSHNER
playwright

A Bright Room Called Day (1986)
The Illusion (adaptor, 1987)
Angels in America Part I: Millennium Approaches (1990; Tony Award; Pulitzer Prize)
Angels in America Part II: Perestroika (1993, Tony Award)
Slavs! (1994)
Dybbuk (adaptor, 1995)
Hydriotaphia (1997)

ANDREW LLOYD WEBBER
composer

Joseph and the Amazing Technicolor Dreamcoat (1968)
Jesus Christ Superstar (1971)
Jeeves (1974; revision *By Jeeves*, 1996)
Evita (1976; Tony Award)
Cats (1982; Tony Award; Grammy Award)
Song and Dance (1982)
Starlight Express (1984)
The Phantom of the Opera (1986)
Aspects of Love (1989)
Sunset Boulevard (1993; Tony Award)
Whistle Down The Wind (1996)

DAVID MAMET
playwright/screenwriter

The Duck Variations (1972)
Mackinac (1974)
Squirrels (1974)
Sexual Perversity in Chicago (1974)
American Buffalo (1975)
The Poet and the Rent (1975)
Marranos (1975)
Reunion (1976)
The Woods (1977)
The Revenge of the Space Pandas, or Binky Rudich and the Two-Speed Clock (1977)
The Water Engine: An American Fable (1977)
A Life in the Theatre (1977)
Lone Canoe, or, The Explorer (1979)
Lakeboat (1980)
The Postman Always Rings Twice (screenplay, 1981)
The Verdict (screenplay, 1982)
Edmond (1982)
Glengarry Glen Ross (1983; Pulitzer Prize; screenplay, 1992)
Red River (adaptor, 1983)
The Cherry Orchard (adaptor, 1985)
The Shawl (1985)
Three Sisters (adaptor, 1985)
The Untouchables (screenplay, 1987)
House of Games (screenplay, 1987)
Things Change (coauthor screenplay, 1987)
Speed-the-Plow (1988)
We're No Angels (screenplay, 1989)
Homicide (screenplay, 1991)
Oleanna (1992; screenplay, 1994)
Hoffa (screenplay, 1992)
The Village (novel, 1994)
The Cryptogram (1994)

TERRENCE MCNALLY
playwright

And Things That Go Bump in the Night (1964)
Next (1967)
Where Has Tommy Flowers Gone (1971)
Whiskey (1973)
Bad Habits (1974)
The Ritz (1974)
It's Only a Play (1985)
The Rink (1985)
Frankie and Johnny in the Claire de Lune (1987; screenplay, *Frankie and Johnny*, 1991)
The Lisbon Traviata (1989)
Andre's Mother (teleplay, 1990; Emmy Award)
Lips Together, Teeth Apart (1991)
Prelude and Liebestod (1991)
A Perfect Ganesh (1993)
Kiss of the Spider Woman (book, 1993; Tony Award)
Love! Valour! Compassion! (1994; Tony Award; screenplay, 1997)
Master Class (1995; Tony Award)
Ragtime (book, 1996)

ARTHUR MILLER
playwright/screenwriter

Honors at Dawn (1936)
No Villain (1936)
The Half-Bridge (written 1943, never produced)
The Pussycat and the Expert Plumber Who Was a Man (radio play, 1943)
William Ireland's Confession (radio play, 1942)
The Man Who Had All the Luck (1944)
That They May Win (1944)
The Story of G.I. Joe (screenplay, 1945)
Grandpa and the Statue (radio play, 1942)
The Story of Gus (radio play, 1942)
All My Sons (1947)
Death of a Salesman (1948; Pulitzer Prize)
An Enemy of the People (adaptor, 1950)
The Crucible (1953; Tony Award; screenplay, 1996)
A View from the Bridge (1955)
A Memory of Two Mondays (1955)
The Witches of Salem (screenplay, 1958)
The Misfits (screenplay, 1961)
After the Fall (1964)
Incident at Vichy (1964)
The Price (1968)
Fame (1971)
The Creation of the World and Other Business (1972; musical version, *Up from Paradise*, 1982)
The Archbishop's Ceiling (1977)
The American Clock (adaptor, 1979)
Playing for Time (adaptor, teleplay, 1981)
Two-Way Mirror (1982)
Danger: Memory (1987)
The Golden Years (radio play, 1987)
Everybody Wins (screenplay, 1990)
The Ride Down Mt. Morgan (1991)
The Last Yankee (1993)
Broken Glass (1994)

MARSHA NORMAN
playwright/screenwriter

Getting Out (1977)
The Pool Hall (1978)
It's the Willingness (teleplay, 1978)
Third and Oak: The Laundromat (1978)
Circus Valentine (1979)
In Trouble at Fifteen (teleplay, 1980)
The Holdup (1980)
'Night, Mother (1983; Pulitzer Prize; screenplay, 1984)
Traveler in the Dark (1984)
The Fortune Teller (novel, 1988)
Sarah and Abraham (1988)
The Secret Garden (book and lyrics, 1991; Tony Award)
Face of a Stranger (teleplay, 1992)
Loving Daniel Boone (1992)
The Red Shoes (book and lyrics, 1993)
Trudy Blue (1995)

HAROLD PINTER
playwright/screenwriter

The Room (1957)
The Birthday Party (1958; screenplay, 1968; teleplay, 1987)
The Dumb Waiter (1960)
The Caretaker (1960)
A Night Out (radio play, 1960)
The Collection (teleplay, 1961)
The Servant (screenplay, 1963)
The Lover (1963)
The Pumpkin Eater (screenplay, 1964)
The Tea Party (1965)
The Quiller Memorandum (screenplay, 1966)
Accident (screenplay, 1967)
The Basement (radio 1967; stage 1969)
Landscape (1968)
The Homecoming (screenplay, 1973)
Silence (1969)
The Go-Between (screenplay, 1970)
The Last Tycoon (screenplay, 1971)
Old Times (1971)
The Proust Screenplay: A la Recherche du temps perdu (screenplay, 1973)
No Man's Land (1975)
Players (radio play, 1975)
Betrayal (1978; screenplay, 1982)
Langrishe, Go Down (adaptor, screenplay, 1978)
The Hothouse (1980)
The French Lieutenant's Woman (screenplay, 1981)
Other Places (1982)
Turtle Diary (screenplay, 1985)
Reunion (screenplay, 1989)
The Comfort of Strangers (screenplay, 1990)
The Handmaid's Tale (adaptor, screenplay, 1990)
Moonlight (1993)
The Trial (screenplay, 1993)
Ashes to Ashes (1996)

SAM SHEPARD
playwright/screenwriter

Up to Thursday (1965)
Dog (1965)
Rocking Chair (1965)
4-H Club (1965)
La Turista (1967)
Forensic and the Navigators (1967)
Me and My Brother (coauthor, screenplay, 1967)
Operation Sidewinder (1969)
The Unseen Hand (1969)
Zabriskie Point (coauthor, screenplay, 1970)
Cowboy Mouth (coauthor, 1971)
Ringaleenio (screenplay, 1971)
The Tooth of Crime (1972)
Blue Bitch (1973)
Nightwalk (coauthor, 1973)
Little Ocean (1974)
Geography of a Horse Dreamer (1974)
The Sad Lament of Pecos Bill on the Eve of Killing His Wife (1976)
Suicide in B Flat (1976)
Angel City (1977)
Curse of the Starving Class (1977)
Inacoma (1977)
Buried Child (1978; Pulitzer Prize)
Seduced (1978)
Tongues (coauthor, 1979)
Savage/Love (coauthor, 1979)
Jackson's Dance (coauthor, 1980)
True West (1980)
Black Bart and the Sacred Hills (1981)
Fool for Love (1983; screenplay, 1985)
Superstitions (1983)
Paris, Texas (coauthor, screenplay, 1984)
A Lie of the Mind (1985)
The War in Heaven: Angel's Monologue (coauthor, teleplay, 1985)
States of Shock (1989)
Far North (screenplay, 1992)
Silent Tongue (screenplay, 1993)
Simpatico (1994)
When the World Was Green (A Chef's Fable) (co-author,1996)

NEIL SIMON
playwright/screenwriter

Adventures of Marco Polo: A Musical Fantasy (book, 1959)
Heidi (book, 1959)
Come Blow Your Horn (1961)
Little Me (book, 1962; revised version, 1982)
Barefoot in the Park (originally *Nobody Loves Me*, 1963; screenplay, 1967)
The Odd Couple (1965; Tony Award; screenplay, 1968; female version, 1985)
Sweet Charity (book, 1966)
The Star-Spangled Girl (1966)
After the Fox (screenplay, 1966)
Promises, Promises (book, 1968)
Plaza Suite (1968; screenplay, 1971)
The Last of the Red-Hot Lovers (1969; screenplay, 1972)
The Gingerbread Lady (1970; revised as *Only When I Laugh*, screenplay, 1982)
The Out-of-Towners (screenplay, 1970)
The Prisoner of Second Avenue (1971; screenplay, 1975)
The Heartbreak Kid (screenplay, 1973)
The Sunshine Boys (1972; screenplay, 1975)
The Good Doctor (1973)
God's Favorite (1974)
California Suite (1976; screenplay, 1978)
Murder by Death (screenplay, 1976)
The Goodbye Girl (screenplay, 1977; book, 1993)
Chapter Two (1977; screenplay, 1979)
The Cheap Detective (screenplay, 1978)
They're Playing Our Song (book, 1979)
I Ought To Be in Pictures (1980; screenplay, 1982)
Seems Like Old Times (screenplay, 1980)
Fools (1981)
Max Dugan Returns (screenplay, 1983)
Brighton Beach Memoirs (1983; Pulitzer Prize; screenplay, 1986)
The Slugger's Wife (screenplay, 1984)
Biloxi Blues (1985; Tony Award; screenplay, 1988)
Broadway Bound (1986)
Rumors (1988)
Lost in Yonkers (1991; Tony Award; Pulitzer Prize; screenplay, 1993)
The Marrying Man (screenplay, 1991)
Broadway Bound (screenplay, teleplay, 1992)
Jake's Women (1992; teleplay, 1996)
Laughter on the 23rd Floor (1993)
London Suite (1995)
Proposals (1997)

A special Tony was awarded to Mr. Simon in 1975 for overall contribution to the theater.

STEPHEN SONDHEIM
composer/lyricist

West Side Story (lyrics, 1957)
Gypsy (lyrics, 1959)
A Funny Thing Happened on the Way to the Forum (music and lyrics, 1962)
Anyone Can Whistle (music and lyrics, 1964)
Do I Hear a Waltz? (lyrics, 1965)
The Mad Show (co-lyricist, 1966)
Company (music and lyrics, 1970; Tony Award)
Follies (music and lyrics, 1971; Tony Award)

MUSICAL THEATER HALL OF FAME

The Musical Theater Hall of Fame, organized by a committee from New York University, announced its first set of inductees (greats from the past) and honorees (still-active legends) in 1993.

INDUCTEES:

Jerome Kern
George and Ira Gershwin
Richard Rodgers
Oscar Hammerstein II
Alan Jay Lerner
Frederick Loewe
Ethel Merman
Irving Berlin
Cole Porter
E. Y. "Yip" Harburg
Mary Martin
Frank Loesser
Dorothy Fields
Abe Burrows
Harold Rome
George M Cohan
Ella Fitzgerald
Harold Arlen
Leonard Bernstein
Eubie Blake
Lorenz Hart

HONOREES:

Carol Channing
Jule Styne
George Abbott
Gwen Verdon
Betty Comden
Adolph Green
Jerry Herman
Burton Lane
Jerome Robbins
John Kander
Fred Ebb

A Little Night Music (music and lyrics, 1973; Tony Award)

Candide (revival, co-lyricist, 1973)

The Frogs (music and lyrics, 1974)

Pacific Overtures (music and lyrics, 1976)

Sweeney Todd (music and lyrics, 1979; Tony Award)

Merrily We Roll Along (music and lyrics, 1981)

Sunday in the Park with George (music and lyrics, 1984; Pulitzer Prize)

Into the Woods (music and lyrics, 1987; Tony Award)

Assassins (music and lyrics, 1991)

Passion (music and lyrics, 1994; Tony Award)

Getting Away with Murder (co-author, 1996)

TOM STOPPARD
playwright

A Walk on the Water (1960)

The Dissolution of Dominic Boot (radio play, 1964)

"M" is for Moon Among Other Things (radio play, 1964)

The Gamblers (1965)

If You're Glad I'll Be Frank (radio play, 1966)

Rosencrantz and Guildenstern Are Dead (1966; Tony Award; screenplay, 1990)

Tango (adaptor, 1966)

A Separate Peace (teleplay, 1966)

Lord Malquist and Mr. Moon (novel, 1966)

Albert's Bridge (radio play, 1967)

Teeth (teleplay, 1967)

Another Moon Called Earth (teleplay, 1967)

Neutral Ground (teleplay, 1968)

The Real Inspector Hound (1968)

After Magritte (1970)

Where Are They Now? (radio play, 1970)

Dogg's Our Pet (1971)

Jumpers (1972)

Artist Descending a Staircase (radio play, 1972; stage, 1988)

The House of Bernarda Alba (adaptor, 1973)

Travesties (1974; Tony Award)

Dirty Linen, and New-found-land (1976)

The Fifteen Minute Hamlet (1976)

Professional Foul (teleplay, 1977)

Every Good Boy Deserves Favour: A Play for Actors and Orchestra (1977)

Night and Day (1978)

Undiscovered Country (1979)

Dogg's Hamlet, Cahoot's MacBeth (1979)

On the Razzle (adaptor, 1981)

The Real Thing (1982; Tony Award)

The Dog It Was That Died (radio play, 1982)

The Love for Three Oranges (adaptor, 1983)

Rough Crossing (adaptor, 1984)

Squaring the Circle: Poland 1980–81 (TV docudrama, 1984)

Dalliance (adaptor, 1986)

Largo Desolato (adaptor, 1986)

Brazil (screenplay, 1987)

Empire Of The Sun (1987)

Hapgood (1988)

The Dog It Was That Died (adaptor,1989)

The Russia House (1989)

Billy Bathgate (film, 1990)

In the Native State (radio play, 1991)

Arcadia (1993)

Indian Ink (1995)

The Invention Of Love (1997)

TOMMY TUNE
director/choreographer/performer

Baker Street (actor, 1965)

A Joyful Noise (actor, 1967)

How Now Dow Jones (actor, 1968)

Seesaw (actor, 1973; Tony)

The Club (director, 1976)

Sunset (director, 1977)

The Best Little Whorehouse in Texas (co-director and choreographer, 1978)

A Day in Hollywood/A Night in the Ukraine (director and choreographer, 1980; Tony Award for best choreographer)

Cloud 9 (director, 1981)

Nine (director and choreographer, 1982; Tony Award for best director)

My One and Only (co-director, co-choreographer, actor, 1983; Tony Awards for best choreographer and best actor)

Stepping Out (director, 1987)

Grand Hotel (1989; Tony Awards for best director and best choreographer)

The Will Rogers Follies (director, choreographer, 1991; Tony Awards for best director and best choreographer)

The Best Little Whorehouse Goes Public (co-director, 1994)

Busker Alley (actor, 1995)

WENDY WASSERSTEIN
playwright/screenwriter

Any Woman Can't (1973)

When Dinah Shore Ruled the Earth (coauthor, 1977)

Uncommon Women and Others (teleplay, 1978)

The Sorrows of Gin (adaptor, teleplay, 1981)

Hard Sell (1980)

Isn't It Romantic? (1981)

Tender Offer (1983)

The Man in a Case (adaptor, 1985)

Miami (coauthor, book, 1985)

Drive, She Said (1988)

The Heidi Chronicles (1988; Pulitzer Prize, Tony Award)

Kiss, Kiss Darling (1991)

The Sisters Rosenzweig (1993)

The Object of My Affection (1994)

AUGUST WILSON
playwright

Black Bart and the Sacred Hills (1981)

Jitney (1982)

Joe Turner's Come and Gone (1983)

Ma Rainey's Black Bottom (1984)

Fences (1985; Pulitzer, Tony)

The Piano Lesson (1987; Pulitzer)

Two Trains Running (1990)

Seven Guitars (1995)

BREAKTHROUGH BRITISH IMPORTS

Some of the most significant and successful shows on Broadway over the last 25 years have been imported from Britain. The following list credits the major figures behind them and gives the year of their American premiere.

Amadeus, Peter Shaffer, director Peter Hall (1980)

An Inspector Calls, J. B. Priestly, director Stephen Daldry (1995)

Arcadia, Tom Stoppard, director Trevor Nunn (1995)

Aspects of Love, Andrew Lloyd Webber, Don Black and Charles Hart, director Trevor Nunn, producer Cameron Mackintosh (1989)

Betrayal, Harold Pinter, director Peter Hall (1980)

Cats, Andrew Lloyd Webber, Trevor Nunn, director Trevor Nunn, producer Cameron Mackintosh (1982)

Equus, Peter Shaffer, director John Dexter (1974)

Evita, Andrew Lloyd Webber and Tim Rice, director Harold Prince (1979)

Hamlet, Shakespeare, director Jonathan Kent, Ralph Fiennes as Hamlet (1995)

Jesus Christ Superstar, Andrew Lloyd Webber and Tim Rice, director Tim O'Horgan (1971)

Joseph and the Amazing Technicolor Dreamcoat, Andrew Lloyd Webber and Tim Rice, director Tony Tanner (1982)

Les Liaisons Dangereuses, Christopher Hampton, Royal Shakespeare Company production, director Howard Davies (1987)

Les Misérables, by Claude-Michel Schönberg, Alain Boublil, Herbert Kretzmer, directors and adaptors Trevor Nunn and John Caird (1987)

Me and My Girl, L. Arthur Rose, Douglas Furber, Noel Gay, director Mike Ockrent (1986)

Miss Saigon, Claude-Michel Schönberg, Alain Boublil, Richard Maltby, director Nicholas Hytner (1991)

Nicholas Nickleby, David Edgar, directors Trevor Nunn and John Caird, producer Cameron Mackintosh (1986)

Noises Off, Michael Frayn, director Michael Blakemore (1983)

The Norman Conquests, Alan Ayckbourn, director Eric Thompson (1975)

Oliver!, Lionel Bart, director Peter Coe, producer Cameron Mackintosh (1984)

The Phantom of the Opera, Andrew Lloyd Webber, Charles Hart, Richard Stilgoe, director Harold Prince (1988)

Plenty, David Hare, director David Hare (1983)

The Real Thing, Tom Stoppard, director Mike Nichols (1984)

The Rocky Horror Show, Richard O'Brien, director Jim Sharman (1975)

Some Americans Abroad, Richard Nelson, director Roger Mitchell, Royal Shakespeare Company production (1990)

Starlight Express, Andrew Lloyd Webber and Richard Stilgoe, director Trevor Nunn (1987)

Sunset Boulevard, Andrew Lloyd Webber, Don Black and Christopher Hampton (1994)

MAJOR SHOWS THAT BEGAN IN REGIONAL THEATERS

Beginning in the '70s, the creative impetus in American drama began to shift away from the increasingly expensive Broadway venues and toward regional and nonprofit theaters. While most major playwrights once wrote directly for Broadway production, regional theaters have more commonly become the place of origination for America's most important plays. The following productions may have gone on to national and even international fame, but all began in regional theaters.

American Buffalo, by David Mamet, Goodman Theater, Chicago

Angels in America, by Tony Kushner, Eureka Theatre Company, San Francisco

Annie, by Thomas Meehan, Martin Charnin, and Charles Strouse, Goodspeed Opera House, East Haddam, Connecticut

Big River, adapted by William Hauptman from Mark Twain, La Jolla Playhouse, La Jolla, California

Buried Child, by Sam Shepard, Magic Theater, San Francisco

California Suite, by Neil Simon, Hartman Theatre, Stamford, Connecticut

Children of a Lesser God, by Mark Medoff, Mark Taper Forum, Los Angeles

The Colored Museum, by George C. Wolfe, Crossroads Theatre Company, New Brunswick, New Jersey

Conversations with my Father, by Herb Gardner, Seattle Repertory Theatre

Crimes of the Heart, by Beth Henley, Actors Theatre of Louisville

Eastern Standard, by Richard Greenberg, Seattle Repertory Theatre

BROADWAY: PRICEY, DICEY, BUT FILLING SEATS

Though Broadway ticket prices have risen with inflation over the past two decades, theater attendance has remained fairly steady. The prices listed below represent the net collected by management after taxes and various deductions; show-goers actually paid about 10% more. (Source: *Variety*)

Year	Average Ticket Price	Attendance	Year	Average Ticket Price	Attendance
1975-76	$9.86	7,181,898	1986-87	$29.74	6,968,277
1976-77	10.60	8,815,095	1987-88	31.65	8,142,722
1977-78	12.05	8,621,262	1988-89	32.88	7,968,273
1978-79	14.02	9,115,613	1989-90	35.24	8,039,106
1979-80	15.29	9,380,648	1990-91	36.53	7,314,138
1980-81	17.97	10,822,324	1991-92	39.69	7,365,528
1981-82	22.07	10,694,373	1992-93	41.71	7,856,727
1982-83	25.07	8,102,262	1993-94	43.87	8,116,031
1983-84	28.68	7,898,765	1994-95	44.92	9,044,763
1984-85	29.06	7,156,683	1995-96	46.06	9,468,210
1985-86	29.20	6,527,498	1996-97	48.40	10,318,217

Fences, by August Wilson, Yale Repertory Theatre, New Haven, Connecticut

The Gin Game, by D. L. Coburn, Long Wharf Theatre, New Haven, Connecticut

Glengarry Glen Ross, by David Mamet, Goodman Theatre, Chicago

The Heidi Chronicles, by Wendy Wasserstein, Seattle Repertory Theatre

I'm Not Rappaport, by Herb Gardner, Seattle Repertory Theatre

In the Belly of the Beast, adapted by Adrian Hall from Jack Henry Abbott, Trinity Repertory Company, Providence, Rhode Island

Into the Woods, by James Lapine and Stephen Sondheim, Old Globe Theatre, San Diego

Jelly's Last Jam, by George C. Wolfe, Jelly Roll Morton, and Susan Birkenhead, Mark Taper Forum, Los Angeles

Joe Turner's Come and Gone, by August Wilson, Yale Repertory Theatre, New Haven, Connecticut

Love Letters, by A. R. Gurney, Long Wharf Theatre, New Haven, Connecticut

Ma Rainey's Black Bottom, by August Wilson, Yale Repertory Theatre, New Haven, Connecticut

"Master Harold"...and the Boys, by Athol Fugard, Yale Repertory Theatre, New Haven, Connecticut

'Night, Mother, by Marsha Norman, American Repertory Theatre, Cambridge, Massachusetts

Prelude to a Kiss, by Craig Lucas, South Coast Repertory, Costa Mesa, California

Quilters, by Molly Newman and Barbara Damashek, Denver Center Theatre Company

Streamers, by David Rabe, Long Wharf Theatre, New Haven, Connecticut

True West, by Sam Shepard, Steppenwolf Theatre Company, Chicago

Two Trains Running, by August Wilson, Yale Repertory Theatre, New Haven, Connecticut

The Wake of Jamey Foster, by Beth Henley, Hartford Stage Company, Hartford, Connecticut

The Who's "Tommy," by Pete Townshend and Wayne Cilento, La Jolla Playhouse, La Jolla, California

How To Succeed in Business Without Really Trying, La Jolla Playhouse, La Jolla, California

Master Class, by Terrence McNally, Philadelphia Theater Company, Pennsylvania

Twilight, by Anna Deavere Smith, Mark Taper Forum, Los Angeles, California

MAJOR REGIONAL THEATERS AND THEIR DIRECTORS

Far from the bright lights of Broadway, vibrant regional theater companies can be found in rural communities, urban neighborhoods, metropolitan centers, and suburbs around the U.S. Their repertoire ranges from the classics to musicals to modern plays to experimental, multi-media, and solo performance works. Despite deeply felt cuts in government funding, these shining companies continue to cast their light from every corner of the country.

Actors Theatre of Louisville, Louisville, Kentucky, Jon Jory, producing director

Alley Theatre, Houston, Gregory Boyd, artistic director

Alliance Theatre Company, Atlanta, Kenny Leon, artistic director

American Conservatory Theater, San Francisco, Carey Perloff, artistic director

American Repertory Theatre, Cambridge, Massachusetts, Robert Brustein, artistic director

Arena Stage, Washington, D.C., Douglas Wager, artistic director

Center Stage, Baltimore, Irene Lewis, artistic director

Dallas Theater Center, Dallas, Richard Hamburger, artistic director

Goodman Theatre, Chicago, Robert Falls, artistic director

Goodspeed Opera House, East Haddam, Connecticut, Michael P. Price, executive director

Guthrie Theater, Minneapolis, Joe Dowling, artistic director

Hartford Stage Company, Hartford, Connecticut, Mark Lamos, artistic director

La Jolla Playhouse, La Jolla, California, Michael Greif, artistic director

Long Wharf Theatre, New Haven, Connecticut, Douglas Hughes, artistic director

Mark Taper Forum, Los Angeles, Gordon Davidson, artistic director

McCarter Theatre Center for the Performing Arts, Princeton, New Jersey, Emily Mann, artistic director

Milwaukee Repertory Theater, Milwaukee, Joseph Hanreddy, artistic director

Old Globe Theatre, San Diego, Jack O'Brien, artistic director

Oregon Shakespeare Festival, Ashland, Oregon, Libby Appel, artistic director

Seattle Repertory Theatre, Seattle, Sharon Ott, artistic director

Shakespeare Theatre, Washington, D.C., Michael Kahn, artistic director

South Coast Repertory, Costa Mesa, California, David Emmes, producing artistic director

Steppenwolf Theatre Company, Chicago, Martha Lavey, artistic director

Trinity Repertory Company, Providence, Rhode Island, Oscar Eustis, artistic director

Yale Repertory Theatre, New Haven, Connecticut, Stan Wojewodski, artistic director

WHAT'S HOT IN HIGH SCHOOL DRAMA

Here's a list of the most popular full-length shows for high school performance in the United States, in 1996 and over the entire post–World War II period through 1984. In the September 1985 issue of *Dramatics* magazine, one theater educator lamented the list's conservatism—its preponderance of musicals, oldies, and relatively unadventurous shows by American playwrights.

1996

1. *Bye Bye Birdie,* Michael Stewart, Charles Strouse, and Lee Adams
2. *A Midsummer Night's Dream,* William Shakespeare
3. *Guys and Dolls,* Frank Loesser, Jo Swerling, and Abe Burrows
4. *The Miracle Worker,* William Gibson
5. *Rumors,* Neil Simon (tie)
5. *You Can't Take It with You,* Moss Hart and George S. Kaufman (tie)
7. *Our Town,* Thornton Wiilder
8. *The Diary of Anne Frank,* Frances Goodrich and Albert Hackett (tie)
8. *Grease,* Jim Jacobs and Warren Casey (tie)
10. *Fiddler on the Roof,* Joseph Stein, Jerry Bock, and Sheldon Harnick (tie)
10. *The Music Man,* Meredith Willson (tie)
12. *Hello, Dolly!,* Michael Stewart and Jerry Herman
13. *Oklahoma!,* Richard Rodgers and Oscar Hammerstein II (tie)
13. *The Wizard of Oz,* various adaptations of the L. Frank Baum novel (tie)
15. *Joseph and the Amazing Technicolor Dreamcoat,* Andrew Lloyd Webber and Tim Rice
16. *Godspell,* Stephen Schwartz and John-Michael Tebelak (tie)
16. *Once upon a Mattress,* Jay Thompson, Marshall Barer, Dean Fuller, and Mary Rodgers (tie)
18. *Arsenic and Old Lace,* Joseph Kesselring (tie)
18. *Crazy for You,* George Gershwin, Ira Gershwin, and Ken Ludwig (tie)
20. *Little Shop of Horrors,* Howard Ashman and Alan Menken (tie)
20. *Much Ado About Nothing,* William Shakespeare (tie)

1945–1984

1. *You Can't Take It with You,* Moss Hart and George S. Kaufman
2. *Our Town,* Thornton Wilder
3. *Arsenic and Old Lace,* Joseph Kesselring
4. *Harvey,* Mary Chase
5. *The Curious Savage,* John Patrick
6. *Oklahoma!,* Richard Rodgers and Oscar Hammerstein II
7. *The Miracle Worker,* William Gibson (tie)
7. *The Diary of Anne Frank,* Frances Goodrich and Albert Hackett (tie)
9. *The Music Man,* Meredith Wilson (tie)
9. *Our Hearts Were Young and Gay,* Jean Kerr (tie)
9. *The Night of January 16,* Ayn Rand (tie)
12. *Bye Bye Birdie,* Michael Stewart, Charles Strouse, and Lee Adams
13. *The Man Who Came to Dinner,* George S. Kaufman and Moss Hart
14. *Up the Down Staircase,* Christopher Serge, from the novel by Bel Kaufman (tie)
14. *You're a Good Man, Charlie Brown,* John Gordon and Clark Gesner (tie)
14. *The Sound of Music,* Richard Rodgers and Oscar Hammerstein II (tie)
17. *Guys and Dolls,* Frank Loesser, Jo Swerling, and Abe Burrows
18. *Godspell,* John Michael Tebelak and Stephen Schwartz
19. *Teahouse of the August Moon,* John Patrick
20. *The Crucible,* Arthur Miller

FAVORITE FICTIONAL CHARACTERS FROM THEATER

Legendary director Peter Brook says that theater, among other things, makes the unseen visible. And thanks to these 12 remarkable roles, we have seen nothing less than ourselves. (Source: *The Encyclopedia of Fictional Characters*, Berkley Publishing Corp. and Seth Godin Productions)

George Berger
Hair
Hates his name; call him Bananaberger. He thinks of himself as a poor young psychedelic teddy bear. He willfully violates P.S. 183's Personal Appearance Code, knowing people will wonder if he's a boy or a girl. Eighteen years old, bright, funny, wild, he's still serious underneath it all. A rapist, pothead, and neurotic liar who lives by the words "This is 1968, not 1967!" Goals: floating around India, being invisible, staying high forever.

Joe Boyd
Damn Yankees
Perennially frustrated fan of the Washington Senators baseball team, he makes a desperate bargain and becomes a Senators superstar. Terrific at the plate, in the field, and with a song. He may yield to temptation for a while, but Joe is true-blue down deep.

Guildenstern
Rosencrantz and Guildenstern Are Dead
A dapper Elizabethan courtier, Guildenstern senses that he and his companion, Rosencrantz, serve a function in the play *Hamlet*, but he can't figure out what it is. Not willing to accept this existential dilemma, Guildenstern seeks to solve it, initially through clever word games, and later, with increasing agitation, by way of soul-searching soliloquies. Guildenstern is so perplexed that at one point he mistakes himself for Rosencrantz. As the pair drift in and out of *Hamlet*, Guildenstern's depression deepens, and he's unable to find solace in Rosencrantz's optimism. He is proven the wiser when the two are executed for reasons beyond their control or understanding.

Willy Loman
Death of a Salesman
He is a tired, aging traveling salesman, who believes devoutly in the notion that success comes to he who is "well liked." Acceptance, however, is only part of Willy's list of desires. After a lifetime on the road, he wants the company for which he has toiled to give him a nontraveling position. He wants to be out from under the weight of debt. He wants his sons, Happy and Biff, to respect the enormous effort he has made to make himself a success. And he wants Happy and Biff to be successful in their own right. Since none of these dreams are anywhere close to fruition, Willy is a frustrated and unhappy man still looking for a way to leave behind something tangible for his family, wanting to believe in a pot of gold at the end of the rainbow, but beginning to realize that he might not find it. "A man is not a piece of fruit."

Jack Jefferson
The Great White Hope
While on his way to becoming the first black heavyweight boxing champion of the world, Jefferson always smiles. But after he wins the title, his smile disappears. He becomes a target for bigots in both the white and black communities, who want him to end his relationship with his white lover, Eleanor. The law and boxing promoters conspire to wrest his title from him. Jefferson leaves America to avoid imprisonment on a trumped-up charge but can find little happiness anywhere else. "I ain't fightin' for no race. I ain't redeemin' nobody. My mama told me Mr. Lincoln done that. Ain't that why they shot him?"

Ouisa Kittredge
Six Degrees of Separation
Her life certainly seems to be dandy. She lives in soigné surroundings with her wealthy art-dealer husband, Flan Kittredge, she dines out every night, her life is a mad social whirl. Then she's charmed by a young black man, Paul Poitier, who claims to be Sidney Poitier's son. When his story is revealed as bogus, she sees that, under the glossy veneer, her life has been a big lie and that she is a "collage of unaccounted-for brush strokes."

Roberto Miranda
Death and the Maiden
Music lover. Also, possibly, a onetime torturer of political prisoners, including Paulina Escobar. He likes to play out difficult situations with a deliberate, thoughtful approach. A lover of drink and conversation, prone to giving wry and mysterious remarks when occasions warrant.

Gaylord Ravenal

Showboat

As skilled in card games as he is in winning the hearts of women, Gaylord uses his good looks and charm to get a job as the leading man on a Mississippi showboat when his luck as a gambler runs out. Soon after joining the company of the Cotton Blossom Floating Palace, Gaylord woos and secretly weds Magnolia Hawks, the leading lady and daughter of the showboat's owners. Unable to persuade Magnolia's mother that he has left behind his seamy past, Gaylord convinces his wife to move to Chicago, where he turns once again to the uncertain and ultimately self-destructive life at the roulette table.

Tevye

Fiddler on the Roof

Resident milkman in the small Russian village of Anatevka. He is married to Golde and the father of five daughters. Tevye is proud of his Jewish heritage, though often subjects God to a grilling in private dialogues. Can be impossibly stubborn at times, particularly in dealing with his family. Given to occasional but hearty singing and dancing when the moment is right. "Would it have spoiled some vast eternal plan if I was a wealthy man?"

Marian Paroo

The Music Man

The River City librarian, Marian Paroo also teaches piano to the town's young 'uns. She lives at home with her mom and younger brother. She's smart and commonsensical, and she sees right through "Professor" Harold Hill when he shows up in town claiming to be a music scholar. But she withholds judgment, because he has a way about him that's quite different from the nice, dull local swains. Soon she's in love with a man she's deep down sure is a swindler, and she blooms like a rose.

Brick Pollitt

Cat on a Hot Tin Roof

The handsome eldest son of the powerful, wealthy Big Daddy is nonetheless filled with self-loathing, because of his unfulfilled life and sexual frustration. A former star high school athlete and the apple of his father's eye, Brick is nursing a broken leg suffered while trying to jump hurdles while drunk. His stubborn, self-destructive nature and loathing of his grasping, conniving family spur his drinking. While most blame his alcoholic intake on unhappy marriage and despondency after the death of his best friend, Brick's beautiful, frustrated wife, Maggie, knows that the roots of his problems run deeper. The true nature of Brick's relationship with his late friend reflects the ambiguity of his sexuality. He senses that, to survive, he must escape his family and the hypocrisy they personify.

Walter Lee "Brother" Younger

A Raisin in the Sun

A chauffeur by trade and a dreamer by nature, Walter Lee lives in frustrating awareness of the gap between what he feels is his due and the actuality of the world and its limitations. He lives with his wife and son in his mother's apartment. As an African American, he does not have the same access to the American Dream as the people for whom he works. Brother dreams of making deals, of gaining material wealth, and thereby getting respect. He desperately wants to give to the people he loves all that they deserve; and he is terribly frustrated by his inability to do it. "And you—ain't you bitter, man? Don't you see no stars gleaming that you can't reach up and grab? You happy? Bitter? Man, I'm a volcano. Bitter? Here I am a giant—surrounded by ants! Ants who can't even understand what I'm talking about."

THE TONY AWARDS

	1947	1948	1949
Actor (Dramatic)	Fredric March, *Years Ago*; José Ferrer, *Cyrano de Bergerac*	Basil Rathbone, *The Heiress*; Henry Fonda, *Mister Roberts*; Paul Kelly, *Command Decision*	Rex Harrison, *Anne of the Thousand Days*
Actress (Dramatic)	Helen Hayes, *Happy Birthday;* Ingrid Bergman, *Joan of Lorraine*	Jessica Tandy, *A Streetcar Named Desire*; Judith Anderson, *Medea*; Katharine Cornell, *Antony and Cleopatra*	Martita Hunt, *The Madwoman of Chaillot*
Supporting Actor (Dramatic)	—	—	Arthur Kennedy, *Death of a Salesman*
Supporting Actress (Dramatic)	Patricia Neal, *Another Part of the Forest*	—	Shirley Booth, *Goodbye, My Fancy*
Play	—	*Mister Roberts*	*Death of a Salesman*
Actor (Musical)	—	Paul Hartman, *Angel in the Wings*	Ray Bolger, *Where's Charley?*
Actress (Musical)	—	Grace Hartman, *Angel in the Wings*	Nanette Fabray, *Love Life*
Supporting Actor (Musical)	David Wayne, *Finian's Rainbow*	—	—
Supporting Actress (Musical)	—	—	—
Musical	—	—	*Kiss Me Kate*
Director	Elia Kazan, *All My Sons*	—	Elia Kazan, *Death of a Salesman*
Score	—	—	Cole Porter, *Kiss Me Kate*
Author (Dramatic)	—	Thomas Heggen and Joshua Logan, *Mister Roberts*	Arthur Miller, *Death of a Salesman*
Author (Musical)	—		Bella and Samuel Spewack, *Kiss Me Kate*
Scenic Designer	—	Horace Armistead, *The Medium*	Jo Mielziner, *Sleepy Hollow; Summer and Smoke; Anne of the Thousand Days; Death of a Salesman; South Pacific*
Costume Designer	—	—	Lemuel Ayers, *Kiss Me Kate*
Choreographer	Agnes de Mille, *Brigadoon*; Michael Kidd, *Finian's Rainbow*	Jerome Robbins, *High Button Shoes*	Gower Champion, *Lend an Ear*
Producer (Dramatic)	—	Leland Hayward, *Mister Roberts*	Kermit Bloomgarden and Walter Fried, *Death of a Salesman*
Producer (Musical)	—	—	Saint-Subber and Lemuel Ayers, *Kiss Me Kate*
Conductor and Musical Director	—	—	Max Meth, *As the Girls Go*
Stage Technician	—	George Gebhardt; George Pierce	—

1950	1951	1952	1953
Sydney Blackmer, *Come Back, Little Sheba*	Claude Rains, *Darkness At Noon*	Jose Ferrer, *The Shrike*	Tom Ewell, *The Seven Year Itch*
Shirley Booth, *Come Back, Little Sheba*	Uta Hagen, *The Country Girl*	Julie Harris, *I Am a Camera*	Shirley Booth, *Time of the Cuckoo*
—	Eli Wallach, *The Rose Tattoo*	John Cromwell, *Point of No Return*	John Williams, *Dial M for Murder*
—	Maureen Stapleton, *The Rose Tattoo*	Marian Winters, *I Am a Camera*	Beatrice Straight, *The Crucible*
The Cocktail Party	*The Rose Tattoo*	*The Fourposter*	*The Crucible*
Ezio Pinza, *South Pacific*	Robert Alda, *Guys and Dolls*	Phil Silvers, *Top Banana*	Thomas Mitchell, *Hazel Flagg*
Mary Martin, *South Pacific*	Ethel Merman, *Call Me Madam*	Gertrude Lawrence, *The King & I*	Rosalind Russell, *Wonderful Town*
Myron McCormick, *South Pacific*	Russell Nype, *Call Me Madam*	Yul Brynner, *The King & I*	Hiram Sherman, *Two's Company*
Juanita Hall, *South Pacific*	Isabel Bigley, *Guys And Dolls*	Helen Gallagher, *Pal Joey*	Sheila Bond, *Wish You Were Here*
South Pacific	*Guys And Dolls*	*The King & I*	*Wonderful Town*
Joshua Logan, *South Pacific*	George S. Kaufman, *Guys and Dolls*	Jose Ferrer, *The Shrike; The Fourposter; Stalag 17*	Joshua Logan, *Picnic*
Richard Rodgers, *South Pacific*	Frank Loesser, *Guys and Dolls*	—	Leonard Bernstein, *Wonderful Town*
T.S. Eliot, *The Cocktail Party*	Tennessee Williams, *The Rose Tattoo*	—	Arthur Miller, *The Crucible*
Oscar Hammerstein II and Joshua Logan, *South Pacific*	Jo Swerling and Abe Burrows, *Guys and Dolls*	—	Joseph Fields and Jerome Chodorov, *Wonderful Town*
Jo Mielziner, *The Innocents*	Boris Aronson, *The Rose Tattoo; The Country Girl; Season in the Sun*	Jo Mielziner, *The King & I*	Raoul Pene du Bois, *Wonderful Town*
Aline Bernstein, *Regina*	Miles White, *Bless You All*	Irene Sharaff, *The King and I*	Miles White, *Hazel Flagg*
Helen Tamiris, *Touch and Go*	Michael Kidd, *Guys and Dolls*	Robert Alton, *Pal Joey*	Donald Saddler, *Wonderful Town*
Gilbert Miller, *The Cocktail Party*	Cheryl Crawford, *The Rose Tattoo*	—	Kermit Bloomgarden, *The Crucible*
Richard Rodgers, Oscar Hammerstein II, Leland Hayward, and Joshua Logan, *South Pacific*	Cy Feuer and Ernest H. Martin, *Guys and Dolls*	—	Robert Fryer, *Wonderful Town*
Maurice Abravanel, *Regina*	Lehman Engel, *The Consul*	Max Meth, *Pal Joey*	Lehman Engel, *Wonderful Town; Gilbert and Sullivan Season*
Joe Lynn, master propertyman, *Miss Liberty*	Richard Raven, *The Autumn Garden*	Peter Feller, master carpenter, *Call Me Madam*	Abe Kurnit, *Wish You Were Here*

	1954	1955	1956
Actor (Dramatic)	David Wayne, *The Teahouse of the August Moon*	Alfred Lunt, *Quadrille*	Paul Muni, *Inherit the Wind*
Actress (Dramatic)	Audrey Hepburn, *Ondine*	Nancy Kelly, *The Bad Seed*	Julie Harris, *The Lark*
Featured/Supporting Actor (Dramatic)	John Kerr, *Tea and Sympathy*	Francis L. Sullivan, *Witness for the Prosecution*	Ed Begley, *Inherit the Wind*
Featured/Supporting Actress (Dramatic)	Jo Van Fleet, *The Trip to Bountiful*	Patricia Jessel, *Witness for the Prosecution*	Una Merkel, *The Ponder Heart*
Play	*The Teahouse of the August Moon*	*The Desperate Hours*	*The Diary of Anne Frank*
Actor (Musical)	Alfred Drake, *Kismet*	Walter Slezak, *Fanny*	Ray Walston, *Damn Yankees*
Actress (Musical)	Dolores Gray, *Carnival In Flanders*	Mary Martin, *Peter Pan*	Gwen Verdon, *Damn Yankees*
Featured/Supporting Actor Role (Musical)	Harry Belafonte, *John Murray Anderson's Almanac*	Cyril Ritchard, *Peter Pan*	Russ Brown, *Damn Yankees*
Featured/Supporting Actress (Musical)	Gwen Verdon, *Can-Can*	Carol Haney, *The Pajama Game*	Lotte Lenya, *The Threepenny Opera*
Musical	*Kismet*	*The Pajama Game*	*Damn Yankees*
Director	Alfred Lunt, *Ondine*	Robert Montgomery, *The Desperate Hours*	Tyrone Guthrie, *The Matchmaker; Six Characters in Search of an Author; Tamburlaine the Great*
Director (Dramatic)	—	—	—
Director (Musical)	—	—	—
Score	Alexander Borodin, *Kismet*	Richard Adler and Jerry Ross, *The Pajama Game*	Richard Adler and Jerry Ross, *Damn Yankees*
Author (Dramatic)	John Patrick, *The Teahouse of the August Moon*	Joseph Hayes, *The Desperate Hours*	Frances Goodrich and Albert Hackett, *The Diary of Anne Frank*
Author (Musical)	Charles Lederer and Luther Davis, *Kismet*	George Abbott and Richard Bissell, *The Pajama Game*	George Abbott and Douglass Wallop, *Damn Yankees*
Scenic Designer	Peter Larkin, *Ondine; The Teahouse of the August Moon*	Oliver Messel, *House of Flowers*	Peter Larkin, *Inherit the Wind; No Time for Sergeants*
Costume Designer	Richard Whorf, *Ondine*	Cecil Beaton, *Quadrille*	Alvin Colt, *The Lark/Phoenix '55/ Pipe Dream*
Choreographer	Michael Kidd, *Can-Can*	Bob Fosse, *The Pajama Game*	Bob Fosse, *Damn Yankees*
Producer (Dramatic)	Maurice Evans and George Schaefer, *The Teahouse of the August Moon*	Howard Erskine and Joseph Hayes, *The Desperate Hours*	Kermit Bloomgarden, *The Diary of Anne Frank*
Producer (Musical)	Charles Lederer, *Kismet*	Frederick Brisson, Robert Griffith, and Harold S. Prince, *The Pajama Game*	Frederick Brisson, Robert Griffith, Harold S. Prince in association with Albert B. Taylor, *Damn Yankees*
Conductor and Musical Director	Louis Adrian, *Kismet*	Thomas Schippers, *The Saint of Bleecker Street*	Hal Hastings, *Damn Yankees*
Stage Technician	John Davis, *Picnic*	Richard Rodda, *Peter Pan*	Harry Green, electrician and sound man, *The Middle of the Night; Damn Yankees*

1957	1958	1959	1960
Fredric March, *Long Day's Journey into Night*	Ralph Bellamy, *Sunrise at Campobello*	Jason Robards Jr., *The Disenchanted*	Melvyn Douglas, *The Best Man*
Margaret Leighton, *Separate Tables*	Helen Hayes, *Time Remembered*	Gertrude Berg, *A Majority of One*	Anne Bancroft, *The Miracle Worker*
Frank Conroy, *The Potting Shed*	Henry Jones, *Sunrise at Campobello*	Charlie Ruggles, *The Pleasure of His Company*	Roddy McDowall, *The Fighting Cock*
Peggy Cass, *Auntie Mame*	Anne Bancroft, *Two for the Seesaw*	Julie Newmar, *The Marriage-Go-Round*	Anne Revere, *Toys In the Attic*
Long Day's Journey into Night	*Sunrise at Campobello*	*J.B.*	*The Miracle Worker*
Rex Harrison, *My Fair Lady*	Robert Preston, *The Music Man*	Richard Kiley, *Redhead*	Jackie Gleason, *Take Me Along*
Judy Holliday, *Bells Are Ringing*	Gwen Verdon, *New Girl In Town*; Thelma Ritter, *New Girl In Town*	Gwen Verdon, *Redhead*	Mary Martin, *The Sound of Music*
Sydney Chaplin, *Bells Are Ringing*	David Burns, *The Music Man*	Russell Nype, *Goldilocks;* cast of *La Plume de ma tante*	Tom Bosley, *Fiorello!*
Edith Adams, *Li'l Abner*	Barbara Cook, *The Music Man*	Pat Stanley, *Goldilocks;* cast of *La Plume de ma tante*	Patricia Neway, *The Sound of Music*
My Fair Lady	*The Music Man*	*Redhead*	*Fiorello!*
Moss Hart, *My Fair Lady*	—	Elia Kazan, *J.B.*	—
—	Vincent J. Donehue, *Sunrise at Campobello*	—	Arthur Penn, *The Miracle Worker*
—	—	—	George Abbott, *Fiorello!*
Frederick Loewe, *My Fair Lady*	Meredith Willson, *The Music Man*	Albert Hague, *Redhead*	Jerry Bock, *Fiorello!*; Richard Rodgers, *The Sound of Music*
Eugene O'Neill, *Long Day's Journey into Night*	Dore Schary, *Sunrise at Campobello*	Archibald MacLeish, *J.B.*	William Gibson, *The Miracle Worker*
Alan Jay Lerner, *My Fair Lady*	Meredith Willson and Franklin Lacey, *The Music Man*	Herbert and Dorothy Fields, Sidney Sheldon, and David Shaw, *Redhead*	Jerome Weidman and George Abbott, *Fiorello!;* Howard Lindsay and Russel Crouse, *The Sound of Music*
Oliver Smith, *A Clearing in the Woods; Candide; Auntie Mame; My Fair Lady; Eugenia; A Visit to a Small Planet*	Oliver Smith, *West Side Story*	Donald Oenslager, *A Majority of One*	Howard Bey, *Toys in the Attic* (Dramatic); Oliver Smith, *The Sound of Music* (Musical)
Cecil Beaton, *Little Glass Clock/ My Fair Lady*	Motley, *The First Gentleman*	Robert Ter-Arutunian, *Redhead*	Cecil Beaton, *Saratoga*
Michael Kidd, *Li'l Abner*	Jerome Robbins, *West Side Story*	Bob Fosse, *Redhead*	Michael Kidd, *Destry Rides Again*
Leigh Connell, Theodore Mann, and Jose Quintero, *Long Day's Journey into Night*	Lawrence Langner, Theresa Helburn, Armina Marshall, and Dore Schary, *Sunrise at Campobello*	Alfred de Liagre, Jr., *J.B.*	Fred Coe, *The Miracle Worker*
Herman Levin, *My Fair Lady*	Kermit Bloomgarden, Herbert Greene, Frank Productions, *The Music Man*	Robert Fryer and Lawrence Carr, *Redhead*	Robert Griffith and Harold Prince, *Fiorello!;* Leland Hayward and Richard Halliday, *The Sound of Music*
Franz Allers, *My Fair Lady*	Herbert Greene, *The Music Man*	Salvatore Dell'Isola, *Flower Drum Song*	Frederick Dvonch, *The Sound of Music*
Howard McDonald (posthumous), carpenter, *Major Barbara*	Harry Romar, *Time Remembered*	Sam Knapp, *The Music Man*	John Walters, chief carpenter, *The Miracle Worker*

	1961	1962	1963
Actor (Dramatic)	Zero Mostel, *Rhinoceros*	Paul Scofield, *A Man for All Seasons*	Arthur Hill, *Who's Afraid of Virginia Woolf?*
Actress (Dramatic)	Joan Plowright, *A Taste of Honey*	Margaret Leighton, *Night of the Iguana*	Uta Hagen, *Who's Afraid of Virginia Woolf?*
Featured/Supporting Actor (Dramatic)	Martin Gabel, *Big Fish, Little Fish*	Walter Matthau, *A Shot in the Dark*	Alan Arkin, *Enter Laughing*
Featured/Supporting Actress (Dramatic)	Colleen Dewhurst, *All the Way Home*	Elizabeth Ashley, *Take Her, She's Mine*	Sandy Dennis, *A Thousand Clowns*
Play	*Becket*	*A Man for All Seasons*	*Who's Afraid of Virginia Woolf?*
Actor (Musical)	Richard Burton, *Camelot*	Robert Morse, *How To Succeed in Business Without Really Trying*	Zero Mostel, *A Funny Thing Happened on the Way to the Forum*
Actress (Musical)	Elizabeth Seal, *Irma La Douce*	Anna Maria Alberghetti, *Carnival*	Vivien Leigh, *Tovarich*
Featured/Supporting Actor (Musical)	Dick Van Dyke, *Bye, Bye Birdie*	Charles Nelson Reilly, *How To Succeed in Business Without Really Trying*	David Burns, *A Funny Thing Happened on the Way to the Forum*
Featured/Supporting Actress (Musical)	Tammy Grimes, *The Unsinkable Molly Brown*	Phyllis Newman, *Subways Are for Sleeping*	Anna Quayle, *Stop the World—I Want To Get Off*
Musical	*Bye, Bye Birdie*	*How To Succeed in Business Without Really Trying*	*A Funny Thing Happened on the Way to the Forum*
Director (Dramatic)	John Gielgud, *Big Fish, Little Fish*	Noel Willman, *A Man for All Seasons*	Alan Schneider, *Who's Afraid of Virginia Woolf?*
Director (Musical)	Gower Champion, *Bye, Bye Birdie*	Abe Burrows, *How To Succeed in Business Without Really Trying*	George Abbott, *A Funny Thing Happened on the Way to the Forum*
Score	—	Richard Rodgers, *No Strings*	Lionel Bart, *Oliver!*
Author (Dramatic)	Jean Anouilh, *Becket*	Robert Bolt, *A Man for All Seasons*	—
Author (Musical)	Michael Stewart, *Bye, Bye Birdie*	Abe Burrows, Jack Weinstock, and Willie Gilbert, *How To Succeed in Business Without Really Trying*	Burt Shevelove and Larry Gelbart, *A Funny Thing Happened on the Way to the Forum*
Scenic Designer	Oliver Smith, *Becket* (Dramatic); Oliver Smith, *Camelot* (Musical)	Will Steven Armstrong, *Carnival*	Sean Kenny, *Oliver!*
Costume Designer	Motley, *Becket;* Adrian and Tony Duquette, *Camelot*	Lucinda Ballard, *The Gay Life*	Anthony Powell, *The School for Scandal*
Choreographer	Gower Champion, *Bye, Bye Birdie*	Agnes de Mille, *Kwamina;* Joe Layton, *No Strings*	Bob Fosse, *Little Me*
Producer (Dramatic)	David Merrick, *Becket*	Robert Whitehead and Roger L. Stevens, *A Man for All Seasons*	Richard Barr and Clinton Wilder, Theatre 1963, *Who's Afraid of Virginia Woolf?*
Producer (Musical)	Edward Padula, *Bye, Bye Birdie*	Cy Feuer and Ernest Martin, *How To Succeed in Business Without Really Trying*	Harold Prince, *A Funny Thing Happened on the Way to the Forum*
Conductor and Musical Director	Franz Allers, *Camelot*	Elliot Lawrence, *How To Succeed in Business Without Really Trying*	Donald Pippin, *Oliver!*
Stage Technician	Teddy Van Bemmel, *Becket*	Michael Burns, *A Man for All Seasons*	—

1964	1965	1966	1967
Alec Guinness, *Dylan*	Walter Matthau, *The Odd Couple*	Hal Holbrook, *Mark Twain Tonight!*	Paul Rogers, *The Homecoming*
Sandy Dennis, *Any Wednesday*	Irene Worth, *Tiny Alice*	Rosemary Harris, *The Lion in Winter*	Beryl Reid, *The Killing of Sister George*
Hume Cronyn, *Hamlet*	Jack Albertson, *The Subject Was Roses*	Patrick Magee, *Marat/Sade*	Ian Holm, *The Homecoming*
Barbara Loden, *After the Fall*	Alice Ghostley, *The Sign In Sidney Brustein's Window*	Zoe Caldwell, *Slapstick Tragedy*	Marian Seldes, *A Delicate Balance*
Luther	*The Subject Was Roses*	*Marat/Sade*	*The Homecoming*
Bert Lahr, *Foxy*	Zero Mostel, *Fiddler on the Roof*	Richard Kiley, *Man of La Mancha*	Robert Preston, *I Do! I Do!*
Carol Channing, *Hello, Dolly!*	Liza Minnelli, *Flora, the Red Menace*	Angela Lansbury, *Mame*	Barbara Harris, *The Apple Tree*
Jack Cassidy, *She Loves Me*	Victor Spinetti, *Oh, What a Lovely War!*	Frankie Michaels, *Mame*	Joel Grey, *Cabaret*
Tessie O'Shea, *The Girl Who Came to Supper*	Maria Karnilova, *Fiddler on the Roof*	Beatrice Arthur, *Mame*	Peg Murray, *Cabaret*
Hello, Dolly!	*Fiddler on the Roof*	*Man of La Mancha*	*Cabaret*
Mike Nichols, *Barefoot in the Park*	Mike Nichols, *Luv/The Odd Couple*	Peter Brook, *Marat/Sade*	Peter Hall, *The Homecoming*
Gower Champion, *Hello, Dolly!*	Jerome Robbins, *Fiddler on the Roof*	Albert Marre, *Man of La Mancha*	Harold Prince, *Cabaret*
Jerry Herman, *Hello, Dolly!*	Jerry Bock and Sheldon Harnick, *Fiddler on the Roof*	Mitch Leigh and Joe Darion, *Man of La Mancha*	John Kander and Fred Ebb, *Cabaret*
John Osborne, *Luther*	Neil Simon, *The Odd Couple*	—	—
Michael Stewart, *Hello, Dolly!*	Joseph Stein, *Fiddler on the Roof*	—	—
Oliver Smith, *Hello, Dolly!*	Oliver Smith, *Baker Street/Luv/The Odd Couple*	Howard Bay, *Man of La Mancha*	Boris Aronson, *Cabaret*
Freddy Wittop, *Hello, Dolly!*	Patricia Zipprodt, *Fiddler on the Roof*	Gunilla Palmstierna-Weiss, *Marat/Sade*	Patricia Zipprodt, *Cabaret*
Gower Champion, *Hello, Dolly!*	Jerome Robbins, *Fiddler on the Roof*	Bob Fosse, *Sweet Charity*	Ronald Field, *Cabaret*
Herman Shumlin, *The Deputy*	Claire Nichtern, *Luv*	—	—
David Merrick, *Hello, Dolly!*	Harold Prince, *Fiddler on the Roof*	—	—
Shepard Coleman, *Hello, Dolly!*	—	—	—
—	—	—	—

	1968	1969	1970
Actor (Dramatic)	Martin Balsam, *You Know I Can't Hear You When the Water's Running*	James Earl Jones, *The Great White Hope*	Fritz Weaver, *Child's Play*
Actress (Dramatic)	Zoe Caldwell, *The Prime of Miss Jean Brodie*	Julie Harris, *Forty Carats*	Tammy Grimes, *Private Lives*
Featured/Supporting Actor (Dramatic)	James Patterson, *The Birthday Party*	Al Pacino, *Does a Tiger Wear a Necktie?*	Ken Howard, *Child's Play*
Featured/Supporting Actress (Dramatic)	Zena Walker, *Joe Egg*	Jane Alexander, *The Great White Hope*	Blythe Danner, *Butterflies Are Free*
Play	*Rosencrantz and Guildenstern Are Dead*	*The Great White Hope*	*Borstal Boy*
Actor (Musical)	Robert Goulet, *The Happy Time*	Jerry Orbach, *Promises, Promises*	Cleavon Little, *Purlie*
Actress (Musical)	Leslie Uggams, *Hallelujah, Baby!*; Patricia Routledge, *Darling of the Day*	Angela Lansbury, *Dear World*	Lauren Bacall, *Applause*
Featured/Supporting Actor (Musical)	Hiram Sherman, *How Now, Dow Jones*	Ronald Holgate, *1776*	Rene Auberjonois, *Coco*
Featured/Supporting Actress (Musical)	Lillian Hayman, *Hallelujah, Baby!*	Marian Mercer, *Promises, Promises*	Melba Moore, *Purlie*
Musical	*Hallelujah, Baby!*	*1776*	*Applause*
Director (Dramatic)	Mike Nichols, *Plaza Suite*	Peter Dews, *Hadrian VII*	Joseph Hardy, *Child's Play*
Director (Musical)	Gower Champion, *The Happy Time*	Peter Hunt, *1776*	Ron Field, *Applause*
Book (Musical)	—	—	—
Score	Jule Styne, Betty Comden, and Adolph Green, *Hallelujah, Baby!*	—	—
Scenic Designer	Desmond Heeley, *Rosencrantz and Guildenstern Are Dead*	Boris Aronson, *Zorba*	Howard Bay, *Cry for Us All*; Jo Mielziner, *Child's Play*
Costume Designer	Desmond Heeley, *Rosencrantz and Guildenstern Are Dead*	Louden Sainthill, *Canterbury Tales*	Cecil Beaton, *Coco*
Lighting Designer	—	—	Jo Mielziner, *Child's Play*
Choreographer	Gower Champion, *The Happy Time*	Joe Layton, *George M!*	Ron Field, *Applause*
Producer (Dramatic)	The David Merrick Arts Foundation, *Rosencrantz and Guildenstern Are Dead*	—	—
Producer (Musical)	Albert Selden, Hal James, Jane C. Nusbaum, and Harry Rigby, *Hallelujah, Baby!*	—	—

	1971	1972	1973	1974
1	Brian Bedford, *The School for Wives*	Cliff Gorman, *Lenny*	Alan Bates, *Butley*	Michael Moriarty, *Find Your Way Home*
2	Maureen Stapleton, *The Gingerbread Lady*	Sada Thompson, *Twigs*	Julie Harris, *The Last of Mrs. Lincoln*	Colleen Dewhurst, *A Moon for the Misbegotten*
3	Paul Sand, *Story Theatre*	Vincent Gardenia, *The Prisoner of Second Avenue*	John Lithgow, *The Changing Room*	Ed Flanders, *A Moon for the Misbegotten*
4	Rae Allen, *And Miss Reardon Drinks a Little*	Elizabeth Wilson, *Sticks and Bones*	Leora Dana, *The Last of Mrs. Lincoln*	Frances Sternhagen, *The Good Doctor*
5	*Sleuth*	*Sticks and Bones*	*That Championship Season*	*The River Niger*
6	Hal Linden, *The Rothschilds*	Phil Silvers, *A Funny Thing Happened on the Way to the Forum* (Revival)	Ben Vereen, *Pippin*	Christopher Plummer, *Cyrano*
7	Helen Gallagher, *No, No, Nanette*	Alexis Smith, *Follies*	Glynis Johns, *A Little Night Music*	Virginia Capers, *Raisin*
8	Keene Curtis, *The Rothschilds*	Larry Blyden, *A Funny Thing Happened on the Way to the Forum* (Revival)	George S. Irving, *Irene*	Tommy Tune, *Seesaw*
9	Patsy Kelly, *No, No, Nanette*	Linda Hopkins, *Inner City*	Patricia Elliot, *A Little Night Music*	Janie Sell, *Over Here!*
10	*Company*	*Two Gentlemen of Verona*	*A Little Night Music*	*Raisin*
11	Peter Brook, *Midsummer Night's Dream*	Mike Nichols, *The Prisoner of Second Avenue*	A.J. Antoon, *That Championship Season*	Jose Quintero, *A Moon for the Misbegotten*
12	Harold Prince, *Company*	Harold Prince and Michael Bennett, *Follies*	Bob Fosse, *Pippin*	Harold Prince, *Candide*
13	George Furth, *Company*	John Guare and Mel Shapiro, *Two Gentlemen of Verona*	Hugh Wheeler, *A Little Night Music*	Hugh Wheeler, *Candide*
14	Stephen Sondheim, *Company*	Stephen Sondheim, *Follies*	Stephen Sondheim, *A Little Night Music*	Frederick Loewe (Music); Alan Jay Lerner (Lyrics), *Gigi*
15	Boris Aronson, *Company*	Boris Aronson, *Follies*	Tony Walton, *Pippin*	Franne and Eugene Lee, *Candide*
16	Raoul Pene du Bois, *No, No, Nanette*	Florence Klotz, *Follies*	Florence Klotz, *A Little Night Music*	Franne Lee, *Candide*
17	H.R. Poindexter, *Story Theatre*	Tharon Musser, *Follies*	Jules Fisher, *Pippin*	Jules Fisher, *Ulysses in Nighttown*
18	Donald Saddler, *No, No, Nanette*	Michael Bennett, *Follies*	Bob Fosse, *Pippin*	Michael Bennett, *Seesaw*
19	Helen Bonfils, Morton Gottlieb, and Michael White, *Sleuth*	—	—	—
20	Harold Prince, *Company*	—	—	—

	1975	1976	1977
Actor (Dramatic)	John Kani and Winston Ntshona, *Sizwe Banzi Is Dead & The Island*	John Wood, *Travesties*	Al Pacino, *The Basic Training of Pavlo Hummel*
Actress (Dramatic)	Ellen Burstyn, *Same Time, Next Year*	Irene Worth, *Sweet Bird of Youth*	Julie Harris, *The Belle of Amherst*
Featured Actor (Dramatic)	Frank Langella, *Seascape*	Edward Herrmann, *Mrs. Warren's Profession*	Jonathan Pryce, *Comedians*
Featured Actress (Dramatic)	Rita Moreno, *The Ritz*	Shirley Knight, *Kennedy's Children*	Trazana Beverley, *For Colored Girls Who Have Considered Suicide/When the Rainbow Is Enuf*
Play	*Equus*	*Travesties*	*The Shadow Box*
Actor (Musical)	John Cullum, *Shenandoah*	George Rose, *My Fair Lady*	Barry Bostwick, *The Robber Bridegroom*
Actress (Musical)	Angela Lansbury, *Gypsy*	Donna McKechnie, *A Chorus Line*	Dorothy Loudon, *Annie*
Featured Actor (Musical)	Ted Ross, *The Wiz*	Sammy Williams, *A Chorus Line*	Lenny Baker, *I Love My Wife*
Featured Actress (Musical)	Dee Dee Bridgewater, *The Wiz*	Carole Bishop, *A Chorus Line*	Delores Hall, *Your Arms Too Short To Box with God*
Musical	*The Wiz*	*A Chorus Line*	*Annie*
Director (Dramatic)	John Dexter, *Equus*	Ellis Rabb, *The Royal Family*	Gordon Davidson, *The Shadow Box*
Director (Musical)	Geoffrey Holder, *The Wiz*	Michael Bennett, *A Chorus Line*	Gene Saks, *I Love My Wife*
Book (Musical)	James Lee Barrett, *Shenandoah*	James Kirkwood and Nicholas Dante, *A Chorus Line*	Thomas Meehan, *Annie*
Score	Charlie Smalls (Music & Lyrics), *The Wiz*	Marvin Hamlisch (Music); Edward Kleban (Lyrics), *A Chorus Line*	Charles Strouse (Music); Martin Charnin (Lyrics), *Annie*
Scenic Designer	Carl Toms, *Sherlock Holmes*	Boris Aronson, *Pacific Overtures*	David Mitchell, *Annie*
Costume Designer	Geoffrey Holder, *The Wiz*	Florence Klotz, *Pacific Overtures*	Theoni V. Aldredge, *Annie;* Santo Loquasto, *The Cherry Orchard*
Lighting Designer	Neil Patrick Jampolis, *Sherlock Holmes*	Tharon Musser, *A Chorus Line*	Jennifer Tipton, *The Cherry Orchard*
Choreographer	George Faison, *The Wiz*	Michael Bennett and Bob Avian, *A Chorus Line*	Peter Gennaro, *Annie*
Reproduction of a Play or Musical	—	—	*Porgy and Bess*

1978	1979	1980	1981
Barnard Hughes, *Da*	Tom Conti, *Whose Life Is It Anyway?*	John Rubinstein, *Children of a Lesser God*	Ian McKellen, *Amadeus*
Jessica Tandy, *The Gin Game*	Constance Cummings, *Wings;* Carole Shelley, *The Elephant Man*	Phyllis Frelich, *Children of a Lesser God*	Jane Lapotaire, *Piaf*
Lester Rawlins, *Da*	Michael Gough, *Bedroom Farce*	David Rounds, *Morning's at Seven*	Brian Backer, *The Floating Light Bulb*
Ann Wedgeworth, *Chapter Two*	Joan Hickson, *Bedroom Farce*	Dinah Manoff, *I Ought To Be in Pictures*	Swoosie Kurtz, *Fifth of July*
Da	*The Elephant Man*	*Children of a Lesser God*	*Amadeus*
John Cullum, *On the Twentieth Century*	Len Cariou, *Sweeney Todd*	Jim Dale, *Barnum*	Kevin Kline, *The Pirates of Penzance*
Liza Minnelli, *The Act*	Angela Lansbury, *Sweeney Todd*	Patti LuPone, *Evita*	Lauren Bacall, *Woman of the Year*
Kevin Kline, *On the Twentieth Century*	Henderson Forsythe, *The Best Little Whorehouse in Texas*	Mandy Patinkin, *Evita*	Hinton Battle, *Sophisticated Ladies*
Nell Carter, *Ain't Misbehavin'*	Carlin Glynn, *The Best Little Whorehouse in Texas*	Priscilla Lopez, *A Day in Hollywood, a Night in the Ukraine*	Marilyn Cooper, *Woman of the Year*
Ain't Misbehavin'	*Sweeney Todd*	*Evita*	*42nd Street*
Melvin Bernhardt, *Da*	Jack Hofsiss, *The Elephant Man*	Vivian Matalon, *Morning's at Seven*	Peter Hall, *Amadeus*
Richard Maltby Jr., *Ain't Misbehavin'*	Harold Prince, *Sweeney Todd*	Harold Prince, *Evita*	Wilford Leach, *The Pirates of Penzance*
Betty Comden and Adolph Green, *On the Twentieth Century*	Hugh Wheeler, *Sweeney Todd*	Tim Rice, *Evita*	Peter Stone, *Woman of the Year*
Cy Coleman (Music); Betty Comden and Adolph Green (Lyrics), *On the Twentieth Century*	Stephen Sondheim (Music & Lyrics), *Sweeney Todd*	Andrew Lloyd Webber (Music); Tim Rice (Lyrics), *Evita*	John Kander (Music); Fred Ebb (Lyrics), *Woman of the Year*
Robin Wagner, *On the Twentieth Century*	Eugene Lee, *Sweeney Todd*	John Lee Beatty, *Talley's Folly*; David Mitchell, *Barnum*	John Bury, *Amadeus*
Edward Gorey, *Dracula*	Franne Lee, *Sweeney Todd*	Theoni V. Aldredge, *Barnum*	Willa Kim, *Sophisticated Ladies*
Jules Fisher, *Dancin'*	Roger Morgan, *The Crucifer of Blood*	David Hersey, *Evita*	John Bury, *Amadeus*
Bob Fosse, *Dancin'*	Michael Bennett and Bob Avian, *Ballroom*	Tommy Tune and Thommie Walsh, *A Day in Hollywood, a Night in the Ukraine*	Gower Champion, *42nd Street*
Dracula	—	Elizabeth I. McCann, Nelle Nugent, Ray Larsen, producers, *Morning's at Seven*	Joseph Papp, producer, *The Pirates of Penzance*

	1982	1983	1984
Actor (Dramatic)	Roger Rees, *The Life and Adventures of Nicholas Nickleby*	Harvey Fierstein, *Torch Song Trilogy*	Jeremy Irons, *The Real Thing*
Actress (Dramatic)	Zoe Caldwell, *Medea*	Jessica Tandy, *Foxfire*	Glenn Close, *The Real Thing*
Featured Actor (Dramatic)	Zakes Mokae, "*Master Harold"...and the Boys*	Matthew Broderick, *Brighton Beach Memoirs*	Joe Mantegna, *Glengarry Glen Ross*
Featured Actress (Dramatic)	Amanda Plummer, *Agnes of God*	Judith Ivey, *Steaming*	Christine Baranski, *The Real Thing*
Play	*The Life and Adventures of Nicholas Nickleby*	*Torch Song Trilogy*	*The Real Thing*
Actor (Musical)	Ben Harney, *Dreamgirls*	Tommy Tune, *My One and Only*	George Hearn, *La Cage Aux Folles*
Actress (Musical)	Jennifer Holliday, *Dreamgirls*	Natalia Makarova, *On Your Toes*	Chita Rivera, *The Rink*
Featured Actor (Musical)	Cleavant Derricks, *Dreamgirls*	Charles "Honi" Coles, *My One and Only*	Hinton Battle, *The Tap Dance Kid*
Featured Actress (Musical)	Liliane Montevecchi, *"Nine"*	Betty Buckley, *Cats*	Lila Kedrova, *Zorba*
Musical	*"Nine"*	*Cats*	*La Cage aux folles*
Director (Dramatic)	Trevor Nunn and John Caird, *The Life and Adventures of Nicholas Nickleby*	Gene Saks, *Brighton Beach Memoirs*	Mike Nichols, *The Real Thing*
Director (Musical)	Tommy Tune, *"Nine"*	Trevor Nunn, *Cats*	Arthur Laurents, *La Cage aux folles*
Book (Musical)	Tom Eyen, *Dreamgirls*	T. S. Eliot, *Cats*	Harvey Fierstein, *La Cage aux folles*
Score	Maury Yeton (Music & Lyrics), *"Nine"*	Andrew Lloyd Webber (Music); T. S. Eliot (Lyrics), *Cats*	Jerry Herman (Music & Lyrics), *La Cage aux folles*
Scenic Designer	John Napier and Dermot Hayes, *The Life and Adventures of Nicholas Nickleby*	Ming Cho Lee, *K2*	Tony Straiges, *Sunday in the Park with George*
Costume Designer	William Ivey Long, *"Nine"*	John Napier, *Cats*	Theoni V. Aldredge, *La Cage aux folles*
Lighting Designer	Tharon Musser, *Dreamgirls*	David Hersey, *Cats*	Richard Nelson, *Sunday in the Park with George*
Choreographer	Michael Bennett and Michael Peters, *Dreamgirls*	Thommie Walsh and Tommy Tune, *My One and Only*	Danny Daniels, *The Tap Dance Kid*
Reproduction of a Play or Musical	Barry and Fran Weissler, CBS Video Enterprises, Don Gregory, producers, *Othello*	Alfred De Liagre Jr., Roger L. Stevens, John Mauceri, Donald R. Seawell, Andre Pastoria, producers, *On Your Toes*	Robert Whitehead, Roger L. Stevens, producers, *Death of a Salesman*

1985	1986	1987	1988
Derek Jacobi, *Much Ado About Nothing*	Judd Hirsch, *I'm Not Rappaport*	James Earl Jones, *Fences*	Ron Silver, *Speed-the-Plow*
Stockard Channing, *Joe Egg*	Lily Tomlin, *The Search for Signs of Intelligent Life in the Universe*	Linda Lavin, *Broadway Bound*	Joan Allen, *Burn This*
Barry Miller, *Biloxi Blues*	John Mahoney, *The House of Blue Leaves*	John Randolph, *Broadway Bound*	B. D. Wong, *M. Butterfly*
Judith Ivey, *Hurlyburly*	Swoosie Kurtz, *The House of Blue Leaves*	Mary Alice, *Fences*	L. Scott Caldwell, *Joe Turner's Come and Gone*
Biloxi Blues	*I'm Not Rappaport*	*Fences*	*M. Butterfly*
—	George Rose, *The Mystery of Edwin Drood*	Robert Lindsay, *Me and My Girl*	Michael Crawford, *The Phantom of the Opera*
—	Bernadette Peters, *Song & Dance*	Maryann Plunkett, *Me and My Girl*	Joanna Gleason, *Into the Woods*
Ron Richardson, *Big River*	Michael Rupert, *Sweet Charity*	Michael Maguire, *Les Misérables*	Bill McCutcheon, *Anything Goes*
Leilani Jones, *Grind*	Bebe Neuwirth, *Sweet Charity*	Frances Ruffelle, *Les Misérables*	Judy Kaye, *The Phantom of the Opera*
Big River	*The Mystery of Edwin Drood*	*Les Misérables*	*The Phantom of the Opera*
Gene Saks, *Biloxi Blues*	Jerry Zaks, *The House of Blue Leaves*	Lloyd Richards, *Fences*	John Dexter, *M. Butterfly*
Des McAnuff, *Big River*	Wilford Leach, *The Mystery of Edwin Drood*	Trevor Nunn and John Caird, *Les Misérables*	Harold Prince, *The Phantom of the Opera*
William Hauptman, *Big River*	Rupert Holmes, *The Mystery of Edwin Drood*	Alain Boublil and Claude-Michel Schönberg, *Les Misérables*	James Lapine, *Into the Woods*
Roger Miller (Music & Lyrics), *Big River*	Rupert Holmes (Music & Lyrics), *The Mystery of Edwin Drood*	Claude-Michel Schönberg (Music); Herbert Kretzmer, and Alain Boublil (Lyrics), *Les Misérables*	Stephen Sondheim (Music & Lyrics), *Into the Woods*
Heidi Landesman, *Big River*	Tony Walton, *The House of Blue Leaves*	John Napier, *Les Misérables*	Maria Bjornson, *The Phantom of the Opera*
Florence Klotz, *Grind*	Patricia Zipprodt, *Sweet Charity*	John Napier, *Starlight Express*	Maria Björnson, *The Phantom of the Opera*
Richard Riddell, *Big River*	Pat Collins, *I'm Not Rappaport*	David Hersey, *Starlight Express*	Andrew Bridge, *The Phantom of the Opera*
—	Bob Fosse, *Big Deal*	Gillian Gregory, *Me and My Girl*	Michael Smuin, *Anything Goes*
The Shubert Organization, Emanuel Azenberg, Roger Berlind, Ivan Bloch, MTM Enterprises, Inc., producers, *Joe Egg*	Jerome Minskoff, James M. Nederlander, Arthur Rubin, Joseph Harris, producers, *Sweet Charity*	Jay H. Fuchs, Steven Warnick, Charles Patsos, producers, *All My Sons*	Lincoln Center Theater, Gregory Mosher, Bernard Gersten, producers, *Anything Goes*

	1989	1990	1991
Actor (Dramatic)	Philip Bosco, *Lend Me a Tenor*	Robert Morse, *Tru*	Nigel Hawthorne, *Shadowlands*
Actress (Dramatic)	Pauline Collins, *Shirley Valentine*	Maggie Smith, *Lettice & Lovage*	Mercedes Ruehl, *Lost in Yonkers*
Featured Actor (Dramatic)	Boyd Gaines, *The Heidi Chronicles*	Charles Durning, *Cat on a Hot Tin Roof*	Kevin Spacey, *Lost in Yonkers*
Featured Actress (Dramatic)	Christine Baranski, *Rumors*	Margaret Tyzack, *Lettice & Lovage*	Irene Worth, *Lost in Yonkers*
Play	*The Heidi Chronicles*	*The Grapes of Wrath*	*Lost in Yonkers*
Actor (Musical)	Jason Alexander, *Jerome Robbins' Broadway*	James Naughton, *City of Angels*	Jonathan Pryce, *Miss Saigon*
Actress (Musical)	Ruth Brown, *Black and Blue*	Tyne Daly, *Gypsy*	Lea Salonga, *Miss Saigon*
Featured Actor (Musical)	Scott Wise, *Jerome Robbins' Broadway*	Michael Jeter, *Grand Hotel, the Musical*	Hinton Battle, *Miss Saigon*
Featured Actress (Musical)	Debbie Shapiro, *Jerome Robbins' Broadway*	Randy Graff, *City of Angels*	Daisy Eagan, *The Secret Garden*
Musical	*Jerome Robbins' Broadway*	*City of Angels*	*The Will Rogers Follies*
Director (Dramatic)	Jerry Zaks, *Lend Me a Tenor*	Frank Galati, *The Grapes of Wrath*	Jerry Zaks, *Six Degrees of Separation*
Director (Musical)	Jerome Robbins, *Jerome Robbins' Broadway*	Tommy Tune, *Grand Hotel, the Musical*	Tommy Tune, *The Will Rogers Follies*
Book (Musical)	—	Larry Gelbart, *City of Angels*	Marsha Norman, *The Secret Garden*
Score	—	Cy Coleman (Music); David Zippel (Lyrics), *City of Angels*	Cy Coleman (Music); Betty Comden and Adolph Green (Lyrics), *The Will Rogers Follies*
Scenic Designer	Santo Loquasto, *Cafe Crown*	Robin Wagner, *City of Angels*	Heidi Landesman, *The Secret Garden*
Costume Designer	Claudio Segovia, Hector Orezzoli, *Black and Blue*	Santo Loquasto, *Grand Hotel, the Musical*	Willa Kim, *The Will Rogers Follies*
Lighting Design	Jennifer Tipton, *Jerome Robbins' Broadway*	Jules Fisher, *Grand Hotel, the Musical*	Jules Fisher, *The Will Rogers Follies*
Choreographer	Cholly Atkins, Henry LeTang, Frankie Manning, Fayard Nicholas, *Black and Blue*	Tommy Tune, *Grand Hotel, the Musical*	Tommy Tune, *The Will Rogers Follies*
Reproduction of a Play or Musical	Lincoln Center Theater, Gregory Mosher, Bernard Gersten, producers, *Our Town*	Barry and Fran Weissler, Kathy Levin, Barry Brown, producers, *Gypsy*	Barry and Fran Weissler, Pace Theatrical Group, *Fiddler on the Roof*

1992	1993	1994	1995
Judd Hirsch, *Conversations with My Father*	Ron Leibman, *Angels in America: Millennium Approaches*	Stephen Spinella, *Angels in America: Perestroika*	Ralph Fiennes, *Hamlet*
Glenn Close, *Death and the Maiden*	Madeline Kahn, *The Sisters Rosensweig*	Diana Rigg, *Medea*	Cherry Jones, *The Heiress*
Larry Fishburne, *Two Trains Running*	Stephen Spinella, *Angels in America: Millennium Approaches*	Jeffrey Wright, *Angels in America: Perestroika*	John Glover, *Love! Valour! Compassion!*
Brid Brennan, *Dancing at Lughnasa*	Debra Monk, *Redwood Curtain*	Jane Adams, *An Inspector Calls*	Frances Sternhagen, *The Heiress*
Dancing at Lughnasa	*Angels in America: Millennium Approaches*	*Angels in America: Perestroika*	*Love! Valour! Compassion!*
Gregory Hines, *Jelly's Last Jam*	Brent Carver, *Kiss of the Spider Woman—The Musical*	Boyd Gaines, *She Loves Me*	Matthew Broderick, *How to Succeed in Business Without Really Trying*
Faith Prince, *Guys and Dolls*	Chita Rivera, *Kiss of the Spider Woman—The Musical*	Donna Murphy, *Passion*	Glenn Close, *Sunset Boulevard*
Scott Waara, *The Most Happy Fella*	Anthony Crivello, *Kiss of the Spider Woman—The Musical*	Jarrod Emick, *Damn Yankees*	George Hearn, *Sunset Boulevard*
Tonya Pinkins, *Jelly's Last Jam*	Andrea Martin, *My Favorite Year*	Audra Ann McDonald, *Carousel*	Gretha Boston, *Show Boat*
Crazy for You	*Kiss of the Spider Woman—The Musical*	*Passion*	*Sunset Boulevard*
Patrick Mason, *Dancing at Lughnasa*	George C. Wolfe, *Angels in America: Millennium Approaches*	Stephen Daldry, *An Inspector Calls*	Gerald Gutierrez, *The Heiress*
Jerry Zaks, *Guys and Dolls*	Des McAnuff, *The Who's Tommy*	Nicholas Hynter, *Carousel*	Harold Prince, *Show Boat*
William Finn and James Lapine, *Falsettos*	Terrence McNally, *Kiss of the Spider Woman—The Musical*	James Lapine, *Passion*	Christopher Hampton and Don Black, *Sunset Boulevard*
William Finn, *Falsettos*	John Kander (Music), Fred Ebb (Lyrics), *Kiss of the Spider Woman—The Musical;* Pete Townshend (Music and Lyrics), *The Who's Tommy*	Stephen Sondheim, *Passion*	Andrew Lloyd Webber (music), Christopher Hampton and Don Black (lyrics) *Sunset Boulevard*
Tony Walton, *Guys and Dolls*	John Arnone, *The Who's Tommy*	Bob Crowley, *Carousel*	John Napier, *Sunset Boulevard*
William Ivey Long, *Crazy for You*	Florence Klotz, *Kiss of the Spider Woman—The Musical*	Ann Hould-Ward, *Beauty and the Beast*	Florence Klotz, *Show Boat*
Jules Fisher, *Jelly's Last Jam*	Chris Parry, *The Who's Tommy*	Rick Fisher, *An Inspector Calls*	Andrew Bridge, *Sunset Boulevard*
Susan Stroman, *Crazy for You*	Wayne Cilento, *The Who's Tommy*	Kenneth McMillan, *Carousel*	Susan Stroman, *Show Boat*
Dodger Productions, Roger Berlind, Jujamcyn Theaters/TV Asahi, Kardana Productions, John F. Kennedy Center for the Performing Arts, *Guys and Dolls*	Roundabout Theatre Company and Todd Haimes, *Anna Christie*	Noel Pearson, the Shubert Organization, Capital Cities/ABC, Joseph Harris, *An Inspector Calls* (Dramatic); Lincoln Center Theater, Andre Bishop, Bernard Gersten, the Royal National Theater, Cameron Mackintosh, the Rodgers & Hammerstein Organization, *Carousel* (Musical)	Lincoln Center Theater, Andre Bishop, Bernard Gersten, *The Heiress* (Dramatic); Livent (U.S.) Inc., *Show Boat* (Musical)

	1996	1997
Actor (Dramatic)	George Grizzard, *A Delicate Balance*	Christopher Plummer, *Barrymore*
Actress (Dramatic)	Zoe Caldwell, *Master Class*	Janet McTeer, *A Doll's House*
Featured Actor (Dramatic)	Ruben Santiago-Hudson, *Seven Guitars*	Owen Teale, *A Doll's House*
Featured Actress (Dramatic)	Audra McDonald, *Master Class*	Lynne Thigpen, *An American Daughter*
Play	*Master Class*	*The Last Night of Ballyhoo*
Actor (Musical)	Nathan Lane, *A Funny Thing Happened on the Way to the Forum*	James Naughton, *Chicago*
Actress (Musical)	Donna Murphy, *Passion*	Bebe Neuwirth, *Chicago*
Featured Actor (Musical)	Wilson Jermain Heredia, *Rent*	Chuck Cooper, *The Life*
Featured Actress (Musical)	Ann Duquesnay, *Bring in 'Da Noise, Bring in 'Da Funk*	Lillias White, *The Life*
Musical	*Rent*	*Titanic*
Director (Dramatic)	Gerald Gutierrez, *A Delicate Balance*	Anthony Page, *A Doll's House*
Director (Musical)	George C. Wolfe, *Bring in 'Da Noise, Bring in 'Da Funk*	Walter Bobbie, *Chicago*
Book (Musical)	Jonathan Larson, *Rent*	Peter Stone, *Titanic*
Score	Jonathan Larson, *Rent*	Maury Yeston, *Titanic*
Scenic Designer	Brian Thomson, *The King and I*	Stewart Laing, *Titanic*
Costume Designer	Roger Kirk, *The King and I*	Judith Dolan, *Candide*
Lighting Designer	Jules Fisher and Peggy Eisenhauer, *Bring in 'Da Noise, Bring in 'Da Funk*	Ken Billington, *Chicago*
Choreographer	Savion Glover, *Bring in 'Da Noise, Bring in 'Da Funk*	Ann Reinking, *Chicago*
Reproduction of a Play or Musical	Lincoln Center Theater, *A Delicate Balance* (Dramatic); Dodger Productions, the John F. Kennedy Center for the Performing Arts, James M. Nederlander, Perseus Productions, John Frost, The Adelaide Festival Center, the Rodgers and Hammerstein Organization, *The King and I* (Musical)	Bill Kenwright, Thelma Holt, *A Doll's House* (Dramatic); Barry Weissler, Fran Weissler, Kardana Productions Inc., *Chicago* (Musical)

TIMELINE

A POP CULTURE TIMELINE OF THE 20TH CENTURY

Here is a selective chronicle of the events and inventions, milestones and hallmarks, people and productions that have entertained us and changed life in our century.

1900

THE BROWNIE BOX CAMERA, the first consumer-oriented camera, is introduced by Eastman Kodak. It sells for $1.

PHILOSOPHER FRIEDRICH NIETZSCHE dies after 11 years of madness.

THE HOT DANCE around the nation is the cake walk, invented by African Americans in the late 18th century.

STAGE ACTRESS SARAH BERNHARDT, 56, makes her film debut in *Hamlet's Duel.* She plays Hamlet.

BOOKER T. WASHINGTON publishes his autobiography, *Up from Slavery.*

FERDINAND VON ZEPPELIN'S famous airship makes its first flight on July 20.

Sarah Bernhardt.

1901

VICTORIA, Queen of England and Ireland, and Empress of India, dies on January 22 at age 82, marking the end of the Victorian Era.

THE VICTOR TALKING MACHINE COMPANY is formed by Emile Berliner and Eldridge Johnson. "His Master's Voice" is the registered trademark for their gramophones, called Victrolas.

1902

BEATRIX POTTER creates the first of her legendary Peter Rabbit children's stories.

1903

THE GREAT TRAIN ROBBERY, starring Max Anderson, is released, marking the debut of the first male movie star.

THE WORLD SERIES is launched, pitting the winners of the National and the American Leagues against each other: this year, the Boston Red Stockings triumph over the Pittsburgh Pirates.

ORVILLE AND WILBUR WRIGHT fly the first powered, heavier-than-air airplane at Kitty Hawk, N.C., on December 17.

1904

HELEN KELLER graduates with honors from Radcliffe, thanks to years of devoted assistance from Anne Sullivan, who will go down in history as the Miracle Worker.

FREUD introduces the idea of neuroses in *The Psychopathology of Everyday Life,* his first major work on psychoanalysis.

THE TEDDY BEAR makes its debut. Created by the German Richard Sterb, it is inspired by President Theodore Roosevelt, who refused to kill a bear cub on a hunting trip.

1905

THE WORLD'S FIRST all-motion picture theater opens in Pittsburgh. The cost is 10¢ for a showing of *Poor But Honest.*

ALBERT EINSTEIN publishes his theory of the photoelectric effect, which is later essential in the development of the TV camera.

1906

Jelly Roll Morton at the piano.

FERDINAND "JELLY ROLL" MORTON, jazz's first great composer, writes "The King Porter Stomp."

THE SAN FRANCISCO EARTHQUAKE kills hundreds on April 18 and causes hundreds of millions of dollars in damage throughout the Bay Area as the city crashes and burns.

UPTON SINCLAIR publishes *The Jungle*, his exposé of the meat-packing industry, which prompts Congress to pass labor reform laws in addition to the Pure Food and Drug Act and the Meat Packing Act of 1906.

1907

FLORENZ ZIEGFELD offers his first version of the *Ziegfeld Follies*, an extravaganza that will continue for 24 years.

HENRY ADAMS'S masterful autobiography, *The Education of Henry Adams*, is published privately; the Nobel Prize for Biography will be awarded to Adams posthumously in 1919.

COLOR PHOTOGRAPHY becomes practical for the first time due to the development of a new method by the brothers Auguste and Louis Lumière.

THE FIRST MOTION PICTURE with both sound and color is shown in Cleveland.

THE RINGLING BROTHERS buy out their archrivals, Barnum and Bailey, although the two circuses will be operated separately until 1919.

1908

A L'ECU D'OR becomes the earliest dated pornographic film.

THE FIRST MODEL T, known as the Tin Lizzy, is produced on October 1 at Ford's Detroit plant.

THE FIRST COMMERCIAL COLOR FILM, G. A. Smith's *A Visit to the Seaside* (Britain), is released.

1909

ROLLER COASTERS become increasingly popular in amusement parks all over the country.

VITAGRAPH'S *Les Misérables* becomes the first feature film produced in the United States.

THE FIRST ANIMATED CARTOON, *Gertie the Dinosaur*, is released.

ROBERT EDWIN PEARY becomes the first person ever to reach the North Pole.

1910

AUTHOR MARK TWAIN (Samuel Longhorne Clemens) dies at 74.

Mark Twain.

THOMAS EDISON demonstrates his "kinetophone," which successfully displays talking motion pictures.

THE BOY SCOUTS OF AMERICA is founded by William D. Boyce, who takes his inspiration from the English program started by Sir Robert Baden-Powell.

T. S. ELIOT writes *Love Song of J. Alfred Prufrock* while a Harvard undergraduate; it becomes one of the seminal works of the Modernist movement when it is published in 1915.

1911

JEAN, Larry Trimble's pet collie, becomes the first canine star on the big screen. Hired by Vitagraph, she earns $10 more per week than Trimble earns as an actor-writer.

IRVING BERLIN writes "Alexander's Ragtime Band," melding the rhythms of black ragtime into American popular music.

1912

SEIZING ON A CRAZE that has millions of Americans doing the tango, the turkey trot, the hesitation waltz, and the one-step, Victor releases a series of recordings intended for dancing.

THE *TITANIC* sinks after hitting an iceberg on April 14, drowning 1,595 people.

ZANE GREY publishes his most famous Western, *Riders of the Purple Sage*.

THE FIRST BLUES SONG is published by W. C. Handy. Originally called "Memphis Blues," it becomes a hit as "Mr. Crump."

PERHAPS THE BEST ALL-AROUND ATHLETE in history, Native American track-and-field star Jim Thorpe dominates the Olympics, winning gold medals for both the pentathlon and the decathlon. But his medals are taken away from him when it is discovered that he played semi-pro baseball two years before.

STUNT FLYING becomes a staple across the country, taking a terrible toll on pioneering aviators.

1913

DUKE ELLINGTON writes his first song, "Soda Fountain Rag," at the age of 14.

BILLBOARD magazine publishes its first song-popularity chart by listing leading songs in vaudeville as well as bestselling sheet music.

THE FIRST CROSSWORD puzzle is published in the *New York World*.

1914

CHARLIE CHAPLIN creates the legendary Little Tramp in his second film, *Kid's Auto Races*.

BERT WILLIAMS, a popular vaudevillian, stars in *Darktown Jubilee*, one of the first movies to use an African American actor rather than white actors in blackface. The movie causes a riot in Brooklyn, N.Y.

THE TARZAN SAGA begins with the publication of *Tarzan of the Apes* by Edgar Rice Burroughs.

ASCAP—the American Society of Composers, Authors, and Publishers—is formed to empower artists to collect fees for the performances and use of their work.

THE PANAMA CANAL opens on May 18.

WORLD WAR I breaks out on July 28. One of the many consequences is that movie production outside of the United States will be suspended, allowing American filmmakers to dominate the industry.

1915

ALBERT EINSTEIN proposes the General Theory of Relativity.

AUDREY MUNSON reveals all as she becomes the first leading lady to appear on the screen nude in *Inspiration*.

MARGARET SANGER is jailed for writing about birth control in her book *Family Limitation*.

THE MOST FAMOUS MOVIE of the silent era, D. W. Griffith's *The Birth of a Nation*, opens in New York City to great success, but is bitterly criticized for its racism.

THE DIVINE Sarah Bernhardt finally faces what appears to be the end of her stage career when her leg is amputated at the age of 71; the next year, however, she stages what proves at last to be her final one-for-the-road, this time playing Portia in *The Merchant of Venice* with an artificial leg.

THE PROVINCETOWN PLAYERS are organized in Massachusetts and become the first to present the works of playwright Eugene O'Neill. The next year the group moves its already highly influential theater to New York where it begins the off-Broadway theater movement.

USING VACUUM TUBES, AT&T introduces long-distance service between New York and San Francisco.

THE MOVIE BUSINESS takes root in Hollywood, California, land of good weather and cheap labor. By 1915, half of all American films are made there.

1916

NOTORIOUS SIBERIAN MONK GRIGORY RASPUTIN is murdered. Rasputin had been a confidant and

Grigory Rasputin.

advisor to the Czarina after using his hypnotic powers to "cure" the Empress's heir, Alexis, of hemophilia.

TWO VERY DIFFERENT major American writers die—action-adventure writer Jack London, author of *Call of the Wild*, and expatriate novelist Henry James, author of *Portrait of a Lady*.

THE DADA MOVEMENT is founded in Zurich as an anti-art, anti-literature protest against the atrocities of the Great War.

1917

"THE DIXIE JAZZ BAND ONE-STEP" by Nick LaRocca's Original Dixieland Jazz Band, a group of white musicians, is the first jazz record to be released in the United States.

MATA HARI, a Dutch dancer, is executed by the French as a spy for Germany.

THE FIRST PULITZER PRIZES are awarded, in the categories of biography, history, and journalism. The award for drama is added the following year.

1918

PRESIDENT WOODROW WILSON proclaims his Fourteen Points for world peace; World War I comes to an end on November 11.

DAYLIGHT SAVINGS TIME is introduced in America.

1919

JACK DEMPSEY, known as the Manassa Mauler, wins the world heavyweight boxing championship.

Mata Hari.

1920

PROHIBITION begins with the enactment of the Eighteenth Amendment, which makes it illegal to produce, sell, or drink alcoholic beverages.

HERCULE POIROT is introduced in Agatha Christie's first novel, *The Mysterious Affair at Styles.*

MAMIE SMITH becomes the first African-American singer to record a vocal blues performance with "Crazy Blues."

THE NATION'S FIRST RADIO stations—KDKA, Pittsburgh and WWJ, Detroit—hit the airwaves.

1921

THE FIRST MISS AMERICA pageant is held on September 9, won by Margaret Gorman, Miss Washington, D.C.

READER'S DIGEST begins publication.

1922

THE FIRST 3-D feature film is released when Nat Deverich creates *Power of Love*.

NANOOK OF THE NORTH by Robert J. Flaherty is released and comes to be regarded as one of the greatest documentaries ever filmed.

THE TECHNICOLOR film process makes its initial successful run.

JAMES JOYCE'S *Ulysses* is published in Paris by the expatriate American Sylvia Beach; though one of the greatest novels of the century, it remains banned in the United States until December 6, 1933, when a judge rules that the book does not contain "the leer of a sensualist."

1923

LEE DEFOREST devises a method of recording sound directly on film. Producers utilize the technology to create vaudevills shorts.

THE COVERED WAGON, the first of the great Western epics, is released to huge success.

TIME magazine begins publication, providing the news in a flavorful, succinct format.

1924

STAGE LEGENDS Alfred Lunt and Lynn Fontanne first appear together as a team in a play called *The Guardsman.*

THE FIRST MILLION-SELLERS in America are instrumentals: Paul Whiteman's *Whispering* and Ben Selvin's *Dardanella*.

NATHAN LEOPOLD and Richard Loeb are tried for the "thrill killing" of 14-year-old Robert Franks; Clarence Darrow's pioneering insanity plea saves them from execution.

THE LITTLE ORPHAN ANNIE comic strip is created by Harold Gray.

1925

THE FIRST national spelling bee is held.

THE AGE OF THE CHARLESTON bounces into dancehalls across America.

THE NEW YORKER is founded on February 21, edited by Harold Ross. The first issue bears the image of Eustace Tilley, who will come to serve as the magazine's unofficial symbol and patriarch.

THE WSM BARN DANCE—renamed the *Grand Ole Opry* in 1928—premieres in November.

THE CLASSIC NOVEL of the Jazz Age, *The Great Gatsby* by F. Scott Fitzgerald, is published.

1926

TELEVISION is invented in Scotland by John Logie Baird, but the Depression and World War II stifle development of the industry until the '50s.

DEFORD BAILEY is the first African American musician to appear on Nashville's *Grand Ole Opry* show. He becomes nationally known as "The Harmonica Wizard," and remains a regular until 1941.

RUDOLPH VALENTINO, the most popular of all male silent film

Rudolph Valentino.

stars and a worldwide sex symbol, dies at age 31 of a ruptured appendix and a gastric ulcer.

NBC RADIO is founded.

NEW YORK talks to London in the first successful transatlantic radiotelephone conversation.

Mae West.

MAE WEST writes and stars in a play called *Sex*; the performance that launches her career as the greatest sex symbol of the era also inspires the police to close the show and sentence West to 10 days in a workhouse.

THE BOOK-OF-THE-MONTH CLUB is founded, the first of the mail-order book programs. The first offering is Sylvia Townsend Warner's novel, *Lolly Willowes.*

MINIATURE GOLF is introduced in Lookout Mountain, Tenn., and from there it expands to over 40,000 courses within three years.

THE SUN ALSO RISES, the classic novel of disillusionment in the postwar years, is written by Ernest Hemingway.

1927

THE AGE OF THE TALKIES arrives with the Warner Bros. release of the wildly successful film *The Jazz Singer*, starring Al Jolson.

THE FIRST CAR RADIOS are introduced.

Charles Lindbergh and his famous plane.

CHARLES LINDBERGH makes the first nonstop solo flight across the Atlantic, from New York to Paris.

1928

TELEVISION comes to a home in Schenectady, N.Y., and begins receiving regularly scheduled broadcasts, three afternoons a week, on its one and one-half-inch screen.

WOMEN COMPETE in the Olympics (in Amsterdam) for the first time.

AMELIA EARHART becomes the first woman to fly across the Atlantic Ocean when she lands in London.

MICKEY MOUSE debuts in Walt Disney's first cartoon, *Plane Crazy*. The public however, first meets him in *Steamboat Willie,* which is released before its progenitor.

1929

THE FIRST ACADEMY AWARDS are presented at the Hollywood Roosevelt Hotel in Los Angeles, May 16. Douglas Fairbanks Sr. presents all of the awards in five minutes. The first winner for Best Picture is the now-forgotten Clara Bow vehicle, *Wings*.

VIRGINIA WOOLF publishes her feminist classic, *A Room of One's Own.*

CBS (Columbia Broadcasting System) is founded by William S. Paley, age 27.

THE MUSEUM OF MODERN ART (MOMA) opens in New York with an exhibition of works by Cezanne, Gaugin, Seurat, and Van Gogh.

ON BLACK THURSDAY, October 24, the stock market crashes, abruptly beginning the transition from the Roaring Twenties to the Great Depression.

KODAK introduces 16mm color movie film.

1930

SINCLAIR LEWIS becomes the first American to win the Nobel Prize for Literature.

THE FIRST SUPERMARKET opens in Queens, N.Y., offering low prices, and a huge selection; it achieves tremendous success overnight.

THE HAYS OFFICE creates a production code to enforce self-censorship in the film business.

Garbo poses.

GRANT WOOD paints *American Gothic.*

GARBO TALKS, in Eugene O'Neill's *Anna Christie*, her first speaking role.

1931

THE WORLD'S TALLEST BUILDING, the Empire State Building, is opened to the public. RCA and NBC install a TV transmitter atop the building.

AL "SCARFACE" CAPONE, all-time great American gangster, goes to jail for tax evasion.

THE WHITNEY MUSEUM, founded by sculptor and railroad heiress Gertrude Vanderbilt Whitney, opens in New York City.

SCRABBLE is invented by New York architect Alfred Butts, but the game is turned down by every manufacturer; not until 1948 is Scrabble widely distributed, and not until 1952 does word of mouth turn it into a bonanza.

1932

THE LINDBERGH BABY is kidnapped on May 1, only to be discovered dead 12 days later, after the parents pay a $50,000 ransom.

OF THEE I SING, a musical comedy written by George and Ira Gershwin with book by George S. Kaufman and Morrie Ryskind, becomes the first musical to win a Pulitzer Prize.

BIG-TIME VAUDEVILLE beginsits final fadeout as the last two-a-day show opens at the Palace on Broadway.

1933

ECSTASY, in which Hedy Lamarr appears nude, becomes the first film in which a sexual experience is depicted.

FRANCES PERKINS becomes the first woman to hold a Cabinet post when she is appointed secretary of labor by Franklin Delano Roosevelt.

THE FIRST DRIVE-IN cinema is built in Camden, N.J., accommodating 400 cars, and opens with *Wife Beware*.

PRESIDENT ROOSEVELT holds the first Fireside Chat on March 12, a radio address to the entire nation.

PROHIBITION is repealed with the ratification of the 21st Amendment on December 5. The watering holes that soon cover the country—bars, saloons, cocktail lounges—have a new feature, the jukebox.

THE FIRST NATIONAL FOOTBALL LEAGUE championship playoff pits the Chicago Bears against the New York Giants on December 17. The Bears win, 23–21.

1934

THE APOLLO THEATRE stages its first live show in Harlem.

BENNY GOODMAN begins his radio show *Let's Dance*, establishing himself as the "King of Swing."

JOHN DILLINGER, Public Enemy No. 1, is gunned down in chicago by FBI agents.

1935

THE FEDERAL THEATRE Project is instituted by Congress as part of the Works Progress Administration. An attempt to assist an ailing theater community hit badly by the Depression, it is disbanded in 1939.

BECKY SHARP, the first full-length color feature film, opens.

THE FIRST NIGHT BASEBALL game in the major leagues is played between the Cincinnati Reds and the Philadelphia Phillies. Cincinnati wins, 2–1.

GEORGE AND DOROTHY GERSHWIN'S opera *Porgy and Bess* opens at Boston's Colonial Theater.

1936

JESSE OWENS wins four gold medals in track events at the Berlin Olympics, infuriating German Chancellor Adolf Hitler,who preaches the mental and physical supremacy of Aryan whites over all other races.

MARGARET MITCHELL'S *Gone with the Wind* is published, selling a million copies in six months and winning the Pulitzer Prize in 1937. It will be her only book.

FRANKLIN DELANO ROOSEVELT is reelected president in the greatest Democratic landslide ever, carrying 48 states.

EUGENE O'NEILL, the great American dramatist, is awarded the Nobel Prize for Literature.

Jesse Owens in gold-medal form.

1937

VENTRILOQUIST EDGAR BERGEN and Charlie McCarthy premiere on NBC. They will remain hugely popular with audiences when the show makes the move from radio to TV.

JOHN STEINBECK'S *Of Mice and Men* is published.

THE FIRST worldwide radio broadcast to be received in the United States brings us the coronation of King George VI of England on May 12.

WALT DISNEY'S *Snow White and the Seven Dwarfs* tops the movie charts, making Disney internationally famous, and goes on to become an all-time classic.

OUR TOWN, by Thornton Wilder, is produced (and not in a high school theater). It wins a Pulitzer.

HEAVYWEIGHT BOXING champion Joe Louis defends his title with a first-round knockout of German boxer Max Schmeling, a Nazi hero who symbolizes the notion of Aryan superiority. His victory is viewed

Joe Louis.

as a triumph both for African Americans and for democracy.

THE DIRIGIBLE *Hindenburg* bursts into flames as it lands in New Jersey on May 6, marking the virtual end of lighter-than-air transportation. Simultaneously, the first coast-to-coast radio broadcast is conducted by Herbert Morrison, who reports on the disaster.

THE RADIO PLAY *War of the Worlds* (based on the novel by H.G. Wells) is broadcast on October 30 by Orson Welles, causing widespread panic among listeners who believe its story of an invasion from Mars.

1939

THE FIRST GOLDFISH is swallowed by a Harvard undergrad, beginning a fad that quickly sweeps across the nation and sets off such variations on the theme as eating light bulbs and biting snakes' heads off.

MARIAN ANDERSON, world-famous African American contralto, is denied permission to sing in Washington D.C.'s Constitution Hall by the Daughters of the American Revolution. Undaunted, she is sponsored by Eleanor Roosevelt in a triumphant performance on the steps of the Lincoln Memorial in front of 75,000 fans.

ROBERT KANE creates the cartoon character Batman.

THE GOLDEN GATE Exposition is held in San Francisco.

LOU NOVA squares off against Max Baer in the first televised prizefight, direct from Yankee Stadium. Nova wins in 11 rounds.

RHETT BUTLER'S infamous declaration in the film version of *Gone with the Wind*, "Frankly, my dear, I don't give a damn," breaks the taboo against cursing in the movies.

AT THE NEW YORK WORLD'S FAIR thousands ogle RCA TV sets featuring a 12-inch screen reflected in a cabinet-lid mirror.

1940

RICHARD WRIGHT'S masterpiece, *Native Son*, is published to wide acclaim; it is later adapted for a successful Broadway run.

A WORKABLE COLOR TV is announced by Peter Goldmark, chief television engineer at CBS.

THE COTTON CLUB, Harlem's famous jazz nightclub, closes down.

CONGRESS passes the Selective Service Act, the first U.S. peacetime draft law ever.

1941

THE FIRST TV AD comes on the air, marking the advent of commercial television; the spot, for Bulova watches, lasts 10 seconds and costs the company $9.

PEARL HARBOR is bombed by Japan on December 7, a day of infamy that ushers the U.S. into World War II.

1942

RODGERS AND HAMMERSTEIN transform the musical comedy

with their production of *Oklahoma!*

PHYSICISTS John Atanasoff and Clifton Berry develop the first fully electronic computer.

CAPITOL RECORDS is launched by Glenn Wallichs, who invents the art of record promotion by sending copies of new record releases to prominent disc jockeys.

BING CROSBY releases "White Christmas," from the film *Holiday Inn*, and it becomes the biggest-selling song from a movie in history.

1943

FRANK LLOYD WRIGHT begins work on the Solomon R. Guggenheim Museum in New York. Founded in 1939 as the Museum of Non-Objective Painting, the building opens its doors in 1959.

GEORGE WASHINGTON CARVER, 81, dies in Tuskegee, Ala. Born into slavery, he developed inventive uses for peanuts, soybeans, and other traditional Southern crops, which proved to be a boon to agriculture in the region.

1944

BILLBOARD introduces the first country music charts, first called "Most-Played Juke Box Hillbilly Records" and then changed to "Folk Records" before being relabeled "Country & Western" in 1949.

PAPER SHORTAGES during World War II force the publishing business to experiment with softcover bindings for its books, with stunning success.

1945

SMELL-O-VISION is created by Swiss inventor Hans E. Laube, who develops a "smell pack" that is stimulated by TV waves to produce an odor to accompany what is being shown on the screen.

WORLD WAR II comes to an end. Germany surrenders on May 8 (V-E Day). The only atomic bombs ever to be used in war are dropped by the U.S. on Hiroshima on August 6 and Nagasaki three days later, leading to the surrender of Japan on August 15 (V-J Day).

1946

DR. BENJAMIN SPOCK revolutionizes the way Americans raise their families with his *Common Sense Book of Baby and Child Care.*

WINSTON CHURCHILL coins the term "iron curtain" in a speech at Westminster College in Missouri.

THE U.S. detonates a nuclear bomb on Bikini Atoll on July 5 in the South Pacific. Five days later, designer Louis Reard commemorates the blast at a fashion show in Paris, where a certain itsy-bitsy, teeny-weeny two-piece bathing suit makes its first appearance.

THE CANNES FILM FESTIVAL premieres in September.

THE FIRST TV SOAP OPERA, *Faraway Hill,* debuts on the DuMont network.

CONSUMERS RUSH to buy the new 10-inch RCA TV set for $375. This "Model T of television" ushers in the TV age.

1947

THE POLAROID Land camera is patented by Dr. Edwin Land, providing prints that develop inside the camera within a minute. It enters the market the following year, selling for $90.

JACKIE ROBINSON becomes the first African American to sign with a major-league baseball team. His first game with the Brooklyn Dodgers is an exhibition game against the New York Yankees.

NBC'S *KRAFT TELEVISION THEATRE* introduces serious drama. Overnight, cheese sales soar and Madison Avenue melts.

FLYING SAUCER! The first sighting is reported on June 25, according to one source.

THE WORLD SERIES is broadcast on TV for the first time and four million baseball fans watch the New York Yankees and the Brooklyn Dodgers battle it out. The Yanks go on to the series.

THE FIRST ANTOINETTE PERRY (TONY) AWARDS for excellence in theater are handed out. No best play award is included, but José Ferrer wins as Best Actor, and Best Actress awards go to Ingrid Bergman and Helen Hayes.

THE TRANSISTOR is invented by Bell Telephone Laboratories; it becomes one of the most significant advances in the history of consumer electronics, paving the way for miniature TV sets, radios, and gear like CD players that haven't yet been invented.

1948

TED MACK'S *THE ORIGINAL AMATEUR HOUR* premieres in January. By year's end the first "ratings sweep" declares it the most popular show on TV.

THE PHONOGRAPH RECORDING market is fraught with competition as companies come up with improvements on the old 78 rpm disks. Columbia introduces the first long-playing commercial record,the 33 ½ rpm disk, and RCA releases the 45.

LEE STRASBERG takes over the Actors Studio, introducing the Method acting techniques that will profoundly influence such students as Marlon Brando, Paul Newman, James Dean, and Marilyn Monroe.

THE MOTORCYCLE CLAN Hell's Angels is formed.

THE ED SULLIVAN SHOW premiers to an initially poor viewer response. The influential variety program will stay on the air until 1971.

THE TERM "COLD WAR" is popularized by a speech before the Senate War Investigation Committee.

TV SET SALES skyrocket, with an estimated 250,000 sets installed every month.

NORMAN MAILER'S first novel, *The Naked and the Dead*, comes out. It remains one of the most important fictional works about World War II.

1949

CHIC YOUNG'S *BLONDIE* is the most popular comic strip in the world.

THE FIRST CABLE television systems go into homes.

ARTHUR MILLER'S play *Death of a Salesman*, the first dramatic tragedy to feature a common man as a protagonist, wins a Pulitzer Prize.

UNERRING *CRUSADER RABBIT* debuts as the first made-for-TV animated cartoon.

1950

GWENDOLYN BROOKS is the first African American to win a Pulitzer Prize, for her work *Annie Allen*.

MCCARTHYISM begins in February when the obscure U.S. senator Joseph McCarthy alleges that the federal government is infested with Communists.

GOOD OL' CHARLIE BROWN enters American culture as Charles Schulz creates the legendary comic strip *Peanuts*.

TELEVISION takes it first late-night variety plunge with *Broadway Open House*, and "dumb blonde" Dagmar (Jennie Lewis) becomes the first boob-tube sex symbol.

THE FIRST AMERICAN TROOPS land in Korea on July 1 after soldiers from North Korea invade South Korea. Although the move is described as a United Nations action, American soldiers comprise the vast majority of foreign troops. With news footage being aired on American TVs, it is also the first living-room war.

HOLLYWOOD buys its first million-dollar property: Columbia acquires the rights to the successful Broadway play *Born Yesterday* from the writer Garson Kanin.

A. C. NIELSEN begins gathering ratings data for TV, employing electronic viewing records along with written logs to determine the popularity of shows.

BELL LABORATORIES and Western Electric create the first telephone answering machine.

THE SITCOM laugh track is introduced on *The Hank McCune Show*, a program that has the added distinction of being canceled midseason.

THE FIRST CREDIT CARD is introduced through the Diners Club.

THE CISCO KID, starring Duncan Renaldo and Leo Carillo, is the first TV series filmed in color. At the time, there are fewer than 100 experimental sets in the U.S.

THE 1949 NOBEL PRIZE for Literature is retroactively awarded to William Faulkner. No prize had been awarded the previous year because none of the candidates had won a majority of the votes.

1951

PAY-PER-VIEW dies a premature death after Zenith begins testing its "Phone-vision" in Chicago. Viewers can dial a phone number and watch a recent feature film for $1. But skittish movie studios decide not to make first-run films available, fearing the consequences.

SENATE HEARINGS on organized crime rivet the nation. Mobster Frank Costello allows only his hands to be shown.

UNIVAC I, the first commercially built computer, goes into operation at the Census Bureau in Philadelphia.

CBS broadcasts the first commercial color telecast on June 25 with a one-hour special from New York to four other cities.

NBC begins the first network coast-to-coast programming.

AMOS 'N' ANDY bows with TV's first all-black cast. Though canceled in 1953, reruns air until 1966, when protests about racial stereotyping force withdrawal of the show from syndication.

I LOVE LUCY debuts to tremendous success, creating the mold for TV sitcoms.

CLEVELAND DJ Alan Freed, the first to introduce black R&B to a white audience on station WJW, coins the term "rock and roll."

CBS debuts its "unblinking eye," which evolves into TV's most famous logo.

GIAN CARLO MENOTTI'S *Amahl and the Night Visitors* becomes the first made-for-TV opera on Christmas Eve. It becomes a perennial seasonal favorite.

1952

THE REVISED STANDARD edition of the Old Testament, only the third authorized Protestant revision in 341 years, becomes a No. 1 bestseller and sets records by selling 1.6 million copies in eight weeks; the old record was held by *Gone with the Wind*, which sold 1 million books in six months.

THE MOUSETRAP, originally a play created by Agatha Christie for the 80th birthday of Britain's Queen Mary, premieres in London.It will become the longest-running theatrical work of all time.

***MAD* MAGAZINE** and the *National Enquirer* make their debuts.

UNIDENTIFIED FLYING OBJECTS capture the imagination of Americans. No longer looked on as simply science fiction, the national fascination with UFOs even prompts the U.S. Air Force to publish possible photographs of the phenomena.

THE FIRST HYDROGEN BOMB is detonated on November 1, and Americans' fear of complete annihilation intensifies.

BWANA DEVIL leads a resurgence of popularity for 3-D movies, Hollywood's attempt to combat the appeal of "free" TV.

PANTY RAIDS occur in epic proportions at college sororities across the nation.

Marilyn Monroe.

TWO OF TELEVISION'S biggest all-time hits—*Today,* hosted by Dave Garroway, and *Guiding Light*—begin broadcasting on NBC and CBS, respectively; both programs are still going strong today.

THE MARILYN MONROE image crystallizes with four film releases, helping movie theaters draw Americans away from their TV sets.

ART LINKLETTER tosses a *House Party* on September 1, and the bash lasts longer (17 years) than any daytime variety show.

VEEP HOPEFUL Richard Nixon makes a politician's first direct TV appeal on September 23, citing his dog, Checkers, in his successful quest to beat fund-misuse charges and save his career.

CHRISTINE JORGENSON returns from Denmark where she had undergone the first publicized sex-change operation.

1953

I LOVE LUCY features the birth of Little Ricky on January 19 as the real Lucille Ball gives birth to Desi Arnaz Jr. The landmark show

Hugh Hefner.

draws a 92 percent share of TV sets in use, or 44 million viewers—a record to date. Turns out the "dual birth" was no happy accident, since Desi Junior was born by a scheduled caesarean section. The event received more media attention than Dwight Eisenhower's inauguration, which took place the following day. Eisenhower and Nixon form the first Republican administration in 24 years.

DESI JR. scores again when the first issue of *TV Guide* is published, featuring him on the cover.

AT AGE 27, Queen Elizabeth II is crowned as England's monarch.

JULIUS AND ETHEL ROSENBERG are executed, the only American civilians ever to receive such a penalty for espionage.

THE DISC JOCKEY Top 40 radio format is established on KOWH, an Omaha station. It features a limited number of records played over and over, hourly news breaks, and sporadic chatter from the announcer.

CINEMASCOPE premieres with *The Robe*, and its widescreen format becomes a huge hit with filmgoers.

***PLAYBOY* MAGAZINE** is founded by 27-year-old Hugh Hefner with a first issue featuring the nude Marilyn Monroe on its cover.

THE FIRST ROCK AND ROLL song hits the Billboard charts: Bill Haley and His Comets' "Crazy, Man, Crazy."

THE RCA compatible color television is approved by the FCC and becomes the industry standard.

HOUSTON'S KUHT debuts as the country's first noncommercial educational TV station; within 10 years there will be 75 other such stations.

1954

MARILYN MONROE marries former New York Yankees star Joe DiMaggio, a second marriage for both. Alas, the match is not meant to be—Marilyn files for divorce nine months later.

TELEVISION JOURNALIST Edward R. Murrow launches the first major attack on Joseph McCarthy's witch-hunt tactics on CBS's *See It Now*, inspiring a groundswell of support for the senator's critics and ultimately precipitating his downfall.

Elvis Presley.

SEGREGATION in schools is declared unconstitutional on May 14 in the landmark case, *Brown vs. Board of Education.*

ELVIS PRESLEY cuts his first record, the double-sided 45 "That's All Right (Mama)"/"Blue Moon of Kentucky."

THE FIRST COLOR TV sets and the first transistor radios are marketed.

TONIGHT!, later known as *The Tonight Show,* premieres with Steve Allen as host.

SWANSON brings out the very first TV dinners—ominously, turkey—for 69¢.

1955

CONTRALTO MARIAN ANDERSON becomes the first African American to sing a major role at the Metropolitan Opera, appearing as Ulrica in Verdi's *Masked Ball*.

A NEW ERA in domestic politics is launched with the first filmed presidential press conference. Both TV and motion picture newsreel photographers cover the event.

WALT DISNEY'S TV show, *Disneyland*, first appears on ABC and quickly becomes one of the most successful programs on the tube. One segment, "Davy Crockett, Indian Fighter," instigates a full-blooded Davy Crockett mania, which sweeps the country. Over 3,000 Crockett-related items sell in crazy numbers, from coonskin caps to Bill Hayes's song "Ballad of Davy Crockett," which rises to the top of the charts.

ANN LANDERS launches her advice column in the *Chicago Sun-Times*.

BILL HALEY and His Comets' "Rock Around the Clock" goes to No. 1 on *Billboard*'s charts on June 6, marking the indisputable ascent of rock and roll.

DISNEYLAND, the first theme amusement park, opens south of Los Angeles in Anaheim.

JAMES DEAN stars in *Rebel Without a Cause,* his second and penultimate starring role before crashing his Porsche later in the year and dying at age 26. His death gives rise to his enduring status as a cult hero, embodying the spirit of rebelliousness so sought after by America's younger generation.

BOB KEESHAN debuts as the Captain on *Captain Kangaroo*, which goes on to become the longest-running kids' show. *The Mickey Mouse Club* begins as well.

IN ONE OF THE greatest record deals of all time, RCA buys Elvis's contract—for an unprecedented $40,000—from Sam Phillips's Sun Records.

COMIC BOOK popularity reaches unprecedented heights, with sales soaring beyond a billion copies. Concern over their violent content increases in due measure, prompting New York State to ban the sale of certain graphic comics to minors.

1956

ACTOR GRACE KELLY retires from Hollywood and marries Prince Rainier III of Monaco, a member of the thousand-year-old Grimaldi dynasty, in one of the most publicized marriages of the century.

BEAT POET ALAN GINSBERG'S *"Howl" and Other Poems*is released and its publisher is promptly brought up on obscenity charges that are later successfully defended in court.

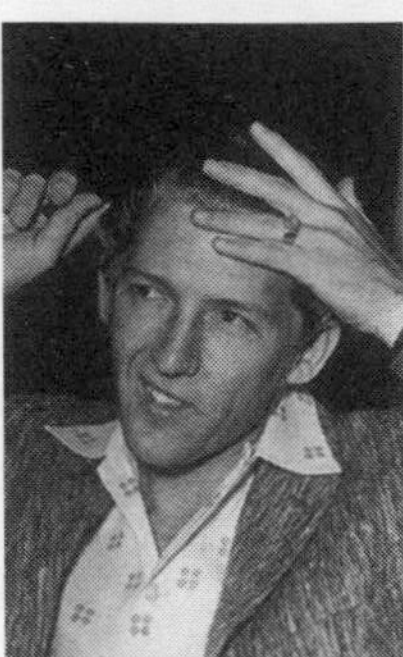

Slick Jerry Lee Lewis.

MARILYN MONROE weds husband No. 3, Pulitzer- and Tony Award-winning playwright Arthur Miller (it's his second marriage). The two are divorced in 1961.

DEAN MARTIN and Jerry Lewis are a team no more. They split on July 25, exactly 10 years after they first appeared together in Atlantic City.

NBC'S Huntley and Brinkley are TV's first co-anchors: "Goodnight, Chet." "Goodnight, David."

IN HIS FIRST YEAR OF stardom, Elvis releases "Don't Be Cruel"/"Hound Dog," a double-sided 45 that becomes the biggest hit of all time on *Billboard's* charts. His appearance on Ed Sullivan's *Toast of the Town* on September 9, shot discreetly above the pelvis, earns the highest rating for any regularly scheduled program, drawing an estimated audience of 50 million people. He also appears in his first movie, *Love Me Tender.*

1957

LEONARD BERNSTEIN is named the first American musical director of the New York Philharmonic.

JERRY LEE LEWIS scandalizes the nation when he marries his 13-year-old cousin, Myra Gale Brown—also committing bigamy by failing to divorce his first wife, Jane Mitcham.

BOBBY FISCHER, 14, wins the U.S. chess championship.

THE HULA HOOP is introduced and takes America by storm, selling over 45 million by 1958.

DICK CLARK'S *American Bandstand* moves from a local Philadelphia station to its national debut on ABC. It becomes the longest-running variety show in TV history.

THE SOVIET UNION launches *Sputnik*, setting off the space race.

LEAVE IT TO BEAVER debuts on CBS, presenting the audience with the most typically American family to date.

THE NAT "KING" COLE SHOW, the first major series with an African American host, is canceled after a year, for lack of a national sponsor.

1958

ALVIN AILEY founds the American Dance Theatre.

BILLBOARD begins its Hot 100 chart; the first No. 1 record is "Poor Little Fool" by Ricky Nelson.

VLADIMIR NABOKOV'S sensational novel *Lolita* is published by Putnam after being rejected as too obscene by four other American publishers.

DEEJAYS AT ST. LOUIS' KWK radio station complete their "Record Breaking Week" when, at the insistence of the management, "undesirable" records are given a final play on the airwaves and then ceremoniously destroyed. Most of the sacrificed recordings are of rock and roll music.

SCIENTISTS at the ESSO Gas Research Center—now EXXON—announce on July 28 that they have found that drivers waste gas when they listen to rock and roll because they tend to jiggle the pedals in time with the beat.

VAN CLIBURN becomes the first American to win a gold medal at the Tchaikovsky International Piano Festival. His subsequent recording of the composer's *Piano Concerto No. 1* is the first classical record to go gold.

THE BROOKLYN DODGERS and the New York Giants move to California, bringing major-league baseball to the West Coast.

THE GRAMMY AWARDS are launched. Ignoring the rising predominance of rock and roll, the organizers present Best Album of the Year to Henry Mancini and name "Volaré" by Domenico Modugno as Best Song.

QUIZ SHOW scandals erupt with an initial investigation of answer-feeding on a program called *Dotto* prompted by a complaint by contestant Eddie Hilgemeier. By the end of the year most quiz shows are pulled off the air.

1959

BUDDY HOLLY, Ritchie Valens, and The Big Bopper are tragically killed in February when their single-engine light aircraft crashes in a snowstorm about 10 minutes after takeoff.

BARBIE is introduced to the toy world, created by Ruth and Elliot Handler, who founded Mattel in 1945. The doll's proportions, if copied on a human scale, would be 33-18-28. Barbie was named for the Handlers' daughter, Barbara, just as their son, Ken, was later honored when his parents created a male companion doll.

ISLAND IN THE SUN, starring James Mason, Dorothy Dandridge, Harry Belafonte, and Joan Fontaine, becomes the first film to portray interracial romance.

THE U.S. POSTMASTER GENERAL bans *Lady Chatterly's Lover* by D. H. Lawrence, but sales skyrocket after courts hold that the book is not obscene.

AMERICANS SEE THE WORLD from a new perspective as *Explorer VI* sends down the first photograph of Earth taken from outer space.

THE TELEPHONE-BOOTH JAMMING fad hits this year and fades almost as quickly. The fad first catches hold on the West Coast and moves quickly across the country, the record being set with 32 squashed students at Modesto Junior College in California.

MOTOWN RECORDS is founded in Detroit by songwriter Berry Gordy Jr.

IS TELEVISION KING? In December, for the first time, TV rings up more in commercial sales ($1.24 billion) than Hollywood cashes in box-office receipts ($1.235 billion).

1960

ELVIS PRESLEY'S army career, which began in March of 1958, comes to a close.

A CONGRESSIONAL investigation into payola determines that radio deejays have been receiving payments from record companies to play their disks. Dick Clark and Alan Freed are the particular focus of allegations, and Freed eventually loses his job.

SMELL-O-VISION hits theaters as Michael

Todd Jr.'s film *Scent of Mystery* is released to general indifference.

PSYCHO, directed by Alfred Hitchcock, sets new movie attendance records and earns a mint as one of the most frightening films ever made.

THE TWIST is introduced by 19-year-old Chubby Checker.

BEN-HUR collects a record 11 Oscars out of 12 nominations.

Master director Alfred Hitchcock.

THE FANTASTICKS debuts May 3. It will become the longest-running off-Broadway show ever, hitting its 14,000th performance on March 2, 1994—and still going strong at the Sullivan Street Playhouse in Greenwich Village. Since its beginning, notable performers have included Kevin Kline, Richard Chamberlain, and Jerry Orbach.

THE FLINTSTONES debuts as prime time's first animated sitcom.

BIRTH CONTROL PILLS become available for widespread use as the FDA approves the public sale of Enovid at $10 to $11 for a month's supply.

1961

THE FIRST FRENCH KISS on the Hollywood big screen takes place between Natalie Wood and Warren Beatty in *Splendor in the Grass*.

SOPRANO LEONTYNE PRICE, 34, debuts at New York's Metropolitan Opera House in *Il Trovatore* and receives a 45-minute ovation.

BOB DYLAN gives his first solo performance, opening for blues musician John Lee Hooker in New York City's Gerde's Folk City.

ABC'S WIDE WORLD OF SPORTS with Jim McKay is introduced and runs on Saturday afternoons, showing us "the thrill of victory and the agony of defeat."

ALAN B. SHEPARD JR. becomes the first American astronaut to go into space on May 5.

Jacqueline Kennedy lights up the White House.

SATURDAY NIGHT AT THE MOVIES debuts as the first regular TV showcase for major motion pictures.

1962

JACQUELINE KENNEDY takes the country on a televised tour of the White House.

THE FIRST USE OF NUDITY in advertising appears in *Harper's Bazaar* in a bare-breasted photo by Richard Avedon.

THE FIRST JAMES BOND movie, *Dr. No*, is released starring Sean Connery, 32.

DIRECT-DIAL long-distance telephone service begins in the United States.

MARILYN MONROE dies of a barbiturate overdose at age 36 on August 5.

THE VIRGINIAN makes its debut as the first 90-minute TV series. In a nine-year run, its cast includes Lee Majors,David Hartman, and Lee J. Cobb as a frontier judge.

JOHNNY CARSON takes over *The Tonight Show* where he will reign as King of Television until he retires in 1992.

1963

WEIGHT WATCHERS enters the market, turning dieting into big business.

POP ART is given its first major show at the Guggenheim Museum in New York. Artists include Andy Warhol, Jasper Johns, and Roy Lichtenstein.

BETTY FRIEDAN publishes her landmark feminist tract, *The Feminine Mystique.*

JULIA CHILD bubbles up on *The French Chef* and becomes public TV's first star; she'll keep TV cooking for the next 10 years.

WHISKEY A-GO-GO opens in Los Angeles, beginning its tenure as Hollywood's longest-lived club devoted to cutting-edge rock music.

Elizabeth Taylor as Cleopatra.

THE BEATLES release their first single in the U.S., "Please Please Me," in February along with their LP *Introducing The Beatles.*

CLEOPATRA, with Elizabeth Taylor and Richard Burton, scores as both the top money-maker of the year and one of the biggest flops in movie history as its vast costs far overrun its huge budget; Taylor alone receives $1.75 million for her participation.

PEBBLES FLINTSTONE is born to parents Wilma and Fred on February 22 at the Bedrock Rockapedia Hospital.

TROLLS are introduced. Billed as good-luck charms, their ugliness is a charm indeed, producing sales in the millions.

THE FUGITIVE debuts September 17; David Janssen runs. He'll catch the one-armed man—and a then record prime-time audience—in the '67 finale. That episode still ranks as the third-most-watched episode of a television series ever..

PRESIDENT JOHN F. KENNEDY, 46, is assassinated in Dallas on November 22. The immediacy of television's coverage of the surrounding events transforms TV into a witness to history and binds together a nation in mourning.

1964

FIVE THOUSAND SCREAMING FANS greet The Beatles at Kennedy Airport in New York on February 7, when the band arrives for its first American tour. Two days later the Fab Four appear on *The Ed Sullivan Show.* They draw an estimated 75 percent of all TV viewers, making it the most-watched hour of television to date. Songs include "All My Loving," "She Loves You," and "I Want To Hold Your Hand."

THE MOOG, the first commercial music synthesizer, is developed.

ELIZABETH TAYLOR finally meets her match, again, as she marries husband No. 5, Richard Burton, just 10 days after getting a divorce from Eddie Fisher. The two had met on the set of *Cleopatra.*

THE HOME VIDEO RECORDER is invented in Japanby the Sony Corporation.

MARSHALL MCLUHAN declares that the "medium is the message" in his book *Understanding Media.* Nobody gets it, but everybody talks about it.

LYNDON B. JOHNSON'S "daisy" campaign spot airs once on September 7, suggesting that Republican opponent Goldwater is nuke-happy. Fallout: LBJ wins in a landslide.

PEYTON PLACE airs September 15 as the first prime-time soap and becomes a smash hit.

G.I. JOE is introduced by Hasbro and sells for $4.

MARTIN LUTHER KING JR. receives the Nobel Peace Prize. Jean-Paul Sartre is awarded the Nobel Prize for Literature and becomes the first person to reject the honor.

1965

SOUPY SALES asks his loyal young viewers to send him "those little green pieces of paper" from dad's wallet, "and I'll send you a postcard from Puerto Rico." The

January 1 stunt draws a big enough response to get Sales suspended by the station, but viewers protest and he is reinstated.

BELL-BOTTOMS grace the nation's hips, and lava lamps make a splash, selling 2.5 million units this year alone.

THE FIRST AMERICAN COMBAT TROOPS not deployed in an advisory capacity land in South Vietnam, urning a local conflict into an undeclared large-scale international war.

THE NATIONAL ENDOWMENT for the Arts and Humanities is established by Congress.

"(I CAN'T GET NO) SATISFACTION," the classic Rolling Stones tune, becomes a No. 1 hit in the United States, sealing the British invasion as one of the dominant musical developments of the decade.

THE BEATLES play before 55,000 fans at New York's Shea Stadium August 15 to open their third U.S. tour.

THE SOUND OF MUSIC is released, eventually overtaking *Gone with the Wind* to rank for a time as the top box-office earner ever.

GO-GO DANCING and its accompanying little white boots quickly wax and then wane in popularity among discotheque goers.

CINEMA'S 34-year rule against nudity is broken when a scene in *The Pawnbroker* is approved by the ratings board as essential to the plot.

CBS AND NBC adopt virtually all-color formats starting with the fall season.

BILL COSBY becomes the first African American TV star, in *I Spy*.

SONY introduces the first commercial home video tape recorder. The size of an overnight bag, it costs $995.

1966

"YESTERDAY," the most recorded song in the history of popular music, is released by Paul McCartney in the first solo by a Beatle. The record label, however, still reads "Beatles."

CINEMA'S BLUE LANGUAGE ban finally falls with *Who's Afraid of Virginia Woolf?*

THE SUPREMES become the first female group to top the U.S. album chart with *Supremes a Go Go*.

JOHN LENNON makes his most infamous remark on August 5 by saying that he and his Beatles bandmembers are "more popular than Jesus." Subsequently radio stations across the country take Beatles songs off the air.

LSD is pulled off the market by its manufacturer, Sandoz Pharmaceuticals after being banned by the government in response to controversy over the hallucinogen's recreational uses.

STAR TREK is launched in September 8 and remains on the air until 1969. It will become one of the few series to be more popular in syndication than in its network run.

"PAUL IS DEAD." For those who believe, November 9 marks the date of the Beatle's supposed decapitation.

STEREO CASSETTE TAPE RECORDERS are introduced, a breakthrough for tape cartridges.

1967

THE FIRST SUPER BOWL is held on January 15, broadcast in color on both CBS and NBC; setting a model for future contests, the Green Bay Packers defeat the Kansas City Chiefs in a lopsided game, 35–10.

THE BLACK PANTHER PARTY is founded in Oakland by Huey Newton and Bobby Seale.

OTIS REDDING, 26, dies in a plane crash in December. One month later, his biggest hit, the chart-topping "Sittin' on the Dock of the Bay," is released.

ELVIS PRESLEY weds Priscilla Beaulieu on May 1 at the Aladdin Hotel in Las Vegas.

THE MONTEREY INTERNATIONAL POP FESTIVAL in California features such performers as Janis Joplin, Jimi Hendrix, and the Grateful Dead.

RIOTING breaks out in Detroit as racial tension builds; over 17,000 people are arrested in what proves to be the worst U.S. riot of the century.

FOLKSINGER PETE SEEGER is finally allowed to appear on TV (on *The Smothers Brothers Comedy Hour*) after having been blacklisted for 17 years for his leftist politics.

HAIR has its off-Broadway premiere at the Public Theatre in New York.

ROLLING STONE magazine begins publication under the direction of 21-year-old Jann Wenner.

PRESIDENT LYNDON B. JOHNSON signs a law insuring federal support for public TV, and the Corporation for Public Broadcasting is created.

THE FIRST WITH SO-CALLED SPAGHETTI WESTERN, Sergio Leone's *A Fistful of Dollars*, is released in the United States. Filmed in 1964, it stars Clint Eastwood.

INTERRACIAL ROMANCE unfolds on TV as Mia and Paulfall for each other on *Love Is a Many-Splendored Thing.*

BOXER MUHAMMAD ALI is stripped of his heavyweight title after refusing to serve in the army during the Vietnam War.

THE FIRST HUMAN HEART TRANSPLANT is performed by Dr. Christiaan Barnard in South Africa on Louis Washkansky, who lives for 18 days.

MAO TSE-TUNG'S QUOTATIONS, better known as the Red Book, is the biggest-selling read in the world this year.

Martin Luther King Jr. giving his famous "I have a dream" speech in Washington D.C.

1968

CARDIGAN-CARRYING MISTER ROGERS opens his Neighborhood February 19, beginning a 27-year run that will establish a PBS record.

MOVIE RATINGS are introduced by the Motion Picture Association of America. The original classifications are G, M (mature audience), R, and X. M is changed to GP two years later, and then PG (parental guidance) a year after that.PG-13 is invented in 1984 as the result of a dispute over the violence in *Gremlins* and *Indiana Jones and the Temple of Doom,* and in 1990 the nefarious X is replaced by NC-17.

ARTHUR CLARKE and Stanley Kubrick's *2001: A Space Odyssey* is released, introducing the evil computer, Hal, an antihero who becomes a cultural icon.

THE EARLIEST-KNOWN HEIDI scandal: With 50 seconds left and the New York Jets leading the Oakland Raiders, NBC cuts from the game to the movie *Heidi*. The Raiders go on to win by scoring two touchdowns in nine seconds.

CIVIL RIGHTS LEADER Martin Luther King Jr. is assassinated April 4 at age 39 on the balcony outside of his motel room in Memphis, Tenn. Days later, many American cities erupt in riots.

ROBERT F. KENNEDY, 42, is assassinated June 5 by Sirhan Sirhan in a Los Angeles hotel after winning the California presidential primary. As a response, David Crosby writes "A Long Time Coming."

AT THE SUMMER OLYMPIC GAMES in Mexico City, American runners Tommy Smith and John Carlos give the black power salute as they receive their gold and bronze medals, resulting in their suspension from competition.

PRESIDENTIAL CANDIDATE Richard Nixon appears on *Laugh-In* and says,"Sock it to me!"

JULIA, premiering September 17, is the first TV series to star a black woman in a non-menial role as Diahann Carroll plays a nurse who is also a single parent.

MIKE WALLACE and Harry Reasoner start grilling as *60 Minutes* starts ticking September 24; the news program will eventually top the ratings.

1969

THE BEATLES stage their last public performance January 30 from a rooftop in London.

JIM MORRISON, lead singer for The Doors, is arrested for lewd and lascivious behavior after exposing himself at a concert in Miami.

DIANA ROSS invites 350 special guests to the trendy Daisy Club in Beverly Hills to see the new Motown act, The Jackson Five.

JOHN LENNON and Yoko Ono tie the knot on Gibraltar March 20.

THE FIRST FULL-FRONTAL male nudity appears in film with Alan Bates and Oliver Reed in Ken Rus-sell's *Women in Love.*

THE ALTAMONT FESTIVAL—starring such acts as The Rolling Stones, Santana, Jefferson Airplane, and Crosby, Stills, Nash & Young—is struck by tragedy when the Hell's Angels security force beats to death an 18-year-old boy.

CAST MEMBERS of the play *Oh! Calcutta!* are arrested for indecent exposure in Los Angeles.

THE SUPREME COURT rules that laws prohibiting the private possession of obscene material by adults are unconstitutional.

PRINCE CHARLES is officially titled Prince of Wales.

UPON WALKING ON THE MOON on July 20, Neil Armstrong proclaims, "That's one small step for a man, one giant leap for mankind."

ACTRESS SHARON TATE, wife of director Roman Polanski, is found murdered along with four others—victims of Charles Manson's cult, known as The Family. Although not present at the house that night, would-be rock musician and psychopath Manson is convicted of the grisly killings and imprisoned.

THE WOODSTOCK Music and Art Festival is held August 15–17 in upstate New York. Playing before an audience of around 400,000, featured performers include The Who, Grateful Dead, Janis Joplin, Joe Cocker, Santana, Jimi Hendrix, Jefferson Airplane, and Crosby, Stills & Nash.

SESAME STREET debuts, starring Big Bird, Oscar, Bert, Ernie, Cookie Monster, Grover, and Kermit; it marks a radical breakthrough for children's TV programming.

TINY TIM marries Miss Vickie before 45 million witnesses on *The Tonight Show.*

1970

RECORDING TOGETHER for the last time, the Beatles cut "I Me Mine" January 3. The historic breakup happens on April 10, when Paul McCartney announces that he will not record with John Lennon again. By the end of the year, John, Paul, George, and Ringo have all released albums of their own.

Jimi Hendrix.

EVERYTHING *You Always Wanted to Know About Sex, but Were Afraid To Ask* by Dr. David Reuben becomes a No. 1 bestseller.

JIMI HENDRIX and Janis Joplin both die drug-related deaths this year at age 27.

THE FILM VERSION OF *M*A*S*H,* with Elliott Gould and Donald Sutherland, is officially banned from military installations for "reducing the conventions and paraphernalia of war to total idiocy."

MIDNIGHT COWBOY is the first and only X-rated film to win Best Picture at the Academy Awards.

MASTERPIECE THEATRE is introduced on National Educational Television, hosted by Alistair Cooke, featuring BBC dramas.

TV'S PARTRIDGE FAMILY records "I Think I Love You," which becomes a smash hit first in the show's story line and then in real life, and makes David Cassidy a teen idol.

WATERBEDS hit the market, and although technical problems often produce flooding, sales skyrocket.

MONDAY NIGHT FOOTBALL takes its bow September 21 (with the New York Jets vs. the Cleveland Browns) and strains U.S. marriages, but Don Meredith, Howard Cosell, and Frank Gifford will boost ABC's ratings.

1971

CIGARETTE ADS are banned January 2 and TV networks lose $200 million in annual advertising.

CBS'S controversial *All in the Family* is introduced, featuring the bigoted Archie Bunker, whose offensive diatribes and hilarious family members drive the show's great popularity.

EXCERPTS FROM THE PENTAGON PAPERS, leaked by Daniel Ellsberg, are published in the *New York Times*, showing that presidential administrations had indeed recognized the futility of the Vietnam War but escalated involvement anyway and then lied about it.The Nixon administration attempts to block publication but the Supreme Court rules in favor of the newspaper on First Amendment grounds.

BILL GRAHAM closes down Fillmore East in New York City and Fillmore West in San Francisco, unable to pay the increasing prices charged by the musicians he has showcased for so long.

MUHAMMAD ALI'S conviction for draft evasion is overturned by the Supreme Court, which rules that the boxer's pacifist religious convictions were sincere.

JIM MORRISON, 27, dies in a bathtub in Paris on July 3.

HOSTED BY GEORGE HARRISON, the Concert for Bangladesh initiates the rise of the celebrity fundraiser. The concert features Ringo Starr, Eric Clapton, and Bob Dylan, but while its success is great, only a small fraction of its proceeds ever reach the starving people of Bangladesh.

LEGENDARY ALLMAN BROTHERS Band member Duane Allman is killed October 29 in a motor- cycle accident near Macon, Ga.

1972

MS., edited by Gloria Steinem, publishes its premiere issue in January.

RECLUSIVE MULTIMILLIONAIRE Howard Hughes exposes as a hoax an upcoming "autobiography" supposedly written with, but actually forged by, author Clifford Irving.

PONG, the first commercial computer game, is created by Atari.

BURT REYNOLDS poses nude for the centerfold of *Cosmopolitan*.

AT THE SUMMER OLYMPICS in Munich, 11 Israeli Olympians are killed by Arab terrorists, and the games are suspended for the first time in history.

JONATHAN LIVINGSTON SEAGULL establishes itself as the best-selling book since *Gone with the Wind*.

DEEP THROAT becomes one of the most successful porn films ever made; produced on a budget of $40,000, it goes on to gross around $40 million.

THE HOME BOX OFFICE cable channel goes on the air in Wilkes-Barre, Pa., with 365 subscribers. The first offering is a Paul Newman movie, *Sometimes a Great Notion*.

1973

ROE V. WADE is upheld by the Supreme Court, legalizing unrestricted abortion in the first trimester of pregnancy.

Marlon Brando as the Godfather.

A CEASE-FIRE agreement is signed on January 27 that essentially ends the Vietnam War.

SACHEEN LITTLEFEATHER refuses Marlon Brando's Oscar for Best Actor on his behalf to protest the treatment of Native Americans. (Brando had been nominated for *The Godfather*.)

PBS'S *STEAMBATH* takes on a taboo as Valerie Perrine becomes the first woman to bare her breasts in a dramatic TV program.

AT THE AGE OF 38, Seiji Ozawa becomes the youngest permanent conductor of the Boston Symphony.

A BREAK-IN at Democratic party headquarters at the Watergate Hotel is discovered, eventually leading to the only resignation of a sitting president in American history when Richard Nixon is forced to leave office on August 9 of the following year.

PUNK/NEW WAVE club CBGB and OMFUG (which stands for Country, Bluegrass, Blues, and Other Music for Uplifting Gourmandizers) opens its doors on Manhattan's divey Bowery, becoming home to such performers as Blondie, Talking Heads, Patti Smith, The Ramones, The Police, Joan Jett, and Sid Vicious. As Joey Ramone put it 20 years later, "It's a birthplace. It's like a big womb there. It's very primitive, very primal."

BILLIE JEAN KING trounces male chauvinist Bobby Riggs in tennis's ballyhooed "Battle of the Sexes."

THE AMERICAN PSYCHIATRIC ASSOCIATION reverses its traditional position and declares that homosexuality is not a mental illness.

1974

THE AUTOBIOGRAPHY OF MISS JANE PITTMAN, starring Cicely Tyson, becomes one of TV's most highly praised and successful special programs, going on to win nine Emmys.

HEIRESS PATRICIA HEARST is kidnapped by the Symbionese Liberation Army, which she later joins and with which she commits a robbery. 19 months after her kidnapping, Hearst is captured and convicted.

AFTER 10 YEARS OF MARRIAGE, Cher files for divorce from her husband and performing partner Sonny Bono. She marries Gregg Allman of the Allman Brothers Band only four days after the divorce is finalized.

PEOPLE magazine, featuring Mia Farrow on the cover, is launched by Time, Inc., in February.

EVEL KNIEVEL fails his attempt to jump the Snake River Canyon on his motorcycle, but survives.

ONE THOUSAND FANS at a David Cassidy concert in London are injured during a frenzy following the teen idol's appearance. One concertgoer dies.

FLORIDA TV commentator Chris Chubbuck announces her own suicide at the end of the news broadcast, and proceeds to shoot herself in the head on the air.

ALEKSANDR SOLZHENITSYN is expelled from Russia for his dissident writings; this year *The Gulag Archipelago* is also published in the West.

STREAKING becomes a momentary fad, primarily on college campuses, although the madness eventually extends to telecasts of the Academy Awards and *The Tonight Show.*

RUSSIAN DANCER EXTRAORDINAIRE Mikhail Barishnikov defects to the West, electrifying the American dance scene.

KAREN SILKWOOD is killed in a suspicious car crash on November 13. A laboratory worker at the Kerr-McGee plutonium plant, she dies on her way to meet with a reporter to discuss safety hazards at her workplace.

Sonny and Cher, before the divorce.

1975

THE VIETNAM WAR officially comes to an end.

JOHN LENNON wins a four-year-long battle against American immigration authorities when they drop his case for humanitarian reasons due to the pregnancy of Yoko Ono.

SATURDAY NIGHT LIVE hits the airwaves from New York City, with guest host George Carlin.

RICHARD BURTON and Elizabeth Taylor marry for the second time, only a year after their divorce.

THE VIDEOCASSETTE recorder/player is introduced by Sony.

MOOD RINGS are introduced and reach their peak in only a few months, selling more than 20 million before passing from popular fancy. Meanwhile, maintenance-free pet rocks also hit the short-term big time.

1976

THE MINISERIES comes to commercial TV, as *Rich Man, Poor Man* airs, starring Peter Strauss, Susan Blakely, and Nick Nolte.

BRITAIN'S PRINCESS MARGARET scandalizes the world with an illicit liaison on the island of Mustique with brewery heir Roddy Llewellyn. She and her husband, Lord Snowden, separate later this year.

GONE WITH THE WIND is telecast over two eveningson NBC, earning the highest ratings to date.

1977

ALEX HALEY'S novel *Roots*, a story of his quest for his ancestors in Africa and America, is made into the most successful miniseries in history. It wins a record nine Emmys, and mesmerizes the country for over a week, drawing approximately 130 million people to watch at least one of its eight episodes.

STUDIO 54 opens its doors in New York, becoming the quintessential glamorous nightclub until owners Steve Rubell and Ian Shrager are arrested for tax evasion in 1980.

GEORGE LUCAS releases *Star Wars*, which becomes the highest-grossing movie of all time until dethroned by *E. T., the Extra-Terrestrial* five years later.

John Travolta strikes the pose that made him famous.

THE KING IS DEAD: Elvis Presley, 42, passes on at Graceland, his palatial estate in Memphis, Tenn., on August 16.

SOAP introduces prime time's first gay character–Billy Crystal as Jodie Dallas.

RONALD ZAMORA, 15, confesses to murder and claims TV made him do it; he will be convicted in the first televised trial.

SATURDAY NIGHT FEVER premieres in New York on December 14, launching the disco era.

1978

FORMER FIRST LADY Betty Ford helps break the stigma of addiction by entering a rehabilitation clinic.

THE WORLD'S FIRST test-tube baby, Louise Brown, is born July 25 in England.

AT 25 HOURS and $25 million, the dramatization of James Michener's *Centennial* is the most outsized program yet produced for TV.

JIM JONES leads his followers to a mass death in Jonestown, Guyana, on November 18. 1,914 of his cult commit suicide or kill each other.

SONY invents the revolutionary Walkman, the first portable cassette player.

1979

RAP MUSIC is ushered into the commercial age when the Sugarhill Gang releases "Rapper's Delight." Earlier in the year a Brooklyn group called The Fatback Band had produced "King Tim III (Personality Jock)," a disk widely regarded as the first rap record.

WHILE THE WOMEN on TV's *Charlie's Angels* changed outfits on average eight times per show, a guest appearance this year by Farrah Fawcett (who left the show in 1977) easily breaks the record: in one hour-long program she changes clothes 12 times.

1980

THE U.S. HOCKEY TEAM beats the Soviet Union during the Winter Olympics at Lake Placid, on their way to winning their first gold medal since 1960—and only their second gold since the Olympics began.

President Ronald Reagan.

POST-IT NOTES enter the market, revolutionizing the office and the refrigerator.

TED KOPPEL'S *Nightline*, begun as an ABC series following the status of U.S. hostages in Iran, brings hard news in the wee hours.

COMEDIAN RICHARD PRYOR is badly burned when a flammable drug mixture used to make "freebase," a cocaine derivative, explodes in his face.

WITH SUCH BLOCKBUSTER musicals as *A Chorus Line, Oh! Calcutta!*, and *Evita* on the boards, Broadway box offices collect almost $200 million, a dramatic increase over a five-year period. Road shows during this period experience an even greater success.

TV'S FIRST ALL-NEWS SERVICE begins with Ted Turner's Cable News Network on June 1. Broadcasting 24 hours a day, the network loses $16 million in a year, but grabs seven million viewers.

HALF THE NATION'S VIEWERS tune in to *Dallas* on November 21 to find out "Who Shot J.R.?," more viewers than for any other single TV show in history.

MARK DAVID CHAPMAN shoots and kills John Lennon on December 8 outside the singer's apartment in New York City.

1981

HOMOSEXUAL MEN across the country are struck down by a wave of cancer and pneumonia that is traced to a mysterious breakdown in the body's disease-fighting system. It will be referred to later as Acquired Immune Deficiency Syndrome, or AIDS.

HILL STREET BLUES premieres.

TICKETS TO BROADWAY'S *The Life and Adventures of Nicholas Nickleby* go on sale at the Plymouth Theatre for a record-setting $100 each.

PRESIDENT RONALD REAGAN is shot in an assassination attempt on March 30 that leaves his press secretary, James Brady, paralyzed for life. John Hinckley apparently undertakes the assassination in an attempt to impress Jodie Foster.

THE VIDEO GAME PAC MAN devours the market as young people everywhere are seized with acute Pacmania.

CHARLES, PRINCE OF WALES, and Lady Diana Spencer are married July 29 at Saint Paul's Cathedral in London.

MTV unveils music for your eyes on August 1. The channel's opener: "Video Killed the Radio Star," by The Buggles.

SANDRA DAY O'CONNOR becomes the first woman Supreme Court justice in U.S. history.

PRIVATE SATELLITE DISHES sprout after the FCC gives them the okay. By the end of the '80s, there will be two million nationwide.

1982

OZZY OSBOURNE bites the head off a live bat thrown at him during a performance on January 20, a moment that is immortalized in heavy metal chronicles.

THE REVEREND SUN MYUNG MOON performs a mass ceremony at Madison Square Garden, marrying some 4,150 of his followers, the "Moonies."

MICHAEL JACKSON'S *Thriller* is released. Selling over 20 million copies in 1983 and 1984 alone, it becomes the biggest-selling album in history.

JOHN BELUSHI dies March 5 of an overdose of cocaine and heroin in a Hollywood hotel room.

CHARLES AND DI produce their first offspring, Prince William, on June 21, the latest heir to the British throne.

PRINCESS GRACE dies on September 14 after an automobile accident.

THE WATCHMAN, Sony's portable microtelevision, is invented.

THE FIRST ARTIFICIAL HEART is transplanted into Barney C. Clark, age 61, in Utah. He lives for 112 days.

1983

CABLE TV subscribers reach the 30 million mark.

SINGER KAREN CARPENTER dies of anorexia nervosa on February 4.

M*A*S*H ends its 11-year, 14-Emmy run with the largest audience ever to watch a single TV show.

ASTRONAUT SALLY RIDE becomes the first american woman in space as she blasts off June 18 with four colleagues aboard the space shuttle *Challenger.*

VANESSA WILLIAMS becomes the first African American to win the Miss America pageant. She relinquishes her title two months before her term ends in 1984, when it is discovered that revealing nude photos of the singer are going to be published in *Penthouse.*

THE CHILLING TV DRAMA *The Day After*, with Jason Robards, explores the aftermath of nuclear war, hardening both pro- and anti-freeze positions.

CABBAGE PATCH DOLLS, introduced by Coleco Industries, become the holy grail of the holiday season.

1984

HOME TAPING OF TV programming is held not to be in violation of copyright law by the Supreme Court, which throws out a suit brought against Sony by MCA and Walt Disney.

SURROGATE CONCEPTION is successful for the first time in California.

GERALDINE FERRARO becomes the first woman to run for vice president as presidential candidate Walter Mondale names the Queens congresswoman as his running mate; the pair lose the election to President Reagan and Vice President George Bush in a landslide.

GYMNAST MARY LOU RETTON wins two gold, two silver, and two bronze Olympic medals for the U.S.

SIDNEY BIDDLE BARROWS is arrested. Known as the Mayflower Madam, she included numerous famous and powerful people among her clients.

Vice-presidential candidate Geraldine Ferraro.

THE COSBY SHOW premieres, becoming the most popular series of the decade before going off the air in 1993.

THE FIRST ALL-RAP RADIO format is introduced by KDAY in Los Angeles.

RUN-DMC becomes the first rap group to have an album—*Run-DMC*—certified gold.

BOB GELDOF and Band Aid's "Do They Know It's Christmas" raises money to help feed the starving people of Africa.

1985

"WE ARE THE WORLD" is recorded by 45 pop music superstars under the auspices of USA for Africa.

CRACK COCAINE hits the streets, further devastating already blighted urban areas.

PIANO MAN BILLY JOEL and supermodel Christie Brinkley tie the knot.

MADONNA begins her road debut, The Virgin Tour, on April 10.

THE MUSIC INDUSTRY'S benefit for African famine relief, Live Aid, is staged in London and Philadelphia and beamed all over the world.

ROCK HUDSON becomes the first major public figure to die of AIDS, at 59, on October 2.

1986

THE SPACE SHUTTLE *CHALLENGER* explodes January 28 shortly after launching, killing everyone on board, including schoolteacher Christa McAuliffe, the first private citizen to go into space.

FILIPINO FIRST LADY Imelda Marcos is revealed to possess 2,700 pairs of shoes.

ARNOLD SCHWARZENEGGER and Maria Shriver are married.

JOHNNY CARSON stops talking to Joan Rivers when she accepts an offer to host a late-night show on the Fox network.

CAROLINE KENNEDY arries artist-designer Edwin Schlossberg.

PRINCE ANDREW marries Sarah Ferguson in London on July 23.

THE OPRAH WINFREY SHOW, originally a local program called *A.M. Chicago*, goes national on September 8. Its host quickly establishes herself as one of the most successful personalities in show business.

TURNER BROADCASTING colorizes black-and-white classics and directors, stars and movie buffs see red. First to run: Jimmy Cagney's *Yankee Doodle Dandy.*

1987

JESSICA HAHN is implicated in a scandal with TV evangelist Jim Bakker.

VAN GOGH'S "Irises" is auctioned at $53.9 million, the highest price ever paid for a painting at the time.

PRINCE CHARLES and Diana begin leading separate lives in March as their marriage starts to deteriorate.

PRESIDENTIAL CANDIDATE Gary Hart's connection with model Donna Rice destroys his political aspirations, and he is forced to withdraw from the race.

GARRISON KEILLOR broadcasts his last radio show, *A Prairie Home Companion*, from Lake Wobegon on June 13 and moves to New York City.

PORN QUEEN CICCIOLINA wins a seat in Italian parliament on June 16.

BRUCE WILLIS and Demi Moore are married November 21 in Las Vegas.

1988

TV PREACHER JIMMY SWAGGART admits his involvement with pornography and prostitutes. His February 21 statement, "I have sinned," deals a serious setback to electronic evangelism.

COMPACT DISCS outsell vinyl albums for the first time: the Recording Industry Association of America reports unit sales of 149.7 million CDs to 72.4 million records.

SONNY BONO is elected mayor of Palm Springs, California.

THE VERY LAST Playboy Club in America closes July 30 in Lansing, Mich.

ACTRESS ROBIN GIVENS files for divorce on October 7 from world heavyweight champion Mike Tyson, claiming that the fighter is violent.

TALK SHOW HOST Phil Donahue wears a dress on November 18 to boost his ratings.

BENAZIR BHUTTO of Pakistan becomes the first woman to lead an Islamic nation.

PAN AM FLIGHT 103 explodes over Lockerbie, Scotland, killing all 259 passengers.

THE ERA of the personal video arrives when Sony introduces the Video Walkman, an ultracompact VCR with a three-inch color screen.

1989

LATE-NIGHT TV gets its first regular African-American host on January 3 with comedian Arsenio Hall.

VIRTUAL REALITY, the term as well as the equipment to achieve it, is invented by Jaron Lanier.

NOVELIST SALMAN RUSHDIE is forced into hiding after a death threat is issued by Islamic militants angry over what they see as sacrilege in his book *The Satanic Verses.*

KIM BASINGER steps in to rescue near-bankrupt Braselton, Ga., by buying the town for a reported $20 million.

LUCILLE BALL, perhaps the most beloved television star in history, dies on April 26.

ACTOR ROB LOWE is identified by Fulton County, Ga. officials in a homemade porn video with an underaged girl.

***PLAYBOY* FOUNDER** Hugh Hefner marries former *Playboy* Playmate Kimberley Conrad.

JOSE MENENDEZ AND his wife, Kitty, are found murdered August 20 in their $4 million Beverly Hills mansion. Their sons, Lyle and Erik, will later be accused of murdering their parents for money, though at their trials the brothers claim that years of sexual and psychological abuse by their parents drove them to kill in self-defense.

PETE ROSE, Cincinnati Reds manager and one of the greatest baseball players in history, is banned from the game for life for gambling.

TV GUIDE boasts a picture on the cover of the newly slim Oprah Winfrey, but the image turns out to be a composite of Oprah's head and Ann-Margret's body.

PRINCESS ANNE issues a palace statement on August 31 that she is officially separating from her husband, Mark Phillips.

THE BERLIN WALL falls on November 9.

SAN FRANCISCO GIANTS pitcher Dave Dravecky retires after an aborted comeback attempt from cancer in his pitching arm.

1990

THE SIMPSONS spins off from *The Tracey Ullman Show* and makes the fledgling Fox network a real contender as a fourth network.

NELSON MANDELA is released from prison after 27 years of incarceration for leading a campaign against the South African government.

"ICE ICE BABY" by Vanilla Ice becomes the first rap record to top the U.S. singles chart.

SONY creates the first portable compact disc player, the Discman.

M. C. HAMMER releases *Please Hammer Don't Hurt 'Em*, which becomes the biggest-selling rap record in history.

DONALD AND IVANA TRUMP divorce.

MILLI VANILLI is accused of fraud for using voices other than its own on its Grammy-winning album, *Girl You Know It's True*. The group is forced to surrender the award.

IN THE FIRST such ruling against a music group in the U. S., a Florida judge declares 2 Live Crew's album *As Nasty As They Wanna Be* obscene and bans all sales of the rap recording to minors. The move ignites a campaign against censorship in the music business.

TWIN PEAKS debuts on ABC as a two-hour movie with limited commercial interruption.

SEINFELD, a show about "nothing," quietly debuts on May 31.

AMERICA RELIVES the war between the states with Ken Burns's indelible PBS documentary *The Civil War*.

IN AN EFFORT to raise money for AIDS research, the *Red Hot & Blue* album is released on October 30, featuring such stars as U2, David Byrne, and The Neville Brothers performing Cole Porter songs.

1991

OPERATION DESERT SHIELD turns into Desert Storm on January 16 as the Allied forces attack Iraq to liberate Kuwait. CNN's Bernard Shaw, Peter Arnett, and John Holliman cover the events for the world, broadcasting from downtown Baghdad.

THE GODFATHER OF SOUL, James Brown, is released from a Georgia prison after serving two years of a six-year sentence for aggravated assault, not stopping for police, and carrying a gun.

RODNEY KING'S beating by Los Angeles police is recorded by an observer with a home video camera on March 3.

DR. JACK KEVORKIAN'S attempts to help people commit suicide first come to light.

WILLIAM KENNEDY SMITH, nephew of Ted Kennedy, is accused of rape by a Florida woman; after a harrowing trial, he is exonerated.

PAUL REUBENS, creator of the much-admired *Pee-wee's Playhouse* and the character Pee-wee Herman, is busted in Florida for indecent exposure.

Paul Reubens, a.k.a. Pee-wee Herman, after his infamous arrest.

LIZ TAYLOR marries husband number seven, 39-year-old Larry Fortensky, a carpenter she met at the Betty Ford Center where they were both being treated for alcohol and drug dependency. The wedding, held on Michael Jackson's estate, draws such guests as Nancy Reagan.

THE ANITA HILL/ CLARENCE THOMAS hearings galvanize the nation with charges of sexual harassment against the Supreme Court nominee; Thomas is narrowly approved for the post.

MAGIC JOHNSON announces his retirement from professional basketball because he has tested positive for the HIV virus.

MEDIA MOGUL Ted Turner and actress-cum-fitness-guru Jane Fonda are married.

1992

ARTHUR ASHE, tennis star and beloved public figure, dies of AIDS.

MIKE TYSON is convicted of raping beauty contestant Desiree Washington. In 1995, Tyson walks out of the Indiana Youth Center in Plainfield, Ohio, a free man. While in prison, Tyson studied the Koran intensely, and has embraced its teachings.

TAMMY FAYE BAKKER files for divorce from husband Jim, who's still in prison on a fraud conviction and not eligible for parole for another three years.

FERGIE AND ANDY separate after six years of marriage.

A *MURPHY BROWN* segment in which the unmarried Murphy gives birth, spurs the wrath of Vice President Dan Quayle and instigates a nationwide debate over family values.

LONG ISLAND TEENAGER Amy Fisher shoots Mary Jo Buttafuoco.

JOHNNY CARSON ends his reign over late-night talk shows on May 22 with his last appearance on *The Tonight Show.*

CANDIDATE BILL CLINTON appears on *The Arsenio Hall Show*, complete with dark shades and saxophone, to perform "Heartbreak Hotel" with the show's "posse."

WOODY ALLEN AND MIA FARROW begin a bitter custody battle over their son Satchel, 4, and two children they adopted together, Moses, 14, and daughter Dylan, 7. The dispute is fueled by Allen's affair with Farrow's adopted daughter Soon-Yi Previn.

THE TORONTO BLUE JAYS become the first non-American team to win that most American of sports championships, the World Series, with a 4–2 series win over Ted Turner's Atlanta Braves.

PRINCE CHARLES and Princess Diana formally serparate.

1993

THE U.S. POSTAL SERVICE releases its commemorative Elvis stamp, featuring the youthful Elvis, the overwhelming selection of the voting public.

BILL WYMAN leaves The Rolling Stones in January. He is 56.

DR. DRE'S album *The Chronic* (named after a very potent form of marijuana) reaches No. 1 on the *Billboard* charts and becomes the most successful hard-core rap album to date.

MICHAEL JACKSON tells interviewer Oprah Winfrey that his lightened skin color is due to a rare skin disease, and says that he is in love with Brooke Shields. Later in the year Jackson is accused of having fondled a 13-year-old Los Angeles boy.

PRINCE, born Prince Rogers Nelson, turns 35 and, in a most confusing commemoration, changes his name to a symbol that no one knows how to pronounce.

JULIA ROBERTS, 25, and Lyle Lovett, 35, wed.

ACTOR RIVER PHOENIX, 23, dies on October 31. The young actor had a reputation for clean living, but coroners find high levels of cocaine and morphine as well as Valium and marijuana in Phoenix's system.

1994

NANCY KERRIGAN is attacked in January by a club-wielding assailant, but battles back from the resulting knee injury to win a silver medal in the Winter Olympics.

MICHAEL JORDAN quits basketball and signs a contract with the Chicago White Sox, fulfilling his childhood dream of becoming a baseball player. He is assigned to the Birmingham Barons, a Class AA team, and finishes the season with a batting average of .202.

STEVEN SPIELBERG finally claims Oscars for Best Picture and Best Director with *Schindler's List*, which receives a total of seven awards. *Jurassic Park* wins another three. Later in the year, Spielberg forms Dreamworks SKG, the first new major studio in 55 years, with record mogul David Geffen and former Disney executive Jeffrey Katzenberg.

KURT COBAIN takes his own life with a shotgun on April 8 in his Seattle-area lakeside home. He joins a long and sad list of fellow rock stars: Janis Joplin, Jimi Hendrix, Jim Morrison—all dead at 27.

JACQUELINE BOUVIER KENNEDY ONASSIS dies at age 64 on May 19. She had been diagnosed just four months before with non-Hodgkin's lymphoma, a cancer of the lymphatic system.

NICOLE BROWN SIMPSON, 35, and Ronald Goldman, 25, are brutally murdered in front of Simpson's Brentwood condominium. After an eerie low-speed chase watched live on television by 95 million people, Nicole's ex-husband O.J. Simpson surrenders to police and is charged with the murders.

NEVERLAND meets Graceland as Michael Jackson and Lisa Marie Presley get hitched in a secret ceremony in the Dominican Republic.

WOODSTOCK '94 is held on the 25th anniversary of the original with acts old (the Allman Brothers Band, Bob Dylan) and new (Green Day, Nine Inch Nails).

GEORGE FOREMAN, 45, recaptures the heavyweight title he lost to Muhammad Ali 20 years ago. He defeats Michael Moore in Las Vegas with a 10th-round knockout.

1995

O.J. SIMPSON is found not guilty of the murders of Nicole Brown Simpson and Ronald Goldman.

OLYMPIC DIVER GREG LOUGANIS discloses to Barbara Walters and readers of his memoirs that "I do have AIDS."

EAZY-E, (a.k.a. Eric Wright), 31, the founder of rap group N.W.A. and president of Ruthless Records, dies of AIDS.

MICHAEL JORDAN resumes his basketball career. Dismayed by the baseball strike, he dons a new basketball jersey, #45, and proceeds to rack up 55 points against the New York Knicks in one of his first games back.

TOUTED AS LATIN MUSIC'S Madonna, the Texas-born singer Selena is killed by her fan club president Yolanda Saldvar, 34, whom she was about to confront for embezzling funds.

AT THE COMMONWEALTH PARK equestrian facility in Culpeper County, Va., Christopher Reeve suffers a tragic accident on the cross-country jumping course, when his 7-year-old chestnut Thoroughbred Eastern Express refuses a fence. Though he is wearing a protective vest and helmet, the fall causes multiple fractures in his spinal column, leaving the actor paralyzed.

THE KING OF POP and his princess go live with Diane Sawyer and draw over 60 million viewers. The combination interview/publicity opportunity includes an answer to fans' most frequently asked question: Do Lisa-Marie and Michael have sex? "Yes, yes, yes," answers Mrs. Presley-Jackson.

HUGH GRANT, parked on a Los Angeles side street, is arrested for engaging in a "lewd act" with Sunset Strip prostitute Divine Brown. News of the British heartthrob's indiscretion shocks his fans, who knew the actor as a clever and charming 34-year-old adored by longtime girlfriend, Estée Lauder model Elizabeth Hurley. Grant soon begins his tour of contrition with a *Tonight Show* appearance that draws the show its third-highest ratings ever.

THE WALT DISNEY COMPANY announces that it's buying Capital Cities/ABC for $19 million. The day after Disney's acquisition, Westinghouse Electric announces its agreement to purchase of CBS for $5.4 billion.

LEGENDARY GRATEFUL DEAD guru Jerry Garcia, 53, dies of an apparent heart attack. To many who have idolized the band from its formation in 1966, it is a sad ending to the "feel good" era that the Dead carried well into the '90s with their record-grossing tours.

NEW YORK YANKEE GREATS gather in Dallas to lay to rest Mickey Mantle, dead of cancer, in a funeral filled with warm memories.

AFTER 10 YEARS IN THE PLANNING, the $92 million I. M. Pei-designed Rock and Roll Hall of Fame and Museum opens in Cleveland, paying tribute to 40 years of rock and to the jazz, blues, and gospel artists who laid down the roots of the genre.

1996

O.J. SIMPSON stands trial in a wrongful death suit filed by the families of Nicole Brown Simpson and Ronald Goldman.

HE WAS THE FIRST TALK show host to invite the audience into the act, but after 29 years, Phil Donahue calls it quits. He was seen in 200 television markets at the height of his popularity, winning 20 Emmys and a Peabody Award along the way.

MAYBE IT WAS JUST A matter of time: Lisa Marie Presley files for divorce from husband of 20 months, Michael Jackson. Divorce papers cite irreconcilable differences.

AFTER TWO HOURS of deliberation, a jury rules that Random House owes Joan Collins further payment on her book contract for *A Ruling Passion*. Saying her 690-page manuscript was unpublishable, Random House had sued Collins, and the *Dynasty* actress had countersued for the balance of her contract, $3.6 million.

THEODORE JOHN KACZYNSKI, 53, the former Berkeley math professor suspected of being the Unabomber, is charged with possessing a partially completed pipe bomb.

JACKIE KENNEDY ONASSIS'S cherished belongings are auctioned off during a four-day sale at Christie's New York. The least expensive item, an etching of Washington, D.C. valued no higher than $30, sells for $2,070. A walnut cigar humidor smokes out $574,500.

EIGHT CLIMBERS ON MOUNT EVEREST become victims in one of the worst tragedies to strike the 29,028-foot Himalayan peak since it was first scaled in 1953.

GYMNAST KERRI STRUG, 18, limps to the gold after her heart-stopping final vault clinches top honors—the first ever—for the U.S. women's team. The Tucson, Ariz., native had to be carried to the medal stand by coach Bela Karolyi, who had coached gold medalist Nadia Comaneci to victory 20 years before.

PRINCESS DIANA and Prince Charles's divorce becomes official in late August.

JOHN F. KENNEDY JR. and Calvin Klein publicist Carolyn Bessette surprise everyone with a secret wedding on Cumberland Island, off the Georgia coast.

THE MATERNAL GIRL'S newest release, born in October, is a daughter: Lourdes Maria Ciccone Leon. Her father is Carlos Leon, Madonna's personal trainer and companion.

PEOPLE EXTRAS

THE MOST INTRIGUING PEOPLE: 1974–PRESENT

Every December, in the Christmas double issue, the People editors single out the 25 most intriguing people of the past year. We reprint here the complete roll of honorees, with a brief description for each, to remind readers of the notable and notorious from the past 23 years.

1974

Gerald Ford—The president copes with an office he didn't seek and savage inflation

Patty Hearst—The kidnapped newspaper heiress turned terrorist might be another face in the crowd—but in disguise

Joe Hirshhorn—He heaps the land with beauty by donating 2,000 sculptures and 4,000 paintings to Smithsonian's new Hirshhorn Museum

Kay Graham—The publisher of the *Washington Post* emerges as the big winner of Watergate

Yasir Arafat—A tough soldier takes the point for Palestine and addresses the United Nations

Faye Dunaway—A panther of an actress springs back to the top in *Chinatown, The Towering Inferno,* and *Three Days of the Condor*

Alexander Solzhenitsyn—The Russian exile's Nobel honors are late but sweet

Nelson Rockefeller—The vice president–elect has his finances questioned by Congress; being rich turns out to be a problem

Leon Jaworski—The Watergate prosecutor knew Nixon was lying, but couldn't say it

Erica Jong—A hit author who is like her uninhibited heroine in *Fear of Flying*

Francis Ford Coppola—*Godfather II* confirms him as cinema's creative king

Muhammad Ali—The title isn't enough for the world heavyweight champ—he wants another son

Pat Nixon—The last First Lady deals stoically with her husband's fall from grace

John Glenn—Could the Ohio senator and former astronaut be the Ike of the '70s?

Sherlock Holmes—He emerges from Victorian England as the most omnipresent literary figure of 1974

Carter Heyward—One of 11 women ordained as Episcopal priests (the ordinations were later declared invalid) defies her church to serve her God

Stevie Wonder—A blind artist brings soul to all his music

Alexander Calder—Now it seems every U.S. city must have one of his mobiles

Charlie Finley—The owner of the Oakland A's doesn't win friends, just the World Series

Ella Grasso—The first woman in American history to capture a governorship without inheriting the office from her husband. In this year of political women, Conn.'s governor–elect is the biggest name of all

J. Kenneth Jamieson—Exxon's chief has big profits and big problems

Jimmy Connors—He catches fire; his romance catches cold

Gunnar Myrdal—Nobel Prize winner in economics is honored for his "pioneering work in the theory of money and economic fluctuations"

Valerie Harper—*Rhoda*'s a winner on her own, and so much for TV taboos

Mikhail Barishnikov—The former Kirov Ballet star defects to Toronto, and ballet is changed forever

1975

Betty Ford—The president's secret weapon is a refreshing First Lady high on being herself

Richard Zanuck—Son of Darryl F., he makes his own name coproducing Hollywood's most toothsome grosser ever (*Jaws*)

Frank E. Fitzsimmons—The boss of 2.2 million teamsters is Nixon's buddy and shows he is "not Hoffa's puppet"

Charles Manson—He's in prison, but may have influenced Squeaky Fromme in her failed assassination attempt on President Ford

Daniel Patrick Moynihan—Fighting Irishman at the U.N. talks tough—and, many Americans feel, talks sense too

James Coleman—The University of Chicago professor blamed for busing says it backfired

Indira Gandhi—After six months of rule in India, her popularity soars

Cher Bono Allman—Move over Liz 'n' Dick, this ricochet bride is the new First Lady of splitsville

Andrei Sakharov—The Nobel Peace Prize winner is a man under siege in his own country

Teng Hsiao-Ping—After years of obscurity, a tough, blunt, outspoken man steps into the big shoes of Chinese leadership

Patty Hearst—Was she a volunteer terrorist or a victim of her captors?

Christina Onassis—The only daughter of the late shipping magnate Aristotle Onassis has the ships and the gold, and marries her father's rival

Leonard Matlovich—The ex–Air Force sergeant is discharged after admitting his homosexuality and sets up the Matlovich Foundation for Civil Rights

Dolly Parton—There's a brain under that beehive of Nashville's new queen-in-waiting

Fred Lynn—An all-American boy dazzles Boston and baseball in his miraculous rookie year

Frank Borman—An ex-astronaut takes the controls of a company in a financial tailspin and gets Eastern Airlines off the ground

Rosemary Rogers—The master of the erotic gothic takes her readers past the bedroom door

Werner Erhard—In the wake of TM and Zen, a former encyclopedia huckster is the smooth guru of est

Woody Allen—A winning klutz moves from snappy one-liners to triple creative threat—actor, director, and author with his latest, *Without Feathers*

Marabel Morgan—The Florida housewife behind *The Total Woman* cashes in on the antifeminist backlash

Jerry Brown—California loves its young governor who avoids the mansion, limos, and labels

Don King—A flashy ex-con turned promoter is the new lord of the rings

Hercule Poirot—Who kills the famed Belgian detective after 55 years? No, not the butler, but Dame Agatha Christie

Anwar Sadat—The president of Egypt opens the Suez Canal, closed since the Six Day War in 1967

Gelsey Kirkland—The prima ballerina of the American Ballet dances a triumphant *Giselle*, highlighting a great year in ballet

1976

Jimmy Carter—The president-elect wants to be the "citizen president"

Farrah Fawcett-Majors—The shape of things to come? The nation watches an "Angel" turn into a star

Andrew Wyeth—Is he America's most popular painter? The thought grieves some critics, who see him as "the rich man's Norman Rockwell"

Betty Williams—After seven bloody years, an anguished mother whose three children were killed starts her own movement and asks Ulster to give peace a chance

Andrew Young—The first black ambassador to the United Nations. When this former congressman speaks, Jimmy Carter listens

Juan Carlos I—The new Spanish king takes aim at Franco's fascist legacy and hands power to the people

Linda Ronstadt—A vagabond grows into country rock's First Lady

Reverend Sun Myung Moon—Troubles build up for the mysterious head of the Unification Church

Bert Jones—A cool, calm Colt is pro football's man with the golden arm

Julius Nyerere—Tanzania's superstar of black African diplomacy acts as a buffer between ruling white Ian Smith's government and the black nationalists of Rhodesia

Carl Sagan—The Viking I expedition on Mars provides vicarious adventure for a would-be space explorer

Fred Silverman—Since TV's superprogrammer switched channels, ABC enjoys Happy Days and Mashes CBS

Liz Ray—The woman whose affair with Representative Wayne Hays set off the steamiest Washington sex scandal in years brings out a book and gets religion

PEOPLE'S COVER CHAMPS

Their fame far exceeded the usual 15 minutes. The saga of their lives held readers rapt. Here are the titleholders for the most times on the cover of PEOPLE.

Personality	Number of Covers
Princess Diana	43
Sarah Ferguson	14
Elizabeth Taylor	14
Michael Jackson	13
Jacqueline Kennedy Onassis	13
Cher	10

C. W. McCall—After "Convoy," the year's bestselling single, Rubberduck is king of the road

Shere Hite—That report on women's sexuality becomes a bestseller, and its author moves on to men

Donald Kendall—With the Soviets part of the Pepski Generation, Pepsico's chief is now waging war on Coke

Vivian Reed—The star of Broadway's *Bubbling Brown Sugar* proves that black is beautiful at the box office

Ron Kovic—Crippled Vietnam veteran turned antiwar activist and author of *Born on the Fourth of July* sells movie rights for $150,000—and is a new breed of Yankee Doodle Dandy

Chevy Chase—He's hot and you're not: *Saturday Night*'s stumblebum says so much for tepid TV

Regine—The queen mother of the disco craze opens clubs all over the globe

Har Gobind Khorana—A shy genius gives the world its first man-made working gene

Nadia Comaneci—The Rumanian Olympic champion prepares for the 1980 games in Moscow. In Montreal she was just about perfect—now she wants even more.

Robert Redford—The actor turns producer with *All the President's Men* and shows he's not just a pretty face

Don Shomron—The Israeli general who led the Entebbe raid to save 105 hostages is a global hero and can't understand why

King Kong—Producer Dino De Laurentis sees and monkey does—$200 million, he hopes

1977

Jimmy Carter—The first year at 1600: he likes it, Rosalynn is chilly, and Amy's adjusting

Diane Keaton—Her gamble on *Looking for Mr. Goodbar* put Woody Allen's flaky foil in the Hollywood catbird seat

General Omar Torrijos—Ratify the canal treaties or bring in the marines, says Panama's strongman

Steven Ross—An impresario of all parlors (originally funeral), the founder-chairman of Warner Communications is the greatest showman on earth

Midge Costanza—Assertive and quick-tongued, she's Carter's pipeline to the people as the assistant for public liaison

Anwar Sadat and Menachem Begin—Is it a possible secret weapon of peace that the president of Egypt and the prime minister of Israel are so much alike?

Ted Turner—After the Americas Cup the sea gets a little choppy for the cable entrepreneur and baseball team owner

Margaret Trudeau—The runaway wife of Canada's prime minister, Pierre Trudeau, says of her old life, "Politics is an ugly and thankless role. What I did was never really appreciated."

Robert Byrd—A self-made fiddler calls the tunes in the world's most exclusive club

Susanne Albrecht—A brutal murder of an old friend makes her the dark queen of German terrorism

Lily Tomlin—The actress/comedian won a Tony for her one-woman show *Appearing Nitely*. "Is this the country to whom I'm speaking?" Happily for America the answer is yes

Billy Carter—President Carter's baby brother and typical southern "sly ole boy" has an agent and a career as spokesman for products such as Billy Beer. He may be a royal pain to some, but his brother is still amused

Anita Bryant—After a *très* ungay year, she's still praising God and passing the orange juice

Shaun Cassidy—The star of *The Hardy Boys* moonlights as a pop star, and preadolescent America is swooning

Jacqueline Onassis—Quits her editor's job at Viking and gets $25 million from stepdaughter Christina Onassis

Jasper Johns—The enigmatic master of pop art—known for depictions of the stars and stripes, targets, alphabets, and lightbulbs—stays on target

Toni Morrison—"O-o-o-ooh she done fly" into the literary top rank with *Song of Solomon*

Dr. Robert Linn—His liquid protein diet has him in fat city, but some unexplained deaths worry the FDA

Tracy Austin—Out of the cradle and onto the courts comes a new tennis wunderkind, at 14 the youngest player ever to be invited to Wimbledon

Rosalyn Yalow—All this: winner of the 1977 Nobel Prize for medicine, first laureate educated only in the United States, sixth woman science winner, second woman medicine winner

Reggie Jackson—Once just a hot dog; now he's a candy bar and a millionaire Yankee hero

Stevie Nicks—A songwriting soprano with fragile vocal cords casts her sexy spell on rock

George Lucas—From the void he created the droid and a new "force" in film

Princess Caroline—Grace and Rainier's grown-up little girl will wed Junot next July

1978

Jimmy Carter—At Camp David he negotiates peace between Egypt and Israel, but back in the White House he looks for antidotes to rising inflation and helps Amy practice her pitch on the violin

Pope John Paul II—A tough Polish priest molds the papacy to his own ebullient personality

Queen Noor al-Hussein—The blue-jeaned American queen says of her king, "I'd be delighted to have his child"

G. William Miller—The chairman of the Federal Reserve says of inflation, in effect, "We have nothing to fear but fear itself"

Teng Hsiao-Ping—The tough vice-premier gives China less of Mao, and more of himself

Brooke Shields—Pretty baby at 13: One horse, three movies, beaucoup bucks, but no beau

Melvin Gottlieb—The dream this Princeton physicist pursues is limitless energy from nuclear fusion

Louise Brown—The first test-tube baby is doing just fine, thank you, but the fuss is far from over

Reverend Jim Jones—When this religious demagogue felt his encampment was threatened by Congress and newsmen, he offered a deadly communion to his followers

John Belushi—With the hit movie *Animal House*, TV's man of mugs is becoming a hard act to outgross—in every way

Jim Fixx—His *The Complete Book of Running,* a how-to book on the simplest sport in the world, is the year's runaway bestseller

Garry Marshall—TV writer and producer of the hits *Laverne and Shirley* and *Happy Days* continues his successful career with *Mork and Mindy*

Arlene Blum—The University of California biochemist who led the first all-woman expedition up Annapurna, the tenth highest peak in the world, loses two fellow climbers

Howard Jarvis—The crusader against high property taxes may have changed the future of U.S. politics following the endorsement of his Proposition 13 by California voters in June

Miss Piggy—The famed Muppet pig states, "I want children, my career, and the frog—not necessarily in that order"

Luciano Pavarotti—It's supertenor, opera's newest sex symbol

Cheryl Tiegs—This model's photos still bring out the beast, and earn her $2,000 for a day's work, but her new goal is survival in the TV jungle

Meat Loaf—Rock's newest (and heftiest) hero takes a Texas-size bite into the music biz

Sir Freddie Laker—The founder of the Skytrain revolutionized air fares with cheap transatlantic flights and has a knighthood to prove his success

Nancy Lopez—The golfer has a fantastic year, finishing first in nine out of 25 tournaments and is named Rookie Player and Golfer of the Year

John Travolta—Stayin' Alive is the word for the solitary new superstar besieged by his fans

James Crosby—The man who brought big-time gambling to Atlantic City hopes for the city's economic rebirth

John Irving—His novel *The World According to Garp* is on the bestseller list and revenues allow the down-to-earth Vermonter to work full-time on his upcoming work, *The Hotel New Hampshire*

Donna Summer—The queen of disco is softening her act, but she'd still love to love you, baby

Burt Reynolds—Life isn't always easy for a star working on a new image: sensitivity

1979

Rosalynn Carter—The First Lady skirts the charge that she is involved in government policy formation, and instead emphasizes the Carters as a family

Aleksandr Godunov—The Russian danseur defects to the United States "to dance more often," but his volatile personality may be the reason he has yet to perform

Marvin Mitchelson—The millionaire divorce lawyer makes "palimony" a household threat

Bo Derek—Shows the world that she's a 10 as costar to Dudley Moore, and is credited with bringing sex back to films

Lee Iacocca—Struggles valiantly to get Chrysler into gear under the threat of bankruptcy

Sly Stallone—Comes off the canvas for the biggest movie purse of the year, *Rocky II,* and is already thinking ahead to *Rocky III*

Megan Marshack—After a year of seclusion, former vice president Nelson Rockefeller's secretary and companion on the night of his death is back in New York

Mani Said al-Otaiba—Leader of OPEC, he writes poetry and tames his Arab colleagues with cordial threats

Joan Kennedy—Impressing the nation, she sobers up to be at Ted's side for the campaign

Johnny Carson—Carson announces that he plans to give up his 17-year reign and $2.5-million contract at NBC and may entertain offers from ABC

PEOPLE'S BEST AND WORST DRESSED

Who are the biggest fashion victors and victims? The following celebrities found themselves on PEOPLE's Best Dressed and Worst Dressed lists most often.

ALL-TIME WINNERS

3 Times

Princess Caroline
Princess Diana
Kevin Costner
Jackie Onassis
Prince William

2 Times

Corbin Bernsen
Delta Burke
Cher
George Clooney
Tom Cruise
Mel Gibson
Don Johnson
Michael Jordan
Angela Lansbury
Cyndi Lauper
Donna Mills
Julia Roberts
Liz Taylor
Bruce Willis

ALL-TIME SINNERS

5 Times

Sarah Ferguson
Madonna

4 Times

Arsenio Hall
Daryl Hannah

3 Times

Paula Abdul
Rosanna Arquette
The Artist Formerly Known As Prince
Kim Basinger
Cher
Demi Moore
Roseanne

2 Times

Justine Bateman
Geena Davis
Princess Diana
Andrea Evans
Goldie Hawn
Elton John
Cybill Shepherd
Princess Stephanie
Liz Taylor
Ivana Trump
Raquel Welch

1997'S BEST AND WORST

10 Best Dressed

Carolyn Bessette Kennedy
Cuba Gooding Jr.
Winona Ryder
Harrison Ford
Celine Dion
Toni Braxton
Mira Sorvino
Bette Midler
George Clooney
Christine Baranski

10 Worst Dressed

Paula Abdul
Pat Boone
Lea Thompson
Woody Harrelson
Justine Bateman
Donald Trump
Mary J. Blige
Andie MacDowell
Eileen Davidson
Matthew McConaughey

Ayatollah Khomeini—The fate of the hostages is still unknown, but Iran's fanatic ruler leads his nation toward chaos with growing social and economic problems

Tom Wolfe—After six years of writer's block, his latest, *The Right Stuff,* is his biggest seller

Joan Baez—The brave anti-warrior raises her voice for the boat people and refugees of Cambodia and is accused of changing her tune on Vietnam

Sebastian Coe—After setting three world records, this British runner takes time out to prepare for the Olympics in Moscow, complete his postgraduate studies, and take a break from all the "razzmatazz"

Gloria Vanderbilt—Living up to her genes, the poor little rich girl brings new chic to a bottom line with her top-grossing designer jeans

Bruce Babbitt—The Arizona governor and member of the presidential commission to investigate Three Mile Island believes nuclear power is a necessary evil

Meryl Streep—A big year for the most intelligent actress now at work, with *Manhattan, Kramer vs. Kramer,* and *The Deer Hunter*

Willie Stargell—Captain of the Pittsburgh Pirates, voted MVP this year, but didn't need an award to get the respect and love of his team

Pope John Paul II—Good receptions all over the world indicate a fine first year for the new pope, although his message is often a bitter pill to swallow.

Paul Volcker—The chairman of the Federal Reserve leads an exemplary frugal life, which he brings to the office

Jesse Jackson—Reverend Jackson jets around the world offering support and often inflammatory statements

Dan Aykroyd—*Saturday Night Live* loses the brilliant actor/writer, who is moving on to make more movies

Margaret Thatcher—The first female prime minister of England is not a promotion for feminist ideals but advocates a nostalgic return "to economic Calvinism: hard work, self reliance, and upward mobility"

William Webster—America's top cop takes aim at a tough target: modernizing and de-Hooverizing the FBI

Deborah Harry—Gentlemen and record buyers prefer this platinum blondie: she switches disco to a new wavelength

1980

Ronald Reagan—He wins the presidency by a landslide

Goldie Hawn—*Private Benjamin* liberates a beloved ding-a-ling, promoting her to captain of her soul

Lech Walesa—An unemployed electrician becomes a working-class hero to Poland and the free world

Colonel Charlie Beckwith—The commander of the failed mission to rescue American hostages in Iran emerges as a quiet hero

Herbert Boyer—If nothing else, his forays into genetic engineering can turn this scientist into a multimillionaire

Mary Cunningham—Blond, beautiful, and no longer at Bendix, she's looking for room at the top

Fidel Castro—He grinned after solving 125,000 problems, but now he faces a new one: Reagan

Mel Weinberg—A king con artist sets up Abscam for the FBI and snares some unsuspecting politicians

Sugar Ray Leonard—Who is the greatest? A tough little man wins the boxing championship and the title

Robert Redford—First time behind the scenes, a superstar directs a fine film and says, "I'll phase out acting"

Jean Harris—Was the death of Scarsdale Diet's Dr. Tarnower an accident or murder? Only the quiet headmistress knows

Stephen King—A mild downeaster discovers terror is the ticket

Grete Waitz—A swift Norwegian teacher gives the cold shoulder to the other women runners in the world

Baron St. Helens—An English diplomat's name lives on as a killer volcano

The Reverend Jerry Falwell—A TV preacher sells America on flag, family, and freedom, of sorts

Pat Benatar—Rock finds its missing lynx: she's doing time in the top 10 for what she calls *Crimes of Passion*

Lee Rich—Like J. R. Ewing's assailant, the producer behind *Dallas* aims to please, and does

Sonia Johnson—In the battle for the Equal Rights Amendment, a Mormon feminist waits for the balloon to go up

Sam Shepard—Mr. Funk of off-Broadway may be the Redford of the '80s—if he can play his way

Richard Pryor—Having been through the fire, he's back with a new self and, he says, no bad habits

Eudora Welty—The critics bow before the small-town tales of a masterly Southern writer

Soichiro Honda—The Henry Ford of the Japanese auto industry is known as "Pop" to his workers

Beverly Sills—Bubbles from Brooklyn has stopped singing and begun bossing the company she once graced, the New York City Opera

Dan Rather—When asked if he can hold Walter Cronkite's audience, the new CBS Atlas shrugs

Brooke Shields—From *Blue Lagoon* to blue ads for blue jeans, nothing is coming between her and success

1981

Ronald Reagan—The president survives an assassination attempt, promises 25% tax cuts over the next three years, and says time will tell if he'll run again in '84

Elizabeth Taylor—Old Violet Eyes gets a Tony nomination for her first Broadway performance, in *The Little Foxes*

Lech Walesa—Poland's patriarch of Solidarity is a man of faith and bold deeds, organizing 10 million Poles to stand up to their government

Bradford Smith—Though his Voyager project took us to the planets, he may face a permanent grounding from Reagan's budget axe

Bryant Gumbel—The new *Today* show host aims to be king of the mountain on morning TV

Crown Prince Fahd—The Saudi heir-apparent works to preserve peace between Israel and radical Arab nations

Rabbit Angstrom—John Updike's fictional hero returns fat, rich, and ready for the '80s

Ted Turner—In his one-man air war, cable's Captain Courageous stares down the big guns of network TV

Princess Diana—A kindergarten teacher becomes a princess, beguiles the world, and produces an heir

YEAR-BY-YEAR, THE BEST (AND WORST) SELLING PEOPLE ISSUES

Here are the regular weekly issues that fared best and worst at the newsstand in our first 23 years.

	Best Seller	Worst Seller
1974	The Johnny Carsons	J. Paul Getty
1975	Cher & Gregg Allman	Liv Ullmann
1976	Cher, Gregg, & Baby	Nancy Reagan
1977	Tony Orlando	Julie Andrews
1978	Olivia Newton-John	Vice President & Mrs. Mondale
1979	A Readers' Poll	Fleetwood Mac
1980	John Lennon, A Tribute	Paul Simon
1981	Charles & Diana	Justice Sandra Day O'Connor
1982	Princess Grace, A Tribute	*Annie,* the musical
1983	Karen Carpenter, A Tribute	America's First Woman in Space, Sally Ride
1984	Michael Jackson	How To Make Your Kid a Star
1985	Rock Hudson	Bisset & Godunov
1986	Andrew & Fergie	The Raid on Libya
1987	Fergie & Di	Michael Caine
1988	Burt & Loni	Our American Hostages
1989	Lucy, A Tribute	Abbie Hoffman, Death of a Radical
1990	Patrick Swayze	Campus Rape
1991	Jeffrey Dahmer	Richard & Jeramie Dreyfuss
1992	Princess Diana	Betty Rollin: "I Helped My Mother Die"
1993	Julia & Lyle, A Wedding Album	Hillary Clinton
1994	O.J. and Nicole, The Shocking Story	Kelsey Grammer
1995	David Smith	Larry Hagman
1996	JFK Jr. & Carolyn Bessette	Hollywood Stars, A Tribute

Gloria Monty—Producing ABC's *General Hospital*, she's behind the biggest bubble in showbiz: soap operas

David Stockman—Reagan's budget director is nearly done in by his own hand, the one that would tighten the nation's belt

Lena Horne—A glamorous grandmother wants audiences to wonder, "how does the old broad do it?"

John McEnroe—He's number one in tennis, but superbrat's score with the public is still love-hate

Edgar Bronfman—Seagram's liquor baron enlivens a year of corporate merger mania

Barbara Mandrell—No hee-haw, a new country queen takes on TV and wins

Thomas Sowell—Ronald Reagan's favorite black intellectual attracts attention and decides he doesn't like it

Wolfgang Amadeus Mozart—After two centuries, Austria's child prodigy has become the world's favorite composer

Tom Selleck—More modest than macho, he's the hot-as-a-pistol heartthrob of *Magnum P.I.*

Mick Jagger—Mr. Rolling Stone finds sweet satisfaction with rock's richest tour ever

Richard Viguerie—The New Right's buoyant fundraiser helps purge the Senate of four of its most powerful Democrats

Nicholas Nickleby—At $100 a seat it could have been a bleak house on Broadway, but Dickens proved a smash

Sandra Day O'Connor—Up at 4 a.m. to read briefs, she learns that a woman justice's work is never done

Harrison Ford—He's the new breed of action star—little ego, medium fame, big bucks

Fernando Valenzuela—Baseball almost struck out, but a Mexican rookie conjures up a magical season

Elizabeth McGovern—A talented beauty soars from high school to stardom as a dippy sex kitten in *Ragtime*

1982

Ronald Reagan—Two years into his term, the president enjoys his "confinement" in the White House

Joan Jett—Rock's latest leading lady earns her stripes with a hard look and her hit song, *I Love Rock and Roll*

Ariel Sharon—Stunned by backlash from the Beirut massacre, the defiant Israeli defense minister battles on

Princess Stephanie—Numbed by her mother's death, a sad teenager has lost her zest for life

Jessica Lange—A talented beauty gets a monkey off her back with two major films, *Tootsie* and *Frances*

Herschel Walker—Forget the Heisman—Georgia's got the trophy that counts: the best running back in football, bar none

Larry Gelbart—After 10 years, *M*A*S*H* departs, but the man who wrote the show has a wacky new hit called *Tootsie*

Margaret Thatcher—With Churchill to inspire her, a dogged prime minister triumphs in a nasty little war in the Falkland Islands

Dr. William DeVries—A surgeon touches the soul with a new machine, the artificial heart

Princess Diana—She may have those newlywed blues, but she's still Britain's darling

Yuri Andropov—Emerging from the shadows of the Soviet KGB, a master spy takes over Brezhnev's Kremlin

George Wallace—Politically recast as a friend of blacks, he seeks their votes and forgiveness—and gets both

Paolo Rossi—A handsome soccer hero leads Italy to the World Cup and wins back the hearts of his countrymen

Randall Forsberg—A Massachusetts scholar sounds a nationwide call to (freeze) arms

Norma Kamali—Wowing Seventh Avenue has been no sweat for fashion's Greta Garbo

E.T.—An alien finds his home in Hollywood

Richard Gere—*Officer* makes a star, if not quite a gentleman, out of a movie maverick

Sam Knox—An authority on the scourge of the sexes offers some consoling facts to legions of herpes victims

Andrew Lloyd Webber—From the Bible to back alleys, Broadway's hottest composer strikes all the right notes

Evelyn Waugh—A curmudgeon's elegy for England's upper crust, *Brideshead Revisited* becomes the TV event of 1982

Barbra Streisand—At 40, the Brooklyn songbird returns to the Old World to conquer a new one—directing *Yentl*

Ted Koppel—A clear-eyed shark surveys war and peace and revolutionizes night-owl journalism on *Nightline*

Kiri Te Kanawa—New Zealand's diva hits the top in opera and wins a royal title by acting nothing like a dame

Reverend Sun Myung Moon—The Unification Church's controversial leader is convicted of tax evasion, but he still wins converts

Paul Newman—*The Verdict* is in: a risky role may win Blue Eyes that elusive Oscar gold

Bill Agee and Mary Cunningham—The Bendix takeover didn't take, but this famous couple makes one merger that works

1983

Ronald Reagan—After harrowing events in Granada and Lebanon, the president finishes a tough year on a tougher note with the bombing of Syrian antiaircraft nests in the mountains east of Beirut

Debra Winger—A Hollywood sexpot turns serious actress and scores on her own *Terms*

Fidel Castro—The aging lion of revolution in Latin America gets savvy—and pulls in his claws

The Cabbage Patch Kids—Glassy of eye and poker of face, this chubby, alien horde masks a plot to take over the planet

Jesse Jackson—An explosive orator's campaign breeds fusion and fission for the Democrats

William Gates—Dropping out of Harvard pays off for a computer whiz kid who's making hard cash from Microsoft software

Sam Shepard—He has it all as a laureate of stage and screen but just wants anonymity

Chun Byung In—The career of an "infallible" pilot ends in the debris of Korean Air Lines flight 007, shot down over Soviet airspace in August

Mr. T—The terror of *The A-Team* is indisputably the show-business maniac of the year

Ben Lexcen—An impish Aussie designer and his magic keel haul the America's Cup Down Under after 132 years of U.S. ownership

Joan Rivers—Where's Johnny Carson? Home, watching a *Tonight Show* guest host skewer guests and boost his ratings

Robert Mastruzzi—A Bronx high school principal won't let his school be less than the best

Eddie Murphy—He makes folks mad, but he's got it made

Matthew Broderick—Oh, to be young and hot in Hollywood; yet instead of acting up, the leader of the brat pack is buttoned-down

Barbara McClintock—After six decades of research, the shy discoverer of biology's "jumping genes" wins her Nobel Prize

Harvey Fierstein—Brooklyn's funny boy takes Broadway on a gay mad whirl with *La Cage aux folles*

Philip Johnson—The grand old man of architecture comes full circle, designing the downfall of his own glass box

Vanessa Williams—A thorny crown goes with the job of being the first black Miss America

Richard Chamberlain—He gets no awards from his peers, but the public hails the king of miniseries

Michael Jackson—Thanks to a *Thriller* album, the former small fry of the Jacksons becomes the biggest star in pop

Rei Kawakubo—Japan's Stravinsky of fashion rocks the West with her atonal, asymmetric sad rags

Konrad Kujau—A Nazi-obsessed amateur forger fakes the Führer's diaries and nearly fools the world

Alice Walker—*The Color Purple*, her protagonist's letters to God, bring her a bestseller and a Pulitzer

Alfred Hitchcock—Three years after his death, five buried treasures from the master of sus pense prove to be the movie event of 1983

Jennifer Beals—Dazzling looks and a ripped wardrobe turn a dancing Yalie into a flashy star

1984

Geraldine Ferraro—A tough, savvy, political pioneer loses the battle for vice president but wins a historic war for women

Bruce Springsteen—*Born in the U.S.A.* reaches for 5 million sales and the Boss transcends mere legend to become a symbol of all that once was right about America

Andrei Gromyko—For nearly half a century, this most durable diplomat has been the poker face of Soviet foreign policy

José Napoleón Duarte—On the broad shoulders of this gutsy president rest El Salvador's hopes of emerging from a nightmare civil war

Mary Lou Retton—L.A.'s golden girl Olympian marches to a new beat as Madison Avenue's million-dollar baby

Richard Gere—This elusive screen actor seems bent on preserving the silence that marks him as a Hollywood enigma

Peter Ueberroth—An organizational wizard turns the L.A. Olympic Games into a glowing personal triumph

Joe Kittinger—In the year's greatest adventure, a hard-nosed pilot transforms a POW fantasy into a dream come true with a solo flight across the Atlantic in a hot-air balloon

Farrah Fawcett—With *The Burning Bed*, her career surges, and at 37 she's a happy mother-to-be—proud papa Ryan O'Neal hopes they're altar-bound

Clint Eastwood—As *Tightrope*'s kinky cop he reveals new and darker dimensions that leave astonished critics cheering

Betty Ford—The former First Lady publicly tackles her problems with alcohol and painkillers—and helps cure a nation's ills

John Malkovich—A versatile young Chicago actor storms Broadway in *Death of a Salesman* and stakes a claim on Oscar in two of the year's best movies, *Places in the Heart* and *The Killing Fields*

John Henry—This equine geriatric marvel has traveled from coast to coast and convincingly proved that the race is not always to the youngest

Sparky Anderson—He managed the Detroit Tigers to victory in the World Series and also leads the league in rough-hewn rhetoric

Tina Turner—After eight years of deep rivers and high mountains, a self-professed "Soul Survivor" strides back into the rock and roll promised land with her new album, *Private Dancer*

William Kennedy—At 56, Albany's patient author watches the work of a lifetime pay off with a Pulitzer Prize, *The Cotton Club*, movie deals, and a $264,000 MacArthur "genius grant"

Lee Iaccoca—With his autobiography riding atop the bestseller list, Chrysler's blunt shirtsleeve philosopher offers a plan to fix the sputtering economy

Vanessa Williams—The first black Miss America's reign is distinguished by dignity, delight, and talent—until the discovery that she had posed nude forces her resignation

Kathleen Turner—The star of *Romancing the Stone* mixes sex and sensitivity to become the hottest actress since Streep

James Baker—President Ronald Reagan remains curiously ageless as his chief of staff grows older quickly—could there be a connection?

Kathleen Morris—A controversial Minnesota prosecutor vows to continue the legal fight against sexual abuse of children

John Torrington—From his ice-shrouded tomb in the Canadian Arctic, a 19th-century explorer sheds new light on the chilling fate of Britain's ill-fated Franklin expedition

Bill Murray—This ghostbuster is the comedy star of the year's biggest box-office hit ($220 million), but if you think it's gone to his head—get outta here

Baby Fae—A wondering world watches as a child with a transplanted baboon heart fights for life

Michael Jackson—PEOPLE ran five covers, 73 photos, and 33,205 words on the singer during 1984—what more is there to say?

1985

Bob Geldof—Moved by scenes of mass starvation, this scruffy Irishman raises a cry with a song and rouses the world to save the hungry

Joe Kennedy—The best-known name in American politics surfaces again as Bobby's eldest son announces for the congressional seat once held by his Uncle Jack

Corazon Aquino—As the ghost of her assassinated husband haunts the rule of Philippine president Ferdinand Marcos, a housewife rides an emotional swell to political prominence

Steven Rosenberg—By energizing the body's natural defenses, a surgeon at the National Cancer Institute may

PEOPLE'S MOST BEAUTIFUL PEOPLE IN THE WORLD

Every year PEOPLE faces the difficult task of choosing only 50 of the most stunning celebrities we've seen all year. Here is the face of beauty in 1997, and a look at the stars who have dazzled their way onto more than one of our Most Beautiful People lists.

ALL-TIME BEAUTIES

5 Times
Tom Cruise
Mel Gibson
John F. Kennedy Jr.

4 Times
Michelle Pfeiffer
Julia Roberts

3 Times
Antonio Banderas
Halle Berry
Kevin Costner
Demi Moore
Brad Pitt
Claudia Schiffer
Denzel Washington

2 Times
Juliette Binoche
Toni Braxton
George Clooney
Cindy Crawford
Whitney Houston
Matt Lauer
Jared Leto
Daniel Day-Lewis
Paul Newman
Paulina Porizkova
Jason Priestley
Isabella Rossellini
Winona Ryder
Katarina Witt

1997'S MOST BEAUTIFUL PEOPLE

Gillian Anderson
Lauren Bacall
Jacinda Barrett
Drew Barrymore
David Baldacci
Toni Braxton
Juliette Binoche
Andre Braugher
Jim Carrey
Deana Carter
David Chokachi
Tom Cruise
Christopher Cuomo
Claire Danes
Oscar De La Hoya
Kamar do los Reyes
Leonardo DiCaprio
Roma Downey
Michael Flatley
Harrison Ford
Tom Ford
Vivica A. Fox
Cuba Gooding Jr.
Jeff Gordon
Mia Hamm
Derek Jeter
Lisa Kudrow
Matt Lauer
Lucy Lawless
Jared Leto
Jennifer Lopez
Pattie Maes
Marie-Chantal of Greece
Jeanine Pirro
Brad Pitt
Rebecca Romijn
Gavin Rossdale
Winona Ryder
Kristin Scott Thomas
Paul Sereno
Spice Girls
(Victoria Adams,
Melanie Brown,
Emma Bunton,
Melanie Chisholm,
Geri Halliwell)
Gwen Stefani
Liv Tyler
Garrett Wang
Oprah Winfrey
Michelle Yeoh

have made the biggest step in 30 years toward a cancer cure

Rambo—His deeds are the stuff of cinema legend from here to Haiphong, but to the folks of one small western town, he's just a local boy with a preposterous set of pecs

Akira Kurosawa—Japan's feisty grand old man of the movies comes back from despair to film *Ran*, a feudal version of *King Lear* that may turn out to be his greatest triumph

Nelson Mandela—Banished behind prison walls since 1964, a legendary black leader may yet save South Africa from the horror of racial war

William Perry—He can block, run, and do endorsements. The 308-pound Refrigerator is the big surprise of the football season

Uli Derickson—TWA Flight 847's flight attendant becomes the heroine of a hijacking

Bernhard Goetz—New York's subway vigilante acted out our angriest fantasies, but a year later the questions remain—is he a hero or a villain, a victim or a criminal?

William Hurt—His risky transvestite role in *Kiss of the Spider Woman* makes him an Oscar favorite as Best Actor, but he'd rather hide from the world than try to be world-famous

Hulk Hogan—The World Wrestling Federation's heavyweight champion's favorite subjects are his biceps, his California home, and milk, his breakfast of champions

Cathleen Webb—The New Hampshire housewife says she faked a rape that sent a man to prison for years, and suddenly finds herself an unlikely celebrity

Madonna—She's a big girl now—rich, famous, and married to actor Sean Penn—but once upon a time, the reigning queen of all things pop was just another wannabe

Rupert Murdoch—The empire-building publisher of the *New York Post* and freshly minted American citizen takes on television, Hollywood, and morality

Dwight Gooden—Vulnerable only to kryptonite, baseball's best pitcher is quiet but deadly, playing a game he hasn't learned how to lose

Don Johnson—Every woman wants his body, every man wants his clothes—that's why he's America's Friday night vice

Princess Diana—No matter where she is she embodies dreams and always looks just like a princess

Mel Fisher—In a season of shipwreck salvagings, Captain Audacious ends a 17-year search for buried treasure, pulling 34 tons of Spanish silver from the Key West waters

Michael J. Fox—The comedy star of the year's No. 1 movie, *Back to the Future*, and the No. 2 TV show, *Family Ties*, puts on the dog as the boy king of Hollywood

Mengele's Bones—Discovery of the moldering remains of the Nazis' infamous "Angel of Death" ends the most intense manhunt of the century

Whoopi Goldberg—She's been on welfare and on Broadway; now she's on-screen in *The Color Purple*

Rock Hudson—His name stood for Hollywood's golden age of wholesome heroics and lighthearted romance—until he becames the most famous person to die of AIDS

The Springsteens—The storybook year of Beauty and the Boss ends on a harmonious note with Bruce and Julianne Phillips at ease at last in New Jersey

Gracie Mansion—A hip gallery owner brings world fame to the brassy, flashy, sometimes trashy art that grows in Manhattan's revitalized East Village

1986

Sarah, Duchess of York—Breaking out of the royal mold, a commoner marries her prince and wins a nation's heart without losing her independent personality

Ivan Boesky—It isn't insight but inside tips that make this risk arbitrageur the demon of Wall Street

Dr. Seuss—*You're Only Old Once!* made us hoot, made us cheer / Seuss wrote it for oldsters, it came out this year

Bette Midler—No longer the wacked-out Divine Miss M, she becomes a mother and mainstream box-office draw in two hugely successful Disney films

David Letterman—The *Late Night* host's askew humor finally finds a home in the heartland

Pat Robertson—A television preacher bids to move from God's House to the White House

Daniel Ortega—The 41-year-old president of Nicaragua wears baseball caps, wields his own AK-47, and bedevils the Reagan state department

Raymond Hunthausen—Seen by the Vatican as the shepherd who strayed, Seattle's progressive archbishop believes he's keeping the faith

Bob Hoskins—A pudgy, pint-size dynamo known as the Cockney Cagney shapes up as the actor of the year with appearances in *Sweet Liberty* and *Mona Lisa*

Oliver North—After a series of bombshell disclosures, the question remains—was the

President's marine a hero or a loose cannon?

Terry Waite—An envoy from the Church of England inspires international trust and obtains freedom for hostages in Beirut

Paul Hogan—An Aussie smoothy makes *Crocodile Dundee* America's favorite easy-watching movie

Howard the Duck—George Lucas's feathered friend turns out to be a turkey, as *Howard the Duck* loses $35 million

Greg LeMond—Becoming the first American to win the Tour de France is no easy feat for the 25-year-old cyclist, who has to battle a mentor's betrayal

Run–D.M.C.—Rap's Kings of (Hollis) Queens persuade skeptical rock fans to "Walk This Way"

Debi Thomas—The U.S. women's figure-skating champion finds the time to study microbiology at Stanford

Helga—A Pennsylvania housekeeper bewitches the art world, as it is revealed that she posed for hundreds of previously unknown Andrew Wyeth paintings

Vanna White—The latest in the line of Lite Celebrities, the letter-turning bombshell of *Wheel of Fortune* rakes in endorsements, writes a book, and leaves some wondering why she's famous at all

Beth Henley—A Mississippi playwright goes Hollywood with a trio of quirky comedies: *True Stories*, *Nobody's Fool*, and *Crimes of the Heart*

Jerome P. Horwitz—AZT, the anticancer drug he developed 22 years ago, is now our best hope in the battle against AIDS

David Byrne—Letting down his avant-garde, the Talking Head celebrates a wondrous, wacky America in his movie *True Stories*

William Rehnquist—In all matters large and small, the new chief justice of the Supreme Court goes his own way

Tom Cruise—A fave rave of the teen scene grows up to be the box-office *Top Gun* of 1986

Max Headroom—With electrons for blood, computers for brains, and an ego as big as all TV, this nonhuman talk show host is Chairman of the Tube

Whitney Houston—Singer Cissy Houston's shy daughter emerges as pop's prettiest commercial monster

1987

Ronald Reagan—Entering his eighth year in office, the president remains vigorous and completes his term with a Hollywood finish

Mikhail Gorbachev—The Russian leader who put a human face on communism takes the West by storm and ushers in an age of optimism

Baby Jessica McClure—Up and running after her fall down a Midland, Texas, well and her televised rescue, she gets on with a normal toddler's life

Gary Hart—Undaunted by negative press on his personal life, the Colorado senator reenters the 1988 presidential race

Oliver North—An all-American marine charms his way through the Iran-Contra hearings. Will he ever pay for his involvement in the arms-for-hostages scandal?

Michael Douglas—Playing a lech in *Fatal Attraction* and a slimy corporate raider in *Wall Street*, Kirk's son steps into the spotlight

Patient Zero—Randy Shilts's book *And the Band Played On* identifies French Canadian Gaetan Dugas as a major transmitter of the AIDS virus. 40 of the 248 homosexuals diagnosed with the disease in 1982 had either had sexual relations with the flight steward or with someone else who had

Donald Trump—Emerging as an icon for the '80s, this real estate mogul is pushing his way around in the media and in the marketplace

Cher—Sonny's onetime partner, who says she "refuses to accept other people's limitations," soars as her roles in *The Witches of Eastwick* and *Moonstruck* bring her power, happiness, and a wider audience

Christian Lacroix—A new designer's whimsical approach to his trade revolutionizes the high-fashion world and caters to the most chic of the stars

Oprah Winfrey—The leading voice among talk show hosts is using television to fight apartheid as well as racism at home

Vincent Van Gogh—Despite bouts with depression so severe they drove him to suicide, Vincent Van Gogh is emerging as the most marketable Postimpressionist of the twentieth century

Magic Johnson—This talented point guard is leading the Los Angeles Lakers to the top of the NBA—and smiling all the way

Church Lady—*Saturday Night Live*'s most biting holy roller flourishes in a year of sex scandals, church scams, and other *special* sins

Princess Diana—Hints of discord follow the princess into her sixth year of marriage, as she and Charles spend more and more time apart and she begins to test the limits of acceptable royal behavior

Donna Fawn Hahn—Rice, Hall, and Jessica, the women who fell with Gary Hart, Ollie

North, and Jim Bakker, are actually all the same person—the three faces of Eve

Bono—Struggling with sainthood, this rock musician spray-paints a work of art in San Francisco and tries to chip away at his heroic status

Brigitte Nielsen—Newly divorced from Sylvester Stallone, she remains notorious for her leggy sexuality and questionable motives in love

Tracey Ullman—Host of her own show on Fox, this British comedian astonishes and delights her audience, always hoping to avoid the bland

Jerry Garcia—Despite more than just a touch of grey, the middle-aged hippie priest is still getting by—and is singing to a new generation of Deadheads

Glenn Close—A 40-year-old actress battles her earth-mother image and becomes a screen siren with fatal attraction

Garrison Keillor—The creator of National Public Radio's *A Prairie Home Companion* is happy with life in the aftermath of his show

William Casey—Dying before he is able to testify in the Iran-Contra hearings, Ronald Reagan's CIA director admitted using any means necessary to defend the free world as he saw it

Dennis Quaid—His sure-footed sex appeal and engaging grin ignite the screen in *The Big Easy*

Tammy Faye Bakker—Hurt by a drug addiction and her husband's alliance with Jessica Hahn, America's most unusual makeup consumer stuns *Nightline* audiences and makes herself a national joke

1988

George Bush—The president-elect is a gentleman of the old school and a family man who is not above a bare-knuckled brawl when it comes to politics

Jodie Foster—No longer haunted by would-be Reagan assassin John Hinckley, she makes an acclaimed comeback as a rape victim who fights back in *The Accused*

Roseanne Barr—Looking at her, it's difficult to distinguish art from life—Roseanne plays the larger-than-life housewife both on and off the small screen

Athina Roussel—Now only three, she will inherit over $1 billion when she turns 18—but money won't buy the love she lost with the death of her mother, Christina Onassis

The Cyberpunk—The nerds rise again, as "misfit" hackers wreak havoc on America's information networks

Florence Griffith Joyner—She may have won four medals as a sprinter at the Seoul Olympics, but she's still got two feet firmly on the ground

Lisa Marie Presley—The King's daughter lives down a princess image by marrying a sober fellow and settling down

Benazir Bhutto—A Radcliffe-and-Oxford-educated feminist becomes prime minister of Pakistan and discovers the challenges posed in being the first woman to lead an Islamic nation

Liz Taylor—In another roller-coaster year, Liz writes an upbeat autobiography, raises millions to fight AIDS, and descends again into a drug addiction so severe that a staffer at the Betty Ford Center calls her the "female version of Elvis"

Michelle Pfeiffer—*Married to the Mob, Tequila Sunrise,* and *Dangerous Liaisons* prove that this actress is more than just a pretty face

Jesse Jackson—He may not have clinched the nomination, but Jesse Jackson's presidential campaign shows that he is a political force to be reckoned with

Phantom of the Opera— Rising from his lonely catacomb, this anguished spirit of the night beguiles us once again with a vision of the tragic depths of love

Merv Griffin—At 63, the former talk show host becomes a billionaire and takes over ownership of Trump's Resorts International, beating Donald at his own game

Anne Tyler—With her new novel *Breathing Lessons* and a film adaptation of her 1985 bestseller, *The Accidental Tourist,* a reclusive novelist is faced by an adoring public

Orel Hershiser—Squeaky clean or tough and mean? Off the diamond he may be an angel, but this World Series MVP is uncompromising when he pitches

Shi Peipu—Posing as a woman throughout his 20-year relationship with French diplomat Bernard Boursicot, a onetime singer with the Peking opera inspires David Hwang's Tony Award–winning play, *M. Butterfly*

Kevin Costner—*Bull Durham*'s down-to-earth romantic lead sends hearts aflutter and critics abuzz

Tracy Chapman—A serious black folk musician sings about a revolution and becomes one of the most successful recording artists of the year

David Hockney—25 years after making the move from England to sunny California, artist David Hockney and his bright canvases are the talk of the art scene

Jessica Rabbit—The hottest woman on celluloid isn't a

woman at all, according to fans of this sultry 'toon

Stephen Hawking—Plagued by Lou Gehrig's disease, a Cambridge University mathematics professor works to unwind the mysteries of the universe—and writes a bestselling book

Tom Hanks—A familiar face hits the *Big* time with his portrayal of a 13-year-old trapped in a 35-year-old's body

Fergie—The Duchess of York's first year with the Windsors is not the fairy tale it had been cut out to be

Mike Tyson—The heavyweight champion's most formidable opponent proves to be his beautiful wife, Robin Givens

Sage Volkman—Thanks to a strong will and the miracles of modern surgery, a six-year-old burn survivor gets back her smile

1989

George and Barbara Bush—After a successful meeting with Gorbachev abroad, George turns his gaze to domestic matters while Barbara helps Millie write her book

Jack Nicholson—As *Batman*'s Joker, he romps in a role that fits him as closely as his white grease paint

Arsenio Hall—This hippest night-owl of them all hops to the top of the talk-show totem pole

Julio Berumen—The San Francisco Bay Area earthquake's pluckiest survivor takes his first steps with a new leg

Princess Anne—Once Britain's least-liked royal, she becomes an object of desire

Mikhail Gorbachev—He shrugs when the Eastern Bloc cracks and proves he's serious about perestroika

Salman Rushdie—For publishing the controversial *The Satanic Verses* he now lives with the threat he'll perish

John Goodman—The TV Barr-tender and newly minted movie star is an extra-large hit in any medium

Gaia—The Greek earth goddess lends her name to James Lovelock's daring theory that the planet itself is alive

Manuel Noriega—The Panamanian dictator gives American leaders fits, but he may be nearing his last hurrah

Michael Milken—A junk bond entrepreneur makes $1.1 billion financing corporate takeovers—but his indictment brings an era to an end

Paula Abdul—No longer just Janet Jackson's footwork coach, she steps out as a song-and-dance sensation

Deborah Gore Dean—As the HUD scandal unravels, it's clear that she saw government as a game show and helped her friends win valuable prizes

Robert Fulghum—His unlikely bestseller, *All I Really Need To Know I Learned in Kindergarten*, goes to the head of the class

Madonna—In another typical year, she irks some Christians, splits from Sean, dallies with Warren, and gets canned by Pepsi

Spike Lee—The director raises a ruckus—and important questions—with his film *Do The Right Thing*

Ellen Barkin—She's tough, vulnerable, smart, very sexy, and doesn't quite add up; which may be why she's so riveting on-screen

Billy Crystal—Learning that an orgasm can be faked, he becomes a genuine sex symbol in *When Harry Met Sally...*

Pete Rose—Charlie Hustle battles bad press, baseball commissioner A. Bartlett Giamatti, and his own demons

THE SEXIEST MAN ALIVE

PEOPLE has honored someone with this title beginning in 1985. Here is a look at the magazine's hunks of the year. Discerning readers will recall the drought of 1994, when no one made the honor roll.

1985
Mel Gibson

1986
Mark Harmon

1987
Harry Hamlin

1988
John F. Kennedy Jr.

1989
Sean Connery

1990
Tom Cruise

1991
Patrick Swayze

1992
Nick Nolte

1993
Richard Gere and
Cindy Crawford
(The Sexiest Couple Alive)

1994
No winner

1995
Brad Pitt

1996
Denzel Washington

Pablo Escobar—A Colombian drug lord markets death by the kilo while evading an outraged citizenry

Michelle Pfeiffer—In *The Fabulous Baker Boys* she adds a dash of hot pepper to a delicious dish

Elizabeth Morgan—Jailed for shielding her daughter from alleged sexual abuse, she is freed at last

Robert Mapplethorpe—The photographer rattles the art world and Jesse Helms with a shocking retrospective

Captain Al Haynes—In crash-landing a crippled DC-10 in Sioux City, Iowa, he saves lives with grit and cool

Donna Karan—Her DKNY collection secures the designer's position as high fashion's newest mogul

1990

George Bush—His place in history insecure, he faces a sea of troubles—and his most daunting crisis lies before him in the treacherous Middle East

Sinead O'Connor—Her haunting rebel voice is heard in an age of flashing legs and lip sync

Julia Roberts—After becoming the first hit female star of the '90s in *Pretty Woman,* she's sitting pretty

Ken Burns—The producer of the 11-hour epic *The Civil War* makes a big bang in an unlikely place—public television

Patrick Swayze—More mesomorphic than ectoplasmic in *Ghost*, he's every woman's dream of a heavenly body

Neil Bush—His questionable involvement with a Denver S&L puts a First Family face on the $500-billion S&L scandal

Delta Burke—She has unkind words for her *Designing Women* producers; the next thing she loses may not be pounds

Saddam Hussein—His invasion of Kuwait—bloody politics as usual for him—brings the world to the brink of war

Michael Ovitz—The man everyone in Hollywood would like to know spins gold out of tinsel

Nancy Cruzan—Finally off life support after eight years in a coma, she dramatizes the need for living wills

Colin Powell—America's top man in uniform raises the world's shield in the desert against Saddam Hussein

Fidel Castro—Cuba's leader stands alone and defiant after watching the lights go out all over the Communist world

Effi Barry—She's a model of wifely decorum as husband Marion, Washington's mayor, goes up in a puff of smoke

Dr. Anthony Fauci—He's used to taking the heat: he's America's point man in the fight against AIDS

M.C. Hammer—He brings showbiz flash and footwork to rap—and cashes in with the year's hottest LP

Bart Simpson—TV's intemperate urchin suits his audience to a T(shirt)—while authority figures have a cow

Nancy Ziegenmeyer—A housewife and rape victim goes public to fight a once-unmentionable crime

Nelson Mandela—He steps from the dim recesses of a South African jail into the harsh reality of freedom

Francis Ford Coppola—The acclaimed director stages the movies' most ambitious mob scene with his sequel *The Godfather, Part III*

Keenan Ivory Wayans—His *In Living Color* brings howls of laughter and out-Foxes the network establishment

Claudia Schiffer—No guesswork about this supermodel's genes—they come from Germany, via Bardot

William Styron—His *Darkness Visible*, an account of his bleak depression, helps fellow sufferers see the light

Laura Palmer—Wasn't washed up when she was washed up—she's the Girl Most Likely To Pique on *Twin Peaks*

Bo Jackson—He can hit, run, rattle, and roll—and score on Madison Avenue

Princess Caroline—Eight years after her mother's death Monaco's First Lady is coping once more with tragedy in the year of her husband's violent death

1991

George and Barbara Bush—The First Couple's first concerns are war, peace, and their kids

Jodie Foster—As an actor she's known as BLT (bossy little thing) because she isn't silent as a lamb, but the first-time director commands respect on the set with *Little Man Tate*

Magic Johnson—He copes with testing HIV-positive by mounting a full-court press against AIDS

Julia Roberts—With a busted engagement and a box-office bust that's no sleeper, she ends the year flying off to Never-Never Land

Luke Perry—This hunk steals not only the *Beverly Hills 90210* spotlight but also the hearts of girls in all zip codes

Anita Hill—Her testimony doesn't stop Clarence Thomas, but it starts a national debate on sexual harassment

Garth Brooks—His country album *Ropin' the Wind* crosses over to lasso the attention of all America

Princess Diana—Surviving digs at her marriage and her AIDS activism, she turns a very regal 30

William Kennedy Smith—He beats a charge of rape, but his famous family may never be the same again

Terry Anderson—Unbowed after nearly seven years as a Beirut hostage, he emerges eager to catch up

Boris Yeltsin—By elbowing aside both Gorby and the Kremlin hard-liners, he becomes Russia's new voice

Kenneth Branagh—Taking a break from the Bard, he goes Hollywood with the hit noir thriller *Dead Again*

Anjelica Huston—Recovered from the loss of a father and a lover, she emerges as Morticia, the *Addams*'s coolest ghoul

Jeffrey Dahmer—His confession could not explain why his grisly serial killings went so long undetected

Elizabeth Taylor—She must be the world's most incurable romantic; will altar trip No. 8 be her last?

Robert Bly—He says there's a bit of "hairy primate" in us all, and *Iron John*'s (mostly male) readers go ape

John Singleton—His *Boyz N the Hood* opens middle-class eyes to inner-city life—not bad for a 23-year-old

Naomi Campbell—With her drop-dead looks and her diva's temperament, she reigns over high-fashion runways

Axl Rose—Lowering the sonic boom onstage and off befits the rock monster who is Guns N' Roses' lead pistol

The 4,600-Year-Old Man—Freed from an Alpine deep freeze, he becomes the modern world's unlikeliest souvenir

Mariah Carey—She becomes pop's queen by sharing her musical *Emotions*, not by truth-or-baring her life

Derek Humphry—His best-selling suicide manual, *Final Exit*, ignites a passionate public debate about the right to die

Pee-Wee Herman—Loses his image at an X-rated theater—but not his public, nor the support of Hollywood

Norman Schwarzkopf—A hero after the Gulf, he now faces the challenges of a post-army career

Jimmy Connors—Written off as a tennis has-been, he defiantly returns to the present tense at the U.S. Open

1992

Bill Clinton—The president-elect and his family recoup from a rough campaign and prepare to leave Little Rock behind for Washington

Hillary Clinton—Barbara's successor is a savvy lawyer who loves her country and her husband and is determined to make a difference

Cindy Crawford—She shows the brains behind the beauty, becoming a video celebrity

Ross Perot—Trying to crash the two major parties, he goes from can-do to quitter and back

Denzel Washington—As a mesmerizing *Malcolm X* he catapults to superstardom

Princess Diana—She dumps her hubby but gets to keep the kids, the perks, and the palace

Woody Allen—His breakup with Mia Farrow is like *Annie Hall Goes Ballistic*

Larry King—*Larry King Live* is the whistle-stop that White House contenders have to visit this year

Barney—The purple dino fossilizes the Ninja Turtles and gives kid-vid a Jurassic spark

Billy Ray Cyrus—All pecs and no talent, said critics, but he's raising Nashville's pulse

Terry McMillan—She can breathe easy now that her novel *Waiting To Exhale* is a surprise smash

Gregory K.—He changes his name and sets legal precedents by divorcing his mother

Desiree Washington—She scores a knockout in court over heavyweight champ Mike Tyson

Diane English—The producer makes *Murphy Brown* a single mom and herself a lightning rod

Madonna—She bares her bod, blankets the media, and leaves fans asking, "What next?"

George Smoot—He finds the missing ripples that confirm the universe began with a Big Bang

Katie Couric—With political know-how and a chipper personality, she boosts the *Today* show

Fabio—Once a fantasy figure on romance-novel covers, he actually moves and speaks

Arthur Ashe—He brings eloquence, guts, and grace to his instructive fight against AIDS

Dana Carvey—Whether he's doing Bush, Perot, or *Wayne*'s Garth, he's always hilariously on target

Bernadine Healy—The first woman to head the National Institute of Health is brash and brainy, and gives women's health research a shot in the arm

Carol Moseley Braun—The first black woman to be a U.S. senator defies naysayers to win a place in the history books

Henri Matisse—Sybarite and family man, this glorious painter has crowds standing in line to see his work

Whoopi Goldberg—The actor is suddenly a Hollywood force more prolific than some studios

Sharon Stone—She shows a *Basic Instinct* for sensuality and stardom—and doesn't sit like a lady

1993

Bill Clinton—The president faces tough issues and a skeptical nation

Hilary Rodham Clinton—She reflects on family life and the value of prayer while heading the committee on health care reform

Princess Diana—She may be out of power in the palace, but she still has a place in Britons' hearts

Michael Jackson—The pop star can moonwalk but he can't hide from career-threatening allegations of child abuse

Yasir Arafat—With a handshake seen around the world, the PLO leader makes peace with his sworn enemy

Oprah Winfrey—This talk show host becomes the world's highest-paid entertainer, sheds 60 pounds, and stays single

Andrew Wiles—A shy Princeton prof you've never heard of awes the great minds of math

David Letterman—Once an after-hour prankster, now he's the leader of the late-night pack

Janet Reno—She wows Washington with her guts and candor, though you can't please everyone

Susan Powter—Her hot *Stop The Insanity!* suggests anger might be the best weight-loss prescription

Howard Stern—Radio's raffish raconteur exposes his *Private Parts,* and everybody wants a peek

Baby Jessica—She focuses our eyes and hearts on the tangled arguments over parental rights

Lyle Lovett—Country's wry specialist in heartache and rue wins the hand of winsome Julia Roberts

Ol' Man River—The Mississippi inspires words of awe and rage, from days gone byto last summer's rampaging floods

Jerry Seinfeld—He's got TV's most buzzed-about sitcom, a hot book—and an 18-year-old girlfriend

Katherine Ann Power—In facing her bloody past she prompts a rethinking of '60s ideals

Eddie Vedder—His hellbound vocals make Pearl Jam jell. Now he's got just one problem—he's a star

Vincent Foster—His suicide brings sadness and self-examination to Clinton's inner circle

Sheik Omar Abdel Rahman—A blind cleric is accused of inciting his U.S. followers to bomb and kill

Michael Jordan—His surprise retirement shows that even the highest fliers need to be well grounded

Rush Limbaugh—He bashes liberals for fun, profit, and the devotion of a fanatic following on air and in print

Shannen Doherty—Unlike *Beverly Hills 90210*'s Brenda, the feisty actress runs amok in several zip codes

Tommy Lee Jones—He's not the man you want on your tail, but you sure want to see him on the big screen

Lorena Bobbitt—She provokes the national imagination with an act few could view with detachment

Tom Hanks—Seen this year in three diverse and challenging roles, this star doesn't get caught up in the glitz of Hollywood

1994

Bill Clinton—Foiled by failed politics and gloating Republicans, the president strives to restore voter confidence

Tim Allen—Good things come in threes for the still-climbing star; with a hit film, book, and sitcom, he has the last ho-ho-ho

O.J. Simpson—Once an All-American, he finds his greatest fame as the murder suspect of the decade

The Pope—Despite failing health he delivers his message to millions in a book that lands at No. 1

Princess Diana—She tries to resume private life amid allegations of adultery and instability

Gerry Adams—The Sinn Fein leader calls for his Irish countrymen to lay down their arms

Shannon Faulkner—The 19-year-old "Lady Bulldog" fights tenaciously to become the Citadel's first female cadet

Michael Fay—In Singapore, the American teen is charged with vandalism and sentenced to a caning that sets off a worldwide debate: Is it spanking or torture?

Whitney Houston—Pop's top songstress takes her show on the road but walks a rocky path at home

Ricki Lake—Less than 3.6 rating points from Oprah, she trounces her competition, walks down the aisle, and lands in jail for an antifur protest

Vinton Cerf—The hearing-impaired Father of the Internet is working toward a universal network—his brainchild has doubled every year for the past six

Michael Jordan—Basketball's king tries the summer game, gracing baseball during the labor strife that threatened to steal the season

Heather Locklear—When not luring living rooms to join sizzling *Melrose Place,* she's planning her real life marriage to Bon Jovi's Richie Sambora

Jim Carrey—He may look *Dumb and Dumber,* but that comic *Mask* shows off rare slapstick style

Tonya Harding—The feisty figure skating champion slides into scandal and ices her dream

Jeffrey Katzenberg—The Disney exec ditches Mickey and Pluto for Spielberg and Geffen

Nadja Auermann—Forget the waif: This year's supermodel is a German import who gives fashion a shot of '30s glamour

Aldrich Ames—For nine years before his arrest, this rogue CIA agent brazenly betrayed his country

Christine Todd Whitman—New Jersey's new governor becomes a darling of G.O.P. moderates and moves up in line for the 1996 ticket

James Redfield—His philosophical thriller, *The Celestine Prophecy,* breathes new life into New Age

Andre Agassi—With Brooke in his court and a win at the U.S. Open, tennis's reformed bad boy serves notice he's back to stay

Liz Phair—Alternative rock's hottest star looks perky and sings dirty, communicating that wholesome girls have prurient thoughts

Power Rangers—Six multicultural teenage superheroes battle evil (and the once invincible Barney), but adults worry they are models of violence

John Travolta—From disco prancing to ponytailed *Pulp Fiction,* he proves to be Hollywood's most durable comeback kid

Newt Gingrich—The new Speaker of the House uses tough talk to tame Democrats

1995

Bill Clinton—Taking on Bosnia and the budget, the rejuvenated President sees approval ratings soar

Princess Diana—With a stunning confession to the BBC, she opens a bid to become "queen of people's hearts"

Christopher Reeve—Injured but not defeated, he finds a new role as inspirational spokesperson

Elizabeth Hurley—Actress, model, and Hugh Grant's better half, this Brit puts her career in high gear and her beau on a leash

Colin Powell—The once and possibly future presidential candidate decides to stay high and dry above the fray

Nicole Kidman—*To Die For* gives birth to a star and puts an end to the "Mrs. Cruise" label

O. J. Simpson—After the verdict, the unsettling image of a fallen idol remains

Marcia Clark—A beleaguered working mother loses the O. J. trial but wins in the court of public opinion

Susan Smith—Convicted of drowning her sons, she's sentenced to a life of punishing memory

Jay Leno—With a new set and gentle bite, Mr. Nice Guy becomes late night's top dog

C. Delores Tucker—Alarmed by what gangsta rap was doing to children, she declares war on media giant Time-Warner—and wins

Jane Austen—Her novel Brit wit makes her hot in Hollywood—178 years after death

Shania Twain—A Canadian honky-tonker sings her hard-luck heart out and watches her fortunes change in Nashville

Brad Pitt—*Seven* proves his appeal to be more than skin-deep

Babe—The sty's no limit to a charming porker who wants to be a real pig star

Louis Farrakhan—Taking a step from hate toward healing, a demagogue tests the mainstream

Ted Turner—The titan cheers his champion Braves and hitches his wagon to Time Warner

Hootie & the Blowfish—What's in a name? For this fun-loving frat band, the sweet sound of success

The Unabomber—America's most mysterious serial killer issues another bomb, more threats and a "manifesto"

Jennifer Aniston—Gen X's Mary Tyler Moore makes *Friends* and influences hairstyles

JFK Jr.—With his own magazine, *George,* a political prince gets focused

Monica Seles—Healed and whole, a leading lady of tennis returns to center court

R. L. Stine—Churning out two dozen bestsellers a year, he gives young readers *Goosebumps*

Selena—Not silenced by death, the Latina Madonna takes *Tejano* mainstream

Cal Ripken Jr.—The Oriole restores the glory to baseball by playing 2,131 consecutive games

1996

Rosie O'Donnell—The Queen of Nice cleans up the talk show

Ted Kaczynski—A Harvard-educated hermit is charged as the Unabomber

Carolyn Bessette Kennedy—She weds JFK Jr. and become's America's most watched woman

Dennis Rodman—Nude, lewd, and heavily tattooed, he cross-dresses for success, but is he all Bull?

Diana—Out of the Palace and into the world, she tried to find her separate peace

George Clooney—The new Batman wages a real-life war against stalkerazzi

Richard Jewell—Cleared as a bombing suspect, he struggles to restore his name

Binta-Jua—The world goes ape over a gorilla with a humanitarian streak

Jenny McCarthy—MTV's rising star looks pretty and acts anything but!

Christopher Reeve—Undeterred by his paralysis, he works tirelessly for the disabled

Kathie Lee Gifford—At first she cried...then pushed to put an end to sweatshops

Dilbert—The office drudge conceived by cartoonist Scott Adams gets the last laugh

Gwyneth Paltrow—For this hot actress, Brad Pitt is just the icing on the cake

Marian Wright Edelman—Fighting for children's rights, she loses a White House ally

Tom Cruise—Mission Accomplished: two blockbusters and three rescues

Alanis Morissette—The pied piper of teen angst sets a music industry record

Shannon Lucid—A working mom logs 188 trailblazing days in space

Brooke Shields—With an unlikely turn to comedy, she's Hollywood's comeback kid

Conan O'Brien—After a stumbling start, he's the big man of the wee small hours

Carolyn McCarthy—A victim of tragedy wins a seat in Congress

Madonna—The people behind her latest reinvention are named Lourdes and Evita

Tiger Woods—No longer a sport just for geezers, golf gets a Gen-X superstar

Goldie Hawn—With two acclaimed movies at 51, her career is golden

Chelsea Clinton—The First Daughter gracefully takes the stage

Bob Dole—He loses his presidential bid but makes 'em laugh on Letterman

CYBERWORLD: 20 ESSENTIAL BOOKMARKS

Some Websites are good for a one-time giggle, and some will have you going back again and again. PEOPLE technology writer Samantha Miller selects some of the best—the useful, the dishy, and the downright indispensable:

1. Yahoo!
(yahoo.com)

Yahoo! breaks down the Web like a card catalog, sorting through sites by subject. So when you search, you'll find what you want—and not a lot of what you don't. The starting point for any Web search expedition.

2. AltaVista
(altavista.digital.com)

The search method of choice among hardcore techies, this turbo-charged search engine scours the Web and Usenet newsgroups for any words you enter—and returns the results in a jif.

3. The Internet Movie Database
(us.imdb.com)

Everything you ever wanted to know about just about every movie ever made. Cast, crew, reviews, release dates, and more—all linked so you can play your own version of Six Degrees of Kevin Bacon.

4. The Weather Channel
(www.weather.com)

A stormy paradise for weather junkies—minus the Muzak. And handy for anyone without a window office.

5. Quote.com
(www.quote.com)

Get stock-market prices 15 minutes after the pros do—the best you can get for free.

6. ESPNet Sportszone
(espnet.sportszone.com)

Whether your pleasure is baseball or roller hockey, this popular site charges for some material but still dishes out more free, up-to-the-minute stats and scores than you can shake a stick (bat, racquet, javelin...) at.

7. Firefly
(www.firefly.com)

Recommends music and movies based on the opinions of other people who like what you like. Sound simple? The heavy-duty technology is actually way cutting-edge—and uncannily accurate. And you can meet the people who think like you do, so some say Firefly doubles as a dating service.

8. Tripod
(www.tripod.com)

Aimed at those headed from college to the real world, this friendly site's tips, discussions, and news you can use (and its free home pages for members) are applicable to browsers of all ages.

9. Four11
(four11.com)

Track down the e-mail addresses of friends, neighbors, high-school buddies, etc.—and maybe electronically rekindle an old flame—at this useful directory.

10. FAQs
(www.cis.ohio-state.edu/hypertext/faq/usenet/top.html)

One of many sites archiving Usenet newsgroups' Frequently Asked Questions lists—one of the great inventions of geek culture.

11. Liszt
(liszt.com)

A directory of the tens of thousands of e-mail discussion groups, for devotees of everything from anime to Zoroastrianism. Forget Usenet newsgroups: Net vets know mailing lists are much more conducive to intelligent conversation.

12. Slate
(www.slate.com)

Pundit Michael Kinsley's Microsoft-sponsored Webzine seems to have slid from an enjoyably eclectic *New Yorker* clone to something more reminscent of the snoozy *New Republic.* But here's always a fascinating—or agenda-setting—article or two in the mix.

13. Salon
(www.salonmagazine.com)

The cream of the mainstream-Webzine crop, with lots of arts and media coverage and a few big-name writers. And, not least, an elegant, easy-to-navigate design with classy graphics.

14. The Drudge Report
(www.drudgereport.com)

Matt Drudge's controversial one-man gossip operation serves as a tip sheet to those seeking breaking entertainment and political dirt.

15. Ain't It Cool News
(www.aint-it-cool-news.com)

Proprietor Harry Knowles commands an army of moles who attend advance movie screenings, providing early dish and perturbing Hollywood execs.

16. The Dilbert Zone
(www.unitedmedia.com/comics/dilbert)

Cartoonist Scott Adams's *Dilbert* books became mega-bestsellers, but he hasn't forgotten his Net fans: His pioneering Website just keeps getting bigger and funnier.

17. CNN
(cnn.com)

Rival MSNBC's 24-hour news site is more stylish, but CNN got there first, and it's a preferred stop for a quick peek at the day's headlines.

18. The Palace
(www.thepalace.com)

A glimpse into the future of the Net. Citizens chat while wandering virtual worlds in the form of an "avatar"—a disembodied smiley face or any image of your choosing.

19. E! Online
(eonline.com)

All sorts of info about celebrities, movies, and other pursuits of people-watchers.

20. PEOPLE Online
(people.com)

Well, duh.

THE MOST BEAUTIFUL PEOPLE ON THE WEB

Every year, PEOPLE's print editors name the 50 Most Beautiful People in the World. PEOPLE Online, meanwhile, asks Web surfers to nominate their own favorites. Here are those who received the most e-mail votes (thanks in part to their online fan clubs' rallying of the troops):

1. Adrian Paul, *Highlander*
2. Larisa Oleynik, *The Secret Life of Alex Mack*
3. Gillian Anderson, *The X-Files*
4. Claire Danes, of *Romeo & Juliet* and *My So-Called Life*
5. David Duchovny, *The X-Files*
6. Peter Wingfield, *Highlander*
7. Hudson Leick, *Xena: Warrior Princess*
8. Renee O'Connor, *Xena: Warrior Princess*
9. Lucy Lawless, star of *Xena: Warrior Princess*
10. Jenny McCarthy, *Jenny* and *Singled Out*

BEST AND WORST OF THE NET

Ten best? Ten worst? Who knows? The jury's still out on the cyber-trends of 1997. Here's our weather report on the year's clouds and silver linings:

1. Censorship Wars

To the jublilation of cyberlibertarians, the U.S. Supreme Court ruled in June that the government couldn't outlaw "indecent" speech online. Bravo—Net censorship would have been neither wise nor enforceable. The alternative approach: raunch-blocking software that parents can control.

BUT...

Such "censorware" isn't all that easy to use, and asking sites to rate their own age-appropriateness still smacks of Big Brotherism. There's no substitute for parental supervision.

2. Scare Stories

Yellow journalism lives in lurid, mostly exaggerated tales of Net addiction, online drug bazaars, marauding hackers, creepy cyberdates, and rampant child porn.

BUT...

Umm, kids, are you sure you don't want to get off the computer and go play outside?

3. Girl Games

Its eyes opened by the success of Barbie CD-ROMs, the computer-game industry discovers that it's been ignoring half of its potential customers: girls.

BUT...

Pink packaging and makeup advice may be an alternative to grisly shoot-'em-ups, but Gloria Steinem would wince.

4. Virtual Pets

Imported from Japan (where else?), the wackiest craze in many a summer is keychain-sized video games featuring pixelated "pets" that require round-the-clock attention. Geek Chic hits the kiddie generation.

BUT...

Some tots were emotionally traumatized when their neglected virtual pets kicked the virtual bucket.

5. No Secrets

New revelations emerge almost every week about personal information that strangers can snoop out online: Social Security numbers, credit histories, etc. And who knows who's watching where you surf on the Net?

BUT...

Like it or not, most of the info was already available well before the Web came into being.

6. On Sale

Buying books, CDs, even groceries over the Net became less a novelty than an everyday convenience. Heck, Web bookseller Amazon.com and real-world chain Barnes & Noble even found enough of an online market to fight over.

BUT...

So Web surfing is finally as exciting as... a trip to the mall.

7. Power to the People

Maverick online gossipmongers like Matt Drudge (The Drudge Report) and Harry Knowles (Ain't It Cool News) stirred up controversy and perturbed Hollywood and D.C. power players.

BUT...

Boring parties where everybody (or everybody with a Net connection) swaps the same gossip.

8. Web TV

Undaunted by the flop of the original WebTV last year, more companies rolled out their own versions of a cheap device to pipe the Net directly to the boob tube.

BUT...

If the second generation manages to catch on, it's a great way to get Grandma into e-mail.

9. Heaven's Gate

When 39 cult members committed mass suicide in March, they left behind Web-sites explaining it all—a big hit among morbid curiosity-seekers.

BUT...

Another great image boost for the Internet.

10. Mars Mission

Up-to-the-minute updates from the Pathfinder mission to Mars sent millions of users to NASA's Web-site—a watershed moment for the Net as a mass news medium, pundits declared.

BUT...

Really, guys, those pictures of rocks weren't all that exciting.

CYBERSPACE'S MOST WANTED

As the Web grows, search engines keep webcrawlers up to date on sites for favorite stars and shows. From March to July 1997, here's who Lycos users sought most on the superhighway.

FEMALE CELEBRITIES

1. Pamela Lee
2. Jenny McCarthy
3. Cindy Crawford
4. Anna Nicole Smith
5. Madonna
6. Demi Moore
7. Alicia Silverstone
8. Carmen Electra (MTV's *Singled Out*)
9. Gillian Anderson
10. Teri Hatcher

MALE CELEBRITIES

1. Brad Pitt
2. Marilyn Manson
3. Michael Jordan
4. Dennis Rodman
5. Tiger Woods
6. Tom Cruise
7. Leonardo DiCaprio
8. Howard Stern
9. Tupac Shakur
10. Michael Jackson

BAND

1. Spice Girls
2. No Doubt
3. Wu-Tang Clan
4. Backstreet Boys
5. Pink Floyd
6. Smashing Pumpkins
7. Grateful Dead
8. Pearl Jam
9. Nine Inch Nails
10. The Beatles

MOVIES AND TV SHOWS

1. Star Wars
2. Star Trek
3. The X-Files
4. The Simpsons
5. Beavis & Butt-head
6. Days of Our Lives
7. Romeo & Juliet
8. Men in Black
9. Monty Python's Flying Circus
10. Batman & Robin

INFORMATION PLEASE

Personality will get you so far—but life on the Web isn't *all* Pamela and Brad. Here are the non-celebrity topics most requested at Lycos between March and July 1997.

1. chat rooms
2. air fares
3. screen savers
4. *Consumer Reports*
5. real estate
6. Mars Pathfinder mission
7. Beanie Babies
8. Heaven's Gate
9. Las Vegas
10. Hale-Bopp Comet

MOST POPULAR WEBSITES

Be warned: ranking the popularity of Web-sites is far from an exact science. One method follows the approach of TV's Nielsen ratings—keep tabs on a bunch of selected surfers and watch where they're clicking. For this June 1997 survey, consulting group Media Metrix followed 9,265 Web users to see which sites they visited most:

TOP NEWS AND ENTERTAINMENT SITES

1. ZDNet, Ziff-Davis computer magazines (www.zdnet.com)
2. Pathfinder, Time Inc. magazines (pathfinder.com)
3. The Weather Channel (www.weather.com)
4. The Walt Disney Co. (www.disney.com)
5. Sony entertainment (www.sony.com)
6. Warner Bros. Online (wb.com)
7. CNET, Computer news and tips (cnet.com)
8. MSNBC (msnbc.com)
9. USA Today (usatoday.com)
10. CNN (cnn.com)
11. ESPN SportsZone (sports zone.com)
12. Intellicast, weather and travel info (www.intellicast.com)
13. ABC News (abcnews.com)
14. Sportsline (sportsline.com)
15. PC World magazine (pcworld.com)
16. AudioNet, live audio and video cybercasts (www.audionet.com)
17. Gamespot, computer-game news and reviews (gamespot.com)
18. NBC (nbc.com)
19. Nascar auto racing (nascar.com)
20. TV Guide (tvguide.com)

TOP SEARCH SITES

1. Yahoo! (yahoo.com)
2. Excite (excite.com)
3. Infoseek (infoseek.com)
4. Lycos (lycos.com)
5. AltaVista (altavista.digital.com)

TOP TRAVEL AND TOURISM SITES

1. CityNet, local entertainment listings (citynet.com)
2. MapQuest, maps and travel directions (mapquest.com)
3. Travelocity, travel info and do-it-yourself bookings (travelocity)
4. American Airlines (www.americanair.com)
5. Delta Airlines (delta-air.com)

TOP SHOPPING SITES

1. Download.com, computer software (download.com)
2. Columbia House, record club (columbiahouse.com)
3. Amazon.com, booksellers (amazon.com)
4. Shareware.com, computer software (shareware.com)
5. Hotfiles.com, computer software (hotfiles.com)

PEOPLE'S EXCLUSIVE POP PROFILES™

Every year, PEOPLE joins forces with a leading social research firm to create POP Profiles™, an exclusive multi-dimensional measure of celebrity power. An extensive poll surveys what you, the public, think of 1,000 top personalities—who is popular, who is trustworthy, whose career is on the move, who possesses the indefinable magic of "cool," and more.

A selection of rankings, scores, and comparisons drawn from the most recent wave of PEOPLE POP Profiles™ is reproduced here, including a ranking of the stars who boast the top POPScores™, an overall statistical measure derived from cumulative totals in 14 celebrity attributes and behavioral measures. Fast-rising newcomers to the "Most Powerful Celebrities" list this year are highlighted in **bold** type. Finishing 1,000th for the second straight year was O. J. Simpson.

THE MOST POWERFUL CELEBRITIES

Name	POPScore™
1. Tom Hanks	125
2. Robin Williams	122
3. Mel Gibson	120
4. Ron Howard	119
5. Sean Connery	119
6. Harrison Ford	119
7. Goldie Hawn	118
8. Carol Burnett	117
9. Bill Cosby	117
10. Sally Field	116
11. Whoopi Goldberg	116
12. Steven Spielberg	115
13. Denzel Washington	115
14. Dustin Hoffman	115
15. Tim Allen	115
16. Oprah Winfrey	115
17. James Earl Jones	114
18. Meg Ryan	114
19. Clint Eastwood	114
20. Jodie Foster	**114**
21. John Travolta	114
22. Tom Cruise	114
23. Michael Richards	**114**
24. Tom Selleck	**114**
25. Sandra Bullock	**114**
26. Bette Midler	113
27. Julia Louis-Dreyfus	**113**
28. Billy Crystal	113
29. Kevin Costner	112
30. Jimmy Stewart	112
31. Katharine Hepburn	112
32. Helen Hunt	**112**
33. Steve Martin	112
34. Danny DeVito	112
35. Arnold Schwarzenegger	112
36. Jane Seymour	**112**
37. Paul Newman	112
38. Al Pacino	**111**
39. Kurt Russell	**111**
40. Andy Griffith	111
41. Whitney Houston	111
42. Michelle Pfeiffer	**111**
43. Chevy Chase	111
44. Reba McEntire	111
45. Christopher Reeve	110
46. Gloria Estefan	**110**
47. Jamie Lee Curtis	110
48. Danny Glover	110
49. Halle Berry	**110**
50. Tina Turner	**110**
51. Demi Moore	110
52. Amy Grant	**110**

Note: Although two or more celebrities may have the same rounded off POPScore™, rankings are determined by POPScore™ calculations carried out to multiple decimal points. Source: PEOPLE POP Profiles™

SEINFELD, ALLEN & OTHER CELEBRITY DUOS

After checking out some sideline questions below—like whom our survey sample would most like to spend a day with, and comparing male and female reactions—turn the page for intriguing comparisons of big names like, say, Jerry Seinfeld vs. Tim Allen or Goldie Hawn vs. Kurt Russell. The average score in each category is 100, so a celebrity scoring a 106 ranks 6% above average in the category, while one scoring a 96 ranks slightly below average. Obviously, higher category scores are better, except for *one*—"Overexposed."

WHOM YOU MOST WANT TO SPEND A DAY WITH

Name	Category Score
Nia Long	139
Salma Hayek	139
Jada Pinkett	134
Mel Gibson	129
Tom Hanks	129
Sean Connery	128
Sandra Bullock	128
Robin Williams	128
Oprah Winfrey	127
Keri Russell	126

WHO'S THE MOST FUN

Name	Category Score
Robin Williams	137
Michael Richards	135
Bill Cosby	134
Tom Hanks	132
Jada Pinkett	132
Cheri Oteri	132
Carol Burnett	131
Nia Long	130
Whoopi Goldberg	130
Goldie Hawn	128

WHO'S THE COOLEST

Name	Category Score
Jada Pinkett	138
Nia Long	133
Salma Hayek	132
Cuba Gooding Jr.	131
Mary J. Blige	129
Robin Williams	128
Mel Gibson	127
Tom Hanks	127
Michael Richards	127
Denzel Washington	127

WHO MEN THINK IS HOT

Name	Category Score
Salma Hayek	157
Jada Pinkett	154
Kate Winslet	150
Keri Russell	150
Nia Long	148
Liv Tyler	145
Jenny McCarthy	145
Niki Taylor	143
Cameron Diaz	140
Hedy Burress	140

WHO WOMEN THINK IS HOT

Name	Category Score
Tom Cruise	145
Brad Pitt	141
Antonio Sabato Jr.	140
Noah Wyle	140
Jada Pinkett	139
Mel Gibson	138
Kevin Costner	137
Oprah Winfrey	136
Nia Long	135
Denzel Washington	135

WHO MEN FIND MOST TRUSTWORTHY

Name	Category Score
Kate Winslet	139
Norman Schwarzkopf	126
Jim Lehrer	123
Itzhak Perlman	122
Keri Russell	122
Ron Howard	122
Christopher Reeve	122
Cal Ripken Jr.	122
Salma Hayek	122
James Earl Jones	122

WHO WOMEN FIND MOST TRUSTWORTHY

Name	Category Score
Oprah Winfrey	133
Katharine Hepburn	129
Matt Lauer	126
Bill Cosby	125
Ron Howard	125
Nia Long	124
Colin Powell	124
Ossie Davis	124
Norman Schwarzkopf	123
Christopher Reeve	123

JERRY SEINFELD

Total POPScore™ 104

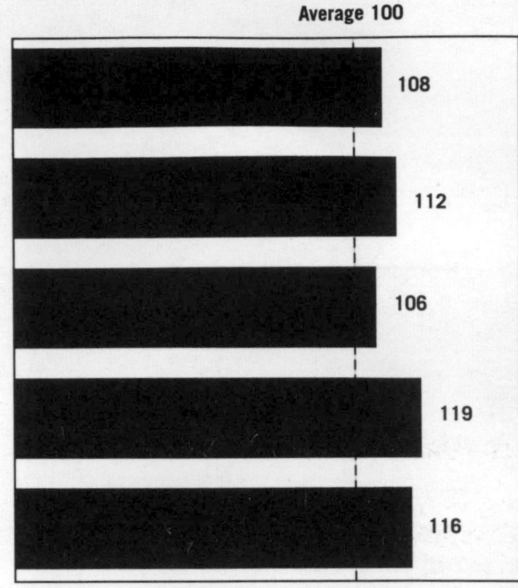

TIM ALLEN

Total POPScore™ 115

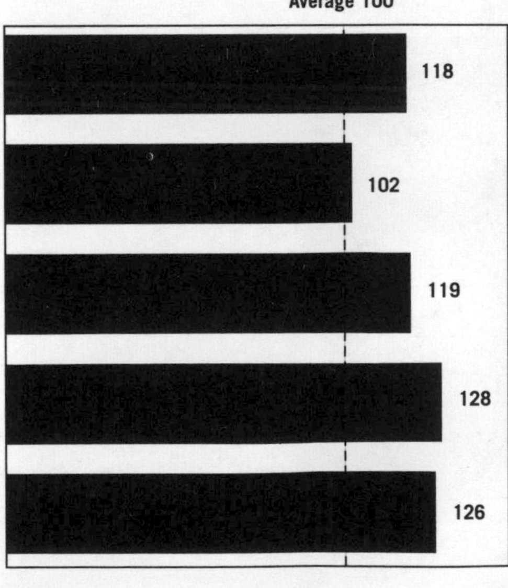

BROOKE SHIELDS

Total POPScore™ 97

Hot

Overexposed

One-of-a-Kind

Believable

Up & Coming

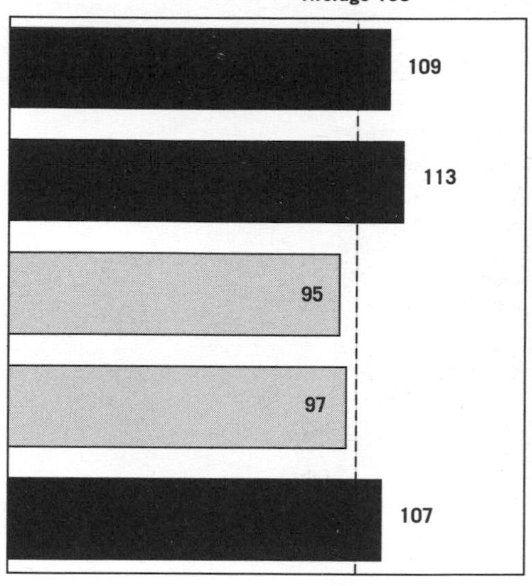

ANDRE AGASSI

Total POPScore™ 98

Hot

Overexposed

One-of-a-Kind

Believable

Up & Coming

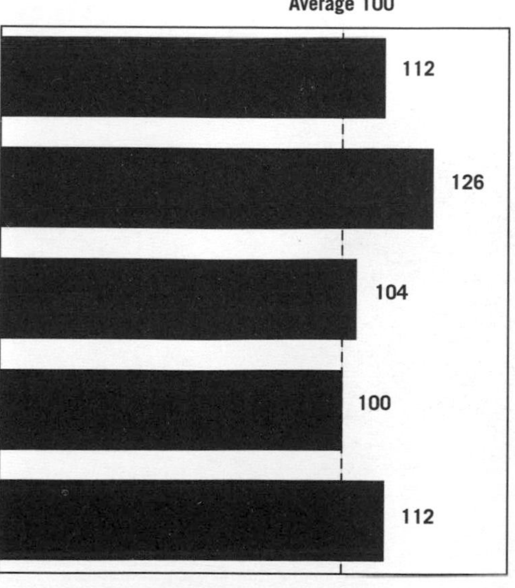

TOM CRUISE

Total POPScore™ 114

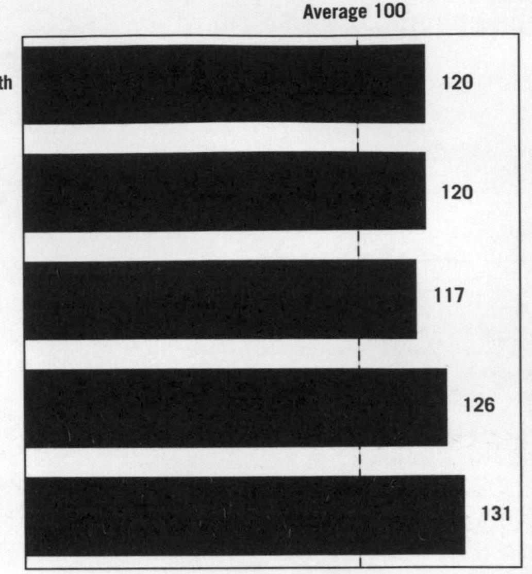

NICOLE KIDMAN

Total POPScore™ 107

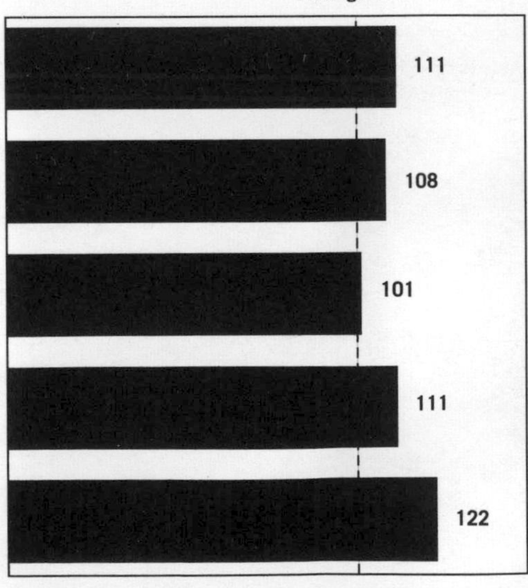

CINDY CRAWFORD

Total POPScore™ 101

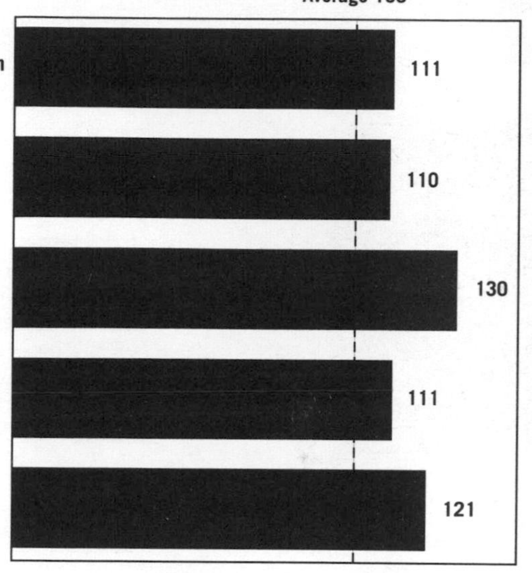

NAOMI CAMPBELL

Total POPScore™ 101

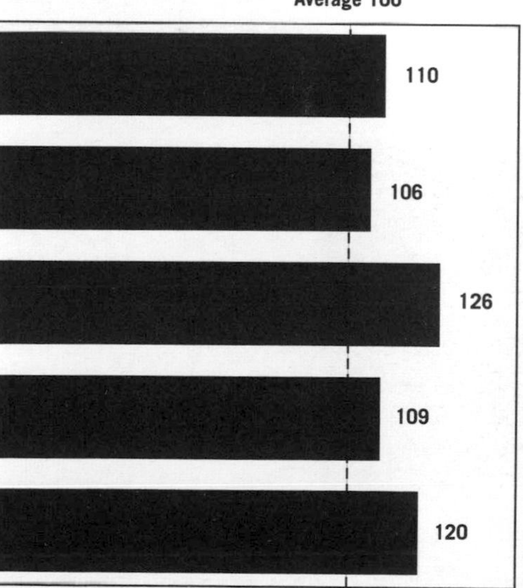

TIGER WOODS

Total POPScore™ 106

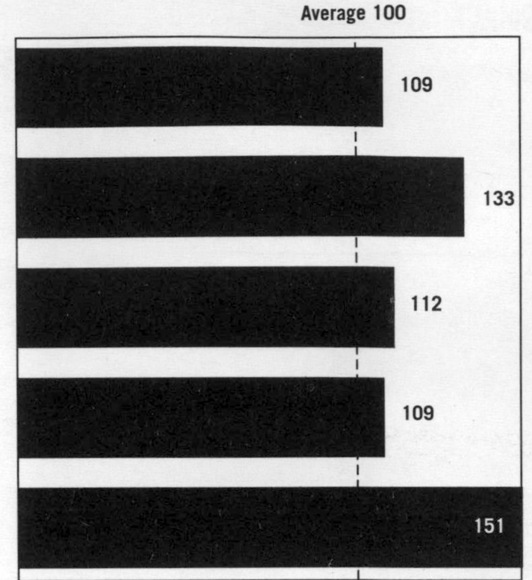

MICHAEL JORDAN

Total POPScore™ 105

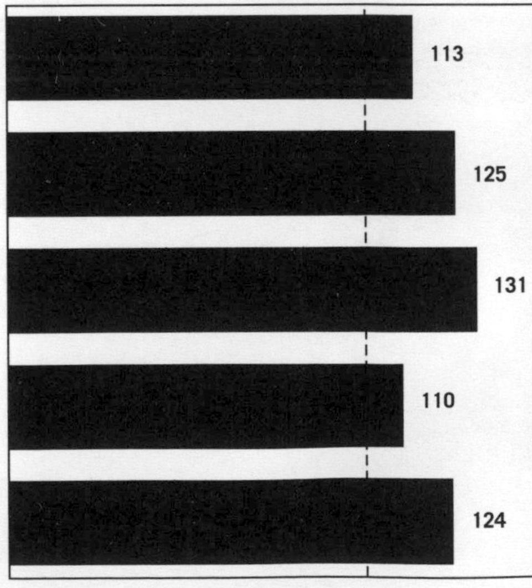

GIORGIO ARMANI

Total POPScore™ 98

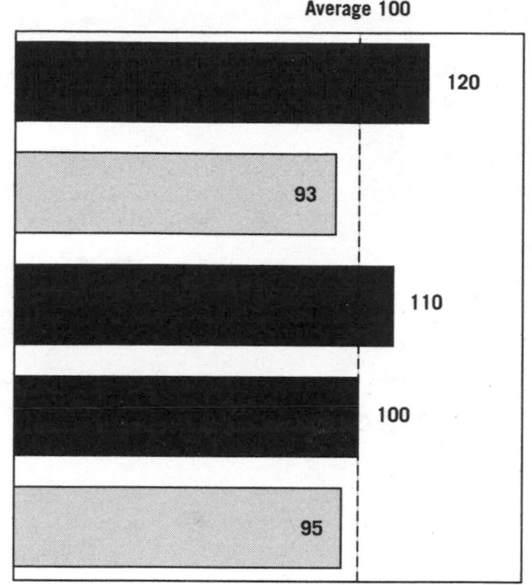

TOMMY HILFIGER

Total POPScore™ 99

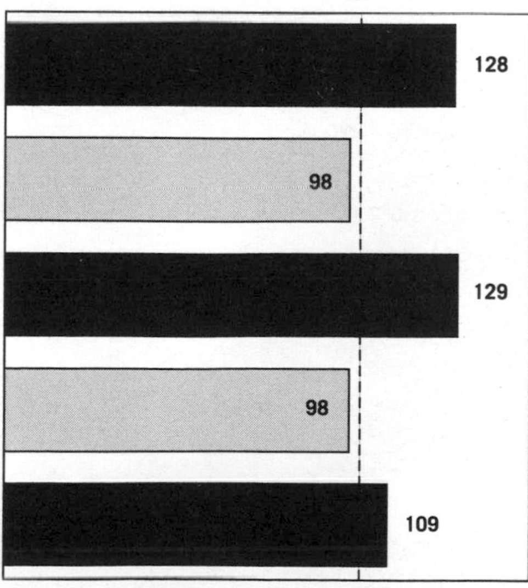

PAUL REISER

Total POPScore™ 107

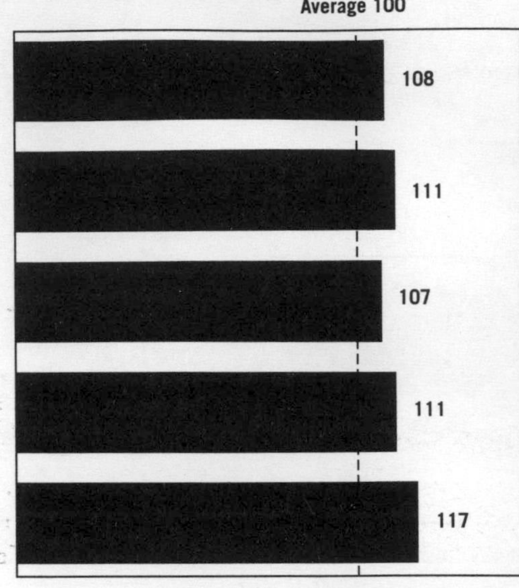

HELEN HUNT

Total POPScore™ 112

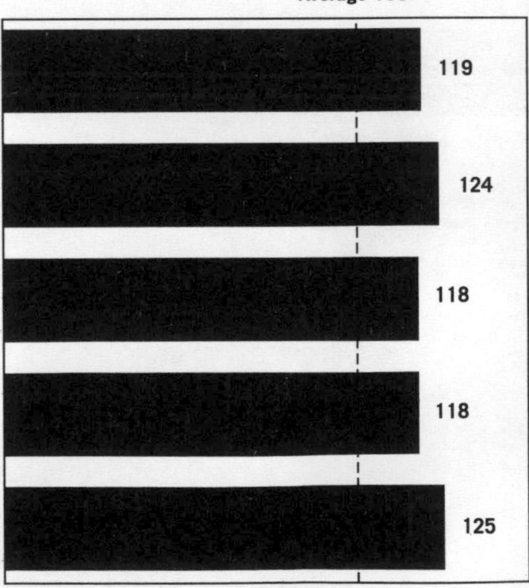

DANNY DEVITO

Total POPScore™ 112

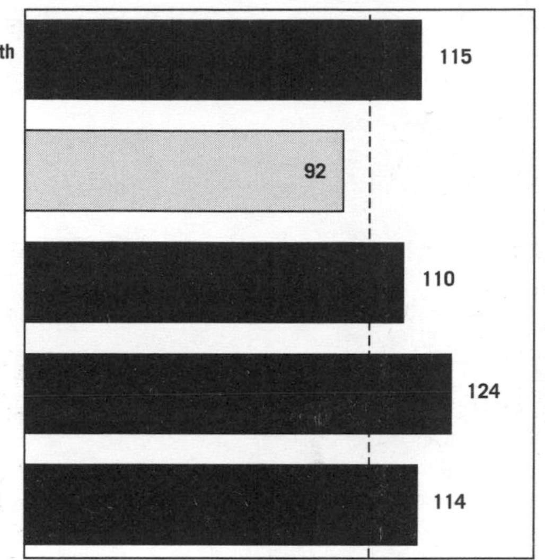

RHEA PERLMAN

Total POPScore™ 109

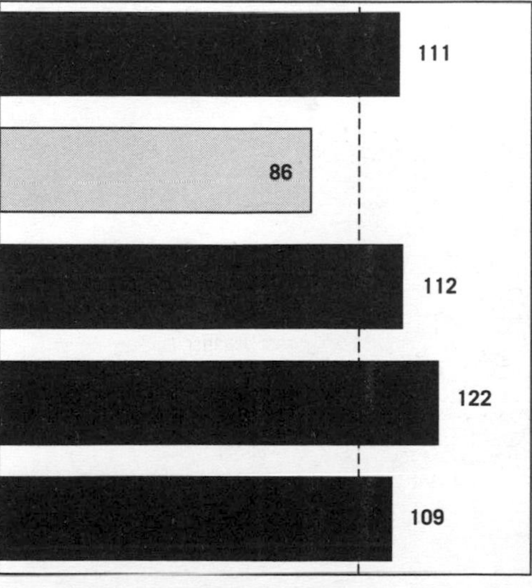

JANE PAULEY

Total POPScore™ 101

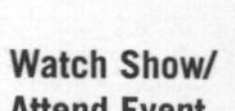

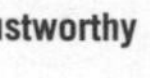
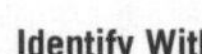
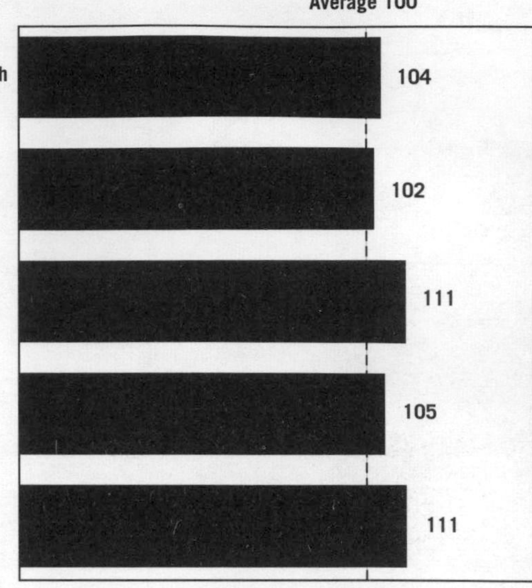

BARBARA WALTERS

Total POPScore™ 101

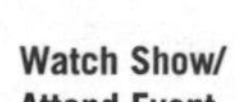

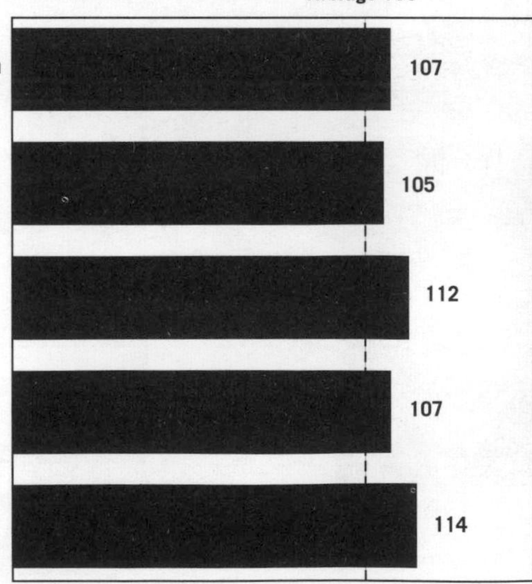

HOWARD STERN

Total POPScore™ 71

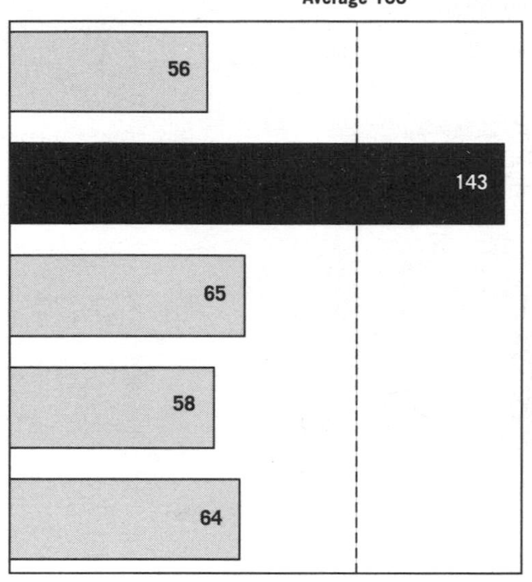

Like

Overexposed

Identify With

Believable

Cool

RUSH LIMBAUGH

Total POPScore™ 76

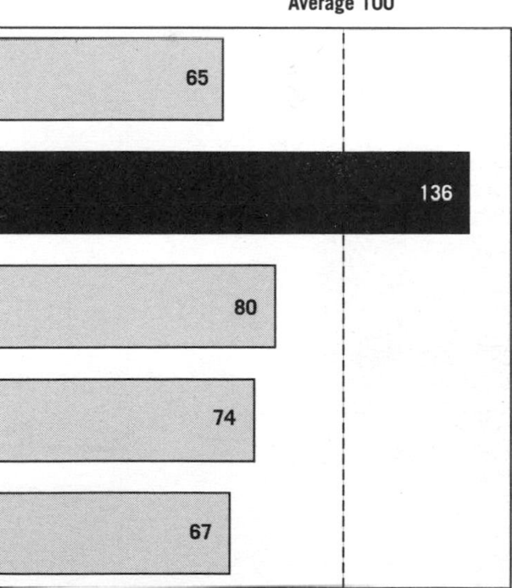

Like

Overexposed

Identify With

Believable

Cool

BILL CLINTON

Total POPScore™ 92

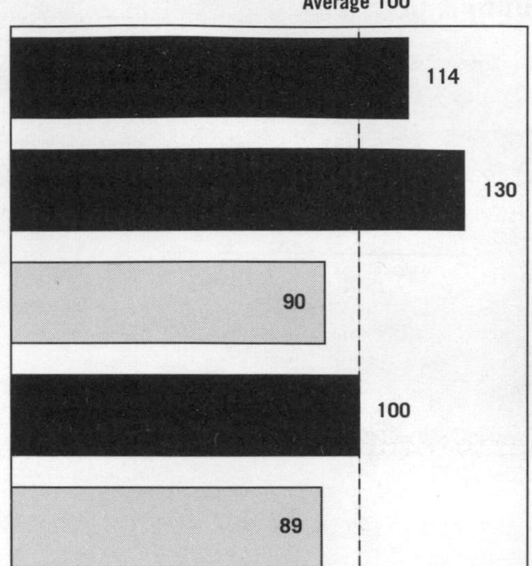

AL GORE

Total POPScore™ 84

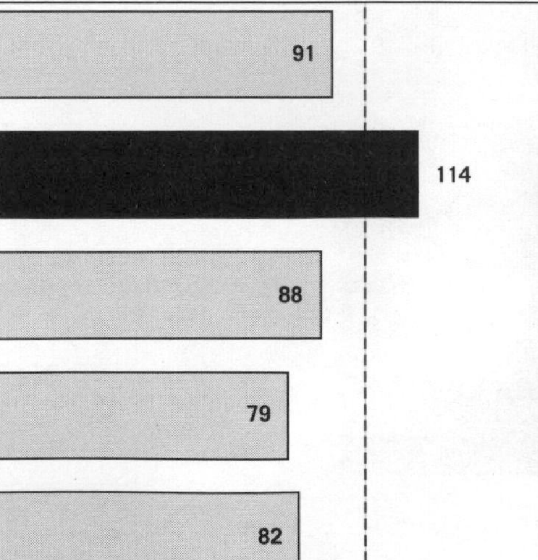

HILLARY RODHAM CLINTON

Total POPScore™ 81

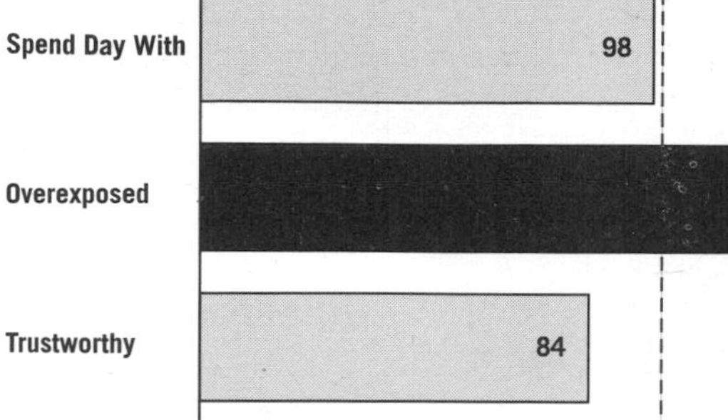

TIPPER GORE

Total POPScore™ 90

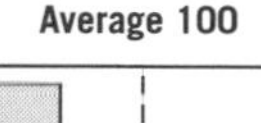

WALTER MATTHAU

Total POPScore™ 108

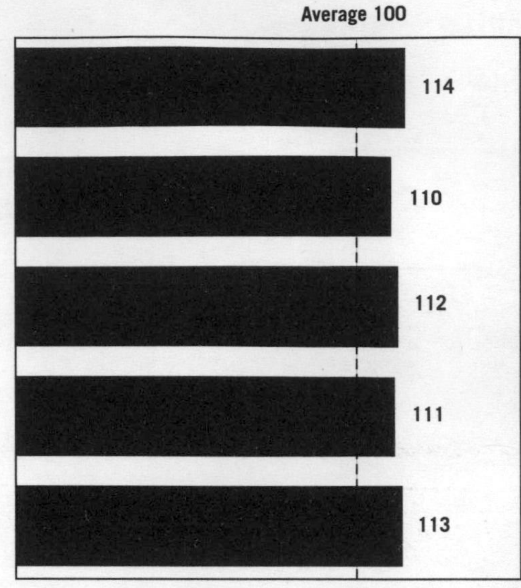

JACK LEMMON

Total POPScore™ 104

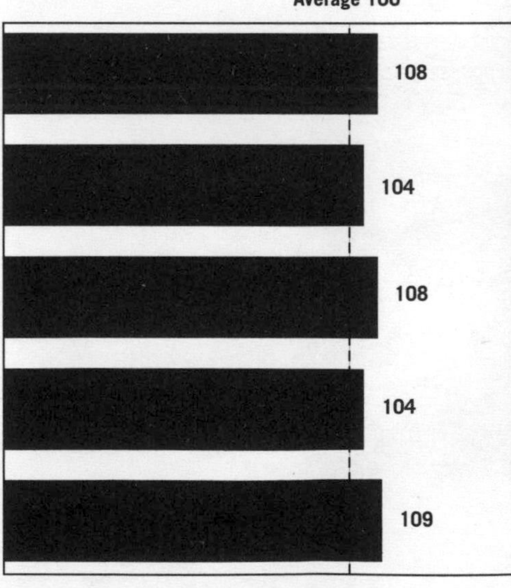

DOLLY PARTON

Total POPScore™ 109

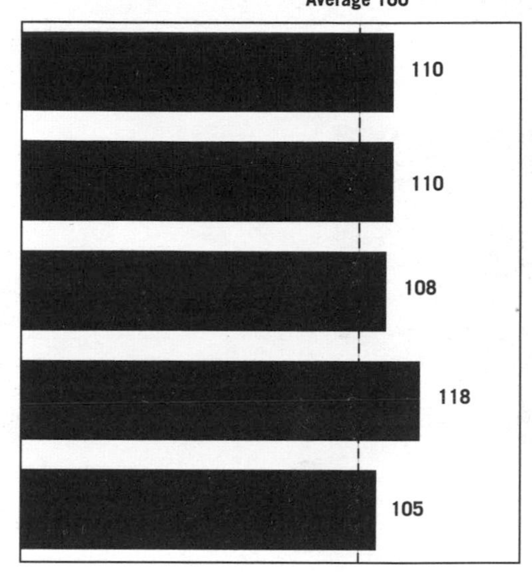

REBA MCENTIRE

Total POPScore™ 111

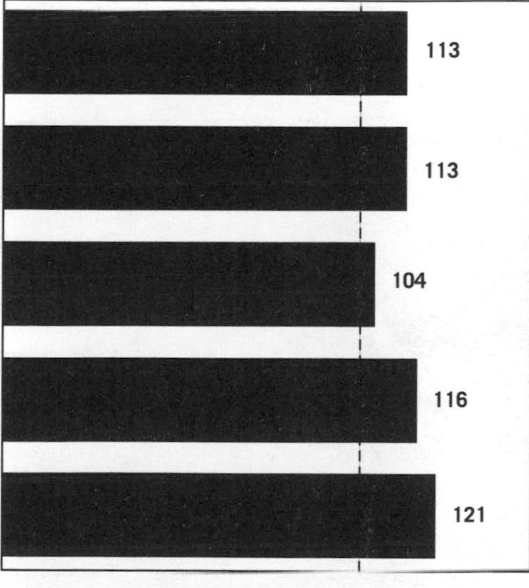

GENE SISKEL

Total POPScore™ 87

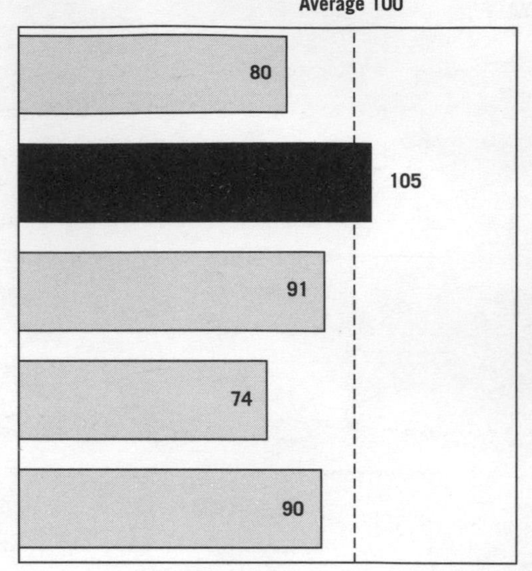

ROGER EBERT

Total POPScore™ 90

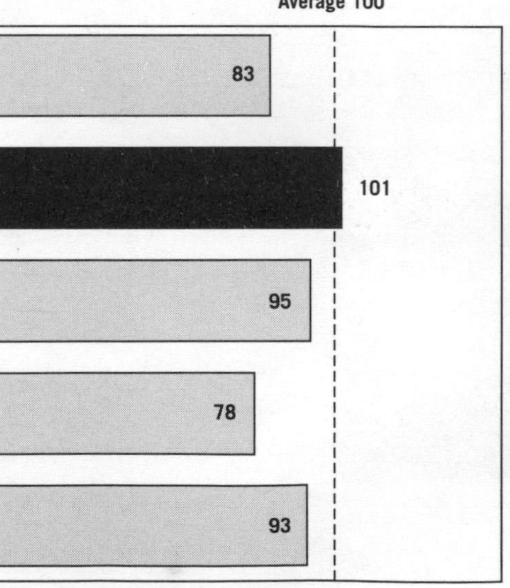

GOLDIE HAWN

Total POPScore™ 118

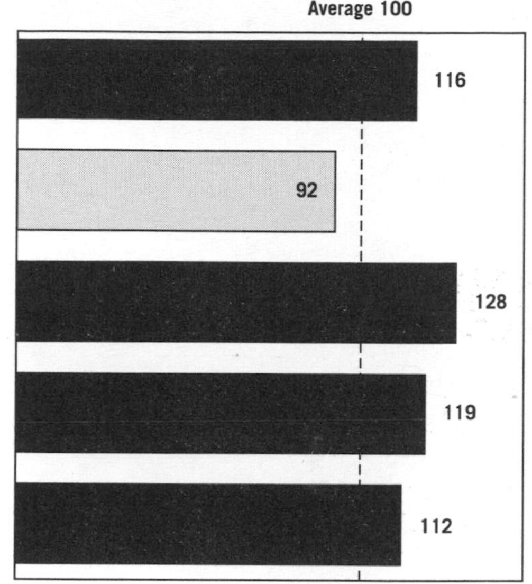

KURT RUSSELL

Total POPScore™ 111

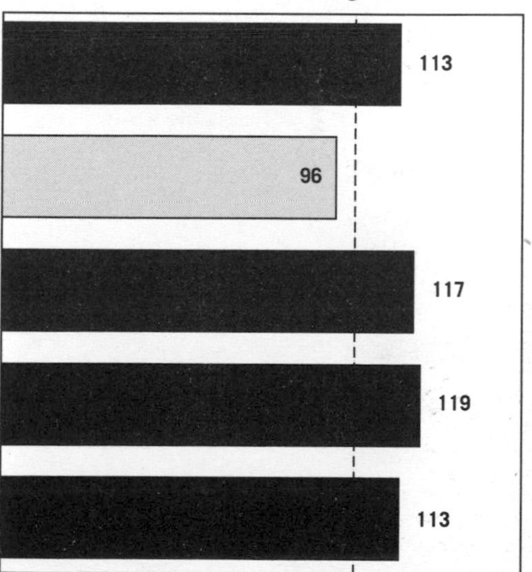

THE PEOPLE REGISTER

THE PEOPLE 400

Each year's Almanac pulls together an imaginary guest list of the 400 most compelling, fastest-rising, and indisputably established stars and starmakers, for a party to put Mrs. Astor's original 400 or Truman Capote's Black and White Ball to shame. With this year's edition we welcome 40 newcomers to our dance, which means an equal number had to sit this one out. Below we preview the comings and goings among our elite. Celebs who are gone (at least temporarily) from the 400 are not forgotten; you can find them (among others) in the Register of Thousands, beginning on page 553.

A HEARTY WELCOME (OR WELCOME BACK)

Beck
Juliette Binoche
Ed Burns
Neve Campbell
Drew Carey
John Cusack
Cameron Diaz
Roma Downey
Jakob Dylan
Matthew Fox
Morgan Freeman
Cuba Gooding Jr.
Melissa Joan Hart
Anne Heche
Lauryn Hill
Jewel
Carolyn Bessette Kennedy
Matt Lauer
Lucy Lawless
George Lucas
Frances McDormand
Tim McGraw
Ewan McGregor
Mike Myers
Edward Norton
Jada Pinkett
LeAnn Rimes
Chris Rock
Gavin Rossdale
Geoffrey Rush
Rene Russo
Gwen Stefani
Kristin Scott Thomas
Billy Bob Thornton
Tanya Tucker
Kate Winslet
Scott Wolf
James Woods
Tiger Woods
Renee Zellweger

AND A FOND FAREWELL

Stephen Baldwin
William Baldwin
Josie Bissett
Bobby Brown
Joey Buttafuoco
Jennifer Capriati
Dana Carvey
Macaulay Culkin
Billy Ray Cyrus
Robert Downey Jr.
Richard Dreyfuss
Fabio
Andy Garcia
James Garner
Melissa Gilbert
Amy Grant
Wayne Gretzky
Don Henley
Chris Isaak
Anthony Kiedis
John Larroquette
Laura Leighton
Juliette Lewis
Meat Loaf
Rob Lowe
Joan Lunden
John Madden
Natalie Merchant
Julia Ormond
Ozzy Osbourne
Chazz Palminteri
Pepa
Liz Phair
Priscilla Presley
Burt Reynolds
Salt
Paul Shaffer
Andrew Shue
Sherry Stringfield
Gianni Versace

THE NUMBERS BEHIND THE LUMINARIES

Are the PEOPLE 400 really different from you and me? We analyzed the stats on registrants, and here's what we found:

Average year of birth	1955	Members currently married	187
Average number of children	1.51	Members currently engaged	15
Members without children	150	Members currently separated/divorced	103
Average number of marriages	1.15	Members never married	108

ANDRÉ AGASSI

Birthplace: Las Vegas, NV
Birthdate: 4/29/70
Occupation: Tennis player
Education: Nick Bollettieri Tennis Academy
Facts: His father was so determined that André would grow up to be a tennis star that he hung a ball and racquet over the infant's crib and, as soon as his son could sit up, gave him a Ping-Pong paddle and a balloon.

Celebrated his fourth birthday by hitting balls for 15 minutes with tennis great Jimmy Connors.

At the end of 1993 he was injured, overweight, and No. 24 in the tennis world. A year later, he bounced back to No. 2.

Infamy: Admitted to using marijuana as a young teen player.
Marriage: Brooke Shields
Famous Relative: Mike Agassi, former Iranian Olympic boxer, father
Tennis Accomplishments: Olympic Gold Medal, 1996; 34 Pro Titles including: Wimbledon '92; U.S. Open '94; Australian Open '95
Address: ATP Tour North America, 200 ATP Tour Blvd., Ponte Vedra Beach, FL 32082

TROY AIKMAN

Birthplace: Cerritos, CA
Birthdate: 11/21/66
Occupation: Football player
Education: University of Oklahoma, UCLA
Signature: Quarterback for the Dallas Cowboys
Facts: Number one pick in the NFL's 1989 draft.

By age 27, he had won two Super Bowls, the youngest of only five quarterbacks in history to do so.

The Cowboys gave him the largest rookie contract in NFL history: six years for $11,037,000.

In the 1990 season, he was hit so often that he was dubbed "Troy Ache-man."

Infamy: In 1993 Aikman became the first player in football history to leave the NFL Pro Bowl early (he had a charity meeting early the next day). NFL Commissioner Paul Tagliabue fined him $10,000 for leaving after the third quarter.
Original Job: Baseball player
Major Award: Named MVP of the 1993 Super Bowl
Address: Dallas Cowboys Football Club, One Cowboy Parkway, Irving, TX 75063

JASON ALEXANDER

Real Name: Jay Scott Greenspan
Birthplace: Newark, NJ
Birthdate: 9/23/59
Occupation: Actor
Education: Boston University
Debut: (Film) *The Burning,* 1981; (TV) *Senior Trip!,* 1981
Signature: *Seinfeld*
Facts: *Seinfeld* creator Larry David modeled the George character after himself.

Is an accomplished dancer and operatic tenor.

Marriage: Daena E. Title
Child: Gabriel
Major Awards: Tony, Best Actor, *Jerome Robbins' Broadway,* 1989; Grammy, Best Cast Show Album, *Jerome Robbins' Broadway* (with others), 1989
Quote: "I started losing my hair when I was a wee kid of 16."
Address: NBC Television, 3000 West Alameda Ave., Burbank, CA 91523

TIM ALLEN

Real Name: Tim Allen Dick
Birthplace: Denver, CO
Birthdate: 6/13/53
Occupation: Comedian, actor
Education: Western Michigan University
Debut: (TV) *Showtime Comedy Club All-Stars II*
Signature: *Home Improvement*
Facts: Has nine brothers and sisters.

Appeared in Mr. Goodwrench commercials.

Provided the voice for Buzz Lightyear in *Toy Story.*

Paid $2 million for 26 acres of Michigan campground with the intention of keeping it in its natural, undeveloped state.

Infamy: He served 28 months in jail in 1978 for attempting to sell cocaine.

Pled guilty to impaired driving in 1997. When stopped by police, Allen failed four sobriety tests, including counting backward and reciting the alphabet.

Original Job: Creative director for an advertising agency
Marriage: Laura Deibel
Child: Kady
Major Award: Golden Globe, Best Actor in a Comedy Series, *Home Improvement,* 1995
Address: *Home Improvement,* Walt Disney Studios, 500 S. Buena Vista St., Burbank, CA 91521

WOODY ALLEN

Real Name: Allen Stewart Konigsberg; legal name Heywood Allen
Birthplace: Brooklyn, NY
Birthdate: 12/1/35
Occupation: Actor, director, writer
Education: New York University, City College of New York
Debut: (Film) *What's New Pussycat?,* 1965
Signature: *Annie Hall*
Facts: Played clarinet every Monday night at Michael's Pub in Manhattan. Missed the Academy

Awards ceremony for *Annie Hall* because it was on a Monday night. Now plays at the Café Carlyle.

Among his many neuroses: won't take showers if the drain is in the middle.

Was suspended from New York University for inattention to his work.
Infamy: After details became known of his affair with Soon-Yi, Mia Farrow's oldest adopted daughter, Farrow accused him of sexual abuse of her younger children. In 1993, he was denied custody but retained visitation rights of their adopted children, Dylan (since renamed Eliza) and Moses, and biological son Satchel (since renamed Seamus).
Original Job: During high school, he supplied comic snippets to newspaper columnists Walter Winchell and Earl Wilson; he later became a hired gag-writer on a retainer of $25 a week.
Marriages: Harlene Rosen (divorced), Louise Lasser (divorced); Soon-Yi Previn (relationship)
Children: Eliza (formerly Dylan, adopted), Moses (adopted), Seamus (formerly Satchel)
Major Awards: Oscar, Best Director, *Annie Hall,* 1977; Oscar, Best Original Screenplay, *Annie Hall,* 1977; Oscar, Best Original Screenplay, *Hannah and Her Sisters,* 1986; Golden Globe, Best Screenplay, *The Purple Rose of Cairo,* 1985
Address: International Creative Management, 40 W. 57th Street, New York, NY 10019

TORI AMOS

Real Name: Myra Ellen Amos
Birthdate: 8/22/64
Occupation: Singer, songwriter
Education: High school
Debut: (Album) *Y Kant Tori Read?,* 1988
Signature: "Crucify"
Facts: She started playing the piano at age three. At age 5 she won a scholarship to study piano in a conservatory in Baltimore but was kicked out by age 11 for refusing to practice.

Father was an evangelical preacher, a fact that figures heavily into her sex-laden lyrics in songs like "Leather" and "God."
Original Job: Piano player in Los Angeles lounges
Relationship: Eric Rosse
Quote: "I have vivid memories of being a prostitute in another life."
Address: Atlantic Records, 75 Rockefeller Plaza, New York, NY 10019

GILLIAN ANDERSON

Birthplace: Chicago, IL
Birthdate: 8/9/68
Occupation: Actor
Education: DePaul University
Debut: (Stage) *Absent Friends*, 1991
Signature: *The X-Files*
Facts: Lived in London during her childhood.

As a teenager smitten by British punk rock, she spiked her hair, pierced her nose, put a safety pin through her cheek, and dated a rock musician almost a decade her senior.

To hide her pregnancy, Anderson wore bulky trench coats and took three episodes off during an alleged alien abduction.

Believes in UFOs, ESP and other paranormal phenomena.

Thousands of male fans have formed an online Gillian Anderson Testosterone Brigade.
Marriage: Clyde Klotz (separated); Rodney Rowland (relationship)
Child: Piper
Major Award: Golden Globe, Best Actress in a Drama Series, *The X-Files*, 1996; Emmy, Best Actress in a Drama Series, *The X-Files*, 1997
Address: William Morris Agency, 151 El Camino Dr., Beverly Hills, CA 90212

JULIE ANDREWS

Birthplace: Walton-on-Thames, England
Birthdate: 10/1/35
Occupation: Actor, singer
Education: High school
Debut: (Stage) *Starlight Roof*, 1947; (Film) *Mary Poppins*, 1964
Signature: *Mary Poppins*
Facts: By age 8, had a fully formed adult throat and a four-octave voice.

The 1965 film *The Sound of Music*, in which she played Maria Von Trapp, was the highest-grossing film of its day.

She and husband Edwards adopted two Vietnamese girls during the war.

Under married name Julie Edwards, wrote two children's books in the 1970s, *Mandy* and *The Last of the Really Great Whangdoodles.*

Before starring in *Victor/Victoria*, was last on Broadway 33 years ago.

Rejected her 1996 Tony award nomination for best actress for *Victor/Victoria* because the show was snubbed in all other categories.
Infamy: Tried to shed *Mary Poppins* image by baring her breasts in 1981's *S.O.B.*
Original Job: Toured from age 12 with mother and alcoholic stepfather in a vaudeville act.
Marriage: Tony Walton (divorced), Blake Edwards
Children: Emma (with Tony Walton), stepdaughter Jennifer, stepson Geoffrey, Joanna (adopted), Amy (adopted)
Major Awards: Oscar, Best Actress, *Mary Poppins*, 1964; Golden Globe, Best Actress, *Mary Poppins*, 1964; Golden Globe, Best Actress, *The Sound of Music*, 1965
Address: William Morris Agency, 151 El Camino Dr., Beverly Hills, CA 90212

MAYA ANGELOU

Real Name: Margueritte Annie Johnson
Birthplace: St. Louis, MO
Birthdate: 4/4/28
Occupation: Writer, actor, singer, dancer
Education: California Labor School

Debut: (Film) *Calypso Heatwave,* 1957
Signature: *I Know Why the Caged Bird Sings*
Facts: Nicknamed "Maya" by her brother, who called her "My" or "Mine."

At age 7, she was raped by her mother's boyfriend. Several days after her testimony at the trial, her assailant was found dead—killed by her uncles. She blamed herself for the death and did not speak for the next five years.

Tried to join the army in the late 1940s, but was turned down after a security check revealed that the California Labor School was listed as subversive.

Has received over 30 honorary degrees.

Read the inaugural poem at President Clinton's inauguration ceremony.

Infamy: In the late 1950s, she worked as a madam, managing two prostitutes in San Diego. Her guilty conscience caused her to quit after only a short stint.
Original Job: The first black—and the first female—streetcar conductor in San Francisco at age 16.
Marriages: Tosh Angelos (divorced), Paul Du Feu (divorced)
Child: Guy Johnson
Major Award: Grammy, Best Spoken Word Recording, *On the Pulse of Morning,* 1993
Address: Wake Forest University, Department of Humanities, P.O. Box 7314, Reynolds Station, Winston-Salem, NC 27106

JENNIFER ANISTON

Birthplace: Sherman Oaks, CA
Birthdate: 2/11/69
Occupation: Actor
Education: High School of Performing Arts
Debut: (TV movie) *Camp Cucamonga,* 1990
Signature: *Friends*
Facts: Actor Telly Savalas was her godfather.

Like her *Friends* character, Aniston worked as a waitress after graduating from school.

The rail-thin Aniston actually used to be fat. When she realized that was keeping her from landing acting parts, she went on the Nutri/System diet and lost 30 pounds.

Because of her often-emulated shag, she was dubbed America's First Hairdo by *Rolling Stone* magazine.

Infamy: Caused a stir in 1996 when she posed nude in *Rolling Stone.*
Relationship: Tate Donovan
Famous Relative: John Aniston, actor, father
Address: Creative Artists Agency, 9830 Wilshire Blvd., Beverly Hills, CA 90212

GIORGIO ARMANI

Birthplace: Piacenza, Italy
Birthdate: 7/11/34
Occupation: Fashion designer
Facts: Entered medical school but after two years decided to join the military.

Designed uniforms for the Italian Air Force (1980).

Original Job: Medical assistant for Italian military, window dresser in a Milan department store
Major Awards: Neiman-Marcus Award, Distinguished Service in the Field of Fashion, 1979; Cutty Sark Award, Outstanding International Designer, 1981
Address: 650 Fifth Ave., New York, NY 10019

TOM ARNOLD

Birthplace: Ottumwa, IA
Birthdate: 3/6/59
Occupation: Actor
Education: Indian Hills Community College
Debut: (TV) *Roseanne*
Signature: *True Lies*
Facts: The 26,000 square foot, 30-room house that the Arnolds shared is the largest residence in Iowa.

Converted to Judaism when he married Roseanne.

After the breakup with Roseanne, started a new production company, Clean Break Productions.

Infamy: He was once arrested for urinating in public at a McDonald's restaurant.

He was a cocaine addict when Roseanne recruited him to work on her show.

Roseanne claimed that he physically abused her during their marriage, a charge he denies.

Original Job: Ham packer at a Hormel plant, box stacker, bartender, bouncer
Marriages: Roseanne Barr (divorced); Julie Champnella
Address: William Morris Agency, 151 El Camino Dr., Beverly Hills, CA 90212

THE ARTIST FORMERLY KNOWN AS PRINCE

Real Name: Prince Rogers Nelson
Birthplace: Minneapolis, MN
Birthdate: 6/7/58
Occupation: Singer, songwriter, actor
Education: High school dropout
Debut: (Album) *For You,* 1978
Signature: *Purple Rain*
Facts: Named after the Prince Roger Trio, a jazz group led by his father.

Can play over two dozen instruments.

Now known as a symbol, or referred to as "The Artist Formerly Known as Prince," sometimes abbreviated to "TAFKAP."

Marriage: Mayte Garcia
Child: name unreported (deceased)
Major Awards: Grammy, Best Rock Performance—Duo or Group, *Purple Rain* (with The Revolution), 1984; Grammy, Best Rhythm and Blues Song, "I Feel for You," 1984; Grammy, Best Soundtrack Album, *Purple Rain* (with The Revolution, John L. Nelson, Lisa & Wendy), 1984; Grammy, Best R&B Duo or Group,

"Kiss" (with The Revolution), 1986; Oscar, Best Original Song, "Purple Rain," 1984
Address: 9401 Kiowa Trail, Chanhassen, MN, 55317

DAN AYKROYD

Birthplace: Ottawa, Canada
Birthdate: 7/1/52
Occupation: Actor, writer
Education: Carleton University
Debut: (TV) *Saturday Night Live,* 1975; (Film) *1941,* 1979
Signature: *Ghostbusters*
Facts: His grandfather was a Mountie.

Was expelled for delinquency from St. Pius X Preparatory Seminary.

Had a cameo role in *Indiana Jones and the Temple of Doom,* 1984.

A police buff, he rides an Ontario Provincial Police motorcycle, collects police badges, sometimes rides shotgun with detectives in squad cars, and owns, in partnership with several Toronto police officers, a Toronto bar called Crooks.

He is very interested in the supernatural and has an extensive collection of books on the subject. He admits, "I've never seen a full apparition, but I once saw what could be termed ectoplasmic light, and that scared the hell out of me."

Co-founder of the House of Blues restaurant/music club chain.
Original Job: Stand-up comedian
Marriages: Maureen Lewis (divorced), Donna Dixon
Children: Oscar, Mark, Lloyd
Major Award: Emmy, Best Writing in a Comedy, Variety, or Music Series, *Saturday Night Live,* 1977
Address: Creative Artists Agency, 9830 Wilshire Blvd., Beverly Hills, CA 90212

KEVIN BACON

Birthplace: Philadelphia, PA
Birthdate: 7/8/58
Occupation: Actor
Education: Manning St. Actor's Theatre, Circle in the Square Theater School
Debut: (Film) *National Lampoon's Animal House*, 1978
Signature: *Footloose*
Facts: Nervous about Bacon's sex appeal, Paramount's Dawn Steel took his photo around the studio when casting *Footloose* asking everyone, "Is this guy f--kable?" (Obviously he was; he got the teen idol part in the 1984 film.)

For *Murder in the First*, went on a 600 calorie-a-day diet, shaved his head and wore uncomfortable contacts which completely covered his eyes. When filming the "dungeon" scenes, he put crickets in his hair (to simulate lice) and got welts from being hit with a leather blackjack.

In 1994, formed band the Bacon Brothers with Emmy-winning composer, older brother Michael.
Marriage: Kyra Sedgwick
Children: Sosie, Travis
Famous Relatives: Michael Bacon, composer, brother
Address: Creative Artists Agency, 9830 Wilshire Blvd., Beverly Hills, CA 90212

ALEC BALDWIN

Real Name: Alexander Rae Baldwin III
Birthplace: Massapequa, NY
Birthdate: 4/3/58
Occupation: Actor
Education: New York University, Lee Strasberg Theatre Institute
Debut: (TV) *The Doctors*
Signature: *The Hunt for Red October*
Facts: He is not naturally tall, dark, and handsome—he dyes his fair hair black.

Originally wanted to be a lawyer.

Was engaged to Janine Turner (*Northern Exposure*); she had the wedding dress ready and the invitations were sent out when they broke up.
Infamy: Was taken to court for assaulting a paparazzo, who had staked out the actor's house for a photo of his newborn; Baldwin's acquittal was applauded weeks later by the audience at the Oscars.
Original Job: Waiter and doorman at Studio 54
Marriage: Kim Basinger
Child: Ireland Elliesse
Famous Relatives: William Baldwin, actor, brother; Stephen Baldwin, actor, brother; Daniel Baldwin, actor, brother
Address: William Morris Agency, 151 El Camino Dr., Beverly Hills, CA 90212

ANTONIO BANDERAS

Birthplace: Málaga, Spain
Birthdate: 1960
Occupation: Actor
Education: School of Dramatic Art, Málaga, Spain
Debut: (Stage) *Los Tarantos,* 1981; (Film) *Labyrinth of Passion,* 1982
Signature: *Philadelphia*
Facts: Modeled for Ralph Lauren and Gucci.

Would love to play the Hunchback of Notre Dame, but thinks he won't be able to because of his good looks.
Original Job: Model, waiter
Marriages: Ana Leza (divorced), Melanie Griffith
Child: Estela del Carmen
Quote: "I thought to myself, 'Oh my God. How disgusting.' Then I went to the first rehearsal and it was...so easy. I didn't lose my fingers, my ear didn't fall down. Nothing happens if you're sure of who you are." (On his first kiss in a role as a homosexual, in the 1988 Almodóvar movie *Law of Desire.*)
Address: Creative Artists Agency, 9830 Wilshire Blvd., Beverly Hills, CA 90212

TYRA BANKS

Birthplace: Inglewood, CA
Birthdate: 12/4/96
Occupation: Model, actor
Education: High school
Debut: (TV) *Fresh Prince of Bel Air,* 1994; (Film) *Higher Learning,* 1995

Facts: The August before she was to enroll in college, she was asked by a French modeling agent to work at the couture shows in Paris. Within a week of that first stroll, "Miss Tyra" (as the fashion cognoscenti call her) had accumulated 25 more bookings.

Became the second-ever black model (Lana Ogilvie was the first) under contract with Cover Girl Cosmetics.

Singleton saw her on the cover of *Essence* and felt she'd be perfect for a part in his *Higher Learning*. He arranged for an audition, and during the drawn-out casting process they fell in love.

Relationship: Seal

Address: IMG, 170 5th Ave, 10th Floor, New York, NY 10010

CHRISTINE BARANSKI

Birthplace: Buffalo, NY

Birthdate: 5/2/52

Occupation: Actor

Education: Juilliard School

Debut: (Stage) *She Stoops to Conquer*, 1976; (Film) *Soup for One*, 1982

Signature: *Cybill*

Facts: Spent two decades performing on New York stages before finally accepting a TV series role in *Cybill*.

Admits she doesn't even own a TV set, and if she did, she wouldn't let her daughters, ages 9 and 12, watch her "adult and sophisticated" show.

Lives in an 18th century Connecticut farmhouse, holing up in an apartment hotel when filming in Los Angeles.

Marriage: Matthew Cowles

Children: Isabel, Lilly

Major Awards: Emmy, Best Supporting Actress, *Cybill*, 1995; Tony, Best Actress (Drama), *The Real Thing*, 1984; Tony, Best Actress (Drama), *Rumors*, 1989

Address: International Creative Management, 40 W. 57th Street, New York, NY 10019

CHARLES BARKLEY

Birthplace: Leeds, AL

Birthdate: 2/20/63

Occupation: Basketball player

Education: Auburn University

Facts: He is the shortest player (6' 6") ever to lead the NBA in rebounding.

At birth, he was anemic and weighed only six pounds, 12 ounces. Doctors administered blood transfusions to keep him alive.

During his college years, he battled a weight problem, at one point exceeding 300 pounds. Schoolmates nicknamed him "Boy Gorge," "The Round Mound of Rebound," and "The Leaning Tower of Pizza."

Turned down offers of over $500,000 from trade shows because he believes that fans should not have to pay for autographs.

Infamy: During the 1989–90 season, he racked up nearly $36,000 in fines, setting an NBA record. His misconduct included spitting on a referee, making a bet with another player, and fighting.

In March 1991 Barkley spit at a fan yelling racial epithets at him, but missed and hit an 8-year-old girl instead.

Basketball Accomplishments: NBA MVP (Season) '93;10 Time NBA All-Star; 5 Time All NBA First Team; Gold Medal at 1992 & 1996 Olympics

Marriage: Maureen

Child: Christiana

Address: Houston Rockets, 2 Greenway Plaza, Suite 400, Houston, TX 77046

DREW BARRYMORE

Birthplace: Los Angeles, CA

Birthdate: 2/22/75

Occupation: Actor

Education: High school dropout

Debut: (Film) *Altered States,* 1980

Signature: *E.T., the Extra-Terrestrial*

Facts: Starred in a TV commercial for Gainsburgers when she was 11 months old.

After drug rehabilitation, she starred in *Fifteen and Getting Straight* (1989), a TV movie about drug abuse, and wrote her own autobiography, *Little Lost Girl,* at age 14 to clear the air. Credits musician David Crosby for helping her get over drugs.

Infamy: Began drinking at age 9 and started taking drugs at 10.

In 1992, posed nude for *Interview* magazine.

In 1995, posed nude for *Playboy.*

While on the *Late Show with David Letterman* in 1995, pulled down her trousers to display tattoos on her behind, then pulled up her shirt and flashed her breasts at Letterman.

Marriage: Jeremy Thomas (divorced), Eric Erlander (relationship)

Famous Relatives: John Barrymore Jr., actor and director, father; Ethel Barrymore, actor, great-aunt; Lionel Barrymore, actor, great-uncle; John Barrymore Sr., actor, grandfather

Major Award: Golden Globe, Best Actress in a Miniseries or Telefilm, *Guncrazy*, 1993

Address: United Talent Agency, 9560 Wilshire Blvd., Suite 500, Beverly Hills, CA 90212

KIM BASINGER

Birthplace: Athens, GA

Birthdate: 12/8/53

Occupation: Actor

Education: University of Georgia

Debut: (Film) *Hard Country,* 1981

Signature: *9 1/2 Weeks*

Facts: Filed for bankruptcy in May 1993 after an $8.1 million verdict was rendered against her in favor of Main Line Pictures, after she dropped out of the movie *Boxing Helena.* Had to limit her monthly living expenses to $10,000 under bankruptcy plan. An appeals court later reversed the verdict, setting the stage for another trial.

Developed agoraphobia while a model. Threw her modeling portfolio off the Brooklyn Bridge.

Was involved with The Artist

Formerly Known as Prince before marrying Alec Baldwin.
Infamy: In 1983, she appeared in an eight-page *Playboy* spread.

Bought Braselton, a town in Georgia, for $20 million in 1989, with plans to develop it into a tourist attraction. Dumped her interest in the town after she declared bankruptcy, leaving residents angry and fearful for their futures.
Original Job: Breck shampoo model, then a Ford model; pursued a singing career under the nom-de-chant Chelsea
Marriages: Ron Britton (divorced), Alec Baldwin
Child: Ireland Elliesse
Address: Creative Artists Agency, 9830 Wilshire Blvd., Beverly Hills, CA 90212

ANGELA BASSETT

Birthplace: New York, NY
Birthdate: 8/16/58
Occupation: Actor
Education: Yale University
Debut: (Film) *F/X,* 1986
Signature: *What's Love Got To Do with It*
Facts: Helped integrate her high school, where she was on the honor roll and the cheerleading squad. Went to college on a scholarship.
Original Job: Hair stylist, photo researcher at *U.S. News and World Report*
Relationship: Courtney B. Vance (engaged)
Major Award: Golden Globe, Best Actress in a Comedy or Musical, *What's Love Got to Do With It,* 1993
Address: Ambrosio/Mortimer & Associates, 9150 Wilshire Blvd., Suite 175, Beverly Hills, CA 90212

KATHY BATES

Real Name: Kathleen Doyle Bates
Birthplace: Memphis, TN
Birthdate: 6/28/48
Occupation: Actor
Education: Southern Methodist University
Debut: (Film) *Taking Off,* 1971; (Stage) *Casserole,* 1975; (TV) *The Love Boat,* 1977
Signature: *Misery*
Facts: She lost the screen roles of characters she originated on the stage (Frankie in *Frankie and Johnny in the Claire de Lune* and Lenny McGrath in *Crimes of the Heart*) to Michelle Pfeiffer and Diane Keaton.

Terrence McNally created the character Frankie (in *Frankie and Johnny in the Claire de Lune*) with her in mind.
Original Job: Singing waitress in the Catskills, cashier in the gift shop of Museum of Modern Art in New York
Marriage: Tony Campisi (divorced)
Major Awards: Oscar, Best Actress, *Misery,* 1990; Golden Globe, Best Actress in a Drama, *Misery,* 1990; Golden Globe, Best Supporting Actress in a Miniseries or Telefilm, *The Late Show,* 1996
Address: c/o S. Smith, 121 N. San Vicente Blvd., Beverly Hills, CA 90211

WARREN BEATTY

Real Name: Henry Warren Beaty
Birthplace: Richmond, VA
Birthdate: 3/30/37
Occupation: Actor, producer, director, screenwriter
Education: Northwestern University
Debut: (Film) *Splendor in the Grass,* 1961
Signature: *Shampoo*
Facts: Rejected football scholarships to go to drama school.

Is famed for his reluctance to do interviews and his tendency to pause for a minute or more before giving a yes or no answer.

The longtime womanizer broke the hearts of many famous actresses, including Natalie Wood, Leslie Caron, and Joan Collins. (Collins even had a wedding dress hanging in a wardrobe for almost a year.)
Original Job: Bricklayer, dishwasher, construction worker, piano player
Marriage: Annette Bening
Children: Kathlyn, Benjamin, Isabel
Famous Relative: Shirley MacLaine, actor, sister
Major Awards: Golden Globe, Most Promising Newcomer—Male, 1962; Golden Globe, Best Actor in a Comedy, *Heaven Can Wait,* 1978; Oscar, Best Director, *Reds,* 1981; Golden Globe, Best Director, *Reds,* 1981
Quote: "For me, the highest level of sexual excitement is in a monogamous relationship."
Address: Creative Artists Agency, 9830 Wilshire Blvd., Beverly Hills, CA 90212

BECK

Real Name: Beck Hansen
Birthplace: Los Angeles, CA
Birthdate: 7/8/70
Occupation: Singer, songwriter
Education: High school dropout
Debut: (Album) *Mellow Gold,* 1994
Signature: *Odelay*
Facts: In 1993, making just four dollars an hour, lived in a rat-infested shed behind a house. *Mellow Gold,* which includes "Loser," was recorded for $500, mostly at his friend's house.

Hung out in New York's East Village in the late '80s, where the "anti-folk scene" convinced him that there are no restrictions on subject matter for songs.

Mom was once a regular at Andy Warhol's Factory.
Original Jobs: Painting signs, moving refrigerators, taking ID photos at New York's YMCA, clerking in a video store
Famous Relatives: Bibbe Hansen, guitarist, mother; Al Hansen, artist, grandfather
Major Awards: Grammy, Best Rock Vocal—Male, "Where It's At," 1996; Grammy, Best Alternative Album, *Odelay,* 1996
Address: DGC Records, 9130 Sunset Blvd., Los Angeles, CA 90069

ANNETTE BENING

Birthplace: Topeka, KS
Birthdate: 5/5/58
Occupation: Actor
Education: Mesa College, San Francisco State University, American Conservatory Theater, San Francisco
Debut: (Stage) *Coastal Disturbances,* 1986; (Film) *The Great Outdoors,* 1988
Signature: *The Grifters*
Fact: Originally cast as Catwoman in *Batman Returns,* she got pregnant and lost the role to Michelle Pfeiffer.
Original Job: Cook on a charter boat for a year, to pay for college
Marriages: Steve White (divorced), Warren Beatty
Children: Kathlyn, Benjamin, Isabel
Address: Creative Artists Agency, 9830 Wilshire Blvd., Beverly Hills, CA 90212

TONY BENNETT

Real Name: Anthony Dominick Benedetto
Birthplace: Astoria, NY
Birthdate: 8/3/26
Occupation: Singer
Education: Manhattan's School of Industrial Art
Debut: (Album) *The Boulevard of Broken Dreams,* 1950
Signature: "I Left My Heart in San Francisco"
Facts: Marched with Martin Luther King Jr. in Selma in 1965 at the urging of Harry Belafonte.

Used the name Joe Bari until Bob Hope introduced him as Tony Bennett in 1950.

Served two years as an infantryman in Europe during World War II.

An avid painter, his works have been exhibited in galleries around the country.
Original Job: Singing waiter
Marriages: Patricia Beech (divorced), Sandra Grant (divorced)
Children: Danny, Daegal, Joanna, Antonia
Major Awards: Grammy, Best Pop Vocal—Male, "I Left My Heart in San Francisco," 1962; Grammy, Record of the Year, "I Left My Heart in San Francisco," 1962; Grammy, Album of the Year, *MTV Unplugged,* 1994; Grammy, Best Traditional Pop Vocal Performance, *MTV Unplugged,* 1994
Address: William Morris Agency, 151 El Camino Dr., Beverly Hills, CA 90212

CANDICE BERGEN

Birthplace: Beverly Hills, CA
Birthdate: 5/9/46
Occupation: Actor, photojournalist
Education: University of Pennsylvania
Debut: (Film) *The Group,* 1966
Signature: *Murphy Brown*
Facts: Her father's puppet, Charlie McCarthy, had a bigger bedroom and more clothes than she did as a child.

As a photojournalist, was published in *Life* and *Playboy.*

Wrote a play, *The Freezer,* which is included in *Best Short Plays of 1968.*
Original Job: Model
Marriage: Louis Malle (deceased)
Child: Chloe
Famous Relative: Edgar Bergen, ventriloquist, father
Major Awards: Emmy, Best Actress in a Comedy Series, *Murphy Brown,* 1989, 1990, 1992, 1993, 1995; Golden Globe, Best Actress in a Comedy Series, *Murphy Brown,* 1989, 1992, 1993
Address: William Morris Agency, 151 El Camino Dr., Beverly Hills, CA 90212

HALLE BERRY

Birthplace: Cleveland, OH
Birthdate: 8/14/68
Occupation: Actor
Education: Cuyahoga Community College
Debut: (TV) *Living Dolls,* 1989
Signature: *Boomerang*
Facts: Elected prom queen her senior year in high school, she was accused of stuffing the ballot box. Was forced to share the title with a "white, blond, blue-eyed, all-American girl."

Raised by her white mother after her black father left when she was four years old.

Lost 80 percent of the hearing in her left ear from an injury sustained from a physically abusive lover. (She rarely wears her hearing aid.)

Learned she was a diabetic when she collapsed in a coma while filming the TV series *Living Dolls.*

She was first runner-up in the 1986 Miss USA pageant.

Played a crackhead in Spike Lee's *Jungle Fever* (1991) and did not bathe for days to prepare for the role.
Infamy: Sued by a Chicago dentist (and former boyfriend) who claims she never repaid the $80,000 she borrowed from him. Refused to settle and, spending $50,000 defending herself, won in court.
Original Job: Model
Marriage: David Justice (divorced)
Address: Creative Artists Agency, 9830 Wilshire Blvd., Beverly Hills, CA 90212

JULIETTE BINOCHE

Birthplace: Paris, France
Birthdate: 3/9/64
Occupation: Actor
Education: Attended Paris's National Conservatory of Dramatic Arts

Debut: (Film) *La Vie de famille,* 1984
Signature: *The English Patient*
Facts: A big star in France, she is known simply as "la Binoche."

Was replaced in the title role of *Lucie Aubrac* while filming was already underway; Binoche felt some of her lines were out of character and wanted to rewrite them.

Her lucrative Lancôme deal requires only 10 working days a year.

Her parents divorced when she was four; grew up shuttling between each parent and a Catholic boarding school.

Relationship: Olivier Martinez
Child: Raphael
Major Awards: Cesar (France's Oscar), Best Actress, *Blue,* 1994; Oscar, Best Supporting Actress, *The English Patient,* 1996
Address: 10 Avenue George V, F-75008, Paris, France

CLINT BLACK

Birthplace: Long Branch, NJ
Birthdate: 2/4/62
Occupation: Singer, songwriter
Education: High school
Debut: (Album) *Killin' Time,* 1989
Signature: "Killin' Time"
Facts: He was the first country artist since Freddy Fender to reach No. 1 with his first charted single.

Recorded an R&B record with The Pointer Sisters, who were surprised at his ability to sing in this genre.

Appeared in the 1994 movie *Maverick.*

Infamy: In 1992 Black fired his manager of five years, Bill Ham, and hired his wife's mother as his personal assistant. Ham filed a breach of contract suit in Los Angeles Superior Court, and Black filed a $2 million countersuit. The case was settled out of court.
Original Job: Construction worker
Marriage: Lisa Hartman
Address: Clint Black International Fan Club, P.O. Box 307125, Nashville, TN 37230

MARY J. BLIGE

Birthplace: Bronx, NY
Birthdate: 1/11/71
Occupation: Singer, songwriter
Education: High school dropout
Debut: (Album) *What's the 411?,* 1992
Signature: "I'm Goin' Down"
Facts: Her father left the family when she was 4, leaving her mother to raise Blige and three siblings in a Yonkers, N.Y., housing project.

While hanging out with buddies at a suburban New York mall, made a karaoke-style recording of an Anita Baker song. That tape found its way to Uptown Records' CEO, who signed her to his label.

This Queen of Hip-Hop Soul has been dubbed the Aretha Franklin of Generation X.

Infamy: Developed a reputation for having an "attitude problem" after being sullen, withdrawn, and even nasty during interviews.

Sued for $1 million by her ex-managers for breach of contract, who claimed Blige was a "selfish artist" who forgot the people who worked to make her a success.

Relationship: Jodeci lead singer K-Ci (engaged)
Major Award: Grammy, Best Rap Performance by a Duo or Group, "I'll Be There for You/You're All I Need To Get By" 1995
Address: International Creative Management, 40 West 57th Street, New York, NY 10019

STEVEN BOCHCO

Birthplace: New York, NY
Birthdate: 12/16/43
Occupation: Producer, screenwriter
Education: Carnegie Institute of Technology
Debut: (TV) *A Fade to Black,* 1967
Signature: *NYPD Blue*
Facts: *Hill Street Blues* won 26 Emmys.

His father, Rudolph Bochco, was a child prodigy violinist who later played with orchestras in Broadway shows and with leading artists at Carnegie Hall.

Wrote material for *Ironside* and was the story editor for *Columbo.*

Turned down the presidency of CBS Entertainment in 1987.

Original Job: Assistant to the head of the story department at Universal Studios
Marriage: Barbara Bosson (separated)
Children: Jesse, Melissa
Famous Relative: Alan Rachins, actor, brother-in-law
Major Awards: Emmy, Outstanding Drama Series, *Hill Street Blues,* 1981, 1982, 1983, 1984; Emmy, Outstanding Drama Series, *L.A. Law,* 1987, 1989, 1990, 1991; George Foster Peabody Award; Edgar Allan Poe Award
Address: Fox Studios, 10201 W. Pico Blvd., Los Angeles, CA 90064

MICHAEL BOLTON

Real Name: Michael Bolotin
Birthplace: New Haven, CT
Birthdate: 2/26/53
Occupation: Singer, songwriter
Education: High school dropout
Debut: (EP) *Blackjack* (with Blackjack), 1979; (Album) *Michael Bolton* (solo), 1983
Facts: Wrote ballads and love songs for other artists, including Laura Branigan, Cher, The Pointer Sisters, and Barbra Streisand.

After the breakup of his band,

Blackjack, he began recording solo in 1983.

In the mid '80s, he was a regular opening act for metal acts such as Ozzy Osbourne and Krokus.

A research library in the New York Medical College was dedicated to him in 1993 for his work as honorary chairman of This Close for Cancer Research.

Infamy: After a two-week trial in 1994, a jury ruled that Bolton's "Love Is a Wonderful Thing" is remarkably similar to the Isley Brothers song "Love Is a Wonderful Thing."
Marriage: Maureen McGuire (divorced)
Children: Isa, Holly, Taryn
Major Awards: Grammy, Best Pop Vocal—Male, "How Am I Supposed to Live Without You," 1989; Grammy, Best Pop Vocal—Male, "When a Man Loves a Woman," 1991; American Music Awards, Favorite Male Vocalist, 1992; American Music Awards, Favorite Pop/Rock Album, 1992
Address: Columbia Records, 1801 Century Park W., Los Angeles, CA 90067

JON BON JOVI

Real Name: John Bongiovi
Birthplace: Sayreville, NJ
Birthdate: 5/2/62
Occupation: Singer, songwriter
Education: High school
Debut: (Album) *Bon Jovi,* 1984
Signature: Bon Jovi
Facts: Polygram executives gave the band a contract with the following conditions: John Bongiovi would become Jon Bon Jovi and only he would be given a contract. The other four members of the band would become Jon Bon Jovi's employees.

His first solo album, *Blaze of Glory* (1990), was "written for and inspired by" the film *Young Guns II,* in which he had a cameo role.

Title of Bon Jovi's album, *7800° Fahrenheit,* refers to the temperature of an exploding volcano.

Infamy: Had a legal dispute with cousin Tony Bongiovi, who owned the Record Plant, a New York City recording studio, over the extent to which Tony had aided his cousin's career. In 1984, Tony brought a lawsuit against Bon Jovi, the outcome of which gave him a producer's credit, a fee, royalties from Bon Jovi's first album, a cash award, and a one percent royalty from the group's next two albums.
Original Job: Floor sweeper at the Record Plant
Marriage: Dorothea Hurley
Children: Stephanie Rose, Jesse James Louis
Major Awards: Golden Globe, Best Song, "Blaze of Glory," 1990; American Music Awards, Best Pop/Rock Single, "Blaze of Glory," 1991
Address: Mercury, 825 8th Ave., New York, NY 10019

BONO

Real Name: Paul Hewson
Birthplace: Dublin, Ireland
Birthdate: 5/10/60
Occupation: Singer, songwriter
Education: High school
Debut: (EP) *U2:3* (with U2), 1979
Signature: U2
Facts: Got his nickname from a billboard advertising Bono Vox, a hearing aid retailer.

In November 1987, U2 opened for themselves at the L.A. Coliseum as the country-rock group The Dalton Brothers.

Infamy: Was the first winner in Grammy history to say "f--k"during its live telecast (1994).
Marriage: Alisa
Children: Eve, Jordan
Major Awards: Grammy, Album of the Year, *The Joshua Tree*, 1987; Grammy, Best Rock Performance—Duo or Group, *The Joshua Tree,* 1987; Grammy, Best Video—Long Form, *Where the Streets Have No Name,* 1988; Grammy, Best Rock Performance—Duo or Group, "Desire," 1988; Grammy, Best Rock Performance—Duo or Group, *Achtung Baby,* 1992; Grammy, Best Alternative Performance, *Zooropa,* 1993
Address: Island Records, 14 East 4th St., New York, NY 10003

KENNETH BRANAGH

Birthplace: Belfast, Northern Ireland
Birthdate: 12/10/60
Occupation: Actor, director
Education: Royal Academy of Dramatic Arts
Debut: (Stage) *Another Country,* 1982
Signature: *Henry V*
Facts: Grew up in poverty in the shadow of a tobacco factory in Belfast.

Co-founded England's Renaissance Theater Company.

To prepare for *Henry V,* Branagh received an audience with Prince Charles to gain insight on being heir to the throne.

Marriage: Emma Thompson (divorced)
Address: Hofflund-Pollone, 9615 Brighton Way, Suite 320, Beverly Hills, CA 90210

MARLON BRANDO

Birthplace: Omaha, NE
Birthdate: 4/3/24
Occupation: Actor
Education: Expelled from Shattuck Military Academy, attended New School for Social Research
Debut: (Stage) *I Remember Mama,* 1944; (Film) *The Men,* 1950
Signature: *The Godfather*
Fact: Exiled himself on his private island, Tetiaroa, near Tahiti, which he bought after filming *Mutiny on the Bounty* there in 1960.

Wrote an autobiography, *Brando: Songs My Mother Taught Me* (1994) to raise money for son Christian's legal fees, but the book was panned for omitting his many wives and

lovers, the latter including Shelley Winters and Rita Moreno.
Infamy: Son Christian killed daughter Cheyenne's boyfriend and served time for manslaughter (1990). Distraught, Cheyenne took her own life in 1995.
Original Job: Tile fitter, elevator operator
Marriages: Anna Kashfi (divorced), Movita Castenada (annulled), Tarita Teripia (divorced)
Children: Christian Devi, Miko, Rebecca, Simon Tehotu, Cheyenne (deceased), Ninna Priscilla
Major Awards: Oscar, Best Actor, *On the Waterfront,* 1955; Golden Globe, Best Actor, *On the Waterfront,* 1955; Oscar, Best Actor, *The Godfather,* 1972; Golden Globe, Best Actor, *The Godfather,* 1972; Emmy, Best Supporting Actor in a Limited Series, *Roots,* 1979; Golden Globe, World Film Favorite—Male, 1956, 1973, 1974
Address: International Creative Management, 8942 Wilshire Blvd., Beverly Hills, CA 90211

BRANDY

Real Name: Brandy Norwood
Birthplace: McComb, MS
Birthdate: 2/11/79
Occupation: Singer, actress
Debut: (Album) *Brandy,* 1994
Signature: "I Wanna Be Down"
Facts: From ages 12 to 14, sang backup for the R&B group Immature.

Brandy's famous braids are styled every two weeks, with fake hair extensions added for thickness, in an eight-hour process.

Before starring in UPN's *Moesha,* played the daughter in the short-lived 1993 TV comedy, *Thea.*

Her dad was choir director at their church, so as a child Brandy was always showcased as a featured singer.

Wasn't allowed to date until she was 16, but her mother/manager did provide her with a $500/week allowance.
Infamy: Sued by a management and production company for $5 million for allegedly breaking an oral contract to represent her.
Famous Relative: Ray-J, actor, singer, brother
Address: International Creative Management, 8942 Wilshire Blvd., Beverly Hills, CA 90211

TONI BRAXTON

Birthplace: Severn, MD
Birthdate: 1968
Occupation: Singer
Education: Bowie State University
Signature: "Breathe Again"
Fact: Learned to sing in a church choir. Her three sisters sing backup vocals on her albums. She and her sisters were only allowed to listen to gospel music, but she would "sneak into empty rooms to watch *Soul Train.*"
Relationship: Curtis Martin
Major Awards: Grammy, Best New Artist, 1993; Grammy, Best R&B Vocal—Female, "Another Sad Love Song," 1993; Grammy, Best R&B Vocal—Female, "Breathe Again," 1994; Grammy, Best Pop Vocal—Female, "Un-break My Heart," 1996; Grammy, Best R&B Vocal—Female, "You're Makin' Me High," 1996
Address: Toni Braxton, P.O.Box 4127, Upper Marlboro, MD 20775

JEFF BRIDGES

Birthplace: Los Angeles, CA
Birthdate: 12/4/49
Occupation: Actor
Education: High school, Herbert Berghof Studio
Debut: (Film) *The Company She Keeps,* 1950; (TV) *Sea Hunt,* 1957
Signature: *The Fabulous Baker Boys*
Facts: Joined the Coast Guard Reserves in 1968 to avoid the draft.

At age 16, he wrote a song included on the soundtrack of the 1969 film *John and Mary,* which starred Dustin Hoffman and Mia Farrow, and sold two compositions to Quincy Jones. To date, he has written over 200 songs.

Has exhibited his paintings and photographs in art galleries.
Infamy: In high school, developed a dependency on marijuana. He joined DAWN (Developing Adolescents Without Narcotics) and kicked the habit.
Marriage: Susan Gaston
Children: Isabelle, Jessica, Hayley
Famous Relatives: Lloyd Bridges, actor, father; Beau Bridges, actor, brother
Address: Creative Artists Agency, 9830 Wilshire Blvd., Beverly Hills, CA 90212

CHRISTIE BRINKLEY

Birthplace: Malibu, CA
Birthdate: 2/2/54
Occupation: Supermodel
Education: UCLA
Debut: (Film) *National Lampoon's Vacation,* 1983
Signature: Cover Girl Cosmetics model
Facts: An avid Francophile, Brinkley transferred from her local high school to the Lycée Français in Los Angeles. She later dropped out of college and worked at odd jobs selling ice cream, clothes, and plants to earn money for a ticket to Paris.

Designed the cover for Billy Joel's *River of Dreams* album.

Married Taubman atop a ski mountain, a symbolic acknowledgment of the helicopter crash they both survived while heli-skiing in 1994.
Original Job: Painter
Marriages: Jean Francois Allaux (divorced), Billy Joel (divorced), Rick Taubman (divorced), Peter Cook
Children: Alexa Ray, Jack Paris
Famous Relative: Don Brinkley, scriptwriter, producer, father
Address: William Morris Agency, 151 El Camino Dr., Beverly Hills, CA 90212

MATTHEW BRODERICK

Birthplace: New York, NY
Birthdate: 3/21/62
Occupation: Actor
Debut: (Stage) *Torch Song Trilogy,* 1982; (Film) *Max Dugan Returns,* 1983
Signature: *Ferris Bueller's Day Off*
Fact: Was heavily influenced by father James Broderick, who played the father in the TV series *Family* and died of cancer in 1982.
Infamy: While on vacation in Northern Ireland in 1987 with his then-girlfriend, actress Jennifer Grey, Broderick suffered a broken leg when the car he was driving collided with another automobile, killing its two occupants. Broderick was acquitted of one count of manslaughter and reckless driving.
Marriage: Sarah Jessica Parker
Famous Relative: James Broderick, character actor, father
Major Awards: Tony, Best Supporting Actor, *Brighton Beach Memoirs,* 1983; Tony, Best Actor (Musical), *How To Succeed in Business Without Really Trying,* 1995
Address: Creative Artists Agency, 9830 Wilshire Blvd., Beverly Hills, CA 90212

TOM BROKAW

Birthplace: Yankton, SD
Birthdate: 2/6/40
Occupation: Anchor, correspondent, managing editor
Education: University of South Dakota
Debut: (TV) KTIV, Sioux City, IA, 1960
Signature: *NBC Nightly News*
Facts: Served as president of high school student body. Also met future wife who became Miss South Dakota in high school.

Began with NBC as their White House correspondent in 1973.

Was the only network anchor present at the collapse of the Berlin Wall in 1989.
Marriage: Meredith
Children: Jennifer, Andrea, Sarah
Address: NBC, 30 Rockefeller Plaza, New York, NY 10112

GARTH BROOKS

Real Name: Troyal Garth Brooks
Birthplace: Tulsa, OK
Birthdate: 2/7/62
Occupation: Singer, songwriter
Education: Oklahoma State University
Debut: (Album) *Garth Brooks,* 1989
Signature: *Ropin' the Wind*
Facts: In 1990 at age 28, Garth became the youngest member of Nashville's Grand Ole Opry.

Brooks met his future wife while working as a bouncer. (He threw her out for fighting.)

In 1991, *Ropin' the Wind* became the first country album ever to reach No. 1 on the *Billboard* pop chart.

The video for "The Thunder Rolls," about a cheating husband shot by his battered wife after coming home drunk, was banned by Country Music Television and The Nashville Network. Thousands of shelters for battered women in America used the video in group counseling sessions.

Brooks' half sister is his bassist, his brother handles the books, and a college roommate is one of his guitarists.

Refused the Artist of the Year title from the American Music Awards in 1996, later explaining "I just couldn't accept it, just out of the love of the fellow musicians. I think we're all one."
Original Job: Bouncer in a nightclub
Marriage: Sandy Mahl
Children: Taylor Mayne Pearl, August Anna, Allie Colleen
Famous Relative: Colleen Carroll, singer, mother
Major Award: Grammy, Best Country Vocal—Male, *Ropin' the Wind,* 1991
Address: 1109 17th Ave. S., Nashville, TN 37212

JAMES L. BROOKS

Birthplace: North Bergen, NJ
Birthdate: 5/9/40
Occupation: Producer, director, actor, screenwriter
Education: New York University
Debut: (TV) *Room 222,* 1969; (Film) *Starting Over,* 1979
Signature: Creator of *The Mary Tyler Moore Show*
Facts: Founded Gracie Films, which produces *The Simpsons,* in 1984.

With fellow writer Allan Burns, created *The Mary Tyler Moore Show* in 1970.
Original Job: Copyboy for CBS News
Marriages: Marianne Catherine Morrissey (divorced), Holly Beth Holmberg
Children: Amy Lorraine, Chloe, Cooper
Major Awards: Emmy, Best Writing in a Comedy Series, *The Mary Tyler Moore Show,* 1971, 1977; Emmy, Best Comedy Series, *The Mary Tyler Moore Show,* 1975, 1976, 1977; Emmy, Best Comedy Series, *Taxi,* 1979, 1980, 1981; Emmy, Outstanding Variety, Music, or Comedy Program, *The Tracey Ullman Show,* 1989; Emmy, Outstanding Animated Program, *The Simpsons,* 1990, 1991; Oscar, Best Director, *Terms of Endearment,* 1983; Oscar, Best Adapted Screenplay, *Terms of Endearment,* 1983; Golden Globe, Best Adapted Screenplay, *Terms of Endearment,* 1983
Address: International Creative Management, 8942 Wilshire Blvd., Beverly Hills, CA 90211

MEL BROOKS

Real Name: Melvin Kaminsky
Birthplace: Brooklyn, NY
Birthdate: 6/28/26
Occupation: Actor, writer, director, producer
Education: Boston College
Debut: (Stage) *Broadway Revue,* 1949; (TV) *Your Show of Shows,* 1950

Signature: *Blazing Saddles*
Facts: Fought in Battle of the Bulge during World War II.

Co-creator of the TV series *Get Smart.*
Original Job: Drummer
Marriages: Florence Baum (divorced), Anne Bancroft
Children: Stephanie, Nicholas, Edward, Maximillian
Major Awards: Emmy, Best Writing in a Variety or Music Program, *Howard Morris Special,* 1967; Oscar, Best Original Screenplay, *The Producers,* 1968; Emmy, Best Guest Actor in a Comedy Series, *Mad About You,* 1997
Address: BrooksFilms 10202 W. Pico Blvd, Bldg. 215, Los Angeles, CA 90035

PIERCE BROSNAN

Birthplace: Navan, County Meath, Ireland
Birthdate: 5/16/52
Occupation: Actor
Debut: (Stage) *Wait Until Dark,* 1976; (Film) *The Mirror Crack'd,* 1980; (TV) *Remington Steele,* 1982
Signature: *Remington Steele*
Facts: Wife, Cassandra (best known for playing Countess Lisl in *For Your Eyes Only,* 1981), introduced Brosnan to Albert Broccoli, producer of the 007 series. Brosnan almost replaced Roger Moore as James Bond, but couldn't get out of his contract with NBC's *Remington Steele.*

In 1995, he finally played Bond in *Goldeneye,* and is credited with helping to revive the then-ailing series.

Ran away with the circus as a fire eater in his teens.
Original Job: Commercial artist
Marriages: Cassandra Harris (deceased), Keely Schaye-Smith
Children: stepdaughter Charlotte, stepson Christopher, Sean, Dylan Thomas
Address: Creative Artists Agency, 9830 Wilshire Blvd., Beverly Hills, CA 90212

JIMMY BUFFETT

Birthplace: Pascagoula, MS
Birthdate: 12/25/46
Occupation: Singer, songwriter
Education: University of Southern Mississippi
Debut: (Album) *Down to Earth,* 1970
Signature: "Margaritaville"
Facts: Has chaired Florida's Save the Manatee Club since its inception in 1981. In 1992, sued the parent Florida Audubon Society for independent control of the club, arguing that the society was "too cozy" with many of the businesses he felt were polluters.

Wrote a children's book, *The Jolly Man,* with his eight-year-old daughter in 1987. Also wrote two novels, including *Tales from Margaritaville* (1989). Has received a $3-million advance for a collection of tropical short stories.

In 1991, four Cuban exiles seeking political asylum swam to Buffett's Florida house. He handed them over to the authorities after offering them refreshments.

Also owns the Margaritaville Cafe franchise.
Original Job: Reviewer for *Billboard* magazine and freelance writer for *Inside Sports* and *Outside* magazines
Marriage: Jane Slagsvol
Children: Savannah, Sarah
Address: Frontline Management, 80 Universal City Plaza, 4th Fl., Universal City, CA 91608

SANDRA BULLOCK

Birthplace: Arlington, VA
Birthdate: 1967
Occupation: Actor
Education: East Carolina University, Neighborhood Playhouse with Sanford Meisner
Debut: (Film) *Fire on the Amazon,* 1990
Signature: *Speed*
Facts: Her mother was a European opera singer, so as a child Bullock shuttled between Austria, Germany, and the U.S.

Played lead actress in the short-lived TV series *Working Girl.*

Her role in *While You Were Sleeping* was originally offered to Demi Moore, whose salary demands were out of reach.
Original Job: Waitress
Famous Relative: Helga Bullock, mother, opera singer
Address: United Talent Agency, 9560 Wilshire Blvd., Beverly Hills, CA 90212

ED BURNS

Birthplace: Valley Stream, NY
Birthdate: 1/29/68
Occupation: Director, actor, writer
Education: Attended Hunter College
Debut: (Film) *The Brothers McMullen,* 1995
Signature: *The Brothers McMullen*
Facts: His first seven screenplays were rejected by agents and producers.

The Brothers McMullen was shot in eight months for around $20,000 (primarily a loan from dad), with Burns's parents' home the principal set.

Then-girlfriend Maxine Bahns was studying to be a classics professor when Burns began casting. Though she originally said no to the part, she decided acting would be good practice for her grad-school oral presentations.
Original Job: Production assistant, *Entertainment Tonight*
Address: International Creative Management, 40 W. 57th Street, New York, NY 10019

BRETT BUTLER

Birthplace: Montgomery, AL
Birthdate: 1/30/58
Occupation: Actor, comedian
Debut: (TV) *Dolly,* 1988
Signature: *Grace Under Fire*
Facts: Writes short stories and poetry in her spare time.

Was named after Lady Brett Ashley in Ernest Hemingway's *The Sun Also Rises.*

During her childhood, her family was so poor they sometimes ate Tootsie Rolls for dinner.

Butler was discovered while working at the Lone Star Cafe Steak House in Georgia. A wealthy club owner asked her to figure a tip, and she responded, "I can't believe you've got 10 million dollars and your I.Q. matches your in-seam." She was hired on the spot.

Before achieving sitcom success, often occupied one of the nine boxes on *The Hollywood Squares.*

Infamy: Arrested for drunken driving in 1981.
Original Job: Cocktail waitress
Marriages: Charles Wilson (divorced), Ken Ziegler
Quote: "I've come to terms with the fact that I'm an interesting broad with a salty past."
Address: International Creative Management, 8942 Wilshire Blvd., Beverly Hills, CA 90211

NICOLAS CAGE

Real Name: Nicholas Coppola
Birthplace: Long Beach, CA
Birthdate: 1/7/64
Occupation: Actor
Education: High school dropout
Debut: (TV) *The Best of Times,* 1980; (Film) *Valley Girl,* 1983
Signature: *Raising Arizona*
Facts: Was expelled from elementary school.

Changed his last name to have an identity independent of his famous uncle. He assumed the name Cage in admiration of the avant-garde composer John Cage and comic-book character Luke Cage.

His method-acting techniques have involved having wisdom teeth removed without Novocaine for his role as a wounded war veteran in *Birdy,* slashing his arm with a knife in *Racing with the Moon,* and eating a live cockroach for *Vampire's Kiss.*

Eight years before marrying Patricia Arquette, Cage proposed to her by volunteering to go on "a quest" for her. When he came up with a few of her chosen items—including J. D. Salinger's signature and a (spray-painted) black orchid—Arquette called off the deal.

Marriage: Patricia Arquette
Child: Weston (by ex-girlfriend Kristina Fulton)
Famous Relatives: Francis Ford Coppola, director, uncle; Talia Shire, actor, aunt
Major Award: Oscar, Best Actor, *Leaving Las Vegas,* 1995; Golden Globe, Best Actor, *Leaving Las Vegas,* 1995
Address: Creative Artists Agency, 9830 Wilshire Blvd., Beverly Hills, CA 90212

DEAN CAIN

Birthplace: Mt. Clemens, MI
Birthdate: 7/31/66
Occupation: Actor
Education: Princeton University
Debut: (Film) *The Stone Boy,* 1983; (TV) *The ABC Saturday Mystery,* 1990
Signature: *Lois & Clark: The New Adventures of Superman*
Facts: As a child, played baseball with Charlie Sheen and football with Chris Penn, and served on the student council with Rob Lowe.

Passed up 17 college football scholarships. He was a star defensive back (set an NCAA Division 1-AA record for interceptions in a season) and dated fellow student Brooke Shields for two years.

Was signed by the Buffalo Bills after his graduation in 1988, but injured his knee three days before his first preseason NFL game.

Had a recurring role in *Beverly Hills 90210,* in 1992, as Brenda Walsh's boyfriend, Rick.

Was turned down for the role of Jake on *Melrose Place.*

Original Job: Professional football player
Relationship: Mindy McCready (engaged)
Famous Relatives: Sarah Thomas, actor, mother; Christopher Cain, director, stepfather
Address: United Talent Agency, 9560 Wilshire Blvd., Suite 500, Beverly Hills, CA 90212

NAOMI CAMPBELL

Birthplace: London, England
Birthdate: 5/22/70
Occupation: Supermodel
Education: London School of Performing Arts
Debut: (Magazine) *British Elle,* 1985
Facts: In an effort to extend her talents beyond her modeling career, she wrote a novel, *Swan,* starred in the movie *Miami Rhapsody,* and recorded an album for Epic Records.

Has been romantically involved with Mike Tyson, Robert De Niro, and U2's Adam Clayton.

Opened Fashion Cafe in 1995 in New York City with fellow supermodels Elle MacPherson and Claudia Schiffer.

Infamy: Staged an impromptu stripping episode during lesbian night at a Manhattan bar.
Relationship: Joaquin Cortes
Address: Ford Models Inc., 334 East 59th St., New York, NY 10022

NEVE CAMPBELL

Birthplace: Guelph, Ontario
Birthdate: 10/3/73
Occupation: Actor
Education: National Ballet School of Canada
Debut: (Stage) Toronto production, *Phantom of the Opera,* 1988; (TV) *Catwalk,* 1992
Signature: *Party of Five*
Facts: Beat out 300 other actors for her *Po5* role.

At age 9, joined the prestigious National Ballet of Canada. Is also trained in jazz, modern, flamenco, and hip-hop.

Drama may be in her blood: her

mother once owned a dinner theater and her father was a high school drama teacher. They divorced when she was a toddler.

Her first name is her mother's Dutch maiden name and means "snow."

Original Job: Ballerina, model
Marriage: Jeff Colt (separated)
Famous Relative: Christian, actor, brother
Address: Fox-TV, P.O. Box 900, Beverly Hills, CA 90213

DREW CAREY

Birthplace: Cleveland, OH
Birthdate: 5/23/58
Occupation: Actor, comedian, writer
Education: Attended Kent State University
Debut: (TV) *Star Search,* 1987
Signature: *The Drew Carey Show*
Facts: Served in the marines for six years.

Got into comedy when a D.J. friend paid him to write some comedy material; Carey decided to try out the jokes himself on stage.

Battled depression for years, stemming from his grief over his father's death from a brain tumor when Drew was 8. Attempted suicide on several occasions.

Original Job: Waiter at Las Vegas Denny's
Address: ABC, 77 W. 66th Street, New York, NY 10023

MARIAH CAREY

Birthplace: New York, NY
Birthdate: 3/27/70
Occupation: Singer
Education: High school
Debut: (Album) *Mariah Carey,* 1990
Signature: "Vision of Love"
Facts: Her vocal range spans five octaves.

Her wedding cost half a million dollars. She watched tapes of the 1981 wedding of Charles and Diana in preparation.

Infamy: Sued by her stepfather in 1992 for failing to share profits from her 1990 album.
Original Job: Waitress, hat checker, restaurant hostess
Marriage: Tommy Mottola (separated)
Major Awards: Grammy, Best Pop Vocal—Female, "Vision of Love," 1990; Grammy, Best New Artist, 1990
Address: Columbia/CBS Records, 51 West 52nd St., New York, NY 10019

MARY CHAPIN CARPENTER

Birthplace: Princeton, NJ
Birthdate: 2/21/58
Occupation: Singer, songwriter, guitarist
Education: Brown University
Debut: (Album) *Hometown Girl,* 1988
Signature: "He Thinks He'll Keep Her"
Facts: Father, Chapin Carpenter, was a high-level *Life* magazine executive, so she spent her youth in Princeton, Tokyo, and Washington, DC.

Goes by the name Chapin, not Mary.

After college, considered music something to do for extra cash until she found her real career. Only after landing a nine-to-five job did she realize how much music meant to her, and began to focus on it.

Wrote Wynonna Judd's hit "Girls with Guitars" and co-wrote Cyndi Lauper's "Sally's Pigeon."

Infamy: Became an alcoholic after performing for years in bars.
Major Awards: Grammy, Best Country Vocal—Female, "Down at the Twist and Shout," 1991; Grammy, Best Country Vocal—Female, "I Feel Lucky," 1992; Grammy, Best Country Vocal—Female, "Passionate Kisses," 1993; Grammy, Best Country Vocal—Female, "Shut Up and Kiss Me," 1994; Grammy, Best Country Album, *Stones in the Road,* 1994
Address: Columbia Records, 51 West 52nd St., New York, NY 10019

JIM CARREY

Birthplace: Jacksons Point, Canada
Birthdate: 1/17/62
Occupation: Actor
Debut: (TV) *The Duck Factory,* 1984; (Film) *Finders Keepers,* 1984
Signature: *Ace Ventura: Pet Detective*
Fact: When his accountant father was laid off, he quit high school to make money doing janitorial work.

His $20 million paycheck for *The Cable Guy* was the highest salary yet paid to a comedian.

A coalition of fire prevention groups demanded that his Fire Marshall Bill sketches on *In Living Color* be taken off the air because of the negative effect they were having on children.

Marriages: Melissa Womer (divorced), Lauren Holly (divorced)
Child: Jane
Address: United Talent Agency, 9560 Wilshire Blvd., Suite 500, Beverly Hills, CA 90212

JOHNNY CARSON

Birthplace: Corning, IA
Birthdate: 10/23/25
Occupation: Talk show host
Education: University of Nebraska
Debut: (TV) *Carson's Cellar,* 1951
Signature: *The Tonight Show*
Facts: Declined role to play lead in the series that became *The Dick Van Dyke Show.*

As a 12-year-old, performed at local parties as "The Great Carsoni."

His son Richard was killed when his car plunged off a road (1991).

Third wife Joanna Holland received $20 million in cash and property in divorce settlement, 1983.

Served with the U.S. Naval Reserve during World War II.

Original Job: Radio announcer, ventriloquist, magician
Marriages: Joan Wolcott (divorced), Joanne Copeland (divorced), Joanna Holland (divorced), Alexis Mass
Children: Christopher, Richard (deceased), Cory
Major Awards: Elected to the Emmy Hall of Fame in 1987; Kennedy Center honoree, 1993
Address: Carson Productions, P.O. Box 5474, Santa Monica, CA 90409

JOHNNY CASH

Real Name: J. R. Cash
Birthplace: Kingsland, AR
Birthdate: 2/26/32
Occupation: Singer, songwriter
Debut: (Song) "Hey Porter," 1955
Signature: "I Walk The Line"
Facts: Cash is one-fourth Cherokee Indian.

He cannot read music.

Created 75 cuts for his 1994 album, produced by Rick Rubin (of Beastie Boys fame), which included songs written for him by Red Hot Chili Pepper Flea and Glenn Danzig.

Known as "the Man in Black," which is the title of his 1975 autobiography. Cash adopted this persona while working in a trio that only wore matching black outfits.

Wrote a novel, *Man in White,* in 1986.

He chose John as a first name when the military wouldn't accept initials.

Infamy: Cash was addicted to Dexadrine in the '60s.
Original Job: Door-to-door appliance salesman, factory worker
Marriages: Vivian Liberto (divorced), June Carter
Children: Rosanne, Kathleen, Cindy, Tara, John Carter, stepdaughter Rebecca Carlene, stepdaughter Rozanna Lea
Major Awards: Grammy, Best Country Performance—Duo or Group, "Jackson" (with June Carter), 1967; Grammy, Best Country Vocal—Male, "Folsom Prison Blues," 1968; Grammy, Best Country Vocal—Male, "A Boy Named Sue," 1969; Grammy, Best Country Performance—Duo or Group, "If I Were a Carpenter" (with June Carter), 1970; Grammy, Best Spoken Word Recording, *Interviews from the Class of '55* (with others), 1986; Grammy, Legend Award, 1991; Grammy, Best Contemporary Folk Album, *American Recordings*, 1994; elected to Country Music Hall of Fame, 1980; elected to the Rock and Roll Hall of Fame, 1992
Address: Agency for the Performing Arts, 9000 Sunset Blvd., Suite 1200, Los Angeles, CA 90069

ROSANNE CASH

Birthplace: Memphis, TN
Birthdate: 5/24/55
Occupation: Singer, songwriter
Education: State Community College; Vanderbilt University and Lee Strasberg Theatre Institute
Debut: (Song) "Blue Moon with Heartache," 1979
Signature: "I Don't Know Why You Don't Want Me"
Fact: Never intended to become a musician. Her original ambition was to become a serious fiction writer.
Infamy: In 1982, entered a drug rehabilitation program for a cocaine dependency she had developed in 1979.
Original Job: Worked in wardrobe department during her father's tour. One day the tour managers asked her to come on stage and sing harmony.
Marriage: Rodney Crowell (divorced)
Children: Hannah, Caitlyn, Chelsea
Famous Relatives: Johnny Cash, country singer, father; June Carter Cash, country singer, stepmother; Carlene Carter, country singer, stepsister
Major Award: Grammy, Best Country Vocal—Female, "I Don't Know Why You Don't Want Me," 1985
Address: Capitol Records, 1750 N. Vine Street, Hollywood, CA 90028

JACKIE CHAN

Real Name: Chan Kwong-Sang
Birthplace: Hong Kong
Birthdate: 4/7/54
Occupation: Actor, writer, producer, director
Education: Chinese Opera Research Institute
Debut: *Big and Little Wong Tin Bar*, 1962; American debut, *The Big Brawl*, 1980
Signature: *Rumble in the Bronx*
Facts: Considered the biggest non-Hollywood movie star in the world; has been in more than 40 Asian action comedies. His fan club once topped 10,000 mostly young-girl members, one of whom killed herself when she read Chan was involved with someone.

His first attempts to break into Hollywood in the early '80s led to movie flops.

Nearly died making a 1986 film, when, leaping from a castle to a tree, he fell nearly 40 feet and broke his skull. He's also broken his jaw, shoulder, fingers and nose three times making movies.

To perfect his comic approach, studied old Hollywood Buster Keaton movies.

Impoverished parents left him at the Chinese Opera Institute at age 7 when they moved to Australia. During this militaristic-type training, he was beaten nearly every day.

Original Job: Stuntman
Marriage: Lin Feng-Chiao (separated)
Child: J. C.
Address: William Morris Agency, 151 El Camino Dr., Beverly Hills, CA 90212

DEEPAK CHOPRA

Birthplace: India
Birthdate: 1949
Occupation: Author
Education: All-India Institute of Medicine
Signature: *Ageless Body, Timeless Mind*
Facts: Was a mainstream endocrinologist, and chief of staff at New England Memorial Hospital, before embracing alternative healing methods.

Dr. Chopra practices a form of ayurvedic medicine called Maharishi Ayur-Veda, named after the Indian spiritual leader who taught transcendental meditation to The Beatles. The system is based on a 5,000-year-old Indian holistic health system involving herbal remedies, massage, yoga, and transcendental meditation. (Ayur-Veda is derived from the Sanskrit roots for "life" and "knowledge.")
Marriage: Rita
Children: Gautama, Mallika
Address: Sharp Institute for Human Potential and Mind Body Medicine, 973B Lomas Santa Fe, Solana Beach, CA 92075

TOM CLANCY

Birthplace: Baltimore, MD
Birthdate: 1947
Occupation: Author
Debut: (Book) *The Hunt for Red October*, 1984
Facts: First short story was rejected by *Analog* science fiction magazine. Had just one article (on the MX missile system) to his credit when *Hunt for Red October* was published.

In the U.S. Army Reserve Officers' Training Corps, his poor eyesight kept him from serving in the Vietnam War.

Part-owner of the Baltimore Orioles, he also led the effort to bring an NFL expansion team to Baltimore for the 1994 season. He was successful, and is now part-owner of the Baltimore Ravens.

Clear and Present Danger was the bestselling book of the '80s.
Original Job: Insurance agent
Marriage: Wanda Thomas (separated)
Children: Michelle, Christine, Kathleen, Tom
Quote: "What do I care if someone reads my books a hundred years from now? I will be dead. And it's kind of hard to make money when you're dead."
Address: G. P. Putnam's Sons, 200 Madison Ave., New York, NY 10016

ERIC CLAPTON

Real Name: Eric Clapp
Birthplace: Ripley, England
Birthdate: 3/30/45
Occupation: Singer, guitarist, songwriter
Education: Kingston Art School
Debut: (Album) *The Yardbirds,* 1963
Signature: "Layla"
Facts: At the Ealing Club in London, occasionally substituted for lead singer Mick Jagger in Blues, Inc.

Earned the nickname "Slowhand" because his powerful playing regularly broke his guitar strings, which he then changed onstage to the accompaniment of a slow handclap from listeners.

The song "Layla" was reportedly inspired by an affair that Clapton had at the time with George Harrison's wife Patti, and was dedicated "to the wife of my best friend."

Tragedy struck in 1991, when his 4-year-old son died in a fall from Clapton's ex-girlfriend's apartment. The song "Tears in Heaven" is a tribute to him.

Was among 1,080 Britons recognized on Queen Elizabeth's honors list at the end of 1994.
Infamy: After release of *Layla and Other Assorted Love Songs* (1970), dropped out of sight for two-and-a-half years because of a heroin addiction. He was brought out of seclusion by Pete Townshend of The Who. A bout with alcoholism followed. Now, he says he hasn't touched a drink since 1987.
Original Job: Construction worker
Marriage: Patricia Anne Boyd-Harrison (divorced)
Child: Conor (deceased)
Major Awards: Grammy, Album of the Year, *The Concert for Bangladesh* (with George Harrison and Friends), 1972; Grammy, Best Rock Vocal—Male, "Bad Love," 1990; Grammy, Album of the Year, *Unplugged,* 1992; Grammy, Best Rock Vocal—Male, "Layla," 1992; Grammy, Record of the Year, Song of the Year, and Best Pop Vocal—Male, "Tears in Heaven," 1992; Grammy, Best Traditional Blues Album, *From the Cradle*, 1994; Grammy, Record of the Year, "Change the World," 1996; Grammy, Best Pop Vocal—Male, "Change the World," 1996
Address: Creative Artists Agency, 9830 Wilshire Blvd., Beverly Hills, CA 90212

GEORGE CLOONEY

Birthplace: Lexington, KY
Birthdate: 5/6/61
Occupation: Actor
Education: Northern Kentucky University
Debut: (TV) *E/R*, 1984
Signature: *ER*
Facts: Got his Hollywood break playing a medical intern on the short-lived CBS comedy series *E/R*, set in a Chicago hospital emergency room. On NBC's *ER*, also set in a

Chicago hospital emergency room, he graduated to full-fledged doctor.

Appeared as Roseanne's boss and Jackie's boyfriend during the first season of *Roseanne.*

Marriage: Talia Balsam (divorced); Celine Balidran (relationship)
Famous Relatives: Rosemary Clooney, singer, aunt; Nick Clooney, TV host, father; Miguel Ferrer, actor, cousin
Address: William Morris Agency, 151 El Camino Dr., Beverly Hills, CA 90212

GLENN CLOSE

Birthplace: Greenwich, CT
Birthdate: 3/19/47
Occupation: Actor
Education: The College of William and Mary
Debut: (Stage) *Love for Love,* 1974; (TV) *Too Far To Go,* 1979; (Film) *The World According to Garp,* 1982
Signature: *Fatal Attraction*
Facts: When she was 13, her father opened a clinic in the Belgian Congo (now Zaire) and ran it for 16 years. During most of that time, the Close children lived alternately in Africa and at boarding schools in Switzerland.

Chosen by Andrew Lloyd Webber to replace Patti LuPone in *Sunset Boulevard,* 1994.

Infamy: When she went on a two-week vacation from *Sunset Boulevard* in 1995, the production company released erroneous box-office figures implying that Close's absence had no effect on ticket sales. Close sent a scathing letter of complaint to composer-producer Andrew Lloyd Webber, which was obtained and published in the media.
Original Job: Toured Europe and the U.S. as a member of Up With People
Marriages: Cabot Wade (divorced), James Marlas (divorced), Steve Beers (engaged)
Child: Annie Maude Starke (from relationship with John Starke)
Major Awards: Tony, Best Actress, *The Real Thing,* 1984; Tony, Best Actress, *Death and the Maiden,* 1992; Tony, Best Actress (Musical), *Sunset Boulevard,* 1995; Emmy, Best Actress in a Miniseries or Special, *Serving in Silence: The Margarethe Cammermeyer Story,* 1995
Address: Creative Artists Agency, 9830 Wilshire Blvd., Beverly Hills, CA 90212

SEAN CONNERY

Real Name: Thomas Connery
Birthplace: Edinburgh, Scotland
Birthdate: 8/25/30
Occupation: Actor
Debut: (Stage) *South Pacific,* 1951
Signature: James Bond
Facts: Connery grew up in a poor, industrial district of Scotland. At age 7, he took a job delivering milk before school, and by age 13 he quit school.

Served in the British Navy from 1947 to 1950. Was discharged due to ulcers.

In 1950, represented Scotland in London's Mr. Universe competition.

Original Job: Lifeguard, milkman, bricklayer, plasterer, coffin polisher, and usher
Marriages: Diane Cilento (divorced), Micheline Roquebrune
Child: Jason
Major Awards: Golden Globe, World Film Favorite, 1972 (with Charles Bronson); Oscar, Best Supporting Actor, *The Untouchables,* 1987; Golden Globe, Best Supporting Actor, *The Untouchables,* 1987
Address: Creative Artists Agency, 9830 Wilshire Blvd., Beverly Hills, CA 90212

HARRY CONNICK JR.

Birthplace: New Orleans, LA
Birthdate: 9/11/67
Occupation: Singer
Education: Loyola University, Hunter College, Manhattan School of Music
Debut: (Album) *Harry Connick, Jr.,* 1987
Signature: "It Had To Be You"
Facts: Performed annually at the New Orleans Jazz & Heritage Festival from the time he was 8.

He also recorded two albums of Dixieland music on little-known labels—the first when he was nine and the second when he was 10.

Learned jazz music from Ellis Marsalis, the patriarch of the Marsalis family at the New Orleans Center for the Creative Arts.

Infamy: Arrested for having a gun in his luggage at New York's JFK airport.
Marriage: Jill Goodacre
Child: Georgia Tatom
Major Awards: Grammy, Best Jazz Vocal—Male, *When Harry Met Sally,* 1989; Grammy, Best Jazz Vocal—Male, "We Are in Love," 1990
Address: Creative Artists Agency, 9830 Wilshire Blvd., Beverly Hills, CA 90212

COOLIO

Real Name: Artis Ivey Jr.
Birthplace: Los Angeles, CA
Birthdate: 1963
Occupation: Rap artist
Education: Compton Community College
Debut: (Album) *It Takes a Thief,* 1994
Signature: "Gangsta's Paradise"
Facts: Nicknamed "Boo."

Formed a foundation to encourage the teaching of black and Hispanic history in public schools.

Owns a hair salon, Whoop-De-Doo, in Long Beach, California.

Teaches ghetto kids the music business at his recording studio.

Infamy: Jailed for seven months at age 17 for trying to cash a money order taken in an armed robbery. Was also hooked on crack, a habit he broke during a job fighting forest fires in the California mountains, a place where, he says, "you can't get drugs."
Relationship: Josefa Salinas (engaged)

Children: daughter Brandy, 5 sons
Major Award: Grammy, Best Rap Solo Performance, "Gangsta's Paradise,"1995
Address: William Morris Agency, 151 El Camino Drive, Beverly Hills, CA 90212

DAVID COPPERFIELD

Real Name: David Kotkin
Birthplace: Metuchen, NJ
Birthdate: 9/16/56
Occupation: Magician
Education: Fordham University
Debut: (TV) *The Magic of ABC,* 1977
Facts: In his act, has levitated a Ferrari, walked through the Great Wall of China, and made the Statue of Liberty disappear. He has also extricated himself from a safe in a building about to be demolished by explosives and a steel box on a raft heading for the Niagara Falls.

By age 12, had performed at local birthday parties for a fee of five dollars, under the name "Davino, the Boy Magician."

In 1982 developed Project Magic, a program designed to help people with physical and mental disabilities by teaching them magic.
Relationship: Claudia Schiffer (engaged)
Address: 9017 Wilshire Blvd., #500, Beverly Hills, CA 90210

FRANCIS FORD COPPOLA

Birthplace: Detroit, MI
Birthdate: 4/7/39
Occupation: Director and writer
Education: Hofstra University, UCLA Film School
Debut: (Film) *Dementia 13,* 1963
Signature: *The Godfather*
Facts: First dreamed of becoming a filmmaker at age 10, while bedridden with polio. He put on shows for himself using puppets, a tape recorder, a film projector, and a television set.

Coppola's interest in producing a film about the automaker Preston Tucker—*Tucker: The Man and His Dream,* (1988)—began when his father invested and lost $5,000 in the automaker's company.

Directed Michael Jackson in the 15-minute Epcot Center feature *Captain EO.*

First son, Gian Carlo, was killed in a boating accident in 1986.

Owns a vineyard in California's Napa Valley. Also owns a restaurant in San Francisco and property in Belize; he hopes to make that country the hub for a huge telecommunications center.
Original Job: Worked for famous B-movie producer/director Roger Corman as dialogue director, sound man, and associate producer
Marriage: Eleanor Neil
Children: Gian Carlo (deceased), Roman, Sofia
Famous Relatives: Talia Shire, actor, sister; Nicholas Cage, actor, nephew
Major Awards: Oscar, Best Original Screenplay, *Patton* (with Edmund H. North), 1970; Oscar, Best Adapted Screenplay, *The Godfather* (with Mario Puzo), 1972; Oscar, Best Director, *The Godfather Part II,* 1974; Oscar, Best Adapted Screenplay, *The Godfather Part II* (with Mario Puzo), 1974; Golden Globe, Best Director, *The Godfather,* 1972; Golden Globe, Best Screenplay, *The Godfather* (with Mario Puzo), 1972; Golden Globe, Best Director, *Apocalypse Now,* 1979; Golden Globe, Best Score, *Apocalypse Now* (with Carmine Coppola), 1979
Address: Creative Artists Agency, 9830 Wilshire Blvd., Beverly Hills, CA 90212

BILL COSBY

Birthplace: Philadelphia, PA
Birthdate: 7/12/37
Occupation: Actor, comedian, producer, author
Education: Temple University; Doctor of Education, University of Massachusetts at Amherst
Debut: (TV) *I, Spy,* 1965; (Film) *Hickey and Boggs,* 1971
Signature: *The Cosby Show*
Facts: Grew up in a housing project in Philadelphia.

A gifted athlete, he was noticed by a scout for the Green Bay Packers.

Has played the drums since he was 11. A jazz aficionado, is president of the Rhythm and Blues Hall of Fame.
Infamy: In 1997, Cosby admitted having an adulterous "rendezvous" with Shawn Thompson in the early 1970s. The one-night stand came to light when Thompson's daughter, Autumn Jackson, threatened to tell the media that Cosby was her father unless he gave her $40 million. Jackson, whose education was charitably financed by the entertainer, was convicted of extortion. Cosby has since submitted to a DNA test to settle paternity issues but at press time Jackson, awaiting sentencing, was withholding her own DNA samples.
Original Job: Shined shoes, delivered groceries
Marriage: Camille Hanks
Children: Erika Ranee, Erinn Charlene, Ennis William (deceased), Ensa Camille, Evin Harrah
Major Awards: Emmy, Best Actor in a Drama Series, *I Spy,* 1966, 1967, 1968; Emmy, *Bill Cosby Special,* 1969; Emmy, *The New Fat Albert Show,* 1981; Emmy, Best Comedy Series, *The Cosby Show,* 1985; Golden Globe, Best Actor in a Comedy Series, *The Cosby Show,* 1985, 1986; elected to the Emmy Hall of Fame, 1991; NAACP Image Award, 1976; Grammy, Best Comedy Recording, *I Started Out as a Child,* 1964; *Why Is There Air,* 1965; *Wonderfulness,* 1966; *Revenge,* 1967; *To Russell, My Brother, Whom I Slept With,* 1968; *Bill Cosby,* 1969; *Those of You with or without Children, You'll Understand,* 1986; Grammy, Best Recording for Children, *Bill Cosby Talks to Kids*

About Drugs, 1971; Grammy, Best Recording for Children, *The Electric Company* (with Lee Chamberlin and Rita Moreno), 1972
Address: William Morris Agency, 151 El Camino Dr., Beverly Hills, CA 90212

ELVIS COSTELLO

Real Name: Declan McManus
Birthplace: London, England
Birthdate: 8/25/55
Occupation: Singer, songwriter
Education: High school dropout
Debut: (Album) *My Aim Is True,* 1977
Signature: Elvis Costello & The Attractions
Fact: Got his first contract with CBS Records by performing on the sidewalk in front of the hotel where the label's sales conference was in progress. Was arrested for disturbing the peace, but achieved his purpose.
Infamy: In a drunken argument in 1979, used racial epithets in referring to Ray Charles and James Brown. American disc jockeys took his records off their playlists, and he received numerous death threats.
Original Job: Computer operator at an Elizabeth Arden cosmetics factory
Marriages: Mary (divorced), Caitlin O'Riordan
Child: Matthew
Famous Relative: Ross McManus, singer, father
Address: Warner Brothers Recording, 3300 Warner Blvd., Burbank, CA 91505

KEVIN COSTNER

Birthplace: Lynwood, CA
Birthdate: 1/18/55
Occupation: Actor, director, producer
Education: California State University at Fullerton
Debut: (Film) *Sizzle Beach,* 1979
Signature: *The Untouchables*
Facts: At 18, built a canoe and paddled down the same rivers that Lewis and Clark had navigated on their way to the Pacific.

As a teenager, he sang in the church choir.

Turned down the leading role in *War Games* (played by Matthew Broderick) to play Alex, the character who commits suicide, in *The Big Chill.* Only two weeks before the film's release, Alex's part was cut. But director Lawrence Kasdan promised Costner that he would write a part for him in another film, and tailored the role of Jake in *Silverado* (1985) for Costner.
Infamy: In February 1995, Costner and his brother Dan began building an entertainment complex in the Black Hills of South Dakota, on land that the Lakota Indians consider sacred and have been trying to recover since 1887. Costner had been made an honorary Lakota in 1990 after working with them on *Dances with Wolves.*
Original Job: Worked in marketing, stage-managed Raleigh Studios in L.A.
Marriage: Cindy Silva (divorced)
Children: Annie, Lily, Joe, Liam
Major Awards: Oscar, Best Director, *Dances with Wolves,* 1990; Oscar, Best Picture, *Dances with Wolves* (produced with Jim Wilson), 1990; Golden Globe, Best Director, *Dances with Wolves,* 1990
Address: William Morris Agency, 151 El Camino Dr., Beverly Hills, CA 90212

KATIE COURIC

Birthplace: Arlington, VA
Birthdate: 1/7/57
Occupation: Broadcast journalist
Education: University of Virginia
Signature: *Today*
Fact: After hearing Couric read a report on the air, the president of CNN banned the young assignment editor from further television appearances, complaining about her high-pitched, squeaky voice. Keeping her spirits, Couric began working with a voice coach.
Original Job: Desk assistant at ABC News in Washington, DC
Marriage: Jay Monahan
Children: Elinor Tully, Caroline
Address: NBC, 30 Rockefeller Plaza, New York, NY 10122

COURTENEY COX

Birthplace: Birmingham, AL
Birthdate: 6/15/64
Occupation: Actor
Education: Mt. Vernon College in Washington, DC
Debut: (TV) *Misfits of Science,* 1985; (Film) *Down Twisted,* 1987
Signature: *Friends*
Facts: Discovered in 1984 Brian De Palma video "Dancing in the Dark" with Bruce Springsteen.

Played Michael J. Fox's girlfriend on *Family Ties* and Jim Carrey's love interest in *Ace Ventura: Pet Detective.*
Original Job: Model
Address: Creative Artists Agency, 9830 Wilshire Blvd., Beverly Hills, CA 90212

CINDY CRAWFORD

Birthplace: De Kalb, IL
Birthdate: 2/20/66
Occupation: Supermodel
Education: Northwestern University
Debut: (Film) *Fair Game,* 1995
Signature: *House of Style*
Facts: Crawford was the valedictorian of her high school class, and received a full scholarship to study chemical engineering in college. There, a professor accused Crawford of cheating after she received a perfect score on a calculus midterm exam.

Supports P-FLAG (Parents and Friends of Lesbians and Gays) and leukemia research (her brother died of the disease at age 3).
Infamy: Posed for the cover of *Vanity Fair* shaving lesbian singer k.d. lang, prompting a renewal of international

rumors she and then-husband Richard Gere were each homosexual and maintained the marriage for appearances only. In May 1994, the couple took out a $30,000 ad in the *Times* of London denying the rumors.
Original Job: Spent summers during high school detasseling corn in fields
Marriage: Richard Gere (divorced); Rande Gerber (relationship)
Address: William Morris Agency, 151 El Camino Dr., Beverly Hills, CA 90212

MICHAEL CRICHTON

Real Name: John Michael Crichton
Birthplace: Chicago, IL
Birthdate: 10/28/42
Occupation: Writer, director, producer
Education: Harvard, Harvard Medical School
Debut: (Book) *Odds On* (under the pseudonym John Lange), 1966; (Film) *Westworld,* 1973
Signature: *Jurassic Park*
Facts: Published a travel article in *The New York Times* when he was 14.

Developed FilmTrak, a computer program for film production, and is creator of the computer game Amazon.
Infamy: In 1974 was fired as screenwriter of the film adaptation of *The Terminal Man* when his screenplay deviated too much from the book.
Original Job: Anthropology professor
Marriages: Joan Radam (divorced), Kathy St. Johns (divorced), Anne Marie Martin
Child: Taylor
Address: Creative Artists Agency, 9830 Wilshire Blvd., Beverly Hills, CA 90212

SHERYL CROW

Birthplace: Kennett, MO
Birthdate: 2/11/63
Occupation: Singer, songwriter
Education: University of Missouri
Debut: (Album) *Tuesday Night Music Club*, 1994
Signature: "All I Wanna Do"
Facts: Her mother and father played piano and trumpet, respectively, with a big band on weekends. Their four children were encouraged to learn music and often practiced on the four pianos in the house simultaneously.

Sang backup for Michael Jackson's 18-month *Bad* tour and, later, for Don Henley.

Went through a severe depression in the late '80s and didn't get out of bed for six months.

Played at Woodstock '94.
Major Awards: Grammy, Record of the Year, "All I Wanna Do," 1994; Grammy, Best New Artist, 1994; Grammy, Best Pop Vocal—Female, "All I Wanna Do," 1994; Grammy, Bet Rock Vocal—Female, "If It Makes You Happy," 1996
Address: William Morris Agency, 151 El Camino Dr., Beverly Hills, CA 90212

TOM CRUISE

Real Name: Thomas Cruise Mapother IV
Birthplace: Syracuse, NY
Birthdate: 7/3/62
Occupation: Actor
Education: High school dropout
Debut: (Film) *Endless Love,* 1981
Signature: *Top Gun*
Facts: Dyslexia put him in remedial reading courses in school, but Cruise proved himself in sports.

At age 14, enrolled in a seminary to become a priest. Dropped out after one year.

Took up acting after losing his place on a high school wrestling team due to a knee injury.

Member of the Church of Scientology.
Infamy: Author Anne Rice publicly criticized David Geffen for casting Cruise in *Interview with a Vampire* in 1994. After Rice saw the film she admitted Geffen had been right.
Original Job: Busboy
Marriages: Mimi Rogers (divorced), Nicole Kidman
Children: Isabella Jane (adopted), Connor Antony (adopted)
Major Award: Golden Globe, Best Actor in a Drama, *Born on the Fourth of July,* 1989; Golden Globe, Best Actor in a Musical or Comedy, *Jerry Maguire*, 1996
Quote: "I'm not the Stanislavski kind of actor. I just want to communicate with the people in the scene."
Address: Creative Artists Agency, 9830 Wilshire Blvd., Beverly Hills, CA 90212

BILLY CRYSTAL

Birthplace: New York, NY
Birthdate: 3/14/47
Occupation: Comedian, actor
Education: Marshall University, Nassau Community College; New York University
Debut: (TV) *Soap,* 1977; (Film) *Rabbit Test,* 1978
Signature: *When Harry Met Sally ...*
Facts: Went to college on a baseball scholarship and hosted a campus-radio talk show.

First theater job as a house manager for *You're a Good Man Charlie Brown,* 1968.

Studied directing under Martin Scorsese at New York University.
Infamy: Walked off the set of his first *Saturday Night Live* appearance after his seven-minute monologue was cut from the show.
Original Job: Substitute teacher, writer
Marriage: Janice Goldfinger
Children: Jennifer, Lindsay
Famous Relative: Milt Gabler, founded Commodore Records and later headed Decca Records, uncle
Major Awards: Emmy, Best Writing in a Variety or Music Program, *Midnight Train to Moscow,* 1990; Emmy, Best Individual Performance in a Variety or Music Program, *The 63rd Annual Oscars,* 1991; Emmy, Best Writing in a Variety or Music

Program, *The 63rd Annual Oscars,* 1991; Emmy, Best Writing in a Variety or Music Program, *The 64th Annual Oscars,* 1992
Quote: "My father used to bring home jazz musicians at Passover. We had swinging seders."
Address: Creative Artists Agency, 9830 Wilshire Blvd., Beverly Hills, CA 90212

JAMIE LEE CURTIS

Birthplace: Los Angeles, CA
Birthdate: 11/22/58
Occupation: Actor
Education: Choate; University of the Pacific
Debut: (TV) *Operation Petticoat,* 1977; (Film) *Halloween,* 1978
Signature: *A Fish Called Wanda*
Facts: Very athletic, Curtis was trained as a dancer and appeared on *Circus of the Stars* as an acrobat.

Curtis became interested in her husband Christopher Guest when she saw his picture in *Rolling Stone.* She gave him her home number through an agent.

When her husband inherited his grandfather's English peerage title, Curtis earned the right to be addressed as "Lady Haden-Guest."
Infamy: Admitted to using cocaine, even with her father, although not abusing it. She quit completely in 1983.
Marriage: Christopher Guest
Children: Annie, Thomas Haden (adopted)
Famous Relatives: Tony Curtis, actor, father; Janet Leigh, actor, mother
Major Awards: Golden Globe, Best Actress in a Comedy Series, *Anything but Love,* 1990; Golden Globe, Best Actress in a Comedy, *True Lies,* 1994
Address: Creative Artists Agency, 9830 Wilshire Blvd., Beverly Hills, CA 90212

JOHN CUSACK

Birthplace: Evanston, IL
Birthdate: 6/28/66
Occupation: Actor, writer, producer
Education: Attended New York University
Debut: (Film) *Class,* 1983
Signature: *Say Anything*
Facts: Grew up in a tightknit Irish Catholic family, always putting on neighborhood plays. Four of the five kids appear in *Grosse Pointe Blank,* which Cusack wrote and produced.

His parents were active in the anti-war and social protest movements; today he chooses most roles with an eye towards their social statements. During the Gulf War, he even wrote an op-ed for the *Chicago Sun-Times* protesting "police brutality" during an anti-war rally outside a rap concert.

At 20, started his own Chicago theater group, New Crime Productions.
Famous Relative: Joan Cusack, actor, sister
Address: William Morris Agency, 151 El Camino Dr., Beverly Hills, CA 90212

CLAIRE DANES

Birthplace: New York, NY
Birthdate: 4/12/79
Occupation: Actor
Debut: (TV) *Law & Order,* 1992; (Film) *Little Women,* 1995
Signature: *My So-Called Life*
Facts: Winona Ryder was so taken with Danes's portrayal of Angela Chase on *My So-Called Life* that she called her *Little Women* director to suggest Danes for the part of Beth.

First auditioned for *My So-Called Life* when she was 13, but it took two more years for the show to get a firm commitment from ABC.
Major Awards: Golden Globe, Best Actress in a TV Drama, *My So-Called Life,* 1995
Address: Creative Artists Agency, 9830 Wilshire Blvd., Beverly Hills, CA 90212

JEFF DANIELS

Birthplace: Georgia
Birthdate: 2/19/55
Occupation: Actor
Education: University of Central Michigan, apprentice at New York's Circle Rep
Debut: (Stage) *The Farm,* 1976; (Film) *Ragtime,* 1981
Signature: *The Purple Rose of Cairo*
Facts: In 1989, played guitar on Don Johnson's album, *Let It Roll.*

While Jim Carrey was paid $7 million for his role in *Dumb and Dumber,* Daniels was reportedly paid just $500,000.
Original Job: Lumberyard worker
Marriage: Kathleen Treado
Child: Ben
Address: International Creative Management, 8942 Wilshire Blvd., Beverly Hills, CA 90211

TED DANSON

Real Name: Edward Bridge Danson III
Birthplace: San Diego, CA
Birthdate: 12/29/47
Occupation: Actor
Education: Stanford University, Carnegie-Mellon University
Debut: (TV) *Somerset,* 1975; (Film) *The Onion Field,* 1979
Signature: *Cheers*
Facts: Father was the director of a local Native American museum.

In 1981, was the Ramis man on TV ads for cologne and men's toiletry products.

While at Stanford, followed a good-looking waitress to an audition "just to be near her" and ended up winning a part.

Tap dances.
Infamy: Appeared at then-companion Whoopi Goldberg's 1993 Friars Club roast in blackface.
Marriages: Randall Lee Gosch (divorced), Casey Coates (divorced), Mary Steenburgen
Children: Kate, Alexis
Major Awards: Golden Globe, Best Actor in a Made-for-TV Movie, *Some-*

thing About Amelia, 1985; Emmy, Best Actor in a Comedy Series, *Cheers,* 1990, 1993; Golden Globe, Best Actor in a Comedy Series, *Cheers,* 1990, 1991
Address: Creative Artists Agency, 9830 Wilshire Blvd., Beverly Hills, CA 90212

GEENA DAVIS

Real Name: Virginia Davis
Birthplace: Wareham, MA
Birthdate: 1/21/57
Occupation: Actor
Education: Boston University
Debut: (Film) *Tootsie,* 1982; (TV) *Buffalo Bill,* 1983
Signature: *Thelma and Louise*
Facts: Six-foot Davis, two inches taller than the cutoff established by professional modeling agencies, worked as a waitress to pay her bills. Finally she lied about her height and was accepted by the Zoli agency.

While working as a saleswoman at Anne Taylor, Davis got a job as a human mannequin in the store window.
Marriages: Richard Emmolo (divorced), Jeff Goldblum (divorced), Renny Harlin (separated)
Major Award: Oscar, Best Supporting Actress, *The Accidental Tourist,* 1988
Address: Creative Artists Agency, 9830 Wilshire Blvd., Beverly Hills, CA 90212

DANIEL DAY-LEWIS

Birthplace: London, England
Birthdate: 4/29/57
Occupation: Actor
Education: Old Vic Theatre School
Debut: (Film) *Sunday, Bloody Sunday,* 1971
Signature: *My Left Foot*
Fact: At 16, accidentally overdosed on migraine medicine and suffered from two weeks of hallucinations. Because of this, he was mistakenly diagnosed as a heroin addict and placed in a mental hospital. To escape, he had to put on his "greatest performance of sanity."
Original Job: Loaded trucks
Marriage: Rebecca Miller
Child: Gabriel Kane (with Isabelle Adjani)
Famous Relatives: C. Day-Lewis, former poet laureate of Britain, father; Sir Michael Balcon, producer, grandfather; Jane Balcon, actress, mother
Major Award: Oscar, Best Actor, *My Left Foot,* 1989
Address: William Morris Agency, 151 El Camino Dr., Beverly Hills, CA 90212

ELLEN DEGENERES

Birthplace: New Orleans, LA
Birthdate: 1958
Occupation: Actor, comedian
Signature: *Ellen*
Facts: Considered becoming a professional golfer.

In the 1980s the Showtime cable network, looking to name someone Funniest Person in America, found DeGeneres at a comedy club in New Orleans. She was given the title, and toured the country in a Winnebago with a big nose above the front bumper. It earned her the scorn of other comics, who thought she received the title undeservedly.

Was the first female comic ever to be invited to sit on Carson's couch in her first appearance on *The Tonight Show.*

Ellen's title character became the first uncloseted TV lead when she declared herself a lesbian; weeks before the "coming out" episode aired, DeGeneres herself did the same.
Original Job: Vacuum cleaner saleswoman, waitress
Relationship: Anne Heche
Major Awards: Emmy, Best Writing in a Comedy Series, *Ellen,* 1997
Address: ABC, 4151 Prospect Ave., Hollywood, CA 90027

ROBERT DE NIRO

Birthplace: New York, NY
Birthdate: 8/17/43
Occupation: Actor
Education: Attended the High School of Music and Art and dropped out, studied at the Dramatic Workshop, the Luther James Studio, the Stella Adler Studio, and the Actor's Studio
Debut: (Film) *Greetings,* 1969
Signature: *Taxi Driver*
Facts: Although commonly regarded as Italian-American, De Niro is more Irish in ancestry.

First acting experience was playing the Cowardly Lion in a Public School 41 production of *The Wizard of Oz.*

Co-owns Rubicon, a San Francisco restaurant, with Francis Ford Coppola.

The pop group Bananarama recorded a song (1984) called "Robert De Niro's Waiting." They originally wanted to use Al Pacino's name, but Pacino refused to let them.

De Niro grew up in New York City's Little Italy, just a few blocks away from his future friend, Martin Scorsese.

Three years after their breakup, De Niro was sperm donor for his ex-girlfriend Toukie Smith; a surrogate mother delivered her twin boys, Aaron and Julian
Marriage: Diahnne Abbott (divorced), Grace Hightower
Children: Raphael; Aaron; Julian
Major Awards: Oscar, Best Supporting Actor, *The Godfather Part II,* 1974; Oscar, Best Actor, *Raging Bull,* 1980; Golden Globe, Best Actor, *Raging Bull,* 1980
Address: Creative Artists Agency, 9830 Wilshire Blvd., Beverly Hills, CA 90212

JOHNNY DEPP

Birthplace: Owensboro, KY
Birthdate: 6/9/63
Occupation: Actor

Education: High school dropout
Debut: (Film) *Nightmare on Elm Street,* 1984
Signature: *21 Jump Street*
Facts: Dropped out of school at age 16 and joined a series of garage bands, one of which (The Kids) opened for Iggy Pop. Moved to L.A., where his ex-wife introduced him to actor Nicolas Cage, who spawned Depp's career.

Once owned a painting of a clown by executed serial killer John Wayne Gacy; now Depp has a pathological fear of clowns.

Tattoos: "Betty Sue" and "Wino Forever" (formerly "Winona Forever").

Co-owns the Viper Room, the '30s-style nightclub in L.A., outside of which River Phoenix died (1994).

Member of the band P, with ex-Sex Pistol Steve Jones and Red Hot Chili Pepper Flea.
Infamy: Charged with trashing a $1,200/night hotel room in New York City in September 1994. He agreed to pay the $9,767.12 in damages.
Original Job: Rock guitarist, sold pens over the phone
Marriages: Lori Anne Allison (divorced), Sherilyn Fenn (engaged, never married), Jennifer Grey (engaged, never married), Winona Ryder (engaged, never married), Kate Moss (relationship)
Address: International Creative Management, 8942 Wilshire Blvd., Beverly Hills, CA 90211

DANNY DEVITO

Birthplace: Neptune, NJ
Birthdate: 11/17/44
Occupation: Actor, director, producer
Education: American Academy of Dramatic Arts
Debut: (Stage) *The Man with a Flower in His Mouth,* 1969
Signature: *Taxi*
Facts: After high school he worked in his sister's hair salon and was known as "Mr. Danny."

Got his part in *One Flew Over the Cuckoo's Nest* (1975) through producer Michael Douglas, whom DeVito had met in summer stock a few years before. Kirk Douglas had directed DeVito in *Scalawag* in 1973.
Original Job: Hairdresser, theatrical makeup artist, valet
Marriage: Rhea Perlman
Children: Lucy Chet, Gracie Fan, Jake Daniel Sebastian
Major Awards: Golden Globe, Best Supporting Actor in a Comedy Series, *Taxi,* 1979; Emmy, Best Supporting Actor in a Comedy Series, *Taxi,* 1981
Address: Creative Artists Agency, 9830 Wilshire Blvd., Beverly Hills, CA 90212

CAMERON DIAZ

Birthplace: San Diego, CA
Birthdate: 8/30/72
Occupation: Actor, model
Education: High school
Debut: (Film) *The Mask,* 1994
Signature: *My Best Friend's Wedding*
Facts: The 5' 9" beauty signed with the Elite Modeling Agency at age 16; as a teen, made up to $2,000 a day.

Says she "nearly killed herself" with her excessive drinking as she traveled the world as a successful —and fun-loving—model.

Since her only acting experience was in a school play, she originally auditioned for the smaller part of a reporter in *The Mask;* she was called back 12 times before snaring the lead.

Her looks spring from a combination of her dad's Cuban ethnicity and her mother's heritage of German, English, and American Indian.
Relationship: Matt Dillon
Quote: " 'Model turned actress' is a silly phrase. People just assume you don't have the capacity to think."
Address: Creative Artists Agency, 9830 Wilshire Blvd., Los Angeles, CA 90212

LEONARDO DICAPRIO

Birthdate: 11/11/75
Occupation: Actor
Debut: (TV) *Romper Room;* (Film) *Parenthood,* 1990
Signature: *What's Eating Gilbert Grape?*
Facts: Rejected by a talent agent when he was 10 years old for having a bad haircut.

First memory is of wearing red-and-yellow tap shoes and being lifted onto a stage by his father to entertain people waiting for a concert.

First acting experience was in a Matchbox car commercial.
Address: c/o Addis Wechsler, 955 S. Carrillo Drive, Suite 300, Los Angeles, CA 90048

CELINE DION

Birthplace: Charlemagne, Canada
Birthdate: 3/30/68
Occupation: Singer
Education: High school dropout
Fact: Celine had nine best-selling French albums behind her before she recorded *Unison* in 1990.
Infamy: In 1990, refused to accept a Quebec music award as anglophone artist of the year, declaring she was "proud to be Quebecoise." The anglophone press criticized her harshly for exploiting the incident for its publicity value.
Marriage: Rene Angelil
Major Awards: Grammy, Best Pop Performance—Duo or Group, "Beauty and the Beast" (with Peabo Bryson), 1992; Grammy, Best Song Written Specifically for a Movie, "Beauty and the Beast" (with Peabo Bryson), 1992
Address: 550 Music/Epic, 550 Madison Ave., New York, NY 10022

MICHAEL DOUGLAS

Birthplace: New Brunswick, NJ
Birthdate: 9/25/44
Occupation: Actor, producer, director

Education: University of California, Santa Barbara
Debut: (TV) *The Experiment,* 1969; (Film) *Hail, Hero!,* 1969
Signature: *Fatal Attraction*
Facts: His film company produced *One Flew over the Cuckoo's Nest* (1975) and *The China Syndrome* (1979), in which he starred.

Directed two episodes of TV show *The Streets of San Francisco,* in which he costarred.

Flunked out of college during his freshman year.

Marriage: Diandra Luker (separated)
Child: Cameron
Famous Relatives: Kirk Douglas, actor, father; Diana Dill, actress, mother; Eric Douglas, comedian, half brother
Major Awards: Oscar, Best Actor, *Wall Street,* 1987; Golden Globe, Best Actor, *Wall Street,* 1987
Address: Creative Artists Agency, 9830 Wilshire Blvd., Beverly Hills, CA 90212

ROMA DOWNEY

Birthplace: Derry, Northern Ireland
Birthdate: 5/6/63
Occupation: Actor
Education: London Drama Studio
Debut: (Stage) *The Circle,* 1989; (TV) *A Woman Named Jackie,* 1991
Signature: *Touched by an Angel*
Facts: An Irish Catholic, was raised in war-torn Northern Ireland, where she sometimes heard gunshots in the night.

Her mother collapsed from a heart attack in front of her when she was 10. Her father died from a heart attack 11 years later.

Turned down for a grant to attend drama school; her tuition was paid by a local theater director and two other teachers who believed in her talent.

Angel costar Della Reese, a minister, officiated at her Salt Lake City wedding, then entertained guests with a jazzy, romantic set.

Marriage: One prior marriage; David Anspaugh
Child: Reilly Marie
Address: CBS, 7800 Beverly Blvd., Los Angeles, CA 90036

DR. DRE

Real Name: Andre Young
Birthplace: Compton, CA
Birthdate: 1965
Occupation: Rap artist, record producer
Debut: (Album) *Boyz N the Hood* (with N.W.A.), 1986; (Album) *The Chronic* (solo), 1993
Signature: *The Chronic*
Facts: Founding member of N.W.A., a group labeled "the Sex Pistols of rap," in his late 20s.

Efil4 Zaggin (with N.W.A.) was the first hardcore rap album to make it to No.1 on the *Billboard* pop charts.

Dre launched the rap career of his brother, Warren G, and his brother's friend, Snoop Doggy Dogg; his label, Death Row Records, released Snoop's debut album.

Took shock value to new levels with 1994 music video with Ice Cube for "Natural Born Killaz," which featured a graphic recreation of the Nicole Simpson/Ron Goldman slayings.

Infamy: Arrested in a New Orleans hotel lobby after a scuffle ended in the battery of an officer.

Former colleague Eazy-E, who died of AIDS, sued Dre under federal racketeering laws.

Convicted of a misdemeanor assault for breaking the jaw of an aspiring record producer.

Sentenced on August 30, 1994, to five months in a halfway house for violating the terms of his probation in a drunk driving incident. Dre was also ordered to pay a $1,053 fine and attend a 90-day alcoholism education program.

In 1995, became the object of a $10 million palimony suit filed by his ex-girlfriend, Vivian Morgan.

Children: Marcel, Summer
Major Award: Grammy, Best Rap Performance—Solo, "Let Me Ride," 1993
Address: Aftermath Records, 15060 Ventura Blvd, Suite 225, Sherman Oaks, CA 91403

FRAN DRESCHER

Birthplace: Queens, NY
Birthdate: 9/30/57
Occupation: Actor
Education: Queens College
Debut: (Film) *Saturday Night Fever,* 1977
Signature: *The Nanny*
Facts: Her husband (since 1979) is a writer and executive producer of *The Nanny.*

Her five-line part in *Saturday Night Fever* included memorably asking John Travolta, "Are you as good in bed as you are on the dance floor?"

Before pursuing acting, went to beauty school to have a profession to fall back on. Uses that knowledge to do her own "AstroTurf of hairdos—nothing can hurt it": first mousse, then gel, then voluminize.

Studied with a vocal coach to lose her accent, but gave that up when she stopped getting acting work.

During the writer's strike in the late '80s, started a gourmet crouton business, a product that recently grossed seven figures annually.

Marriage: Peter Marc Jacobson (separated)
Address: CBS, 7800 Beverly Blvd. Los Angeles, CA 90036

DAVID DUCHOVNY

Birthplace: New York, NY
Birthdate: 8/7/60
Occupation: Actor
Education: Princeton; master's degree from Yale
Debut: (Film) *Julia Has Two Lovers,* 1991
Signature: *The X-Files*
Facts: Duchovny was working on his Ph.D. dissertation, "Magic and Tech-

nology in Contemporary Fiction," when he got his first acting job in a Lowenbrau beer commercial.

Played Denise the transvestite detective on *Twin Peaks,* 1990–91.

America Online has two separate folders devoted to messages about him; as one fan explained, "the drool is too heavy to be confined to one."

Original Jobs: Teaching assistant at Yale, bartender

Marriage: Téa Leoni

Major Award: Golden Globe, Best Actor in a Drama Series, *The X-Files,* 1996

Address: International Creative Management, 8942 Wilshire Blvd., Beverly Hills, CA 90211

BOB DYLAN

Real Name: Robert Zimmerman

Birthplace: Duluth, MN

Birthdate: 5/24/41

Occupation: Singer, songwriter

Education: University of Minnesota

Debut: (Album) *Bob Dylan,* 1961

Signature: "Blowin' in the Wind"

Facts: Took stage name from Dylan Thomas.

His backup band, The Hawks, later evolved into The Band.

Motorcycle crash in July 1966 led to a brief retirement.

Became a born-again Christian in 1979.

Infamy: Sued by Ruth Tryangiel in 1994. She claims she was his lover on and off for 19 years, and that she cowrote much of his music and helped manage his career. The lawsuit asks for $5 million plus damages and palimony.

Original Job: Performed with a Texas carnival

Marriage: Sarah Lowndes (divorced)

Children: Jesse, Maria, Samuel, Anna, Jakob

Major Awards: Grammy, Best Album Cover—Photography, *Bob Dylan's Greatest Hits,* 1967; Grammy, Album of the Year, *The Concert for Bangladesh* (with George Harrison and Friends), 1972; Grammy, Best Rock Vocal—Male, "Gotta Serve Somebody," 1979; Grammy, Lifetime Achievement Award, 1991; Grammy, Best Traditional Folk Album, *World Gone Wrong,* 1994

Address: Columbia Records, 51 West 52nd St., New York, NY 10019

JAKOB DYLAN

Birthplace: New York, NY

Birthdate: 1969

Occupation: Singer, songwriter

Education: Attended Parsons School of Design

Debut: (Album) *The Wallflowers,* 1992

Signature: The Wallflowers

Facts: The youngest of five children, is rumored to be the inspiration for his father's classic "Forever Young." As a child, often went on the road with dad.

Lived with his mother, Sarah Lowndes, after parents' bitter 1977 divorce. In an incident during custody suit, Sarah tried to take Dylan and his siblings out of school, chasing them down the halls and even assaulting an uncooperative teacher.

Had a D average in high school. Began career wearing anonymous knit caps for seven years, playing L.A.'s clubs and delis without identifying himself as Dylan's son.

Having grown up the protected child of a famous celebrity, Dylan says privacy and security are crucial to his own family as well: he won't even reveal his son's first name.

Debut album bombed at only 40,000 copies, causing Virgin Records to drop him; took more than a year to find a new label.

Marriage: Paige

Child: son

Famous Relative: Bob Dylan, singer, songwriter, father

Address: Interscope Records, 10900 Wilshire Blvd., Suite 1230, Los Angeles, CA 90024

CLINT EASTWOOD

Birthplace: San Francisco, CA

Birthdate: 5/31/30

Occupation: Actor, director

Education: Los Angeles City College

Debut: (Film) *Revenge of the Creature,* 1955

Signature: *Dirty Harry*

Facts: He was drafted in 1951 but en route to Korea his plane crashed. He swam miles to shore and was made swimming instructor at a boot camp, where he met actors Martin Milner and David Janssen, who sparked his acting career.

Elected mayor of Carmel, CA, in 1986; reelected in 1988.

Jazz musician and self-taught piano player, he plays three songs in the movie *In the Line of Fire.* Also composed two Cajun-inspired instrumentals for *A Perfect World.*

Has own beer "Pale Rider Ale," named for his 1985 Western *Pale Rider.*

Infamy: Slapped with palimony suit by former lover Sondra Locke.

Original Job: Lumberjack, forest-fire fighter, steelworker

Marriages: Maggie Johnson (divorced); Dina Ruiz

Children: Kyle, Alison, Francesca, Kimber, Morgan

Major Awards: Golden Globe, Cecil B. DeMille Award, 1988; Oscar, Best Picture, *Unforgiven,* 1992; Golden Globe, Best Director, *Unforgiven,* 1992; Oscar, Irving G. Thalberg Memorial Award, 1995

Address: William Morris Agency, 151 El Camino Dr., Beverly Hills, CA 90212

ROGER EBERT

Birthplace: Urbana, IL
Birthdate: 6/18/42
Occupation: Film critic, writer
Education: University of Illinois; University of Cape Town, South Africa; University of Chicago
Debut: Film critic for the *Chicago Sun-Times,* 1967
Signature: *Siskel & Ebert*
Facts: While at the University of Illinois, Ebert was editor of the *Daily Illini* and president of the U.S. Student Press Association, 1963–64.

Ebert wrote the screenplay for the movie version of *Beyond the Valley of the Dolls,* 1970. He also wrote a novel, *Behind the Phantom's Mask,* which was released in 1993.

He is a member of the Studebaker Drivers' Club.
Major Award: Pulitzer Prize, 1975; Emmy, 1979
Marriage: Chaz Hammel-Smith
Address: c/o Chicago Sun-Times, 401 N. Wabash Ave., Chicago, IL 60611

KENNETH "BABYFACE" EDMONDS

Birthplace: Indianapolis, IN
Birthdate: 1958
Occupation: Singer, songwriter, producer
Debut: (Album) *Lovers,* 1989
Facts: While in ninth grade, phoned concert promoters pretending to be his teacher, asking if musicians would grant his gifted young charge—actually himself—an interview. Through this ruse, chatted with Stevie Wonder, the Jackson 5, and Earth, Wind and Fire.

Given his moniker in the early '80s by funk guitarist Bootsy Collins because of his youthful looks.

Has written or produced hits for Mariah Carey, Whitney Houston, Bobby Brown, TLC, Boyz II Men, and Toni Braxton.
Marriages: Denise (divorced), Tracey McQuarn
Major Awards: Grammy, Best R&B Song, "It's No Crime," 1991; Grammy, Album of the Year (producer), *The Bodyguard,* 1993; Grammy, Producer of the Year, "Boomerang" (with L.A. Reid), 1993; Grammy, Best R&B Vocal—Male, "When Can I See You," 1994; Grammy, Best R&B Song, "I'll Make Love to You," 1994; Best R&B Song, "Exhale (Shoop Shoop)," 1996
Address: Epic Records, 2100 Colorado Ave., Santa Monica, CA 90404

ANTHONY EDWARDS

Birthplace: Santa Barbara, CA
Birthdate: 7/19/63
Occupation: Actor
Education: University of Southern California
Debut: (TV) *The Killing of Randy Webster,* 1981; (Film) *Heart Like a Wheel,* 1982
Signature: *ER*
Facts: His classmates at USC included Forest Whitaker and Ally Sheedy.

Played a burnt-out surfer in 1982's *Fast Times at Ridgemont High,* and one of the two head nerds in 1984's *Revenge of the Nerds.*

Somewhat bored with acting, he was planning to direct a low-budget children's feature, *Charlie's Ghost Story,* when he was called for *ER.* Originally turned down the *ER* role when production dates for the two projects initially overlapped.
Original Job: Actor in commercials for McDonald's and Country Time Lemonade
Marriage: Jeanine Lobell
Child: Bailey
Address: United Talent Agency, 9560 Wilshire Blvd., Suite 500, Beverly Hills, CA 90212

NORA EPHRON

Birthplace: New York, NY
Birthdate: 5/19/41
Occupation: Screenwriter, director
Education: Wellesley College
Debut: (Book) *Wallflower at the Orgy,* 1970; (TV) *Perfect Gentleman,* 1978
Signature: *Sleepless in Seattle*
Facts: She was the subject of the play *Take Her, She's Mine,* written by her parents.

Her book *Heartburn* was adapted into a 1986 movie starring Jack Nicholson and Meryl Streep. Wrote screenplays for *Silkwood* and *When Harry Met Sally . . .*
Marriages: Dan Greenburg (divorced), Carl Bernstein (divorced), Nicholas Pileggi
Children: Jacob, Max
Famous Relatives: Henry Ephron, screenwriter, father; Phoebe Ephron, screenwriter, mother; Delia Ephron, writer, sister
Address: International Creative Management, 8942 Wilshire Blvd., Beverly Hills, CA 90211

MELISSA ETHERIDGE

Birthplace: Leavenworth, KS
Birthdate: 5/29/61
Occupation: Singer, songwriter, guitarist
Education: Berklee College of Music
Debut: *Melissa Etheridge,* 1988
Facts: Played in women's bars around L.A. for six years beginning in 1982.

Came out by leaping onstage at one of Bill Clinton's presidential inaugural bashes, kissing cult figure Elvira, and proclaiming herself a proud lifelong lesbian.
Relationship: Julie Cypher
Child: Bailey Jean
Major Awards: Grammy, Best Rock Vocal—Female, "Ain't It Heavy," 1992; Grammy, Best Rock Vocal—Female, "Come to My Window," 1994
Quote: "I like to bring the sexual energy out by seducing the audience, and, when it's there,

building on it. I would like to say that, maybe, going to a concert of mine is like foreplay."
Address: Island Records, 14 East 4th St., New York, NY 10012

CHRIS FARLEY

Birthplace: Madison, WI
Birthdate: 2/15/64
Occupation: Actor
Education: Marquette University
Debut: (Film) *Wayne's World,* 1992
Signature: *Saturday Night Live*
Fact: His childhood heroes were John Belushi, Dan Aykroyd, and Bill Murray, and just like them he started out doing stand-up at Second City in Chicago.
Original Job: Worked at an oil company
Address: Brillstein-Grey Entertainment, 9150 Wilshire Blvd., Suite 350, Beverly Hills, CA 90212

MIA FARROW

Birthplace: Los Angeles, CA
Birthdate: 2/9/45
Occupation: Actor
Education: Marymount in Los Angeles and Cygnet House in London
Debut: (Stage) *The Importance of Being Earnest,* 1963
Signature: *Rosemary's Baby*
Facts: Mother—biological or adoptive—of 13 kids.

Was on first cover of PEOPLE, March 4, 1974.
Infamy: Was awarded custody of the two children she and Woody Allen adopted, as well as their biological son, after a highly publicized case involving allegations of molestation by Allen.
Marriages: Frank Sinatra (divorced), Andre Previn (divorced)
Children: Soon-Yi, Keili-Shea, Tam, Lark, Daisy, Moses, Isaiah Justus, Fletcher, Matthew, Sascha, Seamus (formerly Satchel), Eliza (formerly Dylan), Gabriel Wilk
Famous Relatives: Maureen O'Sullivan, actress, mother; John Farrow, director, father
Address: William Morris Agency, 151 El Camino Dr., Beverly Hills, CA 90201

SALLY FIELD

Birthplace: Pasadena, CA
Birthdate: 11/6/46
Occupation: Actor
Education: Columbia Pictures Workshop, Actor's Studio
Debut: (TV) *Gidget,* 1965
Signature: *The Flying Nun*
Facts: Was a cheerleader in high school.

Won the lead role in *Gidget* from among 150 other finalists.

Though entertaining, *The Flying Nun* discouraged people from thinking of her as a serious actress; the producers of the movie *True Grit* refused even to give her an audition. She was paid $4,000 a week for the television show.

According to PEOPLE's Pop Profile, Field is the female celebrity most appreciated by the public.
Marriages: Steve Craig (divorced), Alan Greisman (divorced)
Children: Peter, Eli, Samuel
Famous Relatives: Mary Field Mahoney, actress, mother; Jock Mahoney, actor, stepfather
Major Awards: Emmy, *Sybil,* 1977; Golden Globe, Best Actress, *Norma Rae,* 1979; Oscar, Best Actress, *Norma Rae,* 1979; Oscar, Best Actress, *Places in the Heart,* 1984
Address: Creative Artists Agency, 9830 Wilshire Blvd., Beverly Hills, CA 90212

RALPH FIENNES

Birthplace: Suffolk, England
Birthdate: 12/22/62
Education: London's Royal Academy of Dramatic Art
Debut: (Film) *Wuthering Heights,* 1992
Signature: *Schindler's List*
Facts: Fiennes gained 28 pounds to play Amon Goeth in *Schindler's List,* 1993. He was chosen for the role after director Steven Spielberg saw Fiennes's performance in the British TV movie *A Dangerous Man: Lawrence After Arabia.*
Marriage: Alex Kingston (separated)
Major Award: Tony, Best Actor (Drama), *Hamlet,* 1995
Address: Creative Artists Agency, 9830 Wilshire Blvd., Beverly Hills, CA 90212

LAURENCE FISHBURNE

Birthplace: Augusta, GA
Birthdate: 7/30/61
Occupation: Actor
Education: Lincoln Square Academy
Debut: (Stage) *Section D,* 1975; (Film) *Cornbread, Earl and Me,* 1975
Signature: *Boyz N the Hood*
Facts: Appeared regularly on soap opera *One Life to Live* for four years starting when he was 9.

At 14, went with his mother to the Philippines for what was supposed to be a three-month shoot for *Apocalypse Now;* the shoot lasted 18 months.

A theater buff, he wrote, directed, and starred in a play, *Riff Raff,* in 1994.
Marriage: Hanja Moss (divorced)
Children: Langston, Montana
Major Awards: Tony, Featured Actor, *Two Trains Running,* 1992; Emmy, Best Guest Actor in a Drama, *Tribeca,* 1993
Address: Paradigm, 10100 Santa Monica Blvd., 25th Fl., Los Angeles, CA 90067

CARRIE FISHER

Birthplace: Burbank, CA
Birthdate: 10/21/56
Occupation: Actor, novelist, screenwriter
Education: Dropped out of Beverly Hills High School, attended Sarah Lawrence College and Central School of Speech and Drama, London
Debut: (Stage) *Irene,* 1972
Signature: *Star Wars*

Facts: Sang in her mother's Las Vegas nightclub act.

Her first public appearance was in a *Life* magazine photograph with her mother shortly after her father had run off to marry Elizabeth Taylor.
Infamy: Was a user of LSD and Percodan; almost overdosed, 1985.
Marriage: Paul Simon (divorced)
Child: Billie
Famous Relatives: Debbie Reynolds, actress, mother; Eddie Fisher, singer, father
Quote: "You find me a kid that thinks he got enough affection and attention as a child and I'll show you Dan Quayle."
Address: Simon & Schuster, 1230 Ave. of The Americas, New York, NY 10020

BRIDGET FONDA

Birthplace: Los Angeles, CA
Birthdate: 1/27/64
Occupation: Actor
Education: New York University, studied at the Lee Strasberg Institute and with Harold Guskin
Debut: (Film) *Aria,* 1987; (TV) *21 Jump Street,* 1989
Signature: *Singles*
Facts: Named after Bridget Hayward, a woman her father had loved who had committed suicide.

Her movie debut was in *Aria,* in which she stripped naked, had sex, then committed suicide during her eight minutes on screen with no dialogue.
Relationship: Eric Stoltz
Famous Relatives: Peter Fonda, actor, father; Susan Brewer, actor, mother; Henry Fonda, actor, grandfather; Jane Fonda, actor, aunt
Address: William Morris Agency, 151 El Camino Dr., Beverly Hills, CA 90212

JANE FONDA

Birthplace: New York, NY
Birthdate: 12/21/37
Occupation: Actor, political activist, fitness instructor
Education: Vassar College, studied method acting in Lee Strasberg's Actors Studio
Debut: (Film) *Tall Story,* 1960
Signature: *Barbarella*
Facts: Mother committed suicide in a sanitarium in 1953.

Jane Fonda's Workout is the best-selling nondramatic video in history.

Spent much of the '70s speaking for the Black Panthers and against the Vietnam War and was almost arrested for treason, earning her the nickname "Hanoi Jane."
Marriages: Roger Vadim (divorced), Tom Hayden (divorced), Ted Turner
Children: Vanessa, Troy, Garrity, Nathalie (stepdaughter)
Famous Relatives: Henry Fonda, actor, father; Peter Fonda, actor, brother; Bridget Fonda, actor, niece
Major Awards: Oscar, Best Actress, *Klute,* 1971; Oscar, Best Actress, *Coming Home,* 1978. Golden Globe, World Film Favorite—Female, 1973, 1979, 1980; Emmy, Lead Actress in a Limited Series or Special, *The Dollmaker,* 1983
Address: Creative Artists Agency, 9830 Wilshire Blvd., Beverly Hills, CA 90201

HARRISON FORD

Birthplace: Chicago, IL
Birthdate: 7/13/42
Occupation: Actor, director
Education: Ripon College
Debut: (Film) *Dead Heat on a Merry-Go-Round,* 1966
Signature: Indiana Jones
Fact: Scar beneath his lower lip is the result of a motorcycle accident.

Ford had his ear pierced at age 54, explaining that he had always wanted one; he was accompanied by already-pierced old friends Jimmy Buffett and Ed Bradley.
Original Job: Carpenter
Marriages: Mary Marquardt (divorced), Melissa Mathison
Children: Willard, Benjamin, Malcolm, Georgia
Quote: "I want to be bald, completely bald. Wouldn't it be great to be bald in the rain?"
Address: Pat McQueeney Management, 10279 Century Woods Dr., Los Angeles, CA 90067

JODIE FOSTER

Real Name: Alicia Christian Foster
Birthplace: Los Angeles, CA
Birthdate: 11/19/62
Occupation: Actor, director
Education: Yale University
Debut: (TV) *Mayberry RFD,* 1969; (Film) *Napoleon and Samantha,* 1972
Signature: *The Silence of the Lambs*
Facts: Started at 3 years old as the bare-bottomed Coppertone child in the then ubiquitous advertisement. She got the job when, too young to wait in the car, she was noticed at her brother's casting call. By age 8, she had appeared in over 40 commercials.

At 13, played a hooker in *Taxi Driver.* Because she was so young, the film's producers hired her sister Constance to double for her in a nude scene. Before she got the role, she had to pass psychological tests. "I spent four hours with a shrink to prove I was normal enough to play a hooker. Does that make sense?"

As valedictorian in high school, she gave her graduation speech in French.
Infamy: Object of would-be presidential assassin John Hinckley's obsession.

Famous Relative: Buddy Foster, actor, brother
Major Awards: Golden Globe, Best Actress, *The Accused,* 1988; Golden Globe, Best Actress, *The Silence of the Lambs,* 1991; Oscar, Best Actress, *The Accused,* 1988; Oscar, Best Actress, *The Silence of the Lambs,* 1991
Address: International Creative Management, 8942 Wilshire Blvd., Beverly Hills, CA 90211

MATTHEW FOX

Birthplace: Crowheart, WY
Birthdate: 7/14/66
Occupation: Actor
Education: Columbia University
Debut: (TV) *Freshman Dorm,* 1992
Signature: *Party of Five*
Facts: Grew up on a 120-acre Wyoming ranch, attending a one-room schoolhouse until the fourth grade.

Pondered becoming a farmer like his father, but dad suggested he go east for college. During a year of prep at Massachusetts' Deerfield Academy, snooty classmates voted him "Most Likely to Appear on *Hee-Haw.*"

Attended college on a football scholarship, where he was wide receiver and an economics major.
Original Job: Model
Marriage: Margherita Ronchi
Child: Kyle Allison
Address: Fox-TV, P.O. Box 900, Beverly Hills, CA 90213

MICHAEL J. FOX

Birthplace: Edmonton, Canada
Birthdate: 6/9/61
Occupation: Actor
Education: High school dropout
Debut: (TV) *Palmerstown, U.S.A,* 1980; (Film) *Midnight Madness,* 1980
Signature: *Family Ties*
Facts: When he got the audition for *Family Ties,* he was $35,000 in debt, living on macaroni and cheese, and had been forced to sell off a sectional couch piece by piece to raise money.

Eric Stoltz was first cast in *Back to the Future,* but when he proved to be "too intense for the comedy," Fox got the role. For seven weeks he played Alex on *Family Ties* by day, then transformed himself into Marty McFly for the film.

Heavy smoker, but asks not to be photographed smoking to avoid becoming a negative role model for his younger fans.
Marriage: Tracy Pollan
Children: Sam Michael, Aquinnah Kathleen, Schuyler Frances
Major Awards: Emmy, Best Actor in a Comedy Series, *Family Ties,* 1985, 1986, 1987, 1988; Golden Globe, Best Actor in a Comedy Series, *Family Ties,* 1989
Address: Creative Artists Agency, 9830 Wilshire Blvd., Beverly Hills, CA 90212

JEFF FOXWORTHY

Birthplace: Hapeville, GA
Birthdate: 9/6/58
Occupation: Comedian, actor
Education: Georgia Tech
***Debut:** (Album) You Might Be a Redneck If...* 1993; (TV) *The Tonight Show,* 1990
Signature: "You Might Be a Redneck If..."
Facts: The idea for the redneck bit came at a comedy club in Detroit, when the bowling alley next door had valet parking and he realized there were rednecks everywhere.

Games Rednecks Play was the best-selling comedy album since Eddie Murphy's a decade earlier.

Was following in his IBM executive father's footsteps when friends made him enter a local comedy club contest. Soon after winning, he quit his job and went on the road.
Original Job: Mainframe computer engineer
Marriage: Pamela Gregg
Children: Jordan, Juliane
Address: Creative Artists Agency, 9830 Wilshire Blvd., Beverly Hills, CA 90212

ARETHA FRANKLIN

Birthplace: Memphis, TN
Birthdate: 3/25/42
Occupation: Singer
Education: High school dropout
Debut: (Song) "Rock-A-Bye Your Baby with a Dixie Melody," 1961
Signature: "Respect"
Facts: Started out as a gospel singer in her father's Baptist church in Detroit in the '50s. Her father was minister of the New Bethel Baptist Church, one of the largest pastorates in the U.S., until 1979, when he went into a coma after being shot in his home by a burglar.
Infamy: Was sued for breach of contract in 1984 when she was unable to open in the Broadway musical *Sing, Mahalia, Sing,* mainly because of her fear of flying.
Marriages: Ted White (divorced), Glynn Thurman (divorced)
Children: Clarence, Edward, Teddy, Kecalf
Major Awards: Grammy, Best Rhythm and Blues Song, "Respect," 1967; Grammy, Best R&B Vocal—Female, "Respect," 1967; Grammy, Best R&B Vocal—Female, "Chain of Fools," 1968; Grammy, Best R&B Vocal—Female, "Share Your Love with Me," 1969; Grammy, Best R&B Vocal—Female, "Don't Play That Song," 1970; Grammy, Best R&B Vocal—Female, "Bridge over Troubled Water," 1971; Grammy, Best R&B Vocal—Female, *Young, Gifted, & Black,* 1972; Grammy, Best R&B Vocal—Female, "Master of Eyes," 1973; Grammy, Best R&B Vocal—Female, "Ain't Nothing Like the Real Thing," 1974; Grammy, Best R&B Vocal—Female, "Hold On I'm Comin'," 1981; Grammy, Best R&B Vocal—Female, "Freeway of Love," 1985; Grammy, Best R&B Vocal—Female, *Aretha,* 1987; Grammy, Best R&B Duo or Group, "I Knew You Were Waiting (For Me)" (with George Michael), 1987; Grammy Legend Award, 1991; inducted into the Rock and Roll Hall

of Fame, 1987; NARAS Lifetime Achievement Award, 1994
Address: William Morris Agency, 151 El Camino Dr., Beverly Hills, CA 90212

DENNIS FRANZ

Birthplace: Chicago, IL
Birthdate: 10/28/44
Occupation: Actor
Debut: (TV) *The Chicago Story,* 1981
Signature: *NYPD Blue*
Facts: Claims he was the "worst postman in the history of the post office" before becoming an actor. "I used to start my route at daybreak, and I would finish long after dark. I'd stop for donuts, I'd play with animals, I'd go home with my bag of mail and just lay around the house a bit."

Served 11 months in Vietnam with an elite Airborne division.
Marriage: Joanie Zeck
Children: Krista (stepdaughter), Tricia (stepdaughter)
Major Awards: Emmy, Best Actor in a Drama Series, *NYPD Blue,* 1994, 1996, 1997; Golden Globe, Best Actor in a Drama Series, *NYPD Blue,* 1995
Address: Paradigm, 200 West 57th St., Suite 900, New York, NY 10019

MORGAN FREEMAN

Birthplace: Memphis, TN
Birthdate: 6/1/37
Occupation: Actor, director
Education: Attended Los Angeles City College
Debut: (Stage, Broadway) *Hello, Dolly,* 1967; (Film) *Brubaker,* 1980
Signature: *Driving Miss Daisy*
Facts: Got his show business start as a dancer at the 1964 New York World's Fair. He had studied ballet, tap, and jazz.

Played Easy Reader for five years in the 1970s on the PBS series *Electric Company.*

Moved from New York City, where he lived for 25 years, to a Mississippi farm. Is raising one of his nine grandchildren there.
Marriage: Jeanette Adair Bradshaw (divorced), Myrna Colley-Lee
Children: Alphonse, Saifoulaye, Deena, Morgana
Address: William Morris Agency, 151 El Camino Drive, Beverly Hills, CA 90212

JANEANE GAROFALO

Birthplace: New Jersey
Birthdate: 9/28/64
Occupation: Actor, comedian
Education: Providence College
Debut: (TV) *The Ben Stiller Show,* 1992; (Film) *Reality Bites,* 1994
Signature: *The Truth About Cats and Dogs*
Fact: Has "Think" tatooed on her arm.
Original Job: Bike messenger, receptionist
Marriage: Rob Cohn (divorced)
Quote: "If I've learned one thing in life, it's that I can always count on pinkeye at the most inappropriate moment."
Address: United Talent Agency, 9560 Wilshire Blvd., Suite 500, Beverly Hills, CA 90212

BILL GATES

Birthplace: Seattle, WA
Birthdate: 10/28/55
Occupation: Computer software entrepreneur-executive
Education: Harvard University
Signature: Microsoft Windows
Facts: After learning how to crash an operating system while a high school student, did it to the Control Data Corporation. Their reprimand caused him to abandon computers for a year.

Formed a company to sell a computerized traffic counting system to cities, which made $20,000 its first year. Business fell off when customers learned Gates was only 14.

Became the youngest billionaire ever at age 31.

As head of fast-growing Microsoft, took a total of six vacation days in the company's first six years.

Owns the Bettmann Archive, one of the world's greatest collections of documentary images.

His former $30 million "smart house" in Lake Washington features a 20-vehicle garage; dining space for 100; and music, artwork, lighting, and TV shows that follow individuals from room to room.
Infamy: Accused by competitors of using clout from operating systems software to quash software competitors.
Marriage: Melinda French
Child: Jennifer Katherine
Address: Microsoft Corp., One Microsoft Way, Redmond, WA 98052

DAVID GEFFEN

Birthplace: Brooklyn, NY
Birthdate: 2/21/43
Occupation: Producer, executive
Education: Dropped out of two colleges
Signature: Geffen Records
Facts: Graduated in the bottom 10 percent of his high-school class.

Diagnosed with terminal cancer in 1976 and retired soon after. Four years later, doctors told him his diagnosis had been a mistake.

Dated Cher and Marlo Thomas. Later claimed to be bisexual and, in 1992, pronounced himself gay.

Has produced such hits as movies *Beetlejuice* and *Risky Business*, and

Broadway musicals *Cats* and *Miss Saigon.*

Sold Geffen Records to MCA in 1990 for 10 million shares of stock (at the time worth $540 million). Eight months later MCA was sold to Matsushita and his shares soared to $710 million.

Was publicly criticized by *Interview with a Vampire* author Anne Rice for casting Tom Cruise in the movie's lead in 1994. After Rice saw the film she admitted Geffen had been right.

His DreamWorks SKG, formed with Jeffrey Katzenberg and Steven Spielberg, is the first completely new movie studio in 50 years.

Infamy: Admits to having been extremely promiscuous with men during his Studio 54 days in the 1970s.

Original Job: Television audience usher, mailroom worker at William Morris Talent Agency

Major Awards: Tony, Best Musical, *Cats,* 1983; Tony, Best Play, *M Butterfly,* 1988

Quote: "I wouldn't rather be smart than lucky. I'll take it however it comes. Because I'd rather win than be right."

Address: Dreamworks, P.O. Box 8896, Universal City, CA 91608

RICHARD GERE

Birthplace: Philadelphia, PA

Birthdate: 8/31/48

Occupation: Actor

Education: University of Massachusetts

Debut: (Film) *Report to the Commissioner,* 1975

Signature: *An Officer and a Gentleman*

Facts: Won a gymnastics scholarship to the University of Massachusetts.

In 1973, first studied the "middle way" of Siddhartha Gotama Buddha as preached by a Japanese sect. In 1982, switched faith to the Tibetan school of Buddhism. In 1986, became a student of the exiled Dalai Lama.

First three big film roles (*Days of Heaven,* 1978, *American Gigolo,* 1980, and *An Officer and a Gentleman,* 1982) were roles turned down by John Travolta.

Infamy: Took out a $30,000 ad with then-wife Cindy Crawford in the *Times* of London in May 1994 denying rumors of their homosexuality.

Original Job: Rock musician

Marriage: Cindy Crawford (divorced)

Address: International Creative Management, 8942 Wilshire Blvd., Beverly Hills, CA 90211

MEL GIBSON

Birthplace: Peekskill, NY

Birthdate: 1/3/56

Occupation: Actor, director

Education: University of New South Wales

Debut: (Film) *Summer City,* 1977

Signature: *Lethal Weapon*

Facts: Father moved the family from New York to Australia in the '60s so his sons wouldn't be drafted.

The night before his audition for *Mad Max,* he got into a barroom fight in which his face was badly beaten, an accident that won him the role.

Took up acting only because his sister submitted an application to the National Institute of Dramatic Art behind his back.

Marriage: Robyn Moore

Children: Hannah, Edward, Christian, Will, Lucian, Meggin

Famous Relative: Eva Mylott, opera singer, grandmother

Major Awards: Oscars for Best Director and Best Picture, *Braveheart,* 1995; Golden Globe for Best Director, *Braveheart,* 1995

Address: International Creative Management, 8942 Wilshire Blvd., Beverly Hills, CA 90211

KATHIE LEE GIFFORD

Real Name: Kathie Epstein

Birthplace: Paris, France

Birthdate: 8/16/53

Occupation: Talk show host, singer

Education: Oral Roberts University

Debut: (TV) *$100,000 Name That Tune,* 1976

Signature: *Live with Regis and Kathie Lee*

Facts: Despite having a Jewish father, became a born-again Christian at age 11.

Organized a folk singing group while at Oral Roberts University.

Named her dog Regis.

Infamy: A human rights crusader accused Gifford's Honduran-manufactured clothing line of using exploitative child labor.

Original Job: Gospel singer

Marriages: Paul Johnson (divorced), Frank Gifford

Children: Cody Newton, Cassidy Erin

Quote: "I am irreverent, I am opinionated, but I'm not perky."

Address: William Morris Agency, 151 El Camino Dr., Beverly Hills, CA 90212

VINCE GILL

Birthplace: Norman, OK

Birthdate: 4/12/57

Occupation: Singer, songwriter, guitarist

Education: High school

Debut: (Song) "Turn Me Loose," 1984

Signature: "When I Call Your Name"

Facts: After high school, contemplated a career as a pro golfer, but dropped that idea when offered a spot in a top progressive bluegrass group, Bluegrass Alliance.

Joined the band Sundance to play with its great fiddler, Bryon Berline; later joined The Cherry Bombs to be with singer-songwriter Rodney Crowell.

Lead singer for Pure Prairie League in the late '70s.

In the 1980s, worked in Nashville as a studio session vocalist and musician with such stars as Bonnie Raitt, Rosanne Cash, and Patty Loveless.

Dubbed "The Benefit King," he sponsors his own pro-celebrity golf tournament and annual celebrity basketball game and concert.

Marriage: Janis Oliver (separated)

Child: Jennifer
Major Awards: Grammy, Best Country Vocal—Male, "When I Call Your Name, "1990; Grammy, Best Country Vocal Collaboration (with Steve Wariner and Ricky Skaggs), "Restless," 1991; Grammy, Best Country Song, "I Still Believe in You" (with John Barlow Jarvis), 1992; Grammy, Best Country Vocal—Male, "I Still Believe in You," 1992; Grammy, Best Country Instrumental "Red Wing" (with Asleep at the Wheel), 1993; Grammy, Best Country Vocal—Male, "When Love Finds You," 1994; Grammy, Best Country Vocal—Male, "Go Rest High on That Mountain," 1995; Grammy, Best Country Song, "Go Rest High on That Mountain," 1995; Grammy, Best Country Vocal—Male, "Worlds Apart," 1996
Address: William Morris Agency, 2100 West End Avenue, Suite 1000, Nashville, TN 37203

SAVION GLOVER

Birthplace: Newark, NJ
Birthdate: 1973
Occupation: Dancer, choreographer
Education: Newark Arts High School
Debut: (Stage) *The Tap Dance Kid,* 1984; (Film) *Tap,* 1989
Signature: *The Tap Dance Kid*
Facts: At age 7, played drums in a band.

Made choreography debut at age 16 at New York's Apollo Theater.

Began a featured run on *Sesame Street* in 1990 as a character also named Savion.

His name is his mother's variation on the word "savior."

Infamy: Arrested in late 1995 for driving under the influence of marijuana and criminal possession of bags of marijuana hiding in his socks. Pled guilty to the reduced charge of disorderly conduct.
Famous Relatives: Yvette Glover, actress and singer, mother
Major Awards: Tony, Best Choreography, *Bring In 'Da Noise, Bring in 'Da Funk,* 1996; Dance Magazine Award, 1996
Address: William Morris Agency, 151 El Camino Dr., Beverly Hills, CA 90212

WHOOPI GOLDBERG

Real Name: Caryn Johnson
Birthplace: New York, NY
Birthdate: 11/13/49
Occupation: Actor, comedian
Education: School for the Performing Arts, New York
Debut: (Film) *The Color Purple,* 1985
Signature: *Ghost*
Facts: Kicked a heroin addiction in the '70s.

Began performing at age 8 with the Helena Rubenstein Children's Theater and later enrolled in the Hudson Guild children's arts program.

Co-owns the West Hollywood restaurant Eclipse with Steven Seagal and Joe Pesci.

Infamy: Was roasted by black-faced companion Ted Danson at a Friars Club event, 1993.
Original Job: Bricklayer, hairdresser, bank teller, and makeup artist for a funeral parlor
Marriages: One prior marriage, David Claessen (divorced), Lyle Trachtenberg (divorced); Frank Langella (relationship)
Child: Alexandra Martin
Major Awards: Grammy, Best Comedy Recording, *Whoopi Goldberg,* 1985; Golden Globe, Best Actress, *The Color Purple,* 1985; Golden Globe, Best Supporting Actress, *Ghost,* 1990; Oscar, Best Supporting Actress, *Ghost,* 1990
Address: William Morris Agency, 151 El Camino Dr., Beverly Hills, CA 90212

JEFF GOLDBLUM

Birthplace: Pittsburgh, PA
Birthdate: 10/22/52
Occupation: Actor
Education: Trained at Sanford Meisner's Neighborhood Playhouse
Debut: (Stage) *Two Gentlemen of Verona,* 1971; (Film) *Death Wish,* 1974
Signature: *The Big Chill*
Facts: Brother Rick died at 23 from a rare virus picked up on a North African trip.

Starred as a stockbroker-turned-P.I. with Ben Vereen in the TV series *Tenspeed and Brownshoe,* 1980.

Marriages: Patricia Gaul (divorced), Geena Davis (divorced)
Address: International Creative Management, 8942 Wilshire Blvd., Beverly Hills, CA 90211

CUBA GOODING JR.

Birthplace: Bronx, NY
Birthdate: 1/2/68
Occupation: Actor
Education: High school dropout
Debut: (Film) *Coming to America,* 1988
Signature: *Jerry Maguire,*
Facts: His first professional job was at age 16, breakdancing with Lionel Richie at the 1984 Olympic Games.

Big money came to his family when Cuba was a child, after his father's band (The Main Ingredient) hit it big with "Everybody Plays the Fool," but dad split two years later (they have since reunited), leaving mom and the kids on welfare.

Became a born-again Christian at age 13.

Original Jobs: Construction worker, busboy
Marriage: Sara Kapfer
Children: Spencer, Mason
Famous Relative: Cuba Gooding, singer, father
Quote: "The first time I saw myself naked in a school locker room, I was like, 'Wow.' After that, everything had to be trimmed, oiled, and together."
Major Awards: Oscar, Best Supporting Actor, *Jerry Maguire*, 1996
Address: William Morris Agency, 151 El Camino Drive, Beverly Hills, CA 90212

JOHN GOODMAN

Birthplace: Afton, MO
Birthdate: 6/20/52
Occupation: Actor
Education: Southwest Missouri State University
Debut: (Film) *Eddie Macon's Run*, 1983
Signature: *Roseanne*
Facts: Made a living doing dinner and children's theater before Broadway debut in 1979 in *Loose Ends*.

Acted in college with Kathleen Turner and Tess Harper.

Appeared in commercials for Coors beer, Crest toothpaste, and 7UP.

Original Job: Bouncer
Marriage: Annabeth Hartzog
Child: Molly
Major Award: Golden Globe, Best Actor in a Comedy Series, *Roseanne*, 1993
Address: Creative Artists Agency, 9830 Wilshire Blvd., Beverly Hills, CA 90212

KELSEY GRAMMER

Birthplace: St. Thomas, Virgin Islands
Birthdate: 2/20/55
Occupation: Actor
Education: Juilliard School
Debut: (TV) *Another World*, 1983
Signature: *Frasier*
Facts: Father and sister were murdered; his two half brothers died in a scuba accident.

His unborn child died when his ex-wife attempted suicide.

Was nominated five times before finally winning an Emmy in 1994.

Infamy: Arrested for driving under the influence of drugs in 1987; failed to show up for two arraignments for a cocaine arrest in 1988; sentenced to community service and 30 days in prison in 1990.

In 1995, faced allegations of sexual assault by a 17-year-old, who claimed they had had sex when she was 15. The New Jersey grand jury declined to charge him.

In 1996, crashed his Viper and wound up in the Betty Ford Clinic.

Original Job: Theatrical painter
Marriages: Doreen Alderman (divorced), Leigh-Anne Csuhany (divorced), Camille Donatucci
Children: Greer, Spencer
Major Awards: Emmy, Best Actor in a Comedy, *Frasier*, 1994, 1995; Golden Globe, Best Actor in a Comedy Series, 1996
Address: Paramount Television Productions, 5555 Melrose Ave., Los Angeles, CA 90038

HUGH GRANT

Birthplace: London, England
Birthdate: 9/9/60
Occupation: Actor
Education: New College, Oxford University
Debut: (Film) *Privileged*, 1982
Signature: *Four Weddings and a Funeral*
Facts: Grant opted not to do a nude scene with Andie MacDowell in *Four Weddings and a Funeral* when a makeup artist asked if he wanted definition painted on his body.

While at Oxford, formed a revue group, The Jockeys of Norfolk.

Grant is very popular in Japan, and there are two books on him published there, *Hugh Grant Vol. 1* and *Hugh Grant Vol. 2*.

Infamy: Arrested in June 1995 in Hollywood for picking up a prostitute. Was sentenced to two years' probation, fined $1,180 (which included court costs), and ordered to complete an AIDS education program.
Relationship: Elizabeth Hurley
Major Award: Golden Globe, Best Actor in a Comedy, *Four Weddings and a Funeral*, 1994
Quote: "So many dogs have their day. I'm having mine now—and though I'd love it to go on and on, I suspect I'll be back doing BBC radio drama next spring."
Address: Creative Artists Agency, 9830 Wilshire Blvd., Beverly Hills, CA 90212

MELANIE GRIFFITH

Birthplace: New York, NY
Birthdate: 8/9/57
Occupation: Actor
Education: Pierce College
Debut: (Film) *Night Moves*, 1975
Signature: *Working Girl*
Facts: Alfred Hitchcock, who was in love with Griffith's mother, gave Melanie a tiny wooden coffin containing a wax replica of her mother, outfitted in the same clothes she had worn in *The Birds*, on her sixth birthday.

At 14, left home to move in with Don Johnson, who was then 22. She married him at 18 and was divorced a year later. In 1988, on her way to the Hazelden Clinic for rehab, she called Don from the plane and renewed their love.

Was clawed in the face by a lioness in the filming of *Roar* (1981).

Infamy: Was addicted to drugs and alcohol in the late '70s and early '80s, and studio executives refused to speak with her. In 1980, she was hit by a car while crossing Sunset Boulevard. She suffered a broken leg and arm, but her doctor said that if she hadn't been so drunk she probably would have been killed.

Original Job: Model
Marriages: Don Johnson (divorced), Steven Bauer (divorced), Don Johnson (divorced), Antonio Banderas
Children: Alexander, Dakota, Estela del Carmen
Famous Relative: Tippi Hedren, actor, mother
Major Award: Golden Globe, Best Actress in a Comedy, *Working Girl,* 1988
Address: Creative Artists Agency, 9830 Wilshire Blvd., Beverly Hills, CA 90212

JOHN GRISHAM

Birthplace: Arkansas
Birthdate: 1955
Occupation: Author
Education: Mississippi State, University of Mississippi Law School
Debut: (Book) *A Time To Kill,* 1989
Signature: *The Firm*
Facts: Little League baseball coach.

Wife edits his books as he writes them.

Was inspired to write *A Time To Kill* by testimony he heard at the De Soto County courthouse from a 10-year-old girl who was testifying against a man who had raped her and left her for dead.

Served as a Democrat in the Mississippi State Legislature for seven years (1983–90).

Shaves only once a week, before church on Sunday.

In 1989 formed Bongo Comics Group.

A 16th cousin of Bill Clinton.
Original Job: Attorney
Marriage: Renee
Children: Ty, Shea
Address: The Gernert Company, 194 Kotonah Ave., Box 144, Kotonah, NY 10536

CHARLES GRODIN

Real Name: Charles Grodinsky
Birthplace: Pittsburgh, PA
Birthdate: 4/21/35
Occupation: Actor, writer
Education: University of Miami, Pittsburgh Playhouse School, studied with Lee Strasberg and Uta Hagen
Debut: (Stage) *Tchin-Tchin,* 1962
Signature: *Midnight Run*
Facts: Grodin was almost cast in the lead role in *The Graduate* but lost it due to an argument with the producers over salary.

Only leases white or gray Cadillac DeVille sedans because he doesn't like to attract attention.

Took his "self-parodying loutishness," as one reviewer called it, to his own cable TV talk show in 1995, to entertaining results.
Marriages: Julia (divorced), Elissa
Children: Marion, Nicky
Quote: On a *Tonight Show* appearance, Grodin told Johnny Carson, "It's hard for me to answer a question from someone who really doesn't care about the answer." Carson banned Grodin from the show.
Address: United Talent Agency, 9560 Wilshire Blvd., Suite 500, Beverly Hills, CA 90212

MATT GROENING

Birthplace: Portland, OR
Birthdate: 2/15/54
Occupation: Cartoonist
Education: Evergreen College
Debut: (Comic Strip) *Life in Hell* (in the *Los Angeles Reader*), April 1980
Signature: *The Simpsons*
Facts: Elected student-body president in high school. Once elected, tried to rewrite the student government constitution to switch absolute power to himself.

In Los Angeles, ghostwrote the autobiography of an elderly film director who also employed him as a chauffeur, and worked as a landscaper for a sewage treatment plant.

The members of the Simpson family bear the same names as members of Groening's family (although Bart is an anagram for brat).

Groening's home in Venice, CA, is near a canal so he can canoe easily.
Original Job: Writer, rock critic
Marriage: Deborah Caplin
Children: Homer, Abraham
Major Award: Emmy, Outstanding Animated Program, *The Simpsons,* 1990, 1991
Address: Fox Broadcasting Co., 10201 West Pico Blvd., Los Angeles, CA 90035

GENE HACKMAN

Birthplace: San Bernardino, CA
Birthdate: 1/30/30
Occupation: Actor
Education: Pasadena Playhouse, University of Illinois, School of Radio Technique in NY
Debut: (Stage) *Any Wednesday,* 1964
Signature: *The French Connection*
Facts: Did his own driving in the car-chase scenes in *The French Connection,* 1971.

At the Pasadena Playhouse, he and classmate Dustin Hoffman were voted the two least likely to succeed.
Original Job: Doorman, truck driver, shoe salesman, soda jerk, furniture mover
Marriages: Faye Maltese (divorced), Betsy Arakawa
Children: Elizabeth, Leslie, Christopher
Major Awards: Oscar, Best Actor, *The French Connection,* 1971; Oscar, Best Supporting Actor, *Unforgiven,* 1992; Golden Globe, Best Actor, *The French Connection,* 1971; Golden Globe, Best Supporting Actor, *Unforgiven,* 1992
Address: Creative Artists Agency, 9830 Wilshire Blvd., Beverly Hills, CA 90212

TOM HANKS

Birthplace: Concord, CA
Birthdate: 7/9/56
Occupation: Actor

Education: Chabot College, California State University–Sacramento
Debut: (Film) *He Knows You're Alone,* 1980
Signature: *Forrest Gump*
Facts: Attended at least five different elementary schools.

After a one-shot guest spot on *Happy Days,* producer Ron Howard asked him to read for a secondary part in *Splash,* but he got the lead instead.

Played Michael J. Fox's alcoholic uncle on the sitcom *Family Ties.*
Marriages: Samantha Lewes (divorced), Rita Wilson
Children: Colin, Elizabeth, Chester, Truman Theodore
Major Awards: Golden Globe, Best Actor in a Comedy, *Big,* 1988; Golden Globe, Best Actor, *Philadelphia,* 1993; Golden Globe, Best Actor, *Forrest Gump,* 1994; Oscar, Best Actor, *Philadelphia,* 1993; Oscar, Best Actor, *Forrest Gump,* 1994
Address: Creative Artists Agency, 9830 Wilshire Blvd., Beverly Hills, CA 90212

WOODY HARRELSON

Real Name: Woodrow Tracy Harrelson
Birthplace: Midland, TX
Birthdate: 7/23/61
Occupation: Actor
Education: Hanover College
Debut: (Film) *Wildcats,* 1986
Signature: *Cheers*
Facts: A hyperactive child, sometimes prone to violence, he was placed in a school for problem students. "Violence was almost an aphrodisiac for me." Took Ritalin.

His absent father was convicted of murdering a federal judge and sentenced to life in prison when Woody was a freshman in college.

Sang and composed for a 10-piece "blues-a-billy" band, Manly Moondog and the Three Kool Kats.

Dated Brooke Shields, Carol Kane, Glenn Close, and Moon Unit Zappa.
Infamy: Admits to having been a sex addict.

Arrested for marijuana possession when he planted four hemp seeds in July 1996 to challenge a state law making it illegal to grow industrial hemp.

Arrested November 1996 for climbing the Golden Gate Bridge. Harrelson was intending to hang banners calling for federal protection for 60,000 acres of redwood trees in Northern California. He was charged with trespassing, being a public nuisance, and failing to obey a peace officer.
Original Job: Claims he had over 17 different jobs in one year, including waiting tables and short-order cooking, and was fired from almost all of them
Marriages: Nancy Simon (divorced), Laura Louie (relationship)
Children: Deni Montana, Zoe
Major Award: Emmy, Best Supporting Actor in a Comedy Series, *Cheers,* 1989
Address: Creative Artists Agency, 9830 Wilshire Blvd., Beverly Hills, CA 90212

ED HARRIS

Birthplace: Tenafly, NJ
Birthdate: 11/28/50
Occupation: Actor
Education: California Institute of the Arts
Debut: (Film) *Coma,* 1978
Signature: *Apollo 13*
Facts: Twelve years before *Apollo 13,* appeared in the space film *The Right Stuff.*

His highly lauded *Apollo* scene where he reacts to the astronauts' splashing down was perfected in a single take.

Played more than 20 film roles in 17 years.
Marriage: Amy Madigan
Child: Lily
Address: Creative Artists Agency, 9830 Wilshire Blvd., Beverly Hills, CA 90212

MELISSA JOAN HART

Birthplace: Sayville, NY
Birthdate: 4/18/76
Occupation: Actor
Education: Attended New York University
Debut: (TV) *The Lucie Arnaz Show,* 1984
Signature: *Sabrina, the Teenage Witch*
Facts: By age five, had already appeared in 22 commercials. In the next few years she would star in more than a hundred.

She was so young at the time of her 1984 performance on *Saturday Night Live* that she couldn't stay up for the entire show.

Her mom developed *Sabrina,* and became its executive producer.
Relationship: James Fields
Address: ABC, 77 W. 66th Street, New York, NY 10023

PHIL HARTMAN

Birthplace: Brantford, Canada
Birthdate: 9/24/48
Occupation: Actor, writer
Debut: (TV) *Our Time,* 1985
Signature: *Saturday Night Live*
Facts: When Hartman left *Saturday Night Live* in 1994, he had set a record for the longest run (eight seasons, 153 shows) by a regular cast member.

Hartman cowrote the film *Pee-wee's Big Adventure* with Paul Reubens, and starred as Kap'n Karl on the TV show *Pee-wee's Playhouse.*

Original Job: Graphic designer (designed the Crosby, Stills, and Nash logo)
Marriages: Two prior marriages; Brynn Omdahl
Children: Sean, Birgen
Major Award: Emmy, Best Writing in a Variety or Music Program, *Saturday Night Live,* 1989
Address: William Morris Agency, 151 El Camino Dr., Beverly Hills, CA 90212

DAVID HASSELHOFF

Birthplace: Baltimore, MD
Birthdate: 7/17/52
Occupation: Actor
Education: California Institute of the Arts
Debut: (TV) *The Young and the Restless,* 1975
Signature: *Knight Rider*
Facts: Hasselhoff is a successful recording star in Europe, and has toured Germany and Austria. He performed a concert in front of 500,000 people at the Berlin Wall.

Baywatch was the first American show to appear in mainland China. It is the most watched show on the planet, seen by almost a billion people every day.
Marriages: Catherine Hickland (divorced), Pamela Bach
Children: Taylor Ann, Hayley Amber
Address: 11342 Dona Lisa, Studio City, CA 91604

TERI HATCHER

Birthplace: Sunnyvale, CA
Birthdate: 12/8/64
Occupation: Actor
Education: De Anza Junior College
Debut: (TV) *The Love Boat,* 1985; (Film) *Tango & Cash,* 1989
Signature: *Lois & Clark: The New Adventures of Superman*
Facts: Played Penny Parker on *MacGyver* in 1985, a role that later became a recurring character.
Infamy: Before *Lois and Clark,* she made an independent film, *Cool Surface,* with nudity and simulated sex scenes.
Original Job: Dancer
Marriage: One prior marriage; Jon Tenney
Quote: "Despite the fact that I have a good-size pair of breasts ... in *Lois & Clark* I have the opportunity to show the world they're not my only attribute."
Address: William Morris Agency, 151 El Camino Dr., Beverly Hills, CA 90212

ETHAN HAWKE

Birthplace: Austin, TX
Birthdate: 11/6/70
Occupation: Actor, director, writer
Education: New York University, studied acting at the McCarter Theatre in Princeton, the British Theatre Association, and Carnegie-Mellon University
Debut: (Film) *Explorers,* 1985; (Stage) *The Seagull,* 1992
Signature: *Dead Poets Society*
Facts: Was seen out drinking and dancing with the married Julia Roberts in April 1994. He claims they were just discussing a possible movie project.

Starred in *Explorers* when he was 14 with River Phoenix.

His own singing was featured in the *Reality Bites* soundtrack.

Dropped out of Carnegie Mellon after two months to act in *Dead Poets Society.*

Co-founded the New York theater company Malaparte.

Raised eyebrows when *The Hottest State,* his first published novel, attracted advance payments much higher than other novice authors'.
Relationship: Uma Thurman
Address: Creative Artists Agency, 9830 Wilshire Blvd., Beverly Hills, CA 90212

GOLDIE HAWN

Birthplace: Takoma Park, MD
Birthdate: 11/21/45
Occupation: Actor
Education: American University
Debut: (Film) *The One and Only Genuine Family Band,* 1968
Signature: *Private Benjamin*
Facts: Discovered while dancing in the chorus of an Andy Griffith TV special in 1967. Became a regular on *Laugh-In.*

Father performed as a musician at the White House.
Original Job: Go-go dancer
Marriages: Gus Trikonis (divorced), Bill Hudson (divorced), Kurt Russell (relationship)
Children: Katie, Oliver, Wyatt
Major Awards: Oscar, Best Supporting Actress, *Cactus Flower,* 1969; Golden Globe, Best Supporting Actress, *Cactus Flower,* 1969
Address: International Creative Management, 8942 Wilshire Blvd., Beverly Hills, CA 90211

ANNE HECHE

Birthplace: Aurora, OH
Birthdate: 5/25/69
Occupation: Actor
Education: High school
Debut: (TV) *Another World,* 1988; (Film) *The Adventures of Huck Finn,* 1993
Signature: *Volcano*
Facts: Her father was a Baptist church choir director who was secretly gay; Heche found out at age 12 when he was dying of AIDS.

The same year her father died, her brother was killed in a car accident. To help support her family while in junior high school, Heche sang in a local dinner theater.

Was asked to be in a soap opera by a Procter & Gamble talent scout who happened to see her in a high school play.

Dated Steve Martin, costar of her film *A Simple Twist of Fate* for two years until she broke it off.
Infamy: Shortly after her lesbian relationship with Ellen DeGeneres was announced, the pair was criticized for nuzzling and hugging

during the annual White House Correspondents' Dinner.
Relationship: Ellen DeGeneres
Quote: "I put a very high premium on honesty. If you don't accept your own sexuality, it will kill you."
Major Awards: Emmy, Outstanding Younger Actress, *Another World,* 1990
Address: Creative Artists Agency, 9830 Wilshire Blvd., Los Angeles, CA 90212

KATHARINE HEPBURN

Birthplace: Hartford, CT
Birthdate: 11/8/07
Occupation: Actor
Education: Bryn Mawr College
Debut: (Stage) *The Czarina,* 1928; (Film) *A Bill of Divorcement,* 1932
Signature: *The African Queen*
Facts: In her strict New England home, where her father was a surgeon and her mother a militant suffragette, Hepburn and her siblings took cold showers every morning.

Since she was considered too much of a tomboy, she was educated by home tutors.

Decided to take up acting once she realized there was little opportunity for a woman to become a doctor.

According to a 1995 biography, she settled for Tracy after her true love, Catholic director John Ford, couldn't get a divorce from his wife.
Original Job: Sold balloons
Marriages: Ludlow Ogden Smith (divorced), Spencer Tracy (relationship, deceased)
Major Awards: Oscar, Best Actress, *Morning Glory,* 1933; Oscar, Best Actress, *Guess Who's Coming to Dinner,* 1967; Oscar, Best Actress, *The Lion in Winter,* 1968; Emmy, Best Actress in a Drama Special, *Love Among the Ruins,* 1975; Oscar, Best Actress, *On Golden Pond,* 1981; Kennedy Center Honor for Lifetime Achievement, 1990
Quote: "I am revered rather like an old building."
Address: William Morris Agency, 151 El Camino Dr., Beverly Hills, CA 90212

LAURYN HILL

Birthplace: South Orange, NJ
Birthdate: 5/25/75
Occupation: Singer
Education: Attended Columbia University
Debut: (Album) *Blunted on Reality,* 1993
Signature: The Fugees
Facts: The group's name springs from the trio's feeling of being refugees from mainstream culture and even hip-hop, and from their sense that they find refuge in the music they make.

Hill met fellow group member Pras Michel when the two attended the same high school. Wyclef Jean, who soon joined forces with them, is Michel's cousin.

Originally called Tranzlator Crew, was forced to change the group's name when a long-forgotten 1980s new-wave act called Translator objected.

Supports a not-for-profit summer camp for city kids, paid through corporate sponsorships of high-profile performance events.
Relationship: Steve Marley
Major Award: Grammy, Best R&B Group with Vocal, "Killing Me Softly," 1996
Address: Ruff House/Columbia Records, 550 Madison Avenue, New York, NY 10022

DUSTIN HOFFMAN

Birthplace: Los Angeles, CA
Birthdate: 8/8/37
Occupation: Actor
Education: Los Angeles Conservatory of Music, Santa Monica City College; studied at the Pasadena Playhouse and the Actor's Studio
Debut: (Stage) *Yes Is for a Very Young Man,* 1960; (Film) *Tiger Makes Out,* 1967
Signature: *The Graduate*
Facts: Played Tiny Tim in junior high school.

Slept on Gene Hackman's kitchen floor while looking for work.

Achieved Ratso's distinctive walk in *Midnight Cowboy* by putting pebbles in his shoe.

When taking the screen test for *The Graduate,* Hoffman said, "I don't think I'm right for the role. He's a kind of Anglo-Saxon, tall, slender, good-looking chap. I'm short and Jewish." During the screen test he forgot his lines and was nervous and clumsy.

Hoffman originally wanted to be a concert pianist. Also studied to be a doctor.
Original Job: Washing dishes, checking coats, waiting tables, cleaning a dance studio, selling toys at Macy's, attendant in a psychiatric institution
Marriages: Anne Byrne (divorced), Lisa Gottsegen
Children: Karina, Jenna, Jacob, Rebecca, Max, Alexandra
Major Awards: Oscar, Best Actor, *Kramer vs. Kramer,* 1979; Oscar, Best Actor, *Rain Man,* 1988; Emmy, Best Actor in a Made-for-TV Movie, *Death of a Salesman,* 1986
Address: Creative Artists Agency, 9830 Wilshire Blvd., Beverly Hills, CA 90212

LAUREN HOLLY

Birthplace: Geneva, NY
Birthdate: 1966
Occupation: Actor
Debut: (Film) *Band of the Hand,* 1986
Signature: *Picket Fences*
Facts: Personal tragedy struck in 1992 when her parents ended their 30-year marriage and, a short time later, her 14-year-old brother died in a house fire.

Her very public 1994 divorce from Anthony Quinn's struggling actor son, Danny, had him claiming that her careless spending squandered their

fortune and her accusing him of having affairs and refusing to work.
Marriages: Danny Quinn (divorced), Jim Carrey (divorced)
Address: Creative Artists Agency, 9830 Wilshire Blvd., Beverly Hills, CA 90212

ANTHONY HOPKINS

Birthplace: Port Talbot, South Wales
Birthdate: 12/31/37
Occupation: Actor
Education: Welsh College of Music and Drama, Royal Academy of Dramatic Art, London
Debut: (Stage) *Julius Caesar,* 1964; (Film) *The Lion in Winter,* 1968
Signature: *The Silence of the Lambs*
Facts: Debuted as conductor with the New Symphony Orchestra at Royal Albert Hall, 1982.

Was knighted in 1993.

Understudied for Laurence Olivier in *Dance Of Death,* 1966.
Infamy: Had a long bout with alcohol addiction.
Original Job: Steelworker
Marriages: Petronella Barker (divorced), Jennifer Ann Lynton
Child: Abigail
Major Awards: Emmy, Best Actor in a Drama or Comedy Special, *The Lindbergh Kidnapping Case,* 1976; Emmy, Best Actor in a Miniseries, *The Bunker,* 1981; Oscar, Best Actor, *The Silence of the Lambs,* 1991
Address: Creative Artists Agency, 9830 Wilshire Blvd., Beverly Hills, CA 90212

WHITNEY HOUSTON

Birthplace: Newark, NJ
Birthdate: 8/9/63
Occupation: Singer
Education: High school
Debut: (Album) *Whitney Houston,* 1985
Signature: "The Greatest Love of All"
Facts: Got her start at age 8 singing in the New Hope Baptist Junior Choir.

Sang backup for Chaka Khan, Lou Rawls, and Dionne Warwick.

As a model, appeared on the cover of *Seventeen.*

Was an actress in her early days, appearing on *Silver Spoons* and *Gimme a Break.*
Original Job: Model
Marriage: Bobby Brown
Child: Bobbi Kristina
Famous Relatives: Cissy Houston, singer, mother; Thelma Houston, singer, aunt; Dionne Warwick, singer, cousin
Major Awards: Emmy, Best Individual Performance in a Variety or Music Program, *The 28th Annual Grammy Awards,* 1986; Grammy, Best Pop Vocal—Female, "Saving All My Love for You," 1985; Grammy, Best Pop Vocal—Female, "I Wanna Dance with Somebody," 1987; Grammy, Best Pop Vocal—Female, "I Will Always Love You," 1993; Grammy, Record of the Year, "I Will Always Love You," 1993; Grammy, Album of the Year, *The Bodyguard Soundtrack,* 1993
Address: William Morris Agency, 151 El Camino Dr., Beverly Hills, CA 90212

RON HOWARD

Birthplace: Duncan, OK
Birthdate: 3/1/54
Occupation: Actor, director, producer
Education: University of Southern California
Debut: (Film) *Frontier Woman*, 1956; (TV) *Playhouse 90, 1959*
Signature: *Cocoon*
Facts: Starred on *The Andy Griffith Show* as Opie when just 6 years old.

The long-running hit *Happy Days* actually struggled in the ratings when it focused mostly on the misadventures of Howard's teenage character; it took off a year later when Henry Winkler's Fonzie became the star.

First directing effort, 1977's *Grand Theft Auto,* was shot in 20 days for $602,000; grossed $15 million.

True to his All-American persona, married his high school sweetheart.
Marriage: Cheryl Alley
Children: Bryce, Jocelyn, Paige, Reed
Famous Relatives: Rance Howard, actor, father; Jean Howard, actor, mother; Clint Howard, actor, brother
Address: Creative Artists Agency, 9830 Wilshire Blvd., Beverly Hills, CA 90212

HELEN HUNT

Birthplace: Los Angeles, CA
Birthdate: 6/15/63
Occupation: Actor
Education: UCLA
Debut: (TV) *The Mary Tyler Moore Show,* 1970; (Film) *Rollercoaster,* 1977
Signature: *Mad About You*
Facts: Hunt studied acting, got an agent, and got a part in the TV movie *Pioneer Woman* by age 9.

Began a two-year romance with actor Matthew Broderick while working on *Project X* (1986).

Played Murray Slaughter's daughter on *The Mary Tyler Moore Show.*
Relationship: Hank Azaria
Famous Relatives: Gordon Hunt, director, father; Peter Hunt, director, uncle
Major Awards: Golden Globe, Best Actress in a Comedy Series, *Mad About You,* 1994, 1995, 1996; Emmy, Best Actress in a Comedy Series, *Mad About You,* 1996, 1997
Address: Creative Artists Agency, 9830 Wilshire Blvd., Beverly Hills, CA 90212

HOLLY HUNTER

Birthplace: Conyers, GA
Birthdate: 3/20/58
Occupation: Actor
Education: Carnegie Mellon University
Debut: (Film) *The Burning,* 1981; (Stage) *Crimes of the Heart,* 1981
Signature: *Broadcast News*
Facts: Director Jane Campion was originally looking for a tall, stat-

uesque Sigourney Weaver type for the lead in *The Piano.*

Youngest of seven children, grew up on a cattle and hay farm in Georgia, where she drove a tractor.

Appeared in pilot for television series *Fame* (1982).

Marriage: Janusz Kaminski

Major Awards: Emmy, Best Actress in a Miniseries, *Roe vs. Wade,* 1989; Emmy, Best Actress in a Miniseries, *The Positively True Adventures of the Alleged Texas Cheerleader-Murdering Mom,* 1993; Oscar, Best Actress, *The Piano,* 1993; Golden Globe, Best Actress, *The Piano,* 1993

Address: International Creative Management, 8942 Wilshire Blvd., Beverly Hills, CA 90211

ELIZABETH HURLEY

Birthplace: Hampshire, England

Birthdate: 6/10/65

Occupation: Actor, model

Education: London Studio Centre

Debut: (Stage) *The Man Most Likely To...,* (Film) *Rowing in the Wind,* 1986

Facts: Long recognized only as actor Hugh Grant's girlfriend. In 1995 when she accompanied Grant on a guest appearance on *The Joan Rivers Show,* Rivers asked, "And who are you?" The two have dated since 1987.

She and Grant started the production company, Simian Films.

At the opening of Grant's movie *Four Weddings and a Funeral,* she wore a Versace dress held together by 24 safety pins.

Replaced Paulina Porizkova as the face of Estée Lauder cosmetics. Defied conventional stardom by beginning as an actor and becoming a supermodel at age 29.

Characterizes herself as an army brat; her father was an army major.

Notorious in her early 20s for her punk-rock phase. She pierced her nose, spiked and painted her hair pink and frequented punk rock bars.

Needlepoint is one of her favorite pastimes.

Was a candidate for the position of ambassador for the United Nations High Commissioner for Refugees.

Infamy: Was expelled from the London Studio Centre after leaving school and going to a Greek Island.

Relationship: Hugh Grant

Address: Creative Artists Agency, 9830 Wilshire Blvd., Beverly Hills, CA 90212-1825

ICE CUBE

Real Name: O'Shea Jackson

Birthplace: Los Angeles, CA

Birthdate: 6/15/69

Occupation: Rap artist, actor

Education: Phoenix Institute of Technology

Debut: (Album) *Boyz N the Hood* (with N.W.A.), 1986; (Album) *Amerikkka's Most Wanted* (solo), 1990

Signature: *Boyz N the Hood*

Facts: Former lyricist of the rap group N.W.A. His 1991 album, *Death Certificate,* stirred controversy because it contained racist attacks on Koreans and called for the murder of a Jewish man.

Began writing rap lyrics at age 14.

Child: O'Shea Jackson Jr.

Quote: "Rap is the network newscast black people never had."

Address: Priority Records, 6430 Sunset Blvd., Hollywood, CA 90028

ICE-T

Real Name: Tracy Morrow

Birthplace: Newark, NJ

Birthdate: 2/16/58

Occupation: Rap artist, actor

Debut: (Single) "The Coldest Rap," 1982; (Film) *Breakin',* 1984;

Signature: *New Jack City*

Facts: Appeared in the films *Breakin'* and *Breakin' II,* among others.

Spent four years running with gangs in South Central Los Angeles.

Served four years as a ranger in the U.S. Army.

Was raised by an aunt in Los Angeles after both of his parents died by the time he was in seventh grade.

Infamy: His controversial song "Cop Killer" caused public outrage.

Relationship: Darlene

Children: Latisha, Ice Jr.

Major Award: Grammy, Best Rap Performance—Duo or Group, "Back on the Block" (with others), 1990

Address: William Morris Agency, 151 El Camino Dr., Beverly Hills, CA 90212

DON IMUS

Real Name: John Donald Imus Jr.

Birthplace: Riverside, CA

Birthdate: 7/23/40

Occupation: Radio talk-show host

Education: High school dropout

Debut: KUTY, Palmdale, CA, 1968

Signature: "Imus in the Morning"

Facts: Fired from an early window dressing job for staging striptease shows with mannequins to amuse passersby.

Once called a fast-food restaurant while on the air and ordered 1,200 specially-prepared hamburgers to go, an incident that contributed to an FCC ruling that DJs must identify themselves when phoning listeners.

Wrote the novel *God's Other Son,* based on his lecherous evangelist radio character. Originally published in 1981, it was reissued in 1994 and hit the bestseller list for 13 weeks.

Infamy: Caused a stir among media members when his jokes insulted Bill and Hillary Clinton during a televised correspondents' dinner.

Had a severe alcohol and cocaine abuse problem, for which he was fired from his New York station in 1977. Finally kicked the habit in 1987, after a nine-day drinking binge scared him into a treatment center.

Original Job: Department store window dresser

Marriage: Harriet (divorced), Deirdre Coleman
Children: Nadine, Toni, Elizabeth, Ashleigh
Major Award: Inducted into the Broadcast Hall of Fame, 1996
Address: International Creative Management, 8942 Wilshire Blvd., Beverly Hills, CA 90211

JEREMY IRONS

Birthplace: Isle of Wight, England
Birthdate: 9/19/48
Occupation: Actor
Education: Bristol Old Vic Theatre School
Debut: (Stage) *Godspell,* 1972
Signature: *The French Lieutenant's Woman*
Facts: At school, excelled at rugby, the fiddle, and clarinet and headed the cadet corps.

Made his mark with the BBC series *Brideshead Revisited,* 1981.

Played a dual role as twin brothers in *Dead Ringers,* a 1988 movie he considers his best work.

Original Job: Housecleaner, gardener, assistant stage manager, busker (singing and playing guitar outside movie theaters)
Marriage: Sinéad Moira Cusack
Children: Samuel James, Maximilian Paul
Major Awards: Tony, Best Actor, *The Real Thing,* 1984; Oscar, Best Actor, *Reversal of Fortune,* 1990; Golden Globe, Best Actor, *Reversal of Fortune,* 1990
Address: Creative Artists Agency, 9830 Wilshire Blvd., Beverly Hills, CA 90212

ALAN JACKSON

Birthplace: Newnan, GA
Birthdate: 10/17/58
Occupation: Singer, songwriter
Education: South Georgia College
Debut: (Album) *Here in the Real World,* 1989
Signature: "Neon Rainbow"
Facts: In 1985, his wife got Jackson his big break. A flight attendant, she cornered Glen Campbell in the Atlanta airport and asked him to listen to her husband's tape.

Started wearing his trademark white Stetson to hide scars above his left eyebrow (a result of a childhood accident with a coffee table).

Original Job: Forklift operator, car salesman, home builder
Marriage: Denise
Children: Mattie, Alexandra, Dani Grace
Address: Arista Records, 6 W. 57th St., New York, NY 10019

JANET JACKSON

Birthplace: Gary, IN
Birthdate: 5/16/66
Occupation: Singer, actor
Debut: (TV) *Good Times,* 1977
Signature: *Control*
Facts: With 1986 song "When I Think of You," she and brother Michael became the first siblings in the rock era to have No. 1 songs as soloists.

Paula Abdul was Janet's choreographer before starting her own career.

Played Charlene DuPrey on the TV series *Diff'rent Strokes.*

Marriages: James DeBarge (annulled), Rene Elizondo (relationship)
Famous Relatives: Michael, singer, brother; La Toya, singer, sister; Tito, singer, brother; Randy, singer, brother; Marlon, singer, brother; Jermaine, singer, brother; Jackie, singer, brother
Major Awards: Grammy, Best Music Video—Long Form, *Rhythm Nation 1814,* 1989; Grammy, Best R&B Song, "That's the Way Love Goes," 1993
Address: Virgin Records, 1790 Broadway, New York, NY 10019

MICHAEL JACKSON

Birthplace: Gary, IN
Birthdate: 8/29/58
Occupation: Singer, songwriter, actor
Debut: (Stage) Mr. Lucky's, Gary, IN (with Jackson 5), 1966
Signature: *Thriller*
Facts: Built amusement park on property and maintains a menagerie of animals including Bubbles the Chimp.

Gave Elizabeth Taylor away at her marriage to Larry Fortensky in 1991.

Surgery includes four nose jobs, two nose adjustments, and cleft put in his chin. Randy Tarraborelli's unauthorized biography claims that Michael had the surgery to avoid resembling his abusive father as much as possible.

Infamy: Settled out of court a civil lawsuit alleging child molestation. The boy then refused to testify in a criminal proceeding, so prosecutors declined to press charges.

Accused of including anti-Semitic lyrcs in his song "They Don't Care About Us" on *HIStory;* to stem the controversy, the offending lines were altered on later pressings.

Famous Relatives: Janet, singer, sister; LaToya, singer, sister; Tito, singer, brother; Randy, singer, brother; Marlon, singer, brother; Jermaine, singer, brother; Jackie, singer, brother
Marriage: Lisa Marie Presley (divorced); Debbie Rowe
Child: Prince
Major Awards: Grammy, Best R&B Vocal—Male, "Don't Stop Till You Get Enough," 1979; Grammy, Album of the Year, *Thriller,* 1983; Grammy, Best Pop Vocal—Male, *Thriller,* 1983; Grammy, Best R&B Song, "Billie Jean," 1983; Grammy, Best R&B Vocal—Male, "Billie Jean," 1983; Grammy, Best Recording for Children, *E.T., the Extraterrestrial,* 1983; Grammy, Record of the Year, "Beat It," 1984; Grammy, Best Pop Vocal—Male, "Beat It," 1984; Grammy, Song of the Year, "We Are the World" (with Lionel Richie), 1985; Grammy, Best Music Video, Short Form, *Leave Me Alone,* 1989; Grammy, Legend Award, 1993; Grammy, Best Music Video, "Scream," 1995
Address: United Talent Agency, 9560 Wilshire Blvd., Suite 500, Beverly Hills, CA 90212

SAMUEL L. JACKSON

Birthplace: Chattanooga, TN
Birthdate: 1949
Occupation: Actor
Education: Morehouse College
Debut: (Film) *Ragtime*, 1981
Signature: *Pulp Fiction*
Facts: Angry at Morehouse College's lack of African-American studies and its control by a white governing body, he participated in a protest involving locking up the school's board of trustees, and was expelled in 1969. He later returned to graduate.

In 1991's *Jungle Fever*, Jackson's performance as crackhead Gator won him the first-ever supporting actor award given by the Cannes Film Festival.

Was Bill Cosby's stand-in for three years on *The Cosby Show*.
Infamy: Had a problem with drugs and alcohol for several years. Ironically, his first role after taking a vow of sobriety was as the crack addict Gator.
Original Job: Security guard
Marriage: LaTanya Richardson
Child: Zoe
Address: International Creative Management, 8942 Wilshire Blvd., Beverly Hills, CA 90211

MICK JAGGER

Birthplace: Dartford, England
Birthdate: 7/26/43
Occupation: Singer, songwriter
Education: London School of Economics
Debut: (Song) "Come On" (cover of Chuck Berry original), 1963
Signature: The Rolling Stones
Facts: Went to elementary school with guitarist Keith Richards but lost touch with him until they met again on a London train in 1960.

Sang backup on Carly Simon's 1973 hit, "You're So Vain."

Co-owned the Philadelphia Furies, a soccer team, with Peter Frampton, Rick Wakeman, and Paul Simon.
Marriages: Bianca Peres Morena de Macias (divorced), Jerry Hall
Children: Karis, Jade, Elizabeth Scarlett, James Leroy Augustine, Georgia May
Major Awards: Grammy, Best Album Package, *Tattoo You* (with the Rolling Stones), 1981; Grammy, NARAS Lifetime Achievement Award, 1986; inducted into the Rock and Roll Hall of Fame (with the Rolling Stones), 1989; Grammy, Best Rock Album, *Voodoo Lounge* (with the Rolling Stones), 1994
Quote: "It's a good way of making a living. I think we'll just keep right on doing it."
Address: The Rolling Stones, 1776 Broadway, #507, New York, NY 10019

PETER JENNINGS

Birthplace: Toronto, Canada
Birthdate: 7/29/38
Occupation: Anchor, senior editor
Education: Carleton University and Rider College
Debut: At age nine, hosted *Peter's People,* a CBC radio show for children, 1947
Signature: *ABC's World News Tonight*
Facts: At 26, was the youngest network anchor ever. ABC removed him after three years. Took over as permanent anchor in 1983.
Original Job: Bank teller and late-night radio host
Marriage: One previous marriage (divorced), Valerie Godsoe (divorced), Kati Marton (divorced); Kayce Freed (engaged)
Children: Elizabeth, Christopher
Famous Relative: Charles Jennings, vice president of programming at CBC, father
Address: ABC, 77 West 66th St., New York, NY 10023

JEWEL

Real Name: Jewel Kilcher
Birthplace: Payson, UT
Birthdate: 5/23/74
Occupation: Singer, songwriter
Education: Interlochen Arts Academy High School
Debut: (Album) *Pieces of You,* 1995
Signature: *Pieces of You*
Facts: Was raised by her father in a log cabin on an 800-acre farm near Homer, Alaska, with no running water, an outhouse for a bathroom, and only a coal stove for heat.

Before they divorced, her parents, Atz and Nedra Kilcher, recorded two LPs as a folk duo.

Jewel has been a crackerjack yodeler since she was a small child; experts told her parents it was supposed to be impossible for someone so young to yodel, since the vocal cords aren't well developed.

When she began singing at coffeehouses, she and her mom lived in adjacent vans, surviving on fruit from nearby orchards and free happy-hour fare from bars.

Ex-boyfriend Sean Penn directed the video for "You Were Meant for Me"; Jewel had it refilmed after their breakup.
Original Job: Restaurant worker
Relationship: Michel Francoeur
Address: Atlantic Records, 75 Rockefeller Plaza, New York, NY 10019

BILLY JOEL

Birthplace: Bronx, NY
Birthdate: 5/9/49
Occupation: Singer, songwriter, piano player
Education: High school
Debut: (Song) "You Got Me Hummin'" (cover of Sam and Dave original, with The Hassles), 1965
Signature: "Piano Man"
Facts: Had a suicidal period when he was in his early 20s; after taking pills and swallowing furniture polish, he spent three weeks in Meadowbrook Hospital.

Wrote "New York State of Mind" within 20 minutes of returning home from California in 1975.
Original Job: Rock critic for *Changes* magazine
Marriages: Elizabeth Weber (divorced), Christie Brinkley (divorced), Carolyn Beegan (relationship)
Child: Alexa Ray
Major Awards: Grammy, Record of the Year, "Just the Way You Are," 1978; Grammy, Song of the Year, "Just the Way You Are," 1978; Grammy, Album of the Year, *Billy Joel,* 1979; Grammy, Best Pop Vocal—Male, *52nd Street*, 1979; Grammy, Best Rock Vocal—Male, *Glass Houses*, 1980; Grammy, Best Recording for Children, *In Harmony 2* (with others), 1982; Grammy, Legend Award, 1991
Address: QBQ Entertainment, 341 Madison Ave., 14th Fl., New York, NY 10017

ELTON JOHN

Real Name: Reginald Kenneth Dwight
Birthplace: Pinner, England
Birthdate: 3/25/47
Occupation: Singer, songwriter, piano player
Education: Royal Academy of Music, London
Debut: (Album) *Come Back Baby* (with Bluesology), 1965
Signature: "Rocket Man"
Facts: Took his name from first names of Bluesology members Elton Deal and John Baldry.

Wrote "Philadelphia Freedom" in 1975 for Billie Jean King.

Is godfather to Sean Lennon.

Along with Tim Rice (of *Little Shop of Horrors* fame), scored the 1994 Disney movie *The Lion King*.

Attended London's Royal Academy of Music but quit three weeks before final exams.

Has donated more than $5.5 million—profits from his singles—to his nonprofit care and education foundation.
Infamy: In 1994, *Star* magazine alleged that he was in a romantic relationship with an Atlanta man. He denied being involved with the man and sued the magazine over the article.
Original Job: Worked at Mills Music Publishers
Marriage: Renate Blauer (divorced)
Major Awards: Grammy, Best Pop Performance—Duo or Group, "That's What Friends Are For" (with Dionne & Friends), 1986; Grammy, Best Pop Vocal Performance—Male, "Can You Feel the Love Tonight," 1994; inducted into the Rock and Roll Hall of Fame, 1994; Golden Globe, Best Original Song, "Can You Feel the Love Tonight," 1994; Oscar, Best Original Song, "Can You Feel the Love Tonight," 1994
Address: c/o Rocket Records, 825 8th Avenue, New York, NY 10019

DON JOHNSON

Birthplace: Flat Creek, MO
Birthdate: 12/15/49
Occupation: Actor
Education: University of Kansas, studied at the American Conservatory Theater in San Francisco
Debut: (Stage) *Fortunes and Men's Eyes,* 1969; (Film) *The Magic Garden of Stanley Sweetheart,* 1970
Signature: *Miami Vice*
Facts: At age 12, seduced his babysitter. At 16, moved out of his dad's place and moved in with a 26-year-old cocktail waitress. At the University of Kansas, became romantically involved with a drama professor.
Infamy: When he was 12, was caught stealing a car and sent to a juvenile detention home.

Admits to having been addicted to alcohol and cocaine. Says he was sober for ten years, but was treated again for a drinking problem in 1994.
Original Job: Worked in a meat-packing plant
Marriages: Melanie Griffith (divorced, remarried, divorced); Jodi O'Keefe (relationship)
Children: Jesse (with Patti D'Arbanville), Dakota
Major Award: Golden Globe, Best Actor in a Drama Series, *Miami Vice,* 1986
Address: International Creative Management, 8942 Wilshire Blvd., Beverly Hills, CA 90211

MAGIC JOHNSON

Real Name: Earvin Johnson
Birthplace: Lansing, MI
Birthdate: 8/14/59
Occupation: Basketball player (retired)
Education: Michigan State University
Facts: On November 7, 1991, announced that he was retiring from basketball after being diagnosed HIV positive. Was diagnosed only months after marrying longtime friend Earletha "Cookie" Kelly, who was in the early stages of pregnancy. Neither Cookie nor the child have tested positive for the disease.

After his diagnosis, became one of the world's major fundraisers and spokesmen for AIDS.

Given his nickname in high school by a local sportswriter after a game in which he scored 36 points and had 18 rebounds.
Infamy: In 1992, admitted he

caught the AIDS virus from "messing around with too many women."
Marriage: Earletha "Cookie" Kelly
Children: Andre, Earvin III, Elisa (adopted)
Major Awards/Titles: MVP, National Collegiate Athletic Association Final Four playoff tournament, 1979; MVP, NBA Finals,'80,'82,'87; 3 Time NBA Regular Season MVP; 9 Time All-NBA First Team; 11 Time NBA All-Star; Olympic Gold Medal 1992; Grammy, Best Spoken Word Album, *What You Can Do To Avoid AIDS* (with Robert O'Keefe), 1992
Address: Magic Johnson Enterprises, 9100 Wilshire Blvd., Suite 1060, W. Beverly Hills, CA 90212

QUINCY JONES

Birthplace: Chicago, IL
Birthdate: 3/14/33
Occupation: Composer, producer
Education: Seattle University; Berklee College of Music, Boston Conservatory
Debut: Trumpeter, arranger, for Lionel Hampton Orchestra, 1950
Signature: Produced *Off the Wall, Thriller,* and *Bad*
Facts: Established his own label, Qwest, in 1981 and founded *Vibe* magazine.

Scored the TV series *Roots* in 1977.

Has worked with many prominent pop and jazz artists, including Ray Charles, Miles Davis, Ella Fitzgerald, Dizzy Gillespie, Ice-T, Chaka Khan, and Sarah Vaughan.

Middle name is Delight.
Marriages: Jeri Caldwell (divorced), Ulla Anderson (divorced), Peggy Lipton (divorced), Donya Fiorentino (relationship)
Children: Jolie, Martina-Lisa, Quincy III, Kidada, Rashida, Kenya
Major Award: Grammy, Album of the Year, *Back on the Block,* 1991; Oscar, Jean Hersholt Humanitarian Award, 1995
Address: Qwest Records, 3800 Barham Blvd., Suite 503, Los Angeles, CA 90068

TOMMY LEE JONES

Birthplace: San Saba, TX
Birthdate: 9/15/46
Occupation: Actor
Education: Harvard University
Debut: (Stage) *A Patriot for Me,* 1969; (TV) *One Life To Live,* 1969; (Film) *Love Story,* 1970
Signature: *The Executioner's Song*
Facts: Roomed with Vice President Al Gore while attending Harvard.

Is a champion polo player.

Raises Black Angus cattle on his ranch in San Antonio.
Original Job: Worked in oil fields
Marriages: Katherine Lardner (divorced), Kimberlea Gayle Cloughley (separated), Dawn Laurel (relationship)
Children: Austin, Victoria
Major Awards: Emmy, Best Actor in a Miniseries, *The Executioner's Song,* 1983; Oscar, Best Supporting Actor, *The Fugitive,* 1993; Golden Globe, Best Supporting Actor, *The Fugitive,* 1993
Quote: "I like to cook. I'm really interested in killing things and eating them."
Address: International Creative Management, 8942 Wilshire Blvd., Beverly Hills, CA 90211

MICHAEL JORDAN

Birthplace: Brooklyn, NY
Birthdate: 2/17/63
Occupation: Basketball player
Education: University of North Carolina
Facts: He was cut from the varsity basketball team in high school.

Though he said, "This is my dream," after hitting his first homer playing professional baseball in the minor leagues, he soon left baseball to return to basketball.

In his first game back against archrival Knicks in 1995, some fans paid scalpers more than $1,000 a ticket. They were not disappointed; he scored 55 points.
Marriage: Juanita Vanoy
Children: Jeffrey, Marcus, Jasmine
Major Awards/Titles: NCAA Colleg Player of the Year 1984; MVP NBA Finals,'91, '92, '93, '96; 4 Time NBA Regular Season MVP; 8 Time All NBA First Team; 10 Time NBA All-Star; 8 Time Winner of NBA Scoring Title; Olympic Gold Medal 1984, 1992
Address: Chicago Bulls, One Magnificent Mile, 980 N. Michigan Ave., Chicago, IL 60611

DONNA KARAN

Real Name: Donna Faske
Birthplace: Forest Hills, NY
Birthdate: 10/2/48
Occupation: Fashion designer
Education: Parsons School of Design
Signature: DKNY clothes
Facts: While in college, worked for designers Chuck Howard and Liz Claiborne.

After serving a long apprenticeship with the Anne Klein collection, at age 26 was given full creative control by the principal owner of the firm after Anne Klein died of cancer in 1974.

Close personal friend to many stars including Barbra Streisand.
Original Job: Sales clerk at a Long Island dress shop
Marriages: Mark Karan (divorced), Stephen Weiss
Child: Gabrielle
Major Awards: Coty Award, 1977, 1981; named to Coty Hall of Fame, 1984
Address: Donna Karan Co., 550 7th Ave., New York, NY 10018

HARVEY KEITEL

Birthplace: Brooklyn, NY
Birthdate: 5/13/39
Occupation: Actor, producer
Education: Studied with Lee Strasberg at the Actor's Studio and Stella Adler
Debut: (Film) *Who's That Knocking at My Door?,* 1968
Signature: *Bad Lieutenant*
Facts: Joined the U.S. Marine Corps at age 16 and served in Lebanon.

Answered a newspaper ad placed by Martin Scorsese, then an NYU student director, seeking actors for his first film in 1965, which started their professional relationship.

Was cast as the lead in *Apocalypse Now,* but had a falling out with director Francis Ford Coppola and was fired on location in the Philippines. He was replaced by Martin Sheen.

As a child, Keitel had a severe stutter.

Unusual among Hollywood actors for his willingness to show frontal nudity in his films *(The Piano, Bad Lieutenant).*

Infamy: Was asked to leave the Alexander Hamilton Vocational School in Brooklyn because of truancy.
Original Job: Shoe salesman
Marriage: Lorraine Bracco (divorced)
Child: Stella
Address: William Morris Agency, 151 El Camino Dr., Beverly Hills, CA 90212

CAROLYN BESSETTE KENNEDY

Birthplace: Greenwich, CT
Birthdate: 1966
Occupation: Socialite
Education: Boston University
Facts: Though made as a gift to the bride, the Narcisco Rodriguez pearl-white gown worn at her secretive wedding was reportedly worth $40,000. The ceremony, on 18-mile-long Cumberland Island, Georgia, took place before 40 relatives and friends.

Stands 6 feet tall; wears size 6 clothes.

Jobs at Calvin Klein included personal shopper for stars like Annette Bening, Diane Sawyer, and Blaine Trump.

Was the cover girl for the 1988 "Girls of B.U." calendar. Her college degree was in elementary education, though she never taught.

Original Job: Publicist, Calvin Klein
Marriage: John Kennedy Jr.
Address: *George,* 1633 Broadway, 41st floor, New York, NY 10019

JOHN F. KENNEDY JR.

Birthplace: Washington, DC
Birthdate: 11/25/60
Occupation: Editor-in-chief of political magazine, *George*
Education: Brown University, New York University Law School
Facts: First baby in the White House since 1893.

Worked in the Peace Corps in Guatemala following a devastating earthquake.

Failed the bar exam twice.

Famous Relatives: John F. Kennedy, president, father; Jacqueline Onassis, first lady, mother; Ted Kennedy, senator, uncle
Marriage: Carolyn Bessette
Address: *George,* 1633 Broadway, 41st Floor, New York, NY 10019

NICOLE KIDMAN

Birthplace: Hawaii
Birthdate: 6/20/67
Occupation: Actor
Education: St. Martin's Youth Theatre, Melbourne, Australia
Debut: (Film) *Bush Christmas,* 1983
Signature: *To Die For*
Facts: Became an overnight star in Australia with her performance in the miniseries *Vietnam,* 1988.

Joined the Church of Scientology, of which husband Cruise is a devoted member.

Marriage: Tom Cruise
Children: Isabella Jane (adopted), Connor Antony (adopted)
Major Award: Golden Globe, Best Actress in a Musical or Comedy, *To Die For,* 1995
Address: Creative Artists Agency, 9830 Wilshire Blvd., Beverly Hills, CA 90212

VAL KILMER

Birthplace: Los Angeles, CA
Birthdate: 12/31/59
Occupation: Actor
Education: Hollywood Professional School, Juilliard
Debut: (Stage) *Slab Boys,* 1983; (TV) *One Too Many,* 1985; (Film) *Top Secret!,* 1984
Signature: *The Doors*
Facts: Grew up in Chatsworth, CA, across the road from the Roy Rogers ranch. Was the middle child of three boys.

His younger brother, Wesley, drowned right before he left for Juilliard.

At 17, was the youngest person ever accepted to Juilliard's drama school. Cowrote a play with Juilliard classmates, *How It All Began;* starred in an off-Broadway production at the New York Shakespeare Festival.

Met Joanne Whalley on the set of *Willow* in 1988. Pursued her persistently until she finally agreed to marry him.

Provided much of the vocals for the film *The Doors.*

Lives in a cabin in Santa Fe, NM. Is part Cherokee and spends his leisure time exploring the Southwest.

Infamy: On the set of *The Island of Dr. Moreau,* Kilmer burned a cameraman's face with a cigarette.
Marriage: Joanne Whalley (divorced)
Children: Mercedes, Jack

Famous Relatives: Joyce Kilmer, poet, second cousin twice removed
Address: Creative Artists Agency, 9830 Wilshire Blvd., Beverly Hills, CA 90212

LARRY KING

Real Name: Lawrence Harvey Zeiger
Birthplace: Brooklyn, NY
Birthdate: 11/19/33
Occupation: Talk show host
Facts: In February of 1992, Ross Perot announced his bid for the presidency on *Larry King Live.*

Father died of a heart attack when he was 10, and he grew up on public assistance.

As a teenager, ran away to get married. Had the ceremony annulled shortly thereafter.

Graduated from high school just one point above passing.
Infamy: In December of 1971, he was arrested for stealing money a financier had given him for the New Orleans D.A.'s investigation into the death of John F. Kennedy. King had used the money to pay taxes after he had blown his own money on Cadillacs, expensive restaurants, and gambling debts. The charge was eventually dropped.
Original Job: Janitor at a local AM radio station in Florida
Marriages: Alene Akins (divorced, remarried, divorced), Mickey Sutphin (divorced), Sharon Leporte (divorced), Julie Alexander (divorced), Shawn Southwick
Child: Chaia
Address: CNN Larry King Live, 820 1st St., NE, Washington, DC 20002

STEPHEN KING

Birthplace: Portland, ME
Birthdate: 9/21/47
Occupation: Author
Education: University of Maine
Debut: (Book) *Carrie,* 1974
Signature: *The Shining*
Facts: Family was deserted by father, who went out for a pack of cigarettes and never returned.

Wrote first short story at age 7.

Had his first story published in a comic book fan magazine, *Comics Review,* in 1965.

Was working as a high school English teacher at Hampden Academy, in Maine, when his first book was published.

Used the pseudonym Richard Bachman for five novels, including *The Running Man* (made into an Arnold Schwarzenegger film, 1987).
Original Job: Laborer in an industrial laundry
Marriage: Tabitha Spruce
Children: Joe, Owen, Naomi
Address: Creative Artists Agency, 9830 Wilshire Blvd., Beverly Hills, CA 90212

GREG KINNEAR

Birthplace: Logansport, IN
Birthdate: 1964
Occupation: Actor
Education: University of Arizona
Debut: (TV) *Movietime,* 1987; (Film) *Sabrina,* 1995
Signature: *Talk Soup*
Facts: Lived in Beirut, Lebanon, with family and then evacuated to Athens, Greece, when the Lebanese civil war broke out.

Worked on the advertising campaigns for such films as *Space Sluts in the Slammer, The Imp,* and the *Ghoulies* series.

Hosted syndicated action game show, *College Mad House.*
Address: Creative Artists Agency, 9830 Wilshire Blvd., Beverly Hills, CA 90212

CALVIN KLEIN

Real Name: Richard Klein
Birthplace: New York, NY
Birthdate: 11/19/42
Occupation: Fashion designer
Education: Fashion Institute of Technology
Facts: Rescued his daughter from kidnappers in 1978.

As a boy in the Bronx, grew up around the corner from Ralph Lifshitz (now Ralph Lauren).

Former junk bond czar Michael Milken issued $80 million in high-interest Klein bonds in the '80s.
Infamy: Was addicted to valium and alcohol in the '80s, and attended a Minnesota rehabilitation center for 31 days in 1988.
Marriages: Jayne Centre (divorced), Kelly Rector (separated)
Child: Marci
Major Awards: Coty Award, 1973, 1974,1975; elected to American Fashion Critics Circle Hall of Fame, 1975; Council of Fashion Designers of America Award, 1994
Quote: "Anything I've ever wanted to do, I've done. Anyone I've wanted to be with, I've had."
Address: Calvin Klein, Ltd., 205 West 39th St., New York, NY 10018

TED KOPPEL

Birthplace: Lancashire, England
Birthdate: 2/8/40
Occupation: Broadcast journalist
Education: Syracuse University, Stanford University
Debut: (Radio) WMCA radio
Signature: *Nightline*
Facts: Author, *Adlai Stevenson: In the National Interest.*

When he joined ABC in 1963, he was the youngest news reporter ever to join a network.

Emigrated to the U.S. from England in 1953.
Marriage: Grace Anne Dorney
Children: Andrea, Deidre, Andrew, Tara
Major Award: Elected to the Emmy Hall of Fame, 1991
Address: ABC, 77 West 66th St., New York, NY 10023

LISA KUDROW

Birthplace: Encino, CA
Birthdate: 7/30/63
Occupation: Actor
Education: Vassar College
Debut: (TV) *Cheers,* 1982
Signature: *Friends*
Facts: Earned her B.S. in sociobiology, intent on being a doctor like her father, a renowned headache expert. Decided to become a comic actor when she saw Jon Lovitz, her brother's childhood friend, make it on *Saturday Night Live.*

Her movie debut in 1990's *Impulse* ended up completely cut from the film. Later, she was hired but soon fired as Roz on the pilot for *Frasier.*

Grew up with a pool table in her house and is something of a pool shark, able to perform many difficult trick shots.
Marriage: Michel Stern
Address: Creative Artists Agency, 9830 Wilshire Blvd., Beverly Hills, CA 90212

KARL LAGERFELD

Birthplace: Hamburg, Germany
Birthdate: 9/10/38
Occupation: Fashion designer
Education: Lycée Montaigne
Debut: First prize, women's coat design, International Wool Secretariat contest, 1954
Signature: Chanel
Facts: Drew illustrations for books as a child. Apprenticed to Pierre Balmain, designing clothes for Sophia Loren, Rita Hayworth, and Gina Lollobrigida.

Led the pret-à-porter wave of designers in the '60s in Paris, working at various times for Fendi furs and Charles Jourdan shoes.

Initiated art deco revival in early '70s.

Created the perfume Chloé for Elizabeth Arden (1975). Under the pen name Minouflet de Vermenou, he reviews books for French *Vogue.*
Infamy: Refused director Robert Altman access to his Paris show to film *Ready to Wear*; sued Altman after the film's release, claiming it referred to Lagerfeld as "a thief of ideas."
Address: 3 West 57th St., New York, NY 10019

RICKI LAKE

Birthplace: New York, NY
Birthdate: 9/21/68
Occupation: Actor, talk show host
Education: Ithaca College
Debut: (Film) *Hairspray,* 1988
Signature: *The Ricki Lake Show*
Facts: This once-dumpy star of John Waters' cult films like *Cry Baby* lost 125 pounds over a three-year period.

Plays the flute, piccolo, clarinet, and piano.
Infamy: Arrested in 1994 for criminal mischief for her part in a People for the Ethical Treatment of Animals attack on the offices of designer Karl Lagerfeld.
Original Job: Cabaret singer, appeared off-Broadway in 1983
Marriage: Rob Sussman
Child: Milo Sebastian
Address: William Morris Agency, 151 El Camino Dr., Beverly Hills, CA 90212

NATHAN LANE

Real Name: Joseph Lane
Birthplace: Jersey City, NJ
Birthdate: 2/3/56
Occupation: Actor
Education: High school
Debut: (Stage) *A Midsummer Night's Dream,* 1978; (Film) *Ironweed,* 1987
Signature: *The Birdcage*
Facts: Took the name Nathan at age 22 after playing Nathan Detroit in a *Guys and Dolls* dinner-theater show, since there was another Joe Lane in Actors' Equity.

His truckdriver father drank himself to death when Lane was 11. Lane, too, had a drinking problem for two decades, one he kicked only a few years ago.

Playwright Terrence McNally wrote several plays specifically for him.

Played the voice of Timon, the wisecracking meerkat in *The Lion King.*
Original Job: Police bail interviewer
Major Award: Tony, Best Actor in a Musical, *A Funny Thing Happened on the Way to the Forum,* 1996
Address: Huvane Baum Halls Public Relations, 8383 Wilshire Blvd., Suite 444, Beverly Hills, CA 90211

K.D. LANG

Real Name: Katherine Dawn Lang
Birthplace: Consort, Canada
Birthdate: 9/2/61
Occupation: Singer, songwriter
Education: Attended college in Red Deer, Alberta, Canada
Debut: (Album) *A Truly Western Experience,* 1984
Signature: "Constant Craving"
Facts: Acted in the movie *Salmonberries,* 1991.

Recorded a duet with Roy Orbison on a remake of his song "Crying" in 1988, shortly before he died.
Infamy: Her recordings have been boycotted in the conservative areas of the South and cattle ranching areas of central Canada because she is a lesbian and an animal rights activist.
Original Job: Performance artist
Relationship: Leisha Hailey
Major Awards: Grammy, Best Country Vocal—Collaboration, "Crying" (with Roy Orbison), 1988; Grammy, Best Country Vocal—

Female, "Absolute Torch and Twang," 1989; Grammy, Best Pop Vocal—Female, "Constant Craving," 1992
Quote: "I have a little bit of penis envy. They're ridiculous, but they're cool."
Address: Sire Records, 75 Rockefeller Plaza, New York, NY 10019

JESSICA LANGE

Birthplace: Cloquet, MN
Birthdate: 4/20/49
Occupation: Actor
Education: University of Minnesota
Debut: (Film) *King Kong,* 1976
Signature: *Frances*
Facts: Raised in a depression-prone family with an alcoholic father who moved the family repeatedly, Lange adopted a full-blown, travel-and-party lifestyle as a young adult.

Had a relationship (and a child) with Mikhail Baryshnikov.

The 1994 film *Blue Sky,* for which she won a best actress Academy Award (after four previous nominations), languished in a bank vault after it was made in 1991 because its studio, Orion Pictures, had declared bankruptcy.
Original Job: Dancer, model
Marriages: Paco Grande (divorced), Sam Shepard (relationship)
Children: Alexandra, Hannah, Walker
Major Awards: Oscar, Best Supporting Actress, *Tootsie,* 1982; Oscar, Best Actress, *Blue Sky,* 1994; Golden Globe, Best Actress, *Blue Sky,* 1994; Golden Globe, Best Actress in a Miniseries or Telefilm, *A Streetcar Named Desire,* 1995
Address: Creative Artists Agency, 9830 Wilshire Blvd., Beverly Hills, CA 90212

ANGELA LANSBURY

Birthplace: London, England
Birthdate: 10/16/25
Occupation: Actor
Education: Webber-Douglas School of Singing and Dramatic Art, Feagin School of Drama and Radio
Debut: (Film) *Gaslight,* 1944
Signature: *Murder, She Wrote*
Facts: Immigrated with her family to the U.S. when the Germans began to bomb London in World War II.

In 1943, went to MGM to audition for *The Picture of Dorian Gray* and was told the studio was looking for someone to play the role of the maid in *Gaslight.* She auditioned and got it.

In the seven years she was under contract to MGM, she appeared in 70 films.
Original Job: Ticket-taker in the theater in which her mother worked, clerk in department store
Marriages: Richard Cromwell (divorced), Peter Pullen Shaw
Children: Anthony Peter, Deidre Angela
Famous Relatives: Moyna McGill, actor, mother; David Lansbury, actor, nephew
Major Awards: Golden Globe, Best Supporting Actress, *The Picture of Dorian Gray,* 1946; Golden Globe, Best Supporting Actress, *The Manchurian Candidate,* 1962; Golden Globe, Best Actress in a TV Series—Drama, *Murder, She Wrote,* 1985, 1987, 1990, 1992; Tony, Best Actress (Musical), *Mame,* 1966; Tony, Best Actress (Musical), *Dear World,* 1969; Tony, Best Actress (Musical), *Gypsy,* 1975; Tony, Best Actress (Musical), *Sweeney Todd,* 1979
Address: William Morris Agency, 151 El Camino Dr., Beverly Hills, CA 90212

QUEEN LATIFAH

Real Name: Dana Owens
Birthplace: East Orange, NJ
Birthdate: 3/18/70
Occupation: Rap artist, actor
Education: High school
Debut: (Album) *All Hail the Queen,* 1989; (TV) *The Fresh Prince of Bel-Air,* 1991; (Film) *Jungle Fever,* 1991
Facts: Was a power forward on two state championship basketball teams in high school.

Trained in karate and use of firearms by her policeman father.

CEO of Flavor Unit, a management and production company whose clients have included Naughty by Nature and FU-Schnickens.

Brother Lance Owens Jr. died at age 24 in a motorcycle accident in 1992; "Winky's Theme" on the album *Black Reign* was dedicated to him.

Starred in sitcom *Living Single.*
Infamy: Charged in a municipal misdemeanor complaint in 1995 after 240 illegally copied tapes were found in a video store she had sold in 1994.

Arrested by California Highway Patrolman in west L.A. and cited for speeding, driving under the influence, carrying a concealed firearm, carrying a loaded firearm, and possession of marijuana.
Original Job: Worked at Burger King, cashier at the Wiz
Major Award: Grammy, Best Rap Solo Performance, *U.N.I.T.Y.,* 1994
Address: Fox Broadcasting Co., 10201 West Pico Blvd., Los Angeles, CA 90035

MATT LAUER

Birthplace: New York, NY
Birthdate: 12/30/57
Occupation: Newscaster, producer
Education: Ohio University
Debut: (TV) WOWK-TV, Huntington, WV, 1980
Signature: *Today*
Facts: Quit college for a TV job four credits shy of graduation in 1979; finally got the degree 18 years later by writing a paper on his work experience.

Hosted *9 Broadcast Plaza,* a low-budget tabloid talk show, for two years, but was fired when he refused to do live commercials during the program. Months later, desperate for a job, he applied for a tree-trimming position in upstate New York. When the phone rang, however, it was

NBC, asking him to host a local news show.

Appeared 150 times as guest-host of *Today* before landing the permanent slot.

Has an impressive 8 handicap in golf.

Marriage: Nancy Alspaugh (divorced)
Address: NBC, 30 Rockefeller Plaza, New York, NY 10112

LUCY LAWLESS

Birthplace: Mount Albert, Auckland, New Zealand
Birthdate: 3/28/68
Occupation: Actor
Education: Attended Auckland University
Debut: (TV) *Funny Business,* 1988
Signature: *Xena: Warrior Princess*
Facts: Got the part of *Xena* when the original actor became ill and the producers needed someone to fill in quickly. They turned to Lawless, who had been cast in bit parts in the show.

Stands at 5' 11".

Original Jobs: Picking grapes along Germany's Rhine River, working a gold mine in Australia.
Marriage: Garth Lawless (divorced), Rob Tapert (relationship)
Child: Daisy
Address: MCA TV, 100 Universal Plaza, Universal City, CA 91608

MARTIN LAWRENCE

Birthplace: Frankfurt, Germany
Birthdate: 4/16/65
Occupation: Actor
Education: High school
Debut: (TV) *What's Happening Now,* 1985; (Film) *Do the Right Thing,* 1989
Signature: *Martin*
Facts: He was a *Star Search* winner, a street performer in Washington Square Park, and a stand-up comedian at the Improv's open-mike night.

Worked at Sears in Queens with Salt-N-Pepa and Kid 'N Play.

Infamy: After a 1994 appearance on *Saturday Night Live* in which he told women to "put a Tic-Tac in your ass" to remain clean, Lawrence was banned from all NBC productions.

Yelled at passersby and brandished a pistol in the middle of a busy L.A. intersection. Tried to board a plane while carrying a Baretta.

In 1997, former *Martin* costar Tisha Campbell filed a suit claiming that he groped and kissed her, among other things, in front of the cast and crew.

Original Job: Gas station attendant, store clerk
Marriage: Patricia Southall (divorced)
Child: Jasmine Page
Address: United Talent Agency, 9560 Wilshire Blvd., Suite 500, Beverly Hills, CA 90212

MATT LEBLANC

Birthplace: Newton, MA
Birthdate: 7/25/67
Occupation: Actor
Education: Wentworth Institute of Technology
Debut: (TV) *TV 101,* 1988
Signature: *Friends*
Facts: First big breaks were in TV commercials, including an award-winning Heinz spot that ran four years.

Actually of mixed heritage—Italian, French, English, Irish, and Dutch—though usually cast as Italian.

After receiving his first motorcycle at age 8, began entering amateur competitions with hopes of racing professionally, a dream his mother quickly quashed.

A passion for landscape photography has taken him all over the world.

Before *Friends,* starred in three TV flops; interest in him soon cooled, and he sold his truck and motorcycle and moved to a smaller apartment to stay afloat financially.

Address: United Talent Agency, 9560 Wilshire Blvd., Suite 500, Beverly Hills, CA 90212

PAMELA LEE

Birthplace: Comox, Canada
Birthdate: 7/1/67
Occupation: Actor
Education: High school
Debut: (TV) *Home Improvement,* 1991; (Film) *Barb Wire,* 1995
Signature: *Baywatch*
Facts: Got her first commercial job after her image was projected on a giant scoreboard screen at a Canadian football game in 1989.

Says her mother encouraged her to pose for her several *Playboy* covers, telling her it was a compliment.

Writes fairy tales and poetry and regularly keeps a dream diary.

Married Mötley Crüe drummer Tommy Lee in Cancun, Mexico, in 1995 wearing a tiny white bikini. (Lee wore white Bermuda shorts.)

Original Job: Beer company spokesmodel
Marriage: Tommy Lee
Child: Brandon Thomas
Address: United Talent Agency, 9560 Wilshire Blvd., Suite 500, Beverly Hills, CA 90212

SPIKE LEE

Real Name: Shelton Lee
Birthplace: Atlanta, GA
Birthdate: 3/20/57
Occupation: Filmmaker, director
Education: Morehouse College, New York University
Debut: (Film) *She's Gotta Have It,* 1986
Signature: *Do the Right Thing*
Facts: Known as an unofficial New York Knick, sitting courtside and shouting out to players on both teams. During the 1994 Eastern Conference Championships, some fans felt that his harassment of an Indiana Pacer caused the player to

score the most points in the game and defeat the Knicks.

Taught at Harvard as a visiting professor in 1992.

A film he made at NYU, *Joe's Barbershop: We Cut Heads,* was the first student work ever selected for Lincoln Center's "New Directors, New Films" showcase and won a student award from the Academy of Motion Pictures Arts and Sciences.

Infamy: Accused by the Anti-Defamation League of B'Nai Brith of fostering anti-Semitism through his films, most notably via his portrayal of two Jewish nightclub owners in *Mo' Better Blues.*
Original Job: Advertising copywriter
Marriage: Tonya Linette Lewis
Children: Satchel Lewis; Jackson Lewis
Address: International Creative Management, 8942 Wilshire Blvd., Beverly Hills, CA 90211

JENNIFER JASON LEIGH

Real Name: Jennifer Morrow
Birthplace: Los Angeles, CA
Birthdate: 2/5/62
Occupation: Actor
Education: Lee Strasberg Institute
Debut: (Film) *Death of a Stranger,* 1971
Signature: *Fast Times At Ridgemont High*
Facts: In order to prepare for roles, she writes a complete imaginary diary for the character.

Dieted down to 86 pounds for her role as an anorexic in the TV movie *The Best Little Girl in the World,* 1981.

When her father, Vic Morrow, was killed in a helicopter accident while filming *Twilight Zone: The Movie,* Leigh and her family reportedly mourned by watching his old films through the night.

Famous Relatives: Vic Morrow, actor, father; Barbara Turner, screenwriter, mother; Mina Badie, actor, half sister
Major Award: Golden Globe, Special Achievement, *Short Cuts,* 1993
Address: International Creative Management, 8942 Wilshire Blvd., Beverly Hills, CA 90211

JAY LENO

Real Name: James Leno
Birthplace: New Rochelle, NY
Birthdate: 4/28/50
Occupation: Talk show host, comedian
Education: Emerson College
Debut: (TV) *The Marilyn McCoo & Billy Davis Jr. Show,* 1977; (Film) *Silver Bears,* 1978
Signature: *The Tonight Show*
Facts: Collects antique cars and motorcycles.

Made his first appearance on *The Tonight Show* in 1977.

While in grade school, Leno executed such pranks as flushing tennis balls down the toilet and hiding a dog in his locker. His fifth grade teacher wrote on his report card, "If Jay spent as much time studying as he does trying to be a comedian, he'd be a big star."

Original Job: Rolls-Royce mechanic, deliveryman
Marriage: Mavis Nicholson
Address: International Creative Management, 8942 Wilshire Blvd., Beverly Hills, CA 90211

TÉA LEONI

Birthplace: New York, NY
Birthdate: 2/25/1966
Occupation: Actor
Education: Sarah Lawrence College
Debut: (TV) *Santa Barbara,* 1984
Signature: *The Naked Truth*
Facts: A sufferer of stage fright, was so nervous shooting the pilot for *The Naked Truth* she threw up five times.

Got into acting when, on a dare, entered a mass audition for the remake of *Charlie's Angels* and was chosen, although the show never aired.

Caused a stir when *The Naked Truth* producer Chris Thompson left his wife and children to date her.

Original Job: Teaching Japanese men how to interact with American women
Marriage: One prior marriage; David Duchovny
Address: International Creative Management, 8942 Wilshire Blvd., Beverly Hills, CA 90211

DAVID LETTERMAN

Birthplace: Indianapolis, IN
Birthdate: 4/12/47
Occupation: Talk show host
Education: Ball State University
Debut: (TV) *The Starland Vocal Band Show,* 1977
Signature: *Late Show with David Letterman*
Facts: While working as a weather announcer at a local TV station, he congratulated a tropical storm on being upgraded to a hurricane.

Was the announcer for the late-night movie program *Freeze Dried Movies.* On the program, he blew up a model of the television station at which he was working.

Infamy: Margaret Ray has continually stalked him at his New Canaan, CT, home. She was caught at or in his home eight times from 1988–1993.
Original Job: TV announcer, weatherman
Marriage: Michelle Cook (divorced), Regina Lasko (relationship)
Major Awards: Emmy, Best Host of a Daytime Variety Series, *The David Letterman Show,* 1981; Emmy, Writing in a Variety or Music Show, *Late Night with David Letterman,* 1984, 1985, 1986, 1987
Address: Worldwide Pants Inc., 1697 Broadway, New York, NY 10019

RUSH LIMBAUGH

Birthplace: Cape Girardeau, MO
Birthdate: 12/12/51
Occupation: Talk show host

Education: Southeastern Missouri State University
Debut: (Radio) *The Rush Limbaugh Show*
Facts: Claims he does not own a pair of blue jeans.

More than 300 "Rush rooms" have opened in restaurants nationwide for the purpose of broadcasting Rush Limbaugh's programs to patrons.

Met his current wife, Marta Fitzgerald, via electronic mail on CompuServe Information Service. They were married by Supreme Court Justice Clarence Thomas.

Infamy: In February 1994, the Florida Citrus Commission advertised orange juice on Limbaugh's show. The ads generated 7,500 calls to the Commission protesting their choice of such a controversial figure to promote their product. The National Organization for Women, as well as various gay and lesbian groups, urged people to boycott Florida orange juice. Meanwhile, about 30 Rush supporters bought out the entire supply of orange juice at an Orlando, Florida store in a counterprotest.
Original Job: Disc jockey, PR man for the Kansas City Royals
Marriages: Roxy Maxine McNeely (divorced), Michelle Sixta (divorced), Marta Fitzgerald
Address: c/o The Rush Limbaugh Show, 2 Penn Plaza, 17th Floor, New York, NY 10121

JOHN LITHGOW

Birthplace: Rochester, NY
Birthdate: 10/19/45
Occupation: Actor
Education: Harvard University, London Academy of Music and Dramatic Arts
Debut: (Film) *Dealing: or The Berkeley-to-Boston Forty-Brick Lost-Bag Blues*, 1972
Signature: *3rd Rock from the Sun*
Facts: His father ran the Antioch Shakespeare Festival, and John had small parts in the plays from early childhood.

Stars in a children's videotape, *John Lithgow's Kid-Size Concert*.

Some years ago he read the book *Forrest Gump* and wanted to acquire the movie rights so he could play the lead, but he didn't get around to it.

Known as a serious dramatic actor, but actually did more than 40 comedies on stage.

Son Ian appears in *3rd Rock* as Professor Solomon's slowest student.
Marriage: Jean Taynton (divorced), Mary Yeager
Children: Ian, Phoebe, Nathan
Major Awards: Tony, Best Supporting Actor (Drama), *The Changing Room*, 1973; Emmy, Outstanding Guest Performance in a Drama Series, *Amazing Stories*, 1986; Golden Globe, Best Actor in a Comedy Series, *3rd Rock from the Sun*, 1996; Emmy, Best Actor in a Comedy Series, *3rd Rock from the Sun*, 1996, 1997
Quote: "God bless television."
Address: Creative Artists Agency, 9830 Wilshire Blvd., Beverly Hills, CA 90212

HEATHER LOCKLEAR

Birthplace: Los Angeles, CA
Birthdate: 9/25/61
Occupation: Actor
Education: UCLA
Debut: (TV) *Dynasty*, 1981
Signature: *Dynasty*
Facts: Served over six years as the spokesperson for the Health and Tennis Corporation of America.

Played officer Stacy Sheridan on the crime drama series *T.J. Hooker* with William Shatner, 1982–87.

When she joined the cast of *Melrose Place*, the series's audience jumped 50 percent.
Marriage: Tommy Lee (divorced), Richie Sambora
Address: Creative Artists Agency, 9830 Wilshire Blvd., Beverly Hills, CA 90212

JULIA LOUIS-DREYFUS

Birthplace: New York, NY
Birthdate: 1/13/61
Occupation: Actor
Education: Northwestern University
Debut: (TV) *Saturday Night Live*, 1982; (Film) *Hannah and Her Sisters*, 1986
Signature: *Seinfeld*
Facts: Parents were divorced when she was only 1 year old.

Met husband in college and worked with him on *Saturday Night Live*.

Her role in *Seinfeld* was not in the original mix created by Jerry Seinfeld and Larry David, but was imposed by the network, which felt a female perspective was needed.
Original Job: Member of the Second City comedy troupe
Marriage: Brad Hall
Child: Henry, Charles
Major Award: Golden Globe, Best Supporting Actress, *Seinfeld*, 1993; Emmy, Best Supporting Actress, *Seinfeld*, 1996
Address: United Talent Agency, 9560 Wilshire Blvd., Suite 500, Beverly Hills, CA 90212

COURTNEY LOVE

Real Name: Courtney Menely
Birthplace: San Francisco, CA
Birthdate: 7/9/64
Occupation: Singer, songwriter
Education: High school dropout
Debut: (Album) *Pretty on the Inside*, 1991
Signature: Hole
Facts: Ran away to Europe at 15; her grandfather's death left her a millionaire.

Mother was the psychologist who examined Katherine Anne Power ('60s radical and fugitive who recently confessed to being an accessory to bank robbery).

Appeared in the film *Straight to Hell*, 1987.

Before founding Hole, Love was lead vocalist for the rock band Faith

No More in the early '80s "for about a week" (before they found Chuck Mosely). She also played with Kat Bjelland of the Minneapolis all-girl band Babes in Toyland and future L7 member Jennifer Finch in Sugar Baby Doll.

Named daughter after the '30s actress Frances Farmer, who is the subject of Nirvana song "Frances Farmer Will Have Her Revenge on Seattle."

Infamy: In her early teens, was sent to a juvenile detention center after stealing a Kiss T-shirt from a department store.

A *Vanity Fair* article described Love as shooting heroin while pregnant. Though she denied the charge, child-welfare authorities temporarily removed the baby after she was born.

Arrested in 1995 for verbally abusing a flight attendant aboard an Australian flight. She was not convicted, but ordered to remain on good behavior for one month.

Original Job: Danced in strip joints in L.A. and Alaska

Marriage: Kurt Cobain (deceased); Edward Norton (relationship)

Child: Frances Bean

Famous Relatives: Linda Carroll, psychologist, mother; Hank Harrison, author, father

Address: Creative Artists Agency, 9830 Wilshire Blvd., Beverly Hills, CA 90212

LYLE LOVETT

Birthplace: Klein, TX

Birthdate: 11/1/57

Occupation: Singer, songwriter

Education: Texas A&M

Debut: (Album) *Lyle Lovett,* 1986

Facts: Played guitar in coffee shops while in college.

Lives in a clapboard house built by his grandparents.

Is afraid of cows.

Marriage: Julia Roberts (divorced); Elizabeth Vargas (relationship)

Major Awards: Grammy, *Lyle Lovett and His Large Band,* 1989; Grammy, Best Pop Vocal Collaboration, "Funny How Time Slips Away" (with Al Green), 1994; Grammy, Best Country Group Performance with Vocal, "Blues for Dixie" (with Asleep at the Wheel), 1994

Address: International Creative Management, 8942 Wilshire Blvd., Beverly Hills, CA 90211

GEORGE LUCAS

Birthplace: Modesto, CA

Birthdate: 5/14/44

Occupation: Director, producer, screenwriter

Education: University of Southern California

Debut: (Film) *THX-1138,* 1971

Signature: *Star Wars*

Facts: Has sold more than $3 billion in licensed *Star Wars* merchandise, money Lucas got to keep because licensing rights were thrown into his contract in exchange for his having given up an extra director's fee (he forfeited the higher fee to ensure that 20th Century Fox would bankroll his sequel).

His empire includes the Industrial Light & Magic special effects firm, LucasArts interactive media, and a group selling his advanced THX theater sound system.

Still writes scripts in longhand, using the same three-ring binder he used in college.

As an 18-year-old, nearly killed himself while joyriding on a country road when his Fiat hit a car, flipped over, and crashed into a tree. He survived only because his seat belt broke and threw him from the car before impact.

Marriage: Marcia (divorced)

Children: Amanda, Katie, Jett (all adopted)

Major Awards: Academy of Motion Pictures Arts and Sciences, Irving Thalberg Award, 1992

Address: Lucasfilm Ltd., Skywalker Ranch, P.O. Box 2009, San Rafael, CA 94912

SUSAN LUCCI

Birthplace: Scarsdale, NY

Birthdate: 12/23/50

Education: Marymount College

Debut: (TV) *All My Children,* 1969

Signature: *All My Children*

Facts: Was nominated 16 times for the best actress in a daytime series, and lost every time.

Made the semifinals in New York State Miss Universe pageant, 1968. Dropped out of the competition to finish her college exams.

As Erica Kane, Lucci has impersonated a nun, been kidnapped, rescued a lover from prison using a helicopter, and stared down a grizzly bear.

Original Job: "Color girl" for CBS, sitting for cameras as a new lighting system for color TV was being developed

Marriage: Helmut Huber

Children: Liza Victoria, Andreas Martin

Address: International Creative Management, 8942 Wilshire Blvd., Beverly Hills, CA 90211

LORETTA LYNN

Real Name: Loretta Webb

Birthplace: Butcher Hollow, KY

Birthdate: 4/14/35

Occupation: Singer, songwriter

Debut: (Single) "Honky Tonk Girl," 1960

Signature: "Coal Miner's Daughter"
Facts: First woman to earn a certified gold country album.

While her kids were still young, her husband gave her a guitar to accompany the singing she did around the house. She taught herself to play.

Her first No. 1 single, "Don't Come Home A-Drinkin' (With Lovin' on Your Mind)" was banned from several stations. Many of her songs have been banned, including "Rated X" and "The Pill."

Married when she was 13. "By the time I was 17, I had four kids, and I had never been anywhere." She was a grandmother at 31, one year after her twins (her last children) were born.

Marriage: Oliver Vanetta Lynn Jr. (deceased)
Children: Betty Sue Lynn Markworth, Jack Benny (deceased), Clara Lynn Lyell, Ernest Ray, Peggy, Patsy
Famous Relative: Crystal Gayle, singer, sister
Major Awards: Grammy, Best Country Performance—Duo or Group, "After the Fire Is Gone" (with Conway Twitty), 1971; Grammy, Best Recording for Children, *Sesame Country* (with others), 1981; inducted into the Country Music Hall of Fame, 1988
Address: P.O. Box 120369, Nashville, TN 37212

ANDIE MACDOWELL

Real Name: Rosalie Anderson MacDowell
Birthplace: Gaffney, SC
Birthdate: 4/21/58
Occupation: Actor
Education: Winthrop College
Debut: (Film) *Greystoke: The Legend of Tarzan, Lord of the Apes,* 1984
Signature: *sex, lies and videotape*
Facts: After *Greystoke* was filmed, MacDowell's part was overdubbed with a British accent provided by Glenn Close.

Played Jimi Hendrix's "Angel" at her wedding.

Original Job: Elite model
Marriage: Paul Qualley
Children: Justin, Rainey, Sarah Margaret
Major Award: Golden Globe, Special Achievement, *Short Cuts,* 1993
Address: International Creative Management, 8942 Wilshire Blvd., Beverly Hills, CA 90211

SHIRLEY MACLAINE

Real Name: Shirley MacLean Beaty
Birthplace: Richmond, VA
Birthdate: 4/24/34
Occupation: Actor, author
Education: Washington School of Ballet
Debut: (Stage) *Oklahoma!,* 1950
Signature: *Terms of Endearment*
Facts: Starred in her own TV series, *Shirley's World* (1971–72).

Was performing with the Washington School of Ballet by the time she was 12, but soon grew too tall to be a ballerina.

Following a showbiz cliché, she got the lead in the 1954 Broadway show *The Pajama Game* when the lead hurt her ankle.

As a young girl, often had to come to the aid of her bookish and picked-on younger brother with fists blazing.

Infamy: Ridiculed for her oft-expressed beliefs in reincarnation, detailed in her best-selling books *Out on a Limb* and *Dancing in the Light.* Satirized herself in the "Pavilion of Former Lives" in the film *Defending Your Life* (1991).

Had an open marriage with husband Parker, but was stunned to learn from a channeler (later confirmed by a private eye) that he had transferred millions of dollars to his girlfriend's account.

Wrote a tell-all book in 1995, detailing how Debra Winger mooned her and broke wind, and describing Frank Sinatra as "a perpetual kid" and "someone who muscled others." Sinatra's response to the book: "It's amazing what a broad will do for a buck."

Original Job: Dancer
Marriage: Steve Parker (divorced)
Child: Stephanie Sachiko
Famous Relative: Warren Beatty, actor, brother
Major Awards: Golden Globe, New Female Star of the Year, 1955; Golden Globe, Best Actress, *Some Came Running*, 1958; Golden Globe, Most Versatile Actress, 1958; Golden Globe, Best Actress in a Comedy, *The Apartment*, 1960; Golden Globe, Best Actress, *Irma la Douce*, 1963; Golden Globe, Best Actress, *Terms of Endearment*, 1983; Golden Globe, Best Actress, *Madame Sousatzka*, 1988; Emmy, Outstanding Comedy-Variety or Musical Special, *Shirley MacLaine: If They Could See Me Now*, 1974; Emmy, Outstanding Comedy-Variety or Musical Special, *Gypsy in My Soul*, 1976; Emmy, Outstanding Writing of Variety or Music Program, *Shirley MacLaine... Every Little Movement*, 1980; Oscar, Best Actress, *Terms of Endearment*, 1983
Address: International Creative Management, 8942 Wilshire Blvd., Beverly Hills, CA 90211

ELLE MACPHERSON

Real Name: Eleanor Gow
Birthplace: Sydney, Australia
Birthdate: 1965
Occupation: Supermodel, actor
Debut: *Sports Illustrated* swimsuit model, (Film) *Sirens*, 1994
Facts: Appeared in every issue of *Elle* magazine from 1982 to 1988.

Launched a designer lingerie line in Australia and New Zealand in 1991.

Opened Fashion Cafe in New York City in 1995 with supermodels Claudia Schiffer and Naomi Campbell.

Marriage: Gilles Bensimon (divorced), Tim Jeffries (relationship)
Address: International Creative Management, 8942 Wilshire Blvd., Beverly Hills, CA 90211

MADONNA

Real Name: Madonna Louise Veronica Ciccone
Birthplace: Bay City, MI
Birthdate: 8/16/58
Occupation: Singer
Education: University of Michigan
Debut: Dancer, Alvin Ailey Dance Company, 1979
Signature: "Material Girl"
Facts: She starred in an exploitation film called *A Certain Sacrifice* in 1980.

Early in her career, posed nude for a New York photographer. Those photos later appeared in *Playboy.*

She appears in a nightclub scene from the 1983 movie *Vision Quest,* singing "Crazy for You" in the background.

Infamy: Swore 14 times while on *The Late Show with David Letterman,* to get revenge for his many jokes at her expense. She also handed Letterman a pair of her panties and told him to smell them.

Her video for "Justify My Love" (1990) was banned from MTV.

Her book *Sex* (1992) was originally banned in Japan, where it is against the law to show pubic hair. Officials eventually relented since the book was being distributed anyway.

Original Job: Model, worked in a doughnut shop
Marriage: Sean Penn (divorced), Carlos Leon (relationship)
Child: Lourdes Maria Ciccone Leon
Major Awards: Grammy, Best Music Video—Long Form, *Madonna—Blonde Ambition World Tour Live,* 1991; Golden Globe, Best Actress in a Musical or Comedy, *Evita,* 1996
Address: International Creative Management, 8942 Wilshire Blvd., Beverly Hills, CA 90211

BILL MAHER

Birthplace: New York, NY
Birthdate: 1/20/56
Occupation: Comedian, talk show host
Education: Cornell University
Debut: *The Tonight Show,* 1982
Signature: *Politically Incorrect*
Facts: Says the most politically incorrect thing he ever did was to say "f--k" in front of the president.

Originally did stand-up on the New York club circuit with other up-and-coming comics, including Jerry Seinfeld and Paul Reiser.

Wrote *True Story: A Comedy Novel.*

Major Award: CableAce, Best Cable Talk Show Host, 1994
Address: Creative Artists Agency, 9830 Wilshire Blvd., Beverly Hills, CA 90212

JOHN MALKOVICH

Birthplace: Christopher, IL
Birthdate: 12/9/53
Occupation: Actor
Education: Eastern Illinois University, Illinois State University
Debut: (Stage) *True West,* 1982
Signature: *Dangerous Liaisons*
Facts: Played football and tuba in high school.

Took up acting in college when he fell for a female drama student.

Co-founded the Steppenwolf Theatre in Chicago, in 1976.

Original Job: Enrolled in Eastern Illinois University with plans of becoming an environmentalist
Marriages: Glenne Headly (divorced), Nicoletta Peyran
Children: Amandine, Lowey
Major Award: Emmy, Best Supporting Actor in a Made-for-TV Movie, *Death of a Salesman,* 1986
Address: International Creative Management, 8942 Wilshire Blvd., Beverly Hills, CA 90211

DAVID MAMET

Birthplace: Chicago, IL
Birthdate: 11/30/47
Occupation: Writer, director
Education: Goddard College, studied at the Neighborhood Playhouse in New York
Debut: (Stage) *The Duck Variations,* 1972
Signature: *Glengarry Glen Ross*
Facts: Has written several books and children's plays, including *Revenge of the Space Pandas, or Binky Rudich and the Two-Speed Clock.*

Has worked as a busboy, driven a cab, worked at *Oui* magazine, and waited tables. Was an assistant office manager for a real estate company and taught drama at Yale, New York University, and the University of Chicago.

Wrote the screenplays for *The Postman Always Rings Twice* (1981), *The Verdict* (1982), and *The Untouchables* (1987).

Published his first novel, *The Village,* in 1994.

Still writes on a '70s manual typewriter and uses a pencil.

Co-founded the Atlantic Theater Company as a summer workshop in Vermont for his NYU students.

Original Job: Worked backstage at the Hull House Theatre in Chicago
Marriages: Lindsay Crouse (divorced), Rebecca Pidgeon
Children: Willa, Clara, Zosia
Major Award: Pulitzer Prize, *Glengarry Glen Ross,* 1984
Address: P.O. Box 381589, Cambridge, MA 02238

JULIANNA MARGULIES

Birthplace: Spring Valley, NY
Birthdate: 6/8/66
Occupation: Actor
Education: Sarah Lawrence College
Debut: (Film) *Out for Justice,* 1991
Signature: *ER*
Facts: Her father was the ad executive who wrote the Alka Seltzer "Plop, plop, fizz, fizz" jingle.

Her parents divorced early, and her mother, a former dancer with the American Ballet Theatre, moved her to Paris and then London.

A perfectionist in high school, once threw a 50-page, illustrated research report into the mud because it got an A-minus.

While waiting for an acting break, waitressed at some of New York's trendiest restaurants.

Major Award: Emmy, Best Supporting Actress (Drama), *ER*, 1995

Address: International Creative Management, 40 West 57th Street, New York, NY 10019

WYNTON MARSALIS

Birthplace: New Orleans, LA

Birthdate: 10/18/61

Occupation: Trumpeter

Education: Attended Juilliard on a full scholarship

Debut: (Band) Art Blakey's Jazz Messengers, 1980

Facts: His first trumpet was a hand-me-down from bandleader Al Hirt.

Played with New Orleans Philharmonic at age 14.

Released his first classical album, *Trumpet Concertos,* in 1983. Was first artist ever to receive—or be nominated for—awards in both jazz and classical categories in a single year.

Relationship: Victoria Rowell

Children: Wynton, Simeon, Jasper Armstrong

Famous Relatives: Ellis Marsalis, musician, father; Branford Marsalis, musician, brother

Major Awards: Grammy, Best Jazz Performance—Soloist, "Think of One," 1983; Grammy, Best Jazz Performance—Soloist, "Hot House Flowers," 1984; Grammy, Best Jazz Performance—Soloist, "Black Codes from the Underground," 1985; Grammy, Best Jazz Performance—Group, "Black Codes from the Underground," 1985; Grammy, Best Jazz Performance—Group, "J Mood," 1986; Grammy, Best Jazz Performance—Group, *Marsalis Standard Time Volume I,* 1987; Pulitzer Prize, *Blood on the Fields*

Address: Sony Music, 550 Madison Avenue, New York, NY 10019

PENNY MARSHALL

Real Name: Carole Penny Marshall

Birthplace: New York, NY

Birthdate: 10/15/42

Occupation: Actor, director

Education: University of New Mexico

Debut: (TV) *The Danny Thomas Hour,* 1967

Signature: *Laverne and Shirley*

Facts: Even though the family was Congregationalist, Marshall's mother was convinced that Jewish men make the best husbands, so she sent Penny to a Jewish summer camp each year.

Lost the part of Gloria on TV's *All in the Family* to Sally Struthers.

Was first woman director to have a film take in more than $100 million at the box office (*Big*).

Original Job: Dance instructor, secretary

Marriages: Michael Henry (divorced), Rob Reiner (divorced)

Child: Tracy Lee

Famous Relatives: Garry Marshall, director, producer, brother; Tony Maschiarelli, producer, father

Address: International Creative Management, 8942 Wilshire Blvd., Beverly Hills, CA 90211

STEVE MARTIN

Birthplace: Waco, TX

Birthdate: 8/14/45

Occupation: Actor, writer

Education: Long Beach State College, UCLA

Debut: (TV) *The Smothers Brothers Comedy Hour,* 1967

Signature: *A Wild and Crazy Guy*

Facts: Lived behind Disneyland and got his start there performing magic tricks and playing the banjo.

Is a dedicated art collector.

Original Job: Sold guidebooks at Disneyland

Marriage: Victoria Tennant (divorced)

Major Awards: Emmy, Best Writing in a Comedy, Variety, or Music Program, *The Smothers Brothers Comedy Hour,* 1969; Grammy, Best Comedy Recording, *Let's Get Small,* 1977; Grammy, Best Comedy Recording, *A Wild and Crazy Guy,* 1978

Address: International Creative Management, 8942 Wilshire Blvd., Beverly Hills, CA 90211

JENNY MCCARTHY

Birthplace: Chicago, IL

Birthdate: 11/1/72

Occupation: Actor

Education: Southern Illinois University

Debut: (TV) *Playboy's Hot Rocks,* 1994

Signature: *Singled Out*

Facts: Raised in an Irish Catholic family, and attended a Catholic school.

Went to college for nursing, but dropped out after two years when she ran out of money.

Was Playboy's 1993 Miss October and Playmate of the Year. Says the nude photos were doctored by a computer.

Excels at karate and kick boxing.

Infamy: Her *Singled Out* episode featuring gay and lesbian couples was bumped out of its regularly scheduled 7:00 p.m. timeslot. It was deemed too explicit by MTV executives. The show was aired at 11:00 p.m. only.

Relationship: Ray Manzella

Address: Hofflund-Pollone, 9615 Brighton Way, Suite 320, Beverly Hills, CA 90210

PAUL MCCARTNEY

Real Name: James Paul McCartney

Birthplace: Liverpool, England

Birthdate: 6/18/42

Occupation: Singer, songwriter, bassist

Education: High school

Debut: Formed the Quarry Men, Moondogs, and the Silver Beatles with John Lennon and George Harrison, 1956–1962

Signature: The Beatles
Facts: When he wanted to use "Yesterday" in his 1984 film *Give My Regards to Broad Street,* he had to apply to the publishers for its use; he no longer owned the copyright of the most recorded song in history (over 2,500 cover versions exist).

Was the first Beatle to quit in 1970, releasing his solo album *McCartney* almost simultaneously with the band's release of *Let It Be.*

His version of "Mary Had a Little Lamb" hit No. 9 on the British charts in June 1972.

In the Paul McCartney Kindergarten in Krakow, Poland, children are taught English through McCartney's songs.

Was knighted by Queen Elizabeth in 1996.
Infamy: Admitted to taking LSD and was arrested numerous times with Linda for possession of marijuana and for growing it at their Scotland farmhouse. Because of this, his application for a U.S. passport was refused many times.
Marriage: Linda Eastman
Children: James, Mary, Stella, Heather (stepdaughter)
Major Awards: Grammy, Best New Artist (with The Beatles), 1964; Grammy, Best Pop Vocal—Duo or Group, *A Hard Day's Night* (with The Beatles), 1964; Grammy, Song of the Year, "Michelle" (with John Lennon), 1966; Grammy, Best Rock Vocal, "Eleanor Rigby," 1966; Grammy, Album of the Year, *Sgt. Pepper's Lonely Hearts Club Band* (with The Beatles), 1967; Grammy, Best Score, *Let It Be* (with The Beatles), 1970; Grammy, Best Pop Performance—Duo or Group, *Band on the Run* (with Wings), 1974; Grammy, Hall of Fame Winner, *Sgt. Pepper's Lonely Hearts Club Band* (with The Beatles), 1992; Oscar, Best Score, *Let It Be* (with The Beatles), 1970; inducted into the Rock and Roll Hall of Fame (with The Beatles), 1988; NARAS Lifetime Achievement Award, 1990; Grammy, Best Pop Vocal, Duo or Group with Vocal, "Free as a Bird" (with the Beatles), 1996
Address: Capitol Records, 1750 N. Vine St., Hollywood, CA 90028

MATTHEW MCCONAUGHEY

Birthplace: Uvalde, TX
Birthdate: 1970
Occupation: Actor
Education: University of Texas
Debut: (Film) *Dazed and Confused,* 1993
Signature: *A Time To Kill*
Facts: Endlessly rereads the motivational book, *The Greatest Salesman in the World.* Used its techniques to sell his talents to get acting parts.

Was cast in *Kill* after executives vetoed Kevin Costner, Keanu Reeves, Val Kilmer and others in a year-long search. Received just $200,000 to play the part.
Address: William Morris Agency, 151 El Camino Dr., Beverly Hills, CA 90212

FRANCES MCDORMAND

Birthplace: Illinois
Birthdate: 6/23/57
Occupation: Actor
Education: Bethany College, Yale Drama School
Debut: (Film) *Blood Simple,* 1984
Signature: *Fargo*
Facts: Born to a Disciples of Christ preacher. The family moved repeatedly throughout the Midwest when she was a child.

Met Holly Hunter when the two studied at Yale. After graduation, Hunter told her she had auditioned for "two weird guys" (the Coen brothers) and that McDormand should too. After repeated failed attempts to get an audition, McDormand finally succeeded. *Blood Simple* not only launched her (and Hunter's) career, it introduced her to future husband Joel.

Was nominated in 1988 for Oscar's best supporting actress (for *Mississippi Burning*), the same year she was also nominated for a Tony for *A Streetcar Named Desire.*
Marriage: Joel Coen
Child: Pedro (adopted)
Famous Relative: Ethan Coen, writer, director, producer, brother-in-law
Major Award: Oscar, Best Actress, *Fargo,* 1996
Address: William Morris Agency, 151 El Camino Dr., Beverly Hills, CA 90212

REBA MCENTIRE

Birthplace: Chockie, OK
Birthdate: 3/28/55
Occupation: Singer, songwriter
Education: Southeastern State University
Debut: (Song) "I Don't Want To Be a One-Night Stand," 1976
Signature: "Is There Life Out There?"
Facts: As a teenager, performed with her siblings in the Singing McEntires. Their first single was a tribute to her grandfather, rodeo rider John McEntire.

Appeared in the 1990 movie *Tremors,* as well as other film and TV roles.

Her longtime tour manager and seven of her band members died in a plane crash in 1991.
Original Job: Cattle rancher, rodeo barrel racer
Marriages: Charlie Battles (divorced), Narvel Blackstock
Child: Shelby Stephen
Major Awards: Grammy, Best

Country Vocal—Female, "Whoever's in New England," 1986; Grammy, Best Country Female Vocalist, 1987; Grammy, Best Country Vocal—Collaboration, "Does He Love You" (with Linda Davis), 1993
Address: MCA Records, 70 Universal City Plaza, Universal City, CA 91608

TIM MCGRAW

Birthplace: Jacksonville, FL
Birthdate: 5/1/66
Occupation: Singer
Education: Attended Northeast Louisiana University
Debut: (Album) *Tim McGraw,* 1993
Signature: *Not a Moment Too Soon*
Facts: Mom Betty was an 18-year-old dancer when she and then bachelor Tug consummated their summer romance while Tug was in baseball camp. Tim learned who his father was only when he found his birth certificate at age 11. Tim met Tug but had little contact until high school, when Tug agreed to help pay for his son's college education.

Started his own management company, Breakfast Table Management, to launch other groups.

The lyrics to his "Indian Outlaw" outraged some Native American groups, who had it banned from radio stations in several states.
Marriage: Faith Hill
Child: Gracie Katherine
Famous Relative: Tug McGraw, baseball player, father
Address: Curb Records, 47 Music Square E., Nashville, TN 37203

EWAN MCGREGOR

Birthplace: Crieff, Scotland
Birthdate: 3/31/71
Occupation: Actor
Education: Attended London's Guildhall School of Music and Drama
Debut: (Film) *Being Human,* 1993
Signature: *Trainspotting*
Facts: Inspired by his uncle, knew he wanted to be in theater at age 9. Left home at 16 to work backstage at Scotland's Perth Repertory Theatre.

Lost nearly 30 pounds and shaved his head for his role in *Trainspotting.* Debated whether to try shooting heroin but decided that it would be disrespectful to the recovering addicts acting as technical advisors to the film.
Marriage: Eve Maurakis
Child: Clara Mathilde
Famous Relative: Dennis Lawson, actor, uncle
Address: Creative Artists Agency, 9830 Wilshire Blvd., Los Angeles, CA 90212

LORNE MICHAELS

Real Name: Lorne Lipowitz
Birthplace: Toronto, Canada
Birthdate: 11/17/44
Occupation: Producer, writer
Education: University of Toronto
Debut: (TV) *Rowan and Martin's Laugh-In,* 1968 (writer)
Signature: *Saturday Night Live*
Facts: In addition to *Saturday Night Live,* Michaels produces *Late Night with Conan O'Brien.* He has also produced the films *Three Amigos* (1986), *Wayne's World* (1992), *Wayne's World 2* (1993), *Coneheads* (1993), *Lassie* (1994), *Stuart Saves His Family* (1995), *Tommy Boy* (1995), *Black Sheep* (1996), and *Brain Candy* (1996).
Marriages: Rosie Shuster (divorced), Susan Forristal (divorced), Alice Barry
Children: Henry Abraham, Edward
Major Awards: Writers Guild of America Awards (4); Emmy, Best Writing in a Comedy, Variety, or Music Special, *Lily,* 1974, 1976; Emmy, Best Writing in a Comedy, Variety, or Music Series, *Saturday Night Live,* 1976, 1977; Emmy, Best Writing in a Comedy, Variety, or Music Series, *The Paul Simon Special,* 1978; Emmy, Best Writing in a Variety or Music Program, *Murderers Among Us,* 1989
Address: Broadway Video, 1619 Broadway, 9th Fl., New York, NY 10019

DEMI MOORE

Real Name: Demetria Guynes
Birthplace: Roswell, NM
Birthdate: 11/11/62
Occupation: Actor
Education: Left high school to model in Europe, studied with Zina Provendie
Debut: (Film) *Choices,* 1981; (TV) *General Hospital,* 1981
Signature: *Ghost*
Facts: Was cross-eyed as a child and had an operation to correct it, wearing a patch over one eye.

Decided to become an actor in high school when she lived in the same building as Nastassja Kinski.

In order to play coke addict Jules in the 1985 movie *St. Elmo's Fire,* she had to sign a contract stipulating that she would stop her own alcohol and drug abuse, an agreement that caused her to turn her life around.

Was engaged to Emilio Estevez.

She and Bruce Willis were married on November 21, 1987, by singer Little Richard.
Infamy: Posed nude and pregnant on the cover of *Vanity Fair.*
Original Job: Model
Marriages: Freddy Moore (divorced), Bruce Willis
Children: Rumer Glenn, Scout Larue, Tallulah Belle
Address: Creative Artists Agency, 9830 Wilshire Blvd., Beverly Hills, CA 90212

ALANIS MORISSETTE

Birthplace: Ottawa, Canada
Birthdate: 6/1/74
Occupation: Singer, songwriter
Education: High school
Debut: (Album) *Alanis,* 1991
Signature: "You Oughta Know"
Facts: At age 10, appeared as a sweet little girl on Nickelodeon's *You Can't Do That on Television.* At 17, was a Queen of Disco, dubbed the Canadian Debbie Gibson.

During her dance pop days, toured with Vanilla Ice.

Has a twin brother, Wade.

Claimed it took 15 to 45 minutes to write most of the songs on *Jagged Little Pill.*

Major Awards: Grammy, Album of the Year, *Jagged Little Pill,* 1995; Grammy, Best Rock Album, *Jagged Little Pill,* 1995; Grammy, Best Female Rock Vocalist, "You Oughta Know," 1995; Grammy, Best Rock Song, "You Oughta Know," 1995

Address: Creative Artists Agency, 9830 Wilshire Blvd., Beverly Hills, CA 90212

TONI MORRISON

Real Name: Chloe Anthony Wofford
Birthplace: Lorain, OH
Birthdate: 2/18/31
Occupation: Author
Education: Howard University, Cornell University
Debut: (Book) *The Bluest Eye,* 1969
Signature: *Beloved*
Facts: Has served as an editor at Random House, helping to publish the works of other black Americans like Toni Cade Bambara, Angela Davis, and Muhammad Ali.

Has taught at Harvard, Yale, and Princeton.

Original Job: Textbook editor
Marriage: Harold Morrison (divorced)
Children: Harold Ford, Slade Kevin
Major Awards: National Book Critics Circle Award, *Song of Solomon,* 1977; Pulitzer Prize, *Beloved,* 1988; Nobel Prize for Literature, 1993
Quote: "Although we women are coming into our own, we still love you men for what you are, just to let you know."
Address: International Creative Management, 8942 Wilshire Blvd., Beverly Hills, CA 90211

VAN MORRISON

Real Name: George Ivan Morrison
Birthplace: Belfast, Northern Ireland.
Birthdate: 8/31/45
Occupation: Singer, songwriter
Education: High school dropout
Debut: (Song) "Don't Start Crying" (with Them), 1964
Signature: "Brown Eyed Girl"
Facts: Was lead singer of Them from 1964 to 1967 and has worked solo ever since.

In 1965, wrote "Gloria," which achieved moderate success but didn't hit the U.S. top ten until it was covered by The Shadows of Knight in 1966.

Marriage: Janet Planet (divorced)
Major Award: Grammy, Best Pop Vocal Collaboration (with the Chieftains), "Have I Told You Lately That I Love You," 1995
Address: Polydor, 825 Eighth Avenue, 27th Floor, New York, NY 10019

EDDIE MURPHY

Birthplace: Hempstead, NY
Birthdate: 4/3/61
Occupation: Actor
Education: Nassau Community College
Debut: (TV) *Saturday Night Live,* 1980
Signature: *Beverly Hills Cop*
Facts: Father was a policeman who died when Eddie was 5.

Was voted most popular at Roosevelt Jr.-Sr. High School in New York, NY.

Created and produced the TV series *The Royal Family,* which was cut short upon the sudden death of the star Redd Foxx.

Co-owns the L.A. restaurant Georgia with Denzel Washington.

Infamy: In May 1997, police tracking a transvestite prostitute pulled Murphy's Toyota over at 4:45 a.m.; police arrested the prostitute and immediately released Murphy, who explained he was only giving the streetwalker a lift. In the aftermath Murphy sued the *National Enquirer* for publishing interviews with transvestite prostitutes claiming to have had sex with Murphy; the suit was eventually dropped.

Original Job: Shoe store clerk
Marriage: Nicole Mitchell
Children: Bria, Myles Mitchell, Christian, Shayne Audra
Major Award: Grammy, Best Comedy Recording, *Eddie Murphy—Comedian,* 1983; Golden Globe, Best Actor, *Trading Places,* 1983
Address: International Creative Management, 8942 Wilshire Blvd., Beverly Hills, CA 90211

BILL MURRAY

Birthplace: Wilmette, IL
Birthdate: 9/21/50
Occupation: Actor, writer
Education: Loyola Academy, Regis College, Second City Workshop in Chicago
Debut: (TV) *Saturday Night Live,* 1977
Signature: *Ghostbusters*
Facts: Was a pre-med student at St. Regis College.

Provided the voice of Johnny Storm, the Human Torch, on Marvel Comics' radio show, *The Fantastic Four.* This is where he was heard by the producers of *Saturday Night Live.*

Bill's son, Homer Banks, is named after legendary Chicago Cub Ernie Banks.

In 1981, performed the song "The Best Thing (Love Song)" for John Waters' *Polyester.*

Original Job: Pizza maker
Marriage: Margaret Kelly
Children: Homer, Luke
Famous Relative: Brian Doyle-Murray, actor, brother
Major Award: Emmy, Best Writing in a Comedy Series, *Saturday Night Live,* 1977
Address: Creative Artists Agency, 9830 Wilshire Blvd., Beverly Hills, CA 90212

MIKE MYERS

Birthplace: Scarborough, Canada
Birthdate: 5/25/63
Occupation: Actor, writer
Education: High school

Debut: (TV) *Mullarkey & Myers,* 1984
Signature: *Wayne's World*
Facts: When he was a child, Myers's comedy-loving father would wake his three sons at night to watch *Monty Python.*

Appeared in a TV commercial with Gilda Radner at age 8.

Modeled his *Saturday Night Live* character Linda "Coffee Talk" Richman on his mother-in-law.

Wrote the script for *Austin Powers* in three weeks.

Started a retro-mod band, Ming Tea.
Marriage: Robin Ruzan
Major Awards: Emmy, Outstanding Writing in a Comedy Series, *Saturday Night Live,* 1989; Emmy, Best Writing in a Variety or Music Program, *Murderers Among Us,* 1989.
Address: Creative Artists Agency, 9830 Wilshire Blvd., Los Angeles, CA 90212

LIAM NEESON

Birthplace: Ballymena, Northern Ireland
Birthdate: 6/7/52
Occupation: Actor
Debut: (Stage) *In the Risen,* 1976; (Film) *Excalibur,* 1981
Signature: *Schindler's List*
Facts: At age 9, joined a boxing team run by a priest. Nose was broken during an early match, and had it set on site by his manager. Quit boxing at age 17.

First starring role was the disfigured hero of the film *Darkman,* 1990.
Original Job: Forklift operator, architect's assistant, amateur boxer
Marriage: Natasha Richardson
Children: Micheál, Daniel Jack N.
Address: International Creative Management, 8942 Wilshire Blvd., Beverly Hills, CA 90211

WILLIE NELSON

Birthplace: Abbott, TX
Birthdate: 4/30/33
Occupation: Singer, songwriter, guitarist, actor
Education: Baylor University
Debut: (Album) *...And Then I Wrote,* 1962; (Film) *The Electric Horseman,* 1979
Signature: "Mamas, Don't Let Your Babies Grow Up To Be Cowboys"
Facts: Nelson taught at Baptist Sunday school until officials objected to him playing in seedy bars.

Sold his first song, "Family Bible," for $50 to feed his family; it became a huge hit, performed by more than 70 country artists.

Organized Farm Aid concerts to help midwestern farmers stricken by drought and threatened with foreclosure.

Began writing songs at age 7.
Infamy: In 1991, after a seven-year dispute with the IRS over $16.7 million in back taxes, the government seized most of Nelson's possessions (country club, recording studio, 44-acre ranch, 20 other properties in four states, instruments, recordings, and memorabilia).

Arrested in 1994 for possession of marijuana. Charges were later dismissed.
Original Job: Janitor, door-to-door salesman (Bibles, encyclopedias, vacuum cleaners, sewing machines), hosted country music shows on Texas radio stations
Marriages: Martha Matthews (divorced), Shirley Collie (divorced), Connie Koepke (divorced), Annie D'Angelo
Children: Lana, Susie, Billy (deceased), Paula Carlene, Amy, Lukas Autry, Jacob Micah
Major Awards: Grammy, Best Country Vocal—Male, "Blue Eyes Cryin' in the Rain," 1975; Grammy, Best Country Vocal—Male, "Georgia on My Mind," 1978; Grammy, Best Country Performance—Duo or Group, "Mamas Don't Let Your Babies Grow Up To Be Cowboys" (with Waylon Jennings), 1978; Grammy, Best Country Song, "On the Road Again," 1980; Grammy, Best Country Vocal—Male, "Always on My Mind," 1982; Grammy, Best Country Song, "Always on My Mind," 1982; Grammy, Legend Award, 1990; inducted into the Country Music Hall of Fame in 1993
Address: Mark Rothbaum & Associates, P.O. Box 2689, Danbury, CT 06813

AARON NEVILLE

Birthplace: New Orleans, LA
Birthdate: 1/24/41
Occupation: Singer
Debut: (Single) "Over You," 1960
Signature: The Neville Brothers
Facts: Worked as a longshoreman on the docks in New Orleans to pay the record company for the studio time he used to record songs like "Over You" and "Tell It Like It Is."

A staunch Catholic, he credits his success to his faith in God. To this day he still offers novenas to St. Jude. "There's always something impossible to pray for."
Infamy: Spent six months in jail for auto theft in 1959.
Marriage: Joel
Children: Ernestine, Ivan, Jason, Aaron Jr.
Famous Relatives: Art Neville, singer, brother; Charles Neville, singer, brother; Cyril Neville, singer, brother
Major Awards: Grammy, Best Pop Vocal—Duo or Group with Vocal, "Don't Know Much" (with Linda Ronstadt), 1989; Grammy, Best Pop Vocal—Duo or Group with Vocal, "All My Life" (with Linda Ronstadt), 1990; Down Beat Blues, Soul, R&B Award, 1990; Grammy, Best Country Vocal Collaboration, "I Fall to Pieces" (with Trisha Yearwood), 1994
Address: William Morris Agency, 151 El Camino Dr., Beverly Hills, CA 90212

PAUL NEWMAN

Birthplace: Cleveland, OH
Birthdate: 1/26/25
Occupation: Actor, director, producer

Education: Kenyon College, Yale School of Drama, Actors Studio
Debut: (Film) *The Silver Chalice,* 1954
Signature: *The Hustler*
Facts: Briefly attended Ohio University and was allegedly asked to leave for crashing a beer keg into the president's car.

The Newman's Own food company he founded in 1987 with writer friend A.E. Hochner has donated more than $60 million to charity.

Has worked on more than nine movies with actor wife Joanne Woodward.

A die-hard, marching liberal, he invested in the leftist opinion-making magazine, *The Nation.*

Is a professional race car driver.
Marriages: Jacqueline Witte (divorced), Joanne Woodward
Children: Scott (deceased), Susan, Stephanie, Elinor "Nell" Teresa, Melissa Steward, Claire Olivia
Major Awards: Golden Globe, World Film Favorite—Male, *Hud,* 1963; Oscar, Lifetime Achievement, 1985; Oscar, Best Actor, *The Color of Money,* 1986; Oscar, Jean Hersholt Humanitarian Award, 1993
Address: Creative Artists Agency, 9830 Wilshire Blvd., Beverly Hills, CA 90212

WAYNE NEWTON

Birthplace: Norfolk, VA
Birthdate: 4/3/42
Occupation: Entertainer
Education: High school dropout
Debut: (TV) *Jackie Gleason and His American Scene Magazine,* 1962; (Film) *80 Steps to Jonah,* 1969
Signature: *Danke Schoen*
Facts: Protégé of Jackie Gleason.

Partly Native American.

Earns $250,000 a week for his Las Vegas performances.
Infamy: In 1992, declared bankruptcy, listing debts of more than $20 million.

In 1994 his creditors again went to court, charging that, despite millions in current earnings, he continued spending lavishly on himself (including a reported $75,000 repairing his home pond for his pet penguins) and made little effort to pay what he owed them.
Marriages: Elaine Okamura (divorced), Kathleen McCrone
Child: Erin
Address: c/o Yellow Ribbon Theater, P.O. Box 7710, Branson, MO 65614

JACK NICHOLSON

Birthplace: Neptune, NJ
Birthdate: 4/22/37
Occupation: Actor, director, producer, screenwriter
Education: Studied with the Players Ring acting group
Debut: (Stage) *Tea and Sympathy,* 1957; (Film) *Cry-Baby Killer,* 1958
Signature: *One Flew Over the Cuckoo's Nest*
Facts: Recorded *The Elephant's Child,* a children's record, with Bobby McFerrin (1987).

Abandoned by his father in childhood, he was raised believing his grandmother was his mother and his real mother was his older sister. The truth was revealed to him years later when a *Time* magazine researcher uncovered the truth while preparing a story on the star.

Has been nominated ten times for the Academy Award.
Infamy: Known for being a ladies' man, Nicholson had a 17-year relationship with actress Anjelica Huston that ended in 1990 when Nicholson revealed that actor Rebecca Broussard, his daughter's best friend, was carrying his child.

During a later two-year falling out period with Broussard, he dated a 20-year-old and reportedly fathered her baby girl.

Reportedly used a golf club to strike the windshield of a '69 Mercedes that had cut him off in traffic in 1994. The driver's civil suit was settled out of court.

Recently admitted the paternity of Caleb Goddard, 25, a New York City producer and writer. The public acknowledgment arose out of a messy civil battle between Nicholson and Goddard's mother, actress Susan Anspach.
Original Job: Office boy in MGM's cartoon department
Marriages: Sandra Knight (divorced)
Children: Jennifer, Caleb, Lorraine, Raymond
Major Awards: Golden Globe, Best Actor, *Chinatown,* 1974; Golden Globe, Best Actor, *One Flew over the Cuckoo's Nest,* 1975; Golden Globe, Best Supporting Actor, *Terms of Endearment,* 1983; Golden Globe, Best Actor in a Comedy, *Prizzi's Honor,* 1985; Oscar, Best Actor, *One Flew over the Cuckoo's Nest,* 1975; Oscar, Best Supporting Actor, *Terms of Endearment,* 1983; Grammy, Best Recording for Children, *The Elephant's Child,* 1987
Address: 15760 Ventura Blvd., Suite 1730, Encino, CA 91426

LESLIE NIELSEN

Birthplace: Regina, Canada
Birthdate: 2/11/26
Occupation: Actor, writer
Education: Lorne Greene's Academy of Radio Arts, Toronto
Debut: (TV) *Actor's Studio,* 1950; (Film) *Forbidden Planet,* 1956
Signature: *The Naked Gun*
Facts: Grew up in a log cabin 200 miles south of the Arctic Circle.

Suffered a childhood case of rickets. Legally deaf.

Served in the Royal Canadian Air Force during World War II.
Original Job: Radio announcer, disc jockey
Marriages: Monica Boyer (divorced), Sandy Ullman (divorced), Barbaree Earl
Children: Thea, Maura
Famous Relative: Eric Nielsen, member of Canadian Parliament, brother
Address: 15760 Ventura Blvd., #1730, Encino, CA 91436

EDWARD NORTON

Birthplace: Columbia, MD
Birthdate: 1969
Occupation: Actor
Education: Yale University
Debut: (Film) *Primal Fear,* 1996
Signature: *Primal Fear*
Facts: When Leonardo DiCaprio dropped out of *Primal Fear,* Paramount launched an international search of 2,100 actors with no success. Costar Richard Gere was ready to walk from the project when Norton wowed them when he read for the part.

Grandfather James designed Boston's Faneuil Hall and New York's South Street Seaport. Father Ed Sr., a lawyer, was a federal prosecutor under Jimmy Carter.

Studied astronomy and Japanese (he's fluent) in college before getting a degree in history.
Original Job: Proofreader, waiter, low-income housing worker
Relationship: Courtney Love
Famous Relative: James Rouse, architect, grandfather
Major Award: Golden Globe, Best Supporting Actor, *Primal Fear,* 1996
Address: International Creative Management, 8942 Wilshire Blvd., Beverly Hills, CA 90211

CONAN O'BRIEN

Birthplace: Brookline, MA
Birthdate: 4/18/63
Occupation: Talk show host
Education: Harvard University
Debut: (TV) *Not Necessarily the News,* 1985
Signature: *NBC's Late Night with Conan O'Brien*
Facts: Has written for *Saturday Night Live* and *The Simpsons.*

While at Harvard, served as president of *The Harvard Lampoon* for two years, the first person to do so since Robert Benchley in 1912.

First TV producing credit was *Lookwell* (1991), a sitcom pilot starring Adam West as a former TV detective who becomes a real cop.
Relationship: Lynn Kaplan
Major Award: Emmy, Best Writing in a Variety or Music Program, *Murderers Among Us,* 1989
Quote: "The nightmare is that you spend the rest of your life being funny at parties and people say, 'Why didn't you do *that* when you were on television?' "
Address: Hofflund-Pollone, 9615 Brighton Way, Suite 320, Beverly Hills, CA 90210

CHRIS O'DONNELL

Birthplace: Chicago, IL
Birthdate: 1970
Occupation: Actor
Education: Boston College, UCLA
Debut: (TV) *Jack and Mike,* 1986; (Film) *Men Don't Leave,* 1990
Signature: *Scent of a Woman*
Facts: Youngest of seven children (four sisters and two brothers), grew up in Winnetka, IL.

Began modeling and appearing in commercials in 1983, at age 13. Appeared in a McDonald's commercial opposite Michael Jordan.

Was 17 when he auditioned for *Men Don't Leave.* His mother had to promise him a new car to get him to try out. He is still waiting for that car.

Originally cast as Barbra Streisand's son in *Prince of Tides,* but she decided to have her real-life son play the role instead.

Took time off from pursuing a degree in marketing from Boston College in order to work with Al Pacino on *Scent of a Woman.*
Marriage: Caroline Fentress
Address: Creative Artists Agency, 9830 Wilshire Blvd., Beverly Hills, CA 90212

ROSIE O'DONNELL

Birthplace: Commack, NY
Birthdate: 1962
Occupation: Actor, comedian
Education: Dickinson College and Boston University
Debut: (TV) *Gimme a Break,* 1986; (Film) *A League of Their Own,* 1992; (Stage) *Grease,* 1994
Signature: *The Rosie O'Donnell Show*
Facts: Won the *Star Search* comedy competition five times.

Fascinated with the blue-collar mundane, she began extensively collecting McDonald's Happy Meal figurines.

Against her agent's advice, she auditioned for—and won—the role of Betty Rizzo in the Broadway revival of *Grease* in 1994. She had no theater experience and says she'd never sung in public before.
Child: Parker Jaren (adopted)
Address: International Creative Management, 8942 Wilshire Blvd., Beverly Hills, CA 90211

ASHLEY OLSEN

Birthdate: 6/13/86
Occupation: Actor
Debut: (TV) *Full House,* 1987
Facts: Two minutes older than

fraternal twin sister Mary-Kate and has a freckle under her nose.

Their mother says, "When they need someone to be more active or emotional, they let Ashley do it."

How is she different from her twin? "My voice is deeper."

Famous Relative: Jamie Olsen, former dancer with the Los Angeles Ballet, mother

Address: Mary Kate & Ashley Fun Club, 13273 Ventura Blvd, Suite 208, Studio City, CA 91604

MARY-KATE OLSEN

Birthdate: 6/13/86

Occupation: Actor

Debut: (TV) *Full House,* 1987

Facts: Wants to be a candymaker or a cowgirl when she grows up.

Both twins earned income not only from the show but also through sale of the talking Michelle doll.

"Mary-Kate is more serious, so she gets the serious lines to do," says her mother.

Famous Relative: Jamie Olsen, former dancer with the Los Angeles Ballet, mother

Address: Mary Kate & Ashley Fun Club, 13273 Ventura Blvd, Suite 208, Studio City, CA 91604

SHAQUILLE O'NEAL

Birthplace: Newark, NJ

Birthdate: 3/6/72

Occupation: Basketball player

Education: Louisiana State University

Facts: His rap album, *Shaq Diesel,* sold more than one million copies. Got his rap start by singing on "What's Up Doc," a song put out in 1993 by his favorite rap group, FU-Schnickens.

He stands seven feet one inch, weighs 303 pounds, and wears size 21 triple-E shoes.

His first name translates, ironically, to "little one."

Spent most of his adolescence in Germany, where his stepfather was an army sergeant.

Major Awards: NBA Rookie of the Year, 1993; 4 Time NBA All-Star; Winner of NBA Scoring Title '95;Olympic Gold Medal 1996

Marriage: Arnetta (engaged)

Children: Tahaera

Address: L.A. Lakers, P.O. Box 10, Inglewood, CA 90306

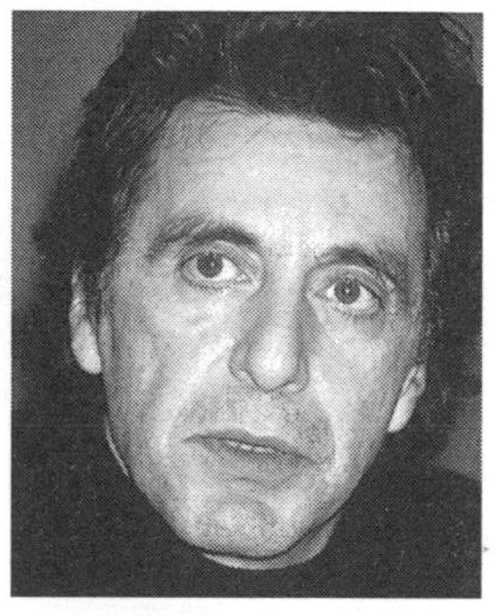

AL PACINO

Real Name: Alfredo James Pacino

Birthplace: New York, NY

Birthdate: 4/25/40

Occupation: Actor

Education: High School of the Performing Arts, Actor's Studio

Debut: (Stage) *The Peace Creeps,* 1966; (Film) *Me, Natalie,* 1969

Signature: *The Godfather*

Fact: Has been involved with actresses Jill Clayburgh, Marthe Keller, and Diane Keaton.

Original Job: Mail deliverer at *Commentary* magazine, messenger, movie theater usher, building superintendent

Relationship: Beverly D'Angelo

Child: Julie Marie

Major Awards: Tony, Best Supporting Actor (Dramatic), *Does a Tiger Wear a Necktie?,* 1969; Tony, Best Actor, *The Basic Training of Pavlo Hummel,* 1977; Golden Globe, Best Actor, *Serpico,* 1973; Golden Globe, Best Actor, *Scent of a Woman,* 1992; Oscar, Best Actor, *Scent of a Woman,* 1992

Address: Creative Artists Agency, 9830 Wilshire Blvd., Beverly Hills, CA 90212

GWYNETH PALTROW

Birthplace: Los Angeles, CA

Birthdate: 9/28/73

Occupation: Actor

Education: University of California, Santa Barbara

Debut: (Film) *Shout,* 1991

Signature: *Emma*

Facts: Nude pictures of her and former beau Brad Pitt that were taken with a telephoto lens while the couple vacationed in privacy in St. Bart's were circulated on the Internet and published in the tabloids. Pitt filed suit against the photographer. The couple split in 1997 after more than two years together.

Says a major goal for her life is to have babies.

Famous Relatives: Blythe Danner, actor, mother; Bruce Paltrow, producer, father; Jake Paltrow, actor, brother

Address: Creative Artists Agency, 9830 Wilshire Blvd., Beverly Hills, CA 90212

SARAH JESSICA PARKER

Birthplace: Nelsonville, OH

Birthdate: 3/25/65

Occupation: Actor

Education: American Ballet Theater, Professional Children's School in New York

Debut: (TV) *The Little Match Girl,* 1973; (Stage) *The Innocents,* 1976

Signature: *Honeymoon in Vegas*

Facts: Sang in Metropolitan Opera productions of *Hansel and Gretel, Cavalleria Rusticana, Pagliacci,* and *Parade.*

Starred as nerdy Patty Green on the CBS TV sitcom *Square Pegs,* 1982–83.

Played Annie in the Broadway musical, 1979–80.

Lived with Robert Downey Jr. for seven years.

Wears a size two.

Original Job: Dancer with Cincinnati

Ballet and the American Ballet Theatre
Marriage: Matthew Broderick
Address: Creative Artists Agency, 9830 Wilshire Blvd., Beverly Hills, CA 90212

DOLLY PARTON

Birthplace: Sevierville, TN
Birthdate: 1/19/46
Occupation: Singer, songwriter
Education: High school
Debut: (Song) "Puppy Love," 1956
Signature: "9 to 5"
Facts: Met her husband in the Wishy Washy laundromat.

Has her own theme park, Dollywood, located in Gatlinburg at the edge of the Smoky Mountains. In her hometown of Sevierville, Tennessee, there is a statue of her on the Sevier County Courthouse lawn.
Marriage: Carl Dean
Major Awards: Grammy, Best Country Vocal—Female, *Here You Come Again*, 1978; Grammy, Best Country Vocal—Female, "9 to 5," 1981; Grammy, Best Country Performance—Duo or Group, *Trio* (with Linda Rondstadt and Emmylou Harris), 1987
Quote: "Left to my own, I'd rather look like trash. I love tacky clothes. My look came from a very serious honest place, and that was a country girl's idea of what glamour was."
Address: International Creative Management, 8942 Wilshire Blvd., Beverly Hills, CA 90211

JANE PAULEY

Real Name: Margaret Jane Pauley
Birthplace: Indianapolis, IN
Birthdate: 10/31/50
Occupation: Broadcast journalist
Education: Indiana University
Debut: (TV) WISH-TV, Indiana, 1972
Signature: *Dateline NBC*
Facts: Succeeded Barbara Walters on the *Today* show two weeks shy of her 26th birthday in 1976; left 13 years later in a controversy over Deborah Norville's role that generated enormous sympathy for Pauley.

Limits her children's TV viewing to one hour a day.
Marriage: Garry Trudeau
Children: Ross, Rachel, Thomas
Address: International Creative Management, 8942 Wilshire Blvd., Beverly Hills, CA 90211

LUCIANO PAVAROTTI

Birthplace: Modena, Italy
Birthdate: 10/12/35
Occupation: Singer
Education: Istituto Magistrale Carlo Sigonio
Debut: (Stage) *La Bohème*, 1961
Facts: Established Opera Company of Philadelphia/ Luciano Pavarotti Vocal Company, 1980.

Makes at least $100,000 per concert. His fortune is estimated to be between $25 and $50 million.

Dreads the anticipation of singing more than singing itself. "The 10 minutes before the performance you wouldn't wish on your worst enemies."

Half a billion people saw the televised "Three Tenors" concert (with Placido Domingo and José Carreras) in 1990.

In 1990, the only musicians who sold more recordings than Pavarotti were Madonna and Elton John.
Infamy: He was sued by the BBC when it found out that a 1992 Pavarotti concert it had bought for broadcast had really been lip-synched.

An ongoing affair to his 26-year old secretary, Nicoletta Mantovani, led to his separation.
Original Job: Elementary school teacher, salesman
Marriage: Adua Veroni (separated); Nicoletta Mantovani (relationship)
Children: Lorenza, Cristina, Giuliana
Major Awards: Grammy, Best Classical Vocal Performance, *Luciano Pavarotti—Hits from London Center*, 1978; Grammy, Best Classical Vocal Performance, *O Sole Mio (Favorite Neapolitan Songs)*, 1979; Grammy, Best Classical Vocal Performance, *Live from Lincoln Center—Sutherland—Horne—Pavarotti* (with Joan Sutherland and Marilyn Horne), 1981; Grammy, Best Classical Vocal Performance, *Luciano Pavarotti in Concert*, 1988; Grammy, Best Classical Vocal Performance, *Carreras, Domingo, Pavarotti in Concert* (with José Carreras and Placido Domingo), 1990
Address: 941 Via Giardini, 41040 Saliceta S. Giuliano, Modena, Italy

BILL PAXTON

Birthplace: Ft. Worth, TX
Birthdate: 5/17/55
Occupation: Actor
Education: New York University
Debut: (Film) *Mortuary*, 1981
Signature: *Twister*
Facts: Spent much of his career making B-grade movies like *Pass the Ammo* and *Brain Dead*.

For his *Mortuary* character's wardrobe, Paxton bought second-hand sweaters, from which he caught scabies.

Directed *Fishheads*, a cult music video that aired on MTV in the early 1980s.

Has had several long bouts of depression that sometimes took months to shake.

Wife is 10 years younger than he is. They met when he followed her onto a bus.
Original Job: Set dresser
Marriage: First wife (divorced), Louise Newbury
Child: James
Address: Creative Artists Agency, 9830 Wilshire Blvd., Beverly Hills, CA 90212

SEAN PENN

Birthplace: Burbank, CA
Birthdate: 8/17/60
Occupation: Actor, director, writer
Education: High school
Debut: (Film) *Taps*, 1981

Signature: *Dead Man Walking*
Facts: His lavish house burned to the ground in the 1993 Malibu brushfires. Rather than rebuilding, he put a 27 1/ foot trailer on the land and moved in there.

Wears a tattoo saying "NOLA deliver me!," a reference to a frightening night spent in New Orleans (the NOLA) after drinking a glass of water spiked with seven hits of acid.

While growing up, his director father was blacklisted as a Communist, and had trouble getting work for years.
Infamy: Punched several photographers attempting to take his picture, and allegedly fired a gun at a hovering helicopter covering his first wedding. Spent 34 days in jail in 1987 for smacking a film extra while on probation for hitting someone who tried to kiss then wife Madonna.

Was so volatile during his marriage to Madonna she called a SWAT team to help her retrieve her possessions. Now says he "was drunk all the time" during their marriage.
Marriage: Madonna (divorced), Robin Wright
Children: Dylan, Hopper
Famous Relatives: Leo Penn, director, father; Eileen Ryan, actor, mother; Christopher Penn, actor, brother
Address: William Morris Agency, 151 El Camino Drive, Beverly Hills, CA 90212

MATTHEW PERRY

Birthplace: Williamstown, MA
Birthdate: 8/19/69
Occupation: Actor, writer
Education: High school
Debut: (Film) *A Night in the Life of Jimmy Reardon*, 1988
Signature: *Friends*
Facts: His father is best known for Old Spice commercials.

Moved to his mother's native Ottawa after his parents split when he was a year old. His journalist mother became press aide to Pierre Trudeau.

An avid tennis player, at 13 was ranked the No. 2 junior player in Ottawa.

Frustrated by the lack of good parts, he and a friend wrote a sitcom about six twentysomethings, which interested NBC. When the network ultimately decided to go with a similar sitcom, *Friends,* Perry decided since he couldn't beat 'em, he'd join 'em.
Infamy: Checked into rehab to overcome addiction to prescription painkillers.
Famous Relative: John Bennett Perry, actor, father
Address: William Morris Agency, 151 El Camino Drive, Beverly Hills, CA 90212

JOE PESCI

Birthplace: Newark, NJ
Birthdate: 2/9/43
Occupation: Actor
Education: High school dropout
Debut: (Radio) *Star Kids,* 1947; (Film) *Hey, Let's Twist!,* 1961
Signature: *My Cousin Vinny*
Facts: Played guitar for Joey Dee and The Starliters.

At age 5 appeared in Broadway musicals and Eddie Dowling plays. At age 10 became a regular on TV's *Star Time Kids* doing impersonations and singing.

Was managing a restaurant in the Bronx when called by Robert De Niro and Martin Scorsese to play Jake LaMotta's brother in *Raging Bull,* 1978.

He appears in some of his films under the psuedonym Joe Ritchie.
Original Job: Has worked as a nightclub singer, stand-up comedian, barber, postal worker, delivery boy, produce manager, answering service worker, and restaurant manager
Marriages: Two prior marriages, Martha Haro
Child: Tiffany
Major Award: Oscar, Best Supporting Actor, *GoodFellas,* 1990
Address: Creative Artists Agency, 9830 Wilshire Blvd., Beverly Hills, CA 90212

TOM PETTY

Birthplace: Gainesville, FL
Birthdate: 10/20/52
Occupation: Singer, songwriter, guitarist
Education: High school dropout
Debut: *Tom Petty and the Heartbreakers*, 1977
Signature: "Free Fallin'"
Facts: Toured for two years as Bob Dylan's backing band.

Recorded two albums with The Traveling Wilburys, comprised of George Harrison, Bob Dylan, Roy Orbison, Jeff Lynne, and Petty.
Marriage: Jane (divorced)
Children: Adria, Anna Kim
Address: Warner Brothers Records, 3300 Warner Blvd., Burbank, CA 91505

MICHELLE PFEIFFER

Birthplace: Santa Ana, CA
Birthdate: 4/29/57
Occupation: Actor
Education: Golden West College and Whitley College for Court Reporting
Debut: (TV) *Delta House,* 1979; (Film) *The Hollywood Knights,* 1980
Signature: *The Fabulous Baker Boys*
Facts: Had one line on TV show *Fantasy Island.*

Got her first break by winning the Miss Orange County Beauty Pageant.

In 1993, she decided to be a single mother and adopted a baby girl, who was given the last name Kelley after Pfeiffer married.

Had the leading role in *Grease 2,* 1982.
Original Job: Supermarket cashier, court reporter, model
Marriages: Peter Horton (divorced), David E. Kelley

Children: Claudia Rose (adopted), John Henry
Famous Relatives: DeDee Pfeiffer, actor, sister
Major Award: Golden Globe, Best Actress, *The Fabulous Baker Boys,* 1989
Address: International Creative Management, 8942 Wilshire Blvd., Beverly Hills, CA 90211

REGIS PHILBIN

Birthplace: New York, NY
Birthdate: 8/25/33
Occupation: Talk show host
Education: University of Notre Dame
Debut: (TV) KOGO news anchor, San Diego, 1960
Signature: *Live With Regis and Kathie Lee*
Facts: Named after Regis High, a Manhattan Catholic boys' school and his father's alma mater.

Son Dan was born with two malformed legs, which were later amputated.

Between 1970 and 1990, hosted nearly a dozen talk and game shows and went through a series of co-hosts before clicking with Kathie Lee.
Marriage: Catherine Faylan (divorced); Joy Senese
Children: Amy, Dan, Joanna, Jennifer
Address: c/o ABC, 77 W. 66th Street, New York, NY 10023

DAVID HYDE PIERCE

Birthplace: Saratoga Springs, NY
Birthdate: 4/3/59
Occupation: Actor
Education: Yale University
Debut: (Stage) *Beyond Therapy,* 1982; (Film) *The Terminator,* 1984; (TV) *Powers That Be,* 1991
Signature: *Frasier*
Facts: Realized he had a strong resemblance to his TV brother Frasier (Kelsey Grammer) after being mistaken for Grammer many times before he even accepted the role. In the original storyline for *Frasier,* Pierce's character (Niles) didn't exist but was added after producers, who saw Pierce in *The Powers That Be,* noticed the resemblance.
Original Job: Clothing salesman, church organist
Major Award: Emmy, Best Supporting Actor in a Comedy Series, *Frasier,* 1995
Address: Paramount Television Productions, 5555 Melrose Ave., Los Angeles, CA 90038

JADA PINKETT

Birthplace: Baltimore, MD
Birthdate: 8/18/71
Occupation: Actor
Education: Attended North Carolina School for the Arts
Debut: (TV) *A Different World,* 1991; (Film) *Menace II Society,* 1993
Signature: *The Nutty Professor*
Facts: Her parents divorced around the time of her birth. She was raised in a rough Baltimore neighborhood by her mother and grandmother.

In addition to acting, has directed rap music videos, performed poetry readings, appeared at inner-city schools as a motivational speaker, and started a mail-order clothing line of T-shirts and dresses bearing feminist slogans.

Five feet tall and just 100 pounds, she often buys her clothes from stores' children's departments.
Infamy: Reportedly gave $100,000 bail to rapper/actor friend Tupac Shakur to gain his release from jail while awaiting an appeal on a sexual abuse conviction.
Relationship: Will Smith
Address: United Talent Agency, 9560 Wilshire Blvd., Suite 500, Beverly Hills, CA 90212

BRAD PITT

Real Name: William Bradley Pitt
Birthplace: Shawnee, OK
Birthdate: 12/18/64
Occupation: Actor
Education: University of Missouri at Columbia, studied acting with Roy London
Debut: (TV) *Dallas*; (Film) *Cutting Class,* 1989
Signature: *Legends of the Fall*
Facts: Got his big break when he was seen in a sexy Levi's TV ad in 1989. Was cast as the hitchhiker in the 1991 movie *Thelma and Louise* only after William Baldwin turned down the role, choosing to star in *Backdraft* instead.

Dated Robin Givens for six months when they both acted in the TV series *Head of the Class.* Also lived with Juliette Lewis for several years; was engaged to Gwyneth Paltrow.

While at college, posed shirtless for a campus fundraising calendar.
Original Job: Chauffeur for Strip-O-Gram women, dressed up as the El Pollo Loco restaurant chicken
Major Award: Golden Globe, Best Supporting Actor, *12 Monkeys,* 1995
Quote: "Being a sex symbol all the time hampers my work."
Address: Creative Artists Agency, 9830 Wilshire Blvd., Beverly Hills, CA 90212

LISA MARIE PRESLEY

Birthplace: Memphis,TN
Birthdate: 2/1/68
Facts: Daughter of Elvis and Priscilla Presley

Will likely inherit $150 million on her 30th birthday.

When Lisa Marie once said she had never seen snow, Elvis flew her to Utah. She also received a tiny mink coat from her father and $100 bills from the Tooth Fairy.

Is a devoted follower of the Church of Scientology.
Marriages: Danny Keough (divorced), Michael Jackson (divorced)
Children: Danielle, Benjamin
Address: William Morris Agency, 151 El Camino Dr., Beverly Hills, CA 90212

DENNIS QUAID

Birthplace: Houston, TX
Birthdate: 4/9/54
Occupation: Actor
Education: University of Houston
Debut: (Film) *September 30, 1955,* 1978
Signature: *The Big Easy*
Fact: Wrote songs for three of his films: *The Night the Lights Went Out in Georgia* in 1981, *Tough Enough* in 1983, and *The Big Easy* in 1987.

Shed 47 pounds over a three-month period before playing the scrawny Doc Holliday in 1994's *Wyatt Earp.*
Infamy: Admitted to having a cocaine addiction, a problem he overcame with help from then girlfriend Meg Ryan.
Marriages: Pamela Jayne Soles (divorced), Meg Ryan
Child: Jack Henry
Famous Relative: Randy Quaid, actor, brother
Address: International Creative Management, 8942 Wilshire Blvd., Beverly Hills, CA 90211

BONNIE RAITT

Birthplace: Burbank, CA
Birthdate: 9/8/49
Occupation: Singer, songwriter
Education: Radcliffe College
Debut: (Album) *Bonnie Raitt,* 1971
Signature: "Something To Talk About"
Facts: Grew up in a Quaker family in L.A.

Got her first guitar for Christmas when she was eight.

Founded the annual Rhythm & Blues Awards, to provide money to deserving R&B stars who may have been cheated in the early days by managers and/or record labels.
Infamy: Was an avid drinker until giving up all alcohol and drugs a decade ago.
Marriage: Michael O'Keefe
Child: One son
Famous Relative: John Raitt, actor, father
Major Awards: Grammies, Album of the Year, Best Rock Vocal—Female, and Best Pop Vocal—Female, "Nick of Time," 1989; Grammy, Best Pop Vocal—Female, "Something To Talk About," 1991; Grammy, Best Rock Vocal—Female, "Luck of the Draw," 1991; Grammy, Best Rock Duo with Vocal, "Good Man, Good Woman" (with Delbert McClinton), 1991; Grammy, Best Pop Album, *Longing in Their Hearts,* 1994
Address: P.O. Box 626, Los Angeles, CA 90078

DAN RATHER

Birthplace: Wharton, TX
Birthdate: 10/31/31
Occupation: Anchor, correspondent, editor
Education: Sam Houston State College
Debut: (TV) KHOU-TV, Houston, 1960
Signature: *CBS Evening News with Dan Rather*
Facts: Succeeded Walter Cronkite in anchoring the evening news upon Cronkite's retirement in 1981.

In his 1994 book, *The Camera Never Blinks Twice,* he devotes less than a page to his former co-anchor Connie Chung.

Was attacked on the street by two men who called him "Kenneth" and repeatedly demanded "What's the frequency?" R.E.M. used the cryptic phrase as a song title and later performed the tune with Rather on *Late Show with David Letterman.*
Infamy: Angry over a delay in the start of the news, he walked off the set, leaving TV screens blank for six minutes. He also had a stormy pre-election interview with then vice-president George Bush in 1988.
Marriage: Jean
Children: Robin, Danjack
Major Awards: Emmy, Correspondent, Coverage of the Watergate Affair, 1973; Emmy, Correspondent, Shooting of Governor Wallace, 1973; Emmy, Correspondent, Agnew Resignation, 1974; Emmy, Correspondent, Watergate, the White House Transcripts, 1974; Emmy, Documentary Correspondent, The Senate and the Watergate Affair, 1974; Emmy, Correspondent, "The Computers Are Coming," 1983; Emmy, Correspondent, Afghanistan, 1984; Emmy, Correspondent, Geneva Summit: Mexican Earthquake, 1985; Emmy, "The Battle for Afghanistan," 1987; Emmy, Correspondent, "Inside Afghanistan," 1987
Address: CBS, 51 West 52nd St., New York, NY 10019

ROBERT REDFORD

Real Name: Charles Robert Redford Jr.
Birthplace: Santa Monica, CA
Birthdate: 8/18/37
Occupation: Actor, director, producer
Education: University of Colorado, Pratt Institute of Design, the American Academy of Dramatic Arts
Debut: (Stage) *Tall Story,* 1959; (Film) *War Hunt,* 1962
Signature: *Butch Cassidy and the Sundance Kid*
Facts: Went to college on a baseball scholarship but lost it due to alcohol abuse. Left school in 1957 to go to Europe; lived in Paris and Florence as a painter.

Founded the nonprofit Sundance Institute in Park City, UT, which sponsors an annual film festival and provides support for independent film production.
Infamy: As a teenager, Redford stole and resold hubcaps.
Original Job: Carpenter, shop assistant, oil field worker
Marriage: Lola Van Wagenen (divorced), Kathy O'Rear (relationship)
Children: Shauna, Amy Hart, David James
Major Awards: Oscar, Best Director, *Ordinary People,* 1980; Golden Globe, New Male Film Star, *Inside Daisy Clover,* 1965; Golden Globe, Male World Film Favorite, 1975, 1977, 1978; Golden Globe, Best Director, *Ordinary People,* 1980;

Golden Globe, Cecil B. DeMille Lifetime Achievement Award, 1994
Address: Creative Artists Agency, 9830 Wilshire Blvd., Beverly Hills, CA 90212

CHRISTOPHER REEVE

Birthplace: New York, NY
Birthdate: 9/25/52
Occupation: Actor
Education: Cornell University, Juilliard graduate program
Debut: (Film) *Gray Lady Down*, 1977
Signature: *Superman*
Facts: While studying at Juilliard under John Houseman, shared an apartment with then-unknown Robin Williams.

Turned down a lucrative offer to do cigarette commericals in Japan in 1990.

Says the accident that fractured his first and second vertebrae happened on an easy jump, when his Thoroughbred Eastern Express suddenly halted and his hands became entangled in the bridle so he couldn't break his fall.

Completely paralyzed, though with some sensation in his left leg, he gets around by motorized wheelchair, which he directs by puffing air through a tube.
Marriage: Dana Morosini
Children: Matthew, Alexandra (both with Gae Exton), Will
Address: William Morris Agency, 151 El Camino Drive, Beverly Hills, CA 90212

KEANU REEVES

Birthplace: Beirut, Lebanon
Birthdate: 9/4/64
Occupation: Actor
Education: High school dropout; studied with Jasper Deeter
Debut: (Film) *Youngblood,* 1986
Signature: *Speed*
Facts: His father is Chinese-Hawaiian and his mother is English.

Hasn't seen his father, who is currently serving a ten-year prison term in Hawaii for cocaine possession, since he was 13.

His first name means "cool breeze over the mountains" in Hawaiian.

Had traveled around the world by the time he was 2 years old.

Was the MVP on his high school hockey team in Toronto. A skilled goalie, Reeves earned the name "The Wall."

Turned down the Al Pacino/Robert De Niro film *Heat* to play Hamlet on stage in Winnipeg, Canada. The February 1995 sold-out run was critically acclaimed.

He plays bass in the band Dogstar.

His mother was a costume designer for rock stars.
Address: Creative Artists Agency, 9830 Wilshire Blvd., Beverly Hills, CA 90212

PAUL REISER

Birthplace: New York, NY
Birthdate: 3/30/57
Occupation: Actor, comedian
Education: SUNY-Binghamton
Debut: (Film) *Diner,* 1982
Signature: *Mad About You*
Facts: Has appeared in several hit films, including *Beverly Hills Cop* (1984), *Aliens* (1986), and *Beverly Hills Cop II* (1987).

Dubbed by reporters as part of the Four Funniest Men in the World Club, which includes Jerry Seinfeld, Larry Miller, and Mark Schiff. The members meet every New Year's Day for lunch (once they even met in London when Reiser was there filming *Aliens*).
Original Job: Health food distributor
Marriage: Paula
Child: Ezra Samuel
Address: United Talent Agency, 9560 Wilshire Blvd., Suite 500, Beverly Hills, CA 90212

TRENT REZNOR

Birthplace: Mercer, PA
Birthdate: 5/17/65
Occupation: Singer, keyboardist
Education: Allegheny College
Debut: (Album) *Pretty Hate Machine*, 1989
Signature: Nine Inch Nails
Facts: Reznor makes all Nine Inch Nails albums himself, using a band only for live shows.

In 1990, misplaced video footage of a half-naked Reznor being thrown from a building landed in the hands of the FBI, who thought it was an actual murder. They led an investigation and found Reznor, alive and well and on tour. The publicity helped put Nine Inch Nails in the spotlight.

Mixed the soundtrack LP for Oliver Stone's film *Natural Born Killers* in 1994.

Lived for a year in the Benedict Canyon, CA, house where Sharon Tate and others were murdered by Charles Manson followers.

In what he says was possibly an unconscious attempt to identify with Woodstock '94 fans, he tripped his guitar player on the way to the stage, who fell flat in the mud and started the whole band in a mud match. They performed covered in the stuff.
Original Job: Odd jobs—including cleaning toilets—at a recording studio
Major Awards: Grammy, Best Metal Performance, "Wish," 1992
Address: Nothing Records, 2337 West 11th St., Suite 7, Cleveland, OH 44113

ANNE RICE

Real Name: Howard Allen O'Brien
Birthdate: 10/4/41
Occupation: Writer
Education: North Texas State University, San Francisco State College
Debut: (Book) *Interview with a Vampire,* 1976
Facts: Is the author of a series of pornographic novels under the name A. N. Roquelaure (which means "cloak").

Is afraid of the dark.

Was originally named after her father and mother's maiden name; changed name to Anne by the time she was in first grade.

In 1972, her six-year-old daughter died of leukemia.

Original Job: Waitress, cook, insurance claims adjuster
Marriage: Stan Rice
Children: Michele (deceased), Christopher
Address: Alfred A. Knopf, 201 East 50th St., New York, NY 10022

MICHAEL RICHARDS

Birthplace: Culver City, CA
Birthdate: 7/21/48
Occupation: Actor
Education: Los Angeles Valley College, California Insitute of the Arts
Debut: (TV) *Fridays,* 1980
Signature: *Seinfeld*
Facts: Has appeared in guest spots on *Hill Street Blues* and *Miami Vice.*

Starred with Weird Al Yankovic in the film *UHF,* 1989.

He was drafted at the height of the Vietnam War in 1970: "When the drill sergeant yelled at me on the first day, I tried to explain the duffel bag was too heavy."

Original Job: Postal worker, schoolbus driver
Marriages: Cathleen (divorced), Ann Talman (relationship)
Child: Sophia
Major Award: Emmy, Best Supporting Actor in a Comedy Series, *Seinfeld,* 1992, 1993, 1997
Address: International Creative Management, 8942 Wilshire Blvd., Beverly Hills, CA 90211

NATASHA RICHARDSON

Birthplace: London, England
Birthdate: 5/11/63
Occupation: Actor
Education: Central School for Speech and Drama
Debut: (Stage) *On the Razzle,* 1983
Signature: *The Handmaid's Tale*
Facts: At age 4, appeared as a bridesmaid of Vanessa Redgrave in *The Charge of the Light Brigade.*

Was named after the heroine in Tolstoy's *War and Peace.*

Marriages: Robert Fox (divorced), Liam Neeson
Children: Micheál, Daniel Jack N.
Famous Relatives: Vanessa Redgrave, actor, mother; Tony Richardson, director, father; Joely Richardson, actor, sister; Lynn Redgrave, actor, aunt
Quote: "I've spent half my life trying to get away from being Vanessa Redgrave's daughter, and now I've got to get away from being Liam Neeson's wife."
Address: International Creative Management, 8942 Wilshire Blvd., Beverly Hills, CA 90211

LEANN RIMES

Birthplace: Flowood, MS
Birthdate: 8/28/82
Occupation: Singer
Debut: (Album) *Blue,* 1996
Signature: *Blue*
Facts: Was singing songs like "Jesus Loves Me"—on pitch—at 18 months. Appeared on *Star Search* at age 8 and signed a major record deal at 11.

"Blue" was actually written for Patsy Cline in 1963 but was never recorded because she died that year. When songwriter Bill Mack heard Rimes sing the "Star-Spangled Banner" at a Texas Rangers game he was so impressed he sent her the tune.

Major Awards: Grammy, Best New Artist, 1996; Grammy, Best Country Vocal—Female, "Blue," 1996
Address: Curb Records, 47 Music Square E., Nashville, TN 37203

GERALDO RIVERA

Birthplace: New York, NY
Birthdate: 7/4/43
Occupation: Broadcast journalist, talk show host
Education: University of Arizona; J.D., Brooklyn School of Law; Columbia Journalism School post-graduate
Debut: (TV) *Eyewitness News,* WABC-TV, New York, 1968
Signature: *Geraldo!*
Facts: In the late '60s was involved with a Latino activist group, the Young Lords. Appeared so many times on the evening news the station eventually hired him as a temporary reporter—a good way to satisfy federal minority hiring quotas.

Was fired from ABC-TV in 1985 when the network tired of his sensationalist style and arrogance. At the time, was making $800,000 a year.

In the late '80s, promised a junior high school class he would pay for their college education. Five years later paid $180,000 for nine of the graduates' schooling.

In 1993, opened the Broadcast Boxing Club fitness center in New York.

Infamy: Arrested several times at demonstrations, as well as at a TV filming of a rally, when he got into a scuffle with a Ku Klux Klansman.

Accused of leading talk shows into the gutter. Once even had his nose broken during a brawl on his show.

Original Job: Attorney
Marriage: Linda (divorced), Edith Bucket Vonnegut (divorced), Sherryl Raymond (divorced), C. C. Dyer
Children: Gabriel, Isabella, Simone, Cruz
Major Awards: 3 national and 4 local Emmy Awards

Address: William Morris Agency, 1350 Avenue of the Americas, New York, NY 10019

JOAN RIVERS

Real Name: Joan Alexandra Molinsky
Birthplace: Brooklyn, NY
Birthdate: 6/8/37
Occupation: Talk show host
Education: Connecticut College for Women, Barnard College
Debut: (TV) *The Tonight Show,* 1965
Facts: Wrote for *Candid Camera* and *The Ed Sullivan Show.*
Original Job: Publicist at Lord & Taylor, fashion coordinator for Bond Clothing Stores, temporary office secretary, syndicated columnist
Marriage: Edgar Rosenberg (deceased), Orin Lehman (relationship)
Child: Melissa
Major Awards: Clio Award, 1976, 1982; Emmy, Best Host of a Talk Show, *The Joan Rivers Show,* 1990
Address: William Morris Agency, 151 El Camino Dr., Beverly Hills, CA 90212

TIM ROBBINS

Birthplace: West Covina, CA
Birthdate: 10/16/58
Occupation: Writer, director, actor
Education: New York University, SUNY-Plattsburgh, and UCLA
Debut: (Film) *No Small Affair,* 1984
Signature: *The Player*
Facts: Was kicked off the hockey team in high school for fighting.

Founded Los Angeles theater group Actors' Gang.

Has been an outspoken political activist and peace advocate.
Original Job: Factory worker
Relationship: Susan Sarandon
Children: Jack Henry, Miles
Major Awards: Golden Globe, Best Actor in a Comedy, *The Player,* 1992; Golden Globe, Special Achievement, *Short Cuts,* 1993
Address: International Creative Management, 8942 Wilshire Blvd., Beverly Hills, CA 90211

JULIA ROBERTS

Real Name: Julie Fiona Roberts
Birthplace: Smyrna, GA
Birthdate: 10/28/67
Occupation: Actor
Education: High school
Debut: (TV) *Crime Story,* 1986
Signature: *Pretty Woman*
Facts: Originally wanted to be a veterinarian.

In 1986, she played opposite her brother (actor Eric Roberts) in the film *Blood Red.*

Was set to marry Kiefer Sutherland in 1991, but canceled the wedding at the last minute with virtually no explanation.
Original Job: Worked in a shoe store and an ice cream shop
Marriage: Lyle Lovett (divorced); Ross Partridge (relationship)
Famous Relatives: Eric Roberts, actor, brother; Lisa Roberts, actor, sister
Major Awards: Golden Globe, Best Supporting Actress, *Steel Magnolias,* 1989; Golden Globe, Best Actress in a Comedy, *Pretty Woman,* 1990
Address: International Creative Management, 8942 Wilshire Blvd., Beverly Hills, CA 90211

CHRIS ROCK

Birthplace: Brooklyn, NY
Birthdate: 2/7/66
Occupation: Actor, comedian
Education: High school dropout (later got his GED)
Debut: (Film) *Beverly Hills Cop II,* 1987; (TV) *Saturday Night Live,* 1990
Signature: *The Chris Rock Show*
Facts: Grew up in Bedford-Stuyvesant but was bused to an all-white grade school in Bensonhurst, where he was often the victim of racial violence and discrimination.

Discovered by Eddie Murphy at age 18 during open-mike night at a New York comedy club.

Created the voice of the Little Penny puppet on the Penny Hardaway Nike ads.
Marriage: Malaak Compton
Major Award: Emmy, Best Writing in a Variety or Music Program, *Chris Rock: Bring the Pain,* 1997
Address: HBO, 1100 6th Avenue, New York, NY 10036

DENNIS RODMAN

Birthplace: Trenton, NJ
Birthdate: 5/13/61
Occupation: Basketball player
Education: Southeastern Oklahoma University
Debut: Detroit Pistons, 1986
Facts: At 5' 9", was too small to make his high school basketball team. Only after graduating did he grow almost another foot, to 6' 8".

Before college, worked as a janitor at Dallas–Fort Worth Airport, and was arrested for stealing watches from an airport boutique.

Sports more than 10 tattoos plus numerous body piercings, including one in his scrotum, though he had to have the silver ring removed when it got infected.

Was $1 million in debt in 1995, despite a $2.5 million salary, due to spending sprees and Las Vegas junkets.
Infamy: Has been known to dress in drag and hang out in gay bars.

Excessively defiant on the basketball court, was fined $20,000 for head-butting a referee. Suspended in

1997 for kicking a TV cameraman, to whom he forked over $200,000.
Marriages: Annie Bakes (divorced), Stacy Yarbrough (relationship)
Child: Alexis
Major Awards: Defensive Player of the Year Award, 1990, 1991; NBA Rebounding leader 1992, 1993, 1994, 1995
Address: International Creative Management, 8942 Wilshire Blvd., Beverly Hills, CA 90211

ROSEANNE

Birthplace: Salt Lake City, UT
Birthdate: 11/3/53
Occupation: Actor
Education: High school dropout
Debut: (TV) *Funny,* 1983; (Film) *She-Devil,* 1989
Signature: *Roseanne*
Facts: Dropped out of high school to hitchhike cross country, landing in a Colorado artists' colony at age 18.

Had cosmetic surgery and weight reduction in 1993. Breasts were reduced from 40DD to 38C.

Had a tattoo on her upper right thigh that read: "Property of Tom Arnold." When the pair split, she tattooed over it with a flying fairy and flowers.

Claims she was physically and sexually abused as a child. Suppressed memory of the abuse until an adult.

Gave up baby girl for adoption at age 18.

Born to Jewish parents but raised as a Mormon in Salt Lake City. Her dad sold crucifixes door to door.
Infamy: Grabbed her crotch, spat, and screeched while singing the national anthem at a San Diego baseball game in 1990.
Original Job: Window dresser, cocktail waitress
Marriages: Bill Petland (divorced), Tom Arnold (divorced), Ben Thomas
Children: Brandi, Jessica, Jennifer, Jake, Buck
Major Awards: Golden Globe, Best Actress in a Comedy Series, *Roseanne,* 1993; Emmy, Best Actress in a Comedy Series, *Roseanne,* 1993
Address: William Morris Agency, 151 El Camino Dr., Beverly Hills, CA 90212

GAVIN ROSSDALE

Birthplace: London, England
Birthdate: 10/30/67
Occupation: Singer, songwriter, guitarist
Education: High school
Debut: (Album) *Sixteen Stone,* 1994
Signature: Bush
Facts: His parents divorced when he was eleven. He lived with his physician father in the well-heeled North London Kilburn district, attending the posh Westminster high school. After graduating, became a regular party animal at London's clubs.

As a teen, played semi-pro soccer in London and even tried out for a top pro team, Chelsea.

His former band, the pop-oriented Midnight, had a record deal in the mid-1980s but produced no hits.

Originally signed by Disney's Hollywood Records, but exec Frank G. Wells, a major fan, was killed in a helicopter crash just as *Sixteen Stone* was completed. Other execs deemed the album unacceptable, so it went into limbo until being rescued by Interscope.
Original Job: Music video production assistant
Relationship: Gwen Stefani
Address: Trauma/Interscope, 10900 Wilshire Blvd., Suite 1000, Los Angeles, CA 90024

DARIUS RUCKER

Birthplace: Charleston, SC
Birthdate: 5/13/66
Occupation: Singer, songwriter, guitarist
Education: University of South Carolina
Debut: (Album) *Cracked Rear View,* 1994
Signature: Hootie & The Blowfish
Facts: Formed the Wolf Brothers to play cover tunes during college, with guitarist and fellow broadcast-journalism major Mark Bryan.

The band's name doesn't refer to Rucker and his group, but rather to the nicknames of two friends.

Before signing with a major label, sold 50,000 copies of an EP—an unprecedented number for an unsigned band.

A huge Miami Dolphins fan, has their emblem tattooed on his body.
Child: Carolyn
Major Awards: Grammy, Best New Artist, Hootie &The Blowfish, 1995; Grammy, Best Pop Group Performance, "Let Her Cry," 1995
Quote: "You know why I don't get tired of being called nice? Because we are."
Address: Atlantic Records, 75 Rockefeller Plaza, New York, NY 10019

GEOFFREY RUSH

Birthplace: Toowoomba, Australia
Birthdate: 7/6/51
Occupation: Actor
Education: University of Queensland, attended Paris's Lacques Lecoq School of Mime, Movement and Theater
Debut: (Stage) *You're a Good Man, Charlie Brown,* 1971; (Film) *Star Struck,* 1982
Signature: *Shine*
Facts: TV didn't arrive in his Australian city until 1959, but vaudeville flourished, so Rush grew up watching mostly live theater.

He and then struggling actor Mel Gibson shared a house in Sydney in 1979 while the pair appeared in a local production of *Waiting for Godot.* Too poor for furniture, they slept on the floor.

Is considered one of Australia's most prolific and accomplished classic stage performers.

In the early '90s he suffered a breakdown due to exhaustion and anxiety; it left him unable to work for two months.

Shine's producers originally had

trouble getting financing for the film because the money people wanted a "name" actor in the lead.
Marriage: Jane Menelaus
Children: Angelica, James
Major Awards: Golden Globe, Best Actor, *Shine,* 1996; Oscar, Best Actor, *Shine,* 1996
Address: Creative Artists Agency, 9830 Wilshire Blvd., Los Angeles, CA 90212

KURT RUSSELL

Birthplace: Springfield, MA
Birthdate: 3/17/51
Occupation: Actor, screenwriter, producer
Education: High school
Debut: (Film) *The Absent-Minded Professor,* 1960
Signature: *Stargate*
Facts: At 12, starred in his own Western series, *The Travels of Jaimie McPheeters,* featuring Charles Bronson and the very young Osmond brothers.

Left acting in 1971 to play minor league baseball. Returned to acting two years later after tearing a shoulder muscle.

His actor father played the sheriff for 14 years on *Bonanza.*
Marriages: Season Hubley (divorced), Goldie Hawn (relationship)
Children: Boston, Wyatt
Famous Relatives: Bing Russell, actor, father
Address: Creative Artists Agency, 9830 Wilshire Blvd., Beverly Hills, CA 90212

RENE RUSSO

Birthplace: Burbank, CA
Birthdate: 2/17/54
Occupation: Actor
Education: High school dropout
Debut: (Film) *Major League,* 1989
Signature: *Lethal Weapon 3*
Facts: Considered herself unattractive as a teen because she wore a body cast to correct a curved spine from ages 10 to 14. Shy and uninterested in school (where high school classmates included Ron Howard), she dropped out in 10th grade and worked in an eyeglass factory.

Was discovered by a modeling agent in the parking lot following a Rolling Stones concert. A few weeks later, she was in New York shooting a Revlon ad with Richard Avedon.

At age 30, depressed by being too old to model, she discovered Christian theology, which she spent the next three years studying. Religion gave her the confidence to try an acting career.

Met her future husband on the set of *Freejack,* a film for which she had originally turned down an acting role and for which Gilroy had originally rejected the job of script rewriting.
Original Job: Supermodel
Marriage: Danny Gilroy (divorced)
Child: Rose
Address: Progressive Artists Agency, 400 S. Beverly Drive, Suite 216, Beverly Hills, CA 90212

MEG RYAN

Real Name: Margaret Hyra
Birthplace: Fairfield, CT
Birthdate: 11/19/61
Occupation: Actor
Education: New York University
Debut: (Film) *Rich and Famous,* 1981; (TV) *As the World Turns, 1983*
Signature: *When Harry Met Sally . . .*
Fact: Became high school homecoming queen when the original queen was suspended.

Her strained relationship with her mother became tabloid-show fodder when her stepfather wrote an article about the pair's discord in a magazine in 1992. Ryan subsequently ended all contact with them.

Met husband Quaid on the set of the comedy film, *Innerspace,* in 1987. A year later, they professionally reunited for the unsuccessful film *D.O.A.*
Marriage: Dennis Quaid
Child: Jack Henry
Address: International Creative Management, 8942 Wilshire Blvd., Beverly Hills, CA 90211

WINONA RYDER

Real Name: Winona Laura Horowitz
Birthplace: Winona, MN
Birthdate: 10/29/71
Occupation: Actor
Education: High school
Debut: (Film) *Lucas,* 1986
Signature: *Beetlejuice*
Facts: Her childhood home in Elk, CA, had no electricity.

In junior high school, was attacked and beaten by fellow students during her first week at a new school, apparently because they mistook her for a boy.

Has read *The Catcher in the Rye* countless times, and travels with a copy.

Dated Christian Slater, was engaged to Johnny Depp.

Timothy Leary, the famous psychologist and countercultural philosopher, was her godfather.
Major Award: Golden Globe, Best Supporting Actress, *The Age of Innocence,* 1993
Address: William Morris Agency, 151 El Camino Dr., Beverly Hills, CA 90212

ADAM SANDLER

Birthplace: Brooklyn, NY
Birthdate: 9/9/66
Occupation: Comedian, actor
Education: New York University
Debut: (TV) *The Cosby Show,* 1987; (Film) *Shakes the Clown,* 1992
Signature: *Saturday Night Live*
Facts: Became a writer for *Saturday Night Live* in 1990, but his sketches were often too eccentric for others to make their own. He soon became a "featured player" doing those skits and, after the success of his Opera Man, became a regular cast member.

As a developing comic, was so taken by Rodney Dangerfield he memorized many of Dangerfield's routines.
Original Job: Stand-up comedian
Relationship: Margaret Ruden (engaged)
Address: c/o Brillstein-Grey, 9150 Wilshire Blvd., Suite 350, Beverly Hills, CA 90212

SUSAN SARANDON

Real Name: Susan Abigail Tomalin
Birthplace: New York, NY
Birthdate: 10/4/46
Occupation: Actor
Education: Catholic University of America
Debut: (Film) *Joe,* 1970
Signature: *Thelma and Louise*
Facts: Her background is Welsh-Italian. Was one of nine children, and attended Catholic school.

Is 12 years older than beau Tim Robbins.

An activist for numerous political, cultural, and health causes, she digressed during her 1991 Academy Awards presentation to speak for a half-minute on behalf of Haitian refugees with AIDS.

Starred in cult classic *The Rocky Horror Picture Show.*
Original Job: While in college, worked in the drama department, modeled, and cleaned apartments
Marriages: Chris Sarandon (divorced), Tim Robbins (relationship)
Children: Eva Maria Livia, Jack Henry, Miles
Major Awards: Oscar, Best Actress, *Dead Man Walking,* 1995
Address: International Creative Management, 8942 Wilshire Blvd., Beverly Hills, CA 90211

DIANE SAWYER

Birthplace: Glasgow, KY
Birthdate: 12/22/45
Occupation: Broadcast journalist
Education: Wellesley College
Debut: (TV) WLKY-TV, Louisville, 1967
Signature: *Primetime Live*
Facts: Was national Junior Miss, largely on the strength of her interview and essays.

As a weathercaster in Louisville, KY, she spruced up forecasts with quotes from her favorite poems.

Served as staff assistant to former President Nixon and helped him research his memoirs.
Marriage: Mike Nichols
Major Awards: Emmy, "PanAm Flight 103," 1990; Emmy, "Murder in Beverly Hills," 1991
Address: ABC, 77 West 66th St., New York, NY 10023

CLAUDIA SCHIFFER

Birthplace: Dusseldorf, Germany
Birthdate: 8/24/71
Occupation: Supermodel
Education: High school
Facts: Tripped during her runway modeling debut in 1990.

Earns as much as $50,000 a day.

Opened Fashion Cafe in New York City in 1995 with fellow supermodels Elle MacPherson and Naomi Campbell.
Relationship: David Copperfield (engaged)
Address: 5 Union Sq., #500, New York, NY 10003

ARNOLD SCHWARZENEGGER

Birthplace: Graz, Austria
Birthdate: 7/30/47
Occupation: Actor, director, bodybuilder
Education: University of Wisconsin
Debut: (Film) *Hercules in New York,* 1969
Signature: *The Terminator*
Facts: After coming to the U.S. in the '60s, founded a bricklaying business, Pumping Bricks, to finance his bodybuilding career.

Won the Austrian Junior Olympic weightlifting championship as well as Junior Mr. Europe and several curling titles.

In 1974, acted in *Happy Anniversary and Goodbye,* an unsold CBS sitcom pilot starring Lucille Ball and Art Carney.

Has killed over 275 people on screen.
Infamy: Named in a 1995 paternity suit by a Texas woman who claims he fathered her daughter 12 years earlier.
Original Job: Managed a Munich health club
Marriage: Maria Owings Shriver
Children: Katherine Eunice, Christina Maria Aurelia, Patrick
Major Award: Golden Globe, Best Newcomer in Films, *Stay Hungry,* 1976
Quote: "Everything I have ever done in my life has always stayed. I've just added to it...But I will not change. Because when you are successful and you change, you are an idiot."
Address: International Creative Management, 8942 Wilshire Blvd., Beverly Hills, CA 90211

DAVID SCHWIMMER

Birthplace: Queens, NY
Birthdate: 11/12/66
Occupation: Actor
Education: Northwestern University
Debut: (TV movie) *A Deadly Silence,* 1989; (Film) *Crossing the Bridge,* 1992
Signature: *Friends*
Facts: His mother is the attorney who handled Roseanne's first divorce. Since his father is also an attorney, he flirted with becoming one before settling on acting.

Appeared in the 1994 Henry Winkler flop, *Monty.*

Started Chicago's Lookingglass Theater Company in 1988 with seven other Northwestern graduates.
Address: NBC, 3000 W. Alameida Ave., Burbank, CA 91523

MARTIN SCORSESE

Birthplace: New York, NY
Birthdate: 11/17/42
Occupation: Director
Education: New York University
Debut: (Film) *Boxcar Bertha,* 1972
Signature: *Taxi Driver*
Facts: Collaborated on the production of Michael Jackson's *Bad* video in 1987.

Was originally enrolled as an English major before switching to film.

Original Job: Faculty assistant and instructor in film department at NYU
Marriages: Larraine Marie Brennan (divorced), Julia Cameron (divorced), Isabella Rosellini (divorced), Barbara DeFina (separated); Illeana Douglas (relationship)
Children: Catherine Terese, Domenica Elizabeth
Major Award: Cannes Film Festival, Palme d'Or, *Taxi Driver,* 1976
Address: Creative Artists Agency, 9830 Wilshire Blvd., Beverly Hills, CA 90212

STEVEN SEAGAL

Birthplace: Lansing, MI
Birthdate: 4/10/51
Occupation: Actor, producer
Education: Orange Coast College
Debut: (Film) *Above the Law,* 1988
Signature: *Hard To Kill*
Facts: Founder, Aikido Ten Shin Dojo, Los Angeles.

First non-Asian to successfully open a martial arts academy in Japan.

In 1968, moved to Japan, where he taught English and wrote articles for Japanese magazines and newspapers.

Organized security for the departure of the Shah's family from Iran.

Commands the title of Shihan (Master of Masters).

Infamy: Was sued by a film assistant for sexual harassment. Paid money to settle out of court in 1990.

Was married to both his first and second wives simultaneously.

Scriptwriter Lars Hansson claimed in 1994 that Seagal threatened him with death after he refused to sell him film rights to a CIA hit-man story.

In 1995, was accused by ex-girlfriend Cheryl Shuman of harassing her. A judge threw out her lawsuit, calling it unintelligible.

Original Job: Martial arts instructor, bodyguard
Marriages: Miyako Fujitani (divorced), Adrienne LaRussa (annulled), Kelly LeBrock; Arissa Wolf (relationship)
Children: Kentaro, Ayako, Anna-lisa, Arissa, Dominick San Rocco, Savannah
Address: International Creative Management, 8942 Wilshire Blvd., Beverly Hills, CA 90211

SEAL

Real Name: Sealhenry Samuel
Birthplace: Paddington, England
Birthdate: 2/19/63
Occupation: Singer, songwriter
Education: High school dropout
Debut: (Album) *Seal,* 1991
Signature: "Kiss from a Rose"
Facts: His name comes from his Brazilian father's custom of having the grandparents select the name (they chose Seal) coupled with his parents' fascination with British royalty (they wanted Henry).

As an infant, lived with a white foster family until his Nigerian mother reclaimed him. When she became ill several years later, went to his father's, whom he says beat him mercilessly.

Plays a six-string guitar upside down; left-handed, learned on guitars borrowed from studios and they were all right-handed.

The scars on his face are remnants of lupus contracted at age 23.

Relationship: Tyra Banks
Major Awards: Grammy, Record of the Year, "Kiss from a Rose,"1995; Grammy, Song of the Year, "Kiss from a Rose," 1995; Grammy, Best Male Pop Vocal Performance, "Kiss from a Rose," 1995
Address: Creative Artists Agency, 9830 Wilshire Blvd., Beverly Hills, CA 90212

JERRY SEINFELD

Birthplace: Brooklyn, NY
Birthdate: 4/29/55
Occupation: Actor, comedian
Education: Queens College
Debut: (Stand-up) Catch a Rising Star, Manhattan, 1976
Signature: *Seinfeld*
Facts: At his first stage appearance, he was so nervous he forgot his routine and only mumbled the words "The beach. Driving. Shopping. Parents," and walked off.

Owns several dozen pairs of sneakers, including a custom pair of "Air Seinfelds."

Has practiced yoga for 20 years and is a strict vegetarian.

Infamy: Created a stir when he began dating 18-year-old Shoshanna Lonstein in 1993. They broke up in 1997.

Original Job: Sought the worst jobs possible, including selling light bulbs over the phone and costume jewelry on the streets of New York, to force himself to succeed at comedy
Major Awards: American Comedy Award, Funniest Male Stand-up, 1988; Emmy, Best Comedy Series, *Seinfeld,* 1993; Golden Globe, Best Actor in a Comedy Series, *Seinfeld,* 1994
Address: Creative Artists Agency, 9830 Wilshire Blvd. Beverly Hills, CA 90212

JANE SEYMOUR

Real Name: Joyce Frankenberg
Birthplace: Hillingdon, England
Birthdate: 2/15/51
Occupation: Actor
Education: Arts Educational School, London
Debut: (Film) *Oh, What a Lovely War,* 1968

Signature: *Dr. Quinn, Medicine Woman*
Facts: Danced with the London Festival Ballet at 13.

Named Honorary Citizen of Illinois by Governor Thompson in 1977.
Original Job: Ballet dancer
Marriages: Michael Attenborough (divorced), Geoffrey Planer (divorced), David Flynn (divorced), James Keach
Children: Katie (stepdaughter), Sean (stepson), Jennifer, Kalen, John, Kristopher
Major Awards: Golden Globe, Best Actress in a Miniseries, *East of Eden,* 1982; Emmy, Best Supporting Actress in a Miniseries, *Onassis,* 1988; Golden Globe, Best Actress in a Drama Series, *Dr. Quinn, Medicine Woman,* 1996
Address: c/o CBS, 7800 Beverly Blvd., Los Angeles, CA 90036

GARRY SHANDLING

Birthplace: Chicago, IL
Birthdate: 11/29/49
Occupation: Actor, writer, comedian
Education: University of Arizona
Debut: (TV) *Sanford & Son,* 1976
Signature: *Larry Sanders Show*
Fact: Wrote for *Sanford & Son, Welcome Back, Kotter,* and *Three's Company.*

Named *The Tonight Show*'s permanent guest host in 1986 and was widely expected to be Johnny Carson's successor, but decided he didn't enjoy it enough so he left.
Infamy: A former co-star sued Shandling for sexual harassment; she claimed her firing from *Sanders* was tied to the break-up of their relationship.
Address: Grant & Tani, 9100 Wilshire Blvd., Suite 1000 West, Beverly Hills, CA 90212

WILLIAM SHATNER

Birthplace: Montreal, Canada
Birthdate: 3/22/31
Occupation: Actor, author, producer, director
Education: McGill University
Debut: (TV) *Goodyear TV Playhouse,* 1956
Signature: *Star Trek*
Facts: Has written a series of books, beginning with *TekWar,* which were turned into movies in which he stars.

Most celebrated pre-*Trek* experience was as a guest on one of the most famous *Twilight Zone* episodes, "Nightmare at 20,000 Feet," in 1963.

One of his leisure activities is breeding horses.

Became CEO of a special effects company, CORE Digital Pictures, in 1995.
Original Job: Novelist
Marriages: Gloria Rand (divorced), Marcy Lafferty (divorced)
Children: Leslie, Lisabeth, Melanie
Address: 100 Wilshire Blvd., Suite 1800, Santa Monica, CA 90401

CHARLIE SHEEN

Real Name: Carlos Irwin Estevez
Birthplace: Los Angeles, CA
Birthdate: 9/3/65
Occupation: Actor
Education: High school dropout
Debut: (TV) *The Execution of Private Slovik,* 1975; (Film) *Grizzly II: The Predator,* 1984
Signature: *Platoon*
Facts: Pitched on the Santa Monica High School baseball team. Was kicked off the team for skipping school.

A Peace of My Mind, a collection of his poetry, was published in 1991.

As a teenager, produced and directed over 200 Super-8 and video short films, some starring future stars such as Sean and Chris Penn, Rob and Chad Lowe, and his brother Emilio Estevez.
Infamy: Admits to having been addicted to drugs and alcohol.

Admits to having paid prostitutes employed by Heidi Fleiss at least $2,000 per encounter between 1991 and 1993.

Divorced after less than six months of marriage, explaining "You buy a used car, it breaks down, what are you going to do?"

Pled "no contest" to allegations that he beat up former lover Brittany Ashland.
Marriage: Donna Peel (divorced)
Child: Cassandra (with Ginger Lynn Allen)
Famous Relatives: Martin Sheen, actor, father; Emilio Estevez, actor, brother; Renee Estevez, actor, sister; Ramon Estevez, actor, brother
Major Awards: Emmy, Best Guest Actor in a Comedy, *Murphy Brown,* 1993
Address: William Morris Agency, 151 El Camino Dr., Beverly Hills, CA 90212

CYBILL SHEPHERD

Birthplace: Memphis, TN
Birthdate: 2/18/50
Occupation: Actor
Education: New York University, University of Southern California
Debut: (Film) *The Last Picture Show,* 1971
Signature: *Cybill*
Facts: Was named for her grandfather Cy and her father Bill, when her parents were disappointed she wasn't a boy.

Became a *Glamour* cover girl at age 19, ultimately appearing there 17 times.

At age 20, began an affair with the older, married director Peter Bogdanovich. His subsequent divorce was blamed on her.

Entered her first and second marriages while pregnant.

After a string of movie flops and a breakup with Bogdanovich in the late 1970s, left the business and moved back to Tennessee. When she decided for a comeback several years later, her then agent told her, "Forget it, you're dead."
Original Job: Model
Marriages: David Ford (divorced); Bruce Oppenheim (divorced); Robert Martin (engaged)
Children: Clementine, Ariel, Zack

Major Award: Golden Globe, Best Actress in a TV Comedy, *Cybill,* 1995
Address: c/o CBS, 7800 Beverly Blvd., Los Angeles, CA 90036

BROOKE SHIELDS

Birthplace: New York, NY
Birthdate: 5/31/65
Occupation: Actor
Education: Princeton University
Debut: (Film) *Alice, Sweet Alice*, 1978
Signature: *Pretty Baby*
Facts: Began her career as an Ivory Snow baby when she was 11 months old. Appeared on more than 30 magazine covers at age 16.

Says now that her overbearing ex-manager stage-mother, Teri, was an alcoholic. Shields was conceived out of wedlock and her father was around only for the first few months of her life.

Has previously been linked romantically to Liam Neeson, Prince Albert of Monaco, George Michael, Michael Bolton, and Michael Jackson.
Infamy: As the 12-year-old star of *Pretty Baby*, played a prostitute in various states of undress.
Original Job: Model
Marriage: André Agassi
Address: William Morris Agency, 151 El Camino Dr., Beverly Hills, CA 90212

ELISABETH SHUE

Birthplace: Wilmington, DE
Birthdate: 6/10/63
Occupation: Actor
Education: Wellesley College, Harvard University
Debut: (Film) *The Karate Kid*, 1984
Signature: *Leaving Las Vegas*
Facts: Admits to drinking heavily and going to class stoned while in high school.

Encouraged her baby brother Andrew to join her in acting.

Older brother Will died in an accident at age 27.
Marriage: Davis Guggenheim
Famous Relatives: Andrew Shue, actor, brother
Address: Creative Artists Agency, 9830 Wilshire Blvd., Beverly Hills, CA 90212

ALICIA SILVERSTONE

Birthplace: San Francisco, CA
Birthdate: 1976
Occupation: Actor
Education: High school equivalency
Debut: (Film) *The Crush*, 1993
Signature: *Clueless*
Facts: Filed for emancipation from her parents at 15 so she could work in films as an adult.

Won MTV's Villain of the Year award in 1993 for her performance as the lovestruck psychopath in *The Crush.*
Quote: "People who say I'm sexy don't really understand what sexy means. I'm always dirty and always in sweats. That's the real me."
Address: c/o Columbia Pictures, First Kiss Productions, 10202 Washington Blvd., Culver City, CA 90232

NEIL SIMON

Real Name: Marvin Neil Simon
Birthplace: Bronx, NY
Birthdate: 7/4/27
Occupation: Playwright, screenwriter, producer
Education: New York University
Debut: (Stage) *Adventures of Marco Polo: A Musical Fantasy,* 1959; (Film) *After the Fox,* 1966
Signature: *The Odd Couple*
Facts: Flew in the U.S. Air Force, 1945–46.

Met his third wife in 1985 when she was handing out perfume samples at the Beverly Hills Neiman Marcus store.

Owns Eugene O'Neill Theatre in New York.

Has written more than 27 Broadway shows.
Original Job: Mail room clerk
Marriages: Joan Baim (deceased), Marsha Mason (divorced), Diane Lander (divorced, remarried, divorced)
Children: Ellen, Bryn, Nancy
Major Awards: Tony, Best Author (Dramatic), *The Odd Couple,* 1965; Tony, Special Award, 1975; Golden Globe, Best Screenplay, *The Goodbye Girl,* 1977; Tony, Best Play, *Biloxi Blues,* 1985; Tony, Best Play, *Lost in Yonkers,* 1991; Pulitzer Prize, Best Play, *Lost in Yonkers,* 1991
Address: c/o Gary DeSilva, 616 Highland, Manhattan Beach, CA 90266

PAUL SIMON

Birthplace: Newark, NJ
Birthdate: 10/13/41
Occupation: Singer, songwriter
Education: Queens College, Brooklyn Law School
Debut: (Song) "Hey Schoolgirl" (with Art Garfunkel, under the name Tom and Jerry), 1957
Signature: *Graceland*
Facts: In sixth grade, he played the White Rabbit to Garfunkel's Cheshire Cat in *Alice in Wonderland.*

Co-owned the Philadelphia Furies, a soccer team, with Mick Jagger, Peter Frampton, and Rick Wakeman.
Marriages: Peggy Harper (divorced), Carrie Fisher (divorced), Edie Brickell
Children: Harper, Adrian Edward, Lulu
Famous Relative: Louis Simon, bassist, father
Major Awards: Grammy, Record of the Year, "Mrs. Robinson" (with Simon & Garfunkel), 1968; Grammy, Best Pop Performance—Duo or Group, "Mrs. Robinson" (with Simon & Garfunkel), 1968; Grammy, Best Soundtrack Album, *The Graduate* (with Dave Grusin), 1968; Grammy, Record of the Year, "Bridge over Troubled Water" (with Simon & Garfunkel), 1970; Grammy, Album of the Year, *Bridge over Troubled Water* (with Simon & Garfunkel), 1970; Grammy, Song of the Year, "Bridge over Troubled Water," 1970; Grammy,

Best Rock/Contemporary Song, "Bridge over Troubled Water," 1970; Grammy, Album of the Year, *Still Crazy After All These Years,* 1975; Grammy, Best Pop Vocal—Male, "Still Crazy After All These Years," 1975; Grammy, Album of the Year, *Graceland,* 1986; Emmy, Best Writing in a Comedy, Variety, or Music Special, *The Paul Simon Special,* 1978; inducted into the Rock and Roll Hall of Fame (with Art Garfunkel), 1990
Address: 1619 Broadway, Suite 500, New York, NY 10019

O.J. SIMPSON

Real Name: Orenthal James Simpson
Birthplace: San Francisco, CA
Birthdate: 7/9/47
Occupation: Football player (retired), actor
Education: City College of San Francisco, University of Southern California
Debut: Halfback, Buffalo Bills, 1969, (Film) *The Klansman,* 1974
Facts: Had rickets as a child, wore braces on his legs.

In 1979, his daughter Aaren drowned in the family swimming pool.

Films include *The Towering Inferno* and *The Naked Gun.*

Infamy: In 1994, was indicted for the murder of ex-wife Nicole and her friend Ronald Goldman. Reports that he had beaten Nicole during their marriage surfaced during the criminal trial; Simpson was found not guilty on all counts. The civil trial resulted in Simpson being found guilty and forced to pay over $20 million to the families of Brown and Goldman.
Major Awards: Heisman Trophy, 1968; set many NFL rushing records including first to gain 2,000 yards in season, 1973; Pro Football Hall of Fame, 1985
Marriages: Marquerite L. Whitley (divorced), Nicole Brown (divorced)
Children: Arnelle, Jason, Aaren (deceased) (with Marguerite Whitley), Sydney, Justin
Address: Little, Brown, & Company, 34 Beacon St., Boston, MA 02106

FRANK SINATRA

Real Name: Francis Albert Sinatra
Birthplace: Hoboken, NJ
Birthdate: 12/12/15
Occupation: Singer, actor
Education: Drake Institute
Debut: (Radio) *Lucky Strike Hit Parade*
Signature: "My Way"
Facts: Provided a voice for the 1988 film *Who Framed Roger Rabbit.*

Weighed over 13 pounds at birth and was mistaken for stillborn until his grandmother held him under a cold water faucet.

Begged executives at Columbia to let him play the key role of Maggio in *From Here to Eternity,* and agreed to play the part for only $8,000.

Has recorded over fifteen hundred songs.

Infamy: Has been reportedly linked to the Mafia.
Original Job: Worked on the news truck of the *Jersey Observer,* later was a copy boy and covered college sports
Marriages: Nancy Barbato (divorced), Ava Gardner (divorced), Mia Farrow (divorced), Barbara Marx
Children: Nancy, Christine, Frank Jr.
Famous Relatives: Nancy Sinatra, singer, actor, daughter; Frank Sinatra Jr., actor, son; Christine Sinatra, producer, daughter
Major Awards: Special Academy Award, 1945; Oscar, Supporting Actor, *From Here to Eternity,* 1953; Grammy, Best Album, *Come Dance with Me,* 1959; Grammy, Best Album, *September of My Years,* 1965; Grammy, Best Album, *Moonlight,* 1966; Grammy, Record of the Year, "Moonlight," 1966; Grammy, Best Male Vocalist, 1959, 1965, 1966; Emmy, Outstanding Musical Special, *Frank Sinatra: A Man and His Music,* 1965; Oscar, Jean Hersholt Humanitarian Award, 1970; Presidential Medal of Freedom, 1985
Address: Warner Brothers Recording, 3300 Warner Blvd., Burbank, CA 91505

SINBAD

Real Name: David Adkins
Birthplace: Benton Harbor, MI
Birthdate: 11/10/56
Occupation: Actor, comedian
Education: University of Denver
Debut: (TV) *Comedy Tonight,* 1985; (Film) *That's Adequate,* 1989
Signature: *A Different World*
Facts: Finalist in the comedy competition on *Star Search* in 1984.

Original dream was to play pro basketball.

Infamy: While in the Air Force, impersonated officers and went AWOL.
Marriage: Meredith (divorced)
Children: Paige, Royce
Address: International Creative Management, 8942 Wilshire Blvd., Beverly Hills, CA 90211

CHRISTIAN SLATER

Real Name: Christian Hawkins
Birthplace: New York, NY
Birthdate: 8/18/69
Occupation: Actor
Education: Dalton School, Professional Children's School
Debut: (TV) *One Life To Live,* 1976; (Film) *The Legend of Billie Jean,* 1985
Signature: *Heathers*
Facts: Began his career in the stage revival of *The Music Man,* at the age of 9.

Dated Winona Ryder, Christy Turlington, and Samantha Mathis.

Was born on the final day of Woodstock.

Infamy: Arrested twice for drunk driving, served ten days in jail in 1990.

Arrested in 1994 for attempting to carry a 9mm pistol through an airport metal detector. He was ordered to spend three days working with homeless children on a plea-bargained misdemeanor charge in 1995.

Was sued in 1995 for palimony seeking $100,000 plus property worth $2 million by ex-fiancée Nina Peterson Huang, who claims she had an agreement with Slater to put her career on hold during their five years of living together. Four months after they got engaged, Huang left the volatile actor and broke off the relationship.

Was arrested in 1997 for assault and battery for acts which encompassed stomach-biting; later admitted to being on alcohol, heroin, and cocaine at the time.

Famous Relatives: Mary Jo Slater, casting director, mother; Michael Hawkins, stage actor, father

Address: Creative Artists Agency, 9830 Wilshire Blvd., Beverly Hills, CA 90212

WILL SMITH

Birthplace: Philadelphia, PA

Birthdate: 9/25/68

Occupation: Actor, rap artist

Education: High school

Debut: Rapper as part of DJ Jazzy Jeff & The Fresh Prince

Signature: *Independence Day*

Facts: Turned down a scholarship to MIT to pursue music.

By 1989 had made and lost his first million dollars, the latter due to excessive spending.

Earned his nickname, the Prince, from a teacher in Overbrook High School because of his regal attitude and ability to talk his way out of difficult situations.

Original Job: Rap artist

Marriage: Sheree Zampino (separated); Jada Pinkett (relationship)

Child: Willard C. "Trey" III

Major Awards: Grammy, Best Rap Performance—Solo, "Parents Just Don't Understand" (with D.J. Jazzy Jeff & The Fresh Prince), 1988; Grammy, Best Rap Performance—Duo or Group, "Summertime" (with D.J. Jazzy Jeff & The Fresh Prince), 1991

Address: Creative Artists Agency, 9830 Wilshire Blvd., Beverly Hills, CA 90212

WESLEY SNIPES

Birthplace: Orlando, FL

Birthdate: 7/31/62

Occupation: Actor

Education: New York City's High School of the Performing Arts, SUNY-Purchase

Debut: (Film) *Wildcats,* 1985

Signature: *New Jack City*

Facts: Has studied martial arts, including the African/Brazilian version Capoeira, since his youth.

Appeared in commercials for Levi's 501 Jeans and Coca-Cola Classic.

Snipes came to director Spike Lee's attention when he played a young punk who threatens Michael Jackson in the Martin Scorsese–directed video *Bad,* 1987.

Infamy: Arrested in 1994 for reckless driving for speeding at up to 120 mph on his motorcycle in Florida, leading state troopers on a 30-mile chase. Sentenced to eighty hours of community service, six months' probation, and $7,000 in fines and court costs.

Original Job: Street and puppet theater in his troupe, Struttin' Street Stuff, installed telephones

Marriages: One marriage (divorced), Roshumba (relationship)

Child: Jelani

Major Award: ACE Award, *Vietnam War Story,* 1989

Address: Starr & Company, 350 Park Avenue, 9th Floor, New York, NY 10022

SNOOP DOGGY DOGG

Real Name: Calvin Broadus

Birthplace: Long Beach, CA

Birthdate: 1971

Occupation: Rap artist

Education: High school

Debut: (Album) *Doggystyle,* 1993

Facts: Nickname "Snoop" was given to him by his mother; "Doggy Dogg" came from a cousin who used to call himself Tate Doggy Dog.

Says his musical heroes are Al Green, Curtis Mayfield, and L. J. Reynolds of the Dramatics.

Infamy: One month after graduating from Long Beach Polytechnic High School, was arrested and incarcerated on a drug charge.

Dogg went on trial for the murder of L.A. gang member Phil Woldemariam; Snoop was driving the Jeep from which his bodyguard fired two fatal gunshots. The two were found not guilty of murder; the jury deadlocked on manslaughter charges and a mistrial was declared.

In 1994, was arrested in Lake Charles, LA, when deputies attempting to deliver civil court papers smelled marijuana outside his hotel room. Charged with possession of marijuana and drug paraphernalia.

Original Job: Sold candy, delivered newspapers, bagged groceries

Marriage: Chantay Taylor
Child: Cordé, a son
Address: International Creative Management, 8942 Wilshire Blvd., Beverly Hills, CA 90211

TOM SNYDER

Birthplace: Milwaukee, WI
Birthdate: 5/12/36
Occupation: Talk show host
Education: Marquette University
Debut: (Radio) WRIT-AM, Milwaukee; (TV) KNBC-TV News, Los Angeles, 1970
Signature: *Late Late Show with Tom Snyder*
Facts: David Letterman, whose company produces Snyder's new late-night talk show, *Late Late Show with Tom Snyder*, is the one who took over Snyder's time slot when NBC dropped *Tomorrow* in 1982.
Marriage: One marriage (divorced)
Child: Anne Marie
Major Award: Emmy, Best Host, *Tomorrow,* 1974
Address: CBS, 51 West 52nd St., New York, NY 10019

STEPHEN SONDHEIM

Birthplace: New York, NY
Birthdate: 3/22/30
Occupation: Composer, lyricist
Education: Williams College
Debut: (Stage) *Girls of Summer,* 1956
Signature: *West Side Story*
Facts: In May 1992, turned down the NEA's Medal of Arts Award, claiming the agency is "a symbol of censorship and repression rather than encouragement and support."

When Sondheim left home at age 15, he was taken in by Oscar Hammerstein II (lyricist of *Oklahoma!*), who taught him how to structure songs.
Original Job: Wrote for *Topper* TV series, 1953, crossword puzzle writer
Major Awards: Pulitzer Prize, Best Play, *Sunday in the Park with George,* 1985; Grammy, Best Cast Show Album, *Company,* 1970; Grammy, Best Cast Show Album, *A Little Night Music,* 1973; Grammy, Song of the Year, "Send in the Clowns," 1975; Grammy, Best Cast Show Album, *Sweeney Todd,* 1979; Grammy, Best Cast Show Album, *Sunday in the Park with George,* 1984; Grammy, Best Cast Show Album, *West Side Story,* 1985; Grammy, Best Cast Show Album *Follies in Concert,* 1986; Grammy, Best Cast Show Album, *Into the Woods,* 1988; Oscar, Best Song, "Sooner or Later (I Always Get My Man)," 1990; Tony, Best Score, *Company,* 1971; Tony, Best Score; *Follies,* 1972; Tony, Best Score, *A Little Night Music,* 1973; Tony, Best Score, *Sweeney Todd,* 1979; Tony, Best Score, *Into the Woods,* 1988; Tony, Best Score, *Passion*, 1994
Quote: "I like neurotic people. I like troubled people. Not that I don't like squared away people, but I prefer neurotic people.... Songs can't develop uncomplicated characters or unconflicted people. You can't just tell the sunny side and have a story with any richness to it."
Address: c/o F. Roberts, 157 W. 57th Street, Pent. A, New York, NY 10019

MIRA SORVINO

Birthplace: Tenafly, NJ
Birthdate: 1969
Occupation: Actor
Education: Harvard University
Debut: (Film) *Amongst Friends*, 1993
Signature: *Mighty Aphrodite*
Facts: The East Asian Studies major speaks fluent Chinese Mandarin.

Discouraged from acting by her father, took up ballet and performed in a professional production of *The Nutcracker* at age 12.

In addition to playing the female in *Amongst Friends*, was casting director and third assistant director.
Original Job: Script reader
Relationship: Quentin Tarantino
Famous Relative: Paul Sorvino, actor, father
Major Awards: Oscar, Best Supporting Actress, *Mighty Aphrodite,* 1995; Golden Globe, Best Supporting Actress, *Mighty Aphrodite,* 1995
Address: William Morris Agency, 151 El Camino Drive, Beverly Hills, CA 90212

KEVIN SPACEY

Birthplace: South Orange, NJ
Birthdate: 7/26/59
Occupation: Actor
Education: Los Angeles Valley College, Juilliard
Debut: (Film) *Heartburn,* 1986
Signature: *Wiseguy*
Facts: Kicked out of a military academy as a kid for hitting a classmate with a tire.

Worked in New York theater in classic Shakespeare, Chekhov and O'Neill roles before coming to Hollywood.
Major Awards: Tony, Best Featured Actor (Drama), *Lost in Yonkers*, 1991; Oscar, Best Supporting Actor, *The Usual Suspects*, 1995
Address: William Morris Agency, 151 El Camino Drive, Beverly Hills, CA 90212

AARON SPELLING

Birthplace: Dallas, TX
Birthdate: 4/22/23
Occupation: Producer, writer
Education: The Sorbonne, Southern Methodist University
Signature: *Beverly Hills 90210*
Facts: Served in U.S. Army Air Force, 1942–45; awarded the Bronze Star and Purple Heart with Oak Leaf Cluster.

In 1969, founded Thomas-Spelling Productions with actor Danny Thomas.

Has produced network hit series such as *The Mod Squad, Starsky and Hutch, S.W.A.T., Charlie's Angels, Family, Dynasty, Beverly Hills 90210,* and *Melrose Place.*
Original Job: Actor

Marriage: Carole Gene Marer
Children: Victoria "Tori" Davey, Randall Gene
Famous Relative: Tori Spelling, actor, daughter
Major Awards: Emmy, Outstanding Drama/Comedy Special, *Day One,* 1989; Emmy, Outstanding Made-for-TV Movie, *And the Band Played On*, 1993
Quote: "I just got tired of the critics saying that I was the master of schlock. It didn't bother me until my kids began growing up and reading it. Well, I'm proud of those entertainment shows they call schlock."
Address: Creative Artists Agency, 9830 Wilshire Blvd., Beverly Hills, CA 90212

STEVEN SPIELBERG

Birthplace: Cincinnati, OH
Birthdate: 12/18/47
Occupation: Director, producer
Education: California State College at Long Beach
Debut: (TV) *Night Gallery,* 1969
Signature: *E.T., the Extra-Terrestrial*
Facts: Made the film *Firelight* at age 16, about the reflecting telescope he made himself, and his father hired a Phoenix, AZ, movie house to show it.

Became a TV director at Universal Pictures at age 20 after finding an empty office and pretending he belonged there.

Was not accepted by the University of Southern California's film department.

Co-owns the L.A. restaurant Dive! with Jeffrey Katzenberg.

A 22-minute film he made in college, *Amblin'*, brought him the attention of Sidney Sheinberg, at the time head of Universal Television. It also provided the name for his production company.

Directed the first episode of *Columbo*, as well as installments of *Marcus Welby, M.D.*

His DreamWorks SKG studio, formed in 1994 with David Geffen and Jeffrey Katzenberg, is the first new studio in 50 years.
Marriages: Amy Irving (divorced), Kate Capshaw
Children: Max, Sasha, Sawyer, Jessica (stepdaughter), Theo (adopted), MikaelaGeorge (adopted), Destry Allyn
Famous Relative: Anne Spielberg, screenwriter, sister
Major Awards: Irving G. Thalberg Memorial Award, 1986; Oscar, Best Director, *Schindler's List,* 1993; Golden Globe, Best Director, *Schindler's List;* 1993, American Film Institute Lifetime Achievement Award, 1995
Address: Creative Artists Agency, 9830 Wilshire Blvd., Beverly Hills, CA 90212

BRUCE SPRINGSTEEN

Birthplace: Freehold, NJ
Birthdate: 9/23/49
Occupation: Singer, songwriter
Education: Ocean City Community College
Debut: (Album) *Greetings from Asbury Park,* 1973
Signature: *Born in the USA*
Facts: E Street Band, formed in 1973, was named after the road in Belmar, NJ, where keyboardist David Sancious's mother lives.

After a 1976 Memphis concert, was caught climbing over the wall to Graceland.

Gave the song "Because the Night" to Patti Smith's producer, who was working in the adjacent recording studio.

In 1986, he rejected a $12-million offer from Lee Iococca to use "Born in the U.S.A." for Chrysler commercials.
Marriages: Julianne Phillips (divorced), Patti Scialfa
Children: Evan, Jessica, Sam
Major Awards: Grammy, Best Recording for Children, *In Harmony 2* (with others), 1982; Grammy, Best Rock Vocal, "Dancing in the Dark," 1984; Grammy, Best Rock Vocal, "Tunnel of Love," 1987; Grammy, Song of the Year, "Streets of Philadelphia," 1994; Grammy, Best Rock Vocal—Male, "Streets of Philadelphia," 1994; Grammy, Best Rock Song, "Streets of Philadelphia," 1994; Grammy, Best Song Written for a Motion Picture, "Streets of Philadelphia," 1994; Oscar, Best Song, "Streets of Philadelphia," 1993; Golden Globe, Best Song, "Streets of Philadelphia," 1993; Grammy, Best Contemporary Folk Recording, *The Ghost of Tom Joad,* 1996
Address: Columbia Records, 1801 Century Park W., Los Angeles, CA 90067

SYLVESTER STALLONE

Birthplace: Hell's Kitchen, New York
Birthdate: 7/4/46
Occupation: Actor, writer, director
Education: American School of Switzerland, University of Miami
Debut: (Film) *Bananas,* 1971
Signature: *Rocky*
Facts: When he was born, the forceps severed a nerve in his face and partially paralyzed his lip, chin, and half of his tongue.

Had rickets as a child.

In high school he played football, fenced, and threw discus.

His paintings have been featured in galleries.

In *Bananas* (1971), played a goon who was thrown off a subway by Woody Allen.

As a boy was kicked out of fourteen schools in eleven years.

In 1971 appeared in a soft-core porn film, *A Party at Kitty & Stud's.*
Infamy: In March 1994, dumped longtime girlfriend Jennifer Flavin via letter sent FedEx. They have since reconciled.

Romanced Janice Dickinson, until DNA tests revealed that her newborn daughter wasn't his. She claimed to be pregnant by him again, then miscarried.

Original Job: Usher, fish salesman, zoo attendant, bookstore detective, teacher at American School of Switzerland.
Marriages: Sasha Czack (divorced), Brigitte Nielsen (divorced), Jennifer Flavin
Children: Sage, Seth (with Sasha Czack); Sophia Rose (with Jennifer Flavin)
Famous Relative: Frank Stallone, musician, brother; Jacqueline Stallone, astrologer, mother
Address: Creative Artists Agency, 9830 Wilshire Blvd., Beverly Hills, CA 90212

DANIELLE STEEL

Real Name: Danielle Schuelein-Steel
Birthplace: New York, NY
Birthdate: 8/14/47
Occupation: Writer
Education: Lycée Français, Parsons School of Design, New York University
Debut: (Book) *Going Home,* 1973
Facts: Wrote over 30 best-selling novels in 20 years, including *The Ring* (1980), *Secrets* (1985), and *Daddy* (1989).
Infamy: Two of her ex-husbands were convicts; she married one while he was still in prison, the other when she was eight months pregnant with his child.
Original Job: Vice president of public relations and new business for Supergirls, Ltd., a PR and ad agency
Marriages: Claude Eric Lazard (divorced), Danny Zugelder (divorced), Bill Toth (divorced), John Traina (separated)
Children: Beatrix, Nicholas (deceased), Samantha, Victoria, Vanessa, Max, Zara
Address: Bantam Doubleday Dell Publishing Group, 1540 Broadway, New York, NY 10036

GWEN STEFANI

Birthplace: Anaheim, CA
Birthdate: 10/3/69
Occupation: Singer, songwriter
Education: Attended California State—Fullerton
Debut: (Album) *No Doubt,* 1992
Signature: No Doubt
Facts: Older brother Eric recruited her in 1986 to sing in the band he formed with his Dairy Queen coworker John Spence, their flamboyant front man who the following year fatally shot himself in a local park. Gwen was eventually encouraged to step out front so the group could continue.

The bouncy group gave away kazoos at the album-release party for their first record. Released at the height of grunge's popularity, the album bombed.

Started wearing the stick-on *pottu* dots, the jewel-like Hindi forehead decoration, when she dated fellow band member Tony Kanal, whose parents are Indian. Many of the songs on *Tragic Kingdom* reflect her distress about their breakup after seven years.
Relationship: Gavin Rossdale
Address: Trauma/Interscope, 10900 Wilshire Blvd., Suite 1000, Los Angeles, CA 90024

HOWARD STERN

Birthplace: New York, NY
Birthdate: 1/12/54
Occupation: Radio DJ
Education: Boston University
Signature: *The Howard Stern Show*
Facts: 1994 Libertarian gubernatorial candidate in New York but dropped out of race before the elections.

Once fired for referring to station management as "scumbags" on the air during a salary dispute.

Practices transcendental meditation each morning in the limo ride to work.
Infamy: After angry listeners provided the FCC with transcripts of Stern's show about masturbating to thoughts of Aunt Jemima and having rough sex with actress Michelle Pfeiffer, the commission fined Infinity Broadcasting, which owns WNBC-New York, $600,000.

Stern made fun of singer Selena Quintanilla Perez after her murder in April 1995, playing her music with sounds of gunfire in the background and parodying her mourners. The League of United Latin American Citizens said it intended to drive Stern's program off the air. Stern later apologized for his conduct.
Marriage: Alison Berns
Children: Emily, Debra, Ashley
Address: K-ROCK-FM (WXRK), 600 Madison Ave., New York, NY 10022

JON STEWART

Real Name: Jon Stuart Liebowitz
Birthplace: Lawrence, NJ
Birthdate: 1963
Occupation: Comedian, actor
Education: College of William and Mary
Debut: (TV) *Short Attention Span Theater,* 1991
Signature: *The Jon Stewart Show*
Facts: Got the idea to do stand-up at age 24, when using puppets to teach schoolkids about disabled people—a gig that honed his prop-wielding skills. Went on the road doing stand-up for the next six years.

His parents divorced when he was 9, and his relationship with his dad became increasingly strained over

the years as Stewart gleefully aired the family's dirty laundry in his club acts.
Original Job: Bartender, bike mechanic, porter in a bakery, research lab assistant
Quote: "As long as I can remember, I wanted to sleep late, stay up late, and do nothing in between."
Address: William Morris Agency, 151 El Camino Dr., Beverly Hills, CA 90212

MARTHA STEWART

Birthplace: Nutley, NJ
Birthdate: 1942
Occupation: Entertainment and lifestyle consultant
Education: Barnard College
Debut: (Book) *Entertaining*, 1981
Signature: *Martha Stewart Living*
Facts: Has published more than a dozen books on entertaining.

Discovered her love for decorating, gardening, and cooking when she and her husband bought a Connecticut farmhouse and fixed it up themselves in 1971. Over the years, she added a barn-turned-party-room, a greenhouse, pool, vegetable gardens, orchards, an English border garden, and beehives, turkeys, chickens, and cats.

Sleeps four hours a night with the lights on so when she wakes up she can get right to work.
Original Job: Model, stockbroker, take-out gourmet food store owner
Marriage: Andy Stewart (divorced)
Child: Alexis
Address: *Martha Stewart Living*, 20 West 43rd St., New York, NY 10036

PATRICK STEWART

Birthplace: Mirfield, England
Birthdate: 7/13/40
Occupation: Actor, writer
Education: Bristol Old Vic Theatre School
Debut: (Stage) *Treasure Island*, 1959
Signature: *Star Trek: The Next Generation*
Facts: Was so sure that he was going to be fired from the initial season of *Star Trek: The Next Generation* that he didn't unpack his bags for six weeks.
Original Job: Journalist
Marriage: Sheila (divorced); Wendy Neuss (relationship)
Children: Sophie, Daniel
Quote: "I was brought up in a very poor and very violent household. I spent much of my childhood being afraid."
Address: International Creative Management, 8942 Wilshire Blvd., Beverly Hills, CA 90211

BEN STILLER

Birthplace: New York, NY
Birthdate: 1966
Occupation: Actor, director
Education: UCLA
Debut: (Film) *Empire of the Sun*, 1987
Signature: *Reality Bites*
Facts: At age 10, began making Super-8 movies about getting revenge on bullies in his neighborhood.

His short film parody of *The Color of Money* landed him a job at *Saturday Night Live* and his own show on MTV.
Relationship: Jeanne Tripplehorn (engaged)
Famous Relatives: Jerry Stiller, comedian, father; Anne Meara, comedian, mother; Amy Stiller, actor, sister
Major Award: Emmy, Best Writing in Variety or Music Program, *The Ben Stiller Show* (with others), 1992
Address: United Talent Agency, 9560 Wilshire Blvd., Suite 500, Beverly Hills, CA 90212

R. L. STINE

Birthplace: Columbus, OH
Birthdate: 10/8/43
Occupation: Teen horror fiction writer
Education: Ohio State University, New York University graduate
Debut: (Book) *The Absurdly Silly Encyclopedia and Flyswatter*, 1978
Signature: *Goosebumps*
Facts: The R.L. stands for Robert Lawrence. Originally wrote under the pen name Jovial Bob Stine.

At one point had more than 90 million volumes in print, outselling John Grisham and Anne Rice.

Churns out his paperbacks at a rate of more than one a month.

Was editing a kids' humor magazine when a book executive asked him to try writing for teens; authored humor books first, then switched to horror.
Original Job: Junior high social studies teacher
Marriage: Jane Waldhorn
Child: Matthew
Quote: "I believe that kids as well as adults are entitled to books of no socially redeeming value."
Address: William Morris Agency, 151 El Camino Dr., Beverly Hills, CA 90212

STING

Real Name: Gordon Matthew Sumner
Birthplace: Newcastle upon Tyne, England
Birthdate: 10/2/51
Occupation: Singer, songwriter, actor
Education: Warwick University
Debut: (Song) "Fall Out" (with The Police), 1977
Signature: The Police
Facts: Rejected the villain role in James Bond film *A View to a Kill.*

He gained his nickname by wearing a black-and-yellow striped shirt, like a bee.

Received a seaman's card and worked as a bass player with The Ronnie Pierson Trio on Princess Cruise Lines at age 17.

Claimed in a 1993 *Rolling Stone* interview that by practicing meditation, he can make love for more than five hours at a time.

Original Job: Teacher, construction worker, clerk for Inland Revenue
Marriages: Frances Eleanor Tomelty (divorced), Trudie Styler
Children: Joseph, Katherine, Mickey, Jake, Coco, Giacomo Luke Sumner
Major Awards: Grammy, Best Rock Performance—Duo or Group, "Don't Stand So Close to Me" (with The Police), 1981; Grammy, Song of the Year, "Every Breath You Take," 1983; Grammy, Best Pop Performance—Duo or Group, "Every Breath You Take" (with The Police), 1983; Grammy, Best Pop Vocal—Male, "Bring On the Night," 1987; Grammy, Best Rock Song/Vocal Performance, "Soul Cages," 1991; Grammy, Best Pop Vocal—Male, "If I Ever Lose My Faith in You," 1993; Grammy, Best Music Video—Long Form, *Ten Summoner's Tales,* 1993
Address: A&M Records Inc., P.O. Box 118, Hollywood, CA 90078

MICHAEL STIPE

Birthplace: Decatur, GA
Birthdate: 1/4/60
Occupation: Singer, songwriter
Education: Southern Illinois University, University of Georgia
Debut: *Chronic Town* (with R.E.M.), 1982
Signature: R.E.M.
Facts: In the early years of R.E.M., traveled to 49 states by the time he was 24.

Planned to record with friend Kurt Cobain. Cobain had tickets to come to Stipe's in Atlanta but called to cancel, and committed suicide soon after.
Infamy: Was rumored to have AIDS because, he says, he is thin, has bad skin, and is sexually ambiguous. He denies being HIV-positive.
Major Awards: Grammy, Best Alternative Performance, *Out of Time,* 1991; Grammy, Best Pop Vocal—Group, "Losing My Religion," 1991
Address: Warner Brothers Recording, 3300 Warner Blvd., Burbank, CA 91505

OLIVER STONE

Birthplace: New York, NY
Birthdate: 9/15/46
Occupation: Director, writer, producer
Education: Yale University, New York University film school
Debut: (Film) *Seizure,* 1974
Signature: *Platoon*
Facts: Served in the U.S. Merchant Marine, 1966; in the Army in Vietnam, 1967–68. Awarded Bronze Star and Purple Heart with Oak Leaf Cluster.

Made acting debut as a bum in *The Hand* (1981), which he wrote and directed.
Infamy: At least 10 real killings were linked to his ode to violence, *Natural Born Killers,* with one 14-year-old decapitator even telling friends he wanted to be famous like the killers in the movie.
Original Job: Taxi driver in New York City, teacher at Free Pacific Institute in South Vietnam
Marriages: Majwa Sarkis (divorced), Elizabeth Burkit Cox (divorced)
Children: Sean, Michael
Major Awards: Oscar, Best Adapted Screenplay, *Midnight Express,* 1978; Oscar, Best Director, *Platoon,* 1986; Golden Globe, Best Director, *Platoon,* 1986; Oscar, Best Director, *Born on the Fourth of July,* 1991; Golden Globe, Best Director, *Born on the Fourth of July,* 1989; Golden Globe, Best Screenplay, *Born on the Fourth of July* (with Ron Kovic), 1989; Golden Globe, Best Director, *JFK,* 1991
Address: Creative Artists Agency, 9830 Wilshire Blvd., Beverly Hills, CA 90212

SHARON STONE

Birthplace: Meadville, PA
Birthdate: 3/10/58
Occupation: Actor
Education: Edinboro State University
Debut: (Film) *Stardust Memories,* 1981
Signature: *Basic Instinct*
Facts: She has an I.Q. of 154.

Between 1977 and 1980, became one of the top 10 models at the Ford Agency.
Infamy: Posed nude for *Playboy* just days after finishing *Total Recall,* 1990.
Original Job: Model
Marriages: George Englund (divorced), Michael Greenburg (divorced), Phil Bronstein (relationship)
Famous Relative: Michael Stone, actor, brother
Major Award: Golden Globe, Best Actress in a Drama, *Casino,* 1995
Quote: "If I was just intelligent, I'd be OK. But I am fiercely intelligent, which most people find threatening.... I have a strong point of view based on my experience. It may or may not be the correct one, but it is an informed one, and I'm willing to fight for it. If I were a petite, brunette, ethnic lawyer then my behavior would be totally acceptable. But we Barbie dolls are not supposed to behave the way I do."
Address: c/o Miramax Films, 375 Greenwich Ave., New York, NY 10013

MADELEINE STOWE

Birthplace: Los Angeles, CA
Birthdate: 8/18/58
Occupation: Actor
Education: USC
Debut: (TV) *Baretta,* 1977; (Film) *Stakeout,* 1987
Signature: *The Last of the Mohicans*
Facts: Starred in first film, *Tropical Snow,* in 1986, but the film was not released until 1989. *Stakeout* was her first released film in 1987.
Marriage: Brian Benben
Major Award: Golden Globe, Special Achievement, *Short Cuts,* 1993
Address: United Talent Agency, 9560 Wilshire Blvd., Suite 500, Beverly Hills, CA 90212

MERYL STREEP

Real Name: Mary Louise Streep
Birthplace: Summit, NJ
Birthdate: 4/22/49
Occupation: Actor
Education: Vassar College; MFA, Yale University
Debut: (Stage) *Trelawny of the Wells,* NY Shakespeare Festival, 1975; (Film) *Julia,* 1977
Signature: *Sophie's Choice*
Facts: When she was 12, began studying with vocal coach Estelle Liebling, who had also taught diva Beverly Sills.

In high school, was a cheerleader and homecoming queen.

Formed a child support group with Annette Bening, Carrie Fisher, and Tracey Ullman, in which they watch each other's children.

When New York theater giant Joseph Papp, who ran Shakespeare in the Park among others, knew he was dying, he asked Streep to succeed him; she turned him down so she could devote more time to her family.
Original Job: Waitress
Marriage: Don Gummer
Children: Henry, Mary Willa, Grace Jane, Louisa Jacobson
Major Awards: Emmy, Best Actress in a Miniseries, *Holocaust,* 1978; Golden Globe, Best Supporting Actress, *Kramer vs. Kramer;* 1979; Golden Globe, Best Actress, *The French Lieutenant's Woman,* 1981; Golden Globe, Best Actress, *Sophie's Choice,* 1982; Oscar, Best Supporting Actress, *Kramer vs. Kramer,* 1979; Oscar, Best Actress, *Sophie's Choice,* 1982
Address: Creative Artists Agency, 9830 Wilshire Blvd., Beverly Hills, CA 90212

BARBRA STREISAND

Real Name: Barbara Streisand
Birthplace: Brooklyn, NY
Birthdate: 4/24/42
Occupation: Singer, actor, director
Education: Yeshiva University
Debut: (Stage) *Another Evening with Harry Stoones,* 1961; (Film) *Funny Girl,* 1968
Signature: "The Way We Were"
Facts: Her father died when she was 15 months old.

She graduated from high school two years early.

Although she had never sung before an audience before, she won a talent contest in a Greenwich Village bar and won a singing job at another bar.

Her Oscar for *Funny Girl* (1968) tied with Katharine Hepburn for *A Lion in Winter,* the only tie for a Best Actress Academy Award.
Original Job: Theater usher, switchboard operator, waitress
Marriage: Elliot Gould (divorced); James Brolin (engaged)
Child: Jason Emanuel
Famous Relative: Roslyn Kind, singer, sister
Major Awards: Emmy, Outstanding Program Achievements in Entertainment, *My Name is Barbra,* 1965; Oscar, Best Actress, *Funny Girl,* 1968; co-recipient Oscar, Best Song, "Evergreen," 1976; Golden Globe, Best Actress, *Funny Girl,* 1968; Golden Globe, Best Director, *Yentl,* 1984; Georgie Award, AGVA, 1977; Grammy, Best Female Pop Vocalist 1963–65, 1977, 1986; Grammy, Best Songwriter (with Paul Williams), 1977; Grammy, Legend Award, 1992; Tony, Special Award, 1970; Emmy, Best Individual Performance in a Variety or Music Program, *Barbra Streisand: The Concert,* 1995.
Address: International Creative Management, 8942 Wilshire Blvd., Beverly Hills, CA 90211

QUENTIN TARANTINO

Birthplace: Knoxville, TN
Birthdate: 3/27/63
Occupation: Director, writer, actor
Education: High school dropout
Debut: (Film) *Reservoir Dogs,* 1992 (writer, director, and actor)
Signature: *Pulp Fiction*
Facts: Studied movies while working at an L.A. video store for four years. Got the idea for *Reservoir Dogs* when he saw that no one had made a heist movie in a long time.

Once played an Elvis impersonator on *The Golden Girls.*

Is said to have an I.Q. of 160.

Had already tried his hand at screenwriting as a teenager, penning *Captain Peachfuzz and the Anchovy Bandit.*
Infamy: Once went to jail for failing to pay his parking tickets.
Original Job: Video sales clerk
Relationship: Mira Sorvino
Major Awards: Cannes Film Festival, Palme d'Or, *Pulp Fiction,* 1994; Oscar, Best Original Screenplay, *Pulp Fiction,* 1994; Golden Globe, Best Screenplay, *Pulp Fiction,* 1994
Quotes: "People ask me if I went to film school. And I tell them, 'No, I went to films.' "
Address: William Morris Agency, 151 El Camino Dr., Beverly Hills, CA 90212

ELIZABETH TAYLOR

Birthplace: London, England
Birthdate: 2/27/32
Occupation: Actor
Education: Byron House, Hawthorne School, Metro-Goldwyn-Mayer School
Debut: (Film) *There's One Born Every Minute,* 1942
Signature: *Cleopatra*
Facts: Almost died from pnuemonia and had an emergency tracheotomy in 1961.

When she was three years old she danced before Queen Elizabeth and Princess Margaret.

After friend Rock Hudson died from AIDS, became the founding chair of the American Foundation for AIDS Research (AMFAR) in 1985.

She met construction worker Larry Fortensky, whom she married in 1992, at the Betty Ford Clinic.

Infamy: Checked herself into the Betty Ford Clinic to overcome alcohol dependency, 1983. Returned in 1988 to overcome painkiller dependency.
Marriages: Nicholas Conrad Hilton Jr. (divorced), Michael Wilding (divorced), Mike Todd (deceased), Eddie Fisher (divorced), Richard Burton (divorced, remarried, divorced), John Warner (divorced), Larry Fortensky (divorced)
Children: Michael, Christopher, Elizabeth, Maria Carson (adopted)
Major Awards: Oscar, Best Actress, *Butterfield 8*, 1960; Oscar, Best Actress, *Who's Afraid of Virginia Woolf*, 1966; Oscar, Jean Hersholt Humanitarian Award, 1992; French Legion of Honor, 1987; American Film Institute Lifetime Achievement Award, 1993
Address: 700 Nimes Road, Los Angeles, CA 90077

JOHN TESH

Birthplace: Garden City, NY
Birthdate: 7/1/53
Occupation: Television host, composer, pianist
Education: Attended Juilliard during high school, North Carolina State University
Signature: *Entertainment Tonight*
Facts: Anchored local TV news in Durham, NC, Orlando, Nashville, and New York before signing with CBS Sports and, in 1986, *Entertainment Tonight.*

An incurable romantic, he proposed to Selleca by reserving an entire Monterey restaurant, hiring a string quartet to serenade her with a song he had written, "Concetta," and arranging for a fireworks display outside the window.

He and Selleca, who pledged to avoid premarital sex during their year-long courtship, starred in a late-night infomercial for a series of videos about relationships.

Composed songs for sporting events he was covering for CBS, including the Tour de France and the Pan-American Games, both of which won Emmys.

His own recording label, GTS Records, has sold more than two million of his CDs. His *Romantic Christmas,* with Selleca, went gold, selling more than 500,000 copies.

Whenever Tesh performs a concert, the event's promoters are contractually bound to provide at least one World Wrestling Foundation action figure for his dressing room.
Original Job: TV reporter
Marriages: Julie Wright (divorced), Connie Selleca
Child: Prima
Major Awards: Emmy, Best Musical Composition for a Sports Program, Pan-American Games, 1983; Emmy, Best Musical Score, Tour de France, 1987
Address: John Tesh Productions, 13749 Riverside Dr., Sherman Oaks, CA 91423

JONATHAN TAYLOR THOMAS

Real Name: Jonathan Weiss
Birthplace: Bethlehem, PA
Birthdate: 9/8/81
Occupation: Actor
Debut: (TV) *The Bradys,* 1990
Signature: *Home Improvement*
Facts: Was the voice of Simba in *The Lion King,* as well as several other characters in kids' cartoons.

Got straight A's when attending public school during breaks in filming.

Has received nearly 50,000 pieces of fan mail a month.
Original Job: Model
Address: International Creative Management, 8942 Wilshire Blvd., Beverly Hills, CA 90211

KRISTIN SCOTT THOMAS

Birthplace: Redruth, Cornwall, England
Birthdate: 5/24/60
Occupation: Actor
Education: Attended London's Central School of Speech and Drama and Paris's Ecole Nationale des Arts et Techniques de Theatre
Debut: (Film) *Under the Cherry Moon,* 1986
Signature: *The English Patient*
Facts: Her father, a naval pilot, was killed in a flying accident when she was 5. Some years later her stepfather, another naval pilot, was killed in a nearly identical crash.

At 16, enrolled in a convent school with aspirations to be a nun.

Was married in Dorset, a beautiful part of England made famous by novelist Thomas Hardy. Two days of ceremonies included one civil and one before a rabbi and a priest (she's Catholic).
Marriage: Francois Oliviennes
Children: Hannah, Joseph
Famous Relative: Serena Scott Thomas, model, actor, sister
Major Award: British Academy of Film and Television Arts Award, Best Actress, *Four Weddings and a Funeral,* 1995
Address: International Creative Management, 8942 Wilshire Blvd., Beverly Hills, CA 90211

EMMA THOMPSON

Birthplace: London, England
Birthdate: 4/15/59
Occupation: Actor
Education: Cambridge University
Debut: (Film) *Henry V,* 1989
Signature: *Howards End*
Facts: Wrote screenplay adaptation of *Sense and Sensibility* by Jane Austen, whose novels she began reading at age 9.

When first met her ex-husband, Kenneth Branagh, she "thought he had strange hair."

Lives on the street on which she was raised, opposite her mother and down the street from her younger sister, Sophie.
Marriage: Kenneth Branagh (divorced); Greg Wise (relationship)

Famous Relatives: Eric Thompson, producer, father; Phyllida Law, actor, mother; Sophie Thompson, actor, sister
Major Award: Oscar, Best Actress, *Howards End*, 1992; Golden Globe, Best Actress, *Howards End*, 1992; Oscar, Best Adapted Screenplay, *Sense and Sensibility*, 1995; Golden Globe, Best Adapted Screenplay, *Sense and Sensibility*, 1995
Address: William Morris Agency, 151 El Camino Drive, Beverly Hills, CA 90212

BILLY BOB THORNTON

Birthplace: Alpine, AR
Birthdate: 8/4/55
Occupation: Actor, screenwriter, director
Education: Attended Henderson State University
Debut: (Film) *Hunter's Blood*, 1986
Signature: *Sling Blade*
Facts: Grew up in a rural area with coal-oil lamps and an outhouse, where supper was whatever grandpa happened to shoot.

Mother Virginia was a psychic, who once predicted that Thornton would work with Burt Reynolds, which he did on *Evening Shade* in 1990.

Broke for years in L.A., he ate nothing but potatoes during a particularly bleak period in 1984, which resulted in nearly fatal heart failure.

Sling Blade's character Karl came to Thornton in 1985 while in a B-movie trailer awaiting his four-line part. The character later appeared in his 1994 short film, *Some Folks Call It a Sling Blade,* a forerunner to the feature.

Terrified of flying, he got distributor Miramax to drive him to the New York Film Festival from L.A. in a limousine.
Original Job: Drummer (one of his bands, Tres Hombres, once opened for Hank Williams Jr.), singer, screen-door factory worker, pizza maker
Marriage: Melissa Lee Gatlin (divorced), Toni Lawrence (divorced), Cynda Williams (divorced), Pietra Dawn Cherniak (divorced), Laura Dern (relationship)
Children: Amanda, William, Harry
Major Award: Oscar, Best Adapted Screenplay, *Sling Blade,* 1996
Address: Miramax, 7966 Beverly Blvd, Los Angeles, CA 90048

UMA THURMAN

Birthplace: Boston, MA
Birthdate: 4/29/70
Occupation: Actor
Education: Professional Children's School
Debut: (Film) *Kiss Daddy Good Night,* 1987
Signature: *Dangerous Liaisons*
Facts: Her father, a professor of Asian religion, named her Uma after a Hindu goddess.

Her Swedish mother, a psychotherapist, was once married to Timothy Leary.

The nearly six-foot actress quit school and headed for New York at age 16. Modeling jobs and movies quickly followed.
Original Job: Model, dishwasher
Marriage: Gary Oldman (divorced); Ethan Hawke (relationship)
Address: Creative Artists Agency, 9830 Wilshire Blvd., Beverly Hills, CA 90212

JOHN TRAVOLTA

Birthplace: Englewood, NJ
Birthdate: 2/18/54
Occupation: Actor
Education: High school dropout
Debut: (Film) *The Devil's Rain,* 1975; (TV) *Welcome Back, Kotter,* 1975
Signature: *Saturday Night Fever*
Facts: Holds the record for the most *Rolling Stone* covers for an actor: four.

An avid flyer since the age of 16, he turned down the lead in *An Officer and a Gentleman*, a part reportedly written for him, because the shooting conflicted with his attendance of American Airlines' month-long jet pilot training school. In 1995, a plane he owns and was piloting lost electrical power over Washington, DC, and had a mid-air near-miss with a commercial jetliner.

His first love, actor Diana Hyland, was 18 years older than the then 22-year-old Travolta. Nine months into the romance she died of cancer—in Travolta's arms.

Languished for nearly a decade in forgettable and/or unpopular films until *Pulp Fiction* restored him to Hollywood's A-list. He earned just $140,000 for his part in the film, far less than the millions-per-picture he once commanded and now receives again.

Has been a member of the Church of Scientology for more than 20 years.
Marriage: Kelly Preston
Child: Jett

Famous Relatives: Ellen Travolta, actor, sister; Joey Travolta, actor, brother
Major Award: Golden Globe, Best Actor in a Comedy or Musical, *Get Shorty,* 1995
Address: William Morris Agency, 151 El Camino Dr., Beverly Hills, CA 90212

TANYA TUCKER

Birthplace: Seminole, TX
Birthdate: 10/10/58
Occupation: Singer
Education: High school dropout
Debut: (Album) *Delta Dawn,* 1972
Signature: "Delta Dawn"
Facts: Her family moved to Las Vegas when she was 12, on the theory that it was a good city to launch a new entertainer. Within two years she had a hit in "Delta Dawn," a $1.5 million record deal, and a cover story in *Rolling Stone.*

High-profile romances included Merle Haggard, Don Johnson, the late Andy Gibb, and Glen Campbell.

Has released more than 30 country albums.

A reported $700,000 advance and the prodding of friends convinced her to write the tell-all, *Nickel Dreams.*
Infamy: Began drinking in her late teens and quickly developed a reputation as a wild party girl. The cocaine, alcohol, and violence that was integral to her 1980 relationship with Glen Campbell became a national symbol of celebrity excess (the pair split in 1981, and Tucker continued her drinking and drugging until entering the Betty Ford clinic in 1988).

In 1997, with a TV crew in attendance to film a *Dateline* profile segment, Tucker flashed her breasts to a roomful of Nashville music-industry partygoers.
Children: Presley Tanita, Beau Grayson (both with Ben Reed)
Address: William Morris Agency, 151 El Camino Dr., Beverly Hills, CA 90212

CHRISTY TURLINGTON

Birthplace: Walnut Creek, CA
Birthdate: 1/2/69
Occupation: Supermodel
Education: UCLA
Facts: Her face was used on mannequins at the Metropolitan Museum of Art's costume galleries.

Dated screenwriter Roger Wilson for seven years and they had a Buddhist service together, though they were never officially married.
Relationship: Jason Patric
Address: Ford Models Inc., 334 East 59th St., New York, NY 10022

KATHLEEN TURNER

Real Name: Mary Kathleen Turner
Birthplace: Springfield, MO
Birthdate: 6/19/54
Occupation: Actor
Education: Studied at London's Central School of Speech and Drama, Southwest Missouri State University, University of Maryland
Debut: (TV) *The Doctors,* 1977; (Stage) *Gemini,* 1978; (Film) *Body Heat,* 1981
Signature: *Romancing the Stone*
Facts: Places pencil erasers at the back of her mouth to practice her sultry voice.

Daughter of a U.S. foreign service officer, she grew up in Canada, Cuba, Washington, DC, and Venezuela before settling in London.
Infamy: Husband was the leaseholder of a building in New York City where 87 people were killed by a fire caused by arson. He pled guilty in 1992 to building code violations, paying $60,000 to be used by a Bronx community service center and performing fifty hours of community service.
Original Job: Waitress
Marriage: Jay Weiss
Child: Rachel Ann
Major Awards: Golden Globe, Best Actress in a Comedy, *Romancing the Stone,* 1984; Golden Globe, Best Actress in a Comedy, *Prizzi's Honor,* 1985
Address: International Creative Management, 8942 Wilshire Blvd., Beverly Hills, CA 90211

TED TURNER

Real Name: Robert Edward Turner III
Birthplace: Cincinnati, OH
Birthdate: 11/19/38
Occupation: Media executive, owner of Atlanta Braves and Hawks
Education: Brown University
Debut: In 1970, bought failing Atlanta TV station, which he turned into WTBS
Signature: CNN
Facts: Won the America's Cup in his yacht, *Courageous,* in 1977.

Interested in owning a major TV network, he made a failed bid for CBS in 1985, and launched negotiations with NBC in 1994 that ultimately broke down.

Owns four bison ranches out west, making him America's largest private bison rancher.
Infamy: Was "asked to leave" Brown University in 1967 for having a girl in his room after hours; was later awarded an honorary degree.
Original Job: Selling space on billboards in family business
Marriages: Judy Nye (divorced), Jane Shirley Smith (divorced), Jane Fonda
Children: Laura Lee, Robert Edward IV, Rhett, Beau, Jennie
Major Award: Elected to the Emmy Hall of Fame, 1991
Address: Turner Broadcasting System, One CNN Center, Atlanta, GA 30348

TINA TURNER

Real Name: Anna Mae Bullock
Birthplace: Nutbush, TN
Birthdate: 11/26/39
Occupation: Singer, actor
Debut: (Song) "Fool in Love," 1960
Signature: "What's Love Go To Do with It?"
Facts: "River Deep, Mountain High"

(1966) was No. 1 in Britain and earned The Ike and Tina Turner Revue the chance to open for The Rolling Stones in 1969.

Became a Buddhist in the early '80s.

Endured years of physical abuse and extramarital affairs by then husband Ike.

Marriage: Ike Turner (divorced), Erwin Bach (relationship)
Children: Stepson Craig, stepson Ronnie, Ike Jr., Michael
Major Awards: Grammy, Best R&B Duo or Group, "Proud Mary" (with Ike Turner), 1972; Grammy, Record of the Year and Best Pop Vocal—Female, "What's Love Got To Do With It?," 1984; Grammy, Best Rock Vocal of the Year, "Better Be Good to Me," 1985; Grammy, Best Rock Vocal of the Year, "One of the Living," 1986; Grammy, Best Rock Vocal of the Year, "Back Where You Started," 1986; Grammy, Best Rock Vocal of the Year, *Tina Live in Europe,* 1988; inducted into Rock and Roll Hall of Fame, 1991
Address: Creative Artists Agency, 9830 Wilshire Blvd., Beverly Hills, CA 90212

SHANIA TWAIN

Real name: Eileen Twain
Birthplace: Windsor, Ontario
Birthdate: 1965
Occupation: Singer, songwriter
Education: High school
Debut: (Album) *Shania Twain*, 1993
Signature: *The Woman in Me*
Facts: Grew up so poor her Canadian family often went without heat.

Says she's of Ojibwa Indian ancestry, but was actually adopted by her Indian stepfather. Shania means "I'm on my way" in Ojibwa dialect.

Raised her three younger brothers after her parents died in an auto accident when she was 21.

Marriage: Robert "Mutt" Lange
Major Award: Grammy, Best Country Album, *The Woman in Me*, 1995
Address: Creative Artists Agency, 9830 Wilshire Blvd., Beverly Hills, CA 90212

LIV TYLER

Birthplace: New York, NY
Birthdate: 7/1/77
Occupation: Actor
Education: High school
Debut: (Film) *Silent Fall*, 1994
Signature: *Stealing Beauty*
Facts: First came to the world's attention as the girl wearing a silver bra in the Aerosmith's 1994 video "Crazy," which also starred Alicia Silverstone.

As a child, believed her father was rocker Todd Rundgren, who was involved with her mother,'70s Playboy Playmate Bebe Buell. But at an Aerosmith concert at age 11, she realized she greatly resembled Steven Tyler.

Original Job: Model
Relationship: Joaquin Phoenix
Famous Relative: Steve Tyler, Aerosmith lead singer, father
Address: Creative Artists Agency, 9830 Wilshire Blvd., Beverly Hills, CA 90212

STEVEN TYLER

Real Name: Steven Tallarico
Birthplace: Boston, MA
Birthdate: 3/26/48
Education: High school dropout
Debut: (Album) *Aerosmith,* 1973
Signature: Aerosmith
Facts: Met future Aerosmith members Joe Perry and Tom Hamilton at Lake Sunapee, NH, where their families had vacation houses.

Seriously injured in a motorcycle accident in 1981, capping a long period of discord and debauchery among band members. "I lay there in the hospital crying and flipping out, knowing some other group was going to step into our space. Through the stupor of my medication, I pictured a spotlight. We walked out of it."

When the band reformed in 1984, they got a contract with Geffen but had to audition first.

Aerosmith co-owns the West Hollywood restaurant House of Blues with Dan Aykroyd and Jim Belushi.

Infamy: Alcohol and drug use including heroin addiction.
Children: Mia (with Cyrinda Tallarico), Liv (with Bebe Buell)
Major Awards: Grammy, Best Rock Performance by a Duo or Group with Vocal, "Janie's Got a Gun," 1990; Grammy, Best Rock Performance by a Duo or Group with Vocal, "Crazy," 1994
Quote: On what is left for his band to accomplish: "I'm looking to be the lounge act on the space shuttle so I can sing 'Walk This Way' on the ceiling."
Address: Columbia Records, 1801 Century Park W., Los Angeles, CA 90067

MIKE TYSON

Birthplace: New York, NY
Birthdate: 7/1/66
Occupation: Boxer
Education: High school dropout
Signature: Youngest heavyweight champion ever, 1986
Facts: Has a 30,000 square-foot mansion near Cleveland with an indoor swimming pool shaped like a boxing glove.

Entered prison in 1992 a doughy 275 pounds, some 50 over his last fighting weight, but emerged a sculpted 216 pounds after patronizing the prison commissary (mostly for milk, cereal, and canned tuna) more than the prison mess.

Born a Catholic and baptized as a Baptist in 1988, he converted to Islam while in prison.

He lined his eight-by-eleven foot prison cell with more than 300 books, and was so impressed by the writings of Arthur Ashe and Mao Tse-tung that he had his biceps inscribed with their portraits by an inmate tattoo artist.

Infamy: Convicted in 1992 of raping

18-year-old beauty contestant Desiree Washington. Spent three years in prison; released on probation in the spring of 1995, with requirements to perform 100 hours of community service each year and undergo counseling for "sex problems."

Bit Evander Holyfield's ear in 1997 rematch. Was fined $3 million by the Nevada Athletic Commission and banned from the ring.
Marriage: Robin Givens (divorced), Monica Turner
Children: Michael, Rayna
Major Awards/Titles: Heavyweight Boxing Champion, 1986–1990
Address: Don King Productions, 32 East 69th St., New York, NY 10021

JOHN UPDIKE

Birthplace: Shillington, PA
Birthdate: 3/18/32
Occupation: Writer
Education: Harvard College, Oxford University
Debut: (Book) *The Carpentered Hen and Other Tame Creatures,* 1958
Signature: *Rabbit, Run*
Facts: Collected Walt Disney comic books.
Marriages: Mary Entwhistle Pennington (divorced), Martha R. Bernhard
Children: Elizabeth, David, Miranda, Michael, three stepchildren
Major Awards: Pulitzer Prize, *Rabbit Is Rich,* 1982, *Rabbit at Rest,* 1991; American Book Award, *Rabbit Is Rich,* 1982
Address: Alfred A. Knopf, 201 East 50th St., New York, NY 10022

JEAN-CLAUDE VAN DAMME

Real Name: Jean-Claude Van Varenberg
Birthplace: Brussels, Belgium
Birthdate: 10/18/60
Occupation: Actor, martial arts expert
Debut: (Film) *Rue Barbare (Barbarous Street),* 1983
Signature: *Kickboxer*
Facts: A middleweight champion in the Professional European Karate Association, he began studying karate at age 11.

Van Damme's fight scenes are so intense that he won't film them in the United States for fear of being sued.

Changed his name to Frank Cujo in 1983; however, changed it again after the release of the Stephen King film *Cujo.*
Infamy: In 1989, was sued for "willfully" gouging the eye of an extra in a swordfight while filming *Cyborg.*
Original Job: Ran the California Gym in Brussels before coming to the U.S. in 1981, worked as a limo and taxi driver, bouncer, carpet installer, and pizza deliveryman
Marriage: Two prior marriages, Gladys Portugues (divorced), Darcy LaPier
Children: Kristopher, Bianca, and Nicolas
Address: United Talent Agency, 9560 Wilshire Blvd., Suite 500, Beverly Hills, CA 90212

EDDIE VAN HALEN

Birthplace: Nijmegen, Holland
Birthdate: 1/26/55
Occupation: Singer, guitarist
Education: Pasadena City College
Debut: (Album) *Van Halen,* 1978
Signature: Van Halen
Facts: When Van Halen wanted to propose to Valerie Bertinelli, he first asked her father for her hand.

Did guitar work on Michael Jackson's "Beat It," free of charge, as a favor.

Formed the group Broken Combs with brother Alex, later changed the name to Mammoth. Formed Van Halen in 1974.

Album, and recording studio that Eddie owns, 5150, is named after the New York police code for the criminally insane.
Infamy: A now reformed alcoholic, he and his band were notorious for backstage partying and obnoxious behavior; they even insisted that all brown M&Ms be removed from candy bowls backstage at their concerts.

Charged with trying to bring a loaded semiautomatic pistol on an airplane in 1995. Fined $1,000 and sentenced to a year of probation.
Marriage: Valerie Bertinelli
Child: Wolfgang
Famous Relative: Alex Van Halen, drummer, brother
Major Award: Grammy, Best Hard Rock Performance, *For Unlawful Carnal Knowledge* (with Van Halen), 1991
Address: Warner Brothers Recording, 3300 Warner Blvd., Burbank, CA 91505

LUTHER VANDROSS

Birthplace: New York, NY
Birthdate: 4/20/51
Occupation: Singer, songwriter
Education: Western Michigan University
Debut: (Song) "Everybody Rejoice (A Brand New Day)" from *The Wiz,* 1978
Signature: "Here and Now"
Facts: Started playing the piano at age 3.

Sister was a member of the '50s group The Crests.

His first group, Listen My Brother, formed while he was a high school student, played at the Apollo and appeared on the first episode of *Sesame Street.*
Original Job: S&H Green Stamp defective-merchandise clerk
Major Awards: Grammy, Best R&B Vocal—Male, "Here and Now," 1990; Grammy, Best R&B Song, "Power of Love/Love Power," 1991; Grammy, Best R&B Vocal—Male, *Power of Love,* 1991; Grammy, Best R&B Vocal—Male, "Your Secret Love," 1996
Address: International Creative Management, 8942 Wilshire Blvd., Beverly Hills, CA 90211

EDDIE VEDDER

Real Name: Eddie Mueller
Birthplace: Chicago, IL
Birthdate: 12/23/64
Occupation: Singer, songwriter
Education: High school
Debut: (Album) *Ten,* 1991
Signature: Pearl Jam
Facts: Vedder, a Red Hot Chili Peppers roadie, was introduced to future Pearl Jam members by Jack Irons.

"Vedder" is his mother's maiden name.

Parents divorced before he was 2, and he grew up thinking his stepfather was his real father. His mother revealed the identity of his biological father only after the man had died. The song "Alive" chronicles his feelings on this discovery.

Voted "most talented" by his high school graduating class. Dropped out of high school his senior year (later passed equivalency exam).

Original Job: Worked at service station, waited tables
Marriage: Beth Liebling
Quote: "I think celebrities suck."
Address: Epic Records, 550 Madison Ave., New York, NY 10022

BARBARA WALTERS

Birthplace: Boston, MA
Birthdate: 9/25/31
Occupation: Broadcast journalist
Education: Sarah Lawrence College
Debut: (TV) *The Today Show,* 1974
Signature: *20/20*
Facts: In 1957, Don Hewitt, now executive producer of *60 Minutes,* told Walters: "You're marvelous, but stay out of television."

Walters was the only woman reporter in the press group that accompanied President Nixon on his historic trip to China in 1972.

Original Job: Intent on becoming a teacher, went for her master's in education while working as a secretary
Marriages: Robert Henry Katz (annulled), Lee Guber (divorced), Merv Adelman (divorced), Sen. John Warner (relationship)
Child: Jacqueline Dena
Major Awards: Emmy, Best Host on a Talk Show, *Today,* 1975; Emmy, Best Interviewer, *The Barbara Walters Show,* 1982; elected to the Television Hall of Fame, 1990
Address: *20/20,* ABC, 77 West 66th St., New York, NY 10023

DENZEL WASHINGTON

Birthplace: Mt. Vernon, NY
Birthdate: 12/28/54
Occupation: Actor
Education: Fordham University, studied acting at the American Conservatory Theatre, San Francisco
Debut: (Film) *Carbon Copy,* 1981
Signature: *Malcolm X*
Facts: Played Malcolm X in *When The Chickens Come Home To Roost* on Broadway, as well as in the 1992 Spike Lee movie.

In college, played football and basketball and wrote poetry before deciding to try acting.

Original Job: Drama instructor
Marriage: Paulette Pearson
Children: John David, Katia, Malcolm, Olivia
Major Awards: Oscar, Best Supporting Actor, *Glory,* 1989; Golden Globe, Best Supporting Actor, *Glory,* 1989
Address: International Creative Management, 8942 Wilshire Blvd., Beverly Hills, CA 90211

WENDY WASSERSTEIN

Birthplace: Brooklyn, NY
Birthdate: 10/18/50
Occupation: Playwright
Education: Mount Holyoke College, City College of New York, Yale University School of Drama
Debut: (Stage) *Any Woman Can't,* 1973
Signature: *The Heidi Chronicles*
Facts: Almost enrolled in business school rather than pursuing drama.

Brother sent her a note prior to a premiere: "Can't come to play tonight. Am buying Nabisco."

Famous Relative: Bruce Wasserstein, investment banking star, brother
Major Awards: Pulitzer Prize, *The Heidi Chronicles,* 1988; Tony, *The Heidi Chronicles,* 1988
Address: Vintage Books, 201 East 50th St., New York, NY 10022

DAMON WAYANS

Birthplace: New York, NY
Birthdate: 1961
Occupation: Comedian, actor, writer, director
Education: High school
Debut: (Film) *Beverly Hills Cop,* 1984; (TV) *Saturday Night Live,* 1985
Signature: *In Living Color*
Facts: Grew up poor as one of 11 children.

Began career performing stand-up in clubs.

Marriage: Lisa
Children: Damon, Michael, Cara Mia, Kyla
Famous Relatives: Keenan Ivory Wayans, actor/producer/writer/director, brother; Kim Wayans, actor, sister; Marlon Wayans, actor, brother; Shawn Wayans, actor, brother
Address: Fox Broadcasting Co., 10201 West Pico Blvd., Los Angeles, CA 90035

SIGOURNEY WEAVER

Real Name: Susan Weaver
Birthplace: New York, NY
Birthdate: 10/8/49
Occupation: Actor
Education: Stanford University; Yale University (MFA)
Debut: (Stage) *The Constant Wife* (with Ingrid Bergman), 1974
Signature: *Alien*
Facts: Took her name from a character in *The Great Gatsby.*

As a senior at Stanford, she dressed as an elf and lived in a treehouse with her boyfriend.

Accepted at Yale Drama School as "Mr." Sigourney Weaver.

Marriage: Jim Simpson
Child: Charlotte
Famous Relatives: Sylvester "Pat" Weaver, president of NBC, father; Elizabeth Inglis, actor, mother
Major Awards: Golden Globe, Best Actress, *Gorillas in the Mist,* 1988; Golden Globe, Best Supporting Actress, *Working Girl,* 1988
Address: International Creative Management, 8942 Wilshire Blvd., Beverly Hills, CA 90211

ANDREW LLOYD WEBBER

Birthplace: London, England
Birthdate: 3/22/48
Occupation: Composer, producer
Education: Magdelen College of Oxford University, Royal Academy of Music, Oxford, Guildhall School of Music, Royal College of Music
Debut: (Stage) *Joseph and the Amazing Technicolor Dreamcoat,* 1968
Signature: *The Phantom of the Opera*
Fact: In 1969, was commissioned by RCA to write an opera based on a single, "Jesus Christ Superstar."
Infamy: After firing Faye Dunaway from the play *Sunset Boulevard* in 1994 because, he said, she couldn't sing, Webber wrote a confidential letter of apology that he then allowed the *London Standard* to print in its entirety. Dunaway, claiming she could indeed sing, sued, and settled for a reported $1.5 million.
Marriages: Sarah Jane Tudor Hugill (divorced), Sarah Brightman (divorced), Madeleine Astrid Gurdon
Children: Nicholas, Imogen, Alastair, Isabella Aurora
Famous Relative: William Webber, London College of Music director, father
Major Awards: Grammy, Best Cast Show Album, *Evita* (with Tim Rice), 1980; Grammy, Best Cast Show Album, *Cats,* 1983; Grammy, Legend Award, 1990; New York Drama Critics Award, *Evita,* 1980; Tony, Best Score, *Evita* (music; Tim Rice, lyrics), 1980; Tony, Best Score, *Cats* (music; T. S. Eliot, lyrics), 1983; Tony, Best Musical, *The Phantom of the Opera,* 1988; Golden Globe, Best Origina Song, "You Must Love Me," (music; Tim Rice, lyrics), 1996; Academy Award, Best Song, "You Must Love Me," (music; Tim Rice, lyrics), 1996
Address: Peter Brown, 909 Third Ave., 8th Fl., New York, NY 10022

ROBIN WILLIAMS

Birthplace: Chicago, IL
Birthdate: 7/21/52
Occupation: Actor
Education: Claremont Men's College, College of Marin, Juilliard
Debut: (TV) *Laugh-In,* 1977
Signature: *Mork and Mindy*
Facts: Grew up on a 30-room estate in Bloomfield Hills, MI.

Spent most of childhood playing with his 2,000 toy soldiers.

Second wife was a former nanny of Robin's children and his personal assistant. She served as a producer for *Mrs. Doubtfire,* 1994.

Infamy: Sued for $6.2 million in 1986 by former companion Michelle Tish Carter, who claimed that he gave her herpes during their two-year relationship. Williams countersued for extortion. The suits were settled out of court for an undisclosed amount.

Shared cocaine with John Belushi only a few hours before Belushi's death.

Original Job: Street mime
Marriages: Valeri Velardi (divorced), Marsha Garces
Children: Zachary, Zelda, Cody Alan
Major Awards: Golden Globe, Best Actor in a Comedy Series, *Mork and Mindy,* 1979; Emmy, Best Individual Performance in a Variety or Music Program, *A Carol Burnett Special,* 1987; Emmy, Best Individual Performance in a Variety or Music Program, *ABC Presents a Royal Gala,* 1988; Golden Globe, Best Actor in a Comedy, *Good Morning, Vietnam,* 1987; Golden Globe, Best Actor in a Comedy, *The Fisher King,* 1991; Golden Globe, Special Achievement, *Aladdin,* 1992; Golden Globe, Best Actor in a Comedy, *Mrs. Doubtfire,* 1993; Grammy, Best Comedy Recording, *Reality...What a Concept,* 1979; Grammy, Best Comedy Recording, *A Night at the Met,* 1987; Grammy, Best Comedy Recording, *Good Morning, Vietnam,* 1988; Grammy, Best Recording for Children, *Pecos Bill,* 1988
Address: Creative Artists Agency, 9830 Wilshire Blvd., Beverly Hills, CA 90212

VANESSA WILLIAMS

Birthplace: New York, NY
Birthdate: 3/18/63
Occupation: Singer, actor
Education: Syracuse University
Debut: (Album) *The Right Stuff,* 1988; (Film) *The Pick-Up Artist,* 1987
Signature: *Kiss of the Spider Woman*
Facts: Was the first black Miss America. Got hate mail from white-supremacist groups and also from blacks claiming she was too white.

Her debut album sold more than 500,000 copies.

Infamy: Forced to resign as Miss America in 1984, after *Penthouse* printed nude photos of her in leather bondage gear with another woman that had been taken several years earlier.
Marriage: Ramon Hervey (separated)
Children: Melanie, Jillian, Devin
Address: William Morris Agency, 151 El Camino Dr., Beverly Hills, CA 90212

BRUCE WILLIS

Real Name: Walter Bruce Willis
Birthplace: Idar-Oberstein, Germany
Birthdate: 3/19/55
Occupation: Actor
Education: Montclair State College
Debut: (Stage) *Heaven and Earth,* 1977
Signature: *Die Hard*
Facts: Was student council president in high school.

The stammer he'd had since childhood disappeared whenever he performed.

Willis and Demi Moore were married on November 21, 1987, by singer Little Richard.

Has his own band, Bruno.

He and his family live in once sleepy Hailey, Idaho, in the Rockies. Attempting to revitalize the town, Willis bought nearly every building on Main Street.

Infamy: During his senior year in high school, was expelled after a racial disturbance and was only permitted to graduate because his father hired an attorney to get him reinstated.
Original Job: Du Pont plant worker, bartender, commercial actor for Levi's 501 jeans
Marriage: Demi Moore
Children: Rumer Glenn, Scout Larue, Tallulah Belle
Major Awards: Emmy, Best Actor in a Drama Series, *Moonlighting,* 1987; Golden Globe, Best Actor in a Comedy Series, *Moonlighting,* 1987
Quote: "Being famous, it's like alcohol—whatever you are, it's just a little more of that. If you're an ---hole, you're more of an ---hole; if you're a nice guy, you're more of a nice guy."
Address: William Morris Agency, 151 El Camino Dr., Beverly Hills, CA 90212

AUGUST WILSON

Real Name: Frederick August Kittel
Birthplace: Pittsburgh, PA
Birthdate: 4/27/45
Education: High school dropout
Occupation: Playwright
Debut: (Play) *Ma Rainey's Black Bottom,* 1981
Signature: *The Piano Lesson*
Fact: Founded the black activist theater company Black Horizon on the Hill in the 1960s.
Marriages: One prior marriage, Judy Oliver (divorced), Constanza Romero
Child: Sakina Ansari
Major Awards: Pulitzer Prize, Best Play, *Fences,* 1987; Pulitzer Prize, Best Play, *The Piano Lesson,* 1990; Tony, Best Play, *Fences,* 1987
Address: 600 First Avenue, Suite 301, Seattle, WA 98104

OPRAH WINFREY

Birthplace: Kosciusko, MS
Birthdate: 1/29/54
Occupation: Talk show host
Education: Tennesee State University
Debut: (Radio Reporter) WVOL, Nashville, 1971–72
Signature: *The Oprah Winfrey Show*
Facts: Delivered Easter sermon to congregation when she was 2 years old.

Once approached Aretha Franklin as she was stepping out of a limo and convinced Franklin that she had been abandoned. Aretha gave her $100, which Oprah used to stay in a hotel.

As a college sophomore, was the first African-American news co-anchor on a local TV station.

In college, won the title of Miss Tennessee and competed in the Miss Black America contest.

After being sexually abused at age 9 by an older cousin and later by a family friend, she ran away from home at age 13.

Original Job: News reporter, WVOL radio, WTVF television, Nashville, TN
Relationship: Stedman Graham (engaged)
Major Awards: Emmy, Best Host of a Talk Show, *The Oprah Winfrey Show,* 1986, 1990, 1991, 1992, 1993, 1994
Address: Harpo Productions, 110 N. Carpenter St., Chicago IL 60607

KATE WINSLET

Birthplace: Reading, England
Birthdate: 10/5/75
Occupation: Actor
Education: High school
Debut: (Film) *Heavenly Creatures,* 1994
Signature: *Sense and Sensibility*
Facts: Her grandparents ran a local repertory theater, where uncle Robert Bridges and father Roger Winslet both worked as actors.

Appeared in a breakfast cereal commercial frolicking with a "honey monster" creature at age 11. By age 17, starred in her first feature film.

Weighing 180 pounds in high school, she had the unhappy nickname Blubber. Finally went on Weight Watchers to drop 50 pounds.

Original Job: Delicatessen worker
Address: William Morris Agency, 151 El Camino Dr., Beverly Hills, CA 90212

SCOTT WOLF

Birthplace: Boston, MA
Birthdate: 6/4/68
Occupation: Actor
Education: George Washington University
Debut: (TV) *Evening Shade,* 1990
Signature: *Party of Five*
Facts: Majored in finance in college.

Played doubles tennis with Tony the Tiger in a long-running early 1990s Frosted Flakes commercial.

Proposed to actress Alyssa Milano

by hiding a 1940s-vintage diamond engagement ring in a pumpkin, getting down on one knee to pop the question, then carving the gourd with a big heart. The pair subsequently broke off their engagement. For a time after, Wolf dated fellow *Po5* costar Paula Devicq.
Address: Fox-TV, P.O. Box 900, Beverly Hills, CA 90213

ELIJAH WOOD

Birthplace: Cedar Rapids, IA
Birthdate: 1/28/81
Occupation: Actor
Debut: (Film) *Back to the Future II,* 1989
Signature: *The War*
Facts: His first acting role was when he was seven, playing the pint-sized executive in Paula Abdul's "Forever Your Girl" video.

Has appeared in more than 15 national commercials.

Gets more than 700 fan letters every week from adoring teenage girls.
Original Job: Model, commercial actor
Address: William Morris Agency, 151 El Camino Dr., Beverly Hills, CA 90212

JAMES WOODS

Birthplace: Vernal, UT
Birthdate: 4/18/47
Occupation: Actor
Education: Massachusetts Institute of Technology
Debut: (Film) *The Visitors,* 1972
Signature: *Ghosts of Mississippi*
Facts: Majored in political science in college. His mother was also interested in politics and was once asked to run for lieutenant governor of Rhode Island, though she declined.

Modeled his voice as Hades for Disney's *Hercules* after an oily William Morris agent he knows.

Left the set of John Savage's *Salvador* in the middle of shooting in a rural Mexican area after an argument with Savage. Walked for five kilometers until Savage finally got in a helicopter and apologized from overhead.
Infamy: He and then fiancé Owens were allegedly the objects of harassment in the late 1980s by actress Sean Young, with whom Woods supposedly had an affair. Hate mail and gifts of mutilated dolls arrived, though nothing was ever proven. After Owens split with Woods following their four-month marriage, she accused him in the tabloids of spousal abuse. Woods countered by saying that Owens had been the one staging the earlier harassment.
Marriage: Kathryn Greko (divorced), Sarah Owens (divorced), Missy Crider (engaged)
Major Awards: Emmy, Best Actor in a Miniseries, *The Promise,* 1986; Emmy, Best Actor in a Special, *My Name Is Bill W,* 1988
Address: International Creative Management, 8942 Wilshire Blvd., Beverly Hills, CA 90211

TIGER WOODS

Real Name: Eldrick Woods
Birthplace: Cypress, CA
Birthdate: 12/30/75
Occupation: Golfer
Education: Attended Stanford University
Facts: Was introduced to golf by his athletic father at nine months; by age 2 had outputt Bob Hope on *The Mike Douglas Show*, by 6 had hit his first hole-in-one, and by 8 had broken 80.

Began listening to subliminal tapes at age 6, featuring such messages as "I believe in me," and "My will moves mountains."

A gifted athlete, is also a switch-hitter in baseball, plays shooting guard in basketball, runs 400-meter track, and has played wide receiver in football.

His ethnicity includes parts African-American, Thai, Chinese, and Indian. On applications requesting ethnic identity, he has described himself as Asian.

The nickname Tiger comes from father Earl's Green Beret army past; it was the moniker of a South Vietnamese officer who saved Earl's life on several occasions.
Major Awards: U.S. Golf Association National Junior Amateur Champion, 1991-1993; U.S. Amateur Golf Champion, 1994-1996; Masters Tournament winner, 1997
Address: International Management Group, 1 Erie View Plaza, Ste. 1300, Cleveland, OH 44114

NOAH WYLE

Birthplace: Los Angeles, CA
Birthdate: 6/2/71
Occupation: Actor
Education: High school
Debut: (TV) *Blind Faith*, 1990
Signature: *ER*
Facts: Is a Civil War buff.

Was given George Clooney's 1960 Oldsmobile Dynamic 88, with the hope that his so-called makeoutmobile would be as lucky for him as it had been for Clooney.

Plays billiards like a pool shark at the Hollywood Athletic Club and at his pool table at home.
Relationship: Tracy Warbin
Address: c/o NBC, 3000 W. Alameda Avenue, Burbank, CA 91523

WYNONNA

Real Name: Christina Claire Ciminella
Birthplace: Ashland, KY
Birthdate: 5/3/64
Occupation: Singer
Education: High school
Debut: (Song) "Had a Dream" (with The Judds), 1984
Signature: *Wynonna*
Facts: Drives a 1957 Chevy and a turquoise Harley-Davidson.

Had asthma as a child.

Adopted her name after the town of Wynona, OK, mentioned in the song "Route 66."

The Judds got their first recording contract when mother Naomi, a nurse, gave a tape to patient Diana Maher, daughter of record producer Brent Maher.

Marriage: Arch Kelley III
Children: Elijah, Pauline Grace
Famous Relatives: Naomi Judd, country singer, mother; Ashley Judd, actor, sister
Major Awards: Best Country Performance by a Group or Duo, "Mama He's Crazy," 1984; "Why Not Me," 1985; "Grandpa (Tell Me 'Bout the Good Old Days)," 1986; "Give a Little Love," 1988; "Love Can Build a Bridge," 1991; Grammy, Best Country Song, "Love Can Build a Bridge," 1991
Address: Curb Records, 47 Music Square E., Nashville, TN 37203

YANNI

Real Name: Yanni Chrysomallis
Birthplace: Kalamata, Greece
Birthdate: 11/4/54
Occupation: Musician, pianist
Education: University of Minnesota
Debut: (Album) *Optimystique,* 1986
Facts: Former member of the Greek National Swimming Team.

Toured with the cult rock band Chameleon.

His music has been used on broadcasts of numerous sporting events, including the Tour de France, the Olympic Games, and the World Series.

Relationship: Linda Evans
Address: Arista Records, 6 W. 57th St., New York, NY 1001

RENEE ZELLWEGER

Birthplace: Katy, TX
Birthdate: 1969
Occupation: Actor
Education: University of Texas
Debut: (Film) *The Texas Chainsaw Massacre 2*, 1986
Signature: *Jerry Maguire*
Facts: Her Texas hometown was so small it had neither a movie theater nor cable television.

Signed up for her first drama class in college simply because she needed the credit to complete her English degree. Fell in love with acting and declared herself a professional actor upon graduation.

Though practically every well-known actress under age 35 auditioned during a four-month hunt for the *Jerry Maguire* part, the relatively obscure Zellweger impressed Tom Cruise and writer Cameron Crowe with her freshness and offbeat quality—and the fact that she wasn't intimidated by her sizzling co-star.

Original Job: Bartender assistant
Relationship: Josh Pate
Address: United Talent Agency, 9560 Wilshire Blvd., Suite 500, Beverly Hills, CA 90212

ROBERT ZEMECKIS

Birthplace: Chicago, IL
Birthdate: 5/14/51
Occupation: Director, producer, screenwriter
Education: University of Southern California
Debut: (Film) *I Wanna Hold Your Hand*, 1978 (directing and cowriting)
Signature: *Forrest Gump*
Facts: Films he directed include *Romancing the Stone*, *Death Becomes Her*, *Who Framed Roger Rabbit,* and the trilogy of *Back to the Futures*. Co-executive-produced HBO's *Tales from the Crypt*.

Is considered one of Hollywood's most accomplished techno-wonk filmmakers, using elaborate special effects in most of his films.

Met his frequent script collaborator Bob Gale at USC film school; in 1979 they wrote the ill-fated *1941* for Steven Spielberg.

Marriage: Mary Ellen Trainor
Child: Alex
Major Awards: Oscar, Best Director, *Forrest Gump*, 1994; Golden Globe, Best Director, *Forrest Gump*, 1995
Address: Creative Artists Agency, 9830 Wilshire Blvd., Beverly Hills, CA 90212

THE REGISTER OF THOUSANDS

Here's a celebrity data base covering the multitudes of shakers and shapers, the near-great and notorious, those who grace the screen and the tube, the page and the stage—a resource to discover the real names, birthdates, birthplaces, occupations, and claims to fame of a large slice of pop culture. Those who are coy about their birthdates or are too new on the scene to be sufficiently well documented have been passed over for this year's list—but stay tuned.

AAMES, WILLIE (Willie Upton). Los Angeles, CA, 7/15/60. Actor. *Eight Is Enough.*
ABBOTT, JIM. Flint, MI, 9/19/67. One-handed baseball pitcher.
ABDUL, PAULA. Los Angeles, CA, 6/19/62. Singer, dancer, choreographer, divorced from Emilio Estevez. "Straight Up."
ABRAHAM, F. MURRAY. Pittsburgh, PA, 10/24/39. Actor. *Amadeus.*
ABRAHAMS, JIM. Milwaukee, WI, 5/10/44. Producer, writer, director. *Airplane!; The Naked Gun.*
ABRAHAMS, MICK. Luton, England, 4/7/43. Guitarist. Jethro Tull.
AD-ROCK, KING (Adam Horovitz). New York, NY, 10/31/66. Rap artist. The Beastie Boys.
ADAMS, BROOKE. New York, NY, 2/8/49. Actor. *Invasion of the Body Snatchers.*
ADAMS, BRYAN. Kingston, Canada, 11/5/59. Singer, songwriter. "(Everything I Do) I Do it for You."
ADAMS, DON. New York, NY, 4/19/26. Actor. Maxwell Smart on *Get Smart.*
ADAMS, DOUGLAS. Cambridge, England, 3/11/52. Novelist. *The Hitchhiker's Guide to the Galaxy.*
ADAMS, EDIE (Elizabeth Edith Enke). Kingston, PA, 4/16/29. Actor. *The Ernie Kovacs Show.*
ADAMS, MAUD (Maud Wikstrom). Lulea, Sweden, 2/12/45. Actor. *Octopussy.*
ADAMSON, STUART (William Adamson). Manchester, England, 4/11/58. Guitarist, singer. Big Country.
ADJANI, ISABELLE. Paris, France, 6/27/55. Actor. *Camille Claudel.*
AGAR, JOHN. Chicago, IL, 1/31/21. Actor, formerly married to Shirley Temple. *The Sands of Iwo Jima.*
AGNEW, PETE. Scotland, 9/14/46. Bassist, singer. Nazareth.
AGUTTER, JENNY. Taunton, England, 12/20/52. Actor. *Logan's Run.*
AIELLO, DANNY. New York, NY, 6/20/33. Actor, writer. *Moonstruck.*
AIKMAN, TROY KENNETH. Cerritos, CA, 11/21/66. Football player. Quarterback for the Dallas Cowboys.
AIMEE, ANOUK (Françoise Soyra Dreyfus). Paris, France, 4/27/32. Actor. *A Man and a Woman.*
AKERS, KAREN. New York, NY, 10/13/45. Cabaret singer.
ALBERT, EDDIE (Eddie Albert Heimberger). Rock Island, IL, 4/22/08. Actor, father of Edward. Oliver Wendell Douglas on *Green Acres.*
ALBERT, EDWARD. Los Angeles, CA, 2/20/51. Actor, son of Eddie. *Midway.*
ALBRECHT, BERNIE (Bernard Dicken). Salford, England, 1/4/56. Guitarist. Joy Division; New Order.
ALDA, ALAN (Alphonso D'Abruzzo). New York, NY, 1/28/36. Actor, writer, director, son of Robert Alda. Benjamin Franklin "Hawkeye" Pierce on *M*A*S*H.*
ALDRIN, BUZZ (Edwin Eugene Aldrin Jr.). Montclair, NJ, 1/20/30. Astronaut, businessman.
ALEXANDER, GARY. Chattanooga, TN, 9/25/43. Singer, guitarist. The Association.
ALEXANDER, JANE (Jane Quigley). Boston, MA, 10/28/39. Actor. *All the President's Men.* Head of the National Endowment for the Arts.
ALI, MUHAMMAD (Cassius Clay). Louisville, KY, 1/17/42. Boxing great.
ALLEN, DEBBIE. Houston, TX, 1/16/50. Choreographer, actor, sister of Phylicia Rashad. *Fame.*
ALLEN, DUANE. Taylortown, TX, 4/29/43. Singer. The Oak Ridge Boys.
ALLEN, JOAN. Rochelle, IL, 8/20/56. Actor. *Compromising Positions.*
ALLEN, KAREN. Carrollton, IL, 10/5/51. Actor. *Raiders of the Lost Ark.*
ALLEN, NANCY. New York, NY, 6/24/50. Actor. *Robocop.*
ALLEN, PAPA DEE (Thomas Allen). Wilmington, DE, 7/18/31. Keyboardist, singer. War.
ALLEN, RICK. Sheffield, England, 11/1/63. One-armed drummer. Def Leppard.
ALLEN, ROD (Rod Bainbridge). Leicester, England, 3/31/44. Bassist, singer. The Fortunes.
ALLEN, STEVE. New York, NY, 12/26/21. Writer, performer, variety show host, husband of Jayne Meadows. *The Steve Allen Show.*
ALLEN, VERDEN. Hereford, England, 5/26/44. Keyboardist. Mott The Hoople.
ALLEY, KIRSTIE. Wichita, KS, 1/12/55. Actor, married to Parker Stevenson. Rebecca Howe on *Cheers.*
ALLISON, JERRY. Hillsboro, TX, 8/31/39. Drummer. Buddy Holly & The Crickets.
ALLMAN, GREGG. Nashville, TN, 12/8/47. Keyboardist, guitarist, singer, formerly married to Cher. The Allman Brothers Band.
ALLSUP, MIKE. Modesto, CA, 3/8/47. Guitarist. Three Dog Night.
ALLYSON, JUNE (Ella Geisman). Westchester, NY, 10/7/17. Actor. *The Dupont Show Starring June Allyson; Lassie.*
ALMOND, MARC (Peter Almond). Southport, England, 7/9/59. Singer. Soft Cell.
ALONSO, MARIA CONCHITA. Cuba, 6/29/57. Actor. *The Running Man.*
ALPERT, HERB.Los Angeles, CA, 3/31/35. Trumpeter, band leader, cofounder of A&M Records. The Tijuana Brass.
ALSTON, BARBARA. Brooklyn, NY, 1945. Singer. The Crystals.
ALSTON, SHIRLEY (Shirley Owens). Passaic, NJ, 6/10/41. Singer. The Shirelles.
ALT, CAROL. Queens, NY, 12/1/60. Supermodel.
ALTMAN, ROBERT. Kansas City, MO, 2/20/25. Director, writer, producer. *The Player.*
ALVARADO, TRINI. New York, NY, 1/10/69. Actor. *Rich Kids.*
AMIN, IDI. Koboko, Uganda, 1/1/25. Political leader, former president of Uganda.
AMIS, SUZY. Oklahoma City, OK, 1/5/61. Actor. *Blown Away.*
AMOS, JOHN. Newark, NJ, 12/27/41. Actor. James Evans on *Good Times.*
AMOS, WALLY JR. Tallahassee, FL, 7/1/36. Business executive. Famous Amos chocolate chip cookies.
ANDERSON, ALFA. 9/7/46. Singer. Chic.
ANDERSON, HARRY. Newport, RI, 10/14/52. Actor. Judge Harry Stone on *Night Court.*
ANDERSON, IAN. Edinburgh, Scotland, 8/10/47. Singer, flautist. Jethro Tull.
ANDERSON, JON. Lancashire, England, 10/25/44. Singer, drummer. Yes.

ANDERSON, KEVIN. Illinois, 1/13/60. Actor. *Sleeping with the Enemy.*
ANDERSON, LAURIE. Chicago, IL, 6/5/50. Singer, performance artist.
ANDERSON, LONI. St. Paul, MN, 8/5/46. Actor. Receptionist Jennifer Marlowe on *WKRP in Cincinnati.*
ANDERSON, MELISSA SUE. Berkeley, CA, 9/26/62. Actor. Mary Ingalls Kendall on *Little House on the Prairie.*
ANDERSON, MELODY. Edmonton, Canada, 1/3/55. Actor. Dale Arden in *Flash Gordon.*
ANDERSON, RICHARD. Long Branch, NJ, 8/8/26. Actor. Oscar Goldman on *The Six Million Dollar Man* and *The Bionic Woman.*
ANDERSON, RICHARD DEAN. Minneapolis, MN, 1/23/50. Actor. *MacGyver.*
ANDERSON, RICK. St. Paul, MN, 8/1/47. Bassist. The Tubes.
ANDERSON, TERRY. 10/27/47. Journalist, former hostage.
ANDERSSON, BENNY (Goran Andersson). Stockholm, Sweden, 12/16/46. Keyboards, singer. Abba.
ANDERSSON, BIBI. Stockholm, Sweden, 11/11/35. Actor. *The Seventh Seal.*
ANDES, MARK. Philadelphia, PA, 2/19/48. Bassist. Spirit.
ANDRESS, URSULA. Berne, Switzerland, 3/19/36. Actor. *Dr. No.*
ANDRETTI, MARIO. Montona Trieste, Italy, 2/28/40. Auto racer.
ANDREW, PRINCE. London, England, 2/19/60. British royalty, son of Queen Elizabeth II.
ANDREWS, ANTHONY. London, England, 1/12/48. Actor. *Brideshead Revisited.*
ANDREWS, BARRY. London, England, 9/12/56. Keyboardist. XTC.
ANDREWS, JULIE (Julia Wells). Walton-on-Thames, England, 10/1/35. Actor, singer. *The Sound of Music.*
ANKA, PAUL. Ottawa, Canada, 7/30/41. Singer, songwriter. "Diana."
ANN-MARGRET (Ann-Margret Olsson). Valsjobyn, Sweden, 4/28/41. Actor, singer. *Viva Las Vegas.*
ANNAUD, JEAN-JACQUES. Draveil, France, 10/1/43. Writer, director. *Quest for Fire; The Lover.*
ANNE, PRINCESS. London, England, 8/15/50. British royalty, daughter of Queen Elizabeth II.
ANSPACH, SUSAN. New York, NY, 11/23/45. Actor. *Five Easy Pieces.*
ANT, ADAM (Stewart Goddard). London, England, 11/3/54. Singer. Adam & The Ants.
ANTHONY, MICHAEL. Chicago, IL, 6/20/55. Bassist. Van Halen.
ANTON, SUSAN. Oak Glen, CA, 10/12/50. Actor, singer. *Goldengirl.*
ANWAR, GABRIELLE. Laleham, England, 2/4/70. Actor. Tangoed with Al Pacino in *Scent of a Woman.*
APPICE, CARMINE. New York, NY, 12/15/46. Drummer. Vanilla Fudge.
APPLEGATE, CHRISTINA. Hollywood, CA, 11/25/72. Actor. Kelly Bundy on *Married ... with Children.*
AQUINO, CORAZON. Tarlac, Philippines, 1/25/33. Political leader. Former president of the Philippines.
ARAFAT, YASIR. Cairo, Egypt, 8/24/29. Political leader. Head of the PLO.
ARCHER, ANNE. Los Angeles, CA, 8/25/47. Actor. Wife of Michael Douglas in *Fatal Attraction.*
ARENHOLZ, STEPHEN. The Bronx, NY, 4/29/69. Actor.
ARGENT, ROD. St. Albans, England, 6/14/45. Keyboardist. The Zombies.
ARKIN, ALAN. New York, NY, 3/26/34. Actor, director, writer, folk singer, member of Second City, father of Adam Arkin (*Chicago Hope*). *The In-Laws.*
ARMATRADING, JOAN. Basseterre, West Indies, 12/9/50. Singer, songwriter. "Me, Myself, I."
ARMSTRONG, BESS. Baltimore, MD, 12/11/53. Actor. Julia Peters on *On Our Own.*
ARMSTRONG, BILLIE JOE Rodeo, CA, 2/17/72, Singer, songwriter, guitrarist, Green Day.
ARMSTRONG, NEIL. Wapakoneta, OH, 8/5/30. Astronaut.
ARNAZ, DESI JR. Los Angeles, CA, 1/19/53. Actor, singer, son of Lucille Ball and Desi Arnaz. *Here's Lucy.*
ARNAZ, LUCIE. Los Angeles, CA, 7/17/51. Actor, daughter of Lucille Ball and Desi Arnaz, married to Laurence Luckinbill. *Here's Lucy.*
ARNESS, JAMES (James Aurness). Minneapolis, MN, 5/26/23. Actor, brother of Peter Graves. *Gunsmoke.*
ARQUETTE, PATRICIA. New York, NY, 4/8/68. Actor, granddaughter of Cliff Arquette, sister of Rosanna. *True Romance.*
ARQUETTE, ROSANNA. New York, NY, 8/10/59. Actor, granddaughter of Cliff Arquette, sister of Patricia, and inspiration for Toto song "Rosanna." *Desperately Seeking Susan.*
ARTHUR, BEATRICE (Bernice Frankel). New York, NY, 5/13/26. Actor. *Maude.*
ASH, DANIEL. 7/31/57. Guitarist, singer. Bauhaus; Love and Rockets.
ASHER, PETER. London, England, 6/22/44. Singer. Peter and Gordon.
ASHFORD, NICKOLAS. Fairfield, SC, 5/4/42. Singer. Ashford and Simpson.
ASHFORD, ROSALIND. Detroit, MI, 9/2/43. Singer. Martha & The Vandellas.
ASHLEY, ELIZABETH (Elizabeth Ann Cole). Ocala, FL, 8/30/39. Actor. *Evening Shade.*
ASNER, EDWARD. Kansas City, KS, 11/15/29. Actor. *Lou Grant.*
ASSANTE, ARMAND. New York, NY, 10/4/49. Actor. *The Doctors.*
ASTBURY, IAN. Heswall, England, 5/14/62. Singer. The Cult.
ASTIN, JOHN. Baltimore, MD, 3/30/30. Actor, formerly married to Patty Duke, father of Sean Astin. Gomez Addams on *The Addams Family.*
ASTIN, SEAN. Santa Monica, CA, 2/25/71. Actor, son of John Astin and Patty Duke. *Encino Man.*
ASTLEY, RICK. Warrington, England, 2/6/66. Singer, songwriter. "Never Gonna Give You Up."
ASTON, JAY. London, England, 5/4/61. Singer. Bucks Fizz.
ASTON, JOHN. England, 11/30/57. Guitarist. Psychedelic Furs.
ATKINS, CHET. Luttrell, TN, 6/20/24. Virtuoso guitarist.
ATKINS, CHRISTOPHER. Rye, NY, 2/21/61. Actor. *The Blue Lagoon.*
ATKINSON, PAUL. Cuffley, England, 3/19/46. Guitarist. The Zombies.
ATTENBOROUGH, RICHARD. Cambridge, England, 8/29/23. Actor, producer, director. *Gandhi.*
ATWOOD, MARGARET. Ottawa, Canada, 11/18/39. Author, poet. *The Handmaid's Tale.*
AUBERJONOIS, RENE. New York, NY, 6/1/40. Actor. Security Chief Odo on *Deep Space Nine.*
NADJA AUERMANN Berlin, Germany, 1971, Supermodel.
AUTRY, ALAN. Shreveport, LA, 7/31/52. Actor. Bubba Skinner on *In the Heat of the Night.*
AUTRY, GENE. Tioga, TX, 9/29/07. Screen's first singing cowboy. *The Gene Autry Show.*
AVALON, FRANKIE (Francis Thomas Avallone). Philadelphia, PA, 9/18/40. Singer, actor. *Beach Blanket Bingo.*
AVORY, MICK. London, England, 2/15/44. Drummer. The Kinks.
AXTON, HOYT. Duncan, OK, 3/25/38. Singer, songwriter, actor. *Gremlins.*
AZNAVOUR, CHARLES (Shahnour Varenagh Aznourian). Paris, France,

5/22/24. Singer, songwriter, actor. *The Tin Drum.*
BACALL, LAUREN (Betty Perske). New York, NY, 9/16/24. Actor, widow of Humphrey Bogart, formerly married to Jason Robards. *Key Largo.*
BACH, BARBARA. Queens, NY, 8/27/47. Actor, married to Ringo Starr. *The Spy Who Loved Me.*
BACHMAN, RANDY. Winnipeg, Canada, 9/27/43. Guitarist, singer. Bachman-Turner Overdrive; The Guess Who.
BACHMAN, ROBBIE. Winnipeg, Canada, 2/18/53. Drummer. Bachman-Turner Overdrive.
BACON, KEVIN. Philadelphia, PA, 7/8/58. Actor, married to Kyra Sedgwick. *Footloose.*
BADANJEK, JOHN. 1948. Drummer. Mitch Ryder & The Detroit Wheels.
BAEZ, JOAN. Staten Island, NY, 1/9/41. Folk singer and songwriter, peace and civil rights activist.
BAILEY, PHILIP. Denver, CO, 5/8/51. Singer, conga player, percussionist. Earth, Wind & Fire.
BAILEY, TOM. Halifax, England, 6/18/57. Singer, keyboardist. Thompson Twins.
BAIN, BARBARA. Chicago, IL, 9/13/34. Actor. *Mission: Impossible.*
BAIO, SCOTT. Brooklyn, NY, 9/22/61. Actor. Charles "Chachi" Arcola on *Happy Days.*
BAKER, ANITA. Detroit, MI, 12/20/57. R&B singer.
BAKER, CARROLL. Johnstown, PA, 5/28/31. Actor. *Kindergarten Cop.*
BAKER, CHERYL (Rita Crudgington). London, England, 3/8/54. Singer. Bucks Fizz.
BAKER, GINGER (Peter Baker). Lewisham, England, 8/19/40. Drummer. Cream; Blind Faith.
BAKER, JOE DON. Groesbeck, TX, 2/12/36. Actor. *Walking Tall.*
BAKER, KATHY. Midland, TX, 6/8/50. Actor. *Picket Fences.*
BAKER, MICKEY (McHouston Baker). Louisville, KY, 10/15/25. Singer. Mickey & Sylvia.
BAKKER, JIM. Muskegon, MI, 1/2/40. TV evangelist, participant in the PTL scandal.
BAKKER, TAMMY FAYE. International Falls, MN, 3/7/42. TV evangelist. Former wife of PTL founder Jim Bakker.
BAKSHI, RALPH. Haifa, Palestine, 10/29/38. Animator, writer, director. *Fritz the Cat.*
BAKULA, SCOTT. St. Louis, MO, 10/9/55. Actor. *Quantum Leap.*
BALABAN, BOB. Chicago, IL, 8/16/45. Actor. Roles in *Midnight Cowboy, Little Man Tate.*
BALDWIN, ADAM. Chicago, IL, 2/27/62. Actor. *My Bodyguard.*
BALDWIN, STEPHEN. Massapequa, NY, 1966. Actor. *Threesome.*
BALDWIN, WILLIAM. Massapequa, NY, 1963. Actor, married to Chynna Phillips. *Backdraft.*
BALIN, MARTY (Martyn Jerel Buchwald). Cincinnati, OH, 1/30/43. Singer. Jefferson Airplane/Starship.
BALL, DAVID. Blackpool, England, 5/3/59. Keyboardist. Soft Cell.
BALL, ROGER. Dundee, Scotland, 6/4/44. Alto and baritone saxophonist. Average White Band.
BALLARD, HANK. Detroit, MI, 11/18/36. Singer/songwriter. "Work with Me Annie."
BALLARD, KAYE (Catherine Gloria Balotta). Cleveland, OH, 11/20/26. Actor, singer.
BALSLEY, PHILIP. 8/8/39. Singer. Kingsmen; Statler Brothers.
BAMBAATAA, AFRIKA. The Bronx, NY, 1958. Rap/hip-hop DJ.
BANALI, FRANKIE. 11/14/55. Musician. Quiet Riot.
BANANA (Lowell Levinger). Cambridge, MA, 1946. Keyboardist, guitarist. The Youngbloods.
BANCROFT, ANNE (Anna Maria Italiano). The Bronx, NY, 9/17/31. Actor. Mrs. Robinson in *The Graduate.*
BANKS, TONY. East Heathly, England, 3/27/51. Keyboardist. Genesis.
BARBATA, JOHN. 4/1/45. Drummer. The Turtles; Jefferson Starship.
BARBEAU, ADRIENNE. Sacramento, CA, 6/11/45. Actor. Carol on *Maude.*
BARBIERI, RICHARD. 11/30/57. Keyboardist. Japan.
BARDOT, BRIGITTE (Camille Javal). Paris, France, 9/28/34. Sex goddess. *And God Created Woman.*
BARGERON, DAVE. Massachusetts, 9/6/42. Trombonist. Blood, Sweat and Tears.
BARKER, BOB. Darrington, WA, 12/12/23. Game show host. *The Price Is Right.*
BARKER, CLIVE. Liverpool, England, 10/5/52. Author. *The Inhuman Condition.*
ELLEN BARKIN. Bronx, NY,4/16/54, Actor, *Sea of Love.*
BARNES, LEO. 10/5/55. Musician. Hothouse Flowers.
BARRE, MARTIN. 11/17/46. Guitarist. Jethro Tull.
BARRERE, PAUL. Burbank, CA, 7/3/48. Lead guitarist. Little Feat.
BARRETT, ASTON. Kingston, Jamaica, 11/22/46. Bassist. Bob Marley & The Wailers.
BARRETT, MARCIA. St. Catherine's, Jamaica, 10/14/48. Singer. Boney M.
BARRETT, RONA. New York, NY, 10/8/36. News correspondent, columnist.
BARRETT, SYD (Roger Barrett). Cambridge, England, 1/6/46. Singer, guitarist. Pink Floyd.
BARRY, MARION. Itta Bena, MS, 3/6/36. Mayor of Washington, served six-month prison term for cocaine possession.
BARRYMORE, JOHN DREW. Beverly Hills, CA, 6/4/32. Actor, father of Drew Barrymore.
BARSON, MIKE. England, 5/21/58. Keyboardist. Madness.
BARTEL, PAUL. New York, NY, 8/6/38. Director, writer, actor. *Eating Raoul.*
BARTHOL, BRUCE. Berkeley, CA, 1947. Bassist. Country Joe & The Fish.
BARYSHNIKOV, MIKHAIL. Riga, Latvia, 1/27/48. Dancer, actor. *White Nights.*
BATEMAN, JASON. Rye, NY, 1/14/69. Actor, brother of Justine. David on *The Hogan Family.*
BATEMAN, JUSTINE. Rye, NY, 2/19/66. Actor, sister of Jason. Mallory Keaton on *Family Ties.*
BATES, ALAN. Allestree, England, 2/17/34. Actor. *An Unmarried Woman.*
BATTLE, KATHLEEN. Portsmouth, OH, 8/13/48. Opera singer.
BAUER, JOE. Memphis, TN, 9/26/41. Drummer. The Youngbloods.
BAUER, STEVEN (Steven Echevarria). Havana, Cuba, 12/2/56. Actor, formerly married to Melanie Griffith. *Wiseguy.*
BAUMGARTNER, STEVE. Philadelphia, PA, 10/28/67. Writer *Permanent Vacation.*
BAXTER, JEFF "SKUNK." Washington, DC, 12/13/48. Lead Guitarist. Steely Dan; The Doobie Brothers.
BAXTER, KEITH. Monmouthshire, Wales, 4/29/33. Actor.
BAXTER, MEREDITH. Los Angeles, CA, 6/21/47. Actor, formerly married to David Birney. Elyse Keaton on *Family Ties.*
BEACHAM, STEPHANIE. Hertfordshire, England, 2/28/47. Actor. Sable Scott Colby on *The Colbys.*
BEAKY (John Dymond). Salisbury, England, 7/10/44. Guitarist. Dave Dee, Dozy, Beaky, Mick and Tich.
BEALS, JENNIFER. Chicago, IL, 12/19/63. Actor. *Flashdance.*
BEARD, FRANK. Dallas, TX, 12/10/49. Drummer. ZZ Top.
BEASLEY, ALLYCE. Brooklyn, NY, 7/6/54. Actor. Agnes Dipesto on *Moonlighting.*
BEATRICE, PRINCESS. London, England, 8/8/88.

British royalty, daughter of Prince Andrew and the Duchess of York.
BEATTY, NED. Lexington, KY, 7/6/37. Actor. *Deliverance.*
BECK, JEFF. Wallington, England, 6/24/44. Guitarist. The Yardbirds; The Jeff Beck Group; The Jan Hammer Group.
BECK, JOHN. Chicago, IL, 1/28/43. Actor. Mark Graison on *Dallas.*
BECK, MICHAEL. Memphis, TN, 2/4/49. Actor. *Xanadu.*
BECKER, BORIS. Liemen, Germany, 11/22/67. Tennis player.
BECKER, WALTER. New York, NY, 2/20/50. Bassist. Steely Dan.
BECKLEY, GERRY. Texas, 9/12/52. Singer, guitarist. America.
BEDELIA, BONNIE. New York, NY, 3/25/46. Actor. *Presumed Innocent.*
BEDFORD, MARK. London, England, 8/24/61. Bassist. Madness.
BEEFHEART, CAPTAIN (Don Van Vliet). Glendale, CA, 1/15/41. Singer, high school friend of Frank Zappa. Captain Beefheart & The Magic Band.
BEERS, GARY. 6/22/57. Bassist, singer. INXS
BEGLEY, ED JR. Los Angeles, CA, 9/16/49. Actor. Dr. Victor Ehrlich on *St. Elsewhere.*
BEL GEDDES, BARBARA New York, NY, 10/31/22. Actor. *Dallas.*
BELAFONTE, HARRY. New York, NY, 3/1/27. Actor, singer, father of Shari. "The Banana Boat Song."
BELAFONTE, SHARI. New York, NY, 9/22/54. Actor, daughter of Harry. *Hotel.*
BELL, ANDY. Peterborough, England, 4/25/64. Singer. Erasure.
BELL, RICKY. Boston, MA, 9/18/67. Singer. New Edition.
BELL, ROBERT. Youngstown, OH, 10/8/50. Bassist. Kool & The Gang.
BELL, RONALD. Youngstown, OH, 11/1/51. Saxophonist. Kool & The Gang.
BELLADONNA, JOEY. Oswego, NY. Singer. Anthrax.
BELLAMY, GEORGE. Sunderland, England, 10/8/41. Guitarist. The Tornados.
BELLAMY, TONY. Los Angeles, CA, 9/12/40. Singer, guitarist. Redbone.
BELLO, FRANK. 7/9/65. Bassist. Anthrax.
BELMONDO, JEAN-PAUL. Paris, France, 4/9/33. Actor. *Breathless.*
BELUSHI, JIM. Chicago, IL, 6/15/54. Actor, brother of late John Belushi. *K-9.*
BENATAR, PAT (Pat Andrzejewski). Brooklyn, NY, 1/10/53. Singer. "Heartbreaker."
BENBEN, BRIAN. Newburgh, NY. Actor. Dream On. Married to Madeline Stowe.
BENEDICT, DIRK (Dirk Niewoehner). Helena, MT, 3/1/45. Actor. Lt. Templeton Peck on *The A-Team.*
BENJAMIN, RICHARD. New York, NY, 5/22/38. Actor, director. *Love at First Bite; Goodbye, Columbus.*
BENNETT, BRIAN. London, England, 2/9/40. Drummer. The Shadows.
BENNETT, ESTELLE. New York, NY, 7/22/44. Singer. The Ronettes.
BENNETT, PATRICIA. New York, NY, 4/7/47. Singer. The Chiffons.
BENSON, GEORGE. Pittsburgh, PA, 3/22/43. Singer, guitarist. "Give Me the Night."
BENSON, RENALDO. Detroit, MI, 1947. Singer. The Four Tops.
BENSON, ROBBY (Robby Segal). Dallas, TX, 1/21/56. Actor, writer, director. *Ice Castles.*
BERENGER, TOM. Chicago, IL, 5/31/50. Actor. *Platoon.*
BERENSON, MARISA. New York, NY, 2/15/47. Actor. *Barry Lyndon.*
BERGEN, POLLY (Nellie Paulina Burgin). Knoxville, TN, 7/14/30. Singer, actor. *The Winds of War.*
BERGER, ALAN. 11/8/49. Bassist. Southside Johnny & The Asbury Jukes.
BERGMAN, INGMAR. Uppsala, Sweden, 7/14/18. Writer, director. *The Silence.*
BERKOWITZ, DAVID. New York, NY, 6/1/53. Serial killer. Son of Sam.
BERLE, MILTON (Milton Berlinger). New York, NY, 7/12/08. Actor. *The Milton Berle Show.*
BERNHARD, SANDRA. Flint, MI, 6/6/55. Actor, singer. *Roseanne.*
BERNSEN, CORBIN. Los Angeles, CA, 9/7/54. Actor, married to Amanda Pays. Arnie Becker on *L.A. Law.*
BERRI, CLAUDE (Claude Langmann). Paris, France, 7/1/34. Actor, director, producer of films.
BERRY, BILL. Hibbing, MN, 7/31/58. Drummer. R.E.M.
BERRY, CHUCK. San Jose, CA, 10/18/26. Rock and Roll legend, singer and guitarist. "Johnny B. Goode."
BERRY, JAN. Los Angeles, CA, 4/3/41. Singer. Jan & Dean.
BERTINELLI, VALERIE. Wilmington, DE, 4/23/60. Actor, married to Eddie Van Halen. Barbara Cooper Royer on *One Day at a Time.*
BETTS, DICKEY. West Palm Beach, FL, 12/12/43. Guitarist, singer. The Allman Brothers Band.
BIALIK, MAYIM. San Diego, CA, 12/12/75. Actor. *Blossom.*
BIEHN, MICHAEL. Anniston, AL, 7/29/56. Actor. *The Terminator.*
BIG FIGURE, THE (John Martin). 1947. Drummer. Dr. Feelgood.
BILLINGSLEY, BARBARA. Los Angeles, CA, 12/22/22. Actor. June Cleaver on *Leave It to Beaver.*
BILLINGSLEY, PETER. New York, NY, 1972. Child actor. *A Christmas Story.*
BILLINGSLEY, RAY. Wake Forest, NC, 7/25/57. Cartoonist. *Curtis.*
BIRD, LARRY. West Baden, IN, 12/7/56. Basketball great. Boston Celtics.
BIRNEY, DAVID. Washington, DC, 4/23/39. Actor, formerly married to Meredith Baxter. *St. Elsewhere.*
BIRRELL, PETE. Manchester, England, 5/9/41. Bassist. Freddie & The Dreamers.
BIRTLES, BEEB (Gerard Birtlekamp). Amsterdam, the Netherlands, 11/28/48. Guitarist. The Little River Band.
BISHOP, JOEY (Joseph Gotllieb). The Bronx, NY, 2/3/18. Actor. *The Joey Bishop Show.*
BISSET, JACQUELINE. Waybridge, England, 9/13/44. Actor. *The Deep.*
BISSET, JOSIE. Seattle, WA, 10/5/69. Actor. *Melrose Place.*
BIVINS, MICHAEL. 8/10/68. Singer. New Edition, Bell Biv DeVoe.
BLACK, CILLA (Cilla White). Liverpool, England, 5/27/43. Singer, TV personality.
BLACK, JET (Brian Duffy). England, 8/26/58. Drummer. The Stranglers.
BLACK, KAREN (Karen Ziegler). Park Ridge, IL, 7/1/42. Actor. *Easy Rider.*
BLACKMON, LARRY. New York, 5/29/56. Singer, drummer. Cameo.
BLACKMORE, RITCHIE. Weston-Super-Mare, England, 4/14/45. Guitarist. Deep Purple; Rainbow.
BLADD, STEPHEN JO. Boston, MA, 7/13/42. Drummer, singer. The J. Geils Band.
BLADES, RUBEN. Panama City, Panama, 7/16/48. Actor, singer. *The Milagro Beanfield War.*
BLAIR, BONNIE. Cornwall, NY, 3/18/64. Speed skater.
BLAIR, LINDA. Westport, CT, 1/22/59. Actor. *The Exorcist.*
BLAKE, ROBERT (Michael Gubitosi). Nutley, NJ, 9/18/33. Actor. *Baretta.*
BLAKELY, SUSAN. Frankfurt, Germany, 9/7/50. Actor. *Rich Man, Poor Man.*
BLAKLEY, ALAN. Bromley, England, 4/1/42. Guitarist. Brian Poole & The Tremeloes.
BLAND, BOBBY. Rosemark, TN, 1/27/30. Singer.
BLASS, BILL. Ft. Wayne, IN, 6/22/22. Fashion designer.

BLEDSOE, TEMPESTT. Chicago, IL, 8/1/73. Actor. Vanessa Huxtable on *The Cosby Show.*
BLOOM, CLAIRE. London, England, 2/15/31. Actor. *Richard III.*
BLOOM, ERIC. Long Island, NY, 12/1/44. Lead guitarist, keyboardist. Blue Öyster Cult.
BLOW, KURTIS (Kurtis Walker). New York, NY, 8/9/59. DJ, rapper.
BLUECHEL, TED JR. San Pedro, CA, 12/2/42. Singer, drummer. The Association.
BLUME, JUDY. Elizabeth, NJ, 2/12/38. Novelist. *Are You There God? It's Me Margaret.*
BLUNSTONE, COLIN. Hatfield, England, 6/24/45. Singer. The Zombies.
BOBBY G. (Bobby Gubby). London, England, 8/23/53. Singer. Bucks Fizz.
BOGARDE, DIRK (Derek Niven van den Bogaerde). Hampstead, England, 3/28/21. Actor. *Death in Venice.*
BOGERT, TIM. Richfield, NJ, 8/27/44. Bassist. Vanilla Fudge.
BOGLE, BOB. Portland, OR, 1/16/37. Guitarist, bassist. The Ventures.
BOGOSIAN, ERIC. Woburn, MA, 4/24/53. Actor, writer. *Talk Radio.*
BOLAN, MARC (Mark Feld). Hackney, England, 9/30/47. Singer, guitarist. T. Rex.
BOLDER, TREVOR. 6/9/50. Bassist. Spiders from Mars; Uriah Heep.
BOLOGNA, JOSEPH. Brooklyn, NY, 12/30/38. Actor. *Chapter Two.*
BONADUCE, DANNY. 8/13/59. Actor, radio personality. Danny on *The Partridge Family.*
BOND, RONNIE (Ronnie Bullis). Andover, England, 5/4/43. Drummer. The Troggs.
BONDS, GARY (Gary Anderson). Jacksonville, FL, 6/6/39. Singer.
BONET, LISA. San Francisco, CA, 11/16/67. Actor, formerly married to Lenny Kravitz. Denise Huxtable on *The Cosby Show.*
BONHAM-CARTER, HELENA. London, England, 5/26/66. Actor. *A Room with a View.*
BONNER, FRANK. Little Rock, AR, 2/28/42. Actor. Herb Tarlek on *WKRP in Cincinnati.*
BONO, CHASTITY. Los Angeles, CA, 3/4/69. Daughter of Sonny and Cher.
BONO, SONNY (Salvatore Bono). Detroit, MI, 2/16/35. Singer, actor, director, congressman, formerly married to Cher, father of Chastity. *The Sonny and Cher Comedy Hour.*
BONSALL, BRIAN. 12/3/82. Child actor. *Family Ties.*
BONSALL, JOE. Philadelphia, PA, 5/18/48. Singer. The Oak Ridge Boys.
BOONE, PAT. Jacksonville, FL, 6/1/34. Singer, actor. *The Pat Boone Show.*
BOONE, STEVE. North Carolina, 9/23/43. Bassist, singer. The Lovin' Spoonful.
BOOTHE, POWERS. Snyder, TX, 6/1/49. Actor. *Guyana Tragedy: The Story of Jim Jones.*
BORGNINE, ERNEST (Ernest Borgnino). Hamden, CT, 1/24/17. Actor. *McHale's Navy.*
BOSSON, BARBARA. Charleroi, PA, 11/1/39. Actor, married to producer Steven Bochco. Fay Furillo on *Hill Street Blues.*
BOSTWICK, BARRY. San Mateo, CA, 2/24/45. Actor. *The Rocky Horror Picture Show.*
BOTTOMS, JOSEPH. Santa Barbara, CA, 4/22/54. Actor. *The Black Hole.*
BOTTOMS, SAM. Santa Barbara, CA, 10/17/55. Actor. *Apocalypse Now.*
BOTTOMS, TIMOTHY. Santa Barbara, CA, 8/30/51. Actor. *Johnny Got His Gun.*
BOTTUM, RODDY. Los Angeles, CA, 7/1/63. Keyboardist. Faith No More.
BOUCHARD, JOE. Long Island, NY, 11/9/48. Bassist, singer. Blue Öyster Cult.
BOWE, RIDDICK. New York, NY, 8/10/67. Boxer, former heavyweight champion of the world.
BOWERS, TONY. 10/31/56. Bassist. Simply Red.
BOWIE, DAVID (David Jones). Brixton, England, 1/8/47. Singer, actor, married to Iman. *Ziggy Stardust and the Spiders from Mars.*
BOX, MICK. London, England, 6/8/47. Guitarist, songwriter. Uriah Heep.
BOXLEITNER, BRUCE. Elgin, IL, 5/12/50. Actor, married to Melissa Gilbert. *Scarecrow and Mrs. King.*
BOY GEORGE (George O'Dowd). Eltham, England, 6/14/61. Singer. Culture Club.
BOYLE, LARA FLYNN. Davenport, IA, 3/24/70. Actor. *Twin Peaks.*
BOYLE, PETER. Philadelphia, PA, 10/18/33. Actor. *Young Frankenstein.*
BRACCO, LORRAINE. Brooklyn, NY, 1955. Actor. *GoodFellas.*
BRADBURY, RAY. Waukegan, IL, 8/22/20. Novelist. *The Martian Chronicles.*
BRAGG, BILLY (Steven Bragg). Barking, England, 12/20/57. Punk/R&B singer, songwriter.
BRAID, LES (William Braid). Liverpool, England, 9/15/41. Bassist. The Swinging Blue Jeans.
BRAMLETT, BONNIE. Acton, IL, 11/8/44. Singer. Delaney & Bonnie.
BRAMLETT, DELANEY. Pontotoc County, MS, 7/1/39. Guitarist, singer. Delaney & Bonnie.
BRANDAUER, KLAUS MARIA. Altaussee, Austria, 6/22/44. Actor. *Out of Africa.*
BRATTON, CREED. Sacramento, CA, 2/8/43. Guitarist. The Grass Roots.
BRAUNN, ERIK. Boston, MA, 8/11/50. Guitarist, singer. Iron Butterfly.
BREATHED, BERKE. Encino, CA, 6/21/57. Cartoonist. *Bloom County.*
BRENNAN, EILEEN. Los Angeles, CA, 9/3/35. Actor. *Private Benjamin.*
BRENNEMAN, AMY. New London, CT, 6/22/64. Actor. *NYPD Blue.*
BRENNER, DAVID. Philadelphia, PA, 2/4/45. Stand-up comedian. *Nightlife.*
BREWER, DONALD. Flint, MI, 9/3/48. Drummer. Grand Funk Railroad.
BRICKELL, EDIE. Oak Cliff, TX, 1966. Singer, songwriter, married to Paul Simon. Edie Brickell and New Bohemians.
BRIDGES, BEAU (Lloyd Vernet Bridges III). Los Angeles, CA, 12/9/41. Actor, director, son of Lloyd, brother of Jeff. *The Fabulous Baker Boys.*
BRIDGES, LLOYD. San Leandro, CA, 1/15/13. Actor, father of Beau and Jeff. *Sea Hunt.*
BRIDGES, TODD. San Francisco, CA, 5/27/66. Actor. Willis Jackson on *Diff'rent Strokes.*
BRIGATI, EDDIE. Garfield, NJ, 10/22/46. Singer, percussionist. The (Young) Rascals.
BRIGGS, DAVID. Melbourne, Australia, 1/26/51. Guitarist. The Little River Band.
BRILEY, ALEX. 4/12/56. Singer. The Village People.
BRIMLEY, WILFORD. Salt Lake City, UT, 9/27/34. Actor. *Cocoon.*
BRINKLEY, DAVID. Wilmington, NC, 7/10/20. Pioneer news journalist and anchor. *This Week with David Brinkley.*
BRIQUETTE, PETE (Patrick Cusack). Ireland, 7/2/54. Bassist, singer. The Boomtown Rats.
BRITTANY, MORGAN (Suzanne Cupito). Los Angeles, CA, 12/5/51. Actor. Katherine Wentworth on *Dallas.*
BRITTON, CHRIS. Watford, England, 6/21/45. Guitarist. The Troggs.
BROLIN, JAMES (James Bruderlin). Los Angeles, CA, 7/18/40. Actor, father of Josh. Dr. Steven Kiley on *Marcus Welby, M.D.*
BRONSON, CHARLES (Charles Buchinsky). Ehrenfield, PA, 11/3/21. Actor, widower of Jill Ireland. *Death Wish.*
BROOKER, GARY. Southend, England, 5/29/45. Singer, keyboardist. Procol Harum.
BROOKS, ALBERT (Albert Einstein). Los Angeles, CA,

7/22/47. Actor, writer, director. *Defending Your Life.*
BROOKS, LALA. Brooklyn, NY, 1946. Singer. The Crystals.
BROTHERS, JOYCE (Joyce Bauer). New York, NY, 10/20/28. Psychologist.
BROWN, BLAIR. Washington, DC, 1948. Actor. *The Days and Nights of Molly Dodd.*
BROWN, BOBBY. Boston, MA, 2/5/69. Singer, dancer. "My Perogative."
BROWN, BRYAN. Panania, Australia, 6/23/47. Actor, married to Rachel Ward. *FX.*
BROWN, DAVID. Houston, TX, 2/15/47. Bassist. Santana.
BROWN, ERROL. Kingston, Jamaica, 11/12/48. Singer. Hot Chocolate.
BROWN, GEORG STANFORD. Havana, Cuba, 6/24/43. Actor. *Colossus: The Forbin Project.*
BROWN, GEORGE. Jersey City, NJ, 1/5/49. Drummer. Kool and The Gang.
BROWN, HAROLD. Long Beach, CA, 3/17/46. Drummer. War.
BROWN, IAN. Sale, England, 2/20/63. Singer. Stone Roses.
BROWN, JAMES. Augusta, GA, 5/3/28. The Godfather of Soul.
BROWN, JIM. St. Simons Island, GA, 2/17/36. Football player, actor. *The Dirty Dozen.*
BROWN, JIMMY. Birmingham, England, 11/20/57. Drummer. UB40.
BROWN, MICHAEL (Michael Lookofsky). New York, NY, 4/25/49. Keyboardist. The Left Banke.
JACKSON BROWNE Heidelberg, Germany, 10/9/48, Singer, songwriter.
BRUCE, JACK. Glasgow, Scotland, 5/14/43. Singer, bassist. Cream.
BRUCE, MICHAEL. 3/16/48. Guitarist, keyboardist. Alice Cooper.
BRUFORD, BILL. London, England, 5/17/48. Drummer. Yes.
BRYAN, DAVID (David Rashbaum). New Jersey, 2/7/62. Keyboardist. Bon Jovi.
BRYON, DENNIS. Cardiff, Wales, 4/14/49. Drummer. Amen Corner.
PEABO BRYSON (Robert Peabo Bryson), Greenville, SC, 4/13/51, Singer.
BRZEZICKI, MARK. Slough, England, 6/21/57. Drummer. Big Country.
BUCHANAN, PAUL. Scotland. Singer, synthesizer player. Blue Nile.
BUCHHOLZ, FRANCIS. 2/19/50. Guitarist. Scorpions.
BUCK, PETER. Athens, GA, 12/6/56. Guitarist. R.E.M.
BUCK, ROBERT. Guitarist. 10,000 Maniacs.
BUCKINGHAM, LINDSEY. Palo Alto, CA, 10/3/47. Guitarist, singer. Fleetwood Mac.
BUCKLER, RICK (Paul Buckler). 12/6/56. Drummer, singer. The Jam.
BUCKLEY, BETTY. Big Spring, TX, 7/3/47. Actor. *Eight Is Enough.*
BUJOLD, GENEVIEVE. Montreal, Canada, 7/1/42. Actor. *Dead Ringers.*
BUNKER, CLIVE. Blackpool, England, 12/12/46. Drummer. Jethro Tull.
BUNNELL, DEWEY. Yorkshire, England, 1/19/51. Singer, guitarist. America.
BURCHILL, CHARLIE. Glasgow, Scotland, 11/27/59. Guitarist. Simple Minds.
BURDEN, IAN. 12/24/57. Synthesizer player. Human League.
BURDON, ERIC. Walker-on-Tyne, England, 5/11/41. Singer, songwriter. The Animals; War.
BURGHOFF, GARY. Bristol, CT, 5/24/43. Actor. Radar O'Reilly on *M*A*S*H.*
BURKE, DELTA. Orlando, FL, 7/30/56. Actor, married to Gerald McRaney. *Designing Women.*
BURKE, SOLOMON. Philadelphia, PA, 1936. Country-gospel-R&B singer, songwriter.
BURNEL, JEAN-JACQUES. London, England, 2/21/52. Bassist. The Stranglers.
BURNETT, CAROL. San Antonio, TX, 4/26/33. Actor. *The Carol Burnett Show.*
BURNS, BOB. Drummer. Lynyrd Skynyrd.
BURR, CLIVE. 3/8/57. Drummer. Iron Maiden.
BURRELL, BOZ (Raymond Burrell). Lincoln, England, 1946. Bassist. Bad Company.
BURROWS, DARREN E. Winfield, KS, 9/12/66. Actor. Ed Chigliak on *Northern Exposure.*
BURSTYN, ELLEN (Edna Rae Gillooly). Detroit, MI, 12/7/32. Actor. *Alice Doesn't Live Here Anymore.*
BURT, HEINZ. Hargin, Germany, 7/24/42. Bassist. The Tornados.
BURTON, LEVAR. Landstuhl, Germany, 2/16/57. Actor. Geordi LaForge on *Star Trek: The Next Generation.*
BURTON, TREVOR. Aston, England, 3/9/44. Lead guitarist. The Move.
BUSEY, GARY. Goose Creek, TX, 6/29/44. Actor. *The Buddy Holly Story.*
TIMOTHY BUSFIELD Lansing, MI, 6/12/57, Actor, *thirtysomething.*
BUSH, BARBARA. Rye, NY, 6/8/25. Former First Lady, married to George Bush.
BUSH, GEORGE. Milton, MA, 6/12/24. Political leader, husband of Barbara. Forty-first president of the U.S.
BUSH, KATE. Bexleyheath, England, 7/30/58. Singer, songwriter.
BUSHY, RONALD. Washington, DC, 9/23/45. Drummer. Iron Butterfly.
BUTKUS, DICK. Chicago, IL, 12/9/42. Football player, actor. *My Two Dads.*
BUTLER, GEEZER (Terry Butler). Birmingham, England, 7/17/49. Bassist. Black Sabbath.
BUTLER, JERRY. Sunflower, MS, 12/8/39. Singer. The Impressions.
BUTLER, JOE. Glen Cove, NY, 9/16/43. Drummer, singer. The Lovin' Spoonful.
BUTLER, RICHARD. Surrey, England, 6/5/56. Singer, lyricist. Psychedelic Furs.
BUTLER, TONY. Ealing, England, 2/13/57. Bassist. Big Country.
BUTTAFUOCO, JOEY. Massapequa, NY. 3/11/56. Mechanic. Had affair with Amy Fisher.
BUTTONS, RED (Aaron Chwatt). New York, NY, 2/5/19. Performer. *The Red Buttons Show.*
BUXTON, GLEN. Akron, OH, 11/10/47. Guitarist. Alice Cooper.
BUZZI, RUTH. Westerly, RI, 7/24/36. Actor. *Laugh-In.*
DAVID BYRNE Dumbarton, Scotland, 5/14/52, Singer, songwriter, director, Talking Heads.
BYRNE, GABRIEL. Dublin, Ireland, 1950. Actor, formerly married to Ellen Barkin. *Miller's Crossing.*
BYRON, DAVID. Essex, England, 1/29/47. Singer. Uriah Heep.
CAAN, JAMES. The Bronx, NY, 3/26/39. Actor. *The Godfather.*
CADDY, ALAN. London, England, 2/2/40. Guitarist. The Tornados; Johnny Kidd & The Pirates.
CAESAR, SID. Yonkers, NY, 9/8/22. Performer. *Your Show of Shows.*
CAFFEY, CHARLOTTE. Santa Monica, CA, 10/21/53. Singer. The Go-Gos.
CAIN, JONATHAN. Chicago, IL, 2/26/50. Keyboardist. Journey.
CAINE, MICHAEL (Maurice Joseph Micklewhite). London, England, 3/14/33. Actor. *Hannah and Her Sisters.*
CALABRO, THOMAS. 2/3/59. Actor. Michael Mancini on *Melrose Place.*
CALE, JOHN. Garnant, Wales, 12/4/40. Bassist, keyboardist, violist, singer. The Velvet Underground.
CALIFORNIA, RANDY (Randy Wolfe). Los Angeles, CA, 2/20/51. Guitarist, singer. Spirit.
CALLOW, SIMON. London, England, 6/15/49. Actor. *A Room with a View.*
CALVERT, BERNIE. Burnley, England, 9/16/43. Bassist. The Hollies.
CAMERON, KIRK. Panorama City, CA, 10/12/70. Actor,

brother of Candace. Mike Seaver on *Growing Pains.*
CAMP, COLLEEN. San Francisco, CA, 1953. Actor. Kristin Shepard on *Dallas.*
CAMPBELL, ALI (Alastair Campbell). Birmingham, England, 2/15/59. Lead singer, guitarist. UB40.
CAMPBELL, BILL. Chicago, IL, 1960. Actor. *The Rocketeer.*
CAMPBELL, BRUCE. Royal Oak, MI, 6/22/58. Actor, producer, screenwriter. *The Adventures of Briscoe County Jr.*
CAMPBELL, GLEN. Delight, AR, 4/22/36. Actor, singer. *The Glen Campbell Goodtime Hour.*
CAMPBELL, MIKE. Panama City, FL, 2/1/54. Guitarist. Tom Petty & The Heartbreakers.
CAMPBELL, ROBIN. Birmingham, England, 12/25/54. Lead guitarist, singer. UB40.
CAMPBELL, TISHA. Oklahoma City, OK, 10/13/70. Actor. *Martin.*
CAMPION, JANE. Wellington, New Zealand, 4/30/54. Director, screenwriter, daughter of Richard and Edith. *The Piano.*
CANN, WARREN. Victoria, Canada, 5/20/52. Drummer. Ultravox.
CANNON, DYAN (Samille Diane Friesen). Tacoma, WA, 1/4/37. Actor. *Bob & Carol & Ted & Alice.*
CAPALDI, JIM. Evesham, England, 8/24/44. Drummer, singer. Traffic.
CAPRIATI, JENNIFER. Long Island, NY, 3/29/76. Tennis player
CAPSHAW, KATE (Kathleen Sue Nail). Ft. Worth, TX, 1953. Actor, married to Steven Spielberg. *Indiana Jones and the Temple of Doom.*
CARA, IRENE. New York, NY, 3/18/59. Actor, singer. *Fame.*
CARAY, HARRY. Saugus, CA, 5/16/21. Announcer for the Chicago Cubs.
CARDIN, PIERRE. Venice, Italy, 7/7/22. Fashion designer.
CARDINALE, CLAUDIA. Tunis, Tunisia, 4/15/39. Actor. *The Pink Panther.*
CAREY, TONY. 10/16/53. Keyboardist. Rainbow.
CARLIN, GEORGE. New York, NY, 5/12/37. Actor. "Seven Dirty Words."
CARLISLE, BELINDA. Hollywood, CA, 8/16/58. Singer, songwriter.
CARLOS, BUN (Brad Carlson). Rockford, IL, 6/12/51. Drummer. Cheap Trick.
CARMEN, ERIC. Cleveland, OH, 8/11/49. Singer. The Raspberries.
CARNE, JUDY (Joyce Botterill). Northampton, England, 3/27/39. Actor. *Laugh-In.*
CARNEY, ART. Mt. Vernon, NY, 11/4/18. Actor and comedian. Ed Norton on *The Honeymooners.*
CAROLINE, PRINCESS. Monte Carlo, Monaco, 1/23/57. Daughter of Princess Grace of Monaco.
CARON, LESLIE. Paris, France, 7/1/31. Actor. *Lili.*
CARPENTER, JOHN. Carthage, NY, 1/16/48. Director, writer. *Halloween.*
CARPENTER, RICHARD. New Haven, CT, 10/15/46. Keyboardist, singer. The Carpenters.
CARR, DAVID. Leyton, England, 8/4/43. Keyboardist. The Fortunes.
CARRACK, PAUL. Sheffield, England, 4/21/51. Singer, songwriter. Squeeze; Ace; Mike and the Mechanics.
CARRADINE, DAVID. Hollywood, CA, 12/8/36. Actor, son of John Carradine, brother of Keith and Robert. *Kung Fu.*
CARRADINE, KEITH. San Mateo, CA, 8/8/49. Actor, son of John, brother of David and Robert, father of Martha Plimpton. *The Will Rogers Follies.*
CARRADINE, ROBERT. Hollywood, CA, 3/24/54. Actor, son of John, brother of David and Keith. *Revenge of the Nerds.*
CARRERA, BARBARA. Managua, Nicaragua, 12/31/51. Model, actor. *Dallas.*
CARROLL, DIAHANN (Carol Diahann Johnson). New York, NY, 7/17/35. Actor, singer, married to Vic Damone. *I Know Why the Caged Bird Sings.*
CARRY, JULIUS. Actor. Mitchell Baldwin on *Murphy Brown.*
CARTER, DIXIE. McLemoresville, TN, 5/25/39. Actor. Julia Sugarbaker on *Designing Women.*
CARTER, JIMMY. Plains, GA, 10/1/24. Political leader. Thirty-ninth president of the U.S.
CARTER, LYNDA. Phoenix, AZ, 7/24/51. Actor. *Wonder Woman.*
CARTER, NELL. Birmingham, AL, 9/13/48. Actor, singer. *Gimme a Break.*
CARTERIS, GABRIELLE. 1/2/61. Actor. Andrea Zuckerman on *Beverly Hills 90210.*
CARTWRIGHT, VERONICA. Bristol, England, 1950. Actor. *Alien.*
CARVEY, DANA. Missoula, MT, 4/2/55. Actor. *Saturday Night Live, Wayne's World.*
CARUSO, DAVID. Queens, NY, 1/17/56. Actor. *NYPD Blue.*
CASADY, JACK. Washington, DC, 4/13/44. Bass guitarist. Jefferson Airplane/Starship.
CASEY, HARRY WAYNE (Harold Casey). Hialeah, FL, 1/31/51. Singer, keyboardist. KC & The Sunshine Band.
CASS, PEGGY (Mary Margaret Cass). Boston, MA, 5/21/24. Actor. Panelist on *To Tell The Truth.*
CASSIDY, DAVID. New York, NY, 4/12/50. Actor, half brother of Shaun, son of Jack, step-son of Shirley Jones. Keith in *The Partridge Family.*
CASSIDY, ED. Chicago, IL, 5/4/31. Drummer. Spirit.
CASSIDY, JOANNA. Camden, NJ, 8/2/44. Actor. Jo Jo White on *Buffalo Bill.*
CASTRO, FIDEL (Fidel Ruz). Mayari, Cuba, 8/13/26. Political leader. President of Cuba.
CATES, PHOEBE. New York, NY, 7/16/63. Actor, married to Kevin Kline. *Fast Times at Ridgemont High.*
CATHERALL, JOANNE. Sheffield, England, 9/18/62. Singer. Human League.
CATTINI, CLEM. 8/28/39. Drummer. Johnny Kidd & The Pirates; Tornados.
CATTRALL, KIM. Liverpool, England, 8/21/56. Actor. *The Bonfire of the Vanities.*
CAVALIERE, FELIX. Pelham, NY, 11/29/44. Singer, keyboardist. The (Young) Rascals.
CAVETT, DICK. Gibbon, NE, 11/19/36. Actor, talk show host. *The Dick Cavett Show.*
CEASE, JEFF. Nashville, TN, 6/24/67. Guitarist. The Black Crowes.
CETERA, PETER. Chicago, IL, 9/13/44. Singer, songwriter. Chicago.
CHADWICK, LES (John Chadwick). Liverpool, England, 5/11/43. Bassist. Gerry & The Pacemakers.
CHAMBERLAIN, RICHARD (George Chamberlain). Los Angeles, CA, 3/31/35. Actor. *Dr. Kildare.*
CHAMBERLAIN, WILT. West Philadelphia, PA, 8/21/36. Basketball great.
CHAMBERS, GEORGE. Flora, MS, 9/26/31. Bassist, singer. The Chambers Brothers.
CHAMBERS, JOE. Scott County, MS, 8/24/42. Guitarist, singer. The Chambers Brothers.
CHAMBERS, LESTER. Flora, MS, 4/13/40. Harmonicist, singer. The Chambers Brothers.
CHAMBERS, MARTIN. Hereford, England, 9/4/51. Drummer. The Pretenders.
CHAMBERS, TERRY. England, 7/18/55. Drummer. XTC.
CHAMBERS, WILLIE. Flora, MS, 3/3/38. Guitarist, singer. The Chambers Brothers.
CHANDLER, GENE (Gene Dixon). Chicago, IL, 7/6/37. Singer, songwriter.
CHANNING, CAROL. Seattle, WA, 1/31/21. Actor. *Hello, Dolly!*

CHANNING, STOCKARD (Susan Williams Antonia Stockard). New York, NY, 2/13/44. Actor. *Grease.*
CHAO, ROSALIND. Los Angeles, CA. Actor. Soon-Lee on *M*A*S*H.*
CHAPLIN, GERALDINE. Santa Monica, CA, 7/31/44. Actor. *Dr. Zhivago.*
CHAPMAN, ROGER. Leicester, England, 4/8/44. Singer. Family.
CHAPMAN, TRACY. Cleveland, OH, 3/30/64. Folk singer, songwriter.
CHAQUICO, CRAIG. 9/26/54. Singer, guitarist. Jefferson Starship.
CHARISSE, CYD (Tula Ellice Finklea). Amarillo, TX, 3/8/22. Actor. *Brigadoon.*
CHARLES, RAY (Ray Robinson). Albany, GA, 9/23/30. Singer, songwriter. "Georgia on My Mind."
CHARLTON, MANUEL. 7/25/41. Guitarist, singer, songwriter. Nazareth.
CHARO. Murcia, Spain, 1/15/51. Actor, singer. *The Love Boat.*
CHASE, CHEVY (Cornelius Crane Chase) New York, NY, 10/8/43, Actor, *National Lampoon's Vacation* movies.
CHECKER, CHUBBY (Ernest Evans). Spring Gulley, SC, 10/3/41. Singer, songwriter. Popularized the Twist and Limbo.
CHER (Cherilyn Sarkisian La Piere). El Centro, CA, 5/20/46. Singer, actor, formerly married to Sonny Bono and Gregg Allman. *Moonstruck.*
CHERRY, NENEH. Stockholm, Sweden, 3/10/64. Rap/pop singer, songwriter.
CHILD, JULIA. Pasadena, CA, 8/15/12. TV chef, author. *Mastering the Art of French Cooking.*
CHILES, LOIS. Alice, TX, 1950. Model, actor. *The Way We Were.*
CHILTON, ALEX. Memphis, TN, 12/28/50. Guitarist, singer. The Box Tops; Big Star.
CHONG, RAE DAWN. Vancouver, Canada, 1962. Actor, daughter of Thomas Chong. *The Color Purple.*
CHONG, THOMAS. Edmonton, Canada, 5/24/38. Singer, actor, writer, director, former partner of Cheech Marin, father of Rae Dawn Chong. *Up in Smoke.*
CHRISTIAN, GARRY. Merseyside, England, 2/27/55. Singer. The Christians.
CHRISTIAN, ROGER. 2/13/50. Singer. The Christians.
CHRISTIAN, RUSSELL. 6/8/56. Singer. The Christians.
CHRISTIE, JULIE. Chukua, India, 4/14/41. Actor. *Dr. Zhivago.*
CHRISTIE, LOU (Lugee Sacco). Glenwillard, PA, 2/19/43. Singer, songwriter. "Lightnin' Strikes."
CHRISTO (Christo Javacheff). Gabrovo, Bulgaria, 6/13/35. Artist. The Umbrellas.
CHRISTOPHER, WILLIAM. Evanston, IL, 10/20/32. Actor. Father Francis Mulcahy on *M*A*S*H.*
CHUCK D. (Charles Ridenhour). 1960. Rap artist. Public Enemy.
CHUNG, CONNIE (Constance Yu-Hwa Chung) Washington, DC, 8/20/46, TV journalist, CBS.
CHURCHILL, CHICK. Mold, Wales, 1/2/49. Keyboardist. Ten Years After.
CIPOLLINA, JOHN. Berkeley, CA, 8/24/43. Guitarist. Quicksilver Messenger Service.
CLAIBORNE, LIZ (Elisabeth Claiborne). Brussels, Belgium, 3/31/29. Fashion designer.
CLARK, ALAN. Durham, NC, 3/5/52. Keyboardist. Dire Straits.
CLARK, DAVE. Tottenham, England, 12/15/42. Drummer. The Dave Clark Five.
CLARK, DICK. Mt. Vernon, NY, 11/30/29. Producer, music/game show host. *American Bandstand.*
CLARK, GRAEME. Glasgow, Scotland, 4/15/66. Bassist. Wet Wet Wet.
CLARK, NEIL. 7/3/55. Guitarist. Lloyd Cole & The Commotions.
CLARK, PETULA. Surrey, England, 11/15/32. Actor, singer. *Downtown.*
CLARK, ROY. Meherrin, VA, 4/15/33. Country singer, songwriter. *Hee Haw.*
CLARK, STEVE. Hillsborough, England, 4/23/60. Guitarist. Def Leppard.
CLARKE, ALLAN (Harold Clarke). Salford, England, 4/5/42. Singer. The Hollies.
CLARKE, EDDIE. 10/5/50. Guitarist. Motörhead.
CLARKE, MICHAEL (Michael Dick). New York, NY, 6/3/44. Drummer. The Byrds.
CLARKE, VINCE. Basildon, England, 7/3/61. Keyboardist. Erasure.
CLAY, ANDREW DICE. Brooklyn, NY, 1958. Actor. *The Adventures of Ford Fairlaine.*
CLAYBURGH, JILL. New York, NY, 4/30/44. Actor. *An Unmarried Woman.*
CLAYTON, ADAM. Ireland, 3/13/60. Bassist. U2.
CLAYTON-THOMAS, DAVID (David Thomsett). Surrey, England, 9/13/41. Lead singer. Blood, Sweat & Tears.
CLEESE, JOHN. Weston-Super-Mare, England, 10/27/39. Actor. *Monty Python's Flying Circus.*
CLIFF, JIMMY (Jimmy Chambers). Somerton, Jamaica, 1949. Reggae singer, songwriter.
CLIFFORD, DOUG. Palo Alto, CA, 4/24/45. Drummer. Creedence Clearwater Revival.
CLINTON, BILL. Hope, AK, 8/9/46. Husband of Hillary Rodham, father of Chelsea. 42nd President of the United States.
CLINTON, CHELSEA. Arkansas, 2/27/80. Daughter of Bill and Hillary.
CLINTON, GEORGE. Kannapolis, NC, 7/22/40. Funk pioneer, singer. Parliament; Funkadelic.
CLINTON, HILLARY RODHAM. Park Ridge, IL, 10/26/47. Wife of Bill, mother of Chelsea. First Lady.
CLOONEY, ROSEMARY. Maysville, KY, 5/23/28. Actor, singer.
CLYDE, JEREMY. England, 3/22/44. Singer, guitarist. Chad & Jeremy.
COBURN, JAMES. Laurel, NE, 8/31/28. Actor. *The Magnificent Seven.*
COCA, IMOGENE. Philadelphia, PA, 11/18/08. Actor. *Your Show of Shows.*
COCHRANE, TOM. 5/14/53. Singer, guitarist. Red Rider.
COCKER, JOE (John Cocker). Sheffield, England, 5/20/44. Singer.
COEN, ETHAN. St. Louis Park, MN, 1958. Director, writer. Brother of Joel. *Raising Arizona.*
COEN, JOEL. St. Louis Park, MN, 1955. Director, writer. Brother of Ethan. *Raising Arizona.*
COGHLAN, JOHN. Dulwich, England, 9/19/46. Drummer. Status Quo.
COHEN, DAVID. Brooklyn, NY, 1942. Keyboardist. Country Joe & The Fish.
COHEN, LEONARD. Montreal, Canada, 9/21/34. Singer, songwriter, poet.
COLE, BRIAN. Tacoma, WA, 9/8/42. Singer, bassist. The Association.
COLE, LLOYD. Derbyshire, England, 1/31/61. Singer, guitarist. Lloyd Cole & The Commotions.
COLE, NATALIE (Stephanie Natalie Maria Cole). Los Angeles, CA, 2/6/49. Singer. *Unforgettable.*
COLEMAN, DABNEY. Austin, TX, 1/3/32. Actor. *Buffalo Bill.*
COLEMAN, GARY. Zion, IL, 2/8/68. Actor. Arnold Jackson on *Diff'rent Strokes.*
COLEY, DORIS. Passaic, NJ, 8/2/41. Singer. The Shirelles.
COLLA, JOHNNY. California, 7/2/52. Saxophonist, guitarist. Huey Lewis & The News.
COLLEN, PHIL. London, England, 12/8/57. Guitarist. Def Leppard.
COLLINS, ALLEN. Jacksonville, FL, 7/19/52. Guitarist. Lynyrd Skynyrd.

COLLINS, GARY. Boston, MA, 4/30/38. Actor, talk show host. *Home.*
COLLINS, JOAN. London, England, 5/23/33. Actor. Alexis Carrington Colby on *Dynasty.*
COLLINS, JUDY. Seattle, WA, 5/1/39. Folk/rock guitarist, singer, songwriter. "Send in the Clowns."
COLLINS, PHIL. Chiswick, England, 1/30/51. Singer, drummer. Genesis.
COLLINS, STEPHEN. Des Moines, IA, 10/1/47. Actor. *Tales of the Gold Monkey.*
COLOMBY, BOBBY. New York, NY, 12/20/44. Drummer, singer. Blood, Sweat & Tears.
COLT, JOHNNY. Cherry Point, NC, 5/1/66. Bassist. The Black Crowes.
COLUMBUS, CHRIS. Spangler, PA, 9/10/58. Director. *Home Alone.*
CONAWAY, JEFF. New York, NY, 10/5/50. Actor. Bobby Wheeler on *Taxi.*
CONNELLY, JENNIFER. New York, NY, 12/12/70. Actor. *The Rocketeer.*
CONNOLLY, BRIAN. Hamilton, Scotland, 10/5/49. Singer. Sweet.
CONNORS, JIMMY. Belleville, IL, 9/2/52. Tennis player.
CONNORS, MIKE (Krekor Ohanian). Fresno, CA, 8/15/25. Actor. *Mannix.*
CONROY, KEVIN. Westport, CT, 11/30/55. Actor. Voice of Batman in *Batman: The Animated Series.*
CONSTANTINE, MICHAEL (Constantine Joanides). Reading, PA, 5/22/27. Actor. *Room 222.*
CONTI, TOM. Paisley, Scotland, 11/22/41. Actor. *Reuben Reuben.*
CONWAY, KEVIN. New York, NY, 5/29/42. Actor. *Slaughterhouse Five.*
CONWAY, TIM (Thomas Daniel Conway). Willoughby, OH, 12/15/33. Actor. *The Carol Burnett Show.*
COODER, RY (Ryland Cooder). Los Angeles, CA, 3/15/47. Folk blues guitarist, composer.
COOK, JEFF. Fort Payne, AL, 8/27/49. Singer, fiddler, guitarist, keyboardist. Alabama.
COOK, NORMAN (Quentin Cook). Sussex, England, 7/31/63. Singer. The Housemartins.
COOK, PAUL. London, England, 7/20/56. Drummer. The Sex Pistols.
COOK, STU. Oakland, CA, 4/25/45. Bassist. Creedence Clearwater Revival.
COONCE, RICKY. Los Angeles, CA, 8/1/47. Drummer. The Grass Roots.
COOPER, ALICE (Vincent Furnier). Detroit, MI, 2/4/48. Singer, songwriter. Alice Cooper.
COOPER, JACKIE (John Cooper Jr.). Los Angeles, CA, 9/15/22. Actor, director. *Superman.*
COPE, JULIAN. Bargoed, Wales, 10/21/57. Singer, bassist. The Teardrop Explodes.
COPELAND, STEWART. Alexandria, Egypt, 7/16/52. Drummer, singer. The Police.
CORBIN, BARRY. Dawson County, TX, 10/16/40. Actor. Maurice Minnifield on *Northern Exposure.*
CORGAN, BILLY. Chicago, IL, 3/17/67. Singer, songwriter, guitarist. Smashing Pumpkins.
CORLEY, PAT. Dallas, TX, 6/1/30. Actor. Phil the bartender on *Murphy Brown.*
CORNELL, CHRIS. Seattle, WA, 7/20/64. Singer, songwriter, drummer. Soundgarden.
CORNICK, GLENN. Barrow-in-Furness, England, 4/24/47. Bassist. Jethro Tull.
CORNISH, GENE. Ottowa, Canada, 5/14/45. Guitarist. The (Young) Rascals.
CORNWELL, HUGH. London, England, 8/28/49. Singer, guitarist. The Stranglers.
CORT, BUD (Walter Edward Cox). New Rochelle, NY, 3/29/50. Actor. *Harold and Maude.*
COSTELL, DAVID. Pittsburgh, PA, 3/15/44. Bassist. Gary Lewis and the Playboys.
COULIER, DAVID. Detroit, MI. Actor. Joey Gladstone on *Full House.*
COVERDALE, DAVID. Saltburn-by-the-Sea, England, 9/22/49. Singer. Whitesnake.
COWSILL, BARRY. Newport, RI, 9/14/54. Bassist, singer. The Cowsills.
COWSILL, BILL. Newport, RI, 1/9/48. Guitarist, singer. The Cowsills.
COWSILL, BOB. Newport, RI, 8/26/49. Guitarist, singer. The Cowsills.
COWSILL, JOHN. Newport, RI, 3/2/56. Drummer. The Cowsills.
COWSILL, PAUL. Newport, RI, 11/11/52. Keyboardist, singer. The Cowsills.
COWSILL, SUE. Newport, RI, 5/20/60. Singer. The Cowsills.
COX, ANDY. Birmingham, England, 1/25/60. Guitarist. Fine Young Cannibals.
COX, RONNY. Cloudcroft, NM, 8/23/38. Actor. *Beverly Hills Cop.*
COYOTE, PETER (Peter Cohon). New York, NY, 1942. Actor. *Jagged Edge.*
CRAIG, MIKEY. Hammersmith, England, 2/15/60. Bassist. Culture Club.
CRAVEN, WES. Cleveland, OH, 8/2/39. Director, novelist. *A Nightmare on Elm Street.*
CRAWFORD, JOHN. 1/17/60. Bassist, singer. Berlin.
CRAWFORD, MICHAEL (Michael Dumble-Smith). Salisbury, England, 1/19/42. Actor, singer. *The Phantom of the Opera.*
CRAWFORD, RANDY (Veronica Crawford). Macon, GA, 2/18/52. Rock-R&B singer, songwriter.
CRAY, ROBERT. Columbus, GA, 8/1/53. Contemporary blues singer, songwriter. "Smoking Gun."
CREGAN, JIM. 3/9/46. Guitarist. Steve Harley & Cockney Rebel.
CREME, LOL. Manchester, England, 9/19/47. Singer, guitarist. 10cc; Godley & Creme.
CRENNA, RICHARD. Los Angeles, CA, 11/30/27. Actor. *Rambo: First Blood Part II.*
CREWSDON, ROY. Manchester, England, 5/29/41. Guitarist. Freddie & The Dreamers.
CRISS, PETER (Peter Crisscoula). Brooklyn, NY, 12/27/47. Drummer, singer. Kiss.
CROFTS, DASH. Cisco, TX, 8/14/40. Singer, guitarist, mandolinist. Seals & Crofts.
CRONIN, KEVIN. Evanston, IL, 10/6/51. Singer. REO Speedwagon.
CRONKITE, WALTER. St. Joseph, MO, 11/4/16. News journalist and anchor. *CBS Evening News.*
CRONYN, HUME. London, Canada, 7/18/11. Actor, writer, director, widower of Jessica Tandy. *The Postman Always Rings Twice.*
CROPPER, STEVE. Willow Springs, MO, 10/21/41. Guitarist. Booker T. & The MG's.
CROSBY, CATHY LEE. Los Angeles, CA, 12/2/49. Actor. *That's Incredible!*
CROSBY, DAVID (David Van Cortland). Los Angeles, CA, 8/14/41. Singer, guitarist. The Byrds; Crosby, Stills, Nash & Young.
CROSBY, DENISE. Hollywood, CA, 1958. Actor, granddaughter of Bing Crosby. *Star Trek: The Next Generation.*
CROSBY, HARRY. Los Angeles, CA, 8/8/58. Actor, singer.
CROSS, BEN. London, England, 12/16/48. Actor. *Chariots of Fire.*
CROSS, CHRIS (Chris St. John). London, England, 7/14/52. Bassist, synthesizer player. Ultravox.
CROSS, CHRISTOPHER (Christopher Geppert). San Antonio, TX, 5/3/51. Guitarist, singer, songwriter. "Ride Like the Wind."
CROUSE, LINDSAY. New York, NY, 5/12/48. Actor. *The Verdict.*
CRYER, JON. New York, NY, 4/16/65. Actor. *The Famous Teddy Z.*

CULKIN, MACAULAY. New York, NY, 8/26/80. Actor. *Home Alone, My Girl.*
CULLIMORE, STAN. Hull, England, 4/6/62. Bassist. The Housemartins.
CULLUM, JOHN. Knoxville, TN, 3/2/30. Actor. Holling Vincoeur on *Northern Exposure.*
CULP, ROBERT. Oakland, CA, 8/16/30. Actor. *I Spy.*
CUMMINGS, BURTON. Winnipeg, Canada, 12/31/47. Singer, keyboardist. The Guess Who.
CUMMINGS, GEORGE. Meridian, MS, 7/28/38. Lead guitarist. Dr. Hook.
CUNNINGHAM, BILL. Memphis, TN, 1/23/50. Bassist, pianist. The Box Tops; Big Star.
CUNNINGHAM, TOM. Glasgow, Scotland, 6/22/65. Drummer. Wet Wet Wet.
CUOMO, MARIO. Queens, NY, 6/15/32. Political leader. Former Governor of New York.
CURRIE, ALANNAH. Auckland, New Zealand, 9/20/59. Singer, saxophonist, percussionist. Thompson Twins.
CURRIE, BILLY. Huddersfield, England, 4/1/52. Synthesizer player, keyboardist. Ultravox.
CURRIE, CHERIE. Los Angeles, CA, 1960. Singer, married to Robert Hays. The Runaways.
CURRY, TIM. Cheshire, England, 4/19/46. Actor. *The Rocky Horror Picture Show.*
CURTIN, JANE. Cambridge, MA, 9/6/47. Actor. *Kate & Allie.*
CURTIS, CHRIS (Chris Crummy). Oldham, England, 8/26/41. Singer, drummer. The Searchers.
CURTIS, SONNY. Meadow, TX, 5/9/37. Guitarist. Buddy Holly & The Crickets.
CURTIS, TONY (Bernard Schwartz). New York, NY, 6/3/24. Actor, father of Jamie Lee Curtis, formerly married to Janet Leigh. *Some Like It Hot.*
CUSACK, CYRIL. Durban, South Africa, 11/26/10. Actor. *Fahrenheit 451.*
CUSACK, JOAN. Evanston, IL, 10/11/62. Actor. *Working Girl.*
CUSACK, SINEAD. Ireland, 2/18/48. Actor, married to Jeremy Irons, daughter of Cyril Cusack.
CYRUS, BILLY RAY. Flatwoods, NY, 8/25/61. Singer, son of politician Ronald Ray Cyrus. "Achy-Breaky Heart."
D'ALEO, ANGELO. The Bronx, NY, 2/3/41. Singer. Dion & The Belmonts.
D'ANGELO, BEVERLY. Columbus, OH, 11/15/54. Actor. *Hair.*
D'ARBY, TERENCE TRENT. New York, NY, 3/15/62. R&B singer, songwriter. "Wishing Well."
DAFOE, WILLEM. Appleton, WI, 7/22/55. Actor. *Mississippi Burning.*
DALE, GLEN (Richard Garforth). Deal, England, 4/2/43. Guitarist, singer. The Fortunes.
DALEY, ROSIE. South Seaville, NJ, 1961. Chef. *In the Kitchen with Rosie.*
DALLIN, SARAH. Bristol, England, 12/17/61. Singer. Bananarama.
DALTON, TIMOTHY. Colwyn Bay, Wales, 3/21/44. Actor. James Bond in *The Living Daylights.*
DALTREY, ROGER. London, England, 3/1/44. Lead singer. The Who.
DALY, GARY. Merseyside, England, 5/5/62. Singer. China Crisis.
DALY, TIMOTHY. New York, NY, 3/1/56. Actor. *Wings.*
DALY, TYNE (Ellen Tyne Daly). Madison, WI, 2/21/46. Actor. *Cagney & Lacey.*
DAMMERS, JERRY (Jerry Dankin). 5/22/54. Keyboardist. The Specials.
DAMONE, VIC (Vito Farinola). Brooklyn, NY, 6/12/28. Singer, married to Diahann Caroll. *The Vic Damone Show.*
DANCE, CHARLES. Worcestershire, England, 10/10/46. Actor. *The Jewel in the Crown.*
DANELLI, DINO. New York, NY, 7/23/45. Drummer. The (Young) Rascals.
DANGERFIELD, RODNEY (Jacob Cohen). Babylon, NY, 11/22/21. Actor. *Back to School.*
DANIEL, JEFFREY. Los Angeles, CA, 8/24/55. Singer. Shalamar.
DANIELS, WILLIAM. Brooklyn, NY, 3/31/27. Actor. *St. Elsewhere.*
DANKO, RICK. Simcoe, Canada, 12/9/43. Bassist, singer. The Band.
DANNER, BLYTHE. Philadelphia, PA, 2/3/43. Actor. *The Prince of Tides.*
DANTE, MICHAEL (Ralph Vitti). Stamford, CT, 1935. Actor. Crazy Horse in *Custer.*
DANZA, TONY. Brooklyn, NY, 4/21/51. Actor. Tony Micelli on *Who's the Boss?*
DAVIDOVICH, LOLITA. Ontario, Canada, 7/15/61. Actor. *Blaze.*
DAVIDSON, JAYE. Riverside, CA, 1967. Actor. *The Crying Game.*
DAVIDSON, JOHN. Pittsburgh, PA, 12/13/41. Game show host. *Hollywood Squares.*
DAVIDSON, LENNY. Enfield, England, 5/30/44. Guitarist. The Dave Clark Five.
DAVIES, DAVE. Muswell Hill, England, 2/3/47. Singer, guitarist. The Kinks.
DAVIES, IVA. Australia, 5/22/55. Guitarist, singer. Icehouse.
DAVIES, RAY. Muswell Hill, England, 6/21/44. Singer, guitarist. The Kinks.
DAVIES, RICHARD. England, 7/22/44. Singer, keyboardist. Supertramp.
DAVIS, BILLY JR. St. Louis, MO, 6/26/40. Singer. The 5th Dimension.
DAVIS, CLIFTON. Chicago, IL, 10/4/45. Actor, singer, composer. *Never Can Say Goodbye.*
DAVIS, JIM. Marion, IN, 7/28/45. Cartoonist. *Garfield.*
DAVIS, MAC (Morris Mac Davis). Lubbock, TX, 1/21/42. Singer, songwriter, actor. *The Mac Davis Show.*
DAVIS, MARTHA. Berkeley, CA, 1/15/51. Singer. The Motels.
DAVIS, OSSIE. Cogdell, GA, 12/18/17. Actor, writer. *Evening Shade.*
DAVIS, PAUL. Manchester, England, 3/7/66. Keyboardist. Happy Mondays.
DAVIS, ROB. Carshalton, England, 10/1/47. Lead guitarist, singer. Mud.
DAVIS, SPENCER. Swansea, Wales, 7/17/42. Guitarist. The Spencer Davis Group.
DAVIS, WILLIE. 1940. Drummer. Joey Dee and the Starliters.
DAY, DORIS (Doris von Kappelhoff). Cincinnati, OH, 4/3/24. Actor, performer. *The Doris Day Show.*
DAY, MARK. Manchester, England, 12/29/61. Guitarist. Happy Mondays.
DE BURGH, CHRIS (Chris Davidson). Argentina, 10/15/48. Singer, songwriter. "Lady in Red."
DE HAVILLAND, OLIVIA. Tokyo, Japan, 7/1/16. Actor. *Gone with the Wind.*
DE LAURENTIS, DINO. Torre Annunziata, Italy, 8/8/19. Producer. *King Kong; Conan the Barbarian.*
DEACON, JOHN. Leicester, England, 8/19/51. Bassist. Queen.
DEAN, JIMMY. Plainview, TX, 8/10/28. Performer. *The Jimmy Dean Show.*
DEBARGE, EL (Eldra DeBarge). Grand Rapids, MI, 6/4/61. Singer, keyboardist, record producer.
DEE, DAVE (Dave Harman). Salisbury, England, 12/17/43. Lead singer, tambourinist. Dave Dee, Dozy, Beaky, Mick and Tich.
DEE, JOEY (Joey DiNicola). Passaic, NJ, 6/11/40. Singer. Joey Dee and the Starliters.
DEE, KIKI. Bradford, England, 3/6/47. Pop singer.
DEE, RUBY. Cleveland, OH, 10/27/24. Actor. *Do the Right Thing.*
DEE, SANDRA (Alexandra Zuck). Bayonne, NJ, 4/23/42. Actor. *Gidget.*
DEFOREST, CALVERT. Brooklyn, NY, 1923. Actor, Larry "Bud" Melman.
DEKKER, DESMOND (Desmond Dacris). Kingston, Jamaica,

7/16/42. Reggae singer, songwriter.
DELANY, DANA. New York, NY, 3/11/56. Actor. *China Beach.*
DELON, ALAIN. Sceaux, France, 11/8/35. Actor. *Is Paris Burning?*
DELP, BRAD. Boston, MA, 6/12/51. Guitarist, singer. Boston.
DELUISE, DOM. Brooklyn, NY, 8/1/33. Actor. *The Dom DeLuise Show.*
DELUISE, PETER. Hollywood, CA, 1967. Actor. Doug Penhall on *21 Jump Street.*
DEMME, JONATHAN. Rockville Centre, MD, 2/22/44. Director, producer, writer. *The Silence of the Lambs; Swimming to Cambodia.*
DEMORNAY, REBECCA. Santa Rosa, CA, 8/29/62. Actor. *The Hand That Rocks the Cradle.*
DEMPSEY, PATRICK. Lewiston, ME, 1/13/66. Actor. *Loverboy.*
DENEUVE, CATHERINE (Catherine Dorleac). Paris, France, 10/22/43. Actor. *Belle de Jour.*
DENNEHY, BRIAN. Bridgeport, CT, 7/9/39. Actor. *Cocoon.*
DENSMORE, JOHN. Los Angeles, CA, 12/1/45. Drummer. The Doors.
DENVER, BOB. New Rochelle, NY, 1/9/35. Actor. Gilligan on *Gilligan's Island.*
DENVER, JOHN (Henry Deutschendorf). Roswell, NM, 12/31/43. Country singer, songwriter, actor. "Country Roads."
DEPARDIEU, GERARD. Chateauroux, France, 12/27/48. Actor. *Green Card.*
DEREK, BO (Mary Cathleen Collins). Long Beach, CA, 11/20/56. Actor, married to John Derek. *10.*
DEREK, JOHN (Derek Harris). Hollywood, CA, 8/12/26. Actor, director, married to Bo Derek. *The Ten Commandments.*
DERN, BRUCE. Chicago, IL, 6/4/36. Actor, father of Laura. *Coming Home.*
DERN, LAURA. Los Angeles, CA, 2/10/67. Actor, daughter of Bruce Dern and Diane Ladd, engaged to Jeff Goldblum. *Jurassic Park.*
DERRINGER, RICK (Richard Zehringer). Fort Recovery, OH, 8/5/47. Singer, songwriter, producer. The McCoys.
DESTRI, JIMMY. 4/13/54. Keyboardist. Blondie.
DEVANE, WILLIAM. Albany, NY, 9/5/37. Actor. Greg Sumner in *Knots Landing.*
DEVITO, TOMMY. Montclair, NJ, 6/19/36. Singer, guitarist. The Four Seasons.
DEVOE, RONALD. 11/17/67. Singer. New Edition; Bell Biv DeVoe.
DEY, SUSAN. Pekin, IL, 12/10/52. Actor. *L.A. Law.*
DEYOUNG, CLIFF. Inglewood, CA, 2/12/45. Actor. *The Hunger.*
DEYOUNG, DENNIS. Chicago, IL, 2/18/47. Singer, keyboardist. Styx.
DIAMOND, NEIL (Noah Kaminsky). New York, NY, 1/24/41. Singer, songwriter. *The Jazz Singer.*
DIAMONDE, DICK (Dingeman Van Der Sluys). Hilversum, Holland, 12/28/47. Bassist. The Easybeats.
DICKEN (Jeff Pain). 4/4/50. Singer. Mr. Big.
DICKERSON, B. B. (Morris Dickerson). Torrance, CA, 8/3/49. Bassist, singer. War.
DICKINSON, ANGIE (Angie Brown). Kulm, ND, 9/30/32. Actor. *Police Woman.*
DICKINSON, BRUCE (Paul Dickinson). Worksop, England, 8/7/58. Singer. Iron Maiden.
DIDDLEY, BO (Otha Bates). McComb, MS, 12/30/28. Legendary blues guitarist, singer, songwriter.
DIFFORD, CHRIS. London, England, 11/4/54. Singer, guitarist. Squeeze.
DILLER, PHYLLIS (Phyllis Driver). Lima, OH, 7/17/17. Actor. *The Phyllis Diller Show.*
DILLON, KEVIN. Mamaroneck, NY, 8/19/65. Actor. *The Doors.*
DILLON, MATT. New Rochelle, NY, 2/18/64. Actor. *The Outsiders.*
DIMAGGIO, JOE. Martinez, CA, 11/25/14. Baseball great. New York Yankees. Once married to Marilyn Monroe.
DIMUCCI, DION. The Bronx, NY, 7/18/39. Lead singer. Dion & The Belmonts.
DIO, RONNIE JAMES. Cortland, NY, 7/10/48. Singer. Rainbow; Black Sabbath.
DITKA, MIKE. Carnegie, PA, 10/18/39. NFL football player, coach.
DIXON, DONNA. Alexandria, VA, 7/20/57. Actor, married to Dan Aykroyd. *Bosom Buddies.*
DOBSON, KEVIN. New York, NY, 3/18/43. Actor. *Knots Landing.*
DOHERTY, DENNY. Halifax, Canada, 11/29/41. Singer. The Mamas and the Papas.
DOHERTY, SHANNEN. Memphis, TN, 4/12/71. Actor. Brenda Walsh on *Beverly Hills 90210.*
DOLENZ, MICKEY (George Dolenz). Los Angeles, CA, 3/8/45. Singer, drummer. The Monkees.
DOMINO, FATS (Antoine Domino). New Orleans, LA, 2/26/28. Legendary singer, songwriter.
DONAHUE, PHIL. Cleveland, OH, 12/21/35. Talk show host.
DONAHUE, TROY (Merle Johnson). New York, NY, 1/27/36. Actor. *Hawaiian Eye.*
DONALDSON, SAM. El Paso, TX, 3/11/34. News reporter and anchor. *Prime Time Live.*
DONEGAN, LAWRENCE. 7/13/61. Bassist. Lloyd Cole & The Commotions.
DONEGAN, LONNIE (Anthony Donegan). Glasgow, Scotland, 4/29/31. Folk/blues guitarist, banjoist, and singer.
DONOVAN (Donovan Leitch). Glasgow, Scotland, 2/10/46. Folk/psychedelic singer, songwriter, father of Ione Skye and Donovan Leitch. "Mellow Yellow."
DONOVAN, JASON. Malvern, Australia, 6/1/68. Singer, actor.
DORMAN, LEE. St. Louis, MO, 9/19/45. Bassist. Iron Butterfly.
DOUGHTY, NEAL. Evanston, IL, 7/29/46. Keyboardist. REO Speedwagon.
DOUGLAS, BUSTER (James Douglas). Columbus, OH, 4/7/60. Boxer. Defeated Mike Tyson.
DOUGLAS, DONNA (Dorothy Bourgeois). Baywood, LA, 9/26/35. Actor. Elly May Clampett on *The Beverly Hillbillies.*
DOUGLAS, KIRK (Issur Danielovitch). Amsterdam, NY, 12/9/16. Actor, producer, father of Michael. *Spartacus.*
DOW, TONY. Hollywood, CA, 4/13/45. Actor. Wally Cleaver on *Leave It to Beaver.*
DOWN, LESLEY-ANN. London, England, 3/17/54. Actor. *Dallas.*
DOWNEY, BRIAN. Dublin, Ireland, 1/27/51. Drummer. Thin Lizzy.
DOWNEY, MORTON JR. 12/9/33. Controversial talk show host, actor.
DOWNEY, ROBERT, JR. New York, NY, 4/4/65. Actor. *Chaplin.*
DOWNS, HUGH. Akron, OH, 2/14/21. Host, actor, commentator. *20/20.*
DOZY (Trevor Davies). Enford, England, 11/27/44. Bassist. Dave Dee, Dozy, Beaky, Mick and Tich.
DRAGON, DARYL. Los Angeles, CA, 8/27/42. Keyboardist. The Captain & Tennille.
DREJA, CHRIS. Surbiton, England, 11/11/44. Guitarist. The Yardbirds.
DREYFUSS, RICHARD. Brooklyn, NY, 10/29/47. Actor. *Close Encounters of the Third Kind.*
DRYDEN, SPENCER. New York, NY, 4/7/38. Drummer. Jefferson Airplane/Starship.
DUBROW, KEVIN. 10/29/55. Lead singer. Quiet Riot.
DUDIKOFF, MICHAEL. Redondo Beach, CA, 10/8/54. Actor. *American Ninja.*
DUFFY, BILLY. 5/12/61. Lead guitarist. The Cult.
DUFFY, JULIA. Minneapolis, MN, 6/27/50. Actor. *Newhart.*
DUFFY, PATRICK. Townsend, MT, 3/17/49. Actor. Bobby Ewing on *Dallas.*
DUKAKIS, OLYMPIA. Lowell, MA, 6/20/31. Actor. *Moonstruck.*

DUKE, DAVID. Tulsa, OK, 1951. White supremacist, politician.
DUKE, PATTY (Anna Marie Duke). New York, NY, 12/14/46. Actor, formerly married to John Astin, mother of Sean Astin. *The Patty Duke Show.*
DUKES, DAVID. San Francisco, CA, 6/6/45. Actor. *Sisters.*
DULLEA, KEIR. Cleveland, OH, 5/30/36. Actor. *2001: A Space Odyssey.*
DUNAWAY, DENNIS. Cottage Grove, OR, 12/9/48. Bassist. Alice Cooper.
DUNAWAY, FAYE. Bascom, FL, 1/14/41. Actor. *Mommie Dearest.*
DUNCAN, GARY (Gary Grubb). San Diego, CA, 9/4/46. Guitarist. Quicksilver Messenger Service.
DUNCAN, SANDY. Henderson, TX, 2/20/46. Actor. *Funny Face.*
DUNN, DONALD. Memphis, TN, 11/24/41. Bassist. Booker T. & The MG's.
DUNN, LARRY. Colorado, 6/19/53. Keyboardist. Earth, Wind & Fire.
DUNNE, GRIFFIN. New York, NY, 6/8/55. Actor. *After Hours.*
DURBIN, DEANNA (Edna Durbin). Winnipeg, Canada, 12/4/21. Actor. *One Hundred Men and a Girl.*
DURNING, CHARLES. Highland Falls, NY, 2/28/33. Actor. *Evening Shade.*
DURY, IAN. Upminster, England, 5/12/42. Singer. Ian Dury & The Blockheads.
DUTTON, CHARLES. Baltimore, MD, 1/30/51. Actor. *Roc.*
DUVALL, ROBERT. San Diego, CA, 1/5/31. Actor. *Tender Mercies.*
DUVALL, SHELLEY. Houston, TX, 7/7/49. Actor, producer. *The Shining.*
DYSART, RICHARD. Brighton, MA, 3/30/29. Actor. Leland McKenzie on *L.A. Law.*
EARLE, STEVE. Fort Monroe, VA, 1/17/55. Country/rock singer, songwriter. Guitar Town.
EASTON, ELLIOT (Elliot Shapiro). Brooklyn, NY, 12/18/53. Guitarist. The Cars.
EASTON, SHEENA (Sheena Orr). Bellshill, Scotland, 4/27/59. Rock/R&B singer.
EBSEN, BUDDY (Christian Ebsen Jr.). Belleville, IL, 4/2/08. Actor. Jed Clampett on *The Beverly Hillbillies.*
ECHOLS, JOHN. Memphis, TN, 1945. Lead guitarist. Love.
EDDY, DUANE. Corning, NY, 4/26/38. Legendary rock guitarist.
EDEN, BARBARA (Barbara Huffman). Tucson, AZ, 8/23/34. Actor. Jeannie in *I Dream of Jeannie.*
EDGE, GRAEME. Rochester, England, 3/30/42. Drummer. The Moody Blues.
EDGE, THE (David Evans). Wales, 8/8/61. Guitarist. U2.
EDMONTON, JERRY. Canada, 10/24/46. Drummer. Steppenwolf.
EDWARD, PRINCE. London, England, 2/19/60. British royalty, son of Queen Elizabeth II.
EDWARDS, BERNARD. Greenville, NC, 10/31/52. Bassist. Chic.
EDWARDS, BLAKE (William Blake McEdwards). Tulsa, OK, 7/26/22. Writer, director. The *Pink Panther* series.
EDWARDS, NOKIE. Washington, DC, 5/9/39. Lead guitarist. The Ventures.
EGGAR, SAMANTHA. London, England, 3/5/39. Actor. *The Collector.*
EIKENBERRY, JILL. New Haven, CT, 1/21/47. Actor. Ann Kelsey on *L.A. Law.*
EKBERG, ANITA. Malmo, Sweden, 9/29/31. Actor. *La Dolce Vita.*
EKLAND, BRITT. Stockholm, Sweden, 10/6/42. Actor. *After the Fox.*
ELIZONDO, HECTOR. New York, NY, 12/22/36. Actor. *Freebie and the Bean.*
ELLERBEE, LINDA. Bryan, TX, 8/15/44. News commentator. *Our World.*
ELLIOTT, BOBBY. Burnley, England, 12/8/42. Drummer. The Hollies.
ELLIOTT, CHRIS. New York, NY, 1960. Comedy writer, actor. *Get a Life.*
ELLIOTT, DENNIS. London, England, 8/18/50. Drummer. Foreigner.
ELLIOTT, JOE. Sheffield, England, 8/1/59. Singer. Def Leppard.
ELLIOTT, SAM. Sacramento, CA, 8/9/44. Actor. *Tombstone.*
ELLIS, RALPH. Liverpool, England, 3/8/42. Guitarist, singer. The Swinging Blue Jeans.
ELMORE, GREG. San Diego, CA, 9/4/46. Drummer. Quicksilver Messenger Service.
ELSWIT, RIK. New York, NY, 7/6/45. Guitarist, singer. Dr. Hook.
ELVIRA (Cassandra Peterson). Manhattan, KS, 9/17/51. Horror film hostess.
ELWES, CARY. London, England, 10/26/62. Actor. *The Princess Bride.*
EMERSON, KEITH. Todmorden, England, 11/1/44. Keyboardist. Emerson, Lake & Palmer.
ENGEL, SCOTT (Noel Engel). Hamilton, OH, 1/9/44. Singer. The Walker Brothers.
ENGLUND, ROBERT. Hollywood, CA, 6/6/49. Actor. Freddie Krueger in *Nightmare on Elm Street* series.
ENNIS, RAY. Liverpool, England, 5/26/42. Lead guitarist, singer. The Swinging Blue Jeans.
ENO, BRIAN. Woodbridge, England, 5/15/48. Synthesizer player, producer. Cofounder of Roxy Music.
ENTNER, WARREN. Boston, MA, 7/7/44. Singer, guitarist. The Grass Roots.
ENTWISTLE, JOHN. Chiswick, England, 10/9/44. Bassist. The Who.
ENYA (Eithne Ni Bhraona). Gweedore, Ireland, 1962. Singer, composer.
ERRICO, GREG. San Francisco, CA, 9/1/46. Drummer. Sly & The Family Stone.
ERVING, JULIUS. Roosevelt, NY, 2/22/50. Basketball great. Philadelphia 76ers.
ESIASON, BOOMER (Norman Julius Esiason Jr.). West Islip, NY, 4/17/61. NFL football player.
ESPOSITO, GIANCARLO. Copenhagen, Denmark, 4/26/58. Actor. *Do the Right Thing.*
ESSEX, DAVID (David Cook). Plaistow, England, 7/23/47. Drummer, singer, songwriter, actor. *Stardust.*
ESTEFAN, GLORIA (Gloria Fajardo). Havana, Cuba, 9/1/57. Latin pop singer. The Miami Sound Machine.
ESTEVEZ, EMILIO. New York, NY, 5/12/62. Actor, writer, divorced from Paula Abdul, son of Martin Sheen. *Repo Man.*
ESTRADA, ERIK. New York, NY, 3/16/49. Actor. Frank "Ponch" Poncherello on *CHiPS.*
EUGENIE, PRINCESS. London, England, 3/23/90. British royalty, daughter of Prince Andrew and the Duchess of York.
EVANGELISTA, LINDA. Canada, 6/10/65. Supermodel, married to Kyle MacLachlan.
EVANS, DALE (Francis Smith). Uvalde, TX, 10/31/12. Actor. *The Yellow Rose of Texas.*
EVANS, LINDA (Linda Evanstad). Hartford, CT, 11/18/42. Actor. *Dynasty.*
EVANS, MARK. Melbourne, Australia, 3/2/56. Bassist. AC/DC.
EVANS, MIKE (Michael Jonas Evans). Salisbury, NC, 11/3/49. Actor. Lionel on *The Jeffersons.*
EVERETT, CHAD (Raymond Lee Cramton). South Bend, IN, 6/11/36. Actor. *Medical Center.*
EVERLY, DON (Isaac Everly). Brownie, KY, 2/1/37. Singer, guitarist. The Everly Brothers.
EVERLY, PHIL. Chicago, IL, 1/19/39. Singer, guitarist. The Everly Brothers.
EVERT, CHRIS. Ft. Lauderdale, FL, 12/21/54. Tennis player.
EVIGAN, GREG. South Amboy, NJ, 10/14/53. Actor. *B.J. and the Bear.*
FABARES, SHELLEY (Michelle Marie Fabares). Santa Monica, CA, 1/19/44. Actor, married to Mike Farrell, niece

of Nanette Fabray. Christine Armstrong on *Coach.*
FABIAN (Fabian Forte). Philadelphia, PA, 2/6/43. Singer, actor. *American Bandstand.*
FABIO (Fabio Lanzoni). Milan, Italy, 3/15/61. Model.
FABRAY, NANETTE (Ruby Nanette Fabares). San Diego, CA, 10/27/20. Actor, aunt of Shelley Fabares. *One Day at a Time.*
FAGEN, DONALD. Passaic, NJ, 1/10/48. Singer, keyboardist. Steely Dan.
FAHEY, SIOBHAN. 9/10/60. Singer. Bananarama.
FAIRBANKS, DOUGLAS JR. New York, NY, 12/9/09. Actor. *Gunga Din.*
FAIRCHILD, MORGAN (Patsy McClenny). Dallas, TX, 2/3/50. Actor. *Falcon Crest.*
FAIRWEATHER-LOW, ANDY. Ystrad Mynach, Wales, 8/8/50. Singer, guitarist. Amen Corner.
FAITH, ADAM (Terence Nelhams). Acton, England, 6/23/40. Singer, actor, financial adviser.
FAITHFULL, MARIANNE. Hampstead, England, 12/29/46. Folk/rock singer.
FAKIR, ABDUL. Detroit, MI, 12/26/35. Singer. The Four Tops.
FALANA, LOLA (Loletha Elaine Falana). Philadelphia, PA, 9/11/43. Singer.
FALCO (Johann Hoelcel). Austria, 2/19/57. Singer, songwriter. "Rock Me Amadeus."
FALCONER, EARL. Birmingham, England, 1/23/59. Bassist. UB40.
FALK, PETER. New York, NY, 9/16/27. Actor. *Columbo.*
FALTSKOG, AGNETHA. Jonkoping, Sweden, 4/5/50. Singer. Abba.
FAMBROUGH, HENRY. 5/10/38. Singer. The (Detroit) Spinners.
FAME, GEORGIE (Clive Powell). Leigh, England, 9/26/43. Singer, keyboardist. Georgie Fame & The Blue Flames.
FARENTINO, JAMES. Brooklyn, NY, 2/24/38. Actor. *Dynasty.*
FARINA, DENNIS. Chicago, IL, 2/29/44. Actor. *Crime Story.*
FARNER, MARK. Flint, MI, 9/29/48. Singer, guitarist. Grand Funk Railroad.
FARR, JAMIE (Jameel Joseph Farah). Toledo, OH, 7/1/34. Actor. Maxwell Klinger on *M*A*S*H.*
FARRAKHAN, LOUIS (Louis Eugene Walcott). New York, NY, 5/11/33. Controversial Muslim minister.
FARRELL, BOBBY. Aruba, West Indies, 10/6/49. Singer. Boney M.
FARRELL, MIKE. St. Paul, MN, 2/6/39. Actor, writer, director, married to Shelley Fabares. B. J. Hunnicutt on *M*A*S*H.*
FARRIS, STEVE. 5/1/57. Guitarist. Mr. Mister.
FARRISS, ANDREW. Perth, Australia, 3/27/59. Keyboardist. INXS.
FARRISS, JON. Perth, Australia, 8/10/61. Drummer, singer. INXS.
FAULKNER, ERIC. Edinburgh, Scotland, 10/21/55. Guitarist. The Bay City Rollers.
FAWCETT, FARRAH. Corpus Christi, TX, 2/2/47. Actor. Jill Munroe on *Charlie's Angels.*
FELDMAN, COREY. Reseda, CA, 7/16/71. Actor. *Stand By Me.*
FELDON, BARBARA (Barbara Hall). Pittsburgh, PA, 3/12/41. Actor. Agent 99 on *Get Smart.*
FELDSHUH, TOVAH. New York, NY, 12/27/53. Actor. *The Idolmaker.*
FELICIANO, JOSE. Lares, Puerto Rico, 9/10/45. Singer, guitarist. *Chico and the Man.*
FELL, NORMAN. Philadelphia, PA, 3/24/24. Actor. Stanley Roper on *Three's Company.*
FENN, SHERILYN. Detroit, MI, 2/1/65. Actor. *Twin Peaks.*
FERGUSON, JAY (John Ferguson). Burbank, CA, 5/10/47. Singer. Spirit.
FERGUSON, LARRY. Nassau, Bahamas, 4/14/48. Keyboardist. Hot Chocolate.
FERGUSON, SARAH. London, England, 10/15/59. Duchess of York. Married to (and separated from) Prince Andrew.
FERRARO, GERALDINE. Newburgh, NY, 8/26/35. Politician, first woman vice-presidential candidate.
FERRER, MEL (Melchor Gaston Ferrer). Elberon, NJ, 8/25/12. Producer, director, actor, formerly married to Audrey Hepburn. *Falcon Crest.*
FERRER, MIGUEL. Santa Monica, CA, 2/7/54. Actor, son of Jose Ferrer and Rosemary Clooney. *Twin Peaks.*
FERRIGNO, LOU. Brooklyn, NY, 11/9/52. Actor, bodybuilder. *The Incredible Hulk.*
FERRIS, BARBARA. London, England, 10/3/40. Actor. *The Strauss Family.*
FERRY, BRYAN. Durham, England, 9/26/45. Singer, songwriter. Roxy Music.
FIEGER, DOUG. Detroit, MI, 8/20/52. Singer, guitarist. The Knack.
FIELDER, JIM. Denton, TX, 10/4/47. Bassist. Blood, Sweat & Tears.
FIELDS, KIM. Los Angeles, CA, 5/12/69. Actor. Dorothy "Tootie" Ramsey on *The Facts of Life.*
FIERSTEIN, HARVEY. Brooklyn, NY, 6/6/54. Actor, writer. *Mrs. Doubtfire.*
FILIPOVIC, ZLATA. Sarajevo, Bosnia-Herzegovina, 12/3/81. Author. *Zlata's Diary.*
FINCH, RICHARD. Indianapolis, IN, 1/25/54. Bassist. KC & The Sunshine Band.
FINER, JEM. Ireland. Banjoist. The Pogues.
FINGERS, JOHNNIE (Johnnie Moylett). Ireland, 9/10/56. Keyboardist, singer. The Boomtown Rats.
FINN, TIM (Te Awamutu). New Zealand, 6/25/52. Singer, keyboardist. Split Enz.
FINNEY, ALBERT. Salford, England, 5/9/36. Actor. *Shoot the Moon.*
FIORENTINO, LINDA (Clorinda Fiorentino). Philadelphia, PA, 3/9/60. Actor. *The Last Seduction.*
FIRTH, COLIN. Grayshott, England, 9/10/60. Actor. *Another Country.*
FISH (Derek Dick). Dalkeith, Scotland, 4/25/58. Singer. Marillion.
FISHER, AMY. New York, NY, 1974. The "Long Island Lolita."
FISHER, EDDIE. Philadelphia, PA, 8/10/28. Singer, formerly married to Debbie Reynolds, Elizabeth Taylor, and Connie Stevens, father of Carrie Fisher. *The Eddie Fisher Show.*
FISHER, MATTHEW. Croydon, England, 3/7/46. Keyboardist. Procol Harum.
FISHER, ROGER. Seattle, WA, 2/14/50. Guitarist. Heart.
FITZGERALD, GERALDINE. Dublin, Ireland, 11/24/14. Actor. *Wuthering Heights.*
FLACK, ROBERTA. Black Mountain, NC, 2/10/39. Pop singer. "The First Time Ever I Saw Your Face."
FLEA (Michael Balzary). Melbourne, Australia. Singer, bassist. The Red Hot Chili Peppers.
FLEETWOOD, MICK. London, England, 6/24/42. Drummer. Fleetwood Mac.
FLEMING, PEGGY. San Jose, CA, 7/27/48. Ice skater. Olympic gold medalist.
FLETCHER, ANDY. Basildon, England, 7/8/60. Keyboardist. Depeche Mode.
FLETCHER, LOUISE. Birmingham, AL, 7/22/34. Actor. *One Flew over the Cuckoo's Nest.*
FLOYD, EDDIE. Montgomery, AL, 6/25/35. R&B singer, songwriter.
FOGELBERG, DAN. Peoria, IL, 8/13/51. Guitarist, singer, songwriter.
FOGERTY, JOHN. Berkeley, CA, 5/28/45. Singer, guitarist. Creedence Clearwater Revival.
FOLLOWS, MEGAN. Toronto, Canada, 3/14/68. Actor. *Anne of Green Gables.*
FONDA, PETER. New York, NY, 2/23/39. Actor, son of Henry Fonda, brother of Jane, father of Bridget. *Easy Rider.*

FONTAINE, JOAN (Joan de Havilland). Tokyo, Japan, 10/22/17. Actor, sister of Olivia de Havilland. *Suspicion.*
FONTANA, WAYNE (Glyn Ellis). Manchester, England, 10/28/40. Singer. Wayne Fontana & The Mindbenders.
FORD, FAITH. Alexandria, LA, 9/14/64. Actor. Corky Sherwood Forrest on *Murphy Brown.*
FORD, FRANKIE (Frankie Guzzo). Gretna, LA, 8/4/40. Singer.
FORD, LITA. London, England, 9/23/59. Lead guitarist. The Runaways.
FOREMAN, CHRIS. England, 8/8/58. Guitarist. Madness.
FOREMAN, GEORGE. Marshall, TX, 1/10/49. Boxer, actor. *George.*
FORSSI, KEN. Cleveland, OH, 1943. Bassist. Love.
FORSTER, ROBERT. Rochester, NY, 7/13/41. Actor. *Banyon.*
FORSYTHE, JOHN (John Freund). Penns Grove, NJ, 1/29/18. Actor. Blake Carrington on *Dynasty.*
FORTUNE, JIMMY. Newport News, VA, 3/1/55. Musician. Statler Brothers.
FORTUNE, NICK (Nick Fortuna). Chicago, IL, 5/1/46. Bassist. The Buckinghams.
FOSTER, MEG. Reading, PA, 5/14/48. Actor. *Cagney and Lacey.*
FOX, JACKIE. California, 1960. Bassist. The Runaways.
FOX, JAMES. London, England, 5/19/39. Actor. *The Loneliness of the Long Distance Runner.*
FOX, SAMANTHA. England, 4/15/66. Singer. "Naughty Girls (Need Love Too)."
FOX, TERRY (Terrance Stanley Fox). Winnipeg, Canada, 7/28/58. Track athlete, fund-raiser.
FOXTON, BRUCE. Woking, Surrey England, 9/1/55. Guitarist. The Jam.
FOXWORTH, ROBERT. Houston, TX, 11/1/41. Actor. Chase Gioberti on *Falcon Crest.*
FRAKES, JONATHAN. Bethlehem, PA, 1952. Actor. Commander William Riker on *Star Trek: The Next Generation.*
FRAME, RODDY. East Kilbride, Scotland, 1/29/64. Singer, guitarist. Aztec Camera.
FRAMPTON, PETER KENNETH. Beckenham, England, 4/22/50. Guitarist, singer, songwriter.
FRANCIOSA, ANTHONY (Anthony Papaleo). New York, NY, 10/25/28. Actor. *The Long Hot Summer.*
FRANCIS, ANNE. Ossining, NY, 9/16/30. Actor, former child model.
FRANCIS, BILL. Mobile, AL, 1/16/42. Keyboardist, singer. Dr. Hook.
FRANCIS, CONNIE (Concetta Franconero). Newark, NJ, 12/12/38. Singer. "Where the Boys Are."
FRANTZ, CHRIS (Charlton Frantz). Fort Campbell, KY, 5/8/51. Drummer. Talking Heads.
FRASER, ANDY. London, England, 8/7/52. Bassist. Free.
FRASER, BRENDAN. Indianapolis, IN, 1967. Actor. *Encino Man.*
FRAZIER, JOE. Beaufort, SC, 1/17/44. Boxer, former heavyweight champ.
FREDRIKSSON, MARIE. Sweden, 5/30/58. Singer. Roxette.
FREEMAN, BOBBY. San Francisco, CA, 6/13/40. Singer, songwriter.
FREEMAN, MORGAN. Memphis, TN, 6/1/37. Actor, director. *Driving Miss Daisy.*
FREHLEY, ACE (Paul Frehley). The Bronx, NY, 4/22/51. Guitarist, singer. Kiss.
FREIBERG, DAVID. Boston, MA, 8/24/38. Bassist. Quicksilver Messenger Service.
FREWER, MATT. Washington, DC, 1/4/58. Actor. *Max Headroom.*
FREY, GLENN. Detroit, MI, 11/6/48. Singer, songwriter. The Eagles.
FRICKER, BRENDA. Dublin, Ireland, 2/17/45. Actor. *My Left Foot.*
FRIPP, ROBERT. Wimborne Minster, England, 1946. Guitarist. King Crimson.
FROST, CRAIG. Flint, MI, 4/20/48. Keyboardist. Grand Funk Railroad.
FRY, MARTIN. Manchester, England, 3/9/58. Singer. ABC.
FUNICELLO, ANNETTE. Utica, NY, 10/22/42. Actor, Mouseketeer. *Beach Blanket Bingo.*
FUNT, ALLEN. New York, NY, 9/16/14. Producer. *Candid Camera.*
FURAY, RICHIE. Yellow Springs, OH, 5/9/44. Singer, guitarist. Buffalo Springfield; Poco.
FURUHOLMEN, MAGS. Oslo, Norway, 11/1/62. Keyboardist, singer. a-ha.
GABLE, JOHN CLARK. Los Angeles, CA, 3/20/61. Actor. Son of Clark Gable.
GABOR, ZSA ZSA (Sari Gabor). Budapest, Hungary, 2/6/17. Actor. *Moulin Rouge.*
GABRIEL, PETER. Cobham, England, 5/13/50. Singer, songwriter. Genesis.
GAHAN, DAVE. Epping, England, 5/9/62. Singer. Depeche Mode.
GAIL, MAXWELL. Derfoil, MI, 4/5/43. Actor. Sergeant Stanley Wojohowicz on *Barney Miller.*
GALLAGHER, PETER. Armonk, NY, 8/19/55. Actor. *sex, lies and videotape.*
GARCIA, ANDY. Havana, Cuba, 4/12/56. Actor. *The Godfather Part III.*
GARDNER, CARL. Tyler, TX, 4/29/27. Lead singer. The Coasters.
GARFAT, JANCE. California, 3/3/44. Bassist, singer. Dr. Hook.
GARFUNKEL, ART. New York, NY, 11/5/42. Singer, actor, former partner of Paul Simon. *Carnal Knowledge.*
GARLAND, BEVERLY. Santa Cruz, CA, 10/17/30. Actor. *My Three Sons.*
GARNER, JAMES (James Baumgarner). Norma, OK, 4/7/28. Actor, producer. *The Rockford Files.*
GARR, TERI. Lakewood, OH, 12/11/49. Actor. *Tootsie.*
GARRETT, BETTY. St. Joseph, MO, 5/23/19. Actor. *All in the Family.*
GARRITY, FREDDIE. Manchester, England, 11/14/40. Singer. Freddie & The Dreamers.
GARTH, JENNIE. Champaign, IL, 4/3/72. Actor. Kelly Taylor on *Beverly Hills 90210.*
GARTSIDE, GREEN (Green Strohmeyer-Gartside). Cardiff, Wales, 6/22/56. Singer. Scritti Politti.
GARY, BRUCE. Burbank, CA, 4/7/52. Drummer. The Knack.
GATES, DAVID. Tulsa, OK, 12/11/40. Keyboardist, singer. Bread.
GATLIN, RUDY. 8/20/52. Singer. The Gatlin Brothers.
GATLIN, STEVE. 4/4/51. Singer. The Gatlin Brothers.
GAUDIO, BOB. The Bronx, NY, 11/17/42. Singer, organist. The Four Seasons.
GAYLE, CRYSTAL (Brenda Webb). Paintsville, KY, 1/9/51. Country singer.
GAYLORD, MITCH. Van Nuys, CA, 1961. Gymnast.
GAYNOR, MITZI (Francesca Marlene Von Gerber). Chicago, IL, 9/4/31. Actor. *Anything Goes.*
GAZZARA, BEN (Biago Gazzara). New York, NY, 8/28/30. Actor. *Inchon.*
GEARY, ANTHONY. Coalville, UT, 5/29/47. Actor. Luke Spencer on *General Hospital.*
GEARY, CYNTHIA. Jackson, MS, 3/21/66. Actor. *Northern Exposure.*
GEILS, J. (Jerome Geils). New York, NY, 2/20/46. Guitarist. The J. Geils Band.
GELDOF, BOB. Dublin, Ireland, 10/5/54. Singer. The Boomtown Rats.
GERARD, GIL. Little Rock, AR, 1/23/43. Actor. *Buck Rogers in the 25th Century.*
GERARDO. Ecuador, 1965. Rap artist. "Rico Suave."
GERTZ, JAMI. Chicago, IL, 10/28/65. Actor. *Less Than Zero.*
GESSLE, PER. 1/12/59. Guitarist, singer. Roxette.

GETTY, BALTHAZAR. 1/22/75. Actor, grandson of J. Paul Getty. *Where the Day Takes You.*
GETTY, ESTELLE. New York, NY, 7/25/23. Actor. Sophia Petrillo on *The Golden Girls.*
GHOSTLEY, ALICE. Eve, MO, 8/14/26. Actor. *Bewitched.*
GIAMMARESE, CARL. Chicago, IL, 8/21/47. Guitarist. The Buckinghams.
GIANNINI, GIANCARLO. Spezia, Italy, 8/1/42. Actor. *Seven Beauties.*
GIBB, BARRY. Isle of Man, England, 9/1/47. Singer, guitarist. The Bee Gees.
GIBB, CYNTHIA. Bennington, VT, 12/14/63. Actor. *Madman of the People.*
GIBB, MAURICE. Manchester, England, 12/22/49. Singer, bassist. The Bee Gees.
GIBB, ROBIN. Manchester, England, 12/22/49. Singer. The Bee Gees.
GIBBINS, MIKE. Swansea, Wales, 3/12/49. Drummer. Badfinger.
GIBBONS, BILLY. Houston, TX, 12/16/49. Guitarist, singer. ZZ Top.
GIBBONS, LEEZA. 3/26/57. TV personality. *Entertainment Tonight.*
GIBBS, MARLA (Margaret Bradley). Chicago, IL, 6/14/33. Actor. Florence Johnston on *The Jeffersons.*
GIBSON, DEBBIE. Long Island, NY, 8/31/70. Singer, songwriter.
GIBSON, HENRY. Germantown, PA, 9/21/35. Actor. Poet from *Laugh-In.*
GIFFORD, FRANK. Santa Monica, CA, 8/16/30. Football player turned sports commentator, married to Kathie Lee Gifford. *Monday Night Football.*
GIFT, ROLAND. Birmingham, England, 5/28/62. Singer. Fine Young Cannibals.
GIGUERE, RUSS. Portsmouth, NH, 10/18/43. Singer, guitarist. The Association.
GILBERT, GILLIAN. Manchester, England, 1/27/61. Keyboardist. New Order.
GILBERT, MELISSA. Los Angeles, CA, 5/8/64. Actor, daughter of Robert and Barbara Crane. *Little House on the Prairie.*
GILBERT, SARA (Rebecca Sara MacMahon). Santa Monica, CA, 1/29/75. Actor, sister of Melissa and Jonathan Gilbert. Darlene Conner on *Roseanne.*
GILES, MIKE. Bournemouth, England, 1942. Drummer. King Crimson.
GILL, PETER. Liverpool, England, 3/8/64. Drummer. Frankie Goes to Hollywood.
GILLAN, IAN. Hounslow, England, 8/19/45. Singer. Deep Purple.
GILLIAM, TERRY. Minneapolis, MN, 11/22/40. Writer, director, actor. *Monty Python and the Holy Grail.*
GILMORE, JIMMIE DALE. Tulia, TX, 1945. Country singer. "Dallas."
GILMOUR, DAVID. Cambridge, England, 3/6/44. Singer, guitarist. Pink Floyd.
GINTY, ROBERT. New York, NY, 11/14/48. Actor. *Baa Baa Black Sheep.*
GIVENS, ROBIN. New York, NY, 11/27/64. Actor, formerly married to Mike Tyson. *Head of the Class.*
GLASER, PAUL MICHAEL. Cambridge, MA, 3/25/43. Actor, director. Det. Dave Starsky on *Starsky and Hutch.*
GLASS, RON. Evansville, IN, 7/10/45. Actor. *Barney Miller.*
GLEASON, JOANNA. Winnipeg, Canada, 6/2/50. Actor, daughter of Monty Hall. *Into the Woods.*
GLENN, SCOTT. Pittsburgh, PA, 1/26/42. Actor. *The Right Stuff.*
GLESS, SHARON. Los Angeles, CA, 5/31/43. Actor. Chris Cagney on *Cagney and Lacey.*
GLITTER, GARY (Paul Gadd). Banbury, England, 5/8/40. Singer, songwriter.
GLOVER, CRISPIN. New York, NY, 9/20/64. Actor. George McFly in *Back to the Future.*
GLOVER, DANNY. San Francisco, CA, 7/22/47. Actor. *Lethal Weapon.*
GLOVER, JOHN. Kingston, NY, 8/7/44. Actor. *Shamus.*
GLOVER, ROGER. Brecon, Wales, 11/30/45. Bassist. Deep Purple.
GOBLE, GRAHAM. Adelaide, Australia, 5/15/47. Guitarist. Little River Band.
GODLEY, KEVIN. Manchester, England, 10/7/45. Singer, drummer. 10cc; Godley & Creme.
GOLD, TRACEY. New York, NY, 5/16/69. Actor. *Growing Pains.*
GOLDEN, WILLIAM LEE. Brewton, AL, 1/12/39. Singer. The Oak Ridge Boys.
GOLDING, LYNVAL. Coventry, England, 7/24/51. Guitarist. The Specials.
GOLDTHWAIT, BOBCAT. Syracuse, NY, 5/1/62. Actor. *Police Academy* series.
GOLDWYN, TONY. Los Angeles, CA, 5/20/60. Actor. *Ghost.*
GOLINO, VALERIA. Naples, Italy, 10/22/66. Actor. *Rain Man.*
GOODALL, JANE. London, England, 4/3/34. Anthropologist, author. *In the Shadow of Man.*
GOODEN, SAM. Chattanooga, TN, 9/2/39. Singer. The Impressions.
GOODING, CUBA JR. The Bronx, NY, 1968. Actor. *Boyz N the Hood.*
GORBACHEV, MIKHAIL. Privolnoye, Russia, 4/2/31. Former leader of the USSR.
GORE, ALBERT JR. Washington, DC, 3/31/48. Vice president of the United States.
GORE, LESLEY. New York, NY, 5/2/46. Singer.
GORE, MARTIN. Basildon, England, 7/23/61. Keyboardist. Depeche Mode.
GORHAM, SCOTT. Santa Monica, CA, 3/17/51. Guitarist. Thin Lizzy.
GORMAN, STEVE. Hopkinsville, KY, 8/17/65. Drummer. The Black Crowes.
GORME, EYDIE. New York, NY, 8/16/32. Singer. Steve and Eydie.
GORRIE, ALAN Perth, Scotland, 7/19/46. Singer, bassist. Average White Band.
GORSHIN, FRANK. Pittsburgh, PA, 4/5/33. Actor. The Riddler on *Batman.*
GOSSETT, LOUIS JR. Brooklyn, NY, 5/27/36. Actor. *An Officer and a Gentleman.*
GOTTI, JOHN. New York, NY, 10/27/40. Reputed mob leader.
GOUDREAU, BARRY. Boston, MA, 11/29/51. Guitarist. Boston.
GOULD, BILLY. Los Angeles, CA, 4/24/63. Bassist. Faith No More.
GOULD, BOON. 3/14/55. Guitarist. Level 42.
GOULD, ELLIOTT (Elliott Goldstein). Brooklyn, NY, 8/29/38. Actor. Formerly married to Barbra Streisand. *Bob & Carol & Ted & Alice.*
GOULD, PHIL. 2/28/57. Drummer. Level 42.
GOULDMAN, GRAHAM. Manchester, England, 5/10/45. Singer, guitarist. 10cc.
GOULET, ROBERT (Stanley Applebaum). Lawrence, MA, 11/26/33. Singer, actor. *Blue Light.*
GRAF, STEFFI. Bruhl, Germany, 6/14/69. Tennis player, youngest woman to win French Open.
GRAHAM, BILLY. Charlotte, NC, 11/7/18. Evangelist. *Billy Graham Crusades.*
GRAHAM, LARRY. Beaumont, TX, 8/14/46. Bass guitarist. Sly & The Family Stone.
GRAMM, LOU. Rochester, NY, 5/2/50. Singer. Foreigner.
GRANDMASTER FLASH (Joseph Saddler). New York, NY, 1958. Rap artist. Grandmaster Flash; Melle Mel & The Furious Five.
GRANDY, FRED. Sioux City, IA, 6/29/48. Actor, politician. Burl "Gopher" Smith on *The Love Boat.*
GRANGER, FARLEY. San Jose, CA, 7/1/25. Actor. *Strangers on a Train.*
GRANT, AMY. Augusta, GA, 11/25/60. Singer. *Age to Age.*
GRANT, EDDY (Edmond Grant). Plaisance, Guyana, 3/5/48. Reggae singer, songwriter.

GRANT, LEE (Lyova Rosenthal). New York, NY, 10/31/27. Actor, mother of Dinah Manoff. *Peyton Place.*
GRANTHAM, GEORGE. Cordell, OK, 11/20/47. Drummer, singer. Poco.
GRATZER, ALAN. Syracuse, NY, 11/9/48. Drummer. REO Speedwagon.
GRAVES, PETER (Peter Aurness). Minneapolis, MN, 3/18/26. Actor, brother of James Arness. Jim Phelps on *Mission: Impossible.*
GRAY, EDDIE. 2/27/48. Guitarist. Tommy James & The Shondells.
GRAY, LES. Carshalton, England, 4/9/46. Singer. Mud.
GRAY, LINDA. Santa Monica, CA, 9/12/40. Actor. *Dallas.*
GRAY, SPALDING. Barrington, RI, 6/5/41. Actor, writer, performance artist. *The Killing Fields.*
GREBB, MARTY. Chicago, IL, 9/2/46. Keyboardist. The Buckinghams.
GREEN, AL (Al Greene). Forrest City, AR, 4/13/46. R&B singer, songwriter.
GREEN, KARL. Salford, England, 7/31/47. Bassist. Herman's Hermits.
GREENAWAY, PETER. Newport, Wales, 4/5/42. Director, writer. *The Cook, the Thief, His Wife and Her Lover.*
GREENFIELD, DAVE. Keyboardist. The Stranglers.
GREENSPOON, JIMMY. Los Angeles, CA, 2/7/48. Organist. Three Dog Night.
GREENWOOD, ALAN. New York, NY, 10/20/51. Keyboardist. Foreigner.
GREGG, BRIAN. Bassist. Johnny Kidd & The Pirates.
GREGORY, GLENN. Sheffield, England, 5/16/58. Singer. Heaven 17.
GRETZKY, WAYNE. Brantford, Canada, 1/26/61. Hockey player.
GREY, JENNIFER. New York, NY, 3/26/60. Actor, daughter of Joel. *Dirty Dancing.*
GREY, JOEL (Joel Katz). Cleveland, OH, 4/11/32. Musical comedy performer, father of Jennifer. *Cabaret.*
GRIER, DAVID ALAN. Detroit, MI, 6/30/55. Actor. *In Living Color.*
GRIER, ROSEY (Roosevelt Grier). Cuthbert, GA, 7/14/32. Football player, actor.
GRIFFITH, ANDY. Mt. Airy, NC, 6/1/26. Actor, writer, producer. *The Andy Griffith Show.*
GRIFFITH, NANCI. Austin, TX, 7/6/53. Singer, songwriter. "From a Distance."
GRILL, ROB. Los Angeles, CA, 11/30/44. Bassist, singer. The Grass Roots.
GROSS, MARY. Chicago, IL, 3/25/53. Actor, sister of Michael. *Saturday Night Live.*
GROSS, MICHAEL. Chicago, IL, 6/21/47. Actor, brother of Mary. Steven Keaton on *Family Ties.*
GRUNDY, HUGH. Winchester, England, 3/6/45. Drummer. The Zombies.
GUCCIONE, BOB. New York, NY, 12/17/30. Publisher, founder of *Penthouse.*
GUEST, CHRISTOPHER. New York, NY, 2/5/48. Actor, writer, married to Jamie Lee Curtis. *This Is Spinal Tap.*
GUEST, LANCE. Saratoga, CA, 7/21/60. Actor. *Knots Landing.*
GUEST, WILLIAM. Atlanta, GA, 6/2/41. Singer. Gladys Knight & The Pips.
GUILLAUME, ROBERT (Robert Williams). St. Louis, MO, 11/30/37. Actor. Benson DuBois on *Soap.*
GUINNESS, ALEC. London, England, 4/2/14. Actor. *The Bridge on the River Kwai.*
GULAGER, CLU. Holdenville, OK, 11/16/28. Actor. *The Last Picture Show.*
GUMBEL, BRYANT. New Orleans, LA, 9/29/48. News show host and sportscaster. *Today.*
GUSTAFSON, KARIN. Miami, FL, 6/23/59. Actor. *Taps.*
GUSTAFSON, STEVEN. Bassist. 10,000 Maniacs.
GUTHRIE, ARLO. New York, NY, 7/10/47. Folk singer, songwriter. "Alice's Restaurant."
GUTTENBERG, STEVE. Brooklyn, NY, 8/24/58. Actor. *Three Men and a Baby.*
GUY, BILLY. Attasca, TX, 6/20/36. Baritone. The Coasters.
GUY, BUDDY (George Guy). Lettsworth, LA, 7/30/36. Blues guitarist.
GUY, JASMINE. Boston, MA, 3/10/64. Actor. Whitley Gilbert on *A Different World.*
HAAS, LUKAS. West Hollywood, CA, 4/16/76. Actor. *Witness.*
HACK, SHELLEY. Greenwich, CT, 7/6/52. Actor. *Charlie's Angels.*
HACKETT, BUDDY (Leonard Hacker). Brooklyn, NY, 8/31/24. Actor. *It's a Mad Mad Mad Mad World; The Love Bug.*
HADLEY, TONY. Islington, England, 6/2/59. Singer. Spandau Ballet.
HAGAR, SAMMY. Monterey, CA, 10/13/47. Singer, guitarist. Van Halen.
HAGERTY, JULIE. Cincinnati, OH, 6/15/55. Actor. *Airplane!*
HAGMAN, LARRY (Larry Hageman). Fort Worth, TX, 9/21/31. Actor, son of Mary Martin. J. R. Ewing on *Dallas.*
HAHN, JESSICA. Massapequa, NY, 7/7/59. *Playboy* model, involved in PTL Jim Bakker scandal.
HAID, CHARLES. San Francisco, CA, 6/2/43. Actor, director, producer. Andrew Renko on *Hill Street Blues.*
HAIM, COREY. Toronto, Canada, 12/23/72. Actor. *The Lost Boys.*
HALE, BARBARA. DeKalb, IL, 4/18/22. Actor, mother of William Katt. Della Street on *Perry Mason.*
HALFORD, ROB. Birmingham, England, 8/25/51. Singer. Judas Priest.
HALL, ANTHONY MICHAEL. Boston, MA, 4/14/68. Actor. *Sixteen Candles.*
HALL, ARSENIO. Cleveland, OH, 2/12/59. Actor, talk show host.
HALL, BRIDGET. Dallas, TX, 12/14/77. Supermodel.
HALL, BRUCE. Champaign, IL, 5/3/53. Bassist. REO Speedwagon.
HALL, DARYL (Daryl Hohl). Pottstown, PA, 10/11/49. Singer, guitarist. Hall & Oates.
HALL, DEIDRE. 10/31/47. Actor. Marlena Evans on *Days of Our Lives.*
HALL, FAWN. Annandale, VA, 1959. Secretary for Oliver North. Iran-Contra scandal.
HALL, MONTY. Winnipeg, Canada, 8/25/24. TV personality. *Let's Make a Deal.*
HALL, TERRY. Coventry, England, 3/19/59. Singer. The Specials.
HAM, GREG. Australia, 9/27/53. Saxophonist, keyboardist, flautist. Men at Work.
HAM, PETE. Swansea, Wales, 4/27/47. Guitarist, pianist, singer. Badfinger.
HAMEL, VERONICA. Philadelphia, PA, 11/20/43. Actor. Joyce Davenport on *Hill Street Blues.*
HAMILL, DOROTHY. Chicago, IL, 7/26/56. Ice skater. Olympic gold medalist.
HAMILL, MARK. Oakland, CA, 9/25/52. Actor. Luke Skywalker in *Star Wars* trilogy.
HAMILTON, GEORGE. Memphis, TN, 8/12/39. Actor. *Love at First Bite.*
HAMILTON, LINDA. Salisbury, MD, 9/26/56. Actor. Sarah Connor in *The Terminator.*
HAMILTON, SCOTT. Haverford, PA, 8/28/58. Ice skater.
HAMILTON, TOM. Colorado Springs, CO, 12/31/51. Bassist. Aerosmith.
HAMLIN, HARRY. Pasadena, CA, 10/30/51. Actor. *L.A. Law.*
HAMLISCH, MARVIN. New York, NY, 6/2/44. Composer. *The Way We Were; The Sting.*
HAMMER (Stanley Kirk Burrell). Oakland, CA, 3/29/63. Rap artist, dancer. *Please Hammer Don't Hurt 'Em.*
HAMMETT, KIRK. 11/18/62. Guitarist. Metallica.
HAMPSHIRE, SUSAN. London, England, 5/12/41. Actor. *The Forsythe Saga.*
HANCOCK, HERBIE. Chicago, IL, 4/12/40. Jazz pianist, composer. "Rockit."
HANNAH, DARYL. Chicago, IL, 12/3/60. Actor. *Splash.*

HARDING, TONYA. Portland, OR, 11/12/70. Figure skater. Pled guilty to hindering prosecution in Nancy Kerrigan attack.
HARDISON, KADEEM. Brooklyn, NY, 7/24/66. Actor. Dwayne Wayne on *A Different World.*
HAREWOOD, DORIAN. Dayton, OH, 8/6/50. Actor. *Roots—The Next Generation.*
HARKET, MORTEN. Konigsberg, Norway, 9/14/59. Lead singer. a-ha.
HARLEY, STEVE (Steve Nice). London, England, 2/27/51. Singer. Steve Harley & Cockney Rebel.
HARMON, MARK. Los Angeles, CA, 9/2/51. Actor. *St. Elsewhere.*
HARPER, JESSICA. Chicago, IL, 10/10/49. Actor.
HARPER, TESS (Tessie Jean Washam). Mammoth Spring, AR, 8/15/50. Actor. *Crimes of the Heart.*
HARPER, VALERIE. Suffern, NY, 8/22/40. Actor. Rhoda Morgenstern on *The Mary Tyler Moore Show.*
HARRINGTON, PAT. New York, NY, 8/13/29. Actor. Dwayne Schneider on *One Day at a Time.*
HARRIS, BARBARA (Sandra Markowitz). Evanston, IL, 7/25/35. Actor. *Family Plot.*
HARRIS, JULIE. Grosse Point, MI, 12/2/25. Actor. *Knots Landing.*
HARRIS, MEL (Mary Ellen Harris). Bethlehem, PA, 7/12/57. Actor. Hope Murdoch Steadman on *thirtysomething.*
HARRIS, RICHARD. Limerick, Ireland, 10/1/30. Actor. *A Man Called Horse.*
HARRISON, BILLY. Belfast, Ireland, 10/14/42. Lead guitarist. Them.
HARRISON, GEORGE. Liverpool, England, 2/25/43. Singer, lead guitarist. The Beatles.
HARRISON, GREGORY. Catalina Island, CA, 5/31/50. Actor. *Trapper John, MD.*
HARRISON, JENILEE. Northridge, CA, 6/12/59. Actor. Jamie Ewing Barnes on *Dallas.*
HARRISON, JERRY. Milwaukee, WI, 2/21/49. Keyboardist. Talking Heads.
HARRISON, NOEL. London, England, 1/29/35. Singer, actor. *The Girl from U.N.C.L.E.*
HARRY, DEBORAH. Miami, FL, 7/1/45. Singer. Blondie.
HART, MARY. Sioux Falls, SD, 11/8/50. TV hostess. *Entertainment Tonight.*
HART, MICKY (Michael Hart). New York, NY, 9/11/44. Drummer, songwriter. Grateful Dead.
HARTLEY, MARIETTE. New York, NY, 6/21/40. Actor. *Peyton Place.*
HARTMAN, DAVID. Pawtucket, RI, 5/19/35. Actor, talk show host. *Good Morning America.*
HARTMAN, JOHN. Falls Church, VA, 3/18/50. Drummer. The Doobie Brothers.
HASSAN, NORMAN. Birmingham, England, 11/26/57. Percussionist. UB40.
HATFIELD, BOBBY. Beaver Dam, WI, 8/10/40. Singer. The Righteous Brothers.
HATTON, BILLY. Liverpool, England, 6/9/41. Bassist. The Fourmost.
HAUER, RUTGER. Breukelen, Netherlands, 1/23/44. Actor. *Blade Runner.*
HAVENS, RICHIE. Brooklyn, NY, 1/21/41. Folk/blues guitarist, singer, songwriter.
HAWKING, STEPHEN. Oxford, England, 1/8/42. Theoretical physicist, author of *A Brief History of Time.*
HAY, COLIN. Scotland, 6/29/53. Singer. Men at Work.
HAY, ROY. Southend, England, 8/12/61. Guitarist, keyboardist. Culture Club.
HAYDOCK, ERIC. Stockport, England, 2/3/42. Bassist. The Hollies.
HAYES, CHRIS. California, 11/24/57. Lead guitarist. Huey Lewis & The News.
HAYES, ISAAC. Covington, TN, 8/20/42. R&B/rock saxophonist, keyboardist, singer, songwriter.
HAYS, ROBERT. Bethesda, MD, 7/24/47. Actor, married to Cherie Currie. *Airplane!*
HAYWARD, JUSTIN. Wiltshire, England, 10/14/46. Singer, songwriter. The Moody Blues.
HEADLY, GLENNE. New London, CT, 3/13/55. Actor, formerly married to John Malkovich. *Dirty Rotten Scoundrels.*
HEADON, NICKY. Bromley, England, 5/30/55. Drummer. The Clash.
HEALEY, JEFF. Toronto, Canada, 1966. Singer, songwriter, guitarist.
HEARD, JOHN. Washington, DC, 3/7/46. Actor. Father in *Home Alone.*
HEATON, PAUL. Birkenhead, England, 5/9/62. Singer, guitarist. The Housemartins.
HEDREN, TIPPI (Natalie Kay Hedren). New Ulm, MN, 1/19/35. Actor. Mother of Melanie Griffith. *The Birds.*
HEFNER, HUGH. Chicago, IL, 4/9/26. Publisher, founder of *Playboy.*
HELL, RICHARD (Richard Myers). Lexington, KY, 10/2/49. Bassist. Television.
HELLER, JOSEPH. New York, NY, 5/1/23. Author, dramatist. *Catch-22.*
HELLIWELL, JOHN. England, 2/15/45. Saxophonist. Supertramp.
HELM, LEVON. Marvell, AR, 5/26/42. Drummer, singer. The Band.
HELMSLEY, HARRY. New York, NY, 3/4/09. Businessman, married to Leona Helmsley.
HELMSLEY, LEONA. New York, NY, 7/4/20. Hotel executive, married to Harry Helmsley. Convicted of tax evasion.
HEMINGWAY, MARIEL. Ketchum, ID, 11/22/61. Actor, granddaughter of Ernest Hemingway, sister of Margaux. *Manhattan.*
HEMSLEY, SHERMAN. Philadelphia, PA, 2/1/38. Actor. George on *The Jeffersons.*
HENDERSON, ALAN. Belfast, Ireland, 11/26/44. Bassist. Them.
HENDERSON, BILLY. Detroit, MI, 8/9/39. Singer. The (Detroit) Spinners.
HENDERSON, FLORENCE. Dale, IN, 2/14/34. Actor. Carol Brady on *The Brady Bunch.*
HENLEY, DON. Linden, TX, 7/22/47. Singer, songwriter, drummer, guitarist. The Eagles.
HENNER, MARILU. Chicago, IL, 4/6/52. Actor. Elaine Nardo on *Taxi.*
HENNING, DOUG. Fort Gary, Canada, 5/3/47. Magician. *The Magic Show.*
HENRIKSEN, LANCE. New York, NY, 5/5/40. Actor. *Aliens.*
HENRY, BUCK (Buck Zuckerman). New York, NY, 12/9/30. Actor, writer. *Get Smart; That Was the Week That Was.*
HENRY, CLARENCE. Algiers, LA, 3/19/37. Singer. "Ain't Got No Home."
HENRY, JUSTIN. Rye, NY, 5/25/71. Actor. *Kramer vs. Kramer.*
HENRY, PRINCE. London, England, 8/15/84. British royalty, son of Prince Charles and Princess Diana.
HENSLEY, KEN. England, 8/24/45. Keyboardist, guitarist, singer, percussionist. Uriah Heep.
HENSLEY, PAMELA. Los Angeles, CA, 10/3/50. Actor. C. J. Parsons on *Matt Houston.*
HERMAN, PEE-WEE (Paul Reubens). Peekskill, NY, 8/27/52. Children's performer. *Pee-Wee's Playhouse.*
HERRMANN, EDWARD. Washington, DC, 7/21/43. Actor. *The Paper Chase.*
HERSHEY, BARBARA (Barbara Herzstein). Hollywood, CA, 2/5/48. Actor. *Hannah and Her Sisters.*
HERVEY, JASON. Los Angeles, CA, 4/6/72. Actor. Wayne Arnold on *The Wonder Years.*
HESSEMAN, HOWARD. Salem, OR, 2/27/40. Actor. Dr. Johnny Fever on *WKRP in Cincinnati.*
HESTON, CHARLTON (Charles Carter). Evanston, IL, 10/4/24. Actor. *The Ten Commandments.*

HETFIELD, JAMES. 8/3/63. Singer, guitarist. Metallica.
HEWETT, HOWARD. Akron, OH, 10/1/55. Singer. Shalamar.
HEYWARD, NICK. Kent, England, 5/20/61. Guitarist, singer. Haircut 100.
HICKS, CATHERINE. New York, NY, 8/6/51. Actor. *Peggy Sue Got Married.*
HICKS, TONY. Nelson, England, 12/16/43. Guitarist. The Hollies.
HILL, ANITA. Tulsa, OK, 7/30/56. Lawyer, law professor. Accused Supreme Court nominee Clarence Thomas of sexual harrassment.
HILL, ARTHUR. Saskatchewan, Canada, 8/1/22. Actor. *Owen Marshall, Counsellor at Law.*
HILL, DAVE. Fleet Castle, England, 4/4/52. Guitarist. Slade.
HILL, DUSTY. Dallas, TX, 5/19/49. Bassist, singer. ZZ Top.
HILL, FAITH. Star, MS, 1968. Singer. "Wild One."
HILL, STEVEN. Seattle, WA, 2/24/22. Actor. *Law and Order.*
HILLERMAN, JOHN. Denison, TX, 12/20/32. Actor. Jonathan Quayle Higgins III on *Magnum P.I.*
HILLERMAN, TONY. Sacred Heart, OK, 5/27/25. Novelist.
HILLMAN, CHRIS. Los Angeles, CA, 12/4/42. Singer, bassist. The Byrds.
HINES, GREGORY. New York, NY, 2/14/46. Actor, dancer. *The Cotton Club.*
HINGLE, PAT (Martin Patterson Hingle). Denver, CO, 7/19/23. Actor. *Gunsmoke.*
HINSLEY, HARVEY. Northampton, England, 1/19/48. Guitarist. Hot Chocolate.
HIRSCH, GARY "CHICKEN." England, 1940. Drummer. Country Joe & The Fish.
HIRSCH, JUDD. New York, NY, 3/15/35. Actor. Alex Rieger on *Taxi.*
HITCHCOCK, RUSSELL. Melbourne, Australia, 6/15/49. Singer. Air Supply.
HO, DON. Kakaako, HI, 8/13/30. Singer. "Tiny Bubbles."
HOBBS, RANDY. 3/22/48. Bassist. The McCoys.
HODGE, PATRICIA. Lincolnshire, England, 9/29/46. Actor. *The Elephant Man.*
HODGSON, ROGER. Portsmouth, England, 3/21/50. Guitarist. Supertramp.
HODO, DAVID. 7/7/50. Singer. The Village People.
HOFFS, SUSANNA. Newport Beach, CA, 1/17/57. Guitarist, singer. The Bangles.
HOGAN, HULK (Terry Gene Bollea). Augusta, GA, 8/11/53. Wrestler, former World Federation heavyweight champion.
HOGAN, PAUL. Lightning Ridge, Australia, 10/8/39. Actor. *Crocodile Dundee.*
HOLBROOK, HAL. Cleveland, OH, 2/17/25. Actor. *All the President's Men.*
HOLDER, NODDY (Neville Holder). Walsall, England, 6/15/50. Guitarist, singer. Slade.
HOLLAND, JOOLS (Julian Holland). 1/24/58. Keyboardist. Squeeze.
HOLLIMAN, EARL. Delhi, LA, 9/11/28. Actor. *Police Woman.*
HOLLIS, MARK. Tottenham, England, 1955. Singer, guitarist, keyboardist. Talk Talk.
HOLM, CELESTE. New York, NY, 4/29/19. Actor. *All About Eve.*
HOLMES, LARRY. Cuthbert, GA, 11/3/49. Boxer. Former heavyweight champ.
HOOK, PETER. Salford, England, 2/13/56. Bassist. Joy Division; New Order.
HOOKER, JOHN LEE. Clarksdale, MS, 8/22/17. Legendary blues guitarist, singer, songwriter.
HOOKS, JAN. Decatur, GA, 4/23/57. Actor. Carlene Frazier Dobber on *Designing Women.*
HOPE, BOB (Leslie Hope). Eltham, England, 5/29/03. Actor, performer for overseas troops. *The Road* movies with Bing Crosby.
HOPE, DAVE. Kansas, 10/7/49. Bassist. Kansas.
HOPKIN, MARY. Pontardawe, Wales, 5/3/50. Singer, discovered by the Beatles. "Those Were the Days."
HOPKINS, TELMA. Louisville, KY, 10/28/48. Singer, actor, former member of Tony Orlando & Dawn. *Family Matters.*
HOPPER, DENNIS. Dodge City, KS, 5/17/36. Actor, director. *Easy Rider.*
HOPPER, SEAN. California, 3/31/53. Keyboardist. Huey Lewis & The News.
HOPWOOD, KEITH. Manchester, England, 10/26/46. Guitarist. Herman's Hermits.
HORNE, LENA. Brooklyn, NY, 6/30/17. Singer, actor.
HORNSBY, BRUCE. Williamsburg, VA, 11/23/54. Singer, keyboardist, accordionist. Bruce Hornsby & The Range.
HOSKINS, BOB. Bury St. Edmunds, England, 10/26/42. Actor. *Who Framed Roger Rabbit.*
HOWARD, ALAN. Dagenham, England, 10/17/41. Bassist. Brian Poole & The Tremeloes.
HOWARD, ARLISS. Independence, MO, 1955. Actor. *Full Metal Jacket.*
HOWARD, KEN. El Centro, CA, 3/28/44. Actor. *The White Shadow.*
HOWE, STEVE. London, England, 4/8/47. Guitarist, singer. Yes; Asia.
HUCKNALL, MICK "RED." Manchester, England, 6/8/60. Singer. Simply Red.
HUDLIN, REGINALD. Centerville, IL, 12/15/61. Director, writer, producer, brother of Warrington. *House Party.*
HUDLIN, WARRINGTON. East St. Louis, IL, 1952. Producer, director, brother of Reginald. *House Party.*
HUDSON, GARTH. London, Canada, 8/2/37. Organist. The Band.
HUGG, MIKE. Andover, England, 8/11/42. Drummer. Manfred Mann.
HUGHES, GLENN. 7/18/50. Singer. The Village People.
HULCE, TOM. White Water, WI, 12/6/53. Actor. *Amadeus.*
HUMPERDINCK, ENGELBERT (Arnold Dorsey). Madras, India, 5/2/36. Pop singer. *The Engelbert Humperdinck Show.*
HUMPHREYS, PAUL. London, England, 2/27/60. Keyboardist. Orchestral Manoeuvres in the Dark (OMD).
HUNT, BILL. 5/23/47. Keyboardist. Electric Light Orchestra (ELO).
HUNT, LINDA. Morristown, NJ, 4/2/45. Actor. *The Year of Living Dangerously.*
HUNTER, IAN. Shrewsbury, England, 6/3/46. Singer, guitarist. Mott The Hoople.
HUNTER, TAB (Arthur Gelien). New York, NY, 7/11/31. Actor. *Damn Yankees.*
HUPPERT, ISABELLE. Paris, France, 3/16/55. Actor. *Entre Nous.*
HURT, JOHN. Shirebrook, England, 1/22/40. Actor. *The Elephant Man.*
HURT, MARY BETH (Mary Beth Supinger). Marshalltown, IA, 9/26/48. Actor, formerly married to William Hurt. *The World According to Garp.*
HURT, WILLIAM. Washington, DC, 3/20/50. Actor, formerly married to Mary Beth Hurt. *Children of a Lesser God.*
HUSSEIN, SADDAM. Tikrit, Iraq, 4/28/37. Leader of Iraq.
HUSSEY, WAYNE. Bristol, England, 5/26/59. Guitarist, singer. The Mission.
HUSTON, ANJELICA. Santa Monica, CA, 7/8/51. Actor, daughter of John Huston. *Prizzi's Honor.*
HUTCHENCE, MICHAEL. Sydney, Australia, 1/22/60. Singer. INXS.
HUTTER, RALF. Krefeld, Germany, 1946. Keyboardist, drummer, singer. Kraftwerk.
HUTTON, DANNY. Buncrana, Ireland, 9/10/42. Singer. Three Dog Night.
HUTTON, LAUREN (Mary Hutton). Charleston, SC, 11/17/43. Actor, model. *American Gigolo.*

HUTTON, TIMOTHY. Malibu, CA, 8/16/60. Actor, director. *Ordinary People.*
HUXLEY, RICK. Dartford, England, 8/5/42. Guitarist. The Dave Clark Five.
HYNDE, CHRISSIE. Akron, OH, 9/7/51. Singer, divorced from Jim Kerr. The Pretenders.
IACOCCA, LEE (Lido Anthony Iacocca). Allentown, PA, 10/15/24. Auto executive, author. *Iacocca.*
IAN, JANIS (Janis Fink). New York, NY, 4/7/51. Folk/rock singer, songwriter.
IDLE, ERIC. Durham, England, 3/29/43. Actor. *Monty Python's Flying Circus.*
IDOL, BILLY (Billy Broad). Stanmore, England, 11/30/55. Singer, songwriter.
IGLESIAS, JULIO. Madrid, Spain, 9/23/43. Pop singer, songwriter.
ILLSLEY, JOHN. Leicester, England, 6/24/49. Bassist. Dire Straits.
IMAN. Mogadishu, Somalia, 7/25/55. Model, married to David Bowie.
INGELS, MARTY. Brooklyn, NY, 3/9/36. Actor, agent, married to Shirley Jones. *The Pruitts of Southampton.*
INGLE, DOUG. Omaha, NE, 9/9/46. Singer, keyboardist. Iron Butterfly.
INGRAM, JAMES. Akron, OH, 2/16/56. R&B singer, songwriter.
INNES, NEIL. Essex, England, 12/9/44. Singer, keyboardist. The Bonzo Dog Doo-Dah Band.
INNIS, ROY. Saint Croix, Virgin Islands, 6/6/34. Civil rights leader.
IOMMI, TONY. Birmingham, England, 2/19/48. Guitarist. Black Sabbath.
IRELAND, KATHY. Santa Barbara, CA, 3/8/63. Model, sister of Mary and Cynthia. *Sports Illustrated* swimsuit cover girl.
IRELAND, PATRICIA. Oak Park, IL, 10/19/45. Political activist. President of NOW.
IRVING, AMY. Palo Alto, CA, 9/10/53. Actor. *Yentl.*
IRVING, JOHN. Exeter, NH, 3/2/42. Author. *The World According to Garp.*
IRWIN, BILL. Santa Monica, CA, 4/11/50. Actor. *Eight Men Out.*
ISAAK, CHRIS. Stockton, CA, 6/26/56. Singer, songwriter, actor. "Wicked Game"
ISLEY, O'KELLY. Cincinnati, OH, 12/25/37. Singer. The Isley Brothers.
ISLEY, RONALD. Cincinnati, OH, 5/21/41. Lead singer. The Isley Brothers.
ISLEY, RUDOLPH. Cincinnati, OH, 4/1/39. Singer. The Isley Brothers.
IVEY, JUDITH. El Paso, TX, 9/4/51. Actor. *Designing Women.*
IVORY, JAMES. Berkeley, CA, 6/7/28. Director, producer. *Howard's End.*
JABS, MATTHIAS. 10/25/56. Guitarist. Scorpions.
JACKEE (Jackee Harry). Winston-Salem, NC, 8/14/56. Actor. *227.*
JACKSON, BO. Bessemer, AL, 11/30/62. Pro football, baseball player.
JACKSON, EDDIE. 1/29/61. Bassist, singer. Queensryche.
JACKSON, FREDDIE. New York, NY, 10/2/56. R&B singer, songwriter.
JACKSON, GLENDA. Birkenhead, England, 5/9/36. Actor. *Women in Love.*
JACKSON, JACKIE (Sigmund Jackson). Gary, IN, 5/4/51. Singer, brother of Michael and Janet Jackson. The Jacksons.
JACKSON, JERMAINE. Gary, IN, 12/11/54. Singer, brother of Michael and Janet. The Jacksons.
JACKSON, JESSE. Greenville, SC, 10/8/41. Civil rights leader, politician. Founded the Rainbow Coalition.
JACKSON, JOE. Burton-on-Trent, England, 8/11/55. Singer, songwriter.
JACKSON, KATE. Birmingham, AL, 10/29/48. Actor. Sabrina Duncan on *Charlie's Angels.*
JACKSON, MARLON. Gary, IN, 3/12/57. Singer, brother of Michael and Janet. The Jacksons.
JACKSON, PERVIS. 5/17/38. Singer. The (Detroit) Spinners.
JACKSON, TITO (Toriano Jackson). Gary, IN, 10/15/53. Singer, brother of Michael and Janet. The Jacksons.
JACKSON, TONY. Liverpool, England, 7/16/40. Singer, bassist. The Searchers.
JACKSON, VICTORIA. Miami, FL, 8/2/58. Actor. *Saturday Night Live.*
JACOBI, DEREK. London, England, 10/22/38. Actor. *The Day of the Jackal.*
JACOBI, LOU. Toronto, Canada, 12/28/13. Actor. *Irma La Douce.*
JAGGER, BIANCA. Managua, Nicaragua, 5/2/45. Socialite, actor. Divorced from Mick Jagger.
JAM MASTER JAY (Jason Mizell). New York, NY, 1965. DJ. Run-D.M.C.
JAMES, CLIFTON. Portland, OR, 5/29/25. Actor. *Cool Hand Luke.*
JAMES, ETTA. Los Angeles, CA, 1/25/38. Singer. Bridged R&B and rock.
JAMES, RICK (James Johnson). Buffalo, NY, 2/1/52. Funk singer, songwriter. "Super Freak."
JAMES, TOMMY (Tommy Jackson). Dayton, OH, 4/29/47. Singer. Tommy James & The Shondells.
JANIS, CONRAD. New York, NY, 2/11/28. Actor, musician. Frederick McConnell on *Mork and Mindy.*
JARDINE, AL. Lima, OH, 9/3/42. Guitarist, singer. The Beach Boys.
JARREAU, AL. Milwaukee, WI, 3/12/40. Jazz singer, sang theme song to *Moonlighting.*
JAZZIE B. (Beresford Romeo). London, England, 1/26/63. Rap artist. Soul II Soul.
JEFFRIES, LIONEL. London, England, 6/10/26. Actor, director. *The Water Babies.*
JENNER, BRUCE. Mount Kisco, NY, 10/28/49. Track athlete, sportscaster. Olympic gold medalist.
JENNINGS, WAYLON. Littlefield, TX, 6/15/37. Country singer, songwriter. *The Dukes of Hazzard* theme song.
JETER, MICHAEL. Lawrenceburg, TN, 8/26/52. Actor. *Evening Shade.*
JETT, JOAN. Philadelphia, PA, 9/22/60. Singer, guitarist. "I Love Rock 'n' Roll."
JILLIAN, ANNE (Anne Nauseda). Cambridge, MA, 1/29/51. Actor. *It's a Living.*
JOHANSEN, DAVID. Staten Island, NY, 1/9/50. Actor, singer, a.k.a. Buster Poindexter. *Scrooged.*
JOHN, DR. (Malcolm Rebennack). New Orleans, LA, 11/21/40. Rock/cajun/ blues singer, songwriter. "Right Place Wrong Time."
JOHN PAUL II, POPE. Wadowice, Poland, 5/18/20. First non-Italian pope since the Renaissance.
JOHNS, GLYNIS. Durban, South Africa, 10/5/23. Actor. *Glynis.*
JOHNSON, ARTE. Benton Harbor, MI, 1/20/29. Actor. *Laugh-In.*
JOHNSON, BEVERLY. Buffalo, NY, 10/13/52. Model, actor.
JOHNSON, HOLLY (William Johnson). Khartoum, Sudan, 2/19/60. Singer. Frankie Goes to Hollywood.
JOHNSON, HOWIE. Washington, DC, 1938. Drummer. The Ventures.
JOHNSON, LADY BIRD. Karnack, TX, 12/22/12. Former First Lady, wife of Lyndon.
JOHNSON, MATT. 8/15/61. Singer, guitarist. The The.
JOHNSON, VAN. Newport, RI, 8/25/16. Actor. *The Caine Mutiny.*
JOHNSON, WILKO (John Wilkinson). 1947. Guitarist. Dr. Feelgood.
JON, JOHN. 2/26/61. Musician. Bronski Beat.
JONES, ALAN. Swansea, Wales, 2/6/47. Baritone saxophonist. Amen Corner.
JONES, BOOKER T. Memphis, TN, 12/11/44. Keyboardist. Booker T. & The MG's.
JONES, DAVY. Manchester, England, 12/30/45. Singer, actor. The Monkees.

JONES, DEAN. Decatur, AL, 1/25/31. Actor. *The Shaggy D.A.*
JONES, GRACE. Spanishtown, Jamaica, 5/19/52. Singer, actor. *A View to a Kill.*
JONES, GRAHAM. North Yorkshire, England, 7/8/61. Guitarist. Haircut 100.
JONES, HOWARD. Southampton, England, 2/23/55. Singer, songwriter.
JONES, JAMES EARL. Arkabutla, MS, 1/17/31. Actor, voice of Darth Vader. *The Great White Hope.*
JONES, JEFFREY. Buffalo, NY, 9/28/47. Actor. Principal Ed Rooney in *Ferris Bueller's Day Off.*
JONES, JENNIFER (Phyllis Isley). Tulsa, OK, 3/2/19. Actor. *The Song of Bernadette.*
JONES, JOHN PAUL (John Paul Baldwin). Sidcup, England, 1/31/46. Bassist. Led Zeppelin.
JONES, KENNY. London, England, 9/16/48. Drummer. The Small Faces.
JONES, MICK. Brixton, England, 6/26/55. Guitarist, singer. The Clash; Big Audio Dynamite.
JONES, MICK. London, England, 12/27/44. Guitarist. Foreigner.
JONES, NEIL. Llanbradach, Wales, 3/25/49. Guitarist. Amen Corner.
JONES, PAUL (Paul Pond). Portsmouth, England, 2/24/42. Singer, harmonicist. Manfred Mann.
JONES, RANDY. 9/13/52. Singer. The Village People.
JONES, RAY. Oldham, England, 10/22/39. Bassist. Billy J. Kramer & The Dakotas.
JONES, RICKIE LEE. Chicago, IL, 11/8/54. Rock/jazz singer, songwriter.
JONES, SAM J. Chicago, IL, 8/12/54. Actor. *Flash Gordon.*
JONES, SHIRLEY. Smithton, PA, 3/31/34. Actor, married to Marty Ingels. *The Partridge Family.*
JONES, STEVE. London, England, 9/3/55. Guitarist. The Sex Pistols.
JONES, TERRY. Colwyn Bay, Wales, 2/1/42. Actor, director, writer. *Monty Python's Life of Brian.*
JONES, TOM (Tom Woodward). Pontypridd, Wales, 6/7/40. Pop singer.
JORDAN, LONNIE (Leroy Jordan). San Diego, CA, 11/21/48. Keyboardist, singer. War.
JOURARD, JEFF. 1955. Guitarist. The Motels.
JOURDAN, LOUIS (Louis Gendre). Marseilles, France, 6/19/19. Actor. *Gigi.*
JOYCE, MIKE. Manchester, England, 6/1/63. Drummer. The Smiths.
JOYNER-KERSEE, JACKIE. St. Louis, IL, 3/3/62. Track athlete. Olympic gold medalist.
JUDD, NAOMI (Diana Judd). Ashland, KY, 1/11/46. Country singer, mother of Wynonna and Ashley. The Judds.
JUMP, GORDON. Dayton, OH, 4/1/32. Actor. Arthur Carlson on *WKRP in Cincinnati.*
JUSTMAN, SETH. Washington, DC, 1/27/51. Keyboardist, singer. The J. Geils Band.
KAHN, MADELINE. Boston, MA, 9/29/42. Actor. *Blazing Saddles.*
KALE, JIM. 8/11/43. Bassist. The Guess Who.
KANE, BIG DADDY. New York, NY, 9/10/68. Rap artist, songwriter. "Long Live the Kane."
KANE, CAROL. Cleveland, OH, 6/18/52. Actor. Simka Graves on *Taxi.*
KANTNER, PAUL. San Francisco, CA, 3/12/42. Guitarist. Jefferson Airplane; Starship.
KAPRISKY, VALERIE. Paris, France, 1963. Actor. *Breathless.*
KARPOV, ANATOLY. Zlatoust, Russia, 5/23/51. Chess player. International grandmaster, world champion.
KARRAS, ALEX. Gary, IN, 7/15/35. Former football player, actor. *Webster.*
KASPAROV, GARRY. Baku, Russia, 4/13/63. Chess player. International grandmaster, world champion.
KATH, TERRY. Chicago, IL, 1/31/46. Guitarist. Chicago.
KATT, WILLIAM. Los Angeles, CA, 2/16/55. Actor, son of Barbara Hale. *The Greatest American Hero.*
KATZ, STEVE. New York, NY, 5/9/45. Guitarist, harmonicist, singer. Blood, Sweat & Tears.
KATZENBERG, JEFFREY. New York, NY, 1950. Studio executive.
KAUKONEN, JORMA. Washington, DC, 12/23/40. Guitarist. Jefferson Airplane; Hot Tuna.
KAVNER, JULIE. Los Angeles, CA, 9/7/51. Actor. Voice of Marge Simpson on *The Simpsons; Rhoda.*
KAY, JOHN (Joachim Krauledat). Tilsit, Germany, 4/12/44. Guitarist, singer. Steppenwolf.
KAYE, STUBBY. New York, NY, 11/11/18. Actor. *Guys and Dolls.*
KAYLAN, HOWARD (Howard Kaplan). New York, NY, 6/22/47. Singer, saxophonist. The Turtles.
KAZURINSKY, TIM. Johnstown, PA, 3/3/50. Actor. *Saturday Night Live.*
KEACH, STACY (William Keach Jr.). Savannah, GA, 6/2/41. Actor. *Mickey Spillane's Mike Hammer.*
KEANE, BIL. Philadelphia, PA, 10/5/22. Cartoonist. *The Family Circus.*
KEATON, DIANE (Diane Hall). Los Angeles, CA, 1/5/46. Actor. *Annie Hall.*
KEATON, MICHAEL (Michael Douglas). Coraopolis, PA, 9/9/51. Actor. *Batman.*
KEEBLE, JON. London, England, 7/6/59. Drummer. Spandau Ballet.
KEEL, HOWARD (Harold Leek). Gillespie, IL, 4/13/17. Actor. Clayton Farlow on *Dallas.*
KEENAN, BRIAN. New York, NY, 1/28/44. Drummer. The Chambers Brothers; Manfred Mann.
KEESHAN, BOB (Robert James Keeshan). Lynbrook, NY, 6/27/27. TV personality, author. *Captain Kangaroo.*
KEFFORD, ACE (Christopher Kefford). Mosely, England, 12/10/46. Bassist. The Move.
KEITH, DAVID LEMUEL. Knoxville, TN, 5/8/54. Actor. *An Officer and a Gentleman.*
KELLER, MARTHE. Basel, Switzerland, 1/28/45. Actor. *Marathon Man.*
KELLERMAN, SALLY. Long Beach, CA, 6/2/37. Actor. Hot Lips in the movie *M*A*S*H.*
KELLEY, DEFOREST. Atlanta, GA, 1/20/20. Actor. Dr. Leonard "Bones" McCoy on *Star Trek.*
KELLEY, KITTY. Spokane, WA, 4/4/42. Unauthorized biographer.
KELLING, GRAEME. Paisley, Scotland, 4/4/57. Guitarist. Deacon Blue.
KELLY, MARK. Dublin, Ireland, 4/9/61. Keyboardist. Marillion.
KELLY, MOIRA. 1968. Actor. *The Cutting Edge.*
KEMP, GARY. Islington, England, 10/16/60. Guitarist, brother of Martin. Spandau Ballet.
KEMP, MARTIN. London, England, 10/10/61. Bassist, brother of Gary. Spandau Ballet.
KENDRICKS, EDDIE. Birmingham, AL, 12/17/39. Singer. The Temptations.
KENNEDY, GEORGE. New York, NY, 2/18/25. Actor. *Cool Hand Luke.*
KENNEDY, TED. Brookline, MA, 2/22/32. Politician, brother of John and Robert.
KENNIBREW, DEE DEE (Dolores Henry). Brooklyn, NY, 1945. Singer. The Crystals.
KENNY G (Kenneth Gorelick). Seattle, WA, 6/5/56. Jazz saxophone player.
KENSIT, PATSY. London, England, 3/4/68. Actor, married to Jim Kerr. *Lethal Weapon 2.*
KERNS, JOANNA (Joanna De Varona). San Francisco, CA, 2/12/53. Actor. Maggie Seaver on *Growing Pains.*

KERR, DEBORAH. Helensburg, Scotland, 9/30/21. Actor. *The King and I.*
KERR, JIM. Glasgow, Scotland, 7/9/59. Singert. Simple Minds.
KERRIGAN, NANCY. Stoneham, MA, 10/13/69. Figure skater. Olympic silver medalist, victim of knee attack.
KHAN, CHAKA (Yvette Marie Stevens). Great Lakes, IL, 3/23/53. Singer. Rufus.
KIDD, JOHNNY (Frederick Heath). London, England, 12/23/39. Singer. Johnny Kidd & The Pirates.
KIDDER, MARGOT. Yellow Knife, Canada, 10/17/48. Actor. Lois Lane in *Superman.*
KIEDIS, ANTHONY. Grand Rapids, MI, 11/1/62. Singer. Red Hot Chili Peppers.
KIEL, RICHARD. Detroit, MI, 9/13/39. Actor. Jaws in *The Spy Who Loved Me.*
KILPATRICK, JAMES JR. Oklahoma City, OK, 11/1/20. Journalist. *60 Minutes.*
KIMBALL, BOBBY (Bobby Toteaux). Vinton, LA, 3/29/47. Lead singer. Toto.
KING, ALAN (Irwin Kniberg). Brooklyn, NY, 12/26/27. Producer, comedian. *The Andersen Tapes.*
KING, B. B. (Riley King). Itta Bena, MS, 9/16/25. Legendary blues guitarist, singer, songwriter.
KING, BEN E. (Ben E. Nelson). Henderson, NC, 9/23/38. Singer. The Drifters.
KING, BILLIE JEAN. Long Beach, CA, 11/22/43. Tennis player.
KING, CAROLE (Carole Klein). Brooklyn, NY, 2/9/42. Singer, songwriter.
KING, CORETTA SCOTT. Marion, AL, 4/27/27. Author, lecturer, widow of Martin Luther King Jr.
KING, DON. Cleveland, OH, 8/20/31. Boxing promoter.
KING, MARK. Isle of Wight, England, 10/20/58. Singer, bassist. Level 42.
KING, PERRY. Alliance, OH, 4/30/48. Actor. Cody Allen on *Riptide.*
KING, WILLIAM. Alabama, 1/30/49. Trumpeter, keyboardist. The Commodores.
KINGSLEY, BEN (Krishna Bhanji). Snaiton, England, 12/31/43. Actor. *Gandhi.*
KINSKI, NASTASSJA (Nastassja Nakszynski). Berlin, Germany, 1/24/60. Actor, daughter of Klaus Kinski. *Cat People.*
KIRBY, BRUNO (Bruce Kirby Jr.). New York, NY, 4/28/49. Actor. *City Slickers.*
KIRKE, SIMON. Wales, 7/28/49. Drummer. Bad Company; Free.
KIRKLAND, SALLY. New York, NY, 10/31/44. Actor. *Anna.*
KIRKMAN, TERRY. Salina, KS, 12/12/41. Singer, keyboardist. The Association.
KIRKPATRICK, JEANE. Duncan, OK, 11/19/26. Diplomat. Former U.S. representative to the U.N.
KISSINGER, HENRY. Fuerth, Germany, 5/27/23. Richard Nixon's secretary of state.
KITT, EARTHA. North, SC, 1/26/28. Actor, singer. *The Mark of the Hawk.*
KLEIN, DANNY. New York, NY, 5/13/46. Bassist. The J. Geils Band.
KLEIN, ROBERT. New York, NY, 2/8/42. Actor. *Comedy Tonight.*
KLEMPERER, WERNER. Cologne, Germany, 3/22/20. Actor. Colonel Wilhelm Klink on *Hogan's Heroes.*
KLINE, KEVIN. St. Louis, MO, 10/24/47. Actor, married to Phoebe Cates. *The Big Chill.*
KLUGMAN, JACK. Philadelphia, PA, 4/27/22. Actor. Oscar Madison on *The Odd Couple.*
KNIGHT, GLADYS. Atlanta, GA, 5/28/44. Singer. Gladys Knight & The Pips.
KNIGHT, JONATHAN. Boston, MA, 11/29/69. Singer. New Kids on the Block.
KNIGHT, JORDAN. Boston, MA, 5/17/71. Singer. New Kids on the Block.
KNIGHT, MERALD. Atlanta, GA, 9/4/42. Singer. Gladys Knight & The Pips.
KNIGHT, MICHAEL E. Princeton, NJ, 5/7/59. Actor. Tad Martin on *All My Children.*
KNIGHT, SHIRLEY. Goessell, KS, 7/5/36. Actor. *The Dark at the Top of the Stairs.*
KNIGHTS, DAVE. Islington, England, 6/28/45. Bassist. Procol Harum.
KNOPFLER, DAVID. Glasgow, Scotland, 12/27/52. Guitarist. Dire Straits.
KNOPFLER, MARK. Glasgow, Scotland, 8/12/49. Singer, guitarist. Dire Straits.
KNOTTS, DON. Morgantown, WV, 7/21/24. Actor. Barney Fife on *The Andy Griffith Show.*
KNOWLES, PATRIC (Reginald Lawrence Knowles). Horstorth, England, 11/11/11. Actor. *How Green Was My Valley.*
KNOX, BUDDY (Wayne Knox). Happy, TX, 4/14/33. Rock/country singer, songwriter.
KNUDSEN, KEITH. Ames, IA, 10/18/52. Drummer, singer. The Doobie Brothers.
KOCH, ED. New York, NY, 12/12/24. Former mayor of New York.
KOENIG, WALTER. Chicago, IL, 9/14/36. Actor, writer, director, producer. Pavel Chekov on *Star Trek.*
KOOL ROCK. (Damon Wimbley). 11/4/66. Rap artist. Fat Boys.
KOPELL, BERNIE. New York, NY, 6/21/33. Actor. Dr. Adam Bricker on *The Love Boat.*
KORMAN, HARVEY. Chicago, IL, 2/15/27. Actor. *The Carol Burnett Show.*
KOSSOFF, PAUL. London, England, 9/14/50. Guitarist. Free.
KOTTO, YAPHET. New York, NY, 11/15/37. Actor. *Live and Let Die.*
KRABBE, JEROEN. Amsterdam, The Netherlands, 12/5/44. Actor. *The Fugitive.*
KRAMER, BILLY J. (Billy J. Ashton). Bootle, England, 8/19/43. Singer. Billy J. Kramer & The Dakotas.
KRAMER, JOEY. New York, NY, 6/21/50. Drummer. Aerosmith.
KRANTZ, JUDITH. New York, NY, 1/9/28. Novelist. *Scruples.*
KRAVITZ, LENNY. New York, NY, 5/26/64. Singer, songwriter, formerly married to Lisa Bonet. "Are You Gonna Go My Way?"
KREUTZMANN, BILL JR. Palo Alto, CA, 5/7/46. Drummer. Grateful Dead.
KRIEGER, ROBBIE. Los Angeles, CA, 1/8/46. Guitarist. The Doors.
KRIGE, ALICE. Upington, South Africa, 6/28/55. Actor. *Chariots of Fire.*
KRISTOFFERSON, KRIS. Brownsville, TX, 6/22/36. Singer, songwriter, actor. *Amerika.*
KUBRICK, STANLEY. The Bronx, NY, 7/26/28. Director, producer, writer. *2001: A Space Odyssey.*
KUHLKE, NORMAN. Liverpool, England, 6/17/42. Drummer. The Swinging Blue Jeans.
KURTZ, SWOOSIE. Omaha, NE, 9/6/44. Actor. *Sisters.*
KWAN, NANCY. Hong Kong, 5/19/39. Actor. *The World of Suzie Wong.*
LABELLE, PATTI (Patricia Holt). Philadelphia, PA, 5/24/44. Pop/soul singer.
LADD, CHERYL (Cheryl Stoppelmoor). Huron, SD, 7/12/51. Actor. Kris Munroe on *Charlie's Angels.*
LADD, DIANE (Diane Ladner). Meridian, MS, 11/29/32. Actor, mother of Laura Dern. *Alice Doesn't Live Here Anymore.*
LAHTI, CHRISTINE. Birmingham, MI, 4/4/50. Actor. *Swing Shift.*
LAINE, DENNY (Brian Hines). Jersey, England, 10/29/44. Singer, guitarist. The Moody Blues.
LAKE, GREG. Bournemouth, England, 11/10/48. Bassist, singer. Emerson, Lake & Palmer; King Crimson.
LAMARR, HEDY (Hedwig Kiesler). Vienna, Austria, 11/9/13. Actor. *Ecstasy.*
LAMAS, LORENZO. Los Angeles, CA, 1/20/58. Actor. Lance Cumson on *Falcon Crest.*

LAMBERT, CHRISTOPHER. New York, NY, 3/29/57. Actor. *Greystoke: The Legend of Tarzan, Lord of the Apes.*
LAMM, ROBERT. New York, NY, 10/13/44. Singer, keyboardist. Chicago.
LANCASTER, ALAN. London, England, 2/7/49. Bassist. Status Quo.
LANDAU, MARTIN. Brooklyn, NY, 6/20/31. Actor. *Mission: Impossible.*
LANDERS, AUDREY. Philadelphia, PA, 7/18/59. Actor. Afton Cooper on *Dallas.*
LANDESBERG, STEVE. The Bronx, NY, 11/3/45. Actor. Detective Arthur Dietrich on *Barney Miller.*
LANDIS, JOHN. Chicago, IL, 8/3/50. Director. *Twilight Zone—The Movie.*
LANE, ABBE. Brooklyn, NY, 12/14/35. Actor, formerly married to Xavier Cugat. *Xavier Cugat Show.*
LANE, CHARLES. New York, NY, 12/5/53. Director. *Sidewalk Stories.*
LANE, DIANE. New York, NY, 1/22/65. Actor. *Rumble Fish.*
LANG, BOB. Manchester, England, 1/10/46. Bassist. Wayne Fontana & The Mindbenders.
LANGE, HOPE. Redding Ridge, CT, 11/28/31. Actor. *The Ghost and Mrs. Muir.*
LANGE, TED. Oakland, CA, 1/5/47. Actor. Isaac Washington on *The Love Boat.*
LANGELLA, FRANK. Bayonne, NJ, 1/1/40. Actor. *Dracula.*
LANIER, ALLEN. 6/25/46. Guitarist, keyboardist. Blue Öyster Cult.
LANSING, ROBERT (Robert Brown). San Diego, CA, 6/5/29. Actor. *The Man Who Never Was.*
LAPREAD, RONALD. Alabama, 9/4/50. Bassist, trumpeter. The Commodores.
LARDIE, MICHAEL. 9/8/58. Musician. Great White.
LARROQUETTE, JOHN. New Orleans, LA, 11/25/47. Actor. *Night Court.*
LARUE, FLORENCE. Pennsylvania, 2/4/44. Singer. The 5th Dimension.
LASSER, LOUISE. New York, NY, 4/11/39. Actor, formerly married to Woody Allen. *Bananas.*
LAUDER, ESTEE. New York, NY, 7/1/08. Fashion designer.
LAUPER, CYNDI. New York, NY, 6/20/53. Singer, actor, professional wrestling promoter. *She's So Unusual.*
LAUREN, RALPH (Ralph Lifshitz). Bronx, NY, 10/14/39. Fashion designer.
LAURENT, YVES SAINT. Oran, Algeria, 8/1/36. Fashion designer.
LAURIE, PIPER (Rosetta Jacobs). Detroit, MI, 1/22/32. Actor. Mother in *Carrie.*
LAVERN, ROGER (Roger Jackson). Kidderminster, England, 11/11/38. Keyboardist. The Tornados.
LAVIN, LINDA. Portland, ME, 10/15/37. Actor, singer. *Alice.*
LAWRENCE, CAROL (Carol Laraia). Melrose Park, IL, 9/5/35. Actor, singer. *West Side Story.*
LAWRENCE, JOEY. Montgomery, PA, 4/20/76. Actor, singer. *Blossom.*
LAWRENCE, VICKI. Inglewood, CA, 3/26/49. Actor. *Mama's Family.*
LAWSON, LEIGH. Atherston, England, 7/21/45. Actor. *Tess.*
LAWTON, JOHN. 6/11/46. Singer. Uriah Heep.
LEA, JIMMY. Melbourne Arms, England, 6/14/52. Bassist, keyboardist, violinist. Slade.
LEACH, ROBIN. London, England, 8/29/41. TV host. *Lifestyles of the Rich and Famous.*
LEACHMAN, CLORIS. Des Moines, IA, 4/30/30. Actor. Phyllis Lyndstrom on *The Mary Tyler Moore Show.*
LEADON, BERNIE. Minneapolis, MN, 7/19/47. Guitarist, singer. The Eagles.
LEAR, NORMAN. New Haven, CT, 7/27/22. Producer, director, formerly married to Frances. *All in the Family.*
LEARNED, MICHAEL. Washington, DC, 4/9/39. Actor. Olivia on *The Waltons.*
LEBON, SIMON. Bushey, England, 10/27/58. Lead singer. Duran Duran.
LEE, ALVIN. Nottingham, England, 12/19/44. Guitarist, singer. Ten Years After.
LEE, ARTHUR. Memphis, TN, 1945. Guitarist, singer. Love.
LEE, BARBARA. New York, NY, 5/16/47. Singer. The Chiffons.
LEE, BEVERLY. Passaic, NJ, 8/3/41. Singer. The Shirelles.
LEE, BRENDA (Brenda Tarpley). Lithonia, GA, 12/11/44. Singer.
LEE, GEDDY. Willowdale, Canada, 7/29/53. Singer, bassist. Rush.
LEE, JASON SCOTT. Los Angeles, CA, 1966. Actor. *Dragon: The Bruce Lee Story.*
LEE, JOHNNY. Texas City, TX, 7/3/46. Singer. "Lookin' for Love."
LEE, MICHELE (Michele Dusiak). Los Angeles, CA, 6/24/42. Actor. Karen Fairgate MacKenzie on *Knots Landing.*
LEE, PEGGY (Norma Delores Egstrom). Jamestown, ND, 5/26/20. Actor, singer. *The Jazz Singer.*
LEE, RIC. Cannock, England, 10/20/45. Drummer. Ten Years After.
LEE, STAN. New York, NY, 12/28/22. Artist, writer, Marvel Comics legend.
LEE, TOMMY (Tommy Bass). Athens, Greece, 10/3/62. Drummer, married to Pamela Anderson, formerly married to Heather Locklear. Mötley Crüe.
LEEDS, GARY. Glendale, CA, 9/3/44. Drummer. The Walker Brothers.
LEESE, HOWARD. Los Angeles, CA, 6/13/51. Keyboardist, guitarist. Heart.
LEEVES, JANE. East Grinstead, England, 4/13/63. Actor. Daphne Moon on *Frasier.*
LEEWAY, JOE. London, England, 1957. Percussionist. Thompson Twins.
LEGUIZAMO, JOHN. Bogota, Columbia, 7/22/65. Actor. *Carlito's Way.*
LEIBMAN, RON. New York, NY, 10/11/37. Actor. *Kaz.*
LEIGH, JANET (Jeannette Helen Morrison). Merced, CA, 7/6/27. Actor, mother of Jamie Lee Curtis. *Psycho.*
LEIGHTON, LAURA (Laura Miller). Iowa City, IA, 7/24/68. Actor. *Melrose Place.*
LEITCH, DONOVAN. 8/16/68. Actor, son of folk singer Donovan, brother of Ione Skye.
LEMAT, PAUL. Rahway, NJ, 9/22/52. Actor. *American Graffiti.*
LEMIEUX, MARIO. Montreal, Canada, 10/5/65. NHL hockey player. Pittsburgh Penguins.
LEMMON, CHRIS. Los Angeles, CA, 1/22/54. Actor, son of Jack Lemmon. *Swing Shift.*
LEMMON, JACK. Boston, MA, 2/8/25. Actor, father of Chris Lemmon. *Some Like It Hot.*
LEMMY (Ian Kilmister). Stoke-on-Trent, England, 12/24/45. Bassist, singer. Motorhead.
LEMON, MEADOWLARK. Wilmington, NC, 4/25/32. Basketball player. Harlem Globetrotters.
LENNON, JULIAN (John Charles Julian Lennon). Liverpool, England, 4/8/63. Singer, songwriter, son of John Lennon.
LENNOX, ANNIE. Aberdeen, Scotland, 12/25/54. Singer, songwriter. Eurythmics.
LEONARD, ROBERT SEAN. Westwood, NJ, 2/28/69. Actor. *Dead Poets Society.*
LEONARD, SUGAR RAY. Wilmington, NC, 5/17/56. Boxer.
LERNER, MICHAEL. Brooklyn, NY, 6/22/41. Actor. *Barton Fink.*
LESH, PHIL (Phil Chapman). Berkeley, CA, 3/15/40. Bassist. Grateful Dead.
LESTER, ROBERT "SQUIRREL." 1/13/30. Singer. The Chi-Lites.
LEVERT, EDDIE. Canton, OH, 6/16/42. Singer. The O'Jays.
LEVIN, DRAKE. Guitarist. Paul Revere & The Raiders.
LEVY, EUGENE. Hamilton, Canada, 12/17/46. Actor, writer. *SCTV.*
LEWIS, AL (Alexander Meister). New York, NY, 4/30/10. Actor. *The Munsters.*
LEWIS, CARL (Carl Frederick Carlton). Birmingham, AL,

7/1/61. Track athlete. Olympic gold medalist.
LEWIS, EMMANUEL. New York, NY, 3/9/71. Actor. Webster Long on *Webster.*
LEWIS, GARY (Gary Levitch). New York, NY, 7/31/46. Singer, drummer, son of Jerry Lewis. Gary Lewis & The Playboys.
LEWIS, HUEY (Hugh Cregg III). New York, NY, 7/5/50. Singer. Huey Lewis & The News.
LEWIS, JERRY (Joseph Levitch). Newark, NJ, 3/16/26. Actor, father of Gary Lewis. *The Nutty Professor.*
LEWIS, JERRY LEE. Ferriday, LA, 9/29/35. Legendary rock keyboardist, singer, songwriter.
LEWIS, JULIETTE. San Fernando Valley, CA, 6/21/73. Actor. *Cape Fear.*
LEWIS, PETER. Los Angeles, CA, 7/15/45. Guitarist, singer. Moby Grape.
LIDDY, G. GORDON. New York, NY, 11/30/30. Watergate participant, talk show host. *The G. Gordon Liddy Show.*
LIFESON, ALEX. Fernie, Canada, 8/27/53. Guitarist. Rush.
LIGHT, JUDITH. Trenton, NJ, 2/9/49. Actor. Angela on *Who's the Boss?*
LIGHTFOOT, GORDON. Orillia, Canada, 11/17/38. Folk guitarist, singer, songwriter.
LINCOLN, ABBEY (Anna Marie Woolridge). Chicago, IL, 8/6/30. Singer, actor. *For Love of Ivy.*
LINDEN, HAL (Hal Lipschitz). The Bronx, NY, 3/20/31. Actor. *Barney Miller.*
LINDES, HAL. Monterey, CA, 6/30/53. Guitarist. Dire Straits.
LINDSAY, MARK. Eugene, OR, 3/9/42. Singer, saxophonist. Paul Revere & The Raiders.
LINDUP, MIKE. 3/17/59. Keyboardist, singer. Level 42.
LINKLETTER, ART. Moose Jaw, Canada, 7/17/12. TV personality. *People Are Funny.*
LINN-BAKER, MARK. St. Louis, MO, 6/17/54. Actor. Cousin Larry Appleton on *Perfect Strangers.*
LINVILLE, LARRY. Ojai, CA, 9/29/39. Actor. Frank Burns on *M*A*S*H.*
LIOTTA, RAY. Newark, NJ, 12/18/55. Actor. *GoodFellas.*
LITHGOW, JOHN. Rochester, NY, 10/19/45. Actor. *The World According to Garp.*
LITTLE EVA (Eva Narcissus Boyd). Bellhaven, NC, 6/29/45. Singer. "The Loco-Motion."
LITTLE RICHARD (Richard Penniman). Macon, GA, 12/5/35. Legendary singer, songwriter.
LIVGREN, KERRY. Kansas, 9/18/49. Guitarist. Kansas.
L.L. COOL J (James Todd Smith). New York, NY, 1/14/68. Rap artist.
LLOYD, CHRISTOPHER. Stamford, CT, 10/22/38. Actor. "Reverend Jim" Ignatowski on *Taxi.*
LLOYD, EMILY. London, England, 9/29/70. Actor. *Wish You Were Here.*
LOCKE, JOHN. Los Angeles, CA, 9/25/43. Keyboardist. Spirit.
LOCKE, SONDRA. Shelbyville, TN, 5/28/47. Actor. *The Gauntlet.*
LOCKHART, JUNE. New York, NY, 6/25/25. Actor. *Lost in Space.*
LOCKWOOD, GARY. Van Nuys, CA, 2/21/37. Actor. *2001: A Space Odyssey.*
LOCORRIERE, DENNIS. Union City, NJ, 6/13/49. Lead singer. Dr. Hook.
LODGE, JOHN. Birmingham, England, 7/20/45. Bassist. The Moody Blues.
LOFGREN, NILS. Chicago, IL, 6/21/51. Guitarist, keyboardist, singer, songwriter.
LOGGIA, ROBERT. Staten Island, NY, 1/3/30. Actor. *Mancuso, FBI.*
LOGGINS, KENNY. Everett, WA, 1/7/48. Singer, songwriter.
LOLLOBRIGIDA, GINA. Subiaco, Italy, 7/4/27. Actor. *Circus.*
LOM, HERBERT. Prague, Czechoslovakia, 1/9/17. Actor. *Spartacus.*
LONG, SHELLEY. Ft. Wayne, IN, 8/23/49. Actor. Diane Chambers on *Cheers.*
LONGMUIR, ALAN. Edinburgh, Scotland, 6/20/53. Bassist. The Bay City Rollers.
LONGMUIR, DEREK. Edinburgh, Scotland, 3/19/55. Drummer. The Bay City Rollers.
LORD, JACK (Jack Ryan). New York, NY, 12/30/30. Actor. *Hawaii Five-O.*
LORD, JON. Leicester, England, 6/9/41. Keyboardist. Deep Purple.
LORDS, TRACY (Norma Kuzma). Steubenville, OH, 5/7/68. Actor, former porn star. *Melrose Place.*
LOREN, SOPHIA (Sophia Scicolone). Rome, Italy, 9/20/34. Actor. *Two Women.*
LOUGANIS, GREG. El Cajon, CA, 1/29/60. Diver. Olympic gold medalist.
LOUGHNANE, LEE. Chicago, IL, 10/21/46. Trumpeter. Chicago.
LOUISE, TINA (Tina Blacker). New York, NY, 2/11/34. Actor. Ginger Grant on *Gilligan's Island.*
LOVE, MIKE. Baldwin Hills, CA, 3/15/41. Singer. The Beach Boys.
LOVELADY, DAVE. Liverpool, England, 10/16/42. Drummer. The Fourmost.
LOVELESS, PATTY. Belcher Holler, KY, 1/4/57 Singer.
LOVITZ, JON. Tarzana, CA, 7/21/57. Actor. *Saturday Night Live.*
LOWE, CHAD. Dayton, OH, 1/15/68. Actor, brother of Rob Lowe. *Life Goes On.*
LOWE, CHRIS. Blackpool, England, 10/4/59. Keyboardist. Pet Shop Boys.
LOWE, ROB. Charlottesville, VA, 3/17/64. Actor. *St. Elmo's Fire.*
LUCIA, PETER. 2/2/47. Drummer. Tommy James & The Shondells.
LUCKINBILL, LAURENCE. Fort Smith, AR, 11/21/34. Actor, married to Lucie Arnaz. *The Boys in the Band.*
LUDLUM, ROBERT. New York, NY, 5/25/27. Novelist, actor, producer. *The Gemini Contenders.*
LUFT, LORNA. Los Angeles, CA, 11/21/52. Actor, half-sister of Liza Minnelli, daughter of Judy Garland. *Where the Boys Are.*
LUKATHER, STEVE. Los Angeles, CA, 10/21/57. Lead guitarist. Toto.
LULU (Marie Lawrie). Glasgow, Scotland, 11/3/48. Singer, actor. *To Sir with Love.*
LUNDEN, JOAN. Fair Oaks, CA, 9/19/50. Host. *Good Morning America.*
LUNDGREN, DOLPH. Stockholm, Sweden, 11/3/59. Actor. *Rocky IV.*
LUPONE, PATTI. Northport, NY, 4/21/49. Actor. *Life Goes On.*
LUPUS, PETER. Indianapolis, IN, 6/17/37. Actor. Willie Armitage on *Mission: Impossible.*
LWIN, ANNABELLA (Myant Aye). Rangoon, Burma, 10/31/65. Singer. Bow Wow Wow.
LYDON, JOHN. London, England, 1/31/56. Singer, a.k.a. Johnny Rotten. The Sex Pistols; Public Image Ltd.
LYNCH, STAN. Gainesville, FL, 5/21/55. Drummer. Tom Petty & The Heartbreakers.
LYNGSTAD, FRIDA (Annl-Frid Lyngstad). Narvik, Sweden, 11/15/45. Singer. Abba.
LYNNE, JEFF. Birmingham, England, 12/30/47. Singer, guitarist. Electric Light Orchestra (ELO).
LYNOTT, PHIL. Dublin, Ireland, 8/20/51. Singer, bassist. Thin Lizzy.
LYONS, LEO. Standbridge, England, 11/30/43. Bassist. Ten Years After.
LYTE, MC. New York, NY, 1971. Rap artist.
MA, YO-YO. Paris, France, 10/7/55. Cello virtuoso.
MACARTHUR, JAMES. Los Angeles, CA, 12/8/37. Actor, son of Helen Hayes. Danny Williams on *Hawaii Five-O.*
MACCHIO, RALPH. Long Island, NY, 11/4/62. Actor. *The Karate Kid.*
MACCORKINDALE, SIMON. Cambridge, England, 2/12/52. Actor. *Falcon Crest.*

MACDONALD, EDDIE. St. Asaph, Wales, 11/1/59. Bassist. The Alarm.
MACDONALD, ROBIN. Nairn, Scotland, 7/18/43. Guitarist. Billy J. Kramer & The Dakotas.
MACGOWAN, SHANE. Kent, England, 12/25/57. Guitarist, singer. The Pogues.
MACGRAW, ALI. Pound Ridge, NY, 4/1/38. Actor. *Love Story.*
MACKAY, ANDY. London, England, 7/23/46. Saxophonist, woodwindist. Roxy Music.
MACKAY, DUNCAN. 7/26/50. Keyboardist. Steve Harley & Cockney Rebel.
MACLACHLAN, KYLE. Yakima, WA, 2/22/59. Actor. *Twin Peaks.*
MACLEAN, BRYAN. Los Angeles, CA, 1947. Guitarist, singer. Love.
MACLEOD, GAVIN. Mt. Kisco, NY, 2/28/31. Actor. Captain Stubing of *The Love Boat.*
MACNAUGHTON, ROBERT. New York, NY, 12/19/66. Actor. *E.T., the Extra-Terrestrial.*
MACNEE, PATRICK. London, England, 2/6/22. Actor. *The Avengers.*
MACNEIL, ROBERT. Montreal, Canada, 1/19/31. Broadcast journalist. *MacNeil/Lehrer Report.*
MACNELLY, JEFF. New York, NY, 9/17/47. Cartoonist. *Shoe.*
MACNICOL, PETER. Dallas, TX, 4/10/54. Actor. *Sophie's Choice.*
MADDEN, JOHN. Austin, MN, 4/10/36. Sportscaster, football analyst.
MADIGAN, AMY. Chicago, IL, 9/11/51. Actor. *Places in the Heart.*
MADSEN, MICHAEL. Chicago, IL, 1959. Actor, brother of Virginia. *Reservoir Dogs.*
MADSEN, VIRGINIA. Winnetka, IL, 9/11/63. Actor, sister of Michael. *Electric Dreams.*
MAGNUSON, ANN. Charleston, WV, 1/4/56. Actor. Catherine Hughes on *Anything but Love.*
MAGUIRE, LES. Wallasey, England, 12/27/41. Keyboardist, saxophonist. Gerry & The Pacemakers.
MAHONEY, JOHN. Manchester, England, 6/20/40. Actor. Father of Dr. Crane on *Cheers* and *Frasier.*
MAJORS, LEE (Harvey Lee Yeary II). Wyandotte, MI, 4/23/40. Actor, formerly married to Farrah Fawcett. *The Six Million Dollar Man.*
MAKEPEACE, CHRIS. Montreal, Canada, 4/22/64. Actor. *My Bodyguard.*
MAKO (Makoto Iwamatsu). Kobe, Japan, 12/10/33. Actor. *The Sand Pebbles.*
MALDEN, KARL (Mladen Sekulovich). Gary, IN, 3/22/14. Actor, American Express spokesperson. *The Streets of San Francisco.*
MALONE, DOROTHY. Chicago, IL, 1/30/25. Actor. *Written on the Wind.*
MALTIN, LEONARD. New York, NY, 12/18/50. Film critic. *Entertainment Tonight.*
MANDEL, HOWIE. Toronto, Canada, 11/29/55. Actor. Dr. Wayne Fiscus on *St. Elsewhere.*
MANDELA, NELSON. Umtata, South Africa, 7/18/18. President of South Africa.
MANDELA, WINNIE. Transkei, South Africa, 9/26/34. Political activist, formerly married to Nelson Mandela.
MANDRELL, BARBARA. Houston, TX, 12/25/48. Country singer. Barbara Mandrell & The Mandrell Sisters.
MANETTI, LARRY. Chicago, IL, 7/23/47. Actor. Rick on *Magnum, P. I.*
MANILOW, BARRY (Barry Alan Pincus). Brooklyn, NY, 6/17/46. Singer, songwriter. *I Write the Songs.*
MANN, MANFRED (Michael Lubowitz). Johannesburg, South Africa, 10/21/40. Keyboardist. Manfred Mann.
MANN, TERRENCE. Kentucky, 1945. Actor. *Les Misérables.*
MANOFF, DINAH. New York, NY, 1/25/58. Actor, daughter of Lee Grant. Carol Weston on *Empty Nest.*
MANSON, CHARLES. Cincinnati, OH, 11/11/34. Murderer, cult leader.
MANTEGNA, JOE. Chicago, IL, 11/13/47. Actor. *The Godfather, Part III.*
MANZANERA, PHIL. London, England, 1/31/51. Guitarist. Roxy Music.
MANZAREK, RAY. Chicago, IL, 2/12/35. Keyboardist. The Doors.
MARCEAU, MARCEL. Strasbourg, France, 3/22/23. Actor, pantomimist. *Bip.*
MARCHAND, NANCY. Buffalo, NY, 6/19/28. Actor. *Lou Grant.*
MARCOS, IMELDA. Talcoban, the Philippines, 7/2/31. Wife of late Ferdinand Marcos.
MARCOVICCI, ANDREA. New York, NY, 11/18/48. Actor, singer. *Trapper John, MD.*
MARGO, MITCH. Brooklyn, NY, 5/25/47. Tenor singer. The Tokens.
MARGO, PHIL. Brooklyn, NY, 4/1/42. Bass singer. The Tokens.
MARIN, CHEECH (Richard Marin). Los Angeles, CA, 7/13/46. Actor, writer, former partner of Tommy Chong. *Up in Smoke.*
MARINARO, ED. New York, NY, 3/31/50. Actor, football player. *Hill Street Blues.*
MARK, MARKY (Mark Wahlberg). Dorchester, MA, 6/5/71. Rap artist, Calvin Klein underwear model, brother of Donny Wahlberg.
MARLEY, ZIGGY (David Marley). Jamaica, 1968. Singer, songwriter, son of Bob Marley. Ziggy Marley & The Melody Makers.
MARR, JOHNNY. Manchester, England, 10/31/63. Guitarist. The Smiths.
MARRIOTT, STEVE. Bow, England, 1/30/47. Singer, guitarist. The Small Faces.
MARS, MICK (Bob Deal). Terre Haute, IN, 4/4/55. Guitarist. Mötley Crüe.
MARSALIS, BRANFORD. Breaux Bridge, LA, 8/26/60. Jazz musician, bandleader, saxophonist. Brother of Wynton Marsalis. Former musical director of *The Tonight Show.*
MARSDEN, FREDDIE. Liverpool, England, 10/23/40. Drummer. Gerry & The Pacemakers.
MARSDEN, GERRY. Liverpool, England, 9/24/42. Singer, lead guitarist. Gerry & The Pacemakers.
MARSH, IAN. Sheffield, England, 11/11/56. Keyboardist. The Human League; Heaven 17.
MARSHALL, E. G. (Everett Marshall). Owatonna, MN, 6/18/10. Actor. *Twelve Angry Men.*
MARSHALL, PETER (Pierre La Cock). Huntington, WV, 3/30/30. TV personality. Host of *The Hollywood Squares.*
MARTELL, VINCE. New York, NY, 11/11/45. Guitarist. Vanilla Fudge.
MARTIN, ANDREA. Portland, ME, 1/15/47. Writer, actor. *SCTV.*
MARTIN, DEWEY. Chesterville, Canada, 9/30/42. Singer, drummer. Buffalo Springfield.
MARTIN, DICK. Battle Creek, MI, 1/30/23. Actor. Cohost of *Laugh-In.*
MARTIN, JIM. Oakland, CA, 7/21/61. Guitarist. Faith No More.
MARTIN, PAMELA SUE. Westport, CT, 1/15/53. Actor. *Dynasty.*
MARTINDALE, WINK (Winston Conrad Martindale). Bells, TN, 12/4/34. TV personality. Host of *Tic Tac Dough.*
MARTINI, JERRY. Colorado, 10/1/43. Saxophonist. Sly & The Family Stone.
MARVIN, HANK (Brian Rankin). Newcastle, England, 10/28/41. Lead guitarist. The Shadows.
MARX, RICHARD. Chicago, IL, 9/16/63. Singer, songwriter.
MASON, DAVE. Worcester, England, 5/10/47. Singer, guitarist. Traffic.
MASON, JACKIE. Sheboygan, WI, 6/9/34. Actor. *Chicken Soup.*
MASON, MARSHA. St. Louis, MO, 4/3/42. Actor. *The Goodbye Girl.*
MASON, NICK. Birmingham, England, 1/27/45. Drummer. Pink Floyd.

MASSI, NICK (Nick Macioci). Newark, NJ, 9/19/35. Singer, bassist. The Four Seasons.
MASTELOTTO, PAT. 9/10/55. Drummer. Mr. Mister.
MASTERSON, MARY STUART. Los Angeles, CA, 6/28/66. Actor, daughter of Peter. *Fried Green Tomatoes.*
MASTERSON, PETER. Houston, TX, 6/1/34. Actor, writer, director, father of Mary Stuart. *The Exorcist.*
MASTRANGELO, CARLO. The Bronx, NY, 10/5/39. Bass singer. Dion & The Belmonts.
MASTRANTONIO, MARY ELIZABETH. Oak Park, IL, 11/17/58. Actor. *The Color of Money.*
MASUR, RICHARD. New York, NY, 11/20/48. Actor. *One Day at a Time.*
MATHERS, JERRY. Sioux City, IA, 6/2/48. Actor. Theodore "Beaver" Cleaver on *Leave It to Beaver.*
MATHESON, TIM. Glendale, CA, 12/31/47. Actor. *National Lampoon's Animal House.*
MATHEWS, DENISE (formerly Vanity). Niagara, Canada, 1/3/63. Former singer and actor (a.k.a. D.D. Winters), now Christian Evangelist, bible student, married to L.A. Raiders defensive end Anthony Smith. *The Last Dragon.*
MATHIS, JOHNNY. San Francisco, CA, 9/30/35. Pop singer.
MATLOCK, GLENN. 8/27/56. Bassist. The Sex Pistols.
MATTHAU, WALTER (Walter Matuschanskayasky). New York, NY, 10/1/20. Actor. *The Odd Couple.*
MATTHEWS, IAN (Ian McDonald). Lincolnshire, England, 6/16/45. Singer, guitarist. Matthew's Southern Comfort.
MATURE, VICTOR. Louisville, KY, 1/29/15. Actor. *Samson and Delilah.*
MAUS, JOHN. New York, NY, 11/12/43. Singer. The Walker Brothers.
MAXFIELD, MIKE. Manchester, England, 2/23/44. Lead guitarist. Billy J. Kramer & The Dakotas.
MAY, BRIAN. Twickenham, England, 7/19/47. Guitarist. Queen.
MAY, ELAINE (Elaine Berlin). Philadelphia, PA, 4/21/32. Actor, director, writer. *Ishtar.*
MAY, PHIL. Dartford, England, 11/9/44. Singer. The Pretty Things.
MAYALL, JOHN. Macclesfield, England, 11/29/33. Singer, keyboardist, harmonicist. The Bluesbreakers.
MAYFIELD, CURTIS. Chicago, IL, 6/3/42. Singer, songwriter, record producer, paralyzed in an accident during a concert. "Superfly."
MAYS, WILLIE. Fairfield, AL, 5/6/31. Baseball player. San Francisco Giants.
MAZAR, DEBI. Queens, NY, 1964. Actor. *Civil Wars; L.A. Law.*
MAZURSKY, PAUL. Brooklyn, NY, 4/25/30. Producer, director, writer, actor. *Down and Out in Beverly Hills.*
M.C. ERIC. 8/19/70. Rap artist. Technotronic.
MCA (Adam Yauch). Brooklyn, NY, 8/15/67. Rap artist. The Beastie Boys.
MCBRIDE, MARTINA. Sharon, KS, 7/29/66. Singer.
MCCALLUM, DAVID. Glasgow, Scotland, 9/19/33. Actor. *The Great Escape.*
MCCARTHY, ANDREW. Westfield, NJ, 11/29/62. Actor. *Less Than Zero.*
MCCARTHY, KEVIN. Seattle, WA, 2/15/14. Actor. *Invasion of the Body Snatchers.*
MCCARTNEY, LINDA (Linda Eastman). New York, NY, 9/24/42. Pianist, singer, percussionist, photographer, married to Paul McCartney.
MCCARTY, JIM. Liverpool, England, 7/25/44. Drummer. The Yardbirds; Mitch Ryder & The Detroit Wheels.
MCCAULEY, JACKIE. Coleraine, Ireland, 12/14/46. Keyboardist. Them.
MCCAULEY, PATRICK. Northern Ireland, 3/17/44. Drummer. Them.
MCCLANAHAN, RUE. Healdton, OK, 2/21/34. Actor. Blanche Devereaux on *The Golden Girls.*
MCCLARY, THOMAS. 10/6/50. Lead guitarist. The Commodores.
MCCLINTON, DELBERT. Lubbock, TX, 11/4/40. Singer, songwriter.
MCCLURG, EDIE. Kansas City, MO, 7/23/50. Actor. *The Hogan Family.*
MCCLUSKEY, ANDY. Wirral, England, 6/24/59. Singer. Orchestral Manoeuvres in the Dark (OMD).
MCCOO, MARILYN. Jersey City, NJ, 9/30/43. Singer, cohost of *Solid Gold.* The 5th Dimension.
MCCREADY, MIKE. 4/5/66. Guitarist. Pearl Jam.
MCCULLOCH, IAN. Liverpool, England, 5/5/59. Singer. Echo & The Bunnymen.
MCDANIELS, DARRYL D. New York, NY, 1964. Rap artist. Run-D.M.C.
MCDONALD, COUNTRY JOE. El Monte, CA, 1/1/42. Guitarist, singer. Country Joe & The Fish.
MCDONALD, IAN. London, England, 6/25/46. Saxophonist. King Crimson.
MCDONALD, MICHAEL. St. Louis, MO, 12/2/52. Singer, songwriter, keyboardist. The Doobie Brothers.
MCDONALD, PAT. 8/6/52. Musician. Timbuk 3.
MCDONNELL, MARY. Ithaca, NY, 1952. Actor. *Dances with Wolves.*
MCDORMAND, FRANCES. Illinois, 1958. Actor. *Mississippi Burning.*
MCDOWALL, RODDY. London, England, 9/17/28. Actor. *Planet of the Apes.*
MCDOWELL, MALCOLM. Leeds, England, 6/19/43. Actor. *A Clockwork Orange.*
MCENROE, JOHN JR. Wiesbaden, Germany, 2/16/59. Tennis player. Formerly married to Tatum O'Neal, relationship with Patty Smyth.
MCFERRIN, BOBBY. New York, NY, 3/11/50. Singer. "Don't Worry, Be Happy."
MCGAVIN, DARREN. Spokane, WA, 5/7/22. Actor. *The Night Stalker.*
MCGEOCH, JOHN. Guitarist. Siouxsie & The Banshees.
MCGILLIS, KELLY. Newport Beach, CA, 7/9/57. Actor. *Witness.*
MCGOVERN, ELIZABETH. Evanston, IL, 7/18/61. Actor. *Ragtime.*
MCGOVERN, MAUREEN. Youngstown, OH, 7/27/49. Singer, actor. "The Morning After."
MCGRAW, TIM. Start, LA, 5/1/67. Singer.
MCGUINN, ROGER "JIM" (James Joseph McGuinn). Chicago, IL, 7/13/42. Singer, guitarist. The Byrds.
MCGUINNESS, TOM. Wimbledon, England, 12/2/41. Bassist. Manfred Mann.
MCINTOSH, LORRAINE. Glasgow, Scotland, 5/13/64. Singer. Deacon Blue.
MCINTYRE, FRITZ. 9/2/58. Keyboardist. Simply Red.
MCINTYRE, JOE. Needham, MA, 12/31/73. Singer. New Kids on the Block.
MCINTYRE, ONNIE. Lennox Town, Scotland, 9/25/45. Guitarist. Average White Band.
MCJOHN, GOLDY. 5/2/45. Organist. Steppenwolf.
MCKAGAN, DUFF ROSE (Michael McKagan). Seattle, WA. Bassist. Guns N' Roses.
MCKEAN, MICHAEL. New York, NY, 10/17/47. Actor, writer. Lenny Kosnowski on *Laverne & Shirley.*
MCKELLAR, DANICA. La Jolla, CA. Actor. Winnie Cooper on *The Wonder Years.*
MCKELLEN, IAN. Burnley, England, 5/25/39. Shakespearian actor.
MCKEON, NANCY. Westbury, NY, 4/4/66. Actor. Jo Polniaczek on *The Facts of Life.*
MCKEOWN, LESLIE. Edinburgh, Scotland, 11/12/55. Singer. The Bay City Rollers.
MCKUEN, ROD. Oakland, CA, 4/29/33. Poet. *Laugh-In.*

MCLAGAN, IAN. England, 5/12/46. Keyboardist. The Faces.
MCLEAN, DON. New Rochelle, NY, 10/2/45. Singer, songwriter.
MCLEMORE, LAMONTE. St. Louis, MO, 9/17/39. Singer. The 5th Dimension.
MCMAHON, ED. Detroit, MI, 3/6/23. Announcer and host. *The Tonight Show; Star Search.*
MCNALLY, JOHN. Liverpool, England, 8/30/41. Singer, guitarist. The Searchers.
MCNEIL, MICK. Scotland, 7/20/58. Keyboardist. Simple Minds.
MCNICHOL, KRISTY. Los Angeles, CA, 9/11/62. Actor. Barbara Weston on *Empty Nest.*
MCPHERSON, GRAHAM. Hastings, England, 1/13/61. Singer. Madness.
MCRANEY, GERALD. Collins, MS, 8/19/48. Actor, married to Delta Burke. John D. "Mac" MacGillis on *Major Dad.*
MCVIE, CHRISTINE (Christine Perfect). Birmingham, England, 7/12/44. Keyboardist, singer. Fleetwood Mac.
MCVIE, JOHN. London, England, 11/26/45. Bassist. Fleetwood Mac.
MEADOWS, JAYNE (Jayne Cotter). Wu Chang, China, 9/27/20. Actor, quiz show regular, married to Steve Allen, sister of Audrey.
MEANEY, COLM. Dublin, Ireland, 1953. Actor. Miles O'Brien on *Star Trek: The Next Generation.*
MEARA, ANNE. Brooklyn, NY, 9/20/29. Actor, partner/married to Jerry Stiller, mother of Ben Stiller. *The Out-of-Towners.*
MEATLOAF (Marvin Lee Aday). Dallas, TX, 9/27/51. Singer. *Bat out of Hell.*
MEDLEY, BILL. Santa Ana, CA, 9/19/40. Singer. The Righteous Brothers.
MEDRESS, HANK. Brooklyn, NY, 11/19/38. Tenor singer. The Tokens.
MEHTA, ZUBIN. Bombay, India, 4/29/36. Conductor.
MEINE, KLAUS. 5/25/48. Singer. Scorpions.
MEISNER, RANDY. Scottsbluff, NE, 3/8/47. Bassist, singer. The Eagles; Poco.
MELLENCAMP, JOHN. Seymour, IN, 10/7/51. Guitarist, singer, songwriter.
MENDOZA, MARK. Long Island, NY, 6/13/54. Bassist. Twisted Sister.
MENKEN, ALAN. New Rochelle, NY, 1949. Composer. *Beauty and the Beast.*
MERCHANT, JIMMY. New York, NY, 2/10/40. Singer. Frankie Lymon & The Teenagers.
MERCHANT, NATALIE. Jamestown, NY, 10/26/63. Singer, songwriter. 10,000 Maniacs.
MESSINA, JIM. Maywood, CA, 12/5/47. Guitarist, singer. Poco.
METCALF, LAURIE. Edwardsville, IL, 6/16/55. Actor. Jackie Conner Harris on *Roseanne.*
METHENY, PAT. Lee's Summit, MO, 8/12/54. Jazz guitarist. "Offramp."
MEYERS, ARI. San Juan, Puerto Rico, 4/6/70. Actor. Emma McArdle on *Kate & Allie.*
MEYERS, AUGIE. San Antonio, TX, 5/31/40. Keyboardist. Texas Tornados.
MIALL, TERRY LEE. England, 11/8/58. Drummer. Adam & The Ants.
MICHAEL, GEORGE (Georgios Kyriacou Panayiotou). London, England, 6/25/63. Singer, songwriter. Wham!
MICK (Michael Wilson). Amesbury, England, 3/4/44. Drummer. Dave Dee, Dozy, Beaky, Mick and Tich.
MIDLER, BETTE. Paterson, NJ, 12/1/45. Actor, singer. "The Rose."
MIDORI. Osaka, Japan, 10/25/71. Violinist.
MIFUNE, TOSHIRO. Tsingtao, China, 4/1/20. Actor. *Throne of Blood.*
MIKE D. (Mike Diamond). New York, NY, 11/20/65. Rap artist. The Beastie Boys.
MILANO, ALYSSA. New York, NY, 12/19/72. Actor. Samantha Micelli on *Who's the Boss?*
MILANO, FRED. The Bronx, NY, 8/26/40. Tenor singer. Dion & The Belmonts.
MILES, SARAH. Ingatestone, England, 12/31/41. Actor. *Ryan's Daughter.*
MILES, SYLVIA. New York, NY, 9/9/34. Actor. *Midnight Cowboy.*
MILES, VERA (Vera Ralston). Boise City, OK, 8/23/29. Actor. *Psycho.*
MILKEN, MICHAEL. Van Nuys, CA, 1946. Financier. Convicted of securities violations.
MILLER, ANN (Lucille Ann Collier). Chireno, TX, 4/12/23. Actor. *On the Town.*
MILLER, CHARLES. Olathe, KS, 6/2/39. Saxophonist, clarinetist. War.
MILLER, DENNIS. Pittsburgh, PA, 11/3/53. TV personality. *Saturday Night Live.*
MILLER, JERRY. Tacoma, WA, 7/10/43. Guitarist. Moby Grape.
MILLER, PENELOPE ANN. Santa Monica, CA, 1/13/64. Actor. *Carlito's Way.*
MILLER, STEVE. Milwaukee, WI, 10/5/43. Singer, guitarist. The Steve Miller Band.
MILLS, HAYLEY. London, England, 4/18/46. Actor, daughter of John Mills, sister of Juliet Mills. *The Parent Trap.*
MILLS, JOHN. Suffolk, England, 2/22/08. Actor, father of Hayley and Juliet Mills. *Ryan's Daughter.*
MILLS, JULIET. London, England, 11/21/41. Actor, daughter of John Mills, sister of Hayley Mills. *Nanny and the Professor.*
MILLS, MIKE. 12/17/58. Bassist. R.E.M.
MILLS, STEPHANIE. New York, NY, 3/22/57. Actor, singer. *The Wiz.*
MILLWARD, MIKE. Bromborough, England, 5/9/42. Guitarist, singer. The Fourmost.
MIMIEUX, YVETTE. Los Angeles, CA, 1/8/39. Actor. *The Black Hole.*
MINNELLI, LIZA. Los Angeles, CA, 3/12/46. Singer, actor, daughter of Vincente Minnelli and Judy Garland, half-sister of Lorna Luft. *Cabaret; The Sterile Cuckoo.*
MINOGUE, KYLIE. Melbourne, Australia, 5/28/68. Actor, singer.
MIOU-MIOU (Sylvette Hery). Paris, France, 2/22/50. Actor. *Going Places.*
MIRABELLA, GRACE. Maplewood, NJ, 6/10/30. Fashion editor, publishing executive. *Mirabella.*
MITCHELL, JONI (Roberta Anderson). Fort McLeod, Canada, 11/7/43. Folk singer, songwriter.
MITCHELL, LIZ. Clarendon, Jamaica, 7/12/52. Singer. Boney M.
MITCHELL, MITCH (John Mitchell). Middlesex, England, 7/9/46. Drummer. The Jimi Hendrix Experience.
MITCHELL, NEIL. Helensborough, Scotland, 6/8/67. Keyboardist. Wet Wet Wet.
MITCHUM, JAMES. Los Angeles, CA, 5/8/41. Actor, son of Robert. *Thunder Road.*
MODINE, MATTHEW. Loma Linda, CA, 3/22/59. Actor. *Vision Quest.*
MOFFAT, DONALD. Plymouth, England, 12/26/30. Actor. *Clear and Present Danger.*
MOLL, RICHARD. Pasadena, CA, 1/13/42. Actor, stands 6' 8". Bailiff Nostradamus "Bull" Shannon on *Night Court.*
MOLLAND, JOEY. Liverpool, England, 6/21/48. Guitarist, keyboardist, singer. Badfinger.
MONARCH, MICHAEL. Los Angeles, CA, 7/5/50. Guitarist. Steppenwolf.
MONDALE, WALTER "FRITZ." Ceylon, MN, 1/5/28. Politician, former Vice President of the United States, former presidential candidate.
MONEY, EDDIE (Eddie Mahoney). Brooklyn, NY, 3/2/49. Singer.

MONTALBAN, RICARDO. Mexico City, Mexico, 11/25/20. Actor. *Fantasy Island.*
MONTANA, JOE. New Eagle, PA, 6/11/56. Football great.
MONTGOMERY, GEORGE (George Letz). Brady, MT, 8/29/16. Actor. *The Texas Rangers.*
MONTGOMERY, JOHN MICHAEL. Lexington, KY, 1/20/65. Country singer.
MOODY, MICKY. 8/30/50. Guitarist. Whitesnake.
MOONEY, KEVIN. England, 5/5/62. Bassist. Adam & The Ants.
MOORE, DUDLEY. Dagenham, England, 4/19/35. Actor. *Arthur.*
MOORE, MARY TYLER. Brooklyn, NY, 12/29/36. Actor. *The Mary Tyler Moore Show.*
MOORE, MELBA (Beatrice Hill). New York, NY, 10/29/45. R&B singer, actor. *Purlie.*
MOORE, ROGER. London, England, 10/14/27. Actor, replaced Sean Connery as James Bond. *Live and Let Die.*
MOORE, SAM. Miami, FL, 10/12/35. Singer. Sam & Dave.
MORAN, ERIN. Burbank, CA, 10/18/61. Actor. Joanie Cunningham on *Happy Days.*
MORANIS, RICK. Toronto, Canada, 4/18/54. Actor, writer. *Honey, I Shrunk the Kids.*
MOREAU, JEANNE. Paris, France, 1/23/28. Actor. *Jules et Jim.*
MORENO, RITA (Rosita Dolores Alverio). Humacao, PR, 12/11/31. Actor. *West Side Story.*
MORGAN, LORRIE (Loretta Lynn Morgan). Nashville, TN, 6/27/59. Singer.
MORIARTY, CATHY. The Bronx, NY, 11/29/60. Actor. *Raging Bull.*
MORIARTY, MICHAEL. Detroit, MI, 4/5/41. Actor. *Law and Order.*
MORITA, NORIYUKI "PAT." Isleton, CA, 6/28/32. Actor. *The Karate Kid.*
MORRIS, STEPHEN. Macclesfield, England, 10/28/57. Drummer. New Order.
MORRISON, VAN (George Ivan Morrison). Belfast, Northern Ireland, 8/31/45. Singer, songwriter. "Brown Eyed Girl."
MORRISSEY (Stephen Morrissey). Manchester, England, 5/22/59. Singer. The Smiths.
MORROW, ROB. New Rochelle, NY, 7/21/62. Actor. *Northern Exposure.*
MORSE, DAVID. Hamilton, MA, 10/11/53. Actor. *St. Elsewhere.*
MORTON, JOE. New York, NY, 10/18/47. Actor. *Terminator 2: Judgment Day.*
MORVAN, FABRICE. Guadeloupe, 5/14/66. "Singer." Milli Vanilli.
MOSLEY, BOB. Paradise Valley, CA, 12/4/42. Bassist. Moby Grape.
MOSS, JON. Wandsworth, England, 9/11/57. Drummer. Culture Club.
MOSS, KATE. London, England, 1/16/74. Supermodel.
MOST, DONNY. New York, NY, 8/8/53. Actor. Ralph Malph on *Happy Days.*
MOSTEL, JOSH. New York, NY, 12/21/46. Actor. *City Slickers.*
MOULDING, COLIN. Swindon, England, 8/17/55. Bassist, singer. XTC.
MOUNT, DAVE. Carshalton, England, 3/3/47. Drummer, singer. Mud.
MOYERS, BILL. Hugo, OK, 6/5/34. Journalist, commentator. *Bill Moyers' Journal.*
MOYET, ALISON (Genevieve Moyet). Basildon, England, 6/18/61. Singer. Yazoo.
MUDD, ROGER. Washington, DC, 2/9/28. Broadcast journalist, newscaster.
MULDAUR, DIANA. New York, NY, 8/19/38. Actor. Capt. Kathryn Janeway on *Star Trek: Voyager.*
MULGREW, KATE. Dubuque, IA, 4/29/55. Actor. *Ryan's Hope.*
MULHERN, MATT. Philadelphia, PA, 7/21/60. Actor. 2nd Lt. Gene Holowachuk on *Major Dad.*
MULL, MARTIN. Chicago, IL, 8/18/43. Actor. *Mary Hartman, Mary Hartman.*
MULLEN, LARRY JR. Dublin, Ireland, 10/31/61. Drummer. U2.
MULLIGAN, RICHARD. New York, NY, 11/13/32. Actor. Dr. Harry Weston on *Empty Nest.*
MUMY, BILLY. El Centro, CA, 2/1/54. Actor. *Lost in Space.*
MURPHY, MICHAEL. Los Angeles, CA, 5/5/38. Actor. *Manhattan.*
MURPHY, PETER. 7/11/57. Singer. Bauhaus.
MURRAY, DAVE. London, England, 12/23/58. Lead guitarist. Iron Maiden.
MUSIC, LORENZO. Brooklyn, NY, 5/2/37. Actor, writer. Carlton the Doorman on *Rhoda.*
NABORS, JIM. Sylacauga, GA, 6/12/32. Actor. Gomer Pyle on *The Andy Griffith Show.*
NADER, RALPH. Winsted, CT, 2/27/34. Political activist, author. *Unsafe at Any Speed.*
NAMATH, JOE. Beaver Falls, PA, 5/31/43. Football great, endorser.
NASH, BRIAN. Liverpool, England, 5/20/63. Guitarist. Frankie Goes to Hollywood.
NASH, GRAHAM. Blackpool, England, 2/2/42. Guitarist. The Hollies; Crosby, Stills, Nash & Young.
NAUGHTON, DAVID. West Hartford, CT, 2/13/51. Actor. *An American Werewolf in London.*
NAUGHTON, JAMES. Middletown, CT, 7/6/45. Actor. *The Good Mother.*
NAVRATILOVA, MARTINA. Prague, Czechoslovakia, 10/10/56. Tennis player.
NEAL, PATRICIA. Packard, KY, 1/20/26. Actor. *Hud.*
NEGRON, CHUCK. The Bronx, NY, 6/8/42. Singer. Three Dog Night.
NEIL, VINCE (Vince Wharton). Hollywood, CA, 2/8/61. Singer. Mötley Crüe.
NEILL, SAM. Ireland, 9/14/47. Actor. *Jurassic Park.*
NELLIGAN, KATE. London, Canada, 3/16/51. Actor. *The Prince of Tides.*
NELSON, CRAIG T. Spokane, WA, 4/4/46. Actor, writer. Hayden Fox on *Coach.*
NELSON, DAVID. New York, NY, 10/24/36. Actor, son of Ozzie and Harriet, brother of Ricky. David Nelson on *The Adventures of Ozzie and Harriet.*
NELSON, JUDD. Portland, ME, 11/28/59. Actor. *The Breakfast Club.*
NELSON, SANDY. Santa Monica, CA, 12/1/38. Rock/jazz drummer.
NELSON, TRACY. Santa Monica, CA, 10/25/63. Actor, daughter of Rick Nelson. *Father Dowling Mysteries.*
NEMES, LES. Surrey, England, 12/5/60. Bassist. Haircut 100.
NESMITH, MIKE (Robert Nesmith). Houston, TX, 12/30/42. Singer, guitarist, actor. The Monkees.
NEVILLE, ART. New Orleans, LA, 12/17/37. Singer, keyboardist. The Neville Brothers.
NEVILLE, CHARLES. New Orleans, LA, 12/28/38. Saxophonist. The Neville Brothers.
NEVILLE, CYRIL. 1/10/48. Singer, percussionist. The Neville Brothers.
NEWHART, BOB (George Newhart). Chicago, IL, 9/5/29. Actor, comedian. *The Bob Newhart Show.*
NEWLEY, ANTHONY. Hackney, England, 9/24/31. Actor, composer. "The Candy Man."
NEWMAN, RANDY. Los Angeles, CA, 11/28/43. Singer, songwriter.
NEWTON, JUICE. Lakehurst, NJ, 2/18/52. Country singer. "Angel of the Morning."
NEWTON-JOHN, OLIVIA. Cambridge, England, 9/26/48. Singer, actor. *Grease.*
NGUYEN, DUSTIN. Saigon, Vietnam, 1962. Actor. *21 Jump Street.*
NICHOL, AL. Winston-Salem, NC, 3/31/46. Guitarist, keyboardist, singer. The Turtles.
NICKS, STEVIE. Phoenix, AZ, 5/26/48. Singer. Fleetwood Mac.

NIELSEN, RICK. Rockford, IL, 12/22/46. Singer, guitarist. Cheap Trick.
NIELSON, BRIGITTE. Denmark, 7/15/63. Actor, formerly married to Sylvester Stallone. *Red Sonja.*
NIMOY, LEONARD. Boston, MA, 3/26/31. Actor, director. Mr. Spock on *Star Trek.*
NOIRET, PHILIPPE. Lille, France, 10/1/31. Actor. *Cinema Paradiso.*
NOLAN, MIKE. Dublin, Ireland, 12/7/54. Singer. Bucks Fizz.
NOLTE, NICK. Omaha, NE, 2/8/40. Actor. *48 Hrs.*
NOONAN, PEGGY. New York, NY, 9/7/50. Author, presidential speechwriter. Responsible for phrase "a kinder, gentler nation."
NOONE, PETER. Manchester, England, 11/5/47. Singer. Herman's Hermits.
NORRIS, CHUCK (Carlos Ray). Ryan, OK, 3/10/40. Karate champion, actor. *Good Guys Wear Black.*
NORTH, OLIVER. San Antonio, TX, 10/7/43. Presidential aide, senatorial candidate. Iran-Contra.
NORTON, KEN. Jacksonville, IL, 8/9/45. Boxer, actor. *The Gong Show.*
NOURI, MICHAEL. Washington, DC, 12/9/45. Actor. *Flashdance.*
NOVAK, KIM (Marilyn Novak). Chicago, IL, 2/13/33. Actor. *Vertigo.*
NOVELLO, DON. Ashtabula, OH, 1/1/43. Actor. Father Guido Sarducci.
NUGENT, TED. Detroit, MI, 12/13/48. Hard rock guitarist, actor.
NUMAN, GARY (Gary Webb). Hammersmith, England, 3/8/58. Singer. "Cars."
O'CONNOR, CARROLL. New York, NY, 8/2/24. Actor. Archie Bunker on *All in the Family.*
O'CONNOR, DONALD. Chicago, IL, 8/28/25. Actor. *Singin' in the Rain.*
O'CONNOR, SANDRA DAY. El Paso, TX, 3/26/30. Supreme Court Justice.
O'CONNOR, SINEAD. Dublin, Ireland, 12/8/66. Singer.
O'HARA, BRIAN. Liverpool, England, 3/12/42. Guitarist, singer. The Fourmost.
O'HARA, CATHERINE. Toronto, Canada, 3/4/54. Actor. Mother in *Home Alone.*
O'HARA, MAUREEN (Maureen FitzSimons). Dublin, Ireland, 8/17/21. Actor. *How Green Was My Valley.*
O'NEAL, ALEXANDER. 11/14/53. Songwriter.
O'NEAL, RYAN (Patrick Ryan O'Neal). Los Angeles, CA, 4/20/41. Actor, father of Tatum O'Neal. *Love Story.*
O'NEAL, TATUM. Los Angeles, CA, 11/5/63. Actor, daughter of Ryan, formerly married to John McEnroe. *Paper Moon.*
O'NEILL, ED. Youngstown, OH, 4/12/46. Actor. Al Bundy on *Married ... with Children.*
O'NEILL, JENNIFER. Rio de Janeiro, Brazil, 2/20/49. Actor, former model. *Summer of '42.*
O'NEILL, JOHN. 8/26/57. Guitarist. The Undertones.
O'SHEA, MILO. Dublin, Ireland, 6/2/26. Actor. *The Verdict.*
O'SULLIVAN, GILBERT (Raymond O'Sullivan). Waterford, Ireland, 12/1/46. Singer, songwriter.
O'SULLIVAN, MAUREEN. Byle, Ireland, 5/17/11. Actor, mother of Mia Farrow. *Hannah and Her Sisters.*
O'TOOLE, ANNETTE (Annette Toole). Houston, TX, 4/1/53. Actor. *Superman III.*
O'TOOLE, MARK. Liverpool, England, 1/6/64. Bassist. Frankie Goes to Hollywood.
O'TOOLE, PETER. Connemara, Ireland, 8/2/32. Actor. *Lawrence of Arabia.*
OAKEY, PHILIP. Sheffield, England, 10/2/55. Singer. The Human League.
OAKLEY, BERRY. Chicago, IL, 4/4/48. Bassist. The Allman Brothers Band.
OATES, JOHN. New York, NY, 4/7/49. Singer, guitarist. Hall & Oates.
OCASEK, RIC (Ric Otcasek). Baltimore, MD, 3/23/49. Singer, guitarist. The Cars.
OCEAN, BILLY (Leslie Charles). Fyzabad, Trinidad, 1/21/50. Rock/R&B singer, songwriter.
OLDFIELD, MIKE. Reading, England, 5/15/53. Bassist, composer. "Tubular Bells."
OLDMAN, GARY. New Cross, England, 3/21/58. Actor, formerly married to Uma Thurman, engaged to Isabella Rossellini. *Bram Stoker's Dracula.*
OLIN, KEN. Chicago, IL, 7/30/54. Actor, director. Michael Steadman on *thirtysomething.*
OLIN, LENA. Stockholm, Sweden, 3/22/55. Actor. *Havana.*
OLMOS, EDWARD JAMES. East Los Angeles, CA, 2/24/47. Actor. Martin Castillo on *Miami Vice.*
ONTKEAN, MICHAEL. Vancouver, Canada, 1/24/46. Actor. *Twin Peaks.*
OPPENHEIMER, ALAN. New York, NY, 4/23/30. Actor. Gene Kinsella on *Murphy Brown.*
ORANGE, WALTER. Florida, 12/10/47. Singer, drummer. The Commodores.
ORBACH, JERRY. The Bronx, NY, 10/20/35. Actor. *Law and Order.*
ORLANDO, TONY (Michael Cassivitis). New York, NY, 4/3/44. Singer. Tony Orlando & Dawn.
ORMOND, JULIA. Epsom, England, 1965. Actor. *Legends of the Fall.*
ORR, BENJAMIN (Benjamin Orzechowski). Cleveland, OH, 8/9/55. Singer, bass guitarist. The Cars.
ORZABAL, ROLAND (Roland Orzabal de la Quintana). Portsmouth, England, 8/22/61. Guitarist, keyboardist. Tears for Fears.
OSBORNE, JEFFREY. Providence, RI, 3/9/48. Singer, songwriter, drummer. L.T.D.
OSBOURNE, OZZY (John Michael Osbourne). Anston, England, 12/3/48. Singer. Black Sabbath.
OSGOOD, CHARLES. New York, NY, 1/8/33. Broadcast journalist, author.
OSKAR, LEE (Oskar Hansen). Copenhagen, Denmark, 3/24/46. Harmonicist. War.
OSMOND, ALAN. Ogden, UT, 6/22/49. Singer, member of the Osmond family. The Osmonds.
OSMOND, DONNY. Ogden, UT, 12/9/57. Singer, member of the Osmond family. *The Donny & Marie Show.*
OSMOND, JAY. Ogden, UT, 3/2/55. Singer, member of the Osmond family. The Osmonds.
OSMOND, MARIE (Olive Marie Osmond). Ogden, UT, 10/13/59. Singer, member of the Osmond family. *The Donny & Marie Show.*
OSMOND, MERRILL. Ogden, UT, 4/30/53. Singer, member of the Osmond family. The Osmonds.
OSMOND, WAYNE. Ogden, UT, 8/28/51. Singer, member of the Osmond family. The Osmonds.
OTIS, CARRE. Model, actor, married to Mickey Rourke.
OTIS, JOHNNY (John Veliotes). Vallejo, CA, 12/28/21. R&B drummer, pianist, and songwriter.
OWEN, RANDY. Fort Payne, AL, 12/13/49. Singer, guitarist. Alabama.
OWENS, SHIRLEY. Passaic, NJ, 6/10/41. Lead singer. The Shirelles.
OVITZ, MICHAEL. Encino, CA, 12/14/46. Studio executive.
OXENBERG, CATHERINE. New York, NY, 9/21/61. Actor. Amanda Carrington on *Dynasty.*
OZ, FRANK. Hereford, England, 5/25/44. Puppeteer, film director. *The Muppet Show.*
PACULA, JOANNA. Tamaszow Lubelski, Poland, 1/2/57. Actor. *Gorky Park.*
PAGE, JIMMY. Heston, England, 1/9/44. Guitarist. Led Zeppelin.
PAICE, IAN. Nottingham, England, 6/29/48. Drummer. Deep Purple.
PAICH, DAVID. Los Angeles, CA, 6/25/54. Keyboardist, singer. Toto.

PALANCE, JACK (Walter Palanuik). Lattimer, PA, 2/18/20. Actor. *City Slickers.*
PALIN, MICHAEL. Sheffield, England, 5/5/43. Actor, writer. *Monty Python's Flying Circus.*
PALMER, BETSY. East Chicago, IN, 11/1/26. Actor, panelist on *I've Got a Secret.*
PALMER, CARL. Birmingham, England, 3/20/51. Drummer. Emerson, Lake & Palmer; Asia.
PALMER, JOHN. 5/25/43. Keyboardist. Family.
PALMER, ROBERT (Alan Palmer). Batley, England, 1/19/49. Singer, songwriter. "Addicted to Love."
PALMINTERI, CHAZZ (Chalogero Lorenzo Palminteri). Bronx, NY, 5/15/51. Actor, playwright, screenwriter. *A Bronx Tale.*
PANKOW, JAMES. Chicago, IL, 8/20/47. Trombonist. Chicago.
PANOZZO, CHUCK. Chicago, IL, 9/20/47. Bassist. Styx.
PAQUIN, ANNA. Wellington, New Zealand, 1982. Actor. *The Piano.*
PARAZAIDER, WALTER. Chicago, IL, 3/14/45. Saxophonist. Chicago.
PARE, MICHAEL. Brooklyn, NY, 10/9/59. Actor. *Eddie and the Cruisers.*
PARFITT, RICK (Richard Harrison). Redhill, England, 10/25/43. Guitarist, singer. Status Quo.
PARILLAUD, ANNE. France, 1961. Actor. *La Femme Nikita.*
PARKER, FESS. Fort Worth, TX, 8/16/25. Actor. *Daniel Boone.*
PARKER, GRAHAM. Deepcut, England, 11/18/50. Singer. Graham Parker & The Rumour.
PARKER, JAMESON. Baltimore, MD, 11/18/47. Actor. *Simon and Simon.*
PARKER, MARY-LOUISE. Ft. Jackson, SC, 8/2/64. Actor. *Fried Green Tomatoes.*
PARKER, RAY JR. Detroit, MI, 5/1/54. Singer, songwriter. "Ghostbusters."
PARSONS, ESTELLE. Lynn, MA, 11/20/27. Actor. *Roseanne.*
PARTRIDGE, ANDY. Malta, 11/11/53. Guitarist, singer. XTC.
PATERSON, GERRY. Winnepeg, Canada, 5/26/45. Drummer. The Guess Who.
PATINKIN, MANDY (Mandel Patinkin). Chicago, IL, 11/30/52. Actor. *Yentl.*
PATRIC, JASON (Jason Patrick Miller). Queens, NY, 1966. Actor. *Rush.*
PATRICK, ROBERT. Marietta, GA, 1959. Actor. Evil T-1000 in *Terminator 2: Judgment Day.*
PATTEN, EDWARD. Atlanta, GA, 8/2/39. Singer. Gladys Knight & The Pips.
PATTERSON, LORNA. Whittier, CA, 6/1/57. Actor. *Private Benjamin.*
PATTERSON, MELODY. Los Angeles, CA, 1947. Actor. Wrangler Jane on *F Troop.*
PATTINSON, LES. Ormskirk, England, 4/18/58. Bassist. Echo & The Bunnymen.
PATTON, MIKE. Eureka, CA, 1/27/68. Lead singer. Faith No More.
PATTON, WILL. Charleston, SC, 6/14/54. Actor. *No Way Out.*
PAYCHECK, JOHNNY (Donald Eugene Lytle). Greenfield, OH, 5/31/41. Singer. "Take This Job and Shove It."
PAYNE, BILL. Waco, TX, 3/12/49. Keyboardist. Little Feat.
PAYS, AMANDA. Berkshire, England, 6/6/59. Actor, married to Corbin Bernsen. *The Flash.*
PAYTON, DENIS. Walthamstow, England, 8/11/43. Saxophonist. The Dave Clark Five.
PAYTON, LAWRENCE. Detroit, MI. Singer. The Four Tops.
PAYTON, WALTER. Columbia, MS, 6/25/54. Football player.
PEARSON, DELROY. Romford, England, 4/11/70. Singer. Five Star.
PEARSON, DENIECE. Romford, England, 6/13/68. Lead singer. Five Star.
PEARSON, DORIS. Romford, England, 6/8/66. Singer. Five Star.
PEARSON, LORRAINE. Romford, England, 8/10/67. Singer. Five Star.
PEARSON, STEDMAN. Romford, England, 6/29/64. Singer. Five Star.
PEART, NEIL. Hamilton, Canada, 9/12/52. Drummer. Rush.
PECK, GREGORY (Eldred Peck). La Jolla, CA, 4/5/16. Actor, producer. *To Kill a Mockingbird.*
PEEK, DAN. Panama City, FL, 11/1/50. Singer, guitarist. America.
PELE, PEROLA NEGRA (Edson Arantes do Nascimento). Tres Coracoes, Brazil, 10/23/40. Soccer legend.
PELLOW, MARTI (Mark McLoughlin). Clydebank, Scotland, 3/23/66. Singer. Wet Wet Wet.
PENA, ELIZABETH. Elizabeth, NJ, 9/23/61. Actor. *La Bamba.*
PENDER, MIKE (Michael Prendergast). Liverpool, England, 3/3/42. Singer, lead guitarist. The Searchers.
PENDERGRASS, TEDDY. Philadelphia, PA, 3/26/50. R&B singer, songwriter, drummer.
PENDLETON, AUSTIN. Warren, OH, 3/27/40. Actor. *What's Up Doc?*
PENDLETON, BRIAN. Wolverhampton, England, 4/13/44. Guitarist. The Pretty Things.
PENGILLY, KIRK. 7/4/58. Guitarist, saxophonist, singer. INXS.
PENN, SEAN. Burbank, CA, 8/17/60. Actor, director, formerly married to Madonna. *Fast Times at Ridgemont High.*
PENNY, JOE. London, England, 9/14/56. Actor. Jake Styles on *Jake and the Fatman.*
PEPA (Sanda Denton). Queens, NY, 9/9/69. Rap artist.. Salt-N-Pepa.
PEREZ, ROSIE. Brooklyn, NY, 1964. Actor, choreographer. *Do the Right Thing.*
PERKINS, CARL (Carl Lee Perkings). Ridgely, TN, 4/9/32. Legendary singer, songwriter. "Blue Suede Shoes."
PERKINS, ELIZABETH. Queens, NY, 11/18/61. Actor. *Big.*
PERLMAN, RHEA. Brooklyn, NY, 3/31/48. Actor, married to Danny DeVito. Carla Tortelli LeBec on *Cheers.*
PERLMAN, RON. New York, NY, 4/13/50. Actor. The Beast in *Beauty and the Beast.*
PEROT, HENRY ROSS. Texarkana, TX, 6/27/30. Self-made billionaire businessman, former presidential candidate.
PERRINE, VALERIE. Galveston, TX, 9/3/43. Actor. *Lenny.*
PERRY, JOE. Boston, MA, 9/10/50. Guitarist. Aerosmith.
PERRY, LUKE (Perry Coy III). Fredericktown, OH, 10/11/66. Actor. *Beverly Hills 90210.*
PERRY, STEVE. Hanford, CA, 1/22/53. Singer. Journey.
PERRY, WILLIAM "THE REFRIGERATOR." Aiken, SC, 12/16/62. Very large football player. Chicago Bears.
PESCOW, DONNA. Brooklyn, NY, 3/24/54. Actor. *Saturday Night Fever.*
PETERS, BERNADETTE (Bernadette Lazzara). New York, NY, 2/28/48. Actor, performer. *Pennies from Heaven.*
PETERS, BROCK. New York, NY, 7/2/27. Actor, singer. *To Kill a Mockingbird.*
PETERS, MIKE. Prestatyn, Wales, 2/25/59. Guitarist, singer. The Alarm.
PETERSEN, WILLIAM. Chicago, IL, 1953. Actor. *To Live and Die in L.A.*
PETERSON, DEBBI. Los Angeles, CA, 8/22/61. Drummer, singer. The Bangles.
PETERSON, SYLVIA. New York, NY, 9/30/46. Singer. The Chiffons.
PETERSON, VICKI. Los Angeles, CA, 1/11/58. Guitarist, singer. The Bangles.
PETERSSON, TOM. Rockford, IL, 5/9/50. Singer, bassist. Cheap Trick.
PETTY, LORI. Chattanooga, TN. Actor. *A League of Their Own.*
PFISTERER, ALBAN. Switzerland, 1947. Drummer, keyboardist. Love.

PHANTOM, SLIM JIM (Jim McDonnell). 3/20/61. Drummer. The Stray Cats.
PHAIR, LIZ. New Haven, CT, 4/17/67. Singer, songwriter. *Exile in Guyville.*
PHILIP, PRINCE (Philip Mountbatten). Corfu, Greece, 6/10/21. Husband of Queen Elizabeth II, Duke of Edinburgh.
PHILLIPS, CHYNNA. Los Angeles, CA, 4/29/68. Singer, half-sister of Mackenzie, daughter of John and Michelle, married to Billy Baldwin. Wilson Phillips.
PHILLIPS, JOHN. Parris Island, SC, 8/30/35. Singer, formerly married to Michelle, father of Mackenzie and Chynna. The Mamas & the Papas.
PHILLIPS, LOU DIAMOND (Lou Upchurch). Philippines, 2/17/62. Actor. *La Bamba.*
PHILLIPS, MACKENZIE (Laura Mackenzie Phillips). Alexandria, VA, 11/10/59. Actor, daughter of John Phillips, half-sister of Chynna. Julie Cooper Horvath on *One Day at a Time.*
PHILLIPS, MICHELLE (Holly Gilliam). Santa Ana, CA, 6/4/44. Actor, formerly married to John, mother of Chynna. Anne Matheson on *Knots Landing.*
PHILTHY ANIMAL (Philip Taylor). Chesterfield, England, 9/21/54. Drummer. Motorhead.
PICKETT, WILSON. Prattville, AL, 3/18/41. Singer, songwriter. "In the Midnight Hour."
PIERSON, KATE. Weehawken, NJ, 4/27/48. Organist, singer. The B-52's.
PILATUS, ROBERT. New York, NY, 6/8/65. "Singer." Milli Vanilli.
PINCHOT, BRONSON. New York, NY, 5/20/59. Actor. Balki Bartokomous on *Perfect Strangers.*
PINDER, MIKE. Birmingham, England, 12/12/42. Keyboardist. The Moody Blues.
PINKNEY, BILL. Sumter, NC, 8/15/25. Bassist. The Drifters.
PIRNER, DAVE. Green Bay, WI, 4/16/64. Singer, songwriter, guitarist. Soul Asylum.
PIRRONI, MARCO. England, 4/27/59. Guitarist. Adam & The Ants.
PISCOPO, JOE. Passaic, NJ, 6/17/51. Actor. *Saturday Night Live.*
PITNEY, GENE. Hartford, CT, 2/17/41. Singer, songwriter.
PLACE, MARY KAY. Tulsa, OK, 9/23/47. Actor. *The Big Chill.*
PLANT, ROBERT. Bromwich, England, 8/20/48. Singer. Led Zeppelin.
PLESHETTE, JOHN. New York, NY, 7/27/42. Actor. Richard Avery on *Knots Landing.*
PLESHETTE, SUZANNE. New York, NY, 1/31/37. Actor. Emily Hartley on *The Bob Newhart Show.*
PLOWRIGHT, JOAN. Brigg, England, 10/28/29. Actor, widow of Laurence Olivier. *Enchanted April.*
PLUMB, EVE. Burbank, CA, 4/29/58. Actor. Jan Brady on *The Brady Bunch.*
PLUMMER, AMANDA. New York, NY, 3/23/57. Actor, daughter of Christopher Plummer. *The Fisher King.*
PLUMMER, CHRISTOPHER. Toronto, Canada, 12/13/27. Actor, father of Amanda Plummer. Baron von Trapp in *The Sound of Music.*
POINTER, ANITA. East Oakland, CA, 1/23/48. Singer. Pointer Sisters.
POINTER, BONNIE. East Oakland, CA, 6/11/51. Singer. Pointer Sisters.
POINTER, JUNE. East Oakland, CA, 11/30/54. Singer. Pointer Sisters.
POINTER, RUTH. East Oakland, CA, 3/19/46. Singer. Pointer Sisters.
POITIER, SIDNEY. Miami, FL, 2/20/27. Actor. *Guess Who's Coming to Dinner.*
POLANSKI, ROMAN. Paris, France, 8/18/33. Director, writer. *Rosemary's Baby.*
POLLACK, SYDNEY. South Bend, Indiana, 7/1/34. Director, producer, actor. *The Way We Were.*
POLLAN, TRACY. New York, NY, 6/22/60. Actor, married to Michael J. Fox. *Family Ties.*
POOLE, BRIAN. Barking, England, 11/2/41. Singer. Brian Poole & The Tremeloes.
POP, IGGY (James Osterburg). Ann Arbor, MI, 4/21/47. Singer, songwriter.
POPCORN, FAITH. New York, NY, 5/11/43. Trend analyst, consultant.
PORCARO, STEVE. Los Angeles, CA, 9/2/57. Keyboardist, singer. Toto.
PORTZ, CHUCK. Santa Monica, CA, 3/28/45. Bassist. The Turtles.
POST, MARKIE. Palo Alto, CA, 11/4/50. Actor. Christine Sullivan on *Night Court.*
POTTER, CAROL. Tenafly, NJ, 5/21/48. Actor. *Beverly Hills 90210.*
POTTS, ANNIE. Nashville, TN, 10/28/52. Actor. Mary Jo Shively on *Designing Women.*
POUNDSTONE, PAULA. Alabama, 12/29/60. Comedian, actor.
POVICH, MAURY. Washington, DC, 1/7/39. Talk show host, married to Connie Chung. *A Current Affair.*
POWELL, BILLY. Florida, 6/3/52. Keyboardist. Lynyrd Skynyrd.
POWELL, COLIN. New York, NY, 4/5/37. Military leader.
POWELL, DON. 9/10/50. Drummer. Slade.
POWERS, STEPHANIE (Stefania Federkiewicz). Hollywood, CA, 11/12/42. Actor. Jennifer on *Hart to Hart.*
POWTER, SUSAN. Sydney, Australia, 1957. Weight-loss expert. *Stop the Insanity!*
PRENTISS, PAULA (Paula Ragusa). San Antonio, TX, 3/4/39. Actor. *What's New Pussycat?*
PRESLEY, PRISCILLA. Brooklyn, NY, 5/24/45. Actor, producer, married and divorced Elvis Presley.
PRESLEY, REG (Reginald Ball). Andover, England, 6/12/43. Singer. The Troggs.
PRESTON, KELLY. Honolulu, HI, 10/13/62. Actor, married to John Travolta. *52 Pick-Up.*
PRICE, ALAN. Fairfield, Durham, 4/19/41. Keyboardist. The Animals.
PRICE, LLOYD. Kenner, LA, 5/9/33. Singer, songwriter.
PRICE, RICK. 6/10/44. Bassist. Wizzard.
PRIDE, CHARLEY. Sledge, MS, 3/18/38. Country singer, songwriter.
PRIEST, STEVE. London, England, 2/23/50. Bassist. Sweet.
PRIESTLEY, JASON. Vancouver, Canada, 8/28/69. Actor. Brandon Walsh on *Beverly Hills 90210.*
PRIESTMAN, HENRY. 7/21/58. Singer. The Christians.
PRIME, JAMES. Kilmarnock, Scotland, 11/3/60. Keyboardist. Deacon Blue.
PRINCE MARK D. 2/19/60. Rap artist. Fat Boys.
PRINCIPAL, VICTORIA. Fukuoka, Japan, 1/3/50. Actor. Pam Ewing on *Dallas.*
PRITCHARD, BARRY. Birmingham, England, 4/3/44. Guitarist, singer. The Fortunes.
PROBY, P. J. (James Smith). Houston, TX, 11/6/38. Singer, actor.
PRYCE, JONATHAN. North Wales, 6/1/47. Actor. *Miss Saigon.*
PRYOR, NICHOLAS. Baltimore, MD, 1/28/35. Actor. *Risky Business.*
PRYOR, RICHARD. Peoria, IL, 12/1/40. Actor. *Stir Crazy.*
PUERTA, JOE. 7/2/51. Bassist, singer. Bruce Hornsby & The Range.
PULLMAN, BILL. Hornell, NY, 1954. Actor. *While You Were Sleeping.*
PURCELL, SARAH. Richmond, IN, 10/8/48. TV personality. Cohost on *Real People.*
QADDAFI, MUAMMAR. Sirta, Libya, 1942. Political leader. Libyan head of state.
QUAID, RANDY. Houston, TX, 10/1/50. Actor, brother of Dennis. *The Last Picture Show.*
QUAIFE, PETE. Tavistock, England, 12/31/43. Bassist. The Kinks.

QUATRO, SUZI (Suzi Quatrocchio). Detroit, MI, 6/3/50. Singer, songwriter, actor.
QUAYLE, DAN. Indianapolis, IN, 2/4/47. Vice president under George Bush.
QUAYLE, MARILYN. Indianapolis, IN, 7/29/49. Lawyer, author, married to Dan. *Embrace the Serpent.*
QUINLAN, KATHLEEN. Mill Valley, CA, 11/19/54. Actor. *Clara's Heart.*
QUINN, AIDAN. Chicago, IL, 3/8/59. Actor. *The Playboys.*
QUINN, ANTHONY. Chihuahua, Mexico, 4/21/15. Actor. *Zorba the Greek.*
QUINN, DEREK. Manchester, England, 5/24/42. Lead guitarist. Freddie & The Dreamers.
QUIVERS, ROBIN. 1953. Radio personality, author. *The Howard Stern Show.*
RABBITT, EDDIE. New York, NY, 11/27/44. Singer, songwriter. "I Love a Rainy Night."
RAFFERTY, GERRY. Paisley, Scotland, 4/16/47. Singer, songwriter. "Baker Street."
RAFFI. Cairo, Egypt, 7/8/48. Singer, songwriter, children's performer. *Everything Grows.*
RAFFIN, DEBORAH. Los Angeles, CA, 3/13/53. Actor. *Once Is Not Enough.*
RALPH, SHERYL LEE. Waterbury, CT, 12/30/56. Actor. *The Distinguished Gentleman.*
RALPHS, MICK. Hereford, England, 3/31/44. Guitarist. Mott The Hoople; Bad Company.
RAMIS, HAROLD. Chicago, IL, 11/21/44. Writer, director, actor. Egon Spengler in *Ghostbusters.*
RAMONE, DEE DEE (Douglas Colvin). Fort Lee, VA, 9/18/52. Bassist. The Ramones.
RAMONE, JOEY (Jeffrey Hyman). Forest Hills, NY, 5/19/52. Singer. The Ramones.
RAMONE, JOHNNY (John Cummings). Long Island, NY, 10/8/48. Guitarist. The Ramones.
RAMONE, TOMMY (Thomas Erdelyi). Budapest, Hungary, 1/29/49. Drummer. The Ramones.
RAMOS, LARRY JR. (Hilario Ramos Jr.). Kauai, HI, 4/19/42. Singer, guitarist. The Association.
RAMPLING, CHARLOTTE. Surmer, England, 2/5/46. Actor. *The Verdict.*
RAMSEY, AL. New Jersey, 7/27/43. Guitarist. Gary Lewis & The Playboys.
RANDALL, TONY (Leonard Rosenberg). Tulsa, OK, 2/26/20. Actor. Felix Unger on *The Odd Couple.*
RAPHAEL, SALLY JESSY. Easton, PA, 2/25/43. talk show hostess. *Sally Jessy Raphäel.*
RAPP, DANNY. Philadelphia, PA, 5/10/41. Lead singer. Danny & The Juniors.
RAREBELL, HERMAN. 11/18/49. Drummer. Scorpions.
RASCHE, DAVID. St. Louis, MO, 8/7/44. Actor. *Sledge Hammer.*
RASHAD, AHMAD. Portland, OR, 11/19/49. Football player, sportscaster, husband of Phylicia.
RASHAD, PHYLICIA. Houston, TX, 6/19/48. Actor, sister of Debbie Allen, wife of Ahmad. Clair Huxtable on *The Cosby Show.*
RATZENBERGER, JOHN. Bridgeport, CT, 4/6/47. Actor. Cliff Claven on *Cheers.*
RAWLS, LOU. Chicago, IL, 12/1/36. R&B singer. "Lady Love."
RAY, JAMES EARL. Alton, IL, 3/10/28. Assassin. Killed Martin Luther King Jr.
REA, CHRIS. Middlesbrough, England, 3/4/51. Singer, songwriter, guitarist.
REAGAN, NANCY. New York, NY, 7/6/21. Former First Lady, married to president Ronald Reagan.
REAGAN, RONALD. Tampico, IL, 2/6/11. Politician, actor, father of Ron Jr., husband of Nancy. Fortieth U.S. president. *Bedtime for Bonzo.*
REAGAN, RONALD JR. Los Angeles, CA, 5/20/58. Performer, son of former president Ronald Reagan.
REASON, REX. Berlin, Germany, 11/30/28. Actor. *This Island Earth.*
RECORD, EUGENE. 12/23/40. Lead singer. The Chi-Lites.
REDDING, NOEL. Folkestone, England, 12/25/45. Bassist, The Jimi Hendrix Experience.
REDDY, HELEN. Melbourne, Australia, 10/25/42. Pop singer. *The Helen Reddy Show.*
REDGRAVE, CORIN. London, England, 6/16/39. Actor, brother of Lynn and Vanessa. *A Man for All Seasons.*
REDGRAVE, LYNN. London, England, 3/8/43. Actor, sister of Corin and Vanessa. *House Calls.*
REDGRAVE, VANESSA. London, England, 1/30/37. Actor, sister of Corin and Lynn. *Playing for Time.*
REED, LOU (Louis Firbank). Long Island, NY, 3/2/43. Singer, songwriter. The Velvet Underground.
REED, OLIVER. Wimbledon, England, 2/13/38. Actor. *The Three Musketeers.*
REED, PAMELA. Tacoma, WA, 4/2/53. Actor. *The Right Stuff.*
REEMS, HARRY (Herbert Streicher). The Bronx, NY, 8/27/47. Actor. *Deep Throat.*
REEVES, MARTHA. Alabama, 7/18/41. Lead singer. Martha & The Vandellas.
REEVES, STEVE. Glasgow, MT, 1/21/26. Actor. *Hercules.*
REGALBUTO, JOE. Brooklyn, NY. Actor. Frank Fontana on *Murphy Brown.*
REID, DON. Staunton, VA, 6/5/45. Musician, brother of Harold. Statler Brothers.
REID, HAROLD. Staunton, VA, 8/21/39. Musician, brother of Don. Statler Brothers.
REID, JIM. East Kilbride, Scotland, 1961. Guitarist, singer. The Jesus & Mary Chain.
REID, TIM. Norfolk, VA, 12/19/44. Actor, producer. Gordon "Venus Flytrap" Sims on *WKRP in Cincinnati.*
REID, WILLIAM. East Kilbride, Scotland, 1958. Guitarist, singer. The Jesus & Mary Chain.
REINER, CARL. New York, NY, 3/20/22. Actor, writer, and director. *The Dick Van Dyke Show.*
REINER, ROB. New York, NY, 3/6/45. Actor, writer, producer, director, son of Carl, formerly married to Penny Marshall. Mike Stivic on *All in the Family.*
REINHOLD, JUDGE (Edward Ernest Reinhold Jr.). Wilmington, DE, 5/21/57. Actor. Rosewood in *Beverly Hills Cop.*
REINKING, ANN. Seattle, WA, 11/10/49. Actor, dancer. *Annie.*
REITMAN, IVAN. Komarno, Czechoslovakia, 10/26/46. Director, producer. *Ghostbusters.*
REVERE, PAUL. Harvard, NE, 1/7/38. Keyboardist. Paul Revere & The Raiders.
REYNOLDS, BERT. Waycross, GA, 2/11/36. Actor, formerly married to Judy Carne and Loni Anderson. *Smokey and the Bandit.*
REYNOLDS, DEBBIE (Mary Frances Reynolds). El Paso, TX, 4/1/32. Actor, formerly married to Eddie Fisher, mother of Carrie Fisher. *Singin' in the Rain.*
RHODES, NICK (Nicholas Bates). Mosely, England, 6/8/62. Keyboardist. Duran Duran.
RIBEIRO, ALFONSO. New York, NY, 9/21/71. Actor, dancer. *Fresh Prince of Bel Air.*
RICH, ADAM. New York, NY, 10/12/68. Actor. Nicholas Bradford on *Eight Is Enough.*
RICHARD, CLIFF (Harry Webb). Lucknow, India, 10/14/40. Singer, drummer. The Shadows.
RICHARDS, KEITH. Dartford, England, 12/18/43. Guitarist. The Rolling Stones.
RICHARDSON, MIRANDA. Lancashire, England, 3/3/58. Actor. *The Crying Game.*
RICHARDSON, SUSAN. Coatesville, PA, 3/11/52.

Actor. Susan Bradford on *Eight Is Enough.*
RICHIE, LIONEL. Tuskegee, AL, 6/20/49. Singer, songwriter. The Commodores.
RICHRATH, GARY. Peoria, IL, 10/18/49. Guitarist. REO Speedwagon.
RICKLES, DON. New York, NY, 5/8/26. Actor. *The Don Rickles Show.*
RICKMAN, ALAN. Hammersmith, England, 1946. Actor. *Die Hard.*
RIDGELEY, ANDREW. Windlesham, England, 1/26/63. Guitarist. Wham!
RIEGERT, PETER. New York, NY, 4/11/47. Actor. *Crossing Delancey.*
RIGBY, CATHY. Long Beach, CA, 12/12/52. Gymnast, actor.
RIGG, DIANA. Doncaster, England, 7/20/38. Actor. Emma Peel on *The Avengers.*
RIGGS, BOBBY. Los Angeles, CA, 2/25/18. Tennis player, defeated by Billie Jean King.
RILEY, PAT. Rome, NY, 3/20/45. Basketball coach. Former New York Knicks coach.
RINGWALD, MOLLY. Sacramento, CA, 2/18/68. Actor. *Sixteen Candles.*
RITTER, JOHN. Burbank, CA, 9/17/48. Actor, producer. Jack Tripper on *Three's Company.*
RIVERA, CHITA. Washington, DC, 1/23/33. Singer.
RIVERA, GERALDO. New York, NY, 7/4/43. Talk show host and reporter. *Geraldo.*
RIVERS, JOHNNY (John Ramistella). New York, NY, 11/7/42. Soul/rock singer, songwriter.
RIZZUTO, PHIL. New York, NY, 9/25/18. Baseball great, sports announcer.
ROBARDS, JASON. Chicago, IL, 7/26/22. Actor, formerly married to Lauren Bacall. *Inherit the Wind.*
ROBERTS, ERIC. Biloxi, MS, 4/18/56. Actor, brother of Julia. *The Pope of Greenwich Village.*
ROBERTS, ORAL. Ada, OK, 1/24/18. Evangelist. Oral Roberts University.
ROBERTS, TANYA (Tanya Leigh). The Bronx, NY, 10/15/55. Actor. *Charlie's Angels.*
ROBERTS, TONY. New York, NY, 10/22/39. Actor. *Play It Again, Sam.*
ROBERTS, XAVIER. Cleveland, GA, 10/31/55. Businessman. Creator of Cabbage Patch Kids.
ROBERTSON, BRIAN. Glasgow, Scotland, 9/12/56. Guitarist. Thin Lizzy.
ROBERTSON, CLIFF. La Jolla, CA, 9/9/25. Actor. *Charly.*
ROBERTSON, PAT (Marion Gordon Robertson). Lexington, VA, 3/22/30. Evangelist, TV personality. Founder of Christian Broadcasting Network.
ROBERTSON, ROBBIE (Jaime Robertson). Toronto, Canada, 7/5/44. Guitarist, singer. The Band.
ROBINSON, CHRIS. Atlanta, GA, 12/20/66. Singer. The Black Crowes.
ROBINSON, CYNTHIA. Sacramento, CA, 1/12/46. Trumpeter. Sly & The Family Stone.
ROBINSON, JAY. New York, NY, 4/14/30. Actor. *The Robe.*
ROBINSON, RICH. Atlanta, GA, 5/24/69. Guitarist. The Black Crowes.
ROBINSON, SMOKEY (William Robinson). Detroit, MI, 2/19/40. Motown singer, songwriter. Smokey Robinson & The Miracles.
ROCK, CHRIS. New York, NY, 1967. Actor. *Saturday Night Live.*
ROCKER, LEE (Leon Drucher). 1961. Double bassist. The Stray Cats.
ROCKWELL (Kenneth Gordy). Detroit, MI, 3/15/64. Singer, son of Berry Gordy. "Somebody's Watching Me."
RODGERS, NILE. New York, NY, 9/19/52. Guitarist. Chic.
RODGERS, PAUL. Middlesbrough, England, 12/17/49. Singer. Free; Bad Company.
ROE, TOMMY. Atlanta, GA, 5/9/42. Singer, songwriter.
ROGERS, KENNY. Houston, TX, 8/21/38. Country singer, actor. "The Gambler."
ROGERS, MIMI. Coral Gables, FL, 1/27/56. Actor. Formerly married to Tom Cruise. *Someone To Watch Over Me.*
ROGERS, MISTER (Fred Rogers). Latrobe, PA, 3/20/28. Children's host, producer. *Mr. Rogers' Neighborhood.*
ROGERS, ROY (Leonard Slye). Cincinnati, OH, 11/5/12. TV cowboy, singer. *Happy Trails with Roy and Dale.*
ROGERS, WAYNE. Birmingham, AL, 4/7/33. Actor. Trapper John on *M*A*S*H.*
ROGERS, WILL JR. New York, NY, 10/20/12. Actor, lecturer. *The Story of Will Rogers.*
ROLLE, ESTHER. Pompano Beach, FL, 11/8/22. Actor. *Driving Miss Daisy.*
ROMAN, RUTH. Boston, MA, 12/23/24. Actor. *The Long Hot Summer.*
RONSTADT, LINDA. Tucson, AZ, 7/15/46. Singer, actor. *The Pirates of Penzance.*
ROONEY, ANDY. Albany, NY, 1/14/20. News commentator. *60 Minutes.*
ROONEY, MICKEY (Joe Yule Jr.). Brooklyn, NY, 9/23/20. Actor. *National Velvet.*
ROSE, AXL (William Bailey). Lafayette, IN, 1962. Singer. Guns N' Roses.
ROSE, PETE. Cincinnati, OH, 4/14/41. Baseball player and manager. Cincinnati Reds.
ROSS, DIANA. Detroit, MI, 3/26/44. Singer, actor, former member of the Supremes. *Lady Sings the Blues.*
ROSS, KATHARINE. Hollywood, CA, 1/29/43. Actor. *The Graduate.*
ROSS, MARION. Albert Lea, MN, 10/25/28. Actor. Marion Cunningham on *Happy Days.*
ROSS, RICKY. Dundee, Scotland, 12/22/57. Singer. Deacon Blue.
ROSSELLINI, ISABELLA. Rome, Italy, 6/18/52. Actor, formerly married to Martin Scorsese, engaged to Gary Oldman. *Blue Velvet.*
ROSSI, FRANCIS. Forest Hill, England, 4/29/49. Guitarist, singer. Status Quo.
ROSSINGTON, GARY. Jacksonville, FL, 12/4/51. Guitarist. Lynyrd Skynyrd.
ROTH, DAVID LEE. Bloomingtom, IN, 10/10/55. Singer. Van Halen.
ROTH, TIM. London, England, 1961. Actor. *Reservoir Dogs.*
ROTHERY, STEVE. Brampton, England, 11/25/59. Guitarist. Marillion.
ROTHWELL, RIC. Stockport, England, 3/11/44. Drummer. Wayne Fontana & The Mindbenders.
ROUNDTREE, RICHARD. New Rochelle, NY, 9/7/42. Actor. *Shaft.*
ROURKE, MICKEY. Schenectady, NY, 7/16/53. Actor, married to Carre Otis. *9 1/2 Weeks.*
ROWLAND, KEVIN. Wolverhampton, England, 8/17/53. Singer, guitarist. Dexy's Midnight Runners.
ROWLANDS, GENA. Cambria, WI, 6/19/34. Actor. *Gloria.*
RUDD, PHILIP. Australia, 5/19/46. Drummer. AC/DC.
RUDNER, RITA. Miami, FL, 9/11/55. Actor, comedian.
RUEHL, MERCEDES. Queens, NY, 2/28/48. Actor. *Lost in Yonkers.*
RUFFIN, DAVID. Meridian, MS, 1/18/41. Singer. The Temptations.
RUNDGREN, TODD. Philadelphia, PA, 6/22/48. Singer, songwriter.
RUSHDIE, SALMAN. Bombay, India, 6/19/47. Author. *The Satanic Verses.*
RUSSELL, GRAHAM. Nottingham, England, 6/1/50. Singer. Air Supply.
RUSSELL, JACK. 12/5/60. Singer. Great White.
RUSSELL, JANE. Bemidji, MN, 6/21/21. Actor, pinup girl. *The Outlaw.*
RUSSELL, LEON (Hank Wilson). Lawton, OK, 4/2/41. Country/blues singer, songwriter.
RUSSELL, NIPSEY. Atlanta, GA, 10/13/24. Actor. *Car 54, Where Are You?*

RUSSELL, THERESA (Theresa Paup). San Diego, CA, 3/20/57. Actor. *Black Widow.*
RUTHERFORD, MIKE. Guildford, England, 10/2/50. Guitarist. Genesis; Mike & The Mechanics.
RUTHERFORD, PAUL. Liverpool, England, 12/8/59. Singer. Frankie Goes to Hollywood.
RUTTAN, SUSAN. Oregon City, OR, 9/16/48. Actor. Roxanne on *L.A. Law.*
RYAN, TOM. Anderson, IN, 6/6/26. Cartoonist. *Tumbleweeds.*
RYDER, MITCH (William Levise Jr.). Detroit, MI, 2/26/45. Singer. Mitch Ryder & The Detroit Wheels.
RYDER, PAUL. Manchester, England, 4/24/64. Bassist. Happy Mondays.
RYDER, SHAUN. Little Hulton, England, 8/23/62. Singer. Happy Mondays.
SABATINI, GABRIELA. Buenos Aires, Argentina, 5/16/70. Tennis player.
SADE (Helen Folasade Adu). Ibadan, Nigeria, 1/16/59. Singer.
SAGAL, KATEY. Los Angeles, CA, 1956. Actor. Peg on *Married ... with Children.*
SAGAN, CARL. New York, NY, 11/9/34. Astronomer. *Cosmos.*
SAGET, BOB. Philadelphia, PA, 5/17/56. Actor. *Full House.*
SAHM, DOUG. San Antonio, TX, 11/6/41. Singer, guitarist. Sir Douglas Quintet.
SAINT, EVA MARIE. Newark, NJ, 7/4/24. Actor. *On the Waterfront.*
SAINT JAMES, SUSAN (Susan Miller). Los Angeles, CA, 8/14/46. Actor. Kate on *Kate & Allie.*
SAJAK, PAT. Chicago, IL, 10/26/46. Game show host. *Wheel of Fortune.*
SALAZAR, ALBERTO. Havana, Cuba, 8/7/58. Track athlete, won New York City Marathon.
SALES, SOUPY (Milton Supman). Franklinton, NC, 1/8/30. TV personality. *The Soupy Sales Show.*
SALINGER, J. D. (Jerome David Salinger). New York, NY, 1/1/19. Author. *The Catcher in the Rye.*
SALT (Cheryl James). Brooklyn, NY, 3/8/64. Rap artist. Salt-N-Pepa.
SALT, JENNIFER. Los Angeles, CA, 9/4/44. Actor. *Midnight Cowboy.*
SAMBORA, RICHIE. 7/11/59. Guitarist, married to Heather Locklear. Bon Jovi.
SAMMS, EMMA. London, England, 8/28/60. Actor. Fallon Carrington Colby on *Dynasty* and *The Colbys.*
SAMPRAS, PETE. Washington, DC, 8/12/71. Tennis player.
SAMWELL-SMITH, PAUL. Richmond, England, 5/8/43. Bassist. The Yardbirds.
SAN GIACOMO, LAURA. Denville, NJ, 11/14/61. Actor. *sex, lies and videotape.*
SANDERS, RICHARD. Harrisburg, PA, 8/23/40. Actor. Les Nessman on *WKRP in Cincinnati.*
SANDS, JULIAN. Yorkshire, England, 1/15/58. Actor. *A Room with a View.*
SANDY, GARY. Dayton, OH, 11/3/46. Actor. Andy Travis on *WKRP in Cincinnati.*
SANFORD, ISABEL. New York, NY, 8/29/17. Actor. Louise on *The Jeffersons.*
SANTANA, CARLOS. Autlan de Navarro, Mexico, 7/20/47. Guitarist, singer. Santana.
SANTIAGO, HERMAN. New York, NY 2/18/41. Singer. Frankie Lymon & The Teenagers.
SARANDON, CHRIS. Beckley, WV, 7/24/42. Actor, former husband of Susan. Leon in *Dog Day Afternoon.*
SASSOON, VIDAL. London, England, 1/17/28. Hairstylist.
SAVAGE, FRED. Highland Park, IL, 7/9/76. Actor, brother of Ben. Kevin Arnold on *The Wonder Years.*
SAVAGE, JOHN (John Youngs). Long Island, NY, 8/25/49. Actor. *The Deer Hunter.*
SAVAGE, RICK. Sheffield, England, 12/2/60. Bassist. Def Leppard.
SAVANT, DOUG. 6/21/64. Actor. *Melrose Place.*
SAWYER, RAY. Chickasaw, AL, 2/1/37. Lead singer. Dr. Hook.
SAYER, LEO (Gerard Sayer). Shoreham-by-Sea, England, 5/21/48. Singer, songwriter. "You Make Me Feel Like Dancing."
SCABIES, RAT (Chris Miller). Kingston-upon-Thames, England, 7/30/57. Drummer. The Damned.
SCACCHI, GRETA. Milan, Italy, 2/18/60. Actor. *Presumed Innocent.*
SCAGGS, BOZ (William Scaggs). Ohio, 6/8/44. Guitarist, singer, songwriter. "Lowdown."
SCALIA, JACK. Brooklyn, NY, 11/10/51. Actor. *Wolf.*
SCARPELLI, GLENN. Staten Island, NY, 7/6/68. Actor. Alex Handris on *One Day at a Time.*
SCHACHER, MEL. Flint, MI, 4/3/51. Bassist. Grand Funk Railroad.
SCHEIDER, ROY. Orange, NJ, 11/10/35. Actor. Chief Brody in *Jaws.*
SCHELL, MAXIMILIAN. Vienna, Austria, 12/8/30. Actor. *Judgment at Nuremberg.*
SCHENKER, RUDOLPH. 8/31/48. Guitarist. Scorpions.
SCHERMIE, JOE. Madison, WI, 2/12/45. Bassist. Three Dog Night.
SCHNEIDER, FRED. Newark, GA, 7/1/51. Keyboardist, singer. The B-52's.
SCHNEIDER, MARIA. Paris, France, 3/27/52. Actor. *Last Tango in Paris.*
SCHNEIDER-ESLEBEN, FLORIAN. Dusseldorf, Germany, 1947. Keyboardist, drummer, singer, woodwindist. Kraftwerk.
SCHOLZ, TOM. Toledo, OH, 3/10/47. Guitarist, keyboardist. Boston.
SCHON, NEAL. San Mateo, CA, 2/27/54. Guitarist. Journey.
SCHORR, DANIEL. New York, NY, 8/31/16. Broadcast journalist. *NPR.*
SCHRODER, RICK. Staten Island, NY, 4/13/70. Actor. *Lonesome Dove.*
SCHULTZ, DWIGHT. Baltimore, MD, 11/24/47. Actor. H. M. "Howling Mad" Murdock on *The A-Team.*
SCHULZ, CHARLES. Minneapolis, MN, 11/26/22. Cartoonist. *Peanuts.*
SCHWARZKOPF, NORMAN. Trenton, NJ, 8/22/34. Retired army general, Gulf War hero.
SCHYGULLA, HANNA. Katlowitz, Germany, 12/25/43. Actor. *Dead Again.*
SCIORRA, ANNABELLA. New York, NY, 1964. Actor. *The Hand That Rocks the Cradle.*
SCOLARI, PETER. New Rochelle, NY, 9/12/54. Actor. *Bosom Buddies.*
SCOTT, ANDY. Wrexham, Wales, 6/30/51. Guitarist. Sweet.
SCOTT, BON (Ronald Scott). Kirriemuir, Scotland, 7/9/46. Singer. AC/DC.
SCOTT, GEORGE C. Wise, VA, 10/18/27. Actor, married to Trish Van Devere. *Patton.*
SCOTT, GORDON (Gordon Werschkul). Portland, OR, 8/3/27. Actor. *Tarzan's Hidden Jungle.*
SCOTT, HOWARD. San Pedro, CA, 3/15/46. Guitarist, singer. War.
SCOTT, MIKE. Edinburgh, Scotland, 12/14/58. Singer, guitarist. The Waterboys.
SCOTT, RIDLEY. South Shields, England, 11/30/37. Director, brother of director Tony. *Thelma and Louise.*
SCOTT, WILLARD. Alexandria, VA, 3/7/34. Weatherman. *Today.*
SEAL, ELIZABETH. Genoa, Italy, 8/28/33. Actor. *Irma La Douce.*
SEALE, BOBBY. Dallas, TX, 10/20/36. Political activist, author. Cofounder of the Black Panthers.
SEALS, JIM. Sidney, TX, 10/17/41. Singer, guitarist, saxophonist, violinist. Seals & Crofts.
SEAVER, TOM. Fresno, CA, 11/17/44. Baseball pitcher.
SEBASTIAN, JOHN. New York, NY, 3/17/44. Singer, guitarist, harmonicist, autoharpist. "The Lovin' Spoonful."
SEDAKA, NEIL. Brooklyn, NY, 3/13/39. Pop singer,

songwriter. "Laughter in the Rain."
SEDGWICK, KYRA. New York, NY, 8/19/65. Actor, married to Kevin Bacon.
SEEGER, PETE. New York, NY, 5/3/19. Folk singer, songwriter, guitarist, social activist. Founded The Weavers.
SEGAL, GEORGE. New York, NY, 2/13/34. Actor. *Look Who's Talking.*
SEGER, BOB. Dearborn, MI, 5/6/45. Singer, songwriter. The Silver Bullet Band.
SELLECCA, CONNIE (Concetta Sellecchia). The Bronx, NY, 5/25/55. Actor, married to John Tesh. *Hotel.*
SELLECK, TOM. Detroit, MI, 1/29/45. Actor. *Magnum, P.I.*
SENDAK, MAURICE. New York, NY, 1/10/28. Author, illustrator. *Where the Wild Things Are.*
SENSIBLE, CAPTAIN (Ray Burns). England, 4/23/55. Bassist. The Damned.
SERAPHINE, DANNY. Chicago, IL, 8/28/48. Drummer. Chicago.
SERGEANT, WILL. Liverpool, England, 4/12/58. Guitarist. Echo & The Bunnymen.
SETZER, BRIAN. 4/10/60. Guitarist, singer. The Stray Cats.
SEVERIN, STEVE. 9/25/55. Bassist. Siouxsie & The Banshees.
SEYMOUR, STEPHANIE. San Diego, CA, 7/23/68. Supermodel.
SHAFFER, PAUL. Toronto, Canada, 11/28/49. Musician, bandleader. *Late Show with David Letterman.*
SHALIT, GENE. New York, NY, 1932. Critic. *Today.*
SHAPIRO, HELEN. Bethnal Green, England, 9/28/46. Singer, actor, cabaret performer.
SHARIF, OMAR (Michel Shalhoub). Alexandria, Egypt, 4/10/32. Actor. *Dr. Zhivago.*
SHARKEY, FEARGAL. Londonderry, Northern Ireland, 8/13/58. Singer. The Undertones.
SHARP, DAVE. Salford, England, 1/28/59. Guitarist. The Alarm.
SHARPTON, AL. Brooklyn, NY, 1954. Politician, activist, clergyman.
SHAVER, HELEN. St. Thomas, Canada, 2/24/51. Actor. *The Amityville Horror.*
SHAW, SANDIE (Sandra Goodrich). Dagenham, England, 2/26/47. Pop singer.
SHAW, TOMMY. Montgomery, AL, 9/11/52. Lead guitarist. Styx.
SHAWN, WALLACE. New York, NY, 11/12/43. Playwright, actor. *My Dinner with Andre.*
SHEA, JOHN. North Conway, NH, 4/14/49. Actor. *Lois & Clark.*
SHEARER, HARRY. Los Angeles, CA, 12/23/43. Actor. *This Is Spinal Tap.*
SHEEDY, ALLY. New York, NY, 6/13/62. Actor. *WarGames.*
SHEEHAN, FRAN. Boston, MA, 3/26/49. Bassist. Boston.
SHEEN, MARTIN (Ramon Estevez). Dayton, OH, 8/3/40. Actor, father of Charlie Sheen and Emilio Estevez. *Apocalypse Now.*
SHEILA E. (Sheila Escovedo). Oakland, CA, 12/12/59. Drummer, singer.
SHELDON, SIDNEY. Chicago, IL, 2/11/17. Novelist, producer. *The Other Side of Midnight.*
SHELLEY, CAROLE. London, England, 8/16/39. Actor. *The Elephant Man.*
SHELLEY, PETE (Peter McNeish). Lancashire, England, 4/17/55. Guitarist, singer. The Buzzcocks.
SHEPARD, SAM (Sam Rogers). Ft. Sheridan, IL, 11/5/43. Playwright, actor. *True West*; *The Right Stuff.*
SHERIDAN, JIM. Dublin, Ireland, 1949. Director, writer. *My Left Foot.*
SHERIDAN, NICOLLETTE. Worthington, England, 11/21/63. Actor, model. *The Sure Thing.*
SHIRE, TALIA (Talia Rose Coppola). Lake Success, NY, 4/25/46. Actor, sister of Francis Ford Coppola. *Rocky I–V.*
SHORROCK, GLENN. Rochester, England, 6/30/44. Singer. The Little River Band.
SHORT, MARTIN. Toronto, Canada, 3/26/50. Actor. Ed Grimley on *Saturday Night Live.*
SHOW, GRANT. Detroit, MI, 2/27/62. Actor. *Melrose Place.*
SHOWALTER, MAX (Casey Adams). Caldwell, KS, 6/2/17. Actor. First Ward Cleaver in the *Leave It to Beaver* pilot, "It's a Small World."
SHRIVER, MARIA. Chicago, IL, 11/6/55. Broadcast journalist, married to Arnold Schwarzenegger. *First Person with Maria Shriver.*
SHUE, ANDREW. South Orange, NJ, 2/20/67. Actor, brother of Elizabeth Shue. *Melrose Place.*
SIEGEL, JAY. Brooklyn, NY, 10/20/39. Baritone singer. The Tokens.
SIKKING, JAMES B. Los Angeles, CA, 3/5/34. Actor. Lt. Howard Hunter on *Hill Street Blues.*
SILLS, BEVERLY. New York, NY, 5/25/29. Opera singer.
SILVER, RON. New York, NY, 7/2/46. Actor, director. *Reversal of Fortune.*
SILVERMAN, JONATHAN. Los Angeles, CA, 8/5/66. Actor. *The Single Guy.*
SIMMONS, GENE (Chaim Witz). Haifa, Israel, 8/25/50. Long-tongued bassist, singer. Kiss.
SIMMONS, JEAN. London, England, 1/31/29. Actor. *The Thorn Birds.*
SIMMONS, JOSEPH. Queens, NY, 1964. Rap artist. Run-D.M.C.
SIMMONS, PATRICK. Aberdeen, WA, 1/23/50. Guitarist, singer. The Doobie Brothers.
SIMMONS, RICHARD. New Orleans, LA, 7/12/48. Health guru. *Sweatin' to the Oldies.*
SIMON, CARLY. New York, NY, 6/25/45. Singer, songwriter, childrens' book author.
SIMONE, NINA. Tryon, NC, 2/21/33. Singer. Soundtrack for *The Crying Game.*
SIMONON, PAUL. Brixton, England, 12/15/55. Bassist. The Clash.
SINGER, LORI. Corpus Christi, TX, 5/6/62. Actor. *Fame.*
SINGLETON, JOHN. Los Angeles, CA, 1/6/68. Director, writer. *Boyz N the Hood.*
SINGLETON, STEPHEN. Sheffield, England, 4/17/59. Saxophonist. ABC.
SIOUX, SIOUXSIE (Susan Dallon). Chiselhurst, England, 5/27/57. Singer. Siouxsie & The Banshees.
SISKEL, GENE. Chicago, IL, 1/26/46. Critic. *Siskel & Ebert & The Movies.*
SIXX, NIKKI (Frank Ferrano). Seattle, WA, 12/11/58. Bassist. Mötley Crüe.
SKERRITT, TOM. Detroit, MI, 8/25/33. Actor. *Picket Fences.*
SKYE, IONE (Ione Leitch). London, England, 9/4/71. Actor, daughter of folk singer Donovan, sister of Donovan Leitch. *Say Anything.*
SLASH (Saul Hudson). Stoke-on-Trent, England, 1965. Guitarist. Guns N' Roses.
SLATER, HELEN. New York, NY, 12/15/65. Actor. *Supergirl.*
SLATER, RODNEY. Lincolnshire, England, 11/8/44. Saxophonist, trumpeter. The Bonzo Dog Doo-Dah Band.
SLEDGE, DEBBIE. Philadelphia, PA, 7/9/54. Singer. Sister Sledge.
SLEDGE, JONI. Philadelphia, PA, 9/13/56. Singer. Sister Sledge.
SLEDGE, KATHY. Philadelphia, PA, 1/6/59. Singer. Sister Sledge.
SLEDGE, KIM. Philadelphia, PA, 8/21/57. Singer. Sister Sledge.
SLEDGE, PERCY. Leighton, AL, 11/25/41. Singer. "When a Man Loves a Woman."
SLICK, GRACE (Grace Wing). Chicago, IL, 10/30/39. Singer. Jefferson Airplane/Starship.
SLIWA, CURTIS. New York, NY, 3/26/54. Founder of the Guardian Angels.

SMIRNOFF, YAKOV (Yakov Pokhis). Odessa, Russia, 1/24/51. Actor. *What a Country!*
SMITH, ADRIAN. Huckney, England, 2/27/57. Guitarist. Iron Maiden.
SMITH, BOB. Buffalo, NY, 11/27/17. Entertainer. *Howdy Doody.*
SMITH, BOBBIE. 4/10/36. Singer. The (Detroit) Spinners.
SMITH, CHARLES MARTIN. Los Angeles, CA, 10/30/53. Actor. *American Graffiti.*
SMITH, CLAYDES (Charles Smith). Jersey City, NJ, 9/6/48. Guitarist. Kool & The Gang.
SMITH, CURT. Bath, England, 6/24/61. Singer, bassist. Tears for Fears.
SMITH, JACLYN. Houston, TX, 10/26/47. Actor. Kelly Garrett on *Charlie's Angels.*
SMITH, JEFF. Seattle, WA, 1/22/39. TV personality, chef, author. *The Frugal Gourmet.*
SMITH, JEROME. Miami, FL, 6/18/53. Guitarist. KC & The Sunshine Band.
SMITH, LARRY. Oxford, England, 1/18/44. Drummer. The Bonzo Dog Doo-Dah Band.
SMITH, LIZ. Fort Worth, TX, 2/2/23. Gossip columnist.
SMITH, MAGGIE. Ilford, England, 12/28/34. Actor. *Sister Act.*
SMITH, MIKE. Neath, Wales, 11/4/47. Tenor saxophonist. Amen Corner.
SMITH, MIKE. Edmonton, England, 12/12/43. Singer, keyboardist. The Dave Clark Five.
SMITH, PATTI. Chicago, IL, 12/31/46. Singer, songwriter.
SMITH, PHIL. 5/1/59. Saxophonist. Haircut 100.
SMITH, ROBERT. Crawley, England, 4/21/59. Guitarist, singer. The Cure.
SMITS, JIMMY. New York, NY, 7/9/55. Actor. Victor Sifuentes on *L.A. Law.*
SMOTHERS, DICK. New York, NY, 11/20/39. Actor, singer, brother of Tom. *The Smothers Brothers Comedy Hour.*
SMOTHERS, TOM. New York, NY, 2/2/37. Actor, singer, brother of Dick. *The Smothers Brothers Comedy Hour.*
SMYTH, PATTY. New York, NY, 6/26/57. Singer, relationship with John McEnroe. "The Warrior."
SNEED, FLOYD. Calgary, Canada, 11/22/43. Drummer. Three Dog Night.
SNODGRESS, CARRIE. Chicago, IL, 10/27/46. Actor. *Diary of a Mad Housewife.*
SOMERS, SUZANNE (Suzanne Mahoney). San Bruno, CA, 10/16/46. Actor. *Three's Company.*
SOMERVILLE, JIMMY. Glasgow, Scotland, 6/22/61. Dance/rock singer, keyboardist.
SOMMER, ELKE (Elke Schletz). Berlin, Germany, 11/5/40. Actor. *A Shot in the Dark.*
SORVINO, PAUL. New York, NY, 4/13/39. Actor. *GoodFellas.*
SOTHERN, ANN (Harriet Lake). Valley City, ND, 1/22/09. Actor. *The Ann Sothern Show.*
SOUL, DAVID (David Solberg). Chicago, IL, 8/28/43. Actor. Kevin "Hutch" Hutchinson on *Starsky and Hutch.*
SOUTH, JOE. Atlanta, GA, 2/28/40. Rock/country guitarist, singer, songwriter.
SOUTHSIDE JOHNNY (Johnny Lyon). Neptune Park, NJ, 12/4/48. Singer. Southside Johnny & The Asbury Jukes.
SPACEK, SISSY (Mary Elizabeth Spacek). Quitman, TX, 12/25/49. Actor. *Coal Miner's Daughter.*
SPADER, JAMES. Boston, MA, 2/7/60. Actor. *sex, lies, and videotape.*
SPANO, JOE. San Francisco, CA, 7/7/46. Actor. Henry Goldblume on *Hill Street Blues.*
SPANO, VINCENT. New York, NY, 10/18/62. Actor. *Rumble Fish.*
SPEAR, ROGER. London, England, 6/29/43. Saxophonist, kazooist. The Bonzo Dog Doo-Dah Band.
SPECTOR, PHIL. New York, NY, 12/26/40. Music producer. Wall of sound.
SPECTOR, RONNIE (Veronica Bennett). New York, NY, 8/10/43. Lead singer. The Ronettes.
SPELLING, TORI. Los Angeles, CA, 5/16/73. Actor, daughter of Aaron Spelling. Donna on *Beverly Hills, 90210.*
SPENCE, ALEXANDER. Windsor, Canada, 4/18/46. Guitarist, lead singer. Moby Grape.
SPENCER, JEREMY. West Hartlepoole, England, 7/4/48. Guitarist. Fleetwood Mac.
SPILLANE, MICKEY (Frank Morrison). New York, NY, 3/9/18. Author. Mike Hammer detective stories.
SPINKS, LEON. St. Louis, MO, 7/11/53. Boxer, former heavyweight champion, brother of Michael.
SPINKS, MICHAEL. St. Louis, MO, 7/29/56. Boxer. Olympic gold medalist, brother of Leon.
SPOCK, BENJAMIN. New Haven, CT, 5/2/03. Physician, author. *Common Sense Book of Baby Care.*
SPOONER, BILL. Phoenix, AZ, 4/16/49. Guitarist. The Tubes.
SPRINGFIELD, DUSTY (Mary O'Brien). Hampstead, England, 4/16/39. Folk/pop singer.
SPRINGFIELD, RICK (Richard Spring Thorpe). Sydney, Australia, 8/23/49. Singer, actor. *General Hospital.*
SQUIER, BILLY. Wellesley, MA, 5/12/50. Singer. "Everybody Wants You."
SQUIRE, CHRIS. London, England, 3/4/48. Bassist. Yes.
SQUIRE, JOHN. Sale, England, 11/24/62. Lead guitarist. The Stone Roses.
ST. JOHN, JILL (Jill Oppenheim). Los Angeles, CA, 8/19/40. Actor, married to Robert Wagner. *Diamonds Are Forever.*
STACK, ROBERT. Los Angeles, CA, 1/13/19. Actor. Eliot Ness on *The Untouchables.*
STAFFORD, JIM. Eloise, FL, 1/16/44. Singer, songwriter. "Spiders and Snakes."
STAMOS, JOHN. Cypress, CA, 8/19/63. Actor. *Full House.*
STAMP, TERENCE. London, England, 7/23/39. Actor. *Superman II.*
STANLEY, PAUL (Paul Eisen). Queens, NY, 1/20/50. Guitarist, singer. Kiss.
STANSFIELD, LISA. Rochdale, England, 4/11/66. Singer, songwriter. "All Around the World."
STANTON, HARRY DEAN. West Irvine, KY, 7/14/26. Actor. *Paris, Texas.*
STAPLES, NEVILLE. 4/11/56. Singer, percussionist. The Specials.
STAPLES, PETE. Andover, England, 5/3/44. Bassist. The Troggs.
STAPLETON, JEAN (Jeanne Murray). New York, NY, 1/19/23. Actor. Edith Bunker on *All in the Family.*
STAPLETON, MAUREEN. Troy, NY, 6/21/25. Actor. *Airport.*
STARR, RINGO (Richard Starkey). Liverpool, England, 7/7/40. Drummer, singer, actor, married to Barbara Bach. The Beatles.
STAUBACH, ROGER. Cincinnati, OH, 2/5/42. NFL football player. Dallas Cowboys.
STAX, JOHN (John Fullegar). London, England, 4/6/44. Bassist. The Pretty Things.
STEEL, JOHN. Gateshead, England, 2/4/41. Drummer. The Animals.
STEELE, DAVID. Birmingham, England, 9/8/60. Keyboardist, bassist. Fine Young Cannibals.
STEELE, MICHAEL. 6/2/54. Bassist, singer. The Bangles; The Runaways.
STEELE, TOMMY (Thomas Hicks). Bermondsey, England, 12/17/36. Guitarist, singer, actor.
STEENBURGEN, MARY. Newport, AR, 2/8/53. Actor, engaged to Ted Danson. *Parenthood.*
STEIGER, ROD. Westhampton, NY, 4/14/25. Actor. *In the Heat of the Night.*
STEIN, CHRIS. Brooklyn, NY, 1/5/50. Guitarist. Blondie.
STEIN, MARK. Bayonne, NJ, 3/11/47. Singer, organist. Vanilla Fudge.

STEINBERG, DAVID. Winnipeg, Canada, 8/9/42. Actor, director. *Paternity.*
STEINEM, GLORIA. Toledo, OH, 3/25/34. Women's rights activist.
STERBAN, RICHARD. Camden, NJ, 4/24/43. Singer, bassist. The Oak Ridge Boys.
STERN, DANIEL. Bethesda, MD, 8/28/57. Actor, narrator of *The Wonder Years. City Slickers.*
STERN, ISAAC. Kreminiecz, Russia, 7/21/20. Violinist.
STERNHAGEN, FRANCES. Washington, DC, 1/13/30. Actor. *Driving Miss Daisy.*
STEVENS, ANDREW. Memphis, TN, 6/10/55. Actor, son of Stella. *Dallas.*
STEVENS, CAT (Steven Georgiou). Soho, England, 7/21/47. Folk singer, songwriter—left recording upon conversion to Islam.
STEVENS, CONNIE (Concetta Ann Ingolia). Brooklyn, NY, 8/8/38. Actor. *Hawaiian Eye.*
STEVENS, FISHER. Chicago, IL, 11/27/63. Actor. *Short Circuit.*
STEVENS, RAY (Ray Ragsdale). Clarksdale, GA, 1/24/39. Singer. *Andy Williams Presents Ray Stevens.*
STEVENS, SHAKIN' (Michael Barratt). Ely, Wales, 3/4/48. Singer, actor.
STEVENS, STELLA (Estelle Eggleston). Hot Coffee, MS, 10/1/36. Actor, mother of Andrew. *Santa Barbara.*
STEVENSON, DON. Seattle, WA, 10/15/42. Drummer. Moby Grape.
STEVENSON, PARKER. Philadelphia, PA, 6/4/52. Actor, married to Kirstie Alley. *Falcon Crest.*
STEWART, AL. Glasgow, Scotland, 9/5/45. Guitarist, singer, songwriter.
STEWART, DAVE. Sunderland, England, 9/9/52. Keyboardist, guitarist. Eurythmics.
STEWART, ERIC. Manchester, England, 1/20/45. Singer, guitarist. 10cc.
STEWART, MARTHA (Martha Haworth). Bardwell, KY, 10/7/22. Actor. *Holocaust.*
STEWART, ROD. Highgate, England, 1/10/45. Singer, songwriter.
STIERS, DAVID OGDEN. Peoria, IL, 10/31/42. Actor. Dr. Charles Emerson Winchester on *M*A*S*H.*
STILES, RAY. Carshalton, England, 11/20/46. Bassist, singer. Mud.
STILLER, JERRY. New York, NY, 6/8/31. Actor, partner/married to Anne Meara, father of Ben Stiller.
STILLS, STEPHEN. Dallas, TX, 1/3/45. Singer, guitarist. Buffalo Springfield; Crosby, Stills, Nash & Young.
STOCKDALE, JAMES. Abington, IL, 12/23/23. Vietnam POW, running mate of presidential candidate Ross Perot.
STOCKWELL, DEAN. Hollywood, CA, 3/5/35. Actor. Al Calavicci on *Quantum Leap.*
STOCKWELL, JOHN (John Samuels). Galveston, TX, 3/25/61. Actor. *My Science Project.*
STOLTZ, ERIC. American Samoa, 9/30/61. Actor. *Mask.*
STONE, DEE WALLACE (Deanna Bowers). Kansas City, MO, 12/14/48. Actor. Mother in *E.T., the Extra-Terrestrial.*
STONE, FREDDIE. Dallas, TX, 6/5/46. Guitarist. Sly & The Family Stone.
STONE, ROSIE. Vallejo, CA, 3/21/45. Singer, keyboardist. Sly & The Family Stone.
STONE, SLY (Sylvester Stewart). Dallas, TX, 3/15/44. Singer, keyboardist, guitarist. Sly & The Family Stone.
STORCH, LARRY. New York, NY, 1/8/23. Actor. *F Troop.*
STORM, GALE (Josephine Cottle). Bloomington, TX, 4/5/22. Actor. *My Little Margie.*
STOWE, MADELEINE. Los Angeles, CA, 8/18/58. Actor. *The Last of the Mohicans.*
STRASSMAN, MARCIA. New York, NY, 4/28/48. Actor. Julie Kotter on *Welcome Back Kotter.*
STRATHAIRN, DAVID. San Francisco, CA, 1949. Actor. *Matewan.*
STRATTON, DENNIS. London, England, 11/9/54. Guitarist. Iron Maiden.
STRAUSS, PETER. Croton-on-Hudson, NY, 2/20/47. Actor. *The Jericho Mile.*
STRINGFIELD, SHERRY. Colorado Springs, CO, 6/24/67. Actor. *ER.*
STRICKLAND, KEITH. Athens, GA, 10/26/53. Drummer. The B-52's.
STRITCH, ELAINE. Detroit, MI, 2/2/25. Actor. *September.*
STRUMMER, JOE (John Mellors). Ankara, Turkey, 8/21/52. Singer, guitarist. The Clash.
STRUTHERS, SALLY. Portland, OR, 7/28/48. Actor. Gloria Bunker Stivic on *All in the Family.*
STRYKERT, RON. Australia, 8/18/57. Guitarist. Men at Work.
STUART, CHAD. England, 12/10/43. Singer, guitarist. Chad & Jeremy.
STUART, HAMISH. Glasgow, Scotland, 10/8/49. Singer, guitarist. Average White Band.
STUBBS, LEVI (Levi Stubbles). Detroit, MI, 6/6/36. Lead singer. The Four Tops.
SUCH, ALEC. 11/14/56. Bassist. Bon Jovi.
SULLIVAN, SUSAN. New York, NY, 11/18/44. Actor. Maggie Gioberti Channing on *Falcon Crest.*
SULLIVAN, TOM. Boston, MA, 3/27/47. Singer, actor, composer. "If You Could See What I Hear."
SUMMER, DONNA (LaDonna Gaines). Boston, MA, 12/31/48. Disco/pop singer. "Love To Love You Baby."
SUMMERS, ANDY (Andrew Somers). Poulton le Fylde, France, 12/31/42. Guitarist, singer. The Police.
SUMNER, BARNEY (Bernard Dicken). Salford, England, 1/4/56. Guitarist, singer. New Order.
SUTHERLAND, DONALD. St. John, Canada, 7/17/34. Actor, father of Kiefer. *Ordinary People.*
SUTHERLAND, KIEFER. Los Angeles, CA, 12/18/66. Actor, son of Donald. *Flatliners.*
SUZMAN, JANET. Johannesburg, South Africa, 2/9/39. Actor. *Nicholas and Alexandra.*
SVENSON, BO. Goreborg, Sweden, 2/13/41. Actor. *Walking Tall.*
SWAGGART, JIMMY. Ferriday, LA, 3/15/35. Evangelist.
SWANN, LYNN. Alcoa, TN, 3/7/52. NFL football player.
SWAYZE, PATRICK. Houston, TX, 8/18/52. Actor, dancer. *Dirty Dancing.*
SWEENEY, D. B. (Daniel Bernard Sweeney). Shoreham, NY, 1961. Actor. *The Cutting Edge.*
SWEET, DERRELL. 5/16/47. Drummer, percussionist, singer. Nazareth.
SWEET, MATTHEW. Lincoln, NE, 10/6/64. Singer, songwriter, guitarist. "Girlfriend."
SWENSON, INGA. Omaha, NE, 12/29/32. Actor. Gretchen Kraus on *Benson.*
SWIT, LORETTA. Passaic, NJ, 11/4/37. Actor. Margaret "Hot Lips" Houlihan on *M*A*S*H.*
SYLVIAN, DAVID (David Batt). Lewisham, England, 2/23/58. Singer, guitarist. Japan.
T, MR. (Lawrence Tero). Chicago, IL, 5/21/52. Actor and wrestler. Bosco "B.A." Baracus on *The A-Team.*
TAJ MAHAL. New York, NY, 5/17/42. Singer, songwriter, composer. "Sounder."
TAKEI, GEORGE. Los Angeles, CA, 4/20/39. Mr. Sulu on *Star Trek.*
TALBOT, MICK. London, England, 9/11/58. Keyboardist. The Style Council.
TALLEY, GARY. Memphis, TN, 8/17/47. Guitarist. The Box Tops/Big Star.
TALLEY, NEDRA. New York, NY, 1/27/46. Singer. The Ronettes.
TAMBLYN, RUSS. Los Angeles, CA, 12/30/34. Actor. *West Side Story.*

TAMBOR, JEFFREY. San Francisco, CA, 7/8/44. Actor. *Hill Street Blues.*
TANDY, RICHARD. Birmingham, England, 3/26/48. Bassist. Electric Light Orchestra (ELO).
TARKENTON, FRAN. Richmond, VA, 2/3/40. Football player, sportscaster. *Monday Night Football.*
TAUPIN, BERNIE. Sleaford, England, 5/22/50. Lyricist. Wrote for Elton John.
TAYLOR, ANDY. Tynemouth, England, 2/16/61. Guitarist. Duran Duran.
TAYLOR, CLIVE. Cardiff, Wales, 4/27/49. Bassist. Amen Corner.
TAYLOR, DICK. Dartford, England, 1/28/43. Lead guitarist. The Pretty Things.
TAYLOR, JAMES. South Carolina, 8/16/53. Lead singer. Kool & The Gang.
TAYLOR, JAMES. Boston, MA, 3/12/48. Folk-oriented singer, songwriter.
TAYLOR, JOHN. Birmingham, England, 6/20/60. Bassist. Duran Duran.
TAYLOR, LARRY. Brooklyn, NY, 6/26/42. Bassist. Canned Heat.
TAYLOR, LILI. Chicago, IL, 1967. Actor. *Mystic Pizza.*
TAYLOR, ROD. Sydney, Australia, 1/11/29. Actor. *The Time Machine.*
TAYLOR, ROGER. King's Lynn, England, 7/26/49. Drummer. Queen.
TENCH, BENMONT. Gainesville, FL, 9/7/54. Keyboardist. Tom Petty & The Heartbreakers.
TENNANT, NEIL. Gosforth, England, 7/10/54. Singer. Pet Shop Boys.
TENNANT, VICTORIA. London, England, 9/30/50. Actor, formerly married to Steve Martin. *L.A. Story.*
TENNILLE, TONI. Montgomery, AL, 5/8/43. Singer. The Captain & Tennille.
TERRANOVA, JOE. 1/30/41. Baritone. Danny & The Juniors.

THICKE, ALAN. Ontario, Canada, 3/1/47. Actor. *Growing Pains.*
THISTLETHWAITE, ANTHONY. Leicester, England, 8/31/55. Saxophonist. The Waterboys.
THOMAS, B. J. (Billy Joe Thomas). Hugo, OK, 8/7/42. Pop singer. "Raindrops Keep Fallin' on My Head."
THOMAS, BETTY. Saint Louis, MO, 7/27/48. Actor. Lucy Bates on *Hill Street Blues.*
THOMAS, DAVE. Saint Catharines, Canada, 6/20/49. Actor. Doug MacKenzie on *SCTV.*
THOMAS, HENRY. San Antonio, TX, 9/8/72. Actor. Elliot in *E.T., the Extra-Terrestrial.*
THOMAS, JAY. New Orleans, LA, 7/12/48. Actor, radio personality. *Murphy Brown.*
THOMAS, MARLO (Margaret Thomas). Detroit, MI, 11/21/38. Actor, married to Phil Donahue, daughter of Danny Thomas. *That Girl.*
THOMAS, MARY. Brooklyn, NY, 1946. Singer. The Crystals.
THOMAS, PHILIP MICHAEL. Columbus, OH, 5/26/49. Actor. Ricardo Tubbs on *Miami Vice.*
THOMAS, RAY. Stourport-on-Severn, England, 12/29/42. Flautist, harmonicist, singer. The Moody Blues.
THOMAS, RICHARD. New York, NY, 6/13/51. Actor. John Boy on *The Waltons.*
THOMPKINS, RUSSELL JR. Philadelphia, PA, 3/21/51. Lead singer. The Stylistics.
THOMPSON, LEA. Rochester, MN, 5/31/61. Actor. *Back to the Future.*
THOMPSON, PAUL. Jarrow, England, 5/13/51. Drummer. Roxy Music.
THOMPSON, SADA. Des Moines, IA, 9/27/29. Actor. *Family.*
THOMPSON, TONY. 11/15/54. Drummer. Chic.
THOMSON, DOUGIE. Glasgow, Scotland, 3/24/51. Bassist. Supertramp.
THORN, TRACEY. Hartfordshire, England, 9/26/62. Singer. Everything but the Girl.

THORNE-SMITH, COURTNEY. 11/8/68. Actor. *Melrose Place.*
THORNTON, BLAIR. Vancouver, Canada, 7/23/50. Guitarist. Bachman-Turner Overdrive.
THOROGOOD, GEORGE. Wilmington, DE, 1951. Singer, guitarist. George Thorogood and the Delaware Destroyers.
TICH (Ian Amey). Salisbury, England, 5/15/44. Lead guitarist. Dave Dee, Dozy, Beaky, Mick and Tich.
TIEGS, CHERYL. Alhambra, CA, 9/25/47. Model, author. *The Way to Natural Beauty.*
TIFFANY (Tiffany Renee Darwish). Norwalk, CA, 10/2/71. Singer.
TILBROOK, GLENN. London, England, 8/31/57. Singer, lead guitarist. Squeeze.
TILLIS, MEL. Pahokee, FL, 8/8/32. Singer, songwriter, father of Pam Tillis.
TILLIS, PAM. Plant City, FL, 7/24/57. Singer, daughter of Mel Tillis.
TILLY, MEG. Texada, Canada, 2/14/60. Actor, sister of Jennifer. *The Big Chill.*
TILTON, CHARLENE. San Diego, CA, 12/1/58. Actor. Lucy Ewing Cooper on *Dallas.*
TIPTON, GLENN. Birmingham, England, 10/25/48. Guitarist. Judas Priest.
TOLHURST, LOL (Laurence Tolhurst). 2/3/59. Keyboardist. The Cure.
TOLKAN, JAMES. Calumet, MI, 6/20/31. Actor. Principal in *Back to the Future.*
TOMEI, MARISA. Brooklyn, NY, 12/4/64. Actor. *My Cousin Vinny.*
TOMLIN, LILY (Mary Jean Tomlin). Detroit, MI, 9/1/39. Actor. *Rowan & Martin's Laugh-In.*
TONE-LOC. Los Angeles, CA, 3/3/66. Rap artist. "Wild Thing."
TOPHAM, ANTHONY "TOP." England, 1947. Guitarist. The Yardbirds.
TORK, PETER (Peter Halsten Thorkelson). Washington, DC, 2/13/44. Keyboardist, bassist, actor. The Monkees.
TORME, MEL. Chicago, IL, 9/13/25. Singer.

TORN, RIP. (Elmore Rual Torn Jr). Temple, TX, 2/6/31. Actor. *Blind Ambition.*
TORRENCE, DEAN. Los Angeles, CA, 3/10/40. Singer. Jan & Dean.
TOWNSEND, ROBERT. Chicago, IL, 2/6/57. Actor. *Hollywood Shuffle.*
TOWNSHEND, PETE. Chiswick, England, 5/19/45. Guitarist. The Who.
TOWNSON, RON. St. Louis, MO, 1/20/33. Singer. The 5th Dimension.
TRAVANTI, DANIEL J. Kenosha, WI, 3/7/40. Actor. Captain Frank Furillo on *Hill Street Blues.*
TRAVERS, BILL. Newcastle-upon-Tyne, England, 1/3/22. Actor, producer, director. *Born Free.*
TRAVERS, BRIAN. Birmingham, England, 2/7/59. Saxophonist. UB40.
TRAVIS, RANDY (Randy Traywick). Marshville, NC, 5/4/59. Country singer, songwriter.
TREBEK, ALEX. Sudbury, Canada, 7/22/40. Game show host. *Jeopardy!*
TRESVANT, RALPH. Boston, MA, 5/16/68. Singer. New Edition.
TREVOR, CLAIRE (Claire Wemlinger). New York, NY, 3/8/09. Actor. *Key Largo.*
TREWAVAS, PETER. Middlesborough, England, 1/15/59. Keyboardist. Marillion.
TRIPPLEHORN, JEANNE. Tulsa, Oklahoma, 1963. Actor. *The Firm.*
TRITT, TRAVIS. Marietta, GA, 2/9/63. Country singer, songwriter.
TROWER, ROBIN. Southend, England, 3/9/45. Guitarist. Procol Harum.
TRUDEAU, GARRY (Garretson Beckman Trudeau). New York, NY, 1948. Cartoonist,married to Jane Pauley. *Doonesbury.*
TRUGOY THE DOVE (David Jolicoeur). 9/21/68. Musician. De La Soul.
TRUMP, DONALD. New York, NY, 6/14/46. Real estate developer, author. Married to Marla

Maples, formerly married to Ivana Winkelmayr Trump.
TRUMP, MARLA MAPLES. 10/27/63. Actor. Married to Donald Trump. *The Will Rogers Follies.*
TUCKER, JIM. Los Angeles, CA, 10/17/46. Guitarist. The Turtles.
TUCKER, MICHAEL. Baltimore, MD, 2/6/44. Actor, married to Jill Eikenberry. *L.A. Law.*
TUCKER, MICK. Harlesden, England, 7/17/49. Drummer. Sweet.
TUCKER, TANYA. Seminole, TX, 10/10/58. Pop singer. "Delta Dawn."
TUFANO, DENNIS. Chicago, IL, 9/11/46. Guitarist, lead singer. The Buckinghams.
TUNE, TOMMY. Wichita Falls, TX, 2/28/39. Actor, director, choreographer, dancer.
TURBO B.(Durron Maurice Butler). Pittsburgh, PA, 4/30/67. Rap artist. Snap.
TURNER, C. F. Winnipeg, Canada, 10/16/43. Bassist, singer. Bachman-Turner Overdrive.
TURNER, IKE. Clarksdale, MS, 11/5/31. Singer, songwriter, formerly married to Tina Turner. Ike & Tina Turner.
TURNER, JANINE (Janine Gauntt). Lincoln, NE, 12/6/63. Actor. *Northern Exposure.*
TURNER, LONNIE. Berkeley, CA, 2/24/47. Bassist, singer. The Steve Miller Band.
TUROW, SCOTT. Chicago, IL, 4/12/49. Author. *The Burden of Proof.*
TURTURRO, JOHN. Brooklyn, NY, 2/28/57. Actor. *Barton Fink.*
TWIGGY (Lesley Hornby). London, England, 9/19/49. Model, actor. *The Boy Friend.*
TWIST, NIGEL. Manchester, England, 7/18/58. Drummer. The Alarm.
TYLER, BONNIE (Gaynor Hopkins). Swansea, Wales, 6/8/53. Singer. "Total Eclipse of the Heart."
TYLER, RICHARD. Sunshine, Australia, 1948. Designer.
TYSON, CICELY. New York, NY, 12/19/33. Actor. *The Autobiography of Miss Jane Pittman.*
UECKER, BOB. Milwaukee, WI, 1/26/35. Actor. *Mr. Belvedere.*
UGGAMS, LESLIE. New York, NY, 5/25/43. Singer, actor. Kizzy in *Roots.*
ULLMAN, TRACEY. Hackbridge, England, 12/30/59. Actor. *The Tracey Ullman Show.*
ULLMANN, LIV. Tokyo, Japan, 12/16/39. Actor. *Persona.*
ULVAEUS, BJORN. Gothenburg, Sweden, 4/25/45. Guitarist, singer. Abba.
UNDERWOOD, BLAIR. Tacoma, WA, 8/25/64. Actor. *L.A. Law.*
URICH, ROBERT. Toronto, Canada, 12/19/46. Actor. *Spenser: For Hire.*
VACCARO, BRENDA. Brooklyn, NY, 11/18/39. Actor. *Midnight Cowboy.*
VADIM, ROGER (Roger Vadim Plemiannikov). Paris, France, 1/26/28. Movie director, formerly married to Jane Fonda.
VALE, JERRY. New York, NY, 7/8/32. Pop singer. "Innamorata."
VALE, MIKE. 7/17/49. Bassist. Tommy James & The Shondells.
VALENTINE, HILTON. North Shields, England, 5/21/43. Guitarist. The Animals.
VALENTINE, SCOTT. Saratoga Springs, NY, 6/3/58. Actor. Nick Moore on *Family Ties.*
VALLI, FRANKIE (Frank Castelluccio). Newark, NJ, 5/3/37. Lead singer. The Four Seasons.
VALLONE, RAF (Raffaele Vallone). Tropea, Italy, 2/17/18. Actor. *Obsession.*
VALORY, ROSS. San Francisco, CA, 2/2/49. Bassist. Journey.
VAN ARK, JOAN. New York, NY, 6/16/43. Actor. Val Ewing *Knots Landing.*
VAN DEVERE, TRISH (Patricia Dressel). Englewood Cliffs, NJ, 3/9/45. Actor, married to George C. Scott. *The Day of the Dolphin.*
VAN DOREN, MAMIE (Joan Lucile Olander). Rowena, SD, 2/6/31. Actor. *Ain't Misbehavin'.*
VAN DYKE, DICK. West Plains, MO, 12/13/25. Actor and performer, brother of Jerry. *The Dick Van Dyke Show.*
VAN DYKE, JERRY. Danville, IL, 7/27/31. Actor, brother of Dick. *Coach.*
VAN HALEN, ALEX. Nijmegen, Holland, 5/8/55. Drummer. Van Halen.
VAN PATTEN, DICK. New York, NY, 12/9/28. Actor. *Eight Is Enough.*
VAN PEEBLES, MARIO. New York, NY, 1/15/57. Actor, director, writer, son of Melvin. *Posse.*
VAN PEEBLES, MELVIN. Chicago, IL, 8/21/32. Actor, writer, composer, father of Mario. *Sweet Sweetback's Badasssss Song.*
VAN ZANDT, DONNIE. Florida, 6/11/52. Singer, guitarist. .38 Special.
VAN ZANDT, STEVIE. Boston, MA, 11/22/50. Bassist. E Street Band.
VANDA, HARRY (Harry Vandenberg). The Hague, The Netherlands, 3/22/47. Guitarist. The Easybeats.
VANDERBILT, GLORIA. New York, NY, 2/20/24. Fashion designer. Gloria Vanderbilt Jeans.
VANIAN, DAVE (David Letts). 10/12/56. Singer. The Damned.
VANNELLI, GINO. Montreal, Canada, 6/16/52. Singer, songwriter. "Living Inside Myself."
VARNEY, JIM. Lexington, KY, 6/15/49. Actor. *Ernest Goes to Camp.*
VAUGHN, ROBERT. New York, NY, 11/22/32. Actor. *The Man from U.N.C.L.E.*
VEE, BOBBY (Robert Velline). Fargo, ND, 4/30/43. Singer, songwriter.
VEGA, SUZANNE. New York, NY, 8/12/59. Folk-oriented guitarist, singer, songwriter. "Luka."
VELEZ, EDDIE (Edwin Velez). New York, NY, 6/4/58. Actor. *Extremities.*
VELJOHNSON, REGINALD. Queens, NY, 8/16/52. Actor. *Family Matters.*
VENDELA (Vendela Kirsebom). Sweden, 1/12/67. Supermodel.
VERDON, GWEN. Culver City, CA, 1/13/25. Actor, dancer, choreographer. *The Cotton Club.*
VEREEN, BEN. Miami, FL, 10/10/46. Actor, performer. Chicken George Moore on *Roots.*
VERLAINE, TOM (Thomas Miller). Mt. Morris, NJ, 12/13/49. Singer, lead guitarist. Television.
VERUSCHKA. 1943. Model, actor. *Blow Up.*
VESTINE, HENRY. Washington, DC, 12/25/44. Guitarist. Canned Heat.
VICKERS, MIKE. Southampton, England, 4/18/41. Guitarist. Manfred Mann.
VIDAL, GORE (Eugene Luther Vidal). West Point, NY, 10/3/25. Author, dramatist. *Lincoln: A Novel.*
VINCENT, JAN-MICHAEL. Denver, CO, 7/15/44. Actor. *The Mechanic.*
VINTON, BOBBY. Canonsburg, PA, 4/16/35. Singer, songwriter.
VIRTUE, MICKEY. Birmingham, England, 1/19/57. Keyboardist. UB40.
VOIGHT, JON. Yonkers, NY, 12/29/38. Actor. *Midnight Cowboy.*
VOLMAN, MARK. Los Angeles, CA, 4/19/47. Singer, saxophonist. The Turtles.
VON BULOW, CLAUS. Copenhagen, Denmark, 8/11/26. Businessman. Subject of the motion picture *Reversal of Fortune.*
VON SYDOW, MAX. Lund, Sweden, 7/10/29. Actor. *The Greatest Story Ever Told.*
VONNEGUT, KURT JR. Indianapolis, IN, 11/11/22. Author. *Slaughterhouse Five.*
WAAKTAAR, PAUL. Oslo, Norway, 9/6/61. Guitarist, singer. a-ha.
WAGGONER, LYLE. Kansas City, KS, 4/13/35. Actor. *Wonder Woman.*
WAGNER, JACK. Washington, MO, 10/3/59. Actor, singer.

Frisco Jones on *General Hospital.*
WAGNER, LINDSAY. Los Angeles, CA, 6/22/49. Actor. *The Bionic Woman.*
WAGNER, ROBERT. Detroit, MI, 2/10/30. Actor, widower of Natalie Wood, married to Jill St. John. Jonathan Hart on *Hart to Hart.*
WAHL, KEN. Chicago, IL, 2/14/56. Actor. Vinnie Terranova on *Wiseguy.*
WAHLBERG, DONNIE. Dorchester, MA, 8/17/70. Singer, brother of Marky Mark. New Kids on the Block.
WAILER, BUNNY (Neville O'Riley Livingston). Kingston, Jamaica, 4/10/47. Singer, percussionist. Bob Marley & The Wailers.
WAITE, JOHN. Lancaster, England, 7/4/54. Singer, songwriter.
WAITS, TOM. Pomona, CA, 12/7/49. Singer, actor, composer. *Short Cuts.*
WALKEN, CHRISTOPHER. Astoria, NY, 3/31/43. Actor. *The Deer Hunter.*
WALKER, ALICE. Eatonton, GA, 2/9/44. Author. *The Color Purple.*
WALKER, CLINT. Hartford, IL, 5/30/27. Actor. *Cheyenne.*
WALKER, DAVID. Montgomeryville, AL, 5/12/43. Keyboardist. Gary Lewis & The Playboys.
WALKER, JIMMIE. New York, NY, 6/25/48. Actor. J. J. Evans on *Good Times.*
WALKER, JUNIOR (Autry DeWalt II). Blytheville, AR, 1942. Saxophonist, singer. Junior Walker & The All-Stars.
WALKER, MORT. El Dorado, KS, 9/3/23. Cartoonist. *Beetle Bailey.*
WALLACE, MIKE (Myron Leon Wallace). Brookline, MA, 5/9/18. News reporter and interviewer, anchor. *60 Minutes.*
WALLACH, ELI. Brooklyn, NY, 12/7/15. Actor. *The Good, the Bad and the Ugly.*
WALLER, GORDON. Braemar, Scotland, 6/4/45. Singer. Peter and Gordon.
WALLER, ROBERT JAMES. Rockford, IA, 8/1/39. Author. *The Bridges of Madison County.*
WALLINGER, KARL. Prestatyn, Wales, 10/19/57. Keyboardist, guitarist. World Party.
WALSH, JOE. Cleveland, OH, 11/20/47. Guitarist, singer. The Eagles; The James Gang.
WALSH, M. EMMET. Ogdensburg, NY, 3/22/35. Actor. *Blood Simple.*
WALSTON, RAY. New Orleans, LA, 11/22/17. Actor. Uncle Martin on *My Favorite Martian.*
WALTER, JESSICA. Brooklyn, NY, 1/31/40. Actor. *Play Misty for Me.*
WALTER, TRACEY. Jersey City, NJ. Actor. Bob the Goon in *Batman.*
WANG, VERA. New York, NY, 1949. Designer.
WARD, BILL. Birmingham, England, 5/5/48. Drummer. Black Sabbath.
WARD, BURT. Los Angeles, CA, 7/6/46. Actor. *Batman.*
WARD, FRED. San Diego, CA, 12/30/42. Actor. *Henry and June.*
WARD, RACHEL. London, England, 1957. Actor. *Against All Odds.*
WARD, SELA. Meridian, MS, 7/11/56. Actor. *Sisters.*
WARDEN, JACK (Jack Warden Lebzelter). Newark, NJ, 9/18/20. Actor. Harry Fox on *Crazy Like a Fox.*
WARE, MARTYN. Sheffield, England, 5/19/56. Synthesizer player. The Human League; Heaven 17.
WARFIELD, MARSHA. Chicago, IL, 3/5/55. Actor. Roz Russell on *Night Court.*
WARNER, DAVID. Manchester, England, 7/29/41. Actor. *The Omen.*
WARNER, JULIE. New York, NY, 1965. Actor. *Doc Hollywood.*
WARNER, MALCOLM-JAMAL. Jersey City, NJ, 8/18/70. Actor. Theo Huxtable on *The Cosby Show.*
WARNES, JENNIFER. Orange County, CA, 1947. Pop singer.
WARREN, LESLEY ANN. New York, NY, 8/16/46. Actor. *Mission: Impossible.*
WARRICK, RUTH. St. Joseph, MO, 6/29/15. Actor. Phoebe Wallingford on *All My Children.*
WARWICK, CLINT (Clinton Eccles). Birmingham, England, 6/25/40. Bassist. The Moody Blues.
WARWICK, DIONNE (Marie Warrick). East Orange, NJ, 12/12/40. Gospel/pop singer.
WATERS, JOHN. Baltimore, MD, 4/22/46. Director, writer, actor. *Hairspray; Pink Flamingos; Serial Mom.*
WATERS, ROGER. Great Bookham, England, 9/9/44. Singer, bassist. Pink Floyd.
WATERSTON, SAM. Cambridge, MA, 11/15/40. Actor. *The Killing Fields.*
WATLEY, JODY. Chicago, IL, 1/30/59. Singer. Shalamar.
WATSON, BRUCE. Ontario, Canada, 3/11/61. Guitarist. Big Country.
WATT, BEN. 12/6/62. Guitarist, keyboardist, singer. Everything but the Girl.
WATTS, CHARLIE. Islington, England, 6/2/41. Drummer. The Rolling Stones.
WATTS, OVEREND (Peter Watts). Birmingham, England, 5/13/49. Bassist. Mott The Hoople.
WAXMAN, AL. Toronto, Canada, 3/2/34. Actor. Bert Samuels on *Cagney and Lacey.*
WAYANS, KEENEN IVORY. New York, NY, 6/8/58. Actor, director, writer. *In Living Color.*
WAYBILL, FEE (John Waldo). Omaha, NE, 9/17/50. Singer. The Tubes.
WAYNE, CARL. Mosely, England, 8/18/44. Singer. The Move.
WAYNE, PATRICK. Los Angeles, CA, 7/15/39. Actor, son of John. *McClintock!*
WEATHERS, CARL. New Orleans, LA, 1/14/48. Actor. Apollo Creed in *Rocky.*
WEAVER, BLUE (Derek Weaver). Cardiff, Wales, 3/3/49. Organist. Amen Corner.
WEAVER, DENNIS. Joplin, MO, 6/4/25. Actor. *McCloud.*
WEAVER, FRITZ. Pittsburgh, PA, 1/19/26. Actor. *Marathon Man.*
WEBB, PAUL. 1/16/62. Bassist. Talk Talk.
WEIDER, JOHN. England, 4/21/47. Bassist. Family.
WEIR, BOB. San Francisco, CA, 10/6/47. Guitarist. Grateful Dead.
WEITZ, BRUCE. Norwalk, CT, 5/27/43. Actor. Mick Belker on *Hill Street Blues.*
WELCH, BRUCE (Bruce Cripps). Bognor Regis, England, 11/2/41. Guitarist. The Shadows.
WELCH, RAQUEL (Raquel Tejada). Chicago, IL, 9/5/40. Actor. *One Million Years B.C.*
WELD, TUESDAY (Susan Weld). New York, NY, 8/27/43. Actor. *Looking for Mr. Goodbar.*
WELLER, PAUL. 5/25/58. Singer, bassist. The Jam.
WELLER, PAUL. Woking, England, 5/25/58. Singer, guitarist. The Style Council.
WELLER, PETER. Stevens Point, WI, 6/24/47. Actor. *Robocop.*
WELLS, CORY. Buffalo, NY, 2/5/42. Singer. Three Dog Night.
WELLS, KITTY (Muriel Deason). Nashville, TN, 8/30/19. Country singer.
WELNICK, VINCE. Phoenix, AZ, 2/21/51. Keyboardist. The Tubes.
WENDT, GEORGE. Chicago, IL, 10/17/48. Actor. Norm Peterson on *Cheers.*
WEST, ADAM (William Anderson). Walla Walla, WA, 9/19/29. Actor. *Batman.*
WEST, JOHN. Uhrichsville, OH, 7/31/39. Guitarist. Gary Lewis & The Playboys.
WEST, RICK. Dagenham, England, 5/7/43. Lead guitarist. Brian Poole & The Tremeloes.
WESTHEIMER, RUTH (Karola Ruth Siegel). Frankfurt, Germany, 6/4/28. Sex therapist. *Ask Dr. Ruth.*

WETTON, JOHN. Derbyshire, England, 7/12/49. Lead singer, bassist. Asia.
WEYMOUTH, TINA. Coronado, CA, 11/22/50. Bassist. Talking Heads.
WHALEY, FRANK. Syracuse, NY, 1963. Actor. *The Doors.*
WHALLEY, JOANNE. Manchester, England, 8/25/64. Actor, formerly married to Val Kilmer. *Willow.*
WHELCHEL, LISA. Fort Worth, TX, 5/29/63. Actor. Blair Warner on *The Facts of Life.*
WHITAKER, FOREST. Longview, TX, 7/15/61. Actor. *The Crying Game.*
WHITAKER, JOHNNY. Van Nuys, CA, 12/13/59. Actor. Jody on *Family Affair.*
WHITE, BARRY. Galveston, TX, 9/12/44. R&B singer, songwriter.
WHITE, BETTY. Oak Park, IL, 1/17/22. Actor. Rose Nylund on *The Golden Girls.*
WHITE, CHRIS. Barnet, England, 3/7/43. Bassist. The Zombies.
WHITE, DAVE (David Tricker). Philadelphia, PA, 9/1/40. Singer. Danny & The Juniors.
WHITE, JALEEL. Los Angeles, CA, 11/27/76. Actor. Steve Urkel on *Family Matters.*
WHITE, MARK. Sheffield, England, 4/1/61. Guitarist. ABC.
WHITE, MAURICE. Memphis, TN, 12/19/41. Singer, drummer, kalimba player. Earth, Wind & Fire.
WHITE, VANNA (Vanna Rosich). North Myrtle Beach, SC, 2/18/57. Letter turner extraordinaire. *Wheel of Fortune.*
WHITE, VERDINE. Illinois, 7/25/51. Singer, bassist. Earth, Wind & Fire.
WHITELAW, BILLIE. Coventry, England, 6/6/32. Actor. *Charlie Bubbles.*
WHITFORD, BRAD. Winchester, MA, 2/23/52. Guitarist. Aerosmith.
WHITMORE, JAMES. White Plains, NY, 10/1/21. Actor. *Will Rogers, USA.*
WHITNEY, CHARLIE. Leicester, England, 6/4/44. Guitarist. Family.
WIEST, DIANNE. Kansas City, MO, 3/28/48. Actor. *Hannah and Her Sisters.*
WILCOX, LARRY. San Diego, CA, 8/8/47. Actor. Officer Jon Baker on *CHiPS.*
WILDE, KIM (Kim Smith). London, England, 11/18/60. Singer, songwriter.
WILDER, ALAN. 6/1/59. Singer, synthesizer player. Depeche Mode.
WILDER, GENE (Jerome Silberman). Milwaukee, WI, 6/11/35. Actor, director, writer, widower of Gilda Radner. *Young Frankenstein.*
WILLIAM, PRINCE. London, England, 6/21/82. British royalty, son of Prince Charles and Princess Diana.
WILLIAMS, ANDY. Wall Lake, IA, 12/3/30. Pop singer. "Where Do I Begin?"
WILLIAMS, BARRY. Santa Monica, CA, 9/30/54. Actor. Greg on *The Brady Bunch.*
WILLIAMS, BILLY DEE. New York, NY, 4/6/37. Actor. *Lady Sings the Blues.*
WILLIAMS, CINDY. Van Nuys, CA, 8/22/47. Actor. Shirley Feeney on *Laverne & Shirley.*
WILLIAMS, CLARENCE III. New York, NY, 8/21/39. Actor. Lincoln Hayes on *The Mod Squad.*
WILLIAMS, CLIFF. Rumford, England, 12/14/29. Bass guitarist. AC/DC.
WILLIAMS, DENIECE (Deniece Chandler). Gary, IN, 6/3/51. Gospel/pop singer.
WILLIAMS, ESTHER. Los Angeles, CA, 8/8/23. Actor, swimmer, widow of Fernando Lamas. *Bathing Beauty.*
WILLIAMS, HANK JR (Randall Hank). Shreveport, LA, 5/26/49. Country singer, songwriter. "Texas Women."
WILLIAMS, JOBETH. Houston, TX, 1953. Actor. *The Big Chill.*
WILLIAMS, JOHN TOWNER. Queens, NY, 2/8/32. Composer, conductor. *Jaws; Star Wars.*
WILLIAMS, MAISIE. Montserrat, West Indies, 3/25/51. Singer. Boney M.
WILLIAMS, MILAN. Mississippi, 3/28/48. Keyboardist, trombonist, guitarist, drummer. The Commodores.
WILLIAMS, MONTEL. Baltimore, MD, 7/3/56. Talk show host. *The Montel Williams Show.*
WILLIAMS, OTIS (Otis Miles). Texarkana, TX, 10/30/49. Singer. The Temptations.
WILLIAMS, PAUL. Birmingham, AL, 7/2/39. Singer. The Temptations.
WILLIAMS, TREAT (Richard Williams). Rowayton, CT, 12/1/51. Actor. *Prince of the City.*
WILLIAMS, WALTER. 8/25/42. Singer. The O'Jays.
WILLIAMS, WENDY O. (Wendy Orlean Williams). Rochester, NY, 1946. Entertainer, singer.
WILLIAMSON, NICOL. Hamilton, Scotland, 9/14/38. Actor. *Excalibur.*
WILLIG, GEORGE. New York, NY, 6/11/49. Actor, stuntman. Climbed World Trade Center.
WILSON, AL "BLIND OWL." Boston, MA, 7/4/43. Guitarist, singer, harmonicist. Canned Heat.
WILSON, ANN. San Diego, CA, 6/19/51. Lead singer. Heart.
WILSON, BARRY J. London, England, 3/18/47. Drummer. Procol Harum.
WILSON, BRIAN. Inglewood, CA, 6/20/42. Bassist, keyboardist, singer, father of Wendy and Carnie. The Beach Boys.
WILSON, CARL. Hawthorne, CA, 12/21/46. Guitarist, singer. The Beach Boys.
WILSON, CARNIE. Los Angeles, CA, 4/29/68. Singer, daughter of Brian, sister of Wendy. Wilson Phillips.
WILSON, CASSANDRA. Jackson, MS, 1955. Jazz singer.
WILSON, CINDY. Athens, GA, 2/28/57. Guitarist, singer. The B-52's.
WILSON, DEMOND. Valdosta, GA, 10/13/46. Actor. *Sanford and Son.*
WILSON, DON. Tacoma, WA, 2/10/37. Guitarist. The Ventures.
WILSON, FLIP (Clerow Wilson). Jersey City, NJ, 12/8/33. Actor. *The Flip Wilson Show.*
WILSON, JOYCE. Detroit, MI, 12/14/46. Singer. Tony Orlando & Dawn.
WILSON, MARY. Greenville, MS, 3/6/44. Singer. The Supremes.
WILSON, NANCY. Chillicothe, OH, 2/20/37. R&B singer.
WILSON, NANCY. San Francisco, CA, 3/16/54. Guitarist, singer. Heart.
WILSON, TOM. Grant Town, WV, 8/1/31. Cartoonist. *Ziggy.*
WILSON, TONY. Trinidad, 10/8/47. Bassist, singer. Hot Chocolate.
WILSON, WENDY. Los Angeles, CA, 10/16/69. Singer, sister of Carnie, daughter of Brian. Wilson Phillips.
WINCHELL, PAUL. New York, NY, 12/21/22. Ventriloquist, actor. *The Paul Winchell-Jerry Mahoney Show.*
WINDOM, WILLIAM. New York, NY, 9/28/23. Actor. *Murder She Wrote.*
WINFIELD, DAVE. Saint Paul, MN, 10/3/51. Baseball player.
WINFIELD, PAUL. Los Angeles, CA, 5/22/40. Actor. *Sounder.*
WINGER, DEBRA (Mary Debra Winger). Cleveland, OH, 5/17/55. Actor. *Terms of Endearment.*
WINKLER, HENRY. New York, NY, 10/30/45. Actor, producer, director. Arthur "The Fonz" Fonzarelli on *Happy Days.*
WINNINGHAM, MARE. Phoenix, AZ, 5/6/59. Actor. *St. Elmo's Fire.*
WINSTON, JIMMY (James Langwith). London, England, 4/20/45. Organist. The Small Faces.
WINTER, EDGAR. Beaumont, TX, 12/28/46. Blues/rock keyboardist, brother of Johnny.
WINTER, JOHNNY. Beaumont, TX, 2/23/44. Blues/rock guitarist, brother of Edgar.

WINTERS, JONATHAN. Dayton, OH, 11/11/25. Actor. *The Jonathan Winters Show.*
WINTERS, SHELLEY (Shirley Schrift). St. Louis, MO, 8/18/22. Actor. *The Poseidon Adventure.*
WINWOOD, MUFF (Mervyn Winwood). Birmingham, England, 6/14/43. Singer, songwriter, bassist. The Spencer Davis Group.
WINWOOD, STEVE. Birmingham, England, 5/12/48. Singer, songwriter. The Spencer Davis Group; Traffic; Blind Faith.
WITHERS, BILL. Slab Fork, WV, 7/4/38. Pop singer, songwriter, guitarist.
WITHERS, JANE. Atlanta, GA, 4/12/26. Actor. Josephine the Plumber on TV commercials.
WOLF, PETER (Peter Blankfield). New York, NY, 3/7/46. Singer. The J. Geils Band.
WOLTERS, JOHN. 4/28/45. Drummer, singer. Dr. Hook.
WOMACK, BOBBY. Cleveland, OH, 3/4/44. Gospel/R&B singer, songwriter, guitarist.
WONDER, STEVIE (Steveland Morris). Saginaw, MI, 5/13/50. Singer, songwriter, formerly married to Syreeta Wright.
WONG, B. D. San Francisco, CA, 10/24/62. Actor. *M. Butterfly.*
WOOD, DANNY. Boston, MA, 5/14/71. Singer. New Kids on the Block.
WOOD, RON. London, England, 6/1/47. Guitarist. The Rolling Stones.
WOOD, ROY (Ulysses Adrian Wood). Birmingham, England, 11/8/46. Singer, guitarist, cellist. Electric Light Orchestra (ELO); Wizzard; The Move.
WOOD, STUART. Edinburgh, Scotland, 2/25/57. Guitarist. The Bay City Rollers.
WOODARD, ALFRE. Tulsa, OK, 11/8/53. Actor. *Cross Creek.*
WOODS, JAMES. Vernal, UT, 4/18/47. Actor. *Salvador.*
WOODWARD, EDWARD. Croydon, England, 6/1/30. Actor. *The Equalizer.*
WOODWARD, JOANNE. Thomasville, GA, 2/27/30. Actor, married to Paul Newman. *The Three Faces of Eve.*
WOODWARD, KEREN. Bristol, England, 4/2/61. Singer. Bananarama.
WORLEY, JO ANNE. Lowell, IN, 9/6/37. Actor, singer. *Laugh-In.*
WRAY, FAY. Alberta, Canada, 9/10/07. Actor. *King Kong.*
WRIGHT, ADRIAN. Sheffield, England, 6/30/56. Projector operator for on-stage slides and films. The Human League.
WRIGHT, LITTLE STEVIE. Leeds, England, 12/20/48. Singer. The Easybeats.
WRIGHT, MAX. Detroit, MI, 8/2/43. Actor. Willie Tanner on *ALF.*
WRIGHT, PAT. Brooklyn, NY, 1945. Singer. The Crystals.
WRIGHT, RICK. London, England, 7/28/45. Keyboardist. Pink Floyd.
WRIGHT, STEVEN.Burlington, MA, 12/6/55. Comedian.
WRIGHT, SYREETA. Pittsburgh, PA, 1946. Singer, songwriter, formerly married to Stevie Wonder.
WUHL, ROBERT. Union City, NJ, 10/9/51. Actor, writer. *Bull Durham.*
WYATT, JANE. Campgaw, NJ, 8/13/12. Actor. *Father Knows Best.*
WYMAN, BILL (William Perks). London, England, 10/24/36. Bassist. The Rolling Stones.
WYMAN, JANE (Sarah Jane Fulks). St. Joseph, MO, 1/4/14. Actor, formerly married to Ronald Reagan. Angela Channing on *Falcon Crest.*
WYNETTE, TAMMY (Virginia Wynette Pugh). Itawamba County, MS, 5/5/42. Country singer. "Stand by Your Man."
YAMAGUCHI, KRISTI. Hayward, CA, 7/12/71. Skater, Olympic gold medalist.
YANKOVIC, WEIRD AL (Alfred Matthew Yankovic). Los Angeles, CA, 10/23/59. Singer, spoof artist. "Like a Surgeon."
YANOVSKY, ZAL. Toronto, Canada, 12/19/44. Guitarist, singer. The Lovin' Spoonful.
YARROW, PETER. New York, NY, 5/31/38. Composer, author, singer. Peter, Paul and Mary.
YEARWOOD, TRISHA. Monticello, GA, 9/19/64. Singer.
YELTSIN, BORIS. Burka, Russia, 2/1/31. Russian political leader.
YESTER, JIM. Birmingham, AL, 11/24/39. Singer, guitarist. The Association.
YOAKAM, DWIGHT. Pikesville, KY, 10/23/56. Country singer. "Honky Tonk Man."
YORK, MICHAEL. Fulmer, England, 3/27/42. Actor. *Logan's Run.*
YORK, PETE. Redcar, England, 8/15/42. Drummer. The Spencer Davis Group.
YOUNG, ANGUS. Glasgow, Scotland, 3/31/59. Guitarist. AC/DC.
YOUNG, GEORGE. Glasgow, Scotland, 11/6/47. Guitarist. The Easybeats.
YOUNG, JAMES. Chicago, IL, 11/14/48. Guitarist. Styx.
YOUNG, JESSE COLIN (Perry Miller). New York, NY, 11/11/41. Guitarist, bassist, singer. The Youngbloods.
YOUNG, LORETTA (Gretchen Young). Salt Lake City, UT, 1/6/13. Actor. *The Farmer's Daughter.*
YOUNG, MALCOLM. Glasgow, Scotland, 1/6/53. Guitarist. AC/DC.
YOUNG, NEIL. Toronto, Canada, 11/12/45. Singer, songwriter, guitarist. Buffalo Springfield; Crosby, Stills, Nash & Young.
YOUNG, PAUL. Luton, England, 1/17/56. Singer, songwriter.
YOUNG, ROBERT. Chicago, IL, 2/22/07. Actor. *Marcus Welby, M.D.*
YOUNG, RUSTY. Long Beach, CA, 2/23/46. Pedal steel guitarist. Poco.
YOUNG, SEAN. Louisville, KY, 11/20/59. Actor. *No Way Out.*
YOUNG MC (Marvin Young). London, England, 1968. Rap artist.
YOUNGMAN, HENNY (Henry Youngman). Liverpool, England, 1/12/06. Actor. "Take my wife... please!"
ZADORA, PIA. New York, NY, 5/4/56. Actor. *Naked Gun 33 1/3.*
ZAHN, PAULA. Naperville, IL, 2/24/56. Broadcast journalist. *CBS This Morning.*
ZAL, ROXANA. Los Angeles, CA, 11/8/69. Actor. *Something About Amelia.*
ZANDER, ROBIN. Rockford, IL, 1/23/53. Singer, guitarist. Cheap Trick.
ZAPPA, DWEEZIL. Los Angeles, CA, 9/5/69. Guitarist, son of Frank, brother of Moon Unit. MTV.
ZAPPA, MOON UNIT. Hollywood, CA, 9/28/68. Singer, daughter of Frank, sister of Dweezil. "Valley Girl."
ZEVON, WARREN. Chicago, IL, 1/24/47. Singer, songwriter. "Werewolves of London."
ZIERING, IAN. 4/30/64. Actor. *Beverly Hills 90210.*
ZIMBALIST, STEPHANIE. Encino, CA, 10/8/56. Actor, daughter of Efrem. Laura Holt on *Remington Steele.*
ZMED, ADRIAN. Chicago, IL, 3/4/54. Actor. Vince Romano on *T. J. Hooker.*
ZUNIGA, DAPHNE. Berkeley, CA, 1962. Actor. *Melrose Place.*

HAPPY BIRTHDAY! THE GREATS' NATAL DATES

JANUARY 1
Idi Amin
Frank Langella
Don Novello
J.D. Salinger

JANUARY 2
Jim Bakker
Gabrielle Carteris
Chick Churchill
Cuba Gooding Jr.
Joanna Pacula

JANUARY 3
Melody Anderson
Dabney Coleman
Mel Gibson
Robert Loggia
Victoria Principal
Stephen Stills
Bill Travers

JANUARY 4
Bernie Albrecht
Dyan Cannon
Matt Frewer
Ann Magnuson
Michael Stipe
Barney Sumner
Jane Wyman

JANUARY 5
Suzy Amis
George Brown
Robert Duvall
Diane Keaton
Ted Lange
Walter Mondale
Chris Stein

JANUARY 6
Syd Barrett
Mark O'Toole
John Singleton
Kathy Sledge
Loretta Young
Malcolm Young

JANUARY 7
Nicolas Cage
Katie Couric
Kenny Loggins
Maury Povich
Paul Revere

JANUARY 8
David Bowie
Stephen Hawking
Robbie Krieger
Yvette Mimieux
Charles Osgood
Soupy Sales
Larry Storch

JANUARY 9
Joan Baez
Bill Cowsill
Bob Denver
Scott Engel
Crystal Gayle
David Johansen
Judith Krantz
Herbert Lom
Jimmy Page

JANUARY 10
Trini Alvarado
Pat Benatar
Donald Fagen
George Foreman
Bob Lang
Cyril Neville
Maurice Sendak
Rod Stewart

JANUARY 11
Mary J. Blige
Naomi Judd
Vicki Peterson
Rod Taylor

JANUARY 12
Kirstie Alley
Anthony Andrews
Per Gessle
William Lee Golden
Cynthia Robinson
Vendela
Henny Youngman

JANUARY 13
Kevin Anderson
Patrick Dempsey
Robert "Squirrel" Lester
Julia Louis-Dreyfus
Graham McPherson
Penelope Ann Miller
Richard Moll
Robert Stack
Frances Sternhagen
Gwen Verdon

JANUARY 14
Jason Bateman
Faye Dunaway
L.L. Cool J
Andy Rooney
Carl Weathers

JANUARY 15
Captain Beefheart
Lloyd Bridges
Charo
Martha Davis
Chad Lowe
Andrea Martin
Pamela Sue Martin
Julian Sands
Peter Trewavas
Mario Van Peebles

JANUARY 16
Debbie Allen
Bob Bogle
John Carpenter
Bill Francis
Kate Moss
Sade
Jim Stafford
Paul Webb

JANUARY 17
Muhammad Ali
Jim Carrey
David Caruso
John Crawford
Steve Earle
Joe Frazier
Susanna Hoffs
James Earl Jones
Vidal Sassoon
Betty White
Paul Young

JANUARY 18
Kevin Costner
David Ruffin
Larry Smith

JANUARY 19
Desi Arnaz Jr.
Dewey Bunnell
Michael Crawford
Phil Everly
Shelley Fabares
Tippi Hedren
Harvey Hinsley
Robert MacNeil
Robert Palmer
Dolly Parton
Jean Stapleton
Mickey Virtue
Fritz Weaver

JANUARY 20
Buzz Aldrin
Arte Johnson
DeForest Kelley
Lorenzo Lamas
David Lynch
Bill Maher
John Michael Montgomery
Patricia Neal
Paul Stanley
Eric Stewart
Ron Townson

JANUARY 21
Robby Benson
Geena Davis
Mac Davis
Jill Eikenberry
Richie Havens
Billy Ocean
Steve Reeves

JANUARY 22
Linda Blair
Balthazar Getty
John Hurt
Michael Hutchence
Diane Lane
Piper Laurie
Chris Lemmon
Steve Perry
Jeff Smith
Ann Sothern

JANUARY 23
Richard Dean Anderson
Princess Caroline
Bill Cunningham
Earl Falconer
Gil Gerard
Rutger Hauer
Jeanne Moreau
Anita Pointer
Chita Rivera
Patrick Simmons
Robin Zander

JANUARY 24
Ernest Borgnine
Neil Diamond
Jools Holland
Nastassja Kinski
Michael Ontkean
Oral Roberts
Yakov Smirnoff
Ray Stevens
Warren Zevon

JANUARY 25
Corazon Aquino
Andy Cox
Richard Finch
Etta James
Dean Jones
Dinah Manoff

JANUARY 26
Jazzie B
David Briggs
Scott Glenn
Wayne Gretsky
Eartha Kitt
Paul Newman
Andrew Ridgeley
Gene Siskel
Bob Uecker
Roger Vadim
Eddie Van Halen

JANUARY 27
Mikhail Baryshnikov
Bobby Bland
Troy Donahue
Brian Downey
Bridget Fonda
Gillian Gilbert
Seth Justman
Nick Mason
Mike Patton
Mimi Rogers
Nedra Talley

JANUARY 28
Alan Alda
John Beck
Brian Keenan
Marthe Keller
Nicholas Pryor
Dave Sharp
Dick Taylor
Elijah Wood

JANUARY 29
David Byron
Ed Burns
John Forsythe
Roddy Frame
Sara Gilbert
Noel Harrison
Eddie Jackson
Anne Jillian
Greg Louganis
Victor Mature
Tommy Ramone
Katharine Ross
Tom Selleck
Oprah Winfrey

JANUARY 30
Marty Balin
Phil Collins
Charles Dutton
Gene Hackman
William King
Dorothy Malone
Steve Marriott
Dick Martin
Vanessa Redgrave
Joe Terranova
Jody Watley

JANUARY 31
John Agar
Harry Wayne Casey
Carol Channing
Lloyd Cole
John Paul Jones
Terry Kath
John Lydon
Phil Manzanera
Suzanne Pleshette
Jean Simmons
Jessica Walter

FEBRUARY 1
Mike Campbell

Don Everly
Dennis Farina
Sherilynn Fenn
Sherman Hemsley
Rick James
Terry Jones
Billy Mumy
Lisa Marie Presley-Jackson
Ray Sawyer
Boris Yeltsin

FEBRUARY 2

Christie Brinkley
Garth Brooks
Alan Caddy
Farrah Fawcett
Gale Gordon
Peter Lucia
Graham Nash
Liz Smith
Tom Smothers
Elaine Stritch
Ross Valory

FEBRUARY 3

Joey Bishop
Thomas Calabro
Angelo D'Aleo
Blythe Danner
Dave Davies
Morgan Fairchild
Eric Haydock
Nathan Lane
Fran Tarkenton
Lol Tolhurst

FEBRUARY 4

Gabrielle Anwar
Michael Beck
Clint Black
David Brenner
Alice Cooper
Florence LaRue
Dan Quayle
John Steel

FEBRUARY 5

Bobby Brown
Red Buttons
Christopher Guest
Barbara Hershey
Jennifer Jason Leigh
Charlotte Rampling
Roger Staubach
Cory Wells

FEBRUARY 6

Rick Astley
Tom Brokaw
Natalie Cole
Fabian
Mike Farrell
Zsa Zsa Gabor
Alan Jones
Patrick Macnee
Ronald Reagan
Rip Torn
Robert Townsend
Michael Tucker
Mamie Van Doren

FEBRUARY 7

David Bryan
Miguel Ferrer
Jimmy Greenspoon
Alan Lancaster
Chris Rock
James Spader
Brian Travers

FEBRUARY 8

Brooke Adams
Brian Bennett
Creed Bratton
Gary Coleman
John Grisham
Robert Klein
Ted Koppel
Jack Lemmon
Vince Neil
Nick Nolte
Mary Steenburgen
John Williams

FEBRUARY 9

Mia Farrow
Carole King
Judith Light
Roger Mudd
Joe Pesci
Janet Suzman
Travis Tritt
Alice Walker

FEBRUARY 10

Laura Dern
Donovan
Roberta Flack
Jimmy Merchant
Mark Spitz
Robert Wagner
Don Wilson

FEBRUARY 11

Jennifer Aniston
Brandy
Sheryl Crow
Conrad Janis
Tina Louise
Leslie Nielsen
Burt Reynolds
Sidney Sheldon

FEBRUARY 12

Maud Adams
Joe Don Baker
Judy Blume
Cliff DeYoung
Arsenio Hall
Joanna Kerns
Simon MacCorkindale
Ray Manzarek
Joe Schermie

FEBRUARY 13

Tony Butler
Stockard Channing
Roger Christian
Peter Hook
David Naughton
Kim Novak
Oliver Reed
George Segal
Bo Svenson
Peter Tork

FEBRUARY 14

Hugh Downs
Roger Fisher
Florence Henderson
Gregory Hines
Meg Tilly
Paul Tsongas
Ken Wahl

FEBRUARY 15

Mick Avory
Marisa Berenson
Claire Bloom
David Brown
Ali Campbell
Mikey Craig
Matt Groening
John Helliwell
Harvey Korman
Kevin McCarthy
Jane Seymour

FEBRUARY 16

Sonny Bono
LeVar Burton
James Ingram
William Katt
John McEnroe Jr.
Andy Taylor

FEBRUARY 17

Billie Joe Armstrong
Alan Bates
Jim Brown
Brenda Fricker
Hal Holbrook
Michael Jordan
Lou Diamond Phillips
Gene Pitney
Rene Russo
Raf Vallone

FEBRUARY 18

Robbie Bachman
Randy Crawford
Sinead Cusack
Dennis DeYoung
Matt Dillon
George Kennedy
Toni Morrison
Juice Newton
Jack Palance
Molly Ringwald
Herman Santiago
Greta Scacchi
Cybill Shepherd
John Travolta
Vanna White

FEBRUARY 19

Mark Andes
Justine Bateman
Francis Buchholz
Lou Christie
Jeff Daniels
Falco
Tony Iommi
Holly Johnson
Smokey Robinson
Seal

FEBRUARY 20

Edward Albert
Robert Altman
Charles Barkley
Walter Becker
Ian Brown
Randy California
Cindy Crawford
Sandy Duncan
J. Geils
Kelsey Grammer
Jennifer O'Neill
Sidney Poitier
Andrew Shue
Peter Strauss
Gloria Vanderbilt
Nancy Wilson

FEBRUARY 21

Christopher Atkins
Jean-Jacques Burnel
Mary Chapin Carpenter
Tyne Daly
David Geffen
Jerry Harrison
Gary Lockwood
Rue McClanahan
Nina Simone
Vince Welnick

FEBRUARY 22

Drew Barrymore
Jonathan Demme
Julius Erving
Ted Kennedy
Kyle MacLachlan
John Mills
Miou-Miou
Robert Young

FEBRUARY 23

Peter Fonda
Howard Jones
Mike Maxfield
Steve Priest
David Sylvian
Brad Whitford
Johnny Winter
Rusty Young

FEBRUARY 24

Barry Bostwick
James Farentino
Steven Hill
Paul Jones
Edward James Olmos
Helen Shaver
Lonnie Turner
Paula Zahn

FEBRUARY 25

Sean Astin
George Harrison
Téa Leoni
Mike Peters
Sally Jessy Raphael
Bobby Riggs
Stuart Wood

FEBRUARY 26

Michael Bolton
Jonathan Cain
Johnny Cash
Fats Domino
John Jon
Tony Randall
Mitch Ryder
Sandie Shaw

FEBRUARY 27

Adam Baldwin
Garry Christian
Chelsea Clinton
Eddie Gray
Steve Harley
Howard Hesseman
Paul Humphreys
Ralph Nader
Neal Schon
Grant Show
Adrian Smith
Elizabeth Taylor
Joanne Woodward

FEBRUARY 28

Mario Andretti
Stephanie Beacham
Frank Bonner
Charles Durning
Phil Gould
Robert Sean Leonard
Gavin MacLeod
Bernadette Peters
Mercedes Ruehl
Bubba Smith
Joe South
Tommy Tune
John Turturro
Cindy Wilson

MARCH 1

Harry Belafonte
Dirk Benedict
Roger Daltrey
Timothy Daly
Jimmy Fortune
Ron Howard
Alan Thicke

MARCH 2

John Cowsill
John Cullum
Mark Evans

John Irving
Jennifer Jones
Eddie Money
Jay Osmond
Lou Reed
Al Waxman

MARCH 3
Willie Chambers
Jance Garfat
Jackie Joyner-Kersee
Tim Kazurinsky
Dave Mount
Mike Pender
Miranda Richardson
Tone-Loc
Blue Weaver

MARCH 4
Chastity Bono
Harry Helmsley
Patsy Kensit
Catherine O'Hara
Paula Prentiss
Chris Rea
Chris Squire
Shakin' Stevens
Bobby Womack
Adrian Zmed

MARCH 5
Alan Clark
Samantha Eggar
Eddy Grant
James B. Sikking
Dean Stockwell
Marsha Warfield

MARCH 6
Tom Arnold
Marion Barry
Kiki Dee
David Gilmour
Hugh Grundy
Ed McMahon
Shaquille O'Neal
Rob Reiner
Mary Wilson

MARCH 7
Tammy Faye Bakker
Paul Davis
Matthew Fisher
John Heard
Willard Scott
Lynn Swann
Daniel J. Travanti
Chris White
Peter Wolf

MARCH 8
Mike Allsup
Cheryl Baker
Clive Burr
Cyd Charisse
Mickey Dolenz
Ralph Ellis
Peter Gill
Randy Meisner
Gary Numan
Aidan Quinn
Lynn Redgrave
Claire Trevor

MARCH 9
Juliette Binoche
Trevor Burton
Jim Cregan
Linda Fiorentino
Martin Fry
Marty Ingels
Emmanuel Lewis
Mark Lindsey
Jeffrey Osborne
Mickey Spillane
Robin Trower
Trish Van Devere

MARCH 10
Neneh Cherry
Prince Edward
Jasmine Guy
Chuck Norris
James Earl Ray
Tom Scholz
Sharon Stone
Dean Torrence

MARCH 11
Douglas Adams
Sam Donaldson
Bobby McFerrin
Susan Richardson
Ric Rothwell
Mark Stein
Bruce Watson

MARCH 12
Barbara Feldon
Mike Gibbins
Marlon Jackson
Al Jarreau
Paul Kantner
Liza Minnelli
Brian O'Hara
Bill Payne
James Taylor

MARCH 13
Adam Clayton
Dana Delany
Glenne Headly
Deborah Raffin
Neil Sedaka

MARCH 14
Michael Caine
Billy Crystal
Megan Follows
Boon Gould
Quincy Jones
Walter Parazaider

MARCH 15
Ry Cooder
David Costell
Terence Trent D'Arby
Fabio
Judd Hirsch
Phil Lesh
Mike Love
Bret Michaels
Rockwell
Howard Scott
Sly Stone
Jimmy Lee Swaggart

MARCH 16
Michael Bruce
Erik Estrada
Isabelle Huppert
Jerry Lewis
Kate Nelligan
Nancy Wilson

MARCH 17
Harold Brown
Lesley-Anne Down
Patrick Duffy
Scott Gorham
Mike Lindup
Rob Lowe
Patrick McCauley
Kurt Russell
John Sebastian

MARCH 18
Bonnie Blair
Irene Cara
Kevin Dobson
Peter Graves
John Hartman
Wilson Pickett
Charley Pride
John Updike
Vanessa Williams
Barry J. Wilson

MARCH 19
Ursula Andress
Paul Atkinson
Glenn Close
Terry Hall
Clarence Henry
Derek Longmuir
Ruth Pointer
Bruce Willis

MARCH 20
John Clark Gable
Holly Hunter
William Hurt
Spike Lee
Hal Linden
Carl Palmer
Slim Jim Phantom
Carl Reiner
Mr. Rogers
Theresa Russell

MARCH 21
Matthew Broderick
Timothy Dalton
Cynthia Geary
Roger Hodgson
Gary Oldman
Rosie Stone
Russell Thompkins Jr.

MARCH 22
George Benson
Jeremy Clyde
Randy Hobbs
Werner Klemperer
Andrew Lloyd Webber
Karl Malden
Marcel Marceau
Stephanie Mills
Matthew Modine
Lena Olin
Pat Robertson
William Shatner
Harry Vanda
M. Emmet Walsh

MARCH 23
Princess Eugenie
Chaka Khan
Ric Ocasek
Marti Pellow
Amanda Plummer

MARCH 24
Lara Flynn Boyle
Robert Carradine
Norman Fell
Lee Oskar
Donna Pescow
Dougie Thomson

MARCH 25
Hoyt Axton
Bonnie Bedelia
Aretha Franklin
Paul Michael Glaser
Mary Gross
Jeff Healey
Elton John
Neil Jones
Sarah Jessica Parker
Gloria Steinem
John Stockwell
Maisie Williams

MARCH 26
Alan Arkin
James Caan
Leeza Gibbons
Jennifer Grey
Vicki Lawrence
Leonard Nimoy
Teddy Pendergrass
Diana Ross
Fran Sheehan
Martin Short
Curtis Sliwa
Richard Tandy
Steven Tyler

MARCH 27
Tony Banks
Mariah Carey
Judy Carne
Andrew Farriss
Austin Pendleton
Maria Schneider
Tom Sullivan
Quentin Tarantino
Michael York

MARCH 28
Dirk Bogarde
Ken Howard
Lucy Lawless
Reba McEntire
Chuck Portz
Salt
Dianne Wiest
Milan Williams

MARCH 29
Jennifer Capriati
Bud Cort
Hammer
Eric Idle
Bobby Kimball
Christopher Lambert

MARCH 30
John Astin
Warren Beatty
Tracy Chapman
Eric Clapton
Richard Dysart
Graeme Edge
Peter Marshall
Paul Reiser

MARCH 31
Rod Allen
Herb Alpert
Richard Chamberlain
Liz Claiborne
William Daniels
Albert Gore
Sean Hopper
Shirley Jones
Ewen McGregor
Ed Marinaro
Al Nichol
Rhea Perlman
Mick Ralphs
Christopher Walken
Angus Young

APRIL 1
John Barbata
Alan Blakley
Billy Currie
Rudolph Isley
Gordon Jump
Ali MacGraw
Phil Margo
Toshiro Mifune
Annette O'Toole
Debbie Reynolds
Mark White

APRIL 2
Dana Carvey
Glen Dale
Buddy Ebsen

Mikhail Gorbachev
Alec Guinness
Linda Hunt
Pamela Reed
Leon Russell
Keren Woodward

APRIL 3
Alec Baldwin
Jan Berry
Marlon Brando
Doris Day
Jennie Garth
Jane Goodall
Marsha Mason
Eddie Murphy
Wayne Newton
Tony Orlando
Barry Pritchard
Mel Schacher

APRIL 4
Maya Angelou
Robert Downey Jr.
Steve Gatlin
Dave Hill
Kitty Kelley
Graeme Kelling
Christine Lahti
Mick Mars
Nancy McKeon
Craig T. Nelson
Berry Oakley

APRIL 5
Allan Clarke
Agnetha Faltskog
Maxwell Gail
Frank Gorshin
Peter Greenaway
Mike McCready
Michael Moriarty
Gregory Peck
Colin Powell
Gale Storm

APRIL 6
Stan Cullimore
Marilu Henner
Jason Hervey
Ari Meyers
John Ratzenberger
John Stax
Billy Dee Williams

APRIL 7
Mick Abrahams
Patricia Bennett
Jackie Chan
Francis Ford Coppola
Buster Douglas
Spencer Dryden
James Garner
Bruce Gary
Janis Ian
Elaine Miles
John Oates
Wayne Rogers

APRIL 8
Patricia Arquette
Roger Chapman
Steve Howe
Julian Lennon

APRIL 9
Jean-Paul Belmondo
Les Gray
Hugh Hefner
Mark Kelly
Michael Learned
Carl Perkins
Dennis Quaid

APRIL 10
Peter MacNicol
John Madden
Steven Seagal
Brian Setzer
Omar Sharif
Bobbie Smith
Bunny Wailer

APRIL 11
Stuart Adamson
Joel Grey
Bill Irwin
Louise Lasser
Delroy Pearson
Peter Riegert
Richie Sambora
Lisa Stansfield
Neville Staples

APRIL 12
Alex Briley
David Cassidy
Claire Danes
Shannen Doherty
Andy Garcia
Vince Gill
Herbie Hancock
John Kay
David Letterman
Ann Miller
Ed O'Neill
Will Sergeant
Scott Turow
Jane Withers

APRIL 13
Peabo Bryson
Jack Casady
Lester Chambers
Jimmy Destri
Tony Dow
Al Green
Garry Kasparov
Howard Keel
Jane Leeves
Brian Pendleton
Ron Perlman
Rick Schroder
Paul Sorvino
Lyle Waggoner

APRIL 14
Ritchie Blackmore
Dennis Bryon
Julie Christie
Larry Ferguson
Anthony Michael Hall
Buddy Knox
Jay Robinson
Pete Rose
John Shea
Rod Steiger

APRIL 15
Claudia Cardinale
Graeme Clark
Roy Clark
Samantha Fox
Emma Thompson

APRIL 16
Edie Adams
Ellen Barkin
Jon Cryer
Lukas Haas
Gerry Rafferty
Bill Spooner
Dusty Springfield
Bobby Vinton

APRIL 17
Boomer Esiason
Liz Phair
Pete Shelley
Stephen Singleton

APRIL 18
Barbara Hale
Melissa Joan Hart
Hayley Mills
Rick Moranis
Conan O'Brien
Les Pattinson
Eric Roberts
Alexander Spence
Mike Vickers
James Woods

APRIL 19
Don Adams
Tim Curry
Dudley Moore
Alan Price
Larry Ramos Jr.
Mark Volman

APRIL 20
Craig Frost
Jessica Lange
Joey Lawrence
Ryan O'Neal
George Takei
Luther Vandross
Jimmy Winston

APRIL 21
Paul Carrack
Tony Danza
Queen Elizabeth II
Charles Grodin
Patti LuPone
Andie MacDowell
Elaine May
Iggy Pop
Anthony Quinn
Robert Smith
John Weider

APRIL 22
Eddie Albert
Joseph Bottoms
Glen Campbell
Peter Kenneth Frampton
Ace Frehley
Chris Makepeace
Jack Nicholson
Aaron Spelling
John Waters

APRIL 23
Valerie Bertinelli
David Birney
Steve Clark
Sandra Dee
Jan Hooks
Lee Majors
Alan Oppenheimer
Captain Sensible

APRIL 24
Eric Bogosian
Doug Clifford
Glenn Cornick
Billy Gould
Shirley MacLaine
Paul Ryder
Richard Sterban
Barbra Streisand

APRIL 25
Andy Bell
Michael Brown
Stu Cook
Meadowlark Lemon
Paul Mazursky
Al Pacino
Talia Shire
Bjorn Ulvaeus

APRIL 26
Carol Burnett
Duane Eddy
Giancarlo Esposito

APRIL 27
Anouk Aimee
Sheena Easton
Pete Ham
Coretta Scott King
Jack Klugman
Kate Pierson
Marco Pirroni
Clive Taylor

APRIL 28
Ann-Margret
Saddam Hussein
Bruno Kirby
Jay Leno
Marcia Strassman
John Wolters

APRIL 29
Andre Agassi
Duane Allen
Stephen Arenholz
Keith Baxter
Daniel Day-Lewis
Lonnie Donegan
Carl Gardner
Celeste Holm
Tommy James
Rod McKuen
Zubin Mehta
Kate Mulgrew
Michelle Pfeiffer
Chynna Phillips
Eve Plumb
Francis Rossi
Jerry Seinfeld
Uma Thurman
Carnie Wilson

APRIL 30
Turbo B
Jill Clayburgh
Gary Collins
Perry King
Cloris Leachman
Al Lewis
Willie Nelson
Merrill Osmond
Bobby Vee
Ian Ziering

MAY 1
Judy Collins
Johnny Colt
Steve Farris
Nick Fortune
Bobcat Goldthwait
Joseph Heller
Tim McGraw
Ray Parker Jr.
Phil Smith

MAY 2
Christine Baranski
Jon Bon Jovi
Lesley Gore
Lou Gramm
Engelbert Humperdinck
Bianca Jagger
Goldy McJohn
Lorenzo Music
Benjamin Spock

MAY 3
David Ball
James Brown
Christopher Cross
Bruce Hall
Doug Henning
Mary Hopkin
Pete Seeger
Pete Staples
Frankie Valli
Wynonna

MAY 4
Nickolas Ashford
Jay Aston
Ronnie Bond

Ed Cassidy
Jackie Jackson
Randy Travis
Pia Zadora

MAY 5
Gary Daly
Lance Henriksen
Ian McCulloch
Kevin Mooney
Cathy Moriarty
Michael Murphy
Michael Palin
Bill Ward
Tammy Wynette

MAY 6
George Clooney
Roma Downey
Willie Mays
Bob Seger
Lori Singer
Mare Winningham

MAY 7
Michael Knight
Bill Kreutzmann Jr.
Darren McGavin
Rick West

MAY 8
Philip Bailey
Rick Derringer
Chris Frantz
Melissa Gilbert
Gary Glitter
David Lemuel Keith
James Mitchum
Don Rickles
Paul Samwell-Smith
Toni Tennille
Alex Van Halen

MAY 9
Candice Bergen
Pete Birrell
James L. Brooks
Sonny Curtis
Nokie Edwards
Albert Finney
Richie Furay
Dave Gahan
Paul Heaton
Glenda Jackson
Billy Joel
Steve Katz
Mike Millward
Tom Petersson
Dave Prater
Lloyd Price
Tommy Roe
Mike Wallace

MAY 10
Jim Abrahams
Bono
Henry Fambrough
Jay Ferguson
Graham Gouldman
Dave Mason
Danny Rapp

MAY 11
Eric Burdon
Les Chadwick
Louis Farrakhan
Faith Popcorn
Natasha Richardson

MAY 12
Stephen Baldwin
Bruce Boxleitner
George Carlin
Lindsay Crouse
Billy Duffy
Ian Dury
Emilio Estevez
Kim Fields
Susan Hampshire
Katharine Hepburn
Ian McLagan
Tom Snyder
Billy Squier
David Walker
Steve Winwood

MAY 13
Beatrice Arthur
Peter Gabriel
Harvey Keitel
Danny Klein
Lorraine McIntosh
Dennis Rodman
Darius Rucker
Paul Thompson
Overend Watts
Stevie Wonder

MAY 14
Ian Astbury
Jack Bruce
David Byrne
Tom Cochrane
Gene Cornish
Meg Foster
George Lucas
Fabrice Morvan
Danny Wood
Robert Zemeckis

MAY 15
Brian Eno
Graham Goble
Mike Oldfield

MAY 16
Pierce Brosnan
Harry Carey Jr.
Tracey Gold
Glenn Gregory
Janet Jackson
Barbara Lee
Gabriela Sabatini
Derrell Sweet
Ralph Tresvant

MAY 17
Bill Bruford
Dennis Hopper
Pervis Jackson
Jordan Knight
Sugar Ray Leonard
Maureen O'Sullivan
Bill Paxton
Trent Reznor
Bob Saget
Taj Mahal
Debra Winger

MAY 18
Joe Bonsall
Pope John Paul II

MAY 19
Nora Ephron
James Fox
David Hartman
Dusty Hill
Grace Jones
Nancy Kwan
Joey Ramone
Philip Rudd
Pete Townshend
Martyn Ware

MAY 20
Warren Cann
Cher
Joe Cocker
Sue Cowsill
Tony Goldwyn
Nick Heyward
Brian Nash
Bronson Pinchot
Ronald Reagan Jr.

MAY 21
Mike Barson
Peggy Cass
Ronald Isley
Stan Lynch
Carol Potter
Judge Reinhold
Leo Sayer
Mr. T
Hilton Valentine

MAY 22
Charles Aznavour
Richard Benjamin
Naomi Campbell
Michael Constantine
Jerry Dammers
Iva Davies
Morrissey
Bernie Taupin
Paul Winfield

MAY 23
Drew Carey
Rosemary Clooney
Joan Collins
Betty Garrett
Bill Hunt
Jewel
Anatoly Karpov

MAY 24
Gary Burghoff
Roseanne Cash
Thomas Chong
Bob Dylan
Patti LaBelle
Priscilla Presley
Derek Quinn
Rich Robinson
Kristin Scott Thomas

MAY 25
Dixie Carter
Anne Heche
Justin Henry
Lauryn Hill
Robert Ludlum
Mitch Margo
Ian McKellen
Klaus Meine
Mike Myers
Frank Oz
John Palmer
Connie Sellecca
Beverly Sills
Leslie Uggams
Paul Weller

MAY 26
Verden Allen
James Arness
Helena Bonham-Carter
Ray Ennis
Levon Helm
Wayne Hussey
Lenny Kravitz
Peggy Lee
Stevie Nicks
Gerry Paterson
Philip Michael Thomas
Hank Williams Jr.

MAY 27
Cilla Black
Todd Bridges
Louis Gossett Jr.
Tony Hillerman
Henry Kissinger
Siouxsie Sioux
Bruce Weitz

MAY 28
Carroll Baker
John Fogerty
Roland Gift
Gladys Knight
Sondra Locke
Kylie Minogue

MAY 29
Annette Bening
Larry Blackmon
Gary Brooker
Kevin Conway
Roy Crewsdon
Melissa Etheridge
Anthony Geary
Bob Hope
Clifton James
Lisa Whelchel

MAY 30
Lenny Davidson
Keir Dullea
Marie Fredriksson
Nicky Headon
Ted McGinley
Clint Walker

MAY 31
Tom Berenger
Clint Eastwood
Sharon Gless
Gregory Harrison
Augie Meyers
Joe Namath
Johnny Paycheck
Brooke Shields
Lea Thompson
Peter Yarrow

JUNE 1
Rene Auberjonois
David Berkowitz
Pat Boone
Powers Boothe
Pat Corley
Jason Donovan
Morgan Freeman
Andy Griffith
Mike Joyce
Peter Masterson
Lorna Patterson
Jonathan Pryce
Graham Russell
Alan Wilder
Ron Wood
Edward Woodward

JUNE 2
Joanna Gleason
William Guest
Tony Hadley
Charles Haid
Marvin Hamlisch
Stacy Keach
Sally Kellerman
Jerry Mathers
Charles Miller
Milo O'Shea
Max Showalter
Michael Steele
Charlie Watts
Noah Wyle

JUNE 3
Michael Clarke
Tony Curtis
Ian Hunter
Curtis Mayfield
Billy Powell
Suzi Quatro
Scott Valentine
Deniece Williams

JUNE 4
Roger Ball
John Drew Barrymore
El DeBarge
Bruce Dern
Michelle Phillips
Parker Stevenson
Eddie Velez
Gordon Waller
Dennis Weaver
Ruth Westheimer
Charlie Whitney
Scott Wolf

JUNE 5
Laurie Anderson
Richard Butler
Spalding Gray
Kenny G.
Robert Lansing
Marky Mark
Bill Moyers
Don Reid
Freddie Stone

JUNE 6
Sandra Bernhard
Gary Bonds
David Dukes
Robert Englund
Harvey Fierstein
Roy Innis
Amanda Pays
Tom Ryan
Levi Stubbs
Billie Whitelaw

JUNE 7
James Ivory
Tom Jones
Liam Neeson
Prince

JUNE 8
Kathy Baker
Mick Box
Barbara Bush
Russell Christian
Griffin Dunne
Mick "Red" Hucknall
Julianna Margulies
Neil Mitchell
Chuck Negron
Doris Pearson
Robert Pilatus
Nick Rhodes
Joan Rivers
Boz Scaggs
Jerry Stiller
Bonnie Tyler
Keenen Ivory Wayans

JUNE 9
Trevor Bolder
Johnny Depp
Michael J. Fox
Billy Hatton
Jon Lord
Jackie Mason

JUNE 10
Shirley Alston
Human Beatbox
Linda Evangelista
Lionel Jeffries
Grace Mirabella
Shirley Owens
Prince Philip
Rick Price
Elisabeth Shue
Andrew Stevens

JUNE 11
Adrienne Barbeau
Joey Dee
Chad Everett
John Lawton
Joe Montana
Bonnie Pointer
Donnie Van Zandt
Gene Wilder
George Willig

JUNE 12
Timothy Busfield
George Bush
Bun Carlos
Vic Damone
Brad Delp
Jenilee Harrison
Jim Nabors
Reg Presley

JUNE 13
Tim Allen
Christo
Bobby Freeman
Howard Leese
Dennis Locorriere
Mark Mendoza
Deniece Pearson
Ally Sheedy
Richard Thomas

JUNE 14
Rod Argent
Boy George
Marla Gibbs
Steffi Graf
Jimmy Lea
Will Patton
Donald Trump
Muff Winwood

JUNE 15
Jim Belushi
Simon Callow
Courteney Cox
Mario Cuomo
Julie Hagerty
Russell Hitchcock
Noddy Holder
Helen Hunt
Waylon Jennings
Jim Varney

JUNE 16
Eddie Levert
Ian Matthews
Laurie Metcalf
Corin Redgrave
Joan Van Ark
Gino Vannelli

JUNE 17
Norman Kuhlke
Mark Linn-Baker
Peter Lupus
Barry Manilow
Jason Patric
Joe Piscopo

JUNE 18
Tom Bailey
Roger Ebert
Carol Kane
E.G. Marshall
Paul McCartney
Alison Moyet
Isabella Rossellini
Jerome Smith

JUNE 19
Paula Abdul
Tommy DeVito
Larry Dunn
Louis Jourdan
Nancy Marchand
Malcolm McDowell
Phylicia Rashad
Gena Rowlands
Salman Rushdie
Kathleen Turner
Ann Wilson

JUNE 20
Danny Aiello
Michael Anthony
Chet Atkins
Olympia Dukakis
John Goodman
Billy Guy
Martin Landau
Cyndi Lauper
Alan Longmuir
John Mahoney
Lionel Richie
John Taylor
Dave Thomas
James Tolkan
Brian Wilson

JUNE 21
Meredith Baxter
Berke Breathed
Chris Britton
Mark Brzezicki
Ray Davies
Michael Gross
Mariette Hartley
Bernie Kopell
Joey Kramer
Juliette Lewis
Nils Lofgren
Joey Molland
Jane Russell
Doug Savant
Maureen Stapleton
Prince William

JUNE 22
Peter Asher
Gary Beers
Bill Blass
Klaus Maria Brandauer
Amy Brenneman
Bruce Campbell
Tom Cunningham
Green Gartside
Howard Kaylan
Kris Kristofferson
Michael Lerner
Alan Osmond
Tracy Pollan
Todd Rundgren
Jimmy Somerville
Meryl Streep
Lindsay Wagner

JUNE 23
Bryan Brown
Adam Faith
Karin Gustafson
Frances McDormand

JUNE 24
Nancy Allen
Jeff Beck
Colin Blunstone
Georg Stanford Brown
Jeff Cease
Mick Fleetwood
John Illsley
Michele Lee
Andy McCluskey
Curt Smith
Sherry Stringfield
Peter Weller

JUNE 25
Tim Finn
Eddie Floyd
Allen Lanier
June Lockhart
Ian McDonald
George Michael
David Paich
Walter Payton
Carly Simon
Jimmie Walker
Clint Warwick

JUNE 26
Billy Davis Jr.
Chris Isaak
Mick Jones
Larry Taylor

JUNE 27
Isabelle Adjani
Julia Duffy
Bob Keeshan
Lorrie Morgan
Henry Ross Perot

JUNE 28
Kathy Bates
Mel Brooks
John Cusack
Dave Knights
Alice Krige
Mary Stuart Masterson
Noriyuki "Pat" Morita

JUNE 29
Maria Conchita Alonso
Gary Busey
Fred Grandy
Colin Hay
Little Eva
Ian Paice
Stedman Pearson
Roger Spear
Ruth Warrick

JUNE 30
David Alan Grier
Lena Horne
Hal Lindes
Andy Scott
Glenn Shorrock
Adrian Wright

JULY 1
Wally Amos Jr.
Pamela Anderson
Dan Aykroyd
Claude Berri
Karen Black
Roddy Bottum
Delaney Bramlett
Genevieve Bujold
Leslie Caron
Olivia De Havilland
Princess Diana
Jamie Farr
Farley Granger
Deborah Harry
Estee Lauder
Carl Lewis
Alanis Morissette
Sydney Pollack
Fred Schneider
John Tesh
Mike Tyson

JULY 2
Pete Briquette
Johnny Colla
Imelda Marcos
Brock Peters
Joe Puerta
Ron Silver
Paul Williams

JULY 3
Paul Barrere
Betty Buckley
Neil Clark
Vince Clarke
Tom Cruise

Johnny Lee
Montel Williams

JULY 4
Leona Helmsley
Gina Lollobrigida
Kirk Pengilly
Geraldo Rivera
Eva Marie Saint
Neil Simon
Jeremy Spencer
John Waite
Al "Blind Owl" Wilson
Bill Withers

JULY 5
Shirley Knight
Huey Lewis
Michael Monarch
Robbie Robertson

JULY 6
Allyce Beasley
Ned Beatty
Gene Chandler
Rik Elswit
Nanci Griffith
Shelley Hack
Bill Haley
Jon Keeble
Janet Leigh
James Naughton
Nancy Reagan
Geoffrey Rush
Glenn Scarpelli
Sylvester Stallone
Burt Ward

JULY 7
Pierre Cardin
Shelley Duvall
Warren Entner
Jessica Hahn
David Hodo
Joe Spano
Ringo Starr

JULY 8
Kevin Bacon
Beck
Andy Fletcher
Anjelica Huston
Graham Jones
Raffi
Jeffrey Tambor
Jerry Valy

JULY 9
Marc Almond
Frank Bello
Brian Dennehy
Tom Hanks
Jim Kerr
Kelly McGillis
Mitch Mitchell
Fred Savage
Bon Scott
O.J. Simpson
Debbie Sledge
Jimmy Smits
John Tesh

JULY 10
David Brinkley
Ronnie James Dio
Ron Glass
Arlo Guthrie
Jerry Miller
Neil Tennant
Max Von Sydow

JULY 11
Giorgio Armani
Tab Hunter
Peter Murphy
Leon Spinks
Sela Ward

JULY 12
Milton Berle
Bill Cosby
Mel Harris
Cheryl Ladd
Christine McVie
Liz Mitchell
Richard Simmons
Jay Thomas
John Wetton
Kristi Yamaguchi

JULY 13
Stephen Jo Bladd
Lawrence Donegan
Harrison Ford
Robert Forster
Cheech Marin
Roger "Jim" McGuinn
Patrick Stewart
Spud Webb

JULY 14
Polly Bergen
Ingmar Bergman
Chris Cross
Matthew Fox
Rosey Grier
Harry Dean Stanton

JULY 15
Willie Aames
Alex Karras
Peter Lewis
Brigitte Nielsen
Linda Ronstadt
Jan-Michael Vincent
Patrick Wayne
Forest Whitaker

JULY 16
Ruben Blades
Phoebe Cates
Stewart Copeland
Desmond Dekker
Corey Feldman
Tony Jackson
Mickey Rourke

JULY 17
Lucie Arnaz
Geezer Butler
Diahann Carroll
Spencer Davis
Phyllis Diller
David Hasselhoff
Art Linkletter
Donald Sutherland
Mick Tucker
Mike Vale

JULY 18
Papa Dee Allen
James Brolin
Terry Chambers
Hume Cronyn
Dion DiMucci
Glenn Hughes
Audrey Landers
Robin MacDonald
Nelson Mandela
Elizabeth McGovern
Martha Reeves
Nigel Twist

JULY 19
Allen Collins
Alan Gorrie
Anthony Edwards
Pat Hingle
Bernie Leadon
Brian May

JULY 20
Paul Cook
Chris Cornell
Donna Dixon
John Lodge
Mike McNeil
Diana Rigg
Carlos Santana

JULY 21
Lance Guest
Edward Herrmann
Don Knotts
Leigh Lawson
Jon Lovitz
Jim Martin
Matt Mulhern
Henry Priestman
Isaac Stern
Cat Stevens
Robin Williams

JULY 22
Estelle Bennett
Albert Brooks
George Clinton
Willem Dafoe
Richard Davies
Louise Fletcher
Danny Glover
Don Henley
John Leguizamo
Alex Trebek

JULY 23
Dino Danelli
David Essex
Martin Gore
Woody Harrelson
Andy Mackay
Don Imus
Larry Manetti
Edie McClurg
Stephanie Seymour
Terence Stamp
Blair Thornton

JULY 24
Heinz Burt
Ruth Buzzi
Lynda Carter
Lynval Golding
Kadeem Hardison
Robert Hays
Laura Leighton
Michael Richards
Chris Sarandon

JULY 25
Ray Billingsley
Manuel Charlton
Estelle Getty
Barbara Harris
Iman
Matt LeBlanc
Jim McCarty
Verdine White

JULY 26
Blake Edwards
Dorothy Hamill
Mick Jagger
Stanley Kubrick
Duncan Mackay
Jason Robards
Kevin Spacey
Roger Taylor

JULY 27
Peggy Fleming
Norman Lear
Maureen McGovern
John Pleshette
Al Ramsey
Betty Thomas
Jerry Van Dyke

JULY 28
George Cummings
Jim Davis
Terry Fox
Simon Kirke
Sally Struthers
Rick Wright

JULY 29
Michael Biehn
Neal Doughty
Peter Jennings
Geddy Lee
Martina McBride
Marilyn Quayle
Michael Spinks
David Warner

JULY 30
Paul Anka
Delta Burke
Kate Bush
Larry Fishburne
Buddy Guy
Anita Hill
Lisa Kudrow
Ken Olin
Rat Scabies
Arnold Schwarzenegger

JULY 31
Daniel Ash
Alan Autry
Bill Berry
Dean Cain
Geraldine Chaplin
Norman Cook
Karl Green
Gary Lewis
Wesley Snipes
John West

AUGUST 1
Rick Anderson
Tempestt Bledsoe
Ricky Coonce
Robert Cray
Dom DeLuise
Joe Elliott
Giancarlo Giannini
Arthur Hill
Yves Saint Laurent
Robert James Waller
Tom Wilson

AUGUST 2
Joanna Cassidy
Doris Coley
Wes Craven
Garth Hudson
Victoria Jackson
Carroll O'Connor
Peter O'Toole
Mary-Louise Parker
Edward Patten
Max Wright

AUGUST 3
Tony Bennett
B.B. Dickerson
James Hetfield
John Landis
Beverly Lee
Gordon Scott
Martin Sheen

AUGUST 4
David Carr
Frankie Ford
Billy Bob Thornton

AUGUST 5
Loni Anderson
Neil Armstrong
Rick Derringer
Rick Huxley
Jonathan Silverman

AUGUST 6
Paul Bartel
Dorian Harewood
Catherine Hicks
Abbey Lincoln
Pat McDonald

AUGUST 7
Bruce Dickinson
Andy Fraser
John Glover
David Rasche
Alberto Salazar
B. J. Thomas

AUGUST 8
Richard Anderson
Philip Balsley
Princess Beatrice
Keith Carradine
Harry Crosby
Dino De Laurentiis
The Edge
Andy Fairweather-Low
Chris Foreman
Dustin Hoffman
Donny Most
Connie Stevens
Mel Tillis
Larry Dee Wilcox
Esther Williams

AUGUST 9
Gillian Anderson
Kurtis Blow
Sam Elliott
Melanie Griffith
Billy Henderson
Whitney Houston
Ken Norton
Benjamin Orr
David Steinberg

AUGUST 10
Ian Anderson
Rosanna Arquette
Antonio Banderas
Veronica Bennett
Michael Bivins
Riddick Bowe
Jimmy Dean
Jon Farriss
Eddie Fisher
Bobby Hatfield
Lorraine Pearson

AUGUST 11
Erik Braunn
Eric Carmen
Hulk Hogan
Mike Hugg
Joe Jackson
Jim Kale
Denis Payton
Claus Von Bulow

AUGUST 12
John Derek
George Hamilton
Roy Hay
Sam J. Jones
Mark Knopfler
Pat Metheny
Pete Sampras
Suzanne Vega
Jane Wyatt

AUGUST 13
Kathleen Battle
Danny Bonaduce
Fidel Castro
Dan Fogelberg
Pat Harrington
Don Ho
Feargal Sharkey

AUGUST 14
Halle Berry
Dash Crofts
David Crosby
Alice Ghostley
Larry Graham
Jackee
Magic Johnson
Steve Martin
Susan Saint James
Danielle Steel

AUGUST 15
Princess Anne
Julia Child
Mike Connors
Linda Ellerbee
Tess Harper
Matt Johnson
MCA
Bill Pinkney
Rose-Marie
Pete York

AUGUST 16
Bob Balaban
Angela Bassett
Belinda Carlisle
Robert Culp
Frank Gifford
Kathie Lee Gifford
Eydie Gorme
Timothy Hutton
Madonna
Fess Parker
Carole Shelley
James Taylor
Reginald Veljohnson
Lesley Ann Warren

AUGUST 17
Robert De Niro
Steve Gorman
Colin Moulding
Maureen O'Hara
Sean Penn
Kevin Rowland
Gary Talley
Donnie Wahlberg

AUGUST 18
Dennis Elliott
Martin Mull
Jada Pinkett
Roman Polanski
Robert Redford
Christian Slater
Madeleine Stowe
Ron Strykert
Patrick Swayze
Malcolm-Jamal Warner
Carl Wayne
Shelley Winters

AUGUST 19
Ginger Baker
Bill Clinton
John Deacon
Kevin Dillon
Peter Gallagher
Ian Gillan
Billy J. Kramer
M.C. Eric
Gerald McRaney
Diana Muldaur
Matthew Perry
Jill St. John
John Stamos

AUGUST 20
Joan Allen
Connie Chung
Doug Fieger
Rudy Gatlin
Isaac Hayes
Don King
Phil Lynott
James Pankow
Robert Plant

AUGUST 21
Kim Cattrall
Wilt Chamberlain
Carl Giammarese
Kenny Rogers
Kim Sledge
Joe Strummer
Melvin Van Peebles
Clarence Williams III

AUGUST 22
Ray Bradbury
Valerie Harper
John Lee Hooker
Roland Orzabal
Debbi Peterson
Norman Schwarzkopf
Cindy Williams

AUGUST 23
Ronny Cox
Barbara Eden
Bobby G.
Shelley Long
Vera Miles
Shaun Ryder
Richard Sanders
Rick Springfield

AUGUST 24
Yasir Arafat
Mark Bedford
Jim Capaldi
Joe Chambers
John Cipollina
Jeffrey Daniel
David Freiberg
Steve Guttenberg
Ken Hensley
Marlee Matlin
Claudia Schiffer

AUGUST 25
Anne Archer
Sean Connery
Elvis Costello
Billy Ray Cyrus
Mel Ferrer
Rob Halford
Monty Hall
Van Johnson
Regis Philbin
John Savage
Gene Simmons
Tom Skerritt
Blair Underwood
Joanne Whalley-Kilmer
Walter Williams

AUGUST 26
Jet Black
Bob Cowsill
Macaulay Culkin
Chris Curtis
Geraldine Ferraro
Michael Jeter
Branford Marsalis
Fred Milano
John O'Neill

AUGUST 27
Barbara Bach
Tim Bogert
Jeff Cook
Daryl Dragon
Pee-Wee Herman
Alex Lifeson
Glenn Matlock
Harry Reems
Tuesday Weld

AUGUST 28
Clem Cattini
Hugh Cornwell
Ben Gazzara
Scott Hamilton
Donald O'Connor
Wayne Osmond
Jason Priestley
LeAnn Rimes
Emma Samms
Elizabeth Seal
Danny Seraphine
David Soul
Daniel Stern

AUGUST 29
Richard Attenborough
Rebecca DeMornay
Richard Gere
Elliott Gould
Michael Jackson
Robin Leach
George Montgomery
Isabel Sanford

AUGUST 30
Elizabeth Ashley
Timothy Bottoms
Cameron Diaz
John McNally
Micky Moody
John Phillips
Kitty Wells

AUGUST 31
Jerry Allison
James Coburn
Debbie Gibson
Buddy Hackett
Van Morrison
Harold Reid
Rudolph Schenker
Daniel Schorr
Anthony Thistlethwaite
Glenn Tilbrook

SEPTEMBER 1
Greg Errico
Gloria Estefan
Bruce Foxton
Barry Gibb
Lily Tomlin
Dave White

SEPTEMBER 2
Rosalind Ashford
Jimmy Connors
Sam Gooden
Marty Grebb
Mark Harmon
Fritz McIntyre
Steve Porcaro
Keanu Reeves

SEPTEMBER 3
Eileen Brennan
Donald Brewer
Al Jardine
Steve Jones
Gary Leeds
Valerie Perrine
Charlie Sheen
Mort Walker

SEPTEMBER 4
Martin Chambers
Gary Duncan
Greg Elmore

Mitzi Gaynor
Judith Ivey
Merald Knight
Ronald LaPread
Jennifer Salt
Ione Skye

SEPTEMBER 5
William Devane
Carol Lawrence
Bob Newhart
Al Stewart
Raquel Welch
Dweezil Zappa

SEPTEMBER 6
Dave Bargeron
Jane Curtin
Jeff Foxworthy
Swoosie Kurtz
Claydes Smith
Paul Waaktaar
Jo Anne Worley

SEPTEMBER 7
Alfa Anderson
Corbin Bernsen
Susan Blakely
Chrissie Hynde
Julie Kavner
Peggy Noonan
Richard Roundtree
Benmont Tench

SEPTEMBER 8
Sid Caesar
Brian Cole
Michael Lardie
David Steele
Henry Thomas
Jonathan Taylor Thomas

SEPTEMBER 9
Doug Ingle
Michael Keaton
Sylvia Miles
Cliff Robertson
Adam Sandler
Dave Stewart
Roger Waters

SEPTEMBER 10
Chris Columbus
Siobhan Fahey
Jose Feliciano
Johnnie Fingers
Colin Firth
Danny Hutton
Amy Irving
Big Daddy Kane
Pat Mastelotto
Joe Perry
Don Powell
Fay Wray

SEPTEMBER 11
Harry Connick Jr.
Lola Falana
Mickey Hart
Earl Holliman
Amy Madigan
Virginia Madsen
Kristy McNichol
Jon Moss
Tommy Shaw
Mick Talbot
Dennis Tufano

SEPTEMBER 12
Barry Andrews
Gerry Beckley
Tony Bellamy
Darren E. Burrows
Linda Gray
Neil Peart
Brian Robertson
Peter Scolari
Barry White

SEPTEMBER 13
Barbara Bain
Jacqueline Bisset
Nell Carter
Peter Cetera
David Clayton-Thomas
Randy Jones
Richard Kiel
Joni Sledge
Mel Torme

SEPTEMBER 14
Pete Agnew
Barry Cowsill
Faith Ford
Morten Harket
Walter Koenig
Paul Kossoff
Sam Neill
Joe Penny
Nicol Williamson

SEPTEMBER 15
Les Braid
Jackie Cooper
Prince Henry
Tommy Lee Jones
Oliver Stone

SEPTEMBER 16
Lauren Bacall
Ed Begley Jr.
Joe Butler
Bernie Calvert
David Copperfield
Peter Falk
Anne Francis
Allen Funt
Kenny Jones
B.B. King
Richard Marx
Susan Ruttan

SEPTEMBER 17
Anne Bancroft
Elvira
Jeff MacNelly
Roddy McDowall
Lamonte McLemore
John Ritter
Fee Waybill

SEPTEMBER 18
Frankie Avalon
Ricky Bell
Robert Blake
Joanne Catherall
Kerry Livgren
Dee Dee Ramone
Jack Warden

SEPTEMBER 19
Jim Abbott
John Coghlan
Lol Creme
Lee Dorman
Jeremy Irons
Joan Lunden
Nick Massi
David McCallum
Bill Medley
Nile Rodgers
Twiggy
Adam West

SEPTEMBER 20
Alannah Currie
Crispin Glover
Sophia Loren
Anne Meara
Chuck Panozzo

SEPTEMBER 21
Leonard Cohen
Henry Gibson
Larry Hagman
Stephen King
Ricki Lake
Rob Morrow
Bill Murray
Catherine Oxenberg
Philthy Animal
Alfonso Ribeiro
Trugoy the Dove

SEPTEMBER 22
Scott Baio
Shari Belafonte
David Coverdale
Joan Jett
Paul LeMat

SEPTEMBER 23
Jason Alexander
Steve Boone
Ronald Bushy
Ray Charles
Lita Ford
Julio Iglesias
Ben E. King
Elizabeth Pena
Mary Kay Place
Mickey Rooney
Bruce Springsteen

SEPTEMBER 24
Phil Hartman
Gerry Marsden
Linda McCartney
Anthony Newley

SEPTEMBER 25
Gary Alexander
Michael Douglas
Mark Hamill
John Locke
Heather Locklear
Onnie McIntyre
Christopher Reeve
Phil Rizzuto
Steve Severin
Will Smith
Cheryl Tiegs
Barbara Walters

SEPTEMBER 26
Melissa Sue Anderson
Joe Bauer
George Chambers
Craig Chaquico
Donna Douglas
Georgie Fame
Bryan Ferry
Linda Hamilton
Mary Beth Hurt
Winnie Mandela
Olivia Newton-John
Tracey Thorn

SEPTEMBER 27
Randy Bachman
Wilford Brimley
Greg Ham
Jayne Meadows
Meat Loaf
Sada Thompson

SEPTEMBER 28
Brigitte Bardot
Jeffrey Jones
Gwyneth Paltrow
Helen Shapiro
William Windom
Moon Unit Zappa

SEPTEMBER 29
Gene Autry
Anita Ekberg
Mark Farner
Bryant Gumbel
Patricia Hodge
Madeline Kahn
Jerry Lee Lewis
Larry Linville
Emily Lloyd

SEPTEMBER 30
Marc Bolan
Angie Dickinson
Fran Drescher
Deborah Kerr
Dewey Martin
Johnny Mathis
Marilyn McCoo
Sylvia Peterson
Victoria Tennant
Barry Williams

OCTOBER 1
Julie Andrews
Jean-Jacques Annaud
Jimmy Carter
Stephen Collins
Rob Davis
Richard Harris
Howard Hewett
Jerry Martini
Walter Matthau
Philippe Noiret
Randy Quaid
Stella Stevens
James Whitmore

OCTOBER 2
Richard Hell
Freddie Jackson
Donna Karan
Don McLean
Philip Oakey
Mike Rutherford
Sting
Tiffany

OCTOBER 3
Lindsey Buckingham
Neve Campbell
Chubby Checker
Barbara Ferris
Pamela Hensley
Tommy Lee
Gwen Stefani
Gore Vidal
Jack Wagner
Dave Winfield

OCTOBER 4
Armand Assante
Clifton Davis
Jim Fielder
Charlton Heston
Chris Lowe
Anne Rice
Susan Sarandon

OCTOBER 5
Karen Allen
Clive Barker
Leo Barnes
Josie Bissett
Eddie Clarke
Jeff Conaway
Brian Connolly
Bob Geldof
Glynis Johns
Bil Keane
Mario Lemieux
Carlo Mastrangelo
Steve Miller
Kate Winslet

OCTOBER 6
Kevin Cronin
Britt Ekland
Bobby Farrell
Thomas McClary

Matthew Sweet
Bob Weir

OCTOBER 7
June Allyson
Toni Braxton
Kevin Godley
Dave Hope
Yo-Yo Ma
John Mellencamp
Oliver North
Martha Stewart

OCTOBER 8
Rona Barrett
Robert Bell
George Bellamy
Chevy Chase
Michael Dudikoff
Paul Hogan
Jesse Jackson
Sarah Purcell
Johnny Ramone
R.L. Stine
Hamish Stuart
Sigourney Weaver
Tony Wilson
Stephanie Zimbalist

OCTOBER 9
Scott Bakula
Jackson Browne
John Entwistle
Michael Pare
Robert Wuhl

OCTOBER 10
Charles Dance
Jessica Harper
Martin Kemp
Martina Navratilova
Alan Rachins
David Lee Roth
Tanya Tucker
Ben Vereen

OCTOBER 11
Joan Cusack
Daryl Hall
Ron Leibman
David Morse
Luke Perry
Grant Shaud

OCTOBER 12
Susan Anton
Kirk Cameron
Sam Moore
Luciano Pavarotti
Adam Rich
Dave Vanian

OCTOBER 13
Karen Akers
Tisha Campbell
Sammy Hagar
Beverly Johnson
Nancy Kerrigan
Robert Lamm
Marie Osmond
Kelly Preston
Nipsey Russell
Demond Wilson

OCTOBER 14
Harry Anderson
Marcia Barrett
Greg Evigan
Billy Harrison
Justin Hayward
Ralph Lauren
Roger Moore
Cliff Richard

OCTOBER 15
Mickey Baker
Richard Carpenter
Chris De Burgh
Sarah Ferguson
Lee Iacocca
Tito Jackson
Linda Lavin
Penny Marshall
Tanya Roberts
Don Stevenson

OCTOBER 16
Tony Carey
Barry Corbin
Gary Kemp
Angela Lansbury
Dave Lovelady
Tim Robbins
Suzanne Somers
C.F. Turner
Wendy Wilson

OCTOBER 17
Sam Bottoms
Beverly Garland
Alan Howard
Margot Kidder
Michael McKean
Howard Rollins Jr.
Jim Seals
Jim Tucker
George Wendt

OCTOBER 18
Chuck Berry
Peter Boyle
Mike Ditka
Russ Giguere
Keith Knudsen
Melina Mercouri
Erin Moran
Joe Morton
Gary Richrath
George C. Scott
Vincent Spano

OCTOBER 19
Richard Dreyfuss
Patricia Ireland
John Lithgow
Karl Wallinger

OCTOBER 20
Joyce Brothers
William Christopher
Alan Greenwood
Mark King
Ric Lee
Jerry Orbach
Tom Petty
Will Rogers Jr.
Bobby Seale
Jay Siegel

OCTOBER 21
Charlotte Caffey
Julian Cops
Steve Cropper
Eric Faulkner
Lee Loughnane
Steve Lukather
Manfred Mann

OCTOBER 22
Eddie Brigati
Catherine Deneuve
Joan Fontaine
Annette Funicello
Jeff Goldblum
Valeria Golino
Derek Jacobi
Ray Jones
Christopher Lloyd
Tony Roberts

OCTOBER 23
Johnny Carson
Freddie Marsden
Perola Negra Pele
Weird Al Yankovic
Dwight Yoakam

OCTOBER 24
F. Murray Abraham
Jerry Edmonton
Kevin Kline
David Nelson
B.D. Wong
Bill Wyman

OCTOBER 25
Jon Anderson
Anthony Franciosa
Matthias Jabs
Midori
Tracy Nelson
Rick Parfitt
Helen Reddy
Marion Ross
Glenn Tipton

OCTOBER 26
Hillary Rodham Clinton
Cary Elwes
Keith Hopwood
Bob Hoskins
Ivan Reitman
Pat Sajak
Jaclyn Smith
Keith Strickland

OCTOBER 27
Terry Anderson
John Cleese
Ruby Dee
Nanette Fabray
John Gotti
Simon LeBon
Marla Maples
Carrie Snodgress

OCTOBER 28
Jane Alexander
Steve Baumgartner
Michael Crichton
Wayne Fontana
Dennis Franz
Bill Gates
Jami Gertz
Telma Hopkins
Bruce Jenner
Hank Marvin
Stephen Morris
Joan Plowright
Annie Potts
Julia Roberts

OCTOBER 29
Ralph Bakshi
Kevin Dubrow
Kate Jackson
Denny Laine
Melba Moore
Winona Ryder

OCTOBER 30
Harry Hamlin
Gavin Rossdale
Grace Slick
Charles Martin Smith
Otis Williams
Henry Winkler

OCTOBER 31
King Ad-Rock
Barbara Bel Geddes
Tony Bowers
Bernard Edwards
Dale Evans
Lee Grant
Deidre Hall
Sally Kirkland
Annabella Lwin
Johnny Marr
Larry Mullen Jr.
Jane Pauley
Dan Rather
Xavier Roberts
David Ogden Stiers

NOVEMBER 1
Rick Allen
Ronald Bell
Barbara Bosson
Keith Emerson
Robert Foxworth
Mags Furuholmen
James Kilpatrick Jr.
Lyle Lovett
Eddie MacDonald
Jenny McCarthy
Betsy Palmer
Dan Peek

NOVEMBER 2
k.d. lang
Brian Poole
Bruce Welch
Alfre Woodard

NOVEMBER 3
Adam Ant
Roseanne Arnold
Charles Bronson
Mike Evans
Larry Holmes
Steve Landesberg
Lulu
Dolph Lundgren
Dennis Miller
James Prime
Gary Sandy

NOVEMBER 4
Art Carney
Walter Cronkite
Chris Difford
Ralph Macchio
Delbert McClinton
Markie Post
Kool Rock
Mike Smith
Loretta Swit

NOVEMBER 5
Bryan Adams
Art Garfunkel
Peter Noone
Tatum O'Neal
Roy Rogers
Sam Shepard
Paul Simon
Elke Sommer
Ike Turner

NOVEMBER 6
Sally Field
Glenn Frey
Ethan Hawke
P.J. Proby
Doug Sahm
Maria Shriver
George Young

NOVEMBER 7
Billy Graham
Joni Mitchell
Johnny Rivers

NOVEMBER 8
Alan Berger
Bonnie Bramlett
Alain Delon
Mary Hart
Rickie Lee Jones
Terry Lee Miall
Bonnie Raitt
Esther Rolle
Rodney Slater

Courtney Thorne-Smith
Roy Wood
Roxana Zal

NOVEMBER 9
Joe Bouchard
Lou Ferrigno
Alan Gratzer
Hedy Lamarr
Phil May
Pepa
Carl Sagan
Dennis Stratton

NOVEMBER 10
Glen Buxton
Greg Lake
MacKenzie Phillips
Ann Reinking
Jack Scalia
Roy Scheider

NOVEMBER 11
Bibi Andersson
Paul Cowsill
Chris Dreja
Stubby Kaye
Patric Knowles
Roger Lavern
Charles Manson
Ian Marsh
Vince Martell
Demi Moore
Andy Partridge
Kurt Vonnegut Jr.
Jonathan Winters
Jesse Colin Young

NOVEMBER 12
Errol Brown
Tonya Harding
John Maus
Leslie McKeown
Stephanie Powers
David Schwimmer
Wallace Shawn
Neil Young

NOVEMBER 13
Whoopi Goldberg
Joe Mantegna
Richard Mulligan

NOVEMBER 14
Frankie Banali
Prince Charles
Freddie Garrity
Robert Ginty

Alexander O'Neal
Laura San Giacomo
Alec Such
Yanni
James Young

NOVEMBER 15
Edward Asner
Petula Clark
Beverly D'Angelo
Yaphet Kotto
Frida Lyngstad
Tony Thompson
Sam Waterston

NOVEMBER 16
Lisa Bonet
Dwight Gooden
Clu Gulager

NOVEMBER 17
Martin Barre
Danny DeVito
Ronald DeVoe
Bob Gaudio
Lauren Hutton
Gordon Lightfoot
Mary Elizabeth Mastrantonio
Lorne Michaels
Martin Scorsese
Tom Seaver

NOVEMBER 18
Margaret Atwood
Hank Ballard
Imogene Coca
Linda Evans
Kirk Hammett
Andrea Marcovicci
Graham Parker
Jameson Parker
Elizabeth Perkins
Herman Rarebell
Susan Sullivan
Brenda Vaccaro
Kim Wilde

NOVEMBER 19
Dick Cavett
Jodie Foster
Larry King
Jeane Kirkpatrick
Calvin Klein
Hank Medress
Kathleen Quinlan
Ahmad Rashad

Meg Ryan
Ted Turner

NOVEMBER 20
Kaye Ballard
Jimmy Brown
Mike D
Bo Derek
George Grantham
Veronica Hamel
Richard Masur
Estelle Parsons
Dick Smothers
Ray Stiles
Joe Walsh
Sean Young

NOVEMBER 21
Goldie Hawn
Dr. John
Lonnie Jordan
Laurence Luckinbill
Lorna Luft
Juliet Mills
Harold Ramis
Nicollette Sheridan
Marlo Thomas

NOVEMBER 22
Aston Barrett
Boris Becker
Tom Conti
Jamie Lee Curtis
Rodney Dangerfield
Terry Gilliam
Mariel Hemingway
Billie Jean King
Floyd Sneed
Stevie "Little Steven" Van Zandt
Robert Vaughn
Ray Walston
Tina Weymouth

NOVEMBER 23
Susan Anspach
Bruce Hornsby

NOVEMBER 24
Donald Dunn
Geraldine Fitzgerald
Chris Hayes
Dwight Schultz
John Squire

NOVEMBER 25
Christina Applegate
Joe DiMaggio
Amy Grant
John F. Kennedy Jr.
John Larroquette
Ricardo Montalban
Steve Rothery
Percy Sledge

NOVEMBER 26
Cyril Cusack
Robert Goulet
Norman Hassan
Alan Henderson
John McVie
Charles Schulz
Tina Turner

NOVEMBER 27
Charlie Burchill
Dozy
Robin Givens
Eddie Rabbitt
Bob Smith
Fisher Stevens
Jaleel White

NOVEMBER 28
Beeb Birtles
Ed Harris
Hope Lange
Judd Nelson
Randy Newman

NOVEMBER 29
Felix Cavaliere
Denny Doherty
Barry Goudreau
Jonathan Knight
Diane Ladd
Howie Mandel
John Mayall
Andrew McCarthy
Garry Shandling

NOVEMBER 30
John Aston
Richard Barbieri
Dick Clark
Kevin Conroy
Richard Crenna
Roger Glover
Rob Grill
Robert Guillaume
Billy Idol
Bo Jackson

G. Gordon Liddy
Leo Lyons
Mandy Patinkin
June Pointer
Rex Reason
Ridley Scott

DECEMBER 1
Woody Allen
Carol Alt
Eric Bloom
John Densmore
Bette Midler
Sandy Nelson
Gilbert O'Sullivan
Richard Pryor
Lou Rawls
Charlene Tilton
Treat Williams

DECEMBER 2
Steven Bauer
Ted Bluechel Jr.
Cathy Lee Crosby
Julie Harris
Michael McDonald
Tom McGuinness
Rick Savage
Howard Stern

DECEMBER 3
Brian Bonsall
Ozzy Osbourne
Andy Williams

DECEMBER 4
Tyra Banks
Jeff Bridges
John Cale
Deanna Durbin
Chris Hillman
Wink Martindale
Bob Mosley
Gary Rossington
Southside Johnny
Marisa Tomei

DECEMBER 5
Morgan Brittany
Jeroen Krabbe
Charles Lane
Little Richard
Jim Messina
Les Nemes
Jack Russell

DECEMBER 6
Peter Buck
Rick Buckler

Tom Hulce
Janine Turner
Ben Watt
Steven Wright

DECEMBER 7
Larry Bird
Ellen Burstyn
Mike Nolan
Tom Waits
Eli Wallach

DECEMBER 8
Gregg Allman
Kim Basinger
Jerry Butler
David Carradine
Phil Collen
Bobby Elliott
Teri Hatcher
James MacArthur
Sinead O'Connor
Paul Rutherford
Maximilian Schell
Flip Wilson

DECEMBER 9
Joan Armatrading
Beau Bridges
Dick Butkus
Rick Danko
Kirk Douglas
Morton Downey Jr.
Dennis Dunaway
Douglas Fairbanks Jr.
Buck Henry
Neil Innes
John Malkovich
Michael Nouri
Donny Osmond
Dick Van Patten

DECEMBER 10
Frank Beard
Kenneth Branagh
Susan Dey
Ace Kefford
Mako
Walter Orange
Chad Stuart

DECEMBER 11
Bess Armstrong
Teri Garr
David Gates
Jermaine Jackson
Booker T. Jones
Brenda Lee

Rita Moreno
Nikki Sixx

DECEMBER 12
Bob Barker
Dickey Betts
Mayim Bialik
Clive Bunker
Jennifer Connelly
Sheila E.
Connie Francis
Terry Kirkman
Ed Koch
Rush Limbaugh
Mike Pinder
Cathy Rigby
Frank Sinatra
Mike Smith
Dionne Warwick

DECEMBER 13
Jeff "Skunk" Baxter
John Davidson
Ted Nugent
Randy Owen
Christopher Plummer
Dick Van Dyke
Tom Verlaine
Johnny Whitaker

DECEMBER 14
Patty Duke
Cynthia Gibb
Bridget Hall
Abbe Lane
Jackie McCauley
Mike Scott
Dee Wallace Stone
Cliff Williams
Joyce Wilson

DECEMBER 15
Carmine Appice
Dave Clark
Tim Conway
Reginald Hudlin
Don Johnson
Paul Simonon
Helen Slater

DECEMBER 16
Benny Andersson
Steven Bochco
Ben Cross
Billy Gibbons
Tony Hicks
William Perry
Liv Ullmann

DECEMBER 17
Sarah Dallin
Dave Dee
Bob Guccione
Eddie Kendricks
Eugene Levy
Mike Mills
Art Neville
Paul Rodgers
Tommy Steele

DECEMBER 18
Ossie Davis
Elliot Easton
Ray Liotta
Leonard Maltin
Brad Pitt
Keith Richards
Steven Spielberg
Kiefer Sutherland

DECEMBER 19
Jennifer Beals
Alvin Lee
Robert MacNaughton
Alyssa Milano
Tim Reid
Cicely Tyson
Robert Urich
Maurice White
Zal Yanovsky

DECEMBER 20
Jenny Agutter
Anita Baker
Billy Bragg
Bobby Colomby
John Hillerman
Chris Robinson
Little Stevie Wright

DECEMBER 21
Phil Donahue
Chris Evert
Jane Fonda
Josh Mostel
Kurt Waldheim
Carl Wilson
Paul Winchell

DECEMBER 22
Barbara Billingsley
Hector Elizondo
Maurice Gibb
Robin Gibb
Lady Bird Johnson
Rick Nielsen
Ricky Ross
Diane Sawyer

DECEMBER 23
Corey Haim
Jorma Kaukonen
Johnny Kidd
Susan Lucci
Dave Murray
Eugene Record
Ruth Roman
Harry Shearer
James Stockdale
Eddie Vedder

DECEMBER 24
Ian Burden
Lemmy

DECEMBER 25
Jimmy Buffett
Robin Campbell
O'Kelly Isley
Annie Lennox
Shane MacGowan
Barbara Mandrell
Noel Redding
Hanna Schygulla
Sissy Spacek
Henry Vestine

DECEMBER 26
Steve Allen
Abdul Fakir
Alan KingDonald Moffat
Phil Spector

DECEMBER 27
John Amos
Peter Criss
Gerard Depardieu
Tovah Feldshuh
Mick Jones
David Knopfler
Les Maguire

DECEMBER 28
Alex Chilton
Dick Diamonde
Lou Jacobi
Stan Lee
Charles Neville
Johnny Otis
Maggie Smith
Denzel Washington
Edgar Winter

DECEMBER 29
Ted Danson
Mark Day
Marianne Faithfull
Mary Tyler Moore
Paula Poundstone
Inga Swenson
Ray Thomas
Jon Voight

DECEMBER 30
Joseph Bologna
Bo Diddley
Davy Jones
Matt Lauer
Jack Lord
Jeff Lynne
Mike Nesmith
Sheryl Lee Ralph
Russ Tamblyn
Tracey Ullman
Fred Ward
Tiger Woods

DECEMBER 31
Barbara Carrera
Rosalind Cash
Burton Cummings
John Denver
Tom Hamilton
Anthony Hopkins
Val Kilmer
Ben Kingsley
Tim Matheson
Joe McIntyre
Sarah Miles
Pete Quaife
Patti Smith
Donna Summer
Andy Summers

1998'S WATERSHED BIRTHDAYS

The following folks will have reason to celebrate (or toast themselves) a little harder this year as they reach birthday milestones.

TURNING 90

Eddie Albert
Milton Berle
Imogene Coca
Buddy Ebsen
Estee Lauder
John Mills

TURNING 80

Ingmar Bergman
Joey Bishop
Art Carney
John Forsythe
Billy Graham
Stubby Kaye
Nelson Mandela
Bobby Riggs
Phil Rizzuto
Oral Roberts
Mickey Spillane
Mike Wallace

TURNING 75

Aaron Spelling
James Arness
Richard Attenborough
Bob Barker
Estelle Getty
Dick Martin
Ed McMahon
Liz Smith
Jean Stapleton
James Stockdale
Larry Storch
Mort Walker
Esther Williams

TURNING 70

Maya Angelou
Dr. Joyce Brothers
James Brown
Rosemary Clooney
James Coburn
Vic Damone
Jimmy Dean
Bo Diddley
Fats Domino
Eddie Fisher
James Garner
James Ivory
Conrad Janis
Eartha Kitt
Judith Krantz
Stanley Kubrick
Nancy Marchand
Walter "Fritz" Mondale
Jeanne Moreau
Roger Mudd
James Earl Ray
Mister Rogers
Marion Ross
Vidal Sassoon
Maurice Sendak
Roger Vadim
Dick Van Patten
Dr. Ruth Westheimer

TURNING 65

Danny Aiello
Jean-Paul Belmondo
Robert Blake
Peter Boyle
Carol Burnett
Michael Caine
Joan Collins
Tim Conway
Dom Deluise
Charles Durning
Louis Farrakhan
Marla Gibbs
Frank Gorshin
Quincy Jones
Larry King
Bernie Kopell
David McCallum
Willie Nelson
Kim Novak
Charles Osgood
Regis Philbin
Roman Polanski
Chita Rivera
Wayne Rogers
Nina Simone
Tom Skerritt
Cicely Tyson
Flip Wilson

TURNING 60

Hoyt Axton
Ralph Bakshi
Paul Bartel
Richard Benjamin
Judy Blume
Joseph Bologna
Thomas Chong
Ronny Cox
Duane Eddy
James Farentino
Connie Francis
Elliot Gould
Sherman Hemsley
Derek Jacobi
Etta James
Peter Jennings
Ben E. King
Karl Lagerfeld
Gordon Lightfoot
Christopher Lloyd
Mako
Diana Muldaur
Charlie Pride
Oliver Reed
Paul Revere
Diana Rigg
Kenny Rogers
Connie Stevens
Marlo Thomas
Jon Voight
Nicol Williamson
Bill Withers
Peter Yarrow

TURNING 50

Anthony Andrews
Mikhail Baryshnikov
Kathy Bates
Kathleen Battle
Ruben Blades
Donald Brewer
Blair Brown
Errol Brown
Jackson Browne
Bill Bruford
John Carter
Nell Carter
Alice Cooper
Bill Cowsill
Sinead Cusack
Ben Cross
Lindsay Crouse
Gerard Depardieu
Ronnie James Dio
Brian Eno
Donald Fagen
Peggy Fleming
Glenn Frey
Richard Gere
Albert Gore Jr.
Fred Grandy
Eddy Grant
Christopher Guest
Bryant Gumbel
Barbara Hershey
Phil Hartman
Telma Hopkins
Mary Beth Hurt
Tony Iommi
Jeremy Irons
Kate Jackson
Donna Karan
Greg Lake
Kenny Loggins
Lulu
Margot Kidder
Perry King
Barbara Mandrell
Andrea Marcovicci
Richard Masur
Jerry Mathers
Gerald McRaney
Olivia Newton-John
Stevie Nicks
Ted Nugent
Jeffrey Osborne
Ozzy Ozbourne
Rhea Perlman
Bernadette Peters
Kate Pierson
Robert Plant
Anita Pointer
Sarah Purcell
Raffi
Johnny Ramone
Phylicia Rashad
John Ritter
Mercedes Ruehl
Todd Rundgren
Susan Ruttan
Leo Sayer
Richard Simmons
Southside Johnny
Chris Squire
Steven Tyler
Dee Wallace Stone
Marcia Strassman
Sally Struthers
Donna Summer
James Taylor
Betty Thomas
Garry Trudeau
Jimmy Walker
Carl Weathers
George Wendt
Dianne Wiest
Steve Winwood
Steven Wright

TURNING 40

The Artist Formerly Known as Prince
Kevin Bacon
Alec Baldwin
Afrika Bambaataa
Mike Barson
Angela Bassett
Annette Bening
Bill Berry
Brett Butler
Kate Bush
Bruce Campbell
Belinda Carlisle
Mary Chapin Carpenter
Andrew Dice Clay
Ethan Coen
Chris Columbus
Jamie Lee Curtis
Denise Crosby
Harry Crosby
Ellen Degeneres
Kenneth "Babyface" Edmonds
Giancarlo Esposito
Terry Fox
Jeff Foxworthy
Matt Frewer
Martin Fry
Grandmaster Flash
Steve Guttenberg
Holly Hunter
Scott Hamilton
Jools Holland
Ice-T
Alan Jackson
Michael Jackson
Victoria Jackson
Lorenzo Lamas
Simon Lebon
Andie MacDowell
Madonna
Frances McDormand
Dinah Manoff
Mike Mills
Gary Numan
Gary Oldman
Eve Plumb
Tim Robbins
Ronald Reagan, Jr.
William Reid
Miranda Richardon
Julian Sands
Sharon Stone
Madeleine Stowe
Feargal Sharkey
Nikki Sixx
Mick Talbot
Charlene Tilton
Tanya Tucker
Scott Valentine
Keenen Ivory Wayans
Paul Weller

TURNING 30

Gillian Anderson
Patricia Arquette
Halle Berry
Michael Bivins
Gary Coleman
Toni Braxton
Celine Dion
Cuba Gooding Jr.
Anthony Michael Hall Jr.
Faith Hill
Big Daddy Kane
Moira Kelly
Patsy Kensit
Ricki Lake
Laura Leighton
Donovan Leitch
L.L. Cool J
Tracy Lords
Chad Lowe
Ziggy Marley
Kylie Minogue
Chynna Philips
Adam Rich
Molly Ringwald
Stephanie Seymore
John Singleton
Courtney Thorne-Smith
Ralph Tresvant
Trugoy the Dove
Carnie Wilson
Young MC
Moon Unit Zappa